- **SCHIZOPHRENIA AND OTHER PSYCHOTIC DISORDERS**

  Schizophrenia
  - Paranoid Type
  - Disorganized Type
  - Catatonic Type
  - Undifferentiated Type
  - Residual Type
  Schizophreniform Disorder
  Schizoaffective Disorder
  Delusional Disorder
  Brief Psychotic Disorder
  Shared Psychotic Disorder
  Psychotic Disorder Due to General Medical Condition
  Substance-Induced Psychotic Disorder

- **MOOD DISORDERS**

  Depressive Disorders
  - Major Depressive Disorder
  - Dysthymic Disorder

  Bipolar Disorders
  - Bipolar I Disorder
  - Bipolar II Disorder
  - Cyclothymic Disorder
  - Mood Disorder Due to General Medical-Condition
  - Substance-Induced Mood Disorder

- **ANXIETY DISORDERS**

  Panic Disorder without Agoraphobia
  Panic Disorder with Agoraphobia
  Agoraphobia without History of Panic Disorder
  Specific Phobia
  Social Phobia
  Obsessive-Compulsive Disorder
  Posttraumatic Stress Disorder
  Acute Stress Disorder
  Generalized Anxiety Disorder
  Anxiety Disorder Due to General Medical Condition
  Substance-Induced Anxiety Disorder

- **SOMATOFORM DISORDERS**

  Somatization Disorder
  Undifferentiated Somatoform Disorder
  Conversion Disorder
  Pain Disorder
  Hypochondriasis
  Body Dysmorphic Disorder

- **FACTITIOUS DISORDERS**

- **DISSOCIATIVE DISORDERS**

  Dissociative Amnesia
  Dissociative Fugue
  Dissociative Identity Disorder
  Depersonalization Disorder

- **SEXUAL AND GENDER IDENTITY DISORDERS**

  Sexual Dysfunctions

  Sexual Desire Disorders
  - Hypoactive Sexual Desire Disorder
  - Sexual Aversion Disorder

  Sexual Arousal Disorders
  - Female Sexual Arousal Disorder
  - Male Erectile Disorder

  Orgasmic Disorders
  - Female Orgasmic Disorder
  - Male Orgasmic Disorder
  - Premature Ejaculation

  Sexual Pain Disorders
  - Dyspareunia
  - Vaginismus

  Sexual Dysfunction Due to a General Medical Condition
  - Substance-Induced Sexual Dysfunction

  Paraphilias
  - Exhibitionism
  - Fetishism
  - Frotteurism
  - Pedophilia
  - Sexual Masochism
  - Sexual Sadism
  - Transvestic Fetishism
  - Voyeurism

  Gender Identity Disorders

- **EATING DISORDERS**

  Anorexia Nervosa
  Bulimia Nervosa

- **SLEEP DISORDERS**

  Primary Sleep Disorders

  Dyssomnias
  - Primary Insomnia
  - Primary Hypersomnia
  - Narcolepsy
  - Breathing-Related Sleep Disorder
  - Circadian Rhythm Sleep Disorder

  Parasomnias
  - Nightmare Disorder
  - Sleep Terror Disorder
  - Sleepwalking Disorder

  Sleep Disorders Related to Another Mental Disorder

  Other Sleep Disorders

- **IMPULSE-CONTROL DISORDERS NOT ELSEWHERE CLASSIFIED**

  Intermittent Explosive Disorder
  Kleptomania
  Pyromania

  Pathological Gambling
  Trichotillomania

- **ADJUSTMENT DISORDERS**

- **PERSONALITY DISORDERS (AXIS II)**

  Paranoid Personality Disorder
  Schizoid Personality Disorder
  Schizotypal Personality Disorder
  Antisocial Personality Disorder
  Borderline Personality Disorder
  Histrionic Personality Disorder
  Narcissistic Personality Disorder
  Avoidant Personality Disorder
  Dependent Personality Disorder
  Obsessive-Compulsive Personality Disorder

- **OTHER CONDITIONS THAT MAY BE A FOCUS OF CLINICAL ATTENTION**

  Psychological Factors Affecting Medical Condition

  Medication-Induced Movement Disorders

  Other Medication-Induced Disorder

  Relational Problems
  - Relational Problem Related to a Mental Disorder or General Medical Condition
  - Parent-Child Relational Problem
  - Partner Relational Problem
  - Sibling Relational Problem

  Problems Related to Abuse or Neglect
  - Physical Abuse of Child
  - Sexual Abuse of Child
  - Neglect of Child
  - Physical Abuse of Adult
  - Sexual Abuse of Adult

  Additional Conditions that May Be a Focus of Clinical Attention
  - Noncompliance w ith Treatment
  - Malingering
  - Adult Antisocial Behavior
  - Child or Adolescent Antisocial Behavior
  - Borderline Intellectual Functioning
  - Age-Related Cognitive Decline
  - Bereavement
  - Academic Problem
  - Occupational Problem
  - Identity Problem
  - Religious or Spiritual Problem .
  - Acculturation Problem
  - Phase of Life Problem

- **ADDITIONAL CODES**

  Unspecified Mental Disorder (nonpsychotic)
  No Diagnosis or Condition on Axis I
  Diagnosis or Condition Deferred on Axis I
  No Diagnosis on Axis II
  Diagnosis Deferred on Axis II

ABNORMAL PSYCHOLOGY

Fifth Edition

MEDIA & RESEARCH UPDATE

ABNORMAL PSYCHOLOGY
Clinical Perspectives on Psychological Disorders

Richard P. Halgin

Susan Krauss Whitbourne
University of Massachusetts at Amherst

McGraw-Hill
Higher Education

Boston   Burr Ridge, IL   Dubuque, IA   New York   San Francisco   St. Louis
Bangkok   Bogotá   Caracas   Kuala Lumpur   Lisbon   London   Madrid   Mexico City
Milan   Montreal   New Delhi   Santiago   Seoul   Singapore   Sydney   Taipei   Toronto

The McGraw-Hill Companies

McGraw-Hill
Higher Education

Published by McGraw-Hill, an imprint of The McGraw-Hill Companies, Inc., 1221 Avenue of the Americas, New York, NY 10020. Copyright © 2008, 2007, 2005, 2003, 2000. All rights reserved. No part of this publication may be reproduced or distributed in any form or by any means, or stored in a database or retrieval system, without the prior written consent of The McGraw-Hill Companies, Inc., including, but not limited to, in any network or other electronic storage or transmission, or broadcast for distance learning.

This book is printed on acid-free paper.

1 2 3 4 5 6 7 8 9 0 DOW/DOW 0 9 8 7

ISBN: 978-0-07-338275-3
MHID: 0-07-338275-2

Editor in Chief: *Michael Ryan*
Publisher: *Beth Mejia*
Sponsoring Editor: *Suzanna Ellison*
Marketing Manager: *James Headley*
Director of Development: *Dawn Groundwater*
Developmental Editor: *Judith Kromm*
Media Project Manager: *Ron Nelms, Jr.*
Production Editor: *Leslie LaDow*

Manuscript Editor: *Chet Gottfried*
Design Coordinator: *Margarite Reynolds*
Text Designers: *Glenda King & Maureen McCutcheon*
Art Editor: *Ayelet Arbel*
Production Supervisor: *Tandra Jorgensen*
Composition: *10/12 Times Roman by Newgen*
Printing: *45 # Matte Plus by R.R. Donnelley & Sons*

Cover Credit: © Digital Vision

Credits: The credits section for this book begins on page C-1 and is considered an extension of the copyright page.

Library of Congress Cataloging-in-Publication Data

Halgin, Richard P.
    Abnormal psychology : clinical perspectives on psychological disorders / Richard P. Halgin, Susan Krauss Whitbourne.—5th ed.
       p. cm.
    Includes bibliographical references and index.
    ISBN-13: 978-0-07-338275-3 (alk. paper)
    ISBN-10: 0-07-338275-2 (alk. paper)
    1. Psychology, Pathological. 2. Mental illness. I. Whitbourne, Susan Krauss. II. Title.

RC454.H334 2007
616.89—dc22

2007936348

The Internet addresses listed in the text were accurate at the time of publication. The inclusion of a website does not indicate an endorsement by the authors or McGraw-Hill, and McGraw-Hill does not guarantee the accuracy of the information presented at these sites.

www.mhhe.com

To our families, with love and appreciation

ABOUT THE AUTHORS

Richard Halgin and Susan Krauss Whitbourne are Professors of Psychology at the University of Massachusetts at Amherst. Both teach large undergraduate classes in addition to teaching and supervising doctoral students in clinical psychology. Their clinical experience has covered both inpatient and outpatient settings. Professors Halgin and Whitbourne are Fellows of the American Psychological Association. They have edited *A Case Book in Abnormal Psychology: From the Files of Experts* (Oxford University Press), containing case studies written by leading international authorities in the field of psychopathology. Both serve on the editorial boards of major professional journals.

Professor Halgin received his PhD from Fordham University and completed a 3-year fellowship in the Department of Psychiatry at New York Hospital-Cornell Medical Center prior to joining the faculty of the University of Massachusetts in 1977. He is a Board-Certified Clinical Psychologist and has had over two decades of clinical, supervisory, and consulting experience. At the University of Massachusetts, his course in Abnormal Psychology is one of the most popular offerings on campus, attracting an enrollment of more than 500 students. He also holds the position of Visiting Professor of Psychology at Amherst College, where he teaches Abnormal Psychology on an annual basis. At the University of Massachusetts, he has been honored with the Distinguished Teaching Award, the Alumni Association's Distinguished Faculty Award, and has been the university's nominee for the Carnegie Foundation's U.S. Professor of the Year Award. His teaching has also been recognized by the Danforth Foundation and the Society for the Teaching of Psychology of the American Psychological Association. Professor Halgin is the author of more than fifty journal articles and book chapters in the fields of psychotherapy, clinical supervision, and professional issues in psychology. He is also the editor of *Taking Sides: Controversial Issues in Abnormal Psychology,* Fourth Edition (McGraw-Hill). Professor Halgin is a member of the Committee of Examiners for the Psychology Graduate Record Examination and has served on the Ethics Committee of the American Psychological Association.

Professor Whitbourne received her PhD from Columbia University and has dual specializations in life-span developmental psychology and clinical psychology. She has taught at the State University of New York at Geneseo and the University of Rochester. At the University of Massachusetts, she received the University's Distinguished Teaching Award and the College of Arts and Sciences Outstanding Teacher Award. In 2001, she received the Psi Chi Eastern Region Faculty Advisor Award and presented the Psi Chi Distinguished Lecture at the Eastern Psychological Association 2001 meeting. In 2002, she received the Florence Denmark Psi Chi National Advisor Award and presented the invited lecture at the Southeastern Psychological Association meeting. She is the Honors Coordinator in the Psychology Department and the Director of the Office of National Scholarship Advisement in the newly established Commonwealth Honors College. The author of fourteen books and over one hundred journal articles and book chapters, Professor Whitbourne is regarded as an expert in the field of personality development in adulthood and old age. She is currently the APA Council Representative of Division 20 of APA (Adult Development and Aging), having also served as Division 20 President and is a member of APA's Committee for the Structure and Function of Council. She also serves as the Division 2 (Teaching of Psychology) Liaison to the APA Committee on Aging and is the Chair of the Student Awards Committee of the Gerontological Society of America. Professor Whitbourne has developed nationally recognized approaches to technological innovations in teaching, and the website she created for her introductory psychology course was selected as a McGraw-Hill Web Cafe "Site of the Month."

Faces *of Abnormal Psychology*
interactive

Media & Research Update

Do you want a resource that

- Facilitates students' exploration of diagnostic processes?
- Improves understanding of clinical practice?
- Trains students to prepare case reports?
- Allows students to interview *real people?*

Welcome to the *Faces of Abnormal Psychology Interactive* Media & Research Update. *Faces of Abnormal Psychology Interactive,* McGraw-Hill's exclusive online resource, includes diagnosis, case history, interview, treatment, and assessment tools for twelve disorders commonly covered in the abnormal psychology course:

Attention-Deficit/Hyperactivity Disorder	Dysthymic Disorder	Paranoid Schizophrenia
Bipolar Disorder	Major Depression	Post-Traumatic Stress Disorder
Bulimia Nervosa	Obsessive Compulsive Disorder	Substance Abuse
Borderline Personality Disorder	Panic Disorder with Agoraphobia	Tourette's Syndrome

Available to all users of this book, *Faces of Abnormal Psychology Interactive* includes more than 14 hours of video featuring *real* people and more than 400 interview questions students can use to elicit diagnostic information. With this information, students complete a case report and become prepared for the built-in assessment on each client. Visit **www.mhhe.com/halgin5** to try out this instructor and student favorite.

This edition of *Abnormal Psychology* also includes the most current research on topics of high interest in this course. See the following pages for **Research Updates** that briefly summarize these topics and provide suggestions for discussion and review.

Faces of Abnormal Psychology Interactive and the **Research Updates** are supported by assessment items and accompanied by Blackboard and WebCT course cartridges for courses taught fully or partially online.

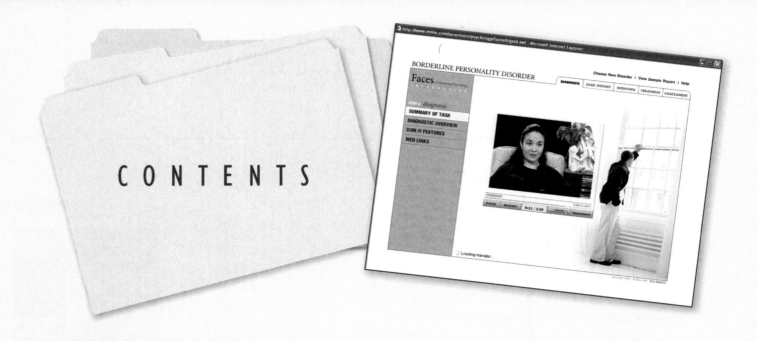

CONTENTS

Chapter 1 Understanding Abnormality: A Look at History and Research Methods

FACES: Major Depressive Disorder

DSM CRITERIA

- Major depressive disorder is a diagnosis assigned to people who have either a single major depressive episode or recurrent episodes with 2 or more months intervening between episodes.
- The major depressive episode is not better explained by another disorder.
- The individual has never had a manic, mixed, or hypomanic episode.

MAJOR DEPRESSIVE EPISODE

- For most of the time during a 2-week period a person experiences at least five of the following symptoms, which involve a change from previous functioning (at least one of the first two symptoms must be present): depressed mood, diminished interest or pleasure in all or most daily activities, significant unintentional weight loss or appetite decrease or increase, insomnia or hypersomnia, psychomotor agitation or retardation, fatigue or energy loss, feelings of worthlessness or inappropriate guilt, concentration difficulty or indecisiveness, or recurrent thoughts of death or suicidality.
- The symptoms are not part of a mixed (manic-depressive) episode and are not attributable to a medical condition, use of a substance, or bereavement.
- The symptoms cause significant distress or impairment.

Brief Case History

Tara's problems with depression began during childhood. In the fourth grade, she hated her teachers and her family. Even at that age, she mostly kept to herself. She described herself as a loner: sad and angry, spending hours isolated in her room in her own fantasy world. In high school, her symptoms worsened. Her boyfriend died, and Tara descended into a dark depression. For almost a year, she slept 20 hours a day, rarely ate, and had persistent thoughts of suicide. The depression persisted when she left for college. She was hospitalized for attempted suicide. During one of these hospitalizations, she was finally diagnosed with major depression.

She has attempted suicide on several more occasions and has been hospitalized, both voluntarily and involuntarily. However, at the time of the interview, Tara said that she was feeling relatively happy. Tara has pursued an aggressive series of treatment options including counseling, medications, and, most recently, an extensive series of electroconvulsive therapy (ECT). Tara has received a total of 24 ECT treatments. At the time of the interview, she was in the middle of a new course of bilateral treatment, which is the most invasive and effective form of ECT. She was also taking antidepressant medications. In spite of her depression, Tara is able to keep a job and perform her professional obligations as a drug abuse counselor. She behaves reflexively—getting up, going to work, and doing her job—all without getting emotionally involved. After work, she sometimes goes shopping—buying things seems to help her mood—and then she goes home, watches television, and goes to bed. She has few other activities in her life and has no interest in becoming involved in a romantic relationship.

Tara remains in contact with her family, and they try to be supportive. Tara insists, however, that they are not. She also regrets the shame that her disorder brings onto her family.

Clinical Questions

Was your childhood depression a "real" depression?

It was real at time! I don't know that I necessarily thought, "Oh, gee. I'm depressed" or "My life is miserable"; I know that we were going through a lot of changes at the time. My parents drank very heavily, and then they just stopped, due to a very religious sort of conversion

when I was 10 and that was also in the fourth grade. And so, I think, just combined with a lot of change.

Has it become easier to control yourself as you have gotten older?

The next time I really remember being majorly depressed was after a boyfriend died. And then that was like, the summer before my senior year. Every single day I tried to figure out how I could kill myself, because I wanted to be with my boyfriend. And that seemed logical to me; that if I died, I could be with him. But I was so depressed, I wouldn't talk to people. I basically hated the world. I don't even know how I survived through that year. I really don't. At least weekly I would make an attempt. Like, pop out in front of a car, or truck; in the middle of the night, go down to the river and just OD on whatever drugs and alcohol I could find. It was a weekly occurrence. I was just very, very depressed. I have no idea how I survived.

When did you first get diagnosed and put on medications?

In college I went to see a counselor, and I, I actually did counseling at that time. And started on antidepressants, but I didn't really take them very well [laughs]. I kinda went on and off of them, and kind of didn't really understand the purpose of them. And I guess it didn't help. I was at a very religious college, and when I went to see the doctor, he said, "You have nothing to be sad about. I don't understand what your problem is. You have everything to live for; you should be happy. But, I guess if you want, I can give you these pills." And so, I didn't really buy into it, and he didn't buy into it, so I didn't really understand. It's not like he helped me to understand that these pills were necessary, and I should take them, even when I felt better.

Do you ever think about killing yourself?

It still goes through my mind a lot. Like, at least several times a week; about killing myself. I really don't really think I have a lot to live for. I haven't got to that point yet, where I think, gee, I really want to live my life, and this is the greatest thing, and I just have everything to live for; I'm really not at that point. But I am at the point where I realize that suicide isn't a good option; it would hurt a lot of people. I don't have any more days left on my insurance plan for the hospital, so I also think about that too; I've used all my days this year, so I can't really try to kill myself, 'cause I'd be in trouble. They'd just let me die. I don't know how that works, if you're out of hospital days. So, I just kinda think it's not an option to kill myself; even though I would kind of like to. I think about different ways. If I see a train, I think, I could just drive in front of that train! I just consistently have suicidal thoughts.

This may sound dumb, but what are you depressed about? You're pretty, you're smart, you're employed. What do you got to be depressed about?

That's the thing, nothing. That's when I realized, it was really a problem. I wasn't depressed about anything, really. It's just like, one day you're doing fine, and then the next day you just kinda shut down. And there's really no reason for it.

Differential Diagnosis

Tara's long history of dysphoric mood, suicidality, and feelings of hopelessness are characteristic symptoms of major depressive disorder. However, the clinician would also consider alternative or additional diagnoses. Her self-injurious behavior might suggest borderline personality disorder; however, her suicidal attempts appear to be genuine, not attempts to draw attention to herself. Although Tara's depression seems to have been triggered by the death of a boyfriend, bereavement does not account for her symptoms. Tara remained depressed for years after his death, and she showed signs of depression prior to his death. Finally, the clinician may consider dysthymic disorder, but Tara's depressive symptoms are more severe than those associated with that disorder.

DISCUSSION QUESTIONS

1. What symptoms might lead someone suffering from major depressive disorder to contemplate suicide?
2. Is it right to involuntarily commit suicidal patients?

RESEARCH: Changes in Mental Health Reimbursement

Changes in the provision of mental health services have been occurring steadily over the past fifty years, following the dramatic changes associated with the deinstitutionalization movement of the 1960s. The introduction of new psychiatric medications has had a particularly large impact on the provision of care. Shedding light on these changes is one of the largest studies ever conducted on epidemiology of psychological disorders, the National Comorbidity Study, conducted between 1990 and 2002 and replicated between 2001 and 2003 (Kessler & Merikangas, 2004). Changes in the reimbursement of mental health services by insurance companies and greater promotion of psychiatric medications have resulted in a decrease in the utilization of psychotherapy services and an increase in the use of medically oriented treatment services (Wang et al., 2006). At present, only two states in the United States have approved prescription privileges for psychologists. Until psychologists are able to prescribe psychiatric medications on a more widespread basis, this trend in the provision of mental health services will undoubtedly continue.

One of the reasons that individuals needing psychological treatment favor medical versus psychological interventions is that there is less stigma attached to seeking help for physically based disorders than for those that reflect psychological disturbance. Researchers investigating this issue have recently begun to think about the impact of stigma on the individual's sense of self. In addition to experiencing the symptoms themselves, people with psychological disorders may come to feel ashamed of their symptoms and, as a result, feel even more distressed than they otherwise would. In one study, two groups of women, one with borderline personality disorder and the other with social phobia, were compared in the tendency to feel stigmatized by their disorder (Rusch et al., 2006). The women with borderline personality disorder were more affected in a negative way by stigmatization primarily due, according to the researchers, to the fact that they had experienced frequent psychiatric hospitalizations compared to the women with social phobia, whose disorder did not result in the need for hospitalization. In addition, women with borderline personality disorder were more likely to have physical scars due to their tendency to engage in suicidal behavior (such as cutting their wrists). These women also were likely to have more serious interpersonal problems. Stigma, then, is a problem that continues to plague individuals with psychological disorders, affecting them on a daily basis and lowering not only their feelings of self-worth but possibly their treatment-seeking behavior.

Kessler, R. C., & Merikangas, K. R. (2004). The National Comorbidity Survey Replication (NCS-R): Background and aims. *International Journal of Methods in Psychiatric Research, 13,* 60–68.

Rusch, N., Holzer, A., Hermann, C., Schramm, E., Jacob, G. A., Bohus, M., Lieb, K., & Corrigan, P. W. (2006). Self-stigma in women with borderline personality disorder and women with social phobia. *Journal of Nervous and Mental Disorder, 194,* 766–773.

Wang, P. S., Demler, O., Olfson, M., Pincus, H. A., Wells, K. B., & Kessler, R. C. (2006). Changing profiles of service sectors used for mental health care in the United States. *American Journal of Psychiatry, 163,* 1187–1198.

Chapter 2   Classification and Treatment Plans

FACES: Bipolar I Disorder

DSM CRITERIA

- People with bipolar disorder have experienced at least one manic episode, with the possibility but not the necessity of a major depressive episode. This contrasts with bipolar II disorder in which an individual experiences recurrent major depressive episodes and has a history of at least one hypomanic episode but no manic episodes.
- The condition is not attributable to another disorder.
- The symptoms cause significant distress or impairment.
- A manic episode is a period of abnormally and persistently elevated, expansive, or irritable mood lasting at least 1 week. During this period, three or more of the following symptoms have persisted (four if the mood is only irritable): inflated self-esteem or grandiosity; decreased need for sleep; increased talkativeness; flight of ideas or racing thoughts; distractibility; increase in goal-directed activity or psychomotor agitation; excessive involvement in pleasurable activities with potentially painful consequences.

Brief Case History

Bernie is a 38-year-old man diagnosed with bipolar disorder at the age of 24. Bernie thinks that the first signs of trouble occurred when he was about 17 years old. He began shutting himself off from people, and his grades became erratic. One semester he was failing, and the next he was on the honor roll. His fluctuations continued for the next few years. One week he was leading school activities, and the next week found him holed up in bed. Things became particularly acute after a girlfriend broke up with him in college. He entered a deep and protracted depression that lasted for several months. When that depression finally relented, he spiraled up and experienced his first full manic episode. At first, he says, it felt great to have energy again. But the energy continued to escalate, and eventually it got out of control. His thoughts were racing, he was unable to sleep, and there was little logic behind his actions. As an

example, during that episode, he saw cans of paint at his mother's house, and without consulting her, he proceeded to paint her house.

Since that first episode, Bernie has continued cycling through a series of depressions and manias, and both emotional extremes have proved dangerous. During his depressions, Bernie sinks into a deep darkness spending days or weeks alone in his apartment. He closes the curtains, talks to no one, seldom bathes, and drinks a lot of alcohol. Those depressions have led to several hospitalizations. The manic episodes are probably even more dangerous. On the one hand, Bernie says he initially enjoys the energy and recklessness. But the mania causes him to make bad decisions, ones that violate his own morals and that get him into trouble with the law.

Over the years, Bernie has gained experience with his disorder, and his cycles have become fairly predictable. The manic phases usually last 1 to 2 weeks, while the depression cycles last up to a month. He sometimes gets a period of 1 to 3 weeks of relative normalcy. Bernie has been prescribed a variety of mood stabilizers and antidepressants. While he continues to cycle through episodes of depression and mania, these medications have reduced the severity of his symptoms. At the time of this interview, however, Bernie was unemployed and without health insurance. As a result, he was unable to afford his medications and he had to suffer through more acute mood changes. In lieu of the medications, Bernie tried to ward off new episodes by leading a healthy lifestyle, avoiding

stress, and attending group support sessions for people who suffer from bipolar disorder.

Clinical Questions

When was your first serious breakdown?

I noticed that when I went to college, um, I was having these really high feelings and emotions and wanting to do things, and it had nothing to do with, with sports. Or even the music. I just had these, these high, high times. And then, you know, I'd be in the bed for a week. Even in college; again, my grades were very erratic. One semester I was on academic probation; next semester I made the dean's list. And people who were around me, centered around me, they wanted to know as well. What was going on? So, you know, after a while I didn't do anything about it, because at that point I had graduated.

When did you begin to recognize that you might suffer from a mental illness?

My supervisor recognized some things in me as well. At that time he called me in to, to the office, and he pulled out some medication of his and said that you gotta go get some help; because I see some things in you that was happening to me. So that's when I really start seeking some help. 'Cause a lot of my co-workers were getting intimidated, and some were getting extremely angry with me because I was short with them. . . . So this supervisor had already filled out the, the leave of absence—medical leave of absence papers for me. And so I just ended up spending about 40 days in the hospital; it was a private hospital I went to. And that's when I got diagnosed.

How do you feel when you are manic?

We were going to our Sunday services, and the light, I knew it was a short light, but I was cursing at the light. Because this is conspiring. This is all against me. You know, how dare this light turn? I was mean. Very, very mean toward simple things. You spilt juice on my shoe, you clumsy idiot! What are you? All thumbs? All the things that again, I'm saying, a crazy person is doing. Hell, I'm doing these things. And I'm, I'm supposed to be,

you know, and I'm working as a social worker in, in, in the prison system. And I'm thinking to myself, maybe the, the system is rubbing off on me.

You say that you have enjoyed being in a manic state. Is there a downside to it?

I have gotten in some minor trouble. I have done some things that—that I'm not proud of. Like for example, I have a tendency to be promiscuous. And that goes against my, my personal and uh, moral fiber. Uh,

and it's never enough, you know, to just be with one person now. And it's like, one conquest after the next. One this morning, two or three this afternoon, and how many can I go and get this evening. You know, that's where I'm at. When I'm that way, I'm really, really, in that frame. And unfortunately I've gotten arrested. And, when the initial shock was over, it didn't make a difference. I went right back out. I'm, this is crazy. This is stupid; why am I going back out there? I just got arrested! And I've only been arrested twice. I shouldn't, shouldn't even be saying only, but the fact of the matter is, that I went right back out, almost in the same area, to do what I just got arrested for. Stupid; crazy. And that's the manic side of it.

Differential Diagnosis

Bernie's mood swings between mania and depression provide a classic illustration of bipolar I disorder. However, in evaluating his symptoms, a clinician would also consider a number of possible alternatives. First, the clinician would determine whether Bernie suffers from a medical condition that would cause mood swings. The next possibility to consider is substance abuse. Third, the clinician would evaluate whether Bernie suffers from cyclothymia, which is characterized by less extreme mood swings. Bernie might also be evaluated for an impulse control disorder as reflected in his impulsivity; however, his episodes of impulsive behavior appear to be related to his mood alterations.

DISCUSSION QUESTIONS

1. People with bipolar disorder often resist staying on their medication. Why might this be the case?
2. Do you think that scientists may eventually be able to diagnose psychological disorders entirely on the basis of brain imaging methods?

RESEARCH: **The Future of Psychiatric Diagnosis**

Individuals in the throes of profound depression speak not only about feelings of sadness but also a sense of agitation and anxiety. Conversely, individuals struggling with intense anxiety feel an accompanying depression and sense of incapacitation. In the *DSM-IV-TR,* a categorical approach is used which pulls for the clinician to assign a diagnosis that focuses on either depression or anxiety. However, panels of nationwide experts working on the development of *DSM-V* are attempting to determine whether the categorical system should remain or be replaced with a dimensional approach.

Widiger and Samuel (2005) delineate two dilemmas inherent in the categorical approach to diagnosis: excessive diagnostic co-occurrence and boundary issues between diagnoses. Diagnostic co-occurrence, called *comorbidity,* refers to situations in which a person experiences symptoms that meet the diagnostic criteria for more than one disorder. Some argue that such co-occurrence is the norm rather than the exception. In the case of depression and anxiety, there may be a shared negative affectivity dimension that is common to mood disorders, anxiety disorders, and certain personality disorders. The second dilemma, problematic boundaries, refers to the overlap among several diagnoses, such as the distinction between oppositional defiant disorder, attention-deficit/hyperactivity disorder, and conduct disorder.

Watson and Clark (2006) propose two possible approaches for *DSM-V.* The first is a reorganization of diagnostic classes that would replace the current categories with a new set that reflect real-world similarities between disorders. Second, the personality disorders would be organized along dimensions rather than into discrete categories.

One dramatic proposal is the possibility of relinquishing a single diagnostic scheme and, instead, embracing the notion of different diagnostic systems for different purposes. In other words, there might be two parallel systems, one for clinicians in practice and the other for researchers in the field of psychopathology (Watson & Clark, 2006).

During the last 30 years, significant gains have been made in refining the psychiatric diagnostic system. With increasing experience and wisdom, however, researchers and clinicians have come to recognize the limitations of the current system and have expressed a commitment to a significant overhaul, such that the psychological disorders of real human beings can be more thoughtfully understood and treated.

Watson, D., & Clark, L. A. (2006). Clinical diagnosis at the crossroads. *Clinical Psychology: Science and Practice, 13,* 210–215.

Widiger, T. A., & Samuel, D. B. (2005). Diagnostic categories or dimensions? A question for the *Diagnostic and Statistical Manual of Mental Disorders — Fifth Edition. Journal of Abnormal Psychology, 114,* 494–504.

Chapter 3 Assessment

RESEARCH: MRI in Assessment

Functional magnetic resonance imaging (fMRI) is quickly becoming an important adjunct to psychological assessment. As the technology of this method increases in sophistication and as it becomes more widely available, researchers are finding more and more applications for its use in a wide range of contexts, from marketing of commercial products to detecting deception in criminals. The fMRI can provide a picture of how people react to stimuli virtually in real time, making it possible to present stimuli to an individual while monitoring the brain's reaction.

The use of MRIs as a correlate of neuropsychological testing seems to be a logical place to start to integrate brain imaging into psychological assessment, as neuropsychological testing attempts to identify brain regions associated with specific behavioral deficits. *Neurological soft signs (NSS)* are minor behavioral abnormalities, such as faulty motor coordination, difficulties in sensation and perception, and problems in sequencing complex motor tasks. Individuals diagnosed with psychotic disorders are known to exhibit NSS, but they are remarkably highly prevalent in healthy individuals, with rates ranging from 0 to 50 percent. However, few studies to date have attempted to identify the neuroanatomical substrate of these abnormalities. Using fMRI, researchers in the UK have now begun to investigate the connection (Dazzan et al., 2006). Individuals ranging in age from 17 to 55 with no evidence of psychotic disorder, head trauma, a neurological disease, or English language problems were given MRIs along with tests of brain function known as the Neurological Evaluation Scale, which assesses sensory functioning, motor coordination, and integration of sensory and motor functioning. Individuals showing greater reduction in the volume of cortical areas involved in attention, auditory, tactile, and language processes or in integration of audio and visual stimuli also showed greater deficits on tests of sensory-motor integration. Interestingly, the pattern of findings in normal (nonpsychotic) individuals was the same as that found in individuals with diagnosed psychotic disorders, suggesting that there is a common set of neuroanatomical changes involved in the development of abnormal neurological test performance.

In addition to using MRIs as assessment tools, researchers are finding that they can be of value in identifying specific brain dysfunctions associated with particular disorders. A team of German researchers compared the MRIs of women with major depressive disorder (MDD) and controls on an emotion learning task, in which objects were paired with faces displaying one of six emotions. The women with MDD had difficulty learning the pairing of faces expressing fear, surprise, and disgust. Moreover, those with MDD had larger volumes of the amygdala, an organ within the limbic system involved in emotional responsiveness. However, when both depressive status and amygdala size were jointly considered, it was only the women with MDD and a larger amygdala who showed impaired performance on the emotion learning task. The emotional memory deficit, then, may be associated with changes in the brain related to the development of MDD (Weniger, Lange, & Irle, 2006).

Of course, watching the brain reacting to stimuli does not tell us what the individual is thinking, only which parts of the brain are active. Nevertheless, to the extent that researchers become able to relate areas of brain activation to behavioral reactions, this technology will undoubtedly revolutionize the field of psychological assessment.

Dazzan, P., Morgan, K. D., Chitnis, X., Suckling, J., Morgan, C., Fearon, P., McGuire, P. K., Jones, P. B., Leff, J., & Murray R. M. (2006). The structural brain correlates of neurological soft signs in healthy individuals. *Cerebral Cortex, 16,* 1225–1231.
Weniger, G., Lange, C., & Irle, E. (2006). Abnormal size of the amygdala predicts impaired emotional memory in major depressive disorder. *Journal of Affective Disorders, 94,* 219–229.

Chapter 4 Theoretical Perspectives

RESEARCH: Panic-Focused Psychodynamic Therapy

The theory and practice of psychoanalysis have undergone radical shifts in the past several decades. From a perspective that emphasized long-term intensive therapy to one that now incorporates brief and focused treatments, psychoanalysis is being incorporated into the range of empirically validated treatments. Although for years disorders involving the experience of anxiety were thought of as amenable only to behavioral or cognitive behavioral therapy, researchers have recently tested a brief psychodynamic intervention that can be successfully applied to the treatment of panic disorder (Milrod et al., 2007).

People who experience panic disorder are vulnerable to panic attacks in which they have a range of physical and psychological symptoms that cause them to feel as though they are in serious danger of being harmed. In panic-focused psychodynamic psychotherapy, therapists attempt to identify core unconscious conflicts that are at the root of the symptoms. These might include issues dealing with separation and autonomy, such as having difficulty being alone or being in control of one's life. The therapist uses transference as a means of approaching and dealing with the conflicts. Unlike traditional psychoanalysis, the therapist attempts to alleviate the problems quickly, and therapy itself is time-limited (12 weeks).

In an empirical test of panic-focused psychodynamic therapy, a team of therapists treated 49 men and women who suffered from a variety of forms of panic disorder. Half of the participants received relaxation training, and the other half received psychodynamic therapy. At the end of the 12-week trial, nearly twice as many of those receiving psychodynamic therapy reported significant improvements in anxiety and panic-related symptoms. For example, one of the study participants had daily panic attacks while studying. A musician, she was so self-critical that she could hardy perform without feeling extreme levels of anxiety. In therapy, her fear of her mother's criticism and high expectations transferred onto the therapist, allowing her to confront those issues and work them through in a therapeutic context.

As researchers continue to explore new variants on cognitive behavioral therapy for clients with the symptoms of panic disorder, such as group-based cognitive behavioral therapy (Galassi et al., 2007) and short (2-day) intensive treatment, the addition of psychodynamic methods to the resources available to clinicians provides a means of addressing the issues involved in this troubling and disabling disorder.

Galassi, F., Quercioli, S., Charismas, D., Niccolai, V., & Barciulli, E. (2007). Cognitive-behavioral group treatment for panic disorder with agoraphobia. *Journal of Clinical Psychology, 63,* 409–416.

Milrod, B., Leon, A. C., Busch, F., Rudden, M., Schwalberg, M., Clarkin, J., Aronson, A., Singer, M., Turchin, W., Klass, E. T., Graf, E., Teres, J. J., & Shear, M. K. (2007). A randomized controlled clinical trial of psychoanalytic psychotherapy for panic disorder. *American Journal of Psychiatry, 164,* 265–272.

Chapter 5 Anxiety Disorders

FACES: Panic Disorder with Agoraphobia

DSM CRITERIA

The diagnosis of panic disorder with agoraphobia is assigned to people who experience panic attacks not due to substances or a medical condition. They experience (1) recurrent, unexpected panic attacks and (2) at least one attack has been followed by at least 1 month during which they experience one or more of the following: persistent concern about having more attacks, worry about the implications of the attack or its consequences, or significant change in behavior related to the attacks.

Agoraphobia is a condition associated with some forms of panic disorder.

- People with agoraphobia experience anxiety about being in places or situations from which escape might be difficult or embarrassing or in which they may not be able to get help should they experience panic.
- People with agoraphobia avoid the feared situations or endure them with marked distress or anxiety about having a panic attack or symptoms, or they insist that someone be present in the event that they panic.

Brief Case History

Annie remembers a normal childhood. However, she alluded to a history of abuse which she was reluctant to discuss. Annie began having significant problems during puberty. She became very uncomfortable around people, and was having difficulties at school. She first visited a psychiatrist when she was 15 years old. Annie's psychiatrist initially diagnosed her as suffering from major depressive disorder. More recently, Annie has been diagnosed as suffering from panic disorder with agoraphobia. Initially, Annie was relieved to hear that there was a name for her condition. Knowing that other people experience the same symptoms gave her a sense of community and hope. Unfortunately,

Annie has not responded well to medical treatment. She was prescribed a variety of medications, but they had little effect on her anxiety. Furthermore, she objects to the side effects that the drugs produce. At the time of the interview, she was not taking any medications. Psychotherapy has proved helpful, but she has been unable to maintain treatment due to the expense. Although she has held jobs in the past, being in a public setting causes her tremendous anxiety. Currently, she is unemployed and is receiving disability payments from the government. She shares a modest home with friends, and relies on them to help her with day-to-day chores such as shopping. She is determined to find a behavioral means for coping with her anxiety. In terms of the future, Annie has a variety of goals. Principally, she wants to gain control over her anxiety. She dreams of attending college or getting a job working with animals. She also hopes to help people better understand psychological disorders.

Clinical Questions

When did you begin experiencing your current problems with anxiety and panic attacks?

Things really broke down for me when I was about 15, and when the hormones were kicking in, I was starting to analyze things within my family and realize all this, just abuse and stuff that was going on, and that was when I started being treated for psychological stuff. I remember my first psychiatrist. I was so relieved just to hear that there was something that they could put a name on. That means other people have this; that means it's something they know what to do with. Talking to my parents, then my parents saying, okay good, there's something wrong with her; it's not really something wrong with the situation. It was a relief to me, and then, I remember thinking when I heard the "medication" thing, there was already just like this stigma sort of attached to it for me. I was to the point where anything . . . if it's gonna help. But my psychiatrist told me that this was going to be my medicine and that I could be on these drugs for the rest of my life, and that's what I remember a lot. That's pretty intense.

Can you describe how it feels to have a panic attack?

All of a sudden time would get real weird, and I'd feel like—first of all, my heart would start speeding up. I'd start hyperventilating. Shaking, can't feel my hands, it's just total—it's terror, and if there was some sort of thing that I was afraid of like a bear, or something, it would be different. It would be a natural terror; I would run. But with the panic attacks, it's this unnamable, like unknown fear.

Your panic attacks sound awful. Do they cause you to experience any other psychological problems?

Well, I've been diagnosed agoraphobic. And from a diagnostic point of view, agoraphobia, I've heard it described as fear of being in a place with a lot of people, or

I guess the root word is from the Greek market, *agora,* or something like that. And I've also heard it described as something that results from panic attacks that kinda manifests itself as like sometimes I'm not able to go back to a place that I've been with panic attacks. If I have a panic attack there, it's almost like this thing that takes over my brain, and that means you're going to have a panic attack again, and I have to do all these things in order to make myself not have a panic attack.

How do you deal with day-to-day chores? For example, what do you do when you need groceries? Is it a problem for you?

What I feel, when I have to go to the grocery store, is usually I have a checklist that I go down. How's my stomach doing? Did I just eat recently? Is there somebody that can go with me, in case I can't wait in line alone? Do I have a mode of transportation? Because I don't take the bus right now, because it just freaks me out. If I take the bus somewhere, and then I get off the bus, I'm not immediately home. I still have to find my way back home. So the car's important. And then somebody being with me is really good. I have friends that have been real good about that. Where it's like, if I need to abandon my shopping cart, use the bathroom, or if I just can't wait in line, then they'll use my money to pay. But it does make me really nervous. And there's some times that I have to ask people if they can just go to the store for me, and a lot of people are real good about that. And I totally appreciate that in people. That they can understand. It's like if they can, they will. 'Cause they know that if I ask, I really can't. But when I know I can't, it's not just that I don't want to. It's

not that at all. There's all these things that are built up in my brain that are not letting me do it. I won't even get out the door—and it's not worth it to me. Because of how terrifying that would be to me.

Differential Diagnosis

Annie clearly shows the symptoms of panic disorder with agoraphobia. The fact that she was misdiagnosed initially as having major depressive disorder might suggest that she also has experienced a major depressive episode, but at the present time, her disorder seems to involve fear of having a panic attack while out in public and unable to seek help.

Clinicians treating individuals with symptoms such as those of Annie would consider other anxiety conditions, such as generalized anxiety disorder (GAD). However, people with GAD experience more constant worry and anxiety that occurs more days than not for at least 6 months.

In determining the presence of agoraphobia, the clinician might rule out social phobia, which shares some similarities. However, social phobia differs from agoraphobia in that the individual is concerned about being scrutinized by other people, rather than being concerned about developing a panic attack.

DISCUSSION QUESTIONS

1. Would the fact that Annie is aware of the irrationality of her fears make her symptoms easier to treat?
2. What treatment options are available for those suffering from agoraphobia?

FACES: Obsessive-Compulsive Disorder

DSM CRITERIA

▪ People with obsessive-compulsive disorder (OCD) suffer from either obsessions or compulsions, which the person recognizes as excessive or unreasonable. The obsessions or compulsions cause

marked distress, continue for more than an hour a day, or significantly interfere with functioning.

▪ Obsessions are defined by the following features: (1) recurrent, persistent thoughts, impulses, or images that feel intrusive and inappropriate and cause anxiety or distress; (2) not simply excessive worries about real-life problems;

(3) attempts to ignore or suppress or replace these with another thought or action; and (4) recognition that these are products of one's own mind.

▪ Compulsions are defined by two features: (1) repetitive behaviors or mental acts that the person feels driven to perform in response to an obsession or to rigid rules and (2) the behaviors or mental acts are intended to prevent or reduce distress or to prevent a dreaded event or situation, but are clearly excessive or not realistically connected with what they are intended to neutralize or prevent.

Brief Case History

Laura and Marna are longtime friends who both suffer from obsessive-compulsive disorder. They obsess over different issues, and their compulsive behaviors are very different. At a deeper level, they share very similar feelings and motivations, and the similarities can help us appreciate the fundamental nature of obsessive-compulsive disorder. Obsessions and compulsions have plagued the two women their entire lives. Marna remembers that, even as a child, she had serious difficulties selecting her clothes. When Laura was a teenager, she would spend up to an hour each day applying mascara. Both women acknowledge a significant history of mental illness in their respective families. Marna states that she was abused as a child. Laura is a checker, spending hours reading the tags on clothes or arranging and rearranging paperwork. Marna has obsessive thoughts about keeping things orderly and spends hours arranging the dishes in her cabinets.

Both women have excellent insight into their disorders. They realize that the obsessions and compulsions are irrational but feel powerless to overcome them. Marna had a career as a professional model, but her disorder made it impossible for her to meet professional demands. For Laura, the OCD has created significant obstacles in both her personal and her professional life.

Both women have also learned compensatory behaviors. For example, Laura has learned to cut the tags off her clothing to prevent herself from checking them. Marna, who has intrusive thoughts of run-

ning over pedestrians at a stoplight, has learned to put her car in neutral as she sits waiting. These women have learned that deferring the compulsive actions in this way helps reduce the symptoms. Marna also finds relief by cross stitching. While it is true that the activity requires careful, almost obsessive action, she says stitching provides a kind of positive relief that is not produced by straightening dishes or her other compulsive behaviors.

Although Marna had exhibited obsessive-compulsive disorder symptoms throughout childhood, she was finally diagnosed at the age of 30, only 3 years prior to this interview. Interestingly, her initial insight occurred during a conversation with Laura. While Marna was describing her thoughts and actions, Laura recognized the patterns and encouraged her to see a psychiatrist.

The two friends find consolation in speaking with each another and use humor as a coping mechanism. Although they suffer from a serious psychological disorder, they are not depressed. They continue to live happy, fulfilling, productive lives. Laura and Marna have explored a variety of treatment options. Both of them are currently taking medications that have helped keep their symptoms under control. They find that learning more about the nature of obsessive-compulsive disorder and participating in support groups have provided them with relief.

Clinical Questions

Do you experience obsessive thoughts?
I have obsessive thoughts that affect my life. It makes it difficult to function or to think about productive things. Or you think about them too much.

Can you give an example of obsessions?
Paperwork, let's say at work that there's filing, or let's say I'm looking for a particular thing. I can find it and pull it out. Usually where I get tripped up is where I'm putting something away. I still hate filing. What I'll do is I'll put it away, and then the, urge, it's almost like a surge that you have to check, I gotta see. Is that other insurance paper behind there? And what's behind that? And, and what's behind that? And what's in the other little portable file, and so I just end up checking all of it.

In my worst days several years back, I would have to cut the tags off my clothes, because I'll check if it's made in Korea. I know brand names for zippers. Y-A-L-O-N, the

Yalon company! Paperwork: I'll check it to see, check and recheck the labels. It says 100 percent silk, but you have to check again.

What does it feel like when you have a compulsion to do something?
It is like a negative energy. I tense up; I gotta check. One time at work I called my boss, who knew that I had OCD. I said, would you open my file cabinet, and check if that piece paper is there, and she just busted up laughing. It's like an urge.

When does the OCD first affect you during the day?
It starts from the moment I wake up; but it's in my dreams as well, so actually, it starts the night before, because, you know, how am I gonna deal with the morning? Functioning . . . in the morning, how am I gonna start the day? I've spent years trying to refine this process. I exercise, so, I finally needed to break it down to that these are the days of the week and the time slot, so that I don't have to think about it anymore.

Laura, what's it like when you have a compulsion, and something prevents you from doing it?
I was starting a filing project; for instance, that I had a bunch of papers I had to file, and I was in the middle of it. I have to stop what I'm doing, and wait, after about 15, 20 minutes, especially like half hour, the urge is either gone, or it's much less. And that's the behavioral, the crust of the behavior modification, with OCD; that's what they try and do; is have you wait, until that urge passes. It gets to a point where you can maybe do something else, or get on with your day.

Differential Diagnosis

The obsessions and compulsions experienced by Laura and Marna fit the diagnostic criteria of obsessive-compulsive disorder. However, the clinician would also attempt to rule out obsessive-compulsive personality disorder, in which the individual exhibits the personality traits of perfectionism and conscientiousness to a degree that interferes with the routines of everyday life.

DISCUSSION QUESTIONS

1. What examples of obsessions and compulsions does Laura discuss?

2. What types of therapeutic approaches would a clinician take with a patient suffering from OCD?

3. What are the differences between OCD and obsessive-compulsive personality disorder?

FACES: Post-Traumatic Stress Disorder

DSM CRITERIA

- Post-traumatic stress disorder (PTSD), which causes significant distress or impairment, is a diagnosis assigned to people who have been exposed to a traumatic event in which (1) they experienced, witnessed, or confronted a life-threatening or seriously injurious threat to themselves or others and (2) they responded with intense fear, helplessness, or horror.

- For at least 1 month, there is a persistent reexperiencing of the traumatic event in at least one of the following ways: (1) recurrent and intrusive distressing recollections of the event; (2) recurrent distressing dreams of the event; (3) acting or feeling as if the event is recurring; (4) intense distress at exposure to internal or external cues that symbolize or resemble an aspect of the event; or (5) physiological reactivity on exposure to internal or external cues that symbolize or resemble an aspect of the event.

- For at least 1 month there is avoidance of stimuli associated with the trauma and a numbing of general responsiveness, indicated by three or more of the following: (1) efforts to avoid thoughts, feelings, or conversations associated with the trauma; (2) efforts to avoid activities, places, or people that evoke recollections; (3) inability to recall important aspects of the trauma; (4) diminished interest or participation in significant activities; (5) feelings of detachment or estrangement; (6) restricted range of affect; or (7) sense of foreshortened future.

- For at least 1 month there are persistent symptoms of increased arousal, as indicated by at least two of the following: (1) difficulty falling or staying asleep; (2) irritability or anger outbursts;

(3) concentration difficulty; (4) hypervigilance; or (5) exaggerated startle response.

Brief Case History

Carl was 17 years old when he volunteered for the army and began his service in Vietnam. One of his first duties involved assigning troops to combat zones. The next day he reviewed the casualty lists and sent out the next round of troops. Because this was profoundly distressing, he volunteered for active combat. In a second assignment, Carl operated a machine gun off the side of a patrol helicopter. The battles were both arousing and terrifying. Carl's psychological problems began to emerge after he returned to the United States. The political climate had turned against the war, and he was condemned by both friends and strangers. Over the next few years, Carl developed PTSD symptoms, including flashbacks, hypervigilance, and emotional detachment. Carl is now a social worker, specializing in helping other veterans cope with PTSD. Looking back over his life, Carl knows that his experiences in Vietnam left him with permanent emotional scars. Yet as an American Indian, he takes consolation in tribal traditions where the warrior walks in front, defending his family at all costs. He believes this tradition is essential to his own survival, as well as the survival of society.

Clinical Questions

How much combat did you experience?
When I went to the quarter-cab, because we were a small unit, basically I worked the night shift; which was from six in the evening till six in the morning. I was available during the day, so if someone needed a break on a helicopter, one of the door gunners, I could fly on a slick, or on a loach, slicks being the ones that were hauling the infantry guys in. The loaches were light observation helicopters, part of the hunter-killer team. Sometimes I volunteered to pack the radio, for the radio operator for the aero-rifle platoon, because he never had a break really, except for when one of us would volunteer. And we knew all the call signs and everything, so it was easy for those who worked in operations to do that. So I started getting out on the field more, and there again when you're on the slick, you're putting people in on a hot LZ [landing zone], and you know, you're coming in, and you're getting a call, and it's gonna be hot. That means that they're taking fire already. Enemy's in position, and actually shooting, and you're coming in a helicopter in line; six helicopters, dropping off infantry guys. You've got a door gunner on one side or the other, or both sides keeping a suppressing fire going, and trying to get the guys off the helicopter, hoping they're not going to shoot a rocket-propelled grenade [RPG], which will take out your helicopter, which happened periodically. Then you lift up outta there, leave the aero-rifle platoon there, and fly off and sit down someplace reasonably safe while they get their butts shot up, and then you go back and help pick up what's left, and hopefully nobody's hurt, and everything goes off smooth. But sometimes you gotta pack up bodies or wounded or whatever, depends on the situation.

Probably the worst situation that we got into was late in November of '69. We went in on a mission that we started getting hit with rocket-propelled grenades. We had 21 actually wounded, out of the 28, and 14 severely, that had to be replaced. Actually, two of those were dead, and uh, 12 were wounded seriously and shipped out. Never saw a gook. It was all RPGs. Every time we'd get people moved around and stacked up, and trying to get the choppers in, they'd lob in three or four more RPGs, and right in amongst the wounded. Getting wounded again, two, and three, four times the same person. Never saw anybody; and no way to return fire. Finally got out of there, and because of that, we felt: "Oh wow. We'll probably get a break now." You know, because we lost 14 guys, and we're an all-volunteer unit. But no, we went right down to Zion, where the guys come in from the first infantry division, and picked up 14 more, and brought 'em straight up, and went on a mission that afternoon. Took them in, and lost two of them, trying to train them on how to get on and off helicopters and do a sweep. One of 'em pulled a trip wire in the hedgerow, and blew himself up and another up, but then it was right back to business. Keep on going. You can't stop; there's no break.

How did the combat experiences change you?

I came back home on a 30-day leave, and saw a bunch of the people I went to school with. They're still hanging out at the Arctic Circle, getting hamburgers, and I realize they were kids. And I wasn't a kid anymore. And I'd never be able to see the world the way they did.

Do you ever have intrusive thoughts?

I had a nightmare for a number of years. A pile of bodies that follows me around. Seeing the eyes, and just this huge, overwhelming pile of bodies.

Do you ever have flashback experiences?

If I was drinking alcohol, I'd probably be more likely to have a flashback. I ended up in a number of situations where I was drunk, and it's just all that stuff that is shut off, that's coming back. And you're in the jungle, and you're feeling threatened, and you don't have a weapon and you're looking for a weapon, and it's really crazy. Someone gets in my face and gets angry, and then doesn't want to take it to the extreme. And people are dragging you away. It's a really scary thing, because when I get in that position, I shut off. I just want to go for it. I want to go to the extreme. Be on top of everything. And alcohol tended to get me there if anybody got in my way. If no one bothered me when I'm feeling—everything was fine. But if anybody confronted me in any way, shape, or form, then all that anger and all that stuff would come out. And then, all of a sudden, there was VC [Viet Cong] around. So I stayed away from alcohol. Smoking pot was okay. Kept me mellow, kept me detached, and kept me so I could

sleep at night. I'd get my four hours of sleep and feel okay.

Differential Diagnosis

Although Carl's symptoms seem clearly connected with his combat experiences while on duty in Vietnam, a clinician might also consider whether he now suffers symptoms of substance dependence, given his chronic use of alcohol and marijuana. Carl also suffers from chronic nightmares, a symptom of sleep terror disorder. Given the connection of both symptoms with the anxiety and his history of involvement in combat, the diagnosis of PTSD seems warranted.

DISCUSSION QUESTIONS

1. Which symptoms of PTSD does Carl describe in this segment?
2. How much do you think Carl's PTSD was exacerbated by the reactions of people in his hometown when he returned?

RESEARCH: Do People Benefit from Trauma? The Question of Post-Traumatic Growth

The wars and terrorist acts in recent years have highlighted the ways in which exposure to life-threatening events profoundly affects traumatized victims. Although there is no question that the exposure has a widespread impact on an individual's functioning, researchers are beginning to find that some people actually grow in important emotional ways following the experience of trauma. The phenomenon is known as *post-traumatic growth.*

At first, it might seem inconceivable that people might feel that they have benefited from being victimized through war, physical assault, accident, or severe illness. However, as pointed out by Zoellner and Maercker (2006), clients can "find their own specific meanings, interpretations, ways of coping and recovery" (p. 650). Although it is important not to minimize the suffering of traumatized clients, they also urge

therapists to view the aftereffects of trauma more broadly than simply focusing on the negative impact of trauma.

In a meta-analysis of nearly 90 investigations, Helgeson, Reynolds, and Tomich (2006) examined the relations of "benefit finding" to psychological and physical health. They identified individuals they labeled "benefit finders" who are able to emerge from a traumatic experience with a more positive sense of well-being. Although less depressed than other trauma victims, benefit finders also tended to experience intrusive and avoidant thoughts about their trauma. In their effort to explain this seeming inconsistency, Helgeson and colleagues suggest that the cognitive processing that goes on in the minds of trauma survivors may actually be attempts to understand the traumatic events rather than a symptom of mental distress. They state that "a period of contemplation and consideration of the stressor" may be necessary for growth to occur (p. 810).

How might clinicians help a traumatized client perceive the beneficial aftereffects of trauma survival? Because traumatic events are usually linked to life threats, clinicians can help their clients become more aware of their own mortality and the fragility of life in general, with the result being a greater appreciation for life in general. Furthermore, traumatized individuals may be consumed by "why did it happen" questions which have no clear answer. No one can explain to the innocent victims of a random terrorist act why it was they who were injured. However, clinicians working with these clients might guide them in a process of deriving at least some meaning from the tragic experience (Zoellner & Maercker, 2006).

Helgeson, V. S., Reynolds, K. A., & Tomich, P. L. (2006). A meta-analytic review of benefit finding and growth. *Journal of Consulting and Clinical Psychology, 74,* 797–816.
Zoellner, T., & Maercker, A. (2006). Posttraumatic growth in clinical psychology—A critical review and introduction of a two component model. *Clinical Psychology Review, 26,* 626–653.

Chapter 6 Somatoform Disorders, Psychological Factors Affecting Medical Conditions, and Dissociative Disorders

RESEARCH: Body Dysmorphic Disorder and Suicide

In a society that values a perfect appearance, self-consciousness about the body can be a tormenting condition for some people. Although body dysmorphic disorder (BDD) is a well-established clinical condition, its prevalence rates have recently been found to be higher than was previously thought. In the largest study to date on the prevalence rates of BDD, Rief and colleagues (2006) surveyed over 4,000 Germans. The prevalence rate of BDD was estimated to be 1.7 percent. The most commonly disliked body parts were skin, hair, breasts (women), and chest (men). The rates of cosmetic surgery among those with body dysmorphic disorder were significantly higher than the rates in the general population. Interestingly, individuals with BDD reported lower income, lower rates of having a partner, and higher unemployment rates than individuals who did not meet the BDD criteria. Individuals with BDD also had elevated rates of suicidal ideation and suicidal attempts.

Supporting Rief and colleagues' findings on the German sample, Phillips and Menard (2006) reported on the results of a prospective observational study of 200 clients with BDD.

From 45 to 70 percent of the individuals in this study reported a history of suicidal ideation. Their mean annual suicidal ideation rate of 57.8 percent is approximately 10 to 25 times higher than that found in the U.S. population as a whole, and the 2.6 percent rate of suicide is between 3 and 12 times higher than in the general population. When variables of age, gender, and geography are factored into the equation, the completed suicide rate for those with BDD is 45 times higher than that found in the general population.

With such potentially dire consequences, it is clear that clinicians must take body dysmorphic disorder very seriously. Clients may not always report bodily dissatisfaction, and so it is therefore incumbent upon clinicians to screen for symptoms of this potentially very disabling condition.

Phillips, K. A., & Menard, W. (2006). Suicidality in body dysmorphic disorder: A prospective study. *American Journal of Psychiatry, 163,* 1280–1282.
Rief, Q., Buhlmann, U., Wilhelm, S., Borkenhagen, A., & Brahler, E. (2006). The prevalence of body dysmorphic disorder: A population-based survey. *Psychological Medicine, 36,* 877-885.

Chapter 7 Sexual Disorders

RESEARCH: Efforts to Understand and Treat Individuals Addicted to Child Pornography

As the Internet has expanded, a countless number of websites devoted to pornography are now online. The sexual exploitation of children for pornographic purposes has provoked international outrage and alarm. The U.S. Department of Justice has aggressively pursued those who produce and those who purchase child pornography (Finkelhor & Ormrod, 2004), yet the deviously innovative ways in which child pornography is disseminated makes the task increasingly difficult. Unfortunately, the stigma associated with this behavior makes it unlikely that people who feel addicted to child pornography seek professional help. Most do so only after receiving a court mandate for treatment.

Although the behavior is notoriously difficult to treat, there are several strategies being developed that appear to have promise. Middleton, Beech, and Mandeville-Norden (2004) suggest that treatment focus on the difficulty in dealing with negative emotions experienced by child pornography offenders. For them, sex is a coping mechanism. According to these researchers, therapy should focus on helping the individuals develop ways to manage negative affect. It is also important to help them acquire greater empathic awareness regarding the child victims of pornography.

Another approach focuses on the personal values (Quayle, Vaughan, & Taylor, 2006). The goal of this type of intervention is to help clients accept negative emotions and commit themselves to generating behavioral goals that help them move toward what they personally value. The task is challenging because the therapist is asking the client to forgo the immediate pleasure and gratification that comes from accessing and using child abuse images.

Distress tolerance is a second therapeutic technique. Clients are taught strategies for tolerating distress in ways that allow them to meet their personal goals. According to Quayle and colleagues (2006), clients can be taught to distract themselves from their addiction, to find ways to comfort themselves when experiencing negative emotions, to restructure

their interpretations of events, and to weigh the pros and cons of tolerating versus not tolerating the distress that they feel.

Clinicians working with pornography-addicted clients, particularly those drawn to child pornography, recognize that the clinical work is challenging and intense. Those professionals who can approach their clients as individuals who usually experience profound conflict and distress about their unacceptable behavior, may be able to help their clients change the course of their lives.

Finkelhor, D., & Ormrod, R. (2004, December). *Child pornography: Patterns from NIBRS* (Juvenile Justice Bulletin NCJ 204911). Washington, DC: U.S. Department of Justice, Office of Justice Programs, Office of Juvenile Justice and Delinquency Prevention.

Middleton, D., Beech, A., & Mandeville-Norden, R. (2004). What sort of a person could do that? Psychological profiles of Internet pornography users. Paper presented at the 5th COPINE Conference, Cork, May 2004.

Quayle, E., Vaughan, M., & Taylor, M. (2006). Sex offenders, Internet child abuse images and emotional avoidance: The importance of values. *Aggression and Violent Behavior, 11,* 1-11.

Chapter 8   Mood Disorders

FACES: **Dysthymic Disorder**

DSM CRITERIA

- For a period lasting at least 2 years people with dysthymic disorder experience depressed mood for most of the day, for more days than not, and experience significant distress or impairment.
- While depressed, these individuals experience at least two of the following: poor appetite or overeating; insomnia or hypersomnia; low energy or fatigue; low self-esteem; poor concentration or difficulty making decisions; and feelings of hopelessness.
- During the 2-year period the individual has never been without these symptoms for 2 consecutive months.
- The individual has not (1) had a major depressive episode during the 2 years; (2) ever had a manic, mixed, or hypomanic episode; (3) met the criteria for cyclothymic disorder; (4) experienced the symptoms during the course of a chronic psychotic disorder; or (5) developed the symptoms as a direct result of a medical condition or use of a substance.

Brief Case History

Robert lives alone in a tiny apartment, has no hobbies, and knows only a few acquaintances. He has been sad for as

long as he can remember. At the time of the interview he was 39 years old. Robert struggles to explain his feelings. Sometimes he says he feels they are rooted in the bullies who picked on him during his childhood. At other times he says that his mother hugged him too much. At still other times he blames the fact that he grew up in poverty. Although the cause is not clear, Robert feels fearful and withdrawn, and has suffered from dysthymia for more than 20 years. Compared to individuals who suffer from major depression, Robert's despair is less severe. He does not dwell on thoughts of suicide, and he seems clearheaded. Although his depression is not severe, it has been persistent, and he has suffered without relief through his entire adult life. Having been diagnosed with dysthymic disorder in his

early twenties, Robert receives monthly disability checks from Social Security. He occasionally works at a sheltered workplace, but spends most of his time by himself, eating, masturbating, and watching television. Over the years, Robert has received a variety of treatments including medication and behavior modification. He has also participated in support networks that attempt to get him involved in community activities. Unfortunately, these treatments have not succeeded. Robert admits that he has not taken his treatment very seriously, and his abuse of recreational drugs has very likely interfered with his ability to benefit from treatment.

Clinical Questions

If you think back, when was the first time you went into depression?

When I started taking drugs. The feeling of being high, and then coming off drugs, and feeling like you're needing the drug, and you need a lift so you go back and do it over, over again. For me, it was when I first started experimenting with marijuana. It was a vicious cycle, and I became so engulfed in it that it literally set me on a whirlwind that I'm still reeling from to this day; you know, and I don't deal with drugs or alcohol, but its impact is tremendous. I would never suggest to anybody to experiment with drugs. It's not worth the risk.

What is causing you to feel this sadness, this dysthymia?

How I am toward myself. How I allow myself to take care of me. I can't seem to take care of me. I can't seem to be loving toward me. I'm in a house, and I'm able to have this, and I don't have to worry financially about it. You'd think that would be enough. I just tend to see the flipside, the dark side; the woe-is-me I feel sorry for myself pity-pity side. It takes a lot of energy; to, to be like this. And it really wipes me out, literally. If you direct your energy to negative things, you're going to get negative. But it's all a matter of what you do with the energy. It can be good; it can be bad. It's where you focus it. And I tend to focus it on a negative level.

What is the worst part of your life?

Having to live with my own limitations. The people who love me know that I'm more than that; and I'm not doing it. And I'm not giving what I should be giving, and the potential that Robert has to give. Not giving what one has. If you have a computer, and it's not giving you what you want, you're not gonna be happy. I'm not happy with my limiting view of myself.

What are some of the other diagnoses of psychiatric difficulties that you've had?

The possibility is that I might be bipolar. They've asked me if I've taken lithium or any other kind of drugs. So I seem to be going through ups and downs, highs and lows, sleep disturbances. When I was first

diagnosed, I was literally a basket case. They fed me Stelazine and I ended up in Mount Sinai hospital in New York, and I stayed there for a month; and I was totally immobilized by the drugs. I've taken a number of different medications, and have different diagnoses over the years, but things change. It's been hard because new medications come on the market. Old ones stop working, or you have to increase them, so there's always flexibility, and you have to take your chances. It's literally a gamble finding what works and using it to your best effort.

Do you ever experience delusions? Can you describe them?

Things are centered around me. I'm an important person 'cause my brother's a big shot in New York connected with academia and politics. So I say that's the reason why they're doing it—to persecute me, to persecute him, or something like that. For something he's doing. Could be gangs, could be homosexuals, could be white

supremacists, could be neo-Nazis; could be anybody that values the difference of my Hispanic-ness, or my maleness, and wants to hurt me.

Differential Diagnosis

Robert's symptoms of depressed mood have persisted for many years. However, throughout the time he has suffered from these symptoms, he has also smoked marijuana. The diagnosis of substance abuse can be comorbid with dysthymic disorder, and although Robert does not seem to be taking drugs at the moment, he may be suffering long-term effects of marijuana use. Dysthymic disorder is not associated with delusions; therefore, Robert's statements that he feels that he is being persecuted by virtue of his brother's position suggests that he may either be experiencing symptoms of a paranoid personality disorder or the effects of long-term psychoactive substance use. The clinician would be careful to assess the nature and history of such symptoms before confirming the diagnosis of dysthymic disorder.

DISCUSSION QUESTIONS

1. How does dysthymic disorder differ from major depressive disorder?
2. How much control do you think Robert has over the way he feels and his inability to overcome the despair associated with dysthymic disorder?
3. What treatment options are available to Robert?

RESEARCH: Do Antidepressant Medications Put Children at Risk of Suicide?

In 2004 the U.S. Food and Drug Administration (FDA) issued a public health advisory warning about the increased risk of suicidal thoughts and behaviors of antidepressant medications for children and adolescents. Pharmaceutical companies were instructed to add a warning about the risks of the medications and the importance of close monitoring of all patients. Although the FDA did not prohibit the prescription of such medications to children, health care professionals were alerted to the risk of suicidality and were urged to balance the risk with consideration of clinical need.

The action of the FDA provoked considerable alarm within the mental health profession and understandable concern on the part of parents. Several epidemiological studies were initiated, but unfortunately they produced conflicting findings.

Kaizar and colleagues (2006) concluded that there is only a weak causal link between antidepressant use and suicidality in children. In contrast, Tiihonen and colleagues (2006) concluded that although antidepressants are not related to suicide attempts and death in adults, there is such a relationship among young people.

There are several considerations to take into account in resolving the conflicting findings. First, it is possible that antidepressants are selectively prescribed to more severely depressed children and adolescents, who are already at increased risk for suicidal behavior. Second, matching of research subjects may not be possible with regard to certain unknown factors, such as family history of suicide, imitation and contagion phenomena, stressful precipitating events, and access to lethal methods. Third, the tracking of prescriptions is not optimally precise due to the fact that some patients obtain free samples from physicians, other patients may take less than prescribed, and others may discontinue taking their prescribed medication. Fourth, the accuracy of the death category "suicide" may be questionable due to social stigma or religious beliefs (Tiihonen et al., 2006).

It is clear that more carefully controlled research is needed on the relationship between suicide and the use of antidepressant medication. In the meantime, clinicians have been advised to proceed cautiously with the recommendation of antidepressant medications for children. The risks and the benefits must be carefully weighed, and such prescriptions should be considered only in the most serious cases in which alternative interventions have first been attempted.

Kaizar, E. E., Greenhouse, J. B., Seltman, H., & Kelleher, K. Do antidepressants cause suicidality in children? *Clinical Trials, 3,* 73–98.

Tiihonen, J. Lonnqvist, J., Wahlbeck, K., Klauukka, T., Tanskanen, A., & Haukka, J. (2006). Antidepressants and risk of suicide, attempted suicide, and overall mortality in a nationwide cohort. *Archives of General Psychiatry, 63,* 1358–1367.

Chapter 9   Schizophrenia and Related Disorders

FACES: Paranoid Schizophrenia

DSM CRITERIA

- People with schizophrenia experience a disturbance that lasts at least 6 months and includes at least 1 month of active symptoms, including at least two of the following: delusions; hallucinations; disorganized speech; disturbed or catatonic behavior; and negative symptoms, such as flat affect or severe lack of motivation.
- For a significant period of time since symptom onset, they have experienced dysfunction in work, relationships, or self-care.
- The symptoms are not due to another disorder, a medical condition, or substances.
- People with paranoid schizophrenia are preoccupied with frequent auditory hallucinations or delusions.

Brief Case History

Throughout her childhood, Valerie felt like a social outcast although she was close to her parents. Valerie graduated from college and married in her midtwenties. Her symptoms first developed when she was 28 years old: She began experiencing delusions that people were plotting against her. Over time, her delusions grew more complex and disturbing, and ultimately, she became highly agitated. Her husband had her involuntarily committed to a psychiatric hospital at that time. While in the asylum, Valerie felt that she was being imprisoned and that the doctors were

performing experiments on her. Her delusional state persisted for many months. Eventually the medications reduced Valerie's psychotic symptoms, and she was released from the hospital. Unfortunately, the medications produced significant side effects, and Valerie often refused to take them. Whenever she stopped her medications, her symptoms worsened, and each time she was institutionalized. Valerie has experienced delusions of persecution (that people were plotting to hurt her and her family), delusions of reference (the television programs were secretly referring to her), and delusions of grandeur (that her actions could help save the world). After over 8 years, Valerie states that she has finally accepted her diagnosis, and is now stabilized on medication, holding down a steady job, and living with her parents. She once had dreams of traveling and earning her PhD but now seems content just to live day to day, going to work, and returning home. She states that she has no particular interest in becoming involved in an intimate relationship.

Clinical Questions

When did you first start to become mentally ill?

I kinda slipped from reality into unreality without any sharp change. It was a gradual thing. I didn't think there was anything wrong with me. But obviously, the people around me did. With most people, mental illness usually hits around like 23 or 25. I didn't get sick until about 28 or 29, which is a little later than the average. I was fortunate. I already had my graduate school education out of the way by the time I got to the point where I was sick. But then once I was sick, I was unable to work for 10 to 12 years. They were trying different medications, and some worked better than others. And I had been hospitalized 10 times. And I had other episodes during those years of terror and fear, and so forth.

Did you experience visual hallucinations, seeing things that weren't there?

Only on two occasions. One time I saw two angels, and one time I saw Christ. Those hallucinations were beautiful. That's the thing with this mental illness. You can have bad ones, and you can have good ones. And the good ones, I wouldn't mind having again! When I saw Christ in the heavens, it was absolutely gorgeous! Beautiful rosy-red sky and Jesus standing there, with a crown on his head, and arms outspread. It was a beautiful vision. I talked to the preacher about it, and he said it was probably 'cause of all the medicine I was on. So who knows.

Your case file describes an incident where there was a conspiracy involving cars and computers. Can you explain that?

I was off my medicine at the time because of the side effects. I couldn't tolerate the side effects. I hadn't completely accepted the fact that I had a mental illness either. It's sort of like AA. You have to come to a point where you realize you have a problem before you start growing and building. At this point in my life, I hadn't totally accepted that I was mentally ill, so I went off the medicine again. I had this hallucination that all the cars in the United States were plugged into a giant computer system that controlled where they went, and how much traffic was going at any given time at any place in the country. [*Note:* She is describing a delusion, not a hallucination.] I had this idea in my mind that if I didn't get out and drive the car for so many hours every day, somebody in my

family would be killed. Me and all people who believed like me in my imaginary world had to go out and do time driving cars, tying up the computer system, and then these other people wouldn't die. At the time, it made perfect sense. I'd get out there and drive for hours. At one point in time, I drove all the way to Idaho. I went three days without sleeping, and finally I ended up in a car accident. I crashed into a rock wall.

What were you thinking and feeling when you were having these delusions?

It seemed very real. There was a terrible fear of death. I was really into the religious thing, and martyrdom, and that I may have to be a martyr and die for my faith because people were against me because of my beliefs. I believed that maybe there'd be a bomb in the car, and the car would blow up, because they'd want to kill me that way, or maybe they'd want to strangle me, or they'd come to my home and drag me off somewhere, and torture me. There was a lot of definite fear, just pure, raw fear.

Have you found any medications that work for you?

The medicine they put me on then was Haldol pills, but they didn't work for me. Today, I take Haldol shots, and the shots work fine without any side effects. I've been on Haldol shots 9 years. At one point, I had a problem finding a provider, and I was unable to get my shots for

3 months. And I started to have one episode. I had this fantasy that I was the Virgin Mary. I knew I wasn't the Virgin Mary, and I knew something was wrong with this hallucination in my head, like I was in charge of the whole psych ward. [*Note:* This was a delusion.] Something inside of me said, "This isn't right. You've gotta get back on the shots." So I redoubled my efforts to find another provider, and I found one right away, and went back on the shots. And I'm fine again.

Differential Diagnosis

Although Valerie shows classic symptoms of paranoid schizophrenia, a clinician would seek to determine if she has a physical condition or has abused substances that may contribute to her delusional beliefs. Valerie meets the criteria for schizophrenia in terms of the length of time she has suffered from delusional symptoms, but the clinician may also wish to consider that she has schizoid personality disorder on Axis II, based on her years of feeling isolated and distant from other people.

DISCUSSION QUESTIONS

1. How does a clinician begin treating a client with delusions?
2. Should someone suffering from schiziophrenia and delusions be held accountable for his or her actions?

RESEARCH: Cognitive-Behavioral Treatment for Schizophrenia

The widespread availability and use of antipsychotic medications beginning in the second half of the twentieth century came at the expense of traditional forms of psychotherapy. Although there is no doubt that the antipsychotic medications, particularly the newer generation of atypical psychotherapeutic agents, have contributed to the alleviation of much suffering associated with chronic schizophrenia, some symptoms of the disorder nevertheless are thought of as more amenable to behavioral treatment. Moreover, we know that there are a number of serious side effects associated with antipsychotic medications and that some symptoms of schizophrenia do not diminish even with medication. If psychotherapy can help reduce some of the symptoms of schizophrenia, it might reduce the extent to which individuals must rely on medications as well as improve their levels of functioning on a daily basis.

Several large-scale analyses of published data suggest that cognitive-behavioral therapy, in which clients are helped to monitor and control their symptoms, can have positive effects above and beyond the reduction of symptoms due to medication. In cognitive-behavioral therapy, clients are taught to identify mistakes in thinking and gain insight into the relationship among thoughts, feelings, and behaviors. Zimmerman and colleagues (2005) analyzed the findings from 14 studies conducted between 1990 and 2004 on nearly 1,500 clients, including those suffering from both acute and chronic schizophrenia. Cognitive-behavioral therapy was found to be effective as an adjunct to medication, particularly when clients were in the acute phase of the disorder. Moreover, the positive effects of therapy persisted over long-term follow-up. Although medication clearly is necessary to control many of the symptoms of this disorder, there are benefits of focusing on treating symptoms through psychotherapy.

Given that cognitive-behavioral therapy may be less effective for treating people with chronic schizophrenia than for those who are in the acute phase of the disorder, are there any interventions that would help long-term sufferers? For many years, social skills training was considered the only adjunct to medication that would help reduce the aberrant behaviors associated with schizophrenia, but it is not particularly effective in reducing psychotic symptoms. Putting together cognitive-behavioral therapy with social skills training would combine the best of both worlds to provide clients with help in changing their thinking while improving their abilities to function in the world. Researchers have in fact found that even among a population of middle-aged and older adults with chronic

schizophrenia and schizoaffective disorder seemingly resistant to improvements from psychotherapy, the combination of the two methods can result in more effective social functioning (Patterson et al., 2006). As challenging as this disorder can be to treat, it is nevertheless possible to see improvements by supplementing medication with psychotherapeutic methods.

Patterson, T. L., Mausbach, B. T., McKibbin, C., Goldman, S., Bucardo, J., & Jeste, D. V. (2006). Functional adaptation skills training (FAST): A randomized trial of a psychosocial intervention for middle-aged and older patients with chronic psychotic disorders. *Schizophrenia Research, 86,* 291–299.

Zimmermann, G., Favrod, J., Trieu, V. H., & Pomini, V. (2005). The effect of cognitive behavioral treatment on the positive symptoms of schizophrenia spectrum disorders: A meta-analysis. *Schizophrenia Research, 77,* 1–9.

Chapter 10 Personality Disorders

FACES: Borderline Personality Disorder

DSM CRITERIA

Borderline personality disorder is a diagnosis assigned to people who show recurrent impulsivity and a pervasive pattern of instability of interpersonal relationships, self-image, and affect as indicated by five or more of the following:

- Frantic efforts to avoid real or imagined abandonment
- A pattern of unstable and intense interpersonal relationships characterized by changes between idealizing and devaluing others
- Identity disturbance: unstable self-image or sense of self
- Impulsivity in at least two areas, such as spending, sex, substance abuse, and reckless driving
- Recurrent suicidal behavior, gestures, threats, or self-mutilating behavior
- Emotional instability, such as intense episodes of sadness, irritability, or anxiety, usually lasting a few hours and sometimes several days
- Chronic feelings of emptiness
- Inappropriate, intense anger or difficulty controlling anger, such as frequent displays of temper, constant anger, or recurrent physical fights
- Occasional stress-related paranoid thinking or dissociative symptoms

Brief Case History

At the time of the interview, Becky was 24 years old, working in customer relations for a large corporation while attending school part time. A bright and ambitious woman, she is also deeply troubled. As an adolescent, she got into vicious fights with her family and friends. She spiraled in and out of relationships, alternating between idolizing and scorning others. She was raised in a Mormon church, and while she once found great meaning in that faith, she now renounces it. Becky has very little sense of who she is and believes that her persona is a fraud. She has received compliments and promotions at work, but somehow she believes that she is not really legitimate. Even when people like and admire her, she feels that she has somehow fooled them. Becky expresses serious self-doubt and internal conflict, sometimes directing this anger toward herself in the form of self-mutilation. Becky is currently living with her father,

and while she admits that this is less than ideal, she knows that it is better than living alone. Although she has problems dealing with people, she is most self-injurious when she is living alone.

Clinical Questions

How do you feel about the world? Do you like people?

The human race never ceases to amaze me with their stupidity. I think mankind will ultimately kill himself off. Whether it be an apocalypse with meteoroids coming down, something out of our control you know. It could be nuclear bombs, it could be computers—I mean, take into account all the different movies, all the different theories, people have thought about this before. The world sucks. People are horrible. They're mean. They're spiteful. . . . It's hard to see any good in it.

Tell us about how you make friends. And do your friendships tend to last?

Once I, once I think that someone is someone I could be friends with, someone I could trust, um, then it's very easy to become my friend. But you have to get through that first barrier. I like people who are honest, I like people who are open. I like people who are kind. And any breach of that, and they're just gone. Once they're in, and they're a friend, um—I can draw them in really fast—with complete, complete devotion, complete attention. Then after about 2 years it's like

all of the newness is gone, and you're getting down to the point where everything's routine, and they're gonna start to notice how you actually deal with things. And so, at that point, they then start to see who you really were. And that just can't happen, so either faze them out, or I just drop 'em cold; just stop talking to them. And I feel horrible, because they ask, What did I do? You know, what did I do that's wrong? And it just kills me inside because I know that I'm hurting them, but I can't stop. I can't stop not . . . being friends with them. And then I move on to the next person, and the same thing happens again.

Is physical contact important to you?

I feed off of physical contact. I'm a very touchy-feely person, if you're in my little circle, or whatever. But, I mean, if I don't get that physical contact, that's another trigger; I'll just start to go off into one of my cutting phases; if I'm feeling like that, it takes a TV show that hits me the wrong way; that triggers me. All of a sudden, before I know it, I'm cutting.

How does sadness lead to your hurting yourself?

Well you start out sad, and you're crying, and you're really upset. So you get up, and you walk around, and you try to do something different and distract yourself, and I went in my room to make my bed. I didn't do it right, so then I'm like, what the hell is wrong with me? And then I start thinking about work, and I start thinking about school, still trying to distract myself, mind you. I'm not as far along in school as I'd like, and I don't like the huge corporation I work for, and so, how the hell am I even functioning out in the real world? And, I don't know, it just gets more grandiose as it goes on, and finally, why am I even here? What the hell is wrong with me, why. . . . What's the point to everything?

Differential Diagnosis

Personality disorders are characterized by patterns of rigid, inflexible, and maladaptive behaviors. The key diagnostic criteria for borderline personality disorder include disturbances in sense of self, instability, difficulties maintaining boundaries in relationships, and patterns of self-injurious behavior. Becky clearly demonstrates those symptoms. However, a clinician diagnosing Becky would con-

sider the possibility that her symptoms result from major depressive disorder, an Axis I disorder, particularly as evident in her low self-esteem. In terms of other personality disorders, Becky might also be considered to have symptoms of narcissistic personality disorder, due to her tendency to regard others as serving her needs. She might also be considered to have symptoms of dependent personality disorder in that she has difficulty maintaining her independence from others, particularly when she perceives that they threaten her with abandonment.

DISCUSSION QUESTIONS

1. What developmental events can contribute to borderline personality disorder?
2. Why might people with borderline personality disorder be difficult people with whom to interact? How would they be in a therapy session?

RESEARCH: Treatment Effectiveness with Borderline Personality Disorder

People with personality disorders have long-standing, deeply entrenched patterns of behavior that do not change easily, thus making psychotherapy a challenging and complex process. Clinicians who treat individuals with borderline personality disorder are cautious about suggesting that their interventions will have dramatic and lasting effects.

In exploring which factors are most predictive of outcome, Gunderson and colleagues (2006) concluded that, not surprisingly, clients who are more seriously disturbed at the outset of therapy are most likely to have poor therapy outcomes. In addition, they identified a history of father-daughter incest or parental brutality as another major predictive factor. Unfortunately, these findings raise questions about the extent to which psychotherapeutic intervention can benefit individuals with

more severe forms of borderline symptomatology and histories of childhood abuse.

One particular finding by Gunderson and colleagues (2006) provides a treatment route with a greater potential for successful intervention. Individuals with borderline personality disorder who are less likely to experience interpersonal instability and impaired relationships with current family members and children are also more responsive to positive therapeutic outcomes. This conclusion is especially helpful to clinicians, because it provides a possible focus that can be incorporated into a treatment plan. The overall benefit of therapy can be enhanced by developing a treatment strategy that tries to addresses troubled relationships and help the client improve the quality and experience of those relationships. Clinicians are urged to conduct a thorough examination of current relationships and past relational history, attending specifically to a history of early childhood maltreatment.

Another finding from recent work on emotion dysregulation provides additional insights into the elements of successful therapy with individuals suffering from borderline personality. Emotion dysregulation refers to a lack of awareness, understanding, or acceptance of emotions; an inability to control the intensity or duration of emotions; an unwillingness to experience emotional distress as an aspect of pursuing goals; and the inability to engage in goal-directed behaviors when experiencing distress (Gratz et al., 2006). Clinicians treating clients with borderline personality disorder can improve the likelihood of more positive outcomes by helping their clients become more aware of their emotions and better able to control them, especially in the context of their interpersonal relationships.

Gratz, K. L., Rosenthal, M. Z., Tull, M. T., Lejuez, C. W., & Gunderson, J. G. (2006). An experimental investigation of emotion dysregulation in borderline personality disorder. *Journal of Abnormal Psychology, 115,* 850–855.

Gunderson, J. G., Daversa, M. T., Grilo, C. M., McGlashan, T. H., Bender, D.S., Dyck, I. R., Mcrey, L. C., Stout, R. L., Zanarini, M. C., Shea, M. T., Skodol, A. E., Yen, S. & Sanislow, C. (2006). Predictors of 2-year outcome for patients with borderline personality disorder. *American Journal of Psychiatry, 163,* 822–826.

Chapter 11 Development-Related Disorders

FACES: Attention-Deficit/ Hyperactivity Disorder

DSM CRITERIA

- With an onset of symptoms before the age of 7 that cause impairment in at least two settings, individuals with attention-deficit/hyperactivity disorder (ADHD) show either a pattern of inattention or hyperactivity-impulsivity.
- Inattention is characterized by a pattern consisting of at least six of the following symptoms, which have persisted for at least 6 months: (1) makes careless mistakes or fails to attend to details; (2) has difficulty sustaining attention; (3) doesn't listen when spoken to; (4) doesn't follow through on instructions or responsibilities; (5) has difficulty organizing activities; (6) avoids tasks requiring sustained mental effort; (7) loses items necessary for tasks; (8) is easily distracted; and (9) is often forgetful.
- Hyperactivity-impulsivity is characterized by symptoms including: (1) often fidgets or squirms; (2) often leaves seat inappropriately; (3) often runs about or climbs excessively when it is inappropriate; (4) often has difficulty playing or engaging in leisure activities; (5) is often "on the go" or acts as if "driven by a motor"; and (6) often talks excessively.
- Impulsivity is characterized by symptoms including: (1) often blurts out answers before questions have been completed; (2) often has difficulty awaiting turn; and (3) often interrupts or intrudes.

- Types include (1) combined type, (2) predominantly inattentive type, and (3) predominantly hyperactive-inattentive type.

Brief Case History

David is a 16-year-old high school sophomore, who for the most part is similar to other boys his age. He is energetic, a bit rebellious, and consumed by sports and video games. David says that he has been hyperactive for as long as he can remember. When David's elementary school teachers complained to his mother about his behavior, she brought him to a professional who prescribed medication, which he has taken intermittently since childhood. During the school year, David takes a combination of Wellbutrin and Ritalin. Although medication has helped David focus and do better in school, he has mixed feelings, asserting that they make him feel hazy and nonsocial. David's ADHD affects most aspects of his life. Because he is so inattentive and hyperactive, his interactions with peers are often strained, leaving him feeling ostracized. He finds it nearly impossible to study, explaining that the words jump around the page. David is embarrassed about being somewhat different from his peers.

Clinical Questions

What is the hardest part of school?

I usually get in trouble 'cause I don't ever shut up. I always talk back to teachers and stuff. And this year, I did really good. I rarely got any like, you know, referrals or whatever those things are. I barely got any. You'd see me in the office once or twice a month; I didn't get in very much trouble at all; except for in math class. I always get sent out in math class, every single day. But I didn't get a referral; I just got sent out, 'cause—for being loud.

Has it become easier to control yourself as you have gotten older?

Once you get older, you find out a way to control it a little bit; sometimes you can't control it; I mean like, you just like make noises or like, bounce off of walls; I mean, you try to be quiet, but then—it's like, you'll be quiet for a couple minutes when that person tells you to, but then a couple minutes later, you're not even realizing— they'll be telling you to be quiet again, 'cause you don't like, always know that you're being annoying or whatever.

Why do you get in trouble?

I talk a lot. Make noises. I don't even do it on purpose sometimes. I just be like, making noises or like humming in my mind or something like that, or just weird noises. And the teacher always tells me to be quiet.

Are you able to learn things in school?

I don't learn like other kids. I only learn about something if I like it. Otherwise, I might remember it for a little while, and then ask me a week later, and I won't even know what you're talking about. I can study all I want, and I won't even remember anything. I could read the chapter five times; I won't remember it. So, I have to find different ways on how to . . . get things in my mind to remember it. I have to make it fun, I guess. Make it so I wanna learn about it.

How does the ADHD interfere with your studying?

You can't like, read like other kids can. You can't sit down in, like, one spot. You start squirming and moving around, and just, I don't know, disrupt other people in the class. And you just can't sit there and try to read. You can only read for like a—I

couldn't read very long. The words'll be bouncing all over the page. I mean it just—literally, they'd be gone, and I can't see 'em—they'd get blurry, and weird. It's just really weird. You can't pay attention very well.

Differential Diagnosis

A clinician consulting with David would most likely diagnose him with ADHD following a careful evaluation, but might also consider the possibility that David has bipolar disorder, a condition that in recent years has been more frequently diagnosed in children and adolescents. In evaluating David's highly energized behavior, the clinician would consider the

diagnostic features of a manic episode, a period of abnormally and persistently elevated, expansive, or irritable mood lasting at least a week. The clinician would also evaluate the possibility that David's behaviors reflect hypomania, rather than full-blown mania. Criteria similar to those that characterize a manic episode would be considered (but in less extreme form). Although David's heightened level of energy might suggest that he has a mood disorder, the assessment data point to a clear-cut diagnosis of ADHD. Even the depression that David experiences can be understood as being related to his ADHD. Rather than chronic or episodic depression, David occasionally feels down because of the frustrations he experiences and encounters in life.

DISCUSSION QUESTIONS

1. If David is aware of his inability to focus and behave, what can he do to help himself change his conduct?
2. Is ADHD overdiagnosed? Is giving this diagnosis an easy way for teachers and parents to explain unacceptable behaviors in children?

FACES: **Tourette's Disorder**

DSM CRITERIA

People with Tourette's disorder experience a combination of chronic movement and vocal tics.

- At some point, though not necessarily at the same time, the individual has had a vocal tic and multiple motor tics.
- For more than a year the tics have occurred many times each day, nearly every day or at intervals.
- During this time, the individual never goes longer than 3 months without tics.
- The symptoms cause distress or impairment.

Brief Case History

Ben began expressing the symptoms of Tourette's disorder when he was only 3 years old. His first symptoms were head twitching and a recurring verbal tic. His

pediatrician assured his mother that everything was normal and that he was just passing through a phase, but his mother was skeptical and insisted on taking Ben to see a specialist. When she did, the neurologist immediately recognized that Ben suffered from Tourette's disorder. (Interestingly, Ben's older brother was also expressing symptoms, and when Ben was diagnosed, his parents realized that his brother also suffered from the disorder.)

Over the years, Ben's symptoms have evolved and grown more severe. Whereas the symptoms were once restricted to head twitching and random sounds, now his entire body can tic and his verbal tics include obscenities. Ben's doctors have experimented with various medications that should reduce his ticking behavior and make it easier for him to mix in society. Unfortunately, the medications are either ineffective or produce such unacceptable side effects as profound lethargy. As a result, Ben and his family have focused on developing behavioral strategies that make it easier for him to cope with his disorder.

The first behavioral strategy is living a healthy lifestyle. Ben's tics reduce when he is active and eating a healthy diet. Second, Ben strives to reduce stress in his life since the tics become more prominent when he is anxious. Third, he is trying to develop social skills that enable him to interact within society in spite of his tics. He finds, for example, that just explaining that he suffers from a neurological disorder often disarms people, and socializing becomes easier.

People with Tourette's disorder seem to lack a neurological mechanism that allows them to eliminate inappropriate actions. Let's face it: We all consider inappropriate words and actions from time to time. But most of us have psychological or biological filters that allow us to suppress those words and actions. Ben lacks such filters. Thus when these inappropriate words come into his mind, he emits them before his conscious mind can suppress them.

Sometimes on public buses racial epithets come into his mind. He said he is unable to purge them from his mind and, despite his best efforts, the words come pouring out of him.

During the interview, I asked Ben about the psychological experience of his tics. What do the tics feel like? Does it feel like an itch, and you need to scratch it? Or is it more like a hiccup that builds or a sneeze that you want to release? Ben thought about it, but seemed confused; his answer was not very helpful. Later on though, his mother observed that for Ben, the tics don't necessarily have any special feeling. To him they are just natural, since the tics have been a part of him since he was an infant. You might as well ask what it feels like to have arms or legs.

In closing, as you may know, the definitions of mental illness evolve over time. People who experienced epileptic seizures, for example, were once considered mentally ill. It was only later, when we were able to clearly identify the neurological defects that caused seizures, that it was considered a disorder of the body and not of the mind. I have to wonder if something similar may happen with Tourette's. As research continues, we will eventually know the particular physiological causes for Tourette's disorder and may even develop a reliable treatment or cure. At that point, Tourette's might be removed from the list of mental illnesses and will be considered a purely medical disorder.

Clinical Questions

When did you first begin ticking?

And . . . um, but what I found, you know, I [tics] uh, it didn't, it didn't really become noticeable until um, about first—first grade, primary—first grade.

What are some of your earliest memories about ticking?

Um, [tic] you know I, I don't remember starting to tic—it was a while back. I—but it probably [tics] if I were to [tic] I would probably st—I would've probably started ticking around first or second grade. Major ticking, like, you know, really noticing them. I mean, there was many different tics, you know. I mean, um, [tic] I would—I used to like, move my head like this, or—and also, I would like, you know, throw my arm out, and, well I mean, not like—not like pssh! But I mean, like, you know—you know, jerk, you know, throw my—flop my arm out like that. Not, not like seizure, I was just, as a tic. Uh [tic] and also [tics] and then my vocal tics would [tics] come on [tics].

Are there different kinds of tics?

You know. I have both physical and [tic]—physical and verbal tics. Personally, I would rather have the physical than the verbal.

What is a thought tic?

It's a thought that's in my head, or, you know, that I didn't mean. Something I—or like, if a thought that I didn't mean like—or, it's maybe something [tic] or it's, it's something that I would not act on it, like—or it's just like an irrational thought. Like, [tic] um [tic] like, for example, example, uh, you know, I might say, oh, I, you know what? Hmm. I, maybe—I just wanna th—I just wanna k—I just wanna kill my brother. Or, I just wanna—I wanna run that dog over. Or, you know, ooh. I just, I have a sick feeling. Ooh. God. These are thoughts. Not feelings. And sometimes I need to remem—sometimes that—sometimes [tic] I may have a thought [tic] or, it's like an overall obsession. That's, that's one thing that the OCD and Tourette's can um, tie together. Uh obsessive—compulsive, you know, um what I have, I—you, you know. It's not like [tics] I used to like [tic], have to touch a square in each corner, you know . . . but um, I—OCD—that's how it ties in.

You know, uh [tic] uh, with—for me, Tourette's—I mean, my th—I might have a thought, I might [tic] be thinking [tics] thinking something I [tics] that might be upsetting me, or keeps staying in my

head, um . . . you—it keeps [stutters] it keeps rolling in my head, and, you know [tics], and sometimes I let my [tic] my, my thoughts, you know, get the best of me.

What is the hardest part of being a teenager with Tourette's disorder?

You know, some—but sometimes, you know, sometimes I do . . . it can be—at times, it can be pretty hard for me. You know? But sometimes I just need to realize that this is something that I have. Sometimes I can't go to movie theaters. You know? My friend—I mean, it's not that my friends don't want me there, or it's not that people wouldn't want me there. I mean, it's not that they don't like me, but, I mean if they pay for a, a movie ticket, they pay, they pay to go see—they go see—to go see a movie, they don't want a, a yippy kid, uh, little—a kid in the movie theater, you know, yipping away. Or, but, but it's not like it's—but it's st—but again, it's not that I can hel—It's not that I can help it or anything, but, you know, but I do need to figure out ways that I can, I can . . . you know, help. You know, help, you know? Like, for example, my mom. She has MS. She's very strong, just a wonderful mother. You know, I—and s—you know, you know she someti—she can't, she can't play tennis like she used to. She can't, she can't run [tic] you know, she can't walk as far, and sometimes she can't go with her friends, doing those things. You know? You know, it's—and it's hard for her sometimes as well. We're all on this one—we all have our things that alter what we do.

Differential Diagnosis

In diagnosing an individual with Tourette's disorder, most clinicians would be fairly confident in the diagnosis because the symptoms are so specific. However, the clinician would probably recommend a full neurological assessment to determine whether the individual might be suffering from an alternative movement disorder or brain damage that would cause the development of vocal and motor irregularities.

DISCUSSION QUESTIONS

1. Does Ben seem fit to participate in certain activities he describes, such as driving?
2. Do you imagine that it would be difficult to be a child with Tourette's disorder? In what ways? How can these issues be remedied?

RESEARCH: Adult Attention-Deficit/Hyperactivity Disorder: A Valid Diagnosis

During the past decade researchers and clinicians have tackled questions about whether the diagnosis of attention-deficit/hyperactivity disorder [ADHD], a condition traditionally diagnosed in children and adolescents, can be applied to adults. Recent epidemiological research provides compelling support for the validity of the ADHD diagnosis in adults, with more than 4 percent of American adults meeting the diagnostic criteria for the disorder (Kessler et al., 2006). Despite the persuasiveness of this statistic, *DSM-IV-TR* presents an overly cautious approach to acknowledging the validity of ADHD in adults. McGough and McCracken (2006) enumerate three complications with *DSM*'s approach. First, *DSM* specifies an age-of-onset criterion that requires that symptoms must have been present before age 7, a fact that can be difficult to verify retrospectively in one's adult years. Second, *DSM* symptoms were selected because of their relevance in identifying the condition in children, and therefore may not be especially relevant to impairments evident in older individuals. Third, *DSM*'s symptom thresholds (e.g., six of nine inattentive or hyperactive-impulsive symptoms) are inconsistent with evidence that adults with fewer symptoms are indeed significantly impaired.

In attempts to address controversies and confusion about the diagnosis of ADHD in adults, researchers have begun to set an agenda for future *DSM* conceptualizations. Faraone and colleagues (2006) focused on the validity of *DSM-IV-TR*'s criteria for age of onset and symptom threshold by comparing four groups of adults: (1) adults with full ADHD, (2) adults with late-onset ADHD who met all criteria except the age-of-onset criterion, (3) adults with subthreshold ADHD who did not meet full symptom criteria for ADHD, and (4) adults without ADHD who did not meet any criteria. Adults who developed ADHD beyond childhood showed similar levels of impairment, as well as similar comorbid psychiatric conditions, and patterns of familial transmission as those adults with full ADHD. Interestingly, the adults with subthreshold ADHD had a milder degree of impairment and different patterns of familial transmission than did adults with the other forms of ADHD. Faraone and his colleagues (2006) concluded that late-onset adult ADHD is valid and that the age-of-onset criterion in *DSM-IV-TR* is too stringent. Particularly striking in their research was the finding that 39 percent of adults with full ADHD and 59 percent of adults with late-onset ADHD had never been treated for ADHD.

In a related research project, Biederman and his colleagues (2006) compared adults with ADHD to adults not having ADHD, and found that adults with ADHD were more likely to have deficits of executive functioning (e.g., working memory, sustained attention, verbal fluency, and processing speed), which resulted in lower academic achievement. In recognition of the serious personal and social impact of an undiagnosed and untreated condition such as ADHD in adults, McGough and McCracken (2006) admonish mental health professionals who resist recognizing and treating adults with ADHD to consider the limitations of this narrow perspective. They argue that future *DSM* field trials should give greater attention to assessing symptoms and domains of impairment that are developmentally appropriate for adults. At the very least, McGough and McCracken recommend that the age-of-onset criterion should be raised to age 12, or possibly be abandoned altogether if empirical support is lacking for identifying a clear age-of-onset point.

Biederman, J., Petty, C., Fried, R., Fontanella, J., Doyle, A. E., Seidman, L. J., et al. (2006). Impact of psychometrically defined deficits of executive functioning in adults with attention deficit hyperactivity disorder. *American Journal of Psychiatry, 163,* 1730–1738.

Faraone, S. V., Biederman, J., Spencer, T., Mick, E., Murray, K., Petty, C., Adamson, J. J., & Monuteaux, M. C. (2006). Diagnosing adult attention deficit hyperactivity disorder: Are late onset and subthreshold diagnoses valid? *American Journal of Psychiatry, 163,* 1720–1729.

Kessler, R. C., Adler, L., Barkley, R., Biederman, J., Conners, C. K., Demler, O., Faraone, S. V., Greenhill, L. L., Howes, M. J., Secnik, K. T., Spencer, T., Ustun, T. B., Walters, E. E., & Zaslavsky, A. M. (2006). The prevalence and correlates of adult ADHD in the United States: results from the National Comorbidity Survey Replication. *American Journal of Psychiatry, 163,* 716–723.

McGough, J. J., & McCracken, J. T. (2006). Adult attention deficit hyperactivity disorder: Moving beyond *DSM-IV*. *American Journal of Psychiatry, 163,* 1673–1675.

Chapter 12   Aging-Related and Cognitive Disorders

RESEARCH: Diagnosis and Understanding of Alzheimer's Disease

The diagnosis of Alzheimer's disease through clinical methods is traditionally done by exclusion, because there is no one specific test or clinical indicator unique to the disorder. A definite diagnosis is possible only through autopsy, which identifies the characteristic neurofibrillary tangles and beta amyloid plaques known to occur in the disease. Of particular interest and importance is the need to differentiate the type of moderate memory loss that may reflect the early form of the disease from what is known as mild cognitive impairment (MCI), a subtle loss of memory and learning abilities (Levey et al., 2006).

With the continued improvement of MRI, which has resulted in a virtual explosion of studies on diagnosis of Alzheimer's disease through brain imaging, it is likely that clinicians will soon have the ability to provide a reliable diagnosis in the early to moderate stages of the disorder. In one investigation, Bouwman and colleagues (2007) measured the degree of atrophy in the temporal lobe along with tau and amyloid-β in the cerebrospinal fluid of individuals who showed mild cognitive impairment. After following them for 2 years, nearly all (94 percent) of the 16 people who had abnormal markers in the brain and spinal fluid developed dementia. In contrast, of the 20 whose markers were both normal, 30 percent developed dementia. Another group of investigators were able to identify abnormalities in the temporal lobe and in brain glucose metabolism in cognitively normal older adults living in the community which after 4 years were associated with the development of Alzheimer's disease (Jagust et al., 2006).

In addition to using brain imaging as a possible adjunct to diagnosis, researchers are gaining a better understanding of the disorder itself at the level of disordered cell functioning, specifically, beta amyloid plaques. Although scientists believed that the plaques were responsible for the damage resulting to the brain in people with Alzheimer's disease, they now think that the brain uses the clumps to rid itself of the harmful beta amyloid fragments. The amyloid fragments that are not cleared from the brain may actually interfere with synaptic communication and therefore lead to the memory loss and other cognitive changes associated with the disorder (Cleary et al., 2005).

Armed with improved diagnostic techniques and understanding of changes at the molecular level within the brain, researchers are seeking ways to improve the treatment of individuals who suffer from Alzheimer's disease. Medications that target acetylcholinesterase, long thought to play a role in causing memory deficits, lack effectiveness in stemming the progress of the disorder. Instead, scientists are experimenting with agents that specifically target the process of amyloid formation. The latest discovery is *scyllo*-cyclohexanehexol, a substance that can be administered orally and potentially could modify the progress of the disease rather than only treating its memory loss symptoms (Townsend et al., 2006). Future research using human and animal models will continue to target molecular changes and at the same time attempt to understand further the role of genetics in the development of this devastating cognitive disorder.

Bouwman, F. H., Schoonenboom, S. N., van der Flier, W. M., van Elk, E. J., Kok, A., Barkhof, F., Blankenstein, M. A., & Scheltens, P. (2007). CSF biomarkers and medial temporal lobe atrophy predict dementia in mild cognitive impairment. *Neurobiology of Aging, 7,* 1070–1074.

Cleary, J. P., Walsh, D. M., Hofmeister, J. J., Shankar, G. M., Kuskowski, M. A., Selkoe, D. J., & Ashe, K. H. (2005). Natural oligomers of the amyloid-beta protein specifically disrupt cognitive function. *Nature Neuroscience, 8,* 79–84.

Jagust, W., Gitcho, A., Sun, F., Kuczynski, B., Mungas, D., & Haan, M. (2006). Brain imaging evidence of preclinical Alzheimer's disease in normal aging. *Annals of Neurology, 59,* 673–681.

Levey, A., Lah, J., Goldstein, F., Steenland, K., & Bliwise, D. (2006). Mild cognitive impairment: An opportunity to identify patients at high risk for progression to Alzheimer's disease. *Clinical Therapeutics, 28,* 991–1001.

Townsend, M., Cleary, J. P., Mehta, T., Hofmeister, J., Lesne, S., O'Hare, E., Walsh, D. M. & Selkoe, D. J. (2006). Orally available compound prevents deficits in memory caused by the Alzheimer amyloid-beta oligomers. *Annals of Neurology, 60,* 668–676.

Chapter 13   Substance-Related Disorders

FACES: Substance Dependence

DSM CRITERIA

During a 12-month period, people with substance dependence show at least three of the following: tolerance; withdrawal; use of the substance in larger amounts or over a longer period than intended; persistent desire or unsuccessful efforts to cut down or control substance use; extensive time devoted to activities involved in obtaining, using, or recovering from substance use; a giving up of or reduction in important activities because of substance use; and continued use despite knowledge of a substance-caused physical or psychological problem.

Brief Case History

By the time Bobbie was 16 years old, she was living on the streets. She was a

heroin addict, and her life revolved around selling her body, buying drugs, and satisfying an overwhelming opiate addiction. When Bobbie was 9 years old, her life was already challenging. Her mother was mostly absent, and Bobbie admits that she was desperate for positive attention. At about this time she was sexually abused by men in her household. In spite of the abuse, she desperately wanted to think of herself as a "good girl." Her life began to crumble when she was about 12 years old. She fell in with an older crowd of kids and began smoking cigarettes and drinking alcohol. At 13 she began to smoke marijuana and ran away from home. In the course of the next 3 years she experimented with a variety of hallucinogens, amphetamines, and barbiturates. In fact, her own mother introduced her to heroin. Bobbie's life quickly spiraled out of her control and remained so for almost 10 years.

At the time of the interview, Bobbie had been sober for about 10 years. She lives quietly with her 5-year-old son and her boyfriend in a small suburban house. Although she is drug-free, she still considers herself an addict and admits she is afraid that she might resume using drugs. Furthermore, she still bears the scars of her previous life. When Bobbie's young son asks her about the track marks on her arms, she explains that she was scratched by a cat. She also carries emotional scars. Bobbie is working hard to maintain a normal life for her small family. She has a part-time job and is learning to cope with the special challenges of living with HIV. In spite of her many challenges, she is determined to live a happy and fulfilling life.

Clinical Questions

What effects did the heroin have on you?

I did crank [a form of methamphetamine] for a long time, to the point where I was psychotic. Staying up for weeks at a time, not eating for weeks at a time. It really does a doozy on your body. But heroin, I could think on it. I wasn't paranoid on it. It took the physical and emotional pain away. It kinda numbed me. And so I became very interested in heroin, regardless of being sick on it all the time. If I didn't have it, I was very sick. That was the progression. I went from smoking cigarettes to heroin in a very short time.

Look back and see 15-year-old Bobbie. What do you want to say to her?

That's hard. Because she's really lost right now, at that time; 'cause she's starting sexual activities now. Her stepbrother has finally, for the last time, left her alone. And then he had sexual intercourse with her, and she's reaching out. All I wanna do is hold her. And just tell her that I love her. At that time, I was having a lot of sex with a lot of different guys, unprotected, and trying to fill a void in my heart. A big void. Felt very lost; very unloved, like I was worthless. What I thought at that time is if the body was liked, the person was loved. I can look at that girl at 15, and I can feel the emotions of lost and scared.

Do you use any drugs now?

Today, it's a matter of pain relief. Actual, real, pain relief. And maybe some emotional pain still. I mean, I'm sure of it. I've had to smoke marijuana in order to take my medicine. I mean, regardless of it being illegal, it did help me. Today, it does. But it's like a medicine for me today. My medicine is my medicine. It's like, my 22 pills a day. One of those pills is methadone. That I take for pain in my legs, so I've always had drugs in my life. Always.

Did you participate in a high-risk behavior that might have exposed you to HIV?

I don't now know how I got it; actually, I don't. It was either through IV drug use, sharing needles, unprotected sex with many different people, men, and women. A lot of times, you know? And it doesn't even take a lot of times. It could've been that one time that I had unprotected sex. Or that one time that I shared a needle with somebody. And—just many different ways: oral sex, vaginal sex—which most of the time—or bisexual sex. With many people, you know. And as I will emphasize again, it only takes once. One time. And it coulda been that one time when I had unprotected sex at 15 years old. You know? I just can't say when. But there are many people I've been involved with, that I know are HIV positive now. Either I gave it to them, or they gave it to me. So I just don't know when. I wish, but it wouldn't change anything today if I knew when. I mean, it really wouldn't. So it doesn't matter. I have it; I'm dealing with it, which is very hard.

Differential Diagnosis

Bobbie's heroin addiction serves as the basis for her diagnosis of substance dependence. However, she also shows symptoms of sexual compulsivity, given the fact that she has had sexual relations with multiple partners at a time. Given her history of sexual abuse, the clinician may also wish to evaluate her for post-traumatic stress disorder.

DISCUSSION QUESTIONS

1. How does Bobbie's story seem like a natural progression from experimentation to substance dependence?
2. What types of risks are associated with drug use and dependence? Which risks does Bobbie not mention?

RESEARCH: The Reinforcing Effect of Stimulant Drugs

Despite vigorous federal and state efforts to reduce, or at least contain, the problem of drug abuse in American society during the past few decades, statistics point to a dismal picture in terms of the prospects of overcoming the problem. Although all drug abuse is of concern, the increase in prevalence of stimulants has become especially troubling. In one recent study, one in five participants reported having used drugs at some point, with a considerably higher rate among males than females (25.9 versus 16.8 percent). Although the majority of these individuals used the drugs on only a few occasions, almost a fourth of the users reached the diagnostic criteria of substance abuse or dependence. Factors correlating with the abuse of stimulants included a history of conduct disorder, exposure to childhood sexual abuse, and a history of mood disorder (Lynskey et al., 2007).

The nonmedical use of prescription medications is especially problematic among secondary school students. In fact, approximately one in five high school adolescents reported that they had used prescription medications for nonmedical purposes, and these individuals were found to be at much higher risk of developing serious problems with drug abuse or dependence. Research findings have highlighted the importance of targeting prescription medication abuse in prevention and intervention efforts aimed at adolescents (McCabe, Boyd, & Young, 2007).

Some efforts to understand the proliferation of stimulant use have focused on the reinforcing effects of stimulants, with an aim of developing new pharmaceutical agents that have less reinforcing properties. Methylphenidate and amphetamine, the most frequently used medications for treating attention-deficit/hyperactivity disorder, are reinforcing because the drugs act upon the dopamine neurotransmitter system. Scientists have been working to develop variants of methylphenidate and amphetamine that lead to slow rates of brain uptake. The goal is to design the substances in such a way that they cannot be snorted or injected (Volkow, 2006).

Lynskey, G., Li, L., Nelson, E. C., Bucholz, K. K., Madden, P. A. F., Statham, D., Martin, N. G., & Heath, A. C. (2007). Stimulant use and symptoms of abuse/dependence: Epidemiology and associations with cannabis use—A twin study. *Drug and Alcohol Dependence, 86,* 147–153.

McCabe, S. E., Boyd, C. J., & Young, A. (2007). Medical and nonmedical use of prescription drugs among secondary school students. *Journal of Adolescent Health, 40,* 76–83.

Volkow, N. D. (2006). Stimulant medication: How to minimize their reinforcing effects? *American Journal of Psychiatry, 163,* 359–361.

Chapter 14 Eating Disorders and Impulse-Control Disorders

FACES: Bulimia Nervosa

DSM CRITERIA

People with bulimia nervosa fall into two groups (purging type or nonpurging type) with the following characteristics:

- They engage in recurrent episodes of binge eating that are characterized by (1) eating an amount of food in a 2-hour period that is substantially larger than what most people would eat and (2) experiencing a lack of control over eating during these episodes.
- They engage in recurrent compensatory behavior aimed at preventing weight gain (e.g., self-induced vomiting, fasting, excessive exercise, or misuse of laxatives, diuretics, or enemas).
- The binge eating and compensatory behaviors both occur on average at least twice a week for 3 months.
- Their self-evaluation is unduly influenced by body weight and shape.

Brief Case History

When she wakes up in the morning, Nancy's first thought is about food. When she helps her child prepare for school, when she drives to work, and when she cleans her house, every aspect of her day is dominated by thoughts of food and her next meal. Nancy traces her obsession with eating back to her childhood. There was a lot of discord in her home, and Nancy discovered that binge-eating calmed her and was an effective means to cope with stress. When she began gaining weight, however, her mother teased her and warned that "no one will like you if you are fat." This in turn attached even more emotional power to food, and eventually, thoughts of eating and of her body image came to dominate her thinking. Then when Nancy was a high school student, she read an Ann Landers article in which a young woman explained that she ate in binges and afterward caused herself to vomit. Although the columnist correctly explained that the behavior is quite risky, Nancy became intrigued with the idea and decided to experiment with it herself. Within a short period of time, the experiment evolved into an ingrained habit. Within a year, she was vomiting at least once a day, and she has continued to do so for the past 17 years. Nancy's obsessive thoughts of food and her compulsive eating have become a ritualized part of her daily schedule. She organizes her schedule to allow time for her binges. As the time approaches, she says that the food takes control over her. She feels compelled to eat quickly and voraciously, and she continues to eat until she feels bloated and physically unable to continue. Nancy estimates that she regularly consumes 5,000 calories in a single binge episode. She sometimes binges three or four times in a day. Like many people with this disorder, Nancy is quite concerned about her appearance, and she acts compulsively to avoid gaining weight. In addition to vomiting after each binge, Nancy exercises for several hours every day and often fasts for protracted periods. This repeated binging and purging has created some serious health problems for Nancy. The acid passing through her esophagus has created a throat condition, has ruined her teeth, and may have compromised her heart. In addition, Nancy acknowledges that her disorder has put a great deal of strain on her marriage and her family. She is no longer able to conceal her disorder, and she is terrified that she has passed her eating obsession on to her 9-year-old son who also suffers from a weight problem. Nancy is profoundly frustrated that she has been unable to overcome her disorder and is ashamed of her behavior. She seemed bewildered when asked about her hobbies, explaining that "for the past 17 years I have been too preoccupied with my eating disorder to develop any hobbies."

Clinical Questions

When did you begin vomiting? What brought it on the first time?

I learned at an early age that being overweight was not a good thing. Life was not good for overweight people. When I was about 18, I had lost quite a bit of weight—I had my wisdom teeth taken out, and I had lost weight—and I felt really good, and I liked that feeling a lot. I wanted to get back to that point, and I just couldn't do it; I couldn't do it. Then I was

over at my grandmother's house. In an Ann Landers article, there was an article about a girl who talked about how she lost weight, through putting her hand down her throat and vomiting. And I thought, wow, that's kinda sounds like a good idea, so I'd go over to my grandmother's house and make cookies, and I remember I thought, well I'm gonna try it. So I ate a whole bunch of cookie dough. And went into her bathroom, threw it up, and I thought, this is great. I went over to my girlfriend's house, told her about it, told her to try it. You know, I mean, I was like, thinking I had something going on here! You know? And my girlfriend was like, this is so disgusting. And she couldn't do it. But I kept doing it..

How do you decide whether you are going to begin a binge and purge episode?

I hear a voice in my head. The best way for me to describe it is, it's my mom that I hear. I just go back to when I was young, and her telling me I was overweight, you can't have that food, that I'm going to lose my husband if I keep getting bigger. She pops up in my head all of the time. So sometimes I'll fight with her. I'll say, Marilyn, shut up! That's my mom's name. I think, if I just say, "be quiet," maybe she'll just calm down. And she has sometimes. But sometimes she hasn't. She's been very, very vocal.

How do you feel right after you purge?

I feel like, thank god I could get this all out. That's a big concern for me; that I can't get all of my food out. And then, I start thinking well, I know some of the food has stayed in me; and so I try and figure out how much has stayed in me. So then I can kind of figure out how much I can eat for the rest of the day; or how much I need to go work out. Sometimes I get a powerful feeling from it. Because I think, I'm not gonna gain weight, but I got to eat all of that food. Then I'm totally exhausted. My thought is I gotta get some rest here. Then, when I wake up, I'm okay. I can start all over.

Have you ever used laxatives?

Yeah, I took laxatives. I took Epsom salts which, in the best way I can describe, taking Epsom salts is pouring yourself a glass of Clorox bleach, and drinking it. And, I took those for about three years. And then, when I was reading a book, it talked about

how Epsom salts and laxatives cause kidney damage. I had kidney problems as a kid, and so I really got freaked out about it. So I was able to cut that. So I never went back to that. Was for those three years, taking those Epsom salts—I had to hide them from my husband. I'd buy the quart size of Epsom salts, and he found them several times, and I told him I was using them for a bath. I always had a story for everything, and unfortunately I'd have to run to the bathroom, all of the time. I'd have to make sure there was a bathroom close by. So that got to be a little annoying. Then, at the end, they burned my throat so bad, and I could just feel it, into my stomach, burning it. So, you know, it must have done something to my lining down there. So I did do the Epsom salts, which I do not recommend. But I did quit that on my own.

Why is it so important to you to be thin? Is it just to look more attractive?

Everything else in our life is based on how thin we are. I would [think] that the skinnier I was, I knew my marriage was going to get better; I just knew it was. When that's not true. But that's my thinking.

Differential Diagnosis

Nancy's binging and purging are classic symptoms of bulimia nervosa. A clinician might consider the possibility that Nancy has anorexia nervosa, but she does not show the symptoms of that disorder involving distortion of body image. Nancy desires to be thinner than she is, but she does not perceive herself to be overweight. A clinician would also evaluate Nancy for major depressive disorder, given her low self-esteem, but she shows no other symptoms and her mood does not appear to be dysphoric.

DISCUSSION QUESTIONS

1. Is it an issue that Nancy picked up her bulimic practices from an Ann Landers article, material available to all adolescents?

2. An underlying theme is the idea of control. Does Nancy have any control? When has she lost it?

3. What symptoms here are similar to the symptoms of other disorders involving impulse control?

RESEARCH: **An Epidemic of Self-Injurious Behavior?**

Dramatic increases have occurred in the last decade in the prevalence of self-injurious behavior, particularly among female adolescents and young adults. Self-injurious behaviors differ from the behaviors of individuals who are intent on completing the act of suicide. The terms used to describe self-injurious behaviors that are not socially recognized or sanctioned include *deliberate self-harm, self-injury, self-mutilation,* and *cutting.*

Researchers have devoted considerable attention to efforts to understanding the predictors and correlates of self-injurious behavior. Gratz (2006) examined the role of childhood maltreatment, emotional inexpressivity, and affect intensity/reactivity among college students. A history of childhood abuse has long been established as a correlate of psychopathology later in life, so it is not surprising to see a relationship between childhood maltreatment and subsequent self-injurious behavior. The relationship between self-injurious behavior and emotional inexpressivity, however, is an intriguing one because of the suggestion that one function of self-harm may be to release pent-up emotions that the individual has felt unable to communicate in healthy ways. Although support was found for the relationship between childhood maltreatment and self-harm, maltreatment alone did not emerge as a significant predictor of self-harm frequency among women with a history of self-injurious behavior. Instead, emotional inexpressivity played a prominent role in the maintenance of self-harming behavior.

During the past decade there has been a proliferation of Internet message boards and blogs, including hundreds of such venues devoted to discussion of self-injurious behavior. In one study of Internet websites pertaining to self-injuring behavior, Whitlock, Powers, and Eckenrode (2006) analyzed 406 message boards on this topic. Several themes characterized the message boards, including self-injurious behavior triggered by conflict with important others, perceived depression, school or work stress, loneliness, and sexual abuse or rape. The message boards seemed to provide a powerful vehicle for bringing together self-injurious adolescents in such a way that they can obtain support, share personal stories, and voice opinions and ideas. On the negative side, vulnerable adolescents easily became caught up in a subculture in which self-injury is normalized and encouraged, with the most disturbing aspect being the sharing of techniques.

In light of the fact that emotional inexpressivity plays such a significant role in self-injurious behavior, it is not surprising to find a proliferation of Internet websites in which young people are calling out anonymously in the hope of communicating their pain and discussing their experiences. If professional help could be extended to some of those individuals, it is possible that they would be less inclined to harm themselves. Gratz (2006) highlights the treatment implications that emerge from recognizing the connection between emotional inexpressivity and self-harm frequency. In treatment with self-harming clients, clinicians can give clients more effective ways to express their emotions and to emphasize more effective ways to increase the experience of positive emotions.

Gratz, K. L. (2006). Risk factors for deliberate self-harm among female college students: The role and interaction of childhood maltreatment, emotional inexpressivity, and affect intensity/reactivity. *American Journal of Orthopsychiatry, 76,* 238–250.

Whitlock, J. L., Powers, J. L., & Eckenrode, J. (2006). The virtual cutting edge: The Internet and adolescent self-injury. *Developmental Psychology, 42,* 407–417.

Chapter 15 **Ethical and Legal Issues**

RESEARCH: **The Controversy of Outpatient Commitment**

People who are at risk of seriously harming themselves or others can legally be involuntarily committed to psychiatric hospitals. Although such commitment is within the scope of the law, the decision to commit such at-risk individuals to institutions inevitably provokes debate about civil rights of the individual. Furthermore, such hospitalizations are financially costly. Efforts to protect personal rights and reduce costs have led to alternative solutions, the most notable of which is outpatient commitment, a procedure with its own share of controversies.

Outpatient commitment is a civil court procedure in which individuals are mandated to participate in outpatient treatment in an attempt to reduce the likelihood of relapse, hospital readmission, and incarceration. Most states have statutes regarding outpatient commitment, and rely predominantly on criteria similar to those used for inpatient commitment. In most cases individuals are required to comply with a recommended outpatient treatment program that stops short of permitting forced medication of legally competent people. When individuals fail to comply with the treatment regimen, law enforcement officers are empowered to transport them to a facility for evaluation and possible inpatient commitment (Swartz, Swanson, Kim, & Petrila, 2006).

A storm of controversy has arisen during the past 20 years about outpatient commitment (Geller, 2006). The debate has involved polarizing viewpoints. Those arguing in favor of outpatient commitment argue that people who refuse to comply with treatment are mentally ill, and the symptoms of their illness reduce autonomy. If they are ignored, untreated, and psychotic, they are not really free at all but are actually deprived of living their lives fully. Proponents insist that outpatient commitment actually increases treatment effectiveness in a number of ways, such as being proactive rather than reactive. On the other hand, those who speak against outpatient commitment see this procedure as a social control mechanism in the guise of benevolent coercion. There is the risk that treatments of dubious value will be forced on marginally difficult individuals.

Debate about outpatient commitment will undoubtedly continue for years. Geller (2006) advocates research on the issue of outpatient commitment with a focus on determining from a clinical perspective exactly which kinds of individuals can benefit from outpatient commitment. Other experts (Swanson, Van Dorn, Monahan, & Swartz, 2006) assert that the debate over outpatient commitment has followed similar debates of the past regarding involuntary inpatient commitment. The "dangerousness" criterion for inpatient civil commitment has metamorphosed into a rationale for preventive outpatient commitment aimed at preventing future dangerousness. As with the controversy over inpatient commitment, there will always be outcries of concern about protecting the rights of individuals while trying to protect the well-being of those individuals.

Geller, J. L. (2006). The evolution of outpatient commitment in the USA: From conundrum to quagmire. *International Journal of Law and Psychiatry, 29,* 234–248.

Swanson, J. W., Van Dorn, R. A., Monahan, J., & Swartz, M. S. (2006). Violence and leveraged community treatment for persons with mental disorders. *American Journal of Psychiatry, 163,* 1404–1411.

Swartz, M. S., Swanson, J. W., Kim, M., & Petrila, J. (2006). Use of outpatient commitment or related civil court treatment orders in five U.S. communities. *Psychiatric Services, 57,* 343–349.

BRIEF CONTENTS

CONTENTS

Chapter 5

Chapter 6

Somatoform Disorders, Psychological Factors Affecting Medical Conditions, and Dissociative Disorders 178

Chapter 7

Chapter 15

"Illness is the night-side of life, a more onerous citizenship. Everyone who is born holds dual citizenship, in the kingdom of the well and in the kingdom of the sick."

—Susan Sontag, *Illness as Metaphor*

All human beings experience the duality of illness and wellness. Those who suffer from mental illnesses experience the "night-side" of life more intimately. By providing information on abnormal psychology, we hope students will learn about how individuals understand, cope with, and recover from psychological disorders. Our goal in writing this text is to share our understanding with students who come to this course from a variety of socioeconomic and cultural backgrounds, as well as academic pursuits. In our revisions for this fifth edition of *Abnormal Psychology,* we have focused our efforts on transcending those boundaries to reach our readers on a purely human level. We begin by sharing with you the following stories:

Katya developed a deep interest in abnormal psychology after hearing about friends' and family's immigrant experiences. An immigrant herself, Katya firmly believes that migration can adversely affect human behavior. For example, how does geographical displacement contribute to the onset of major depression? How crucial a factor is "culture shock" in the manifestation of psychological disorders? These are the things Katya seeks to explore.

Chung, an English major and aspiring writer, appreciates the fluctuations in human behavior. He is especially fascinated by and sensitive to its vast range because he knows that characters cannot be written solely from the imagination. A credible character should reflect an individual one would meet on the street, at the local bar, or in the workplace. Thus, it is important to Chung to be as informed as possible about all sides of human behavior.

Jason's reason for taking a course in abnormal psychology is far more personal. A young man whose mother has long been suffering from schizophrenia, Jason seeks to learn more about the disorder so that he can better understand what his mother must endure daily, and to ensure that she is receiving the treatment most suitable for her. He also realizes that he might be genetically susceptible to developing the illness, so he is also interested in the course for his own well-being.

Like Katya, Chung, and Jason, many students find themselves studying abnormal psychology to deepen their own understanding, to satisfy a personal curiosity, or both. Whatever the specific reason, our goal as instructors and authors continues to be to engage students in the study of abnormal psychology from a clinical and human perspective.

In this fifth edition, we are pleased to include a powerful addition to our clinically based approach. *Nothing to Hide: Mental Illness in the Family* captures in photographs and prose the compelling stories of individuals and families whose lives have been affected by a psychological disorder. These excerpts from the book *Nothing to Hide: Mental Illness in the Family,* by Peggy Gillespie, Jean Beard, and Gigi Kaeser, set the stage for the explorations of psychological disorders in the text. As students read each story, they are certain to be moved by the artistic photographs and the words of real people.

Themes

Clinical Perspectives on Psychological Disorders

The study of abnormal psychology is strongly founded on clinical research. The subtitle of this fifth edition reflects our efforts to respond to the need for greater and clearer representation and articulation of disorders and their diagnostic features. We have expanded the wide presentation of case studies. Each disorder comes to life through a mini case, accompanied by a listing of the newly revised *DSM-IV-TR* diagnostic criteria associated with that disorder. Rather than merely list the criteria, we have paraphrased the features into language that is easily understood.

The Biopsychosocial Approach

An understanding of psychological disorders requires a biopsychosocial approach that incorporates biological, psychological, and sociocultural contributions to understanding causes and developing treatments. The disorders are as various as the students who take this course. We have written this text with that thought in mind and address the issue of diversity throughout the book. Each chapter concludes with a section that discusses the chapter's topic from the biopsychosocial perspective—weaving the multiple dimensions into an integrative statement about the interactions among biology, psychology, and the social context as they affect individuals who have psychological disorders.

The Life-Span Approach

Individuals grow and evolve throughout life, and we feel it is essential to capture this development dimension in our book. Therefore, we have incorporated research and theories that provide relevant understandings of how the disorders we cover vary by age. Given that the *DSM-IV-TR* is primarily focused on adulthood, most of this emphasis is reflected in our inclusion of middle age and aging when we examine epidemiology, etiology, and treatments.

The Human Experience of Psychological Disorders

Above all, the study of abnormal psychology is the study of profoundly human experiences. To this end, we have developed a feature entitled "Real Stories." These boxes present biographies and first-person quotations that give students insight into the feelings of people who have a disorder covered in the chapter. Many of the Real Stories boxes are about individuals who are recognizable to undergraduates, and so their stories will have special relevance. Each biography is also tied into the content of the chapter so that it has a sound substantive base. In addition, the MindMAP Plus CD-ROM that accompanies this text contains seven clips of real people living with a disorder. Students who view these clips will see firsthand how people live with and suffer from disorders. We hope that students will take from this course the understanding that abnormal behavior is a very real part of our society, our humanity, and our world, and that it needs to be addressed with compassion and understanding.

The Scientist-Practitioner Framework

We have developed this text using a scientist-practitioner framework. While emphasizing empirically supported research, we share with the student stories of real people who are suffering from compelling personal problems and serious psychological disorders. Our hope is that, as students take this course and long after they have moved on to their respective careers, they will have learned to approach the study of abnormal psychology with the dispassionate eye of a scientist and the compassionate heart of a practitioner.

Organization

The table of contents reflects a building block approach. The first four chapters provide the fundamentals of history and research methods (Chapter 1); diagnosis, classification, and treatment planning (Chapter 2); assessment (Chapter 3); and theories (Chapter 4). These chapters provide a foundation for subsequent discussions regarding the understanding and treatment of psychological disorders.

From here, we move on to a consideration of the disorders, beginning with those on Axis I of *DSM-IV-TR*. Progressing through the major categories of psychological disorders, we begin with anxiety disorders and end with eating disorders and impulse-control disorders. Using a biopsychosocial approach, theory and treatment are both discussed in each chapter. For example, we examine anxiety disorders in terms of biological, psychological, and sociocultural influences that cause and maintain these conditions. We also discuss intervention in terms of the relative contributions offered by each perspective. In the final chapter of the text (Chapter 15), we cover ethical and legal issues.

Changes in the Fifth Edition

This new edition is packaged with a student CD-ROM, MindMAP Plus, which contains two types of multimedia enhancements to the book's content: (1) interactive exercises that give students firsthand exposure to key concepts and (2) video segments from interviews with clients as well as relevant clips from the Discovery Channel. Students are cued into each multimedia unit with a

MindMAP icon. For the instructor, a Media Resources Guide summarizes these activities and film segments and provides related discussion and test questions. We are excited to be able to offer this unique opportunity to bring to life many fascinating aspects of abnormal psychology.

The burgeoning of research in psychopathology in the last several years has prompted us to draw from rich new empirical sources that document the scientific basis for the diagnosis and treatment of disorders. References that are no longer relevant have been deleted; the classic sources in the literature have been retained. Expanded epidemiological databases now accessible via the Internet have also helped improve this edition. Ultimately, our goal is to offer a contemporary and concise approach to the field.

A number of changes in the text reflect new research directions, feedback from reviewers and student readers, and experience from our teaching of abnormal psychology. The fifth edition represents a much more focused approach than previous editions. With the goal of presenting only the most relevant research and clinical material, we have reduced the length of the text. We have accomplished this by deleting outdated content and by integrating into the chapter the material previously presented in boxes (i.e., Research Focus, Social Context). We are confident that students and instructors will find this approach more appealing and more educationally effective. Below is a summary of the most significant changes in each chapter.

CHAPTER 1. Understanding Abnormality: A Look at History and Research Methods
This fifth edition expands the discussion of challenges involved in characterizing abnormal behavior. By using Rosenhan's classic study as a launching pad, more contemporary points are explored which have emerged from recent considerations of what should be considered abnormal. The topic of stigma is also discussed in greater depth, as are the social problems associated with mentally ill individuals in prison.

CHAPTER 2. Classification and Treatment Plans
This edition includes a discussion of issues pertaining to the development of upcoming *DSM-V* and presents current epidemiological data on the international prevalence of mental disorders. The chapter also includes an expanded discussion of the debate regarding evidence-based treatments.

CHAPTER 3. Assessment
This chapter includes new material on structured and semistructured interviews, as well as discussion of the most recent editions of several assessment instruments (e.g., *Stanford-Binet Fifth Edition, Conners Ratings Scales–Revised,* and *The Neuropsychological Assessment Battery*).

CHAPTER 4. Theoretical Perspectives
This chapter has been substantially revised, such that only the most relevant theoretical perspectives and clinical approaches are discussed. Within the biopsychosocial perspective, recent

research advances that bring together divergent perspectives are explored, and findings on genetic causes for psychological disorders are discussed in depth. The discussion of the humanistic approach now incorporates consideration of motivational interviewing, and the section on cognitive perspectives includes discussion of significant advances in theory and technique which have emerged in recent years.

CHAPTER 5. Anxiety Disorders

This chapter expands discussion of the ways in which the biopsychosocial perspective applies to the understanding and treatment of anxiety disorders. For example, the influence of genetics in the development of anxiety disorders and the role of neurotransmitters in the experience of symptoms are explored. The discussion of PTSD has been significantly revamped in light of recent international events related to trauma, such as terrorism, war, and natural disasters.

CHAPTER 6. Somatoform Disorders, Psychological Factors Affecting Medical Conditions, and Dissociative Disorders

This chapter more explicitly discusses the challenges involved in the diagnosis of and treatment of somatoform disorders, health-related psychological conditions, and dissociative disorders. Critical analyses are incorporated into the chapter regarding debates about the validity of diagnoses within this group of disorders, as well as claims about the relationship between early abuse and the development of dissociative disorders.

CHAPTER 7. Sexual Disorders

This chapter includes updated information about the diagnosis and treatment of sexual disorders, and also addresses some of the controversies related to these conditions. For example, the chapter discusses the debate about characterizing the dysphoria related to gender identity as a disorder, particularly in the case of children. Also, increasing attention is given to the treatment of sexual dysfunction in women.

CHAPTER 8. Mood Disorders

Substantial revision of the chapter has been done in order to discuss several phenomena arising from research and clinical practice, such as the increasingly common diagnosis of bipolar disorder in children. In addition, a critical discussion of treatment techniques includes an analysis of controversies related to the use of antidepressant medications, particularly the prescription of SSRIs to young people. The discussion of suicide has been expanded in order to include more contemporary statistics and consideration of the factors that contribute to suicide.

CHAPTER 9. Schizophrenia and Related Disorders

This chapter includes an expanded discussion of emerging research regarding predictors of schizophrenia, such as the biobehavioral abnormalities that are linked to genetic and neurobiological causes. In addition, the chapter discusses abnormalities in cognitive processes that are being increasingly recognized as clues to the biological underpinnings of the development of schizophrenia. Emerging intervention trends are also explored, such as more recently introduced medications and the development of more effective social skills training programs.

CHAPTER 10. Personality Disorders

This edition includes an expanded discussion of the extent to which personality disorders should be considered as dimensional rather than categorical entities. Additional discussion also focuses on contributors to the development of personality disorders, particularly antisocial and borderline personality disorders.

CHAPTER 11. Development-Related Disorders

In light of significant recent advances in the understanding and treatment of attention-deficit/hyperactivity disorder, this chapter has been substantially revised. An expanded discussion of ADHD in adults is now included, with particular attention to differential symptom presentation between adults and children. An expanded discussion of interventions, both pharmacological and psychological, is included and contains specific techniques for addressing the symptoms of this condition.

CHAPTER 12. Aging-Related and Cognitive Disorders

In this edition, a new condition, traumatic brain injury (TBI), has been added to the discussion. TBI is of particular relevance in light of the increasing number of people developing brain-related disorders as a result of injuries received in war and terrorist acts. The chapter also includes expanded coverage of contemporary theories about the etiology of Alzheimer's disease (e.g., Caspase theory).

CHAPTER 13. Substance-Related Disorders

In addition to incorporating the most recent data about the extent to which substances are being used and abused, the chapter also adds discussion of substances that have become especially problematic in recent years (e.g., methamphetamine and OxyContin). There is also expanded discussion of etiological factors associated with the development of substance dependence and the most effective treatment interventions.

CHAPTER 14. Eating Disorders and Impulse-Control Disorders

This chapter expands discussion of biological and sociocultural contributors to the development of eating disorders. In addition, the chapter contains a new section on Internet addiction.

CHAPTER 15. Ethical and Legal Issues

This chapter includes discussion of legal issues that have been affected by recent legislative and judicial decisions (e.g., mandated reporting of self-neglecting elders; duty to warn statutes pertaining to the clinician's responsibility in situations not involving a specific identifiable victim). The chapter also introduces Guidelines for Practice with Older Adults and considers several recent cases that are relevant to legal and ethical issues.

A Brief Note to the Instructor

Like us, most instructors have students like Katya, Chung, and Jason and are aware of the challenge that this heterogeneity of students presents. We want to excite aspiring researchers like Katya to pursue their goals and become immersed in this fascinating and rapidly changing field of abnormal psychology. However, even those of you who are extremely research oriented realize the importance of including ample clinical material in order to make the scientific material understandable. For students like Chung who come to the course with broader interests, we want to capture for them the fascinating and multifarious aspects of abnormal behavior. This includes highlighting interesting clinical phenomena and incorporating them with ideas derived from empirically supported research. Our goal is to infuse teaching with credible and validated scholarship. Students like Jason present the greatest teaching challenge because their concerns are of such a personal nature. As instructors, we need to keep in mind the importance of not creating a therapy context in the classroom. At the same time, we must recognize that emotionally provocative information can be discussed in a way that is informative and responsive to individual needs.

In writing this textbook, we speak to these various types of students in a manner that is informative, scholarly, and engaging. The scientist-practitioner framework is geared toward emphasizing current empirically supported research while conveying the compelling personal problems and serious psychological disorders of real people through case studies. The pedagogy is developed to communicate this framework as well. We believe that, by carefully blending scientific findings with clinical material, we have created a textbook that will serve the needs of a diverse student body as well as the instructors who teach them.

Ancillaries

The following ancillaries are available to accompany *Abnormal Psychology,* Fifth Edition. Please contact your McGraw-Hill sales representative for details concerning policies, prices, and availability, as some restrictions may apply.

For the Instructor

Classroom Performance System Guide and CD-ROM allows instructors to immediately determine what students are learning during lectures. With this Classroom Performance System (CPS) from **eInstruction,** instructors can ask questions, take polls, host classroom demonstrations, and get instant feedback. In addition, CPS makes it easy to take attendance, give and grade pop quizzes, or give formal paper-based class tests with multiple versions of the tests using CPS for immediate grading. For instructors who want to use CPS in the classroom, we offer a guide containing strategies for implementing the system, specific multiple-choice questions designed for in-class use, and classroom demonstrations for use with this system. For a quick, easy demonstration of CPS, go to www.mhhe.com/wmg/cps/psychology.

The *Instructor's Manual* by Michele Catone-Maitino of Hudson Valley Community College provides many tools useful for teaching the fifth edition. For each chapter, the *Instructor's Manual* includes an overview of the chapter, teaching objectives, suggestions and resources for lecture topics, classroom activities, and essay questions designed to help students develop ideas for independent projects and papers. The *Instructor's Manual* is available on the password-protected instructor's side of the Online Learning Center (www.mhhe.com/halgin5).

The latest *Test Bank* by Timothy P. Tomczak of Genesee Community College contains over 2,000 testing items. All testing items are classified as conceptual or applied, and referenced to the appropriate learning objective. The questions are available on the password-protected instructor's side of the Online Learning Center both as Word files and in computerized format.

The **Computerized Test Bank** runs on both Macintosh and Windows computers and includes an editing feature that enables instructors to import their own questions, scramble items, and modify questions to create their own tests.

The **Online Learning Center** for instructors by Kim Dielman of the University of Central Arkansas houses downloadable versions of the *Instructor's Manual,* PowerPoint presentation slides, *Test Bank,* a sample chapter, and a variety of other text-specific instructor resources, including a library of more than 300 images.

For the Student

MindMAP plus Student CD-ROM brings to life many fascinating aspects of abnormal psychology. It contains two types of multimedia enhancements to the book's content: (1) interactive exercises that give students firsthand exposure to key concepts and (2) video segments from interviews with clients as well as relevant clips from the Discovery Channel. Students are cued into each multimedia unit with a MindMAP icon. For the instructor, the *Media Resources Guide* summarizes these activities and film segments and provides related discussion and test questions.

The *Student Study Guide,* by Barbara Bowman of Washburn University, includes the learning objectives from the book, detailed chapter outlines, guided reviews of the major concepts covered in the chapter, and multiple-choice practice tests. Answers to the practice tests are provided.

The Online Learning Center (www.mhhe.com/halgin5) is the official website for the fifth edition of *Abnormal Psychology.* It contains chapter outlines, practice quizzes, interactive exercises, virtual flashcards, links to relevant psychology sites, an Internet primer, a career appendix, and a statistics primer.

Faces Interactive, created by Arthur J. Kohn of Portland State University, is a unique web-based learning environment that provides students with an opportunity to observe real patients through a series of case studies on twelve different psychological disorders. The disorders studied in *Faces Interactive* include Attention-Deficit/Hyperactivity Disorder, Bipolar Disorder, Borderline Personality Disorder, Bulimia Nervosa, Dysthymic Disorder, Major Depression, Obsessive Compulsive Disorder, Panic Disorder with Agoraphobia, Paranoid Schizophrenia, Post-Traumatic Stress Disorder, Tourette's Syndrome, and Substance Dependence. Each case study takes students through five stages of a patient's experience: the diagnosis, case history, an interview, treatment, and assessment. Students are able to explore diagnostic processes, improve their understanding of clinical practice, and gain experience documenting their findings in a case study report project. After using *Faces Interactive,* students will have a wealth of information about, and a humanistic outlook on, these disorders. This product is available at the Online Learning Center (www.mhhe.com/halgin5).

Acknowledgments

The following instructors were instrumental in the development of the text, offering their feedback and advice as reviewers:

Jo Ann Armstrong, *Patrick Henry Community College, Virginia*

Jacqueline A. Conley, *Chicago State University*

Joanne Davila, *State University of New York*

John K. Hall, *University of Pittsburgh, Pennsylvania*

Frances Haemmerlie, *University of Missouri at Rolla*

Angela J. C. LaSala, *Community College of Southern Nevada*

Pamela Mulder, *Marshall University, West Virginia*

Joseph Palladino, *University of Southern Indiana*

Susan K. Pollock, *Mesa Community College, Arizona*

Kathy Sexton-Radek, *Elmhurst College, Illinois*

Daniel Segal, *University of Colorado at Colorado Springs*

Jerome Short, *George Mason University, Virginia*

Lee Skeens, *Southeastern Community College, Iowa*

Irene Staik, *University of Montevallo, Alabama*

Francis Terrell, *University of North Texas*

Timothy P. Tomczak, *Genesee Community College, New York*

Theresa Wadkins, *University of Nebraska at Kearney*

Thomas Weatherly, *Georgia Perimeter College*

Our most heartfelt appreciation goes to our families, whose encouragement and patience gave both of us the energy to follow through on a task that consumed countless hours. The loving support of our spouses, Lucille Halgin and Richard O'Brien, was inspiring and energizing throughout the revision process. The perspectives of our children, Daniel and Kerry Halgin, and Stacey Whitbourne and Jennifer O'Brien, helped keep before us the goal of writing in a way that would appeal to interested students.

A great book can't come together without a great publishing team. We'd like to thank our editorial team, all of whom worked with us through various stages of the publishing process. Special gratitude goes to Dawn Groundwater, Director of Development, Psychology. We are also indebted to Melissa Caughlin, Marketing Director, who possesses a sophisticated understanding of the needs of instructors and students. With thoughtfulness and good humor, Melissa provided us with recommendations that enhance the text in many important ways. Other members of the McGraw-Hill team also deserving an expression of our appreciation are Mary Lee Harms, Freelance Developmental Editor; Leslie LaDow, Production Editor; and Srdjan Savanovic, Designer.

We are also indebted to Justin Smith for his thoughtful contributions to the development of the *Nothing to Hide* sections, and his bibliographic research. Thanks also to Alana Klarman for bibliographic research pertaining to the Media & Research Update section.

Very special thanks to Michelle Whitaker for her outstanding work recruiting all the models, preparing them for their portraits, and coordinating the photo shoot. Special thanks to the individuals who served as models for the chapter cases: K. Anderson, B. Clifford, C. Colletta, A. Costello, C. Cronin, E. Elgin, F. Ge, B. Hait, A. Koske, K. Mills, A. Spring, S. Subramony, D. Teffer, M. Teffer, and S. Wright. We are grateful to these models for allowing their images to be used to bring life to the case material, but want to make it clear that they have no real-life relationship to the character or the disorder described in the corresponding case.

On a personal note, we want to thank each other for a wonderful collaborative relationship. Even the fifth edition of a textbook requires countless discussions and compromises, all of which were managed in a friendly and collegial manner. We are thrilled to see how successful our efforts have been for more than a decade.

Chapter Outline

Each chapter begins with an outline of its content setting the stage for and serving as an overview of the chapter.

Case Report

Opening each chapter is a case report from the files of Dr. Sarah Tobin. The cases detail the history of patients who are dealing with mental health issues covered in the chapters. The clinical perspective and descriptions of real people's experiences provide a window into how chapter material is observed and applied in practice.

Mini Case

This boxed feature, often found several times in each chapter, presents a brief hypothetical case study, accompanied by an outline of the *DSM-IV-IR* criteria that relates to the case. This combination helps readers to recognize a disorder's symptoms and offers them a window into what psychology professionals look for when they make diagnoses.

---

162 Anxiety Disorders

Mini Case

GENERALIZED ANXIETY DISORDER

Gina is a 32-year-old single mother of two children seeking professional help for her long-standing feelings of anxiety. Despite the fact that her life is relatively stable in terms of financial and interpersonal matters, she worries most of the time that she will develop financial problems, that her children will become ill, and that the political situation in the country will make life for her and her children more difficult. Although she tries to dismiss these concerns as excessive, she finds it virtually impossible to control her worrying. Most of the time, she feels uncomfortable and tense, and sometimes her tension becomes so extreme that she begins to tremble and sweat. She finds it difficult to sleep at night. During the day she is restless, keyed up, and tense. She has consulted a variety of medical specialists, each of whom has been unable to diagnose a physical problem.

Diagnostic Features

- This diagnosis is assigned to people who experience excessive anxiety and worry occurring more days than not for at least 6 months, pertaining to a number of events or activities, such as work or school.
- Their anxiety, worry, or related physical symptoms cause significant distress or impairment.
- They find it difficult to control their worry.
- Their anxiety and worry are associated with at least three of the following:
  - Restlessness
  - Being easily fatigued
  - Concentration difficulty
  - Irritability
  - Muscle tension
  - Sleep disturbance

Characteristics of Obsessive-Compulsive Disorder

The obsessions and compulsions that characterize OCD greatly interfere with life and trap the individual in a cycle of distressing, anxiety-provoking thought and behavior. The symptoms of OCD are time-consuming, irrational, and distracting, and the individual may desperately wish to stop them. You can imagine how distressing it is for people whose thoughts are filled with concerns about contamination (e.g., germs), doubts (e.g., leaving the gas on), or aggression (e.g., fear of harming another person).

The most common compulsions involve the repetition of a specific behavior, such as washing and cleaning, counting, putting items in order, checking, or requesting assurance. Another compulsion that has caught the attention of experts in this area involves hoarding (Steketee & Frost, 2003), in which an individual stores useless items such as outdated newspapers, mail, shopping bags, and empty food containers. When other people urge them to discard any of the items, they respond with concern that the item may be needed later for some reason. Of particular concern to public health officials are those individuals who compulsively hoard live animals in their homes, such as cats, dogs, farm animals, wild animals, or birds. Dozens, or even as many as 100 animals, are sometimes kept in the most unhygienic of conditions by these individuals.

In the movie *As Good as It Gets*, Jack Nicholson plays a man with obsessive-compulsive disorder. Even expressing affection to a pet is complicated by his need to wear protective gloves.

Real Stories

For every chapter, a "Real Stories" box highlights an individual's own account of what it is like to have a disorder. These people, many of them well-known public figures, openly share their personal thoughts and feelings and, in doing so, help bridge the gap between the stigma of mental illness and empathetic understanding.

Nothing to Hide: Mental Illness in the Family

Nothing to Hide: Mental Illness in the Family introduces families whose lives have been changed by mental illness. These families are from diverse racial, ethnic, religious, and socioeconomic backgrounds. They live in areas both urban and rural, from Los Angeles to a small town in Tennessee. Clearly, mental illness knows no boundaries.

"When a debilitating illness, either physical or mental, strikes a child, an adolescent, or an adult, it has an impact on the entire family. A diagnosis of mental illness, however, carries with it an additional challenge: the pervasive and destructive burden of stigma. Stigma gives rise to myths, stereotypes, and misunderstandings about people who have psychiatric disorders and their family members. The primary goal of Nothing to Hide is to dispel common misconceptions about mental illness in order to decrease stigma."

—Jean J. Beard and Peggy Gillespie, Amherst, Massachusetts

"People sometimes ask, "Why are these people smiling?" I can't answer that question. But I know the question betrays a notion that most of us have about mental illness: that those who have it are different from us. Slowly, we think, they don't feel what we feel; they don't express it in the same way. Now, please take another look."

—Gigi Kaeser (photographer)

Return to the Case

This end-of-chapter feature revisits the case report presented at the beginning of the chapter. After learning about the disorder in more detail from studying the chapter, the reader can then fully appreciate the in-depth coverage of the patient's history and Dr. Tobin's official assessment, diagnosis, case formulation, treatment plan, and clinical conclusions.

Interactivity

An icon guides the reader to an interactivity related to a specific topic discussed in the text. The interactivity can be found on the MindMAP Plus CD-ROM that is included with each new textbook.

Video Segment

A photo from each video segment on the MindMAP Plus CD-ROM provides a visual cue to launch the CD-ROM and view the video.

Concept Map
This visual guide presents a quick, "at-a-glance" view of the chapter.

Guided Review
This is a fill-in-the-blank summarizing exercise that appears in each chapter.

CHAPTER 2
CLASSIFICATION, TREATMENT PLANS, ETHICS, AND LEGAL ISSUES

CLASSIFICATION AND TREATMENT

DIAGNOSIS
Client's Symptoms
Diagnostic Criteria
Final Diagnosis
Case Formulation
Cultural
Formulation

DSM-IV
Development
Assumptions
The Five Axes

TREATMENT
Planning Goals
Planning Site
Planning Modality
Implementing
Treatment
Treatment Course
Treatment Outcome

LEARNING OBJECTIVES

1.0 Psychological Disorder: Experiences of Client and Clinician (pp. 87-92)
  1.1 Distinguish the concept of a client from that of a patient as the individual who is the focus of psychological treatment. (p. 88)
  1.2 Describe the prevalence of psychological disorders in the United States. (pp. 89-90)
  1.3 Describe the types of clinicians who provide psychological treatment. (p. 91)
2.0 The Diagnostic and Statistical Manual of Mental Disorders (pp. 92-108)
  2.1 Outline the history of the development of DSM-IV. (pp. 93-96)
  2.2 Define the term mental disorder as it is used in DSM-IV. (pp. 97-99)
  2.3 Explain the assumptions underlying the DSM-IV, including the medical model, a theoretical orientation, categorical approach, and multiaxial system. (pp. 99-103)
  2.4 Define the five axes of DSM-IV: (pp. 103-108)
    Axis I: Clinical Disorders (pp. 103-104)
    Axis II: Personality Disorders and Mental Retardation (pp. 104-105)
    Axis III: General Medical Conditions (pp. 105-106)
    Axis IV: Psychosocial and Environmental Problems (pp. 106-107)
    Axis V: Global Assessment of Functioning (pp. 107-108)
3.0 The Diagnostic Process (pp. 108-117)
  3.1 Explain how the clinician obtains the clients reported symptoms. (p. 109)
  3.2 Indicate how the diagnostic criteria of DSM-IV are used in identifying a possible diagnosis, including the role of the decision tree. (pp. 109-111)

REVIEW AT A GLANCE

Nearly (1)_____ the population is afflicted with a diagnosable psychological disorder at some time in life. Approximately (2)_____ percent of these people seek professional help from clinicians, (3)____ percent from other professional sources. The remainder turn to informal sources of support or go without help. Clinicians are found within several professions such as (4)_____, (5)_____, (6)_____, (7)_____, and (8)_____ counseling.

Clinicians and researchers use the (9)_____, which contains descriptions of all psychological disorders. In recent editions the authors have tried to meet the criterion of (10)_____ so that a given diagnosis will be consistently applied to anyone showing a particular set of symptoms. Researchers have also worked to ensure the (11)_____ of the classification system that that the various diagnoses represent real and distinct clinical phenomena. The DSM-IV is based on a (12)_____ model orientation in which disorders are viewed as (13)_____. Diagnoses are categorized in terms of relevant areas of functioning called (14)_____. Axis I includes (15)_____; Axis II, (16)_____; Axis III, (17)_____; Axis IV, (18)_____; and Axis V contains the (19)_____ scale.

The diagnostic process involves using all relevant information to arrive at a label that characterizes a client's disorder. After attending to a client's reported and observable symptoms, the clinician uses the DSM-IV criteria and a strategy known as a (20)_____. The clinician rules out (21)_____ and tries to assign a (22)_____. After the diagnostic process, clinicians develop a (23)_____, in an effort to understand the processes and factors that might have influenced the client's current psychological status. Once diagnosis is determined, a (24)_____ plan is developed, which includes issues pertaining to (25)_____, (26)_____, and (27)_____. A (28)_____ is recommended. Possibilities include a (29)_____, (30)_____, (31)_____, (32)_____ or other appropriate setting. The treatment (33)_____ is specified, and may involve (34)_____, (35)_____, (36)_____, or (37)_____ therapy. After a plan is developed, clinicians implement treatment with particular attention to the fact that the (38)_____ is a crucial determinant of whether therapy will succeed.

Learning Objectives
These goals help students focus their studying efforts on the key information in each chapter.

Exercises

In addition to matching, identifications, and applicable games, each chapter contains critical thinking questions that relate back to the Dr. Sarah Tobin Case Reports in each chapter.

FOCUSING ON RESEARCH

Answer the following questions concerning the Research Focus entitled "How Do Reports Determine if a Treatment is Really Work?"

1. Compare and contrast the goals and research methods of efficacy research and effectiveness research in terms of analyzing psychotherapy.

2. Briefly summarize Seligman's argument that efficacy studies don't tell the whole story about the value of psychotherapy.

3. As a potential consumer of psychotherapy, which types of study would you pay most attention to and why?

FROM THE CASE FILES OF DR. SARAH TOBIN: THINKING ABOUT PETER'S CASE

Answer the following questions about the case of Peter Dickinson.

1. Briefly list Peter's symptoms reported by Peter and his brother, Don.

2. What symptoms did Dr. Tobin observe in Peter?

3. What was Dr. Tobin's diagnosis of Peter?

4. Describe the course of Peter's treatment, both in the hospital and after discharge.

5. Concerning the outcome of Peter's treatment, would you characterize his treatment as effective? Why or why not?

HOW ARE WE DIFFERENT?

Answer these questions about "How People Differ: Are Minorities Really More Vulnerable to Psychological Disorders?"

1. What evidence is there to suggest that persons of African-American heritage might be more likely to suffer from certain psychological disorders?

What particular disorders might have a higher prevalence in this population?

Chapter 2   3   Classification, Treatment Plans, Ethics, and Legal Issues

---

ANSWERS

MATCHING

1.	i	4.	j	7.	m	10.	c	13.	h
2.	k	5.	f	8.	o	11.	d	14.	n
3.	l	6.	b	9.	a	12.	e	15.	g

Assumption about "mental disorder"	Explanation
The disorder is clinically significant	Symptoms must be present to a significant degree and for a significant period of time.
The disorder is reflected in a syndrome	Individual symptoms or problematic behaviors are not sufficient for diagnosis as a mental disorder.
The disorder is associated with present distress, impairment, or risk	The behaviors or symptoms must involve some type of personal or social cost.
The disorder is not culturally sanctioned	The disorder is not expectable for ones society or culture.

FOCUSING ON RESEARCH

1. Efficacy research takes place under experimental conditions, usually in university-based clinics where therapists are carefully selected, trained, and monitored. Patients with multiple problems are usually excluded. Effectiveness studies are conducted in the "field"--in real world therapy settings, where clients are not assigned to random groups, for fixed durations, and treated according to a predetermined script.

2. Efficacy studies do not take into account real world situations. Client's diagnoses often do not fit neatly into one clearly delineated category, which can be treated with a predetermined script. Efficacy studies don't take into account one of the main reasons why therapy is successful (when it is)--the client-therapist relationship.

3. Probably both. Efficacy studies have a place because they are conducted under experimental conditions. But I would also want to know about real-life experiences from effectiveness studies.

HOW DO WE DIFFER?

1. African-Americans suffer more from the effects of stressors accompanying poverty and social disadvantage.

2. Alcohol dependence, phobias, and generalized anxiety disorder.

3. Racial discrimination, lack of economic resources to pay for mental health care, and different attitudes toward consulting mental health professionals.

Chapter 2   5   Classification, Treatment Plans, Ethics, and Legal Issues

---

Answer Keys

At the end of each chapter, full explanations are provided for each of the multiple-choice items. Possible answers are supplied for the cases through essay and short-answer items, and the answers to the matching, identification, review at a glance, and games are also provided.

Instructor's Manual

Chapter Overview
This visual guide presents the chapter outline as a concept map. Each section is self-contained and includes a topic summary and related learning objectives.

Teaching Objectives
Identical to the learning objectives that appear in the student study guide, these objectives are meant to guide instructors' chapter syllabi.

Demonstrations and Classroom Exercises and Video and Films
Includes various demonstrations and exercises to be used in class as well as a list of videos related to chapter content.

Supplementary Lecture/Discussion Topics and Controversies
Includes additional lecture topics and discussion questions linked to learning objectives. These also reflect the main text case features.

Guide to Video Segments on MindMAP Plus Student CD-ROM
For each video segment, the Instructor's Manual includes an introduction to the segment, a transcript, teaching notes, and discussion questions to engage students in the subject of the video.

---

2 Classification and Treatment Plans

CHAPTER OVERVIEW

CLASSIFICATION AND TREATMENT PLANS

DIAGNOSIS
Client's Symptoms
Diagnostic Criteria
Final Diagnosis
Case Formulation
Cultural Formulation

DSM-IV
Development
Assumptions
The Five Axes

TREATMENT
Planning Goals
Planning Site
Planning Modality
Implementing Treatment
Treatment Course
Treatment: Outcome

TEACHING OBJECTIVES

1.0 Psychological Disorder: Experiences of Client and Clinician (pp. 87-92)
  1.1 Distinguish the concept of a client from that of a patient as the individual who is the focus of psychological treatment. (p. 88)
  1.2 Describe the prevalence of psychological disorders in the United States. (pp. 89-90)
  1.3 Describe the types of clinicians who provide psychological treatment. (p. 91)
2.0 The Diagnostic and Statistical Manual of Mental Disorders (pp. 92-108)
  2.1 Outline the history of the development of DSM-IV. (pp. 93-96)
  2.2 Define the term mental disorder as it is used in DSM-IV. (pp. 97-99)
  2.3 Explain the assumptions underlying the DSM-IV, including the medical model, a theoretical orientation, categorical approach, and multiaxial system. (pp. 99-103)
  2.4 Define the five axes of DSM-IV: (pp. 103-108)
      Axis I: Clinical Disorders (pp. 103-104)
      Axis II: Personality Disorders and Mental Retardation (pp. 104-105)
      Axis III: General Medical Conditions (pp. 105-106)
      Axis IV: Psychosocial and Environmental Problems (pp. 106-107)
      Axis V: Global Assessment of Functioning (pp. 107-108)
3.0 The Diagnostic Process (pp. 108-117)
  3.1 Explain how the clinician obtains the client's reported symptoms. (p. 109)
  3.2 Indicate how the diagnostic criteria of DSM-IV are used in identifying a possible diagnosis, including the role of the decision tree. (pp. 109-111)

Demonstrations & Classroom Exercises

Divide students into groups and give each group a brief case description, highlighting a hypothetical client's symptoms. Then have students prepare a group report on how they might arrive at a diagnosis and how they might plan a treatment for the client. The steps highlighted in the text can serve as guidelines for the students.

Videos & Films

Abnormal Behavior: A Mental Hospital, provides students with a glimpse inside the walls of a mental hospital. The film shows several therapy sessions as well as an ECT treatment. This film provides a good overview of the medical model. (McGraw-Hill/CRM; 28 min., color).

Interrupted Lives demonstrates the plight of clients with long-term mental illnesses and how they struggle to reestablish themselves in the community. (Boston University Center for rehabilitation Research and Training in Mental Health, 1019 Commonwealth Ave., Boston, MA 02215; 60 min., color).

Larry is the dramatization of an actual case of a man mistakenly institutionalized who struggles to conquer the effects of years of harsh treatment. (Learning Corporation of America; 78 min., color).

Madness and Medicine is a two-part film, which shows a mental institution and deals with the issues of drug therapy, ECT and psychosurgery from both the patients' and the doctors' perspectives. (CRM; 49 min., color).

Titicut Follies is a documentary filmed at a state hospital in Massachusetts. It illustrates many of the difficult conditions that characterized mental hospitals in the sixties. (Zipporah; 90 min., b/w).

One Flew Over the Cuckoo's Nest is a feature film which tells the story of McMurphy, a rebellious patient in a mental institution that is subjected to nearly ever treatment in the book. It is an interesting Hollywood look at life in a mental hospital. This movie can be rented at most video rental stores like Blockbuster Video. (129 min., color).

Supplementary Lecture/Discussion Topics and Controversies

Linked to Objective 3.6
Since many forms of psychological disorders are intimately tied with the culture in which they occur, it should not be surprising that diagnostic systems developed in the west, like the DSM are culturally based. There are several reports of a disorder characterized by confusion and dramatic excitement that is often brief in duration that has been observed in West Africa, the Caribbean and New Guinea and has been referred to by researchers as transient psychosis, acute confusional state or bouffée délirante aigue. Some researchers argue that this particular syndrome does not fit neatly into any of the standard psychiatric diagnoses established by the American Psychiatric Association (Draguns, 1980, p.138). In some instances, other cultures do not have diagnostic labels for syndromes that we recognize in our culture. The Inuit of Alaska have no word or label to conveniently describe anxiety (Murphy, 1976, p. 1024). These facts lead many to criticize the reliability, validity and the basic utility of the DSM.

Draguns, J. G. (1980). Psychological disorders of clinical severity. In H.C. Triandis, & J. Draguns (Eds.), *Handbook of cross-cultural psychology* (Vol. 6). Boston: Allyn & Bacon.

Murphy, J.M. (1976). Psychiatric labeling in cross-cultural perspective. *Science, 191,* 1019-1028.

Linked to Objective 3.6
It is now well recognized that culture has an impact on the way in which certain psychological disorders are manifest in individuals. Yet culture itself is a very broad construct that encompasses a wide range of factors. Researchers have recently turned their interest to the specific cultural factors that may lead to differences in disorders that are observed between different ethnic and racial groups. Okazaki (1997) hypothesized that one potential factor that might lead to some well-documented differences in social anxiety and depression between Asian-Americans and White Americans is the ethnic difference in self-construals. Okazaki notes that Asian-Americans typically have more interdependent self-construals; that is, there self-definition is based more on their relationships with significant others. White Americans typically have independent self-construals—their self-definition is based more on individual and personal factors. By using multivariate techniques, Okazaki correlated Asian-American and White American students' scores on measures of self-construal, depression and fear of negative evaluation. Although no differences were found on measures of depression, ethnic differences were found on measures of social anxiety. The author suggests that ethnic differences in self-construal might predispose Asian-Americans to certain types of disorders that have social anxiety (e.g., social phobia). Okazaki also points out that the current findings shed light on a culture-bound syndrome observed in Japan called *Taijin Kyofusho* characterized by avoidance of social situations due to a fear of offending or embarrassing others. More researchers will need to focus on the specific cultural factors that may lead to ethnic differences in psychopathology.

Okazaki, S. (1997). Sources of ethnic differences between Asian-American and white American college students on measures of depression and social anxiety. *Journal of Abnormal Psychology, 106,* 52-60.

Supplementary Topics/Lecture Launcher Discussion Questions

Case Report
In the case of Peter Dickinson, why do you think Peter was so resistant to the idea that he might need help? In Peter's own view, do you think he felt he needed help? What aspect of Peter's case most clearly indicates that Peter has a problem?

Research Focus
From a research standpoint, what advantages are there to conducting what Seligman calls efficacy studies as opposed to effectiveness studies? What are some of the disadvantages?

Video Segment 1.1 - History of mental illness
Summary of beliefs about the causes of psychological disorders from ancient times to the present.

CAPTION:
History is filled with a variety of attempts to understand and manage the symptoms of psychological disorders. These efforts ranged from the bizarre and barbaric to the scientific and humanitarian. Segment 1.2 provides vivid illustrations of views about the causes of psychological disorders from ancient to contemporary times.

INTRODUCTION:
This segment, from the Discovery program, "Schizophrenia: Stolen Lives, Stolen Minds," provides vivid illustrations of views about the causes of psychological disorders from ancient to contemporary times. The segment focuses on the experiential aspects of psychological disorders.

TRANSCRIPT:
Insanity is an ancient affliction, perhaps as old as humanity itself. For much of history, the only thing as painful as the madness was the way mankind tried to deal with it. We've tried to lock it away, cut it out, shock it or burn it out, but the nightmare refuses to disappear. Madness has stayed with us. In ancient cultures, it was seen as an imbalance of four bodily fluids. Brain was an organ of the mind, susceptible to disease. In the middle ages, it was seen as a sign of the devil, punishment by god. Between 1460-1680 thousands of people, mostly women, were burned at the stake. In the middle ages, they were shackled and chained and left to rot in their own waste. By the 19th century, madness had become a subject of science. Still new techniques for study, confinement and suppression of lunacy were little more humane and no more productive that what had come before. With 20th century and birth of psychiatry, schizophrenia was defined and named. Schizophrenia, the affliction of the fragmented mind. Modern therapies, like lobotomy and shock, were still abusive. The first real break through came in 1951 with discovery of neuroleptic drugs in France. Powerful medications that diminished the experience of psychosis. Numbed by powerful drugs, they could live outside the institution. Medication can only modify the symptoms. The person is captive to a brain unable to tell the difference between what is real and what is imagined. Imagine a world in which a busy restaurant feels like the front lines of a battlefield, where every sound, every voice, every noise of music, were all firing at you at the same volume. Imagine that in every glance, you felt people were reading your mind, injecting thoughts into your head. That all of these imagined voices inside your head are screaming all at once, in a language you don't understand. Imagine being trapped in a world with no boundaries between self and others. No border between your thoughts and the thoughts of others. For millions of people around the globe, this is everyday life. Life in the world of schizophrenia. Normal people can block out normal conversations but people with schizophrenia can't. When schizophrenics are in a crowded room with a lot of

http://www.mhhe.com/halgin5

Welcome to the
Halgin/Whitbourne
*Abnormal Psychology
Updated 5e website!*

About the Book

- **Overview**
  Provides a quick synopsis of the edition and the material covered.

- **Table of Contents**
  Lists the entire contents.

- **What's New**
  Introduces the new features of the textbook.

- **Supplements**
  Includes title and ISBN information for all accompanying student and instructor supplements.

- **Faces of Abnormal Psychology Video**
  Links to a downloadable demo of McGraw-Hill's latest abnormal psychology video containing new segments on real people with real disorders. FACES is free to adopters.

About the Authors

Meet the Authors

Have questions or comments concerning the text? E-mail the authors!

Richard Halgin
rhalgin@psych.umass.edu

Susan Whitbourne
swhitbo@psych.umass.edu

Student Resources

- **Online Learning Center**
  Links to every text chapter containing learning objectives, quizzes, flashcards, Internet exercises, and more!

- **Internet Primer**
  Links to the McGraw-Hill Internet Guide providing students with valuable information on Internet navigation.

- **Careers in Psychology**
  Links to a list of resources for students interested in a career in psychology.

- **Statistics Primer**
  Provides a quick overview of statistics.

- **Web Resources**
  Links to interesting and useful psychology sites.

Instructor's Resources

- **Online Learning Center**
  Go here to see a web version of the *Instructor's Manual* and downloadable PowerPoint slide presentations for each chapter. This area is password protected. Please contact your McGraw-Hill representative for the password.

- **PageOut**
  FREE to adopters, PageOut is designed for the professor just beginning to explore website options. In just a few minutes, even the novice computer user can have a course website up and running.

- **Psych in the News**
  Links to issues of the *Psychwatch: Newsletter.*

ABNORMAL PSYCHOLOGY

CHAPTER 1

Understanding Abnormality

A Look at History and Research Methods

Twenty years of clinical practice had not prepared me for my encounter with Rebecca Hasbrouck. Working in the outpatient department of a large psychiatric facility, I had encountered hundreds of people whose stories would move me, but, for some reason, Rebecca's seemed unusually troubling. Perhaps it was her similarity to me in so many ways that stirred me up. Like me, she was in her midforties and had mothered two sons when she was in her early thirties. She had been raised in a middle-class family and had attended excellent schools. In fact, when I first spoke with Rebecca, my attention was drawn to the faded Polaroid photo that she grasped tightly in her fist. It was the picture of a jubilant 22-year-old Rebecca on the day of her graduation from an Ivy League university. She stood beside her parents and her older sister, everyone gleaming with pride about all that she had accomplished and filled with the greatest of expectations about all that would lie ahead for her. I later learned that she was planning to attend one of the most prominent law schools in the country, where she would pursue a specialization in maritime law. Everyone, including Rebecca, assumed that a life of happiness and personal fulfillment would lie ahead.

Before telling you the rest of Rebecca's story, let me tell you more about my initial encounter with her. It was the Tuesday morning following Labor Day weekend. The summer was over, and I was returning from a restful vacation, burdened somewhat by the prospects of the correspondence, the messages, and the new responsibilities that awaited me. I had arrived early that morning, even before the receptionist, with the hope of getting a head start on my work. As I approached the clinic's entrance, I was shocked, however, to find a disheveled woman lying up against the locked door. Her hair was dirty and knotted, her clothes torn and stained. She looked up at me with piercing eyes and spoke my name. Who was this woman? How did she know my name? The sight of countless home-less people on the streets of the city every day had made me numb to the power of their despair, but I was suddenly startled to have one of them call me by name.

After unlocking the door, I asked her to come in and take a seat in the waiting room. As she emerged from a state of seeming incoherence, this woman told me that her name was "Rebecca Hasbrouck." She explained that an old college friend whom she had phoned had given her my name and address. Rebecca's friend apparently recognized the seriousness of her condition and urged her to get some professional help.

I asked Rebecca to tell me how I could be of assistance. With tears streaming down her face, she whispered that she needed to "return to the world" from which she had fled 3 years earlier. I asked her to tell me what that "world" was. The story that unfolded seemed unbelievable. She explained that just a few years earlier she was living a comfortable life in an upper-middle-class suburb. Both she and her husband were very successful attorneys, and their two sons were bright, attractive, and athletically gifted. Oddly, Rebecca stopped there, as if that were the end of her story. Naturally, I asked her what happened then. Upon hearing my question, her eyes glazed over as she drifted into a detached state of apparent fantasy. I continued to speak to her, but she did not seem to hear my words. Several minutes went by, and she returned to our dialogue.

Rebecca proceeded to tell me the story of her journey into depression, despair, and poverty. Interestingly, the turning point in Rebecca's life was almost 3 years to the day of our encounter. As she and her family were returning from a vacation in the mountains, a large truck violently rammed their car, causing the car, which Rebecca was driving, to careen off the road and roll over several times. Rebecca was not sure how her body was propelled from the wreckage, but she does recall lying near the burning vehicle as fire consumed the three most important people in her life. For the weeks that she spent in the hospital, recovering from her own serious injuries, including brain trauma, she wandered in and out of consciousness, convinced all the while that her experience was merely a bad dream from which she would soon awaken.

On her release from the hospital, she returned to her empty home but was tormented relentlessly by the voices and memories of her sons and husband. Realizing that she was in emotional turmoil, she turned to her mother for support and assistance. Sadly, Rebecca's mother was also struggling with one of her recurring episodes of severe depression and was unable to help Rebecca in her time of need. In fact, her mother sternly told Rebecca never to call again, because she did not want to be "burdened by" Rebecca's difficulties. Adding to Rebecca's dismay was the fact that she received a similar distancing response from the parents of her deceased husband, who told Rebecca that it was too painful for them to interact with the woman who had "killed" their son and grandchildren.

Feeling that she had no one to whom she could turn for help, Rebecca set out in search of her lost family members. In the middle of a cold October night, she walked out the front door of her home, dressed only in a nightgown and slippers. Walking the 4-mile distance into the center of town, she called out the names of these three "ghosts" and searched for them in familiar places. At one point, she went to the front door of the police chief's home and screamed at the top of her lungs that she wanted her sons and husband "released from prison." A police car was summoned, and she was taken to a psychiatric emergency room. However, during the process of her admission, she cleverly slipped away and set out on a path to reunite with her family members, who were "calling out" to her. During the 3 years that followed this tragic episode, Rebecca had fallen into a life of homelessness, losing all contact with her former world.

Sarah Tobin, PhD

In each chapter of this book, you will read a case study written in the words of Dr. Sarah Tobin, who is a composite of many of the qualities found in a good clinical psychologist. At the beginning of each chapter, Dr. Tobin tells us about her initial encounter with a client who has a problem pertinent to the content of that chapter. At the end of the chapter, after you have developed a better understanding about the client's disorder, we will return to Dr. Tobin's detailed discussion of the case. We believe that you will find each case to be an exciting opportunity to hear the thoughts of a clinician and you will develop an appreciation for the complexity and challenges involved in the diagnosis and treatment of psychological disorders.

The field of abnormal psychology is filled with countless fascinating stories of people who suffer from psychological disorders. In this chapter, we will try to give you some sense of the reality that psychological disturbance is certain to touch everyone, to some extent, at some point in life. As you progress through this course, you will almost certainly develop a sense of the pain and stigma associated with psychological problems. You will find yourself drawn into the many ways that mental health problems affect the lives of individuals, their families, and society. In addition to becoming more personally exposed to the emotional aspects of abnormal psychology, you will learn about the scientific and theoretical basis for understanding and treating the people who suffer from psychological disorders.

This woman claims that her telephone conversations are being recorded by someone who wants to harm her. If you were her friend, how would you go about assessing whether her concerns are legitimate or whether her thinking is disturbed?

What Is Abnormal Behavior?

Think about how you would feel if you were to see someone like Rebecca walking around your neighborhood. You might be shocked, upset, or afraid, or you might even laugh. Why would you respond in this manner? Perhaps Rebecca would seem abnormal to you. But think further about this. On what basis would you judge Rebecca to be abnormal? Is it her dress, the fact that she is mumbling to herself, that she sounds paranoid, or that she is psychologically unstable? And what would account for your emotional responses to seeing this woman? Why should it bother you to see Rebecca behaving in this way? Do you imagine that she will hurt you? Are you upset because she seems so helpless and out of control? Do you laugh because she seems so ridiculous, or is there something about her that makes you nervous? Perhaps you speculate on the causes of Rebecca's bizarre behavior. Is she physically ill, intoxicated, or psychologically disturbed? And, if she is psychologically disturbed, how could her disturbance be explained? You might also feel concerned about Rebecca's welfare and wonder how she might be helped. Should you call the police to take her to a hospital? Or should you just leave her alone, because she presents no real danger to anyone? You may not have experienced a situation involving someone exactly like Rebecca, but you have certainly encountered some people in your life whom you regard as "abnormal," and your reactions to these people probably have included the range of feelings you would experience if you were to see Rebecca.

Conditions like Rebecca's are likely to touch you in a very personal way. Perhaps you have already been affected by the distressing effects of psychological disorders. Perhaps you have been unusually depressed, fearful, or anxious, or maybe the emotional distress has been a step removed from you: your father struggles with alcoholism, or your mother has been hospitalized for severe depression; a sister has an eating disorder, or your brother has an irrational fear. If you have not encountered a psychological disorder within your immediate family, you have very likely encountered one in your extended family and circle of friends. You may not have known the formal psychiatric diagnosis for the problem, and you may not have understood its nature or cause. But you knew that something was wrong and that professional help was needed.

Until they are forced to face such problems, most people believe that "bad things" happen only to other people. Other people have car accidents, other people get cancer, and other people become severely depressed. We hope that reading this textbook will help you go beyond this "other people" syndrome. Psychological disorders are part of the human experience, touching the life—either directly or indirectly—of every person. As you read about these disorders and the people who suffer with them, you will find that most of these problems are treatable, and many are preventable.

What is "abnormal" behavior? You may have read this word in the title of the book without giving it much thought. Perhaps you told a friend that you were taking a course in "abnormal" psychology. Think about what you had in mind when you read or used the word *abnormal* as applied to human behavior. How would you define "abnormal" behavior? Read the following examples. Which of these behaviors do you regard as abnormal?

- Finding a "lucky" seat in an exam
- Being unable to sleep, eat, study, or talk to anyone else for days after a lover says, "It's over between us"
- Breaking into a cold sweat at the thought of being trapped in an elevator
- Swearing, throwing pillows, and pounding fists on the wall in the middle of an argument with a roommate
- Refusing to eat solid food for days at a time in order to stay thin
- Having to engage in a thorough hand-washing after coming home from a ride on a bus
- Believing that the government has agents who are listening in on telephone conversations
- Drinking a six-pack of beer a day in order to be "sociable" with friends after work

What is your basis for deciding between "normal" and "abnormal"? As you can see from this exercise, this distinction is often difficult to make. It may even seem arbitrary, yet it is essential that you arrive at a clear understanding of this term to guide you in your study of the many varieties of human behavior discussed in this book.

Defining Abnormality

Let's take a look at four important ways in which we will be discussing abnormality throughout the remainder of this book. These criteria are based on the current diagnostic procedures used in the mental health community. Abnormality could also be defined in terms of infrequency (such as left-handedness) or deviation from the average (such as extremes in height). In abnormal psychology, such statistical criteria typically are not considered relevant.

Distress   The story of Rebecca is that of a woman whose life was thrown into emotional chaos following a traumatic event in which she witnessed the death of her husband and sons. The horror of this image propelled her into a state of profound psychological turmoil, as she looked for ways to cope with the loss of the most important people in her life. Distress, the experience of emotional or physical pain, is common in life. At times, the level of pain becomes so great that an individual finds it difficult to function. As you will see in many of the conditions discussed in this book, psychological pain, such as deep depression or intense anxiety, may be so great that some people cannot get through the tasks of daily life.

The anxiety about public speaking experienced by this woman may cause such a high level of tension that she becomes unable to continue her presentation.

Impairment   In many instances, intense distress leads to a reduction in a person's ability to function, but there are also instances in which a person's functioning is deficient but he or she does not feel particularly upset. Impairment involves a reduction in a person's ability to function at an optimal or even an average level. For example, when a man consumes an excessive amount of alcohol, his perceptual and cognitive functioning is impaired, and he would be a danger behind the wheel of a car. He might not describe himself as feeling distressed, however; on the contrary, he may boast about how great he feels. For some of the conditions that you will read about, people feel fine and describe themselves with positive terms; however, others would regard them as functioning inadequately in primary spheres of life, such as at work or within their families. In the case of Rebecca, we see a woman who is both distressed and impaired.

Risk to Self or Other People   Sometimes people act in ways that cause risk to themselves or others. In this context, *risk* refers to danger or threat to the well-being of a person. For example, we would describe a severely depressed woman, such as Rebecca, as being at risk of committing suicide. In other situations, an individual's thoughts or behaviors are threatening to the physical or psychological welfare of other people. Thus, people who abuse children or exploit other people create a risk in society that is considered unacceptable and abnormal. Rebecca Hasbrouck certainly engaged in behavior that put her at risk, as she lived a life of a homeless person; out of contact with reality and loved ones, she roamed the streets, looking for the family members who had been killed.

Socially and Culturally Unacceptable Behavior   Our final criterion for abnormality is behavior that is outside the norms of the social and cultural context within which it takes place. For example, it wouldn't be odd to see people with painted faces and bizarre outfits cheering inside a college basketball arena, but such behavior would be abnormal in a college classroom. In this

Do you think that wearing such unusual headgear to run in the Boston marathon is normal or abnormal behavior?

example, the social context calls for, and permits, very different kinds of behavior; people who deviate from the expected norms are regarded as abnormal.

Some behavior that is regarded as odd within a given culture, society, or subgroup may be quite common elsewhere. For example, some people from Mediterranean cultures believe in a phenomenon called *mal de ojo*, or evil eye, in which, they contend, the ill will of other people can affect them in profound ways. As a result, they may experience various bodily symptoms, such as fitful sleep, stomach distress, and fever. People expressing such beliefs in contemporary American culture might be regarded as odd, possibly a bit paranoid, or overly emotional. Returning to the case of Rebecca, her attempts to contact deceased loved ones would be considered bizarre in the United States but would not be considered unusual in other cultures where communication with the dead is an accepted cultural norm. As you can see, the context within which a behavior takes place is a critical determinant of whether it is regarded as abnormal. Although any one of the above four criteria could serve as the basis for defining abnormality, often there is an interaction. For example, a deeply distressed person will customarily be impaired and may even be a risk to self or others.

Challenges Involved in Characterizing Abnormal Behavior

The four criteria just discussed might lead you to imagine that defining abnormality is a fairly straightforward process. However, you will learn as you read this book and study about various conditions that there is rarely a clear delineation between what is normal and what is abnormal. Even experienced clinicians and researchers disagree about what constitutes a psychological disorder, as we will discuss in more depth in the next chapter.

The complexity of diagnosing abnormal psychological conditions was highlighted in a classic study conducted by David Rosenhan in 1973, the conclusions of which continue to resonate in the mental health field. Rosenhan reported the findings of a study in which eight people successfully fooled the staffs of 12 psychiatric hospitals located across the United States. These people were all "sane" and were employed in a variety of mostly professional occupations. They each presented themselves at a hospital's admissions office, complaining that they had been hearing voices that said, "Empty," "Hollow," and "Thud." The kind of "existential psychosis" that these symptoms were supposed to represent had never been reported in the psychiatric literature, which is why those symptoms were chosen. No other details about the lives of the "pseudopatients" (except their names and employment) were changed when they described themselves; consequently, their histories and current behaviors outside of their symptoms could not be considered abnormal in any way. All the hospitals accepted the pseudopatients for treatment. Once admitted to the hospitals, the pseudopatients stopped fabricating any symptoms at all. None of the staff in any of the hospitals detected the sanity of the pseudopatients and, instead, interpreted the ordinary activities of the pseudopatients on the hospital wards as further evidence of their abnormality. One of the most troubling experiences for the pseudopatients was a feeling of dehumanization, as they felt that no one on the staff cared about their personal issues and needs. Further, despite their efforts to convince the staff that they were normal, no one believed them, with the interesting exception of some of the patients who guessed that they might be either reporters or researchers trying to get an inside look at mental hospitals.

It took from 7 to 52 days for the pseudopatients to be released from the hospitals. By the time they left, each had been given a diagnosis of schizophrenia "in remission"; in other words, their symptoms were no longer evident, at least for the time being. Rosenhan concluded that the misattribution of abnormality was due to a general bias among hospital staff to call a healthy person sick: "better to err on the side of caution, to suspect illness even among the healthy" (p. 251).

Rosenhan's study was criticized on both ethical and methodological grounds. Ethical concerns were raised about the fact that the study involved the deception of the mental health professionals whose job it was to diagnose and treat the pseudopatients. Methodological questions were raised by the fact that no attempt was made to exercise the usual experimental controls on a study of this nature, such as having a comparison group (Spitzer, 1975). Other criticisms pertained to diagnostic issues. The pseudopatients were reporting serious symptoms (hallucinations) that would understandably lead most clinicians to a provisional diagnosis of a serious psychological condition such as schizophrenia. At the point of discharge, the fact that the pseudopatients were labeled as being in remission implied that they were symptom-free. Technically, the staff probably felt reluctant to label these individuals as "normal" in light of the fact that the pseudopatients had previously complained of schizophrenia-like symptoms (Farber, 1975).

Despite these criticisms, Rosenhan's results and the debates that followed in the study's aftermath were part of the momentum in the late 1960s and early 1970s to change attitudes toward institutionalization of psychologically disturbed individuals. At the same time, mental health professionals were in the process of changing the system for diagnosing many disorders, including schizophrenia. The point of the study, however, is still pertinent today. When a patient in a psychiatric hospital claims to be "the sane one in an insane place," would anyone believe the patient?

In the decades since Rosenhan conducted this controversial study, much has changed in the mental health field. The pendulum seems to have swung to the other extreme—many people with diagnosable forms of psychosis are finding it difficult to gain admission to mental health facilities. Scribner (2001) studied the experience of seven people with long, well-documented histories of chronic schizophrenia, each of whom was in the midst of an acute episode of symptoms. When they presented themselves for admission, six of the seven people were denied treatment. Scribner concluded that would-be consumers of mental health services now face many bureaucratic impediments to receiving care.

To test out the extent to which things may have changed in the field of psychiatry in the four decades since Rosenhan's study, author-psychologist Lauren Slater (2004) made several attempts to replicate the experience of Rosenhan's pseudopatients. She went to emergency rooms with the complaint that she was hearing a voice saying "thud" but had no other symptoms. In every instance she was denied admission. Most commonly, she was diagnosed as having depression with psychotic symptoms and then prescribed medication and sent on her way. Slater contrasts her experiences with those of Rosenhan's pseudopatients by noting that, although she was mislabeled, she was not "locked up." She also notes another experience that differed from that of the pseudopatients in that she was treated with "palpable kindness" by every medical professional, and she never felt diminished by their diagnoses.

Although there are many methodological and ethical debates related to research involving pseudopatients, the research by David Rosenhan served to initiate dialogue that has lasted for decades about what constitutes abnormal behavior, and how mental health clinicians should and actually do respond to people presenting symptoms outside of normal experience.

What Causes Abnormality?

Now that we have discussed criteria for defining abnormality, we can turn our attention to its causes. In trying to understand why people act and feel in ways that are regarded as abnormal, social scientists look at three dimensions: biological, psychological, and sociocultural. In other words, abnormal behavior arises

from a complex set of determinants in the body, the mind, and the social context of the individual. Throughout this book, you will see that all three of these domains have relevance to the understanding and treatment of psychological disorders. In Chapter 4, we will discuss in much greater depth the theoretical approaches associated with these general causal categories.

Biological Causes In their efforts to understand the causes of abnormal behavior, mental health experts carefully evaluate what is going on in a person's body that can be attributed to genetic inheritance or disturbances in physical functioning. As a routine component of every evaluation, Dr. Tobin assesses the extent to which a problem that seems to be emotionally caused can be explained in terms of biological determinants. Understanding the important causal role of biology also alerts Dr. Tobin to the fact that she may need to incorporate biological components, such as medication, into her intervention.

As is the case with many medical disorders, various psychological disorders run in families. Major depressive disorder is one of these disorders. The odds of a son or daughter of a depressed parent developing depression are statistically greater than they are for offspring of nondepressed parents. In the case of Rebecca Hasbrouck, Dr. Tobin would attend to the fact that Rebecca's mother suffers from recurring episodes of depression. Might Rebecca carry within her body a genetic vulnerability to developing a similar mood disorder?

In addition to considering the role of genetics, clinicians also consider the possibility that abnormal behavior may be the result of disturbances in physical functioning. Such disturbances can arise from various sources, such as medical conditions, brain damage, or exposure to certain kinds of environmental stimuli. Many medical conditions can cause a person to feel and act in ways that are abnormal. For example, a medical abnormality in the thyroid gland can cause wide variations in mood and emotionality. Brain damage resulting from a head trauma, even a slight one, can result in bizarre behavior and intense emotionality. Similarly, the ingestion of substances, either illicit drugs or prescribed medications, can result in emotional and behavioral changes that mimic a psychological disorder. Even exposure to environmental stimuli, such as toxic substances or allergens, can cause a person to experience disturbing emotional changes and behavior.

Psychological Causes If biology could provide all the answers, then we would regard mental disorders as medical diseases. Obviously, there is more to the story. Disturbance commonly arises as a result of troubling life experiences. Perhaps an event an hour ago, last year, or in the early days of a person's life has left its mark in ways that cause dramatic changes in feelings or behavior. For example, a demeaning comment from a professor can leave a student feeling hurt and depressed for days. A disappointment in an intimate relationship can evoke intense emotionality that lasts for months. A trauma that took place many years ago may continue to affect a person's thoughts, behavior, and even dreams. Life experiences may also contribute to

REAL STORIES

KELSEY GRAMMER: RECOVERING FROM TRAUMA

The case of Rebecca Hasbrouck, which opens this chapter, tells the story of a woman who has survived a trauma that changed her life. Witnessing the death of her beloved sons and husband provoked such havoc in her mind that Rebecca lost touch with reality. The enduring effects of traumatic experiences have been discussed in recent years by people, some quite famous, who have stepped forward to share their stories chronicling the residual effects of these intensely disturbing experiences. The life of actor Kelsey Grammer, who is known throughout the world for his television role as Dr. Frasier Crane on the sitcom *Frasier,* is an example of how intensely troubling family experiences can impair one's functioning in life for years.

Grammer's bouts with tragedy began very early in his life. When Grammer was 12, his father was shot and killed by a man who was found not guilty by reason of insanity. Even though he had not been close to his father during his childhood, this trauma left him feeling vulnerable in many ways; in particular, he came to feel that life could not be trusted. Eight years after the murder of his father, Grammer's sister was abducted, raped, and murdered. It was Grammer's task to identify her body. The nightmare continued when, at the age of 25, Grammer found himself once again mourning family members—his two half-brothers had died in a scuba diving accident.

Like so many people devastated by profound personal losses and hurts, Grammer sought ways to relieve his pain and became involved in substance abuse and troubled intimate relationships. In 1988 he was arrested for drunken driving and cocaine possession.

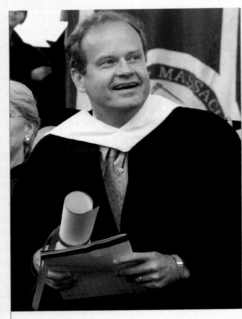

Kelsey Grammer

In 1990 he was arrested again and sentenced to 30 days in jail when he failed to appear in court. In 1996, he flipped his sports car in an alcohol-related incident, after which he sought professional help for his substance-abuse problems at the Betty Ford Center.

The story of Grammer's intimate relationships mirrored the internal chaos with which he was struggling, as he became involved with women he describes in negative terms. His first marriage, to a woman named Doreen, was short-lived, as Grammer became increasingly dissatisfied. He moved on to involvement with Agnes, a woman who made several suicide attempts, and later entered a relationship with another volatile woman, Cerlette. Subsequently, he married Leigh-Anne, a woman who Grammer asserts abused him verbally and physically until he finally ended the marriage.

In his autobiographical book, *So Far . . .* , Grammer speaks with emotion-

ally charged words about his experiences following the death of his father.

"The truth is, life at home was awful. It seemed that my grandmother and my mother, and even my sister at times, were members of a bizarre conspiracy, its sole purpose to ensure that I fulfill their needs.

No matter what I was doing, they could call at any time and make me stop. Not because there was a big problem, but maybe just because they were having a fight. I was the glue, the man of the family."

In speaking about his sister's murder, Grammer writes:

"I walked back to the house in a kind of daze. Karen was dead. I had trouble letting that sink in. It was too much to comprehend. Murdered.

I stood searching helplessly for an appropriate response. I should be crying, I thought. I entered the kitchen and went back to cooking. Yes, I thought, I should be crying, and so I tried. But it didn't work. Something strange was going on. It was as if I were split in two, and one half of me was watching the other. One a victim, and the other an observer, noting from the distance like a stranger what was happening to me.

It's difficult to explain what I was going through. The one who was watching said, What the hell is wrong with you? Your sister's dead. Why aren't you crying? Didn't you love your sister?

Of course I did, the other said, feeling guilty the tears would just not come, and fearing if they did the watching one would say that they weren't real." (p. 80)

Source: Excerpted from So *Far . . .* by Kelsey Grammer, copyright ©1995 by Kelsey Grammer. Reprinted by permission of Dutton, a division of Penguin Putnam, Inc.

psychological disorder by causing the individual to form negative associations to certain stimuli. For example, an irrational fear of small spaces may arise from being trapped in an elevator.

The trauma experienced by Rebecca Hasbrouck was so intense that her life was thrown into chaos and profound disturbance that would last for years. For Dr. Tobin to understand the nature of Rebecca's disorder, it would be important that she have a grasp of the extent of the trauma; such an understanding would also inform the treatment plan that she would develop to help Rebecca.

Thus, in evaluating psychological causes for abnormality, social scientists and clinicians consider a person's experiences. Most experiences are interpersonal—events that take place in interactions with other people. But people also have intrapsychic experiences, those that take place within thoughts and feelings. As you will see later in the text, emotional problems can arise from distorted perceptions and faulty ways of thinking. Take the case of a college student, Matt, who inferred that his girlfriend was angry with him because she failed to return his phone call. For more than a day he was affected by feelings of anger, which led to feelings of depression. He later found out that his answering machine had malfunctioned when his girlfriend called back. After discussing the situation with his roommate, he realized that his response had been irrational. As he thought about it, he realized that his reaction was probably related to a long history of disappointments with his parents, who had hurt him countless times with their unreliability. Having internalized the notion that important people tend to disappoint, Matt now expected this to happen, even when the facts did not support his conclusion. Just as biology can lead to the development of abnormality, so can the psychologically significant events in a person's life.

Sociocultural Causes   So much of who we are is determined by interpersonal interactions that take place in the concentric circles of our lives. The term *sociocultural* refers to the various circles of social influence in the lives of people. The most immediate circle is comprised of those people with whom we interact on the most local level. For the typical college student, this would be a roommate, co-workers, and classmates who are seen regularly. Moving beyond the immediate circle are those people who inhabit the extended circle of relationships, such as family members back home or friends from high school. A third circle is comprised of the people in our environments with whom we interact minimally, and rarely by name, perhaps residents of our community or campus, whose standards, expectations, and behaviors influence our lives. A fourth social circle is the much wider culture in which we live, such as American society.

Abnormality can be caused by events in any or all of these social contexts. Troubled relationships with a roommate or family member can cause a person to feel deeply distressed. A failed relationship with a lover might lead to suicidal depression. Involvement in an abusive relationship may initiate an interpersonal style in which an abused person becomes repeatedly caught up with people who are hurtful and damaging. Being raised by a sadistic parent may cause a person to establish a pattern of close relationships characterized by control and emotional hurt. Political

turmoil, even on a relatively local level, can evoke emotions ranging from disturbing anxiety to incapacitating fear. For some people, the cause of abnormality is much broader, perhaps cultural or societal. For example, the experience of discrimination has profound impact on a person who is part of a minority group, whether involving race, culture, sexual orientation, or disability.

Some social critics have taken an unorthodox stand in pointing out ways in which they believe that society can be at the roots of what is regarded and labeled as abnormal. Noted British psychiatrist R. D. Laing (1964) stirred up a debate that has lasted several decades by contending that modern society dehumanizes the individual, and that people who refuse to abide by the norms of this society are psychologically healthier than those who blindly accept and live by such restrictive social norms. Along similar lines, American psychiatrist Thomas Szasz (1961) argued that the concept of mental illness is a "myth" created by modern society and put into practice by the mental health profession. Szasz proposed that a better way to describe people who cannot fit into society's norms is that they have "problems in living." Such terminology avoids labeling people as "sick" and, instead, indicates that their difficulties stem from a mismatch between their personal needs and society's ability to meet those needs.

Criticisms of the mental health establishment, such as those raised by Laing and Szasz, became more credible when researcher David Rosenhan conducted a radical study, discussed earlier, that caused many people in the scientific community to take a second look at institutionalization.

Although most mental health professionals now regard the ideas of Laing and Szasz as simplistic and the Rosenhan study as methodologically flawed, their ideas have caused mental health professionals to weigh the issues that these theorists have raised. The mental health community as a whole seems more sensitive today than in decades past to the need to avoid labeling people with psychological disorders as socially deviant. Such views also help promote social acceptance of people with emotional problems.

Returning to the case of Rebecca, there are two ways in which sociocultural influences can be seen as playing a role in her depression. First, as the child of a depressed mother, Rebecca grew up in a family in which maternal impairment may have left its mark on her. Second, following the accident, Rebecca was profoundly affected by the decision of her mother and in-laws to distance themselves from her. Although these significant people in her life did not directly cause Rebecca's symptoms, they played a role in aggravating her impairment because of their emotional distancing.

Abnormality: A Biopsychosocial Perspective

The three categories of the causes of abnormality are summarized in Table 1.1. Disturbances in any of these areas of human functioning can contribute to the development of a psychological disorder. However, the causes of abnormality cannot be so neatly divided. There is often considerable interaction among the three sets of influences. Social scientists use the term **biopsychosocial** to refer to the interaction in which biological,

TABLE 1.1 Causes of Abnormality

Biological	Genetic inheritance
	Medical conditions
	Brain damage
	Exposure to environmental stimuli
Psychological	Traumatic life experiences
	Learned associations
	Distorted perceptions
	Faulty ways of thinking
Sociocultural	Disturbances in intimate relationships
	Problems in extended relationships
	Political or social unrest
	Discrimination toward one's social group

psychological, and sociocultural factors play a role in the development of the individual. As you will see when reading about the conditions in this textbook, the degree of influence of each of these variables differs from disorder to disorder. For some disorders, such as schizophrenia, biology plays a dominant role. For other disorders, such as stress reactions, psychological factors predominate. For other conditions, such as post-traumatic stress disorder, that are associated with experiences under a terrorist regime, the cause is primarily sociocultural.

Related to the biopsychosocial model is a very important concept that sheds light on the biopsychosocial approach. Many research articles and scholarly writings are based on the **diathesis-stress model,** according to which people are born with a predisposition (or "diathesis") that places them at risk for developing a psychological disorder. Presumably, this vulnerability is genetic, although some theorists have proposed that the vulnerability may also be acquired due to early life events, such as traumas, diseases, birth complications, and even family experiences (Meehl, 1962; Zubin & Spring, 1977). When stress enters the picture, the person who carries such vulnerability is at considerable risk of developing the disorder to which he or she is prone. Rebecca Hasbrouck is a woman with a diathesis in the form of a genetic vulnerability to the development of a mood disorder. However, it was only following the experience of an intense life stress, the accident and family deaths, that the depression emerged. When we turn to the discussion of schizophrenia, you will read about the fascinating finding that this disorder, with a prominent genetic loading, cannot be fully explained by genetics. For example, in identical twin pairs, one twin may have the disorder while the other does not, even in instances involving a clear family history. As you will see, scientists believe that the affected twin must have been exposed to a stressor not encountered by the unaffected twin.

The bottom line, of course, is that psychological disorders arise from complex interactions involving biological, psychological, and sociocultural factors. Special kinds of vulnerability, such as genetic vulnerability, increase the likelihood of developing given disorders. However, certain life experiences can protect people from developing conditions to which they are vulnerable. Protective factors, such as loving caregivers, adequate health care, and early life successes, reduce one's vulnerability considerably. By contrast, low vulnerability can be heightened when a person receives inadequate health care, engages in risky behaviors (such as using drugs), and gets involved in dysfunctional relationships. Some researchers provide quantitative estimates of the relative contributions of genes and environment to the development of a psychological disorder (McGue & Bouchard, 1998). When we talk later in this book about specific disorders, such as schizophrenia, we will summarize the theories that scientists propose to explain the role of diathesis and stress in the development of each disorder.

Abnormal Psychology Throughout History

Now that you know about the complexities of defining and understanding abnormality, you can appreciate how very difficult it is to understand its causes. The greatest thinkers of the world, from Plato to the present day, have struggled to explain the oddities of human behavior. In this section, we will look at how the mental health field has arrived at current understandings of the causes and treatments of psychological disorders. You will see how ideas about psychological disorders have taken a variety of twists and turns throughout recorded history. There is every reason to expect that these concepts will continue to evolve.

Three prominent themes in explaining psychological disorders recur throughout history: the mystical, the scientific, and the humanitarian. Mystical explanations of psychological disorders regard abnormal behavior as the product of possession by evil or demonic spirits. The scientific approach looks for natural causes, such as biological imbalances, faulty learning processes, or emotional stressors. Humanitarian explanations view psychological disorders as the result of cruelty, nonacceptance, or poor living conditions. Tension among these three approaches has existed throughout history; at times, one or another has dominated, but all three have coexisted for centuries. Even in today's scientific world, the humanitarian and mystical approaches have their advocates. As you read about the historical trends in understanding and treating psychological disorders, see if you can identify which theme is most prevalent at each stage.

Prehistoric Times: Abnormal Behavior as Demonic Possession

There is no written record of ideas regarding psychological disorders in prehistoric times, but there is mysterious archeological evidence dating back to 8000 B.C. during the Stone Age: skulls with holes drilled in them. Furthermore, there is evidence that the bone healed near these holes, which is taken to indicate that the procedure was surgical and that people survived it (Piek, 1999). Why would prehistoric people perform such bizarre surgery?

Anthropologists have wondered whether this kind of surgery, called **trephining,** was performed as a way of treating psychological disorders. They theorize that prehistoric people thought that evil spirits that were trapped inside the head caused abnormal behavior and that releasing the evil spirits would cause the person to return to normal. Another interpretation is that trephining was used to treat medical problems. For all we know, the procedure might have been an effective treatment for some psychological disturbances caused by physiological imbalances or abnormalities. In any case, the skulls are the only evidence we have from that period of history, and we can only speculate about their meaning (Maher & Maher, 1985).

Surprisingly enough, the practice of trephining did not end in the Stone Age (Gross, 1999). It was also practiced all over the world from ancient times through the eighteenth century, for various purposes from the magical to the medical. Evidence of trephining has been found from many countries and cultures, including the Far and Middle East, the Celtic tribes in Britain, ancient and recent China, India, and various peoples of North and South America, including the Mayans, Aztecs, Incas, and Brazilian Indians. The procedure is still in use among certain tribes in Africa for the relief of head wounds.

Another practice that was used in ancient times was the driving away of evil spirits through the ritual of exorcism. Although intended as a cure through the conjuring of spirits, the procedures involved in exorcism seem more like torture to our contemporary eyes. The possessed person might be starved, whipped, beaten, and treated in other extreme ways, with the intention of driving the evil spirits away. Some were forced to eat or drink foul-tasting and disgusting concoctions, which included blood, wine, and sheep dung. Some were executed, because they were considered a burden and a threat to their neighbors. These practices were carried out by a shaman, priest, or medicine man—a person thought by the community to possess magical powers. Although these practices are associated with early civilizations, variants of shamanism have appeared throughout history. The Greeks sought advice from oracles believed to be in contact with the gods. The Chinese practiced magic as a protection against demons. In India, shamanism flourished for centuries, and it still persists in Central Asia.

Had Rebecca lived at a time or in a culture in which exorcism was practiced, her symptoms might have been interpreted as signs of demonic possession. The voices she heard could have been devils speaking to her. Her bizarre behavior would have been perceived as evidence that she was under the control of a supernatural force. Frightened and disturbed by behaviors they could not understand, her neighbors might have sent her to a shaman, who would carry out the rites of exorcism. As you will see, such ideas played a prominent role in the understanding and treatment of psychological disorders for centuries to follow.

Ancient Greece and Rome: The Emergence of the Scientific Model

Even though their theories now may seem strange, early Greek philosophers established the foundation for a systematic approach to psychological disorders. Hippocrates (*ca.* 460–377 B.C.), whom many people consider the founder of modern medicine, was concerned not only with physical diseases but with psychological problems as well. He believed that there were four important bodily fluids that influenced physical and mental health: black bile, yellow bile, phlegm, and blood. An excess of any of these fluids could account for changes in an individual's personality and behavior. For example, an excess of black bile would make a person depressed ("melancholic"), and an excess of yellow bile would cause a person to be anxious and irritable ("choleric"). Too much phlegm would result in a calm disposition bordering perhaps on indifference ("phlegmatic"). An overabundance of blood would cause a person to experience unstable mood shifts ("sanguine"). Treatment of a psychological disorder, then, involved ridding the body of the excess fluid through such methods as bleeding, purging (forced excretion), and administering emetics (nausea-producing substances) and establishing a healthier balance through proper nutrition.

As unlikely as it sounds, Hippocrates' classification of four types of fluid imbalances resurfaced in modern explanations of personality types. The classification proposed by Hans Eysenck (1967), shown in Figure 1.1, is based on a psychological test that provides scores on various personality dispositions. The two dimensions of neurotic–normal and introvert–extrovert interact to produce the four personality types shown in the figure. The resurfacing of ancient ideas in the form of a modern psychological theory suggests that, despite the very different philosophies that underlie these systems, there might be something to the notion that there are some enduring dimensions of personality.

The views of Hippocrates dominated medical thinking on the topic of psychological disorders for 500 years. However, these views were countered by the more popular belief in spiritual possession and the cruel treatment of psychologically disturbed people. The next significant advances in the medical approach were made by two Greek physicians living in Rome, separated by 200 years, who introduced new and more humane ideas about psychological disorders.

In the first century B.C., Aesclepiades rebelled against the Hippocratic belief that the imbalance of bodily substances caused psychological disorders. Instead, he recognized that emotional disturbances could result in psychological problems. Two hundred years later, Claudius Galen (A.D. 130–200) developed a system of medical knowledge that revolutionized previous thinking about psychological as well as physical disorders. Rather than rely on philosophical speculation, Galen studied anatomy to discover answers to questions about the workings of the human body and mind. Unfortunately, although Galen made important advances in medicine, he essentially maintained Hippocrates' beliefs that abnormality was the result of an imbalance of bodily substances. Nevertheless, the writings of Hippocrates and Galen formed the

FIGURE 1.1 Four temperaments
An illustration of Eysenck's explanation of personality types. The two dimensions of neurotic–normal and introvert–extrovert interact to produce the four types described by Hippocrates.

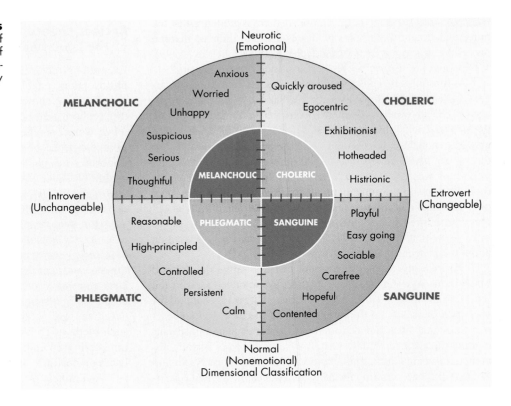

The Middle Ages and Renaissance: The Re-emergence of Spiritual Explanations

The Middle Ages are sometimes referred to as the "Dark Ages." In terms of the approaches to psychological disorders, this was indeed a dark period. No scientific or medical advances occurred beyond those of Hippocrates and Galen. In the rare cases in which people with psychological disorders sought medical treatment, the physician could offer little beyond the barbaric methods of purging and bleeding, ineffectual attempts to manipulate diet, or the prescription of useless drugs.

During the Middle Ages, there was a resurgence of primitive beliefs regarding spiritual possession. People turned to superstition, astrology, and alchemy to explain many natural phenomena, including psychological and physical illnesses. Magical rituals, exorcism, and folk medicines were widely practiced. Beliefs in demonic possession were also used to account for abnormal behavior, and people who sought help from the clergy were treated as sinners, witches, or embodiments of the devil. The punishment and execution of people accused of being witches became more widespread toward the end of the Middle Ages, especially during the Renaissance.

The dominance of religious thinking in the Middle Ages had both positive and negative effects on the care of psychologically disturbed individuals. Beliefs in spiritual possession and the treatment of people as sinners had harmful effects. By contrast, ideas about Christian charity and the need to help poor and sick people formed the basis for more humanitarian approaches to treatment. Monasteries began to open their doors to give these people a place to stay and receive whatever primitive treatments the monks could offer. Poorhouses, or homes for people who could not pay their living expenses, were built all over Europe. Many of them sheltered people who were emotionally disturbed.

Later, the poorhouses became known as **asylums.** One of the most famous of these asylums was the Hospital of St. Mary of Bethlehem in London. Originally founded as a hospital for poor people in 1247, by 1403 it began to house people referred to at the time as "lunatics." In the centuries to follow, the term *bedlam,* a derivative of the hospital's name, became synonymous with the chaotic and inhumane housing of psychologically disturbed people who languished unattended for years (MacDonald, 1981). As the hospital became more crowded and its occupants increasingly unruly, the hospital workers resorted to chains and other punishments to keep the inhabitants under control. Similar conditions prevailed in other asylums as they became more and more crowded. Unfortunately, the original intention of enlisting clergy to treat psychologically disturbed individuals with humanitarian methods had disastrous consequences. Not until several centuries later were the humanitarian ideals reinstated.

In contrast to what you might learn in a history class about the Renaissance as a period of enlightenment, this period was far from enlightened with regard to psychological disorders. There were virtually no scientific or humanitarian advances during this entire period, and demonic possession remained the prevalent

Hieronymous Bosch's *Removal of the Stone of Folly* depicted a medieval "doctor" cutting out the presumed source of madness from a patient's skull. The prevailing belief was that spiritual possession was the cause of psychological disorder.

The inhumane treatment at the Hospital of St. Mary of Bethlehem in London is shown in William Hogarth's *The Madhouse.*

explanation for abnormal behavior of any kind. Some historical accounts have proposed that witch hunts, conducted on a wide scale throughout Europe and later in North America, were directed at people with psychological disturbances. These acts were seen as justified by the publication of the *Malleus Malificarum,* an indictment of witches written by two Dominican monks in Germany in 1486, in which witches were denounced as heretics and devils who must be destroyed in the interest of preserving Christianity. The "treatment" it recommended was deportation, torture, and burning at the stake. Women, particularly old women, as well as midwives, were the main targets of persecution. Once a woman was labeled a witch by the Church, there was no escape for her.

Were Rebecca to be treated during this era, she might have been regarded as a witch, especially if she were heard to refer to the devil or any other supernatural force. However, if she were lucky, someone might consult a medical practitioner. In the midst of the witch hunt frenzy, some voices of reason were starting to be heard, and, in the 1500s, the idea began to spread that people

who showed signs of demonic possession might be psychologically disturbed. In 1563, a physician named Johann Weyer (1515–1588) wrote an important book called *The Deception of Demons,* in which he tried to debunk the myth that psychologically disturbed people were possessed by the devil. Although Weyer did not abandon the notion of demonic possession, his book represented the first major advance since the time of Galen in the description and classification of forms of abnormal behavior. Weyer's approach also formed the basis for what later became a renewal of the humanitarian approach to psychologically disturbed people. However, at the time of his writing, Weyer was severely criticized and ridiculed for challenging the views held by the powerful and influential religious and political leaders of the time. However, in another part of Europe, Weyer's "radical" ideas were being echoed by an Englishman, Reginald Scot (1538–1599), who deviated even further from the prevalent ideologies by denying the very existence of demons.

Europe and the United States in the 1700s: The Reform Movement

The eighteenth century was a time of massive political and social reform throughout Europe. By this point, public institutions housing individuals with psychological disorders had become like dungeons, where people were not even given the care that would be accorded an animal. The living conditions for poor people were miserable, but to be both psychologically disturbed and poor was a horrible fate. People with psychological disorders lived in dark, cold cells with dirt floors and were often chained to straw beds and surrounded by their own excrement. It was widely believed that psychologically disturbed people were insensitive to extremes of heat and cold or to the cleanliness of their surroundings. The "treatment" given to these people involved bleeding, forced vomiting, and purging. It took a few courageous people, who recognized the inhumanity of the existing practices, to bring about sweeping reforms.

The leader of the reform movement was Vincenzo Chiarugi (1759–1820). Fresh from medical school, at the age of 26, he was given the responsibility of heading *Ospitdale di Bonifacio*, the newly built mental hospital in Florence. Within a year of taking charge of the hospital, he instituted a set of revolutionary standards for the care of mental patients. These standards were a landmark in creating general principles for care of the mentally ill, including a detailed history for each patient, high hygiene standards, recreational facilities, occupational therapies, minimal use of restraints, and respect for individual dignity. In 1793–1794, Chiarugi published a major work on the causes and classification of "insanity," which he regarded as due to impairment of the brain. Thus, Chiarugi made important contributions to both the humanitarian and scientific models of abnormality.

More attention was given, however, to the reforms of Philippe Pinel (1745–1826) in La Bicêtre, a hospital in Paris with conditions like those faced by Chiarugi. On his appointment as a hospital physician in 1792, a hospital worker, Jean-Baptiste Pussin, who had begun the process of reform, influenced Pinel. Together, they made changes to improve the living conditions of the patients. When Pinel left La Bicêtre 2 years later, Pussin stayed behind. It was then that Pussin made the bold gesture of freeing patients from their chains, an act for which Pinel is mistakenly given credit. After leaving La Bicêtre, Pinel became

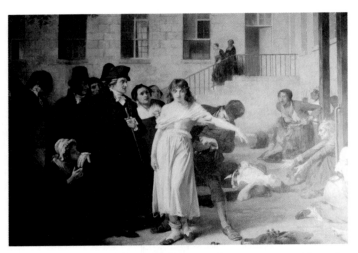

This painting shows Philippe Pinel having the irons removed from the inmates at La Salpêtrière Hospital. It was actually Pinel's employer, Jean-Baptiste Pussin, who performed this liberating gesture.

director of La Salpêtrière Hospital, where he and Pussin continued to spread these reforms.

England was the third country to see major reforms in its treatment of psychologically disturbed individuals. In 1792, an English Quaker named William Tuke established the York Retreat, an institution based on the religious humanitarian principles of the Quakers. Tuke's work was carried on by succeeding generations of his family. Their methods became known as **moral treatment** and were based on the philosophy that the mentally ill deserved to be treated with humanity. Underlying this approach was the philosophy that, with the proper care, people can develop self-control over their own disturbed behaviors. Restraints were used only if absolutely necessary, and even in those cases the patient's comfort came first.

At the time of Europe's revolutionary reforms, similar changes in the care of psychologically disturbed people were being initiated in the United States. Benjamin Rush (1745–1813) became known as the founder of American psychiatry for his rekindling of interest in the scientific approach to psychological disorders. His text, *Observations and Inquiries upon the Diseases of the Mind,* written in 1812, was the first psychiatric textbook printed in the United States. Rush, who was one of the signers of the Declaration of Independence, achieved fame outside psychiatry as well. He was a politician, statesman, surgeon general, and writer in many diverse fields, ranging from philosophy to meteorology. Because of his prestigious role in American society, he was able to influence the institution of reforms in the mental health field. In 1783, he joined the medical staff of Pennsylvania Hospital. Rush was appalled by the poor conditions in the hospital and by the fact that psychologically disturbed patients were placed on wards with the physically ill. He spoke out for changes that were considered radical at the time, such as placing psychologically disturbed patients in separate wards, giving them occupational therapy, and prohibiting visits from curiosity seekers who frequented the hospital for entertainment.

If Rebecca were living in New England during the height of the Salem witch trials, she might have suffered the fate of the woman in this picture who is shown here being arrested.

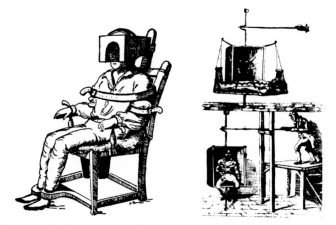

Benjamin Rush's methods of treatment, based on what he thought were scientific principles, would be considered barbaric by today's standards.

In evaluating Rush's contributions, we must also mention that he advocated some of what we now regard as barbaric interventions that were accepted conventions at the time. For example, Rush supported the use of bloodletting and purging in the treatment of psychological disorders. Some of his methods were unusual and seem sadistic now—such as the "tranquilizer" chair, to which a patient was tied. The chair was intended to reduce stimulating blood flow to the brain by binding the patient's head and limbs. Rush also recommended that patients be submerged in cold shower baths and frightened with threats that they would be killed. Other physicians at the time used similar techniques, such as surprise immersions into tubs of cold water and the "well-cure," in which a patient was placed at the bottom of a well as water was slowly poured into it. Rush and his contemporaries thought that the fright induced by these methods would counteract the overexcitement responsible for their violent and bizarre behavior (Deutsch, 1949). It is ironic that, in the spirit of reform, methods just as primitive as those of the Middle Ages continued to be developed.

Despite the more humane changes Rush advocated, conditions in asylums worsened over the next 30 years with continued overcrowding. The psychologically disturbed patients were often forced to live in poorhouses and jails, where conditions were even less conducive to treatment than in the asylums. By 1841, when a Boston schoolteacher named Dorothea Dix (1802–1887) made her first venture into these institutions, conditions had become ripe for another round of major reforms. She was shocked and repulsed by scenes that were reminiscent of the horrifying conditions that European reformers had faced in the previous century. Her first encounter was with the prison system, in which many psychologically disturbed people were incarcerated. Inmates were chained to the walls, no heat was provided for them, and they were forced to live in filth. Viewing these conditions was enough to set Dix off onto an investigative path. She traveled throughout Massachusetts,

visiting jails and poorhouses and chronicling the horrors she witnessed. Two years later, Dix presented her findings to the Massachusetts Legislature, with the demand that more state-funded public hospitals be built to care specifically for the psychologically disturbed. Dix believed, furthermore, that the proper care involved the application of moral treatment. From Massachusetts, Dix spread her message throughout North America, and even to Europe. She spent the next 40 years campaigning for the proper treatment of psychologically disturbed people. She was a very effective champion of this cause, and her efforts resulted in the growth of the state hospital movement.

In the century to follow, scores of state hospitals were built throughout the United States. Once again, as in the Middle Ages, the best intentions of the mental health reformers became lost and ultimately backfired. These new state hospitals became so overcrowded and understaffed that treatment conditions deteriorated. The wards in these hospitals overflowed with people whose symptoms included violent and destructive behaviors. Under these circumstances, there was no way to fulfill Dix's goal of providing moral therapy. Instead, the staff resorted to the use of physical restraints and other measures that moral therapy was intended to replace. However, there were some reforms, such as allowing patients to work on the hospital grounds and to participate in various forms of recreation. At the same time, though, these institutions became custodial facilities where people spent their entire lives, an outcome that Dix had not anticipated. It simply was not possible to "cure" people of these serious disorders by providing them with the well-intentioned

Dorothea Dix worked throughout the late 1800s to move psychologically disturbed people from jails and poorhouses to state-funded hospitals, where they could receive more humane treatment.

but ineffective interventions proposed by moral therapy. Furthermore, over the course of several decades, the emphasis of this form of treatment had shifted almost solely toward disciplinary enforcement of the institution's rules and away from the more humane spirit of the original idea.

Even though moral therapy was a failure, the humanitarian goals that Dix advocated had a lasting influence on the mental health system. Her work was carried forward into the 1900s by advocates of the "mental hygiene" movement—most notably, Clifford Beers. In 1908, Beers wrote the autobiographical *A Mind That Found Itself,* which recounted in alarming detail his own harsh treatment in psychiatric institutions. Beers had become so enraged by the inhumane treatments that he established the National Committee for Mental Hygiene, a group of people who worked to improve the treatment of those in psychiatric institutions.

The 1800s to the 1900s: Development of Alternative Models for Abnormal Behavior

While Dix was engaged in her reform campaign, the superintendents of existing state mental hospitals were also trying to develop better ways to manage patients. In 1844, a group of 13 mental hospital administrators formed the Association

MindMAP Segment 1.1 provides vivid illustrations of views about the causes of psychological disorders from ancient to contemporary times.

History is filled with attempts to understand and manage the symptoms of psychological disorders. These efforts ranged from the bizarre and barbaric to the scientific and humanitarian.

of Medical Superintendents of American Institutions for the Insane. The name of this organization was eventually changed to the American Psychiatric Association. The founding of this organization gave rise to the **medical model,** the view that abnormal behaviors result from physical problems and should be treated medically.

The goals of the American Psychiatric Association were furthered by the publication in 1845 of a book on the pathology and treatment of psychological disorders by William Greisinger, a German psychiatrist. Greisinger focused on the role of the brain, rather than spirit possession, in abnormal behavior. Another German psychiatrist, Emil Kraepelin, was also influential in the development of the American psychiatric movement. Kraepelin carried further Greisinger's ideas that brain malfunction caused psychological disorder. He is perhaps better known, however, for his efforts to improve the way that psychological disorders were classified. Kraepelin's ideas continue to be influential even today, and some of the distinctions he introduced are reflected in contemporary systems of psychiatric diagnosis. For example, Kraepelin's concept of manic-depression was a precursor to what is now called bipolar disorder; his concept of dementia praecox (premature degeneration) is now known as schizophrenia.

At the same time that the medical model was evolving, a very different approach to understanding psychological problems was also taking root. The **psychoanalytic model,** which seeks explanations of abnormal behavior in the workings of unconscious psychological processes, had its origins in the controversial techniques developed by Anton Mesmer (1734–1815), a Viennese physician. Mesmer gained notoriety for his dramatic interventions involving hypnotic techniques. Expelled from Vienna for what were regarded as false claims of cure, Mesmer traveled to Paris, where the same misfortune befell him. Wherever he went, the medical establishment regarded him as a fraud because of his unbelievable assertions and questionable practices. In 1766, Mesmer published a book called *The Influence of the Planets,* which promoted the idea that magnetic fluid filled the universe and, therefore, was in the bodies of all living creatures. He maintained that physical and psychological disturbances were the result of an imbalance in this magnetic fluid, called animal "magnetism." These disturbances could be corrected by a device Mesmer invented called a "magnetizer." So many people became interested in this cure that Mesmer began to treat them in groups. Mesmer's patients held hands around a "baquet," a large oak tub containing water, iron filings, and glass particles, while he walked around them, stroking them with a magnetic wand. This practice became exceptionally popular in Paris because of reports of beneficial effects. Hundreds of sick individuals, particularly women, went to Mesmer's clinic. The medical establishment decided to investigate Mesmer's practices, which aroused suspicion due to their questionable scientific basis. In 1784, the French government invited Benjamin Franklin to head a commission to investigate animal magnetism. The investigation lasted 7 years and concluded that the effects of magnetism were due to "excitement of the imagination" (Baker, 1990).

An English physician, James Braid (1795–1860), was intrigued by what he heard about magnetism's popularity in France and decided to investigate how such a questionable method could actually produce such dramatic benefits. Braid became convinced that whatever positive effects occurred were unrelated to animal magnetism. Instead, Braid proposed that changes took place in people's minds, outside their conscious awareness, that could explain the "cures" attributed to mesmerism. In 1842, Braid introduced the term **hypnotism** to describe the process of being put into a trance, which he believed to be the cause of Mesmer's ability to effect changes in the minds of his subjects. He reasoned that some people treated by Mesmer's method improved because they were in a hypnotic state and were open to suggestions that could result in the removal of their symptoms. The term **mesmerized,** in fact, refers to this state of heightened suggestibility brought about by the words and actions of a charismatic individual. Braid's explanation of hypnosis played an important role in leading practitioners to realize how powerful the mind can be in causing and removing symptoms.

Two decades later, Ambrose-Auguste Liébault (1823–1904), a French doctor, began to experiment with mesmerism. Many of Liébault's patients were poor farmers, whom Liébault treated in his clinic in Nancy, France. Liébault discovered that he could use hypnotic sleep induction as a substitute for drugs. Liébault's clinic eventually became well known for innovative treatments. In 1882, another physician, Hippolyte-Marie Bernheim (1837–1919), who became one of the major proponents of hypnotism in Europe, visited Liébault. Bernheim was seeking Liébault's help in treating a patient with severe back pains for whom other forms of therapy were unsuccessful. Liébault's cure of this patient convinced Bernheim that hypnosis was the wave of the future.

From their work at the Nancy clinic, Bernheim and Liébault gained international attention for advances in the use of hypnosis as a treatment for nervous and psychological disorders. At the

French neurologist Jean-Martin Charcot is shown demonstrating a hypnotic technique during a medical lecture.

same time, an esteemed neurologist in Paris, Jean-Martin Charcot (1825–1893), was testing similar techniques in La Salpêtrière Hospital. However, Charcot's Salpêtrière "school" of hypnosis differed sharply in its explanation of how hypnosis worked. Charcot believed that hypnotizability was actually a symptom of a neurological disorder and that only people who suffered from this disorder could be treated by hypnosis. You can see how Charcot's notion that hypnosis involved physical changes in the nervous system was a radical departure from the Nancy school's position. The weight of evidence, however, was in favor of the Nancy school, and eventually Charcot adopted its position. Hypnosis was clearly understood as a psychological process that could be very instrumental in resolving certain kinds of disorders. In particular, hypnosis became the treatment of choice for **hysteria,** a disorder in which psychological problems become expressed in physical form. A girl whom Mesmer "cured" of her blindness was probably suffering from hysteria; in other words, a psychological conflict was converted into an apparent sensory deficit. Other forms of hysteria became widely known in the medical establishment, including various forms of paralysis, pain disorders, and a wide range of sensory deficits, such as blindness and hearing loss.

The development of hypnosis went on to play a central role in the evolution of psychological methods for treating psychological disorders. In fact, Sigmund Freud (1856–1939) was heavily influenced by both Charcot and Bernheim in his early work with hysterical patients. Freud originally studied medicine in Vienna, where he trained as a neurologist. After graduating from the University of Vienna, Freud traveled to France to learn about hypnosis, a method of treatment that fascinated him. In *Studies in Hysteria* (Breuer & Freud, 1895/1982), written with his colleague, Josef Breuer (1842–1925), Freud analyzed the famous case of "Anna O." and other women suffering from hysteria. Freud and Breuer described how Anna O. was cured of her many and varied hysterical symptoms by the use of hypnosis. In addition, however, Anna O. urged Breuer, who was actually the

Anton Mesmer claimed that, by redistributing the magnetic fluids in the patient's body, he could cure psychological disorders. Mesmer, sitting in the left side of the room, is holding a wand while his patients hold metal rods.

one treating her, to allow her to engage in "chimney sweeping," which she also called the "talking cure." When she was allowed simply to talk about her problems, she felt better, and her symptoms disappeared. Freud and Breuer called this the "cathartic method," a cleansing of the mind's emotional conflicts through talking about them. The cathartic method was the forerunner of **psychotherapy,** the treatment of abnormal behavior through psychological techniques. This discovery eventually led Freud to develop **psychoanalysis,** a theory and system of practice that relied heavily on the concepts of the unconscious mind, inhibited sexual impulses, and early development, as well as the use of the "free association" technique and dream analysis.

In the early 1900s, Freud attracted a variety of brilliant minds and courageous practitioners from across the Atlantic Ocean and all over Europe, who came to work with him at his home in Vienna. Although many of these people eventually broke rank and went on to develop their own theories and training schools, Freud's legacy continues to maintain an important position throughout the world.

At the same time as these developments were taking place in Vienna, the Russian physiologist Ivan Pavlov (1849–1936) discovered principles of classical conditioning in his experiments on salivation in dogs. Some of his experiments included studies of learned neurotic behavior in dogs and provided a model of the learning of abnormal behavior through control of environmental conditions. Pavlov's approach became the basis for the behaviorist movement begun in the United States by John B. Watson (1878–1958), who applied principles of classical conditioning to the learning of abnormal behavior in humans. Watson became best known in this country for the advice he gave to parents on childrearing. At around the same time, Edward L. Thorndike (1874–1949) developed the "law of effect," which proposed that organisms will repeat behavior that produces satisfying consequences; this was the basis for operant conditioning. Building on this work, B. F. Skinner (1904–1990) formulated a systematic approach to operant conditioning, specifying the types and nature of reinforcement as a way to modify behavior. Classical and operant conditioning models are now incorporated into many forms of therapeutic interventions.

Throughout the twentieth century, there emerged alternative models of abnormal behavior based on various experimental approaches. The most prominent among these were the social learning theory of Albert Bandura (1925–), the cognitive model of Aaron Beck (1921–), and the rational-emotive therapy approach developed by Albert Ellis (1913–). In Chapter 4, we will go into greater depth in the discussion of these theories and their use in treatment.

The Late Twentieth Century: The Challenge of Providing Humane and Effective Treatment

When first encountering the various historical approaches to understanding and treating psychological disorders, you may wonder how it could be possible for people to have such extreme beliefs as demonic possession and to propose such seemingly naïve treatments as moral therapy and the use of mechanical devices as cures. However, if you look around at the popular media and perhaps even in your local bookstore, you can readily find examples of spiritual, mystical, or "New Age" approaches to physical and psychological treatment. For the most part, mainstream contemporary society takes a more scientific approach to understanding and treating psychological disorders. The scientific approach, rooted in the ideas of ancient Greek philosophers and physicians, began to be applied systematically in the mid-1900s and is now the predominant view in Western culture.

In the 1950s, scientists introduced medications that controlled some of the debilitating symptoms of severe psychological disturbance. Because of the many reports of dramatic reduction in symptoms, these medicines were quickly incorporated into the treatment regimens of mental hospitals. They were seen as an easy solution to the centuries-old problem of how to control the harmful and bizarre behaviors of psychologically disturbed people and possibly even to cure them. The initial hopes for these "miracle drugs" were naïve and simplistic. No one realized that these medications could have harmful physical side effects, some of which could cause irreversible neurological damage. Swept away by early enthusiasm, mental health professionals often became caught up in the indiscriminate and unselective use of large doses of powerful drugs. An extreme overemphasis on the medical model also had the unanticipated effect of inattention to the other mental health needs of these patients.

Until the 1970s, despite the growing body of knowledge about the causes of abnormal behavior, the actual practices used in the day-to-day care of psychologically disturbed people were sometimes as barbaric as those used in the Middle Ages. Even people suffering from the least severe psychological disorders were often housed in what were known as the "back wards" of large and impersonal state institutions, without adequate or appropriate care. Although patients were not chained to the walls of their cells, they were frequently severely restrained by the use of powerful tranquilizing drugs and straitjackets, coats with sleeves long enough to wrap around the patient's torso. Even more radical was the indiscriminate use of behavior-altering brain surgery or the application of electrical shocks—so-called treatments that were often used as punishments intended to control unruly patients (see more on these procedures in Chapter 2).

Public outrage over these abuses in mental hospitals finally led to a more widespread realization that dramatic changes were needed in the provision of mental health services. The federal government took emphatic action in 1963 with the passage of groundbreaking legislation. The Mental Retardation Facilities and Community Mental Health Center Construction Act of that year initiated a series of changes that would affect mental health services for decades to come. Legislators began to promote policies designed to move people out of institutions and into less restrictive programs in the community, such as vocational rehabilitation facilities, day hospitals, and psychiatric clinics. People were placed in halfway houses after their discharge from the hospital, which provided a supportive environment in which they could learn the social skills needed to reenter the community. By the mid-1970s, the state mental hospitals, which had once been overflowing with patients, were practically deserted (see Figure 1.2). Hundreds of thousands of people who had been confined to dreary institutions were freed, to begin living with greater dignity and autonomy.

Unfortunately, like all other supposed breakthroughs in the treatment of psychologically disturbed people, the **deinstitutionalization movement** that promoted the release of psychiatric clients into community treatment sites did not completely fulfill the dreams of its originators. Rather than abolishing inhumane treatment, deinstitutionalization created another set of woes. Many of the promises and programs hailed as alternatives to institutionalization ultimately failed to come through because of inadequate planning and insufficient funds. Patients were often shuttled back and forth between hospitals, halfway houses, and shabby boarding homes, never having a sense of stability or respect. Some social critics have questioned whether the almost indiscriminate release of psychologically disturbed people was too radical a step that took place too rapidly. Although the intention of releasing patients from psychiatric hospitals was to free people who had been deprived of basic human rights, the result may not have been as liberating as many had hoped. In contemporary American society, many people who would have been found inside the walls of psychiatric hospitals three decades ago are being moved through a circuit of shelters, rehabilitation programs, jails, and prisons, with a disturbing number of these individuals spending long periods of time as homeless and marginalized members of society (Haugland, Siegel, Hopper, & Alexander, 1997).

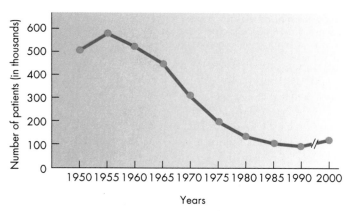

FIGURE 1.2 The number of patients in psychiatric hospitals, 1950–2000 The number of patients in psychiatric hospitals in the United States has dropped since 1960.
Source: U.S. Bureau of the Census, 2005.

Although many of the reports regarding the effects of deinstitutionalization have been negative, some investigators have asserted that moving people out of institutions has been beneficial when the resources have been carefully reallocated. One researcher, Robert Okin (1995), compared patients who had been moved out of state hospitals in Massachusetts between the years 1978 and 1993. He compared communities in which there was greater reliance on returning disturbed individuals to the hospital with communities that made greater use of comprehensive community services. He found that the total expenditures per capita were roughly the same. Even though community care is very expensive, it is not cumulatively more expensive than the unnecessary use of inpatient care.

Emphasizing the importance of community follow-up, Okin and his colleagues (Okin, Borus, & Baer, 1995) found some striking results in their longitudinal study of 53 chronically mentally ill people following their discharge from a state hospital into structured group home settings. Seven and a half years after discharge, 57 percent of these individuals continued to live in residential settings, and more than one fourth had moved on to independent living. Although more than half had to be readmitted to the hospital for some period of time, the amount of time spent in the hospital was relatively brief. Most important were the findings that almost all the individuals expressed a clear preference for life outside the hospital, with many showing impressive improvements in functioning.

Integral to the success of a community program are approaches that help individuals help themselves. The field is moving toward a recovery-oriented mental health system in which community support is viewed as crucial in helping seriously disturbed people cope with psychological disorders. Recovery from psychological disorder can be viewed as comparable to recovery from a physical condition. In both cases, there is a difference between cure and recovery. Even though people who have suffered an affliction may continue to have

 MindMAP Segment 1.2 covers the aspects of Freud's theory relevant to the science of the mind, dream interpretation, hysteria, and his assumptions about human nature.

The impact of Freud's role in understanding the role of the unconscious has continued to be important for more than a century.

Group therapy provides a context for clients to share their stories with others and, in doing so, obtain support while going through difficult experiences, such as grief over the loss of someone close.

symptoms, they can develop coping strategies that help them adapt and move on with their lives. An important component of this approach is the notion that people can recover without professional intervention. Presumably, mental health professionals facilitate the recovery of a person with a psychological disorder, but it is really up to the client, who is called a consumer in this model, to take the steps toward recovery, usually by reaching out to others. Essential to recovery is the availability of people who are concerned about and supportive of the struggling individual, especially in times of active symptoms or intense stress. Self-help can be derived through contact with relatives, friends, groups, and churches. Although the recovery model rests on some lofty ideals, influential changes have emerged from this framework, along with recommendations for new ways of responding to the needs of psychologically troubled people in the years to come.

Although deinstitutionalization has had a profound effect on the delivery of mental health services to severely disturbed people, most communities have not yet resolved the dilemma about how to deal with individuals who are unable to care for themselves, and may indeed be in danger of perishing from inadequate self-care. Some communities rely on procedures involving mandatory outpatient commitment of such individuals, yet this approach is quite controversial because of lively debate about social policy, legal, and philosophical issues (O'Reilly, 2004). Some experts contend that involuntary outpatient commitment is an effective and necessary response in high-risk situations (Swartz & Swanson, 2004), but others argue that personal rights can easily be infringed upon in situations in which a person's autonomy is restricted. You can imagine how complex such issues are, as society faces the challenge of assessing the extent to which some people are able to care for themselves and taking action even in instances in which help is ardently rejected.

In recent years, changes in the insurance industry have had a tremendous effect on the provision of mental health care. Managed health care has become the standard by which third-party payers, such as insurance companies, oversee reimbursement for health services. In a managed care system, all medical and mental health procedures are evaluated to ensure that they provide the best therapeutic value at the least financial cost. For example, if you are in need of a dental filling for a cavity, a dental managed care company will reimburse your dentist for a routine filling, but it would be unwilling to pay for monthly cleanings, because they would be viewed as unnecessary. In the field of mental health care, insurers also want to be certain that the care provided to clients is effective, inexpensive, and limited to what is absolutely necessary.

The rationale of managed care rests on the notion that everyone involved saves money when excessive costs are contained. Unfortunately, many practitioners feel that the ideals on which health maintenance organizations and related provider systems were developed three decades ago have been compromised by recent changes aimed at short-term cost savings with little foresight about the long-term effects on clients and society (Karon, 1995). For example, 15 years ago, a seriously depressed client might have remained in the hospital for several weeks of treatment, but today he or she might be released after a few days, because an insurance company would regard extended inpatient treatment as unnecessary and too expensive. What does this mean for the many individuals who suffer from chronic psychological disorders? In the worst-case scenario, they are released to the community, where they may be at risk of deterioration and neglect.

In a survey of nearly 16,000 licensed psychologists, four out of every five respondents reported that managed care was negatively affecting their clinical practice (Phelps, Eisman, & Kohout,

1998). Of particular concern are the ethical dilemmas raised by working within a managed care system (Murphy, DeBernardo, & Shoemaker, 1998; Rothbaum et al., 1998). For example, clinicians are concerned about the compromise of confidentiality standards, as is the case when they must submit detailed personal information about their patients to seemingly anonymous utilization staff at the managed care company's central office. Many clinicians also complain that managed care decisions commonly lead to the provision of inadequate care or inappropriate treatment—decisions that are based on cost rather than clinical need.

In recent years, consumers have joined with providers in expressing their alarm about inadequacies in the health care system, and some promising changes have taken place. State legislatures have responded to public concern by enacting laws that regulate managed care practices and decisions, ranging from specifying the minimum number of hospital days following the birth of a baby to determining the minimum number of sessions provided for psychological disorders (Heldring, 1998).

At the beginning of the new century, we still face the prospect of many seriously disturbed people wandering homeless in the streets without adequate care and perhaps moving in and out of jails and shelters. Ironically, this situation is not unlike that which confronted Dorothea Dix 165 years ago. Like Dorothea Dix, some contemporary advocates have suggested new forms of compassionate treatment for people who suffer from psychological disorders. In particular, methods of collaboration between the mental health establishment and "consumers" of services are being developed in which the consumers are encouraged to take an active role in choosing their treatment. The community, in turn, can provide greater financial and emotional support, so that those with psychological disorders can survive more effectively outside the institution. In accord with these concerns, the U.S. government has set as an objective for the year 2010 improvements in care that will reduce homelessness among the mentally ill (SAMHSA, 2005).

In response to growing concerns about privacy of health records, particularly those pertaining to mental health treatment, in December 2000 the U.S. Department of Health and Human Services issued the first comprehensive federal rules protecting the privacy of medical information. These rules are intended to initiate long-overdue protections of patient rights and specify to whom information could be disclosed. For example, psychotherapy notes cannot be disclosed without the client's specific written authorization; furthermore, health plans cannot require an individual to authorize such disclosure in order to become eligible for benefits.

In the decades to come, experts and laypeople will continue to struggle to find the proper balance between providing asylum for those in need and incarcerating people in institutions beyond the point at which they are helped. At the same time, scientific researchers will continue to search for the causes of abnormal behavior and the most effective forms of treatment. In the next section, we will examine research methods used by scientists to deal with these crucial issues.

Research Methods in Abnormal Psychology

Psychological disorders are such a fascinating and mysterious aspect of human behavior that people feel compelled to offer explanations, even without adequate support. Popular books claiming that psychological problems are due to everything from diet to radioactivity are regularly published. You can pick up almost any newspaper and read simplistic speculations about the profile of a murderer or a person who has committed suicide. Such easy explanations can be misleading, because they lack a grounding in psychological theory and scientific data.

The Scientific Method

Claims about the cause and treatment of abnormal behavior must be made on the basis of solid, scientific research rather than speculation. We will explain briefly the essentials of scientific methods as applied to abnormal psychology. In this process, we will discuss topics that you may have learned in introductory psychology or in a psychological methods course. Our review of this topic will explain the aspects of research methods that apply specifically to the study of abnormal psychology. This review will equip you to read reports in newspapers and magazines with an eye for scientific standards. An overview of research methods in abnormal psychology is contained in Table 1.2.

The essence of the scientific method is objectivity, the process of testing ideas about the nature of psychological phenomena without bias before accepting these ideas as adequate explanations. Taking a farfetched example, let's say you suspect that people who live on the East Coast are more stable psychologically than people who live on the West Coast (or vice versa, if you live on the West Coast). You should test this suspicion systematically before accepting it as "fact." As you set about this process, you would certainly want to hold open the possibility that your initial hunch was in error. The potential to discard an erroneous idea is an essential ingredient of the scientific method.

The underlying logic of the scientific method involves three concepts: observation, hypothesis formation, and the ruling out of competing explanations through proper controls. You have probably already used the scientific method yourself without referring to it in these terms. You may have found, for example, that it seems that every time you have a caffeinated drink, such as coffee, after 6 P.M. you have trouble falling asleep. What would you need to do to test this possibility? You might go through the **observation process,** in which you mentally keep track of the differences between the nights you drink coffee and the nights you do not. The **hypothesis formation process** would be the step of predicting that drinking coffee causes you to stay awake at night. To test this hypothesis, you could try experimenting with drinking coffee on some nights but not on others. Next, you must rule out competing explanations. You must be careful not to drink coffee on a night that you have just watched a scary television program, for example. Otherwise, you would have no way of knowing whether your

TABLE 1.2 Research Methods in Abnormal Psychology

Type of Method	Application to Studying Depression
Experimental	The effectiveness of an antidepressant drug is evaluated by comparing the scores on a test of depression of people who receive the drug with those of people who do not. Purpose: To establish whether the drug works better than no drug. Advantages: If the group receiving the drug improves and the other group does not, the experimenter can conclude quite confidently that the drug had a therapeutic effect. Disadvantages: It can be difficult to withhold treatment from people who are depressed.
Quasi-experimental	People who differ in the number of friends they have are compared on a measure of depression. Purpose: To determine whether groups that differ in number of friends differ in level of depression. Advantages: It is useful when people are being compared on characteristics that cannot be manipulated. Disadvantages: Since people were not assigned randomly to groups, the experimenter cannot be sure that they actually were similar on all but the relevant variable.
Correlational	People who become depressed are tested on self-esteem to see if they have negative views about themselves. Purpose: To study the relationship of depression with other psychological states. Advantages: The experimenter can determine what other psychological qualities characterize depressed people. Disadvantages: The experimenter cannot determine whether depression causes people to have low self-esteem or whether low self-esteem is a cause of depression.
Survey	Anonymous questionnaires are sent to thousands of people, asking them to indicate whether they have symptoms of depression. Purpose: To obtain responses from a representative sample so that findings can be generalized to the population. Advantages: The responses of large samples of people can be obtained at relatively low cost. Disadvantages: Questions asked of respondents tend to be limited in depth.
Case study	A person with a history of depression is described in detail with particular emphasis on this person's development of the disorder. Purpose: To provide an in-depth analysis of one person to gain unique insight into the particular disorder. Advantages: Many circumstances in the person's life and psychological status can be explored in an attempt to gain a thorough understanding of that individual. Disadvantages: What characterizes one individual may not characterize others with depression.
Single-subject design	A depressed person is given a trial run of a treatment and is tested after this treatment to measure its effectiveness. Then the treatment is discontinued, and depression is measured again. This cycle is repeated one or more times. Purpose: To use one case for studying the effects of alterations in conditions on behavior. Advantages: By comparing the person receiving the treatment with himself or herself rather than with other individuals, differences between people in their life histories or current circumstances can be ruled out. Disadvantages: It can be emotionally draining for the individual to be run through a cycle of on-again, off-again treatments. Later treatments may be influenced by the outcome of earlier ones.

sleep problems were due to the coffee or to the anxiety created by the program.

Although the coffee-drinking example may seem rather simple, it highlights the basic issues involved in most of the research we will encounter in this book. Researchers in abnormal psychology begin by observing a phenomenon of interest, form hypotheses to explain it, and then design ways to eliminate as many competing explanations as possible. This last step often is the most difficult, because abnormal behavior is such a multifaceted phenomenon.

To help make these important decisions, researchers rely on statistical procedures in which probability is a central concept.

Probability refers to the odds, or likelihood, that an event will happen. The probability of a coin toss turning up heads is .5; that is, if a coin is tossed 100 times, it should show heads one half of the time because there are only two possibilities. All conclusions about the correctness of hypotheses are framed in terms of probability, because it is almost impossible to study every individual whose responses might be relevant to the question under study. For example, if you are studying people with serious depression, you cannot obtain data from every person in the world who is depressed. You can study only some people from this very large group. In other words, you would choose a **sample,** or selection, from the **population,** or entire group, of depressed people. After you have studied the sample, you would proceed to draw conclusions about the larger population. For example, you might find that, in your sample of 50 depressed people, most of them have a disturbance in their appetite. You could then infer that appetite disturbance is a common feature of serious depression. However, you would have to be careful to state this inference in terms of probabilities. After all, you did not sample every depressed person in the population. Assuming your results were statistically "significant," there would be at most a 5 percent probability that your results were due to chance factors.

All statistics rely on some very important assumptions about the samples on which the results are based—namely, that the sample is representative of the whole population and that it was randomly selected. **Representativeness** is the idea that your sample adequately reflects the characteristics of the population from which it is drawn. For example, if you interview only 50 men, you cannot draw conclusions about men and women. Random selection increases the likelihood that your sample will not be contaminated by a selective factor. Ideally, every person who is representative of the population of depressed people should have an equal likelihood of being selected for the sample. Let's say you have identified 1,000 potential participants for your study who are representative of the population of depressed people. Of these 1,000, you have resources to interview only 50. To ensure that your final sample is randomly selected you need to use a method, such as drawing names out of a hat. You can see how it would be a mistake to select your final sample by choosing the first 50 people who responded to your initial request for participants. These people might be unusually compulsive or desperate in pursuit of relief from their depression. Either of these attributes might bias your sample so that it no longer represents the full spectrum of people with depression.

The Experimental Method

The purpose of psychological research is to develop an understanding of how and why people differ in their behavior. The dimensions along which people, things, or events differ are called **variables.** For example, depression is a variable. Some people are more depressed than others; if given a test of depression, some people would receive high scores and others would receive low scores. The purpose of research on depression is to find out what accounts for these differences among people.

The experimental method is one approach to discovering the source of differences among people on psychological variables. The **experimental method** involves altering or changing the conditions to which participants are exposed and observing the effects of this manipulation on the behavior of the participants. In research involving this method, the experimenter attempts to determine whether there is a cause–effect relationship between two kinds of variables. The experimenter adjusts the level of one variable, called the **independent variable,** and observes the effect of this manipulation on the second variable, called the **dependent variable.** In our example about the effects of coffee on sleep patterns, the independent variable would be the caffeine in the coffee, and the dependent variable would be ease of falling asleep. In depression research, the independent variable would be a factor the researcher has hypothesized causes depression. For example, a current hypothesis is that some people in northern climates become more depressed in the winter, when the daylight hours are shorter and the light is less intense. To test this hypothesis, you would need to create an artificial situation in which you could manipulate light exposure (independent variable) for at least several days and observe the effect on depression scores (dependent variable) in your participants.

The experimental method usually involves making comparisons between groups exposed to varying levels of the independent variables. The simplest experimental design has two groups: an experimental and a control group. In this design, the **experimental group** receives the "treatment" thought to influence the behavior under study and the **control group** does not. Returning to the coffee example, you would test the hypothesis that caffeine causes sleeplessness by designing an experiment in which the experimental group is given caffeine and the control group is not given caffeine. By comparing sleep patterns in the two groups, you would be able to determine whether caffeine causes sleeplessness.

Many studies involve a special kind of control group—a "placebo" condition. In the **placebo condition,** people are given an inert substance or treatment that is similar in all other ways to the experimental treatment. Thus, to test the caffeine hypothesis, you might give one group of participants a sugar pill that has no caffeine in it but looks identical to the caffeine pill you give the experimental participants. What is the purpose of the placebo condition? Think about your own experience in taking pills or in exposing yourself to other treatments that supposedly affect your behavior or health. Sometimes you feel better (or, perhaps, worse) just knowing that you have taken a substance that you think might affect you. The purpose of a placebo is to eliminate the possibility that a participant will experience a change that could be attributed to his or her expectations about the outcome of a treatment. Again, in the case of the caffeine example, if you wanted to test the effects of coffee (as opposed to caffeine), you might give the experimental group a cup of caffeinated coffee and the placebo group a cup of decaffeinated coffee. That way, people in both groups would be drinking a hot, brown beverage.

This woman is participating in an experimental study on the therapeutic effects of light therapy for alleviating depression. She is a participant in the treatment group, which receives exposure from a light source.

You might compare their sleeping patterns, then, with those of the "no treatment" control group, who drink nothing before going to sleep.

In abnormal psychology, studies on the effectiveness of various therapeutic treatments should, ideally, include a placebo condition. For example, researchers who are investigating whether a new medication will be effective in treating a certain psychological disorder must include a group receiving a placebo to ensure that any therapeutic benefit in the treatment group can be attributed to the active ingredients in the medication. If the medication was found to be an effective treatment or if the researcher was interested in establishing further control, the researcher might then make medication available to the people in the placebo and other control conditions and test the effect of the intervention at that point. Comparable procedures would be carried out in investigating the effects of certain kinds of psychotherapy. In these cases, however, the task of providing a placebo treatment is much more complicated than in the case of medication studies. What would a placebo treatment be for psy-

chotherapy? Ideally, the researchers would want the placebo participants to receive treatments of the same frequency and duration as the experimental group participants who are receiving psychotherapy. As you might imagine, this would provide a real challenge for the researchers, who would be faced with trying to devise a method in which the people in the placebo condition would be meeting with a "therapist" but not participating in a therapeutic interaction. Perhaps they would talk about the weather or politics, but even such apparently neutral conversations might have some therapeutic effect.

Researchers in the field of abnormal psychology must also make allowances for the **demand characteristics** of the experimental situation. People in an experiment have certain expectations about what is going to happen to them and about the proper way they should respond, particularly when these people suspect that the research may reveal something very personal about themselves. For example, if you know that you will be given caffeine, you might anticipate difficulty falling asleep that night. Similarly, if the experimenter knows that you have been given caffeine, he or she might make comments that could further influence how easily you fall asleep. The "demand" in this situation is the pull toward responding in ways based not on the actual effects of caffeine but on how you or the experimenters *think* the caffeine will affect you. Imagine how seriously the demand characteristics could bias an experiment on the effects of an antianxiety medication. An experimenter administers a drug and tells participants that they will feel relaxed in a little while. The chances are that they will feel more relaxed, but there is no way of knowing whether this is the result of the experimenter's leading comments or a true response to the medication. Or perhaps a participant notices labeling on the bottle, indicating that the pill is an antianxiety drug. This alone might have some influence on how the participant feels.

To control for demand characteristics on both sides, most researchers use a **double-blind technique,** in which neither the person giving the treatment nor the person receiving the treatment knows whether the participant is in the experimental or the control group. Even if this technique cannot be applied, as in the case of research on the effects of psychotherapy on depression, a minimal requirement for methodologically sound research is that neither the experimenter nor the participant knows the study's hypotheses. Otherwise, they will behave in ways that fulfill the expectations of the research.

In all of these cases, it is essential that the experimenter assign participants to conditions in a totally random manner. You would not want to put all the people with sleep problems in the coffee-drinking group, or vice versa. Instead, the researcher would place people in groups according to a predetermined method of random assignment.

The experimental method can be a powerful way to determine cause–effect relationships. However, it is not always possible to manipulate a variable in an experiment by assigning participants randomly to conditions. For instance, you cannot use "number of friends" as an independent variable, because there is no practical way you can control how many friends someone has. In this case, you would use a **quasi-experimental design,** one that looks a bit like an experimental design but lacks the key ingredient of random assignment (Cook & Campbell, 1979; Cook, Campbell, & Peracchio, 1990). You would choose groups that appear to be as similar as possible, except on the characteristic of number of friends, and then compare them on the dependent variable of interest. The problem with this method is that, because people are not assigned randomly to groups, you cannot be sure that they actually are similar on all but the relevant variable. Any pre-existing differences between the groups may affect the outcome of the study. For instance, the group with few friends may have poor social skills, compared with the group with many friends. If the dependent variable is depression, it may be differences in social skills rather than number of friends that account for differences in their depression scores. Despite these problems, it is necessary to use a quasi-experimental design in research in which groups whose characteristics have been predetermined are compared. For example, comparisons of males vs. females, older vs. younger individuals, or people of different ethnicities would all involve this type of quasi-experimental design.

Similarly, when participants in a research study choose one of the treatment conditions rather than being randomly assigned to a group, a quasi-experimental method is the only available design. Many studies on psychotherapy use quasi-experimental designs to enable clients to select the intervention they want. However, it is possible to develop statistical methods of controlling for this design problem in studies of the effectiveness of psychotherapy (Shadish, Matt, Navarro, & Phillips, 2000).

The Correlational Method

It is not always possible or desirable to frame a research problem in experimental or even quasi-experimental terms. In such cases, researchers use the correlational method. A **correlation** is an association, or co-relation, between two variables. The relationship described in the previous section between depression and number of friends is a perfect example of a correlation. The advantage of using a correlational procedure is that the researcher can study areas that are not easily tested by the experimental method. For example, it is theorized that people who have depressive disorders think very negatively about themselves and have very low levels of self-esteem. The most direct way to test this theory is to measure the levels of depression and

self-esteem in people and see if the scores are correlated, or related to each other.

The correlation statistic is expressed in terms of a number between +1 and -1. Positive numbers represent positive correlations—meaning that, as scores on one variable increase, scores on the second variable increase. For example, because one aspect of depression is that it causes a disturbance in normal sleep patterns, you would expect, then, that scores on a measure of depression would be positively correlated with scores on a measure of sleep disturbances. Conversely, negative correlations indicate that, as scores on one variable increase, scores on the second variable decrease. An example of a negative correlation is the relationship between depression and self-esteem. The more depressed people are, the lower their scores are on a measure of self-esteem. In many cases, there is no correlation between two variables. In other words, two variables show no systematic relationship with each other. For example, depression is unrelated to height.

Just knowing that there is a correlation between two variables does not tell you whether one variable causes the other. The correlation simply tells you that the two variables are associated with each other in a particular way. Sleep disturbance might cause a person to score higher on a measure of depression, just as a high degree of depression can result in disturbed sleep patterns. Furthermore, a third variable that you have not measured could account for the correlation between the two variables that you have studied. Both depression and sleep disturbance could be due to an unmeasured physical problem, such as a biochemical imbalance. People who use correlational methods in their research are always on guard for the potential existence of unmeasured variables influencing the observed results. Furthermore, new methods involving complex correlational analyses with multiple variables are leading to improved and better-controlled correlational designs in research on abnormal psychology. For example, researchers have assessed the relative contributions of genetics, personality, and attitudes to the development of alcohol abuse (Finn, Sharkansky, Brandt, & Trucotte, 2000).

The Survey Method

Almost every day you can pick up a newspaper or magazine and read the results of the most recent survey report on any aspect of human behavior. It might be nationwide surveys of people's attitudes toward the guilt or innocence of a major figure in the news, a campuswide survey about satisfaction with dormitory food, or a report in a newsmagazine comparing sexual practices in America with those in Europe. The **survey method** is a research tool used to gather information from a sample of people considered representative of a particular population. The reason there are so many surveys published in the news is that people are interested in what other people think and do. Sometimes the most interesting surveys are the ones that do not seem to "fit" with what you might

MindMAP Segment 1.3: Correlational Research

Researchers gain a better understanding of psychological disorders, such as depression, through surveys in which they assess the prevalence of the condition in certain segments of the population.

expect, or the ones that pertain to a particular issue that is on people's minds. Surveys vary, of course, in their scope and relevance, with some pertaining more to political attitudes and others to the general health and well-being of a large segment of the population. Although they have the advantage that they can be administered to thousands of people, they tend to be limited in depth, especially when they rely on the self-reports of respondents.

In abnormal psychology, the surveys that have the most relevance are those that focus on the mental health of the population, reporting the frequency of various psychological disorders. Other aspects of human behavior are also of interest, such as the frequency of drug use, sexual experiences, and child abuse and the use of mental health services.

In the pages to follow, you will read many statistics about the frequency of psychological disorders. Researchers gather information about these disorders by conducting surveys. The statistics they obtain fall into two categories: incidence and prevalence. The **incidence** of a disorder is the frequency of new cases within a given time period. For example, the public health commissioner in a large city may be interested in the number of newly reported cases of AIDS during the month of January. This number would represent the 1-month incidence of AIDS cases for the population of that city. In other cases, incidence may be based on a 1-year period, so that the number represents all new cases reported during that 12-month period. Sometimes researchers do not have access to the entire population in attempting to determine the number of people who develop the disorder in a given time period. In this case, incidence rates are based on a sample that is assumed to be representative of the entire population. For example, researchers interested in estimating the incidence of depression in a 1-month period may base their figures on interviews in which they ask people if they have begun to experience symptoms of depression within the past month.

The **prevalence** of a disorder is the number of people who have ever had the disorder at a given time or over a specified period. The time period could be the day of the survey (the "point"

prevalence), the month preceding the study, or the entire life of the respondent. The period of time on which the prevalence rate is based is important to specify. Lifetime prevalence rates are higher than point prevalence rates, because the chances of a person developing a disorder increase with age. People in their fifties, for example, are more likely to have a higher lifetime prevalence rate of alcohol dependence, because they have lived longer than people in their twenties. Interestingly, the incidence rate for the disorder might actually be higher for the 20-year-olds than for the 50-year-olds, even though the lifetime prevalence might be lower. New cases of alcohol dependence are more likely to arise in the younger group.

The Case Study Method

Sometimes a researcher is interested in studying a condition that is very rare but has compelling features that make it worth investigating. For example, transsexualism is a disorder in which people feel that they are trapped in the body of the wrong gender. This disorder affects a fraction of 1 percent of the population, so researchers would not have access to sufficient numbers to conduct a statistically rigorous study. Instead, they would perform a case study. The **case study method** allows the researcher to describe a single case in detail. For example, a therapist treating a transsexual client would describe the client's developmental history, psychological functioning, and response to interventions. Other clinicians and researchers reading about this case would have the opportunity to learn about a rare phenomenon to which they might otherwise not have access. Furthermore, case studies can be particularly useful in helping others develop hypotheses about either psychological disorders or treatment.

In response to criticisms that case studies are commonly unsystematic and possibly biased reports, some experts (Fishman, 1999, 2001; Fishman & Messer, 2004) have proposed the **pragmatic case study** method, an organized approach for the development and accumulation of case study material that focuses on practical results. The pragmatic case study has a specified structure that fosters systematic, reflective processing of taped sessions or extensive progress notes and the collection of quantitative feedback from client questionnaires. The common framework for case write-ups facilitates the development of a cumulative science of cases. Such a collection of cases would enable scholars and clinicians to organize case studies with similar presenting problems and intervention approaches into searchable databases (Fishman & Messer, 2004).

Single-Subject Design

A **single-subject design** adds an experimental component to the study of the individual. In this type of research, one person at a time is studied in both the experimental and control conditions. Often, this method is used in research in which the focus is really on treatment. For example, suppose a school psychologist wants to assess the effectiveness of a particular approach to treating a kindergartner named Bruce for aggressive outbursts. She could use a four-phase variant of the single-subject design called the "A-B-A-B" method. The "A" phase is the **baseline,** the period in which Bruce is observed but given no treatment for a fixed period of time. During phase "B," the treatment is administered. In Bruce's case, this might consist of sending Bruce to the "time-out" corner. The baseline and treatment conditions are repeated at least once to provide greater assurance that improvements in behavior during treatment were due to the intervention and not other, chance factors. To show this method in its simplest form, the schedule for the experiment might be conducted as follows:

Week 1:   Condition A is followed. The frequency of Bruce's aggressive incidents is observed, but no attempt is made to regulate them.

Week 2:   Bruce is put on a time-out program. This is Condition B. Bruce's aggressive incidents continue to be monitored, but, every time one occurs, he spends 10 minutes in the time-out corner of the classroom.

Week 3:   The time-out program is discontinued (Condition A).

Week 4:   The time-out program is reinstituted (Condition B).

Throughout this period, the frequency of Bruce's aggressive outbursts is monitored. If the treatment is effective, the number of aggressive incidents should be less frequent in the "B" periods than in the "A." You can see from the graph in Figure 1.3 how an A-B-A-B design would look.

Sometimes the withdrawal of treatment in the A-B-A-B design would be considered unethical. In Bruce's case, this would be true if Bruce were physically harming himself or other children. The psychologist would not want to suspend treatment that was regarded as effective. As an alternative, the psychologist could use a **multiple baseline approach.** This method involves observing different dependent variables in the same person over the course of treatment. The intervention would be introduced at different times and its impact evaluated on multiple dependent variables. In Bruce's case, a baseline would be established for verbal outbursts, the treatment introduced, then his number of verbal outbursts measured. Another baseline would be established at a different point for another type of aggressive behavior, such as punching his fists. The time-out procedure would be introduced and the frequency of punching measured. A similar process would be repeated for another type of aggressive behavior, such as kicking. If the time-out procedure is working, then it should result in reduced frequency of all three dependent variables.

Single-subject designs are most appropriate for studying behaviors that are easily observed and measured and are particularly useful in evaluating the effects of therapeutic interventions (Morgan & Morgan, 2001). The emotional state associated with stress would be difficult to study using this procedure, but specific behaviors, such as the amount of alcohol consumed when a person feels stressed, can be studied in this manner (Tennen, Affleck, Armeli, & Carney, 2000). One advantage of this method is that it allows the investigator to make precise manipulations whose effect can be carefully measured. The disadvantage is that the study is carried out on only one individual, thus limiting its generalizability. To avoid this problem, some researchers report the results of several single-subject designs in one study.

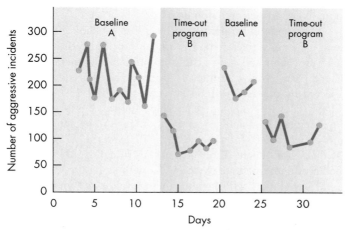

FIGURE 1.3 An example of an A-B-A-B design This graph shows the frequency of aggressive incidents recorded during 20-minute morning observation periods of a child in a classroom.

Source: From J. S. Bailey, H. M. Hutchinson, & H. A. Murphy, "Behavioral school psychology goes outdoors: The effect of organized games on playground aggression" in *Journal of Applied Behavior Analysis*, 16:33. Copyright ©1983. Used by permission of the *Journal of Applied Behavior Analysis*.

Studies of Genetic Influence

So far, we have been discussing psychological methods of research. Although psychological research provides valuable information about the causes and treatment of abnormal behavior, it cannot answer all the questions. In fact, there has been a tremendous amount of excitement over the past decade as researchers have plunged into new areas of inquiry that focus on the genetic transmission of behavioral characteristics. We all know that we inherit many physical characteristics from our parents, but, as researchers discover more about genetics, it is becoming apparent that behavioral characteristics have a strong genetic component as well (McGue & Bouchard, 1998). In the chapters to follow, you will see that many psychological disorders are being examined from a genetic perspective. Depression, schizophrenia, alcoholism, and panic disorder are just a few that geneticists and psychologists are actively researching.

Most researchers begin the search for genetic causes of a disorder by establishing that the disorder shows a distinct pattern of family inheritance. This process requires obtaining complete family histories from people who are identified as having symptoms of the disorder. Their genealogy must be traced in order to calculate the prevalence of the disorder among blood relatives.

Another way to trace inherited causes of psychological disorders is to compare the **concordance rate,** or agreement ratios, between people diagnosed as having the disorder and their relatives. For example, a researcher may observe that out of a sample of 10 twin pairs, the members of 6 pairs each has the same diagnosed psychological disorder. This would mean that, among this sample, there is a concordance rate of .60 (6 out of 10). An inherited disorder would be expected to have the highest concordance between **monozygotic,** or identical, **twins** (whose genes are the same), with somewhat lower rates between siblings and **dizygotic,** or fraternal, **twins** (who are no more alike genetically than siblings of different ages), and even lower rates among more distant relatives.

A more powerful way to determine whether a disorder has a genetic basis is the study of families in which an adoption has taken place. The most extensive evidence gathered from these studies comes from the Scandinavian countries, where the governments maintain complete records for the population. Two types of adoptions are studied in this research. In the first, simply called an **adoption study,** researchers look at children whose biological parents have diagnosed psychological disorders but who are adopted by "normal" parents. In the second and rarer kind of adoption situation, called a **crossfostering study,** researchers look at children who are adopted by parents with psychological disorders but whose biological parents are psychologically healthy.

These kinds of studies enable researchers to draw strong inferences about the relative contributions of biology and family environment to the development of psychological disorders. Take the example of a boy who is born to two seriously depressed parents but who is adopted by two parents with no diagnosed psychological disorder. If this child also develops serious depression later in life, it makes sense to infer that he is genetically predisposed. When researchers study many dozens of people in similar situations and observe a heightened prevalence rate of psychological disorders among these children, they are able to draw these conclusions with a high degree of certainty. Conversely, consider the case of a girl born to parents with no diagnosed psychological disorder who is adopted and whose adoptive parents later become psychologically disturbed. If she develops the adoptive parents' psychological disorder, family environment would be one logical cause.

Researchers trying to understand the specific mechanisms involved in models of genetic transmission have found it helpful to study measurable characteristics whose family patterns parallel the pattern of a disorder's inheritance, called **biological markers.** For example, hair color would be a biological marker if a certain hair color always appeared in people within a family who have the same disorder. Other marker studies involve **genetic mapping,** a process researchers currently use in studying a variety of diseases thought to have a hereditary basis. Using this method, in the early spring of 2001 a team of genetic researchers mapped the entire sequence of genes in humans. In the chapters to follow, we will explore many of the important discoveries about a variety of psychological disorders that have been made using these methods.

The Human Experience of Psychological Disorders

As researchers continue to make progress in understanding the causes of psychological disorders, interest and attention have become increasingly focused on the impact of these disorders on every level—the family, community, and society. The widespread distribution of information, such as research findings, along with society's increased openness to confronting the concerns of people with psychological disorders, has led to a dramatic increase in public awareness of how psychological disorders affect many aspects of life. Psychological problems touch upon many facets of human experience. Not only is the individual with the problem deeply troubled; the family is disturbed, the community is moved, and society is affected.

Impact on the Individual: Stigma and Distress

One of your reactions to seeing people like Rebecca Hasbrouck might be to consider them as very different from you. You may even feel a certain degree of contempt or disgust for them. Many people in our society would react to her in such disdainful ways, not fully realizing the powerful impact of their discriminatory response. Such reactions are common, and they are the basis for the discrimination and stigma experienced by many people with severe psychological disturbance. A *stigma* is a label that causes certain people to be regarded as different, defective, and set apart from mainstream members of society. The phenomenon of stigma was brought to public attention in the writings of famous sociologist Erving Goffman in the 1960s, and, several decades later, stigma continues to be a major focus in publications and discussions pertaining to the rights and treatment of psychologically disturbed individuals.

It is common for people with serious psychological disorders, especially those who have been hospitalized, to experience profound and long-lasting emotional and social effects. These "survivors" commonly report feeling isolated and rejected by others. In time, they come to think less of themselves, take less advantage of opportunities for growth and development, and actually come to believe in society's myths and expectations for the mentally ill (Wright, Gronfein, & Owens, 2000) (see Table 1.3). Unfortunately, the popular media often perpetuate these myths with stereotyped portrayals of individuals with mental illness (Salter & Byrne, 2000). For example, when it is reported that a man with schizophrenia has attacked a stranger, the public is led to believe that most individuals with schizophrenia are prone to such violent behavior. As a result, it is no surprise to find that a large percentage of people in the United States are fearful of people with mental illness and do not wish to be associated with them (Link et al., 1999). Individuals with psychological disorders, especially severe conditions such as schizophrenia, often find

TABLE 1.3 Goals for the Future of Mental Health

The serious problem of stigma has caught the attention of the federal government, which established a Commission on Mental Health. This Commission disseminated a report in 2003 spelling out six goals for the future of mental health:

1. Americans need to understand that mental health is essential to overall health:
   - many people with mental illnesses go untreated
   - stigma impedes people from getting the care they need
   - better coordination is needed between mental health care and primary health care

2. Mental health care needs to be consumer and family driven:
   - the complex mental health system overwhelms many consumers
   - consumers and families do not control their own care
   - consumers and families need community-based care

3. Disparities in mental health services should be eliminated:
   - minority populations are underserved
   - minorities face barriers to receiving appropriate care
   - rural America needs improved access to mental health services

4. Early mental health screening, assessment, and referral to services should be common practice:
   - early assessment and treatment are critical across the life span
   - if untreated, childhood disorders can lead to a downward spiral
   - schools can help address mental health problems

5. Excellent mental health care should be delivered and research should be accelerated:
   - the delay is too long before research reaches practice
   - too few benefit from available treatment
   - reimbursement policies do not foster converting research to practice

6. Technology should be used to access mental health care and information:
   - access to care is a concern in rural and other underserved areas
   - information technology can now enhance medical records systems
   - consumers may not have access to reliable health information

Source: http://www.mentalhealthcommission.gov/reports/Finalreport/downloads/FinalReport.pdf

that other people resist living with them, socializing with them, renting to them, or giving them jobs (Corrigan & Penn, 1999; Penn & Martin, 1998).

Although tremendous efforts have been undertaken to humanize the experiences of patients within psychiatric institutions, for most people the process of hospitalization is deeply upsetting, and possibly traumatizing. A number of institutional procedures are seen as dehumanizing and contributing to stigma. For example, patients who are out of control may be physically restrained. Others may be forced to give up personal possessions or to limit their contact with loved ones, even by telephone. They are expected to participate in group activities, such as occupational or recreational therapy, and to share their private concerns in group therapy. While such structures are designed to be therapeutic, some individuals find them too intrusive and controlling. Even clinic routines that require patients to wait for appointments can be dehumanizing, causing them to feel that they are less important than the staff. Loss of privacy, inadequate access to information about diagnosis and treatment, patronizing or infantilizing speech, offensive slang, and language with a medical orientation are additional objectionable practices that stigmatize individuals. Finally, being forced to accept a psychiatric label may be experienced as stigmatizing. The individual may be made to feel as though he or she cannot argue or dispute the diagnosis once it has been given. In the words of one patient, "The whole system is set up . . . to create and preserve stigma" (Reidy, 1994, p. 5).

Most people would outwardly espouse an understanding and a tolerance for people with psychological disorders. Reflected more subtly in their language, humor, and stereotypes, however, are usually some fairly negative attributions. Watch television for an hour, or listen to the everyday conversation of those around you, and you will probably encounter some comments about emotional illness. Colloquialisms relating to emotional illness abound in our language. Statements about being "nuts," "crazy," "mental," "maniac," "flaky," "off-the-wall," "psycho," "schizo," or "retarded" are quite common. Popular humor is filled with jokes about "crazy people." Imagine the response of a group of teenagers walking past Rebecca; they might make derogatory comments and jokes about her appearance and behavior. What toll do you think this would take on Rebecca's already unstable sense of self?

Considering the tremendous impact of psychological disorder on the individual, why are some people so cruel as to joke about a person's distressed state? One reason might be that people often joke about issues that make them anxious. There is something very frightening about a psychological disorder that makes people want to distance themselves from it as much as possible, perhaps feeling frightened about the prospect of losing control over their own behavior and thoughts. Consequently, they joke about oddities in other people's behavior.

A leading researcher on the topic of stigma, Patrick Corrigan (2004) contends that stigma is particularly problematic because it deters people in need of treatment from seeking or sticking with treatment. Corrigan frames the stigma process in terms of four social cognitive processes: (1) cues, (2) stereotypes, (3) prejudice, and (4) discrimination. Cues include four kinds of information that can fuel inferences about mental illness: (a) psychiatric symptoms (e.g., inappropriate affect or bizarre behavior); (b) social skills deficits (e.g., impaired understanding of socially appropriate behavior); (c) physical appearance (e.g., unkempt clothing or poor hygiene); and (d) labels (e.g., being psychiatrically diagnosed, or even being seen coming out of a mental health clinic).

According to Corrigan (2004), cues elicit stereotypes such as, "All people with mental illness are dangerous." Stereotypes commonly yield prejudice such as, "People with mental illness are dangerous, and I am afraid of them." The result of such thinking and behavior is discrimination, such as, "I do not want to be near them or hire them for a job." The progression of public stigma from stereotype to prejudice to discrimination has a parallel in the self-stigma of the individual with a psychological disorder. For example, a woman with a psychological disorder may hold the stereotype that all people with mental illness are incompetent. Her prejudice is expressed in the thought, "I have a mental illness, so I must be incompetent," and in the notion of discrimination: "Why should I even try to get a job if I'm just an incompetent mental patient?"

What about your attitudes? Imagine the following scenario. An urgent message is waiting for you when you return to your room. It is from the mother of Jeremy, your best friend in high school. You call Jeremy's mother, who says she wants you to meet her at the psychiatric hospital in your hometown as soon as possible. Jeremy has just been admitted there and says that he has to see you, because only you can understand what he is going through. You are puzzled and distressed by this news. You had no idea that he had any psychological problems. What will you say to him? Can you ask him what's wrong? Can you ask him how he feels? Do you dare inquire about what his doctors have told him about his chances of getting better? What will it be like to see him in a psychiatric hospital? Do you think you could be friends with someone who has spent time in such a hospital?

Now imagine the same scenario, but instead you receive news that Jeremy has just been hospitalized for treatment of a kidney dysfunction. As you imagine yourself going to visit him, you will probably not think twice about how you will respond to him. Of course, you will ask him how he feels, what exactly is wrong with him, and when he will be well again. Even though you might not like hospitals very much, at least you have a pretty good idea about what hospital patients are like. It does not seem peculiar to imagine Jeremy as a patient in this kind of hospital. Your friend's physical illness would probably be much easier to understand and accept than his psychological disorder, and you would probably not even consider whether you could be friends with him again after he is discharged.

Apart from the distress created by stigma is the personal pain associated with the actual psychological disorder. Think about Rebecca and the dramatic turn that her life took as she was shaken from her successful and stable existence. Not only was she devastated by the trauma of losing her family, but she lost her own identity and sense of purpose as well. By the time she

reached out for help, she no longer had even the remnants of her former self. Think about how you would feel if everything you had were suddenly gone in the course of a few weeks—your family, your home, your identity. For many people who develop a serious psychological disorder, whatever the cause, the symptoms themselves are painful and possibly terrifying. The sense of loss of control over one's thoughts and behaviors adds to one's torment.

Of course, not all cases of psychological disorder are as severe as Rebecca's, nor do they necessarily follow from an identifiable event. In the chapters to follow, you will read about a wide range of disorders involving mood, anxiety, substance abuse, sexuality, and thought disturbance. The case descriptions will give you a glimpse into the feelings and experiences of people who have these disorders, and you may find that some of these individuals seem similar to you or to people you know. As you read about the disorders, put yourself in the place of the people who have these conditions. Consider how they feel and how they would like to be treated. We hope that you will realize that our discussion is not about disorders but about the people with these disorders.

Impact on the Family

Typically, even before a person with a psychological disorder has been seen by a professional, the family has been affected by the person's behavior and distress. The degree of the impact depends in part on the nature of the problem and in part on the dynamics of the family.

Most commonly, family members are touched by the pain of a relative who is wounded emotionally. For example, a mother loses sleep for many months as she struggles to understand what role she might have played in the development of her teenage daughter's suicidal depression. A father worries that his son might once again drink insecticide as he responds to visions of giant insects crawling down his throat. A wife feels anxious every time the phone rings, wondering whether it might be the police or an acquaintance calling to tell her that her husband has passed out in a drunken stupor at the neighborhood bar.

The stigma of a psychological disorder also taints the family. Many families speak of the shame and embarrassment they feel when neighbors, schoolmates, and co-workers discover that someone in the family is schizophrenic, depressed, addicted to drugs, or abusive. You can imagine how Rebecca's relatives might have felt when news of her wandering and disruptive behavior with the police was broadcast on the local media.

For much of the twentieth century, the mental health profession in general was unsympathetic regarding the impact of psychological disorder on the family. Not only were families kept uninformed about treatment, but they were often blamed for the problem. Theories of many disorders, such as schizophrenia, depression, and sexual problems, typically blamed families—usually mothers. Families found themselves distressed by the

As a kickoff to National Mental Health Month, several thousand people joined in a Washington march to bring attention to the concerns of people with mental illness.

turbulence caused by the problems of one of their relatives, hurt, and confused by what they heard as accusations from mental health professionals. Much of that has changed in recent years, as some prominent mental health professionals, such as psychiatrist E. Fuller Torrey, have recognized the distress of these families and have written books specifically directed to them (Torrey, 1995), letting them know that they are not alone; in fact, their worries, concerns, and problems are similar to those experienced by millions of other Americans.

Families also have banded together for support and mutual education. Across the country, families of people with serious psychological disorders have formed organizations, such as the National Alliance for the Mentally Ill (NAMI). These groups have helped many families better understand the nature of the problems they face, and the organizations have also served an important political function. Such family advocacy groups have played a crucial role in ensuring that psychiatrically hospitalized people are properly treated, that their legal rights are respected, and that adequate posthospitalization care is planned.

Impact on the Community and Society

Anyone who has lived in a community where a state psychiatric hospital is located knows that there are many challenges involved in accommodating the mental health care needs of psychologically disturbed people following their discharge from the hospital. As we discussed earlier, beginning in the 1970s, there has been a national movement toward relocating psychiatric inpatients from hospitals to less restrictive environments. It was commonplace in the mid-1970s for a state hospital to house several thousand patients. By the start of the twenty-first century, those numbers had dwindled. (Review Figure 1.2.) Many institutions had closed; others were left open but operated at a far

smaller scale. Some of the discharged individuals moved back to the homes of their families, but most moved into community-based homes with several other deinstitutionalized people. In some programs and communities, these people are adequately cared for; however, in many areas, particularly large cities, there are dozens, even hundreds of formerly institutionalized people who go without homes, food, or health attention.

A particularly disturbing fact associated with the lack of appropriate care and attention given to mentally ill individuals is the alarming number of mentally ill individuals who are winding up in jail or prison. Some experts contend that the rapid release of patients over the course of decades from mental hospitals, associated with inadequate follow-up, has resulted in a phenomenon in which approximately 16 percent of inmates in the United States are identified as mentally ill, a statistic that is considered an underestimate of the true number (Lamberg, 2004).

Also striking is the fact that ethnic minority persons are unlikely to receive mental health services appropriate to their needs. Even those who have access to some mental health services have little guarantee that the services will be of high quality (Snowden & Yamada, 2005). In the report of the President's New Freedom Commission on Mental Health, conclusions highlighted access problems associated with racial, cultural, and ethnic variables. Various explanations for such disparities have been proposed over the years, including factors such as cultural mistrust, stigma, differences in the way symptoms are expressed and managed, insurance limitations, and even the preference of many people for alternative interventions (e.g., acupressure, chiropractic care, Tai Chi). The fact remains, however, that there are striking ethnic and cultural disparities in the utilization of mental health services, and that continuing research is needed in order to understand such differences and to propose changes in the health care delivery system (Snowden & Yamada, 2005).

In an attempt to tackle the question about why members of ethnic minority groups are less likely than white middle-class people to seek professional treatment for mental health problems such as depression, one researcher (Karasz, 2005) noted that ethnic minority individuals, in this case South Asian immigrants, are likely to view symptoms of depression as social problems or emotional reactions to situations, while European-American white individuals are more likely to view depression as some form of disease warranting professional treatment. Other researchers (Roberts, Alegria, Roberts, & Chen, 2005) have studied the different ways in which members of several ethnic groups view the problems of adolescents, and found that European-American youths and their caregivers are twice as likely as members of minority groups to define problems in mental health terms or to seek help for such problems.

The impact of psychological disorders on society is not easily measured, but there is agreement among mental health professionals and public health experts that psychological problems exact a tremendous toll on society (Callahan, 1999).

Families are often torn apart and communities are divided. Once again, consider Rebecca's story. The loss of her productivity and participation in the community can be considered costs to society. More directly measured are the actual financial costs of her rehabilitation. Her treatment will require intensive therapy, inpatient hospitalization, relocation within the community, and follow-up support. The expenses of her treatment must be weighed against the human cost of the continued suffering she would experience if she were not able to receive proper care. When you think of the fact that there are hundreds of thousands of people like Rebecca on the streets of America, you can appreciate the tragedy of the unfulfilled lives that takes its toll on society.

Reducing Stigma

Stigma is a phenomenon that adds to the burden of psychologically distressed people in several ways. In addition to increasing the burden for them and for their loved ones, stigma deters people from obtaining badly needed help, and thereby perpetuates a cycle in which many people in need become so much worse. Corrigan (2004) discusses three approaches that may diminish aspects of public stigma experienced by such individuals: protest, education, and contact. When people speak out against inaccurate or hostile representations of mental illness, those delivering such messages are often forced to stop, listen, and revise. For example, when a company produced a Valentine's Day teddy bear clothed in a straitjacket, holding commitment papers, and emblazoned with the message "crazy for you," the public outcry was tremendous.

Educational efforts are also important in providing information to the public about the nature of psychological disorders and the effectiveness of mental health interventions. Articles in newspapers and magazines, programs on radio and television, and the vast store of information available on the Internet serve very important roles in enlightening the public about conditions and their treatments.

Contact with people with mental health problems can be especially effective in changing attitudes and reducing stigma. When people become aware of the fact that life goes on for millions of people with serious psychological disorders and that it is possible to be successful in life even while contending with challenging problems, stigma diminishes.

Various advocacy groups have worked tirelessly to change the way the public views mentally ill people and how they are dealt with in all settings of society. These groups include the National Alliance for the Mentally Ill, which we mentioned earlier, as well as the Mental Health Association, the Center to Address Discrimination and Stigma, and the Eliminate the Barriers Initiative. In recent years, the U.S. federal government has also become involved in antistigma programs as part of efforts to improve the delivery of mental health services through the President's New Freedom Commission (Hogan, 2003). Certainly those who have been affected by serious psychological disorder, either directly or indirectly, will welcome efforts to understand and to assist those whose lives have been touched by mental illness.

Bringing It All Together: Clinical Perspectives

As you come to the close of this chapter, you now have an appreciation of the issues that are central to your understanding of abnormal psychology. We have tried to give you a sense of how complex it is to define abnormality, and you will find yourself returning to this issue as you read about many of the disorders in the chapters to follow. The historical perspective we have provided will be elaborated on in subsequent chapters as we look at theories of and treatments for specific disorders. Currently, developments are emerging in the field of abnormal psychology at an unbelievable pace due to the efforts of researchers applying the techniques described here. You will learn more about some of these research methods in the context of discussions regarding specific disorders. You will also develop an understanding of how clinicians, such as Dr. Sarah Tobin, look at the range of psychological disorders that affect people throughout the life span. We will give particular attention to explaining how disorders develop and how they are best treated. Our discussion of the impact of psychological disorders forms a central theme for this book, as we return time and again to consideration of the human experience of psychological disorders.

Course and Outcome

My professional relationship with Rebecca provided a powerful glimpse into the mind and experiences of a woman who had been emotionally devastated by a personal trauma. Little did I expect that my encounter with her on that Tuesday morning in September would be the start of psychotherapy that would prove to be so instrumental in helping a troubled woman set on a new life course, nor did I anticipate the impact that this year-long therapy would have on my other professional work with my other clients. Somehow, this relationship helped me increase my level of empathy and responsiveness to my clients.

I often think back to the first hour I spent with Rebecca and how I was called on to make some important decisions regarding her needs. Of immediate concern was Rebecca's physical health and comfort. I escorted her to the admissions office of the psychiatric unit, where a nurse welcomed her to the unit and assisted her in washing and dressing in clean clothes. I recall being startled, on returning to speak with Rebecca later in the day, to find a woman who looked so dramatically different from the helpless figure I had encountered only a few hours earlier. Although she continued to have a look of numbness, she seemed much more responsive in her interactions with me. She asked me what would happen to her. At one point, she became agitated for a few moments, telling me that she really should be on her way. I asked her to be patient and to listen to my recommendations. Although she could not be retained in the hospital against her will, it made sense for her to rest and recuperate, so that a plan could be developed to return her to a "normal life."

I explained to Rebecca that I would be her therapist during her stay in the hospital, which I expected to last approximately 2 weeks. During that time, I would collaborate with a social worker, Beverly Mullins, who would focus on helping Rebecca reenter the world she had fled 3 years ago. Practical matters would be planned, such as where Rebecca would live and how she would gain access to the financial resources she had left behind. My task would be to help Rebecca understand what had happened to her emotionally—to return to the trauma of the car accident and to develop a basic understanding of how this trauma and the loss of her husband and sons had precipitated a flight from reality. I would try to help her develop some of the psychological strength she would need to recover from her 3 years of torment.

During the first few days of Rebecca's stay in the hospital, the medical staff conducted a comprehensive assessment of her physical health. The list of her physical maladies was lengthy and included gastrointestinal problems, skin infections, and head lice. I also requested a full neurological evaluation, particularly important in light of the fact that Rebecca had suffered a brain trauma in the car accident, which probably contributed to her dysfunction. By the end of the first week, her medical needs were being treated, and she was on a nutritional regimen designed to address various deficiencies. Concurrent with attention to her physical condition, the clinical staff and I formulated a treatment plan to address her psychological state. During her 14 days in the hospital, Rebecca met with me six times and attended group therapy each day. She also met several times with Beverly Mullins, who contacted Rebecca's sister and parents to involve them in developing a plan of action. I joined Bev Mullins for the initial meeting of Rebecca and her family members. The emotion that filled the room was overwhelming; Rebecca was greeted as a person "coming back from the grave."

In my own work with Rebecca in those six sessions during her inpatient stays, we reviewed in painful detail Rebecca's memories of what had happened to her during the past 3 years. Much of this period was blotted out, perhaps in part due to neurological damage, but Rebecca did remember the accident and her psychological devastation in the weeks that followed. She recalled her desperate pursuit of her lost loved ones, and she spoke in disbelief about how she thought she had heard their voices calling out to her. The depth of her depression was so great that Rebecca had become immobilized after losing her children and husband. She spent nights and days for many months crying constantly and wandering the streets of the city. As strange as it came to seem to Rebecca, she found comfort in the community of other homeless people who befriended her. These people became her "family" and taught her the ways of the streets.

Rebecca was never quite sure what prompted her to emerge from the dismal life she had come to live. Perhaps it was the anniversary of the car accident that caused her to think about what was happening to her life and to consider the possibility of returning to the world from which she had tried to escape. Perhaps healing within her traumatized brain was taking place.

The intensity of Rebecca's connection with me was evident from our very first sessions. As we planned her discharge from the hospital, she asked me if she could continue to see me until her functioning was more stable. I agreed.

Bev Mullins was able to arrange a posthospital placement for Rebecca in a halfway house for women who were capable of working and gradually assuming independent control of their lives. Although none of the other six clients in the halfway house had stories as dramatic as that of Rebecca's, each had suffered a serious break with reality and was trying to return to an independent life in the community.

RETURN TO THE CASE
(continued)

Rebecca remained in the halfway house for a month. During that time, she worked out her financial situation with an attorney and took an apartment not far from her sister's house so that she could be near a relative until she felt more comfortable returning to a normal life.

Both during her stay in the halfway house and for 11 months following her departure from the house, Rebecca came to see me twice a week for outpatient therapy. Although dealing with her grief always remained a component of our work, in time we refocused our attention on tapping her talents and abilities so that she could return to work and social involvement with other people.

Rebecca felt that she had fallen out of touch with the practice of law, and she had little desire to return to that kind of work. She also continued to experience cognitive problems that impaired her attention, concentration, and memory. Because of a large insurance settlement, she did not feel pressured to find a high-paying position, but she realized that it was important for her psychological health

to be active and to work. Always having had an affinity for writing, Rebecca decided to pursue a career as a freelance writer of feature articles for popular magazines. This route seemed ideal for her, because it permitted her to work in a more private space, in which she would feel less burdened by having to interact with people who would inquire about her personal life.

The success story that unfolded for Rebecca seemed to have a fairy tale quality to it. Her writing was very well received, and she returned to a healthy psychological state over the course of a year, although mild cognitive dysfunction caused considerable frustration at times. In our work together, she slowly reacquired a sense of her identity and learned to compartmentalize her traumatic experience, so that it would be less intrusive in her day-to-day life. We also developed techniques aimed at compensating for her mild problems with memory.

After a year of regular therapy sessions, Rebecca decided that she was ready to end therapy. I suggested

that she might wish to gradually reduce the frequency of sessions, a practice I have found useful with other long-term clients. Although Rebecca initially considered this possibility, she decided against it, because she felt it important to make a "clean break" in order to prove to herself that she could be truly independent. In the years that followed, I heard from Rebecca only once. About 4 years after we had terminated, I received an engraved announcement of her wedding on which she wrote, "Thanks for everything. I've now come back to the world." Because there was no return address, I concluded that Rebecca did not need, or wish, for me to respond. Her note did mean a great deal to me, however. I was now able to have a sense of completion about our work, and, in contrast to many other cases with less-than-happy outcomes, I was able to feel a sense of comfort that my efforts with Rebecca were instrumental in bringing her "back."

Sarah Tobin, PhD

SUMMARY

- We are defining abnormality in terms of four criteria: distress, impairment, risk to self or others, and behavior that is outside the norms of the social and cultural context within which it takes place.

- In trying to understand why people act and feel in ways that are regarded as abnormal, social scientists look at three dimensions— biological, psychological, and sociocultural—and use the term *biopsychosocial* to characterize the interactions among these three dimensions. Related to the biopsychosocial approach is the diathesis-stress model, according to which people are born with a predisposition (or "diathesis") that places them at risk for developing a psychological disorder.

- The history of understanding and treating people with psychological disorders can be considered in terms of three recurring themes: the mystical, the scientific, and the humanitarian. The

mystical theme regards abnormality as due to demonic or spirit possession. This theme was prevalent during prehistoric times and the Middle Ages. The scientific theme regards abnormality as due to psychological or physical disturbances within the person. This theme had its origins in ancient Greece and Rome, and it has predominated since the nineteenth century. The humanitarian theme regards abnormality as due to improper treatment by society; this theme predominated during the reform movements of the eighteenth century and is still evident in contemporary society.

- Researchers use various methods to study the causes and treatment of psychological disorders. The scientific method involves applying an objective set of methods for observing behavior, making an hypothesis about the causes of behavior, setting up proper conditions for studying the hypothesis, and drawing conclusions about its validity. In the experimental method, the researcher alters the level of the independent variable and observes its effects on the dependent variable. The quasi-experimental method is a variant of this procedure and is used to compare groups that differ on a predetermined characteristic. The correlational method studies associations, or co-relations, between variables. The survey method enables researchers to estimate the incidence and prevalence of psychological disorders. In the case study method, one individual is studied intensively, and a detailed and careful analysis of that individual is conducted. In the single-subject design, one person at a time is studied in both the experimental and control conditions, as treatment is applied and removed in alternating phases.

- Psychological disorders affect not only the people who suffer from them but also the family, community, and society. Individuals with psychological disorders suffer great stigma, which adds to their emotional problems. Family members are affected by the distress of their loved ones, and also share a sense of stigma. On a broader level, the social and financial costs of mental health problems are inestimable. In this book, we will use a clinical perspective rooted within a life-span approach to gain an understanding of the range of psychological disorders and the methods used to treat people with these conditions.

KEY TERMS

See Glossary for definitions

Adoption study   28
Asylums   12
Baseline   27
Biological markers   28
Biopsychosocial   9
Case study method   26
Concordance rate   28
Control group   23
Correlation   25
Crossfostering study   28
Deinstitutionalization movement   19
Demand characteristics   24
Dependent variable   23
Diathesis-stress model   10
Dizygotic twins   28

Double-blind technique   24
Experimental group   23
Experimental method   23
Genetic mapping   28
Hypnotism   17
Hypothesis formation process   21
Hysteria   17
Incidence   26
Independent variable   23
Medical model   16
Mesmerized   17
Monozygotic twins   28
Moral treatment   14
Multiple baseline approach   27
Observation process   21

Placebo condition   23
Population   23
Pragmatic case study   26
Prevalence   26
Probability   23
Psychoanalysis   18
Psychoanalytic model   16
Psychotherapy   18
Quasi-experimental design   25
Representativeness   23
Sample   23
Single-subject design   26
Survey method   25
Trephining   11
Variable   23

 ## INTERNET RESOURCE

To get more information on the material covered in this chapter, visit our website at **www.mhhe.com/halgin5.** There you will find more information, resources, and links to topics of interest.

CHAPTER 2

Classification and Treatment Plans

It was an unbearably hot and humid Friday afternoon in July. As I was wrapping up my work for the week, feeling relieved that I would be able to leave the office on time, I received the seemingly inevitable call from the admissions unit. The head nurse on the unit, Hank Mahar, emphasized that I should get right down to the unit because "this guy's out of control!"

I entered the admitting room and came face to face with Peter, who leaped out of his chair and tried to give me a hug. With ardent enthusiasm in his voice, Peter said, "Thank God you've arrived. Please tell my idiot brother that I don't need to be in this looney bin!" Peter's brother, Don, sat quietly nearby and softly spoke to Peter, "Please calm down so that we can tell the doctor what has been going on."

After settling down a bit, Peter agreed to answer my questions about his background and to tell me what had been going on in his life during the days and weeks prior to being brought to the hospital. He explained that he was 23 years old and divorced. Explaining that he worked as a janitor at a bank and lived in a rooming house, he quickly interjected that he would soon be "moving up in the world as soon as the contract arrived from the recording company." I decided to wait to ask him what he meant by this, feeling that it was more important at that moment to focus on specific symptoms.

In response to my questions about how he had been feeling, Peter did acknowledge that he had been recently having "bouts of anxiety," which caused him to feel "hyper" and restless. In fact, throughout our interview, Peter showed a great deal of edginess as he became intermittently irritable and annoyed with me. He also mentioned that 4 months previously he had experienced a serious depression in which he felt as if he wanted to kill himself. Peter became defensive when discussing the depression, as he explained that the depression was understandable in

light of all that he had gone through. Peter's wife, Christine, had thrown him out of the house and had filed for divorce, because she felt he was a "loser with a lousy job and no future."

This deep depression had lasted about a month, and somehow Peter managed to pull himself out of it. He characterized the depression as "a living hell" and stated with stern emphasis that he "would never become depressed again." At this point, Peter insisted on leaving the room to go out into the hallway for a cigarette. He told me that, if I wanted information, I should talk to his brother.

Don agreed that Peter had been acting "hyper" for several weeks and had been causing quite a disturbance for the preceding several days. Peter's mother had called Don to tell him that Peter seemed to be heading toward a psychological crisis similar to the kind that she had struggled with earlier in her life. Mrs. Dickinson had received a call from the owner of Peter's rooming house, who had become increasingly concerned about Peter's odd behavior. He had been staying up all night, playing his electric guitar, writing what he described as his "first million-dollar recording hit." On several occasions, he ran from room to room in the middle of the night, waking everyone up, urging them to come and "witness a creative genius at work." From what Don could tell, Peter was operating on "nervous energy," as he hadn't slept or eaten anything for several days. There were no signs that Peter had been drinking or abusing drugs, and he had no history of substance abuse. Night after night, Peter had been working on his song. He devoted 4 or 5 daytime hours to making countless telephone calls to recording company executives in an effort to sell his song. He had called one company more than 40 times, insisting that someone listen to him play his song over the phone.

Peter's strange behaviors were also evident outside the rooming house. He had stopped going to

work. When he wasn't calling the record companies, he was pursuing outlandish purchases. For example, he had gone to a luxury car dealership and had submitted a credit application to buy a $75,000 car. He also went to a realtor, who spent many hours showing him expensive homes in the belief that Peter was about to come into a large amount of money. In the evenings, Peter spent time at bars, reportedly looking for a talented singer who would be willing to record his songs. Peter had met a woman, Marnie, who was captivated by Peter's dramatic tales of past success and future potential. They spent 48 hours together and decided to get married, but Marnie never showed up for their planned meeting at city hall to apply for a marriage license. Peter was devastated and infuriated. He made threatening comments about Marnie, although Don felt that there was no real likelihood that Peter would harm her. For one thing, he had no way of finding her; furthermore, he was the kind of individual whose "bark was worse than his bite," Don commented.

Peter was certainly an interesting individual. I was struck by his air of bravado, while at the same time believing that he had many endearing qualities. Beneath his loud and demanding demeanor, there seemed to be a man who was terrified by what he had been experiencing since the day his wife, Christine, left him. I was confident that the hospital treatment staff could help Peter, but I wasn't sure whether he would let us. In as calming a manner as possible, I asked Peter for his cooperation, explaining that it was my sense that he had been through very difficult times since his wife had left him. I also explained that it would take only a couple of weeks to get him back to a normal level of function—somewhere between the deeply depressed and the highly energized extremes he had experienced in recent months.

Sarah Tobin, PhD

You have just read the case of a young man whose life was thrown into havoc by the experience of extreme psychological symptoms ranging from deep depression to frenzied hyperactivity. Imagine that you are a professional and are faced with the responsibility of treating an individual like Peter. How would you begin? One of the first things you might try to do is establish a working relationship, so that you can gain a better understanding of what is going on with Peter and how you might be of assistance to him. In addition, you would attempt to determine which diagnostic label might best apply to his symptoms, so that you could implement the most appropriate treatment. In this chapter, we will take you through the issues that clinicians face every time they encounter a new client.

Psychological Disorder: Experiences of Client and Clinician

The field of abnormal psychology goes beyond the academic concern of studying behavior. It encompasses the large range of human issues involved when a client and a clinician work together to help the client resolve psychological difficulties. Throughout this text, we will continually return to these human issues and focus on the individual experiences of the client and the clinician, as well as the drama that unfolds when they interact. Here, we will orient you to these issues with a discussion of who these people are.

The Client

We use the term *client* in this text to refer to a person seeking psychological services. This term conveys certain meanings that are important to clarify at the outset of our discussion. After providing clarification on the meaning of the term, we will go on to another major point that underlies this book: the "client" can be anyone. Because psychological disorders are so prevalent, we should be aware of the fact that many people in our lives will at some point seek psychological help.

Definitions   What do you think when you hear that someone you know is in psychotherapy? Do you think of the person being treated as a "patient"? This is a common view, with roots in the medical model, and it is reinforced by popular characterizations of therapy on television and in films. **Patient** is a term used to refer to someone who is ill and, consistent with the medical model, someone who passively ("patiently") waits to be treated. Some people, including those who provide as well as those who receive treatment, object to the term *patient* because of its association with illness. They prefer to use an alternative term, *client*. In this sense, **client** refers to the person seeking psychological treatment, to reflect the fact that psychotherapy is a collaborative endeavor. Although these are the terms most commonly used, in recent years, other terms have been suggested, such as *resident,*

In therapy, the client and clinician work jointly to help the client resolve psychological problems.

consumer, and *member.* It may be helpful for you to think about how you would want to be referred to if you were seeking professional psychological services. In this book, we will use the term *client,* except in instances in which other terms have been more commonly used, as in the phrases "outpatient treatment" and "patients' rights."

While we are on the topic of appropriate terms, it is important to understand that people are not disorders. By calling someone a "schizophrenic," one implies that the individual is synonymous with the disorder, and it hides the person's identity as an individual behind the label. A more sensitive phrase is "a person with schizophrenia." Even though this may sound unwieldy, it communicates respect for the individual by putting the person first.

Prevalence of Psychological Disorders   Although this book focuses on people with severe psychological problems, it is important to keep in mind that everyone faces crises, dilemmas, or a desire for greater self-understanding. The Surgeon General's report on mental health (U.S. Department of Health and Human Services, 1999) cites the statistic that 21 percent of all Americans have experienced a mental disorder during the preceding year. Two comprehensive investigations in recent years have provided ample documentation of the extent to which people of all ages and walks of life experience psychological disturbance at some point. We will refer to these studies throughout this book when we provide epidemiological data on each of the disorders.

Researchers at the National Institute of Mental Health designed the Epidemiological Catchment Area (ECA) study to determine the prevalence of psychological disorders in the United States (Robins & Regier, 1991). More than 20,000

TABLE 2.1 Twelve-Month Prevalence of World Mental Health Composite International Diagnostic Interview/*Diagnostic and Statistical Manual of Mental Disorders, Fourth Edition*

Country	Anxiety	Mood	Impulse-Control	Substance	Any
Americas					
Colombia	10.0	6.8	3.9	2.8	17.8
Mexico	6.8	4.8	1.3	2.5	12.2
United States	18.2	9.6	6.8	3.8	26.4
Europe					
Belgium	6.9	6.2	1.0	1.2	12.0
France	12.0	8.5	1.4	0.7	18.4
Germany	6.2	3.6	0.3	1.1	9.1
Italy	5.8	3.8	0.3	0.1	8.2
Netherlands	8.8	6.9	1.3	3.0	14.9
Spain	5.9	4.9	0.5	0.3	9.2
Ukraine	7.1	9.1	3.2	6.4	20.5
Middle East and Africa					
Lebanon	11.2	6.6	1.7	1.3	16.9
Nigeria	3.3	0.8	0.0	0.8	4.7
Asia					
Japan	5.3	3.1	1.0	1.7	8.8
People's Republic of China					
Beijing	3.2	2.5	2.6	2.6	9.1
Shanghai	2.4	1.7	0.7	0.5	4.3

Source: Adapted from the WHO: World Mental Health Association, 2004. Percentage represents the midpoint of a 95 percent confidence interval.

people from five U.S. communities were given structured interview protocols to assess their psychological symptoms. In contrast to many earlier studies, which had relied on samples of individuals already being treated for psychological problems, the ECA study drew on a community sample and allows us to estimate how frequently various disorders occur in the general public (Adebimpe, 1994; Narrow et al., 1993). The lifetime prevalence of any psychological disorder was 32 percent, and about 20 percent of the sample had experienced symptoms within the previous year.

The second study, the National Comorbidity Survey, provided even more impressive evidence of the extent to which psychological disorders appear in so-called normal samples (Kessler, 1997). This study was conducted on a representative sample of more than 8,000 adults from across the United States, with the intention of documenting the extent to which psychiatric disorders are **comorbid,** or co-existing. The results, in fact, confirmed the suspicions of the investigators, who were following up on some intriguing leads from the ECA study, in which it had been reported that 54 percent of the respondents with one psychiatric disorder had a second diagnosis as well at some point in life. Interestingly, a similar rate of comorbidity emerged from this more focused study. Of the respondents with a lifetime history of one psychiatric disorder, over half of the sample had at least one other diagnosis. The most common comorbidities involve drug and alcohol abuse with other psychiatric disorders.

As you read about the conditions described in this book, it will be important for you to keep in mind these facts about the frequency of psychological disorders. Furthermore, obtaining help from others is a normal and natural part of life. Some people receive help from friends, family, or other helpers, such as teachers or clergy. Others turn to mental health professionals in pursuit of assistance, and still others are mandated to obtain help, possibly by a court or an employer. Each of these situations involves one person, a client, accepting assistance from another person in changing troubling or maladaptive behavior or emotional experiences.

The Clinician

Many people respond in an understandably defensive manner to the idea of consulting a mental health professional. They fear being scrutinized and labeled by a total stranger who is in a position to judge them as being "crazy." This negative view of the clinician accounts in part for the resistance some people express about seeing a "shrink."

Optimally, however, a clinician is an astute observer of human nature, an expert in human relations, a facilitator of growth, and a resource who aids others in making crucial life choices. A good clinician assesses others, not out of arrogance and insensitivity, but out of concern for understanding and responding to the problems of people seeking help. There are many types of clinicians, who approach clinical work in a variety of ways, based on their training and orientation. In the early 1900s, people in need of psychological help saw physicians or **psychiatrists**—medical doctors (MDs) with advanced training in treating people with psychological disorders. During World War II, the mental health needs of the nation increased, necessitating an expansion of the mental health provider network. University-based doctoral (PhD) psychology programs were created to increase the number of mental health professionals with training in the behavioral sciences who provided direct service to clients. Along with the growth of PhD programs has been the development of programs that are called "professional schools" of psychology, some of which offer a PhD and some of which offer a newer degree, the doctor of psychology (PsyD). Individuals trained in either type of doctoral program are known as **clinical psychologists.** Some psychologists are trained within the field of counseling psychology, where the emphasis is on normal adjustment and development, rather than on psychological disorders.

Psychiatrists and clinical psychologists currently predominate in the mental health field. An important distinction between them is that psychiatrists are licensed to administer medical treatment, and psychologists are not. In addition to providing psychotherapy, then, psychiatrists are responsible for prescribing medication for the treatment of psychological disorders when necessary. Psychologists and other mental health professionals often work closely with psychiatrists and consult with them when a client needs medication. Another difference is that clinical psychologists are trained in conducting **psychological testing,** a broad range of measurement techniques, all of which involve having people provide scorable information about their psychological functioning.

In addition to doctorally trained professionals, several other groups of professionals provide mental health services, including counseling and school psychologists, psychiatric social workers, nurse clinicians, and marriage and family counselors. The mental health field also includes a large group of individuals who do not have graduate-level training but serve a critical role in the functioning and administration of the mental health system. Included in this group are the thousands of nurses, occupational therapists, recreational therapists, and counselors who devote their careers to working with emotionally troubled people in institutions, agencies, schools, and homes.

We realize that abstract discussions may not enable you to appreciate fully who the clinician is and what the clinician does. Consequently, throughout this book, we will use examples involving one clinician and some of the cases she has treated. This clinician, whom we call Dr. Sarah Tobin, is a composite of many of the qualities found in a good clinical psychologist. Her cases are similar to those in psychological clinics and psychiatric institutions. As you read about Dr. Tobin's work, think of yourself as her apprentice or intern. Imagine yourself discussing the cases with her and consulting with her about the diagnosis and treatment of each client. At the beginning of each chapter, you will read a case report that relates to the content of that chapter. As you read the chapter, use an inquisitive and problem-solving approach to develop your own understanding of the case. Try to form your own hypotheses about the most appropriate diagnosis, the cause of the client's problems, and ways that the client might best be treated.

The *Diagnostic and Statistical Manual of Mental Disorders*

In making a diagnosis, mental health professionals use the standard terms and definitions contained in the ***Diagnostic and Statistical Manual of Mental Disorders (DSM),*** a publication that is periodically revised to reflect the most up-to-date knowledge concerning psychological disorders. The title of this book, and the diagnostic system it contains, is abbreviated as *DSM;* this is followed by an indication, in roman numerals, of the edition currently in use (now the *DSM-IV*). This diagnostic system was originally developed in 1952, when the American Psychiatric Association published the first *DSM.* In the years since then, the *DSM-II, DSM-III, DSM-III-Revised, DSM-IV,* and *DSM-IV-TR* (text revision) (American Psychiatric Association, 2000) have reflected advances and refinements in the system of diagnosis that is most commonly used in the United States. We will discuss the history of the development of this system later, but first it is important for you to have a grasp of what we mean by a diagnostic system, or "nomenclature," as it is sometimes called.

The *DSM-IV* contains descriptions of all psychological disorders, alternatively referred to as mental disorders. In developing recent editions of the *DSM,* various task forces have been appointed, each consisting of a group of expert clinicians and researchers knowledgeable about a particular subset of disorders. Based on their research, these experts have listed several hundred disorders, ranging from relatively minor adjustment problems to long-term chronic and incapacitating disorders. The *DSM-IV* provides both clinicians and researchers with a common language for delineating disorders, so that they can feel relatively confident that diagnostic labels have accepted meanings.

The authors of recent versions of the *DSM* have taken an atheoretical approach. In other words, they have attempted to describe psychological disorders in terms that refer to observable phenomena, rather than presenting the disorders in terms of their possible causes. In describing an anxiety disorder, for example, various psychological and physical symptoms associated with the experience of anxiety are listed, without consideration of whether the cause is physical or emotional.

By characterizing a client's symptoms in terms of a *DSM-IV* diagnosis, the clinician can use that system of knowledge as the basis for a treatment plan. For example, a clinician would plan a very different kind of treatment for a person with an anxiety disorder than for a person with schizophrenia. Furthermore, the clinician often is asked to provide a diagnosis, with the accompanying *DSM-IV* numerical code, to help a client obtain insurance payments to cover the cost of treatment.

The authors of the *DSM-IV* continued in the footsteps of their predecessors to arrive at a system that would be scientifically and clinically accurate (Millon, 1991). They had to ensure that the diagnoses would meet the criterion of **reliability,** meaning that a given diagnosis will be consistently applied to anyone showing a particular set of symptoms. Returning to the case of Peter, if he were to describe his symptoms to a clinical psychologist in Spokane, Washington, that psychologist should be able to use the *DSM-IV* to arrive at the same diagnosis as would a psychiatrist seeing Peter in Baton Rouge, Louisiana. Further, any knowledgeable mental health professional should be able to use the criteria specified in the *DSM-IV* to make a diagnosis, regardless of that professional's theoretical orientation or particular experience with clients. Working toward reliability of diagnoses, the authors of successive versions of the *DSM* have refined the criteria for disorders. At the same time, teams of researchers throughout the United States have continued to investigate the **validity** of the classification system, meaning that the diagnoses represent real and distinct clinical phenomena. In all of these efforts, experts have had to keep in mind the **base rate** of a disorder, the frequency with which it occurs in the general population. The lower the base rate of a disorder, the more difficult it is to establish the reliability of the diagnosis because there are so few cases to compare.

How the *DSM* Developed

The first edition of the American Psychiatric Association's *DSM,* which appeared in 1952, was the first official psychiatric manual to describe psychological disorders and, as such, was a major step forward in the search for a standard set of diagnostic criteria. Although a step in the right direction, these criteria were very vague and had poor reliability. A second limitation of the *DSM-I* was that it was based on the theoretical assumption that emotional problems or "reactions" caused the disorders it described. The second edition, or the *DSM-II,* was published in 1968. This was the first classification of mental disorders based on the system contained in the International Classification of Diseases (ICD). The *DSM-II* represented a movement away from the conceptualization of most psychological disorders as being emotional reactions. The authors of this edition tried to use diagnostic terms that would not imply a particular theoretical framework, but, in retrospect, it is clear that they based their criteria on psychoanalytic concepts. Furthermore, these criteria were sufficiently loose that a clinician with a particular theoretical preference could fit in a client's diagnosis with his or her theory, rather than with the client's actual condition.

To overcome these problems with low reliability, in 1974 the American Psychiatric Association appointed a task force of eminent scholars and practitioners to prepare a new and more extensive classification system that would reflect the most current information on mental disorders. The task force was directed to develop a manual that would have an empirical basis and be clinically useful, reliable, and acceptable to clinicians and researchers of different orientations.

When the *DSM-III* was published in 1980, it was widely heralded as a major improvement over its predecessors. It provided precise rating criteria and definitions for each disorder. These criteria enabled clinicians to be more quantitative and objective in assigning diagnoses. However, the *DSM-III* had some problems. For example, in some instances the manual did not go far enough in specifying criteria. Because of these limitations, the American Psychiatric Association tried once again to improve and refine the diagnostic system. The *DSM-III-R* by the American Psychiatric Association in 1987 was published with the intention that it would serve as an interim manual until a more complete overhaul, the *DSM-IV,* could be introduced in 1994.

Shortly after the publication of the *DSM-III-R,* the American Psychiatric Association established the Task Force on the *DSM-IV* with the intent of providing an empirical base for the diagnoses in the new manual. Work groups investigating specific disorders were appointed to conduct a three-stage process involving further reliability and validity testing of the diagnoses. In Stage 1 of this process, comprehensive reviews of the published research were conducted. Stage 2 involved thorough analyses of research data, some of which had not previously been published. Criteria from the *DSM-III-R* were rigorously applied to these analyses, with the intention of adding or changing criteria on the basis of the analytical findings. Stage 3 was the largest and most ambitious phase of the project, involving field trials in which interviewers evaluated thousands of people with diagnosed psychological disorders. These field trials were attempts by researchers to establish the reliability and validity of the new diagnostic criteria. In reliability testing, pairs of clinicians provided independent ratings of clients through videotaped interviews. Evaluating the validity of diagnostic categories was an even more challenging task. Clinicians conducted focused field trials in which individuals diagnosed as having specific disorders were studied. The purpose of these field trials was to determine the number and nature of the criteria needed for clients to be diagnosed with specific disorders. As you will see later in this book, diagnoses are made on the basis of the kind and number of relevant symptoms. The field trials were used to provide an empirical basis for deciding which symptoms and how many of those symptoms would be necessary for the diagnosis to be applied. For example, for a diagnosis of major depressive disorder, the client must demonstrate at least five symptoms out of a possible list of nine, including such symptoms as disturbed sleep, recurrent thoughts of death, and feelings of worthlessness.

In 2000 the American Psychiatric Association published a "text revision" of *DSM-IV*, called the *DSM-IV-TR* (American Psychiatric Association, 2000), which included several editorial revisions: correction of minor factual errors that had been identified in the *DSM-IV*, updates to the content, and other refinements intended to enhance the educational value of the volume. Although the latest version is officially abbreviated *DSM-IV-TR*, many professionals prefer the simpler designation *DSM-IV*.

Work has begun on the development of *DSM-V*, which probably will not appear in print for several years. As was the case in developing previous editions, a considerable amount of preparation and research is needed for such a complicated process. After research work groups were formed, a series of papers were published with the goal of establishing a research agenda (Kupfer, First, & Regier, 2002). The next step in the process has involved a series of international conferences focusing on particular issues emerging from the research planning work groups; such international collaboration is considered especially important because of the plan to coordinate *DSM-V* with the next edition of the *International Classification of Diseases* (Widiger, 2004).

Controversial Issues Pertaining to the *DSM*

All editions of the *DSM* have generated considerable controversy, and the fifth edition is certain to provoke great debate. Particularly contentious will be the argument about whether "disease, illness, and disorder are scientific biomedical terms or are sociopolitical terms that necessarily involve a value judgment" (Rounsaville et al., 2002, p. 3). Some critics (Kirk & Kutchins, 1992; Kutchins & Kirk, 1997) have argued for years that the *DSM* unfairly labels people and is a highly politicized, money-making publication of the American Psychiatric Association that is laden with problems of reliability and validity. Kutchins and Kirk (1997) note the extent to which the *DSM* diagnoses reflect the politics and culture of the time. For example, they contend that because of pressure from outside groups, homosexuality was dropped and post-traumatic stress disorder was added when *DSM-III* was published in 1980. The very fact that homosexuality had previously been listed in *DSM-II* provides some insight into the complex and potentially biased processes by which "mental disorders" have been defined. It took nearly 10 years of debate for the American Psychiatric Association to conclude that pathologizing people because of sexual orientation was absurd. In discussing post-traumatic stress disorder, Kutchins and Kirk contend that pressure from Vietnam veterans forced the *DSM-III* authors to recognize that the constellation of symptoms experienced by thousands of survivors of traumatic events, such as combat, represented a disorder.

Other critics have argued that the *DSM* system is biased against women and have questioned why women are more likely than men to be assigned particular diagnoses, such as mood and personality disorders. They suggest that gender bias results in feminine personality characteristics being perceived as pathological. Kupers (1997) asserts that people in a position of power (in the case of psychiatry, mostly men) determine what constitutes a mental disorder among those over whom they wield power. In response to such criticism, professionals who were pivotally involved in the development of *DSM-IV* (Ross, Frances, & Widiger, 1997) dismiss such notions, asserting that the *DSM-IV* development process involved serious attempts to base decisions on a fair and balanced interpretation of the available data pertaining to gender issues in diagnoses.

As work continues on the development of *DSM-V*, those professionals involved in the process know that they must listen carefully to the criticisms that have arisen in recent years. Particular attention must be given to making the new manual usable and less reductionistic than previous editions (Banzato, 2004), and that revisions to the diagnostic manual be based on empirical demonstrations of clinical utility; in other words, the advantages of changing diagnostic criteria should clearly outweigh potential negative consequences (First et al., 2004).

Definition of "Mental Disorder"

In Chapter 1, we discussed the alternate conceptions of abnormality and how difficult it is to define what constitutes abnormal behavior or, for that matter, how it should be labeled. The authors of the *DSM* had to confront the task of defining "mental disorder" and arrived at a definition that serves as the foundation for every diagnosable condition within the manual. According to this definition, a mental disorder is "a clinically significant behavioral or psychological syndrome or pattern that occurs in an individual and that is associated with present distress (e.g., a painful symptom) or disability (i.e., impairment in one or more important areas of functioning) or with a significantly increased risk of suffering death, pain, disability, or an important loss of freedom. In addition, this syndrome or pattern must not be merely an expectable and culturally sanctioned response to a particular event, for example, the death of a loved one" (American Psychiatric Association, 2000, p. xxxi). The concept of mental disorders is central to the whole enterprise of diagnosis and treatment. Let's take a closer look at the definition given in the *DSM-IV-TR* and its implications.

In MindMAP Segment 2.1, Bernie discusses his highs and lows in ways that would lead a clinician to diagnose a mood disorder known as Bipolar Disorder.

As clients discuss their symptoms, clinicians are attentive to their characterizations of behaviors and feelings because such information is critical in developing an accurate diagnosis.

A mental disorder is "clinically significant." For each disorder, the *DSM-IV-TR* specifies the length of time during which the symptoms must be present for the diagnosis of a disorder. Thus, a fleeting thought or mood, an occasional strange behavior, or a temporary feeling of instability or confusion does not constitute a mental disorder. You probably can think of a time when you felt emotionally distraught following an upsetting event in your life. Such experiences are common and would not be regarded as mental disorders, unless they are so severe that they result in serious consequences. To be considered "clinically significant," the disorder must be consistently present over time and have enough impact that the person's life is dramatically affected.

The disorder is reflected in a behavioral or psychological "syndrome." A **syndrome** is a collection of symptoms that forms a definable pattern. A behavioral or psychological syndrome is a collection of observable actions and the client's reported thoughts and feelings. Thus, an isolated behavior or a single thought or feeling would not constitute a disorder. Rather, a diagnosable condition is an organized unit that manifests itself in a wide range of thoughts, feelings, and behaviors. If you feel sad for a few days, and this feeling is your only symptom, a diagnosis of depression would be inappropriate.

The disorder is associated with present distress, impairment in life, or serious risk. In other words, a disorder involves personal or social cost. For example, a woman's fear of leaving the house may cause her to be very distressed. She wishes she could overcome her extreme fearfulness but feels incapable of changing her behavior. Her syndrome, then, in addition to being severe, is also causing her a great deal of personal distress. In addition, her functioning is impaired, because she is unable to hold a job or take care of household errands.

Not everyone with a psychological disorder is distressed. Consider a man who has developed an unusually cold, constricted, and impersonal style of relating to other people because of a disturbed view of interpersonal relationships. Although this man might not be bothered by this style, it will make it difficult, if not impossible, for him to develop intimate relationships. Moreover, unless he has a job that involves absolutely no social interaction (and there are not many such jobs), this style of relating to others will invariably hurt his chances of having a productive career.

Some disorders can lead a person to commit suicide or inflict severe physical pain through self-mutilation. Other disorders place the individual at risk, because they lead to acts involving physical peril. A man in a hyperexcited state of euphoria may go out and rent a hang glider, because he feels like flying, unconcerned that he lacks the proper training. Still other disorders threaten the individual with physical harm, because they lead to the adoption of an unhealthy lifestyle. A person who is driven to work excessively hard without taking time for relaxation is likely, over a period of years, to suffer from heart problems due to stress. Finally, a psychological disorder can lead a person to give up personal freedom if it leads to criminal acts, resulting in punishment or incarceration.

The disorder is not an expectable and culturally sanctioned response. Some behaviors and emotional reactions are understandable, given the circumstances. For example, in an oppressive political system, one might expect people to be on the alert for danger, perhaps to the point of seeming paranoid. Such individuals would not be regarded as having a mental disorder

Severe depression can be so devastating that some people consider suicide their only option.

because their reaction is expectable. Another example would be a woman who becomes depressed following the death of her partner. She may lose sleep, cry frequently, and have difficulty eating or concentrating. Her symptoms would not constitute a mental disorder. In some cultures, reactions to the death of a loved one may involve rituals and behaviors that might seem bizarre to outsiders but are acceptable within the culture.

Assumptions of the *DSM-IV-TR*

Throughout the history of the *DSM* system, its authors have debated a number of complex issues, including the theoretical basis of the classification system. Each edition of the manual has represented thousands of hours of discussion among experts in several related fields from very different theoretical backgrounds. The *DSM-IV* today contains the result of these discussions, and underlying its structure and organization are several important assumptions.

Medical Model   One of the most prominent assumptions of the *DSM-IV-TR* is that this classification system is based on a medical model orientation, in which disorders, whether physical or psychological, are viewed as diseases. In fact, as we mentioned earlier, the *DSM-IV-TR* corresponds to the *International Classification of Diseases,* a diagnostic system developed by the World Health Organization to provide consistency throughout the world for the terms that are used to describe medical conditions. For example, proponents of the medical model view major depressive disorder as a "disease" that requires treatment. The use of the term *patient* is consistent with this medical model.

Also consistent with the medical model is the use of the term *mental disorder*. If you think about this term, you will notice that it implies a condition that is inside one's "mind." This term has been used historically to apply to the types of conditions studied within psychiatry, as in the terms *mental hospital* and *mental health*. For many professionals, though, the term *mental disorder* has negative connotations, because it has historically implied something negative. In this book, we use the term *psychological disorder* in an attempt to move away from some of the negative stereotypes associated with the term *mental disorder;* we also wish to emphasize that these conditions have an emotional aspect. For example, a person who has unusually low sexual desire would have a diagnosable condition within the *DSM-IV-TR* called "hypoactive [low] sexual desire disorder." Does it make sense to refer to such a condition as a mental disorder?

Atheoretical Orientation   The authors of the *DSM-IV* wanted to develop a classification system that was descriptive rather than explanatory. In the example of hypoactive sexual desire disorder, the *DSM-IV-TR* simply classifies and describes a set of symptoms without regard to their cause. There might be any number of explanations for why a person has this disorder, including relationship difficulties, inner conflict, or a traumatic sexual experience.

Previous editions of the *DSM* were based on psychoanalytic concepts and used such terms as *neurosis,* which implied that many disorders were caused by unconscious conflict. Besides carrying psychodynamic connotations, these terms were vague and involved subjective judgment on the part of the clinician. **Neurosis** is not part of the official nomenclature, or naming system, but you will still find it in many books and articles on abnormal psychology. When you come across the term, it will usually be in reference to behavior that involves some symptoms that are distressing to an individual and that the person recognizes as unacceptable. These symptoms usually are enduring and lack any kind of physical basis. For example, you might describe your friend as neurotic because she seems to worry all the time over nothing. Assuming that she recognizes how inappropriate her worrying is, your labeling of her behavior as neurotic might be justified. However, a mental health practitioner might diagnose her as having an anxiety disorder, a more precise description of her constant worrying behavior. Mental health professionals still use the term *neurotic* informally to refer to a person who experiences excessive subjective psychological pain and to distinguish such conditions from those referred to as psychotic.

The term **psychosis** is used to refer to various forms of behavior involving loss of contact with reality. In other words, a person showing psychotic behavior might have bizarre thoughts and perceptions of what is happening. This might involve delusions (false beliefs) or hallucinations (false perceptions). The term *psychotic* may also be used to refer to behavior that is so grossly disturbed that the person seems to be out of control. Although not a formal diagnostic category, *psychotic* is retained in the *DSM-IV-TR* as a descriptive term.

Categorical Approach   Implicit in the medical model is the assumption that diseases fit into distinct categories. For example, pneumonia is a condition that fits into the category of diseases involving the respiratory system. The *DSM-IV-TR,* being based on a medical model, has borrowed this strategy. Thus, conditions involving mood fit into the category of mood disorders, those involving anxiety fit into the category of anxiety disorders, and so on. However, the authors of the *DSM-IV-TR* are the first to acknowledge that there are limitations to the categorical approach. For one thing, psychological disorders are not neatly separable from each other or from normal functioning. For example, where is the dividing line between a sad mood and diagnosable depression? Furthermore, many disorders seem linked to each other in fundamental ways. In a state of agitated depression, for example, an individual is suffering from both anxiety and saddened mood.

The difficulty of establishing clear boundaries between psychological conditions prompted the *DSM-IV* Task Force to consider adopting a dimensional rather than a categorical model. In a dimensional model, people would be rated according to the degree to which they experience a set of fundamental attributes. Rather than being classified as "depressed" or "nondepressed," individuals would be rated along a continuum. At one end would be no depression, and at the opposite extreme would be severe incapacitation, with varying degrees in between. In the current system, the many separate categories for depressive disorders lead to a proliferation of diagnoses. A dimensional system with numerical ratings would provide a cleaner and perhaps more accurate representation of psychological disorders (Livesley, Schroeder, Jackson, & Jang, 1994). The categorical system has been retained, however, because the *DSM-IV-TR* authors believe that it is less confusing for clinicians and researchers to think in terms of disorders as clustering into discrete groups.

Multiaxial System In the *DSM,* diagnoses are categorized in terms of relevant areas of functioning within what are called axes. There are five axes, along which each client is evaluated. An **axis** is a class of information regarding an aspect of an individual's functioning. The **multiaxial system** in the *DSM-IV-TR* allows clients to be characterized in a multidimensional way, accommodating all relevant information about their functioning in an organized and systematic fashion.

As you might imagine, when a clinician is developing a diagnostic hypothesis about a client, there may be several features of the individual's functioning that are important to capture. For most of his life, Greg has had serious personality problems characterized by an extreme and maladaptive dependence on other people. These problems have been compounded by a medical condition, ulcerative colitis. Six months ago, Greg's girlfriend was killed in an automobile accident. Before then, he was managing reasonably well, although his personality problems and colitis sometimes made it difficult for him to function well on his job. Each fact the client presents is important for the clinician to take into account when making a diagnosis, not just the client's immediate symptoms. In Greg's case, the symptom of depression is merely one part of a complex diagnostic picture. As we saw earlier, most clients, such as Greg, have multiple concerns that are relevant to diagnosis and treatment. Sometimes there is a causal relationship between comorbid disorders. For example, a man with an anxiety disorder may develop substance abuse as he attempts to quell the terror of his anxiety by using drugs or alcohol. In other situations, the comorbid conditions are not causally related, as would be the case of a woman who has both an eating disorder and a learning disability.

The Five Axes of the *DSM-IV-TR*

Each disorder in the *DSM-IV-TR* is listed on either Axis I or Axis II. The remaining axes are used to characterize a client's physical health (Axis III), extent of stressful life circumstances (Axis IV), and overall degree of functioning (Axis V).

Axis I: Clinical Disorders The major clinical disorders are on Axis I. In the *DSM-IV-TR* system, these are called "clinical syndromes," meaning that each is a collection of symptoms that constitutes a particular form of abnormality. These are the disorders, such as schizophrenia and depression, that constitute what most people think of as psychological disorders. As you can see from Table 2.2, however, there are a wide variety of disorders encompassing many variants of human behavior.

Another set of disorders in Axis I is adjustment disorders. These are reactions to life events that are more extreme than would normally be expected given the circumstances. To be considered an adjustment disorder, this reaction must persist for at least 6 months and must result in significant impairment or distress for the individual. Adjustment disorders manifest themselves in several forms: emotional reactions, such as anxiety and depression; disturbances of conduct; physical complaints; social withdrawal; or disruptions in work or academic performance. For example, a woman may react to the loss of her job by developing a variety of somatic symptoms, including headaches, backaches, and fatigue. A man may respond to a diagnosis of a serious illness by becoming reckless, self-destructive, and financially irresponsible. In these cases, the individual's reaction can be temporally linked to the occurrence of the life event. Moreover, the reactions are considered out of proportion to the nature of the stressful experience.

Some conditions are the focus of clinical attention but are not psychological disorders. In the *DSM-IV-TR,* these conditions are referred to as "V [vee] codes" and include a variety of difficulties, such as relational problems, bereavement reactions, and the experience of being abused or neglected. When these problems are the primary focus of clinical attention, they are listed on Axis I. When these problems are evident but are not the primary focus of concern, they are noted on Axis IV, which you will read about later in this section.

Axis II: Personality Disorders and Mental Retardation Axis II includes sets of disorders that represent enduring characteristics of an individual's personality or abilities. One set of disorders is the personality disorders. These are personality traits that are inflexible and maladaptive and that cause either subjective distress or considerable impairment in a person's ability to carry out the tasks of daily living. The second component of Axis II is mental retardation. Although not a "disorder" in the sense of many of the other conditions found in the *DSM-IV-TR,* mental retardation nevertheless has a major influence on behavior, personality, and cognitive functioning.

To help you understand the differences between Axis I and Axis II, consider the following two clinical examples. One case involves Juanita, a 29-year-old woman who, following the birth of her first child, becomes very suspicious of other people's intentions to the point of not trusting even close relatives. After a month of treatment, she returns to normal functioning and her symptoms disappear. Juanita would receive a diagnosis of an Axis I disorder, because she has a condition that could be considered an overlay on an otherwise healthy personality. In contrast, the hypersensitivity to criticism and fear of closeness shown by Jean, another 29-year-old woman, is a feature of her way of viewing the world that has characterized her from adolescence. She has chosen not to become involved in intimate relationships and steers clear of people who seem overly interested in her. Were she to seek treatment, these longstanding dispositions would warrant an Axis II diagnosis.

An individual can have diagnoses on Axes I and II. For example, Leon is struggling with substance abuse and is

TABLE 2.2 Axis I Disorders of the *DSM-IV-TR*

Category	Description	Examples of Diagnoses
Disorders usually first diagnosed in infancy, childhood, or adolescence	Disorders that usually develop during the earlier years of life, primarily involving abnormal development and maturation	■ Learning disorders ■ Motor skills disorders, communication disorders, pervasive developmental disorders (e.g., autistic disorder) ■ Attention-deficit disorders and disruptive behavior disorders ■ Feeding and eating disorders of infancy and early childhood ■ Tic disorders ■ Elimination disorders
Delirium, dementia, amnestic, and other cognitive disorders	Disorders involving impairments in cognition that are caused by substances or general medical conditions	■ Delirium ■ Dementia (e.g., Alzheimer's type) ■ Amnestic disorder
Mental disorders due to a general medical condition	Conditions characterized by mental symptoms judged to be the physiological consequence of a general medical condition	■ Personality change due to a general medical condition ■ Mood disorder due to a general medical condition ■ Sexual dysfunction due to a general medical condition
Substance-related disorders	Disorders related to the use or abuse of substances	■ Substance use disorders (e.g., substance dependence and substance abuse) ■ Substance-induced disorders (e.g., substance intoxication and substance withdrawal)
Schizophrenia and other psychotic disorders	Disorders involving psychotic symptoms (e.g., distortion in perception of reality; impairment in thinking, behavior, affect, and motivation)	■ Schizophrenia ■ Schizophreniform disorder ■ Schizoaffective disorder ■ Delusional disorder ■ Brief psychotic disorder
Mood disorders	Disorders involving a disturbance in mood	■ Major depressive disorder ■ Dysthymic disorder ■ Bipolar disorder ■ Cyclothymic disorder
Anxiety disorders	Disorders involving the experience of intense anxiety, worry, or apprehension that leads to behavior designed to protect the sufferer from experiencing anxiety	■ Panic disorder ■ Agoraphobia ■ Specific phobia ■ Social phobia ■ Obsessive-compulsive disorder ■ Post-traumatic stress disorder ■ Generalized anxiety disorder

TABLE 2.2 Axis I Disorders of the *DSM-IV-TR* (continued)

Category	Description	Examples of Diagnoses
Somatoform disorders	Disorders involving recurring complaints of physical symptoms or medical concerns not supported by medical findings	■ Somatization disorder ■ Conversion disorder ■ Pain disorder ■ Hypochondriasis ■ Body dysmorphic disorder
Factitious disorders	Conditions in which physical or psychological symptoms are intentionally produced in order to assume a sick role	■ Factitious disorder ■ Factitious disorder by proxy
Dissociative disorders	Disorders in which the normal integration of consciousness, memory, identity, or perception is disrupted	■ Dissociative amnesia ■ Dissociative fugue ■ Dissociative identity disorder ■ Depersonalization disorder
Sexual and gender identity disorders	Disorders involving disturbance in the expression or experience of normal sexuality	■ Sexual dysfunctions (e.g., sexual arousal disorder, orgasmic disorder, sexual pain disorder) ■ Paraphilias (e.g., fetishism, pedophilia, voyeurism) ■ Gender identity disorder
Eating disorders	Disorders characterized by severe disturbances in eating behavior	■ Anorexia nervosa ■ Bulimia nervosa
Sleep disorders	Disorders involving recurring disturbance in normal sleep patterns	■ Dyssomnias (e.g., insomnia, hypersomnia) ■ Parasomnias (e.g., nightmare disorder, sleep-walking disorder)
Impulse-control disorders	Disorders characterized by repeated expression of impulsive behaviors that cause harm to oneself or others	■ Intermittent explosive disorder ■ Kleptomania ■ Pyromania ■ Pathological gambling ■ Trichotillomania
Adjustment disorders	Conditions characterized by the development of clinically significant emotional and behavioral symptoms within 3 months following the onset of an identifiable stressor	■ Adjustment disorder with anxiety ■ Adjustment disorder with depressed mood ■ Adjustment disorder with disturbance of conduct
Other conditions that may be a focus of clinical attention	Conditions or problems for which a person may seek or be referred for professional help	■ Relational problems ■ Problems related to abuse or neglect ■ Psychological factors affecting medical condition ■ Other conditions (e.g., bereavement, academic or occupational problem, religious problem, phase of life problem)

TABLE 2.3 Axis IV of the *DSM-IV-TR*

Problem Category	Examples
Problems with primary support group: childhood	Death of parent Health problems of parent Removal from the home Remarriage of parent
Problems with primary support group: adult	Tensions with partner Separation, divorce, or estrangement Physical or sexual abuse by partner
Problems with primary support group: parent-child	Neglect of child Sexual or physical abuse of child Parental overprotection
Problems related to the social environment	Death or loss of friend Social isolation Living alone Difficulty with acculturation Adjustment to life cycle transition (such as retirement)
Educational problems	Academic problems Discord with teachers or classmates Illiteracy Inadequate school environment
Occupational problems	Unemployment Threat of job loss Difficult work situation Job dissatisfaction Job change Discord with boss or co-workers
Housing problems	Homelessness Inadequate housing Unsafe neighborhood Discord with neighbors or landlord
Economic problems	Extreme poverty Inadequate finances Serious credit problems
Problems with access to health care services	Inadequate health insurance Inadequate health care services
Problems related to interaction with the legal system/crime	Arrest Incarceration Victim of crime
Other psychosocial problems	Exposure to disasters Loss of important social support services

Source: Reprinted with permission from the *Diagnostic and Statistical Manual of Mental Disorders*, Fourth Edition, Text Revision. Copyright © 2000 American Psychiatric Association.

characteristically very dependent on others. Leon would probably be diagnosed on both Axis I and Axis II. On Axis I, he would be assigned a diagnosis pertaining to his substance abuse; on Axis II, he would receive a diagnosis of dependent personality disorder. In other words, his substance abuse is considered to be a condition, and his personality disorder is considered to be part of the fabric of his character.

Axis III: General Medical Conditions Axis III is for documenting a client's medical conditions. Although these medical

One of the first steps in the clinical process is the establishment of a sound working alliance between the clinician and the client.

conditions are not the primary focus of the clinician, there is a solid logic for including Axis III as part of the total diagnostic picture. At times, physical problems can be the basis of psychological problems. For example, a person may become depressed following the diagnosis of a serious physical illness. Conversely, such conditions as chronic anxiety can intensify physical conditions, such as a stomach ulcer. In other cases there is no obvious connection between an individual's physical and psychological problems. Nevertheless, the clinician considers the existence of a physical disorder to be critical, because it means that something outside the psychological realm is affecting a major facet of the client's life.

The clinician must keep Axis III diagnoses in mind when developing a treatment plan for the client. Take the example of a young man with diabetes who seeks treatment for his incapacitating irrational fear of cars. Although his physical and psychological problems are not apparently connected, it would be important for the clinician to be aware of the diabetes, because the condition would certainly have a major impact on the client's life. Furthermore, if the clinician considers recommending a prescription of antianxiety medication, the young man's physical condition and other medications must be taken into account.

Axis IV: Psychosocial and Environmental Problems On Axis IV, the clinician documents events or pressures that may affect the diagnosis, treatment, or outcome of a client's psychological disorder. Examples of Axis IV stressors are shown in Table 2.3. As you can see, Axis IV conditions include the negative life events of losing a job, having an automobile accident, and breaking up with a lover. All of these conditions are stressors

that can cause, aggravate, or even result from a psychological disorder. A depressed man might get into a serious traffic accident because he is so preoccupied with his emotions that he does not concentrate on his driving. Alternatively, a person may become clinically depressed in the aftermath of a serious car accident. As you can see, the same life event can be either the result or the cause of a psychological problem.

For the most part, the life events on Axis IV are negative. However, "positive" life events, such as a job promotion, might also be considered stressors. A person who receives a major job promotion may encounter psychological difficulties due to the increased responsibilities and demands associated with the new position.

Axis V: Global Assessment of Functioning Axis V is used to document the clinician's overall judgment of a client's psychological, social, and occupational functioning. Ratings are made for the client's current functioning at the point of admission or discharge, or the highest level of functioning during the previous year. The rating of the client's functioning during the preceding year provides the clinician with important information about the client's **prognosis,** or likelihood of recovering from the disorder. If a client has functioned effectively in the recent past, the clinician has more reason to hope for improvement. The prognosis may not be so bright if a client has a lengthy history of poor adjustment.

The **Global Assessment of Functioning (GAF) scale,** which is the basis for Axis V, allows for a rating of the individual's overall level of psychological health. The full scale is shown in Table 2.4.

The Diagnostic Process

The diagnostic process involves using all relevant information to arrive at a label that characterizes the client's disorder. This information includes the results of any tests given to the client, material gathered from interviews, and knowledge about the client's personal history. The end result of the diagnostic process is a diagnosis that can be used as the basis for the client's treatment.

Although this definition makes the diagnostic process sound straightforward, it usually is not so simple. In fact, the diagnostic process can be compared to the job of a detective trying to solve a complicated case. A good detective is able to piece together a coherent picture from many bits and pieces of information, some of which may seem insignificant or even random to the untrained observer. Similarly, a good clinician uses every available piece of information to put together a coherent picture of the client's condition. Fortunately, some of this information is readily available, such as the client's age, gender, and ethnicity. This background data can help the clinician gauge the likelihood that a client has a particular disorder. For example, if a 20-year-old were to seek treatment for symptoms that appeared to be

TABLE 2.4 Axis V: Global Assessment of Functioning Scale

Rating	Level of Symptoms	Examples
91–100	Superior functioning; no symptoms	
81–90	No symptoms or minimal symptoms; generally good functioning in all areas; no more than everyday problems	Occasional worries such as feeling understandably anxious before taking examinations or feelings of disappointment following an athletic loss
71–80	Transient, slight symptoms that are reasonable responses to stressful situations; no more than slight impairment in social, occupational, or school functioning	Concentration difficulty following an exciting day; trouble sleeping after an argument with partner
61–70	Mild symptoms, or some difficulty in social, occupational, or school functioning	Mild insomnia; mild depression
51–60	Moderate symptoms or moderate difficulties in social, occupational, or school functioning	Occasional panic attacks; conflicts with roommates
41–50	Serious symptoms or any serious impairment in social, occupational, or school functioning	Suicidal thoughts; inability to keep job
31–40	Serious difficulties in thought or communication or major impairment in several areas of functioning	Illogical speech; inability to work; neglect of responsibilities
21–30	Behavior influenced by psychotic symptoms or serious impairment in communication or judgment or inability to function in almost all areas	Delusional and hallucinating; incoherent; preoccupied with suicide; stays in bed all day every day
11–20	Dangerous symptoms or gross impairment in communication	Suicide attempts without clear expectation of death; muteness
1–10	Persistent danger to self or others or persistent inability to maintain hygiene	Recurrent violence; serious suicidal act with clear expectation of death
0	Inadequate information	

Source: Reprinted with permission from the *Diagnostic and Statistical Manual of Mental Disorders*, Fourth Edition, Text Revision. Copyright © 2000 American Psychiatric Association.

those of schizophrenia, the clinician's ideas about diagnosis would be different than if the individual were 60 years old. Schizophrenia often makes its first appearance in the twenties, and, with a client of this age who shows possible symptoms of schizophrenia, the diagnosis is plausible. On the other hand, if the client were 60 years old and showing these symptoms for the first time, other disorders would seem more likely. Similarly, the client's gender can provide some clues for diagnosis. Some conditions are more prevalent in women, so the clinician is more likely to consider those when diagnosing a woman. Finally, the individual's social and cultural background may provide some clues in the diagnostic process. The clinician may find it helpful to know about the religious and ethnic background of clients if these are relevant to the kind of symptoms they are exhibiting. For example, a client from a country in which the voodoo religion is practiced might complain that she has been "cursed." Without knowing that such a belief is perfectly acceptable within the voodoo religion, the clinician may mistakenly regard this statement as evidence of a serious psychological disorder. We will talk more about the role of culture when we examine the issue of cultural formulations later in the chapter.

We will return now to Peter's symptoms and will discuss the diagnostic process Dr. Tobin would use to evaluate him. You will see how she uses the tools of the detective to arrive at the diagnosis.

The Client's Reported and Observable Symptoms

Remember that Peter first describes his symptoms as involving "bouts of anxiety." When Dr. Tobin hears the word *anxiety,* she immediately begins thinking about the *DSM-IV-TR* criteria for what is called an anxiety disorder. This is the first step in the diagnostic process. Dr. Tobin listens for a key word or phrase in the client's self-report of symptoms and observes how the client acts. That gives her a clue about what to look for next. In the process of following up on this clue, Dr. Tobin will gain more information about the symptoms that Peter reports.

In addition to listening to the client's description of symptoms, the clinician also attends to the client's behavior, emotional expression, and style of thinking. For example, a client with very severe depression may be immobilized and unable to verbalize, leaving the clinician to infer that the client is depressed.

Diagnostic Criteria and Differential Diagnosis

The next step is to obtain as clear an idea as possible of the client's symptoms and to determine the extent to which these symptoms coincide with the diagnostic criteria of a given disorder. What does Peter mean when he says that he has "bouts of anxiety"? After Dr. Tobin asks him this question, she listens to determine whether any of his symptoms match the *DSM-IV-TR* criteria for "anxiety." Do his hands tremble? Does he get butterflies in his stomach? Does he feel jittery and irritable or have trouble sleeping? Dr. Tobin keeps a mental tally of Peter's symptoms to see if enough of the appropriate ones are present before she decides that his state is, in fact, anxiety and that he might therefore have an anxiety disorder.

As she listens to Peter's symptoms, Dr. Tobin discovers that he has also experienced severe depression within the past few months. This discovery leads her to suspect that perhaps Peter does not have an anxiety disorder after all. Now, as she sorts through the facts of his story, she starts to see his highly energized behavior as the classic symptoms of a mood disturbance. Based on this decision, Dr. Tobin then turns to a guide that she will follow to sort through the information she has gathered. This guide takes the form of a **decision tree,** a series of simple yes/no questions in the *DSM-IV-TR* about the client's symptoms that lead to a possible diagnosis. Like the branches of a tree, the assessment questions proposed by the clinician can take different directions. There are different decision trees for many of the major disorders. Dr. Tobin can use the decision tree for mood disorders to narrow down the possible diagnoses and make sure that she has considered all the options in Peter's case.

The decision tree with the specifics of Peter's case is shown in Figure 2.1. Although there are many more steps in this tree than represented here, you can see the basic logic of the process in this simplified version. Dr. Tobin begins with the mood disturbance decision tree, because she has already decided that Peter's symptoms might fit the diagnostic criteria for a mood disorder. Going through the steps of the decision tree, Dr. Tobin begins with the recognition that Peter has been depressed and that his mood is now both expansive and irritable. Although she will request a complete medical workup, there is no evidence at the moment that his symptoms are physiological effects of a medical condition or drugs. She then focuses on the nature of the present mood episode and concludes that Peter may be experiencing a manic episode. It also appears that Peter has suffered a major depressive episode as well. Now, the question is whether Peter has psychotic symptoms at times other than during these episodes. Assuming he does not, it means that Peter should be

Diagnostic questions

Depressed, elevated, expansive, or irritable mood?

☑ Yes
☐ No

Due to the direct physiological effects of a general medical condition?

☐ Yes
☑ No

Due to the direct physiological effects of a substance?

☐ Yes
☑ No

Manic episode: Elevated, expansive, or irritable mood, at least 1-week duration; marked impairment?

☑ Yes
☐ No

Major depressive episode: At least 2 weeks of depressed mood or loss of interest plus associated symptoms?

☑ Yes
☐ No

Psychotic symptoms occur at times other than during manic episodes?

☐ Yes
☑ No

Final Diagnosis: Bipolar I Disorder

FIGURE 2.1 Dr. Tobin's decision tree for Peter Decision trees provide choices for the clinician based on the client's history and symptoms. Follow the choices made by Dr. Tobin throughout the tree for mood disturbances, the area that seems most appropriate for Peter.

diagnosed as having bipolar disorder (formerly referred to as manic depression), a mood disorder that involves the experience of a manic episode and very commonly a depressive episode. If he did have psychotic symptoms at times other than during his mood episodes, Peter would be diagnosed as suffering from another disorder related to schizophrenia.

The final step in the diagnostic process is for Dr. Tobin to be sure that she has ruled out all possible alternative diagnoses, either by questioning Peter or by reviewing the information she has already collected. This step, called **differential diagnosis,** will probably have been completed already, because Dr. Tobin has been through the decision tree process. However, Dr. Tobin must be confident that Peter fits the diagnostic criteria for bipolar disorder.

One of the questions that Dr. Tobin might have is whether Peter's symptoms might be due to drug use or to an undiagnosed medical condition. If Peter had been abusing amphetamines, he might have had symptoms like those of a manic episode. Alternatively, a person with a brain tumor might show mood disturbances similar to those of a person with mania. In the process of differential diagnosis, the clinician must ensure that there is not a physiological basis for the symptoms. Virtually all the diagnoses on Axis I of the *DSM-IV-TR* specify that the clinician should rule out this possibility. There is an entire category of disorders on Axis I termed "mental disorders due to a general medical condition." Another category applies to disorders due to the abuse of psychoactive substances.

The diagnostic process often requires more than one session with the client, which is why some clinicians prefer to regard the first few psychotherapy sessions as a period of evaluation or assessment. While some therapeutic work may be accomplished during this time, the major goal is for the client and clinician together to arrive at as thorough an understanding as possible of the nature of the client's disorder. This paves the way for the clinician to work with the client on an agreed-upon treatment plan.

Peter's diagnosis was fairly straightforward; however, there are many people whose problems do not fit neatly into a diagnostic category. The problems of some individuals meet the criteria for two or more disorders. The most common instance is when a person has a long-standing personality disorder as well as another more circumscribed problem, such as depression or a sexual disorder. It is also possible for an individual to have two concurrent Axis I diagnoses, such as alcoholism and depression. When clinicians use multiple diagnoses, they typically consider one of the diagnoses to be the **principal diagnosis**—namely, the disorder that is considered to be the primary reason the individual is seeking professional help.

Final Diagnosis

The final diagnosis that Dr. Tobin assigned to Peter incorporates all the information gained during the diagnostic phase of his treatment. Clinicians realize the importance of accuracy in designating a final diagnosis, as this label will set the stage for the entire treatment plan. Dr. Tobin's diagnosis of Peter appears in her records as follows:

Axis I: 296.43 Bipolar I Disorder, most recent episode manic, severe without psychotic features

Axis II: Diagnosis deferred (no information yet available on Peter's long-standing personality traits)

Axis III: No physical conditions reported

Axis IV: Problems with primary support group (divorce)

Axis V: Current Global Assessment of Functioning: 43 Highest Global Assessment of Functioning (past year): 80

Case Formulation

Once the formal diagnosis is made, the clinician is still left with a formidable challenge—to piece together a picture of how the disorder evolved. A diagnosis is a categorical judgment, and, although it is very informative, it does not say much about the client as an individual. To gain a full appreciation of the client's disorder, the clinician develops a **case formulation:** an analysis of the client's development and the factors that might have influenced his or her current psychological status. The formulation provides an analysis that transforms the diagnosis from a set of code numbers to a rich piece of descriptive information about the client's personal history. This descriptive information helps the clinician design a treatment plan that is attentive to the client's symptoms, unique past experiences, and future potential for growth.

Let's return to Peter's case. Having diagnosed Peter as having bipolar disorder, Dr. Tobin uses the next two therapy sessions with him to obtain a comprehensive review of his presenting problem as well as his life history. Based on this review, Dr. Tobin makes the following case formulation:

> Peter is a 23-year-old divorced White male with a diagnosis of bipolar disorder. He is currently in the middle of his first manic episode, which follows his first major depressive episode by about 4 months. The precipitant for the onset of this disorder several months ago seems to have been the turbulence in his marriage and the resulting divorce. Relevant to Peter's condition is an important fact about his family—his mother has been treated for a period of 20 years for bipolar disorder. Peter's diagnosis appears to be a function of both an inherited predisposition to a mood disorder and a set of experiences within his family. The younger child of two boys, Peter was somehow singled out by his mother to be her confidant. She told Peter in detail about her symptoms and the therapy she was receiving. Whenever Peter himself was in a slightly depressed mood, his mother told him that it was probably the first sign of a disorder he was bound to inherit from her. Her involvement in his emotional problems creates another difficulty for Peter in that it has made him ambivalent about seeking therapy. On the one hand, he wants to get help for his problems. Counteracting this desire is Peter's reluctance to let his mother find out that he is in therapy, for fear that this information will confirm her dire predictions for him.

This case formulation gives a more complete picture of Peter's diagnosis than does the simple diagnosis of bipolar disorder. Having read this case formulation, you now know some important potential contributions to Peter's current disorder. In effect, in developing a case formulation, a clinician proposes an hypothesis about the causes of the client's disorder. This hypothesis gives the clinician a logical starting point for designing a treatment and serves as a guide through the many decisions yet to be made.

Cultural Formulation

As American culture becomes increasingly diverse, experienced clinicians must broaden their understanding of ethnic and cultural

Clinicians go through a process of differential diagnosis in which they consider all possible alternative diagnoses.

contributions to psychological problems. To middle-class White clinicians, some conditions might seem strange and incomprehensible without an awareness of the existence of these conditions within certain other cultures. Consequently, with clients from culturally diverse backgrounds, it is important for clinicians to go beyond the multiaxial diagnostic process of the *DSM-IV* and to evaluate conditions that might be culturally determined. In these cases, a cultural formulation is developed. This is a formulation that takes into account the client's degree of identification with the culture, the culture's beliefs about psychological disorder, the ways in which certain events are interpreted within the culture, and the cultural supports available to the client.

The individual's degree of involvement with the culture is important for the clinician to know, because it indicates whether the clinician should take into account cultural influences on the client's symptoms. Clients who do not identify with their culture of origin would not be expected to be as affected by cultural norms and beliefs as would those who are heavily involved in their culture's traditions. The client's familiarity with and preference for using a certain language is one obvious indicator of cultural identification. Second, assuming that the client does identify with the culture, it is necessary to know about cultural explanations of the individual's symptoms. In certain cultures, psychological disorders may be expressed as particular patterns of behavior, perhaps reflecting predominant cultural themes that date back for centuries, known as **culture-bound syndromes.** For example, "ghost sickness" is a preoccupation with death and the deceased that is reported by members of American Indian tribes. This phenomenon includes a constellation of extreme bodily and psychological reactions (see Table 2.5). Such symptoms would have a different meaning if reported by a middle-class White person, rather than an American Indian. Third, the clinician takes into account how events are interpreted within the individual's cultural framework. An event may be extremely stressful to members of a given culture who attribute significant meaning to that event. By contrast, members of

another cultural group may have a more neutral interpretation of that event. For example, within certain Asian cultures, an insult may provoke the condition known as "amok," in which a person (usually male) enters an altered state of consciousness in which he becomes violent, aggressive, and even homicidal.

The cultural supports available to the client form the fourth component of the cultural formulation. Within certain cultures, extended family networks and religion provide emotional resources to help individuals cope with stressful life events.

By including culture-bound syndromes, the authors of the *DSM-IV-TR* took a first step toward formal recognition of variations across cultures in the definition of abnormal behavior. Critics believe that the *DSM-IV-TR* did not go far enough, and that in the future these syndromes should be incorporated into the more general diagnostic nomenclature. Such a step requires further research specifically aimed at taking a multicultural approach both to diagnosis and treatment (Mezzich et al., 1999).

In recent years there have been important advances in understanding how cultural factors influence mental health. In fact, advances have been made in the very definition of "culture." Prior to the 1990s, researchers in the area of cultural psychopathology tended to view a given expression of distress as residing within the specific ethnocultural group. More recent conceptualizations of culture attend much more to people's social world than past views of culture. Cultural investigators now focus on "people's daily routines and how such activities are tied to families, neighborhoods, villages, and social networks" (Lopez & Guarnaccia, 2000, p. 574). In this newer conceptualization of culture, researchers and clinicians move away from flat, unidimensional notions of culture and focus instead on a richer kind of cultural analysis—paying attention to how factors like social class, poverty, and gender affect mental health.

In practical terms, it would be insufficient for a clinician writing a cultural formulation to simplistically attribute certain

In the process of developing a case formulation, clinicians know that it is important to be aware of the ways in which the client's age, gender, and ethnicity may be salient.

TABLE 2.5 Culture-Bound Syndromes in the *DSM-IV-TR*

Certain psychological disorders, such as depression and anxiety, are universally encountered. Within particular cultures, however, idiosyncratic patterns of symptoms are found, many of which have no direct counterpart to a specific *DSM-IV-TR* diagnosis. These conditions, called culture-bound syndromes, are recurrent patterns of abnormal behavior or experience that are limited to specific societies or cultural areas.

Culture-bound syndromes may fit into one or more of the *DSM-IV-TR* categories, just as one *DSM-IV-TR* category may be thought to be several different conditions by another culture. Some disorders recognized by the *DSM-IV-TR* are seen as culture-bound syndromes, because they are specific to industrialized societies (e.g., anorexia nervosa).

This table describes some of the best-studied culture-bound syndromes and forms of distress that may be encountered in clinical practice in North America, as well as the *DSM-IV-TR* categories they most closely resemble.

Term	Location	Description	DSM-IV-TR *Disorders*
Amok	Malaysia	Dissociative episode consisting of brooding followed by violent, aggressive, and possibly homicidal outburst. Precipitated by insult; usually seen more in males. Return to premorbid state following the outburst.	
Ataque de nervios	Latin America	Distress associated with uncontrollable shouting, crying, trembling, and verbal or physical aggression. Dissociation, seizure, and suicidal gestures possible. Often occurs as a result of a stressful family event. Rapid return to premorbid state.	Anxiety Mood Dissociative Somatoform
Bilis and colera	Latin America	Condition caused by strong anger or rage. Marked by disturbed core body imbalances, including tension, headache, trembling, screaming, and stomach disturbance. Chronic fatigue and loss of consciousness possible.	
Boufée delirante	West Africa and Haiti	Sudden outburst of agitated and aggressive behavior, confusion, and psychomotor excitement. Paranoia and visual and auditory hallucinations possible.	Brief psychotic
Brain fag	West Africa	Difficulties in concentration, memory, and thought, usually experienced by students in response to stress. Other symptoms include neck and head pain, pressure, and blurred vision.	Anxiety Depressive Somatoform
Dhat	India	Severe anxiety and hypochondriacal concern regarding semen discharge, whitish discoloration of urine, weakness, and extreme fatigue.	
Falling out or *blacking out*	Southern United States and the Caribbean	A sudden collapse, usually preceded by dizziness. Temporary loss of vision and the ability to move.	Conversion Dissociative
Ghost sickness	American Indian tribes	A preoccupation with death and the deceased. Thought to be symbolized by bad dreams, weakness, fear, appetite loss, anxiety, hallucinations, loss of consciousness, and a feeling of suffocation.	
Hwa-byung (wool-hwa-byung)	Korea	Acute feelings of anger resulting in symptoms including insomnia, fatigue, panic, fear of death, dysphoria, indigestion, loss of appetite, dyspnea, palpitations, aching, and the feeling of a mass in the abdomen.	
Koro	Malaysia	An episode of sudden and intense anxiety that one's penis or vulva and nipples will recede into the body and cause death.	
Latah	Malaysia	Hypersensitivity to sudden fright, usually accompanied by symptoms including echopraxia (imitating the movements and gestures of another person), echolalia (irreverent parroting of what another person has said), command obedience, and dissociation, all of which are characteristic of schizophrenia.	

TABLE 2.5 Culture-Bound Syndromes in the *DSM-IV-TR* *(continued)*

Term	Location	Description	DSM-IV-TR *Disorders*
Mal de ojo	Mediterranean cultures	Means "the evil eye" when translated from Spanish. Children are at much greater risk; adult females are at a higher risk than adult males. Manifested by fitful sleep, crying with no apparent cause, diarrhea, vomiting, and fever.	
Pibloktog	Arctic and sub-Arctic Eskimo communities	Abrupt dissociative episode associated with extreme excitement, often followed by seizures and coma. During the attack, the person may break things, shout obscenities, eat feces, and behave dangerously. The victim may be temporarily withdrawn from the community and report amnesia regarding the attack.	
Qi-gong psychotic reaction	China	Acute episode marked by dissociation and paranoia that may occur following participation in qi-gong, a Chinese folk health-enhancing practice.	
Rootwork	Southern United States, African American and European populations, and Caribbean societies	Cultural interpretation that ascribes illness to hexing, witchcraft, or sorcery. Associated with anxiety, gastrointestinal problems, weakness, dizziness, and the fear of being poisoned or killed.	
Shen-k'uei or *Shenkui*	Taiwan and China	Symptoms attributed to excessive semen loss due to frequent intercourse, masturbation, and nocturnal emission. Dizziness, backache, fatigue, weakness, insomnia, frequent dreams, and sexual dysfunction. Excessive loss of semen is feared, because it represents the loss of vital essence and therefore threatens one's life.	
Shin-byung	Korea	Anxiety and somatic problems followed by dissociation and possession by ancestral spirits.	
Spell	African American and European American communities in the southern United States	Trance state in which communication with deceased relatives or spirits takes place. Sometimes connected with a temporary personality change.	
Susto	Latinos in the United States and Mexico, Central America, and South America	Illness caused by a frightening event that causes the soul to leave the body. Causes unhappiness, sickness (muscle aches, stress headache, and diarrhea), strain in social roles, appetite and sleep disturbances, lack of motivation, low self-esteem, and possibly death. Healing methods include calling the soul back into the body and cleansing to restore bodily and spiritual balance.	Major depressive Post-traumatic stress Somatoform
Taijin kyofusho	Japan	Intense fear that one's body parts or functions displease, embarrass, or are offensive to others regarding appearance, odor, facial expressions, or movements.	
Zar	Ethiopia, Somalia, Egypt, Sudan, Iran, and other North African and Middle Eastern societies	Possession by a spirit. May cause dissociative experiences characterized by shouting, laughing, hitting of one's head against a hard surface, singing, crying, apathy, withdrawal, and change in daily habits.	

mental health problems to the client's ethnicity. Consider the anxiety condition reported in Latinos known as *ataque de nervios,* which involves various dramatic expressions of distress such as trembling, crying, and uncontrollable shouting in response to a disturbing life event related to family or significant others. Researchers initiated systematic investigations of *ataque de nervios,* focusing on how the social world interacts with psychological and physical processes in the individual. Particularly interesting was the finding that this condition is not actually a cultural syndrome or clinical entity residing in individuals, but is rather "a common illness that reflects the lived experience largely of women with little power and disrupted social relations" (Lopez & Guarnaccia, 2000, p. 581).

Apart from the role of cultural factors in the formulation, clinicians must also take cultural factors into account when conceptualizing the treatment relationship they will have with clients. The clinician should take care not to make assumptions about how the client would like to be treated, based on the clinician's own cultural background. Seemingly minor aspects of the relationship, such as how familiar the clinician acts toward the client, may have tremendous bearing on the rapport that is established in their relationship. In some cultures, for example, it would be regarded as rude for the clinician to use an individual's first name. Another aspect of the relationship that can be affected by cultural factors is the role of eye contact. The clinician should be aware of whether people within the client's culture make eye contact during conversation. It would be erroneous for the clinician to assume that a client's lack of eye contact implies disrespect.

Attention to all of these factors helps the clinician formulate a diagnosis and treatment that are sensitive to cultural differences. Going a step further, clinicians can benefit from becoming familiar with the culture-bound syndromes such as those in Table 2.5. If some of these seem bizarre to you, think about how someone from another culture might regard conditions that are prevalent in Western culture, such as eating disorders. You might also think about the meaning of these culture-bound syndromes for our understanding of abnormal behavior. The fact that psychological disorders vary from one society to another supports the claim of the sociocultural perspective that cultural factors play a role in influencing the expression of abnormal behavior.

Treatment Planning

We have discussed the steps through which a clinician develops an understanding of a client's problem. This understanding provides the basis for the clinician's next phase, which is to plan the most appropriate treatment for the client. In an optimal situation, the clinician has the client's cooperation in addressing several questions regarding treatment choices: What are the goals of the treatment? What would be the best treatment setting? Who should treat the client? What kind of treatment should be used?

What kind of treatment is financially feasible and available? Finally, what theoretical orientation would be best suited to the client's particular needs? All of these considerations would form Dr. Tobin's treatment plan for Peter as she moves from the diagnostic phase toward the treatment phase.

Goals of Treatment

The first phase of treatment planning is to establish treatment goals, which are the objectives the clinician hopes to accomplish in working with the client. These goals range from the immediate to the long term. To understand this critical phase of the process, put yourself into the shoes of a clinician for the moment and think of an analogous situation in which you are trying to help a friend through a crisis. Although you are not "treating" your friend in a professional sense, the steps you take would be very much like the approach a clinician takes with a client in developing a treatment plan. Let's say this friend knocks on your door late one night, in tears because she has had another of her many arguments on the phone with her father. Because of her problems with her father, she has had academic difficulties all semester. Tomorrow she has an important exam, and she is panic-stricken.

Now, consider what you would do in helping your friend. Your first reaction would be to help her calm down. You might talk to her and try to get her in a better frame of mind, so that she will be able to take the exam. However, you would also realize that she has other problems, which she will need to attend to after she gets through the next day. In the short term, she needs to catch up on the rest of her course work. Over the long term, she will need to deal with the difficulties that recur between her and her father. A clinician treating a client would also think in terms of three stages—immediate management, short-term goals, and long-term goals.

In dealing with immediate management, the clinician addresses the most pressing needs at the moment. Short-term goals involve change in the client's behavior, thinking, or emotions but do not involve a major personality restructuring. Long-term goals include more fundamental and deeply rooted alterations in the client's personality and relationships.

These three stages imply a sequential order, and in many cases this is the way a treatment plan is conceived. First the clinician deals with the crisis, then handles problems in the near future, and finally addresses issues that require extensive work well into the future. However, in other cases, there may be a cyclical unfolding of stages. New sets of immediate crises or short-term goals may arise in the course of treatment. Or there may be a redefinition of long-term goals as the course of treatment progresses. It is perhaps more helpful to think of the three stages not as consecutive stages per se, but as implying different levels of treatment focus.

Immediate management, then, is called for in situations involving intense distress or risk to the client or others. A person experiencing an acute anxiety attack would most likely be treated

PATTY DUKE: MOOD DISTURBANCE

Patty Duke

At the beginning of this chapter, you began reading about Peter Dickinson, a man whose wild mood swings caused him to lose control over his thinking and behavior. Peter was experiencing the symptoms associated with a serious mood disturbance called bipolar disorder. This technical label might not be familiar to you; the condition is more commonly, in nonprofessional discussions, called manic depressive illness. Patty Duke, a legendary star of stage and screen, brought international attention to the seriousness and prevalence of this condition when she began speaking and writing publicly about her own struggles with it.

The story of Patty Duke's fame dates back to her early childhood, when her managers renamed the young Anna Marie in an attempt to make her sound "perkier." Patty/Anna became a celebrity while starring on Broadway as Helen Keller in *The Miracle Worker* and subsequently in a popular television series, *The Patty Duke Show*, in which she played the dual role of identical cousins. She was a very talented and prolific actress, appearing in more than 50 films and winning numerous awards, including a People's Choice Award and an Oscar.

Although she achieved an enormous level of success both on stage and in the movies, Patty Duke's personal life was turbulent for more than three decades. Her father suffered from alcoholism and had trouble holding down jobs. He left home when Patty was 6 and she rarely saw him afterward. He died at the age of 50, leaving Patty to carry an emotional pain she still feels. Patty also speaks of her mother's depression, which was so severe that her mother repeatedly threatened to kill herself and had to be hospitalized. Patty also describes her mother as having an explosive temper that occasionally led to physical abuse, particularly of Patty's brother Raymond.

As a child, Patty Duke was interested in becoming a nun and had very little interest in acting, until she was signed by professional managers, John and Ethel Ross, a demanding duo who insisted that Patty's career would go nowhere without their direction. In the early days of her working with the Ross couple, Patty would go to their luxurious apartment after school for coaching. Eventually she moved in with them, and at their insistence, Patty's contact with her family diminished; eventually the only times Patty saw her mother were when she came to the Ross household to do housework or to baby-sit for Patty.

In her adult years, Patty Duke had a number of troubled relationships and two failed marriages. Perhaps partly due to her turbulent childhood, she experienced wild mood swings that often left her feeling either sad and hopeless or energetic and agitated. Her mood disorder was finally diagnosed when Patty was 35, and she came to understand the nature of her swings between suicidal depression and the soaring manic highs. Once she began taking lithium, she began to feel "normal" for the first time in her life. She also decided to revert to her birth name, Anna.

In the passages that follow, taken from her autobiography *A Brilliant Madness: Living with Manic Depressive Illness*, Anna/Patty describes some of her experiences.

In the depressions, I was interested only in pleasing, but even that didn't make me feel satisfied. For instance, let's say I would cry all Friday night, Saturday night, Sunday—then Monday, get up and go to work, do a good job, but on the way home Monday night I'd be crying again, more fearful, more fretful.

There were times when this leveled off, but I never knew what made it stop, what made the crying stop, what made me not be afraid that day. I also didn't question it. Once things seemed to be okay, I didn't mess with it. This was also a way to deal with the shame attached to that kind of behavior. It's everyone's shame, the family's as well. It's as if we said, "Oh, okay, it's stopped now, let's not talk about it anymore." Number one, talking might bring it back, and number two, it's just too embarrassing to look at. But the depressions always came back. They defined my life. During this time I became very clever about how to obtain and stockpile pills—tranquilizers, usually Valium. At home, I picked fights with Harry; then I would fly into the bathroom and swallow half a bottle of whatever pills I had. . . .

The mania started with insomnia and not eating and being driven, driven to find an apartment, driven to "do" New York, driven to see everybody, driven to never shut up. The first weekend I was there, Bobby Kennedy was assassinated. . . . I had an overwhelmingly out-of- proportion reaction to his assassination. I know those were insane times and we all had enormous reactions to those assassinations, but for me it was as if he had been *my* brother or *my* father. This is not an exaggeration—at least two weeks went by without sleep.

At this suicide hotline, telephone counseling is available 24 hours a day.

on the spot with antianxiety medication. A client who is severely depressed and suicidal may need to be hospitalized. In the case of Peter, Dr. Tobin decides that Peter's possible dangerousness to others warrants hospitalization. Furthermore, his manic symptoms of irrational behavior and agitation suggest that he needs intensive professional care. Not all clinical situations require that action be taken in the immediate management stage, but it is important for the clinician to think about various options to help the client deal with pressing concerns of the moment.

When a client's most troubling symptoms are under control, it is possible for the clinician to work with the client in developing more effective ways of resolving current difficulties. The plan at this point might include establishing a working relationship between the clinician and client, as well as setting up specific objectives for therapeutic change. If Dr. Tobin is to treat Peter's mood disorder, she must establish rapport with him, and he, in turn, must feel committed to working with her. Another short-term goal might be to stabilize Peter on medication, so that his symptoms will be alleviated.

Long-term goals are the ultimate aims of therapeutic change. Ideally, the long-term goals for any client are to overcome the problem and to develop a strategy to prevent recurrence. In reality, these goals are difficult to achieve. The restructuring of a personality can be a lifelong endeavor. With the help of Dr. Tobin, Peter will need to plan his life, taking his disorder into account. For example, Dr. Tobin may advise Peter to take medication aimed at preventing a recurrence of his symptoms. He may also need to prepare himself for some of the ways this disorder may affect his life. In addition, Peter will have to work with Dr. Tobin to deal with the emotional scars he has suffered as a result of his own disorder and the troubled childhood caused by his mother's disorder.

A treatment plan, then, includes a set of goals for short- and long-range interventions. Having established these goals, the clinician's next task is to specify how to implement the plan. This requires decisions regarding the optimal treatment site, the treatment modality, and the theoretical perspective on which the treatment is based.

Treatment Site

The severity of the client's problem is one of the first issues a clinician considers in deciding what kind of treatment site to recommend. Treatment sites vary in the degree to which they provide a controlled environment and in the nature of the services they offer to clients. Treatment sites include psychiatric hospitals, outpatient treatment settings, halfway houses and day treatment centers, and other treatment sites, such as the school or workplace, that provide mental health services. The more serious the client's disturbance, the more controlled the environment that is needed and the more intense the services.

The severity of the client's symptoms is assessed on several dimensions. Is the client suicidal, at risk of harming others, delusional, or otherwise incapable of maintaining control? Does the client have physical problems, such as those that might result from a brain dysfunction, an eating disorder, or illness? What is the client's support system at home? Are people there who can help the client deal with the problems caused by the disorder and its symptoms? Further, the clinician must be sensitive to the financial resources available to the client. In an age in which cost-effectiveness is of major concern to insurance companies, treatment decisions are commonly dictated by decisions to pursue the least expensive care. The clinician's recommendation of a treatment site is also based on the match between the client's needs and the services provided in a particular treatment setting. Depending on how clinical and financial issues are addressed, the clinician will recommend a psychiatric hospital, outpatient treatment, or a halfway house or group home that provides a combination of services.

Psychiatric Hospitals   The decision to hospitalize a client depends largely on the risk the client presents. A clinician usually recommends that the client be admitted to a psychiatric hospital when the client is at risk of harming self or others or seems incapable of self-care. Although some clients choose inpatient psychiatric care quite willingly, there must be demonstrable clinical need and evidence that the client presents a risk in order for this very expensive form of treatment to be covered by insurance or public programs. Often, clients who are at high risk of harm to self or others are involuntarily hospitalized by a court order until their symptoms can be brought under control (this is discussed in more detail in Chapter 15).

Hospitalization is also recommended for clients who have disorders that require medical interventions and intensive forms of psychotherapeutic interventions. Some medical interventions, such as a trial on a new drug regimen, are best done in a hospital setting, where the risks of potential side effects and treatment efficacy can be monitored continuously. Some psychotherapeutic interventions are also best done in a setting where the contingencies of the client's behavior can be monitored and reinforced by trained personnel. For example, a young man prone to violent outbursts may require an environment in which he is rewarded when he is quiet and is responded to aversively when he loses control.

In some cases, the clinician might recommend a specialized inpatient treatment center. Such a treatment site would be appropriate for adults with substance abuse problems or for children and adolescents who need professional treatment in a residential setting.

Returning to the case of Peter, a hospital would be the treatment site of choice, because he is a threat to others, he needs medication monitoring, and the hospital could offer him various forms of therapy. As he improves, Dr. Tobin will develop a discharge plan that will undoubtedly include outpatient care.

Outpatient Treatment   Because hospitalization is such a radical and expensive intervention, most clients receive outpatient treatment, in which they are treated in a private professional office or clinic. Professionals in private practice offer individual or group sessions, usually on a weekly basis. Some prepaid health insurance plans cover the cost of such visits, either to a private practitioner or to a clinician working in a health maintenance organization (HMO). Outpatient treatment may also be offered in agencies supported partially or completely by public funds. **Community mental health centers (CMHCs)** are outpatient clinics that provide psychological services on a sliding fee scale for individuals who live within a certain geographic area.

Outpatient services are, by necessity, more limited than those in a hospital, in terms of both the time involved and the nature of the contact between client and clinician. However, additional services may be made available to clients who need vocational counseling, help with domestic management, group therapy, or the support of a self-help organization, such as Alcoholics Anonymous.

Halfway Houses and Day Treatment Programs   Clients with serious psychological disorders who are able to live in the community need more services than can be provided through conventional outpatient treatment. For such individuals, halfway houses and day treatment programs are the most appropriate treatment sites. These facilities may be connected with a hospital, a public agency, or a private corporation. **Halfway houses** are designed for clients who have been discharged from psychiatric facilities but who are not yet ready for independent living. A halfway house provides a living context with other deinstitutionalized people, and it is staffed by professionals who work with clients in developing the skills they need to become employed and to set up their own living situations. **Day treatment programs** are designed for formerly hospitalized clients as well as for clients who do not need hospitalization but do need a structured program during the day, similar to that provided by a hospital. Many day treatment programs are based on a social club model. Some of the clients who participate in day treatment programs reside in halfway houses and some live independently, with relatives or in apartments supervised by paraprofessional mental health workers.

Psychological treatment is also provided in settings other than hospitals and clinics. This high-school counselor is talking with a student about drug abuse.

Other Treatment Sites   Psychological treatment is also provided in settings not traditionally associated with the provision of mental health services, such as the schools and the workplace. Guidance counselors and school psychologists are often called on to intervene in cases in which a student is emotionally disturbed or is upset by a pathological living situation. These professionals handle much of the intervention in the school, but they often find it necessary to refer the student or family for outside professional help. In the workplace, many employers have recognized the importance of intervening in the lives of employees whose emotional problems are interfering with their job performance and could possibly result in termination from employment. A common program is the Employee Assistance Program (EAP) provided by most large companies. The EAP provides the employee with a confidential setting in which to seek help for emotional problems, substance abuse difficulties, or relationship problems. Often the EAP professional can work with the employee toward a resolution of the problem; at times, the EAP professional can help the employee locate appropriate treatment resources for the problem at hand.

Modality of Treatment

The **modality,** or form in which psychotherapy is offered, is another crucial component of the treatment plan. In **individual psychotherapy,** the therapist works with the client on a one-to-one basis. Typically, the therapist and client meet on a regular schedule—most commonly, once a week for about an hour. In couple therapy, partners in a relationship both participate, and,

In family therapy, all available members of a family are involved in treatment.

in **family therapy,** several or all of the family members are involved in the treatment. In family therapy, one person may be identified by family members as being the "patient." The therapist, however, views the whole family system as the target of the treatment. **Group therapy** provides a modality in which troubled people can openly share their problems with others, receive feedback, develop trust, and improve interpersonal skills.

Milieu therapy, which has been found to be helpful for hospitalized clients, is based on the premise that the milieu, or environment, is a major component of the treatment; a new setting, in which a team of professionals works with the client to improve his or her mental health, is considered to be better than the client's home and work environments, with their stresses and pressures. Ideally, the milieu is constructed in such a way that clients will perceive all interactions and contexts as therapeutic and constructive. In addition to traditional psychotherapy, other therapeutic endeavors are made through group or peer counseling, occupational therapy, and recreational therapy.

The clinician's decision to recommend a particular modality of treatment is based, again, on a match between the client's specific needs and the treatment's potential to meet these needs. For example, a teenage girl with an eating disorder may be seen in both individual therapy and family therapy if the clinician believes that the eating disorder is rooted in disturbed parent-child interactions. As this example illustrates, the clinician has the option of recommending multiple modalities, rather than being restricted to one form of therapy. We will discuss the modalities in more detail in Chapter 4, along with their conceptual underpinnings.

In Peter's case, three treatment modalities would be recommended, at least in the initial phase of his treatment. Along with his individual therapy needs, Peter would benefit from both family therapy and group therapy. Family therapy would be useful in helping Peter develop his support system with his mother and brother, and group therapy would provide Peter with the

opportunity to interact with and derive support from other clients who have similar disorders.

Determining the Best Approach to Treatment

Whatever modality of treatment a clinician recommends, it must be based on the choice of the most appropriate theoretical perspective or the most appropriate aspects of several different perspectives. Many clinicians are trained according to a particular set of assumptions about the origins of psychological disorders and the best methods of treating these disorders. Often, this theoretical orientation forms the basis for the clinician's treatment decisions. However, just as frequently, clinicians adapt their theoretical orientation to fit the client's needs. Further, the growing movement toward integrating diverse theoretical models in treatment planning is addressing the concerns of clinicians who feel that a single theoretical model is too narrow. Increasingly, clinicians are combining the best elements of various theoretical orientations in tailoring the treatment plan to have the greatest likelihood of success for a given client (Chambless & Ollendick, 2001).

Determining the approach for treating each disorder is a complex matter, about which there has been considerable debate in the past several decades. You might assume that most psychotherapists treating a given disorder would use a standard intervention, but, in fact, this is not the case. Consider a client with major depressive disorder. Some clinicians would recommend a brief intervention that focuses on the client's distorted thoughts. Other clinicians would suggest that the client engage in lengthy psychotherapy to explore early life experiences that caused or contributed to adult depression. Still others would dispense with "talk therapy" and recommend antidepressant medication. And others would integrate components of each of these approaches.

Which treatment method is the most effective, and how can effectiveness be measured? In an effort to answer these questions, psychotherapy researchers have devoted considerable effort in recent years to reviewing all published outcome studies on specific disorders. From these efforts to identify empirically supported treatments have emerged treatment recommendations called "practice guidelines" (Nathan, 1998). Although the process of developing practice guidelines might seem straightforward and relatively uncontroversial, these efforts have unleashed a storm of controversy.

Even though efforts to designate the most effective treatments have been admirable, these efforts have not yielded the simple solutions that experts had hoped would be found. To shed some light on the complexity of the issues, Martin Seligman, a leading psychotherapy researcher, has attempted to highlight some of the differences between research that is conducted in laboratory settings (called efficacy research) and outcome studies involving people who have sought professional help in a traditional helping context (effectiveness research) (Seligman, 1995). Efficacy studies are commonly conducted in university-based clinics, where therapists are carefully selected, trained, and monitored; furthermore, patients are also carefully screened in order to exclude those with multiple problems (DeRubeis & Crits-Cristoph, 1998).

Seligman contends that what is measured in efficacy studies has only a slight resemblance to what takes place in a real-world therapy setting. In the real world, clients are not assigned to random groups for fixed durations and treated according to a predetermined script. Furthermore, rarely does a client's diagnosis fit neatly into one clearly delineated category. For example, a client with major depressive disorder may also have a personality disorder, an eating disorder, and a sexual dysfunction. In such a case, which practice guidelines would be followed? Seligman points out that, in effectiveness research, investigators study therapy as it is practiced in the field. Therapy is conducted without a manual; patients may have several presenting problems, and they are choosing therapists in whom they believe.

Dialogue regarding the usefulness of empirically supported treatments has heated up in recent years as experts in the field of psychotherapy have evaluated the various sources of data on psychotherapy efficacy. Chambless and Ollendick (2001) reviewed the following five criticisms of empirically supported treatments (ESTs) and reached some important conclusions.

1. *"ESTs should be ignored because many of these interventions have emerged from recommendations put forth by a small group of biased psychologists."* Chambless and Ollendick reject this claim, pointing out that multiple groups of research reviewers have reached impressively reliable conclusions about various interventions.

2. *"Quantitative research is not an appropriate paradigm for psychotherapy research; rather, qualitative and observation methods are more appropriate."* Chambless and Ollendick note that this argument is based in "a schism of paradigms": extremists make such arguments so vehemently that there is no room for dialogue.

3. *"EST research is based on treatment manuals, which when used to train therapists will lead to lower-quality psychotherapy."* Chambless and Ollendick reply that no empirical studies support this claim.

4. *"There is no difference in efficacy among various forms of psychotherapy; therefore, the identification of ESTs is unnecessary."* While not dismissing this argument, Chambless and Ollendick note that the question of specificity (i.e., which specific intervention is most effective for each specific disorder) is a complex question that needs further exploration.

5. *"EST research should be ignored because it will not generalize to clinical practice involving real-life clients, therapists, clinical settings, and treatment goals."* Chambless and Ollendick acknowledge that some of this concern is legitimate, but they emphasize that an impressive body of data suggests that ESTs are effective in clinical settings with a diverse group of clients.

Wampold (2001) joined the debate about what makes psychotherapy work by comprehensively reviewing decades of psychotherapy research. Wampold concluded that common factors, rather than specific technical ingredients, are most important. In other words, the many specific types of psychotherapeutic treatment achieve comparable benefits because of a common core of curative processes. Following a harsh critique of empirically supported treatments, Wampold recommends that therapists and supervisors should deemphasize manual-based treatments and instead choose the therapy that accords with a client's worldview.

As you are reading about various disorders in this book, and the treatments that have been demonstrated as most effective, it will be important to keep in mind the empirical basis for the treatment conclusions. Findings from efficacy studies shed light on appropriate interventions, but they are insufficient for making conclusive determinations about what is most effective with real people with complex problems.

Wampold and Bhati (2004) assert that the evidence-based movement has overemphasized treatments and treatment differences and ignored aspects of psychotherapy that have been shown to be related to outcome, such as variations among psychotherapists, and the quality of the relationship between the client and the clinician.

Although naive adherence to a narrow clinical approach that has the aura of validity is unwise, experienced clinicians recognize the importance of implementing treatments that have, time and again, been shown to be effective. McCabe (2004) recommends a four-step approach by which intelligent decisions based on scientific knowledge should be used in the treatment process. The clinician should (1) formulate a clear clinical question by conceptualizing the client's problem with sufficient specificity to match the treatment with the most relevant practice guidelines, (2) search the literature for relevant clinical-research articles, (3) appraise the scientific rigor of the research, and (4) replicate the intervention with as much fidelity to the original approach as possible.

Treatment Implementation

When the diagnostic process and treatment planning have taken place, the clinician then implements the treatment. Despite all the thinking and preparation that have gone into this plan, though, the exact way in which treatment unfolds varies according to the characteristics of the clinician, the client, and the interaction between the two. There are many individual variations among both clients and clinicians. Consequently, the potential for variation is virtually unlimited in the interactions between any one client and any one clinician. Some common issues, though, characterize all therapeutic interactions.

Above and beyond whatever techniques a clinician uses to treat a client's problems, the quality of the relationship between the client and clinician is a crucial determinant of whether therapy will succeed or not. A good clinician does more than coldly and objectively "administer" treatment to a client. A good clinician infuses a deep personal interest, concern, and respect for the client into the therapeutic relationship. In this regard, psychotherapy is as much an art as a skill.

The Course of Treatment

The way that treatment proceeds is a function of the contributions made by the clinician and the client. Each has a part to play in determining the outcome of the case, as does the unique interaction of their personalities, abilities, and expectations.

The Clinician's Role in Treatment   One of the skills the clinician develops is an ability to scan the client-clinician interaction for meaningful cues that will provide insight into the nature of the client's problems. An important piece of information the clinician gathers is the way the client seems to respond to the clinician. Let's use Dr. Tobin as an example to illustrate this point. Dr. Tobin is a woman in her early forties. Each of her clients forms a unique impression of the kind of person she is. One client thinks of Dr. Tobin as an authority figure, because Dr. Tobin's mannerisms and appearance remind him of his seventh-grade teacher. Another client perceives Dr. Tobin as a peer, because they are about the same age and professional status. A third client is in his sixties, and Dr. Tobin reminds him of his daughter. Thus, the same clinician is perceived in three different ways by three different clients. With each client, Dr. Tobin has a markedly different basis for a therapeutic relationship.

Not only do clients have unique responses to Dr. Tobin, but she also has individualized responses to each client. As a professional, Dr. Tobin is trained to examine her reactions to each client and to try not to let her reactions interfere with her ability to help. Moreover, she has learned how to use her perception of each client and the way she thinks she is perceived as aids in diagnosing the client's disorder and in embarking on a therapeutic procedure.

The Client's Role in Treatment   In optimal situations, psychotherapy is a joint enterprise in which the client plays an active role. It is largely up to the client to describe and identify the nature of his or her disorder, to describe personal reactions as treatment progresses, and to initiate and follow through on whatever changes are going to be made.

The client's attitudes toward therapy and the therapist are an important part of the contribution the client makes to the therapeutic relationship. There is a special quality to the help that the client is requesting; it involves potentially painful, embarrassing, and personally revealing material that the client is not accustomed to disclosing to someone else. Most people are much more comfortable discussing their medical, legal, financial, and other problems outside the realm of the emotions.

Social attitudes toward psychological disorders also play a role. People may feel that they should be able to handle their emotional problems without seeking help. They may believe that, if they can't solve their own emotional problems, it means they are immature or incompetent. Moreover, having to see a clinician may make a person believe that he or she is "crazy." You would not hesitate to tell your friends that you have an appointment with a physician because of a sore knee. Most people would, though, feel less inclined to mention to acquaintances that they are in psychotherapy for personal problems. The pressure to keep therapy secret usually adds to a client's anxiety about seeking professional help. To someone who is already troubled by severe problems in living, this added anxiety can be further inhibiting. With so many potential forces driving the troubled individual away from seeking therapy, the initial step is sometimes the hardest to take. Thus, the therapeutic relationship requires the client to be willing to work with the clinician in a partnership and to be prepared to endure the pain and embarrassment involved in making personal revelations. Moreover, it also requires a willingness to break old patterns and to try new ways of viewing the self and relating to others.

The Outcome of Treatment

In the best of all possible worlds, the treatment works. The client stays through the treatment, shows improvement, and maintains this improved level of functioning. Many times, though, the road is not so smooth, and either the goals of the treatment plan are never attained or unanticipated problems arise. Some of the obstacles that clinicians face in their efforts to help clients include some curious and frustrating realities. The most frustrating involve the client who is unwilling to change. It may sound paradoxical, but, even though a client may seem terribly distressed by a problem, that client may fail to follow through on a very promising treatment. Mental health professionals know that change is very difficult, and many clients have become so accustomed to living with a problem that the effort needed to solve the problem seems overwhelming. At times, clinicians also face frustration over financial constraints. They may recommend a treatment that they are quite confident can succeed but that is financially infeasible. In other cases there may be an involved party, such as a lover or parent, who refuses to participate in the treatment, even though he or she plays a central role. Other pragmatic issues can disrupt therapy: clients may move, lose jobs, or lack consistent transportation to the clinic. Over time, those in the mental health field learn that they are limited in how effective they can be in changing the lives of people who go to them for help.

RETURN TO THE CASE

Treatment Plan

After only a brief interaction with Peter during our first encounter, I knew that he needed to be hospitalized. As is common when dealing with individuals in a manic state, there was a tremendous amount of resistance to such a suggestion, however. I realized that Peter would balk at my recommendation, so I was prepared to make my viewpoint as unambiguous as possible. In my thoughts, I realized that there was no way that I would feel comfortable sending Peter back out onto the streets. Of particular concern was the intensity of his anger toward Marnie. Might he threaten to harm her in some way? It seemed unlikely, but possible. What did seem likely, however, was that Peter would not be able to take adequate care of himself in this disordered state of mind.

I explained to Peter that I was deeply concerned about his psychological state and that I was prepared to commit him. Not only did I consider him to be a possible danger to others, but I feared for his physical and psychological well-being. As I had anticipated, Peter began ranting and raving in response to this. At one point, he jumped up and began yelling that I had no authority to push him around. I knew that it was important for me to let him know that I was not intimidated. In a gentle but determined voice, I explained to Peter that I was prepared to take this action, which I was quite clear was in his best interest. Even I was surprised, however, by Peter's sudden turnaround. Apparently, on some level, he recognized that he was out of control. He was then able to accept help in regaining his stability. Peter admitted to me that the disturbed reaction of his brother, Don, to his outlandish behavior had helped him realize that "something was seriously wrong."

Peter admitted himself voluntarily to the hospital, asking me to "promise" that he would be discharged within 2 weeks. I explained that a 2-week time frame seemed reasonable, but providing a guarantee was too difficult, because I was not sure how quickly he would respond to treatment.

My treatment recommendations for Peter were relatively straightforward. First, he needed medication to help control his manic symptoms. Beginning Peter on lithium made sense, because this medication has proven to be effective in the treatment of mania. Second, Peter needed to begin a course of psychotherapy that would have several components. In individual therapy, Peter could work with me in developing an understanding of the nature and causes of his psychological disturbance. We would also discuss choices he could make to reduce the amount of stress in his life and to manage his symptoms over the longer course. In addition to individual therapy, I suggested that Peter's mother and brother join Peter for a few family therapy sessions to be conducted by Bev Mullins, the treatment unit's social worker. Family therapy would focus on establishing a more stable source of emotional connection between Peter and his immediate family. The benefits of such an improved alliance would be multiple. Those most concerned about Peter could be available for support in the event that his disturbance reappeared. Furthermore, his mother's personal experience with the same disorder could serve as an invaluable source of insight into the nature and treatment of this condition. Group therapy was the third form of therapy I recommended to Peter. During his stay on the treatment unit, he would participate in three groups per week, during which he would share his own experiences with others who were also struggling with the powerful experiences associated with a psychological disorder. With expressions of reluctance, Peter agreed to go along with my plan.

Outcome of the Case

As it turned out, Peter's stay in the hospital lasted precisely 14 days. He had shown dramatic improvement after only 4 days on lithium, at which point he expressed relief that he was now calmer and "getting back to normal." For the first time in several weeks, he was able to get some sound sleep and return to normal eating habits.

In his sessions with me, Peter told the story of a troubled childhood, having been raised by a mother with extreme and unpredictable mood variations. Making matters worse, his mother saw Peter, the younger of the two boys, as the son in whom she could confide. By doing so, she set up an uncomfortable alliance with him, and he felt unduly responsible for her well-being.

After graduating from high school, Peter didn't choose the college route taken by most of his classmates; instead, he eloped with his girlfriend and took a job at a local convenience store. Peter and his wife fought almost constantly—mostly about money issues—for the 4 years of their marriage, but they had developed an emotional dependence on each other that made separation seem too difficult. When his wife finally threw him out of the house, he was devastated and found himself burdened by feelings of depression and rage. In the weeks that followed the breakup, he "bottomed out." He couldn't work, eat, sleep, or think clearly. At one point, he came close to making a suicide attempt one night while driving alone in his car. Instead of acting on his impulse, he pulled over to the side of the road and cried until dawn. Eventually, over subsequent weeks, the depression subsided. Following a period of relative serenity, however, he found himself unbelievably energized and traveling down the path to mania.

During Peter's stay in the hospital, we met six times. In these sessions, he was able to see how stressors in his life brought on a mood disorder to which he was biologically predisposed. His ongoing interpersonal and financial difficulties placed him at increased risk, and, when his marriage broke up, the psychological turmoil reached a level too intense for him to tolerate.

In the three family sessions Bev Mullins conducted, Peter's mother and brother were remarkably responsive in communicating their concern and support. For the first time that Peter could remember, Mrs. Dickinson acknowledged the turmoil that her mood disorder must have created for Peter, as well as the pressures she placed on her young son to help her solve her problems. In an emotionally charged session, all three family members were brought to tears as they spoke of the hurt and confusion of years past. They also became closer to each other, as they spoke of ways they would try to make their relationships different in the months and years to come.

As successful as individual and family therapy proved to be for Peter, the same was not true for group therapy. Although the group was scheduled to meet three times each week, Peter refused to attend the meetings during the second week of his stay in the hospital. He asserted that, since his symptoms had gone away, he had nothing in common with the "psychos in the therapy group." This issue had the potential of becoming the basis of a power struggle between Peter and the treatment staff.

Peter realized that he would be forfeiting some unit privileges, but he was firm in his insistence. Although I would have preferred that he participate, I realized that on some level he was trying to make a statement about his need to be autonomous. Because he was so cooperative in every other way, and he did not balk about the administrative consequences of his choice, I decided to let the issue rest.

As we approached the point of discharge, I asked Peter what his preference would be regarding aftercare. He asked me if I would be willing to continue seeing him for "a couple more weeks." I believe that Peter realized that his condition warranted a longer term of follow-up therapy. I pointed out to Peter that he had been through a bout with a major psychological disorder. Even though he was feeling fine, he was still vulnerable, and ongoing treatment made sense. I remember the tone of his sarcasm as he asked me, "So how many weeks of therapy do I need, Dr. Tobin?" I responded that 6 months of regular follow-up sessions, perhaps one every other week, would be most helpful. At that point, we would re-evaluate and make a decision about subsequent treatment. He went along with my plan and responded quite positively in our work, every other week, for the following 6 months. He continued to take lithium, and there was no evidence of mood symptoms throughout that period.

At the end of 6 months, Peter had made some important life changes. He had applied for a job as a bank teller, and he had enrolled in an educational support program in which the bank subsidized part-time college courses. Once he had made this move, Peter communicated that he was "feeling OK" and that he wanted to reduce the frequency of sessions to once a month. I concurred with this plan. What I was less comfortable with, however, was Peter's decision to stop taking lithium. He felt that he was over his "sickness" and that he didn't want to take medication he no longer needed. I reviewed the risks with him, but I respected his right to make his own decision. Five months went by, and Peter was doing very well, when suddenly he found himself feeling energized and "high." He called me with a tone of euphoria in his voice to cancel our session, and I sensed that he might once again become manic. He responded to my urgent request that he come in for a session that day. With great ambivalence, he followed my recommendation to resume his medication.

We met monthly for another year, and now Peter contacts me, usually with a brief phone call once every year, on the day after his birthday, to let me know that "all's well."

Sarah Tobin, PhD

SUMMARY

- Nearly half the population is afflicted with a diagnosable psychological disorder at some point in their lives. Approximately 25 percent of these people seek professional help from clinicians, 15 percent from other professional sources; the remainder from informal sources of support or go without help. Clinicians are found within several professions, such as psychiatry, psychology, social work, nursing, and family counseling. They are professionals who are trained to be objective observers of

behavior, facilitators of growth, and resources for people facing difficult situations.

- Clinicians and researchers use the *Diagnostic and Statistical Manual of Mental Disorders,* fourth edition (*DSM-IV-TR*), which contains descriptions of all psychological disorders. In recent editions, the authors of the *DSM* have strived to meet the criterion of reliability, so that a given diagnosis will be consistently applied to anyone showing a particular set of symptoms. At the same time, researchers have worked to ensure the validity of the classification system, so that the various diagnoses represent real and distinct clinical phenomena. The development of the most recent edition, the *DSM-IV-TR,* involved a three-stage process, including a comprehensive review of published research, thorough analyses of the research data, and field trials. The authors of the *DSM* consider a phenomenon a mental disorder if it is clinically significant; if it is reflected in a behavioral or psychological syndrome; if it is associated with distress, impairment, or risk; and if it is not expectable or culturally sanctioned. The *DSM-IV-TR* is based on a medical model orientation, in which disorders, whether physical or psychological, are viewed as diseases. The classification system is descriptive rather than explanatory, and it is categorical rather than dimensional. Diagnoses are categorized in terms of relevant areas of functioning, called axes: Axis I (Clinical Disorders), Axis II (Personality Disorders and Mental Retardation), Axis III (General Medical Conditions), Axis IV (Psychosocial and Environmental Problems), and Axis V (Global Assessment of Functioning).

■ The diagnostic process involves using all relevant information to arrive at a label that characterizes a client's disorder. Clinicians first attend to a client's reported and observable symptoms. The diagnostic criteria in *DSM-IV-TR* are then considered, and alternative diagnoses are ruled out by means of a differential diagnostic process. Going beyond the diagnostic label, clinicians develop a case formulation, an analysis of the client's development and the factors that might have influenced his or her current psychological status. Clinicians also attend to ethnic and cultural contributions to a psychological problem.

■ Once a diagnosis is determined, a treatment plan is developed. The treatment plan includes issues pertaining to immediate management, short-term goals, and long-term goals. A treatment site is recommended, such as a psychiatric hospital, an outpatient service, a halfway house, a day treatment program, or another appropriate setting. The modality of treatment is specified and may involve individual psychotherapy, couple or family therapy, group therapy, or milieu therapy. The clinician will also approach the treatment within the context of a given theoretical perspective or a combination of several perspectives. After a plan is developed, clinicians implement treatment, with particular attention to the fact that the quality of the relationship between the client and the clinician is a crucial determinant of whether therapy will succeed. Although many interventions are effective, some are not. Mental health professionals know that change is difficult and that many obstacles may stand in the way of attaining a positive outcome.

KEY TERMS

See Glossary for definitions

Axis   45
Base rate   41
Case formulation   52
Client   38
Clinical psychologist   40
Community mental health center
  (CMHC)   59
Comorbid   39
Culture-bound syndromes   53
Day treatment program   59
Decision tree   51

*Diagnostic and Statistical Manual of
  Mental Disorders (DSM)*   40
Differential diagnosis   51
Family therapy   60
Global Assessment of Functioning
  (GAF) scale   49
Group therapy   60
Halfway house   59
Individual psychotherapy   59
Milieu therapy   60
Modality   59

Multiaxial system   45
Neurosis   44
Patient   38
Principal diagnosis   52
Prognosis   49
Psychiatrist   40
Psychological testing   40
Psychosis   44
Reliability   41
Syndrome   43
Validity   41

 ## INTERNET RESOURCE

To get more information on the material covered in this chapter, visit our website at **www.mhhe.com/halgin5.** There you will find more information, resources, and links to topics of interest.

CHAPTER 3

Assessment

Wednesday afternoons provided me with interesting opportunities outside of the psychiatric institution where I worked most of my week. My half-day of consultation at the nearby university's counseling center afforded a different perspective on clinical work. Not only did I supervise some of the graduate student trainees, but I also taught a seminar in psychological testing. For the seminar, I relied on the assessment material that I collected from testing clients in the counseling center.

It was a Wednesday afternoon early in October when Ben Robsham, a 21-year-old college junior, stopped by the clinic during walk-in hours. My schedule was completely full for the afternoon, but my 2:00 supervision student was running late. Marie Furcolo, the clinic's receptionist, came down to my office and asked me if I could possibly spend a few minutes with a young man, Ben Robsham, who was in the waiting room. Marie explained that she felt bad for Ben, because this was the third time he had stopped by the clinic during walk-in hours. Each time he had been turned away, because the clinician on duty was busy with clinical crises and was unable to meet with him to answer a few questions he had about psychological testing. Despite my hectic schedule, I felt it important to be responsive to Ben, thinking in the back of my mind that his simple request might be a cover for a serious problem.

The testing case of Ben was different from the customary assessments I had conducted and presented to my class. Most of the assessment clients were individuals about whom there were diagnostic or treatment planning questions. I couldn't think of an instance of a person coming to the clinic requesting testing because he was "interested in finding out what psychological tests were like."

When I approached Ben in the waiting room to introduce myself, I was struck by my initial impression of him. He was sitting in a distant corner of the room, staring intently at the floor. It seemed that he was muttering something, but I wasn't sure if he was talking to himself or humming a song. His clothing was the typical casual clothing commonly worn by college students—jeans and a plaid shirt—but there were a few aspects of his appearance that seemed odd. Although it was a relatively warm afternoon, Ben wore a wool knit hat over his hair and ears. On his hands he wore sleek black leather gloves, the kind that athletes use in sports, such as golf and handball. In introducing myself, I reached out my hand, which Ben firmly grasped without removing his glove. He stared intensely into my eyes and said with a tone of fear in his voice, "Can we please go to your office, and get out of this public place?" Although his request seemed emphatic and intense, it is not uncommon for clients who come to the counseling center to feel self-conscious and concerned that they might be embarrassed if someone they know were to see them seeking professional help.

As we walked down the hallway, it was evident that Ben was not interested in small talk but, rather, was eager to get right to the business at hand. Even in the few moments since we had met, I had been able to develop a fairly clear impression that Ben had more on his mind than just curiosity about the nature of psychological testing. I quickly came to the conclusion that I was interacting with a young man who was experiencing emotional instability and was feeling needy and frightened.

As soon as Ben took a seat in my office, he got right to the point. He had heard from one of his friends that psychological testing was done in the counseling center, and he had become curious about what it would be like to be tested. He stated that he might even learn some "neat stuff" about himself. Although many people are intrigued by psychological testing, there was a strange quality about the way in which Ben discussed the testing issue. He asked me whether "the police" would have access to the testing results. When I asked why he would have such a concern, he claimed that police officers had been following him for several months, since the day he had collided with a police car while rid-ing his bike. Apparently, a police officer had been quite stern with him that day, yelling at Ben as he lay in the street with a minor concussion. No citation was written, nor did Ben suffer any lasting injury, but he grew increasingly concerned that there would be legal repercussions. After hearing this story and Ben's concerns, I reassured him that the test results would be kept confidential. At the same time, I felt a certain level of alarm about the fact that he was troubled by such worries. My concern intensified after asking him why he was wearing a hat and sports gloves. At first, Ben hesitated, apparently reluctant to share the reason for this strange attire, but he then cautiously proceeded to explain. Almost as if he was joking, he said, "It's a good idea to cover up some of your identifying characteristics, just in case . . ." When I asked him, "In case of what?" he responded, "I know it sounds far out to you, but in case someone is trying to identify you for something they think you've done—like a crime or something." I continued to probe about why Ben thought it possible that he could be perceived as a criminal, but he laughed it off and said that he was "just kidding."

By this point in my dealings with Ben, it was evident that this young man had more on his mind than just some questions about psychological testing. Rather, it was quite likely that he was suffering from a psychological disorder and was using the pretext of psychological testing as a route by which to gain access to professional help. I gently raised this possibility with Ben, to which he responded with annoyance by saying, "Can't you shrinks just take something at face value, without reading all sorts of weird meanings into it?" Rather than be offended by what Ben said, I decided to put it aside and accommodated his request for psychological testing. For whatever reason, this was the route Ben was choosing to reach out for help, and I felt I might be able to make a difference in his life.

Sarah Tobin, PhD

As you read the opening case report about Ben's request for psychological testing, certain questions probably came to mind. Perhaps you wondered whether the police might actually be following Ben. Maybe you thought that Ben seemed paranoid. Perhaps it crossed your mind that Ben was actually looking for professional help. If you were Dr. Tobin, how would you go about finding the answers to these questions? First, you would want to talk with Ben and find out more about his concerns. You would possibly find, however, that talking with him did not really answer your questions. He could sound very convincing and present you with "facts" to document his concerns about the police. At the end of your interview, you still would not know whether his concerns were legitimate. You would want to gather more data that would include a careful study of how Ben thinks, behaves, and organizes his world. You would also want to know about his personality and emotional stability. The most efficient way to gather this information is to conduct what is called a psychological assessment.

A clinician uses the clinical interview to gather information and establish rapport with a client.

What Is a Psychological Assessment?

When you meet people for the first time, you usually "size them up." You may try to figure out how smart they are, how nice they are, or how mature they are. In certain circumstances, you may be trying to solve other puzzles, such as whether a car salesperson really has your best interests in mind or is trying to take advantage of your naiveté. Perhaps you are trying to decide whether to accept a classmate's invitation to go on a date. You will probably base your decision on your appraisal of that person's motives and personality. Or consider what you would do if a professor suggests that members of the class pair up to study. You are faced with the task of judging the intelligence of the other students to find the best study partner. All of these scenarios involve **assessment,** a procedure in which a clinician evaluates a person in terms of the psychological, physical, and social factors that have the most influence on the individual's functioning.

Clinicians approach the tasks of assessment with particular goals in mind. These goals can include establishing a diagnosis for someone with a psychological disorder, determining a person's intellectual capacity, predicting a person's appropriateness for a particular job, and evaluating whether someone is mentally competent to stand trial. Depending on the questions to be answered by the assessment, the clinician selects the most appropriate tools. For example, a psychologist asked by a teacher to evaluate a third-grader's mathematical ability would use a very different kind of assessment technique than if asked to evaluate the child's emotional adjustment.

The kinds of techniques used in assessment vary in their focus and degree of structure. There are assessment tools that focus on brain structure and functioning, others that assess personality, and still others that are oriented toward intellectual functioning. These tools range from those that are very structured and follow carefully defined instructions and procedures to those that allow for flexibility on the part of the examiner.

Clinical Interview

The clinical interview is the most commonly used assessment tool for developing an understanding of a client and the nature of the client's current problems, history, and future aspirations. An assessment interview consists of a series of questions administered in face-to-face interaction. The clinician may construct the questions as the interview unfolds or may follow a standard set of questions designed prior to the interview. Methods of recording the interview also vary. The interview may be audio- or videotape-recorded, written down during the interview, or reconstructed from the clinician's memory following the interview. In clinical settings, two kinds of interviews are used: the unstructured interview and the structured interview.

Unstructured Interview

The **unstructured interview** is a series of open-ended questions aimed at determining the client's reasons for being in treatment, symptoms, health status, family background, and life history. The interview is called "unstructured," because the interviewer adjusts the exact content and order of the questions rather than following a preset script. The interviewer formulates questions during the interview on the basis of the client's verbal responses to previous questions. Other information the clinician uses to construct questions includes nonverbal behaviors, such as eye contact, body position, tone of voice, hesitations, and other emotional cues.

The way the clinician approaches the interview depends, in part, on what kind of information the clinician is seeking. If the clinician seeks to make a diagnosis, for example, the interview questions would concern the precise nature of the client's symptoms and behaviors, such as mood disturbances, changes in eating or sleeping patterns, or levels of anxiety. However, as you saw in Chapter 2, some people seek professional psychological help for problems that are not diagnosable psychological disorders. For example, when interviewing a woman who is dissatisfied with her job and her deteriorating marriage, the clinician may feel that it is inappropriate to focus entirely on diagnosis. Instead, the clinician works toward developing insight into what factors are causing this woman's current distress.

An important part of the unstructured interview is history taking, in which the clinician asks the client to provide family information and a chronology of past life events. The main objective of history taking is to gain a clear understanding of the client's life and family. History taking should provide the clinician with enough information to write a summary of the major turning points in the client's life and the ways in which the client's current symptoms or concerns fit into this sequence of events. In some cases, clear links can be drawn between the current problem and an earlier event, such as childhood trauma. Most of the time, however, the determinants of current problems cannot be identified this precisely, and the clinician attempts to draw inferences about the possible contributors to current problems. For example, a man told a college counselor that he was looking for help in overcoming his intense anxiety in situations involving public speaking. The counselor first looked for connections between the student's problem and specific events related to this problem, such as a disastrous experience in high school. Finding no clear connection, the counselor inquired about possible relationships between the student's current problem and a more general pattern of insecurity throughout childhood and adolescence.

In most cases, history taking covers the client's personal history and family history. Personal history includes important events and relationships in the client's life. The clinician asks about experiences in such realms as school performance, peer relationships, employment, and health. **Family history** covers major events in the lives of the client's relatives, including those who are closest to the client as well as more distantly related family members. The questions asked about family history may be particularly important when attempting to determine whether a client may have inherited a diathesis for a disorder with strong genetic components. For example, the fact that a client has relatives going back several generations who suffered from serious depression would be an important piece of information for a clinician to use in evaluating a client who is showing symptoms of depression.

Let's return to the case of Ben, so that you can get an idea of what might take place in an unstructured interview. Read the excerpt from Dr. Tobin's interview focusing on Ben's history (Table 3.1). Take note of how her questions follow naturally from Ben's answers and how there appears to be a natural flow in the dialogue. Imagine yourself interviewing someone like Ben, and try to think of some of the questions you might want to ask in your effort to understand his needs and concerns. What features of this interview stand out? You probably notice that Ben seems quite fearful and evasive as he talks about some matters, particularly his current experiences. He is particularly concerned about the issue of privacy, more so than might be warranted, given the confidential nature of the professional context. At the same time, he is unduly worried about the possibility that he may sound so disturbed that hospitalization might be considered, yet he has very unusual beliefs and perceptions that might lead you to wonder whether he is, in fact, out of touch with reality. As he describes some of his relationships, even the one with his father, you may notice some seemingly paranoid thinking. All of these issues are of considerable concern to Dr. Tobin in her effort to understand the nature of Ben's problems.

Structured and Semistructured Interviews

The **structured interview** consists of a standardized series of questions, with predetermined wording and order. The items are formally written, and the sequence of questioning is prescribed, thus involving less reliance on the clinical experience and judgment of the interviewer. The **semistructured interview** consists of a standardized series of questions in which the interviewer has the discretion to ask follow-up questions that will clarify the person's responses. The purpose of a semistructured interview is to elicit responses that can subsequently be rated according to predetermined criteria. In clinical practice, the delineation between structured and semistructured interviews may not always be precise, due to the fact that clinicians may adapt these instruments in some situations. The evaluation of structured and semistructured interviews is based on objective, predetermined criteria and, consequently, differs from unstructured interviews, which differ substantially from one interviewer to the next.

Structured and semistructured interviews are designed to help researchers and clinicians attain precise accuracy in diagnosing clients. While some interviews cover a range of possible disorders, others have a narrow focus, with the goal of determining whether the interviewee has a given disorder, such as schizophrenia, a mood disorder, or an anxiety disorder.

An example of a commonly used structured interview is the Anxiety Disorders Interview Schedule for *DSM-IV* (ADIS-IV) (Dinardo, Brown, & Barlow, 1994). Examples of semistructured interviews (despite the word "structured" in the instrument's name) are the Structured Clinical Interview for *DSM-IV-TR* Axis I disorders (SCID-I) (First, Spitzer, Gibbon, & Williams, 1997) and the Structured Clinical Interview for *DSM-IV* Personality Disorders (SCID-II) (First, Gibbon, Spitzer, & Williams, 1997). There are variations of the SCID for use in research, as

---

TABLE 3.1 Excerpts from Ben's History Taking

DR. TOBIN: Can you tell me what brings you here today?

BEN: I'd like to take some of the psychological tests I've heard about.

DR. TOBIN: Explain to me what you mean.

BEN: Well, my psychology teacher said that these tests can help you tell whether you're crazy or not.

DR. TOBIN: Is that a concern for you?

BEN: I've had some pretty strange experiences lately, and, when I tell other people about them, they tell me I'm nuts.

DR. TOBIN: Tell me about these experiences.

BEN: Well, sometimes . . . [pause] . . . I don't know if I should tell you this, but . . . [pause] . . . I know that as soon as you hear this you'll want to lock me up . . . but, anyway, here goes. For the past few months, the police have been following me. It all started one day when I was walking by a student demonstration on campus where people were being arrested. I stayed away from the action, because I didn't want to get involved, you know, but I know that the police were watching me. A few days after the demonstration, I saw Nazi soldiers out in my backyard taking pictures of my house and looking in through the windows. You know, this sounds so crazy, I'm not sure I believe it myself. All I know is, it scares the hell out of me, so can I please have the testing to see if I'm losing my mind or not?

DR. TOBIN: We can talk about that a little bit later, but right now I'd like to hear more about the experiences you're having.

BEN: I'd really rather not talk about them anymore. They're too scary.

DR. TOBIN: I can understand that you feel scared, but it would be helpful for me to get a better sense of what you're going through.

BEN: [pause] . . . Well, OK, but you're sure no one else will hear about this? . . .

[Later in the interview, Dr. Tobin inquired about Ben's history.]

DR. TOBIN: I'd like to hear something about your early life experiences, such as your family relationships and your school experiences. First, tell me something about your family when you were growing up.

BEN: Well . . . there's me and my sister, Doreen. She's 2 years older than me. And we haven't ever really gotten along.

My mother . . . well . . . Doreen claims that my mother treated me better than Doreen. Maybe that's true, but not because I wanted it that way.

DR. TOBIN: Tell me more about your relationship with your mother.

BEN: I hated the way she . . . my mother . . . hovered over me. She wouldn't let me make a move without her knowing about it. She always worried that I would get sick or that I would hurt myself. If I was outside playing in the backyard, she would keep coming outside and telling me to be careful. I would get so mad. Even my father would get angry about the way she babied me all the time.

DR. TOBIN: What about your relationship with your father?

BEN: I can't say that I had much of one. No one in the family did. He always came home late, after we had gone to bed. Maybe he was trying to avoid the rest of us or something. I don't know, maybe he was working against the family in some way.

DR. TOBIN: What do you mean, "working against the family"?

BEN: I don't want to get into it.

[Later in the interview]

DR. TOBIN: I'd like to hear about the things that interested you as a child.

BEN: You mean like hobbies, friends, things like that?

DR. TOBIN: Yes.

BEN: I was a loner. That's what Doreen always called me. She would call me a "loser and a loner." I hated those names, but she was right. I spent most of the time in my room, with earphones on, listening to rock music. It was sort of neat. I would imagine that I was a rock star, and I would get lost in these wild thoughts about being important and famous and all. Staying home was OK. But going to school stunk.

DR. TOBIN: Let's talk about your experiences in school.

BEN: Teachers hated me. They liked to embarrass me . . . always complaining that I wouldn't look them in the eye. Why should I? If I made the smallest mistake, they made a federal case out of it. One time . . . we were studying state capitals and the teacher, Mrs. Edison, asked me to name the capital of Tennessee. I didn't know what a capital was. I said, "I don't know anything about capitalism." She got pissed off and called me a "wise guy."

---

well as clinical contexts, and for administration to patients and nonpatients. Major parts of the SCID have been translated into Spanish, French, German, Danish, Italian, Hebrew, Zulu, Turkish, Portuguese, and Greek.

Researchers and clinicians working within the U.S. Alcohol, Drug, and Mental Health Administration (ADAMHA) and the World Health Organization (1997) have developed assessment instruments that can be used cross-culturally. The Composite International Diagnostic Interview (CIDI), which has been translated into many languages, is a comprehensive standardized instrument for the assessment of mental disorders that facilitates psychiatric epidemiological research throughout the world. Table 3.2 contains some sample items from this instrument. New applications and developments of the CIDI have taken place in recent years, as experts have continued their efforts to gather cross-cultural assessments

TABLE 3.2 Sample Items from the CIDI

These questions are from the section of the CIDI concerning symptoms related to animal phobias. They illustrate both the scope and the depth of the items on this structured diagnostic interview. Similar questions on this interview concern other DSM-IV Axis I disorders, including substance abuse, mood disorders, schizophrenia, other anxiety disorders, and sleep disorders.

Modified Sample CIDI Anxiety Disorder Questions

A. There are things that make some people so afraid that they avoid them, even when there is no real danger. Have you ever had an unusually strong fear or needed to avoid things like animals, heights, storms, being in closed spaces, and seeing blood?

If Yes:

1. Have you ever had an unusually strong fear of any of these living things, such as insects, snakes, birds, or other animals?
2. Have you ever avoided being near insects, snakes, birds, or other animals, even though there was no real danger?
3. Did the (fear/avoidance) of insects, snakes, birds, or other animals ever interfere with your life or activities a lot?
4. Was your (fear/avoidance) of insects, snakes, birds, or other animals ever excessive, that is, much stronger than in other people?
5. Was your (fear/avoidance) of insects, snakes, birds, or other animals ever unreasonable, that is, much stronger than it should have been?
6. Were you ever very upset with yourself for (having the fear of/avoiding) insects, snakes, birds, or other animals?

7. When you had to be near insects, snakes, birds, or other animals, or thought you would have to be, did you usually become very upset?

B. When you were near insects, snakes, birds, or other animals, or thought you would have to be . . . (the following questions are asked until two are answered "no").

1. Did your heart pound or race?
2. Did you sweat?
3. Did you tremble or shake?
4. Did you have a dry mouth?
5. Were you short of breath?
6. Did you feel like you were choking?
7. Did you have pain or discomfort in your chest?
8. Did you have nausea or discomfort in your stomach?
9. Were you dizzy or feeling faint?
10. Did you feel that you or things around you were unreal?
11. Were you afraid that you might lose control of yourself, act in a crazy way, or pass out?
12. Were you afraid that you might die?
13. Did you have hot flushes or chills?
14. Did you have numbness or tingling sensations?

C. When was the (first/last) time you (were afraid of/avoided) insects, snakes, birds, or other animals?

D. Between the first time and the last time, was this (strong fear/ avoidance) of insects, snakes, birds, or other animals usually present whenever you were near them or thought you would have to be near them?

Source: From Composite International Diagnostic Interview (CIDI) 1997. Reprinted by permission of World Health Organization. Geneva. Switzerland.

of psychological disorders (Kessler et al., 2004; Kessler & Ustun, 2004).

The International Personality Disorder Examination (IPDE), another cross-cultural instrument, was developed by Armand Loranger and his colleagues (Loranger et al., 1994) to assess the personality disorders that are listed in the *DSM-IV* and the International Classification of Diseases. The authors have demonstrated that this instrument is remarkably accurate in assessing personality disorders (Lenzenweger, Loranger, Korfine, & Neff, 1997), and stable over time (Lenzenweger, 1999). These findings are especially impressive in light of the fact that it relies on self-report. The researchers developed this scale by using the structure of an earlier instrument that had been designed for use in North America. The international version provided a valuable opportunity for the standardized assessment of personality disorders in different cultures and

countries, and it has been published in many languages, including German, Hindi, Japanese, Norwegian, Swahili, Italian, Spanish, Russian, and Estonian. The test developers were concerned about consistency in the administration of this instrument, but they found it was important to acknowledge that departures would have to be made from the literal text to maintain communication with illiterate subjects and those speaking a regional or tribal dialect.

Because the intent of the IPDE is to assess personality disorders, the focus of the instrument is on the subjects' behaviors and characteristics that have been enduring, defined by the authors as having been present for at least a 5-year period. The interviewer begins by giving the subject the following instructions: "The questions I am going to ask concern what you are like most of the time. I'm interested in what has been typical of you throughout your life, and not just recently." The interviewer then moves into six realms of inquiry: work, self, interpersonal relationships, affects, reality testing, and impulse control.

Instruments such as the IPDE present challenges because of their reliance on the respondent's self-report. Sometimes people are unaware of personal characteristics that are regarded as objectionable, or they may be reluctant to admit to negative personal aspects. To offset this problem, clinicians can use additional sources of data, such as information from relatives, other mental health professionals, and clinical records.

Although structured and semistructured interviews are very important in research contexts, some experts question their utility in the typical clinical situation. Some authors contend that, in some circumstances, diagnoses based on therapy sessions will be more accurate than diagnoses based on formalized instruments, because clinicians have the opportunity to observe the client and interact with the client over time (Garb, 2005).

A clinician conducts a mental status examination.

Mental Status Examination

Clinicians use the term mental status (or present status) to refer to what the client thinks about and how the client thinks, talks, and acts. Later, when we discuss particular psychological disorders, we will frequently refer to symptoms reflecting disturbances in mental status. A clinician uses the **mental status examination** to assess a client's behavior and functioning, with particular attention to the symptoms associated with psychological disturbance (Trzepacz & Baker, 1993).

The term *examination* implies that this is a formal instrument, but in reality it is an informal evaluation in which the clinician assesses a client. There are, however, a few specialized mental status examinations that focus on the diagnosis of specific disorders. The Mini-Mental State Examination (Folstein, Folstein, & McHugh, 1975) is one example of a structured mental status instrument shown to have success in the psychological assessment of individuals with Alzheimer's disease and other brain syndromes that are difficult to identify through other assessment methods (Folstein & Folstein, 2000).

In conducting a mental status examination, the clinician takes note of the client's behavior, orientation, content of thought, thinking style and language, affect and mood, perceptual experiences, sense of self, motivation, intelligence, and insight. The report of a mental status examination incorporates both the client's responses to specific questions and the clinician's objective observations of how the client looks, behaves, and speaks.

Appearance and Behavior

What do you notice when you meet someone for the first time? In all likelihood, you attend to the way the person responds to you, whether there are any oddities of behavior, and even how

the individual is dressed. Similarly, in gathering data about the total picture of the individual, the clinician takes note of the client's appearance, level of consciousness, mannerisms, attire, grooming, activity level, and style of interaction. Consider one of Dr. Tobin's cases, a 20-year-old man whom she assessed in the emergency room. Dr. Tobin was struck by the fact that Pierre looked at least 10 years older, that he was dressed in torn and tattered clothing, and that he had a crusty wound on his forehead. In her report, she also made note of the fact that Pierre maintained a stiff posture, refused to remove his hands from his jacket pockets, and never made eye contact with her. In response to Dr. Tobin's questions, Pierre mumbled some unintelligible comments under his breath. These are odd behaviors in our culture that might be important pieces of information as Dr. Tobin develops a more comprehensive understanding of Pierre. Some of these behaviors are found in people with certain forms of psychosis.

Although every bit of information can have diagnostic significance, the movements of a person's body and level of activity are especially noteworthy. The term *motor behavior* refers to the ways in which a client moves. Even clients who are unwilling or unable to speak can communicate a great deal of important information through their bodily movements. For example, one man may be so restless that he cannot stop pacing, whereas another man is so slowed down that he moves in a lethargic and listless manner. **Hyperactivity** involves abnormally energized physical activity, characterized by quick movements and fast talking. Sometimes hyperactivity is evidenced by **psychomotor agitation,** in which the individual appears to be restless and stirred up. In contrast, **psychomotor retardation** involves abnormally slow movements and lethargy.

Perhaps the individual shows some oddities of behavior that are not particularly bizarre but are nevertheless notable, and possibly diagnostically important. These include unusual mannerisms, such as dramatic gesturing or a facial tic in which the individual blinks rapidly when speaking.

Abnormalities of bodily movements can take extreme forms, such as rigid posturing or immobilization. **Catatonia** refers to extreme motor disturbances in a psychotic disorder not attributable to physiological causes. In some instances of catatonia the individual appears to be in a coma, with rigid and unmovable limbs. In other cases, the catatonic person may be extremely flexible and responsive to being "molded" into position by someone else. Consider the case of Alice, who sits motionless all day long in a catatonic state. Even if someone were to stand in front of her and shout or try to startle her, she would not respond. There are other forms of catatonia, in which the individual engages in excited, usually repetitive behavior, such as repeated flailing of the arms. Later in this book, you will read about certain disorders that are characterized by various forms of catatonia.

Another disturbance of behavior is a **compulsion,** a repetitive and seemingly purposeful behavior performed in response to uncontrollable urges or according to a ritualistic or stereotyped set of rules. Compulsions, which involve unwanted behaviors, can take over the individual's life, causing considerable distress. A compulsion can be a simple repetitive action, such as a clap of the hand before speaking, or it can be a complex series of ritualized behaviors. For example, before opening any door, a woman feels that she must scratch her forehead and then clean the doorknob with her handkerchief five times prior to turning the knob. There are many types of compulsive behavior, and you will learn more about them in the chapters in which we discuss certain anxiety and personality disorders.

Orientation

People with some kinds of disorders are disoriented and out of touch with basic facts about themselves and their surroundings. **Orientation** is a person's awareness of time, place, and identity. Disturbances in orientation are used in diagnosing disorders associated with some forms of brain damage and disease, such as amnesia and dementia. They may also be signs of psychotic disorders, such as schizophrenia.

Content of Thought

The **content of thought,** or ideas that fill a client's mind, is tremendously significant in the assessment process. The clinician must carefully seek out information about the various types of disturbing thought content that can be associated with many psychological disorders. Some of this inquiry takes place in the flow of clinical conversation with the client, but, in some parts of the mental status examination, the clinician may ask pointed questions, especially when there is some suggestion of serious thought disturbance. The clinician may ask a question, such as "Do you have thoughts that you can't get out of your head?" Or the clinician may follow up on something that seems odd or idiosyncratic about what the client has reported, as when a client reports having had previous occupations that cannot possibly have a basis in reality. A man who has spent his adult life in a state hospital but believes he is a famous movie actor may answer questions about his occupation that are consistent with his belief, and in the process he may reveal his particular disturbance of thought content. Clinicians listen for these kinds of clues to develop a better understanding of the nature of the client's disorder.

Of particular interest to the clinician are disturbances of thought content known as obsessions. An **obsession** is an unwanted thought, word, phrase, or image that persistently and repeatedly comes into a person's mind and causes distress. No amount of effort can erase this obsession from the individual's thinking.

Most people have experienced transient obsessional thinking, such as following a breakup with a lover or even a heated argument in which the dialogue of the argument recurrently intrudes into consciousness. One common form of obsession involves torturous doubt about an act or a decision, usually of a trivial nature, such as whether one paid too much for a 20 dollar item. Unlike these ordinary occurrences, clinically significant obsessions are enduring and can torment a person for years.

Another common obsession is an individual's irrational concern that he or she has done or is about to do something evil or dangerous, such as inadvertently poisoning others. Obsessions and compulsions often go hand in hand, as in the case of a man who was obsessively worried that a car accident might take place outside his apartment. Consequently, he walked to the window every 10 minutes to make sure that the streetlight had not burned out. He was afraid that a burned-out streetlight would increase the likelihood of cars colliding in the darkness.

Obsessions are certainly irrational, but even further removed from reality are **delusions,** which are deeply entrenched false beliefs that are not consistent with the client's intelligence or cultural background (Table 3.3 gives some examples of delusions). Despite the best efforts of others to convince an individual that these beliefs are irrational, people who have delusions are highly resistant to more realistic views. In determining the presence of delusional thinking, the clinician needs to be aware of the person's intelligence and cultural background. For example, a very religious woman may believe in miracles, which people who are not familiar with her religion might regard as delusional.

Sometimes a person has very unusual ideas that are not so extreme as to be regarded as delusional. **Overvalued ideas** are thoughts that have an odd and absurd quality but are not usually bizarre or deeply entrenched. For example, a man believes

TABLE 3.3 Examples of Delusions

All of these delusions involve a form of *false belief*; that is, they are inconsistent with external reality, and have no validity to anyone except the person who believes in them.

Type of Delusion	Description
Grandeur	A grossly exaggerated conception of the individual's own importance. Such delusions range from beliefs that the person has an important role in society to the belief that the person is actually Christ, Napoleon, or Hitler.
Control	The feeling that one is being controlled by others, or even by machines or appliances. For example, a man may believe that his actions are being controlled by the radio, which is "forcing" him to perform certain actions against his will.
Reference	The belief that the behavior of others or certain objects or events are personally referring to oneself. For example, a woman believes that a soap opera is really telling the story of her life. Or a man believes that the sale items at a local food market are targeted at his own particular dietary deficiencies.
Persecution	The belief that another person or persons are trying to inflict harm on the individual or on that individual's family or social group. For example, a woman feels that an organized group of politically liberal individuals is attempting to destroy the right-wing, political organization to which she belongs.
Self-blame	Feelings of remorse without justification. A man holds himself responsible for a famine in Africa because of certain unkind or sinful actions that he believes he has committed.
Somatic	Inappropriate concerns about one's own body, typically relating to a disease. For example, without any justification, a woman believes she has brain cancer. Adding an even more bizarre note, she believes that ants have invaded her head and are eating away at her brain.
Infidelity	A false belief usually associated with pathological jealousy involving the notion that one's lover is being unfaithful. A man lashes out in violent rage at his wife, insisting that she is having an affair with the mailman because of her eagerness for the mail to arrive each day.
Thought broadcasting	The idea that one's thoughts are being broadcast to others. A man believes that everyone else in the room can hear what he is thinking, or possibly that his thoughts are actually being carried over the airways on television or radio.
Thought insertion	The belief that thoughts are being inserted into one's mind by outside forces. For example, a woman concludes that her thoughts are not her own but that they are being placed there to control her or upset her.

that a credit card that ends in an odd number will cause him to have bad luck. Each time he submits an application for a new credit card, he explains to the issuer that he will refuse to accept the card unless the last digit is an even number. In **magical thinking,** there is also a peculiar and illogical content to the individual's thought, but in this case there is a connection in the individual's mind between two objects or events that other people would see as unrelated. For example, a woman believes that, every time she takes her clothes to the dry cleaners, a natural disaster occurs somewhere in the world within the following day. Although the presence of overvalued ideas or magical thinking does not provide evidence that a person has a psychotic disorder, clinicians make note of these symptoms, because they can be signals that a client is psychologically deteriorating.

Violent ideation is another important area to assess. Clinicians assess the possibility of violent thoughts, either in the form of suicidal thinking or thoughts about harming, and possibly killing, someone else. As you will see later in this book, when we discuss the assessment of suicide in Chapter 9, clinicians are usually quite direct when inquiring about self-injurious intentions, particularly with depressed clients.

Thinking Style and Language

In addition to listening to what a person thinks, the clinician also listens for evidence of **thinking style and language** to indicate how a person thinks. This includes information on the client's vocabulary use and sentence structure. For example, when conversing with a man who is psychotic, you may have a difficult time grasping his words or meaning. His language may be illogical and unconnected. In listening to him during a mental status examination, a clinician would suspect that he has a

TABLE 3.4 Examples of Thought Disorder

Types of Thought Disorder	Description
Incoherence	Speech that is incomprehensible. For example, a client who is asked how he is feeling responds, "The gutter tree ain't here go far."
Loosening of associations	A flow of thoughts that is vague, unfocused, and illogical. In response to the question about how he is feeling, a man responds, "I'm feeling pretty good today, though I don't think that there is enough good in the world. I think that I should subscribe to *National Geographic*."
Illogical thinking	Thinking characterized by contradictions and erroneous conclusions. For example, a client who likes milk thinks that she must be part cat, because she knows that cats like milk.
Neologisms	Words invented by a person, or distortions of existing words to which a person has given new personalized meanings. For example, a woman expresses concerns about her homicidal fantasies, saying, "I can't stand these *gunly* thoughts of *murdeviousness*."
Blocking	The experience in which a person seemingly "loses" a thought in the midst of speaking, leading to a period of silence, ranging from seconds to minutes.
Circumstantiality	Speech that is indirect and delayed in reaching the point because of irrelevant and tedious details. In response to a simple question about the kind of work he does, a man responds with a long-winded description of his 20-year work history.
Tangentiality	Going completely off the track and never returning to the point in a conversation. For example, when asked how long she has been depressed, a woman begins speaking about her unhappy mood and ends up talking about the inadequacy of care in the United States for people who are depressed.
Clanging	Speech in which the sound, rather than the meaning of the words, determines the content of the individual's speech. When asked why he woke up so early, a man responds, "The bell on my clock, the smell from the sock, and the well was out of stock."
Confabulation	Fabricating facts or events to fill in voids in one's memory. These are not conscious lies but are attempts by the individual to respond to questions with answers that seem to approximate the truth. For example, although a client is not fully sure of whether or not he had eaten breakfast that morning, he gives a description of a typical breakfast in his household rather than a confident reporting of precisely what he had eaten that morning.
Echolalia	Persistent repetition or echoing of words or phrases, as if the person is intending to be mocking or sarcastic. When a woman is asked by her roommate, "What's the time?" she responds, "The time, the time, the time."
Flight of ideas	Fast-paced speech that, while usually intelligible, is marked by acceleration, abrupt changes of topic, and plays on words. A man rapidly speaks: "I have to go to work. I have to get there right away. I have to earn some money. I'll go broke."
Pressure of speech	Speech that is so rapid and driven that it seems as though the individual is being inwardly compelled to utter a stream of nonstop monologue. Flight of ideas usually involves pressure of speech.
Perseveration	Repetition of the same idea, word, or sound. A woman says, "I have to get dressed. I have to get dressed. My clothes, my clothes, I have to get dressed."

thought disorder, a disturbance in thinking or in using language. Examples of thought disorders are shown in Table 3.4.

Affect and Mood

Affect is an individual's outward expression of emotion. A feeling state becomes an affect when others can observe it. Clinicians attend to several components of affect, including appropriateness, intensity, mobility, and range.

In assessing affect, the clinician takes note of **inappropriate affect,** the extent to which a person's emotional expressiveness fails to correspond to the content of what is being discussed. For example, affect would be considered inappropriate if a woman were to giggle when asked how she feels about a recent death in her family.

The **intensity of affect,** or strength of emotional expression, provides important clinical clues that the clinician uses in forming a diagnosis. To describe abnormally low affective intensity, the clinician uses such terms as *blunted affect* (minimal expressiveness) and *flat affect* (complete lack of reactivity). By contrast, when the individual's affect seems abnormally strong, the clinician uses such terms as *exaggerated, heightened,* and *overdramatic affect.*

Affect is also described in terms of **range of affect,** or the extent and variety of emotional expression. Most people have a broad range of affect and are able to communicate sadness, happiness, anger, agitation, or calmness as the situation or discussion warrants. People with restricted affect show very few variations in their emotional responsiveness. This would be the case of a woman who remains tearful and sad in her emotional expressiveness, regardless of what is taking place or being discussed.

In contrast to affect, which is behavior that is outwardly expressed, **mood** refers to a person's experience of emotion, the way the person feels "inside." Some examples of emotions are depression, elation, anger, and anxiety. A clinician is particularly interested in assessing a client's mood, because the way the client characteristically feels has great diagnostic and treatment significance. A **normal,** or **euthymic, mood** is one that is neither unduly happy nor sad but shows day-to-day variations within a relatively limited and appropriate range. **Dysphoric mood** involves unpleasant feelings, such as sadness and irritability. **Euphoric mood** is more cheerful and elated than average, possibly even ecstatic. Although your mood might be elevated after succeeding at an important task, euphoric mood is a state in which you feel an exaggerated sense of happiness, elation, and excitement.

In addition to the characterizations of mood as normal, low, or high, there are other clusters of mood, including anger,

Affect is inferred from a person's facial expressions. What does this man's facial expression tell about his emotional state?

apprehension, and apathy. As you might infer, angry mood is experienced as feelings of hostility, rage, sullenness, and impatience. Apprehension connotes feeling anxious, fearful, overwhelmed, panicky, and tense. Those who are apathetic have feelings of dullness and blandness and are lacking motivation and concern about anything.

Perceptual Experiences

Individuals with psychological disorders often have disturbances in perception. A clinician would find out whether a client has these disturbances by asking questions such as whether he or she hears voices or sees things of which other people are not aware. **Hallucinations** are false perceptions not corresponding to the objective stimuli present in the environment. Unlike illusions, which involve the misperception of a real object, such as misperceiving a tree at night to be a man, hallucinations involve the perception of an object or a stimulus that is not there. As you can imagine, the experience of a hallucination can be distressing, even terrifying. Clinicians carefully scrutinize a client's experience of hallucinations, knowing that this symptom may be caused by a range of conditions, including reaction to trauma, the effect of substance intoxication or withdrawal, or a neurological condition, such as Alzheimer's disease or temporal lobe epilepsy.

Hallucinations are defined by the sense with which they are associated. **Auditory hallucinations,** which are the most common, involve hearing sounds, often voices or even entire conversations. With **command hallucinations,** an individual hears an instruction to take an action. For example, one man reported that, while eating at a lunch counter, he heard a voice that directed him to punch the person sitting next to him. Other common auditory hallucinations involve hearing voices making derogatory comments, such as "You're stupid."

Visual hallucinations involve the false visual perception of objects or persons. For some people, the visual hallucination may be chronic, as is reported in some individuals with Alzheimer's disease. For example, a woman claimed that she saw her deceased husband sitting at the table whenever she entered the kitchen.

Olfactory hallucinations, which are relatively uncommon, pertain to the sense of smell, possibly of an unpleasant odor, such as feces, garbage, or noxious gases. **Somatic hallucinations** involve false perceptions of bodily sensations, the most common of which involve tactile experiences. For example, a man reported the feeling that insects were crawling all over his body. **Gustatory hallucinations** are the least commonly reported and involve the false sensation of taste, usually unpleasant.

It is common for hallucinations to be associated with delusions. For example, a man who had a delusion of persecution also had olfactory hallucinations in which he believed that he constantly smelled toxic fumes that he believed were being piped into his room by his enemies.

Sense of Self

A number of psychological disorders alter the individual's personal identity or sense of "who I am." Clinicians assess this altered sense of self by asking clients to describe any strange bodily sensations or feelings of disconnectedness from their body. **Depersonalization** refers to an altered experience of the self, such as a feeling that one's body is not connected to one's mind. At times, the person may not feel "real." Other disturbances in sense of self become apparent when the clinician discovers that a client is experiencing **identity confusion,** which is a lack of a clear sense of who one is. This experience can range from confusion about one's role in the world to actual delusional thinking in which one believes oneself to be under the control of an external person or force.

Motivation

The clinician assesses motivation across a wide range of areas by asking the client to discuss how strongly he or she desires a lasting personality change or relief of emotional distress. With some psychological disorders, the client's motivation is so severely impaired that even ordinary life tasks seem insurmountable, much less the process of embarking on the time-consuming and effortful course of therapy. As surprising as it may seem, some individuals seem to prefer to remain in their present familiar state of unhappiness, rather than risk the uncertainty of facing a new and unknown set of challenges.

Cognitive Functioning

In a mental status examination, a clinician attempts to gauge a client's general level of intelligence as evidenced by level of general information, attention and concentration, memory, physical coordination, and capacity for abstraction and conceptualization. For example, a woman with an IQ significantly above average might use unusual or abstract words that give the impression that she has a thought disorder. Or a man's memory may be so impaired that the clinician hypothesizes that he is suffering from a neurological condition, such as Alzheimer's disease. In the mental status examination, the clinician's task is not to conduct a formal IQ test but, rather, to develop a general idea about the client's cognitive strengths and deficits.

Insight and Judgment

In a mental status examination, the clinician also attempts to assess a client's ability to understand the nature of his or her disorder. Along these lines, the clinician needs to determine a client's receptivity to treatment. A woman who has no understanding of the debilitating nature of her paranoid delusions is certainly not going to be very receptive to intervention by a mental health professional. She may even resist any such attempts because she regards them as proof that others are trying to control or hurt her.

Insight is understanding and awareness about oneself and one's world. For example, a college student notices that she becomes depressed on most Friday afternoons as she prepares to return home for weekend visits. On discussing her reaction with her roommate, she develops insight into the fact that she resents her father treating her like a child. In more serious clinical contexts, the client's level of understanding about the nature of problems and symptoms will set the stage for treatment. A man who is paranoid, but unable to see how his defensive style with others creates interpersonal distance, is not likely to be open to changing his behavior in order to become more emotionally accessible to others.

Judgment is the intellectual process in which an individual considers and weighs options in order to make a decision. Every day, each of us makes many judgments, some of which are inconsequential and others of which may have long-lasting effects. You have probably encountered people who have very poor judgment and make choices that are obviously unwise. Perhaps you know someone who repeatedly gets intimately involved with abusive partners and seems to lack the ability to make an objective assessment of these people before becoming involved. Or you may know someone who, when intoxicated, says or does things that are dramatically different from his or her behavior in a sober state. Similarly, people who are seriously disturbed lack the ability to make choices in their lives that are constructive or wise. They may put their physical health and safety at risk, and in some cases it is necessary for others to step in and help them make decisions that are self-protective.

Psychological Testing

Psychological testing covers a broad range of measurement techniques, all of which involve having people provide scorable information about their psychological functioning. The information that test-takers provide may concern their intellectual abilities, personalities, emotional states, attitudes, and behaviors that reflect lifestyle or interests.

It is very likely that you have had some form of psychological testing in your life and that your scores on these tests had a bearing on decisions made by you or about you, since psychological tests have become increasingly important in contemporary society. Because of this importance, psychologists have devoted intensive efforts to developing tests that accurately measure what they are designed to measure.

What Makes a Good Psychological Test?

Many popular magazines and newspapers publish so-called psychological tests. Items on these tests claim to measure such features of your personality as your potential for loving, how lonely you are, how devoted your romantic partner is, whether you have "too much anger," or whether you worry too much. These tests contain a number of scorable items, accompanied by a scale to tell you what your responses indicate about your personality. Although interesting and provocative, most tests published in the popular press fail to meet accepted standards for a good psychological test.

To show you the issues involved in developing a good psychological test, we will take an in-depth look at each criterion that plays a role in the process. These criteria are covered by the general term **psychometrics,** whose literal meaning, "measurement of the mind," reflects the goal of finding the most suitable tests for the psychological variables of interest to the researcher and clinician.

Reliability and validity are generally considered to be the two features most essential to determining a test's psychometric qualities. **Reliability** indicates the consistency of test scores, and **validity** the extent to which a test measures what it is designed to measure. Table 3.5 describes the types of reliability and validity.

A good psychological test is also one that follows standardized, or uniform, procedures for both test administration and scoring. For example, a national college entrance examination is supposed to be given under strict standardized conditions. The room should be quiet and well lit, the seats should be comfortable for test-taking, proctors should monitor the students so that no one has any unfair advantages, and the same instructions should be given to everyone. A standardized psychological test is intended to follow the same guidelines. Particularly important is the requirement that each person taking the test receives the same instructions. At times, because people with certain psychological disorders have problems focusing on test items or following instructions, the examiner may need to provide extra assistance or encouragement to complete the test. However, the examiner must not suggest how the test-taker should answer the questions or bias the test-taker's performance in any way. It is also important that the

Many magazines contain "personality" tests. This woman is completing a quiz to measure her self-esteem.

examiner not stretch the time limits beyond those allowed for the test.

Standardization also applies to the way tests are scored. The most straightforward scoring method involves adding up responses on a multiple-choice test or a test with items that are rated on numerical scales. Less straightforward are tests that involve judgments on the part of raters who must decide how to score the test-taker's responses. For the scoring to be standardized, the examiner must follow a prescribed set of rules that equates a given response with a particular score. The examiner must be sure not to let any biases interfere with the scoring procedure. This is particularly important when only one person does the scoring, as is the case with many established tests whose reliability has already been documented. When scoring an intelligence test, for example, it may be tempting for the examiner to try to give the test-taker the benefit of the doubt if the test-taker is someone who seems to have been trying hard and wants to do well. Conversely, examiners must be sensitive to their negative biases regarding certain types of clients and not inadvertently penalize them by scoring them lower than they deserve. To minimize such problems, people who administer and score standardized psychological tests receive extensive training and supervision in all of these procedures.

The term *standardization* is also used to refer to the basis for evaluating scores on a particular test. The college entrance examination, for example, has been given to vast numbers of high-school seniors over the years, and there is a known distribution of scores on the parts of this test. When evaluating a student's potential for college, the student's scores are compared with the national scores for the student's gender, and a percentile score is given. This percentile score indicates what percentage of students scored below a certain number. Such a score is considered to be an objective indication of the student's college potential and is preferable to basing such an evaluation on the personal judgment of one individual. As you will see in our discussion of intelligence tests, however, there are many questions about the appropriateness of percentile scores when the person taking the test differs in important ways from the people on whom the test was standardized.

In addition to determining a test's reliability and validity, it is important to take into account its applicability to test-takers from a diversity of backgrounds. For example, assessment instruments may need to be adapted for use with older adults, who may require larger print, slower timing, or special writing instruments that can be used for those who have arthritis (Edelstein, 2000). Another concern relates to the wording of test items. Scores may be distorted by items that reflect the existence of physical conditions rather than psychological disorder. A person with a spinal cord injury may agree with the item "At times, I cannot feel parts of my body," an item that would ordinarily contribute to a high score on a measure of psychotic thinking or drug use.

TABLE 3.5 Criteria for a Good Psychological Test

	Reliability: The Consistency of Test Scores	
Type of Reliability	*Definition*	*Example*
Test-retest	The degree to which test scores obtained from people at one time (the "test") agree with the test scores obtained from those people at another time (the "retest")	A test of intelligence should yield similar scores for the same person on Tuesday and on Thursday, because intelligence is a quality that is assumed not to change over short time periods.
Interjudge	The extent to which two or more people agree on how to score a particular test response	On a 5-point scale of thought disorder, two raters should give similar scores to a psychiatric patient's response.
Internal consistency	How well items on a test correlate with each other	On a test of anxiety, people answer similarly to the items designed to assess how nervous a person feels.

	Validity: How Well the Test Measures What It Is Designed to Measure	
Type of Validity	*Definition*	*Example*
Content	How well the test reflects the body of information it is designed to tap	The professor's abnormal psychology exam concerns knowledge of abnormal psychology, rather than familiarity with music from the 1960s.
Criterion	The extent to which the test scores relate in expected ways to another benchmark	(See more specific examples below.)
Concurrent	How well scores on a test relate to other measures taken at the same time	A test of depression should produce high scores in people with known diagnoses of depression.
Predictive	The extent to which test scores relate to future performance	People who receive high scores on college entrance examinations are expected to achieve high grade-point averages in college.
Construct	The extent to which a test measures a theoretically derived psychological quality or attribute	A test of depression should correlate with recognized characteristics of depression, such as low self-esteem, guilt, and feelings of sadness.

Source: Kazdin, 1998.

Once the psychometric qualities of a measurement instrument have been established, the measure becomes one of many types and forms of tests that the clinician can incorporate into an assessment. Psychologists then choose measurement instruments on the basis of the assessment goals and theoretical preferences. We will examine each of the various types of assessment devices from the standpoint of its most appropriate use in assessment, its theoretical assumptions, and its psychometric qualities.

Intelligence Testing

Psychologists have long been interested in studying intelligence because of its wide-ranging influence on many aspects of an individual's functioning. Psychologists and others have made many attempts to define the elusive quality of

Standardized tests are sometimes administered in group settings for personnel selection. These people have applied for jobs in a small business.

intelligence. Although debate continues, for all practical purposes, current intelligence tests are based on the concept of "g," the proposal by psychologist Charles Spearman (Spearman, 1904) that there is a broad quality ("general" intelligence) that underlies the individual's ability to "see relations." The quality of "g" is theorized to reflect in part the individual's inherited capability and in part the influence of education and other experiences. Tests that assess intelligence reflect, to varying degrees, the individual's level of "g."

Intelligence tests serve various purposes. One important purpose is to help educators determine whether certain students might benefit from remedial or accelerated learning opportunities. Intelligence tests can also be useful for employers who wish to know whether a prospective employee has the intellectual capacity to carry out the duties of a given job. For the mental health professional, intelligence tests provide crucial information about a client's cognitive capacities and the relationship between these capacities and the expression of emotional problems. For example, an exceptionally bright young woman might make very esoteric but bizarre associations on a test of personality. Knowing that this young woman is highly intelligent can provide the clinician with an understanding that such associations are probably not due to a psychological disorder. Alternatively, a man whose intelligence is significantly below average might say or do things that give the appearance of a psychotic disorder.

Intelligence tests can yield fairly specific information about a person's cognitive deficits or strengths, which can be helpful to a therapist working on a treatment plan. Clients who have little capacity for abstract thinking are likely to have difficulty in insight-oriented psychotherapy. Instead, a clinician treating a client with such cognitive deficits would focus on practical, day-to-day problems.

Some intelligence tests are designed to be administered to relatively large groups of people at a time. These tests are more commonly used in nonclinical settings, such as psychological research, schools, personnel screening, and the military. Most of these tests use a multiple-choice question format, and scores are reported in terms of separate subscales assessing different facets of intellectual functioning. Group tests are used because they allow mass administration and are easily scored, with no special training required of the examiner. However, clinicians fault these tests for their impersonality and their insensitivity to nuances in the test-taker's answers. A test-taker may give a creative but wrong answer to a question that the computer simply scores as incorrect, without taking into account the originality of the response.

Individual testing methods have the advantage of providing rich, qualitative information about the client. Open-ended answers to questions regarding vocabulary, which cannot conveniently be obtained in group testing, may reveal that the client's thoughts follow a rather bizarre chain of associations. This sort of information would be lost in a group intelligence test, which does not provide any opportunities to scrutinize the client's thought processes and judgment.

Stanford-Binet Intelligence Test   The first intelligence test was developed in 1905 by Alfred Binet (1857–1911) and Theophile Simon (1873–1961), whose work for the French government involved screening mentally retarded children and adults. In 1916, Stanford University psychologists Lewis Terman and Maude Merrill revised the original Binet-Simon test, and scales were added in an effort to increase the test's reliability and validity. The version published in 1986 is known as the Stanford-Binet Fifth Edition (SB5) (Roid, 2003).

Scores on the Stanford-Binet tests have traditionally been expressed in terms of **intelligence quotient (IQ).** When Lewis Terman originally proposed this term in 1916, it literally referred to a ratio measure or quotient—namely the individual's "mental age" (calculated on the basis of test performance) compared with the individual's chronological age. An IQ of 80, in this system, meant that a child had a mental age of 8 and a chronological age of 10, or was moderately retarded. An IQ of 100 indicated average intelligence; in other words, a child's mental age was equal to his or her chronological age. This scoring system worked reasonably well for children, but it created problems with adults, because 16 is the highest achievable mental age on the Stanford-Binet.

The developers of recent editions of the Stanford-Binet have moved away from this approach, and toward the approach common in other intelligence testing instruments which rely on the concept of **deviation IQ.** The deviation IQ is calculated by converting a person's actual test score to a score that reflects how high or low the score is, compared with the scores of others of similar age and gender. Thus, the SB5 has a standard score of 100 and a standard deviation of 15.

The SB5, which is used to assess intelligence in people from 2 to 85 or more years of age, yields a Full Scale IQ, a Verbal IQ, and a Nonverbal IQ. The SB5 also provides more specific measurement of five factors, which inform

The Block Design is one of the subtests of the Wechsler Adult Intelligence Scale III (WAIS-III).

MindMAP Segment 3.1 illustrates the similarities and differences in behavioral characteristics between identical twins and dramatically presents the issues faced when researchers attempt to tease apart the relative contributions of heredity and environment.

Twin studies provide crucial insights into understanding the relative contributions of nature and nurture in the development of intelligence.

the assessment process: Fluid Reasoning, Knowledge, Quantitative Reasoning, Visual-Spatial Reasoning, and Working Memory.

Wechsler Intelligence Scales More widely used than the Stanford-Binet test are the three Wechsler scales of intelligence published by Psychological Corporation. In 1939, psychologist David Wechsler developed the Wechsler-Bellevue Intelligence Scale to measure intelligence in adults. The format of the Wechsler-Bellevue has persisted until the present day, serving as the basis for revisions of the original adult test and the addition of tests for younger age groups: the Wechsler Adult Intelligence Scale–Third Edition (WAIS-III) (Wechsler, 1997), the Wechsler Intelligence Scale for Children–Fourth Edition (WISC-IV) (Wechsler, 2003), and the Wechsler Preschool and Primary Scale of Intelligence–Third Edition (WPPSI-III) (Wechsler, 2002).

Because Wechsler's tests were initially designed for adults, they required a different method of scoring than the traditional IQ formula, which relies on the ratio of mental to chronological age. Wechsler realized that the concept of mental age was not appropriate for adults, and it was he who developed the method of scoring known as the deviation IQ. As mentioned above, not only is the deviation IQ concept used with the Wechsler scales, but it has also been used with the Stanford-Binet since 1960.

All Wechsler tests share a common organization in that they are divided into two scales: Verbal and Performance. The Verbal scale includes measures of vocabulary, factual knowledge, short-term memory, and verbal reasoning. The Performance subtests measure psychomotor abilities, nonverbal reasoning,

and the ability to learn new relationships. On the basis of the Verbal IQ and the Performance IQ, a Full Scale IQ is computed as a more comprehensive intelligence quotient. In addition to the three IQ scores, the WAIS-III provides four characterizations of intelligence based on more refined domains of cognitive functioning: Verbal Comprehension, Perceptual Organization, Working Memory, and Processing Speed.

Intelligence tests, such as the Wechsler scales, are used for various purposes, including psychoeducational assessment, the diagnosis of learning disabilities, the determination of giftedness or mental retardation, and the prediction of future academic achievement. IQ tests are also sometimes used in the diagnosis of neurological and psychiatric disorders, in which cases they are a component of a more comprehensive assessment procedure. Finally, IQ tests may be used in personnel selection when certain kinds of cognitive strengths are especially important.

Although IQ numbers provide valuable information, they do not tell the whole story; consequently, clinicians know that they must evaluate many factors that may contribute to a subject's test performance and scores. A low IQ may reflect a low level of intellectual functioning, but it may also be the result of the subject's intense anxiety, debilitating depression, poor motivation, oppositional behavior, sensory impairment, or even poor rapport with the examiner. The case of Ben, whom you read about earlier in this chapter, provides an interesting example of how a clinician would use subtle findings from IQ testing to formulate some hypotheses that go beyond intellectual functioning. Dr. Tobin noted that Ben has average intelligence, with no striking strengths or deficits. She also took note of the fact that, even though Ben was distressed at the time of testing, he was able to function adequately on the various subtests of the WAIS-III. From this, Dr. Tobin concluded that, when tasks are clear and structure is provided, Ben is able to respond appropriately. At the same time, Dr. Tobin wondered why Ben's IQ was not as high as might be expected in an academically successful college junior; perhaps emotional problems, such as anxiety or depression, were interfering with Ben's test performance. She would keep these concerns in mind as she continued to collect assessment data from Ben.

Cultural Considerations in Intelligence Testing When conducting an assessment, psychologists must take into account the person's cultural, ethnic, and racial background. In recent years, the publishers of psychological tests, especially those measuring intelligence, have worked to remove culture-specific items, such as definitions that would be familiar primarily to middle- or upper-middle-class White Americans. Going a step further, test publishers have developed specialized tests to provide culture-fair assessments of individuals from diverse backgrounds. Researchers and clinicians have debated for years about using common psychological tests for assessing individuals from diverse cultural and ethnic backgrounds. Questions have been raised about how valid such tests are with people other than middle-class White Americans. Some experts contend that many personality and cognitive tests are biased against minorities, who are more likely to receive lower IQ scores and higher psychological disturbance scores than Whites. Is the issue one of intelligence, or is the issue one of flawed assessment? Are members of minority groups more psychologically disturbed, or is the measurement of such variables problematic?

The SOMPA, or System of Multicultural Pluralistic Assessment (Mercer, 1979), provides a method for the cognitive assessment of children that takes cultural and linguistic differences into account. The SOMPA includes three categories of assessment: medical, social, and pluralistic. For the medical section, the examiner assesses the child's physical dexterity, perceptual ability, physical maturity, vision, hearing, and health history. The social section includes measures of general knowledge and an assessment of the ways in which the child conforms to or deviates from the norms of his or her culture. The pluralistic section is still more specific to ethnic and cultural background. Children complete "sociocultural scales" to determine the extent to which their culture differs from the dominant, Anglo-American culture. Scores on the sociocultural scales are translated into "estimated learning potential" scores, predictions of IQ relative to a child's cultural and ethnic background. Researchers have reported modest success in using the SOMPA to predict academic placement and achievement (Figueroa & Sassenrath, 1989), but controversy also exists about the validity of this test for assessing cognitive abilities.

Another commonly used test is the Test of Nonverbal Intelligence-3 (TONI-3) (Brown, Sherbenou, & Johnsen, 1997), a language-free measure of intelligence, aptitude, abstract reasoning, and problem solving. The respondent is required to provide only a gesture, such as a point or nod, to indicate response choices. The instructions are also presented nonverbally. There are no words, numbers, pictures, or symbols, so that the test can be given to anyone regardless of cultural background or reading ability.

Personality and Diagnostic Testing

Personality and diagnostic tests provide additional means to understand a person's thoughts, behaviors, and emotions. Sometimes these tests are used independently, and at other times they supplement clinical or research interviews. For example,

MindMAP Segment 3.2: How anxious are you?

Dr. Tobin completed an interview with a new client, Vanessa, and hypothesized two possible diagnoses that both seemed plausible. Vanessa explained that she was "penniless and had no hope of ever earning a cent." Dr. Tobin, realizing that Vanessa was delusional, wondered whether this delusion of poverty reflected severe depression or whether it was a symptom of serious personality disorganization. Vanessa's responses on personality tests that Dr. Tobin selected to help make this differential diagnosis led her to conclude that Vanessa was suffering from pervasive personality disorganization.

There are two main forms of personality tests: self-report and projective. These tests differ in the nature of their items and in the way they are scored.

Self-Report Clinical Inventories A **self-report clinical inventory** contains standardized questions with fixed response categories that the test-taker completes independently, "self"-reporting the extent to which the responses are accurate characterizations. The scores are computed and usually combined into a number of scales, which serve as the basis for constructing a psychological profile of the client. This type of test is considered "objective" in the sense that scoring is standardized and usually does not involve any judgment on the part of the clinician. However, the clinician's judgment is needed to interpret and integrate the test scores with the client's history, interview data, behavioral observations, and other relevant diagnostic information. The clinician's judgment is also required in determining whether the diagnostic conclusions from computer-scored tests are accurate, keeping in mind that computerized tests have both strengths and limitations.

A major advantage of self-report inventories is that they are easy to administer and score. Consequently, they can be given to large numbers of people in an efficient manner. Extensive data are available on the validity and reliability of the more well-known self-report inventories because of their widespread use in a variety of settings.

MMPI and MMPI-2 The most popular self-report inventory for clinical use is the Minnesota Multiphasic Personality Inventory (MMPI), published in 1943, and a revised form, the MMPI-2, published in 1989. The original MMPI, which was cited in thousands of research studies, had flaws, such as psychometric limitations and a narrow standardization sample that did not reflect the contemporary population diversity of the United States. In response to these criticisms, in 1982 the University of Minnesota Press embarked on a restandardization project and commissioned a team of researchers to develop the MMPI-2 (Hathaway & McKinley, 1989). The focus of this effort was on maintaining the test's original purpose while making changes in individual items to translate them into contemporary terms. To test the validity of the new items and improve the test's generalizability, data were collected from a sample of 2,600 persons all across the United States who were chosen to be representative of the general population in terms of regional, racial, occupational, and educational dimensions. Additional data from various clinical groups were also obtained, including people in psychiatric hospitals and other treatment settings.

The MMPI-2 consists of 567 items containing self-descriptions to which the test-taker responds "true" or "false." These self-descriptions refer to particular behaviors (for example, alcohol use), as well as thoughts and feelings (such as feelings of sadness or self-doubt). The MMPI-2 yields a profile of the test-taker's personality and psychological difficulties, as well as three scales that provide the clinician with information about the validity of each individual's profile.

The MMPI and MMPI-2 provide scores on 10 "clinical" scales and 3 "validity" scales. The clinical scales provide the clinician with a profile of an individual's personality and possible psychological disorder. The validity scales provide the clinician with important information about how defensive the test-taker was and whether the individual might have been careless, confused, or intentionally lying during the test. Scales 1–10 (or 1–0) are the clinical scales, and the remaining 3 are the validity scales (see Table 3.6). An additional scale—the "?," or "Can't say," scale—is the number of unanswered questions, with a high score indicating carelessness, confusion, or unwillingness to self-disclose.

Let's return once again to the case of Ben. As you study his MMPI-2 profile (see Figure 3.1), you will notice that there are several extremely high scores. First, look at the validity scale scores, which give some important clues to understanding the clinical scales. Ben's high F tells us that he reports having many unusual experiences, thoughts, and feelings. This could be due to a deliberate attempt on Ben's part to make himself appear "sick" for some ulterior motive. On the other hand, an exaggeration of symptoms sometimes reflects a person's desperation, a "call for help." Looking next at Ben's K scale, you can see that he is not particularly defensive; however, recall that Ben appeared to be quite guarded in the opening phase of his interview with Dr. Tobin. How would you reconcile these seemingly conflicting impressions? Perhaps the more anonymous nature of the MMPI-2 allowed Ben to be self-disclosing. The validity scales yield important information, then, about Ben's personality, as well as the fact that Ben's clinical profile is a valid one. The clinical scales show a picture of severe disturbance. The highest elevations are on scales 7 and 8, which measure obsessional anxiety, social withdrawal, and delusional thinking. He also has physical concerns and depression, and very possibly sexual conflicts.

In summary, Ben's MMPI-2 profile is that of a young man on the verge of panic. He is extremely alarmed by very unusual thoughts, feelings, and conflicts. He is calling out for help, while at the same time he feels conflicted about asking for it. Keep these observations about Ben in mind when you read about his responses on the other tests.

Other Self-Report Inventories There are literally hundreds of self-report clinical inventories, many of which have been developed for specific research or clinical purposes. Several are used as adjuncts to the MMPI-2, providing information on personality functioning apart from or in addition to data that might be diagnostically useful. The NEO Personality Inventory (Revised), known as the NEO-PI-R (Costa & McCrae, 1992), is a 240-item questionnaire that measures personality along five personality dimensions, or sets of traits. These traits, the authors theorize, can be seen as underlying all individual differences in personality. Some authors have proposed that the traits measured by the NEO-PI-R provide a better way to classify personality disorders than the current system. Measures such as the NEO-PI-R would be instrumental in providing such a classification. Whether or not such changes in classification come to pass, the NEO-PI-R provides useful data on personality functioning. The five dimensions include three labeled N, E, and O (hence the title of the measure), plus two additional scales added as the result of empirical testing of the original measure. These scales, then, consist of Neuroticism (N), Extraversion (E), Openness to Experience (O), Agreeableness (A), and Conscientiousness (C). The scales can be completed by individuals rating themselves (Form S) as well as by others who know the individual, such as spouses, partners, or relatives (Form R). Within each of the five dimensions or trait domains, six underlying facets are also rated. For example, the O scale includes the six facets of openness to fantasy, aesthetics, feelings, actions, ideas, and values. Profiles based on the NEO-PI-R allow the clinician to evaluate relative scores on the five domains of personality, as well as the six facets within each domain.

The Personality Assessment Inventory (PAI) (Morey, 1991, 1996), another objective inventory of adult personality, has become one of the assessment instruments most frequently used in clinical practice and training (Piotrowski, 2000). The PAI consists of 344 items constituting 22 scales covering the most relevant constructs associated with the assessment of psychological disorders: 4 validity scales, 11 clinical scales, 5 treatment scales, and 2 interpersonal scales. Clients with basic reading skills can usually complete the PAI in less than one hour by rating each of the items on a 4-point scale ranging from false to very true. This instrument is especially appealing to clinicians because it yields both diagnostic hypotheses as well as considerations for treatment.

Researchers and clinicians interested in a quantitative measure of an individual's symptoms might use the SCL-90-R (Derogatis, 1994), a self-report measure in which the respondent indicates the extent to which he or she experiences 90 physical and psychological symptoms. The scales derived from these symptoms include somatization, obsessive-compulsiveness, interpersonal sensitivity, depression, anxiety, hostility, phobic anxiety, paranoid thinking, and psychoticism. There are also general symptom index scales that can be used to assess overall functioning. The SCL-90-R is used to measure current symptoms and can therefore be given on multiple occasions. For example, the SCL-90-R might be used to evaluate whether a

TABLE 3.6 Clinical and Validity Scales of the MMPI-2, with Adapted Items

Scale	Scale Name	Content	Adapted Item
1	Hypochondriasis	Bodily preoccupations, fear of illness and disease, and concerns.	I have a hard time with nausea and vomiting.
2	Depression	Denial of happiness and personal worth, psychomotor retardation and withdrawal, lack of interest in surroundings, somatic complaints, worry or tension, denial of hostility, difficulty controlling thought processes.	I wish I were as happy as others appear to be.
3	Hysteria	Hysterical reactions to stress situations. Various somatic complaints and denial of psychological problems, as well as discomfort in social situations.	Frequently my head seems to hurt everywhere.
4	Psychopathic deviate	Asocial or amoral tendencies, lack of life satisfaction, family problems, delinquency, sexual problems, difficulties with authorities.	I was occasionally sent to the principal's office for bad behavior.
5	Masculinity-femininity	Extent to which individual ascribes to stereotypic sex-role behaviors and attitudes.	I like reading romantic tales (male item).
6	Paranoia	Paranoid symptoms, such as ideas of reference, feelings of persecution, grandiosity, suspiciousness, excessive sensitivity, rigid opinions and attitudes.	I would have been a lot more successful had others not been vindictive toward me.
7	Psychasthenia	Excessive doubts, compulsions, obsessions, and unreasonable fears.	Sometimes I think thoughts too awful to discuss.
8	Schizophrenia	Disturbances of thinking, mood, and behavior.	I have had some rather bizarre experiences.
9	Hypomania	Elevated mood, accelerated speech and motor activity, irritability, flight of ideas, brief periods of depression.	I become excited at least once a week.
0	Social introversion	Tendency to withdraw from social contacts and responsibilities.	I usually do not speak first. I wait for others to speak to me.
L	Lie scale	Unrealistically positive self-presentation.	
K	Correction	Compared with the L scale, a more sophisticated indication of a person's tendency to deny psychological problems and present oneself positively.	
F	Infrequency	Presenting oneself in an unrealistically negative light by responding to a variety of deviant or atypical items.	

Source: MMPI-2™ (Minnesota Multiphasic Personality Inventory-2™) Manual for Administration and Scoring. Copyright ©1942, 1943, 1951, 1967 (renewed 1970), 1989 by the Regents of the University of Minnesota. All rights reserved. Used by permission of the University of Minnesota Press.

certain kind of therapy is effective in reducing symptoms by administering it before and after therapy.

For every clinical issue and syndrome, there are inventories that can be used for the purposes of assessment. Sometimes researchers and clinicians want to assess a clinical phenomenon or theory for which there is no published scale, and they may be faced with the challenge of developing one that fits their needs. Examples of scales developed in this way measure such varied phenomena as eating disorders, fears,

impulsivity, attitudes about sexuality, hypochondriasis, homophobia, assertiveness, depressive thinking, personality style, and loneliness.

Projective Testing We have discussed several tests that are based on the premise that an effective method of understanding psychological functioning involves a highly structured task in which the test-taker provides self-report information. In many instances, such information is sufficient to understand the

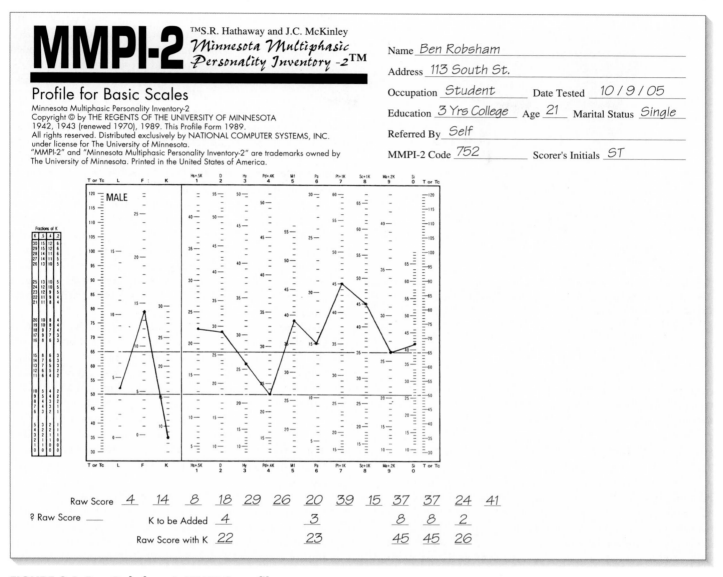

Raw Score   4   14   8   18   29   26   20   39   15   37   37   24   41

? Raw Score ____

K to be Added   4   3   8   8   2

Raw Score with K   22   23   45   45   26

FIGURE 3.1 Ben Robsham's MMPI-2 profile

Source: MMPI-2™ (Minnesota Multiphasic Personality Inventory-2™) Profile for Basic Scales. Copyright 1942, 1943 (renewed 1970), 1989 by the Regents of the University of Minnesota. All rights reserved. Used by permission of the University of Minnesota Press.

individual. However, many clinicians take the theoretical position that unconscious issues exist below the surface of conscious awareness. Projective tests were developed with the intention of gaining access to these unconscious issues. A **projective test** is a technique in which the test-taker is presented with an ambiguous item or task and is asked to respond by providing his or her own meaning. Presumably, the test-taker bases this meaning on unconscious issues or conflicts; in other words, he or she "projects" unconscious meanings onto the item. It is assumed that the respondent will disclose features of his or her personality or concerns that could not easily be reported accurately through more overt or obvious techniques. For example, take the case of a client named Barry, who, in response to items on a self-report

inventory about interpersonal relationships, says that he gets along very well with other people. In contrast, his responses on a projective technique reveal hidden hostility and resentment toward others.

The most famous of the projective techniques is the Rorschach Inkblot Test. This technique is named after Swiss psychiatrist Hermann Rorschach, who created the test in 1911 and in 1921 published his results of 10 years of using this technique in the book *Psychodiagnostik*. Rorschach constructed the inkblots by dropping ink on paper and folding the paper, resulting in a symmetrical design. Before arriving at the final set of 10 inkblots, Rorschach experimented with many hundreds, presumably until he found ones that produced the most useful

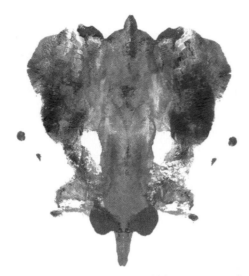

Ben's perception of this Rorschach-like inkblot was "An evil mask that's jumping out to get you. Also a seed, some kind of seed which is dividing itself into two equal halves. It could be a sign of conception and yet it's dying. It's losing part of itself, falling apart, raging."

responses. Although Rorschach did not invent the inkblot technique (it had been proposed by Binet in 1896), he was the first to use standardized inkblots as the basis for assessing psychological disorder. Unfortunately, Rorschach did not live long after the publication of his book; he died a year later, in his late thirties.

The Rorschach test consists of a series of 10 cards showing inkblots. Half of these inkblots are colored, and half are black-and-white. The test-taker is instructed to look at each inkblot and respond by saying what the inkblot looks like. After explaining the procedure, the examiner shows the inkblots one at a time, without giving any guidance as to what is expected, except that the test-taker should indicate what each inkblot looks like. The examiner is trained to provide no clues as to how the inkblot will be scored. The test-taker is then asked to describe what about the inkblot makes it look that way. While the test-taker is talking, the examiner makes a verbatim record of his or her response and how long it takes to respond.

An objective evaluation of the Rorschach leads to the conclusion that this instrument has both limitations and assets. In a critique of projective tests in general, a team of psychometric researchers reviewed the empirical literature and raised serious questions about the validity of how such instruments are scored and used (Lilienfeld, Wood, & Garb, 2000). The debate regarding these instruments is certain to go on for years because many clinicians maintain that the Rorschach provides a wealth of information.

You may be wondering how responses to a set of inkblots can be used to help understand an individual's personality. The Rorschach test is one of several types of projective

techniques that can be integrated with the more objective information gained from a self-report clinical inventory. Let's return to the case of Barry mentioned earlier, who responded in different ways on self-report and projective techniques regarding his attitudes toward other people. The clinician working with his test data would look for ways to integrate these divergent views and might conclude that Barry deludes himself into believing that he feels more positively about other people than might be the case. This hypothesis about Barry's personality could be tested with other projective methods, a clinical interview, or more specific self-report inventories focusing on interpersonal styles.

It is important to remember that the theoretical stand of the clinician influences the choice of what test to incorporate in a battery. Projective techniques are most commonly associated with approaches that focus on unconscious determinants of behavior. In contrast, a clinician who is more interested in conscious and overt behaviors would select a very different battery of tests to assess a client with serious disturbance.

Ben's response to Rorschach Card I shows that the ambiguity of the projective test stimulated a variety of unusual and idiosyncratic perceptions. He sees in this card an "evil mask." Many people look at this card and see a mask; however, Ben sees this mask as "evil," a more ominous image than simply a mask. Furthermore, Ben sees the mask as "jumping out to get you." Not only does the mask have ominous elements, but it is seen as an attacker. In his next response to the same card, Ben sees the inkblot as "a seed . . . which is . . . losing part of itself, falling apart, raging." Is Ben talking about himself in this description?

Ben's response to another card, which contains color, reflects an even more extreme trip into fantasy. By the time Ben saw this card, which came near the end of the test, he had become preoccupied with fantasies of people and objects coming together and splitting apart. His responses had become increasingly bizarre and unconnected with the stimuli. When unusual responses such as these are paired with Ben's MMPI-2 profile, the clinician would hypothesize that Ben is losing control and feels panicked by the experience of losing control.

The Thematic Apperception Test (TAT), another projective test, works on the same premise as the Rorschach; when presented with ambiguous stimuli, test-takers reveal hidden aspects of their personalities. Instead of inkblots, the stimuli are black-and-white ink drawings and photographs that portray people in a variety of ambiguous contexts. The instructions for the TAT request the respondent to tell a story about what is happening in each picture, including what the main characters are thinking and feeling, what events preceded the depicted situation, and what will happen to the people in the picture. Some test-takers become very involved in telling these stories, as the pictures lend themselves to some fascinating interpersonal dramas.

Ben told the following story about this TAT card: "This is a story of a woman who has lived too long with her mother. She wants to break away but knows she can't. Her whole life is wrapped up in her mother and the house. She's a successful businesswoman and yet she feels like a failure because she can't break out because of what she sees going on outside the house. She is looking out at the sky and sees a plane about to make a crash landing on the street. Across the street she sees a man about to jump off the top of a six-story building, but he stops when someone comes to rescue him. Because of all the crazy things going on outside, the woman thinks that maybe it is better to stay with her mother." Source: Reprinted by permission of the publisher from Henry A. Murray, *Thematic Apperception Test,* Cambridge, Mass., Harvard University Press. Copyright ©1943 by the President and Fellows of Harvard College, copyright ©1971 by Henry A. Murray.

The TAT was originally conceived by Christiana Morgan and Henry Murray (Morgan & Murray, 1935), working at the Harvard Psychological Clinic, and was published as a method of assessing personality several years later (Murray, 1938; Murray, 1943).

One of the advantages of the TAT is its flexibility. The pictures lend themselves to a variety of interpretations that can be used for both research and clinical purposes. In one clever adaptation of the TAT, psychologist Drew Westen has developed a comprehensive theoretical framework for understanding TAT responses. This framework is based on object relations theory, a perspective you will read about in Chapter 4, which is based on contemporary psychodynamic theory. Westen's system, called the Social Cognition and Object Relations Scale (SCORS) (Westen, 1991a, 1991b), involves scoring the TAT

along dimensions that incorporate the quality of descriptions of people and their relationships. For example, affect-tone is assessed by analyzing how people in the TAT stories are portrayed; at one extreme people may be described as malevolent or violent, and at the opposite extreme they may be portrayed as positive and enriching. The scoring manual for this system involves specific procedures for assigning scores along these dimensions, ensuring that the measure has high reliability (Westen, Lohr, Silk, & Kerber, 1994).

The themes that emerge from Ben's TAT responses are consistent with the issues identified in the other personality tests, in that they reflect such concerns as family problems, depression, and fears about what is going on around him. Ben describes a character who is frightened by the chaos in her environment. In Ben's story, the character observes someone being rescued from a suicide attempt. One might wonder whether Ben's description of the relationship between the character and her mother is a parallel of his own relationship with his mother. Interestingly, the character describes leaving home as "breaking out," as if home were a prison from which to escape. He pessimistically concludes that the character will not be able to fulfill the wish to separate. In the report at the end of this chapter, Dr. Tobin will integrate the data from this test with the other test results, as she puts together the pieces of Ben's puzzle.

Behavioral Assessment

So far, we have discussed forms of assessment that involve psychological testing. These forms of assessment are the ones that most people think about when they imagine how a psychologist approaches the task of diagnosing psychological disorder. Another form of psychological assessment has emerged since the late 1960s, and it relies on a very different set of assumptions than those of projective testing. **Behavioral assessment** includes a number of measurement techniques based on a recording of the individual's behavior. Clinicians use these techniques to identify problem behaviors, to understand what maintains these behaviors, and to develop and refine appropriate interventions to change these behaviors.

As originally conceived, behavioral assessment relied almost exclusively on recording observable behaviors—namely, actions carried out by the individual that other people could watch. This was in large part a reaction against traditional models that rely on inferences about hidden causes, such as unconscious determinants or unobservable personality traits. Since the late 1970s, though, behavioral assessments have increasingly come to include the recording of thoughts and feelings as reported by the individual, or the observation of the individual's behavior by a trained observer, in addition to outward actions. Commonly used approaches include the behavioral self-report of the client and the clinician's observation of the client.

Behavioral Self-Report

Behavioral self-report is an assessment method in which the client provides information about the frequency of particular behaviors. The rationale underlying behavioral self-report techniques is that information about troublesome behavior should be derived from the client, who has the closest access to information critical for understanding and treating the problem behavior. This information can be acquired in a number of ways, including interviews conducted by the clinician, the client's self-monitoring of the behavior, and the completion of any one of a number of checklists or inventories specifically designed for this purpose.

It is commonly accepted within clinical contexts that the best way to find out what troubles clients is to ask them; the interview is the context within which to undertake such inquiry. Behavioral interviewing is a specialized form of interviewing in which the clinician focuses on the behavior under consideration, as well as what preceded and followed the behavior. Events that precede the behavior are referred to as antecedents, and events following the behavior are called consequences.

Behavioral interviewing has long been regarded as an integral part of behavioral assessment and therapy, for it is within this context that the clinician works to understand the problem under consideration. When interviewing the client about the problem behavior, the clinician gathers detailed information about what happens before, during, and after the enactment of the behavior. For example, take the case of Ernesto, a young man who develops incapacitating levels of anxiety whenever it begins to rain while he is driving his car. In interviewing Ernesto, the clinician tries to develop as precise an understanding as possible of the nature of these attacks of anxiety and asks very specific questions pertaining to the time, place, frequency, and nature of these attacks. Although the clinician wants to obtain some background information, in most cases this is limited to information that seems relevant to the problem behavior. In this example, the clinician would be more likely to focus on particular experiences in Ernesto's history that relate to fears of driving under risky conditions than to ask about early life relationships.

Within the behavioral interview, the clinician not only tries to understand the precise nature of the problem but also seeks to collaborate with the client in setting goals for intervention. What is it that the client wants to change? In the example of the anxiety attacks, presumably the client wants to be able to continue driving after the rain starts, without being impaired by the anxiety that had previously afflicted him. The clinician tries to ascertain whether the client's goal is realistic or not. If the young man asserts that he wants to work toward a goal of never feeling any anxiety while in a car, the clinician would consider

Psychologists using behavioral methods often ask clients to monitor the frequency of target behaviors, as in the case of this young man trying to quit smoking.

such a goal unrealistic and would help the client set a more attainable objective.

Self-monitoring is another behavioral self-report technique in which the client keeps a record of the frequency of specified behaviors, such as the number of cigarettes smoked or calories consumed, or the number of times in a day that a particular unwanted thought comes to the client's mind. Perhaps a woman is instructed to keep a diary of each time she bites her fingernails, documenting the time, place, and context of the **target behavior,** the behavior that is of interest or concern in the assessment. With such careful attention to the troubling behavior, she may come to realize that she is prone to biting her nails primarily in certain situations. For example, she may notice that her nail-biting is twice as likely to occur when she is speaking on the telephone.

Self-monitoring procedures have some limitations. Such habits as nail-biting are so deeply ingrained that people are almost unaware of engaging in the behavior. Another problem with self-monitoring procedures is that the individual must have the discipline to keep records of the behavior. As you might imagine, it could be quite disruptive for the nail-biter to take out a note pad each time she raises her fingernails to her mouth. In response to such concerns, some clinicians acknowledge that the measurement of the behavior in and of itself may be therapeutic.

Behavioral checklists and inventories have been developed to aid in the assessment or recording of troubling behaviors. In completing a behavioral checklist or inventory, the client checks off or rates whether certain events or experiences have transpired. For example, the Conners Ratings Scales-Revised (CRS-R) (Conners, Erhardt, & Sparrow, 1997) consist of instruments that use observer ratings and self-report ratings to assess attention-deficit/hyperactivity disorder and evaluate problem behavior in children and adolescents. Various CRS-R versions solicit assessment data from different sources, including parents, teachers, caregivers, and the young person who is capable of reading and understanding the items (i.e., an adolescent). Computerized versions and a Spanish language form of the CRS-R are also available. Another commonly used behavioral inventory is the Fear Survey Schedule (Wolpe & Lang, 1977), in which an individual is asked to indicate the extent to which various experiences evoke feelings of fear. Checklists and inventories such as these often appeal to both clinicians and clients, because they are relatively economical and easy to use.

However, in many instances it is important to observe and measure the behavior that is the focus of concern. A client can tell a clinician about the nature and frequency of a troubling behavior, but a person may have trouble reporting a behavior that is embarrassing or otherwise upsetting.

Behavioral Observation

Observation of the client's behavior is an important component of behavioral assessment. In **behavioral observation,** the clinician observes the individual and records the frequency of specific behaviors, along with any relevant situational factors. For example, the nursing staff on a psychiatric unit might be instructed to observe and record the target behavior of an individual who bangs his head against a wall every time something out of the ordinary occurs. Or a classroom observer of a hyperactive boy might count the number of times each minute the boy gets out of his seat. The consequences of each behavior would also be recorded, such as the number of times the teacher tells the child to sit down.

The first step in behavioral observation is to select the target behaviors that are of interest or concern. In the example of the hyperactive child, the target behavior would be the boy's getting up from his desk at inappropriate times. The second step is to define the target behavior clearly. Vague terms are not acceptable in a behavioral observation context. For example, a target behavior of "restlessness" in the hyperactive boy is too vague to measure. However, a measurement can be made of the number of times he jumps out of his seat.

Ideally, behavioral observation takes place in the natural context in which the target behavior occurs. This is called *in vivo* **observation.** For the hyperactive boy, the classroom setting is particularly problematic, so it is best that his behavior be observed and measured there, rather than in a laboratory. However, many challenges are involved in conducting such assessments, including overcoming the possible effects of the observer's presence. It is possible that the boy's behavior will be affected by the fact that he knows he is being observed, a phenomenon behaviorists refer to as reactivity.

To deal with some of the limitations of *in vivo* observation, the clinician or researcher may conduct an analog observation, which takes place in a setting or context specifically designed for observing the target behavior. For example, the hyperactive boy may be taken to the clinician's office, where his behavior can be observed through a one-way mirror. Perhaps other children will be included, so that the boy's interactions can be observed and certain target behaviors measured. Analog observation has its limits, however, primarily because the situation is somewhat artificial.

Environmental Assessment

In evaluating an individual, it is often helpful to obtain a perspective on his or her social or living environment. As you read about various approaches to understanding psychological disorders, you will see that some emphasize the role of the individual's family or social context in the development and continuation of symptoms. **Environmental assessment scales** ask the individual to rate certain key dimensions hypothesized to influence behavior. Psychologist Rudolf Moos has been influential in developing such instruments, which include ratings of the family environment, the school, the community setting, or a long-term care institution. For example, the Family Environment Scale (Moos & Moos, 1986) involves having individuals rate their families along dimensions including the quality of relationships, the degree of personal growth the family promotes, and the activities in which the family engages to maintain the system. Within the relationship domain, separate scales assess how much cohesion or commitment exists among family members, how expressive family members are to each other, and how much conflict they express. Specific items on these scales ask about what might seem to be mundane family experiences, such as when the dishes are washed and what family members do together for recreation. Other questions tap into more sensitive issues, such as whether family members hit each other when they are angry and whether family members share religious beliefs.

The Family Environment Scale can be used to assess the quality of, for example, a delinquent adolescent's home life or the degree of supportiveness family members show during a crisis. Such a scale can provide important information to mental health professionals about the influence of the social environment on the individual's adaptation.

In recent years there have been efforts to develop cross-cultural scales to evaluate family environment. For example, the Global Family Environment Scale (Rey et al., 1997; see Table 3.7) quantifies the adequacy of the family environment in which a child is reared. The scale assesses variables such as the family's ability to provide the child with good physical and emotional care, secure attachment relationships, consistency, and appropriate, nonpunitive limit-setting. Rey and colleagues (2000) found impressive agreement among mental health professionals

REAL STORIES

FREDERICK FRESE: PSYCHOSIS

The case report on Ben Robsham at the start of this chapter is the story of an individual becoming overwhelmed by psychotic experiences. It might surprise you to find that psychosis can also be experienced by highly functioning people, like Dr. Frederick Frese, a successful psychologist.

Frederick Frese, PhD, has spent considerable time in mental institutions as a patient diagnosed with paranoid schizophrenia. He was first diagnosed with a psychiatric disorder when he was a 25-year-old Marine Corps captain and experienced a psychotic episode. Frese was guarding atomic weapons in Jacksonville, Florida, when he developed an overwhelming paranoia that enemy nations had hypnotized American leaders in an effort to take over the U.S. weapon supply. Despite repeated hospitalizations for his condition throughout the next decade, Frese completed graduate work in both psychology and management, and in 1978 he earned a doctorate in psychology. While a graduate student at Ohio University, Frese met his wife, Penny, with whom he had four children.

Since earning his doctorate, Frese has worked in both clinical and administrative positions in the Ohio Department of Mental Health. From 1980 to 1995, he served as Director of Psychology at Western Reserve Psychiatric Hospital in Ohio, part of the same hospital system in which he had earlier been a patient. Frese has traveled extensively, giving hundreds of presentations to people all over the world. Frese went on to hold the office of first vice president of the National Alliance for the Mentally Ill (NAMI), a well-known

Frederick Frese

advocacy organization for people with mental illnesses.

The accomplishments of Dr. Frese are especially impressive in light of the struggles with mental illness that have so frequently disrupted his life. Particularly impressive is his willingness to openly share his experiences about his own mental illness:

I, too, am a person with schizophrenia. I am not currently psychotic but I have been in the state of psychosis frequently enough to have become somewhat familiar with trips there and back. After years of keeping my experiences with schizophrenia a secret, a few years ago I decided to become open about my condition. . . . I cannot tell you how difficult it is for a person to accept the fact that he or she is schizophrenic. Since the time when we were very young we have all been conditioned to accept the fact that if something is crazy or insane, its worth to us is automatically dismissed. We live in a world

that is held together by rational connections. That which is logical or reasonable is acceptable. That which is not reasonable is not acceptable. The nature of this disorder is that it affects the chemistry that controls your cognitive processes. It affects your belief system. It fools you into believing that what you are thinking or what you believe is true and correct, when others can usually tell you that your thinking processes are not functioning well. I had been hospitalized five times before I was willing to consider the possibility that something was wrong with me. . . .

From the viewpoint of the person with the disorder, however, the phenomenon can be very much like a mystical experience. . . . Often these mystical experiences can be most seductive. One has the feeling that he is having special insights and even special powers. One is no longer restricted by the rigid control of rationality. . . .

Persons with serious mental illness are disabled, just like people who are blind, deaf, or crippled. Like others who are disabled we can be helped by artificial support. Where the blind may have a cane or a seeing eye dog, the deaf may be helped with a hearing aid, the crippled may be helped with a wheelchair or crutch, we, too, can be helped by artificial means. Because our disability is one of a biochemical imbalance, it is reasonable that our "crutch" is chemical. For us, our crutch is the neuroleptic medications that we take. In order to keep our brain's neurochemical processes properly balanced, we need the assistance of helpful chemical, prescribed medications. Certainly without having such medications available, I would not be able to function as I do today. . . .

REAL STORIES

FREDERICK FRESE (continued)

Often when you visit a psychiatric hospital you will see patients who seem to be talking to people who are not there. In their one-sided conversations they will often become quite animated. Because they are talking to people who are not there, it is usually assumed that they must be hearing voices and talking back to them. Although this may sometimes be the case, often something quite different is at play. Those of us with schizophrenia are very sensitive to having our feelings hurt. Insults, hostile criticism and other forms of psychological assault wound us deeply, and we bear the scars from these attacks to a much greater degree than do our normal friends. Because we have this hypersensitivity, naturally enough we try to protect ourselves and prepare ourselves from possible future attacks. . . . We rehearse or replay situations over and over in our minds, and we often find ourselves speaking in audible fashion when we are doing this. . . . Many years ago my wife became so bothered by my tendency to do this, that we worked out an agreement that I would try to engage in this behavior only when I was in the shower in the morning and while I was mowing the lawn. The lawn mower motor tended to drown out the sound of my mumbling. . . .

Persons with schizophrenia should realize that they can become overstimulated by exciting circumstances as well as stressful circumstances. We need to develop techniques to limit the effects that overstimulation may have on our systems. I find that when I begin to become overstimulated it is often helpful to politely excuse myself from the situation. If I am at a conference I can withdraw to my room or if I am at a mall I can withdraw to a less stimulating environment. . . . When I find myself being faced with unfair criticism I will present the person doing the criticism with my card, which has these words written on it: "Excuse me. I need to tell you that I am a person suffering from a mental disorder. When I am berated, belittled, insulted, or otherwise treated in an oppressive manner I tend to become mentally ill. Could I ask that you restate your concern in a manner that does not tend to disable me? Thank you for your consideration."

While normal [people] can speak openly and even casually about cancer or heart disease, the topic of schizophrenia elicits primarily emotional reactions like fear or derisive humor. Normals are not comfortable with the thought of a seriously mentally ill person living in their neighborhood, being in school with them, or being in their workplace. We still frighten them. They do not know what to expect from us. . . . For those of us who have returned to work and found we are not as welcome as we would like to be, we have a challenge. We must work together to change the image we have with those in what I sometimes refer to as "the chronically normal community." As more and more of us are becoming open about the nature of our disability, we have an obligation to share with others as much as we can about mental illness so that there is less fear and greater understanding and acceptance.

Source: From Frederick J. Frese in *Innovations and Research*, 2(3), 1993. Reprinted by permission of Psychiatric Rehabilitation Journal.

in various countries, including Malaysia. Spain, Australia, Indonesia, the United States, Denmark, and Singapore. The fact that clinicians from different cultures seem to be able to make global ratings of the family environment with only minimal training is especially important for mental health researchers in this increasingly globalized community.

Physiological Assessment

Many psychological disorders occur in the presence of physiological disturbances that must either contribute to or at least may have a bearing on the individual's condition. Sometimes the disturbance is localized in the brain, perhaps in the form of a structural abnormality. Or perhaps a person has a physical disorder, such as diabetes, AIDS, or hyperthyroidism (an overactive thyroid), that causes the individual to experience altered psychological functioning. Increasingly, as psychological disorders are being found to have accompanying physiological abnormalities, the evaluation of the individual's physiological status has become a central aspect of a complete psychological assessment. In some cases, abnormalities of physiological functioning become a central feature of diagnosis.

Psychophysiological Assessment

Since the early days of behavior therapy, many clinicians and researchers have been interested in assessing changes in the

---

TABLE 3.7 Global Family Environment Scale

Raters are instructed to consider family environment on a hypothetical continuum from 1 to 90, by giving an overall rating of the lowest quality of family environment to which the child was exposed during a substantial period of time (at least 1 year) before the age of 12. Information should be obtained from a variety of sources, which are as objective as possible. Having a single parent or a nontraditional family by itself is not rated negatively in the absence of other detrimental factors.

Range 81–90 Adequate Family Environment

Stable, secure, and nurturing for the child, with consistent care, affection, discipline, and reasonable expectations.

Range 71–80 Slightly Unsatisfactory Environment

Mainly stable and secure, but there are some conflicts and inconsistencies about discipline and expectations (e.g., one parent may be often absent or unavailable because of illness or work; a child may be singled out for special treatment); some changes of residence and school.

Range 51–70 Moderately Unsatisfactory Environment

Moderate parental discord (which may have resulted in separation or divorce), inadequate or moderate conflict about discipline and expectations, moderately unsatisfactory parental supervision or care, frequent changes of residence or school.

Range 31–50 Poor Family Environment

Persistent parental discord, hostile separation with problems with custody, exposure to more than one stepparent, substantial parental inconsistency or inadequate care, some abuse (by parental figures or siblings) or neglect, poor supervision, very frequent changes of residence or school.

Range 11–30 Very Poor Environment

Several, usually short-lived parental figures (e.g., de facto fathers), severe parental conflict, inconsistency or inappropriate care, evidence of substantial abuse (e.g., cruel discipline) or neglect, or grave lack of parental supervision.

Range 1–10 Extremely Poor Environment

Very disturbed family environment, often resulting in the child being made a ward of the state, institutionalized, or placed in foster care more than once; evidence of severe abuse, neglect, or extreme deprivation.

Source: Rey et al., 1997.

body that are associated with psychological or emotional experiences, especially changes in a person's cardiovascular system, muscles, skin, and brain. To measure these changes, they use psychophysiological assessment procedures, which provide a wealth of information about the bodily responses of an individual to a given situation.

The cardiovascular system is composed of the heart and blood vessels. As you know from thinking about any situation in which you have felt frightened, your heart rate can change drastically in a short period of time. Even thinking about something that frightens you can cause changes in your cardiovascular system. Various measurement devices are used to monitor cardiovascular functioning, the most common of which is the electrocardiogram (ECG), which measures electrical impulses that pass through the heart and provides an indication of whether the heart is pumping blood normally. Blood pressure is a measure of the resistance offered by the arteries to the flow of blood as it is pumped from the heart. Assessments of cardiovascular functioning may be used to provide information about a person's psychological functioning, as well as his or her level of risk for developing various stress-related conditions that affect the heart and arteries.

Muscular tension, another physiological indicator of stress, is assessed by means of electromyography (EMG), a measure of the electrical activity of the muscles. This technique is used in the assessment and treatment of tension-related disorders, such as headaches, that involve severe and continuous muscle contractions.

An individual's skin also provides important information about what the person is experiencing emotionally. Many people sweat when they feel nervous, which causes electrical changes in the skin called the electrodermal response. This response, also called the **galvanic skin response (GSR),** is a sensitive indicator of emotional responses, such as fear and anxiety.

Brain Imaging Techniques

The growth of increasingly powerful computer technology in the 1980s led to the development of a new generation of physiological measures of brain structure and activity. These techniques have made it possible for psychologists, psychiatrists, and neurologists to gain greater understanding of the normal brain and the brain's changes as a function of various physical and psychological disorders.

One of the earliest techniques to assess the living brain was the **electroencephalogram (EEG),** which measures electrical activity in the brain, an indication of the individual's level of arousal. An EEG recording is taken by pasting electrodes (small metallic discs) with an electricity-conducting gel to the surface of the scalp. A device called a galvanometer, which has an ink-pen attached to its pointer, writes on the surface of a continuously moving paper strip, producing a "wave" drawing on the paper.

EEG activity reflects the extent to which an individual is alert, resting, sleeping, or dreaming. The EEG pattern also shows particular patterns of brain waves when an individual engages in particular mental tasks. For diagnostic purposes, EEGs provide valuable information for determining diseases of the brain, such as epilepsy (convulsions caused by a chaotic activity of neurons), sleep disorders, and brain tumors. When clinicians detect abnormal EEG patterns, they may use this information as preliminary evidence of brain abnormalities that can be investigated further with more in-depth physical and psychological assessments.

In recent years, computerized interpretations of EEG patterns have replaced the subjective interpretations of technicians and clinicians. A computer can translate wave patterns into color-coded plots of activity, such as black and blue to indicate areas of low EEG amplitude and yellow and red to indicate higher amplitude. This approach yields an easily comprehensible view of the patterns of electrical rhythm and amplitude across the surface of the brain. Animations of these images make it even easier to appreciate variations in brain activity patterns, particularly when computer graphing techniques are used to generate three-dimensional video images.

The EEG, particularly the computerized version, provides a "picture" of the living brain that can be extremely useful for diagnosis. Other imaging techniques of the brain provide X-ray like images that can be used to diagnose abnormalities in brain structure caused by disease, tumors, or injury.

A **computed axial tomography (CAT or CT scan)** (*tomo* means "slice" in Greek) is a series of X-rays taken from various angles around the body which are integrated by a computer to produce a composite picture. During a CT exam, the individual lies with his or her head in a large X-ray tube. A beam of X-rays is shot through the brain; as it exits on the other side, the beam is blunted slightly, because it has passed through dense areas of living tissue. Very dense tissue, such as bone, causes the greatest bending of the beam, and fluid causes the least. X-ray detectors collect readings from multiple angles around the circumference of the scanner, and a computerized formula reconstructs an image of each slice. This method can be used to provide a cross-sectional slice of the brain from any angle or level. CT scans provide an image of the fluid-filled areas of the brain, the ventricles. As you will see later in this book, such as in the discussion of schizophrenia, this kind of information is very valuable in determining the structural brain differences between people with this disorder and nonschizophrenic individuals.

Another imaging technique used to assess brain structure is **magnetic resonance imaging (MRI),** which uses radiowaves rather than X-rays to construct a picture of the living brain based on the water content of various tissues. The person being tested is placed inside a device that contains a powerful electromagnet. This causes the nuclei in hydrogen atoms to transmit electromagnetic energy (hence the term *magnetic resonance*), and activity from thousands of angles is sent to a computer, which produces a high-resolution picture of the scanned area. The picture obtained from the MRI delineates

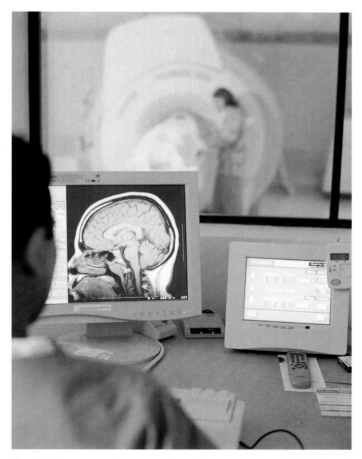

The MRI is a scanning procedure that uses magnetic fields and radiofrequency pulses to construct an image of the brain.

areas of white matter (nerve fibers) from gray matter (nerve cells) and is useful for diagnosing diseases that affect the nerve fibers that make up the white matter. Tumors that cannot be seen on a CT scan can sometimes be seen in an MRI. In a variant of the traditional MRI, which produces static images, **functional magnetic resonance imaging (fMRI)** makes it possible to construct a picture of activity in the brain while the individual is processing information.

Another neuroimaging technique used to assess abnormalities of brain function is the **positron emission tomography (PET) scan** or a variant of this technique known as **single photon emission computed tomography (SPECT).** In this method, radioactively labeled compounds are injected into a person's veins in very small amounts. The compounds travel through the blood into the brain and emit positively charged electrons called positrons, which can then be detected much like

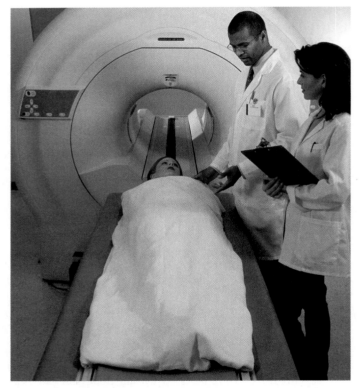

fMRIs are increasingly important in helping professionals pinpoint abnormalities associated with psychological disorders.

MindMAP Segment 3.3 presents imaging techniques and their application to understanding brain-behavior relationships. Scientists at Massachusetts General Hospital record a patient's brain activity while he performs a variety of cognitive and perceptual tasks.

X-rays in a CT. The images, which represent the accumulation of the labeled compound, can show blood flow, oxygen or glucose metabolism, and concentrations of brain chemicals. These vibrant colors at the red end of the spectrum represent higher levels of activity, and colors at the blue-green-violet end of the spectrum represent lower levels of brain activity. What is so intriguing about this process is that the PET scan can show where in the brain specific mental activities are taking place; this is accomplished by assessing the increase in blood flow to a given region. Thus, a thought or specific mental task causes a region of the brain to light up. In addition to the utility of the PET scan in measuring mental activity, this procedure is valuable in studying what happens in the brain following the ingestion of substances, such as drugs.

Sophisticated physiological assessment techniques are not routinely included in a battery because of the tremendous expense involved. At the same time, however, astute clinicians recognize the importance of evaluating the possibility that a medical abnormality may be causing or contributing to an individual's psychological disorder. Although at the present time it would be unlikely for brain imaging techniques to be incorporated into typical clinical practice, all this may change in the near future. As technology, particularly involving fMRI, develops, reliance on such brain imaging techniques in clinical settings will probably be common practice ("Official position of the division of clinical neuropsychology [APA Division 40] on the role of neuropsychologists in clinical use of fMRI: approved by the Division 40 Executive Committee July 28, 2004," 2004).

Let's return to the case of Ben. Recall how he told Dr. Tobin that his concern about the possibility of the police following him dated back to the time that he suffered a minor injury following a bike collision with a police car. As Dr. Tobin attempted to understand the nature of Ben's symptoms, she considered the possibility that he might have sustained a previously undiagnosed brain injury in this accident. Consequently, she recommended that Ben consult with a neurologist for an evaluation. In this procedure, an MRI was done; although the results showed no diagnosable brain damage, the neurologist did note some slight brain abnormalities in the form of enlarged ventricles. Although a clinician would not make a psychiatric diagnosis on the basis of this information, Dr. Tobin did make a mental note of the fact that enlarged ventricles are sometimes associated with schizophrenia.

Neuropsychological Assessment

As valuable as physical assessment techniques are in pinpointing certain kinds of abnormalities in the brain or other parts of the body, they have limitations. Often the clinician needs information about the kind of cognitive impairment that has resulted from a brain abnormality, such as a tumor or brain disease. Perhaps information is needed about the extent of the deterioration that the individual has experienced to that point.

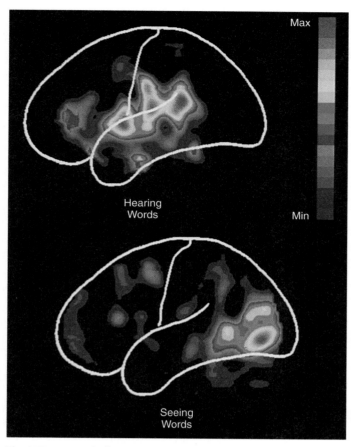

The PET scan on the bottom shows the two areas of the brain (red and yellow) that became particularly active when volunteers read words on a video screen: the primary visual *cortex* and an additional part of the visual system, both in the back of the left hemisphere. Other brain regions became especially active when the subjects heard words through earphones, as seen in the PET scan on the top.

may affect the individual's performance. Also, the WAIS-III may be administered in order to gather information on overall cognitive functioning.

Although the Halstead-Reitan is regarded as an extremely valuable approach to neuropsychological assessment, some clinicians prefer the more recently developed Luria-Nebraska Neuropsychological Battery. A. R. Luria was a well-known Russian neuropsychologist who developed a variety of individualized tests intended to detect specific forms of brain damage. These tests were put into standardized form by a group of psychologists at the University of Nebraska (Golden, Purisch, & Hammeke, 1985). This battery comprises 269 separate tasks, organized into 11 subtests, including motor function, tactile function, and receptive speech. It takes less time to administer than the Halstead-Reitan; furthermore, its content, administration, and scoring procedures are more standardized. A research version of this instrument, known as the Luria-Nebraska III (LNNB-III), is being tested to expand the range of items present on the original battery and to permit its use for patients with motor or speech impairments (Crum, Teichner, Bradley, & Golden, 2000; Teichner, Golden, Bradley, & Crum, 1999).

Though the Halstead-Reitan and the Luria-Nebraska are regarded as impressively precise, their administration involves very sophisticated skills and training. With increased attention to the need for neuropsychological assessment instruments that can be efficiently administered, scored, and interpreted, test publishers have introduced new batteries. The Neuropsychological Assessment Battery (NAB) (Stern & White, 2003) is a comprehensive, integrated instrument comprised of 33 tests that assess a wide array of neuropsychological skills and functions in adults. The tests are grouped into six modules: (1) Attention, (2) Language, (3) Memory, (4) Spatial, (5) Executive Functions, and (6) Screening, a

Neuropsychological assessment is the process of gathering information about a client's brain functioning on the basis of performance on psychological tests.

The most well-known neuropsychological assessment tool is the Halstead-Reitan Neuropsychological Test Battery, a series of tests designed to measure sensorimotor, perceptual, and speech functions. This battery was developed by psychologist Ralph Reitan, based on the earlier work of an experimental psychologist, Ward Halstead (Halstead, 1947). Each test in the battery involves a specific task that measures a particular hypothesized brain-behavior relationship. Clinicians can choose from an array of tests, including the Halstead Category Test, Tactual Performance Test, Rhythm Test, Speech-Sounds Perception Test, and Finger Oscillation Task. These tests were developed by comparing the performance of people with different forms of brain damage as determined through independent measures, such as skull X-rays, autopsies, and physical examinations. In addition to these tests, the battery may include the MMPI-2 as a measure of personality variables that

Psychologists use neuropsychological tests to assess such cognitive functions as the perception and comprehension of words and sentences.

module that allows the clinician to determine which of the other five modules are appropriate to administer to each individual. The NAB is appealing because the assessment can usually be completed in less than 4 hours.

Putting It All Together

At the end of the assessment period, the clinician should have a broad-based understanding of the client as a total individual, as well as an understanding of the client's specific areas of concern. The clinician puts together a "case" that describes the client's current situation and background in a comprehensive, detailed fashion. Using the biopsychosocial model, the clinician would evaluate the extent to which biological, psychological, and sociocultural factors have contributed to and maintained a person's problem. Thus, the clinician is faced with the formidable task of discerning a multitude of possible

factors. When we return to the case of Ben, you will see the ways in which Dr. Tobin considers the three major sets of factors. In the biological realm, Dr. Tobin wonders about the extent to which Ben's problem has been genetically influenced. She also questions the possibility that his minor biking injury might have contributed to his problems. Did he suffer a closed head injury that might have been the cause of his current abnormal thinking and behavior? Or might this accident have been a stress on the already brittle structure of his vulnerable personality? In the psychological realm, Dr. Tobin questions the extent to which past and current emotional difficulties may be contributing to Ben's problems. Finally, she evaluates sociocultural factors, such as family problems, difficulties with peers, and other social forces, that might be causing or adding to Ben's disturbance. As you will see in reading the assessment report about Ben, Dr. Tobin attends to the complex biopsychosocial issues that may be affecting his thoughts, emotions, and behavior.

RETURN TO THE CASE

Case Report
Ben Robsham

Reason for Testing
Although Ben Robsham had stated that his reason for requesting psychological testing was his curiosity about the nature of these tests, it was apparent that he had concerns about his psychological state. Unable to express these concerns in a clear way, it seemed that Ben saw psychological testing as a context within which his disturbance would become apparent, thus opening the door to his obtaining professional help.

Two facts justified the administration of a battery of psychological tests, as well as a neurological evaluation. First, Ben had expressed ideas that sounded delusional, including his belief that the police might be following him. Second, he described an accident in which he sustained minor injuries, possibly including an undiagnosed head injury.

Identifying Information
At the time of the assessment, Ben was 21 years old, living with his family, and working part-time in a supermarket. He was completing his junior

year in college, majoring in political science with career aspirations of eventually running for public office.

Behavioral Observations
Ben was casually dressed in typical college student clothing, except for the fact that he wore a wool hat covering his hair and ears, as well as black leather gloves similar to those worn by athletes playing golf or handball. He was initially tense and ostensibly concerned about the possibility of being seen in the counseling center by people who knew him. In subsequent meetings, this concern diminished. For the most part, Ben was well-mannered and cooperative. During testing, Ben made frequent comments, such as "this really makes you take a good look at yourself." At times, he seemed defensive about his responses. For example, when questioned about the meaning of two unclear sentences on the Incomplete Sentences Blank, he curtly responded, "That's what I meant." In several instances, he responded tangentially to test and

conversational questions, relating personal incidents that had little to do with the task or topic.

Relevant History
Ben Robsham grew up in a middle-class family. He described his early childhood years as being troubled, both at home and at school. Most of Ben's time was spent in solitary hobbies such as listening to rock music. He had no close friends and preferred to stay at home rather than to socialize. He described an antagonistic relationship with his sister, Doreen, who is 2 years older. Ben spoke of how he fought almost constantly with Doreen and how Mrs. Robsham invariably sided with Ben in any dispute. This reflected what Ben believed to be his mother's overprotective parenting style. In describing his mother, Ben spoke of her as a "nut case, who would go ranting and raving about crazy stuff all the time." He also noted that she had been psychiatrically hospitalized at least twice during his childhood for what was described as a "nervous

RETURN TO THE CASE
(continued)

breakdown." Ben described his father as having been minimally involved with the rest of the family, especially in the years following his wife's first hospitalization.

Ben recalls how, from the earliest grades, his teachers repeatedly commented about his failure to look people in the eyes. They were also bewildered when he responded to classroom questions with answers that they found difficult to understand. Ben clearly remembers one incident in which he was asked to name the capital of Tennessee and he replied, "I don't know anything about capitalism." His teacher became angry with him for sounding like a "wise guy," although Ben did not intend to make a joke. Despite his idiosyncrasies, Ben managed to get through high school and get accepted into college.

Several months before the assessment, Ben was involved in a minor traffic collision with a police car while riding his bike. In the accident, he fell off his bike and injured himself slightly. Greater than the physical hurt, however, was the intense fear he felt when confronted by the officer driving the car. The officer spoke sternly to Ben about his careless biking, causing Ben to feel frightened. In the months that followed, Ben's worries about the police intensified. For example, he described one incident in which he was walking by a student demonstration protesting a campus research project that was being funded by the Central Intelligence Agency. On seeing a police officer, Ben became alarmed and feared that he might be arrested. In the following days and weeks, he grew more fearful. He began to worry that his phone might be tapped, his mail read, and his food treated with truth serum. Since that time, Ben reported, he has continued to worry that he was being followed by the police and that they were trying to put together trumped-up charges against him. According to Ben, on several occasions he saw "Nazi agents who were sent by the police" to trail him.

Evaluation Procedures

Diagnostic interview, WAIS-III, MMPI-2,
Rorschach, and TAT
Neurological evaluation
    conducted by Mariel
    Machmer, MD, including an MRI

Impressions and Interpretations

Ben Robsham is a very troubled young man who is desperately seeking help. He is beginning to show signs of thought disorder, emotional instability, and loss of contact with reality.

Ben is of average intelligence, with no exceptional strengths or deficits. However, the quality of many of his responses reflects unusual thought processes. For example, when asked to define the word *winter,* he responded, "It means death." It is possible that conflicts and unusual thought processes, as reflected by this response, interfere with his intellectual test performance, which is lower than the norm for college students.

Ben suffers from intense anxiety, and he is frightened by his gradual loss of touch with reality. In this state of near panic, he is calling out for help. Ben sees the world as an ominous place, filled with people who are either evil or on the verge of a horrible calamity. To cope with his fright, Ben escapes into fantasy, in which he imagines that he will be cared for, that people will live in happiness, and that conflict will disappear.

Ben keeps his distance from other people. His feelings about women are characterized by ambivalence. On the one hand, he wishes for women to be nurturant caretakers yet, on the other hand, sees them as controlling and seductive. This ambivalence about women is further aggravated by his confusion about his own sexuality. He speaks of a secret problem that he is finally admitting to himself. Although he is not explicit about this problem, there are many allusions in his responses to concerns about his sexual orientation.

Several sets of factors seem to be contributing to Ben's disturbance. Ben's mother has a history of psychiatric disturbance. Although no diagnosis is available for this woman, the history and behavior that Ben describes in his mother is that commonly found in people with schizophrenia. Compounding Ben's vulnerability is the fact that he has experienced a lifelong history of feeling socially isolated and unhappy. These feelings are rooted in a family system characterized by disharmony, tension, and psychological disorder. The stresses of adolescence and college achievement may have seemed tremendous for him, intensifying his feelings of vulnerability. Ben's slight accident several months ago may have caused physical and emotional injury, which pushed him to the brink of losing control over his thoughts, behavior, and emotions. Although neurological assessment (MRI) data have yielded no diagnosable brain injury, Dr. Machmer did make note of slight brain abnormalities in the form of enlarged brain ventricles.

In summary, this young man is on the verge of a break with reality and is in immediate need of professional help. Ben needs regular psychotherapy at this time and should be immediately evaluated regarding the possibility of prescribing medication that can address his deteriorating mental health and his heightened level of anxiety.

Recommendations

I will refer Ben for a psychiatric consultation. I recommend that he be evaluated for antipsychotic medication to treat his emerging signs of severe psychological disturbance: delusional thinking, hallucinations, and extreme anxiety. I will also refer Ben for long-term psychotherapy that focuses on helping him develop more appropriate adaptive behaviors, such as social skills and coping strategies.

Sarah Tobin, PhD

SUMMARY

- Assessment is a procedure in which a clinician evaluates a person in terms of the psychological, physical, and social factors that influence the individual's functioning. Some assessment tools focus on brain structure and functioning, others assess personality, and still others are oriented toward intellectual functioning.

- The clinical interview is the most commonly used assessment tool for developing an understanding of a client and the nature of the client's current problems, history, and future aspirations. An unstructured interview is a series of open-ended questions aimed at determining the client's reasons for being in treatment, symptoms, health status, family background, and life history. The structured interview, which is based on objective criteria, consists of a standardized series of questions, with predetermined wording and order.

- Clinicians use the mental status examination to assess a client's behavior and functioning, with particular attention to the symptoms associated with psychological disturbance. Clinicians assess the client's appearance and behavior, orientation, thought content, thinking style and language, affect and mood, perceptual experiences, sense of self, motivation, cognitive functioning, and insight and judgment.

- Psychological testing covers a broad range of techniques in which scorable information about psychological functioning is collected. Those who develop and administer psychological tests attend to psychometric principles, such as validity, reliability, and standardization. Intelligence tests, particularly the Wechsler scales, provide valuable information about an individual's cognitive functioning. Personality tests, such as self-report clinical inventories (e.g., MMPI-2) and projective techniques (e.g., Rorschach), yield useful data about a person's thoughts, behaviors, and emotions.

- Behavioral assessment includes measurement techniques based on the recording of a person's behavior, such as behavioral self-report, behavioral interviewing, self-monitoring, and behavioral observation. In environmental assessment, ratings are provided about key dimensions, such as family environment, that influence behavior. Psychophysiological and physiological techniques assess bodily functioning and structure. Psychophysiological techniques include such measures as ECG, blood pressure, EMG, and other measures of emotional responses. Physiological measures include brain imaging techniques, such as EEG, CT scan, MRI, PET, and other techniques for assessing abnormalities in the body, particularly the brain. Neuropsychological assessment techniques provide additional information about brain dysfunction based on data derived from an individual's performance on specialized psychological tests such as the Halstead-Reitan Neuropsychological Test Battery.

KEY TERMS

See Glossary for definitions

Affect   75
Assessment   68
Auditory hallucination   76
Behavioral assessment   87
Behavioral observation   89
Behavioral self-report   88
Catatonia   73
Command hallucination   76
Compulsion   73
Computed axial tomography (CAT or CT scan)   93
Content of thought   73
Delusions   73
Depersonalization   77
Deviation IQ   80
Dysphoric mood   76
Electroencephalogram (EEG)   93
Environmental assessment scales   89
Euphoric mood   76
Family history   69
Functional magnetic resonance imaging   94

Galvanic skin response (GSR)   92
Gustatory hallucination   76
Hallucination   76
Hyperactivity   72
Identity confusion   77
Inappropriate affect   75
Insight   77
Intelligence quotient (IQ)   80
Intensity of affect   76
In vivo observation   89
Magical thinking   74
Magnetic resonance imaging (MRI)   93
Mental status examination   72
Mood   76
Neuropsychological assessment   95
Normal (or euthymic) mood   76
Obsession   73
Olfactory hallucination   76
Orientation   73
Overvalued idea   73

Positron emission tomography (PET) scan   94
Projective test   85
Psychometrics   78
Psychomotor agitation   72
Psychomotor retardation   72
Range of affect   76
Reliability   78
Self-monitoring   88
Self-report clinical inventory   82
Semistructured interview   69
Single photon emission computed tomography (SPECT)   94
Somatic hallucination   76
Structured interview   69
Target behavior   88
Thinking style and language   74
Unstructured interview   68
Validity   78
Visual hallucination   76

INTERNET RESOURCE

To get more information on the material covered in this chapter, visit our website at **www.mhhe.com/halgin5.** There you will find more information, resources, and links to topics of interest.

CHAPTER 4

Theoretical Perspectives

A year prior to contacting me for therapy, Meera Krishnan had been a student in a large undergraduate abnormal psychology course that I had taught at the state university. More than 300 students were enrolled in this course, and I often regretted the fact that I had so little opportunity to get to know them. However, I did recall Meera, due to the tragedy that she experienced midway through the semester.

I first learned of the terrible events in Meera's life when I received a phone call from Joanne MacKimmie, the Dean of Students, who told me that she had just received news that Meera's father had committed suicide. As is customary in such exceptional circumstances, the Dean urged me to give Meera every possible consideration regarding the fulfillment of course requirements. As told to Dean MacKimmie by a family member, Meera's father was 47 years old, reportedly a "healthy and happy man," to whom she was especially close. He had hanged himself in the family home without any warning. One of Meera's sisters had reportedly discovered Mr. Krishnan's body, as well as the very disturbing suicide note that he had written. In the note, he mentioned the name of his wife and each of his four daughters, stating that he felt so "unloved" by them that he felt that there was no option but to end his life.

The day after Meera received news of this terrible event, she approached me after class, explained what had happened, and in a matter-of-fact manner asked if she could reschedule the examination that was to be given later that week, because she would have to attend her father's funeral. I immediately reacted with sympathy and solicitous concern, stating that we could, of course, work something out. With a notable lack of emotion in her voice, Meera thanked me and began to walk away. I was stunned by the numbness of her emotional state, yet at the same time I realized that Meera was responding to her personal crisis with emotional distancing, a response that is common in people who have experienced a trauma.

I suggested that she come to my office and talk for a while, an invitation she accepted. As soon as I closed my office door, she broke down in tears and blurted out that she didn't want to go on living. After meeting for more than an hour, she agreed to follow my suggestion that she meet with a clinician at the mental health service, so we phoned for an appointment that afternoon.

The following week, I approached Meera after class and asked how she was doing. All she said was "Fine, thanks." From that point on, she made it clear—mostly through nonverbal cues, such as avoiding eye contact—that she did not wish to talk to me about personal matters, and I respected her wish for privacy. For the subsequent 7 weeks of the semester, she dressed completely in black and sat in a place far removed from her classmates.

In light of the manner in which she had chosen to keep her distance from me for the duration of that semester, I was surprised and perplexed that a year later she chose to pursue therapy under my care. When she phoned me, she began the discussion by stating, "I'm sure that you have no recollection of me, but I was in your class last year." She seemed genuinely surprised when I told her that indeed I did recall her and that I remembered what a difficult time it had been for her.

Meera was now 23 years old, and she was seeking therapy to deal with her feelings of "isolation and loneliness." She didn't use the word *depression*, but there was a profound sadness in the tone of her voice. While speaking to me on the phone, Meera asked me whether she might be "untreatable." When I stated that I wasn't sure what she meant, Meera explained her worry that these feelings of sadness may have become a "part of" her personality. I suggested that we hold off discussion of this concern until we could talk face to face. We set an appointment for later that week.

On meeting Meera in the reception room on the day of our first appointment, I immediately noticed the black clothing she was wearing. The image took me back to the sight of her, a year earlier, as she sat in a remote corner of the auditorium during the weeks following her father's death. It had been apparent to me a year ago that she was in a state of mourning, and even after all these months she continued to suffer from unrelenting feelings of sadness. With a faint smile, she meekly responded to my invitation to proceed into my office. Despite my effort to walk beside her, she paced her steps in such a way that she became a follower.

Meera began our first session by telling me she had lived through the "worst year" of her life. On graduating from college, she had found a job as a housewares buyer for a large department store, but she felt this job was not particularly gratifying. She explained that she viewed herself as a "failure" because of her "low salary" and the lack of a boyfriend, or "any friends, for that matter." In fact, she had spent social time with no one since the day she graduated, other than a few "compulsory" visits with her mother. When her former college friends invited her to go to concerts with them, she turned them down, explaining that she felt too busy and exhausted.

In our interview, I returned to the issue of her father's death and inquired about the ways in which that traumatic event continued to affect her. At first, she stated that it was something she had "gotten over," but then admitted she thought of him several times every day, sometimes feeling very sad and at other times feeling "furious about what he did."

Sarah Tobin, PhD

When you were reading Meera's case, you probably formed your own hunches about the causes of her behavior. Dr. Tobin would have done the same from the first moments that she observed Meera acting in unusual ways. Her thinking would have been influenced by the beliefs and assumptions she has developed about human behavior and abnormality. These beliefs and assumptions are based on a **theoretical perspective,** an orientation to understanding the causes of human behavior and the treatment of abnormality.

The Purpose of Theoretical Perspectives in Abnormal Psychology

Theoretical perspectives influence the ways in which clinicians and researchers interpret and organize their observations about behavior. In this chapter, we will examine abnormal behavior from the five major theoretical perspectives that have shaped the field as it is today. We will see what answers each perspective provides to questions regarding abnormal behavior. What is the underlying model of human nature on which the perspective is based? How does the perspective explain human behavior? What are the perspective's implications for research? What treatment approaches would follow from the perspective, and how well do these treatments work?

When it comes to actual practice, experienced clinicians do not adhere strictly to one theoretical perspective but integrate techniques and perspectives from multiple approaches. As you read this chapter, you will find it helpful to recall our discussion in Chapter 1 of the biopsychosocial model, keeping in mind that most disorders have a complex set of causes, warranting a multidimensional treatment.

Psychodynamic Perspective

The **psychodynamic perspective** is the theoretical orientation that emphasizes unconscious determinants of behavior. You will recall from Chapter 1 that Sigmund Freud's (1856–1939) view of psychological disorders focused on unconscious motives and conflicts. His ideas about the cause and treatment of psychological disorders form the foundation for the psychodynamic perspective. As you will see, this theory has come a long way from Freud's original formulations.

Freudian Psychoanalytic Theory

Freud theorized that disorders of the mind produce bizarre and exotic behaviors and symptoms and that these behaviors and symptoms can be scientifically studied and explained. The term *psychoanalytic* is identified with Freud's original theory and approach to therapy. The term *psychodynamic* refers more broadly to the perspective that focuses on unconscious processes

Psychoanalyst Sigmund Freud with his daughter, psychoanalyst Anna Freud, in 1928.

and incorporates a wider variety of theoretical perspectives on personality and treatment.

Freud's Background   Freud is known for saying the "child is father to the man," meaning that early life experiences play a formative role in personality. This observation stemmed from analyzing his own childhood (Gay, 1988; Jones, 1953). When in his thirties and forties, Freud came to the dramatic realization that the events of his early childhood had taken root in the deepest level of awareness, the region of the mind he called the "unconscious." He came to this conclusion through extensive analysis of his dreams and of the thoughts and memories they triggered (Freud, 1900). In the process of this self-analysis, he found that he was able to obtain relief from a variety of disturbing symptoms, such as a fear of trains he developed during a traumatic ride from his hometown to Vienna at the age of 4.

Freud's medical training led him to the convictions that an understanding of disorders of the mind could be achieved by using scientific methods, and that all psychological phenomena could be traced to physiological processes. The scientific approach was also evident in his work, as he sought to confirm his theory through observation and analysis of his patients.

Freud's Structural Model of Personality   According to Freud (1923) the mind has three structures: the id, the ego, and the superego. The three structures constitute the psyche (the Greek word for "soul"), and they are continuously interacting with one another in a "dynamic" fashion. Freud coined the term **psychodynamics** to describe the process of interaction among the personality structures that lie beneath the surface of observable behavior. The **id** is the structure of personality that contains sexual and aggressive instincts, what Freud called a "seething cauldron." Inaccessible to conscious awareness, the id lies entirely in the "unconscious" layer of the mind. The id follows the **pleasure principle,** a motivating force oriented toward the immediate and total gratification of sensual needs and desires. According to Freud, pleasure can be obtained only when the

MindMAP Segment 4.1 puts into larger context the abstract notions of the id, ego, and superego.

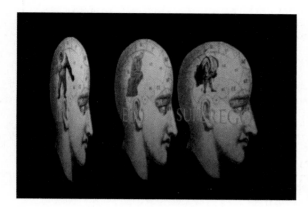

Freud developed a theory of the mind which proposed that personality is made up of three basic structures.

an injured hand. The secondary process thinking of her ego eventually comes into play, and she searches for a more practical solution, such as borrowing some change from a friend.

In Freud's theory, the ego has no motivating force of its own. All of the ego's energy is derived from the energy of the id, a pressure for gratification that Freud called the **libido.** The ego performs the functions that allow the id's desires to be gratified in reality, not just in fantasy. The id, then, is the ego's taskmaster.

Although the ego is the center of consciousness, not all of the ego's contents are accessible to conscious awareness. The unconscious part of the ego contains memories of experiences that reflect unfavorably on the individual's conscious self. These experiences include events in which the individual acted selfishly, behaved in sexually inappropriate ways, or was unnecessarily cruel and violent.

The **superego** is, as the name implies, "over" the ego, controlling the ego's pursuit of the id's desires. Freud believed that, without a superego, people would pursue for pleasure the satisfaction of the "taboo," or socially unacceptable, desires of the id such as rape, murder, and incest. In addition to serving as one's conscience, the superego also serves an inspirational function. It includes the ego ideal, which is the individual's model of how the perfect person should be.

Psychodynamics In the personality of a healthy individual, according to Freud (1923), the id achieves instinctual desires through the ego's ability to navigate in the external world within the confines placed on it by the superego. Psychodynamics, or the interplay among the structures of the mind, is the basis for both normal and abnormal psychological functioning.

Defense Mechanisms To protect against anxiety, people use various tactics to keep unacceptable thoughts, instincts, and feelings out of conscious awareness, tactics that Freud called **defense mechanisms.** According to Freud, everyone uses defense mechanisms on an ongoing basis to screen out potentially disturbing experiences. It is when defense mechanisms become used in a rigid or extreme fashion that they are the source of a psychological disorder.

Current views on defense mechanisms place them into categories or groups based on theoretical considerations and empirically demonstrated relationships to overall mental health (Vaillant, 1994). Based on this approach, the authors of the *DSM-IV* developed a categorical scheme called the Defensive Functioning Scale. These categories provide a helpful way to think about the defense mechanisms and the way they are manifested in various psychological disorders. Examples of some of these defense mechanisms are presented in Table 4.1.

Psychosexual Development Freud (1905) proposed that there is a normal sequence of development through a series of what he called **psychosexual stages.** Each stage focuses on a different sexually excitable zone of the body (erogenous zone); the way the child learns to fulfill the sexual desires associated with each stage becomes an important component of the child's

tension of an unmet drive is reduced. The way the id attempts to achieve pleasure is not necessarily through the actual gratification of a need with tangible rewards. Instead, the id uses "wish fulfillment" to achieve its goals. Through wish fulfillment, the id conjures up an image of whatever will satisfy the needs of the moment.

Freud (1911) used the phrase **primary process thinking** to describe the id's loosely associated, idiosyncratic, and distorted cognitive representation of the world. In primary process thinking, the thoughts, feelings, and desires related to sexual and aggressive instincts are represented symbolically with visual images that do not necessarily fit together in a rational, logical way. Time, space, and causality do not correspond to what happens in real life. Primary process thinking is best illustrated in dreams.

The center of conscious awareness in personality is the **ego.** The ego's function is to give the individual the mental powers of judgment, memory, perception, and decision making, which enable the individual to adapt to the realities of the external world. Recall that the id is incapable of distinguishing between fantasy and reality. The ego is needed to transform a wish into real gratification. Freud (1911) described the ego as being governed by the **reality principle,** a motivational force that leads the individual to confront the constraints of the external world.

In contrast to the id's illogical primary process thinking, the ego functions are characterized by **secondary process thinking,** which is involved in logical and rational problem solving. Imagine a hungry student, working late in the library, who goes to a coin-operated vending machine, inserts her last quarter, and finds that the machine fails to respond. Primary process thinking leads her to bang angrily on the machine, achieving nothing but

TABLE 4.1 Categories and Examples of Defense Mechanisms

Defense Mechanism	Definition	Example
High Adaptive Defenses	*Healthy responses to stressful situations*	
Humor	Emphasizing the amusing aspects of a conflict or stressful situation	Maria jovially reenacted the humiliating experience in which she slipped on the ice while a group of guys watched.
Self-assertion	Dealing with difficult situations by directly expressing feelings and thoughts to others	Pedro told his father that he was disappointed and angry when his father stated that he was too busy to attend Pedro's graduation.
Suppression	Avoiding thoughts about disturbing issues	Maureen made a conscious decision to avoid thinking about financial problems while studying for her final exams.
Mental Inhibitions	*Unconscious tactics that help people keep out of conscious awareness disturbing thoughts, feelings, memories, wishes, and fears*	
Displacement	Shifting unacceptable feelings or impulses from the target of those feelings to someone less threatening or to an object	After his boss criticized him, Fred remained quiet but later barked at one of his subordinates for no good reason.
Dissociation	Fragmenting of the usually integrated cognitive, perceptual, and motor processes in a person's functioning	While being publicly humiliated by his coach in front of the entire hockey team for getting a penalty, Tim "spaced out" by thinking about a party later that night.
Intellectualization	Resorting to excessive abstract thinking in response to issues that cause conflict or stress	Rather than focus on the upsetting aspects of placing her mother in a nursing home, Gabrielle spoke at length about the limitations of the social security system.
Reaction formation	Transforming an unacceptable feeling or desire into its opposite in order to make it more acceptable	Jared, who was secretly addicted to pornography, publicly criticized his daughter's high-school teacher for assigning a classic novel with a sexual theme.
Repression	Unconsciously expelling disturbing wishes, thoughts, or experiences from awareness	Janine was unable to recall any of the details associated with her traumatic automobile accident.
Minor Image-Distorting Defenses	*Distortions in the image of the self, the body, or others in order to regulate self-esteem*	
Devaluation	Dealing with emotional conflict or stress by attributing negative qualities to oneself or others	Patrick claimed that the communication difficulties with his girlfriend were due to her immaturity, low IQ, and lack of sophistication.
Idealization	Dealing with emotional conflict or stress by attributing exaggerated positive qualities to others	Kathleen disregarded her husband's inattentiveness by convincing herself and others that he was absorbed in thoughts of genius and creativity.
Omnipotence	Responding to stress by acting superior to others	The greater the tension in his job as a stockbroker, the more likely it was that Norman would speak in demeaning ways to his co-workers.

TABLE 4.1 Categories and Examples of Defense Mechanisms (continued)

Defense Mechanism	Definition	Example
Disavowal Defenses	Keeping unpleasant or unacceptable stressors, thoughts, feelings, impulses, or responsibility out of awareness	
Denial	Dealing with emotional conflict or stress by refusing to acknowledge a painful aspect of reality or experience that would be apparent to others	Rather than contend with the painful emotions about her cancer diagnosis, Candace acted matter-of-factly as though she were unaffected.
Projection	Attributing undesirable personal traits or feelings to someone else to protect one's ego from acknowledging distasteful personal attributes	Unaware of her reputation for being selfish and miserly, Isabel often complained about the cheapness of others.
Rationalization	Concealing true motivations for thoughts, actions, or feelings by offering reassuring or self-serving but incorrect explanations	To deal with his disappointment about not making the baseball team, Pete convinced himself that he really didn't want to be on "such a weak team" anyway.
Major Image Distorting Defenses	Gross distortion of oneself or others	
Splitting	Compartmentalizing opposite affect states and failing to integrate positive and negative qualities of self or others into cohesive images	Although she had idealized a professor for the entire semester, immediately following a test on which she received an A– Marianne began to view him as an "evil and hostile person."
Defenses Involving Action	Responses to conflict or stress that involve an action or withdrawal	
Acting out	Dealing with emotional conflict or stress by actions rather than thoughts or feelings	Rather than tell his wife that he was hurt by her resistance to sexual intimacy, Rafael decided that he would get even by having an affair with a co-worker.
Passive aggression	Presenting a facade of overcompliance to mask hidden resistance, anger, or resentment	Kevin's resentment about his job as a janitor was reflected in his "overdoing" the office cleaning chores in such a way that the executives were repeatedly distracted by the noise and commotion when he cleaned.
Regression	Dealing with emotional conflict or stress by reverting to childish behaviors	Following even the most minor of disagreements with her co-workers, Adrianne rushed off to the bathroom in tears and waited until someone came to soothe her hurt feelings.
Defenses Involving Breaks with Reality	Responses to stress or conflict that involve bizarre thought or behavior	
Delusional projection	Delusionally attributing undesirable personal traits or feelings to someone else to protect one's ego from acknowledging distasteful personal attributes	Although it was Harry who disdained everyone he encountered, he convinced himself that his neighbors hated him so much that they intended to murder him.
Psychotic distortion	Dealing with emotional conflict or stress by resorting to delusional misinterpretation of reality	As his college grades continued to fall, Yev developed the belief that all his professors were intentionally grading him harshly because of their wish to rid the university of Russian immigrants.

personality. According to Freud, failure to pass through these stages in the normal manner causes various psychosexual disturbances and character disorders.

Freud based his description of the psychosexual stages almost entirely on his observations of adults he treated in psychotherapy, whose recollections convinced him that their difficulties stemmed from repressed sexual instincts left over from their early years (Freud, 1925). According to Freudian theory, the notions of regression and fixation are central to the development of psychological disturbance. An individual may regress to behavior appropriate to an earlier stage or may become stuck, or fixated, at that stage. In **fixation,** then, the individual remains at a stage of psychosexual development characteristic of childhood.

During the **oral stage** (0–18 months) the main source of pleasure for the infant is stimulation of the mouth and lips. This stage is divided into two phases. The first is the oral-passive, or receptive phase, in which pleasurable feelings come from nursing or eating. In the second phase, called oral-aggressive, pleasure is derived from gumming and biting anything the infant can get into the mouth. Regression to or fixation at the oral-passive phase results in excessive reliance on oral sources of gratification (thumb-sucking, cigarette smoking, overeating). People who regress to or fixate at the oral-aggressive phase are hostile and have a critical (biting) attitude toward others.

During the **anal stage** (18 months–3 years) the toddler's sexual energy focuses on stimulation in the anal area from holding onto and expelling feces. The person who becomes fixated at this stage may have an overcontrolled, hoarding type of character structure, called anal retentive, relating to the world by holding back. Conversely, fixation at the anal stage may result in a sloppy, impulsive, and uncontrolled character, called anal expulsive. In regression to the anal stage, the individual may become excessively sloppy or, conversely, excessively neat. For example, a woman who cleans out her dresser drawers in a frenzied manner every time she has an argument with her husband is regressing to anal-like behaviors.

In the **phallic stage** (3–5 years) the genital area of the body is the focus of the child's sexual feelings. Freud believed that the fate of the child's future psychological health was sealed during this phase, when the child must deal with the most important issue of early life. During the phallic stage, the child becomes sexually attracted to the opposite-sex parent. Freud (1913) called this scenario in boys the Oedipus complex, after Oedipus, the tragic character in ancient Greek literature who unknowingly killed his father and married his mother. Freud described a parallel process in girls, the Electra complex, based on Electra, the ancient Greek character who conspired to kill her mother. Freud believed there were important sex differences in how the crisis is resolved but that, for both sexes, it is resolved favorably when the child identifies with the same-sex parent. The child acquires a superego, which enforces society's taboo against incest and sets the stage for all later struggles in dealing with unacceptable sexual and aggressive desires. Freud believed that failure to

During the oral stage of development, infants put anything they can find into their mouth.

resolve the Oedipus complex, as it is now referred to for both sexes, becomes the major source of neurosis.

Following the turmoil of the Oedipus complex, the child's sexual energies recede entirely according to Freud. During **latency** (5–12 years) the child interacts with peers and imitates the behavior of parents and other adults of the same sex as the child. With sex presumably out of the picture, little that is of psychological interest happens during this stage.

In the **genital stage** (12 years through adulthood), coinciding with the resurfacing of sexual energy just prior to puberty, sexual feelings associated with the Oedipus complex begin to reappear. The adolescent must learn to transfer feelings of sexual attraction from the parent figure to opposite-sex peers. Adult genitality, the ability to express sexual feelings in a mature way and in appropriate contexts, is reached when an individual is able to "work and love" (in Freud's words) with another person. Any prior fixations and regressions, however, restrict the individual's ability to complete this stage satisfactorily.

Freud's Place in History You can probably imagine that Freud's theories created a great deal of controversy, especially since he wrote in the early 1900s, when sex was not as openly discussed as it is today. Freud himself often compared his role to that of a conqueror and explorer, paving the way for revolutionary approaches to understanding the mind. During his lifetime, Freud experienced rejection and derision from his colleagues in the medical establishment. By the time he died, however, he had achieved international renown, and his work was beginning to have a major impact on many fields besides psychology.

Even though Freud's ideas have been influential, his theory is far from perfect. As you read further, you will see that important refinements came from both his followers and his critics. However, we must not lose sight of the major role that Freud played in redefining ways of understanding human behavior.

Post-Freudian Psychodynamic Views Post-Freudian theorists departed from Freudian theory, contending that Freud overemphasized sexual and aggressive instincts as the root of personality. Instead, they focused on interpersonal and social needs and the role of sociocultural factors. Carl Jung (1875–1961) developed a theory that differed radically from Freud's emphasis on sexuality (Jung, 1961) and in the conceptualization of the unconscious. According to Jung, the deepest layer of the unconscious includes images common to all human experience, which he called archetypes. Some of these archetypes include images of "good" versus "evil," the "hero," rebirth, and the self. Jung believed that people respond to events in their daily lives on the basis of these archetypes, because they are part of our genetic makeup. For example, Jung asserted that archetypal characters (such as today's Batman and Superman) are popular because they activate the hero archetype. Jung (1916) believed that the goal of healthy personality development involves the integration of the unconscious life with conscious thoughts, and that psychological disorders result from an imbalance between these parts of the personality.

Alfred Adler (1870–1937) and Karen Horney (1885–1952) made important contributions to psychodynamic theory in their emphasis on the ego and the self-concept. People are motivated to maintain a consistent and favorable view of the self, according to these theorists, and they develop psychological defenses to protect this positive self-view. Both Adler and Horney also emphasized social concerns and interpersonal relations in the development of personality. Close relationships with friends and family and an interest in the life of the community are seen as gratifying in their own right, not because a sexual or an aggressive desire is indirectly satisfied in the process. According to these theories, the "neurotic" adult is someone who feels very inferior or unworthy, feelings that originated in childhood.

Erik Erikson (1902–1994) proposed that personality development proceeds throughout the life span in a series of eight "crises" (Erikson, 1963). Each "crisis" is a critical period during which the individual is maximally vulnerable to two opposing forces: one that pulls the person to healthy, age-specific ego-functioning and one that pulls the person to unhealthy functioning. Depending on how the crisis is resolved, the individual's ego will acquire a new "strength" unique to that crisis stage. When the forces of a particular crisis pull the individual toward the unhealthy resolution of that issue, the individual becomes more vulnerable to the development of subsequent problems. Crisis resolutions have a cumulative effect—if one stage is unfavorably resolved, it becomes more likely that succeeding stages

Erik Erikson's psychosocial development theory was the first to incorporate a life-span perspective.

will also be unfavorably resolved. Failure to resolve the early psychosocial issues has particularly serious consequences for later development.

Object Relations Theories Rejecting Freud's belief that the instinctual desire for sexual and aggressive release of tension is the sole basis for the formation of personality, object relations theorists proposed instead that interpersonal relationships lie at the core of personality (Greenberg & Mitchell, 1983). These theorists, including Melanie Klein (1882–1960), D. W. Winnicott (1896–1971), and Heinz Kohut, believed that the unconscious mind contains images of the child's parents and of the child's relationships to the parents. These internalized images remain at the foundation of personality throughout life. This perspective is called **object relations** in keeping with Freud's use of the term *object* to refer to anyone or anything that is the target (object) of an individual's instinctual desires.

Integrating the work of these theorists with systematic observations of infants and young children, Margaret Mahler (1897–1985) and her co-workers sketched out a timetable for the emergence of phases in the development of object relations (Mahler, Bergman, & Pine, 1975). Psychological disturbance, according to Mahler's theory, can result from problems arising during development.

Treatment

The main goal of traditional psychoanalytic treatment as developed by Freud (Freud, 1913–14/1963) is to bring re-pressed, unconscious material into conscious awareness. This is accomplished largely through two therapeutic methods. In **free association,** the client speaks freely in therapy, saying whatever comes to mind. **Dream analysis** involves the client relating the events of a dream to the clinician and free associ-ating to these events. The psychoanalyst attempts to interpret the meaning of the dream both from its content and from the associations the client makes to the dream. These methods of accessing the unconscious mind were best accomplished, ac-cording to Freud, by having the client recline on a couch in as relaxed a state as possible.

According to Freud, the psychoanalytic process is stimu-lated by **transference** in which the client presumably relives conflictual relationships with his or her parents by transferring feelings about them onto the clinician. The clinician best pro-motes the transference by maintaining an attitude of neutrality, not providing any information that would reveal the clinician's preferences, personal background, or reactions to the client's revelations in therapy.

Once conflictual feelings about parents are aroused by evok-ing transference feelings, the clinician can help the client begin the difficult process of **working through.** In this process, the client is helped to achieve a healthier resolution of these issues than had actually occurred in the early childhood environment. For example, the client might transfer onto the clinician the feel-ings of having been neglected as a child. With these feelings brought out into the open within the therapeutic relationship, the clinician can explore with the client the reasons for feeling neg-lected. Over time, the client may learn that it is possible to trust a parent figure (the clinician, in this case), and this realization will help the client feel more secure in relationships outside therapy.

The client's **resistance,** or holding back within the therapy, often impedes the progress of therapy. Confronting unconscious fears and desires is a painful and difficult process, and clients may forget important material, refuse to free associate, or stop therapy altogether to protect themselves from the anxiety asso-ciated with this process. An important part of the clinician's job is to help the client overcome resistance through the process of interpretation. For example, if a client consistently arrives late for therapy appointments, the clinician would try to help the client realize that this behavior may reflect an unconscious de-sire to avoid anxiety.

Although psychoanalysts who broke with the Freudian tradition developed their own theories of personality, their methods of therapy nevertheless relied heavily on Freud's

Attachment theorists believe that a child transfers emotional bonding from the primary caregiver to an object, such as a teddy bear, and eventually from this object to people outside the family.

principles of encouraging the client to explore unconscious personality dynamics. Contemporary clinicians who are psy-chodynamically oriented are likely to base much of their work on object relations views, in which therapy is viewed as an effort to reverse the destructive processes that occurred in the client's early life by providing a new kind of relationship. The clinician attempts to restore, through good "parenting," the client's sense of self and control over the boundaries that define the self.

Some clinicians are attuned to the personality types and prominent defense mechanisms of their clients and adapt their therapeutic approach to the particular styles of each client. They are especially attuned to their own reactions to a client and use this information to form their intervention (McWilliams & Weinberger, 2003).

Evaluation of Psychodynamic Theories

The psychodynamic perspective, just over 100 years old, is still evolving today. Clinicians, researchers, and theorists continue to debate basic issues, such as the role of instincts in shaping the unconscious mind and personality dynamics, the influence of early childhood on later adult functioning, and the role of the clinician in promoting psychological change. The debate centers

Psychodynamic Approaches to Treating Meera

A clinician working from a psychodynamic perspective would assume that her difficulties stem from conflicts in early life. Examining the various elements of Meera's case shows which themes would be important to each of the theorists we have covered. Freud would focus on Meera's unconscious guilt about feeling angry toward her father for abandoning her through death (Freud, 1917). Interpreting Meera's resistance to confronting her feelings of grief would also be important. Jung would attempt to help Meera overcome her conscious unwillingness to speak about her father's death by exploring the symbolic meaning of archetypal images in Meera's dreams. Adler would suggest that perhaps it is time for Meera to move on to use her talents and education in a more productive way and to try to establish new friendships. He might see Meera's lengthy period of unrelenting grief over her father's death as an excuse for not getting involved in a more challenging career or in an intimate relationship.

Horney would help Meera realize that part of her unhappiness comes from following various "shoulds": she "should" have a higher salary, she "should" be involved in a steady relationship, she "should" have recovered from her father's death. By accepting the reality of her situation, Meera can become more comfortable with who she really is. Erikson would approach Meera's depression as being due to unresolved identity and intimacy issues.

The object relations theorists would focus on Meera's early relationships to her parents, both as she perceived these relationships then, and as she perceives them now. A clinician working within this perspective would be alert to problems in early attachment relationships that might be affecting her current difficulty in developing a sense of identity and direction in life.

on several fundamental issues; although these issues are not likely to be resolved in the near future, the writings and research stimulated by this debate have helped refine and clarify some of Freud's most important teachings.

Freud is often given credit for having developed the first comprehensive psychological theory and the first systematic approach to psychotherapy. Although trained in neurology, Freud discovered early in his career that physical symptoms could have psychological causes, and these discoveries formed the cornerstone of a revolutionary approach to understanding the nature and treatment of psychological disorders. Freud can also be credited with introducing into popular culture some important psychological concepts that have given people insights into their behavior and have changed the way that Western society views itself.

Just as Freud's theory led to radical alterations in the way psychological disorder was conceptualized, it also led to intense debates in academic circles regarding its scientific validity. Perhaps the most serious charge levied against psychoanalysis is that its major premises are difficult to test through empirical research. Yet, recently, neuroscientists are finding that such Freudian concepts as unconscious motivation, repression, the pleasure principle, instinctual mechanisms, and the meaning of dreams may have their correspondence in neuronal activity (Solms, 2004). For example, the phenomenon of implicit memory, in which a person cannot remember the details of an event but nevertheless appears to be influenced by it, would seem to support the notion of the "unconscious." Implicit memory would be tested in the laboratory by asking a person to judge whether words in a list are pleasant or unpleasant. Then, when asked to recall those words, the person's memory is typically very good for those items. In cases of people with certain kinds of brain damage, implicit memory is actually better than when the person is told ahead of time that recall of the words is going to be tested. Thus, at some level, memories are formed even when the person is not consciously aware. Nevertheless, on logical grounds, Freud's theory contains many assumptions that are difficult to disprove. For instance, if you challenge the Freudian position that anxiety over sexual impulses lies at the root of defense mechanisms, a Freudian might tell you that it is your own anxiety over sexuality that keeps you from acknowledging the role of sexuality in personality.

Freud believed that people need defense mechanisms to protect themselves from the anxiety and stress of everyday life.

MindMAP Segment 4.2: Secure attachment

Mary Ainsworth, shown on the right, in the laboratory conducting research on infant attachment.

Other criticisms of psychodynamic theory concern the way Freud characterized women. Feminists have argued strongly against Freud's teachings about women, a position articulated by Horney during Freud's lifetime (Horney & Paris, 2000) and carried further by contemporary feminist critics (Chodorow, 1978; Dinnerstein, 1976; Mitchell, 1974; Sayers, 1991). Specifically, critics argue that Freud's theory placed too much emphasis on male development. Furthermore, his views that females desire to possess male genitals ("penis envy") and that "anatomy is destiny" are seen as biased against women.

Post-Freudians broadened the scope of psychodynamic theory to include the relationship between the individual and society. They set the stage for many later theorists and researchers to explore the role of cognitive processes, interpersonal relationships, and social context in the development of personality and psychological disorder. Many studies involving object relations theory have been conducted during the past few decades, particularly on the social behavior of infants and young children. Especially interesting and important has been the work of the late psychologist Mary Salter Ainsworth (1913–1999) and her associates (Ainsworth, Blehar, Waters, & Wall, 1978), who developed characterizations of infants according to **attachment style,** or the way of relating to a caregiver figure. Ainsworth and her colleagues found dramatic evidence pointing to the relationship between the attachment style of infants and subsequent development of competence in social relationships. For example, in one follow-up study of adolescents, those who by the age of 18 had insecure attachment styles as infants were more likely to develop anxiety disorders than those who had shown secure attachment style in early childhood (Warren, Huston, Egeland, & Stroufe, 1997).

Researchers have also adapted the concept of infant attachment style to the ways that individuals relate as adults to significant figures in their lives, such as a romantic partner (Bartholomew, 1997; Hatfield & Rapson, 1994). In one adaptation (Hazan & Shaver, 1994), individuals are classified on the basis of how they say they feel about romantic love relationships. People are classified into one of three attachment styles: secure, ambivalent (or preoccupied), and avoidant (which includes fearful and dismissive). People with a secure attachment style find it easy to relate to others in close relationships and are comfortable with emotional interdependencies. Ambivalent, or preoccupied, individuals seek closeness with others but worry that others will not value them in relationships. For people with a fearful attachment style, relationships create conflict because of the potential for being hurt by rejection, betrayal, or disloyalty within the relationship. Finally, dismissing individuals have little interest in emotional relationships and prefer to remain self-sufficient. Measuring attachment style involves having respondents rate each of these four approaches to relationships as they apply to themselves (see Table 4.2).

Attachment styles have been studied across the adult years, providing an important life-span perspective to this theoretical framework. As part of the National Comorbidity Study (NCS), respondents ranging in age from 15 to 54 years were asked to complete the three-category Hazan and Shaver (1987) attachment style measure (Mickelson, Kessler, & Shaver, 1997). Approximately 60 percent across all age groups rated themselves as securely attached. The oldest sample (45 to 54 years) was half as likely as the youngest group (15 to 24 years) to rate itself as anxiously attached. In another large-scale study of adults, respondents rated themselves on the Bartholomew and Horowitz (1991) four-category attachment style questionnaire (Diehl, Elnick, Bourbeau, & Labouvie-Vief, 1998). As in the NCS, far more respondents in the youngest group (20 to 39) than in the oldest group (60 to 88 years) rated themselves as insecurely attached. Interestingly, the oldest group also contained the largest percentage of dismissing respondents. One interpretation of these findings is that older adults do not wish to appear dependent on others, and responded to the questionnaire from that perspective rather than from the perspective of being insecurely attached. When older adults are studied in the context of a relationship, they seem to be just as capable of expressing and experiencing strong emotions as younger adults are (Carstensen, Gottman, & Levenson, 1995). Over time, older adults with secure attachment styles are also more likely to experience higher levels of well-being and a better ability to cope (Zhang & Labouvie-Vief, 2004).

Attachment style is increasingly being studied in relation to psychological disorders. Individuals with insecure attachment styles are more likely to receive high scores on measures of depression (Shaver, Schachner, & Mikulincer, 2005) and to experience depressive symptoms (Reis & Grenyer, 2004). One possible explanation is that people who are insecurely attached are

TABLE 4.2 Attachment Style Questionnaire

Each of the items below is first rated on a 7-point scale. Then the respondent chooses the one item from the four that best applies to how he or she feels in romantic love relationships.

ATTACHMENT STYLE: *Fearful*

1. I am uncomfortable getting close to others. I want emotionally close relationships, but I find it difficult to trust others completely, or to depend on them. I worry that I will be hurt if I allow myself to become too close to others.

ATTACHMENT STYLE: *Preoccupied*

2. I want to be completely emotionally intimate with others, but I often find that others are reluctant to get as close as I would like. I am uncomfortable being without close relationships, but I sometimes worry that others don't value me as much as I value them.

ATTACHMENT STYLE: *Dismissing*

3. I am comfortable without close emotional relationships. It is very important to me to feel independent and self-sufficient, and I prefer not to depend on others or have others depend on me.

ATTACHMENT STYLE: *Secure*

4. It is easy for me to become emotionally close to others. I am comfortable depending on others and having others depend on me. I don't worry about being alone or having others not accept me.

Source: From C. Hazan and P. R. Shaver, "Attachment as an organizational framework for research on close relationships" in *Psychological Inquiry* 5:1-22. Copyright ©1994. Used by permission of Lawrence Erlbaum Associates, Inc.

more likely to focus on negative information about themselves and more likely to see themselves as being at fault for negative events in their lives (Pereg & Mikulincer, 2004). However, it is important to bear in mind that the concept of attachment is based on Western values regarding personality, relationships, and meaning, and it might have limited relevance in non-Western cultures. For example, in looking at various aspects of Japanese culture that are considered adaptive, contemporary theorists (Rothbaum et al., 2000) have questioned the applicability in that culture of notions like autonomy, individuation, and exploration. When applying powerful constructs such as those found in attachment theory, it is very important to use an approach that is attuned to a person's culture.

The impact of psychodynamic viewpoints continues to be evident in treatment methods involving brief interventions. One approach involves the development of forms of treatment that, while relying on interpretation of transference relationships, focus the therapy more intensely on specific issues of current concern to the client (Grenyer & Luborsky, 1996; McCullough-Vaillant, 1997; Messer, 2000, 2001). Instead of trying to reconstruct the client's personality, the clinician helps the client overcome disappointment in a romantic relationship, or the stress of adjusting to a major life change such as parenthood. A client may participate in weekly therapy for a prearranged period up to 3 to 4 months. At the end of this period, the client uses the strengths developed in treatment to attempt to cope independently with the life stress or issue. The client may seek therapy again later, when new circumstances arise or the gains from therapy have eroded.

Humanistic Perspective

At the core of the **humanistic** perspective is the belief that human motivation is based on an inherent tendency to strive for self-fulfillment and meaning in life. According to humanistic theories of personality, people are motivated by the need to understand themselves and the world and to derive greater enrichment from their experiences by fulfilling their unique potential.

The work of humanistic theorists was heavily influenced by existential psychology, a theoretical position that emphasizes the importance of fully appreciating each moment as it occurs (May, 1983). According to existential psychology, people who are tuned in to the world around them and experience life as fully as possible in each moment are psychologically healthy. Psychological disorders arise when people are unable to experience this kind of living "in the moment." It is not a fundamental flaw in human nature that causes psychological disorders; rather, people become disturbed because they must live within the restrictions on human freedom that modern society imposes (Frankl, 1963; Laing, 1959).

By the mid-twentieth century, psychologists who were disenchanted with the major theoretical approaches to understanding human behavior and psychological disorder had come to believe that psychology had lost its contact with the "human" side of human behavior. These humanists joined together to form the "third force" in psychology, with the intention of challenging psychoanalysis and behaviorism. Two of the most prominent theorists within this tradition were Carl Rogers and Abraham Maslow.

Person-Centered Theory

The **person-centered theory** of Carl Rogers (1902–1987) focuses on the uniqueness of each individual, the importance of allowing each individual to achieve maximum fulfillment of potential, and the individual's need to confront honestly the reality of his or her experiences in the world. In applying the person-centered theory to the therapy context, Rogers (1951) used the term **client-centered** to reflect his belief that people are innately good and that the potential for self-improvement lies within the individual rather than in the therapist or therapeutic techniques.

A central feature of Rogers' theory is the idea that a well-adjusted person's self-image should match, or have congruence with, the person's experiences. When this happens, a person is said to be fully functioning, with an accurate view of the self and experiences. The term *fully* implies that the individual is putting psychological resources to their maximal use. Conversely, a psychological disorder is the result of a blocking of one's potential for living to full capacity, resulting in a state of incongruence—a mismatch between a person's self-perception and reality.

As an example of incongruence, consider Noah, a high-school boy who believes he is unpopular but fails to recognize that most of his classmates like him. According to Rogers, Noah's view of himself is "incongruent" with the reality of his situation. By telling himself that he is unpopular, Noah keeps from his awareness the fact that other people try to approach him in an effort to be friendly. You can see how such a situation would lead to problems over time because of his distorted perceptions of reality. These distortions cause Noah to interact with others in ways that lead to frustration rather than happiness.

Rogers regarded the fully functioning person as being in a process of continual evolution and movement, rather than in a static, or fixed, place. The development of these qualities has been an important focus of Rogers' theory (1959) and is the basis for the application of this theory in schools, parent education, and counseling. According to Rogers, a psychological disorder develops in an individual who, as a child, is subjected to parents who are too critical and demanding. The child feels overanxious about doing things that will be disapproved of. In this case, the parents are setting up what Rogers referred to as conditions of worth or conditions in which the child receives love only when he or she fulfills certain demands. The parents, in effect, tell the child, "If you want us to love you, you have to meet our conditions. That is the only way we will treat you as a worthy person." Children then become so fearful of being punished that they cannot admit to having done something "wrong," and the stage is set for a lifetime of low self-esteem.

Self-Actualization Theory

Related to Rogers' views of the fully functioning person is the theory Abraham Maslow (1962) developed, which centers on the notion of **self-actualization,** the maximum realization of the individual's potential for psychological growth. It is perhaps because of this focus on healthy human functioning that Maslow's

According to Rogers, when a parent communicates the message that a child must be "good" to be loved, the child becomes insecure and anxious.

theory has gained popularity as a guide to optimal living in such contexts as personnel management and human resources. Maslow's theory also focuses on motivation, in that he wanted to draw attention to the experiences that propel people toward realizing their fullest potential. According to Maslow, self-actualized people are accurate in their self-perceptions and are able to find rich sources of enjoyment and stimulation in their everyday activities. They are capable of *peak experiences* in which they feel a tremendous surge of inner happiness, as if they were totally in harmony with themselves and their world. But these individuals are not simply searching for sensual or spiritual pleasure. They also have a philosophy of life that is based on humanitarian and egalitarian values.

Maslow's theory is best known, perhaps, for its pyramid-like structure, which he called the **hierarchy of needs,** which describes the order in which human needs must be fulfilled.

The basic premise of the hierarchy is that, for people to achieve a state of self-actualization, they must have satisfied a variety of more basic physical and psychological needs. Needs that are lower on the hierarchy are called deficit needs, because they describe a state in which the individual seeks to obtain something that is lacking. An individual who is still struggling to meet those needs cannot progress to the top of the pyramid. Maslow would contend that a philosopher who is hungry is unable to philosophize. Of course, there are exceptions, in which people sacrifice their lower-order needs, even their lives, to achieve self-actualization. People who climb Mt. Everest, take off on a space mission, go on a hunger strike, or risk their lives to protest unjust military leaders are risking a variety of deficit needs. The underlying assumption is still that at some point in their lives these individuals satisfied their deficit needs, and for the purpose of achieving self-actualization, were able to set them aside.

Like Rogers, Maslow (1971) defined *psychological disorder* in terms of the degree of deviation from an ideal state and had similar views about the conditions that hamper self-actualization. To progress beyond the "deficit" needs, children must feel a stable sense of being physically cared for, safe from harm, loved, and esteemed. They must also be allowed to express the higher-level needs required to achieve actualization. For example, a person who is raised in an environment of dishonesty is deprived in satisfaction of the need for truth and becomes cynical and mistrusting as a result.

Treatment

According to Rogers' client-centered approach, therapy should focus on the needs of the client, rather than on the predetermined views of the clinician. A clinician's job is to help clients discover their inherent goodness and in the process to help each client achieve greater self-understanding. To counteract the problems caused by conditions of worth in childhood, Rogers recommended that therapists treat clients with **unconditional positive regard.** This method involves total acceptance of what the client says, does, and feels. As clients feel better about themselves, they become better able to tolerate the anxiety associated with acknowledging weaknesses. The clinician tries to be as empathic as possible and attempts to see the client's situation as it appears to the client.

Therapists working within the client-centered model often use such techniques as reflection and clarification. In reflection, the therapist mirrors back what the client has just said, perhaps rephrasing it slightly. For example, the client might say, "I'm really down today, because last week my girlfriend told me to get lost." The therapist's reflection of this statement might be, "So, when your girlfriend threatens to leave you, it makes you feel sad." In clarification, the therapist clarifies a vague or poorly formulated statement the client makes about how he feels. If the client says, "I'm really mad at my girlfriend for the lousy way she treated me," the therapist might say, "And perhaps you're very sad about that too."

Rogers also maintained that clinicians should provide a model of genuineness and willingness to disclose their personal weaknesses and limitations. Presumably, clients can learn a great deal from observing these behaviors in the therapist. Ideally, the client will see that it is acceptable and healthy to be honest in confronting one's experiences, even if those experiences have less than favorable implications. For example, the Rogerian clinician might admit to having experiences similar to those the client describes, such as feeling anxious about speaking before a group.

In contrast to the detailed therapy methods Rogers described, Maslow did not specify a particular model of therapy, because he developed his ideas in an academic context, rather than through clinical observation and treatment. His theory presents more of a map for optimal human development than a concrete basis for treatment of psychological disorders.

In more recent conceptualizations (Elliott, 2001), humanistic and experiential therapists have emphasized the importance of using clinical methods that go beyond the dated caricature of nondirective therapy in which the therapist merely restated the

MindMAP Segment 4.3 shows participants in an "Eco-Challenge" as they forge dangerous rivers and cliffs for the sake of winning a grueling competition.

In efforts to achieve self-actualization, some people engage in death-defying endeavors that test their physical and mental endurance.

client's words. Contemporary humanistic and experiential therapists emphasize the importance of entering the client's world and experience, and try to grasp what is most crucial for the client at the moment. Building on Rogers' premise, effective therapists look for ways to communicate empathy and acceptance, and to involve the client in setting treatment goals and defining therapeutic tasks.

Evaluation of Humanistic Theories

The humanistic approach has generated a considerable body of research based on the ideas of both Rogers and Maslow. Much of this research was conducted by the originators of these theories, both of whom were interested in translating their ideas into measurable concepts. Maslow developed his theory on the basis of case studies, gathered from 60 individuals, which involved combining biographical information about each individual's life with extensive interviews. His sample was purposefully limited to individuals showing signs of optimal psychological functioning, because Maslow maintained that psychology had ignored the study of healthy individuals in favor of those who suffered from various forms of psychopathology (Maslow, 1954–1970). Maslow's ideas have been widely applied in industry and business, as in the notion that worker productivity can be enhanced by satisfying self-actualization needs; if workers feel personally involved in what they do, they will presumably be happier and more productive.

Rogers was interested in researching two central facets of the client-centered approach: self-concept and the therapy process. In his research on self-concept, Rogers focused on the extent to which a person experiences incongruence between the "actual self" and the "ideal self." The aim of therapy would be to reduce incongruence between a client's self-concept and the person he or she would like to be. Rogerian concepts about therapy emphasized the factors that contribute to successful psychotherapy, such as the therapist's empathy. Many contemporary clinicians, irrespective of theoretical orientation, acknowledge the importance of empathy (Kahn & Rachman, 2000). The teaching of empathic communication styles has become integrated into current models of self-help, counseling, and advising programs.

Building upon the work of Carl Rogers, contemporary theorists have developed such techniques as **motivational interviewing (MI),** a directive, client-centered therapeutic style for eliciting behavior change by helping clients explore and resolve ambivalence. Like Rogers, those clinicians using motivational interviewing techniques rely on reflective listening in which they seek to stimulate change from within the client. The therapist attempts to elicit the client's own intrinsic motivation for change by emphasizing the individual's autonomy and ability to choose whether, when, and how to change (Hettema, Steele, & Miller, 2005).

Research on the effectiveness of client-centered therapy has not gone without criticism. Lacking in this research are some of the fundamental requirements for a scientific approach, such as using appropriate control groups or adopting acceptable levels of statistical significance in evaluating outcome. Although some advocates of the client-centered model are open to the importance of research, they have not been particularly successful at ensuring that their work is scientifically rigorous. There are several reasons for this; some have to do with the fact that the humanistic perspective relies heavily on the individual's self-report of psychological functioning, rather than objective assessment.

In response to criticism about the limitations of research on humanistic and experiential therapies, reviews of existing research have been written and new investigations have been initiated (Elliott, 2001). Although no striking conclusions have been drawn suggesting the superiority of experiential approaches, some interesting emerging trends suggest the utility of specific experientially based techniques in certain situations. For example, experiential clinicians have demonstrated the value of using in-session tasks such as relationship repair (Safran & Muran, 2000) and self-soothing.

Humanistic theorists and clinicians saw their ideas as a radical departure from the traditional focus of psychology, which minimized the role of free will in human experience. These theorists also saw human behavior in much more positive terms and viewed psychological disorders as the result of restricted growth potential. It is clear today that, although humanistic theories have limitations and do not play a central role in the understanding of psychological disorders, their influence has been widespread and is felt in many indirect ways.

Humanistic Approaches to Treating Meera

As an approach to treating a client like Meera, humanistic therapists would focus on providing her with a secure sense of positive self-regard. Consistent with Carl Rogers' emphasis on becoming more aware of one's feelings, Meera would be encouraged to experience more fully her feelings regarding her father's death and to link her sadness about his passing with her overall dissatisfaction with her life. In this process, the clinician would help Meera identify her feelings and accept them without undue self-criticism. In keeping with the concept of therapist self-disclosure, the clinician might share with Meera personal reactions to losses or feelings of sadness in hearing Meera talk about the hurt she has experienced.

Sociocultural Perspective

Theorists within the **sociocultural perspective** emphasize the ways that individuals are influenced by people, social institutions, and social forces in the world around them. As we discussed in Chapter 1, these influences can be organized into those that have an immediate impact on the person, such as the family, and more far-reaching circles, such as society. Unlike the other theoretical perspectives covered in this chapter, the sociocultural perspective is a more loosely connected set of orientations. Theorists within this perspective tend to focus on one or more realms of influence, but all share an emphasis on factors external to the individual as the cause of psychological disorders.

Family Perspective

Proponents of the **family perspective** see abnormality as caused by disturbances in the patterns of interactions and relationships that exist within the family. Although there are distinct theories within the family perspective, all share a focus on **family dynamics,** the interactions among family members. There are four major approaches within the family perspective: intergenerational, structural, strategic, and experiential (Sharf, 1996). Murray Bowen's intergenerational approach emphasizes the ways in which the parents' experiences in their own families of origin affect their interactions with their children; parents who experienced family dysfunction in their own childhoods are likely to repeat these disturbed patterns when raising their children. In the structural approach, Salvador Minuchin assumes that, in normal families, parents and children have distinct roles, and there are boundaries between the generations; problems can arise when family members are too close or too distant. Jay Haley proposed the strategic approach, in which the focus is placed on the resolution of family problems, with particular attention to power relationships within the family. Within the experiential approach, such theorists as Carl Whitaker emphasize the unconscious and emotional processes of families; dysfunctional behavior results from interference with personal growth.

REAL STORIES

WILLIAM STYRON: DEPRESSION

At the beginning of this chapter you read about Meera Krishnan's profound depression. Depression is experienced by everyone, and intense debilitating forms of depression have led many people to the point of considering suicide. One such person is the award-winning author William Styron, who divulged personal secrets pertaining to his own depression and suicidality. Well known for his skill and power as a writer, Styron has won numerous literary awards for his novels, including the prestigious Pulitzer Prize for novels such as *The Confessions of Nat Turner,* about the slave revolt in 1831, and *Sophie's Choice,* which described the experience of a Polish survivor of the Auschwitz concentration camp. While many of his novels focus on people burdened by struggle, his book *Darkness Visible* was a more personal view of tribulation, dealing with his own battle with severe depression.

Styron was born in 1925 in Virginia and began writing short stories at the age of 11. His mother died when he was 13, and he carried this pain through his adult years. He attended Duke University, where he published numerous stories in the literary magazine. At the age of 27, Styron married Rose Burgunder, with whom he had four children. His depression descended upon him slowly, but by the summer of 1985 it was clear that something was wrong. Styron recalls lying awake for hours, unable to sleep, tormented by feelings

William Styron

of loss and hopelessness. During his daytime hours, he found that his all-encompassing depression impaired his ability to concentrate. In fact, his efforts to write became so difficult and exhausting that he finally stopped trying. The pain became so intense that Styron contemplated suicide; after he had drafted a suicide note, he found the courage to talk to his wife about the extent of his problems. He then entered a psychiatric hospital where he began the difficult process of disentangling himself from the ominous grasp of profound depression.

In *Darkness Visible,* Styron writes about his depression:

The pain is unrelenting, and what makes the condition intolerable is the foreknowledge that no remedy will come—not in a day, an hour, a month, or a minute. If there is mild relief, one knows that it is only temporary; more pain will follow. It is

hopelessness even more than pain that crushes the soul. So the decision-making of daily life involves not, as in normal affairs, shifting from one annoying situation to another less annoying—or from discomfort to relative comfort, or from boredom to activity—but moving from pain to pain. One does not abandon, even briefly, one's bed of nails, but is attached to it wherever one goes. And this results in a striking experience—one which I have called, borrowing military terminology, the situation of the walking wounded. For in virtually any other serious sickness, a patient who felt similar devastation would be lying flat in bed, possibly sedated and hooked up to the tubes and wires of life-support systems, but at the very least in a posture of repose and in an isolated setting. His invalidism would be necessary, unquestioned and honorably attained. However the sufferer from depression has no such option and therefore finds himself, like a walking casualty of war, thrust into the most intolerable social and family situations. There he must, despite the anguish devouring his brain, present a face approximating the one that is associated with ordinary events and companionship. He must try to utter small talk, and be responsive to questions, and knowingly nod and frown and, God help him, even smile. But it is a fierce trial attempting to speak a few simple words.

Family theorists have made important contributions to the understanding and treatment of people with various disorders. Consider the examples of eating disorders and schizophrenia. As you will read in Chapter 14, some experts on eating disorders have suggested that the girls and young women who starve themselves are acting out a wish to assert their independence from their parents. Eating disorders may also arise from other family disturbances, such as conflictual relationships, parental

According to family systems theories, the cause of psychological disorder lies in family relationships.

withholding of affection, or familial chaos. In Chapter 10, you will read how some researchers believe that a person with schizophrenia can be profoundly affected by a disturbed pattern of interactions within the family. Thus, in a family in which members are critical, hostile, and emotionally overinvolved with each other, a person with schizophrenia is more likely to experience symptoms of the disorder.

Neglect and abuse are also important factors that increase vulnerability to psychological disorder. For example, some theorists contend that dissociative identity disorder, formerly known as "multiple personality disorder," is a response to early abuse; in this condition alternate identities emerge from a fantasy world markedly different from the horrors of the real home life. Researchers attempting to understand personality disorders also focus on the early life experiences of these individuals, especially circumstances involving trauma and abuse within the family. For example, many people with borderline personality disorder (a condition involving a pervasive pattern of instability in relationships) are thought to have difficulty with intimate adult relationships, because they fear they will be subjected to the same harsh treatment they experienced as children.

Social Discrimination

It is an unfortunate but well-recognized fact that many people experience discrimination because of gender, race, or age and that stresses associated with such discrimination can cause psychological problems. For example, as long ago as the 1950s, social scientists assessing the personal effects of discrimination showed that psychological disturbance is more commonly diagnosed among people of lower social class (Hollingshead & Redlich, 1958). In trying to explain this relationship, researchers have focused on the fact that people of

lower social class experience many economic hardships and have limited access to quality education, health care, and employment. Many people within the lower classes are also members of ethnic or racial minorities, for whom the power of socioeconomic discrimination is compounded. Furthermore, the stressful environments in which they live—with high rates of poverty, crime, substance abuse, and unemployment—make matters even worse. The intense stress with which they contend on a daily basis adversely affects their physical and mental health, and for many it leads to premature death (Lantz et al., 1998). Although discriminatory processes associated with social class differ from those pertaining to gender and age, the impact can be similar. When people are given few opportunities or when they encounter oppression because of unalterable human characteristics, they are likely to experience inner turmoil, frustration, and stress, which lead to the development of psychological symptoms.

Social Influences and Historical Events

In addition to personal attributes, such as gender or social class, we can all be adversely affected by general societal forces. For example, Theodore Millon (1998), a major researcher in the area of personality disorders, contends that fluid and inconsistent societal values have contributed to the increase in these disorders in Western society. He believes that social instability and a lack of clear cultural norms make their way into the home, causing children to feel that life is unpredictable and causing them to become more prone to developing psychological disorders later in life.

Psychological disorders can also emerge as a result of destructive historical events, such as the violence of a political revolution, the turmoil of a natural disaster, or the poverty of a nationwide depression. Since World War I, American psychologists have conducted large-scale studies of the ways in which war negatively affects psychological functioning. As you will read in Chapter 6, people who are traumatized as the result of exposure to battle, persecution, or imprisonment are at risk for developing serious anxiety disorders. Similarly, fires and natural disasters, such as earthquakes, tornadoes, and hurricanes, leave more than physical destruction in their wake.

Treatment

How do clinicians intervene with people suffering from conditions caused or exacerbated by sociocultural factors? Clearly, it is not possible to "change the world." However, clinicians can play a crucial role in helping people come to grips with problems that have developed within a family system, the immediate environment, or extended society.

Family Therapy In family therapy, the family is encouraged to try new ways of relating to each other or thinking about their problems. The family therapist, sometimes working with a co-therapist, meets with as many family members as possible. To facilitate communication, family therapists commonly use techniques that would be considered unusual in individual psychotherapy. For example, it is not unusual for the therapist to move around the room, sitting next to one family member for a period of time and then getting up to sit near another. The purpose of doing so may be to draw attention to individual family members or to establish an emotional alliance with a family member who appears to be resistant to the therapy process. At other times, the therapist may initiate a conversation between two family members and "coach" them as they talk to one another, so that the family begins to see their relationship from the therapist's perspective. Some family therapists conduct sessions in rooms with one-way mirrors, so that colleagues can observe and provide ideas and suggestions for improvements.

Gurman (2001) enumerates several ways the work of therapists specializing in work with families or couples differs from the work of clinicians working with clients in individual therapy. Rather than focusing on an individual's problems or concerns, family and couples therapists help clients define treatment goals in the relational patterns that maintain a particular problem or symptom. They also use a life-cycle perspective in which they consider the developmental issues, not only of each individual, but of the entire family or couple. Furthermore, family and couples therapists see the continuing relationships among the family members as potentially more healing than the relationship between clinicians and clients.

The particular techniques used in the therapy depend greatly on the training and theoretical approach of the family therapist. An intergenerational family therapist might suggest drawing a genogram, a diagram of all relatives in the recent past, in an effort to understand the history of family relationships and to use this understanding to bring about change. A structural family therapist might suggest that one of the family members enact a disagreement as if they were characters in a play about the family. Strategic family therapists would work with family members to develop solutions to the issues that are causing difficulty. An experiential family therapist might work with the family members to develop insight into their relationships with each other.

Group Therapy   For many troubled people, the experience of sharing their stories and experiences with other, similar people can be life changing. Irvin Yalom (1995), a prominent group therapy theorist, speaks of several factors in the group experience that are therapeutic. Clients in therapy groups commonly find relief and hope in the realization that their problems are not unique. In the group, they can acquire valuable information and advice from people who share their concerns. Furthermore, in the process of giving to others, people generally find that they themselves derive benefit. For some individuals, the group can compensate for painful and unsatisfactory experiences in their families of origin, as clients have the opportunity to develop more appropriate social skills and to imitate the successful

behavior of peers in a context that facilitates corrective and cathartic emotional experiences.

Often the best advice can be provided by other people experiencing the same condition. This principle has been well documented with peer groups—such as Alcoholics Anonymous, in which people recovering from alcoholism share their histories of substance abuse and the methods they use to abstain from drugs and alcohol. Group therapy in a more formal structure also has been a component of the treatment protocol for many other conditions. For example, people with pedophilia, who have sexually abused children, can benefit from group therapy, which is especially effective in confronting denial and rationalizations. Group therapy provides such individuals with a supportive context conducive to frank discussions of their urges and methods of self-control (Berlin, 1998).

Some clinicians find it particularly valuable to include a group therapy component in the treatment of people with eating disorders. Hearing the stories of people like themselves whose capacity for understanding the nature of the condition is especially insightful.

An extensive meta-analysis of research on the effectiveness of group therapy as a treatment for people with nonpsychotic depression found that this intervention is no less effective than individual psychotherapy (McDermut, Miller, & Brown, 2001). Proponents of group therapy recommend that group therapy for depression should be the frontline intervention for depressed outpatients, possibly supplemented later with individual therapy or medication if there is a need for either (Peterson & Halstead, 1998). Group therapy is preferred, not only because of its effectiveness, but also because of pragmatic benefits such as savings in time and money.

Multicultural Approach   As we discussed in Chapter 2, clinicians have a responsibility to be attuned to ethnic and cultural contributions to psychological problems. When working with clients from culturally diverse backgrounds, they know that they must go beyond the multiaxial diagnostic process in order to evaluate conditions that might be culturally influenced. Treatment must involve three major components: awareness, knowledge, and skills. Awareness involves recognition of sociocultural context as it affects both the client and the clinician. For example, they need to be sensitive to the ways in which the client's cultural background interacts with his or her specific life experiences and family influences. Knowledge is characterized by a commitment to learning about the cultural, ethnic, and racial group of their clients and how these factors play a role in assessment, diagnosis, and treatment. Skills involve culture-specific therapy techniques that are responsive to the unique characteristics of the clients whom they are treating.

Milieu Therapy   Another form of therapy that is based on intervention in the environment, rather than with the individual alone, is **milieu therapy,** in which staff and clients in a treatment setting work as a therapeutic community to promote positive functioning in clients. Members of the community participate in

Sociocultural Approaches to Treating Meera

Family therapists treating Meera would focus on various aspects of her family, both before and after her father's suicide. Most family therapists would prefer that Meera be treated not as an individual client but as a member of a family; as such, they would suggest that Meera's mother and three sisters participate in the therapy. Regardless of the specific approach, her father's powerful suicide message, that he "felt unloved," would play a central role in understanding and treating this dysfunctional system.

Regardless of the specific therapeutic techniques, therapists would be especially attentive to cultural issues relating to the treatment of Meera. These issues would include a sensitivity to the ways in which psychological problems are expressed and treated within the client's culture. For example, it would be important for the therapist to have an understanding of how the act of suicide is viewed in the Indian culture with a Hindu religious background and how the family members should be approached by a mental health professional.

An intergenerational theorist, such as Murray Bowen, would focus on the childhood experiences of Meera's patterns in an attempt to understand how the stage was set for the tragedy that unfolded in Meera's immediate family. The therapist might suggest drawing a genogram in an effort to understand the history of family relationships to use this understanding to bring about change.

Salvador Minuchin would focus on the structure of the family before and after the suicide. A structural therapist might ask one or more of the family members to enact a conflict in the family therapy session, such as an argument that might have taken place just prior to the suicide.

A strategic therapist would return to Jay Haley's problem-solving approach and help Meera's family members look for ways to move beyond their current state of grief and dysfunction.

Carl Whitaker would take a more humanistic and experiential approach to treating Meera and her family by trying to help the family grow beyond the tragedy, learn how to express their feelings, and to appreciate the unique aspects of each family member.

In addition to recommending family therapy for Meera, a clinician, such as Irvin Yalom, might also suggest that she participate in group therapy, particularly with a focus on bereavement. By hearing the stories and experiences of others who have lost loved ones, Meera might come to the realization that her reactions are not unique. The insights shared by others might help her move out of her grief. Furthermore, the help she provides others might prove to be therapeutically beneficial to Meera.

therapist, nurse, or paraprofessional, takes part in the overall mission of providing an environment that supports positive change and appropriate social behaviors. The underlying idea behind milieu therapy is that the pressure to conform to conventional social norms of behavior discourages a severely disturbed client, such as a person with schizophrenia, from expressing problematic symptoms. The "normalizing" effects of such an environment are intended to help the individual make a smoother and more effective transition to life outside the therapeutic community.

Evaluation of the Sociocultural Perspective

For the past several decades, clinicians have recognized the role of contextual factors in causing and maintaining abnormality, while also realizing that changing systems can be extremely difficult. For example, the detrimental effects of discrimination are widely recognized, but the solutions to this divisive social problem are not apparent. On a more local level, a client's family may play a central role in causing or aggravating a psychological problem, but these other people may be resistant to or unavailable for participation in treatment. In such cases, family therapy would not be possible, even if it were the treatment of choice. Although group therapy may be beneficial, many individuals are unwilling to disclose their problems to people they perceive to be strangers, because they feel ashamed or too shy. In the context of individual psychotherapy, clinicians can begin to address these issues by learning to adapt their approach to the specific cultural backgrounds of their clients (e.g., Bracero, 1998).

As important as the sociocultural model is to understanding the causes and treatment of psychological disorders, this perspective does have significant limitations. In recent years, the importance of biological determinants has resulted in a devaluing of the role of family systems as factors for certain disorders. For example, no credible contemporary theorist would support theories, considered tenable earlier in the century, that schizophrenia could be caused by disturbed family relationships. Science has certainly gone beyond such naive assumptions. At the same time, however, as previously noted, some experts believe that disturbed family communication can aggravate schizophrenic symptomatology. For most psychological disorders, the sociocultural perspective provides a valuable lens for looking at psychological disorders, but most conditions are best viewed from a viewpoint that also includes attention to psychological and biological forces.

group activities, ranging from occupational therapy to training classes. Staff members encourage clients to work with and spend time with other residents, even when leaving on passes. The entire community is involved in decision making, sometimes including an executive council, with elected members from units of the treatment setting. Every staff person, whether a

Behavioral and Cognitively Based Perspectives

In this section, we will discuss two perspectives that focus on behaviors and thought processes. According to the **behavioral perspective** abnormality is caused by faulty learning experiences,

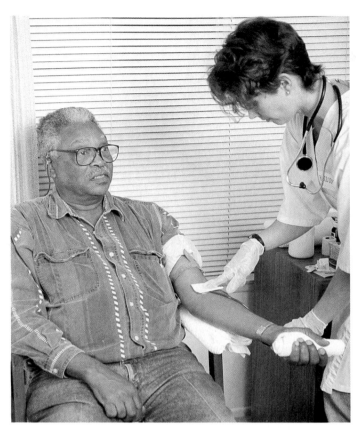

A frightening experience with a medical procedure during childhood can provoke intense fears that last throughout life.

and, according to the **cognitive-behavioral perspective** abnormality is caused by maladaptive thought processes, which result in dysfunctional behavior. The cognitive-behavioral perspective is sometimes referred to simply as "cognitive," although most people who work in this field prefer "cognitive-behavioral" (Craighead, Craighead, Kazdin, & Mahoney, 1994).

As you read the sections that follow, you will see how early behaviorists focused exclusively on observable behaviors, but over time they expanded their views to include a broader consideration of the relationship between thoughts and behaviors. The early behavioral psychologists resisted elaborate speculations about the "whys" of behavior, preferring to look at the "whats." In looking for "what" behaviors occur, they attempted to determine the functional relationships between events in the environment and the individual's behaviors. We will begin with a review of the principles of classical and operant conditioning, which lie at the heart of the behavioral perspective on psychological disorders.

Classical Conditioning

According to behaviorists, many of our automatic, emotional reactions are acquired through the process of **classical conditioning,** in which we associate a reflexive response with an

MindMAP Segment 4.4: Classical Conditioning

unrelated stimulus. For instance, the smell of a certain brand of cologne may make you feel unaccountably sad, until you realize that this was the cologne you wore when you saw the movie *Titanic*. In this example, you formed an association between an originally neutral stimulus (the cologne) and a naturally evoking stimulus (seeing the romantic hero die), which produces an emotional reaction (becoming teary-eyed). This connection is formed through repeated pairings of the two kinds of stimuli. The neutral stimulus is called the **conditioned stimulus,** because only after conditioning does it cause the response. The naturally evoking stimulus is called the **unconditioned stimulus,** because it produces the response before any conditioning takes place. The emotional reaction, once it has become associated with the conditioned stimulus (cologne), is called the **conditioned response.** Prior to conditioning, this reflex is called the **unconditioned response,** because no learning is necessary for you to cry when you witness the death of the heroine's lover.

As an explanation of psychological disorders, the classical conditioning paradigm accounts for acquiring or learning, through conditioning, the emotional reactions that interfere with a person's ability to carry out everyday tasks. For example, 6-year-old Jerry has been accidentally locked in a dark closet. The next time he needs something from that closet, he might feel nervous, almost panicky. His problem will become exacerbated through generalization, the expansion of learning from the original situation to one that is similar. For example, he may feel uncomfortable when he has to ride in an elevator, another enclosed space. This kind of reaction, called **stimulus generalization,** takes place when a person responds in the same way to stimuli that have some common properties. By contrast, discrimination is the process in which learning becomes increasingly specific to a given situation. Perhaps Jerry comes to realize that he will not be harmed if he rides the elevator, because it is not the same as a dark, locked closet. Differentiating between two stimuli that possess similar but essentially different characteristics is called **stimulus discrimination.**

One of the best known examples of conditioned fear is "Little Albert," an 11-month-old infant who was studied by John B. Watson (1878–1958), one of the most prominent early behaviorists. Watson and his associate, Rosalie Rayner, conducted an infamous set of experiments in which Albert was exposed to a loud noise while he petted a white rat; Albert subsequently acquired a fear of white rats. Their experiment represented a form of **aversive conditioning,** in which an aversive or a painful stimulus (the noise) was paired with an initially neutral stimulus (the rat). Albert's conditioned fear of rats generalized to other white, furry objects. Fortunately, this kind of experiment is now forbidden by ethical guidelines for research on human subjects; furthermore, its scientific merits have been questioned.

Even though Watson's analysis may have been misguided, we can draw inferences from it regarding how people acquire irrational fears. You can probably think of instances when you were exposed to a similar kind of aversive conditioning. Perhaps you ate too much pizza and became ill shortly afterward. The following week, when going by a pizzeria, you started to feel queasy. The pizza, previously a neutral or positive stimulus, acquired an aversive meaning for you. This particular principle is very useful in certain forms of behavior therapy, as in the treatment of alcoholism. As you will see in Chapter 13, one form of treatment involves giving a person a medication that causes nausea when alcohol is consumed. The individual then learns to associate alcohol with nausea; theoretically, this should reduce the frequency of alcohol consumption.

Operant Conditioning

Operant conditioning is a learning process in which an individual acquires a set of behaviors through reinforcement. In contrast to classical conditioning, operant conditioning involves the learning of behaviors that are not automatic. The learner tries to become proficient at performing behaviors that will lead to a positive outcome, such as attention, praise, or the satisfaction of a biological need. The "positive" outcome could also consist of the removal of an unpleasant or aversive circumstance. If your next-door neighbor's stereo is blasting, you may "operate" on the environment by making a phone call requesting that it be turned down. Your behavior results in the removal of an aversive stimulus.

The principles of operant conditioning were developed by B. F. Skinner, who, like Freud, is one of the best-known names in psychology. Of course, Skinner's theory is diametrically opposed to Freud's, because it holds that observable behavior is the only appropriate subject matter for psychology. Yet, Skinner's ideas about behavior also became the basis for a broad-ranging philosophy about human nature.

Reinforcement is the principle that underlies Skinner's model of operant conditioning. *Reinforce* means "to strengthen"; think of **reinforcement** as the "strengthening" of a behavior, increasing the likelihood that the behavior will be performed again. You can probably recall many examples in which your own behavior was reinforced. Perhaps a friend responded positively to an expression you used in conversation. Soon you realize you are using that expression quite often. Your friend's

Burrhus Frederick Skinner (1904–1990) demonstrates the principles of operant conditioning that he developed in his laboratory work with animals.

laughter served as a positive reinforcer that increased the frequency of your remark-making behavior. Extending this principle to psychological disorders, you can see how a disturbed behavior that is reinforced may become ingrained in a person. For example, an overprotective parent may inadvertently reinforce a child's pathological dependency by consoling the child with hugs, kisses, and cookies every time the child expresses a minor fear.

As these examples imply, there can be many kinds of reinforcers. The ones that satisfy a biological need (hunger, thirst, relief from pain, sex) are called **primary reinforcers,** because they are intrinsically rewarding. Behavior is also driven by **secondary reinforcers,** which derive their value from association with primary reinforcers. Money is a good example of a secondary reinforcer, because its value comes from the fact that it can be used to obtain primary reinforcers. As you will see later, some forms of behavior therapy use "tokens" as reinforcers, which are like money in that they can be used to purchase special treats or privileges.

Other kinds of secondary reinforcers do not have material value but are reinforcing for other reasons. Praise, attention, and recognition are rewarding to us as adults because earlier in our lives they were associated with the pleasurable feelings of

MindMAP Segment 4.5: Operant Conditioning

being fed and held by a parent. The value of secondary reinforcers extends beyond the family, in such areas as school, work, hobbies, and athletics. Secondary reinforcers can also be involved in the acquisition of various forms of abnormal behavior. For example, a hypochondriacal person who exaggerates the severity of normal physical signs may derive secondary reinforcement in the form of attention from family, friends, or health care professionals.

In operant, as in classical, conditioning, reinforcement can have a pleasurable or unpleasurable effect. So far, our discussion has focused on **positive reinforcement,** in which a person repeats a behavior that leads to a reward. Sometimes, individuals operate on the environment to remove an unpleasant stimulus, as in the case of your request that the neighbor turn the stereo down. The removal of the unpleasant stimulus is called **negative reinforcement.**

It is easy to confuse negative reinforcement with the idea that a person is being penalized for engaging in a certain behavior. However, **punishment** involves applying an aversive stimulus, such as scolding, which is intended to reduce the frequency of the behavior that preceded the punishment. When a parent scolds a misbehaving boy, the presumption is that the scolding will cause the child to stop misbehaving. If you receive a speeding ticket, this punishment is intended to stop you from speeding in the future.

The purpose of negative reinforcement is to increase, not decrease, the frequency of the behavior that preceded it. For example, the parent of the misbehaving boy may tell him that, as soon as he does what he is told, the scolding will stop. Your call to the neighbor stops the aggravating noise of the stereo. Negative reinforcement makes it more likely that you will repeat the behavior that succeeded in removing the unpleasant stimulus. Behaviorists prefer negative reinforcement to punishment, because research has shown that punishment has unpredictable effects on behavior. For example, a child who is spanked may rebel, learn to fear the parent, or even imitate the parent by being physically aggressive with peers and siblings.

In the absence of reinforcement, most learned behaviors tend to diminish and finally cease. If you go to your favorite music store and find that it is unexpectedly closed for the afternoon, you might return one or two more times, but, if this keeps happening, eventually you will stop going there. **Extinction** is the term used to describe the cessation of behavior in the absence of reinforcement. In treating a behavior problem, such as that of a girl who yells out answers in the classroom, the teacher might attempt to extinguish the behavior by ignoring the child, thereby withholding the reinforcement provided by attention. At the same time, the teacher would strengthen appropriate behaviors by attending to the child only when she raises her hand to answer a question.

We have discussed the learning of relatively simple behaviors. However, operant conditioning is also intended to apply to the acquisition of skilled new behavior, such as learning language or becoming a proficient musician. **Shaping** is the process of reinforcing increasingly complex behaviors that come to resemble a desired outcome. It is the method an animal trainer uses, for example, to teach a dolphin to jump through a hoop. The dolphin does not naturally perform this behavior but is capable of doing so with the right incentives. The trainer establishes this "operant" behavior in stages until the desired response sequence is completely established. Shaping is an important component in certain behavioral treatments when combined with other methods of reinforcement, as you will see shortly.

Social Learning and Social Cognition

Many parents object to their children watching television programs with violent or adult content, particularly in recent years, in which murders committed by high-school students have raised national attention. The concern is that children will see that violent behavior produces outcomes desirable to the perpetrator and, therefore, will be inclined to act in a similar fashion. The process of acquiring new responses by imitating the behavior of another person, called **modeling,** has been studied by behaviorists who focus on social learning. Theorists who work within social learning theory are interested in understanding how people develop psychological disorders through their relationships with others and through observation of other people. Some theorists within this perspective also focus on social cognition, the factors that influence the way people perceive themselves and others and form judgments about the causes of behavior. According to these perspectives, not only do direct reinforcements influence behavior, but so do indirect reinforcements, which people acquire by watching others engaging in particular behaviors and seeing them being rewarded or punished.

According to social learning theorist Albert Bandura (b. 1925), when you watch someone else being reinforced for a behavior, you receive **vicarious reinforcement** because you identify with that person (called the "model") and put yourself in that person's place. When the model is reinforced, it is as if you are being reinforced as well. This kind of reinforcement is the underlying process through which advertisements have their effect. People in beer commercials seem to be having a good time with their attractive friends, so, if you want to have a good time and be popular, you should drink that beer!

Social learning theory was considered revolutionary when it was first proposed, because it expanded the realm of influence of learning from direct consequences of behavior to the many indirect reinforcements that exist in life. Furthermore, social learning theory added the idea that people acquire "expectancies" for reinforcement as part of the learning process. This was a step toward a more cognitively oriented form of behavioral theory, which focuses on the role of thoughts and ideas in influences on behavior. Gradually, social learning theory has come to be known as social cognitive theory because of its increased focus on thought processes and how they influence overt behavior.

The process of vicarious reinforcement, according to social learning theorists, accounts for children acquiring the behaviors of adults through imitation.

One important contribution of the social learning and social cognitive theories was to show how maladaptive behaviors are learned through observing other people engaging in these behaviors and seeing them receive rewards. The process of vicarious reinforcement can explain why parents who were abused as children are more likely to be physically violent with their own children. A boy who observes his father beating his mother may batter his own wife years later.

Bandura has also become known for his work on **self-efficacy,** the individual's perception of competence in various life situations. According to Bandura, people will try harder to succeed in difficult tasks if they are confident that they can complete these tasks. The concept of self-efficacy can be applied to a variety of psychological phenomena, including motivation, self-esteem, addictions, interpersonal relations, delinquent behavior, and health (Bandura, 2004; Bandura et al., 2003; Bandura & Locke, 2003). For example, in the area of health, if individuals do not believe they can control their diet, they will be less likely to follow through on the activities needed to help them achieve desirable body weight. People who lack self-efficacy in a given situation can be trained to increase their confidence in their abilities to succeed, thus enhancing their feelings of self-worth.

Cognitively Based Theory

Cognitively based theory focuses on the contribution of the individual's thoughts to maladaptive emotions and behavior. Aaron Beck (b. 1921) is one of the leading advocates of this approach, having developed it as a way of understanding depressive disorders. In addition, David Barlow developed a version of cognitive-behavioral therapy that specifically examines the role of cognitions in anxiety disorders. Each of these approaches emphasizes not only the fact that our thoughts can produce our emotions but also that by changing our thoughts and our behaviors, we can change our emotions.

According to Beck, a pervasive feature of many psychological disorders is the existence of **automatic thoughts**—ideas so deeply entrenched that the individual is not even aware that they lead to feelings of unhappiness and discouragement. (Beck drops the word *behavioral*, referring to his approach simply as cognitive theory.) Automatic thoughts appear to arise spontaneously and are difficult to ignore. For example, in conversation with a friend, a person might start to think, "What a boring person I am," "That was a dumb thing to say," or "Why can't I be more clever and interesting?" Beck compared automatic thoughts to the "shoulds" described by Horney, which lead the person to try to achieve unrealistic goals of perfection. In the case of depression, automatic thoughts are inevitably followed by sadness, because these thoughts are so discouraging (Beck, Rush, Shaw, & Emery, 1979).

Automatic thoughts are the product of **dysfunctional attitudes,** personal rules or values people hold that interfere with adequate adjustment. These attitudes prime the individual who is prone to depression to interpret experiences in negative ways through faulty logical processes, as shown in Figure 4.1. Automatic thoughts emerge from this process, leading to the negative emotion of depression. In other psychological disorders, automatic thoughts of a different nature prevail. However, whatever form of disorder is involved, the process through which negative emotions follow from these thoughts remains the central focus of cognitive theory.

Barlow proposes that a combination of physiological, cognitive, and behavioral phenomena contribute to the experience of dysfunctional emotions, such as the type of anxiety that is not rationally tied to the realities of the situation. For example, a physiological contributor to anxiety is hyperventilation, in which the individual breathes so rapidly that he or she feels deprived of oxygen. A cognitive contribution to the emotion of anxiety is a misperception of the seriousness or danger represented in a situation. Behaviorally, individuals who experience dysfunctional levels of anxiety have formed associations between certain stimuli and the feelings of panic and a desire to avoid the feared situation (Barlow, 2002).

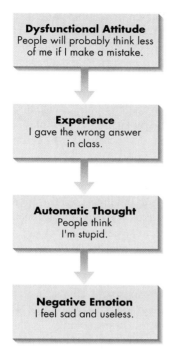

FIGURE 4.1 The relationship among dysfunctional attitude, experience, automatic thought, and negative emotion

Source: Adapted from A. T. Beck, A. J. Bush, B. F. Shaw, & G. Emery in *Cognitive Therapy of Depression.* Copyright ©1979 Guilford Publications, Inc. Reprinted by permission.

Treatment

According to behavioral and cognitively based perspectives, abnormality arises from faulty learning and thinking and can be changed by methods that address these processes. In interventions based on behavioral theory, clinicians use behavioral analysis in which they attempt to provide a precise understanding of the factors that maintain the behavior before proposing methods that are likely to be effective (Mueser & Liberman, 1995). In cognitive therapies, the clinician works with the client to change maladaptive thought patterns.

Conditioning Techniques   Behavior therapists use both classical conditioning and operant conditioning, relying on such mechanisms as positive reinforcement, negative reinforcement, punishment, and extinction. These methods are combined in various procedures that involve helping the client "unlearn" the maladaptive behaviors and replace them with ones that will allow them to move on with their lives.

One method that is particularly useful in treating irrational fears is based on **counterconditioning,** the process of replacing an undesired response to a stimulus with an acceptable response. Counterconditioning is particularly effective when the new response is incompatible with the existing one. The assumption underlying counterconditioning is that, if the undesired response was learned, it can be unlearned, and

the acceptable response can be acquired through the same process.

Physician Joseph Wolpe (1915–1997) is the primary figure in the development of counterconditioning approaches. After classically conditioning cats to experience "anxiety" in a room in which they had been shocked, Wolpe developed methods to inhibit the anxiety by training them to associate the room with eating rather than shocks. From this experiment, Wolpe speculated that the counterconditioning of anxiety could serve as a basis for a radically new therapy model. His insights (Wolpe, 1958, 1973) have had a major impact on behavioral therapy as it is practiced today.

Counterconditioning might be used to help a client overcome a fear of handling knives. The client would be reinforced to feel relaxed while holding a knife, so that relaxation replaces the undesirable response of fear. The therapist would train the client in relaxation techniques and provide rewards for showing a relaxation response instead of fear when presented with a knife. Over time, the pairing of rewards with relaxation in the presence of the previously feared stimulus should establish the new response and reduce or eliminate the old one.

A variant of counterconditioning is **systematic desensitization,** in which the therapist presents the client with progressively more anxiety-provoking images of stimuli while the client is in a relaxed state. This is considered to be a form of counterconditioning in that, in each successive presentation, the therapist encourages the client to substitute the desired response for the undesired one—relaxation rather than anxiety. This technique is used when the clinician believes that having to confront the actual stimulus that has provoked the undesirable behavior would overwhelm the client. For example, if this client has a full-blown anxiety reaction at the sight of a knife, it might be unwise to use counterconditioning, because relaxation would be impossible under these circumstances. Instead, the therapist exposes the client to the knife gradually, in steps, developing a list, or "hierarchy," of images associated with the fear. At each step, the therapist helps the client enter a relaxed state while looking at or handling the feared object. Eventually, the client reaches the point of being able to handle a knife without panicking. However, at any point, if the client suffers a setback, the therapist must move back down the hierarchy until the client is ready to move on.

Another counterconditioning technique developed by Wolpe (1973) is assertiveness training, in which the client is taught to express justified anger, rather than to be anxious and intimidated when other people are exploitive, unduly demanding, or disrespectful. As in counterconditioning, the underlying rationale is that a person cannot experience opposing emotions

MindMAP Segment 4.6: Systematic Desensitization

In a token economy, clients are given tangible rewards, or "tokens," which they exchange for desired activities or privileges.

(anger and anxiety, in this case). By strengthening the desired emotion (anger), the opposite emotion (anxiety) is unlearned in that situation. At the same time, the client learns effective communication methods to manage difficult situations more effectively.

Contingency Management Techniques   Another category of behavioral therapy techniques uses a simple principle that many people follow in their daily lives; that is, desired behavior can be established through rewards, and undesirable behavior can be eliminated by removing its rewards. **Contingency management** is a form of behavioral therapy that involves this principle of rewarding a client for desired behaviors and not providing rewards for undesired behaviors. This treatment teaches the client to connect the outcome of the behavior with the behavior itself, so that a contingency, or connection, is established.

In everyday life, people use contingency management to stop smoking, control their weight, discipline their children, or develop better study habits. Some people turn to therapy if their own contingency management efforts have failed to change undesirable behaviors. A therapist can help monitor the client's behavior and suggest alternative ways to try to control it. A common form of contingency contracting used in psychiatric hospitals is the **token economy,** in which residents who perform desired activities earn plastic chips that can later be exchanged for a tangible benefit (Ayllon & Azrin, 1965).

Modeling and Self-Efficacy Training   In the behavioral therapy methods we have discussed so far, clients directly experience reinforcement for actions they carry out in the context of therapy. However, we have seen from Bandura's research that people can learn new behaviors vicariously. Bandura, in fact, successfully applied the principle of vicarious reinforcement to behavioral therapy by exposing clients to videotapes or real-life models who were being rewarded for demonstrating the desired behaviors (Bandura, 1971). In this approach, a girl who is afraid

of dogs might be shown a videotape of a girl happily petting a dog and playing ball with it. By seeing the videotape, the client presumably develops the idea that playing with dogs can be fun and, more important, need not be dangerous. Going one step further, the therapist might use **participant modeling,** a form of therapy in which the therapist first shows the client a desired behavior and then guides the client through the behavior change. The therapist might first play with the dog and then have the girl do the same while the therapist offers encouragement.

Another form of behavioral therapy relies on Bandura's concept of self-efficacy. According to Bandura, maladaptive responses, such as irrational fears, arise from the perception that one lacks the resources for handling a potentially threatening situation. If the client's feelings of self-efficacy are strengthened, then the client should be able to overcome the irrational fear (Bandura, 1991). Self-efficacy training can also help clients gain control over undesired habits, such as smoking (Shiffman et al., 2000). In this approach, emphasis is placed on helping clients feel that they have the emotional strength to follow through on their wish to stop smoking.

Cognitive Therapies   The principles of cognitive and cognitive-behavioral therapies are straightforward and follow logically from the premise that dysfunctional emotions are the product of dysfunctional thoughts. One of the fundamental techniques is **cognitive restructuring,** in which the clinician helps the client alter the way he or she views the self, the world, and the future. In this method, the therapist reframes negative ideas into more positive ones to encourage the development of more adaptive ways of coping with emotional difficulties. The therapist questions and challenges the client's dysfunctional attitudes and irrational beliefs, and makes suggestions that the client can test in behavior outside the therapy session.

One form of cognitive-behavioral treatment that addresses a particular form of anxiety disorder known as panic disorder is **panic control therapy (PCT),** which consists of cognitive restructuring, exposure to bodily cues associated with panic attacks, and breathing retraining (Barlow, 2002). PCT proceeds through a series of steps. First, clients are given educational information about the physiology of panic attacks in which they learn about the changes in the body that accompany the sensation of acute distress that occurs in one of these attacks. Hyperventilating during a panic attack is addressed by training clients to avoid overbreathing and learning to relax their respiratory response. Behavioral methods similar to those used in counterconditioning are applied to help weaken the association between the feared stimuli and the emotion of anxiety. The cognitive component of PCT involves teaching clients to learn to recognize when their appraisals of situations are unrealistically contributing to the emotion of anxiety. Throughout this process, clients are expected to monitor their reactions and also to be able to identify situations, behavior, or people who make them feel "safe." Eventually, it is hoped that clients will no longer need

Behavioral and Cognitively Based Approaches to Treating Meera

Although Meera's psychological condition is a type not generally treated with strict behavioral methods, she might benefit from interventions that focus on interpersonal skills and communication. For example, Wolpe might suggest that Meera could benefit from assertiveness training, in which she would be taught to express her feelings and needs to others, such as her supervisors at work and her family.

Cognitive therapists would focus on the aspects of Meera's thought processes that contribute to her unrelenting depression. Beck would help Meera see the ways in which her automatic thoughts lead to feelings of unhappiness, and he would work toward the goal of helping her change her views of self, the world, and her future through cognitive restructuring.

these supports as they gain control over their dysfunctional behaviors, thoughts, and emotions. Additional features that may accompany PCT are involvement of partners or other family members and assistance in discontinuing the use of antianxiety medications.

Evaluation of the Behavioral and Cognitively Based Perspectives

Perhaps the main appeal of the behavioral perspective is its relative simplicity and reliance on concepts that can be translated into objective measures. This perspective uses a limited set of empirically based principles and circumvents sticky philosophical questions by not proposing complex structures that underlie behavior. The very simplicity of the behavioral perspective is also its undoing, in the minds of many psychologists. Humanists contend that, by restricting the definition of *psychology* to the study of observable behavior, behaviorists have failed to capture the complexity of human nature and have portrayed free will as a negligible influence on humans, compared with outside forces in the environment. Psychoanalysts argue that the de-emphasis on unconscious influences, which is characteristic of behavioral approaches, leaves out most of what is interesting and unique about human beings.

Cognitively oriented theorists have come closest to satisfying both sets of criticism, in that they regard thought processes as worthy of studying (satisfying the humanist concerns) and propose that behavior can be influenced by unstated assumptions about the self (satisfying the psychoanalytic contentions). However, even the cognitively oriented theorists fail to provide an overall explanation of personality structure, restricting their observations to particular problem areas.

Although not comprehensive, the behavioral and cognitive theories have a strong empirical base. Each of the major theoretical approaches has been grounded in research from its

inception. The methods of therapy proposed by these theories were tested from and developed through controlled studies. When studies have failed to provide supportive evidence, the theory or proposed method of therapy has been revised accordingly. As a result, contemporary researchers continue to broaden the applications of these theories to a variety of clients and settings. Behavioral treatment is used for disorders ranging from alcoholism to sexual dysfunction, as well as a variety of anxiety disorders, and for social skills training in schizophrenia. You will see many instances throughout this book in which the contributions of behavioral and cognitive theorists play prominent roles in understanding and treating various psychological disorders. Even though clinicians may not adhere entirely to behavioral or cognitive approaches, most would recognize that certain strategies within these models have special advantages.

Biological Perspective

Within the **biological perspective,** disturbances in emotions, behavior, and cognitive processes are viewed as being caused by abnormalities in the functioning of the body. As you will read in the following sections, the nervous system and endocrine systems play important roles in determining abnormality, as does the genetic makeup of an individual.

The Nervous System and Behavior

Complex behaviors, thoughts, and emotions are the result of activities of the central nervous system. The central nervous system consists of the brain and the nerve pathways going to and from the brain through the spinal cord. You can think of the central nervous system as a core information processing unit within the body, transmitting information regarding the body's current state to various decision-making centers, and then carrying these decisions back to the body as the basis of action. These activities occur at a rate of speed that exceeds even the most sophisticated computer and involves millions of decisions every second in which trillions of cells participate.

Neurons and Synapses   A neuron, or nerve cell, is the basic unit of structure and function within the nervous system. The neuron is a communicator, whose job it is to transmit information.

The transmission of information throughout the nervous system takes place at synapses, or points of communication

MindMAP Segment 4.7: Neural Functioning

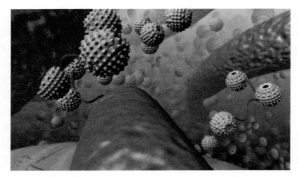

MindMAP Segment 4.8 uses lively animations to demonstrate how several neurotransmitters operate in the brain.

Scientists have made great advances in understanding the role and function of neurotransmitters in the past decade.

between neurons. Electrical signals containing information are transmitted chemically across the synapse from one neuron to the next. Through this transmission, neurons form interconnected pathways, along which information travels from one part of the nervous system to another.

Synapses can have one of two effects—either "turning on" or "turning off" the neuron that receives information. An excitatory synapse is one in which the message communicated to the receiving neuron makes it more likely to trigger a response. By contrast, an inhibitory synapse decreases the activity of the receiving neuron. At any given moment, the activity of a neuron, and whether it sends off a signal to other neurons in its pathway, depends on the balance between excitatory and inhibitory synapses. In this way, each neuron integrates information from all the signals feeding into it, and it responds according to which of these signals is stronger.

Right now, as you read the words on this page, millions of electrochemical transmissions are taking place in your brain. What are these transmissions like? You might imagine something like the set of electrical wires that connects the components of your stereo system. As the signal passes from one wire to another, the sound is transmitted until it finally reaches the speaker. The nervous system is like this, but with one important difference: there are no "hard-wire" connections between the neurons. The neurons do not touch; instead, there is a gap at the juncture between neurons, called the synaptic cleft. The transmission of information from the axon of one neuron to the dendrites of other neurons involves chemical and electrical activities occurring across the synaptic cleft. (The fact that synapses do not involve direct connections will prove to be particularly im-

portant later, when we discuss how psychoactive medications affect the brain.) A chemical substance is released from the transmitting neuron into the synaptic cleft, where it drifts across the synapse and is absorbed by the receiving neuron. This substance is called a *neurotransmitter* (see Figure 4.2).

There are several kinds of neurotransmitters, which differ in their chemical composition. Some of the more important ones are acetylcholine (ACh), gamma-aminobutyric acid (GABA), serotonin, dopamine, norepinephrine, and enkephalins. Other chemicals involved in the regulation of neural activity are hormones, growth factors, and various proteins, such as amino acids and neuropeptides. Some neurotransmitters are excitatory, in that they increase the likelihood that the receiving neuron will trigger a response. Norepinephrine is generally considered an excitatory neurotransmitter, and a deficit in this substance is thought to be a causal factor in depression. Other neurotransmitters, such as GABA, have an inhibitory effect when they pass through the synapse. Some tranquilizers work by facilitating GABA activity—which, in effect, "slows down" the nervous system. The enkephalins have received particular attention since the early 1980s, because they have been recognized as the body's naturally produced painkillers. Abnormalities in other neurotransmitters are considered likely sources of some forms of abnormal behavior. For example, researchers hypothesize that serotonin is involved in a variety of disorders, including obsessive-compulsive disorder, depression, and eating disorders. An excess of dopamine activity has been hypothesized to cause symptoms of schizophrenia. Conversely, a dopamine deficit causes trembling and difficulty walking, which are symptoms of Parkinson's disease.

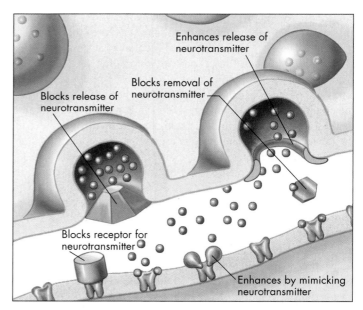

FIGURE 4.2 Action of drugs at the synapse Different drugs affect different parts of the nervous system and brain, and each drug functions in one of these specific ways.

You can see by these examples that neurotransmitters play a central role in affecting a variety of behaviors. Other disorders, particularly those that respond to medication, may someday be found to have their source in neurotransmitter imbalances. The potential that this approach offers to the understanding and treatment of psychological disorders cannot be overemphasized, because it suggests relatively direct, simple interventions that can reduce the toll these disorders take on the quality of human life. However, it is unlikely that a "magic" cure will be found that, like penicillin for bacterial diseases, can eliminate a broad spectrum of serious mental disorders.

Genetic Influences on Behavior

Many people have an intuitive understanding of the genetic influences on behavior. It is common for parents to scrutinize their children to see which of their own characteristics have emerged, from the father's long fingers to the mother's small nose. Relatives often engage in ample speculation about the origins of this or that characteristic in the younger generation. Perhaps an aunt or uncle has told you that you have your grandmother's smile or that you are as mischievous as your father was when he was young. Apart from these informal assessments, most people would find it difficult to trace precisely the genetic routes through which offspring come to acquire the behaviors, appearance, mannerisms, and personality traits that have made their way through the family tree. There is good reason for this. The mechanisms of genetic inheritance often stump even the most sophisticated researcher.

Basic Concepts in Genetics When we speak of inherited characteristics, we are talking about the components of the **genome,** the complete set of instructions for "building" all the cells that make up an organism. The human genome is found in each nucleus of a person's many trillions of cells. As is true for any building plan, things can change as a result of environmental factors. This interaction of the gene with the environment is reflected in the **phenotype,** which is the external expression of the genes. We will return to this crucial point later.

The genome for each living creature consists of tightly coiled threads of the molecule **deoxyribonucleic acid (DNA).** The DNA resides in the nucleus of the body's cells as 23 sets of paired strands each spiraled into a double helix, a shape that resembles a twisted ladder. There are four nitrogen-containing chemicals, called bases, that appear like beads of a necklace on each strand of DNA and form a particular sequence. This sequence of bases contains the information the cells need to manufacture protein, the primary component of all living things. Another function of DNA is to replicate itself before the cell divides. This makes it possible for each new cell to have a complete copy of the DNA's vital message, so that it can continue the process of protein manufacturing carried out by the original cell.

A **gene** is a functional unit of a DNA molecule carrying a particular set of instructions for producing a specific protein. There are about 32,000 genes, and every gene is made up of 2 million pairs of chemical units called nucleotide bases. Human genes vary widely in length, often extending over thousands of bases, but only about 10 percent of the genome actually contains sequences of genes used to code proteins. The rest of the genome contains sequences of bases that code for nothing of known value.

The genome is organized into **chromosomes**—distinct, physically separate units of coiled threads of DNA and associated protein molecules. (See Figure 4.3) Each chromosome contains hundreds to thousands of genes. In humans, there are two sets of chromosomes, one set contributed by each parent. Each set has 23 single chromosomes: 22 are called "autosomes" and contain nonsex-linked information, and the twenty-third is the X or Y sex chromosome. A normal female has a pair of X chromosomes, and a male has an X and Y pair. Although each chromosome always has the same genes on it, there is often no rhyme or reason to the distribution of genes on chromosomes. A gene that produces a protein that influences eye color may be next to a gene that is involved in cellular energy production.

Chromosomes can be seen under a light microscope and, when stained with certain dyes, reveal a pattern of light and dark bands. These bands reflect variations in the amounts of the four bases. Each chromosome has a characteristic size and banding pattern that can be seen through the microscope. This sort of inspection can reveal a few types of major chromosomal abnormalities—such as a missing or an extra copy of a chromosome, as in Down syndrome, a cause of mental retardation in which the individual has a third copy of chromosome 21. Most chromosomal abnormalities, however, are too subtle to be detected by this fairly crude method and require more sophisticated forms of analysis.

Genes undergo alterations, called mutations, some from faulty copying when a cell reproduces itself, some from chemical alterations by sunlight or carcinogens. Significant changes in DNA can result that cause faulty functioning of proteins. Genetic mutations can be either inherited from a parent or acquired over the course of one's life. Inherited mutations originate from the DNA of the cells involved in reproduction (sperm and egg). When reproductive cells containing mutations are combined in one's offspring, the mutation will be in all the bodily cells of that offspring. Inherited mutations are responsible for such diseases as cystic fibrosis and sickle cell anemia and may predispose an individual to cancer, major psychiatric illnesses, or other complex diseases.

Acquired mutations are changes in DNA that develop throughout a person's lifetime. Remarkably, cells possess the ability to repair many of these mutations. If these repair mechanisms fail, however, the mutation can be passed along to future copies of the altered cell.

The Human Genome Project (HGP) began in the United States in 1990 as a joint project of the National Institutes of

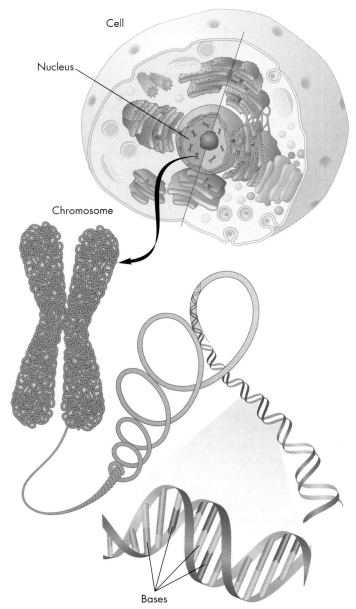

Cell

Nucleus

Chromosome

Bases

FIGURE 4.3 The human genome Every human cell (with the exception of mature red blood cells, which have no nucleus) contains the same DNA. Each cell has 46 molecules of double-stranded DNA. Each DNA molecule is made up of 50 to 250 million bases housed in a chromosome.

Health and the U.S. Department of Energy. Joining forces with international partners, HGP scientists are attempting to decipher the massive amount of information contained in the genomes of humans. In 2001, two rival teams of scientists produced the first complete maps of human DNA; one team was led by J. Craig Venter of Celera Genomics (a private biotech company) (Venter et al., 2001), and the other was led by Eric Lander, head of the Whitehead/MIT Genome Center (International Human Genome Sequencing Consortium, 2001). The

next steps will be equally challenging: namely, to determine the characteristic controlled by each of these genes or gene sequences. These discoveries will be crucial eventually to the treatment of psychological disorders thought to have a genetic basis. Chromosome 21 was the first human chromosome to be completely mapped (Hattori et al., 2000). This is an important chromosome because it is implicated as a cause of both Alzheimer's disease, a form of dementia, and Down syndrome, a form of mental retardation.

Models of Genetic Transmission   Recall that the cells of the body contain two sets of chromosomes, one inherited from the mother and one from the father. Each set of chromosomes has the same genes, but many of these genes come in different variants, called alleles. Genetically based traits (such as hair color and eye color) are determined by the combination of the gene's two alleles that the individual inherits. Alleles are described as either dominant or recessive, depending on whether one or both must be present in the individual's genome for the trait to be expressed. A dominant allele always expresses the trait that it codes, no matter what the other allele is. A recessive allele is expressed only if it is paired with another recessive allele.

Certain genetic disorders are based on a dominant pattern of inheritance. In this case, a person has inherited a "normal" allele and a "disease" allele. Since the disease allele is dominant, it is expressed in the individual, who is likely to become afflicted with the disorder. The affected individual, therefore, carries one normal and one disease allele. Let's say the affected individual is a male. When he has children, each of his children has a 50 percent chance of inheriting the disease allele and, therefore, has a 50 percent chance of developing the disorder. Another pattern of disease inheritance involves altered recessive genes. In this case, both parents carry one normal allele and one disease allele. Although neither parent has the disease, each is a "carrier." Think of the alleles as "ND" and "ND," with "N" for normal and "D" for disease. Two NDs can produce four possible combinations: NN, ND, DN, and DD. Therefore, each child has a 1/4 chance of being diseased, a 1/4 chance of being normal, and a 2/4 (1/2) chance of being a carrier, like the parents.

When scientists attempt to determine the genetic origins of particular psychological and physical characteristics, they often begin with the assumption that a characteristic was acquired through this type of dominant-recessive pattern of transmission. Although this model is complex, only a limited number of factors can influence the inheritance of a characteristic from generation to generation; with the right tools, it is possible to trace the route of genetic transmission by knowing which genes are dominant and which are recessive. Infinitely more challenging is the process of determining patterns of inheritance when the pattern does not follow one of dominant-recessive transmission. Complex traits are characteristics that reflect an inheritance pattern that does not follow the simple rules of dominant and recessive combination. This inheritance pattern follows a **polygenic** model of genetic inheritance, in which two or more genes participate to determine a characteristic. In a polygenic model, multiple genes are assumed to play a role in combining, perhaps at different levels, to determine the overall expression of a characteristic. The combined pattern of as many as 10 or 100 genes determines whether the individual acquires a polygenetically determined characteristic, such as body size.

Researchers have come to accept the notion that an interaction of "nature" and "nurture" causes most forms of psychological disorders. As we saw in Chapter 1, current models propose interactions between genetic and environmental contributors to behavior in which nature and nurture have reciprocal influences on each other. Let's take a look at these interactions in more depth.

Consider the example of extraversion (outgoing behavior), which researchers have claimed to be a partially inherited characteristic (Loehlin, McCrae, Costa, & John, 1998; Saudino et al., 1999). A girl born with "extraversion" genes may trigger friendly responses from people in her environment that encourage her to be even more extraverted, leading to the growth of this trait within her personality. A variation on this model is that people select environments that are consistent with their genetically determined interests and abilities and that these environments, in turn, further influence the expression of these qualities (Scarr, 1992). According to this model, genetically based characteristics are enhanced by experiences that people have chosen because they possess these interests. Estimates of **heritability,** the proportion of the offspring's phenotype that is due to genetic causes, have been applied to traits as diverse as religiosity, political orientation, job satisfaction, leisure interests, proneness to divorce, subjective well-being, and even perceptions of one's talents or abilities. Theorists claim that these characteristics have a strong genetic component as indicated by high heritability indices (Bouchard et al., 1990; Diener & Lucas, 1999; McGue, Hirsch, & Lykken, 1993; Plomin & Caspi, 1999).

Another interactive view of the relationship between genes and the environment is the **diathesis-stress model,** a proposal that people are born with a genetic predisposition ("diathesis") or acquire a vulnerability very early in life due to such formative events as traumas, diseases, birth complications, and even family experiences (Zubin & Spring, 1977). Such vulnerability places individuals at risk for the development of a psychological disorder. A dramatic illustration of the diathesis-stress model comes from a large study extending over a period of nearly 20 years. Biological parents with and without psychiatric disorders and their offspring were assessed through extensive interviews and ratings to determine the risk to the offspring of developing psychiatric disorders (Johnson et al., 2001). A key variable in this study was the presence of maladaptive parental behavior. Children who developed psychiatric disorders were found to be living in homes characterized by high levels of maladaptive behaviors by parents, whether or not the parents themselves had psychiatric disorders. The children of parents who had psychiatric disorders developed psychiatric disorders only when the parents had a history of maladaptive behavior. The diathesis of having parents with psychiatric disorders led to the development of disorders in children only when combined with the stress of living in a home with parents having disturbed behavior.

Complicating the gene-environment equation even further is the fact that, as pointed out earlier, the genome is not always expressed in the phenotype, or observed characteristics of the individual. Some people with a genotype that would predispose them to developing a certain disease may not manifest the disease, a phenomenon referred to as incomplete **penetrance.** Such factors as age, gender, environment, and other genes influence the degree of penetrance of a genetically inherited characteristic. In other cases, a person may develop a disease due to environmental or random causes, without having inherited a predisposition for that disease.

Another perspective on genetic factors is provided by the **multifactorial polygenic threshold** model (Gottesman, 1991; DiLalla, Gottesman, & Carey, 2000; Moldin & Gottesman, 1997). Researchers who hold to this model maintain that several genes with varying influence are involved in the transmission of a disorder or characteristic. The vulnerability for a disease is seen as ranging from low to high, depending on the combination of genes that the individual inherits. The disorder's symptoms are produced when the accumulation of genetic and environmental factors exceeds a certain threshold value. Most contemporary researchers agree that this model provides a better explanation for the actual patterns of family incidence than does the single gene model or others based on simpler mechanisms of genetic inheritance.

Which model is correct? It is possible that all hold partial answers, depending on the modifiability of the characteristic being considered. A person with a "tallness" genotype does not become taller by playing basketball, but a person with artistic talent may become more proficient with training. Physical characteristics may also vary in the degree to which they can be modified; a person with "heavy" genes may maintain an average weight through careful dieting and exercise. Similarly, a person who is genetically predisposed to inherit heart disease may lower the risk of acquiring the disease through careful monitoring of dietary intake. However, blue eyes cannot be changed to brown, no matter what the person looks at or does. Apart from such obviously restricted physical characteristics, the idea of modifying the expression of genetically acquired traits or health problems through the control of lifestyle factors represents an exciting possibility.

Treatment

Therapies that follow from the biological perspective are primarily oriented to reducing or alleviating the symptoms of a disorder. **Somatic** (bodily) **therapies** involve treatments that act on known or presumed causes of the disorder.

Psychosurgery The first form of somatic therapy is in some ways the most extreme: surgical intervention on the brain, also known as **psychosurgery.** The most typical form of psychosurgery involves disconnecting the frontal lobes from the rest of the brain. The basic procedure of this type of surgery was developed by the Portugese neurosurgeon Egas Moniz in 1935 as a way to relieve the symptoms of people with severe psychosis. The technique was considered a major breakthrough at the time, and Moniz received a Nobel Prize in 1949 for his work. After the development of antipsychotic medications in the 1950s, psychosurgery as a widespread practice was discontinued. Even though psychosurgery is rarely performed today, some mental health professionals still recommend this procedure to treat people with otherwise intractable forms of obsessive-compulsive disorder and major depressive disorder who do not respond to medications (Marino-Junior & Cosgrove, 1997).

Electroconvulsive Therapy Less extreme than psychosurgery, but also controversial, is **electroconvulsive therapy (ECT)** for the treatment of severe depression. In ECT, an electric shock is applied through electrodes attached across the head, producing bodily convulsions. This method was developed in 1937 by Ugo Cerletti, an Italian neurologist who developed the procedure through his work in the field of treatment for epilepsy, a brain seizure disorder. Cerletti noticed in his experiments that dogs who were induced to undergo convulsions from electroshocks were much calmer afterward. At about the same time, other physicians in Europe were using chemicals to produce convulsions, but Cerletti felt these methods were too risky and uncontrollable. The attempt to treat severe psychological disorders by causing radical alterations in the brain's environment was based on the notion that these chemical changes would stimulate beneficial changes in the neurons, thus reducing the patient's symptoms. As ECT began to spread throughout Europe, refinements were added that reduced the risk of muscle injury during the convulsions.

As ECT's popularity grew in the 1940s and 1950s, so did the criticisms against it, in part because it was often abused as a means of controlling disruptive patients in hospitals. This was the image depicted in Ken Kesey's *One Flew over the Cuckoo's Nest*. As a result of the controversy surrounding ECT, the method had largely fallen into disuse by the mid-1970s. However, it was still used for treating a narrow range of disorders, and the National Institutes of Health (1985) issued a statement in support of its limited application to these disorders. In recent years, there has been a resurgence of interest in ECT as a method of treatment for severe depression (Gagné, Furman, Carpenter, & Price, 2000; Sobin et al., 1996; Thase & Kupfer, 1996). It has also been used successfully with severely depressed older adults (Kelly & Zisselman, 2000), people in the manic phase of bipolar disorder (Kusumakar et al., 1997), and individuals suffering from psychotic symptoms and depression (Coryell, 1998), and for the short-term relief of symptoms in some individuals with schizophrenia (Tharyan, 2000). However, the procedure is more common in certain areas of the United States, where there is a greater proportion of psychiatrists and more private hospital beds. Practitioners are not in total agreement about its value as a clinical tool. As we discuss in Chapter 9, considerable controversies persist regarding the use of ECT, with particular concern about the commonly reported side effect involving disruption of some forms of memory (Lisanby et al., 2000).

Transcranial Magnetic Stimulation In **transcranial magnetic stimulation (TMS),** a powerful electromagnet is placed on the individual's scalp and a current is passed through the cortex. This procedure is generally used repeatedly (rTMS), with the goal of increasing or decreasing the excitability of the neurons in the targeted area. The current is not limited to the cortex, but seems to have its effect more generally to structures in the subcortical areas of the brain. There is hope that rTMS will ultimately replace ECT in the treatment of major depressive disorder, but it is still too soon to tell (Couturier, 2005). Nevertheless, rTMS seems to be an effective treatment when combined with medications such as amitryptiline (Rumi et al., 2005).

Medication The most common somatic intervention is medication. As we discuss many disorders later in this book, we will also describe the medications demonstrated to be effective in alleviating the symptoms of these disorders. These medications typically alter body chemistry in ways that affect the levels and actions of brain neurotransmitters. During the past decade, major advances in psychopharmacology have resulted in the introduction of medications that are dramatically more effective than those previously in use. As you will read later in this book, medications called **selective serotonin reuptake inhibitors (SSRIs)** (e.g., fluoxetine/Prozac) have been remarkably effective in treating the symptoms associated with depression and obsessive-compulsive disorder. As you will read in the chapter on mood disorders, selective serotonin reuptake inhibitors block the reuptake of serotonin at the synapse, enabling more of this neurotransmitter to be available at the receptor sites. For clients suffering from schizophrenia, the recently introduced atypical antipsychotic medications (e.g., clozapine/Clozaril) have changed the lives of people whose debilitating cognitive, emotional, and behavioral symptoms had previously caused havoc. Clozapine blocks serotonin, as well as dopamine to a lesser degree.

A summary of psychotherapeutic medications and their modes of action is given in Table 4.3. We will discuss these medications in the appropriate sections of each chapter.

Biofeedback In **biofeedback,** a somatic intervention is combined with behavioral principles with the goal of providing clients with the means of controlling their own physiological responses. These responses can be ones that are under voluntary control, such as the actions of the skeletal muscles that are controlled by the central nervous system. More

TABLE 4.3 Common Psychotropic Medications

Substance (Trade Name)	Method of Action	Disorder
Selective Serotonin Reuptake Inhibitors (SSRIs)		
Citalopram (Celexa) Escitalopram (Lexapro) Fluoxetine (Prozac) Fluvoxamine (Luvox) Paroxetine (Paxil) Sertraline (Zoloft)	Block serotonin reuptake mechanism, resulting in increased levels of serotonin	Depression, anxiety disorders including obsessive-compulsive disorder, social phobia, panic disorder, PTSD, generalized anxiety disorder, and eating disorders; may be used to control symptoms of borderline personality disorder
Atypical Antipsychotic Medications		
Clozapine (Clozaril) Olanzapine (Zyprexa) Olanzapine-fluoxetine (Symbyax) Quetiapine (Seroquel) Risperidone (Risperdal) Ziprasidone (Geodon)	Block serotonin receptors as well as dopamine receptors (to a lesser extent) in the limbic system	Schizophrenia as well as symptoms of Alzheimer's disease
Benzodiazepines		
Alprazolam (Xanax) Chlodiazepoxide (Librium) Clonazepam (Klonopin) Clorazepate (Tranxene) Diazepam (Valium) Halazepam (Paxipam) Lorazepam (Ativan) Oxazepam (Serax) Prazepam (Centrax)	Bind to receptor sites of gamma-aminobutyric (GABA) neurons, which inhibit brain sites involved in producing symptoms of anxiety such as panic attacks	Anxiety disorders
Anxiolytics		
Buspirone (BuSpar)	Mimics the effect of serotonin, stimulating the serotonin receptors	Anxiety disorders, particularly generalized anxiety disorder
Mood Stabilizers		
Lithium carbonate (Lithium)	Alters metabolism of neurotransmitters, including catecholamines and serotonin	Bipolar disorder
Valproate (Depakote)	Increases release of GABA	Mania and bipolar disorder
Tricyclic Antidepressants		
Amitriptyline (Elavil) Clomipramine (Anafranil) Desipramine (Norpramin) Imipramine (Tofranil) Nortriptyline (Pamelor)	Block reuptake of norepinephrine and serotonin, increasing their excitatory effect on the postsynaptic neurons	Depression, obsessive-compulsive disorder
Monoamine Oxidase Inhibitors (MAOIs)		
Isocarboxazid (Marplan) Phenelzine (Nardil) Tranylcypromine (Parnate)	Inhibit the monoamine oxidase enzyme, which converts norepinephrine, serotonin, and dopamine into inert substances	Depression

(continued)

TABLE 4.3 Common Psychotropic Medications *(continued)*

Substance (Trade Name)	Method of Action	Disorder
Neuroleptics		
Low potency (require large doses): Chlorpromazine (Thorazine) Mesoridazine (Serentil) Thioridazine (Mellaril)	Block dopamine receptors, reducing the frequency of psychotic symptoms but also interfering with movement and endocrine function	Schizophrenia and also used in treatment of symptoms of Alzheimer's disease
Middle potency (require moderate doses): Aripiprazole (Abilify) Loxapine (Loxitane) Molindone (Lindone, Moban) Perphenazine (Trilafon) Thiothixene (Navane) Trifluoperazine (Stelazine) Trifluopromazine (Vesprin)		
High potency (require low doses): Fluphenazine (Permitil, Prolixin) Haloperidol (Haldol)		
Stimulants		
Methylphenidate (Ritalin) Amphetamine (Adderall)	Increase norepinephrine and dopamine levels by blocking reuptake and assisting release	Attention-deficit/hyperactivity disorder and narcolepsy
Selective Norepinephrine Reuptake Inhibitor (NRI)		
Atomoxetine (Strattera)	Blocks norepinephrine mechanism, resulting in increased levels of norepinephrine	Attention-deficit/hyperactivity disorder
Norepinephrine Dopamine Reuptake Inhibitor (NDRI)		
Bupropion (Wellbutrin)	Increases norepinephrine and dopamine levels by blocking reuptake and assisting release	Depression
Noradrenaline and Specific Serotonergic Agent (NaSSA)		
Mirtazapine (Remeron)	Increases norepinephrine and serotonin levels by blocking reuptake and assisting release	Depression
Serotonin 2 Antagonist/ Reuptake Inhibitor (SARI)		
Trazodone (Desyrel)	Blocks serotonin mechanisms, resulting in increased levels of serotonin	Depression

important, clients can also learn to control the so-called visceral functions of the autonomic nervous system and the hormonal responses of the endocrine system, including heart rate, blood pressure, contractions of the intestinal muscles, and galvanic skin response. In cases where physical symptoms are the result of disturbances in autonomic functions, the ability to control such functions can help the individual achieve tremendous relief. For example, biofeedback can be used to treat migraine headaches, insomnia, pain from injured muscles,

asthma, high blood pressure, intestinal disorders, and heart rhythm abnormalities.

The basis for biofeedback was largely in the pioneering work in the 1960s and 1970s conducted by Rockefeller University psychologist Neal E. Miller. Based on extensive experimental work on the instrumental (operant) conditioning of laboratory animals (Miller & Banuazizi, 1968), Miller concluded that it was possible to use reinforcement to alter physiological responses. He further theorized that some physiological symp-

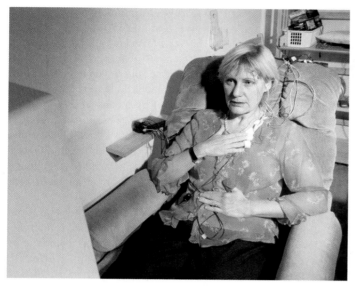

In biofeedback, a person learns to regulate autonomic functions by attending to bodily changes registered on recording instruments connected to specialized computers.

toms in humans resulted from misinterpretations of the cues from their bodies (Miller & Dworkin, 1977). Biofeedback allows clients to learn to "read" their bodily signals more clearly and then go on to the next step, which is to alter them through instrumental conditioning. For example, clients could be taught to recognize the presence of tense muscles and then learn to relax them.

The training methods used in biofeedback are relatively simple, as they are based on principles of learning and reinforcement, and the client can easily carry them outside of the clinician's office. However, the initial training requires very sophisticated instruments to provide precise measurements of bodily responses.

Biological Approaches to Treating Meera

An extreme procedure, such as psychosurgery, would not even be considered for a client such as Meera. Neither would electroconvulsive treatment, unless Meera's depression became so incapacitating that the usual therapeutic efficacy period of antidepressant medication was deemed to be too long and too risky.

Because most clinicians would view Meera's depression as stemming from the trauma caused by her father's suicide, treating Meera just with antidepressant medication would be unlikely. Some clinicians might consider the possibility of including medication, such as a selective serotonin reuptake inhibitor, into a more comprehensive treatment plan if Meera complained about severe symptoms, such as appetite disturbance, sleep disturbance, and incapacitating sadness. In such a treatment regimen, the medication would be a single facet of a broader psychotherapeutic intervention.

After determining what treatment method is best suited to the client's symptoms (such as muscle relaxation for tension headaches), the clinician hooks up the client to an instrument whose output can be easily read. When a desirable outcome is achieved (such as a reduction of muscle tension), reinforcement is provided (such as a light or music going off). Shaping is used, so that initially the thresholds are easily within the client's reach, and gradually, they become more challenging. The goal is for the client to be able to accurately read bodily signals without the machine and then be able to control the response at will.

Evaluation of the Biological Perspective

Biology is the foundation on which all behavior is based. Ultimately, any psychological approach to abnormal behavior must consider the role of biology. Researchers have increasingly realized that, for decades, many disorders that had been explained in psychological terms may have had biological components. In some cases, it is being recognized that the connection between biology and psychology is reciprocal. For example, such emotions as anxiety can cause changes in the body, such as increased heart rate and sweating. These changes can interfere with a number of psychological processes, such as concentration. The realization that one is not concentrating well can lead to even greater anxiety. Chronic anxiety, in turn, can cause physical changes that create long-standing health problems. Cases such as that of Meera raise some fascinating questions about the role of biology in psychological disorders. Many people reading Meera's story would regard the traumatic loss of her father as the direct cause of her depression. However, as you will discover in the chapter on mood disorders, depression often has a prominent biological component. Many people who develop depression have a family history in which one or more relatives have also suffered from mood disturbance. Having this information available, clinicians can develop hypotheses about the kind of mood disorder that is most likely.

The search for genetic contributions to psychological characteristics and disorders is progressing rapidly with the development of new technologies for unlocking biological secrets. Complicating this search, however, is the fact that most psychological characteristics follow a polygenic rather than Mendelian pattern of inheritance. As genetic technologies and understanding increase regarding the complexities of the gene-environment equation, improved understanding of and treatments for genetically based disorders will not be far behind.

Biopsychosocial Perspectives on Theories and Treatments: An Integrative Approach

Now that you have read about the major perspectives on abnormal behavior, you probably can see value in each of them. Certain facets of various theories may seem particularly useful and

Integrative Approach to Treating Meera

An integrative therapist, such as Dr. Tobin, would face several choices in treating a client such as Meera. Perhaps Meera's depression is rooted in lifelong conflicts that would warrant some exploratory work. At the same time, Meera might benefit from cognitive strategies aimed at helping her change her views of herself, her world, and her future. Although Meera's depression is not so severe as to warrant extreme biologically based interventions, some clinicians might consider suggesting antidepressant medication if her symptoms worsened. Furthermore, the therapist might suggest that Meera's family participate in the therapy, because Meera's depression developed in response to a family trauma. The family therapy decision would rest primarily on Meera's preference; some clients feel strongly about limiting their psychotherapy to a private endeavor, uncomplicated by involving family members. Regardless of the therapeutic techniques tapped, a skilled clinician would base Meera's therapy on a foundation of empathy, acceptance, and support. When we return to the case at the end of this chapter, you will see just what Dr. Tobin chose to include in her work and how her integrative approach played out.

interesting. In fact, you may have a hard time deciding which approach is the "best." However, as we have said repeatedly, most clinicians select aspects of the various models, rather than adhering narrowly to a single one. In fact, in recent decades, there has been a dramatic shift away from narrow clinical approaches that are rooted in a single theoretical model. Most clinicians now identify themselves as integrative, or eclectic. The therapist views the needs of the client from multiple perspectives and develops a treatment plan that responds to these particular concerns. Some cases might involve focusing on the client's family; others may call for a more detailed analysis of the client's early development. One client may need a great deal of direction and education from the therapist, whereas another client may benefit from support and nurturance. Similarly, in the course of therapy, components of several different models may be integrated.

Let's take a look at three ways in which clinicians integrate different therapeutic models (Goldfried & Norcross, 1995): (1) technical eclecticism, (2) theoretical integration, and (3) the common factors approach. Those adhering to technical eclecticism seek to match a specific intervention to each client and presenting problem (Beutler, Consoli, & Williams, 1995). These therapists do not affiliate with the particular theoretical models but are willing to acknowledge that a particular technique is effective for a certain kind of problem. For example, a therapist who does not often use behavioral techniques may recognize the value of systematic desensitization in treating a phobic client, while using exploratory techniques to understand the developmental roots of the client's fears and dependent style.

Theoretical integration involves formulating a psychotherapeutic approach that brings divergent models together on a consistent basis in one's clinical work (Wachtel, 1977, 1997). For example, a clinician may consistently choose two theoretical bases, such as family systems and cognitive behaviorism, from which to develop an intervention model. In a way, the clinician is developing his or her own model by means of a conceptual synthesis of the contributions of previously established models. Somewhat independent of the presenting problem, this therapist would consistently look for ways in which both the family system and maladaptive cognitions have contributed to the client's distress. The intervention would be based on an approach that brings these two models together.

When using the common factors approach to integration, the clinician develops a strategy by studying the core ingredients that various therapies share and choosing the components that have been demonstrated over time to be the most effective contributors to positive outcomes in psychotherapy. Strong support has emerged in recent years regarding the importance of the relationship between a client and therapist in determining treatment efficacy. Following a sophisticated scientific analysis of psychotherapy outcome studies, Wampold (2001) concluded that common factors, rather than specific techniques, are what make psychotherapy work. In fact, he considers the working alliance as the key component of psychotherapy: "The alliance appears to be a necessary aspect of therapy, regardless of the nature of the therapy" (p. 158). Some clinicians combine elements of three integrative approaches, yielding what is referred to as a mixed model of integration. One such example is the innovative work of McCullough (2001), who maintains a psychodynamic focus while importing components of other theories in formulating affect phobia therapy (APT). According to McCullough, many clients have conflicts or intense fears about their feelings, a phenomenon she refers to as affect phobias. For example, people who are afraid to experience grief may chuckle to lighten up or try desperately to choke back tears. Or individuals who are too embarrassed to show tenderness may put up a tough front. To treat such clients, McCullough uses a kind of systematic desensitization, or stepwise exposure, to feelings. She may also tap an array of techniques derived from a variety of models such as cognitive, behavioral, and experiential. The advances of experts such as McCullough highlight the fact that the entire field of psychotherapy continues to evolve. Even within integrative approaches, new models are being developed from the contributions of a long list of theorists and clinicians from the past several decades.

When reading Dr. Tobin's cases throughout this text, you will see how she approaches her work from an integrative framework. In addition to incorporating techniques from various models into her treatment approach, Dr. Tobin is attuned to the importance of attending to certain common factors in her clinical work. For example, you will read about the emphasis Dr. Tobin places on her working relationship with her clients.

She realizes that the most effective of techniques will be worthless unless she and her clients are allied in a collaborative working relationship.

As you read about the various psychological disorders in the chapters to follow, imagine the approach you might take if you were treating people with these disorders. Think of the extent to which you might rely on psychodynamic, humanistic, family systems, behavioral, cognitive, and biological models in understanding and treating these conditions. We will discuss the current state of the science regarding which explanations and interventions are regarded as most appropriate and effective. At the same time, it is important for you to keep in mind that knowledge about many of these conditions and the efficacy of certain interventions is still limited. The science of psychopathology and the art of psychotherapy are still evolving.

Case Report

Meera Krishnan

RETURN TO THE CASE

Meera's History

Until the day of her father's death, Meera had thought of her family as "typical, American, and middle class." She was the youngest of four girls, each of whom had reportedly gone on to successful careers and marriages. Meera's parents owned their own real estate business, which they had started prior to the birth of any of the children.

Meera's parents had emigrated from India several decades ago in order to study at an American university. A few years after settling in the United States, they became American citizens and maintained relatively little contact with relatives in India. Although they described themselves as adherents of Hinduism, they gradually moved away from the religion and most customs of their country of origin. Having become acculturated to Western society, Meera's parents did not raise their children within any religion. They placed considerable importance on personal achievements in each child's life.

Meera remembered that, from a very early age, she perceived her three older sisters as being "great" at everything they did. Succeeding at academics, sports, and social pur-

suits, life seemed to be so easy for them. Her mother had similar expectations for Meera, and she made her displeasure evident whenever Meera failed to attain her mother's predefined goals. Even in the early grades of school, Meera recalls feeling an inner pressure to do well and an accompanying feeling of fright that she would not succeed. In time, she developed perfectionistic tendencies about which her sisters and mother frequently chided her. Everything had to be just right—every homework assignment, every piece of clothing, even the placement of the things in her room. Her father responded differently to Meera's perfectionistic style, however. He took a softer approach, in which he tried to talk to her about the ways in which she was getting herself "too upset" by trying to make everything perfect. He tried to communicate his appreciation of what she did and who she was and that "perfect wasn't necessarily the best."

As the years went by, Meera found herself taking comfort in her father's words, and she learned how to accept healthy compromises. She didn't feel compelled to attend an Ivy League college or to have a large cir-

cle of friends. She participated in activities, such as the marching band and intramural sports, because she found them to be fun, and she liked the other people who were attracted to these activities. Even Meera was able to acknowledge that, for most of her college years, she felt happy and healthy, both physically and psychologically. Although she had not been involved in an intimate relationship, she felt confident that the "right guy" would come along sooner or later.

Meera's sense of psychological stability and serenity was dramatically shaken on that day in March of her senior year, when she received the "still unbelievable" phone call from her sister with the news of her father's death. In the months that followed, Meera became consumed by feelings of sadness and loss, and she pulled away from her friends and family. She managed to finish her academic courses, although her grade point average for that semester was the lowest of her college career. Despite her mother's urging that Meera participate in commencement, Meera chose to stay away from the festivities, stating that it would be too emotional for her to be at the event without her father being present.

During the summer months following Meera's completion of college, she remained in her apartment and made halfhearted attempts to find a job. When fall approached, her depression began to lift, and she realized that she would have to find a means of support. The job as a buyer was one of the first for which she applied, and she was surprised to land the position.

In her year in the job, she performed her duties quite adequately. She received high performance evaluations and corresponding salary raises. As with anything positive that happened in her life, Meera did not take much satisfaction in these successes. She went about her work, mostly in a solitary manner, interacting with others only when the circumstance necessitated doing so. As the months passed, however, this solitary style of living became increasingly unbearable, so she decided to contact me to initiate psychotherapy.

Assessment

Meera's case provided an interesting assessment challenge. In some ways, her issues seemed very evident; she was suffering from unresolved grief associated with the tragic death of her father. However, I felt that Meera's clinical issues were far more complicated, as is so often the case. I wanted to get a better grasp of subtle interpersonal issues, especially those pertaining to early development and family relationships. At the same time, I wanted to understand the extent to which Meera's low self-esteem was impeding her satisfaction in life. In addition to an extensive clinical interview, I decided to administer two assessment procedures that are markedly different but complementary: the Thematic Apperception Test and the Beck Depression Inventory-II.

As I might have expected, Meera's TAT stories were filled with themes of loss and interpersonal

pain. However, somewhat surprising was the depth of rage that characterized the interactions between the people in her TAT stories. One of the TAT cards is a drawing of an older woman who dressed in black, standing behind a younger woman [see Chapter 3]. Meera described this scenario as follows: "The two women are attending the funeral of a friend, Adam. They are standing outside the church as the coffin is being carried out. The younger woman is feeling annoyed, actually furious, that the older woman even came to the funeral. In her mind she is thinking, 'Who the hell is she to be here! She didn't even like Adam.' She is also irked that the woman is standing so close to her, breathing down her neck. After a couple of moments, she turns around and gives her a nasty look, then walks away."

The relevance of Meera's TAT story to events in her life was evident. Touching upon the most obvious themes, it was reasonable to interpret that Meera was identifying with the younger figure in the picture, attending the funeral of a close one (her father), accompanied by someone else (possibly her mother) in the background. Perhaps she felt resentful of her mother's emotionally distant relationship with her father and angered by a woman whom she perceived to be "breathing down her neck" in life. Similar conflictual themes characterized Meera's other stories, but in most instances there was little resolution to the conflict. Instead, the person in the story evaded the conflict while internalizing some intense feelings about other people.

The information from Meera's Beck Depression Inventory-II confirmed my impression that she was seriously depressed. On this measure, Meera's responses reflected sadness, pessimism, loss of pleasure, and self-criticalness. Although she expressed no suicidal thoughts or wishes, I was concerned about the extent and depth of Meera's depression.

Diagnosis

Meera was certainly depressed, but her depression was not severe enough to warrant a diagnosis of major depressive disorder or the duration long enough for the diagnosis of dysthymic disorder. The *DSM-IV* does provide the option of assigning the diagnosis of "bereavement" for the period following the death of a loved one, but the length and nature of Meera's condition made this diagnosis inappropriate. In light of the profound nature of Meera's depression, I viewed her as suffering from an unspecified mood disorder.

In addition to her depression following the loss of her father, Meera was struggling with questions about her long-term goals in life, specifically pertaining to the role of intimate relationships and career development. Meera needed to develop a sense of herself in the present and a vision of herself for the future. She was trying to delineate an identity that was a good fit.

Axis I:	Mood Disorder Not Otherwise Specified (296.90) Identity Problem (313.82)
Axis II:	None
Axis III:	No medical diagnosis
Axis IV:	Bereavement issues pertaining to unresolved feelings about the death of her father
Axis V:	Global Assessment of Functioning (current): 68.

Highest Global Assessment of Functioning (past year): 68; some difficulties in social functioning but satisfactory work involvement and performance.

Case Formulation

I was impressed by Meera's recognition of the central issues that had been upsetting her. She knew, as did I, that the suicide of her father would be a focal point of our work but that her issues were deeper and more long-lasting. Feelings of personal inadequacy had been a part of Meera's emotional life for as long as she could remember. Fears of not being accepted, particularly by her mother and sisters, led Meera to feel particularly vulnerable in any close relationship.

Meera's lack of closeness with her mother early in life initiated a pattern of insecurity in other important relationships. For much of her life, she was able to compensate by turning to her father for support and affection. His suicide traumatized Meera, leading her to panic about whether anyone would be there to help her through the next phase of her life. Insecurities that had always haunted her became explosive. Not knowing how to deal with others, even close friends and relatives, she retreated into a world of emotional isolation. Without consciously realizing what she was doing, she dismissed the important people from her life and felt unable to develop new relationships. In her heart was the fear that if she were to become close to another person, she might once again be abandoned.

Treatment Plan

I felt that the nature of Meera's issues warranted a psychotherapy that integrated exploratory, supportive, and cognitive techniques. It was important for Meera to understand the developmental antecedents of her current emotional problems. An approach rooted in an object relations framework would enable me to help Meera understand how her unsatisfying relationship with her mother and sisters throughout life might be interfering with the establishment of intimacy in adult life. I wanted our work together to focus on the sequence of life events, particularly in her family, that brought her to such a stage of unhappiness.

In addition to exploratory work, Meera needed someone to help her feel good about herself once again. Having become so reliant on her father for positive feedback, she was emotionally starved for someone to respect her and take joy in her accomplishments. Ideally, this role would eventually be filled by an intimate partner. For the time being, however, Meera would benefit from a humanistic component to the therapy characterized by a strong positive regard and acceptance.

Complementing the exploratory and supportive work, I would also incorporate cognitive techniques focusing on the ways in which Meera's dysfunctional emotions were the product of dysfunctional thoughts. Through the process of cognitive restructuring, Meera could alter the ways she viewed herself, her family, and other significant people in her world. She could learn how to reframe negative ideas into positive ones that would facilitate the development of more adaptive coping strategies.

I also considered the possibility of medication as well as a family therapy component in my work with Meera, but I ruled out both of these interventions. As for family therapy, Meera explained that it was important to her to have an opportunity to have a therapeutic relationship that was a private and safe place in which she could openly explore family issues, without the pressure to contend with her sisters and mother in the therapy context. As for medication, it was my sense that her depression was not so incapacitating as to warrant antidepressant medication; furthermore, Meera explained that she preferred to tackle her depression psychotherapeutically. I agreed with her, explaining that we could come back to the medication issue if her depression deepened.

Outcome of the Case

My work with Meera, which lasted 3 months, stands out in my mind as having been very special. I saw myself as a "provocative guide" in her evolving sense of herself. At first our work focused on dealing with her feelings about the death of her father. In particular, Meera wanted and needed an opportunity to be openly expressive of her sadness about the loss of this relationship and her anger toward her father for having taken his life. Following the assessment sessions, during which I conducted a clinical interview and administered the TAT and Beck Depression Inventory-II, we moved into a discussion of her depression and unresolved rage.

For several sessions, Meera told me stories of the warm and nurturing relationship she had with her father. With tears streaming down her face, she put forth unanswerable questions, such as "Why did he do this?" There was no clear answer to this query, particularly in light of the fact that her father's cryptic suicide note provided no clues about his life-ending decision, other than the accusatory comment directed to his family members.

By the end of our first month of working together, I felt that Meera had experienced a certain "cleansing" of her emotions relating to pent-up feelings about her father's death. She and I both realized that she would never be able to fully put her father's suicide behind her; nevertheless, she did respond to my notion that she "file it away" for the time being. As I explained to her at the time, there are many past events in each of our lives that we can't change; however, we do have some control over the extent to which they intrude into our lives. With a supportive and affirming style, we incorporated cognitive techniques to help Meera perceive herself as strong and competent and to find ways for her to take power over this past hurt, rather than being controlled by painful memories.

During the second and third months of our work together, the integrative therapy that I was conducting tapped more developmental aspects. With an approach rooted in object relations theory, we explored Meera's early life relationships and the impact of these family relationships on her current life. At the same

RETURN TO THE CASE *(continued)*

time, Meera learned the techniques of cognitive restructuring, in which she was able to alter her thoughts about those relationships and thereby change the feelings about important people in her past and in her present. I helped Meera realize how her interactions with others were being defined by her trauma. Since her father's suicide, Meera had come to expect that any important person in her life would eventually abandon her, so she retreated from any possible intimacy. By capturing this understanding of what she was doing, Meera felt free to venture into new relationships.

In time, not only did Meera's self-perception improve, but so also did her interactions with others. She was able to let go of some of her perfectionistic traits, while coming to view her relationships with others in more positive terms. Meera came to understand how she had desperately pursued acceptance in her family, all the while feeling like an outsider. The distance between her and her mother, whatever the basis,

had caused her to approach intimate relationships with caution and distrust. By using Meera's transference to me, I was able to point out the ways in which she seemed to approach me with fear and apprehension. I broadened this interpretation to other important relationships in Meera's life, including her interactions with co-workers and friends. In a remarkably short period of time, Meera came to see how the template of her interpersonal style had been established early in life and how she had adhered to that style for the past two decades.

By the end of 3 months of work together, Meera was clearly happier. Her approach to other people had changed dramatically. She had begun to accept the invitations from her friends and had begun to date a man who worked with her.

It was rewarding to see Meera grow and change. I realized that I would have liked to continue working with her, because I found the work so rewarding; however, I recognized that my own countertrans-

ference was the basis for this kind of thinking. I guess I was gratified by the success that she was achieving, and I wanted to continue to witness Meera's growth, but my own curiosity would not be justification for recommending that she continue in treatment. I realized that it was important for Meera to separate from me—in a way that felt good to her, that helped her feel she had the emotional strength to leave her work with me when the time seemed right. We mutually agreed after 3 months of progress that the time was, indeed, right.

Several years have passed since Meera's therapy with me. Each December, she sends me a holiday greeting and provides a brief sketch of what has happened in her life—usually happy and upbeat accomplishments but also a few comments about difficult events, experiences, and choices. Meera has found herself.

Sarah Tobin, PhD

SUMMARY

- Theoretical perspectives influence the ways in which clinicians and researchers interpret and organize their observations about behavior. In this chapter, we discussed five major theoretical perspectives: psychodynamic, humanistic, sociocultural, behavioral and cognitively based, and biological; we concluded the discussion with a consideration of an integrative approach in which theorists and clinicians bring together aspects and techniques of more than one perspective.

- The psychodynamic perspective is a theoretical orientation that emphasizes unconscious determinants of behavior and is derived from Freud's psychoanalytic approach. The term *psychodynamics* is used to describe interaction among the id, the ego, and the superego. According to psychodynamic theorists, people use defense mechanisms to keep unacceptable thoughts, instincts, and feelings out of conscious awareness. Freud proposed that there is a normal sequence of development through a series of what he called psychosexual stages, with each stage focusing on a different sexually excitable zone of the body: oral,

anal, phallic, and genital. Post-Freudian theorists, such as Jung, Adler, Horney, and Erikson departed from Freudian theory, contending that Freud overemphasized sexual and aggressive instincts. Object relations theorists, such as Klein, Winnicott, Kohut, and Mahler, proposed that interpersonal relationships lie at the core of personality, believing that the unconscious mind contains images of the child's parents and of the child's relationships to the parents. Treatment within the psychodynamic perspective may incorporate such techniques as free association, dream analysis, analysis of transference, and analysis of resistance. Considerable debate about the tenets and techniques of the psychodynamic perspective continues to take place; much of this debate focuses on the fact that psychodynamic concepts are difficult to study and measure and that some Freudian notions are now regarded as irrelevant in contemporary society. Newer approaches, based on object relations theory, have adapted the concept of infant attachment style to understanding the ways that adults relate to significant people in their lives.

■ At the core of the humanistic perspective is the belief that human motivation is based on an inherent tendency to strive for self-fulfillment and meaning in life, notions that were rooted in existential psychology. Carl Rogers' person-centered theory focuses on the uniqueness of each individual, the importance of allowing each individual to achieve maximum fulfillment of potential, and the need for the individual to confront honestly the reality of his or her experiences in the world. Maslow's self-actualization theory focuses on the maximum realization of the individual's potential for psychological growth. In client-centered therapy, Rogers recommended that therapists treat clients with unconditional positive regard and empathy, while providing a model of genuineness and a willingness to self-disclose.

■ Theorists within the sociocultural perspective emphasize the ways that individuals are influenced by people, social institutions, and social forces. Proponents of the family perspective see the individual as an integral component of the pattern of interactions and relationships that exists within the family. The four major approaches are intergenerational, structural, strategic, and experiential. Psychological disturbance can also arise as a result of discrimination associated with such attributes as gender, race, or age or of pressures associated with economic hardships. People can also be adversely affected by general social forces, such as fluid and inconsistent values in a society and destructive historical events, such as political revolution, natural disaster, or nationwide depression. Treatments within the sociocultural perspective are determined by the nature of the group involved. In family therapy, family members are encouraged to try new ways of relating to each other and thinking about their problems. In group therapy, people share their stories and experiences with other, similar people. Milieu therapy provides a context in which the intervention is the environment, rather than the individual, usually consisting of staff and clients in a therapeutic community.

■ According to the behavioral perspective, abnormality is caused by faulty learning experiences; according to the cognitive-behavioral (sometimes called cognitive) perspective, abnormality is caused by maladaptive thought processes. Behaviorists contend that many emotional reactions are acquired through classical conditioning. Operant conditioning, with Skinner's emphasis on reinforcement, involves the learning of behaviors that are not automatic. The process of acquiring new responses by observing and imitating the behavior of others, called modeling, has been studied by social learning theorists. The cognitive theories of Beck emphasize disturbed ways of thinking. In interventions based on behavioral theory, clinicians focus on observable behaviors, while those adhering to a cognitive perspective work with clients to change maladaptive thought patterns.

■ Within the biological perspective, disturbances in emotions, behavior, and cognitive processes are viewed as being caused by abnormalities in the functioning of the body, such as the brain and nervous system or the endocrine system. A person's genetic makeup can play an important role in determining certain disorders. In trying to assess the relative roles of nature and nurture, researchers have come to accept the notion of an interaction between genetic and environmental contributors to abnormality. Treatments based on the biological model involve a range of somatic therapies, the most common of which is medication. More extreme somatic interventions include psychosurgery and electroconvulsive treatment. Biofeedback is a somatic intervention in which clients learn to control various bodily reactions associated with stress.

■ In contemporary practice, most clinicians take an integrative approach, in which they select aspects of various models rather than adhering narrowly to a single one. Three ways in which clinicians integrate various models include technical eclecticism, theoretical integration, and the common factors approach.

KEY TERMS

See Glossary for definitions

INTERNET RESOURCE

To get more information on the material covered in this chapter, visit our website at **www.mhhe.com/halgin5.** There you will find more information, resources, and links to topics of interest.

NOTHING TO HIDE: MENTAL ILLNESS IN THE FAMILY

Nothing to Hide: Mental Illness in the Family introduces families whose lives have been changed by mental illness. These families are from diverse racial, ethnic, religious, and socioeconomic backgrounds. They live in areas both urban and rural, from Los Angeles to a small town in Tennessee. Clearly, mental illness knows no boundaries.

When a debilitating illness, either physical or mental, strikes a child, an adolescent, or an adult, it has an impact on the entire family. A diagnosis of mental illness, however, carries with it an additional challenge: the pervasive and destructive burden of stigma. Stigma gives rise to myths, stereotypes, and misunderstandings about people who have psychiatric disorders and their family members. The primary goal of *Nothing to Hide* is to dispel common misconceptions about mental illness in order to decrease stigma.

—Jean J. Beard and Peggy Gillespie, Amherst, Massachusetts

People sometimes ask, "Why are these people smiling?" I can't answer that question. But I know the question betrays a notion that most of us have about mental illness: that those who have it are different from us. Surely, we think, they don't feel what we feel; they don't express it in the same way. Now, please take another look.

—Gigi Kaeser (Photographer)

In addition to this segment containing five case stories, you will find a segment following Chapter 9 containing 6 more stories, and a final segment following Chapter 14 with 5 stories.

NOTHING TO HIDE

THE CAMPBELL FAMILY

Jaime reflects about being stigmatized and accepting her schizophrenia

Back row: Meland, Annie, Mike, and Jaime. Seated: Jodi

I have schizophrenia and if anybody gets close to me, they're going to know about my illness. I always say, "I'm Jaime first, but Jaime has a mental illness." It's not all of who I am, but it is definitely a part of me.

• • • •

My boyfriend was the only person out of my entire group of friends who stood by me when I got sick. My other friends would say things like, "You're just too weird." One friend even called me a "schizoid." I had been there for them when they were failing in school or having family troubles. Then, when I needed them the most, they were gone. That was the hardest part of my journey—losing my peer group when I most needed it. For me, this was the clearest example of the stigma of being mentally ill.

For me, having schizophrenia is a warning sign that I need to take good care of myself. It's part of me, and it's a lifestyle. It's a disorder that often causes me to be out of touch with what other people perceive to be reality, but I'm not about to say that it's not my reality. I feel that it's a different kind of reality.

Actually, it's a different kind of living, and a different kind of life. It's not something that you can just walk into and then walk out of. Having schizophrenia is life-transforming. This illness will be with me all of my life.

I still have hallucinations. I hear birds calling me to them and I see fingers in trees. I see four little men that I call "mushroom men." This doesn't mean that these things aren't "real" for me, it just means that other people don't see them. The "mushroom men," for instance, have been a part of my reality ever since I first saw them. They have created a little space in my life.

Sometimes I feel like they're watching me off in the distance. This is probably one of the most vivid hallucinations I've ever had. The first time I saw them, I was coherent enough to know that "mushroom men" shouldn't be standing next to a pine tree. They weren't scary, but not knowing where they came from was weird. I've actually become rather attached to all of my hallucinations because they are an integral part of me.

NOTHING TO HIDE

THE MARGOSIAN FAMILY

Alexandra, Armené, and Abraháni

Everything was falling out from underneath me. I was overwhelmed, and I started to feel very bad about myself. I was all alone with two young children and I had no one to turn to for support. Although I have had depression most of my life, this time it was far more profound. I decided to go to the local mental health clinic, where I requested therapy for both my daughter and myself. Alex was only three years old, but she had observed the beatings I had sustained by her father. I felt we had been through so much that I wanted to make sure she was okay emotionally. The staff at the mental health center told me that Alex didn't need therapy. As for me, they said that I had accomplished so much during the past nine months, why would I need any therapy? They couldn't understand why I was so depressed, and I couldn't really explain it. Those of us who are poor and mentally ill can get treated pretty shabbily by the mental health system.

• • • •

I finally got permission from the clinic staff to see a therapist there. After seeing him for a few weeks, I wasn't feeling any better. One day, I told my therapist that I was afraid to leave his office because I wanted to attempt suicide. He didn't believe me! He said, "Well, you've survived so far. You'll survive another week." When I left the session, I bought over-the-counter sleeping pills and then went home. I cooked dinner, bathed the children, and read them a bedtime story. After they were asleep, I took out some photographs of them

and thought, "These are the most perfect and beautiful children. Anybody would want to take them in after I'm gone." I wrote them a long letter saying good-bye, and I took the pills.

I ended up in the ICU. From there, I admitted myself into the psychiatric unit. While I was there, I kept asking the doctors for antidepressants. They said I didn't need them, and that I had my intellect to fall back on! They thought that my depression was only situational.

• • • •

A few months later, I found a psychiatrist at a different mental health center. She realized that I needed medication to stabilize my condition. In fact, she couldn't believe what I had gone through. She knew that I was a good mother and that I needed some help to get better. The medication she put me on helped to save my life.

• • • •

Given everything that we've been through together, I'm amazed that my children are thriving. Although I'm on state assistance and we live in poverty, I've managed to have the children attend an excellent private school. In the end, it was my children who saved my life. They are my true heroes. They've taught me what is really important in life.

Sometimes my children say things like, "Mommy, I don't see why you have to go to therapy! You don't need therapy! You're fine the way you are." And I always say, "I'm fine *because* I go to therapy!"

THE JAURA/CHAN FAMILY

Marco, Maria, Luz Maria, and Julio

I had the all-American family until five years ago. I was married and had two children, a boy and a girl. I had a good job as a salesman in wholesale produce, and I was making good money. I was hardworking, responsible, and very successful. I had a nice car and a nice house. I wasn't in need of anything. Every once in a while, I might get a little blue here and there, but never to the point where I needed medication or therapy or anything like that. I thought that I was invincible, like Superman. My life was good.

When I was thirty-four, I had a divorce with my wife. The divorce didn't come from me; it came from her. What really took me apart was when I went into the court system, I felt like a victim. I felt like I was raped, crucified, and taken advantage of. I couldn't do anything about it. I just gave up on life. I didn't see any reason to go on, and I quit wanting to live. Depression kicked in, and I've been fighting it ever since.

I would sometimes get the feeling that my friends and family thought that I was faking it. They didn't really know what to make of me; they just didn't understand. My employers didn't understand, either. I couldn't make it to work on time, and there were days when I would even miss work. Lots of people said to me, "Well, you look fine and you seem fine. Why aren't you functioning? Just get over it! Get on with your life." It was hard for me to explain to them that it wasn't quite that easy.

My emotions were out of control to the point where I even became suicidal. One of the biggest problems for me was that I would wake up in the morning with no desire to get out of bed. I had no ambition. I was even off work for a while. When I went back to my job, I struggled. I was much better, but I still had difficult times when the depression would hit me hard and take over my whole being, my feelings, and my emotions. I had a lot of anxiety and stress. My mind was scrambling.

My depression still continues to be a problem for me. I think my mental condition has actually worsened. I don't want to have the depression. I don't want to feel the way I feel. I'm always looking for answers and for help. I go to my psychiatrist; I go to my therapist; I go to support groups; I take my medication. I don't want to vegetate in a room somewhere and let my life go to waste.

I don't know what lies in the future for me, but I hope that someday soon I can return back to my normal self.

Tracey speaks about her agoraphobia and how it has made her a stronger person

THE BAPTISTE FAMILY

Paige, Jacqueline, Tracey, and Cara

I was the first person in my immediate family to experience mental illness. When I was twelve, I started having symptoms of what I now know was an anxiety disorder, but I had no idea what was happening to me. I didn't tell anyone for over a year. I hid my illness until I got to the point where I could no longer function.

I had panic attacks. I would have a sudden, terrifying feeling that everything was unreal. When this happened, I didn't even feel like I was in my body. I would go completely numb, and my heart and mind wouldn't stop racing. I felt as if I were going to die at any moment.

• • • •

Without treatment, my panic attacks led to severe agoraphobia, a type of anxiety disorder. It literally means a fear of open spaces. Just seeing the sky was too much for me to negotiate. It got to the point where any public space terrified me. When I was fourteen, I spent the entire year inside my house, rarely leaving my room. I was shut off from the world.

• • • •

The worst thing was not knowing what was wrong with me. I thought I was the only person on earth experiencing such terror and disorientation. I assumed I was completely insane. The only future I could imagine for myself was eventual confinement in an institution. I lived in fear of the day my mother could no longer care for me.

• • • •

It's nearly impossible to adequately describe the complexity of my ultimate recovery. This last relapse seemed, for me, a necessary final step. I had to let myself experience the terror again to truly learn that it had no power over me. I still occasionally experience symptoms, especially when I'm extremely tired or stressed, symptoms that in the past would have escalated into an anxiety attack. I now know how to handle those sensations.

• • • •

Ironically, agoraphobia has emboldened me. Perhaps because my life was once so severely restricted, I now strive to transcend limits and fully experience life. People who know me now have a difficult time imagining that I was once so disabled. I rarely think about that part of my life anymore. It's not that I'm avoiding it— it just feels over. I no longer fear that my illness will come back.

THE CUMMINGS FAMILY

Ann discusses her son's suicide, her severe depression, and her inability to control her illness alone

Three weeks after he stopped taking his medication, my son committed suicide. He hung himself in the backyard of my mom's house. I have a lot of anger and resentment about this. When I think about the millions of dollars that were spent on President Clinton's affair with Monica Lewinsky, I wonder why I couldn't get decent psychiatric help for my son. It could have saved his life. He was a good, kind, intelligent, wonderful human being. His life was worth saving.

• • • •

Before Brent died, I had gone off my medications because none of them were working. After he died, I was hospitalized immediately, and then entered various treatment facilities to help me with my depression and grief. In 1995, I was in a residential treatment facility that encouraged its clients to return to school. I signed up for classes that fall, but the week they started was the one-year anniversary of my son's death. I was hospitalized again for six weeks and had sixteen electroshock sessions to treat my severe depression. I not only forgot who I was, but also where I was, where I lived, my enrollment at school, and even the fact that my son had died. As my memory slowly returned, I had to relive his death all over again. I was not fully functional or cognizant at that time.

Depression is an oppressive darkness and gloom. No happiness. No spark for life. It is sitting in a corner unable to move. It literally felt as if a physical weight prevented me from being able to do ordinary, everyday things, like brushing my teeth or organizing my medications. The simplest aspects of living that most people take for granted, like decid-

Standing: Jenny and Ann. *Sitting:* Jane

ing what shirt to wear, became impossible for me. I wasn't capable of cleaning my house, taking a shower, or taking care of myself at all. I had absolutely no concentration. I had difficulty speaking and talking. I couldn't formulate sentences. I stuttered. I isolated myself, stayed in my room for days at a time, and didn't go out or talk to anyone. I was angry a lot of the time.

• • • •

A turning point in my recovery came when I turned over the decision-making about my illness to professionals. I finally acknowledged that, not unlike an alcoholic, I wasn't in control of my illness and that I needed to give other people control over my treatment in order to get better. When I met my current psychiatrist, I began to do this, but I didn't do it all at once. It was a gradual process of letting go. I slowly learned to let the clinic staff help make decisions for me. It was very difficult to accept their input at first, but I soon saw that their advice helped me pull my life back together again.

• • • •

Since I've become stable, I am a more loving, calm, and logical person. I'm not as reactionary as I used to be. In the past, I would overreact to certain situations in our family. It was a hardship for my children because I would respond so inappropriately. At the time, I was angry, irritable, and not functioning most of the time. But, thank God, I kept looking for help.

I have to protect my stability, and my family helps me do that by reducing my stress, by not letting me take on too much, and by keeping my life balanced physically, mentally, emotionally, and spiritually. My mother and my daughter, and even my sister, who lives in another city, all assist me in maintaining that balance. I constantly turn to them and say, "I'm considering this. Please help me with this decision."

Anxiety Disorders

Before I left my office to meet Barbara Wilder for the first time, the clinic receptionist, Marie, pulled me aside in the hallway to warn me about the situation in the waiting room. Marie explained that Barbara's friend, who had come along for support, offered the reassuring words that Barbara was fine and that she commonly had these kinds of "attacks." Even with her warning, the scene would leave a lasting mark in my memory—in a distant corner of the otherwise empty waiting room, Barbara was writhing on the floor in what appeared to be a convulsion. Her friend knelt next to her, offering soothing words that had a powerful impact on helping Barbara regain control of herself.

As I walked across the waiting room, I sorted through a number of options about how I would enter this very dramatic situation. I momentarily wondered if I should return to my office and wait until Barbara had calmed down, but I felt it might appear as though I was intimidated by Barbara's behavior. Instead, I reached out my hands to Barbara and, in a reassuring voice, introduced myself and helped her rise from the floor and take a seat in a nearby chair. For a moment, Barbara continued to gasp for breath but gradually recovered as she sat between her friend and me. She seemed like a frightened child whose fears were contained by the presence of caregivers sitting beside her. I sat there for 5 minutes and offered calming words in an effort to offer her further comfort. Barbara then looked into my eyes and said, "I'm really sorry for all this drama. I hope you'll understand that this condition is beyond my control." I told Barbara that I realized this and that I also recognized how disturbing and frightening such reactions could be. I asked her to come with me to my office. At first, she asked if her friend could join us but quickly reconsidered and stated, "Actually, I think I should try to do this on my own."

As Barbara walked alongside me, my occasional glances caused me to wonder about whether I had correctly recalled her age. How could this woman be only 22 years old? The way she carried her body and shuffled her feet, along with the look of worry on her face, caused me to think that she must be at least in her midthirties. I wondered whether she was suffering from a medical problem, such as arthritis, that caused her to walk and move her body with such rigidity. The more we talked, the more I realized that her bodily tension was telling the story of inner turmoil rather than physical impairment. Barbara began her story by telling me how the preceding 6 months had been "pure hell." It all began one evening when she was waiting in a crowded airport lounge to fly home to visit her parents, her first visit since starting her new job. She suddenly felt incredibly dizzy, and the words on the page of her paperback novel began to dance in front of her eyes. She felt a roaring sound in her ears and a sudden stabbing pain in her chest. Her heart pounded wildly, and she broke out into a cold sweat. Her hands trembled uncontrollably. Just that day, Barbara had heard about the sudden death of a young woman due to a rare heart condition. Struggling to overcome the choking sensation in her throat, she was convinced that she was about to die.

In what seemed to Barbara to be an absolute miracle, the woman next to her saw what was happening and summoned paramedics. Neither they nor the physicians who examined Barbara could find anything physically wrong. The doctor told Barbara that she was probably exhausted and that the airport lounge must have been too stuffy. She spent the night at the hospital and was released the next morning.

Barbara had to cancel her visit to her parents, but her alarm about the incident gradually subsided. Two weeks later, though, the same thing happened again. She was shopping at the mall for a present for her roommate, who was to be married in a few days. Once again, a medical exam showed no physical abnormalities. Barbara began to suspect that the physicians were hiding something from her about the seriousness of her condition. Over the next several months, Barbara went from physician to physician, searching in vain for someone who could diagnose her illness and put her on a proper course of therapy. All they did, though, was advise her to get some rest. One physician prescribed a mild tranquilizer, but it offered no relief from her attacks, which became even more intense, occurring once every 2 weeks.

Little by little, Barbara found herself staying away from situations in which she would be trapped if she were to have an attack. She quit her job, because she was terrified that she would have an attack in the elevator while riding up to her office on the 26th floor. Eventually, Barbara became virtually a total recluse. She could not even walk out of her front door without feeling an overwhelming sense of dread. The only time she left the house was when her former roommate, who was now married, took her to the grocery store or for a walk. At this friend's suggestion, Barbara sought help at the mental health clinic. This young woman appeared to others, for much of her early years, to be an individual who functioned quite well. They did not realize, however, that within Barbara's hidden emotional life she was tremendously insecure and felt intensely dependent on others. When confronted with the challenging life transitions of her first job, she became caught up in overwhelming anxiety.

Sarah Tobin, PhD

Everyone becomes anxious from time to time—an examination, a sporting match, a meeting with an important person, and concern over a new relationship can all create feelings of apprehension. Often a person's anxieties are about the future, whether long-term concerns about a career or more immediate worries about a Saturday night date. Think about your own experiences involving anxiety. Perhaps you were so nervous while taking an examination that your mind went blank, or you were so "wound up" while playing in a close basketball game that you missed an easy shot. The anxiety of giving an oral presentation in class may have left you tongue-tied and embarrassed. As upsetting as any of these experiences may be, none would be considered abnormal functioning. It is even possible that such experiences had beneficial aspects. You may have developed ways to calm yourself, which you then found useful in other circumstances, or your anxiety may have energized you to overcome obstacles and perform more effectively. Thus, in moderation, anxiety may serve some positive functions.

Although the terms fear and anxiety are commonly used interchangeably, psychologists make a distinction between them in a clinical context. **Fear** refers to an innate, almost biologically based alarm response to a dangerous or life-threatening situation. People who suffer from the disorders covered in this chapter experience "false alarms," in which harmless stimuli or situations are regarded as dangerous (Street & Barlow, 1994). **Anxiety,** by contrast, is more future-oriented and global, referring to the state in which an individual is inordinately apprehensive, tense, and uneasy about the prospect of something terrible happening. Anxiety has both cognitive and affective components. When you are anxious, you have a feeling that something terrible will happen and that you are powerless to change it. You start to focus on your inner concerns, while becoming hypervigilant, or overly watchful, regarding the possibility of danger or threat.

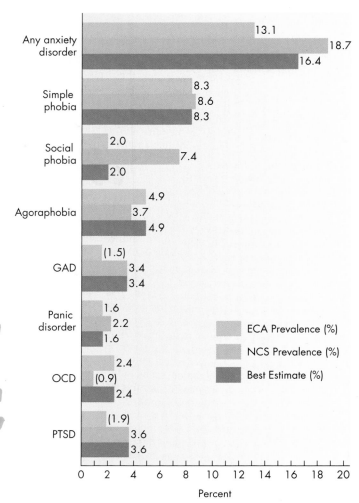

FIGURE 5.1 Best-estimate 1-year prevalence rates based on ECA and NCS, for persons 18 to 54 years old Figures for best estimates were based on a conservative procedure that took into account statistical considerations. Numbers in parentheses indicate the prevalence of the disorder without comorbidity.
Source: U.S. Department of Health and Human Services, 1999.

Anxiety becomes a source of clinical concern when it reaches such an intense level that it interferes with the ability to function in daily life, as a person enters a maladaptive state characterized by extreme physical and psychological reactions. These intense, irrational, and incapacitating experiences are the basis of the anxiety disorders, which affect as many as 19 percent of Americans every year (U.S. Department of Health and Human Services, 1999) (see Figure 5.1).

The Nature of Anxiety Disorders

People with **anxiety disorders** are incapacitated by chronic and intense feelings of anxiety, feelings so strong that they are unable to function on a day-to-day basis. Their anxiety is unpleasant and

Sometimes anxiety can be so overwhelming that people feel unable to cope with the ordinary demands of life.

Diagnostic Features of Panic Attack

A panic attack is a period of intense fear or discomfort, during which a person experiences four or more of the following symptoms, which develop abruptly and reach a peak within 10 minutes:

- Palpitations, pounding heart, or accelerated heart rate
- Sweating
- Trembling or shaking
- Sensations of shortness of breath or smothering
- Feeling of choking
- Chest pain or discomfort
- Nausea or abdominal distress
- Feelings of dizziness, unsteadiness, lightheadedness, or faintness
- Feelings of unreality (derealization) or a sensation of being detached from oneself (depersonalization)
- Fear of losing control or going crazy
- Fear of dying
- Sensation of tingling or numbness
- Chills or hot flushes

makes it difficult for them to enjoy many ordinary situations, but, in addition, they try to avoid situations that cause them to feel anxious. As a result, they may miss opportunities to enjoy themselves or to act in their own best interest. For example, people who are afraid to fly in airplanes face job problems if their work requires air travel. You may have heard of John Madden, the sportscaster who travels around the country by bus because he experiences severe panic attacks in airplanes. The lives of people whose anxiety prevents them from even the more ordinary task of leaving the house are even more disrupted. It is perhaps because of the disabling nature of anxiety and related disorders that prescription drugs for anxiety are among the most widely used in the United States.

Panic Disorder

People with **panic disorder** experience **panic attacks,** periods of intense fear and physical discomfort, in which they feel overwhelmed and terrified by a range of bodily sensations that causes them to feel they are losing control. These attacks have a sudden onset and usually reach a peak within a 10-minute period. The sensations the person experiencing a panic attack feels include shortness of breath or the feeling of being smothered, hyperventilation, dizziness or unsteadiness, choking, heart

palpitations, trembling, sweating, stomach distress, feelings of unreality, sensations of numbness or tingling, hot flashes or chills, chest discomfort, and fear of dying, "going crazy," or losing control. While this is happening, the individual has a sense of impending doom and feels an overwhelming urge to escape. If you have ever had any of the symptoms of a panic attack, even to a small degree, you can imagine how upsetting it must be to someone who experiences a full-blown episode.

For panic disorder to be diagnosed in an individual, at least some of the person's panic attacks must arise "out of the blue," meaning that there is no situational cue or trigger. Such an attack is called an **unexpected (uncued) panic attack.** An individual may also experience a panic attack in anticipation of confronting a particular situation or immediately following exposure to a specific stimulus or cue in the environment. For example, every time Jonathan hears an ambulance siren, he begins to experience the symptoms of a panic attack. This is an example of a **situationally bound (or cued) panic attack.** In cases in which the person has a tendency to have a panic attack in the situation but does not have one every time, the episode is referred to as a **situationally predisposed panic attack.** For example, Samantha may occasionally have a panic attack when she is riding in a subway car, but she does not have a panic attack on every occasion that she rides the subway.

When evaluating the situation of a client who experiences panic attacks, the clinician must consider the possibility that the client has a medical condition that causes the symptoms. Physical disorders, such as hypoglycemia, hyperthyroidism, insulin-secreting tumors, and cardiovascular or respiratory diseases, can cause panic-like symptoms. Some drugs can also cause reactions that mimic panic attacks. People who are intoxicated with cocaine, amphetamines, or even caffeine may appear to be experiencing a panic attack, when, in fact, they are having a toxic reaction to the substances in their bodies.

Characteristics of Panic Disorder

The diagnosis of panic disorder is made when panic attacks occur on a recurrent basis or when a month has elapsed since the first panic attack but the individual has continued to feel apprehensive and worried about the possibility of recurring attacks. A fairly high percentage of Americans, as many as 15 percent, have experienced one or more panic attacks. However, the diagnosis of panic disorder is fairly uncommon, with estimates of lifetime prevalence rates ranging from 1.4 percent to 2.9 percent both in the United States and in other countries around the world (Weissman et al., 1997).

Though panic disorder is relatively uncommon in the general population, it is common in clinical settings. In fact, panic disorder is diagnosed in approximately 10 percent of people who are referred for mental health consultation, and the percentage is even more dramatic in general medical settings. For example, 60 percent of the patients seen in cardiology clinics meet the criteria for panic disorder, primarily because people with bodily symptoms associated with heart problems experience physical symptoms that can be terrifying due to their fatal potential (American Psychiatric Association, 2000).

Most cases of panic disorder develop in people who are around the age of 20, with a second, smaller group of cases arising among people in their midthirties. Although some children and adolescents experience symptoms of panic attacks, the disorder is relatively rare among this age group. Adolescents who do experience panic attacks are at a much greater risk of developing psychological disorders than individuals without panic attacks. These disorders range from mood disorders, other anxiety disorders, substance use disorders, and, in the most extreme cases, psychotic conditions (Goodwin, Fergusson, & Horwood, 2004). Like other anxiety disorders, panic disorder is less likely to arise in later adulthood (Scogin, Floyd, & Forde, 2000). Women are approximately twice as likely to be diagnosed with this disorder (Eaton, Kessler, Wittchen, & Magee, 1994).

Panic disorder, if left untreated, has a variable course. For some individuals, panic attacks occur only periodically, sometimes with months or years between episodes. Then, suddenly and without warning, an attack strikes. More typically, however, the disorder creates continuous problems for many years. People who suffer from these symptoms are faced with the daily uncertainty that they may experience a panic attack when they are not in a position to find someone who can help them. It is the unpredictability of the symptoms that is particularly distressing to these individuals. Researchers have found that people who are able to predict that a panic attack will occur, based on specific cues in the environment, experience less distress (Craske, Glover, & DeCola, 1995).

A person with agoraphobia becomes overwhelmed and panicky in situations that feel unsafe, such as crowds.

> ### Diagnostic Features of Agoraphobia
>
> ■ People with this condition experience anxiety about being in places or situations from which escape might be difficult or embarrassing, or in which they may not be able to get help should they have panic symptoms or a panic attack. Common agoraphobic fears involve such situations as being outside the home alone, being in a crowd or standing in line, being on a bridge, and traveling in a bus, train, or car.
>
> ■ People with this condition avoid the feared situations, or they endure them with marked distress or anxiety about having a panic attack or panic symptoms, or they insist that a companion be present in the event that they panic.

Over time, people with panic disorder learn to avoid places where they fear they may be trapped, such as elevators, crowded stores, or movie theaters. However, such avoidance can lead to the development of a related condition, **agoraphobia,** which is intense anxiety about being trapped, stranded, or embarrassed in a situation without help if a panic attack were to occur. Although panic disorder is usually linked with agoraphobia, it is possible for people to experience agoraphobia without panic disorder, or panic disorder without agoraphobia. These conditions vary in their severity and impact. People with agoraphobia commonly find the condition severely disruptive, while many whose diagnosis is panic disorder without agoraphobia are able to function adequately in their daily lives (Goisman et al., 1994). By contrast, the lifetime prevalence of agoraphobia without panic disorder is surprisingly high, with estimates of 5 percent of the adult population and twice as many women as men suffering from the condition at some point in life (Kessler et al., 1994). Women are also more likely to have symptoms of panic disorder with agoraphobia, while men are more likely to have uncomplicated panic disorder. Furthermore, compared with men, women are more likely to suffer recurring symptoms of panic disorder over time (Yonkers et al., 1998).

Common fears of people with agoraphobia involve such situations as being home alone, in a crowd, on a bridge, or in a moving vehicle. Public transportation is the most frequently cited location of a first panic attack (Shulman et al., 1994). Because people with agoraphobia become so fearful of panic attacks, they develop idiosyncratic personal styles and behaviors in order to avoid these situations. If forced to be in the dreaded situation, they experience intense distress about the possibility that they will experience a panic attack or panic-like symptoms. For example, they may refuse to leave the house unless they are accompanied by someone who knows about their disorder and will be ready to help if needed. They go to extremes to avoid being in a crowd or going to an unfamiliar place. Even when they are not experiencing feelings of immediate danger, people with agoraphobia constantly worry about unexpectedly being put into what they perceive as risky situations. It is common for people

Mini Case

PANIC DISORDER WITH AGORAPHOBIA

Frieda is a 28-year-old former postal worker who sought treatment because of recurrent panic attacks, which have led her to become fearful of driving. She has become so frightened of the prospect of having an attack on the job that she has asked for a medical leave. Although initially she would leave the house when accompanied by her mother, she now is unable to go out under any circumstances, and her family is concerned that she will become a total recluse.

Diagnostic Features

This diagnosis is assigned to people who experience panic attacks not due to the physiological effects of substances or to a medical condition, and who do not have the symptoms of agoraphobia. They experience both of the following:

■ Recurrent, unexpected panic attacks

■ At least one of the attacks has been followed by at least one month during which they experience one of the following: persistent concern about having more attacks, worry about the implications of the attack or its consequences (e.g., fear that they will lose control, have a heart attack, or "go crazy"), significant change in behavior related to the attacks.

with agoraphobia to seek out "safety cues," such as a "safe person," who, the individual believes, can be of help in case of a panic attack. Other safety cues might be medication, a pet, or the home itself (Street & Barlow, 1994).

Theories and Treatment of Panic Disorder and Agoraphobia

In trying to understand the causes of panic disorder and agoraphobia, researchers have tended to discuss both phenomena together, although some give more emphasis to one than to the other. The available theories suggest that both disorders have psychological and physiological components, but it is unclear whether psychological factors cause physiological changes, or vice versa. In the following paragraphs, we will focus on both biological and psychological perspectives, because these are regarded as most relevant to the understanding and treatment of the conditions of panic disorder and agoraphobia.

In considering biological contributors to the development of panic disorder, researchers have been struck by the fact that biological relatives of individuals with panic disorder are 8 times more likely to develop this condition; furthermore, people who develop panic disorder before the age of 20 are 20 times more likely than others to have first-degree relatives with the condition (American Psychiatric Association, 2000).

One set of biological theories focuses on abnormalities in the levels of particular neurotransmitters. According to one view, people with panic disorder have an excess of norepinephrine

in the brain (Hoehn, Braune, Scheibe, & Albus, 1997). Norepinephrine, a neurotransmitter, is activated when the individual is placed under stress or in a dangerous situation. When a drug that increases norepinephrine activity is administered to people with a history of panic disorder, they are more likely than people without the disorder to experience a panic attack. Another theory involving neurotransmitters proposes that people with this disorder suffer from a defect in gamma-aminobutyric acid (GABA), a neurotransmitter with inhibitory effects on neurons. Supporting this theory is evidence of diminished response of GABA receptors in the cortex of individuals with panic disorder (Goddard et al., 2004). According to this theory, the anxiety that people with panic disorder experience is due to underactivity of the GABA neurotransmitter system. Neurons in the subcortical parts of the brain involved in panic attacks become more active with less GABA to inhibit them.

Researchers have also focused on a system in the brain that signals when there is insufficient air available to breathe. According to **anxiety sensitivity theory,** people with panic disorder tend to interpret cognitive and somatic manifestations of stress and anxiety in a catastrophic manner. They are thought to have a hypersensitive "suffocation" mechanism, so that they feel as though they cannot breathe, even though others would feel nothing unusual in that situation. This false alarm mechanism causes the individual to hyperventilate, and the individual is thrown into a panic state. Irregularities in the respiratory system may make these people particularly vulnerable to these sensations of suffocation and choking (Caldirola et al., 2004).

In research testing anxiety sensitivity theory, individuals with panic disorder were subjected to a condition in which they breathed into an instrument that forced them to rebreathe their own air over a 5-minute period. Over the duration of the period, levels of carbon dioxide gradually increased, a condition that could trigger suffocation fear. Both anxiety sensitivity and suffocation fear predicted anxious responding to this condition, but suffocation fear was more strongly related to the feelings of panic that respondents experienced. The findings suggested that both physical and psychological factors are important in understanding the causes of panic disorder (Rassovsky, Kushner, Schwarze, & Wangensteen, 2000). It is possible that there is a genetic component to the phenomenon of anticipatory anxiety; in other words, children may inherit a predisposition in which they overreact to the threat that they may be deprived of oxygen (Pine et al., 2005). The unpredictability of an aversive event may be particularly critical in triggering a panic attack in highly anxious individuals (Lejuez, Eifert, Zvolensky, & Richards, 2000).

As is suggested by the previous discussion of the misinterpretation of bodily cues among people with panic disorder, any physiological disturbances that account for this disorder interact with psychological processes. One approach that focuses on psychological factors regards **conditioned fear reactions** as contributing to the development of panic attacks. This means the individual associates certain bodily sensations with memories of the last panic attack, causing a full-blown panic attack to develop even before measurable biological changes have occurred. Over

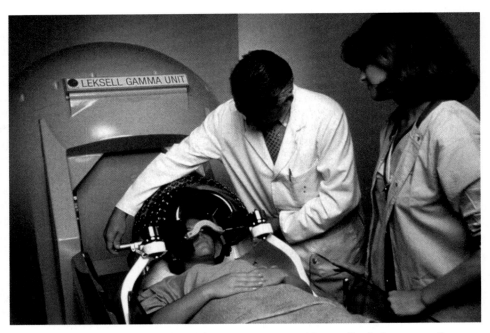

The Gamma Knife, which is used in radiosurgery, contains 201 small cobalt sources of gamma rays that aim radiation to a common focal point for the treatment of various neuropsychiatric conditions, including obsessive-compulsive disorder. These procedures stem from the work of Swedish neurosurgeon Lars Leksell, who developed stereotactic devices in the 1950s to guide the gamma rays, and from the work of Swedish physicist Borje Larsson, who built the first Gamma Knife in 1968. Courtesy Kenneth Oh, MD.

time, the individual begins to anticipate the panic attack before it happens, leading to the avoidance behavior seen in agoraphobia.

In a cognitive-behavioral model of anxiety disorders, psychologist David Barlow and his co-workers proposed that anxiety becomes an unmanageable problem for an individual through the development of a vicious cycle. The cycle begins with the individual's experiencing the sensation of highly negative feelings (such as unpleasant bodily sensations in a panic attack), which in turn causes the person to feel that what is happening is unpredictable and uncontrollable. As these feelings increase in intensity, they draw the individual's attention like a magnet. The individual is now left awash in these unpleasant sensations and cannot do anything else except think about them. Faulty cognitions and the misperception of cues, both within the person's body and in the environment, further contribute to the sensation of anxiety, as in the case of phobias. Cognitive factors also play a role, as the individual develops distorted beliefs, which add to the anxious apprehension of a panic attack occurring in an uncontrollable manner in the future (Bouton, Mineka, & Barlow, 2001).

Given that biological factors play at least some role in causing panic disorder, many clinicians recommend treatment with medications. The most effective antianxiety medications are **benzodiazepines.** These medications bind to receptor sites of GABA neurons, which then become activated by this stimulation, leading to the inhibition of the brain sites involved in panic attacks. Some commonly prescribed benzodiazepines are chlordiazepoxide (Librium), diazepam (Valium), chlorazepate (Tranxene), and alprazolam (Xanax). To be effective in treating panic disorders, these medications must be taken for at least 6 months, and possibly as long as a year. Because these medications often lose their therapeutic efficacy and lead to physiological or psychological dependence, clinicians have sought alternatives, including antidepressants and serotonin reuptake inhibitors, such as fluoxetine (Prozac) and fluvoxamine (Luvox). Sertraline (Zoloft) may also be beneficial with individuals who have chronic and recurrent symptoms (Pollack et al., 2000).

As useful as medications are in alleviating the symptoms of panic, they are regarded as insufficient in the treatment of panic disorder. Experts are now most inclined to recommend that, when medication is prescribed, a psychotherapeutic intervention should also be incorporated into the treatment.

Relaxation training is one behavioral technique used in the treatment of panic disorder and agoraphobia. In this approach, the client learns to systematically alternate tensing and relaxing muscles all over the body, usually starting at the forehead and working downward to the feet. After training, the client should be able to relax the entire body when confronting a feared situation.

Hyperventilation, a common symptom in panic attacks, is sometimes treated with a form of counterconditioning. In this approach, the client hyperventilates intentionally and then begins slow breathing, a response that is incompatible with hyperventilation. Following this training, the client can begin the slow breathing at the first signs of hyperventilation. Thus, the client learns that it is possible to exert voluntary control over hyperventilation.

Although relaxation training and counterconditioning have some appeal, experts now recognize that more comprehensive interventions involving cognitive techniques are necessary. The focus in recent years has been on treatments geared to giving the individual a sense of being able to control the attacks. Experts generally recommend *in vivo* exposure when treating individuals with panic disorder, especially for those suffering with agoraphobia. The assumption is that treatment is most effective when clients can confront the dreaded situation. When this intervention was initially developed in the 1970s, intensive exposure was recommended. However, more recently, experts have suggested the use of graduated exposure, a procedure in which clients gradually expose themselves to increasingly greater anxiety-provoking situations. For example, Martha finds visits to large shopping malls to be emotionally overwhelming. Martha's therapist would recommend that her exposure to stressful environments begin with a small shop in which she feels safe and relatively anxiety free. Step by step, Martha would progress to environments that are higher on her list of anxiety-provoking settings.

Barlow and his colleagues developed the most comprehensive model for treating clients with panic disorder with agoraphobia. **Panic control therapy (PCT)** consists of cognitive restructuring, the development of an awareness of bodily cues associated with panic attacks, and breathing retraining (Barlow, Craske, Cerny, & Klosko, 1989). Studies of this model have demonstrated that clients treated with PCT show marked improvement, at levels comparable to the improvement shown by clients treated with antianxiety medication. Interestingly, how-

ever, later assessments of these clients showed that a greater percentage of those treated with PCT remained symptom free (Klosko, Barlow, Tassinari, & Cerny, 1990). In another comparison of cognitive therapy with other forms of treatment (relaxation and antidepressant medication) and control conditions, cognitive therapy was reported to be particularly beneficial for clients suffering from panic, anxiety, and associated avoidance, both at the end of the treatment and at follow-up (Street & Barlow, 1994). The model proposed by Barlow has stimulated a growing body of research, both in his clinic and elsewhere throughout the world, with dramatic data supporting the efficacy of cognitive-behavioral treatments for panic disorder (Barlow, Esler, & Vitali, 1998).

Although panic disorder and agoraphobia are not viewed as socioculturally caused, clinicians treating clients with these conditions recognize the importance of including in the treatment partners and others intimately involved in the person's life. For example, a professional might recommend the addition of marital communications and problem-solving training to standard exposure-based couples treatment (Street & Barlow, 1994).

Specific Phobias

Everyone has fears about or unpleasant responses to certain objects, situations, or creatures. Perhaps you shrink away from the sight of a spider, rodent, or snake. Or maybe looking down from a high place causes you to tremble and feel nauseated. Standing in a crowded hallway may lead you to feel uncomfortable, even a bit edgy, and you seek an open space. Such responses of discomfort or dislike, called **aversions,** are common and are not much cause for concern. However, if a person's response to one of these experiences is far out of proportion to the danger or threat posed by the stimulus, the person is considered to have a phobia. A **specific phobia** is an irrational and unabating fear of a particular object, activity, or situation that provokes an immediate anxiety response, causes significant disruption in functioning, and results in avoidance behavior. Specific phobias are relatively common, with prevalence rates in community samples ranging from 4 to 8.8 percent (American Psychiatric Association, 2000).

Characteristics of Specific Phobias

You have probably heard the word *phobia* many times, perhaps in a humorous context, such as when someone jokes about having a phobic reaction to computers. For people with genuine phobias, however, their condition is not a humorous matter. Rather, they live with an intense level of anxiety about the prospect of encountering the object of their dread, and they often go to great lengths to avoid contact with it. In circumstances in which they must come face-to-face with the phobic stimulus, their anxiety level intensifies as they come closer to the stimulus,

In MindMAP Segment 5.1, Annie talks about her fear of having a panic attack in a public setting and being totally out of control.

Agoraphobia arises when people fear that they will have a panic attack, and hence they avoid public places where they will be unable to escape or receive assistance.

Crossing this suspension bridge with acrophobia (fear of heights) makes this person feel panicky.

Mini Case

SPECIFIC PHOBIA

Herbert is a 32-year-old lawyer seeking treatment for his irrational fear of thunderstorms. He has had this phobia since the age of 4, and throughout life he has developed various strategies for coping with his fear. Whenever possible, he avoids going outside when a storm is forecast. Not only will he stay within a building, but he will ensure that he is in a room with no windows and no electrical appliances. As his job has grown in responsibility, Herbert has found that he can no longer afford to take time off because of his fear, which he knows is irrational.

Diagnostic Features

- This diagnosis is assigned to people who experience marked and persistent fear that is excessive or unreasonable, and that is brought on by the presence or anticipation of a specific object or situation (e.g., flying, heights, animals, injections, the sight of blood).

- When they encounter the phobic stimulus, they experience immediate anxiety, possibly in the form of a panic attack.

- They recognize that the fear is excessive or unreasonable.

- They avoid the situation or endure it with intense anxiety or distress.

- The condition causes distress or disruption in normal routines and functioning, activities, or relationships.

or as the possibility of escaping the feared situation decreases. For example, in the case of a man with a fear of airplanes, his anxiety increases as he drives to the airport and boards the plane, and it peaks after takeoff, when he realizes that he cannot exit the plane. When phobic individuals confront the object of their fear, or anticipate that they will, they become intensely anxious, occasionally to such an extent that they experience a full-blown panic attack. They are overwhelmed by the prospect of such encounters and often imagine the dire consequences that would result. For example, the prospect of seeing someone else bleeding terrifies Maria. There is no real danger that anything would happen to her if she saw someone else's blood, but her fear of this situation (hematophobia) causes her to avoid any circumstance in which she fears she might see blood, such as watching certain movies. Her anxiety is so intense that, if she inadvertently faces this situation, as when her child cuts his hand, she feels faint, panicky, and breathless. Phobias fall into several categories, with the most commonly reported phobias being those pertaining to animals, the natural environment, and blood or injury.

You may be wondering whether it is appropriate to refer to a feared situation as a phobia if it is avoidable and causes no significant anxiety for an individual. In fact, such a circumstance would not meet the criteria for this condition. For example, an urban woman who is terrified by the prospect of encountering a snake (ephidiophobia) can be fairly confident that she will be able to avoid such encounters if she stays away from the countryside. Therefore, she would rarely have cause for concern about this matter, and her condition would not be clinically significant.

Intense irrational fears are quite common in the general population, yet only those conditions that cause considerable distress or impairment would meet the diagnostic criteria for specific phobia. Lifetime prevalence rates are estimated between 7.2 and 11.3 percent (American Psychiatric Association, 2000).

Some phobias—such as animal phobias, blood-injury phobias, claustrophobia, and dental phobias—can be traced back to childhood. In fact, in one study of children between the ages of 4 and 12, a sizable proportion (17.6 percent) met the full diagnostic criteria for specific phobia (Muris & Merckelbach, 2000). Children do experience certain fears, such as fear of the dark, of strangers, of death, and of imaginary creatures; however, most of these dissipate on their own (Emmelkamp, 1982). Other phobias, such as choking phobia, may arise in response to a traumatic episode of choking on food (McNally, 1994). Females are more likely than males to have specific phobias and to develop phobic symptoms earlier (age 10 for females and age 14 for males) (Dick et al., 1994).

Specific phobias sometimes arise in conjunction with another psychological disorder. For example, almost two thirds of people who have panic disorder with agoraphobia also suffer from a specific phobia, such as situational phobia, dental phobia, blood injection-injury phobia, natural environment phobia, and death-related phobia (fear of funerals, dead bodies, and cemetaries). Many of these phobias preceded the development of panic disorder with agoraphobia by many years, except for death-related phobias, which appear closer in time to the onset of panic disorder.

Theories and Treatment of Specific Phobias

As you have just seen, there are many types of specific phobias, ranging from the common to the relatively obscure. However, the fact that they are grouped together suggests that there is a common theme or element that underlies their cause and potentially their treatment. As is true for panic disorder, the primary explanations of specific phobias rely on biological and psychological perspectives. Nevertheless, as is also true for panic disorder, the existence of a specific phobia in an individual can have a significant impact on those who are close to that person. Consequently, treatment sometimes involves partners and family members.

The primary biological perspective on specific phobias involves the notion that humans are essentially preprogrammed to fear certain situations or stimuli that could threaten our survival (Lang, Davis, & Ohman, 2000). According to this view, there is an evolutionary advantage to the fear of death, disaster, or injury. This "biological preparedness" theory is based on the assumption that there might be a biological "wiring" that causes people to react with fear to threatening situations (Seligman, 1971). Such a biological propensity might explain how people can so rapidly acquire irrational fears that are so resistant to extinction. Adding support to the hypothesis that biology plays a determining role in the development of specific phobias is research that has been conducted with male twins. Using personal interviews, Kendler and his colleagues (2001) assessed 1,198 male-male twin pairs and reported genetic contributions ranging from 25 to 37 percent in the etiology of phobias and the irrational fears associated with phobias. Furthermore, it has been found that family members seem to share similar phobias; for example, first-degree biological relatives of people with animal phobias share this kind of phobia, although not necessarily to the same kind of animal. Similarly, individuals with blood-injury phobias or those with situational phobias are likely to have biological relatives who share similar specific phobias (American Psychiatric Association, 2000).

Speculation about the psychological causes of phobias goes back at least as far as the time of Freud. Although Freud did not initially consider phobias to be psychologically based, his later writings reflect his notion of phobias as psychological symptoms that defend the ego against anxiety. Around the time that Freud was writing on the topic, behavioral psychologists, such as Watson, were demonstrating in the laboratory that animals and humans alike could acquire phobic behavior through conditioning, which led to the conclusion that phobias resulted from maladaptive learning. Current conceptualizations add to this behavioral model the notion that the individual's thoughts also play a role in acquiring and maintaining specific phobias. Many people with phobias report that they had an aversive experience during childhood that has remained with them, or

whose parents, and even grandparents, displayed phobic behavior when confronted with the feared object (Fredrikson, Annas, & Wik, 1997; Merkelbach & Muris, 1997).

Cognitive-behavioral theorists (Beck, Emery, & Greenberg, 1985) view anxiety disorders, such as specific phobias, as rooted in and maintained by the client's cognitive styles. According to this view, phobic individuals have overactive "alarm systems" to danger, and they perceive things as dangerous because they misinterpret stimuli. Their perceptions are based on faulty inferences and overgeneralizations. Consider the case of Roberto, a 30-year-old man who experiences a fear of dying that is triggered by unexpected physical sensations. He interprets the physical sensations as a sign of a physical disease and becomes anxious; in this way, a chain reaction is set up. Roberto then generalizes in such a way that everything looks dangerous. His attention becomes "stuck" on potentially dangerous stimuli, leaving him with less ability to think rationally. Roberto begins to think that he is losing his mind, and this makes matters worse.

Some people have feelings or beliefs about a stimulus that set the stage for developing a phobia. For example, the perception of an object or a situation as uncontrollable, unpredictable, dangerous, or disgusting is correlated with feelings of vulnerability. These attributions might explain the common phobia of spiders, an insect about which people have many misconceptions and apprehensions (Armfield & Mattiske, 1996). In another common phobia, that of blood-injury-injection, disgust and fear of contamination play a prominent role (Sawchuk et al., 2000). People with phobias also tend to overestimate the likelihood of a dangerous outcome after exposure to the feared stimulus (de Jong & Merckelbach, 2000). As you can see, in addition to being associated with prior aversive experiences, specific phobias can also arise from a person's thoughts and perceptions, which heighten the individual's feelings of vulnerability.

Behavioral therapy is highly effective because symptoms are relatively easy to identify and the stimuli are limited to specific situations or objects. Systematic desensitization, described in Chapter 4, rests on the premise that an individual can best overcome maladaptive anxiety by approaching feared stimuli gradually, while in a relaxed state. A therapist might decide, though, that systematic desensitization is either too time consuming, impractical, or unnecessary. Consider the case of Florence, a medical student who sees a therapist in desperation one week before she starts an anatomy course. She has fainted on past occasions when watching videotapes of surgical procedures and is sure that she will make a fool of herself in anatomy class. One week is not enough time to go through the systematic desensitization procedure. Furthermore, Florence's anxiety is not so severe as to be terrifying. Her therapist, therefore, decides to use a behavioral technique called **flooding,** in which the client is

MindMAP Segment 5.2: Systematic Desensitization

Behavioral treatment of a person with claustrophobia sometimes involves live exposure to the feared situation.

totally immersed in the sensation of anxiety, rather than being more gradually acclimated to the feared situation. Florence's therapist chooses a variant of flooding called **imaginal flooding,** in which Florence listens to someone read several vivid descriptions of the dissection of human cadavers. Florence is told to imagine exactly what these scenes look like. Exposure to the threatening stimulus while in a safe context will condition her to confront the target of her phobia without feeling unduly anxious.

Both of the behavioral techniques described so far use imagery in conditioning the client to feel less anxious toward the phobic stimulus. An alternative to imagery, and one that is generally more effective (Craske & Rowe, 1997), is actually exposing the client to the feared object or situation until the client no longer feels anxious. Obviously, this *in vivo* method requires that the therapist have ready access to the phobic stimulus. Florence's therapist could just as easily show her a surgical videotape as encourage her to imagine the sight of blood. However, if the client fears flying in an airplane, it would be impractical for the therapist to embark on *in vivo* treatment by accompanying the client on an airplane ride (although cases of such treatment are occasionally reported). Increasingly, clinicians are taking advantage of new technologies, such as computer simulation (Gilroy et al., 2000) and virtual reality (Anderson, Rothbaum, & Hodges, 2001) to provide the experience of immersion.

In vivo flooding is probably the most stressful of any of the treatments described. An alternative is a graded *in vivo* method, involving a graduated exposure to increasingly anxiety-provoking stimuli. In the **graduated exposure** method, clients initially confront situations that cause only minor anxiety and then gradually progress toward those that cause greater anxiety (Street & Barlow, 1994). Often the therapist tries to be encouraging and to model the desired nonanxious response. In treating a client

named Tan, who has a fear of enclosed spaces, the therapist could go with him into smaller and smaller rooms. Seeing his therapist showing no signs of fear could lead Tan to model the therapist's response. The therapist could also offer praise, to further reinforce the new response that Tan is learning. As illustrated in Table 5.1, behavioral treatments vary according to the nature of the client's exposure to the phobic stimulus (live or imagined) and the degree of intensity with which the stimulus is confronted (immediate full exposure or exposure in graduated steps).

Positive reinforcement is implicit in all behavioral techniques. The therapist becomes both a guide and a source of support and praise for the client's successes. The therapist may also find it useful to incorporate some techniques from the cognitive perspective into the behavioral treatment, because maladaptive thoughts are often part of the client's difficulties. Cognitive-behavioral treatment focuses on helping the client learn more adaptive ways of thinking about previously threatening situations and objects.

Cognitive restructuring, described in Chapter 4, can help the client view the feared situation more rationally by challenging his or her irrational beliefs about the feared stimulus. For example, a therapist may show Victor, who has an elevator phobia, that the "disastrous" consequences he believes will result from riding in an elevator are unrealistic and exaggerated. Victor can also learn the technique of "talking to himself" while in this situation, telling himself that his fears are ridiculous, that nothing bad will really happen, and that he will soon reach his destination.

In **thought stopping,** the individual learns to stop anxiety-provoking thoughts. In therapy, the client is supposed to alert the therapist when the anxiety-provoking thought is present; at that point, the therapist yells, "Stop!" Outside therapy, the client mentally verbalizes a similar shout each time the anxiety-provoking thought comes to mind.

Through stress inoculation, the client can learn coping self-statements (Meichenbaum, 1985), another cognitive-behavioral method. The client prepares a list of statements to use when confronting the feared situation, which provides reassurance that he or she can adequately manage the situation. Examples of such statements are "I can cope with this," "It is irrational for me to feel so scared," "I've gotten through difficult situations before, so I can get through this one," and "Don't think about my fear."

TABLE 5.1 Methods of Exposure Used in Behavioral Therapy of Phobias

	Graduated Exposure	Immediate Full Exposure
Imagery	Systematic	Imaginal flooding, desensitization
Live	Graded *in vivo*	*In vivo* flooding

These statements increase the individual's sense that he or she can conquer the situation.

Bolstering the client's sense of self-efficacy is a related therapy component (Bandura, 1986) that helps the client feel more confident about being able to manage the phobic stimulus. For example, Florence, whose blood-injury phobia was described earlier, could learn through self-efficacy training to see herself as successfully handling her fears. She may observe or imagine observing someone else treating patients who are bleeding, using vicarious reinforcement to change her beliefs about her own ability to come close to a bleeding person. As Florence herself is put into actual situations with increased exposure to blood or injury, she can practice telling herself that she has the capability to cope with the situation, until she no longer experiences anxiety.

Social Phobia

Many people become nervous or jittery before speaking in front of a group, appearing in a musical performance, or participating in an athletic contest or a game. People with **social phobia,** however, feel tremendous anxiety not only in these situations but also in virtually all situations in which others might be observing them.

Characteristics of Social Phobia

The primary characteristic of social phobia is an irrational and intense fear that one's behavior in a public situation will be mocked or criticized by others. People with this disorder recognize that their fears are unreasonable, yet they cannot stop themselves from worrying that others are scrutinizing them. Although people with social phobia go to extremes to avoid such public situations, there are situations in which they have no choice; when this happens, they become crippled with anxiety.

People who have social phobia have many fears about such situations as speaking in public. They are afraid they will do or say something embarrassing, that their minds will go "blank," that they will be unable to continue speaking, will say foolish things or not make any sense, or will show signs of anxiety, such as trembling or shaking (Stein, Walker, & Forde, 1996). Even if their fears are not confirmed and their performance goes smoothly, people with social phobia doubt their ability to do well in these situations and fear that others will expect more of them in the future as a result (Wallace & Alden, 1997).

It may be understandable to think of becoming overwhelmed with fear regarding a public performance, but people with social phobia can have these experiences in seemingly innocuous situations, such as while eating in a restaurant. The simple act of picking up a fork or swallowing food can be seen as an insurmountable task for people with this disorder, who fear that others will laugh at how they hold their fork or swallow their food. They dread the possibility that they will blush, sweat, drop something, choke on their food, or vomit. These fears evaporate

Mini Case

SOCIAL PHOBIA

Ted is a 19-year-old college student who reports that he is terrified at the prospect of speaking in class. His anxiety about this matter is so intense that he has enrolled in very large lecture classes, where he sits in the back of the room, slouching in his chair to make himself as invisible as possible. On occasion, one of his professors randomly calls on students to answer certain questions. When this occurs, Ted begins to sweat and tremble. Sometimes he rushes from the classroom and frantically runs back to the dormitory for a few hours and tries to calm himself down.

Diagnostic Features

- People with this diagnosis experience marked or persistent fear of social or performance situations in which they will encounter unfamiliar people or the scrutiny of others. They fear that they will appear anxious or act in embarrassing or humiliating ways.

- When they encounter the feared situation, they experience anxiety, possibly in the form of a panic attack.

- They recognize that the fear is excessive or unreasonable.

- The condition causes distress or disruption in normal routines and functioning, activities, or relationships.

when the individual is alone or unobserved, because it is the public aspect of the situation that causes the individual to experience anxiety. In addition to their fears about appearing foolish or clumsy, people with social phobia have low self-esteem and underestimate their actual talents and areas of competence (Uhde, Tancer, Black, & Brown, 1991). They also tend to be perfectionistic and believe that others expect perfect performance of them (Bieling & Alden, 1997). They may ruminate for as long as a week, thinking repeatedly about how they could have acted differently in what they felt was an embarrassing social event (Abbott & Rapee, 2004).

Social phobia can have effects similar to agoraphobia in that fears about public embarrassment may prevent the individual from leaving the house. However, the two disorders differ in that the anxiety that people with social phobia experience is specific to certain situations, whereas agoraphobia tends to be more generalized.

Although social phobia occurs in both children and adults, there are differences in the experience of the disorder. First, children are not necessarily aware that their fear is unreasonable. Secondly, children do not have the freedom that adults do to avoid anxiety-provoking situations, such as having to speak publicly in school. Because they have no escape, they may express their anxiety in indirect ways, such as poor school performance or refusal to interact with other children. Unfortunately, many who suffer with social phobia during childhood and adolescence will experience the symptoms of this disorder in adulthood (Pine et al., 1998). In one 29-year follow-up study, children who showed symptoms similar to social phobia (school phobia,

REAL STORIES

DONNY OSMOND: SOCIAL PHOBIA

At the beginning of this chapter you read about Barbara Wilder, a woman suffering with intense symptoms of anxiety. Barbara Wilder is like so many people who find themselves incapacitated by terrifying emotional and physical symptoms. Some of these individuals are remarkably successful people whose careers revolve around public appearances but who are tormented by anxiety symptoms so intense that they meet the diagnostic criteria of an anxiety disorder. The popular singer-actor Donny Osmond is one such celebrity who has spoken openly about his difficulties with social phobia.

Osmond's success in the entertainment industry began at a very early age. With Donny as a child singing sensation during the 1960s and 1970s, his family singing group sold millions of albums. Donny grew wildly popular, received huge amounts of fan mail, and had to be protected by bodyguards whose job it was to fend off shrieking fans.

Donny has been active in the entertainment business for more than three decades, although he has had his share of ups and downs. His greatest claim to fame was the successful television variety show that he and his sister Marie hosted during the 1970s. On *The Donny and Marie Show*, these two attractive and appealing stars sang, danced, acted, and interviewed other celebrities. More recently, Donny landed the lead role in Andrew Lloyd Webber's Broadway musical *Joseph and the Amazing Technicolor Dreamcoat.*

Donny Osmond

During the mid-1990s, Donny began feeling an anxiety that was unlike anything he had ever experienced before. At first, the disturbing feelings of tension and apprehension affected him only prior to going on stage for a performance. In time, however, he began feeling overwhelmed by the disruptive anxiety while at home. The symptoms of social phobia that had overtaken Osmond's life are described in his autobiography, *Life Is Just What You Make It:*

Unless you've experienced a panic attack yourself, you might find it hard to understand what it feels like, but bear with me as I try to explain. Once the fear of embarrassing myself grabbed me, I couldn't get loose. It was as if a bizarre and terrifying unreality had replaced everything that was familiar and safe. I felt powerless to think or reason my way out of the panic. It had a whole, strange, hallucinatory quality to it; for example, I could see myself up as if I were flying above it all, but I couldn't get back "inside" myself and take control. In the grip of my wildest fears, I was paralyzed, certain that if I made one wrong move, I would literally die. Even more terrifying, I'd have felt relieved to die. . . .

Something was definitely wrong, and at first I clung to a "reasonable explanation": the schedule, the commuting back and forth, the fact that I was living so much of my life away from Debbie and the boys, my responsibility to a successful show. But deep inside, I knew that none of it made sense. I'd performed under every adverse condition imaginable. I'd carried a good deal of responsibility since I was a child. Why couldn't I do it now? I wasn't on tour. I knew the show backwards and forwards. The audience was back; they accepted me just fine. So why was everything suddenly so terribly wrong? . . .

The anxiety waxed and waned. Some nights I went on and everything was fine. I confided in Debbie, of course, over the phone, and in Jill Willis, who was there in Minneapolis. They could see that I needed help, but what? I was nervous, but after thirty years of going on stage, how could that be possible?

Osmond's recognition of his problem led him finally to seek help. For other people with his condition, his sharing of his story also provided insight into the nature of this potentially disabling disorder.

Source: From Donny Osmond in *Life Is Just What You Make It* (1999). Reprinted by permission of Hyperion Books.

separation anxiety, and school refusal) were more likely as adults to live with their parents, less likely to have children of their own, and more likely to have psychiatric symptoms (Flakierska-Praquin, Lindstrom, & Gillberg, 1997). For some people, the disorder arises gradually during childhood and adolescence within personalities that are shy and inhibited. For other people, social phobia arises suddenly, perhaps as the result of a humiliating public experience, such as a disastrous piano recital or embarrassing incident of public speaking. The stage is then set for the person to experience subsequent feelings of vulnerability in similar situations. For many people with this disorder, the anxiety creates significant impairment in everyday life (Lang & Stein, 2001; Yonkers, Dyck, & Keller, 2001) for many years. Social phobia has a lifetime prevalence estimated at 3 percent of the general population for severe symptoms and a range of 8.5 to 13.3 percent for nonsevere symptoms. The lifetime prevalence of the disorder is somewhat higher in females than in males (Kessler et al., 1994; Robins & Regier, 1991; Weissman et al., 1996).

Social phobia may appear in a generalized or a specific form, depending on whether the phobia occurs in *any* public situation or whether it is associated with one specific type of situation. Individuals with generalized social phobia dread all interactions with others, not just situations in which they must perform or be observed. Individuals with the more specific type of social phobia have fears only in certain situations, such as public speaking (Kessler, Stein, & Berglund, 1998). In both forms of social phobia, the individual's occupational and social functioning are impaired by the disorder. For example, people with musical talent might steer away from careers as musicians because of the anxiety their social phobia engenders. However, the more generalized form of social phobia imposes many limitations, as individuals with this condition avoid careers with the potential for public exposure. They also are limited in their ability to enjoy many kinds of social relationships and social roles. Individuals with this severe form of social phobia are also more likely to have coexisting conditions—notably, depression, agoraphobia, alcohol abuse, and suicidal thinking and attempts (Lecrubier & Weiller, 1997).

Theories and Treatment of Social Phobia

Although social fears and anxieties have always existed, social phobia was not understood as a separate category of the anxiety disorders until relatively recently. More and more attention is being paid to this disorder, as increasing numbers of clients seek professional help for the symptoms of this condition that interferes with the quality of life (Weissman et al., 1996).

Risk factors in childhood are suggested by investigations of childhood adversities and their relationship to the subsequent development of social phobia. Family difficulties, such as lack of close relationships with parents, conflict between parents, and frequent family moves were identified in one large Canadian study. Also identified as risk factors are involvement with the juvenile and child welfare systems, physical and sexual abuse in child-

hood, violent behavior, school difficulties, and running away from home (Chartier, Walker, & Stein, 2001; Mason et al., 2004). Genetic contributions to social phobia are suggested by findings that the parents of children with this disorder are more likely to be diagnosed with major depression (Biederman et al., 2001).

Recent interest in the topic of social phobia is leading to a greater understanding of the disorder as a biopsychosocial phenomenon. Biological theories focus on abnormalities in neurotransmitters such as serotonin (Furmark et al., 2004) and norepinephrine. In the case of norepinephrine, researchers are beginning to identify genetic markers linking social phobia with this neurotransmitter (Gelernter, Page, Stein, & Woods, 2004). Some researchers have found evidence of left-hemisphere dysfunction in people with social phobia. This finding is important in light of the role of verbal processes in social interactions. Perhaps this dysfunction contributes to the stress that people with social phobia feel in interpersonal situations (Bruder et al., 2004).

Psychological perspectives on social phobia revolve around understanding the thought processes of people with the disorder. As already noted, individuals with this disorder have a variety of maladaptive thoughts about their abilities to perform, and these thoughts can cause them to become distracted from the task at hand. Think about a time when you were called on to perform in public, such as hitting a baseball, delivering a speech, or giving a solo musical performance. Perhaps your hands shook and your heart pounded as you prepared to go into the spotlight. You may have imagined hearing the laughter or criticism of others if you made a mistake. Once you started performing the action, though, chances are that you forgot about these distractions and concentrated on doing the best job you possibly could. According to cognitively oriented explanations of social phobia, people with this disorder are unable to take the step of shifting their attention away from anticipated criticism and onto their performance. They fear making a mistake while performing or speaking, and, because their concentration is impaired, they are likely to make that dreaded mistake. Their fears acquire a solid basis in experience each time this happens, and these people soon avoid similar situations. Even if the individual manages to keep from making a mistake, the unpleasantness of the situation is so intense that it creates a desire to avoid repetition.

Information on sociocultural variations in social phobia is slowly beginning to emerge as this phenomenon gains more attention. For example, Taijin Kyofusho (TKS) is a form of social anxiety found in Japan, in which individuals are concerned about offending others through their appearance or behavior. In a study comparing Japanese and American college students on scores on scales derived from both the *DSM-IV* definition of social phobia and the definition of TKS, there was a high degree of overlap, with half the people in the sample receiving high scores on one scale also receiving high scores on the other (Kleinknecht et al., 1997). Such findings suggest that there are similarities in the expression of this disorder across cultures. Epidemiological studies also suggest that the disorder has similar patterns of prevalence and comorbidity in other countries (Lecrubier & Weiller, 1997; Weissman et al., 1996).

People with generalized anxiety disorder have many worries and physical symptoms that prevent them from enjoying life.

Treating people with social phobia involves helping them learn more appropriate responses to the situations they fear. Behavioral and cognitive-behavioral techniques, such as those used to treat people with specific phobias, are particularly helpful in reaching this goal (Heimberg, 2001). Social phobics need to develop new ways of thinking about their interactions with others. Combining such techniques as cognitive restructuring and *in vivo* exposure can have impressive results (Clark & Agras, 1991; Heimberg & Barlow, 1988). Another treatment approach involves social skills training to help social phobics learn methods for coping with interpersonal stress, so that they can feel more confident and comfortable in their interactions (Ost, Jerremalm, & Johansson, 1984).

A more traditional biological approach examines alterations in neurotransmitter levels, including pathways in the brain involving GABA, serotonin, dopamine, and norepinephrine (Li, Chokka, & Tibbo, 2001). Medications including SSRIs, such as sertraline (Zoloft) (Van Ameringen et al., 2001) and paroxetine (Paxil), are regarded as effective psychopharmacological treatment (Schneier, 2001), as are benzodiazepines, particularly when combined with cognitive-behavioral therapy (Fedoroff & Taylor, 2001).

Generalized Anxiety Disorder

Sometimes anxiety is not associated with a particular object, situation, or event but seems to be a constant feature of a person's day-to-day existence. The diagnosis of **generalized anxiety disorder** applies to this category of anxiety-related experiences.

Characteristics of Generalized Anxiety Disorder

People with generalized anxiety disorder struggle with uncontrollable anxiety much of the time. Efforts to control their worry are usually unsuccessful, and they are afflicted with a number of symptoms, both physical and psychological, which interfere with social, occupational, and general life functioning. They are prone to feeling restless and keyed up much of the time and find it difficult to concentrate, sometimes feeling so tense that their mind goes blank. At night, they find it difficult to fall or stay asleep; during the day, they are likely to feel fatigued, irritable, and tense. As you will learn later in this text, many of the symptoms of this disorder are also associated with other Axis I disorders. For example, the physiological effects of some substances and the psychological components of mood disorder or a psychotic disorder may cause symptoms similar to those of generalized anxiety disorder.

The bodily reactions, feelings, and thoughts associated with generalized anxiety disorder often have no direct connection with a discernible issue in the person's life. If the individual does verbalize specific fears or concerns, these are usually unrealistic and extend to several domains. For example, Ben may worry that his college-age son, who is in good health, will develop a life-threatening disease, and he may worry about going bankrupt, even though his business is thriving. Both sets of worries are without grounds, yet Ben finds himself consumed with anxiety and distracted from his daily responsibilities.

The worries that people with generalized anxiety disorder experience can linger for years. In fact, these individuals often state that at no time in their lives have they *not* felt tense and anxious. Other people tend to see them as "worrywarts."

Generalized anxiety disorder is more common in women. In the general population, the sex ratio is approximately two-thirds female; in clinical settings, 55 to 60 percent of clients diagnosed with this condition are women (American Psychiatric Association, 2000). There are other interesting factors that are associated with higher rates of this disorder, such as having a history of previous marriage, being a homemaker without outside employment, and living in the Northeast section of the United States. As with all studies of the relationship between variables, it is important to keep in mind that these are correlations but do not explain the causes of the disorder. Most people with generalized anxiety disorder also have at least one other disorder, particularly a depressive disorder (Pini et al., 1997).

Generalized anxiety disorder is the most prevalent anxiety disorder in older adults, with a lifetime prevalence of 6 percent (Snyder et al., 2000). Often, this disorder co-occurs with depression, making it more difficult to diagnose in this population

(Hopko et al., 2000). Most cases begin in early life, but stressful events in later adulthood can lead to the appearance of symptoms. For effective diagnosis and treatment, clinicians must take symptoms seriously and not dismiss older adults' reports of worry as natural phemomena associated with the aging process (Scogin et al., 2000).

When the disorder appears in children, the anxieties and fears they express often relate to their performance in school or athletic activities. They worry incessantly that they will not do well in schoolwork or sports, even in situations in which their performance is not evaluated. Some children may worry more about potentially tragic matters, such as the possibility that there will be a nuclear war or an unlikely natural disaster that will affect them or their parents.

Theories and Treatment of Generalized Anxiety Disorder

Despite the fact that so many people suffer from this disorder, generalized anxiety disorder has not been extensively researched, and there are relatively few explanations for how it develops. From a biological perspective, it is suggested that people with this disorder have a biological abnormality similar to that proposed to account for other anxiety disorders involving abnormalities of GABA, serotonergic, and noradrenergic systems (Nutt, 2001). Support for the notion that there is a biological component to generalized anxiety disorder is the finding of an overlap in genetic vulnerability with the personality trait of neuroticism. In other words, people who are prone to developing this disorder have inherited an underlying neurotic personality style (Hettema, Prescott, & Kendler, 2004).

From a cognitive-behavioral perspective, generalized anxiety is seen as resulting from cognitive distortions that arise in the process of worrying (Aikins & Craske, 2001). People with generalized anxiety disorder also appear to become easily distressed and worried by the minor nuisances and small disruptions of life. If something goes wrong in their day-to-day existence, such as car trouble, an argument with a co-worker, or a home repair problem, they magnify the extent of the problem and become unduly apprehensive about the outcome. Their attention shifts from the problem itself to their own worries; as a result, their concern becomes magnified. As a result of their constant worrying, they are less efficient in their daily tasks and, consequently, develop more to worry about as more goes wrong for them. For whatever reason, once the anxiety is initiated, it begins to spiral out of control. Particularly damaging is the individual's lack of confidence in his or her ability to control or manage anxious feelings and reactions, as well as a lack of confidence in the ability to manage daily tasks effectively.

Finally, it is important to recognize the role of sociocultural factors in generalized anxiety disorder. Life stresses can significantly increase the basis for a person's tendency to experience chronic anxiety.

When people with generalized anxiety disorder turn for professional help, many are likely to seek out medical care. Astute physicians recognize the importance of differentiating this condition from a medical problem and usually suggest psychotropic medications or refer the patient to a mental health professional. Although benzodiazepines and newer antianxiety drugs such as buspirone (Buspar) have been used to treat the symptoms of anxiety associated with this disorder, they are being replaced by SSRIs, including paroxetine (Paxil) (Pollack et al., 2001), sertraline (Zoloft) (Allgulander et al., 2004), and the mixed reuptake inhibitor venlafaxine (Effexor) (Fricchione, 2004). Antidepressants may be used to help individuals taper off from antianxiety drugs after long-term use (Rickels et al., 2000) or to treat the symptoms of depression often associated with the disorder (Davidson, 2001).

An alternative to medication is cognitive-behavioral therapy (Borkovec & Ruscio, 2001), in which clients learn how to recognize anxious thoughts, to seek more rational alternatives to worrying, and to take action to test out these alternatives. The emphasis is on breaking the cycle of negative thoughts and worries. Once this cycle is broken, the individual can develop a sense of control over the worrying behavior and become more proficient at managing and reducing anxious thoughts. Over the long run, the benefits of therapy may outweigh those of psychopharmacological interventions (Falsetti & Davis, 2001). It is a well-established principle that active treatments are better than nondirective approaches. In particular, cognitive-behavioral therapy that combines relaxation exercises and cognitive therapy seems to help clients bring their worry under control.

Obsessive-Compulsive Disorder

If you have ever had a thought that you could not seem to force out of your consciousness, you have some insight into the experience of an **obsession**—a persistent and intrusive idea, thought, impulse, or image. People with obsessions recognize the fact that these cognitions arise within their own disturbed thought processes. They desperately try to ignore or suppress these intrusive thoughts, and in some cases they try to neutralize them by taking an action or thinking about something else. To get a sense of obsessive thought, think of a time when you had an argument with someone important in your life, which you relived in your thoughts for hours, even days, afterward. Even as you tried to attend to other matters, you found your mind returning time and again to the argument. Perhaps you tried desperately to erase these thoughts by engaging in an activity that might distract you. Multiply this experience dozens of times in intensity, such that most of every day is filled with similar experiences, and you will have a sense of the experience of clinical obsession.

Many people with obsessions also struggle with compulsions. A **compulsion** is a repetitive and seemingly purposeful behavior performed in response to uncontrollable urges or according to a ritualistic or stereotyped set of rules. Unlike obsessions, which cause anxiety, compulsions are carried out in an effort to reduce anxiety or distress. The disorder known as **obsessive-compulsive disorder (OCD)** involves both components of recurrent obsessions and compulsions that interfere significantly with an individual's daily life.

Mini Case

GENERALIZED ANXIETY DISORDER

Gina is a 32-year-old single mother of two children seeking professional help for her long-standing feelings of anxiety. Despite the fact that her life is relatively stable in terms of financial and interpersonal matters, she worries most of the time that she will develop financial problems, that her children will become ill, and that the political situation in the country will make life for her and her children more difficult. Although she tries to dismiss these concerns as excessive, she finds it virtually impossible to control her worrying. Most of the time, she feels uncomfortable and tense, and sometimes her tension becomes so extreme that she begins to tremble and sweat. She finds it difficult to sleep at night. During the day she is restless, keyed up, and tense. She has consulted a variety of medical specialists, each of whom has been unable to diagnose a physical problem.

Diagnostic Features

- This diagnosis is assigned to people who experience excessive anxiety and worry occurring more days than not for at least 6 months, pertaining to a number of events or activities, such as work or school.

- Their anxiety, worry, or related physical symptoms cause significant distress or impairment.

- They find it difficult to control their worry.

- Their anxiety and worry are associated with at least three of the following:
  - Restlessness
  - Being easily fatigued
  - Concentration difficulty
  - Irritability
  - Muscle tension
  - Sleep disturbance

Characteristics of Obsessive-Compulsive Disorder

The obsessions and compulsions that characterize OCD greatly interfere with life and trap the individual in a cycle of distressing, anxiety-provoking thought and behavior. The symptoms of OCD are time-consuming, irrational, and distracting, and the individual may desperately wish to stop them. You can imagine how distressing it is for people whose thoughts are filled with concerns about contamination (e.g., germs), doubts (e.g., leaving the gas on), or aggression (e.g., fear of harming another person).

The most common compulsions involve the repetition of a specific behavior, such as washing and cleaning, counting, putting items in order, checking, or requesting assurance. Another compulsion that has caught the attention of experts in this area involves hoarding (Steketee & Frost, 2003), in which an individual stores useless items such as outdated newspapers, mail, shopping bags, and empty food containers. When other people urge them to discard any of the items, they respond with concern that the item may be needed later for some reason. Of particular concern to public health officials are those individuals who compulsively hoard live animals in their homes, such as cats, dogs, farm animals, wild animals, or birds. Dozens, or even as many as 100 animals, are sometimes kept in the most unhygienic of conditions by these individuals.

In the movie *As Good as It Gets*, Jack Nicholson plays a man with obsessive-compulsive disorder. Even expressing affection to a pet is complicated by his need to wear protective gloves.

TABLE 5.2 Examples of Obsessions and Compulsions

Obsessions	Compulsions
A student has the urge to shout obscenities in a quiet classroom while listening to a lecture.	She feels driven to screw and unscrew the cap of a ballpoint pen exactly five times each time she thinks of an obscene word.
A woman cannot get the thought out of her mind that she might accidentally leave her gas stove turned on, causing her house to explode.	Each day before leaving for work, she feels the irresistible urge to check the stove exactly 10 times.
A 9-year-old boy worries incessantly that something terrible might happen to his mother while his family is sleeping.	On his way to bed each night, he insists that he must climb the stairs according to a fixed sequence of three steps up, followed by two steps down, in order to ward off danger.
A young woman is constantly terrified by the image that cars might careen onto the sidewalk and run her down.	She feels that she must walk as far from the street pavement as possible, and she always wears red clothes when in town, so that she will be immediately visible.
A man is tormented by the concern that he might inadvertently contaminate food as he cooks dinner for his family each night.	On a daily basis, he sterilizes all cooking utensils in boiling water, scours every pot and pan before placing food in it, and wears rubber gloves while handling food.

As you have probably figured out, a compulsion often goes hand-in-hand with an associated obsession. The man obsessed with a concern that he has left a pot on the stove is compelled to return repeatedly to the kitchen to make sure the stove is turned off. Compulsions may also take the form of mental rituals, such as counting up to the number 15 every time an unwanted thought intrudes. Or perhaps a person conjures up a particular image in response to obsessive fears (Steketee, 1994).

In general, there appear to be four major dimensions to the symptoms of OCD: obsessions associated with checking compulsions, the need to have symmetry and to put things in order, obsessions about cleanliness associated with compulsions to wash, and hoarding-related behaviors (Mataix-Cols, do Rosario-Campos, & Leckman, 2005). Table 5.2 lists examples of common obsessions and compulsions experienced by people with this disorder.

In Chapter 10, you will read about a condition with a similarly sounding name, obsessive-compulsive personality disorder. The person with obsessive-compulsive personality disorder is a rigid and inflexible worrier who does not engage in the extremely disturbed kinds of thinking and behaving that characterize people with obsessive-compulsive disorder. For example, a man with an obsessive-compulsive personality disorder may have a very rigid classification system for all of his books and become very upset if anyone puts a book back in the wrong place. By contrast, the person with obsessive-compulsive disorder may have a compulsion to check the order of the books on the shelf many times a day to ensure that they have not somehow been moved. If anything interferes with his checking of the books, he feels a great deal of distress. As you can see, there is some relationship between these two disorders, but there are also some important differences. Only about one third of all people with OCD also have obsessive-compulsive personality disorder (Diaferia et al., 1997).

Epidemiologists have documented that obsessive-compulsive disorder has a lifetime prevalence rate of 2 percent, a figure derived from various places around the world (Sasson et al., 1997). Some researchers argue for caution in accepting this figure, however, because when conservative screening instruments are used, the prevalence estimate drops to less than 1 percent (Stein, Forde, Anderson, & Walker, 1997). Compounding the problem of estimating prevalence is the fact that, in the Epidemiological Catchment Area study, most of the people who met the diagnostic criteria for OCD when first tested no longer fit the diagnosis when they were retested 1 year later (Nelson & Rice, 1997). Males are likely to develop OCD between the ages of 6 and 15; females tend to develop the condition between 20 and 29 years of age (American Psychiatric Association, 2000).

OCD usually first appears in childhood and adolescence. However, it is interesting to note that not all children who develop compulsive rituals retain them; many lose them by adolescence (Zohar & Bruno, 1997). Many of the children who do develop OCD show a unique pattern of characteristics—they are more likely to be male, to have a family history of OCD, to lack insight into their symptoms, and to suffer from other conditions, such as attention-deficit/hyperactivity disorder (Geller et al., 1998).

Theories and Treatment of Obsessive-Compulsive Disorder

OCD is increasingly being understood as a genetic disorder (Jonnal, Gardner, Prescott, & Kendler, 2000; Pato, Schindler, & Pato, 2001), reflecting abnormalities in the basal ganglia, subcortical areas of brain involved in the control of motor movements. Specifically, systems involving glutamate, dopamine,

In MindMAP Segment 5.3, Leslie discusses a number of behaviors in which she engages on a regular basis. Performing simple actions, such as filing an important paper, can induce a spiral of compulsive behaviors. These behaviors, which can be highly ritualized, can occupy an entire day.

The compulsive behaviors found in people with OCD are usually inordinately time-consuming and distressing.

serotonin, and acetylcholine may be involved, affecting the functioning of the prefrontal cortex (Carlsson, 2001). Thus, the brain circuitry connecting the subcortical and cortical regions of the brain specific to inhibition of behavior seems to function abnormally in this disorder (Saxena & Rauch, 2000).

People with OCD are seen as having thoughts and actions that they literally cannot inhibit, as though the brain structures involved in this process are, in essence, "working overtime" to try to control them (Rosenberg, Dick, O'Hearn, & Sweeney, 1997). Consistent with their PET scans, people with OCD have heightened levels of activity in the brain motor control centers of the basal ganglia and frontal lobes (Leocani et al., 2001; Mataix-Cols et al., 2004).

Other disorders involving abnormal serotonin levels are also thought to be related to obsessive-compulsive disorder along a continuum or spectrum (Stein, 2000). This spectrum includes a wide range of disorders involving dissociation, somatization, hypochondriasis, eating disorders, pathological gambling, borderline personality disorder, and disorders that involve uncontrollable impulses, such as hair pulling, face picking, compulsive shopping, and gambling (Bellodi et al., 2001; Christensen, Mackenzie, & Mitchell, 1991). There may also be a relationship between OCD and Tourette's syndrome (discussed in detail in Chapter 11), in which an individual exhibits a pattern of abnormal motor symptoms, such as uncontrollable twitches, vocalizations, and facial grimaces. When these disorders overlap, the symptom picture tends to be much more severe than is found

when just one of the conditions is diagnosed (Coffey et al., 1998). However, anxiety is a feature that is unique to obsessive-compulsive disorder, even among people who have Tourette-like symptoms (Cath et al., 2001).

As important as biological notions are to the understanding and treatment of OCD, they do not tell the entire story, and the behavioral perspective adds an important dimension. Behaviorally oriented theorists have long focused on the possibility that the symptoms of OCD become established through a process of conditioning, in which their behaviors become associated with the momentary relief of anxiety (Foa, Steketee, & Ozarow, 1985).

The cognitive-behavioral perspective focuses on maladaptive thought patterns as contributing to the development and maintenance of OCD symptoms (Steketee, 1994). Individuals with OCD may be primed to be overreactive to anxiety-producing events in their environment (Kumari et al., 2001). It is assumed that these clients are disturbed by thoughts related to the need to be perfect, the belief that they are responsible for harm to others, and concerns over the possibility of danger (Jones & Menzies, 1997; Salkovsis et al., 2000; Shafran, 1997). They struggle with disturbing images related to these thoughts and try to suppress or counteract them through engaging in compulsive rituals. The more they try to suppress these thoughts, the greater their discomfort and inability to stop them (Salkovskis et al., 1997).

Treatment The most promising interventions for people with obsessive-compulsive disorder are rooted in biological and psychological approaches, which are commonly combined in an integrative treatment (Jenike, 2004). Advances in psychopharmacology during the past three decades have been especially important. In the mid-1970s, it was discovered that an antidepressant medication, clomipramine (Anafranil), had the unanticipated effect of reducing obsessions in depressed people. This led investigators to wonder whether clomipramine would be an effective treatment for nondepressed people suffering from obsessive-compulsive disorder. Extensive experimental tests of this medication yielded very encouraging results, and researchers began to hypothesize that at least for some people, obsessive-compulsive disorder might have biological rather than psychological origins. Researchers noted that serotonin activity was reduced in people who responded favorably to clomipramine. From this they inferred that serotonin probably played a central role in causing the symptoms of this debilitating disorder (Rapaport, 1990). Individuals with these disorders are responsive to a category of medications that make larger amounts of serotonin available within the brain.

So far, treatment with clomipramine or other serotonin reuptake inhibiting medications, such as fluoxetine (Prozac) or sertraline (Zoloft), has proven to be the most effective biological treatment available for obsessive-compulsive disorder (Foa et al., 2005). The excitement generated by success stories with these medications has led to the development of newer medications, which have shown promising results for people who do not respond to clomipramine or fluoxetine. In particular, fluvoxamine (Luvox), which has milder side effects than other medications,

TABLE 5.3 Sample Items from the Yale-Brown Obsessive-Compulsive Symptom Checklist

Scale	Sample Items
Aggressive obsessions	Fear might harm self Fear of blurting out obscenities Fear will be responsible for something else terrible happening (e.g., fire, burglary)
Contamination obsessions	Concerns or disgust with bodily waste or secretions (e.g., urine, feces, saliva) Bothered by sticky substances or residues
Sexual obsessions	Forbidden or perverse sexual thoughts, images, or impulses Sexual behavior toward others (aggressive)
Hoarding/saving obsessions	Distinguish from hobbies and concern with objects of monetary or sentimental value
Religious obsessions	Concerned with sacrilege and blasphemy Excess concern with right/wrong, morality
Obsession with need for symmetry or exactness	Accompanied by magical thinking (e.g., concerned that another will have an accident unless things are in the right place)
Miscellaneous obsessions	Fear of saying certain things Lucky/unlucky numbers Colors with special significance Superstitious fears
Somatic obsessions	Concern with illness or disease Excessive concern with body part or aspect of appearance (e.g., dysmorphophobia)
Cleaning/washing compulsions	Excessive or ritualized hand-washing Excessive or ritualized showering, bathing, toothbrushing, grooming, or toilet routine
Checking compulsions	Checking locks, stove, appliances, etc. Checking that nothing terrible did not/will not harm self Checking that did not make mistake completing a task
Repeating rituals	Rereading or rewriting Need to repeat routine activities (e.g., in/out door, up/down from chair)
Counting compulsions	(Check for presence)
Ordering/arranging compulsions	(Check for presence)
Hoarding/collecting compulsions	Distinguish from hobbies and concern with objects of monetary or sentimental value (e.g. carefully reads junk mail, sorts through garbage)
Miscellaneous compulsions	Excessive list making Need to tell, ask, or confess Need to touch, tap, or rub Rituals involving blinking or staring

Source: From W. K. Goodman, L. H. Price, S. A. Rasmussen, C. Mazure, P. Delgado, G. R. Heninger, and D. S. Charney (1989a), "The Yale-Brown Obsessive-Compulsive Scale II. Validity" in *Archives of General Psychiatry,* 46, pp. 1012–1016. Reprinted with permission of Wayne Goodman.

works in similar fashion to allow more serotonin to be available at receptor sites in the brain (Laird, 1995). People who do not respond to these medications may benefit from risperidone (Risperdal) (McDougle et al., 2000).

Many clinicians recommend psychological interventions instead of, or in addition to, medication (Foster & Eisler, 2001). For example, thought stopping is recommended to help some clients reduce obsessional thinking, as is exposure to situations that provoke compulsive rituals or obsessions. Response prevention may also be used, in which the clinician instructs the client to stop performing compulsive behaviors, either totally or in graded steps (Salkovskis & Westbrook, 1989). Several experts advocate treatment that contains both exposure to the feared obsessions and prevention of the rituals that accompany the obsessions (Franklin et al., 2000). Steketee (1998) explains that exposure helps reduce the obsessive anxiety, while the prevention

Mini Case

OBSESSIVE-COMPULSIVE DISORDER

Mark is a 16-year-old high-school student referred for treatment by his teacher, who became disturbed by Mark's irrational concern about the danger posed by an electrical outlet at the front of the classroom. Mark pleaded daily with the teacher to have the outlet disconnected to prevent someone from accidentally getting electrocuted while walking by it. The teacher told Mark that his concerns were unfounded, but he remained so distressed that he felt driven, when entering and leaving the classroom, to shine a flashlight into the outlet to make sure that a loose wire was not exposed. During classtime, he could think of nothing else but the outlet.

Diagnostic Features

- People with this disorder suffer from either obsessions or compulsions, which the person recognizes at some point as excessive or unreasonable. These obsessions or compulsions cause marked distress, consume more than an hour a day, or significantly interfere with normal routine, functioning, or social activities or relationships.

- Obsessions are defined by the following four features:
  - Recurrent and persistent thoughts, impulses, or images that sufferers recognize as intrusive and inappropriate and that cause marked anxiety or distress
  - Not simply excessive worries about real-life problems
  - Attempts to ignore or suppress these thoughts, impulses, or images or to replace them with another thought or action
  - Recognition that these are products of his or her own mind (rather than the delusional belief that they are thoughts being inserted into the mind)

- Compulsions are defined by the following two features:
  - Repetitive behaviors (e.g., hand-washing, checking, putting items in order) or mental acts (e.g., counting, silent repetition of words) that the person feels driven to perform in response to an obsession or according to rigid rules
  - The behaviors or mental acts are intended to prevent or reduce distress or to prevent a dreaded event or situation, but they are clearly excessive or not connected in a realistic way with what they are intended to neutralize or prevent

of responses controls a person's rituals. For example, Steketee describes her treatment of a woman who compulsively checked faucets and the buttons on her child's clothing, as she was obsessed with the notion that certain numbers and activities were connected with the devil. Steketee helped the client identify her obsessive ideas and accompanying rituals; that information was used to construct a hierarchy of increasingly obsessive situations and associated rituals. Specific situations—such as fastening children's clothing snaps or having angry thoughts about the children or even reading about devils and demons—were selected for exposure. Each step of the way, the client agreed not to use any ritual, such as checking or repeating, that would have previously relieved her anxiety. In an effort to confront her tremendous difficulty with words associated with the devil, she engaged in some interesting forms of exposure; namely, she began to serve devil's food cake and deviled eggs, as well as to write the words *devil* and *satan* in her appointment book. Although there was not a rapid or miraculous cure, over time this woman reported that she felt 80 to 90 percent improved, compared with when she had first come for treatment.

Unfortunately, for some people, neither pharmacological nor psychotherapeutic interventions offer any relief. In extreme cases involving people with debilitating symptoms, the radical intervention of psychosurgery may be used. Cingulotomy involves the precise lesioning of the cingulate bundle, an area of the brain that researchers have implicated in the development of anxiety and compulsive behavior. Small holes, less than 2 centimeters in diameter, are drilled into the skull, and electrodes are carefully positioned in each cingulate bundle. Correct positioning is sometimes verified with magnetic resonance imaging. Electric current is then passed through the electrodes to create

lesions between 1 and 2 centimeters in diameter, which ideally results in a reduction in obsessions and compulsions. Some individuals for whom daily life is torturous consider this a viable option. Although reports of efficacy offer some hope, ethical factors and technical limitations have made it impossible to conduct control studies to establish with certainty the effectiveness of these neurosurgical interventions (Rauch & Jenike, 1998).

Acute Stress Disorder and Post-Traumatic Stress Disorder

A **traumatic experience** is a disastrous or an extremely painful event that has severe psychological and physiological effects. Traumatizing events include such personal tragedies as being involved in a serious accident, being the victim of violence, or experiencing a life-threatening calamity. At the other end of the spectrum are life-threatening events that affect large numbers of people, such as fires, earthquakes, riots, and war.

Each traumatic event takes its toll in human suffering, as the survivors cope with the loss of close ones who were victims of the disaster, with the loss of property when homes are destroyed, or with the sense of personal violation after being assaulted or raped. Survivors must cope with the painful memories of the traumatic event, which often involve vivid images of seeing other people killed or seeing their own lives nearly ended.

Some people develop an **acute stress disorder** soon after a traumatic event. In this condition, the individual develops intense fear, helplessness, or horror. Dissociative symptoms may appear, such as feeling numb, unreal, or detached, and amnesia about the event may develop. These individuals continue to reexperience the event in images, thoughts, dreams, and flashback episodes. They go to extremes to avoid anything that reminds them of the horrific event, whether it is a place, a person, an activity, or even a thought, feeling, or conversation, because these may evoke intense distress or a sense of reliving the trauma. Intensely anxious much of the time, they are likely to find it difficult to sleep or concentrate. They often become irritable and hypervigilant, perhaps easily startled by a minor noise or disruption.

Despite the extreme nature of the symptoms of acute stress disorder, most people are able to return to relatively normal functioning within days or weeks. Others, however, do not. They go on to develop **post-traumatic stress disorder (PTSD),** a diagnosis that is appropriate when the symptoms persist for more than a month.

Characteristics of Post-Traumatic Stress Disorder

In the aftermath of an acute stress disorder, the symptoms of PTSD may start to take hold and take on a chronic and unremitting course. Reminders of the trauma, either in the person's own thoughts or in the environment, evoke intense levels of psychological or physiological distress. Even the anniversary of the

Mini Case

ACUTE STRESS DISORDER

Brendan is a 19-year-old college freshman who was well-liked, psychologically healthy, and quite successful in life until 2 weeks ago when he experienced a traumatic event that seemed to change every aspect of his functioning. The life-changing event involved a devastating dormitory fire from which Brendan barely escaped. In fact, his roommate perished from smoke inhalation. Since the fire Brendan has been tormented by graphic images of waking to see his room filled with smoke, as flames encompassed the overstuffed chair in which his roommate had fallen asleep while smoking a cigarette. Tears come to his eyes as he recalls the experience of grabbing his roommate's leg and dragging the unconscious body out of the room only to realize that he was pulling a corpse. Feeling helpless and terrified, he screamed cries of horror, while suddenly becoming drenched by a sprinkler system that became activated several minutes too late. Brendan spent the days following the tragedy in the university health center where he was treated for smoke inhalation and several psychological symptoms. He described himself as feeling in a daze, as if in a dream state that was more like a nightmare. Despite the efforts of family and friends to connect emotionally with him, Brendan was emotionally unresponsive and seemingly numb. In fact, he found it difficult to talk with people because his thoughts were filled with intrusive images of the fire. After being discharged from the health service, he was unable to go anywhere near the dorm building for fear that he would "really lose it," and ultimately decided to withdraw from school because he felt too anxious and distressed.

event may stir up intense psychological and physical disturbance. These symptoms are so painful that people who suffer from PTSD intentionally go to great lengths to avoid anything that may remind them of the trauma. For example, a woman avoids driving by the site where her house burned to the ground several years ago, because she knows that even a fleeting reminder of the trauma will result in great psychological distress, nightmares, and physical symptoms of anxiety and dread.

Post-traumatic stress disorder is a relatively common diagnosis, with a lifetime prevalence rate of approximately 8 percent of the U.S. population. Of course, the rate is dramatically higher among at-risk individuals—for example, groups of people who have been exposed to specific traumatic incidents such as floods, tornadoes, hurricanes, combat, or ethnic violence (American Psychiatric Association, 2000).

Many people with this disorder seem to "shut down" in a sort of numbness, which causes them to be generally unresponsive in most situations. For example, a woman finds that she is unable to feel or express the love for her husband that was so evident prior to the trauma. A traumatized man loses interest in the activities that had been pleasurable for so much of his life. For an extended period of time, these individuals feel an increased level of arousal that is evident in sleep difficulty,

Diagnostic Features

- This disorder, which occurs within a month of a traumatic event, causes clinically significant distress or impairment that lasts between 2 days and 4 weeks. The diagnosis is assigned to people who experience significant distress or impairment associated with exposure to a traumatic event in which
  - They experienced, witnessed, or confronted event(s) involving actual or threatened death or serious injury, or a physical threat to themselves or others.
  - They responded with intense fear, helplessness, or horror.
- Either during or after the event, the individual has three or more of the following dissociative symptoms:
  - Sense of detachment, numbing, or lack of emotional responsiveness
  - Reduced feeling of awareness of surroundings, as if in a daze
  - Feelings of unreality (derealization)
  - Sensation of being detached from oneself (depersonalization)
  - Inability to recall an important aspect of the trauma (dissociative amnesia)
- The traumatic event is reexperienced through recurrent images, thoughts, dreams, illusions, flashback episodes, or a sense of reliving the experience, or the person feels intense distress when exposed to reminders of the event.
- The individual avoids stimuli that evoke recollections of the trauma.
- The individual experiences symptoms of anxiety or increased arousal, such as difficulty sleeping, irritability, poor concentration, hypervigilance, exaggerated startle response, and restlessness.

Following the September 11, 2001, disaster at the World Trade Center, many people developed symptoms of post-traumatic stress disorder.

anger outbursts, concentration problems, an exaggerated startle response, or general hypervigilance.

The symptoms of PTSD seem to fall into two related clusters. The first, called "intrusions and avoidance," includes intrusive thoughts, recurrent dreams, flashbacks, hyperactivity to cues of the trauma, and the avoidance of thoughts or reminders. The second cluster, "hyperarousal and numbing," includes symptoms that involve detachment, a loss of interest in everyday activities, sleep disturbance, irritability, and a sense of a foreshortened future. Thus, intrusive thoughts give rise to the avoidance of disturbing reminders, and hyperarousal leads to a numbing response (Taylor et al., 1998).

Sometimes it is not until days or months following the trauma that intruding thoughts first emerge. Some people find that the traumatic event repeatedly intrudes into consciousness in

the form of a flashback, a recurrence of a powerful feeling or perceptual experience from the past, sometimes involving graphic and terrifying illusions and hallucinations. Nightmares and unwanted thoughts about the event may plague the individual during this phase, along with physical symptoms, such as a racing heartbeat or heavy sweating. Consider a young man, Gary, who was in a car accident that killed his friend. Gary had recurrent images of the scene of the fatal crash. When riding in cars, he overreacted to every approaching car, repeatedly bracing himself for another imagined crash. He thought he could hear the voice of his deceased friend crying, "Watch out!" For weeks following the accident, he repeatedly "saw" his friend's face when he tried to sleep. He could not get out of his mind the thought that he should have done something to prevent his friend's death.

In the 1980s, when the diagnosis of PTSD was added to the *DSM*, the media drew attention to the psychological aftereffects of combat experienced by Vietnam War veterans. The Vietnam War was the most publicized, but certainly not the only, war to produce psychological casualties. Reports of psychological dysfunction following exposure to combat emerged after the Civil War (Hyams, Wignall, & Roswell, 1996). Following World War I and World War II, there were numerous reports of psychological impairment described with such terms as "shell shock," "traumatic neurosis," "combat stress," and "combat fatigue." Concentration camp survivors were also reported to suffer long-term psychological effects, including the "survivor syndrome" of chronic depression, anxiety, and difficulties in interpersonal relationships.

Television reports brought the Vietnam War, and the horrors of combat, into American living rooms each night, perhaps leading to greater concern on the part of the public and professionals about the lasting effects of war on those involved. Many studies about the post-traumatic effects of the war were initiated, several of which continue decades after the end of the conflict. The statistics emerging from these studies are not always consistent, however, with estimates of the incidence of PTSD among Vietnam veterans ranging from 19 to 30 percent of those exposed to low levels of combat, and 25 to 70 percent of those exposed to high levels. Although the customary image of the Vietnam veteran is a male, there were also many women involved in the conflict, many of whom have also suffered from PTSD (Zatzick et al., 1997).

Because of all that was learned from the Vietnam War era about PTSD, major efforts were made from the outset of the Afghanistan and Iraq wars on the part of the Department of Defense and the U.S. Veterans Administration to assess the impact of combat and to develop interventions that are aimed at reducing long-lasting psychological disturbance (Friedman, 2004).

Our understanding of PTSD became more sophisticated in the wake of the tragic events associated with terrorism and the natural disasters of the past decade. Very soon after events such as the 9/11 attacks, researchers were studying the extent and nature of PTSD symptoms in survivors and aid workers. Approximately one year later, 11 percent of New Yorkers were reported to have probable PTSD, compared with 2.7 percent of people living in the metropolitan Washington area (Schlenger et al.,

In MindMAP Segment 5.4, Carl talks about the problems he faced after returning home from his tours of duty in Vietnam.

Especially profound in the experience of PTSD are symptoms that wreak havoc in the life of the traumatized individual.

2002). Soon after the event, mental health workers began to intervene with survivors in an effort to reduce the debilitating effects of exposure to widespread trauma. The 2004 tsunami in Southeast Asia, one of the most devastating natural disasters in recorded history, resulted in the development of very serious psychological problems. Again, though, learning from previous disasters, relief workers were trained in methods of helping people cope with the psychological toll of devastation.

Theories and Treatment

Biological Perspectives Although by definition PTSD has its origins in life experiences, researchers have increasingly been turning up evidence linking its symptoms to biological abnormalities. Researchers have formulated the theory that, once a traumatic experience has occurred, parts of the individual's nervous system become primed or hypersensitive to possible danger in the future. Subcortical pathways in the central nervous system, as well as structures in the sympathetic nervous system, are permanently on "alert" for signs of impending harm; people who develop PTSD following exposure to trauma are more likely to have had a predisposition in the form of exaggerated "startle" responses (eyeblinks and skin conductance) (Guthrie & Bryant, 2005). Altered neurotransmitter functioning would play a role in this scenario. For some individuals with PTSD, alterations seem to occur in the norepinephrine pathways, while in others abnormalities in the serotonin pathways are more likely (Southwick et al., 1997). Dopamine, particularly in neurons in the prefrontal area that are sensitive to stress, may also be in-

volved in the symptoms of PTSD (Horger & Roth, 1996).

It seems that even the structure of the brain can change as a result of trauma; for example, researchers have noted that these changes in the hippocampus may result from hyperarousal of the amygdala, a limbic system structure that mediates emotional responses (Villarreal & King, 2001). Finally, genetic predisposition may also play a role in the development of PTSD. In one study of more than 4,000 twin pairs who fought in Vietnam, genetic factors seemed to play an important role in their susceptibility to the development of reexperiencing, avoidance, and arousal symptoms (True et al., 1993). Evidence has also emerged that people with first-degree relatives with a history of depression have an increased vulnerability to developing PTSD in response to traumatic life events (American Psychiatric Association, 2000).

Psychological Perspectives It is clear that psychological factors play a central role in the development of PTSD. Theorists have discussed and studied human responses to trauma for many decades. Freud described symptoms such as those in the disorder currently labeled PTSD as representing a flooding of the ego's defenses, with uncontrollable anxiety originating from the intense and threatening experiences. The experiences themselves may be traumatic enough to cause this reaction, or they may trigger painful memories of earlier unresolved unconscious conflicts and may cause anxiety to overflow as a result of an inability to keep these memories repressed. For example, the experience of killing another person in battle may stimulate the emergence of previously repressed aggressive impulses. Anxiety over the expression of these impulses could trigger the stress reaction.

According to classical behavioral approaches, it is assumed that the person with PTSD has acquired a conditioned fear to the stimuli that were present at the time of the trauma. Because of a learned association, the individual experiences anxiety when these or similar stimuli are present, even in the absence of the traumatizing experience. Presumably, such reactions lead to avoidance. To escape, at least in fantasy, from the traumatic event becomes reinforcing for the individual, and this reinforcement then strengthens the withdrawal reaction seen in PTSD victims.

Cognitive-behavioral theorists (Foa, Steketee, & Rothbaum, 1989) have incorporated the concept of how people's beliefs about a traumatic event influence how they cope with it. Thoughts that are likely to have a detrimental effect, and can ultimately lead to PTSD, include excessive self-blame for events that are beyond personal control, as well as guilt over the outcome of these events (Kubany, 1994; Ramsay, Gorst-Unsworth, & Turner, 1993). The individual's unsuccessful attempts to reduce the stress experienced in the aftermath of the event can also increase the risk for PTSD. Some of these problematic coping methods include avoidance of problems for long periods of time, blaming and lashing out at other people, adopting a cynical and pessimistic view of life, catastrophizing or exaggerating the extent of current difficulties, isolating oneself socially, and abusing drugs and alcohol (Hobfall et al., 1991).

Clearly, not everyone exposed to traumatic experiences, combat-related or otherwise, suffers from PTSD. What are the

Years after the Vietnam War ended and their physical wounds healed, many veterans are still tormented by the emotional scars of combat and grief.

factors that increase the likelihood that a particular individual will become one of the victims of trauma-related symptoms? One has to do with the nature of the traumatic experience itself. A general principle that emerges from a variety of studies on trauma victims is that there is a direct relationship between the severity of the trauma and the individual's risk of developing PTSD later (Davidson & Foa, 1991). Of particular significance is the experience of bodily injury. In one study, injured soldiers were more likely to develop PTSD than their noninjured comrades who participated in the same combat (Koren et al., 2005). In another study involving victims of terrorist bombings, PTSD was much more likely to arise in those with severe initial injuries (Lamberg, 2004; Verger et al., 2004). Rape is another experience that can lead to PTSD. In comparing women who were victims of physical assault or injury with women who were victims of rape, researchers found that the rape victims were much more likely to develop PTSD as well as other serious psychological problems. The sexual nature of rape added a dimension that increased their vulnerability (Faravelli, Giugni, Salvatori, & Ricca, 2004).

Individuals vary in their propensity to suffer from PTSD. One factor that mediates the relationship between the extent of trauma and PTSD symptoms is the individual's state of mind while the trauma is occurring. People who experience a period of dissociation during the traumatic episode are more likely to be the ones who will develop PTSD after the trauma has ended (Koopman, Classen, & Spiegel, 1994; Marmar et al., 1994; Shalev, Peri, Canetti, & Schreiber, 1996).

A sense of optimism can help mediate the response to trauma. In a study of rescuers working at the site of an airplane crash, researchers found that those with optimistic personality traits were more likely to seek social support, which in turn reduced their experience of stress. Optimism further contributed to reduced stress by leading to more effective use of problem-focused coping (Dougall et al., 2001).

Sociocultural Perspectives As mentioned, the devastating wars in the second half of the twentieth century—most notably, the conflict in Vietnam—brought many cases of PTSD to the attention of clinicians and researchers, and they provided important opportunities to understand some sociocultural contributions to the development of this disorder. Investigators were particularly attuned to the fact that, for many Vietnam soldiers, symptoms did not emerge until they returned home. In explaining this phenomenon, researchers point out that the Vietnam War was not politically popular. Instead of receiving a hero's welcome on their return home, many soldiers felt that their efforts were neither valued nor respected. This lack of social support, rather than the combat experience itself, may have contributed to the development of the disorder (Sparr & Pankratz, 1983).

Two decades later, approximately 8 percent of those returning from Operation Desert Storm developed PTSD symptoms (Stretch et al., 1996). As with the veterans of the Vietnam War, lack of support on their return from action seemed to play a role in the Gulf War veterans' development of PTSD symptoms (Viola, Hicks, & Porter, 1993). The stigma of seeking mental health services for combat-related psychological problems is yet another obstacle that stands in the way of recovering from stress-related conditions. In one study of combat operations in Iraq and Afghanistan, concern about stigma was greatest among those most in need of help from mental health services (Hoge et al., 2004).

Other sociocultural factors, such as education, income level, and social status, provide additional pieces to the puzzle of PTSD. In assessing the role of sociocultural factors in the determination of PTSD, investigators have been particularly interested in the ways that disadvantaged economic settings may set the stage for increased vulnerability. It has been established that people who live in certain sociocultural contexts are more likely to be victimized (Ensink, Robertson, Zissis, & Leger, 1997). Living in high-crime

Mini Case

POST-TRAUMATIC STRESS DISORDER

For the past 25 years, Steve has suffered from flashbacks, in which he relives the horrors of his 9 months of active duty in Vietnam. These flashbacks occur unexpectedly in the middle of the day, and Steve is thrown back into the emotional reality of his war experiences. These flashbacks, and the nightmares he often suffers from, have become a constant source of torment. Steve has found that alcohol provides the only escape from these visions and from the distress he feels. Often, Steve ruminates about how he should have done more to prevent the deaths of his fellow soldiers, and he feels that his friends, rather than he, should have survived.

Diagnostic Features

- This disorder, which causes clinically significant distress or impairment, is assigned to people who have been exposed to a traumatic event in which

  - They experienced, witnessed, or confronted an event involving actual or threatened death or serious injury, or a physical threat to themselves or others.

  - They responded with intense fear, helplessness, or horror.

- For at least 1 month, there is a persistent reexperiencing of the traumatic event in one or more of the following ways:

  - Recurrent and intrusive distressing recollections of the event

  - Recurrent distressing dreams of the event

  - Acting or feeling as if the event were recurring (e.g., a reliving of the experience, illusions, hallucinations, dissociative flashbacks)

  - Intense distress at exposure to internal or external cues that symbolize or resemble an aspect of the event

  - Physiological reactivity on exposure to internal or external cues that symbolize or resemble an aspect of the event

- For at least 1 month, there is avoidance of stimuli associated with the trauma and a numbing of general responsiveness, as indicated by at least three of the following:

  - Efforts to avoid thoughts, feelings, or conversations associated with the trauma

  - Efforts to avoid activities, places, or people that evoke recollections of the trauma

  - Inability to recall an important aspect of the trauma

  - Markedly diminished interest or participation in significant activities

  - Feelings of detachment or estrangement from others

  - Restricted range of affect (e.g., inability to experience loving feelings)

  - Sense of foreshortened future (e.g., pessimism about career, family, and life)

- For at least 1 month, there are persistent symptoms of increased arousal, as indicated by at least two of the following:

  - Difficulty falling or staying asleep

  - Irritability or outbursts of anger

  - Concentration difficulty

  - Hypervigilance

  - Exaggerated startle response

---

urban neighborhoods increases the likelihood of exposure to traumatizing events and makes it difficult for individuals to receive services, particularly for low-income women (Bassuk et al., 2001). Living in impoverished locales in developing countries, the inadequacy of support and mental health services in the event of a disaster can aggravate the psychological responses of large numbers of people (Lima, Pai, Santacruz, & Lozano, 1991).

Cultural factors are also evident in the ways that people from various ethnic groups respond to traumatic events, such as disasters or devastation (de Silva, 1993b). In some groups, tremendous stigma is associated with the idea of seeking professional psychological help, regardless of the severity of the distress. Lacking sufficient emotional support, in the family and in one's social group, can aggravate the experience of PTSD symptoms for some.

Treatment Within the biological perspective, clinical investigators have reported the successful treatment of PTSD symptoms with a variety of medications, with the choice relying primarily on the client's particular symptoms. For example, clients with symptoms involving hyperexcitability and startle reactions may benefit from antianxiety medications, such as benzodiazepines. Those contending with irritability, aggression, impulsiveness, or flashbacks may find anticonvulsants, such as carbamazepine or valproic

The psychological impact of the fighting in the war in Iraq will not truly be known for years.

acid, helpful. Antidepressants, such as selective serotonin reuptake inhibitors and monoamine-oxidase inhibitors, are often therapeutic

Hurricane Katrina, the most devastating natural disaster in American history, ravaged several southern states in 2005, traumatizing thousands of people who will contend with the emotional aftereffects of this trauma for years to come.

in treating the symptoms of numbing, intrusion, and social withdrawal (Londborg et al., 2001; Seedat et al., 2001).

Even though medications can provide some symptom relief, it would be naive to think that medication alone is sufficient for ameliorating the distressing psychological and interpersonal problems that burden those with PTSD. Consequently, clinicians recommend ongoing psychotherapy, not only to deal with emotional issues but also to monitor the individual's reactions to medical treatments (Davidson, Stein, Shalev, & Yehuda, 2004). The most effective psychological treatments for PTSD involve a combination of "covering" and "uncovering" techniques. "Covering" techniques, such as supportive therapy and stress management, help the client seal over the pain of the trauma. They may also help the client reduce stress more effectively and, in the process, eliminate some of the secondary problems that the symptoms cause. For example, PTSD victims who isolate themselves from friends and family are cutting themselves off from social support, which is an important therapeutic agent. By learning alternate coping methods, clients can become better able to seek out this kind of support.

"Uncovering" techniques, which involve a reliving of the trauma, include the behavioral treatments of imaginal flooding and systematic desensitization. Exposing the person with PTSD to cues that bring back memories of the event in a graded fashion, or in a situation in which the individual is taught simultaneously to relax, can eventually break the conditioned anxiety reaction. Other treatments, such as psychodrama, can also be useful in bringing to conscious awareness, under a controlled setting, repressed memories of the traumatic event.

In an analysis of the results of 26 studies on the treatment of PTSD, researchers compared the efficacy of the major forms of psychotherapy on more than 1,500 patients. They concluded that the majority of patients treated with psychotherapy for PTSD recover or improve, although many patients continue to have substantial residual symptoms that persist long after treatment (Bradley et al., 2005). Clearly, although treatment can be effec-

tive, continued follow-up is necessary to help these clients maintain their treatment gains over the long term.

PTSD victims can also learn to reduce stress by approaching their situations more rationally and by breaking down their problems into manageable units. They can work toward achieving a better balance between self-blame and avoidance. Individuals who feel excessively guilty for their role in the traumatic incident can learn to see that their responsibility was not as great as imagined. Conversely, those who feel they have no control over what happens to them and, therefore, avoid confronting problems can learn to feel a greater sense of mastery over the course of their lives (Hobfall et al., 1991).

Donald Meichenbaum (1998) describes a six-step cognitive-behavioral therapy plan that incorporates strategies he has found beneficial for clients suffering from PTSD:

1. Establish a good working relationship with clients, characterized by nurturance and compassion.

2. Encourage clients to view their symptoms in a more positive light; for example, numbing can be viewed as a way of slowing the pace in order to deal with intense levels of distress.

3. Help clients translate global problem descriptions into specific, problem-solving terms.

4. Take behavioral steps, such as confronting the feared situation, in thoughts and in real settings.

5. Confront barriers in the form of feelings (e.g., fears, guilt, depression) and distorted beliefs (e.g., negative self-views) that get in the way of implementing change and mustering hope.

6. Help clients anticipate possible lapses (e.g., a recurrence of flashbacks, bouts of anxiety or depression).

Anxiety Disorders: The Biopsychosocial Perspective

As you can see, anxiety disorders cover a broad spectrum of problems, ranging from very specific, seemingly idiosyncratic responses to diffuse and undifferentiated feelings of dread. These disorders involve an intriguing intertwining of biological, psychological, and sociocultural phenomena. Fortunately, relatively straightforward behaviorally based treatments are available that can successfully alleviate the symptoms of anxiety for many people who suffer from these disorders. Furthermore, a number of other strategies involving cognitive, insight-oriented, and psychopharmacological interventions can enhance the effectiveness of behavioral techniques. Knowledge gained from research on the causes and treatment of anxiety disorders can also have some practical benefits for managing lesser difficulties.

Barbara's History

As Barbara shared her life history with me, the flow of her speech frequently was interrupted by sobs and pleas that I be patient with her. As Barbara's story unfolded, I came to understand how the emotional scars left by growing up in a dysfunctional family plagued her throughout childhood and adolescence.

Barbara was raised almost exclusively by her mother. Her father spent very little time at home, because he worked as a sales representative for a company that had branch offices spread across a three-state area. When he was home, he was almost always inebriated. Barbara's mother was very protective of her, restricting almost all social and after-school activities. Barbara remembers feeling somewhat resentful of her mother's strong control over her, but she justified her mother's behavior, because "after all, she couldn't count on my father to help her, and, besides, I was a pretty difficult kid and she didn't want me getting into trouble."

Barbara's father was known to have out-of-town affairs with women, and everyone regarded him as a failure in his job. However, no one discussed these problems openly. Barbara remembers being frightened of her father because, when he was drinking, he became furious over even her slightest failure to respond instantly to his instructions. Usually, he gave unclear or contradictory instructions, so she could not predict when he would yell at her and when he would be satisfied with her response. When she tried to apologize, he criticized her even more. Barbara learned that the best way to deal with him was to stay out of his way.

Barbara explained to me that it was not only her father who struggled with psychological impairment. Her mother had, for most of her adult years, an intense fear of leaving the house alone, and she experienced deep depression related to her unhappy marriage. Going back a generation, Barbara's grandmother was considered by most people to be peculiar. She insisted on living the life of a recluse and acted toward her husband in ways that others considered domineering, bordering on sadistic. Barbara's maternal grandfather put up with the abuse, never complaining, always appearing to others as a quiet, accommodating "gentleman." It was quite a shock to the whole community when, at the age of 62, he asphyxiated himself and left a note filled with rage about his "miserable marriage."

In her senior year of high school, Barbara began to write away to a number of colleges for applications. It never occurred to her that her parents would object to her going to college, as long as she realized that she would have to support herself. Since Barbara's grades were excellent, she felt quite certain that she would earn some kind of financial aid. One day, her mother stopped Barbara as she was leaving the house to mail a stack of envelopes and asked Barbara what she was doing. When Barbara explained, her mother burst into tears. She told Barbara that it was time for them to have a talk. They sat down in the kitchen, and Barbara's mother poured forth an amazing "confession." Ever since Barbara was a child, it had been very important for her mother to have Barbara with her at home. That was why she found it so hard to let Barbara go out with her friends and do things after school. She said that Barbara's father had been so impossible that she was unhappy almost all the time. She couldn't even leave the house to run a simple errand unless she had Barbara with her. She begged Barbara not to go away to school, saying that she could not bear the thought of her leaving. Barbara was stunned. She did not realize how much she meant to her mother. There was no way she could even consider going away to school under these circumstances. Barbara threw away all her letters and applied to the community college located 10 miles away from home.

After college, Barbara took a job in an insurance company, where she became a top-notch typist and receptionist. When her boss was transferred to another city, he told Barbara that he wanted her to move also. She could enroll in the university and take courses there to complete her bachelor's degree, all at company expense. According to her boss, Barbara had a lot of potential to advance in a career if she had the proper training. Concerned about leaving her mother, Barbara asked her what she should do. Barbara's mother assured her that she would "manage somehow." Barbara made the move, and all seemed to be going well. She felt particularly lucky to have found a roommate with whom she shared many common interests, ideas, and feelings. They soon became inseparable. Unfortunately, however, things did not remain so serene for Barbara; the ghosts of unresolved conflicts and pain reappeared and took the form of her current emotional crisis.

Assessment

Although I had some reasonable hypotheses about the nature of Barbara's disorder, important gaps needed to be filled in. Of particular concern was the possibility that Barbara might be suffering from a medical problem. It is not uncommon for people with certain medical problems, such as hypoglycemia, hyperthyroidism, or insulin-secreting tumors, to have symptoms that are strikingly similar to those found in anxiety disorders. However, the physician who conducted the physical examination found no physiological basis for Barbara's problems. Drugs and alcohol were ruled out as well. Barbara had never abused drugs, and she only occasionally drank alcohol in desperate attempts to calm herself down.

Because of the prominent features of anxiety in Barbara's presentation, I recommended that she meet with one of my colleagues, Dr. Michelle Herter, for a comprehensive behavioral assessment. Dr. Herter's assessment protocol consisted of three segments: (1) a symptom-focused interview, (2) the administration of a questionnaire, and (3) Barbara's collection of self-monitoring data.

In her interview, Dr. Herter collected extensive information about the frequency, intensity, and duration of Barbara's bodily and cognitive reactions to her periods of panic. She also discussed with Barbara the quality of her relationships, particularly those with her immediate family members. In her report, Dr. Herter described Barbara as a "well-dressed and attractive young woman who looked self-conscious and nervous throughout the interview." She felt that nothing about Barbara suggested intellectual impairment or a personality disorder, but she did discuss Barbara's prominent style of dependency, passive acquiescence to other people's demands, and discomfort in situations involving interpersonal conflict.

Barbara completed the Body Sensations Questionnaire and Agoraphobia Cognitions Questionnaire (Chambless & Goldstein, 1982), which provided compelling data about the nature of her overpowering fear of having disturbing bodily sensations, such as rapid heartbeat and feelings of dizziness. Furthermore, Barbara's responses suggested that she genuinely feared that she was losing her mind.

For the self-monitoring portion of the assessment, Barbara kept a Panic Attack Record (Barlow et al., 1994), on which she documented the time, duration, and intensity of each panic attack. She indicated who was with her at the time, as well as the specific symptoms she experienced. The assessment picture that emerged from these sources of data was that of a woman who was overcome by intense and incapacitating episodes of panic that occurred primarily in situations involving conflict or minor stress, especially when she was alone.

Diagnosis

The most striking feature of Barbara's presenting problems was the occurrence of panic attacks. After experiencing several of these on a frequent basis, Barbara could not leave her apartment because of her fears of having an attack in public. After ruling out the possibility of a physically based disorder on the basis of the medical workup, I felt confident in the diagnosis of an anxiety disorder involving panic attacks and agoraphobia. I focused my attention on Barbara's symptoms during the episodes she described to me and to Dr. Herter, which included experiences of dizziness, speeded-up heart rate, uncontrollable trembling, sweating, choking sensations, chest discomfort, and fear of dying. I was secure in the belief that these episodes constituted panic attacks, because they involved sudden, unexpected periods of intense fear. Compounding the distress for Barbara was the fact that symptoms of agoraphobia accompanied these panic attacks.

Axis I:	Panic Disorder with Agoraphobia
Axis II:	Rule out Personality Disorder. Not otherwise specified
Axis III:	No physical disorders or conditions
Axis IV:	Problems with primary support group (family tensions) Occupational problems (job transitions)
Axis V:	Current Global Assessment of Functioning: 37 Highest Global Assessment of Functioning (past year): 83

Case Formulation

As I pondered what factors might have contributed to Barbara's developing such a troubling and incapacitating disorder, I considered her genetic history as well as her family system. In evaluating genetic contributions, my thoughts were drawn to the problems that both her mother and her grandmother experienced. Their problems seemed similar to Barbara's, leading me to hypothesize that Barbara had inherited a biological propensity to develop panic attacks.

In reviewing information about Barbara's family, I noted her stories of being so distraught about her father's frequent absences, and her resentment toward her overcontrolling mother, who could not protect her from the tyrannical ways of her unreliable and unpredictable father. The family did not air conflicts, and Barbara learned that the best way to get along with people was to do what they wanted or to stay out of their way. At a time when Barbara should have been allowed to begin her independent life, her mother made it virtually impossible for her to do so. When Barbara finally did leave her mother, she experienced considerable guilt when she realized how much her mother depended on her.

As her life went on, Barbara came to realize more and more that she could not please everyone. Perhaps her first panic attack grew out of this unresolvable conflict. Indeed, all of Barbara's early panic attacks were connected with some kind of emotional conflict in her life. The second attack occurred when Barbara was about to experience separation from the roommate to whom she had become so attached. Other panic attacks occurred when Barbara was going to her office, as thoughts of leaving her mother filled her mind. Although the panic attacks started in situations that had a link to an emotional conflict, they eventually generalized to all places outside Barbara's apartment. Barbara came

RETURN TO THE CASE
(continued)

to fear not the situations themselves but the attacks, which caused her to experience an excruciating degree of pain, embarrassment, and terror.

Treatment Plan

As I wrote up my treatment recommendations for Barbara, I realized that she would benefit most from an intervention that tapped behavioral and cognitive-behavioral techniques. Although I was familiar with these techniques, I felt that Barbara's needs would best be served by a clinician who specialized in interventions for people with anxiety disorders. Michelle Herter had offered her services, should such a recommendation seem appropriate, and I chose to accept her offer. I explained to Barbara that Dr. Herter was a leading expert in the kind of treatment she needed. Barbara made it clear that she was committed to obtaining the very best treatment available, even though she expressed disappointment that I would not be her therapist.

I called Dr. Herter and we reviewed the impressions of Barbara that each of us had derived. As we spoke about this case, Dr. Herter put forth a treatment approach not commonly used by most other clinicians. She thought it would be a good idea to begin the therapy in Barbara's home, a nonthreatening context in which she could begin establishing a trusting alliance with Barbara. In time, Dr. Herter would introduce *in vivo* techniques and graded exposure training, in which she would guide Barbara step-by-step through situations that more closely approximated those that had terrified her in the past. At the same time, Dr. Herter planned to work with her in restructuring her beliefs about her inability to control her panic attacks.

Dr. Herter told me that, as time went on, she might also incorporate assertiveness training.

Outcome of the Case

I concurred with Dr. Herter's initial optimism about the likelihood that Barbara would show fairly quick improvement once treatment was begun. Barbara responded very positively to Dr. Herter's willingness to provide home-based therapy. During the first 3 weeks, which included six sessions, Dr. Herter took a comprehensive history of the problem and developed a relationship with Barbara that facilitated the initiation of behavioral techniques during the second phase. In the beginning of the second phase, Dr. Herter taught Barbara techniques she could use to change the way she thought about panic-arousing situations. For example, Barbara was to imagine herself conquering her fear and feeling a sense of increased self-esteem following her success. She became able to envision herself as competent in situations that previously had seemed so threatening. In the third phase, Dr. Herter accompanied Barbara outside her apartment to a nearby convenience store. Step by step, in the weeks that followed, Dr. Herter introduced situations that were increasingly more threatening, culminating in Barbara's successful trip to a crowded shopping mall unaccompanied by her therapist.

Along with conquering her fears of leaving home, Barbara also began to gain some insight into the connection between interpersonal conflicts and her panic attacks. Several weeks into treatment, Barbara reported that her mother was telephoning her more and more frequently. Barbara's mother had developed terrible headaches that made her incapable

of doing anything for hours at a time. Although she did not ask directly, Barbara felt very strongly that her mother was hinting for Barbara to move back home. Barbara missed a session, something that was very unusual for her. Dr. Herter became concerned that Barbara was experiencing a relapse. A call to Barbara confirmed this. Barbara had experienced another panic attack during the week and was unable to leave her apartment. The cognitive techniques she had practiced so faithfully had failed to work. Barbara had wanted to call Dr. Herter but felt too ashamed. After discussing this situation, Barbara was able to understand how this particular panic attack had been provoked by interpersonal conflict; this insight proved useful in motivating Barbara to resume and follow through with her treatment program.

In time, Barbara's mother began making fewer demands on her, and Barbara was able to recover the gains she had made in individual therapy prior to the most recent panic attack. Barbara and Dr. Herter continued to meet for another 6 months, during which time Barbara's progress was cemented. Soon after Barbara terminated with Dr. Herter, she sent me a note to thank me for the referral. In the note, she boasted about her success in overcoming the problem that had been so threatening and devastating for her. She explained how she had developed new ways of solving her problems, whether they pertained to possible panic attacks or to the difficulties she was likely to encounter in her relationship with her mother.

Sarah Tobin, PhD

SUMMARY

- Anxiety disorders are characterized by the experience of physiological arousal, apprehension or feelings of dread, hypervigilance, avoidance, and sometimes a specific fear or phobia.

- Panic disorder is characterized by frequent and recurrent panic attacks—intense sensations of fear and physical discomfort. This disorder is often found in association with agoraphobia, the fear of being trapped or unable to escape if a panic attack occurs. Biological and cognitive-behavioral perspectives have been particularly useful for understanding and treating this disorder. Some experts explain panic disorder as an acquired "fear of fear," in which the individual becomes hypersensitive to early signs of a panic attack, and the fear of a full-blown attack leads the individual to become unduly apprehensive and avoidant of another attack. Treatment based on the cognitive-behavioral perspective involves such methods as relaxation training and *in vivo* or imaginal flooding as a way of breaking the negative cycle initiated by the individual's fear of having a panic attack. Medications can also help alleviate symptoms, with the most commonly prescribed being antianxiety and antidepressant medications.

- Specific phobias are irrational fears of particular objects or situations. Cognitive behaviorists assert that previous learning experiences and a cycle of negative, maladaptive thoughts cause specific phobias. Treatments recommended by the behavioral and cognitive-behavioral approaches include flooding, systematic desensitization, imagery, *in vivo* exposure, and participant modeling, as well as procedures aimed at changing the individual's maladaptive thoughts, such as cognitive restructuring, coping self-statements, thought stopping, and increases in self-efficacy. Treatment based on the biological perspective involves medication.

- A social phobia is a fear of being observed by others acting in a way that will be humiliating or embarrassing. Cognitive-behavioral approaches to social phobia regard the disorder as due to an unrealistic fear of criticism, which causes people with the disorder to lose the ability to concentrate on their performance, instead shifting their attention to how anxious they feel, which then causes them to make mistakes and, therefore, to become more fearful. Behavioral methods that provide *in vivo* exposure, along with cognitive restructuring and social skills training, seem to be the most effective in helping people with social phobia. Medication is the treatment recommended within the biological perspective for severe cases of this disorder.

- People who are diagnosed as having generalized anxiety disorder have a number of unrealistic worries that spread to various spheres of life. The cognitive-behavioral approach to generalized anxiety disorder emphasizes the unrealistic nature of these worries and regards the disorder as a vicious cycle that feeds on itself. Cognitive-behavioral treatment approaches recommend breaking the negative cycle of worry by teaching individuals techniques that allow them to feel they control the worrying. Biological treatment emphasizes the use of medication.

- In obsessive-compulsive disorder, individuals develop obsessions, or thoughts they cannot rid themselves of, and compulsions, which are irresistible, repetitive behaviors. A cognitive-behavioral understanding of obsessive-compulsive disorder regards the symptoms as the product of a learned association between anxiety and the thoughts or acts, which temporarily can produce relief from anxiety. A growing body of evidence supports a biological explanation of the disorder, with the most current research suggesting that it is associated with an excess of serotonin. Treatment with medications, such as clomipramine, seems to be effective, although cognitive-behavioral methods involving exposure and thought stopping are quite effective as well.

- In post-traumatic stress disorder, the individual is unable to recover from the anxiety associated with a traumatic life event, such as tragedy or disaster, an accident, or participation in combat. The aftereffects of the traumatic event include flashbacks, nightmares, and intrusive thoughts that alternate with the individual's attempts to deny that the event ever took place. Some people experience a briefer but very troubling response to a traumatic event; this condition, called acute stress disorder, lasts from 2 days to 4 weeks and involves the kinds of symptoms that people with PTSD experience over a much longer period of time. Cognitive-behavioral approaches regard the disorder as the result of negative and maladaptive thoughts about one's role in causing the traumatic events to happen, feelings of ineffectiveness and isolation from others, and a pessimistic outlook on life as a result of the experience. Treatment may involve teaching people with PTSD new coping skills, so that they can more effectively manage stress and reestablish social ties with others who can provide ongoing support. A combination of "covering" techniques, such as supportive therapy and stress management, and "uncovering" techniques such as imaginal flooding and desensitization, is usually helpful.

KEY TERMS

See Glossary for definitions

INTERNET RESOURCE

To get more information on the material covered in this chapter, visit our website at **www.mhhe.com/halgin5.** There you will find more information, resources, and links to topics of interest.

CHAPTER 6

Somatoform Disorders, Psychological Factors Affecting Medical Conditions, and Dissociative Disorders

Late on a Friday afternoon, I received a call from Dr. Thompson, one of the hospital's emergency room physicians, asking me to conduct an evaluation of Rose Marston, a 37-year-old woman who had become a frequent visitor to the emergency room with an array of physical problems. The story Dr. Thompson told me about Rose was similar to previous histories he had told me about other problematic patients. I found myself completing some of his sentences as he described the frustrations the emergency room staff felt in their dealings with Rose. Dr. Thompson was convinced that Rose's recurrent "physical problems" were attributable to psychological rather than physical factors.

During the preceding year, Rose had come to the emergency room on 15 occasions and each time complained about what seemed like serious medical problems. Doctors conducted extensive medical testing and consulted specialists, but no diagnosable medical conditions had ever been confirmed. Her medical chart included complaints about gastrointestinal problems, such as vomiting, nausea, and bloating; complaints of pain in her chest, back, joints, and hands; neurological symptoms, including double vision and dizziness; and problems of irregular menstruation. On occasion, she had fainted, and several times she could not move her legs.

Dr. Thompson shared with me his own distress about his most recent emergency room contact with Rose. Following one of Rose's customary listings of physical complaints, Dr. Thompson told Rose he had come to believe that her problems were emotionally based, rather than medical in origin. Moments later, Rose collapsed on the floor in what appeared to be an epileptic seizure. When she became conscious, Rose stated that she remembered nothing of what had just happened and, indeed, could not even recall how she had gotten to the emergency room. When Dr. Thompson reviewed the situation with Rose, she became enraged and yelled out with a voice that echoed through the corridors, "I know you wish I would go away. Maybe you'd be relieved if I'd just kill myself!" After calming down, Rose reluctantly agreed to take Dr. Thompson's recommendation to consult with me about her problems.

When Rose first contacted me to arrange the intake appointment, she insisted that our first meeting take place at my office in the hospital, rather than in the more customary outpatient setting in which I see my clients. When I asked Rose her reasons for this request, she stated rather emphatically that it "made sense" to be near medical personnel in the event of a physical crisis she might have. I was initially uncomfortable with the idea of agreeing to this request, feeling that I might reinforce her maladaptive behavior. After some thought, however, I agreed; perhaps it would help Rose establish an alliance with me if she viewed me as responsive to her concerns and worries.

Even with the concession I had made about the place of our first meeting, I could sense in our approaching encounter that Rose was approaching me with considerable skepticism. Her first words were "I guess they've tried to convince you that I'm some kind of hypochondriac crackpot." I assured Rose that I wanted to hear what she had to tell me about her problems. Although I would ask for her permission to speak to the medical staff, I wanted her to know that I was committed to helping her find a way to feel better, both psychologically and physically. I tried tactfully to point out that people often develop physical problems when they are upset about something and that real physical problems become aggravated during times of stress. I could tell that she was cautious about speaking with me, but nevertheless she seemed willing to give it a try.

Though I was eager to proceed with the interview, I found myself wondering about what might be inside the large picnic basket Rose kept on her lap. Rose seemed a bit irked when I inquired about the contents but went on to say, "I guess you should learn about my conditions right away, so you'll be able to understand how serious my medical problems are." She lifted the top of the basket to expose what seemed to be a mini pharmacy—a thermometer, a box of bandages and gauze pads, several tubes and jars of ointment, and a dozen medication bottles. With her face reddening, either from embarrassment or annoyance, Rose emphasized her need to be prepared for the aches and pains that commonly afflict her without warning. I wasn't quite sure how to respond to this display but chose to move right into our discussion of the history of her medical problems.

Rose explained that many of her physical problems dated back to childhood. In fact, she had come to believe that she suffered some bodily problems that "ran in the family." When I asked for clarification, Rose explained that her younger sister, Emily, had been born with serious medical problems and actually died from them during her teenage years. Although Rose was relatively healthy as a young child, she began to develop physical problems of her own, which caused her to wonder whether she was "catching some of Emily's medical problems." By the time she reached adolescence, Rose's problems had worsened; even a common cold or flu would cause her mother to comment that Rose seemed to get "much sicker than other people." In fact, Rose's mother frequently had to stay home from work to nurse Rose back to health. Over time, Rose's problems worsened, as she went from doctor to doctor, seeking answers to the disturbing mysteries of her bodily afflictions. Rose's frustration with the medical profession increased over the years because of the inability of physicians, even leading specialists, to determine what was wrong with her. Rose ultimately came to believe that she had unusual medical problems for which science and medicine did not yet have the answers.

Sarah Tobin, PhD

In this chapter, we will focus on three sets of disorders: somatoform disorders, conditions in which psychological factors affect medical conditions, and dissociative disorders. In each of these sets of disorders, the body expresses psychological conflict and stress in unusual, and sometimes bizarre, fashion. These conditions have an important role in the history of abnormal psychology because they alerted the medical community of the 1800s to the role that psychological processes can play in causing otherwise unexplained symptoms. Recall our discussion in Chapter 1 about hysteria and how medical experts with training in neurology were confused and astounded by case after case of patients with mysterious "physical" symptoms that seemed to have no physical basis. Freud's insight that these physical symptoms could have a psychological basis led to a revolution in the understanding and treatment of many unusual disorders. Although somatoform and dissociative disorders are relatively uncommon today, these disorders have not disappeared, and they remain one of the more fascinating areas of abnormal behavior. Situations in which psychological factors affect medical conditions, on the other hand, seem to be receiving increased attention in contemporary medical circles, as health professionals develop their understanding of the interactions between stress and a variety of medical problems.

Somatoform Disorders

Imagine the following scenario. A classmate of yours, a star hockey player, wakes up one morning complaining that he is unable to move his hand. He then says in an oddly indifferent manner that the situation is very unfortunate, because he has an important game that night. He casually dismisses the problem as "bad luck" and goes back to bed. You may be perplexed at his lack of alarm but would nevertheless presume that there was something physically wrong with his hand. But might there be more to the story? Perhaps you are wondering whether your classmate's problem is "all in his head." Maybe he is very concerned about his performance in the game and is "faking" his injury. Or, on a deeper level, perhaps his anxiety is so great that he does not consciously make the connection between his inability to move his hand and his concern about playing in the game.

Somatoform disorders include a variety of conditions in which psychological conflicts become translated into physical problems or complaints that cause distress or impairment in a person's life. The term *somatoform* comes from the Greek word *soma,* meaning "body." However, somatoform disorders are considered psychological rather than physical disorders, because there is no physical abnormality that can explain the bodily complaint. If your classmate's condition is due to a somatoform disorder, his dysfunctional hand will not produce abnormal responses on neurophysiological testing. In fact, the pain or stiffness he feels would probably not correspond to the symptoms of any known physical disorder.

Increasing recognition is being given to "medically unexplained symptoms" in which an individual complains of a condition such as pain or numbness for which no physical counterpart can be observed. Although the large majority of people who report these symptoms do not have a somatoform disorder, as many as one quarter may meet the *DSM-IV-TR* criteria for this disorder. In addition, people who have medically unexplained symptoms

In high stakes situations such as sports, an athlete's inability to continue in the game can be due to physical injury, psychological stress, or a combination of both.

are more likely to suffer from depression and anxiety (de Waal, Arnold, Eekhof, & van Hemert, 2004; Smith et al., 2005).

Conversion Disorder

As the example of the hockey player illustrates, psychological conflict can be converted into physical problems in some very dramatic ways. **Conversion disorder** involves this translation of unacceptable drives or troubling conflicts into bodily motor or sensory symptoms that suggest a neurological or other kind of medical condition. The essential feature of this disorder is an involuntary loss or alteration of a bodily function due to psychological conflict or need, causing the individual to feel seriously distressed or to be impaired in social, occupational, or other important areas of life. The person is not intentionally producing the symptoms; however, clinicians cannot establish a medical basis for the symptoms, and it appears that the person is "converting" the psychological conflict or need into a physical problem.

In the mid-1800s, a French physician named Paul Briquet systematically described and categorized the symptoms of hysteria based on his review of more than 400 patients. In the latter part of the nineteenth century, French neurologist Jean Martin Charcot used hypnosis to show that psychological factors played a role in the physical symptoms of hysteria. In a person who was under hypnosis, hysterical symptoms could be produced or removed at the hypnotist's suggestion. A student of Charcot's, Pierre Janet, theorized that this difference between normal and hysterical people was due to the presence, in hysterics, of dissociated contents of the mind. According to Janet, these parts of the mind had become dissociated because of hereditary degeneration of the brain. The ideas and functions within the dissociated part of the mind took autonomous hold over the individual and created symptoms that appeared to be beyond the person's voluntary control. Hippolyte Marie Bernheim, another French neurologist, maintained that hypnotizability could be demonstrated in both normal and hysterical people.

The work of Janet and Bernheim attracted attention all over Europe, and Freud became fascinated with their ideas. Through contact with Janet and Bernheim, Freud eventually developed a radically different theory of hysteria in his work with Breuer in the 1890s. Freud called conversion disorder **hysterical neurosis,** implying that it was a physical reaction to anxiety (neurosis).

The mechanism through which the symptoms of conversion disorder arise is still as much in dispute as it was in Freud's day. What is fascinating about conversion symptoms is the way in which they shed light on the relationship between psychological processes and the workings of the body. It is known that many physical disorders can be produced or aggravated by emotional problems that place undue demands on a part of the body or on a particular organ system. Similarly, conversion symptoms are also the physical expression of a psychological disturbance, but the translation from "mind" to "body" occurs in a way that defies medical logic.

An intriguing feature of a conversion symptom for many people with this disorder is that, once the symptom is moved from the realm of the psychological to the realm of the physical, it no longer poses a threat to the individual's peace of mind. The individual may pay little attention to the symptom and dismiss it as minor, even though it may be incapacitating. This phenomenon is called **la belle indifférence,** or the "beautiful" lack of concern, to indicate that the individual is not distressed by what might otherwise be construed as very inconveniencing physical problems. Once thought to be a criterion for diagnosing conversion disorder, la belle indifference is now regarded as an interesting but not defining aspect. In fact, many individuals with conversion disorder present in a very dramatic manner.

Conversion symptoms fall into four categories, each involving mystifying and very different kinds of disturbances: (1) motor symptoms or deficits, (2) sensory symptoms or deficits, (3) seizures or convulsions, and (4) mixed presentations. In motor functioning, the individual may experience such problems as impaired coordination or balance, paralysis or specific weakness, swallowing difficulties, speaking difficulty, and urinary retention. Sensory problems include feelings that one has lost a sense of touch or the ability to experience physical pain, as well as double vision, blindness, or deafness. Some individuals experience dramatic seizures or convulsions that lack a physiological basis, and others have a combination of symptoms or deficits from the other symptom subtypes.

Conversion disorder is a rare phenomenon, affecting 1 to 3 percent of those referred for mental health care. The disorder, which often runs in families, generally appears between the ages

Anna O. (Bertha Pappenheim). Anna's bizarre symptoms of what would now be called conversion disorder were treated by what was an early version of psychoanalysis.

Mini Case

CONVERSION DISORDER

Tiffany, a 32-year-old banker, thought she had already suffered more stress than one person could handle. She had always thought of herself as a person to whom weird things usually happened, and she commonly made more out of situations than was warranted. Driving down a snowy road one night, she accidentally hit an elderly man who was walking on the side of the road, causing a near fatal injury. In the months that followed, she became caught up in lengthy legal proceedings, which distracted her from her work and caused tremendous emotional stress in her life. On awakening one Monday morning, she found herself staggering around the bedroom, unable to see anything other than the shadows of objects in the room. At first, she thought she was just having a hard time waking up. As the morning went on, however, she realized that she was losing her vision. She waited 2 days before consulting a physician. When she did go for her medical appointment, she had an odd lack of concern about what seemed like such a serious physical condition.

Diagnostic Features

- This diagnosis is assigned to people with one or more symptoms or deficits that affect voluntary motor or sensory function that suggest a neurological or general medical condition.

- Psychological factors are judged to be associated with the condition, which began or was aggravated following a conflict or stressor.

- The condition is not intentionally produced or faked.

- After appropriate investigation, the condition cannot be attributed to a general medical condition, substance use, or culturally sanctioned behavior or experience.

- The condition causes significant distress or impairment, or it warrants medical evaluation.

- The condition is neither limited to pain or sexual dysfunction nor better explained by another mental disorder.

- Types are (1) with motor symptom or deficit, (2) with sensory symptom or deficit, (3) with seizures or convulsions, and (4) with mixed presentation.

---

of 10 and 35, and is more frequently observed in women and people with less education. Although conversion disorder is rare by any standards, more attention is being given to this condition. Clinicians recognize that the symptoms can range considerably from person to person. Conditions that might be diagnosed as chronic fatigue syndrome or fibromyalgia (unexplained muscle and joint pain) may represent forms of conversion disorder (Richardson & Engel, 2004). The condition usually appears suddenly and dissipates in less than 2 weeks. The symptoms may recur, however, within a year of their initial development. Symptoms involving paralysis, speaking problems, and blindness have a better prognosis than others. Perhaps as many as half of individuals with conversion disorder also suffer from a dissociative disorder. Clinicians need to be alert to the fact that their condition is more likely to be chronic and severe (Sar et al., 2004).

As you can imagine, it is very difficult for a health professional to diagnose conversion disorder. One concern about helping a person who shows conversion-like symptoms is that a real physical or cognitive problem may be wrongly attributed to psychological causes, and the client may not receive prompt medical attention. Indeed, as many as one half of those who are diagnosed as having conversion disorder are sometimes years later found to have had a physical illness not apparent when they were first seen for treatment (Couprie et al., 1995). Given these difficulties in diagnosis, clinicians recommend that clients suspected to have conversion disorder be given a thorough neurological examination in addition to follow-up to determine whether a client's symptoms represent an underlying medical condition (Hurwitz, 2004).

Somatization Disorder and Related Conditions

Like conversion disorder, **somatization disorder** involves the expression of psychological issues through bodily problems that cannot be explained by any known medical condition or as being due to the effects of a substance. The difference between somatization disorder and conversion disorder is that somatization disorder involves multiple and recurrent bodily symptoms, rather than a single physical complaint. This condition, which usually first appears before the age of 30, results in serious social, occupational, and interpersonal functioning problems. The individual seeks help from physicians, often several different ones simultaneously over the course of years, with seemingly exaggerated physical complaints. In a small number of cases, the individual suffers from a diagnosable medical condition, but his or her complaints are far in excess of what is customarily associated with the condition, and the level of the person's impairment is also much more extreme. Although it may appear that people with this diagnosis are intentionally "faking" a complex medical problem, they actually are not consciously attuned to the ways in which their psychological problems are being expressed physically.

In most cases, somatization disorder first appears during adolescence and progresses to a fluctuating, lifelong course, during which stressful events can cause episodic intensification of the symptoms. Individuals with somatization disorder rarely go through a year without seeking medical treatment for an undiagnosable physical problem. These people go to extreme lengths, compulsively seeking medical and surgical treatment for their vague and unsubstantiated physical problems. Not surprisingly, the disorder can cause significant work and social impairment.

Somatization disorder is relatively rare. Estimates of its prevalence in the general U.S. population are .23 percent in women and .02 percent in men (Swartz et al., 1991). People with somatization disorder tend to be from lower socioeconomic classes, with relatively little education or psychological sophistication. They may have come from a culture that gives less emphasis to the expression of emotions than to the expression of bodily symptoms. Many grew up in a home where they witnessed frequent sickness in a parent and suffered from physical illnesses themselves. In many cases, their home life was lacking in emotional support and was disturbed by alcoholic or antisocial problems on the part of one or both parents. These people generally experienced school problems during their youth, and in many cases they have records of delinquency. As they grew into adolescence, many were sexually promiscuous and married at a young age into unstable relationships with spouses who were substance abusers. Often, they themselves have a history of substance abuse problems. Some individuals who suffer from somatization disorder may also be at risk for suicide, even if they do not suffer from a comorbid condition such as a depressive or personality disorder (Chioqueta & Stiles, 2004).

Because they do not consider their difficulties to have an emotional cause, people with somatization disorder do not voluntarily seek psychotherapy. Only on the insistence of a physician are they likely to do so; even then, they make it clear to the psychotherapist that they feel misunderstood and that their physical problems have not been adequately assessed. The therapist tries to help the client draw the connections between physical problems and psychological conflicts; however, even in the best of these therapies the chances for success are slim.

Pain disorder is yet another related condition. In contrast to the multisymptomatic picture of somatization disorder, in **pain disorder,** a form of pain (which causes intense personal distress or impairment) is the predominant focus of the client's medical complaint. As with all the conditions in this group, the client is not faking the experience of pain. People with pain disorder find that their life becomes consumed by the experience of their pain and the pursuit of relief. In many cases, a diagnosable medical condition exists, but the nature of the pain complaint is regarded as being intricately associated with psychological issues. In other cases, no diagnosable medical condition exists. Researchers have suggested that chronic pain disorder may be on a spectrum of what are called "internalizing" disorders, which include mood, anxiety, and somatization disorder (Krueger, Tackett, & Markon, 2004). In other words, people with such disorders do not express outwardly their emotional conflicts but rather experience them internally.

The diagnosis of pain disorder is particularly complicated in cases in which a medical condition is evident, such as hernias, arthritis, and tumors—which certainly cause a good deal of pain. However, for people with this disorder, much more than the medical condition seems to be associated with the onset, severity, intensification, and maintenance of their pain. In many instances, these individuals have other psychological disorders, such as a mood disorder or an anxiety disorder, conditions that can become intricately intertwined with the experience and complaint of pain.

People struggling with chronic pain can find themselves in an endless pursuit of relief, spending considerable time and money looking for a cure. People with pain disorder are likely to become dependent on substances, either illicit drugs or prescription medications, in their efforts to alleviate their discomfort. In fact, it is estimated that one quarter of patients prescribed

Mini Case

SOMATIZATION DISORDER

Helen, a 29-year-old woman, is seeking treatment because her physician said there was nothing more he could do for her. When asked about her physical problems, Helen recited a litany of complaints, including frequent episodes when she could not remember what has happened to her and other times when her vision is so blurred that she could not read the words on a printed page. Helen enjoys cooking and doing things around the house, but she becomes easily fatigued and short of breath for no apparent reason. She often is unable to eat the elaborate meals she prepares, because she becomes nauseated and is prone to vomit any food with even a touch of spice. According to Helen's husband, she has lost all interest in sexual intimacy, and they have intercourse only about once every few months, usually at his insistence. Helen complains of painful cramps during her menstrual periods, and at other times says she feels that her "insides are on fire." Because of additional pain in her back, legs, and chest, Helen wants to stay in bed for much of the day. Helen lives in a large, old Victorian house, from which she ventures only infrequently "because I need to be able to lie down when my legs ache."

Diagnostic Features

■ This diagnosis is assigned to people who, even before they reach the age of 30, have many physical complaints for years, for which they seek treatment or experience impairment in social, occupational, or other important areas of functioning.

■ These individuals experience symptoms in each of the following four categories:

- ◆ Pain: history of at least four pain symptoms (e.g., in head, abdomen, back, joints, chest, rectum)

- ◆ Gastrointestinal: history of at least two gastrointestinal symptoms (e.g., nausea, bloating, vomiting, diarrhea)

- ◆ Sexual: history of at least one sexual or reproductive symptom other than pain (e.g., erectile or ejaculatory dysfunction, irregular menstruation, menstrual bleeding)

- ◆ Pseudoneurological: history of at least one symptom or deficit suggesting a neurological condition not limited to pain (e.g., conversion symptoms, such as impaired coordination or balance, paralysis or localized weakness, difficulty swallowing, hallucinations, loss of touch or pain sensation, dissociative symptoms)

■ Either: (1) the symptoms cannot be fully attributed to a known medical condition or substance use or (2) when there is a medical condition, the physical complaints or impairment is in excess of what would be expected.

■ The symptoms are not intentionally produced.

Mini Case

PAIN DISORDER

Brian, a 48-year-old store manager, has complained for more than 3 years of constant pain in two distant parts of his body: his teeth and his feet. At times, the pain is so severe that he spends the entire day flat on his back at home. He has visited numerous dentists and podiatrists, who are unable to find any medically diagnosable cause of these complaints. Although several of the doctors pointed out that these symptoms first appeared soon after Brian's painful divorce, he is unable and unwilling to acknowledge that there might be a connection. Brian has missed an extensive amount of work and is at risk of losing his job. The thought of this terrifies him for both financial and emotional reasons. He has worked since the age of 19, beginning his career in merchandising as a shipping clerk for a large retail discount chain. He advanced to his current managerial position and fears that he would never be able to find another job or return to successful employment again.

Diagnostic Features

- People with this condition complain of pain in one or more places that is of sufficient severity to warrant clinical attention.
- The pain causes significant distress or impairment.
- Psychological factors are judged to have an important role in the onset, severity, aggravation, or maintenance of the pain.
- The pain is not intentionally produced or faked.
- The condition is not better accounted for by another mental disorder.
- Types are (1) acute if of less than 6 months' duration or (2) chronic if 6 months or longer.

painkilling medication for treatment of chronic pain develop problems with substance abuse or dependence (American Psychiatric Association, 2000).

Body Dysmorphic Disorder

Perhaps, like most people, you are self-conscious about one aspect of your body, such as your height, your weight, your shape, the size of your nose, or something about your hair. If you confide in friends, they may tell you that they are also self-conscious about a feature of their bodies. In fact, many people have distorted negative concerns about their body (Phillips, 1996); for example, in one study of college students, as many as 70 percent of the group complained of some dissatisfaction with an aspect of their appearance (Fitts, Gibson, Redding, & Deiter, 1989). People with **body dysmorphic disorder** are not just dissatisfied but preoccupied, almost to the point of being delusional, with the idea that a part of their body is ugly or defective. They are so consumed with distress about their bodily problem that their work, social life, and relationships are impaired. They may believe that there is something wrong with the texture of their skin, that they have too much or too little facial hair, or that there

is a deformity in the shape of their nose, mouth, jaw, or eyebrows (Eisen, Phillips, Coles, & Rasmussen, 2004).

A surprising number of people express significant concerns about the appearance of one feature of their body. In a survey of more than 2,000 British adults, women under age 60 and young adult men reported the highest frequency of concern over physical appearance. The greatest numbers of concern were with the nose, weight, and skin. Women were most preoccupied with breasts and abdomens, and men with premature balding. Approximately 19 percent of men and 25 percent of women had scores on the measure of concern about appearance that exceeded those of patients about to undergo cosmetic and reconstructive surgery (Harris & Carr, 2001). Among individuals with body dysmorphic disorder, men are more likely to be preoccupied with their body build, their genitals, and the thinning of their hair (Phillips & Diaz, 1997). The most recent edition of the *DSM* (American Psychiatric Association, 2000) adds muscularity and body build to the list of preoccupations.

In one variation of body dysmorphic disorder, individuals become obsessed with a desire to enhance their body's appearance.

For the most part, the defects these people are concerned about are imaginary. In other instances, there really is something abnormal about the body part, but the person's concern is grossly exaggerated. Mirrors and other reflecting surfaces are commonly problematic. The urge to stare at their "deformity" may be irresistible; they may have a special mirror with focused lighting that enables them to scrutinize the flaw, and they spend long periods of time trying to mask the body part that causes them such great distress. In one study of 13 individuals with this disorder, each person engaged in compulsive behaviors associated with their preoccupation for long durations, usually 3 hours or more each day (Neziroglu & Yaryura-Tobias, 1993). Others go to great lengths to avoid any reflection of their "grotesque" problem, covering mirrors in a hotel room or crossing the street to avoid a reflecting store window. At times, their thinking borders on paranoia, as they imagine that others are talking about them or staring. Perhaps they take some measures to conceal the object of their concerns. For example, a woman who is distressed by her brittle hair texture wears a baseball hat all the time. A man who is distressed by a pock mark on his face grows a beard, which he dyes a deep color to mask the flaw that others hardly notice.

People with body dysmorphic disorder may seek cosmetic surgery or other medical treatment to correct their imagined defect. It is estimated that approximately 5 percent of patients seeking cosmetic surgery have this disorder (Veale, De Haro, & Lambrou, 2003). Not surprisingly, the surgery typically does not relieve their bodily dissatisfaction (Honigman, Phillips, & Castle, 2004).

In one of the first in-depth investigations of people with the disorder, Katherine Phillips and colleagues described specific characteristics and symptoms among 30 cases (Phillips, McElroy, Keck, & Pope, 1993). In more than a third of those clients, who ranged in age from 17 to 80, their preoccupation with their bodily concern was of delusional proportion. The average age of onset for the condition was 15. The impact on their lives was dramatic, with 97 percent reporting that they avoided normal social and work involvements; a third remained housebound. Serious associated psychological disorders occurred in most of these individuals at some point in life, with 93 percent experiencing a major mood disorder, 73 percent an anxiety disorder, and 33 percent a psychotic disorder. Almost a fifth of the clients had made suicide attempts. Their efforts to obtain relief through medical procedures were generally unsuccessful and included surgical, dermatological, and dental treatments. Later studies have documented the co-existence in these individuals of other Axis I disorders, including major depressive disorder, social phobia, obsessive-compulsive disorder, and substance abuse or dependence (Grant et al., 2005; Gunstad & Phillips, 2003).

Medications that are effective in treating obsessive-compulsive disorder and serious depression include SSRIs such as fluoxetine (El-khatib & Dickey, 1995; Heimann, 1997; Phillips & Taub, 1995), fluvoxamine (Phillips, Siniscalchi, & McElroy, 2004), and citalopram (Phillips & Najjar, 2003). Cognitive-behavioral group therapy, in which participants with the disorder

Mini Case

BODY DYSMORPHIC DISORDER

Lydia is a 43-year-old woman who was referred to the mental health clinic by a local surgeon. For the past 8 years, Lydia has visited plastic surgeons across the country to find one who will perform surgery to reduce the size of her hands, which she perceives as being "too fat." Until she has this surgery, she will not leave her house without wearing gloves. The plastic surgeon concurs with Lydia's family members and friends that Lydia's perception of her hands is distorted and that plastic surgery would be inappropriate and irresponsible.

Diagnostic Features

- People with this condition are preoccupied with an imagined defect in their appearance. Even if a slight abnormality is present, their concern is excessive.

- Their preoccupation causes significant distress or impairment.

- Their preoccupation is not better accounted for by another mental disorder, such as anorexia nervosa.

give each other feedback about their actual appearance, can also be successful, as can training in behavioral methods, such as thought stopping, relaxation, and exposure therapy with response prevention (McKay, Todaro, Neziroglu, & Campisi, 1997; Rosen, Reiter, & Orosan, 1995). The effectiveness of combined medication and psychotherapy is also being investigated (Allen & Hollander, 2000).

Researchers are beginning to suspect that body dysmorphic disorder might be part of a spectrum of disorders including obsessive-compulsive disorder, eating disorders, trichotillomania (compulsive hair-picking), social phobia, and certain personality disorders (Eisen et al., 2004; Nestadt et al., 2003; Nierenberg et al., 2002; Schneier, Blanco, Antia, & Liebowitz, 2002). In the case of personality disorders, a study of nearly 150 patients with body dysmorphic disorder revealed that more than half had one or more personality disorders. In addition, people with body dysmorphic disorder received high scores on the personality trait of neuroticism and low scores on extraversion and conscientiousness (Phillips & McElroy, 2000). Interestingly, compared with individuals who develop other "spectrum" disorders, those who develop body dysmorphic disorder are more likely to show an interest in art and aesthetics (Veale, Ennis, & Lambrou, 2002). It is not clear from this finding whether people with body dysmorphic disorder become fascinated with physical beauty because they are studying art, or whether they are drawn to the study of art because of certain personality characteristics that lead them to focus on aesthetics.

Hypochondriasis

People with the somatoform disorder known as **hypochondriasis** believe or fear that they have a serious illness, when in fact

A hypochondriac may spend a small fortune on unnecessary medications to treat imagined bodily disorders.

they are merely experiencing normal bodily reactions. For example, a stomachache that lasts for more than a day might lead a hypochondriacal woman to worry that she has an advanced case of stomach cancer. Or a recurrent headache might lead a hypochondriacal man to infer that he has a brain tumor. Even the most minor of bodily changes, such as itching skin, can cause the person with hypochondriasis to urgently seek medical attention. To the dismay of people with hypochondriasis (approximately 1 to 5 percent of the general population), medical tests

fail to confirm their assumptions that they have a serious medical illness.

Unlike conversion disorder or somatization disorder, hypochondriasis does not involve extreme bodily dysfunction or unexplainable medical symptoms. Instead, the person with hypochondriasis misinterprets or exaggerates normal bodily occurrences. Hypochondriacs sometimes become so alarmed about their symptoms that they appear to be on the verge of panic. Further, unlike some of the disorders we have seen so far, a characteristic of hypochondriasis is the person's intense preoccupation with the perceived abnormality of functioning, despite medical evaluations and reassurances that nothing is wrong. No amount of reassurance from medical authorities can relieve their fears, yet these fears are not delusional, because the individual is aware of the possibility that the fears are unfounded or exaggerated. Thus, people with hypochondriasis do not show la belle indifférence, experienced by some people with conversion disorders. In fact, rather than being unaffected by their medical concerns, many individuals suffer from intense symptoms of anxiety or depression (Gureje, Ustun, & Simon, 1997), and quite a few ruminate considerably about their imagined symptoms (Fink et al., 2004; Hiller, Leibbrand, Rief, & Fichter, 2005).

There are a number of explanations for the exaggeration of bodily symptoms seen in people with hypochondriasis. One possibility is that these individuals are more sensitive to what is happening inside their bodies, such as their heart rate and other somatic processes (Barsky, Brener, Coeytaux, & Cleary, 1995; Haenen, Schmidt, Kroeze, & van den Hout, 1996). Furthermore, they can be so concerned with trying to maintain good health that they become almost fanatical about their bodies (Lecci, Karoly, Ruehlman, & Lanyon, 1996). Their focus on abnormal bodily sensations seems to be related to a heightened perceived risk for developing various medical diseases (Barsky et al., 2001).

Mini Case

HYPOCHONDRIASIS

Beth is a 48-year-old mother of two children, both of whom have recently moved away from home. Within the past year, her menstrual periods have become much heavier and more irregular. Seeking an explanation, Beth began to spend days reading everything she could find on uterine cancer. Although medical books specified menstrual disturbance as a common feature of menopause, one newspaper article mentioned the possibility of uterine cancer. She immediately made an appointment with her gynecologist, who tested her and concluded that her symptoms were almost certainly due to menopause. Convinced that her physician was trying to protect her from knowing the awful "truth," Beth visited one gynecologist after another, in search of someone who would properly diagnose what she was certain was a fatal illness. She decided to give up her job as a department store clerk for two reasons. First, she was concerned that long hours of standing at the cash register would

aggravate her medical condition. Second, she felt she could not be tied down by a job that was interfering with her medical appointments.

Diagnostic Features

- People with this disorder are preoccupied with fears of having, or the idea that they have, a serious disease, due to their misinterpretation of bodily symptoms.
- Their preoccupation persists, despite appropriate medical evaluation or reassurance.
- Their concern is neither of delusional intensity nor related exclusively to a concern about appearance.
- Their preoccupation causes significant distress or impairment.
- The disturbance lasts at least 6 months.
- Their preoccupation is not better accounted for by another mental disorder.

Hypochondriasis may also represent the expression of high levels of the personality trait of neuroticism (Noyes et al., 2005; Noyes et al., 2004). Recall from our discussion in Chapter 3 that people who are high on the trait of neuroticism are characteristically worried and unhappy.

Physicians as well as mental health professionals regard the treatment of hypochondriasis as difficult. The course of hypochondriasis tends to be stable over time, particularly in people who also suffer from anxiety and depressive disorders (Simon, Gureje, & Fullerton, 2001). Because clients with this condition often react with anger and impatience when they feel their concerns are not taken seriously, they often provoke intense frustration and exasperation in those trying to help them recognize the psychological origins of their concerns. Some experts recommend that, when treating people with hypochondriasis, especially older individuals, it is best to conceptualize the intervention as care rather than cure; in this approach, the health professional helps the client cope with, rather than eliminate, the symptoms (Barsky, 1996). In some cases, such medications as fluoxetine are of value, particularly in reducing obsessional worrying about health concerns (Demopulos et al., 1996; Fallon, 2004). Cognitive-behavioral therapy can be effective, in individual (Barsky & Ahern, 2004) or group form (Lidbeck, 2003). The focus of this kind of therapy is teaching individuals to restructure their maladaptive beliefs about their physical symptoms.

Conditions Related to Somatoform Disorders

Malingering involves deliberately feigning the symptoms of physical illness or psychological disorder for an ulterior motive. Returning to the example of the hockey player with the seemingly paralyzed hand, we might consider the possibility that he has fabricated the complaint to avoid playing in a game his team is certain to lose. Another example of a malingerer is the person who feigns a physical problem in order to obtain financial gain, such as disability benefits. Sometimes a person wants to appear psychologically disturbed for a hidden motive, such as financial benefit. For example, Alex, who was involved in a minor car accident, may claim that he has sustained serious memory dysfunction, or that he has developed the symptoms of post-traumatic stress disorder.

The question of possible malingering presents a challenge for clinicians. On the one hand, clinicians want to believe their clients' stories and problems. On the other hand, clinicians need to maintain an objectivity that permits them to assess the possibility that a client may have an ulterior motive. In recent years, psychologists have developed various assessment methods that help clinicians determine whether someone is malingering (Etherton, Bianchini, Greve, & Ciota, 2005). Many clinicians rely on the validity scales of the MMPI-2 to help them determine whether clients are malingering, or "faking bad" (Dearth et al., 2005). Another instrument is the *Validity Indicator Profile* (Frederick, 1998), which consists of verbal and nonverbal tasks designed to determine whether a subject is responding legiti-

Mini Case

MALINGERING

Linda is a 33-year-old janitor who had an accident at work 1 year ago. She slipped on a freshly mopped floor and badly bruised her right knee; since the accident, she has fabricated the claim that she is unable to bend her knee or to support her weight on that leg. Consequently, she has used crutches and even a wheelchair. Linda has undergone numerous medical assessments, but no physical basis for her problems has been found. She has been unable to work and has filed a worker's compensation claim that would provide disability benefits. Linda states that this accident occurred at the worst possible time in her life, because her husband recently left her, and she is concerned about her ability to support herself and her 2-year-old daughter. She is comforted by the thought that, if she is awarded disability benefits, she would have permanent financial security and would be able to remain at home to take care of her daughter. She is annoyed by her physician's doubt that she has a real physical disability, and she has vowed to find the "best orthopedic surgeon in the country" to support her claim. If necessary, she will sue her employer and the worker's compensation insurance company to get her benefits.

Diagnostic Features

- People who malinger intentionally produce false or grossly exaggerated physical or psychological symptoms.

- They are motivated by such incentives as avoiding military duty, avoiding work, obtaining financial compensation, evading criminal prosecution, and obtaining unneeded medications.

---

mately or is trying to look impaired. Subjects are presented with verbal items, such as one in which they are asked to match a word (e.g., *house*) with one of two presented words that comes closest to it in definition (e.g., *home, shoe*). As you might guess, a person trying to appear impaired would choose the wrong word. Researchers have come across some interesting stylistic aspects of malingerers; for example, in one study of people presenting symptoms of amnesia, researchers asked 40 amnestic subjects and 40 individuals faking amnesia to count backward under differing levels of distraction. The fakers tended to exaggerate their memory deficit relative to those with genuine amnesia (Baker et al., 1993). In cases of amnesia, clinicians can use the Test of Memory Malingering in which malingerers are identified as people who do not put forth sufficient effort when they undergo neuropsychological testing (Gavett, O'Bryant, Fisher, & McCaffrey, 2005).

In **factitious disorder,** people fake symptoms or disorders, not for the purpose of any particular gain but because of an inner need to maintain a sick role. The symptoms may be either physical or psychological, or they may be a combination of both. In some instances, the person fabricates a problem, such as excruciating headaches. In other instances, the individual inflicts physical harm, perhaps creating body bruises with a hammer. In other situations, the person makes an actual medical condition

Mini Case

FACTITIOUS DISORDER

Jon is a 27-year-old man who has not completed his undergraduate degree, even though he had been continuously enrolled in college for 9 years. Only three credits short of his bachelor's degree, Jon tearfully presented himself each semester to the professor of his final college course with stories about physical illnesses that prevented him from finishing his last assignment, a three-page paper. One time, he appeared with cuts and bruises on his face and arms, explaining that he had fallen down a flight of stairs. Another time, he sat in his professor's office, gasping for breath and asserting that he had been suffering repeated bouts of pneumonia. In response to Jon's apparently serious health problems, Jon's professor told him that the final paper could be waived; to the professor's surprise, Jon declined the offer, stating that he preferred to do the work. Although Jon's professor agreed, he became suspicious about Jon's health issues when Jon

presented a letter on a physician's stationery, stating that Jon had just been diagnosed with colon cancer. Suspecting that Jon was not telling the truth, his professor sent a copy of the letter to the physician, who called immediately, exclaiming that he had never met Jon and that Jon had somehow gotten his letterhead and typed a fraudulent letter. When Jon's professor confronted him, Jon ran out of the office, never to return to discuss the issue or to complete his college degree.

Diagnostic Features

- This label applies to people who intentionally produce or fake physical or psychological symptoms.
- The motivation of these individuals is to assume a sick role.
- There are no external incentives, such as economic gain or the avoidance of legal responsibility.
- Symptoms may be predominantly psychological, physical, or a combination of both.

---

worse, as in the case of a person intentionally aggravating a skin infection by rubbing it with dirt.

What makes factitious disorder so intriguing is that the individual has no ulterior motive, such as economic gain or the avoidance of responsibilities. Rather, these individuals relish the notion of being ill and may go to great lengths either to appear ill or to make themselves sick. For some, the thought of undergoing surgery is appealing, and they gladly submit themselves to multiple invasive procedures. A man may inject saliva into his skin to produce abscesses, or a woman who is allergic to penicillin may willingly accept an injection to induce a reaction. The medical and mental health literature contains numerous accounts each year of almost unbelievable instances of factitious disorder. For example, in one case, a 29-year-old nurse was treated for septic arthritis in the knee, a condition brought on when she injected contaminated material into her knee joint to cause an infection (Guziec, Lazarus, & Harding, 1994).

These individuals present themselves as dramatically as possible, trying to create scenarios in which their illness plays a starring role. They may simulate a heart attack, appendicitis, kidney stone pain, or fevers of unknown origin. If no one believes them, however, they may become incensed and immediately seek medical help elsewhere, possibly flying all over the country to different medical centers, where their baffling diseases can become the center of concern. Many develop an impressive level of medical knowledge to ensure that their story corresponds to the technical aspects of the disorder about which they are complaining. Some go to great lengths to create a medical profile, possibly even stealing a physician's stationery and writing a "medical report" for others to read. Researchers examining the demographic variables associated with these disorders have come upon interesting correlates of the disorder. In a retrospective examination of the records of 93 patients diagnosed over a period of 21 years, the people most likely to have factitious disorder with physical symptoms were women in their forties working in health care settings (Krahn, Li, & O'Connor, 2003).

Munchausen's syndrome is a type of factitious disorder. This syndrome is named after Baron von Munchausen, a retired German cavalry officer in the 1700s known for his "tall tales" (Asher, 1951). **Munchausen's syndrome** involves chronic cases in which the individual's whole life becomes consumed with the pursuit of medical care. These individuals usually spend an inordinate amount of time inflicting injury on themselves in order to look so "sick" that hospitalization is necessary. Their medical symptoms are limited only by their level of medical knowledge and imagination. Although factitious disorder is generally more common in females, the most chronic and severe cases of Munchausen's syndrome tend to appear in males (American Psychiatric Association, 2000).

In factitious disorder with psychological symptoms, the individual feigns psychological problems, such as psychosis or depression. In such cases, the individual's symptoms tend to be vague and fail to correspond to any particular psychological disorder. However, such individuals tend to be suggestible and to take on new symptoms, which a clinician inadvertently implies are commonly associated with the hypothesized psychological disorder. Those trying to present themselves as psychologically disturbed may take drugs that produce such symptoms as restlessness, insomnia, or hallucinations, in an attempt to mimic psychological disorders.

At times, clinicians encounter an especially intriguing form of factitious disorder. In **factitious disorder by proxy** (or **Munchausen's syndrome by proxy**), a person induces physical symptoms in another person who is under that individual's care. For example, Loretta caused her young daughter to become sick by feeding her toxic substances; she then went from physician to physician with this sick and helpless child and used her daughter to gain access to medical attention and concern. The symptoms of the disorder often go unrecognized because the child, like other abuse victims, is too frightened to speak out about the true cause of the symptoms (Gushurst, 2003). For the most part, this disorder is reported in women, although increased familiarity

Following the jury verdict of guilty for the murder of her five children, Waneta Hoyt looks perplexed while her son Jay reacts with despair. Cases such as this have brought attention to the disorder of factitious disorder by proxy.

with factitious disorder by proxy has alerted professionals to the possibility that men may have this condition. In one reported case, a father repeatedly produced symptoms of illness in his infant daughter during the first 6 months of her life, and he sought medical help for her while denying he knew the cause of her problems. The father finally admitted that he had been holding his daughter so tightly that she would become breathless, at which point he would revive her (Jones, Badgett, Minella, & Schuschke, 1993).

Some cases of factitious disorder by proxy are so extreme that murder takes place. One case that captured the attention of the nation was that of Waneta Hoyt, an upstate New York woman who was convicted of murdering five of her children (Firstman & Talan, 1997). Health professionals thought that Hoyt's children were dying from sudden infant death syndrome (SIDS) and looked at this family as providing evidence that SIDS deaths can run in families. Only years later did the fact come to light that Hoyt had murdered her own offspring, seemingly for no other reason than to get attention from health professionals. Such cases have led researchers to scrutinize unexplained infant deaths and to come to some very disturbing conclusions. Using covert videotaping of suspicious medical cases in two British hospitals, David Southall and his colleagues taped 39 children to investigate suspicions of induced illness (Southall et al., 1997). They reported shocking instances of abuse in 33 of the 39 suspected cases, and they observed the efforts of 33 parents to suffocate their young children, who ranged in age from 2 to 44 months. They also observed attempts to poison, fracture, or otherwise abuse these children. The 39 children being secretly observed had 41 siblings, 12 of whom had previously died suddenly and unexpectedly, presumably from sudden infant death syndrome.

Why would people exert such extreme effort to present themselves or their children as being ill or having died for unexplainable reasons? In addition to wanting to be the center of attention, they seem to be motivated by a desire to be nurtured in a medical setting; some are also driven by a bizarre wish to inflict pain on others or to experience it themselves. Yet another precipitant may be postpartum depression, in which the mother becomes severely depressed following the birth of the child (Gojer & Berman, 2000). Looking into the childhood backgrounds of these individuals, it appears that many were physically abused. Disease or an experience with the medical profession may also have figured into their childhood experiences, possibly creating a diathesis that set the stage for them to perceive professional attention and the hospital environment as positively reinforcing (Trask & Sigmon, 1997).

Although professionals may find it difficult to be sympathetic with these clients, clinicians realize that this strange behavior is often beyond their volition. Many of these individuals have an impaired sense of reality and a poorly consolidated sense of self. When they feel inner distress, they reach out for help in the only way they know, by seeking care in a relatively safe, structured context. Professionals may question whether they should take a confrontative approach in which the client is "accused" of faking; in cases in which the physical health of the client or the client's child is at stake, dramatic responses will be needed. However, a nonconfrontational approach seems preferable, in which the clinician attempts to help the client integrate reality and fantasy, while supporting the client's strengths and avoiding rewards for the client's acting-out behavior (Parker, 1993).

Theories and Treatment of Somatoform Disorders

To understand what motivates people to be "sick," it is helpful to look at what psychologists call the primary gain and secondary gain associated with sickness. **Primary gain** is the avoidance of burdensome responsibilities because one is "disabled." Going back to the case of the hockey player, his primary gain is the avoidance of playing in a game that entails high risk, in terms of both physical injury and loss of self-esteem. **Secondary gain** is the sympathy and attention the sick person receives from other people. For example, the hockey player might be secretly gratified by the solicitous concern of his friends and teammates.

Many potential costs are involved in adopting the sick role, however. Disability can result in lost or reduced wages, and the incapacitation it causes may engender others' annoyance or anger, not sympathy. However, people who take on the sick role find that more rewards than costs become available to them. Society also tends to make it more acceptable for people to receive care for a physical illness than for stress-related problems that seem to be more under voluntary control.

Somatoform disorders can best be explained as an interplay of biological factors, learning experiences, emotional factors, and faulty cognitions. According to this integrative approach, childhood events set the stage for the later development of symptoms. As children, people with this disorder may have had parents who dealt with stress by complaining about various unfounded physical ailments. As adults, they are primed to react to emotional stress with physical complaints. Some of these complaints may have a basis in reality, in that stress can cause muscle tension in parts of the body, such as the head, back, or gastrointestinal system. Although too subtle to show up on diagnostic tests, these symptoms of muscle tension create discomfort, on which the individual focuses attention and concern. A cycle is established, in which concern over these physical sensations becomes magnified, creating more tension and leading to more distress. Reinforcing this process are the rewards the individual stands to gain from being sick, such as disability benefits or attention from friends and family members.

Most contemporary approaches to treating somatoform disorders involve exploring a person's need to play the sick role, evaluating the contribution of stress in the person's life, and providing clients with cognitive-behavioral techniques to control their symptoms. Developing a supportive and trusting relationship with a client who has a somatoform disorder is also very important. In some cases, medication may be added to the treatment plan. For example, for some patients with somatization disorder, antidepressant medications serve an important role in the treatment (Mai, 2004). Negative reinforcement is suggested as the basis for behavioral treatment of conversion disorder in children (Campo & Negrini, 2000). Irrespective of the specific techniques the therapist uses, developing a supportive and trusting relationship with a client who has a somatoform disorder is very important. As was true for Rose Marston, whose case was presented at the outset of this chapter, a client may become upset if a disbelieving therapist challenges physical symptoms that seem very real and troubling.

Psychological Factors Affecting Medical Conditions

Most people are aware that bodily conditions can be adversely affected by psychological factors. For example, intense emotional stress can increase one's vulnerability to getting sick and can seem to slow down recovery from an ailment. Various bodily problems can be brought on or aggravated by the experience of anxiety, depression, and even anger. In some circumstances, the condition is quite serious and warrants clinical attention. There is a special *DSM-IV-TR* diagnostic category, called psychological factors affecting medical conditions, that addresses conditions in which there is a marked relationship between psychological and bodily disturbance.

 MindMAP Segment 6.1: Stress and Life Events

Illness may elicit secondary gain in the form of receiving sympathy and concern from others.

TABLE 6.1 Sleep Disorders

The *DSM-IV* category of sleep disorders includes a number of conditions highlighting the relationship between psychological and bodily disturbance. For some people, conflict and stress are expressed through disturbed sleep. For others, sleep disturbance caused by a neurological problem creates considerable emotional disturbance. Sleep disorders are chronic conditions that cause a great amount of emotional distress and interfere with normal life functioning. At times, these conditions might cause so much fatigue that an individual is in danger while performing the normal tasks of life, such as driving (Roth, Roehrs, & Rosenthal, 1994). Although sleep disorders do not technically fall into the category of psychological factors affecting medical conditions, they are relevant to our discussion of these topics.

Disorder	Symptoms
Dyssomnias	Disturbances in the amount, quality, or timing of sleep
Primary insomnia	Chronic difficulty with sleeping, taking various forms: trouble falling asleep, frequent awakening, or getting a full night's sleep but not feeling rested
Primary hypersomnia	An excessive need for sleep, expressed in having difficulty getting out of bed, yearning for sleep during the day, sneaking naps, and unintentional dozing off
Circadian rhythm sleep disorder	Disturbance in both sleep and daytime functioning caused by disruptions in the normal sleep-wake cycle, usually due to rotating work shifts or jet lag
Breathing-related sleep disorder	Excessive sleepiness during the day caused by frequent awakening during the night because of breathing problems (e.g., loud snoring, gasping for breath, or breathing interruptions)
Parasomnias	Conditions involving abnormal behavior or bodily events occurring during sleep or sleep-wake transitions
Nightmare disorder	The experience of recurrent vivid dreams from which a person awakes and has detailed recollection of extended frightening images
Sleep terror disorder	Condition in which an individual repeatedly wakes up suddenly and in a panic from a sound sleep, causing feelings of intense anxiety, confusion, and disorientation, for which there will be no recall in the morning
Sleepwalking disorder	Condition involving recurrent episodes of arising from sleep, usually walking about with a blank stare and lack of responsivity to other people, with amnesia for the episodes the following morning
Narcolepsy	The experience of irresistible attacks of sleep that can take place at any time and any place, usually lasting between 10 and 20 minutes

Characteristics of the *DSM-IV-TR* Category of Psychological Factors Affecting Medical Conditions

The *DSM-IV-TR* diagnostic category **psychological factors affecting medical conditions** includes situations in which psychological or behavioral factors have an adverse effect on a medical condition. The psychological factors include the following: Axis I disorders (e.g., major depressive disorder), psychological symptoms (e.g., anxiety that aggravates asthma), personality traits (e.g., hostility), maladaptive health behaviors (e.g., unhealthy diet), stress-related physiological responses (e.g., stress-related aggravation of an ulcer), and less specific psychological factors (e.g., interpersonal problems).

This diagnosis is given to clients who suffer from a recognized medical condition that is adversely affected by emotional factors that influence the course of the medical condition, interfere with treatment, create additional health risks, or aggravate its symptoms. An example is the case of Joachim, a man with a history of panic disorder whose recovery from heart surgery is impeded because of his intense bouts with anxiety. Sometimes personality traits or coping style adversely affects an individual's health. For example, Marissa, who is characteristically hostile and impatient, experiences recurrent bodily problems, such as high blood pressure and gastrointestinal discomfort. Some medical conditions are quite sensitive to stress. For example, Alec knows that his asthma is likely to flare up during periods of intense stress.

Emotional and psychological factors can aggravate just about any physical problem. Researchers have conducted extensive investigations of such relationships in trying to better understand cancer, cardiovascular disease, skin conditions, endocrine problems, and difficulties affecting the stomach, breathing, kidney, and neurological functioning. Health professionals now are aware that psychological factors can initiate, aggravate, and prolong medical diseases and problems, and they continue to develop interventions that help enhance both physical and psychological well-being.

Mini Case

PSYCHOLOGICAL FACTORS AFFECTING MEDICAL CONDITIONS

Brenda is a 41-year-old manager of a large discount chain store. Despite her success, she struggles with an agitated depression, which causes her to feel impatient and irritable most of the time. She recognizes that her emotional problems relate to issues with her parents, and she resents the fact that she chronically suffers from an inner tension that has always been part of her personality. The youngest in a family of four children, she perceived that throughout her childhood she had to do "twice as much" as her siblings to gain her parents' attention and affection. Now, as an adult, she is caught up in a drive toward success that literally makes her physically sick. She has intense headaches and stomachaches on most days, yet she is reluctant to seek medical help, because she doesn't want to take time away from her work.

Diagnostic Features

■ This diagnosis is applied to people who have a medical condition and for whom psychological factors adversely affect the medical condition in one of the following ways:

◆ There is a close relationship in time between psychological factors and the beginning of a medical condition, the worsening of the condition, or the delay in recovering from the condition.

◆ The psychological factors interfere with the treatment of the condition.

◆ The psychological factors create additional health risks for the individual.

◆ Stress-related bodily responses bring on or worsen the symptoms of the medical condition.

■ Psychological factors can be represented in various ways, such as psychological symptoms (e.g., depression that delays recovery from surgery, anxiety that aggravates asthma), personality traits (e.g., hostility that contributes to heart disease), maladaptive health behaviors (e.g., overeating), and stress-related physiological response (e.g., tension headache).

Theories and Treatment of the *DSM-IV-TR* Category of Psychological Factors Affecting Medical Conditions

When you have an upset stomach or bad headache during exam time or when an important assignment is due, you probably recognize that there is a connection between what is happening in your emotions and what is happening in your body. Although the connection seems simple on the surface, it is more complex than you might think. Researchers who study the "mind-body" relationship attempt to determine why some people develop physiological or medical problems when their lives become busy, complicated, or filled with unpleasant events.

Stress Most researchers use the term **stress** to refer to the unpleasant emotional reaction a person has when he or she perceives an event to be threatening. This emotional reaction may include heightened physiological arousal due to increased reactivity of the sympathetic nervous system. The **stressor** is the event itself, which may also be called a stressful life event. When a person experiences stress, he or she is likely to try to reduce this unpleasant feeling. Making an effort to reduce stress is called **coping.** It is when coping is unsuccessful, and the stress does not subside, that the individual may seek clinical attention for medical or psychological problems that have developed as a consequence of the constant physiological arousal caused by chronic stress.

Let's take a closer look at all of these components, beginning with the nature of stressful life events. Researchers in this area have developed measures that quantify the degree to which an individual has been exposed to difficult life situations. One of

When stress is high, many people develop physical ailments for which they seek medical care without giving much thought to the role that emotions play in the development of health problems.

the most well known of these is the Social Readjustment Rating Scale (SRRS) (Holmes & Rahe, 1967), which assesses life stress in terms of "life change units" (LCU). Events are given LCU scores, based on how strongly they are associated with physical illness. The rationale behind this measure is that, when people experience a large number of LCUs in a relatively brief period of time, they are at greater risk for developing a major illness within a 2-year period. You can assess your own stressful life events score by taking a scale developed for college students (see Table 6.2), the College Undergraduate Stress Scale (CUSS) (Renner & Mackin, 1998), which was developed to assess the kinds of stressors most familiar to traditional-age college

TABLE 6.2 Items from the College Undergraduate Stress Scale

The number next to each item represents the "stress rating" that each was given by large samples of undergraduates. See how many have applied to you in the past year and then add up your score. The average score reported by the scale's authors is 1,247, with scores ranging from 182 to 2,571. A "normal" range would be between 800 and 1,700.

Event	Stress Ratings	Your Items
Being raped	100	
Finding out that you are HIV-positive	100	
Being accused of rape	98	
Death of a close friend	97	
Death of a close family member	96	
Contracting a sexually transmitted disease (other than AIDS)	94	
Concerns about being pregnant	91	
Finals week	90	
Concerns about your partner being pregnant	90	
Oversleeping for an exam	89	
Flunking a class	89	
Having a boyfriend or girlfriend cheat on you	85	
Ending a steady dating relationship	85	
Serious illness in a close friend or family member	85	
Financial difficulties	84	
Writing a major term paper	83	
Being caught cheating on a test	83	
Drunk driving	82	
Sense of overload in school or work	82	
Two exams in one day	80	
Cheating on your boyfriend or girlfriend	77	
Getting married	76	
Negative consequences of drinking or drug use	75	
Depression or crisis in your best friend	73	
Difficulties with parents	73	

Event	Stress Ratings	Your Items
Talking in front of class	72	
Lack of sleep	69	
Change in housing situation (hassles, moves)	69	
Competing or performing in public	69	
Getting in a physical fight	66	
Difficulties with a roommate	66	
Job changes (applying, new job, work hassles)	65	
Declaring a major or concerns about future plans	65	
A class you hate	62	
Drinking or use of drugs	61	
Confrontations with professors	60	
Starting a new semester	58	
Going on a first date	57	
Registration	55	
Maintaining a steady dating relationship	55	
Commuting to campus, or work, or both	54	
Peer pressures	53	
Being away from home for the first time	53	
Getting sick	52	
Concerns about your appearance	52	
Getting straight A's	51	
A difficult class that you love	48	
Making new friends; getting along with friends	47	
Fraternity or sorority rush	47	
Falling asleep in class	40	
Attending an athletic event (e.g., football game)	20	
Total		

Source: From M. J. Renner and R. S. Mackin in *Teaching of Psychology*, 25, 46–48. Copyright ©1998. Used by permission of Lawrence Erlbaum Associates, Inc.

students (90 percent of the people in the sample were under the age of 22 years).

Although the assessment of stress by the use of life events scales has merits, there is one problem in this kind of measurement instrument. Scales, such as the SRRS and the CUSS, are based on the assumption that the same event is equally stressful to all individuals who experience it. Although there may be compelling reasons for making this assumption, it does not fit with commonsense notions about stressful events or the views of researchers. According to cognitive models of stress, it is not just the event itself, but also the way it is interpreted that determines its impact. One person may view the death of a spouse as a horrible calamity; another person may see it as distressing but not devastating. Further, the context of the event plays a role in determining its impact. For example, if the death of a spouse follows a long, debilitating illness, the survivor may feel a sense of relief.

Coping   Another factor in the mind-body equation is how people attempt to reduce the sensation of stress through coping. There are many ways to think about coping, but one of the most useful is that which distinguishes between **problem-focused coping** and **emotion-focused coping** (Lazarus & Folkman, 1984). In problem-focused coping, the individual reduces stress by acting to change whatever it is that makes the situation stressful. The person might make alternative plans or find a new and better way to correct the situation. In either case, the individual makes the attempt to "fix things." By contrast, in emotion-focused coping, a person does not change anything about the situation itself but, instead, tries to improve his or her feelings about the situation. "Thinking positively" is one emotion-focused coping method people use to make themselves feel better under stressful conditions. Avoidance is another emotion-focused strategy. This coping method is similar to the defense mechanism of denial, in which the individual refuses to acknowledge that a problem or difficulty exists. In extreme form, avoidance as a coping strategy can involve escape into drugs or alcohol and can lead to additional problems in the person's life.

Which coping style more effectively reduces stress depends on the nature of the stressor itself. In some cases, particularly when there is nothing one can do about a problem, feeling as good about it as possible is probably best. Consider the case of Elena, who broke her ankle while roller-blading. Dealing with the stress may become more tolerable if she reframes the temporary disability as an opportunity to slow down her hectic life. When the situation is more controllable, problem-focused coping is more adaptive (Folkman, Lazarus, Gruen, & DeLongis, 1986). For example, if Leonard is refinancing his mortgage, he may become very upset because the interest rates suddenly rise. Rather than save money, he stands to lose thousands of dollars. Problem-focused coping would involve Leonard's developing alternative financial plans to resolve his monetary problems.

As people get older, they are able to use more functional coping strategies. In comparing a sample of community-dwelling older adults with college undergraduates, Segal and colleagues (2001) found that younger adults received higher

People who use emotion-focused coping strategies often resort to escape through drugs or alcohol to handle the stress in their lives.

scores on the dysfunctional coping strategies of focusing on and venting emotions, mentally disengaging, and using alcohol and drugs. Older adults, by contrast, were more likely to use impulse control and turning to their religion as coping strategies. These findings are in keeping with those of other researchers (Labouvie-Vief & Diehl, 2000), which indicated that older adults use more problem-focused coping and other strategies that allow them to channel their negative feeling into productive activities.

Coping strategies can play an important role in whether or not an individual will suffer health problems. A person who is able to manage stress effectively experiences fewer adverse consequences of stress. Furthermore, as you may know from personal experience, situations that create high levels of activation in a person do not always have negative consequences. Some people thrive on a lifestyle filled with challenges and new experiences, feeling energized by being under constant pressure (DeLongis, Folkman, & Lazarus, 1988). Perhaps you perform (or think you perform) at your best when you are facing an urgent deadline.

Stress and the Immune System   We still have not addressed the questions of why and how the experience of stress can lead to physiological abnormalities. To look into this issue, we can draw from the field of **psychoneuroimmunology,** the study of the connections among stress *(psycho),* nervous system functioning *(neuro),* and the immune system *(immuno).* To an increasing degree, researchers in medicine and psychology are beginning to understand such disorders as heart and respiratory disease, some forms of diabetes, and gastrointestinal disorders as being influenced by stress-related responses initiated in the central nervous system. It is becoming clearer that experiences of stress, negative affect, depression, lack of social support, and repression and denial can influence immune status and function (Schneiderman, Ironson, & Siegel, 2005).

A stressful event can initiate a set of reactions within the body that lower its resistance to disease. These reactions can also aggravate the symptoms of a chronic, stress-related physical disorder. One explanation of these relationships is that stress stimulates hormones regulated by the hypothalamus, and these hormones lower the activity of the immune system. With less protection, the body is less resistant to infection, allergens, and the more serious intruders, such as carcinogens. Nervous system reactions also alter immune system functioning through nerve endings in the parts of the body involved in the immune system, such as the lymph nodes, thymus, and spleen. Stress also raises the levels of cortisol, a hormone involved in mobilizing the body's response to a threat or a challenge. These processes appear to account for a wide range of physical disorders, including cancer, hypertension, and rheumatoid arthritis (Costa & VandenBos, 1996). Severe life stress and depression can accelerate the symptoms in people who have HIV disease (Evans et al., 1997; Leserman et al., 1997).

Researchers have used some innovative methods to assess the relationship between illness and stress. For example, Sheldon Cohen, a researcher at Carnegie Mellon University, conducted an intensive study of the relationship between stress and the common cold (Cohen et al., 1998). In this study, 276 volunteers completed a life stressor interview and psychological questionnaires, and they provided blood and urine samples. After the subjects were injected with common cold viruses, the researchers monitored them and found that severe chronic stressors that lasted at least a month were associated with a greater likelihood of their becoming ill; however, stressful events lasting less than a month did not seem to have this negative effect on health. The most salient stressors were employment problems and enduring interpersonal problems with family or friends. In a subsequent investigation, Cohen and his colleagues (2003) found that people who are inherently less sociable, based on personality test scores, were more susceptible to developing a cold, regardless of how good their social interactions were on a daily basis.

The relationship between stress and health goes both ways. People under stress also tend to neglect good health habits, possibly smoking more, drinking more alcohol, eating less nutritious meals, and getting less sleep. When in a state of stress, most people are more susceptible to becoming sick, possibly due to an increased vulnerability to infectious diseases. They turn to other people for support, and, ironically, their increased social interaction with others increases their exposure to viruses and infectious agents. Some people in states of stress seek out sexual intimacy, possibly indiscriminately and with inadequate attention to safe sex practices. If stressed individuals become sick, regardless of the cause, they are less likely to comply with recommended treatment, putting themselves at even greater physical risk (Cohen & Williamson, 1991).

Emotional Expression The inhibition of emotional expression seems to be another key ingredient in the relationship between psychological functioning and health.

If emotional suppression is unhealthy, it seems reasonable to conclude that expressing emotion is beneficial to one's physical and mental well-being. Research connecting emotional expression with immune system functioning is bearing out the common belief that you should "get it off your chest" when you feel unhappy or upset. In a series of innovative experiments, psychologist James Pennebaker and his colleagues have shown that actively confronting emotions that arise from an upsetting or a traumatic event can have long-term health benefits (Pennebaker, 1997a, 1997b). For example, writing about a distressing experience facilitates coping and contributes to physical health. In one study, researchers asked college freshmen to write about the experience of coming to college and asked a control group of students to write about superficial topics. Although those who wrote about their college adjustment experiences reported higher levels of homesickness than the control subjects, they made fewer visits to physicians. By the end of the year, the experimental subjects were doing as well as or better than the control subjects in terms of grade point average and the experience of positive moods. The researchers concluded that confronting feelings and thoughts regarding a stressful experience can have long-lasting positive effects, even though the initial impact of such confrontation may be disruptive (Pennebaker, Colder, & Sharp, 1990). Pennebaker and his colleagues have expanded their findings to a variety of populations. For example, in one study, psychiatric prison inmates were less likely to visit the infirmary when placed in an experimental condition in which they wrote about their past traumatic experiences (Richards, Beal, Seagal, & Pennebaker, 2000).

Personality Style People who frequently feel a sense of impatience, irritability, or pressure to get something done in a hurry may be at risk for developing heart problems. This pattern of being hard-driving, competitive, impatient, cynical, suspicious of and hostile toward others, and easily irritated, is described as Type A (see Table 6.3). Oddly, although individuals with a Type A personality are highly competitive, they seem driven by an internal set of standards; compared with more relaxed individuals (Type B), Type A individuals are less likely to cheat in academic situations (Davis et al., 1995). They want to do well based on their own abilities rather than take the easy way out.

Converging evidence from several large studies points to the higher risk that people with Type A behavior patterns have for developing hypertension and associated heart problems (Smith, Glazer, Ruiz, & Gallo, 2004), problems that increase their mortality rate. Type A individuals tend to react explosively to stressful situations; in doing so, they set off "alarms" throughout their bodies. The sympathetic nervous systems of Type A people are in a state of alert, which puts physiological stress on sensitive bodily organs, which can result in coronary heart disease, cerebral atherosclerosis ("hardening" of the blood vessels in the brain), and atherosclerosis in other parts of the body (Treiber et al., 2003). In fact, some researchers maintain that Type A personality attributes can reliably predict not only if but when an individual

MindMAP Segment 6.2: Type A Behavior

TABLE 6.3 Are You Type A?

The Jenkins Activity Survey assesses the degree to which a person has a coronary-prone personality and behavior pattern. People with high scores, referred to as Type A, tend to be competitive, impatient, restless, aggressive, and pressured by time and responsibilities. In the items below, you can see which responses would reflect these characteristics.

Do you have trouble finding time to get your hair cut or styled?

Has your spouse or friend ever told you that you eat too fast?

How often do you actually "put words in the person's mouth" in order to speed things up?

Would people you know well agree that you tend to get irritated easily?

How often do you find yourself hurrying to get to places even when there is plenty of time?

At work, do you ever keep two jobs moving forward at the same time by shifting back and forth rapidly from one to the other?

Source: From C. D. Jenkins, S. J. Zyzanski and R. H. Rosenman, *The Jenkins Activity Survey*. Copyright ©1965, 1966, 1969, 1979 by The Psychological Corporation, © 2001 by C. D. Jenkins, S. J. Zyzanski and R. H. Rosenman. Reprinted by permission of the author.

will develop coronary heart disease (Gallacher et al., 2003). Associated psychological attributes, including hostility and the need to dominate others, appear to heighten the risk of heart disease for people with the Type A behavior pattern.

People with Type A behavior patterns, particularly those with high levels of hostility, commonly engage in unhealthy behaviors, such as smoking and consuming large amounts of alcohol, behaviors that are well established as detrimental. They also are more likely to engage in high-risk behaviors, such as reckless driving, so it is no surprise that many of these individuals die in accidents and violent situations (Magnavita et al., 1997). Even those who are not especially wild are prone to contend with intense levels of anger, vexed by even the slightest annoyance, an emotional style that has been shown to play a role in provoking a heart attack (Verrier & Mittleman, 1996).

Researchers are now beginning to focus on a new personality type—the Type "D" (distressed) personality. These are individuals who are at increased risk for heart disease due to their tendency to experience negative emotions while inhibiting the expression of these emotions when they are in social situations. In addition to being at higher risk of becoming ill or dying from heart disease, these individuals suffer reduced quality of daily life and benefit less from medical treatments. The link between personality and heart disease for these people is thought to be, in part, due to an impaired immune response to stress (Pedersen & Denollet, 2003; Sher, 2005).

Sociocultural Factors   Sociocultural factors also play a role in causing and aggravating stress-related disorders. For example, living in a harsh social environment that threatens a person's safety, interferes with the establishment of social relationships, and involves high levels of conflict, abuse, and violence are conditions related to lower socioeconomic status. Chronic exposure to the stresses of such an environment can lead to chronically higher cortisol levels, but also, paradoxically, a reduced ability to respond to new threats or challenges (Kristenson et al., 2004). In one large-scale longitudinal study of nearly 1,400 adults ranging in age from 15 to 74 years, a team of Dutch investigators found that low occupational level and income predicted loss of physical mobility. These declines were observed even when controlling for such factors as severity of disease and health-related behavior (Koster et al., 2005). Furthermore, environmental stressors related to racial conflict and discrimination may interact with genetic factors to increase the risk of hypertension. African Americans living in the United States have higher rates of hypertension than Blacks living in other parts of the world where there is less racial discrimination (Cooper, Rotimi, & Ward, 1999).

Treatment   Because the conditions in the category of psychological factors affecting medical conditions include such a vast array of physical problems, no single treatment model exists. During the past two decades, clinicians have increasingly realized that medical treatments alone are insufficient and that they must also introduce and reinforce new health behaviors (Charney, 2004). Psychologists have collaborated with physicians to develop an interdisciplinary approach to these conditions known as **behavioral medicine** (Compas et al., 1998; Gentry, 1984). Behavioral medicine techniques are rooted in behavioral theory and use learning principles to help the client gain psychological control over unhealthy bodily reactions. Clients learn to take responsibility for their health, to initiate and maintain health-producing behaviors, and to terminate

For a person with a Type A behavior pattern, minor frustrations, such as a traffic jam, can evoke a storm of outrage with accompanying physical and psychological disturbance.

unhealthy ones. They learn to be alert to unhealthy bodily processes and to take action to avoid or modify circumstances in which they are likely to become sick. Individuals learn to monitor early signs of mounting tension and to initiate steps to avert the further development of pain, including learning various emotion and problem-focused coping strategies, such as leaving a stressful situation or reframing one's perspective on a situation that is inescapable.

Behavioral medicine techniques are being incorporated into standard medical treatments, as in the case of insomnia, chronic pain (Jacobs, Benson, & Friedman, 1996), and chronic migraine headaches (Kropp et al., 1997). Patients with chronic disorders that require constant medical management can also benefit from behavioral techniques to increase compliance, as in the case of diabetes (Jenkins, 1995).

The successful treatment of people whose physical problems are associated with the Type A behavior pattern integrates education, training in coping strategies, and behavioral interventions (Friedman et al., 1996; Roskies et al., 1989). The educational component includes helping clients understand coronary problems and the relationship between these problems and Type A behavior. The coping strategies include relaxation training and cognitive restructuring techniques. For example, instead of responding with anger to standing in line at the bank, a person could learn to be more relaxed about it. Imaging is a behavioral intervention in which the client learns to imagine a troublesome situation and to practice adaptive coping strategies for managing stress in that situation. Behavior modification gives individuals opportunities to rehearse more adaptive behaviors to use when provoked (Nunes, Frank, & Kornfeld, 1987). Such interventions can be reasonably effective, particularly if the client is given sufficient opportunity to incorporate relaxation exercises into his or her everyday life (Carlson & Hoyle, 1993).

Other treatment approaches involve preventive strategies. People can learn that exercising and taking advantage of available social supports help offset the harmful effects of stress on the body. Psychologists are also studying methods of intervention that can promote the resilience individuals can develop to living in stressful conditions such as urban environments with high crime rates (Wandersman & Nation, 1998). Applying principles from the emerging field of positive psychology, clinicians are designing interventions that enhance feelings of well-being and reduce depression by cultivating pleasure, engagement, and meaning (Duckworth, Steen, & Seligman, 2005).

Ongoing research within the field of psychoneuroimmunology is evaluating the effectiveness of psychological interventions on immune system functioning (Miller & Cohen, 2001). A meta-analysis of more than 85 studies on interventions including stress management, relaxation training, disclosure interventions, hypnosis, and behavioral (conditioning) techniques revealed only modest effects on key immune system variables. Hypnosis and conditioning were found to have the greatest effectiveness. However, limiting the demonstration of effects from most of these studies was the fact that the participants were either med-

Exercise can help relieve potentially harmful effects of stress on the body.

ically ill or not experiencing stressors severe enough to affect their immune systems. The effects of psychological interventions will be more dramatically shown when these interventions are applied to individuals with conditions known to affect the immune system, such as dermatological conditions and allergies. Stepping outside the field of psychoneuroimmunology, there may nevertheless be mental health benefits to the methods suggested by this model for treatment of individuals with stress-related clinical problems.

Dissociative Disorders

The conditions you have read about so far in this chapter involve a range of disorders involving emotions, such as anxiety and stress, that have varying degrees of disturbance and impact on a person's life. Dissociative disorders are far more extreme, involving anxiety or conflict so severe that part of the individual's personality actually separates from the rest of his or her conscious functioning. The individual with a dissociative disorder experiences a temporary alteration in consciousness involving a loss of personal identity, decreased awareness of immediate surroundings, and odd bodily movements. Once the dissociation has occurred, the contents of the dissociated part become inaccessible to the rest of the client's conscious mind.

Psychologists have learned some fascinating clues to understanding normal personality functioning from studying individuals with dissociative disorders. We generally take for granted the idea that within one person's body, only one personality can exist. However, dissociative disorders show that this assumption about human nature does not apply to everyone.

Dissociative Identity Disorder

In **dissociative identity disorder,** the assumption is that a person develops more than one self or personality. These personalities are referred to as **alters,** in contrast to the core personality, called the **host.** This condition was formerly called multiple personality disorder, a term that continues to be used by some lay authors and even a few health professionals. The disorder was made famous in novels and movies, such as *Sybil* (Schreiber, 1973) and *The Three Faces of Eve* (Thigpen & Cleckley, 1957), each of which tells the fantastic story of a woman who had several distinct "personalities." As you will see in the sections that follow, considerable controversy has emerged about the validity of the multiple personality phenomenon. Even the famous cases of Sybil and Eve, regarded by some as prompting the tremendous increase in the incidence of this diagnosis during the past few decades, have been contested by some psychiatric historians who regard the cases as exaggeration and possible fabrication. In dissociative identity disorder, each alter is understood to be a consistent and enduring pattern of perceiving, relating to, and thinking about the environment and the self.

Characteristics of Dissociative Identity Disorder
The individual with dissociative identity disorder has at least two distinct identities or personality states, each with its own pattern of perceiving, thinking, and relating, as well as its own style of behavior, personal history, and self-image. Most cases involve fewer than 10 identities, but reports range well into the hundreds. At different times, one of these identities or personality states takes control of the person's behavior. People with dissociative personality disorder have a primary identity associated with their given name. This primary identity, or host, is customarily passive and dependent, possibly also depressed and guilty. The alters are usually strikingly different, possibly acting in ways that are hostile, demanding, or self-destructive. They may have different ages, races, levels of intelligence, and affective styles, and they may even be of the opposite gender. The transition from one alter to another is usually sudden, triggered by

Mark Peterson, a 31-year-old grocery worker from Oshkosh, Wisconsin, defends himself in court against a rape charge brought against him by Sarah, a woman with multiple personality disorder. He met 26-year-old "Franny" at a bar and asked her for a date. Franny told Peterson about fun-loving, 20-year-old "Jennifer," and, reportedly, he summoned Jennifer and invited her to have sex with him. During intercourse, 6-year-old "Emily" emerged; he reportedly told Jennifer to keep her activites secret from Sarah. But Franny and Emily told Sarah, who pressed charges against him. Although the jury voted to convict Peterson, the judge overturned the verdict on the grounds that the defense was not allowed to have Sarah examined by a psychiatrist before the trial.

psychosocial stress or a personally salient stimulus. At any given moment, only one alter interacts with the external environment, although the others may actively perceive what is happening or influence what is going on. Most of the personalities have a sense of lost or distorted experiences of time. An alter may piece together memories to make up for unaccounted gaps, or an alter may have access to memories of the other alters.

Psychiatrist Richard Kluft played a major role in disseminating information about dissociative identity disorder in the scientific community. Kluft described several key features of this disorder, including the nature of the personalities that reside within the same individual and their relationships to each other. The classic host personality, who seeks professional help, tends to be depressed, anxious, compulsively "good," masochistic, and moralistic. The most frequently seen alters include children, "protectors," "helpers," expressers of forbidden impulses, personalities based on lost loved ones, carriers of lost memories or family secrets, avengers who express anger over abusive experiences, and defenders of the abusers (Kluft, 1984a).

People with dissociative identity disorder also experience a form of amnesia, in which they have gaps in their memory about some aspects of their personal history. Some individuals have gaps that span years, or even a decade or more. This inability to recall important personal information cannot be explained by ordinary forgetfulness. Sometimes only when other people tell them about events do they become aware of something they have done or said. For example, the husband of a woman with dissociative identity disorder witnessed his wife going to the hardware store and buying a set of tools, yet she insisted that someone else must have purchased them and couldn't fathom what he was talking about.

In 1980, the condition that was then called multiple personality disorder began to gain a great deal of recognition, with the publication of four major papers on the topic (Bliss, 1980; Coons, 1980; Greaves, 1980; Rosenbaum, 1980). That year, the disorder was first included in the *DSM* and was defined in such a way that it was no longer reserved for cases as extreme as those of Eve and Sybil. The diagnosis could then be applied in situations in which a person experienced a disorganization of the self and attributed discrepant experiences to separate individuals residing within the self. Along with this broadening of the definition came a proliferation of cases of multiple personality disorder, to the point that it became referred to as an "epidemic" (Boor, 1982). In the 50 years prior to 1970, only a handful of cases had been reported, but since 1970, the number of reports increased astronomically, into the thousands. In fact, more cases of this disorder were reported during one 5-year period in the 1980s than had been documented in the preceding two centuries (Putnam et al., 1986). Clinicians and researchers began to wonder if this increase was actually due to the increased prevalence of the disorder or whether it was an artificial phenomenon due to the broadening of the definition of the disorder. Some maintained that popular first-person characterizations of the disorder, media attention, and efforts by dedicated clinicians and people claiming to have had this disorder contributed to an inappropriate degree of emphasis on this rare but fascinating condition (Frankel, 1996).

Considerable skepticism about this diagnosis has emerged in recent years, particularly within certain mental health groups. For example, in one survey (Lalonde, Hudson, Gigante, & Pope, 2001), only one of every seven Canadian psychiatrists felt that the validity of dissociative diagnoses was supported by scientific evidence. The Canadian psychiatrists were much more critical than American psychiatrists.

A leading skeptic on the topic of multiple personality disorder (MPD) was the late Canadian psychologist Nicholas Spanos, who believed that social factors shape the display of MPD. Following exhaustive reviews of twentieth-century reports and studies of multiple personality disorder, Spanos asserted that this condition became a legitimate way for people to rationalize their failures and manipulate the sympathy of others (Spanos, 1996). Even more alarming is the question raised by Spanos and others (Orne, Dinges, & Orne, 1984; Simpson, 1989) about whether psychotherapists play a central role in generating and maintaining the symptoms of multiple personalities. Are some clients responding to their therapists' suggestions that their problems are attributable to dissociative identity disorder, rather than more common disorders, such as depression or personality disorder? According to this view, some clients are highly sug-

gestible and may pick up on cues from their therapist to construe their problems as resulting from dissociation. Sometimes, without even realizing it, therapists engage in leading and suggestive procedures that persuade some clients to develop the notion of multiplicity (Merskey, 1992). Hypnotic interviews are the most common procedure for eliciting multiple personalities, and it is not uncommon during such exercises for the therapist to suggest explicitly that the alter come forth. Over time, the clients tell stories about alternate personalities and may actually develop behaviors that fit these different personalities.

Following on the heels of professional attention to the possibility of overdiagnosis were reports in the media of individuals fabricating the diagnosis to seek external gain, such as being excused from responsibility for a crime. These reports further questioned the validity of a diagnosis that apparently could be so easily faked. These sensationalistic reports aside, some experts maintained that the increase in reported prevalence of a multiple personality condition was a valid phenomenon due to the fact that diagnostic standards for the disorder had improved in the 1980s. To help refine and standardize the diagnosis of this disorder, psychiatrist Marlene Steinberg (1994) developed the Structured Clinical Interview for *DSM-IV* Dissociative Disorders–Revised (SCID-D-R). Some of the key questions, reproduced in Table 6.4, give further insight into the nature of the symptoms associated with this disorder.

The emergence of new diagnostic instruments led clinicians and researchers to discover what they presumed were previously undiagnosed cases of the disorder. One study reported that 300 people who ultimately were diagnosed as having this disorder had experienced symptoms for an average of almost 7 years until they received a diagnosis of multiple personality disorder. During those years, these individuals were given many other diagnoses, including depression, "neurotic disorder," personality disorder, schizophrenia, "hysterical schizophrenia," substance abuse, bipolar disorder, and epilepsy (Putnam et al., 1986; Ross et al., 1990).

Admittedly, the diagnosis of dissociative identity disorder presents a challenge to clinicians. Dissociative or dissociative-like symptoms can occur in epilepsy, major depressive disorder, schizophrenia, somatoform disorder, borderline personality disorder, and post-traumatic stress disorder (Brodsky, Cloitre, & Dulit, 1995; Devinsky et al., 1989; Kluft, 1987a; Lauer, Black, & Keen, 1993; Shalev et al., 1998). The problem of diagnosis is complicated because the symptoms are not consistent over time, the individual might attempt to hide the symptoms, and the dissociative symptoms might be mixed with a mood disturbance or personality disorder. Some individuals might have a high level of functioning in various areas of life, and the symptoms of dissociative identity disorder might never be suspected (Kluft, 1986). Careful diagnosis to distinguish dissociative conditions from disorders involving clear physical causes, such as epilepsy, is therefore considered crucial (Bowman & Coons, 2000).

As a way to put to rest some of the arguments, pro and con, about the existence of the disorder, the authors of the *DSM-IV* chose to apply the label "dissociative identity disorder" rather than

TABLE 6.4 Items from the SCID-D-R

Scale	Item
Amnesia	Have you ever felt as if there were large gaps in your memory?
Depersonalization	Have you ever felt that you were watching yourself from a point outside of your body, as if you were seeing yourself from a distance (or watching a movie of yourself)? Have you ever felt as if a part of your body or your whole being was foreign to you? Have you ever felt as if you were two different people, one going through the motions of life, and the other part observing quietly?
Derealization	Have you ever felt as if familiar surroundings or people you knew seemed unfamiliar or unreal? Have you ever felt puzzled as to what is real and what's unreal in your surroundings? Have you ever felt as if your surroundings or other people were fading away?
Identity confusion	Have you ever felt as if there was a struggle going on inside of you? Have you ever felt confused as to who you are?
Identity alteration	Have you ever acted as if you were a completely different person? Have you ever been told by others that you seem like a different person? Have you ever found things in your possession (for instance, shoes) that belong to you, but you could not remember how you got them?

Source: From M. Steinberg, "Structured Clinical Interview for DSM-IV Dissociative Disorders—Revised (SCID-D-R)." Copyright © 1994 American Psychiatric Publishing, Inc. Reprinted with permission.

the more popular term "multiple personality disorder." The new term captures the essence of an individual's detachment and disorganization without getting caught up in the issue of multiplicity. Adding the criterion of amnesia to the list of symptoms further refined the diagnostic label (Cardena & Spiegel, 1996). In the section "Dissociative Identity Disorder and the Legal System," we discuss recent efforts to determine the validity of this diagnosis and establish criteria and standards for assessing this condition.

Theories and Treatment of Dissociative Identity Disorder

The primary explanation of dissociative identity disorder focuses on disturbances in childhood in the development of the sense of self. As children, most of us develop a sense of self through interactions with parents and peers; in this process, we maintain a sense of continuity over time. People with dissociative identity disorder fail to develop an integrated and continuous sense of self, because they were severely traumatized at some point in their childhood. Many, if not most, clients with dissociative identity disorder report having been victims of childhood sexual or physical abuse. (Ellason, Ross, & Fuchs, 1996; Kluft, 1997; Lewis et al., 1997; Lussier, Steiner, Grey, & Hansen, 1997; Scroppo, Drob, Weinberger, & Eagle, 1998; Simeon et al., 2001). Intensive studies of hundreds of individuals who meet the diagnostic criteria for the disorder reveal a common history of extreme abuse in childhood (Coons, Bowman, Pellow, & Schneider, 1989; Ross et al., 1990; Terr, 1991; van der Hart, Boon, & Heijtmajer Jansen, 1997; Wilbur & Kluft, 1989). Some critics of such research findings, however, contend that the data are based on retrospective reports in which connections

are made between current disturbance and memories of trauma. The problem with this premise is that most people can think of traumatic events that could be construed as contributors to current psychological problems; even when the trauma is striking, it is difficult to determine with certainty that the trauma is the cause of the dissociation or amnesia (Kihlstrom, 2005).

Theorists on the other side of the debate assert that there is a compelling argument for the notion that there is a connection between childhood trauma and the development of dissociated identity. They contend that perhaps such traumatized children develop alters as an escape, through fantasy, from the horrors of their daily reality. They learn to enter a dissociative, self-hypnotic state filled with fantasy and thoughts of being someone else. According to one theorist, the "I" disappears into the background in the child's perceptual experience (Beere, 1995). Repeated victimization might lead the child to enter this state more and more frequently. As this happens, the split-off, dissociated parts of experience and memory develop independently, and the child's personality and sense of self fail to become integrated (Ross, 1997b). Biological factors may also play a role, as the extreme stress to which the child was exposed during incidents of abuse may have triggered alterations in brain functioning (Bremner, Krystal, Charney, & Southwick, 1996).

As compelling as this explanation might be, some cautions are warranted. Only a small percentage of traumatized children develop such dissociative disorders. Although many people with dissociative identity disorder have a history of abuse, the converse does not necessarily hold true. Researchers do not yet understand

The terror of family violence can drive some children into a dissociative state in which their fantasies provide them with an escape from the harsh realities of their lives.

what makes certain children vulnerable to developing this disorder. An unknown factor, which could be either biological or psychological, seems to predispose a subset of traumatized children to develop different personalities in response to their experiences of abuse, whereas others are able to cope successfully and develop normal personalities (Binder, McNiel, & Goldstone, 1996). One group of researchers has noted that people who develop pathological dissociative symptoms are especially hypnotizable, leading them to hypothesize that hypnotizability may increase vulnerability to this disorder, particularly in instances when such individuals experience acute stress (Butler et al., 1996).

Earlier, criticisms by Spanos and others of the concept of dissociate identity disorder were mentioned as part of the recent history of the diagnosis. In line with their critique, proponents of Spanos' ideas have put forth the **sociocognitive model of dissociative identity disorder** (Lilienfeld et al., 1999). According to this model, clients enact the roles that they feel (consciously or unconsciously) are demanded by the situation. Social attention to the condition of dissociative identity disorder, along with unintentional prompting by therapists, can lead to the development of this disorder in vulnerable individuals. According to the sociocognitive model, these individuals may in fact have suffered abuse as children, but many other factors, socially determined, operate to create the dissociative symptoms in the adult.

Joining the debate about treatment for dissociative conditions are critics of the theory that dissociation arises from the experience of trauma, quite commonly in the form of childhood sexual abuse. These critics argue that there really is no compelling evidence that childhood sexual abuse is related to the development of amnesia or dissociation; thus, if there is no causal

link, they assert that it is "pointless to focus therapy on the recovery and working through of traumatic experiences that may well be false or distorted" (Kihlstrom, 2005, p. 236).

Yet another issue that is vehemently debated in discussions about psychogenic dissociation is the concept of repressed memories, the notion that some individuals are so overwhelmed by trauma that the experience is self-protectively pushed out of awareness. Some professionals insist that repressed memories of childhood abuse are common, and that individuals can "recover" these memories in a way that is therapeutic. Those on the other side of the debate believe that working with clients to recover memories may actually involve ethical violations if clients are led to believe that events occurred that cannot be substantiated.

Empirical research on the phenomenon of repressed or blocked memories is complicated by the retrospective nature of such investigations, yet some experts who have reviewed the literature assert that research provides quite adequate support for the validity of the notions of memory blocking and recovery (Gleaves, Smith, Butler, & Spiegel, 2004). On the other side are theorists who assert that there is considerable "folklore" about the notion that certain experiences are so overwhelmingly traumatic that many victims dissociate their memory from the experience. These critics contend that misguided clinicians may be misinterpreting impaired-memory phenomena that occur following a traumatic event. They suggest that perhaps the memory loss is medically rather than emotionally caused; perhaps it is due to ordinary forgetfulness rather than an inability to remember the trauma; perhaps it is a choice to avoid thinking about something rather than an inability to remember it (McNally, 2004).

REAL STORIES

ANNE HECHE: DISSOCIATIVE SYMPTOMS

As you are aware from reading about dissociative identity disorder, this diagnosis has engendered considerable controversy in the mental health field. On one side of the debate are clinicians who view dissociative identity disorder as a very real condition experienced by many people, particularly individuals who develop separate identities following horrific experiences of abuse. On the other side are those professionals who assert that the diagnosis is bogus, perpetuated by misguided clinicians who induce multiple personalities in suggestible clients. Some of the complex issues associated with this diagnosis are evident in the life story of award-winning actress Anne Heche, who has spoken openly about her experiences of a different identity and personality. Although some of Heche's close relatives have raised significant doubts about Anne's claims, her powerful story captures the essence of what makes the diagnosis of dissociative identity disorder so difficult. In thinking about Heche's story, keep in mind the challenge professionals encounter when responding to stories for which there is no substantiation other than the words of the person telling the story. For the sake of the current discussion, it is reasonable to believe the accuracy of Heche's report, primarily because of the emotional pain and turmoil that she associates with her traumatic memories.

In Heche's autobiography, *Call Me Crazy* (2001), she describes horrific experiences that she believes caused her to escape into another personality in order to feel safe. Heche suggests that the personality served as a haven to which she could escape from recurrent sexual abuse by her father, which she states took place from the time she was a toddler until she was 12.

The public persona of her father was that of an upright citizen who was highly regarded in his role as a choir director in a Baptist church. However, according to Heche, her father also had a secret "second life" as a promiscuous man who ultimately died from AIDS in the early 1980s when Heche was 13 years old. Heche contends that she feared for her life when she learned that her father had AIDS, particularly in light of the fact that she believed she had contracted herpes from him during the episodes when he molested her.

Heche tells a story of a family that lived a lie. To other people, the Heche family seemed like the ideal American family, but the inner picture was quite different. They had so little money that they were evicted from their home and forced to spend one year living with neighbors. Heche felt unloved and exploited during her childhood, and she turned to acting in an attempt to escape.

Anne Heche

REAL STORIES

ANNE HECHE (continued)

At age 17 Heche landed a role play ing twins on the soap opera *Another World,* for which she won an Emmy. Al- though she was now distanced from the pain of her childhood, Heche was still experiencing its effects. By the time she was 25, Heche says, her personality be- gan to fragment into another personality named Celestia, who spoke a different language and had special powers.

Despite Heche's troubled youth and her self-described "insanity," she man- aged to climb the ladder of success in the film industry, acting in well-known movies such as *Donnie Brasco,* the re- make of *Psycho, Wag the Dog,* and *Six Days, Seven Nights.* To the world, she was a star who had it all. In her private life, however, she was riding an emo- tional roller-coaster in which the resid- ual impact of a troubled childhood was causing havoc. She moved from an inti- mate relationship with comedian Steve Martin, 24 years older than her, to a highly publicized lesbian relationship with actress Ellen DeGeneres.

The essence of Heche's dissociative condition is captured in her own com- pelling words:

By the time I finished shooting *Six Days, Seven Nights* I felt like three completely different people, all exist-

ing at the same time. I was Anne-n- Ellen, the second half of the most fa- mous gay couple in the world. I was Anne Heche, the closeted abuse vic- tim with the burning desire to be a successful actress, writer and direc- tor. And I was Celestia, a spirit be- ing from the fourth dimension here to teach the world about love. The fight to keep all of me alive over the next three and a half years almost killed me. . . .

When I didn't get the love I needed, I became Celestia.

In her book Heche describes a psychotic-like experience following her breakup with Ellen DeGeneres. Heche believed that she was supposed to drive to a random house in Fresno, California, to take the drug Ecstasy. She then took Ecstasy after the drive to Fresno to wait for a spaceship that would come for her. When Heche arrived at the house, the people living there called the police to report that a strange woman had come to their home. Heche describes her interactions with the police during this disturbing episode:

"Anne? Anne Heche?" I was still massaging the woman's feet when the cops came through the door.

"Yes," I said as I turned around. "How can I help you?"

"You are Anne Heche? Is that correct?"

"I was Anne, yes. Now I'm Celestia."

"Could you take your hands off that woman please?"

"Certainly." I said. "I wasn't hurt- ing her, you know that, right?"

"Could you stand up and put your hands behind your back?"

"Certainly, I can." I slowly stood up and put my hands behind my back. "But I don't understand, Offi- cer. What seems to be the prob- lem?" As the officer cuffs my hands I begin to get afraid.

"Do you know where you are, Anne?"

"Yes, I know, Officer."

"Where are you? Could you tell me please?"

"Certainly I can. I am at this nice house where I am waiting for my spaceship. They have been lovely enough to host me until the arrival."

Despite all these debates, some clinicians have reported considerable success in treating individuals presenting disso- ciative symptoms by using an approach that rests on the no- tion that dissociative identity disorder is a response to trauma. Kluft contends that treatment is a form of post-traumatic ther- apy, in which the clinician works with the client to recover. Therapy involves helping the client integrate the alters into a unified whole and develop adequate coping strategies to deal with the painful memories of the past and the stresses of cur- rent life without resorting to fragmentation. The most com- mon treatment approach involves techniques derived from psychoanalytic psychotherapy, often including **hypnother- apy,** in which the client is hypnotized and encouraged to re-

call painful past experiences while in a trance state. Clinicians using this approach contend that the various alters with their associated memories are brought out one-by-one and are uni- fied into a consistent whole. Each alter may require a separate treatment, and the therapist may need to establish a positive working relationship with each. Because some alters may be abrasive and antagonistic, while others may be dependent and seductive, each may respond differently to alternate interven- tions (Kluft, 1984b).

It is important to note that use of hypnosis in this context is quite controversial. In fact, some theorists and researchers assert that hypnosis may actually cause the emergence of symptoms that characterize dissociative identity disorder (Powell & Gee,

Mini Case

DISSOCIATIVE IDENTITY DISORDER

Myra is a young single woman who works as a clerk in a large bookstore. She lives by herself, never goes out socially except to see her relatives, and dresses in a conservative manner, which her associates ridicule as "prudish." In her early teens, she was involved in an intimate relationship with a middle-aged man who was quite abusive toward her. Although others remind her of this troubled relationship, Myra claims that she has no recollection of that person, and she has even wondered at times whether others have made up the story to annoy her. At the age of 25, Myra says that she is "saving" herself sexually for marriage, yet she seems totally uninterested in pursuing any close relationships with men. So far, this describes Myra as her work acquaintances and family know her. However, alters reside within Myra's body, and they go by other names and behave in ways that are totally incongruous with "Myra's" personality. "Rita" is flamboyant, outgoing, and uninhibited in her sexual passions. She has engaged in numerous love affairs with a variety of unsavory characters she picked up in nightclubs and discotheques. "Rita" is aware of "Myra" and regards her with extreme disdain. A third personality, "Joe," occasionally emerges from "Myra's" apartment. Dressed in a man's three-piece business suit, "Joe" goes downtown to do some shopping. According to "Joe," "Rita" is nothing but a "slut," who is heading for "big trouble someday." Myra's alters are oblivious to the details of her life.

Diagnostic Features

- This diagnosis is given to people who experience two or more distinct identities or personality states, each with an enduring pattern of perceiving, relating to, and thinking about the environment and the self.

- At least two of the identities or personality states recurrently take control of the person's behavior.

- The person is unable to recall important personal information, well beyond what could be explained by ordinary forgetfulness.

- The disturbance is not due to substance use or a medical condition.

1999). In other words, critics assert that clinicians who use hypnotic techniques with certain kinds of clients are more likely to produce symptoms that conform to the characteristics of dissociative identity disorder, particularly the experience of child alters or protective alters (Powell & Gee, 2000).

Some clinicians prefer to use cognitive-behavioral techniques instead of or in addition to hypnotherapy in an effort to change the client's dysfunctional attitudes (Fine, 1996; Ross, 1997a). These attitudes, arising from the client's history of abuse, include the beliefs that different parts of the self are separate selves, that the victim is responsible for abuse, that it is wrong to show anger or defiance, that the host cannot handle painful memories, that one of the alters hates the parents (but the primary personality loves them), that the host must be punished, and that neither the self nor others can be trusted. According to Ross (1997b), each of these core beliefs carries with it a set of assumptions that further guides the individual's behavior. Although countering these beliefs is not considered sufficient for treating dissociative identity disorder, it would seem to be an important component of an overall treatment plan.

Hypnotherapy is often used in treating clients with dissociative disorders to help the client achieve an integrated personality.

Another aspect of cognitive-behavioral therapy that might be helpful is to bolster the individual's sense of self-efficacy through a process called temporizing (Kluft, 1989), in which the client controls the way that the alters make their appearance. This may be accomplished through hypnosis in an effort to help the client develop coping skills that can be used when dealing with stress, which otherwise might precipitate a personality shift.

As more reliable information becomes available on dissociative identity disorder, improved methods of treatment are certain to be developed. Nevertheless, several factors contribute to difficulty in treating this disorder in addition to the controversies pertaining to the validity of the diagnosis and the notion of repressed memories. First, this is a very broadly defined disorder that ranges from cases such as those of Sybil and Eve to people who show far less dramatic symptoms. Second, clinicians and researchers have ascertained that most people with this disorder also suffer from other psychological problems, such as mood disorders or personality disorders. Third, repairing the damage done by abuse and trauma that took place decades earlier in the client's life can be very difficult. Finally, consider what it must be like for the clinician to work with a client whose problems and style of presentation are so diverse and contradictory. Given all these obstacles, you can see why it can take many years to reach the desired goal of personality integration. Even so, experts in this area have been inspired by the fact that some recent research points to positive outcome in the treatment of people with dissociative identity disorder. In one study of 135 individuals with this disorder, 54 were located and reassessed after a 2-year period and continued to show significant improvement, compared with their status at admission (Ellason & Ross, 1997). Kluft asserts that his work with dissociative clients has been quite successful; in fact, he notes that he has brought over 160 individuals to integration (Kluft, 1998).

Dissociative Identity Disorder and the Legal System

Dissociative identity disorder has become a vexing problem for forensic psychologists and other participants in the legal system who are confronted with criminal defendants using the disorder as an explanation for their offenses (Kihlstrom, 2005). One dramatic legal case brought to light some of the complexities involved in the multiple personality disorder defense. Kenneth Bianchi, a serial murderer also known as the Hillside Strangler, faked multiple personality disorder in an attempt to avoid criminal prosecution for his offenses (Orne et al., 1984; Watkins, 1984). Forensic psychologists and other members of the judicial system are faced with the difficult task of differentiating a true dissociative disorder from instances of malingering.

Individuals who seek to explain their crimes as products of alter personalities typically invoke an insanity defense or claim that they are not competent to stand trial (Slovenko, 1993; Steinberg, Bancroft, & Buchanan, 1993). Defendants who claim insanity assert that symptoms of the disorder precluded

their appreciation and understanding of criminal actions. Those who make the case that they are not competent to stand trial argue that their symptoms would interfere with their participation in court proceedings. In the more dramatic case of the insanity defense, the accused may admit to having committed the crimes, but under the control of an alter personality. They may claim that the offense was committed in a state of dissociation, and that they have no recall of what happened. The more credible these reports of dissociation and amnesia are, the more likely it is that the court will accept the insanity defense (Serban, 1992).

The accurate diagnosis of a psychologically disturbed defendant can lead to appropriate treatment; by contrast, an improper diagnosis can have dire effects for the individual and for the legal system. A missed diagnosis may deprive a person of potentially effective psychological treatment. An incorrect diagnosis of dissociative identity disorder could allow a dangerous individual to escape the consequences of his or her criminal behavior. Psychologists must typically rely on their clinical skills to detect malingering among defendants who claim they have dissociative identity disorder, and some have argued that the differential treatment of these defendants is contrary to sound legal and therapeutic practice. According to Ross (1989), the legal system favors malingering as a means for avoiding responsibility and consequences for criminal actions. Similarly, defendants who successfully use the insanity defense jeopardize their ability to make progress in therapy, which typically emphasizes the acceptance of responsibility for all of one's actions, even those carried out by alter personalities.

Although there is no foolproof way to detect malingering in a claim of multiple personalities, there are some strategies that can be used (Brick & Chu, 1991). Legal experts have found it helpful to work with psychologists using sophisticated assessment techniques, such as the Structured Clinical Interview for *DSM-IV* Dissociative Disorders–Revised (SCID-D-R; Steinberg, 1994; see Table 6.4). This instrument has been particularly useful in evaluating the severity of dissociative symptoms and in diagnosing dissociative disorders in both psychiatric and legal contexts (Steinberg & Hall, 1997). In genuine cases of this disorder, new personalities may be discovered during the course of therapy. When this happens, clinicians should regard these with skepticism. The client may be motivated by the belief that additional personalities could create a stronger legal defense. More reliable evidence can come from diaries or journals that the client kept, as well as testimony from relatives and friends. These sources may reveal information about periods of amnesia, personality change, and other aspects of fragmented experience that either support or contradict the diagnosis. Another distinction pertains to the nature of the symptoms involved in dissociative identity disorder. True cases of this disorder are often a product of extreme abuse in childhood. Furthermore, the symptoms create troublesome interference in the client's everyday life. The malingerer, however, shows none of the emotional scars of early abuse and appears to be suspiciously at ease when discussing actions of alter personalities and past instances of trauma. In other words, malingerers do not experience the acute psychological reactions typical of genuine dissociative identity disorder.

Although dissociative identity disorder is relatively easy to fake, malingerers generally find it difficult to maintain a consistent facade of dissociated feelings, thoughts, and memories that they can then associate with different personality states. Unlike clients who truly have the disorder, malingerers rarely have histories marked by confused and fragmented experiences and failed treatment attempts. Malingerers may describe stereotypical personalities that carry out bad or criminal actions, but their alter and host personalities are less likely to be explainable in terms of their traumatic experiences. Clients who truly have dissociative identity disorder may feel strange and ashamed of their disorder, whereas malingerers play up their symptoms for greater attention, especially from legal authorities (Kluft, 1987b).

In response to growing concerns about the diagnosis of dissociative identity disorder, Steinberg and her colleagues developed criteria for assessing the validity of dissociative symptoms within the context of clinical and forensic evaluations (Steinberg, Hall, Lareau, & Cicchetti 2001). They recommend the use of the SCID-D-R, which has been rigorously standardized and includes a careful structuring, presentation, and scoring of questions. The professionals who developed and conducted research on this instrument emphasize that it must be administered and scored only by experienced clinicians and evaluators who understand dissociative diagnosis and treatment issues. When malingering is part of the evaluation process, it is imperative that the examiner (1) be experienced; (2) obtain a lifetime history of the onset, duration, nature, and impairment resulting from the dissociative symptoms; and (3) use other sources of corroborative data, including a review of past treatment records and interviews with reliable people familiar with the individual's history. It is important to note that the SCID-D-R intentionally excludes questions about abuse or trauma, in order to see if individuals bring up such issues spontaneously rather than in response to leading questions.

Steinberg and her colleagues are well aware of the controversy pertaining to the diagnosis of dissociative identity disorder, and have therefore tried to establish high standards for all procedures pertaining to the diagnosis of this condition. Time will tell whether their efforts to emphasize the importance of high standards and precisely defined assessment techniques will resolve some of the controversy, and either validate this diagnosis or redefine it.

Other Dissociative Disorders

Although dissociative identity disorder is the most dramatic form of dissociative disorder, there are several other related conditions that are equally compelling in terms of impact on the individual's life.

Dissociative Amnesia In **dissociative amnesia,** formerly called psychogenic amnesia, the individual is unable to remember important personal details and experiences usually associated with traumatic or very stressful events. This memory loss is not attributable to brain dysfunction associated with brain damage or drugs, nor is it a matter of common forgetfulness. People who develop dissociative amnesia most commonly describe a gap or series of gaps in their memory about past troubling events or parts of their lives. Dissociative amnesia is rare, yet it is the most common of the dissociative disorders. It received a great deal of attention following the two world wars, in which many individuals with combat-related trauma experienced amnesia (Kardiner & Spiegel, 1947).

There are four forms of dissociative amnesia, each associated with the nature of a person's memory loss. In **localized amnesia,** the most common form, the individual forgets all events that occurred during a specified time interval. Usually, this interval immediately follows a very disturbing event, such as a car accident, fire, or natural disaster. In **selective amnesia,** the individual fails to recall some, but not all, details of events that have occurred during a given period of time. The survivor of a fire may remember the ambulance ride to the hospital, but not having been rescued from the burning house. **Generalized amnesia** is a syndrome in which a person cannot remember anything at all from his or her life. **Continuous amnesia** involves a failure

 In MindMAP Segment 6.3, Stephen discusses his symptoms and his awareness of the presence of two different alters.

The symptoms of dissociative identity disorder are experienced in various ways by people with this condition.

Mini Case

DISSOCIATIVE AMNESIA

In a daze, Norma entered the mental health crisis center, tears streaming down her face. "I have no idea where I live or who I am! Will somebody please help me?" The crisis team helped her search her purse but could find nothing other than a photograph of a blond-haired little girl. Norma appeared to be exhausted and was taken to a bed, where she promptly fell asleep. The crisis team called the local police to find out if there was a report of a missing person. As it turned out, the little girl in the photograph was Norma's daughter. She had been hit by a car in the parking lot of a shopping center. Although badly injured with a broken leg, the child was resting comfortably in the pediatrics ward of the hospital. Her mother, however, had disappeared. Norma had apparently been wandering around for several hours, leaving her wallet and other identifying papers with the hospital social worker in the emergency room. When Norma awoke, she was able to recall who she was and the circumstances of the accident, but she remembered nothing of what had happened since.

Diagnostic Features

- People with this disorder experience one or more episodes during which they are unable to recall important personal information, usually of a traumatic or stressful nature, that is well beyond ordinary forgetfulness.

- The disturbance does not occur as a result of another mental disorder, the use of substances, or a medical or neurological condition.

- The symptoms cause significant distress or impairment.

to recall events from a particular date up to and including the present time. For example, a war veteran may remember his childhood and youth until the time he entered the armed services, but he may have forgotten everything that took place after his first tour of combat duty.

Dissociative amnesia is very difficult for clinicians to diagnose, because there are so many possible causes of memory loss. For example, as you will see in later chapters, amnesia can be caused by a physical dysfunction due to brain injury, psychoactive substance abuse, or epilepsy. Alternatively, other psychological disorders have symptoms that may cause the individual to appear amnestic. For example, a catatonic person who does not communicate may be construed to be amnestic. When the individual is questioned, though, it may be possible to elicit some information about the person's past.

As is sometimes the case with other dissociative disorders, a person might fake symptoms to gain certain benefits or advantages. For example, a man who has committed a serious crime may claim that he remembers nothing of the incident or even who he is. As is true for the issue of repressed memories, there are legal implications when such cases reach trial. Juries tend to be skeptical when defendants in criminal cases claim to have dissociative amnesia for the events surrounding their alleged crimes (Porter, Birt, Yuille, & Herve, 2001). A related situation involves neonaticide, in which a mother kills her newborn child on the day of its birth. In a study of 16 cases of women charged with homicide, nearly all were found to exhibit symptoms of depersonalization as well as other dissociative symptoms (Spinelli, 2001). Clinicians are becoming increasingly sensitive to the need to diagnose these conditions accurately as well as to predict who is at risk for committing such crimes.

Dissociative Fugue   You may have read newspaper accounts or heard news stories of the fascinating story of a person who has found his way to a community far away from home, with no idea of how he got there or who he is. Although such cases are rare, they capture our attention because they seem so unbelievable. Many of the people in such stories are experiencing a **dissociative fugue,** formerly called psychogenic fugue, a condition in which a person who is confused about personal identity suddenly and unexpectedly travels to another place. The venture may be brief, lasting only hours or days, or it may last for weeks or months. People in a fugue state are unable to recall their own history or identity, and a few may even assume a new identity. If a person assumes a new identity, he or she is likely to appear to be much more outgoing than the core personality of the individual and may even go so far as to create a new name, find a place to live, get a job, and interact with others in ways that do not suggest anything out of the ordinary. In fact, in many cases, others do not suspect anything unusual, because the person in the fugue state appears very normal. After the fugue state has passed, the individual often has no recall of what took place during the fugue.

A fugue is rare and usually passes quickly. The disorder is more likely to occur at certain times, such as during a war or following a natural disaster. Personal crises or extreme stress, such as financial problems, the desire to escape punishment (Spiegel & Cardena, 1991), or the experience of a trauma (Classen, Koopman, & Spiegel, 1993) can also precipitate fugue states.

Depersonalization Disorder   You may be able to think of a time when you had a feeling of being "unreal." Perhaps you had not slept or eaten for a long period of time and had the sensation that you were an outsider observing the movements of your body, as if in a dream. The phenomenon of depersonalization includes alterations of mind-body perception, ranging from detachment from one's experiences to the feeling that one has stepped out of one's body. Depersonalization experiences occur in normal people when they are placed under great stress or when they use mind-altering drugs, such as marijuana or LSD.

Mini Case

DISSOCIATIVE FUGUE

George was an administrator at a small college in a rural town. He was a reliable worker, keeping mostly to himself and rarely discussing his personal life with his colleagues. All they knew about him was that he lived with his wife, Judy, and their two teenage children. Family life was quiet until one afternoon, when Judy received a telephone call from George's secretary, asking if she knew George's whereabouts. He had not shown up at work in the morning, nor had he called in sick. The secretary was concerned that George might be very upset, because the college president had announced on the previous day that the college would be closing permanently at the end of the academic year. Judy was startled by the news, because George had not mentioned it at dinner the evening before. No one heard from George for 3 weeks following the date of his mysterious disappearance. During that time, he traveled to Stanford University, with the intention of applying for a position as a philosophy professor. One day, he woke up in a California hotel room and was mystified about how he had gotten there.

Diagnostic Features

- People with this disorder travel suddenly and unexpectedly away from home or job and are unable to recall their past.

- They are confused about personal identity, or they assume a partial or complete new identity.

- The disturbance does not occur as a result of another mental disorder, the use of substances, or a medical or neurological condition.

- The symptoms cause significant distress or impairment.

In **depersonalization disorder,** however, distortions of mind-body perceptions happen repeatedly and without provocation by drugs. Periods of extreme stress, such as the time immediately following an accident, can also precipitate an episode of depersonalization in a vulnerable individual. Some experts have noted that the experience of depersonalization commonly follows a stressful event and emerges in the "calm following the storm" (Shader & Scharfman, 1989). Once considered quite rare, depersonalization disorder is now being diagnosed with increasing frequency (Kihlstrom, 2005).

People with depersonalization disorder feel as though they are not "real," that their body is changing in shape or size, or that they are being controlled by forces outside of themselves, as if they were an automaton or a robot. At the same time, however, they realize that they are not really robotic, but that something odd is happening in their body and mind. At times, the individual may experience "conversations" between an observing self and a participating self (Steinberg, 1991). People with this disorder are aware that something is wrong with them, and this awareness is a further source of distress; however, they may be reluctant to tell other people about their experiences, because they fear they will sound "crazy." Therefore, they can feel quite alone and isolated from others, as well as frightened about their loss of contact with reality. Understandably, people with this disorder often experience symptoms of depression (Lambert et al., 2001).

The onset of depersonalization disorder typically occurs in adolescence or early adulthood. The disorder tends to be chronic, with remissions and exacerbations that are triggered by anxiety, depression, or stress.

Theories and Treatment of Dissociative Amnesia, Dissociative Fugue, and Depersonalization Disorder Most experts agree that dissociative disorders may be the end product of intensely traumatic experiences during childhood, especially

Sometimes people with depersonalization disorder look as though they are on drugs. They may feel like they are in a dreamlike state, observing their own actions.

those involving abuse (Maldonado, Butler, & Spiegel, 1998) or other forms of emotional maltreatment (Simon et al., 2001). However, in addition to childhood abuse experiences, other kinds of traumatic events can also result in dissociative experiences, some of which are transient and some of which are longer-lasting. In the discussion of reactions to traumatic events in Chapter 5, we pointed out that people who dissociate during a traumatic event are at higher risk for the later development of PTSD.

Treatments for dissociative disorders are varied, in great part because the conditions themselves are so variable. As you can tell from reading the preceding sections, dissociative identity disorder is a markedly different phenomenon from depersonalization disorder. Nevertheless, a central goal in the treatment of clients with dissociative symptoms is to bring stability and integration into their lives. Essential to their treatment is the

Mini Case

DEPERSONALIZATION DISORDER

Robert entered the psychiatrist's office in a state of extreme agitation, almost panic. He described the terrifying nature of his "nervous attacks," which began several years ago but had now reached catastrophic proportions. During these "attacks," Robert feels as though he is floating in the air, above his body, watching everything he does but feeling totally disconnected from his actions. He reports that he feels as if his body is a machine controlled by outside forces: "I look at my hands and feet and wonder what makes them move." Robert's thoughts are not delusions, though; he is aware that his altered perceptions are not normal. The only relief he experiences from his symptoms comes when he strikes himself with a heavy object until the pain finally penetrates his consciousness. His fear of seriously harming himself adds to his main worry that he is losing his mind.

Diagnostic Features

- This diagnosis is given to people with persistent or recurrent experiences of feeling detached from their mental processes or body, as if in a dream or as if they were external observers.

- During the depersonalization experience, they are in touch with reality.

- The symptoms cause significant distress or impairment.

- The disturbance does not occur as a result of another mental disorder, the use of substances, or a medical or neurological condition.

---

establishment of a safe environment, away from the threatening stressors that presumably evoked dissociation. In this security of the treatment context, the clinician will introduce soothing techniques, some psychotherapeutic and others psychopharmacological. Psychotherapeutic techniques include hypnosis to help the client recover repressed or dissociated memories at a pace that the client can tolerate. Some clinicians would also add medications to the intervention, also aimed at enhancing a state of calm. The most commonly used medications are sodium pentobarbital and sodium amobarbital, which facilitate the interview process, particularly in clients with dissociative amnesia or dissociative fugue. Once amnesia has been reversed, the clinician helps the client figure out what events and factors evoked the amnesia. While these medications can help with some forms of dissociation, they are not particularly helpful with clients who have dissociative identity disorder, for which there is no easy cure for core symptoms of fragmentation (Maldonado et al., 1998).

The dissociative disorders provide a unique opportunity to appreciate the complexity of the human mind and the very unusual ways in which people respond to stressful life experiences. As fascinating as they are, it is important to keep in mind that these disorders are very rare and very difficult to treat. Although

current explanations rely heavily on psychological perspectives, in the future perhaps more will be learned about a biological substrate for the development of these conditions.

Somatoform Disorders, Psychological Factors Affecting Medical Conditions, and Dissociative Disorders: The Biopsychosocial Perspective

At this point, it should be clear why, historically, disorders involving somatization and dissociation were regarded as neuroses rather than psychoses. People with these disorders have experienced conflict or trauma during their lives, and these circumstances have created strong emotional reactions that they could not integrate into their memory, personality, and self-concept. The symptoms of somaticizing and dissociating represent not a loss of contact with reality, but a translation of these emotions into terms that are less painful to acknowledge than is the original conflict or trauma.

Stressful events can trigger maladaptive responses in physical functioning, ranging from a variety of physical conditions to sleep dysfunctions to the more elusive disorders involving somatization. Stress-related factors, not repressed sexuality, are currently regarded as central in understanding somatoform disorders. In addition, learning seems to play a strong role, particularly as individuals with these disorders develop secondary gain from their symptoms. With regard to dissociative disorders, experts now believe that actual, rather than imagined, trauma is the source of such symptoms as amnesia, fugue, and multiple identities. Cognitive-behavioral explanations of stress-related disorders add to these understandings. Low feelings of self-efficacy, lack of assertiveness, and faulty ideas about the self can all be contributing factors to somatoform and dissociative disorders. For example, believing that one must be sick to be worthy of attention is a dysfunctional attitude that could underlie a somatoform disorder. Similarly, faulty beliefs about the self and the role of the self in past experiences of trauma seem to be important cognitive factors in dissociative disorders. Adding to these psychological components are the biological factors that may contribute to an individual's vulnerability to developing these maladaptive thoughts or susceptibility to trauma.

A variety of treatment modalities for the disorders covered in this chapter are being explored. To varying degrees, these focus on the management of intense and intrusive stress. Supportive therapy aimed at gradual exploration of the role of stress or trauma in the individual's life is important. Cognitive-behavioral methods of enhancing the individual's feelings of self-efficacy, assertiveness, and awareness of dysfunctional thinking patterns are also being incorporated into an integrative treatment approach.

Rose's History

I remember feeling surprised when Rose returned to see me for the second session we had scheduled. People with stories involving numerous undiagnosable medical problems rarely come back after the intake meeting with a mental health clinician. In our second session, Rose told me a life story that gave me the basis for some reasonable hunches about the nature of her problems.

The older of two daughters, Rose grew up in the center of a city, close to the factory where her father worked. Rose vividly remembers the day her younger sister, Emily, was born, 2 days after Rose's seventh birthday. All the excitement surrounding Rose's birthday celebration and the birth of a baby in the family abruptly deteriorated to emotional chaos when Rose's parents were informed, hours after the birth, that Emily had serious abnormalities. This bad news about Emily caused Rose to become extremely worried, particularly about her father, whose drinking problem was apparent to her even at her young age and had already threatened the stability of the family. Rose began to fear that, with the added stress of Emily's health problems, her father might drift further into his alcoholic ways.

In the years that followed, Rose's parents were forced to devote most of their attention to her disabled sister. Feeling obliged to help her parents, Rose spent all her available time tutoring her sister, playing with her, and protecting her from the jeers of neighborhood children. When I inquired about Rose's remarkable level of devotion to her sister, she confided that it was largely the result of her intense feeling of guilt about being so much "luckier" than Emily. Tragically, Rose's sister died from heart trouble in her teenage years. Prior to this, Rose had planned to go to college and become a special education teacher, but her attempts to carry out this ambition were hampered after her sister's death by a

series of unexplainable illnesses and ailments, none of which were very serious but which caused her to drop out of college.

After leaving college, Rose took a job as a cosmetics consultant in a department store, but she had to quit after a short time, due to her nagging and incapacitating physical symptoms. Because of her inability to work, Rose had recently applied for disability benefits from the government, and she told me that she lived from day to day in dread that she may be denied these benefits.

When I inquired about intimate relationships in her life, Rose became uncomfortable as she told me about her "lousy batting average" with men. Citing a long list of brief relationships, Rose explained that these relationships generally fell apart because her physical problems constantly got in the way. Recurrently frustrated by the lack of sympathy on the part of the men whom she had met, Rose concluded that she is "probably better off without them."

Assessment

Although the information provided by both Dr. Thompson and Rose gave me the basis for a diagnostic hypothesis, I was intrigued by the unconscious factors within Rose that might relate to her problems. Rose, who had submitted to countless medical tests in the past, was open to the psychological assessment I recommended. She did express some reservations about the validity of tests, pointing out that dozens of medical tests had been unable to pinpoint any of her problems.

Psychological testing showed Rose to be a bright woman, with an IQ in the above-average range. Her cognitive functioning was consistent across the subscales of the WAIS-III, although she did show some evidence of difficulty in breaking down a problem into component parts and in understanding social situations. Rose's MMPI-2 profile was pre-

dictable, with elevations on Scales 1 (Hypochondriasis), 2 (Depression), and 3 (Hysteria), suggesting the likelihood that Rose defends against depression by using denial and by dwelling on possible physical problems. Rose's TAT responses revealed a highly romanticized, superficial view of intimate relationships, with many unrealistic "happy endings" to her stories. There was also a strong element of jealousy in the relationships between female figures. On the Rorschach test, Rose's first few responses were quite creative and potentially very rich in content, but she seemed unable to sustain this high level of production and quickly reverted to simple images. Throughout testing, Rose complained frequently of various physical problems, which made it necessary to interrupt testing. What struck me as odd about this was that Rose seemed to develop a physical symptom just at the point of becoming immersed in the assessment tasks.

Diagnosis

As I worked toward confirming a diagnosis, my thoughts focused on Rose's lengthy history of unsubstantiated medical complaints. Although I am reluctant to conclude that any person's medical complaints are without physical basis, the evidence supporting the assumption of a psychological, rather than medical, basis was substantial. For a brief moment, I considered the possibility that Rose might be malingering. But for what benefit? I did not believe she wanted to be "sick" just to collect disability benefits. Rose's problems and complaints predated any concern about financial support. Might Rose be a hypochondriac? Certainly, some facets of her story might lead to such a diagnosis, but a major difference was that Rose truly believed she was suffering from physical diseases. My sense was that, even though her problem was psychologically rooted, the discomfort and incapacitation Rose suffered were very real to her. Her lengthy list of recurrent bodily complaints and chronic pursuit of medical help for conditions that lacked any medical basis led me to diagnose Rose as having somatization disorder.

Axis I:	Somatization Disorder
Axis II:	Deferred. Rule out Histrionic Personality Disorder
Axis III:	No diagnosable physical disorders or conditions
Axis IV:	Problems related to the social environment (isolation) Occupational problems (disability)
Axis V:	Current Global Assessment of Functioning: 70 Highest Global Assessment of Functioning (past year): 70

Case Formulation

Rose's history was similar to that of the few other people with somatization disorder I had seen in my clinical practice. She was an individual with a long history of medical complaints, which had brought her much attention from others. As I thought about the possible origins of this psychological disorder, I noted that her physical complaints first developed after the death of her younger sister, an event that Rose described as devastating. It is my sense that Rose struggled with guilt about being more intelligent, more capable, and healthier than her sister. By taking over a parental role in relation to her sister, perhaps Rose was able to relieve some of this guilt. Also, as a result of her physical problems, Emily's parents naturally devoted more time, energy, and attention to her. Rose, with her feelings of guilt, found it difficult to acknowledge any of the jealous feelings she harbored. Thus, early in life, Rose had to cope with powerful feelings of guilt and jealousy; given her youth, she turned

to the immature defense of denial. Had Rose's sister survived her illness, Rose might very well have learned to express her feelings in a more mature fashion. However, her sister's death cut this process off prematurely. Indeed, when her sister died, Rose's physical symptoms began. One hypothesis about the cause of the symptoms at this time was that Rose identified with her sister and took on symptoms that bore a superficial resemblance to those that characterized Emily's fatal medical problems. The symptoms also incapacitated Rose so that she could have a legitimate reason not to live up to her own potential. By punishing herself, she could unconsciously resolve her guilt over having been more capable and healthier than her sister and, at the same time, having been ineffective in saving her.

Rose's symptoms also served a function in the family. For years, Rose's parents had turned all their energies as a couple toward caring for their disabled child. This allowed them to deflect their attention away from their own marital problems, which centered around Mr. Marston's alcoholism. With the death of their ill child, they needed a substitute to serve a similar function in the marriage. Perhaps Rose's symptoms served, in this sense, as unconscious compliance with the needs of her parents. Additionally, Rose's symptoms gave her secondary gain in the form of attention and concern from her parents, reactions she had not gotten from them for many, many years.

Treatment Plan

I made my decision to accept Rose into psychotherapy with some ambivalence. I was well aware of the low odds for success, yet at the same time I was touched by Rose's willingness to give therapy a chance. From the outset, she acknowledged her skepticism about the usefulness of psychotherapy, particularly in light of her belief that her medical prob-

lems were genuine. At the same time, she acknowledged that she might derive some benefit if we directed our attention to stress management. I agreed that this should be a component of the treatment, but I also felt that a broad, integrative therapy was necessary. I believed that, for Rose's life to change for the better, psychotherapy would have to focus on some of the unconscious conflicts underlying her symptoms, the secondary gain she has received as reinforcement, and the problems in Rose's current family life that have maintained her disorder.

I recommended individual outpatient psychotherapy on a weekly basis; however, I also realized that individual psychotherapy for people with such problems is usually insufficient. Ideally, they should be seen in multiple contexts, including group therapy, family therapy, and vocational counseling. Rose agreed to participate in a therapy group with another therapist and a group of seven clients dealing with life stresses in general and with problems with close relationships more specifically. As for family therapy, she told me emphatically that her father would not agree to any kind of professional "intrusion."

Outcome of the Case

In the initial weeks of therapy, Rose tried to redirect my attention away from psychological concerns to her somatic complaints. Gently but firmly I tried to make it clear that our work must focus on emotional rather than medical matters, but Rose was not receptive to my efforts. After a few sessions, she began to question openly the value of therapy, and 2 weeks later she announced she had found a "cure" for her symptoms and was going to discontinue therapy. A friend had told Rose about a new technique of pain management through hypnosis, and Rose was sure it would be right for her.

Several months later, I received a note from the emergency room staff informing me that Rose had been admitted to the psychiatric unit following a suicide attempt involving an overdose of pain medication. She told the physician she was looking for a way to escape her physical problems and pains. After a brief hospital stay, Rose was released from inpatient care and agreed to resume psychotherapy under my care.

In her second round of therapy, Rose made some progress in terms of coming to understand the psychological causes of her symptoms. However, Rose's denial of conflict was firmly entrenched, and she never seemed very convinced of the connection between her physical problems and the difficulties in her emotional life. Whatever gains Rose started to make were wiped out when she had a car accident and required a series of minor operations. Rose phoned me several months later to say that she would not be returning for psychotherapy. She explained that she would not have time, because the physical problems she had sustained in the accident would require many months of intensive medical care and rehabilitation. I wondered to myself whether Rose had finally achieved what she had come to desire for so long—clearly diagnosable medical problems and the attention that would accompany these problems.

Sarah Tobin, PhD

SUMMARY

- This chapter covered three sets of conditions: somatoform disorders, medical conditions affected by psychological factors, and dissociative disorders. In each of these sets of disorders, the body expresses psychological conflict and stress in an unusual fashion.

- Somatoform disorders include a variety of conditions in which psychological conflicts become translated into physical problems or complaints which cause distress or impairment in a person's life. Conversion disorder is the translation of unacceptable drives or troubling conflicts into bodily motor or sensory symptoms that suggest a neurological or medical condition. Somatization disorder involves the expression of psychological issues through bodily problems that have no basis in physiological dysfunction. In pain disorder, some kind of pain, which causes intense personal distress or impairment, is the predominant focus of the client's medical complaint. People with body dysmorphic disorder are preoccupied, almost to the point of being delusional, with the idea that a part of their body is ugly or defective. Individuals with hypochondriasis believe or fear that they have a serious illness, when in fact they are merely experiencing normal bodily reactions. Phenomena sometimes associated with somatoform disorders are malingering and factitious disorders. Malingering involves deliberately faking the symptoms of physical illness or psychological disorder for an ulterior motive. In factitious disorder, people fake symptoms or disorders not for the purpose of any particular gain but because of an inner need to maintain a sick role. In factitious disorder by proxy, a person induces physical symptoms in another person under the individual's care.

- In trying to understand the basis for the development of somatoform disorders, theorists consider issues of primary and secondary gain. Somatoform disorders can also be viewed as developing as a result of an interplay of biological factors, learning experiences, emotional factors, and faulty cognitions. A combination of treatment techniques may be used, in which a clinician strives to develop a supportive and trusting relationship with the client with a somatoform disorder.

- The *DSM-IV-TR* diagnostic category of psychological factors affecting medical conditions includes situations in which psychological or behavioral factors have an adverse effect on a medical condition. The psychological factors include Axis I disorders, psychological symptoms, personality traits, maladaptive health behaviors, stress-related physiological responses, and less specific psychological factors. Researchers and clinicians have focused on the processes by which people learn to deal with disruptive emotional experiences, and they have developed sophisticated theories and techniques pertaining to coping. In the field of psychoneuroimmunology, experts are finding answers to complex questions regarding the nature of the mind-body relationship.

- Dissociative disorders involve expressions of conflict that are so severe that part of the individual's personality actually separates from the rest of conscious functioning. In dissociative identity disorder, a person develops more than one self or personality. Although considerable controversy exists regarding the nature and prevalence of a condition involving multiple personalities, the *DSM-IV-TR* includes the diagnosis of dissociative identity disorder to capture the essence of intense detachment, disorganization, and amnesia reported by many clients. In dissociative amnesia, the individual is unable to remember important personal details and experiences, usually associated with traumatic or very stressful events. Dissociative fugue is a condition in which a person who is confused about personal identity suddenly and unexpectedly travels to another place. In depersonalization disorder, distortions of mind-body perceptions happen repeatedly and without provocation.

■ Experts agree that dissociative disorders commonly arise as the result of intense trauma usually associated with experiences of

abuse during childhood. Treatment depends on the nature of the dissociative disorder, with the goal being integration of the fragmented components of the individual's personality and cognition. Hypnotherapy and other psychotherapeutic techniques are commonly used to attain this goal.

KEY TERMS

See Glossary for definitions

Alters 198
Behavioral medicine 196
Body dysmorphic disorder 184
Continuous amnesia 206
Conversion disorder 181
Coping 192
Depersonalization disorder 208
Dissociative amnesia 206
Dissociative fugue 207
Dissociative identity disorder 198
Emotion-focused coping 194
Factitious disorder 187
Factitious disorder by proxy (Munchausen's syndrome by proxy) 188

Generalized amnesia 206
Host 198
Hypnotherapy 203
Hypochondriasis 185
Hysterical neurosis 181
La belle indifférence 181
Localized amnesia 206
Malingering 187
Munchausen's syndrome 188
Pain disorder 183
Primary gain 189
Problem-focused coping 194
Psychological factors affecting medical conditions 191

Psychoneuroimmunology 194
Secondary gain 190
Selective amnesia 206
Sociocognitive model of dissociative identity disorder 202
Somatization disorder 182
Somatoform disorders 180
Stress 192
Stressor 192

 ## INTERNET RESOURCE

To get more information on the material covered in this chapter, visit our website at **www.mhhe.com/halgin5.** There you will find more information, resources, and links to topics of interest.

CHAPTER 7

Sexual Disorders

When I first read the note on the intake form for Shaun Boyden, I felt a sense of uneasiness as I prepared to meet him in the intake interview. The words on the form were blunt and startling: "Pedophile . . . 46 years old . . . raped a 10-year-old boy. Court-ordered treatment following 6 months in prison." Perhaps I was struck and troubled by the fact that a tragedy of such proportions could be reduced to a few terse phrases. At the same time, I was aware of the difficult issues involved in treating pedophiles, many of whom are resistant to change and tend to regress to their molesting behavior. I knew that I would not be Shaun's therapist, because it was clinic procedure to assign such cases to Dr. Stephanie Draper, a staff psychologist with expertise in treating sex offenders. Frankly, I was relieved that I would not have responsibility for treating this client, feeling that it would be personally very difficult to sustain a relationship with a person who had exploited a child. As a mother, I found the notion of child abuse so despicable that I feared being unable to approach the client with empathy. In addition to my personal sensitivity to the issue, I felt pressures arising from my sense of social conscience; I have little patience with people who take advantage of those less powerful than themselves. I realized that these were issues that I should discuss in my ongoing consultation with my peer supervisor. Even though my interaction with Shaun Boyden would be limited to one or two sessions, I knew that it was important for me to approach these meetings with a mindset of objectivity, neutrality, and understanding. With a commitment to this kind of stance, I felt I would be able to conduct a professional evaluation of Shaun Boyden to determine if he was an appropriate candidate for the clinic's treatment program. My task was to conduct an intake evaluation and psychological assessment to assist Dr. Draper in formulating an appropriate treatment plan for Shaun.

In my initial encounter with Shaun, I found it difficult to view him as a 46-year-old man. His style of dress seemed more like the clothing of a teenager, while the harsh characteristics of his face made him seem at least a decade older than his age. He wore a dark, bulky sweatshirt with the hood creating shadows that obscured his facial features. His oversized pants hung so loosely from his waist that the top of his colorful boxer shorts was clearly visible. On his feet were stylish red Timberland work boots without a scuff or mark on them. At first, I thought it odd that he would come to a professional appointment so casually dressed, but I quickly came to recognize that he desperately wanted to be perceived as youthful and athletic. By contrast, however, his face was engraved with deep wrinkles, which reflected premature aging and exposure to the sun. I had the sense that Shaun fought an ongoing battle with the process of aging on one side and his fantasy of himself as a teenager on the other side.

In my meeting with Shaun, he was ostensibly uncomfortable. Using such words as *humiliated* and *mortified,* Shaun tried to describe his deep feelings of distress about his uncontrollable urges to seduce young boys. A married man, Shaun described himself as the devoted father of two young daughters. He spoke of his relationship with the girls in the most endearing of terms, weeping as he uttered his fears that they might be taken away from him. When I asked him about his marriage, he said that he was at a loss for words and had been unable to face his wife to try to explain his behavior. Adding to his intense anxiety was his realization that with an arrest record for this kind of offense, he would lose his job as a bank teller and would probably never be able to land another job.

When I asked Shaun to tell me the details of these sexual urges and inappropriate behavior, he began to cry, and only after a long delay could he speak about what had happened. Shaun had often volunteered his time to take disadvantaged youths on overnight camping trips to a state park. While sleeping in the tent one night, he became overwhelmed with sexual desire and began to fondle the genitals of one of the boys. Shaun covered the boy's mouth to prevent him from screaming, and he mounted the child in an attempt at anal intercourse. Terrified, the young boy finally managed to scream, causing an adult in a nearby tent to rush over and witness what was taking place.

When I asked Shaun if anything like this had ever happened before, he immediately said no, but I sensed that he was not telling me the truth. Gazing at the floor, Shaun once again began to weep, and in his weeping I could hear the hint of stories involving other seductions. As he struggled to regain his composure, he proceeded to tell me that on many previous camping trips he had fondled boys who were sleeping in his tent, but they had always remained asleep, and Shaun had never attempted intercourse before.

Shaun's wife knew nothing of his problem, although he had struggled with these urges since adolescence. Until a few years ago, he had limited himself to sexual fantasies about young boys while masturbating. However, when being so close to sleeping youngsters, the urges became irresistible.

By the end of the intake hour with Shaun, I felt drained, and I realized that we needed to meet at least once more to gather information about his history before proceeding to the psychological testing. In my mind, the images of the boys who had been exploited were intertwined with the tormented face of this middle-aged man. His problem had been long-standing and had become so enmeshed with his psychological and sexual functioning that only an extreme form of intervention could provide any hope of altering this tragic life course. I sensed that Shaun's honesty about the nature and duration of his problem was rooted in his desperate wish to escape from this nightmarish struggle.

Sarah Tobin, PhD

Sexual functioning is an essential aspect of human existence that can be a very rewarding or upsetting part of a person's life. Sexuality involves such a driving force in human nature, and is such an emotionally charged phenomenon, that it is not surprising that there are problems associated with this facet of human behavior.

What Is Abnormal Sexual Behavior?

How would you define abnormal sexual behavior? What criteria do you use in labeling sexual behaviors "abnormal"? For the sake of our discussion, we will assume that a sexual behavior is a psychological disorder if (1) it causes harm to other people, or (2) it causes an individual to experience persistent or recurrent distress or impairment in important areas of functioning. According to the first criterion, sexual molestation of a child is clearly a psychological disorder. According to the second criterion, a distressing, ongoing aversion to sexuality is a psychological disorder. But what about cases in which the individual finds a behavior pleasurable that society regards as unacceptable or deviant? As you will see in this chapter, the distinction between normal and abnormal in the sexual domain of behavior is complicated and far from clear.

When evaluating the normality of a given sexual behavior, the context is extremely important, as are customs and mores, which change over time. Many attitudes and behaviors related to sex have changed in recent decades. For example, the kinds of magazines, videos, and Internet images featuring explicit sexual behavior that are now commonplace would have been grounds for arrest in most American communities just 25 years ago.

For most of the twentieth century, surprisingly little factual evidence was available about sexual disorders because of such restrictive social attitudes. Much changed in the 1960s and 1970s, partly as a result of the dramatic and candid accounts of human sexual behavior published by world-renowned experts on human sexuality William Masters and Virginia Johnson (Masters & Johnson, 1966, 1970), whom you will read about later in the chapter. Following their pioneering efforts, researchers and clinicians made drastic changes in the way they explained sexual disorders and treated people with these conditions.

Some sophisticated survey and interview studies have been conducted that shed light on the complex behaviors associated with human sexuality. In a major study conducted at the National Opinion Research Center (NORC) at the University of Chicago, researchers conducted 90-minute interviews with more than 3,000 randomly chosen individuals between the ages of 18 and 59 in a survey called the National Health and Social Life Survey (NHSLS) (Laumann, Gagnon, Michael, & Michaels, 1994; Smith, 1996). Using sophisticated statistical analyses, these investigators provided some of the most comprehensive data about human sexuality since Alfred Kinsey's groundbreaking research more than four decades earlier (Kinsey, Pomeroy, & Martin, 1948; Kinsey, Pomeroy, Martin, & Gebhard, 1953). In the study, behaviors that would have been considered abnormal or deviant a

Sexually provocative websites are the most commonly visited sites on the Internet and, for some people, can become such an obsession that they put a person at risk both at work and in relationships.

few decades ago had become part of mainstream sexuality. Least surprising was their finding that, among young people, only 5 percent of the women and 2 percent of the men waited until marriage to have their first sexual intercourse experience, in contrast to 45 percent of the women and 17 percent of the men in the older group. The researchers found similar generational differences regarding the frequency of oral sex, with the younger people engaging more commonly in this form of sexual intimacy. As we begin our discussion of sexual disorders, it is important to realize that what is regarded as "deviant" changes over time.

Paraphilias

The term *paraphilia* (*para* meaning "faulty" or "abnormal," and *philia* meaning "attraction") literally means a deviation involving the object of a person's sexual attraction. **Paraphilias** are

TABLE 7.1 Examples of Paraphilias

Telephone scatologia	Making obscene phone calls, such as describing one's masturbatory activity in great detail, threatening to rape the victim, or trying to find out about the victim's sexual activities
Necrophilia	Deriving sexual gratification from viewing or having sexual contact with a corpse
Zoophilia	Having sex with animals or having recurrent fantasies of sex with animals
Coprophilia	Deriving sexual pleasure from contact with feces
Klismaphilia	Deriving sexual pleasure from the use of enemas
Urophilia	Deriving sexual pleasure from contact with urine
Autagonistophilia	Having sex in front of others
Somnophilia	Having sex with a sleeping person
Stigmatophilia	Deriving sexual pleasure from skin piercing or a tattoo
Autonepiophilia	Wearing diapers for sexual pleasure

disorders in which an individual has recurrent, intense sexually arousing fantasies, sexual urges, or behaviors involving (1) non-human objects, (2) children or other nonconsenting persons, or (3) the suffering or humiliation of oneself or a partner.

Characteristics of Paraphilias

There are several paraphilias (see Table 7.1), but all share the common feature that people who have these disorders are so psychologically dependent on the target of desire that they are unable to feel sexual gratification unless this target is present in some form. For some, the unusual sexual preferences occur in occasional episodes, such as during periods in which the individual feels especially stressed. Keep in mind that paraphilias are not fleeting whims or daydreams about unusual sexual practices but are conditions that last for at least 6 months. People with paraphilias find themselves recurrently compelled to think about or carry out their unusual behavior. Even if they do not actually fulfill their urges or fantasies, they are obsessed with them to the point of experiencing considerable personal distress. A paraphilia can become so strong and compelling that the individual loses sight of any goals other than the achievement of sexual fulfillment. By definition, paraphilias cause intense personal distress or impairment in social, work, and other areas of life functioning. Except for sexual masochism, almost all cases of paraphilia involve males.

To illustrate these points, let us compare the cases of Brian, who has a paraphilia, and Charles, who does not. Brian is extremely upset by his preoccupation with the sight and smell of women's leather gloves, is tormented by his intense arousal when he sees women wearing gloves, and can achieve sexual fulfillment only if he masturbates while fondling a leather glove. Brian has a paraphilia (namely, fetishism). Conversely, Charles finds it sexually stimulating when his girlfriend wears high heels to bed, but it is not necessary for her to wear these in order for

him to be stimulated to orgasm. His attraction seems a little "kinky" to him, but not particularly unusual. Charles does not have a paraphilic disorder. Such distinctions are important to keep in mind as you read about the paraphilias.

Information about the incidence of paraphilias is limited, primarily because people with these disorders are so ashamed or embarrassed that they rarely seek psychological help. The extent to which paraphilias exist may be inferred indirectly by considering the large commercial market in pornographic magazines, movies, and objects sold in adult bookstores and over the Internet.

As you begin to read about the paraphilias, you may question the extent to which they cause distress for an individual, or even for others. In fact, some people with paraphilias insist that neither they nor others are bothered by their unusual sexual practices; they insist that the negative reaction of an unaccepting society is what causes their behavior to be viewed as dysfunctional. Others, however, are tormented by guilt and shame, as they find their lives being consumed by the pursuit of sexual gratification in ways that they view as unacceptable.

Pedophilia We begin our discussion of paraphilias with the most disturbing disorder you will study in this book—**pedophilia,** a paraphilia in which an adult (16 years or over) has uncontrollable sexual urges toward sexually immature children. Sometimes these stories take on gruesome proportions, as when children are submitted to horrifying forms of victimization, such as kidnapping and sexual abuse, that persist for months or even years. Although these extreme cases are rare, the prevalence of child sexual abuse is disturbingly high in the United States. Among children about whom reports of maltreatment are made, approximately 10 percent involve cases of sexual abuse involving forced fondling, sodomy, or penetration with an object (U.S. Department of Health and Human Services, 2005). In fact, when sexual assault statistics for the entire population are reviewed, the statistics are quite alarming, in that two thirds of all sexual assault victims are children and adolescents. Among adolescents (12–17), 14-year-olds are the most commonly abused; among children (under the age of 12), 4-year-olds are the most common victims. Nearly two thirds of the victims are females, the vast majority of perpetrators are male, and approximately one third of the offenders are relatives of the victimized children (Snyder, 2000).

Types of Pedophilia   Although pedophiles are by definition attracted to children, their sexual preferences and behavior vary a great deal. Some do not act out their impulses but have disturbing fantasies and inclinations to molest children. Those who do act on their pedophilic impulses commit such acts as undressing the child, touching the child's genitals, coercing the child to participate in oral-genital activity, and attempting vaginal or anal intercourse.

Researchers have used various systems to classify pedophiles. A particularly useful one (Lanyon, 1986) involves the distinction among situational molesters, preference molesters, and child rapists. Situational molesters have a history of normal sexual development and interests; as adults, they are primarily interested in relationships with other adults. However, in certain contexts, such as during a stressful time, they are overcome by a strong impulse to become sexual with a child. Rather than feeling relieved after the incident, though, situational molesters feel distress. For the preference molester, pedophilic behavior is ingrained into his personality and lifestyle, and he has a clear preference for children, especially boys. He will marry only out of convenience, to be near children or as a cover for his disorder. The preference molester sees nothing wrong with his behavior; if anything, he feels that society is too critical of what he regards as simply a variant of sexual expression. The child rapist is a violent child abuser whose behavior is an expression of hostile sexual drives.

Another model applies to the behavior of sexual aggressors in general, but it seems particularly well suited for understanding pedophilia. According to this model (Hall, Shondrick, & Hirschman, 1993), there are four subtypes of sexual aggressors: physiological, cognitive, affective, and developmentally related. The physiological aggressor, who experiences deviant sexual arousal patterns, is more likely to choose male children and to have multiple victims, while refraining from physical violence and nonsexual aggression. The cognitive aggressor plans his sexual aggression, which is more likely to be acquaintance rape or incest that is less impulsive and violent than found in the other subtypes. The affective aggressor, who lacks affective control, engages in sexual aggression that is opportunistic, unplanned, and often violent. Affective aggressors who violate children are more prone to suffer from depression, while those who victimize adults tend to be more angry. Sexual aggressors with developmentally related personality problems tend to have a long history of personality and adjustment difficulties, family and interpersonal conflicts, and childhood victimization, and they tend to engage in violent forms of sexual aggression. This last group has the poorest treatment prognosis.

A playground can be the setting for a pedophile to target a potential victim.

Theories and Treatment of Pedophilia   Because of the extreme harm caused innocent victims that results from pedophilic behavior, it is one of the most widely investigated of the paraphilias. We will devote greater attention to the understanding and treatment of this disorder in this section and then return to more general theories and treatments of the other paraphilias later in the chapter. As you will see, the biopsychosocial model of pedophilia is particularly appropriate because of the complex interactions of physiological, psychological, and sociocultural influences on its development.

Clinicians and researchers working within a biological perspective take less interest in understanding the causes of pedophilia than in finding a somatic treatment that will reduce the individual's sexual urges. Consequently, a number of approaches are aimed at the endocrine system, such as administering the female hormone progesterone to reduce the pedophile's sex drive by lowering his level of testosterone. Another approach is the administration of antiandrogens, which are intended to have the same effect. Most recently, researchers have developed a treatment that involves administering a substance that reduces testosterone secretion by inhibiting the action of the pituitary gland. Although such an intervention appears to have positive effects, it is nevertheless considered necessary to combine medical treatments with psychotherapy (Rosler & Witztum, 2000).

The most radical medical interventions involve surgery. Castration, or removal of the testes, is intended to eliminate the production of testosterone (Weinberger, Sreenivasan, Garrick, & Osran, 2005). Another surgical intervention is hypothalamotomy, or destruction of the ventromedial nucleus of the hypothalamus. This procedure is intended to change the individual's sexual arousal patterns by targeting the source of these patterns in the central nervous system. Hypothalamotomies have been used most frequently in Germany, but with limited effectiveness. Researchers in Germany have also experimented with lutenizing hormone–releasing hormone (LHRH) a substance normally present in women that triggers the production of female sex hormones. This treatment was reported to reduce the incidence of penile erection, ejaculation, masturbation, sexually deviant impulsiveness, and fantasies (Briken, Nika, & Berner, 2001). The problem with all of these procedures, in addition to their side effects, is that they do not eliminate the man's ability to be sexually aroused and to have intercourse or masturbate. They may reduce the level of testosterone and, thus, help curb the pedophile's sex drive, but the issue of the inappropriateness of his choice of a partner must also be addressed. Therefore, any of these somatic treatments must be combined with psychotherapy (Prentky, 1997).

Keep in mind that surgical treatments for sex offenders are performed very rarely and represent extreme forms of intervention. But it is also important to consider why these alternatives are even regarded as viable methods of treatment. The men for whom these treatments are recommended are incorrigible individuals who have repeatedly exploited and seriously harmed vulnerable individuals. Even though it may be difficult for some people to understand or support the use of such radical interventions, it is also disturbing to consider the alternatives, which may include life imprisonment as the only means of preventing these men from repeating their offenses against children.

Psychological theorists focus on the early life experiences of people with this disorder. Some researchers have described a "victim-to-abuser cycle" (Bagley, Wood, & Young, 1994; Haywood et al., 1996), which leads childhood victims of sexual abuse to perpetrate similar acts of sexual abuse when they reach adulthood. Establishing such a connection would provide some greater insight into the minds of those who commit these disturbing crimes, and it might lead to the development of effective treatment programs for pedophiles. Unfortunately, the relationship between being victimized and becoming a victimizer is not quite so clear.

Although some researchers have found that many pedophiles were sexually abused as children, other researchers have observed that the rate of childhood sexual abuse among pedophiles is only marginally higher than that found among individuals who commit sexual offenses against adults or violent offenses against a variety of victims (Freund, Watson, & Dickey, 1990). These researchers suggest that pedophiles might be motivated to minimize responsibility for their offenses and offer the quasi-excuse that their own experience of having been victimized led to their exploitive behavior.

Other researchers have broadened their scope beyond looking specifically at abuse to investigate more general familial and developmental antecedents of pedophilia and sexual aggression. They note that sexual abuse of children is rarely an isolated event; instead, it often occurs in the context of families struggling with considerable emotional and physical conflict.

Serious family disturbance may lay the groundwork for both sexual victimization and for offending later in life. Alexander (1992) suggested that parents' insecure patterns of attachment, their disturbed style of relating, and their sexually abusive behavior become models for the individual who later goes on to be sexually abusive himself. Sexually abusive parents are impaired in their ability to meet their relationship needs in mature and appropriate ways, and they are less able to seek assistance to stop abusive behavior. Thus, pedophiles come to view others, adults and children alike, as acting on their own desires and needs, while denying the effects of sexual transgressions on their victims. Similarly, Prentky and his colleagues (1989) determined that early relationship disturbances with caregivers, accompanied by sexual deviation within the family, are characteristics of the most violent sexual offenders. Lacking adequate models for relationships and for controlling aggressive and sexual impulses, sexual offenses become "acceptable" outlets for the feelings of isolation, anger, and sexual arousal these individuals experience.

Some intriguing factors within early life that may affect the development of pedophilia are beginning to draw the attention of researchers. Birth order may also play a role in predisposing an individual to developing homosexual versus heterosexual pedophilia. Men with pedophilia who had a greater number of older brothers were more likely to become attracted to boys (Blanchard et al., 2000).

Another approach focuses on the psychological factors that lead to pedophilia by zeroing in on the personality traits of sex offenders. In one study (Serin, Malcolm, Khanna, & Barbaree, 1994), researchers found a strong relationship between psychopathy, or antisocial personality disorder, and deviant sexual arousal in a group of 65 offenders, some of whom were rapists and others child molesters. The pedophiles who preyed on unrelated children showed the strongest relationship between psychopathy and deviant sexual arousal. Next in degree of psychopathy were the rapists, followed by the incest offenders (those whose victims were relatives). Thus, there appears to be a strong antisocial element in the personalities of child molesters. In a study of the Rorschach responses comparing men with antisocial personality disorder, a history of sexual homicide, and pedophilia, men with pedophilia were more likely to show evidence of feelings of anger stemming from feelings of inadequacy, introversion, and cognitive rigidity (Gacono, Meloy, & Bridges, 2000).

Both the diagnosis and treatment of pedophilia may be assisted by the use of a measure called a penile plethysmograph, an instrument that measures the blood flow in the penis and, hence, objectively registers the degree of a man's sexual arousal. This procedure, called phallometry, is an accurate technique for determining pedophilic responses in males that is far more reliable than self-report. Child molesters, for example, experience changes in penile circumference when shown stimuli depicting sexual scenes involving children.

In contrast, sexual offenders who have had sexual contact with the highest number of women have the lowest probability

PEDOPHILIA

Shortly following his marriage, Kirk began developing an inappropriately close relationship with Amy, his 8-year-old stepdaughter. It seemed to start out innocently, when he took extra time to give her bubble baths and backrubs. But, after only 2 months of living in the same house, Kirk's behavior went outside the boundary of common parental physical affection. After his wife left for work early each morning, Kirk invited Amy into his bed on the pretext that she could watch cartoons on the television in his bedroom. Kirk would begin stroking Amy's hair and gradually proceed to more sexually explicit behavior, encouraging her to touch his genitals, saying that it would be "good" for her to learn about what "daddies" are like. Confused and frightened, Amy did as she was told. Kirk reinforced compliance to his demands by threatening Amy that, if she told anyone about their secret, he would deny everything and she would be severely beaten. This behavior continued for more than 2 years, until one day Kirk's wife returned home unexpectedly and caught him engaging in this behavior.

Diagnostic Features

- For a period lasting at least 6 months, people with this disorder have recurrent, intense sexually arousing fantasies, sexual urges, or behaviors involving sexual activity with a prepubescent child or children (generally 13 years old or younger).

- The person has acted on these urges, or the sexual urges or fantasies cause significant distress or impairment.

- The individual with this disorder is at least 16 years old and at least 5 years older than the victimized child or children.

- The individual's pedophilic behavior may be characterized by sexual attraction to males, females, or both sexes.

- The pedophilic behavior is characterized by whether or not it is limited to incest.

- The pedophilic behavior is characterized by whether or not sexual attraction is exclusive to children.

of being diagnosed with pedophilia based on their phallometric response (Blanchard et al., 2001). Phallometry can also be used to distinguish homicidal child molesters from nonhomicidal child molesters, and both from nonoffenders (Firestone, Bradford, Greenberg, & Nunes, 2000). However, there are limits to physiological testing alone, and clinicians recommend that phallometry be combined with more comprehensive psychological assessments (Marshall & Fernandez, 2000).

In addition to looking at factors that predict pedophilic behavior, researchers have attempted to determine which offenders are more likely to repeat their acts. There appears to be a pattern or constellation of factors that leads to high rates of repeating pedophilic behavior among convicted offenders. In examinations of the records of 269 convicted child molesters, researchers found that, compared to nonrepeaters, those who were likely to offend repeatedly had higher scores on measures of pedophilia, a history of previous sexual charges, were younger, tended to prey on male victims (frequently from outside the family), and were more likely to be living alone (Proulx et al., 1997). In a similar study of conviction records, another team of researchers also found that individuals who had a paraphilia besides pedophilia were more likely to engage repeatedly in pedophilic acts (Prentky, Knight, & Lee, 1997). Overall, the reconviction rate for pedophilia was 13 percent.

The psychological treatments of pedophilia involve behavioral methods, cognitive-behavioral techniques, and biological interventions. Within the behavioral realm, clinicians use a variety of techniques. Electroshock is a form of aversive therapy rooted in classical conditioning; it involves the administration of shock in response to sexual arousal in response to a deviant stimulus, such as a depiction of a sexual situation involving a child. In another technique, the clinician attempts to replace the pedophile's attraction to a child as a sexual target with an appropriate adult object. For example, while masturbating using his customary fantasies of sexual activity with a child, the pedophile may be instructed to replace the child image with an adult image as he approaches the point of orgasm. Other behavioral techniques involve principles of aversive conditioning, with the stimulus being a child's picture or image. Alternatively, the pedophile might be instructed to talk about his sexual practices to an "audience" of other clients or clinicians who criticize and deride him. The behavioral techniques are intended not only to extinguish the inappropriate behavior and replace it with appropriate sexual behavior but also to reinforce socially acceptable ways of relating to other adults.

Cognitive interventions are another psychological treatment used for pedophilia. In relapse prevention, the therapist helps the client strengthen self-control by providing methods for identifying and analyzing problem situations and by developing strategies that help the client avoid and cope more effectively in these circumstances. Cognitive therapy for depression or anger may also be used in cases in which the pedophile has associated disorders.

There is no one best approach to treating people with pedophilia. The fact that people with this disorder are likely to repeat their behavior, even after long-term intensive treatment, has led clinicians and researchers to conclude that a multifaceted approach is needed (Barbaree & Seto, 1997). Especially promising have been treatment approaches involving a combination of techniques, with particular attention to the inclusion of a group therapy component. Berlin (1998) describes an approach that has been successful in reducing repeated offenses to less than 8 percent of those participating. In this program, Berlin and his colleagues incorporate group therapy, which is combined in some cases with medications aimed at lowering sex drive. In the group therapy, efforts are made to confront denial and rationalizations, while providing a supportive context that is conducive to a frank discussion of desires and conflicts. Yet another component of this approach is the development of a family- and community-based support system to help the pedophile stick to his determination to remain healthy (Berlin, 1998).

Exhibitionism In **exhibitionism,** a person has intense sexual urges and arousing fantasies involving the exposure of genitals to a stranger. The exhibitionist actually does not expect a sexual reaction from the other person but finds the sight of shock or fear in the onlooker to be arousing. Some exhibitionists have the fantasy, however, that the onlooker will become sexually aroused. When discussing exhibitionistic behavior, it is important to differentiate this psychological disorder from exhibiting behaviors that are associated with a neurological condition in which an individual lacks normal inhibitory capacity. The paraphilia of exhibitionism is also different from socially sanctioned display (Hollender, 1997) as would be found at a nudist beach or strip club. People with this paraphilia feel they cannot control their behavior or feel driven to this behavior in a desperate attempt to get attention; the result is emotional torment and significant disruption in life.

In trying to understand how people, most of whom are men, become so compulsively driven to display their genitals, it is useful to consider early developmental experiences having to do with comparable situations. According to one view, the exhibitionist is motivated to overcome chronic feelings of shame and humiliation. His exhibitionistic behavior provides a temporary reprieve from his feelings of incompetence by bolstering feelings of personal adequacy (Silverstein, 1996). A more behavioral explanation regards the exhibitionistic behavior as a product of learning experiences in childhood, when the individual was sexually aroused while displaying himself and was excited by the distress that his inappropriate behavior caused in other people. Over time, repetition of this behavior is reinforced

Exhibitionists usually target unsuspecting strangers.

Mini Case

EXHIBITIONISM

Ernie is in jail for the fourth time in the past 2 years for public exposure. As Ernie explained to the court psychologist who interviewed him, he has "flashed" much more often than he has been apprehended. In each case, he has chosen as his victim an unsuspecting teenage girl, and he jumps out at her from behind a doorway, a tree, or a car parked at the sidewalk. He has never touched any of these girls, instead fleeing the scene after having exposed himself. On some occasions, he masturbates immediately after the exposure, fantasizing that his victim was swept off her feet by his sexual prowess and pleaded for him to make love to her. This time, seeing that his latest victim responded by calling the police to track him down, Ernie felt crushed and humiliated by an overwhelming sense of his own sexual inadequacy.

Diagnostic Features

- This diagnosis is assigned to people who, for a period lasting at least 6 months, have intense sexually arousing fantasies, sexual urges, or behaviors involving genital exposure to unsuspecting strangers.
- The person has acted on these urges, or the sexual urges or fantasies cause significant distress or impairment.

to such an extent that it becomes addictive. In fact, exhibitionists often prefer this form of behavior to sexual intercourse, because they have come to associate intense feelings of sexual gratification with the display of their genitals to alarmed strangers (Money, 1984). Their behavior enhances their feelings of masculinity and power, especially as the shock value of their behavior is so strong and easily observed in the victim.

The treatment of exhibitionists takes a multifaceted approach (Maletzky, 1997), often involving a reliance on learning principles, such as counterconditioning or aversive conditioning. The person must unlearn the connection between sexual pleasure and the exhibitionistic behavior, either through creating new associations between sexuality and appropriate stimuli or through associating pain and embarrassment, instead of pleasure, with exhibitionistic behavior. For example, the therapist might use **covert conditioning,** a behavioral method in which the client imagines a great deal of shame when his acquaintances observe him engaging in his exhibitionistic behaviors. In addition to psychological interventions, there is some clinical evidence that paroxetine (Paxil) might help reduce the compulsive behaviors seen in exhibitionism (Abouesh & Clayton, 1999).

Fetishism A **fetish** is a strong, recurrent sexual attraction to a nonliving object. People with the paraphilia of **fetishism** are preoccupied with an object, and they become dependent on this object for achieving sexual gratification, actually preferring it over sexual intimacy with a partner. It is difficult to estimate how common fetishism is, because fetishists, virtually all of whom are men, are unlikely to seek treatment for their disorder.

The most common fetishistic objects are ordinary items of clothing, such as underwear, stockings, shoes, and boots; however, there are also reports in the psychiatric literature of a wide range of fetishes, including rubber items, leather objects, diapers, safety pins, and even amputated limbs. Some fetishes involve very specific attractions—for example, brown boots lined with fur. **Partialism** is another paraphilia, which some experts regard as a variant of fetishism; people with partialism are interested solely in sexual gratification from a specific body part, such as feet. Cases in which a man's sexual excitement is dependent on female clothing used for cross-dressing fall into another category, transvestic fetishism, which we will discuss later. Also, behavior is not regarded as fetishistic when it involves the use of an object specifically designed for increasing sexual excitation, such as a vibrator.

A fetishist becomes sexually excited by the object. Some fondle or wear the fetishistic object. Some are aroused by smelling the object, rubbing against it, or observing other persons wearing it during sexual encounters. In some cases, the fetishist may not even desire to have intercourse with the partner, preferring instead to masturbate with the fetishistic object. Some men find that they are unable to attain an erection unless the fetishistic object is present. Some fetishists engage in bizarre behavior, such as sucking it, rolling in it, burning it, or cutting it into pieces.

When discussing fetishes, it is important to keep in mind the difference between what is considered "normal" sexual behavior and what would be considered deviant. Fantasies and behaviors that occasionally enhance a person's sexual excitement are different from the ritualistic preoccupations seen in true fetishism. Fetishism involves a compulsive kind of behavior that seems beyond the control of the individual, and it can be the source of considerable distress and interpersonal problems. Although some people with fetishes incorporate their fetishistic behavior into their sexual relationship with a partner who accepts this divergent behavior, more often the fetishistic behavior interferes with normal sexual functioning.

Fetishism appears to develop in a way similar to exhibitionism, in that early life experiences result in a connection between sexual excitation and a fetishistic object. As the person grows older, he becomes conditioned to associate sexual gratification with the object, rather than with another person. For example, fetishists who prefer baby-related objects, such as diapers, crib sheets, or rubber diaper pants, may have developed an intense association in early childhood between pleasurable genital feelings and the touching of these objects. To test this learning hypothesis (in experiments that would be regarded as unethical by today's standards), one group of researchers reported that they could condition male subjects to acquire a fetish (Rachman, 1966; Rachman & Hodgson, 1968). In one of these studies, the researchers showed men pictures of nude or scantily dressed women (unconditioned stimulus) paired with pictures of fur-lined boots (conditioned stimulus) and used an apparatus to measure the men's erectile response. After repeated pairings of the pictures of women and boots (and other footwear), the men became aroused by the pictures of footwear alone (conditioned stimulus). Extinction of this behavior was then achieved by

Mini Case

FETISHISM

For several years, Tom has been breaking into cars and stealing boots or shoes, and he has come close to being caught on several occasions. Tom takes great pleasure in the excitement he experiences each time he engages in the ritualistic behavior of procuring a shoe or boot and going to a secret place to fondle it and masturbate. In his home, he has a closet filled with dozens of women's shoes, and he chooses from this selection the particular shoe with which he will masturbate. Sometimes he sits in a shoe store and keeps watch for women trying on shoes. After a woman tries on and rejects a particular pair, Tom scoops the pair of shoes from the floor and takes them to the register, explaining to the clerk that the shoes are a gift for his wife. With great eagerness and anticipation, he rushes home to engage once again in his masturbatory ritual.

Diagnostic Features

- For a period lasting at least 6 months, people with this condition have recurrent, intense sexually arousing fantasies, sexual urges, or behaviors involving nonliving objects.

- The fantasies, sexual urges, or behaviors cause significant distress or impairment.

- The fetish objects are not limited to female clothing used in cross-dressing or devices used for tactile genital stimulation, such as a vibrator.

repeatedly showing the shoes and boots without the pictures of women. Over time, the men lost interest in these objects, which no longer had sexual associations.

As controversial as this study was, it provided a model for the treatment of fetishes, and researchers have established that extinction and other behavioral methods are effective treatment strategies. One technique is aversion therapy, in which the individual is subjected to punishment, such as taking a vomit-inducing drug or being hypnotized to feel nauseated, while masturbating with the fetishistic object.

Orgasmic reconditioning is another behavioral method geared toward a relearning process. In this procedure for treating paraphilias, an individual is instructed to arouse himself with a fantasy of the unacceptable object, then masturbate while looking at an appropriate sexual stimulus, such as a picture of an adult partner. If his arousal decreases, he may return to the fantasy of the unacceptable object, but he is to attain orgasm only while focusing on the acceptable stimulus. In time, the individual presumably relies less and less on the unacceptable object for sexual excitement and increasingly on the desired sexual stimulus.

Frotteurism The term **frotteurism** is derived from the French word *frotter* (meaning "to rub"), and it refers to masturbation that involves rubbing against another person. A **frotteur** has recurrent, intense sexual urges and sexually arousing fantasies of rubbing against or fondling another person. The target of the frotteur is not a consenting partner but a stranger. The frotteur

Mini Case

FROTTEURISM

Bruce, who works as a delivery messenger in a large city, rides the subway throughout the day. He thrives on the opportunity to ride crowded subways, where he becomes sexually stimulated by rubbing up against unsuspecting women. Having developed some cagey techniques, Bruce is often able to take advantage of women without their comprehending what he is doing. As the day proceeds, his level of sexual excitation grows, so that by the evening rush hour he targets a particularly attractive woman and only at that point in the day allows himself to reach orgasm.

Diagnostic Features

- For a period lasting at least 6 months, people with this condition have recurrent, intense sexually arousing fantasies, sexual urges, or behaviors involving touching and rubbing against nonconsenting people.

- The person has acted on these urges, or the sexual urges or fantasies cause significant distress or impairment.

A crowded subway provides an opportunity for the frotteur to become sexually excited by rubbing against other people.

seeks out crowded places, such as buses or subways, where he can select an unsuspecting victim and then usually rubs up against the person until he ejaculates. While rubbing against or touching the person, the frotteur may fantasize that they are involved in a close, intimate relationship. To avoid detection, he acts quickly and is prepared to run before his victim realizes what is happening. Customarily, it is a very brief encounter and the victim may be unaware of what has just taken place.

As with other paraphilias, learning theory provides a useful model for understanding the development of frotteurism. According to this view, at a point in the frotteur's life, this behavior was acquired through a pleasurable, perhaps inadvertent experience, and each repetition of the behavior provides additional reinforcement. Treatment involves an unlearning of these associations through such methods as extinction and covert conditioning.

Sexual Masochism and Sexual Sadism The term **masochism** comes from the name of nineteenth-century Austrian writer Leopold Baron von Sacher-Masoch (1836–1895), known for his novels about men who were sexually humiliated by women. A masochist is someone who seeks pleasure from being subjected to pain. The term *sadism* comes from the name of eighteenth-century French author Marquis de Sade (1740–1814), who wrote extensively about obtaining sexual enjoyment from inflicting cruelty. The psychiatric terms *masochism* and *sadism* were coined by Krafft-Ebing (1840–1903), a German physician who pioneered the scholarly approach to understanding the broad range of human sexual behavior in his book *Psychopathia Sexualis* (Krafft-Ebing, 1886/1950).

Sexual masochism is a disorder marked by an attraction to achieving sexual gratification by having painful stimulation applied to one's own body, either alone or with a partner. Men and women with this disorder achieve sexual satisfaction by such means as binding with cloth or ropes, injuring the skin with pins or knives, or administering electric shocks. Some sexual masochists do not act on their fantasies, but they feel recurrent urges and may feel distressed by the power of these urges.

Sexual sadism is the converse of sexual masochism in that it involves deriving sexual gratification from activities that harm, or from urges to harm, another person. Seeing or imagining another's pain excites the sadist. In contrast to sexual masochism, which does not require a partner, sexual sadism clearly does require a partner to enact sadistic fantasies.

People with these disorders may alternate playing sadistic and masochistic roles. In some sexual activities, one of the partners acts in a very submissive role and begs to be hurt and humiliated. In other activities, the partners reverse the roles such that the previously submissive person now inflicts the pain and dominates the interaction. The term **sadomasochist** refers to people who derive sexual pleasure from both inflicting and receiving pain.

The specialized nature of their sexual activities and their desire to meet other people with similar preferences lead some sadomasochistic individuals to join organizations designed to cater to their needs, such as the Till Eulenspiegel Society in New York City or the Janus Society in San Francisco. They may use the Internet to find others who share their interests using chat rooms or emails to communicate with people around the world. Obviously, it is difficult to conduct research on people with this disorder. In a rare survey of sadomasochists who were members of such a society, researchers found the most prevalent sadistic sexual interests to be spanking, master-slave relationships, extremely restrictive bondage, humiliation, and restraint. Less common were infliction of pain, whipping, verbal abuse, less

Mini Case

SEXUAL SADISM AND SEXUAL MASOCHISM

For a number of years, Ray has insisted that his wife, Jeanne, submit him to demeaning and abusive sexual behavior. In the early years of their relationship, Ray's requests involved relatively innocent pleas that Jeanne pinch him and bite his chest while they were sexually intimate. Over time, however, his requests for pain increased and the nature of the pain changed. At present, they engage in what they call "special sessions," during which Jeanne handcuffs Ray to the bed and inflicts various forms of torture. Jeanne goes along with Ray's requests that she surprise him with new ways of inflicting pain, so she has developed a repertoire of behaviors, ranging from burning Ray's skin with matches to cutting him with razor blades. Jeanne and Ray have no interest in sexual intimacy other than that involving pain.

Diagnostic Features of Sexual Sadism

- For a period lasting at least 6 months, people with this condition have recurrent, intense sexually arousing fantasies, sexual urges, or behaviors involving real or simulated acts in which they are sexually excited by the psychological or physical suffering or humiliation of another person.

- The person has acted on these sexual urges with a nonconsenting person, or the sexual urges or fantasies cause significant distress or impairment.

Diagnostic Features of Sexual Masochism

- For a period lasting at least 6 months, people with this condition have recurrent, intense sexually arousing fantasies, sexual urges, or behaviors involving real or simulated acts of being humiliated, beaten, bound, or made to suffer in other ways.

- The fantasies, sexual urges, or behaviors cause significant distress or impairment.

---

severe bondage, and enemas and other toilet-related activities. Some people act out dramatic scenarios, such as being led around on a collar and leash and ordered to act like a submissive puppy who may be spanked for slight misbehaviors. Interestingly, women and men reported similar levels of interest in most of these behaviors, with somewhat higher percentages of women indicating interest in bondage and verbal abuse (Breslow, Evans, & Langley, 1985).

Activities such as cutting, bondage, pricking, and shocking can be dangerous, and this danger adds to the excitement sadomasochists feel. Even more extreme, however, is strangling to the point of oxygen deprivation, wearing a mask or plastic bag over the head, placing a noose around one's neck, or ingesting a nitrate

gas, which causes asphyxiation. This type of activity, which some individuals practice while alone, is usually accompanied by fantasies of near escapes from death; however, such fantasies sometimes become reality when the limits are pushed too far.

One avenue to understanding sexual sadism and sexual masochism is to consider the role that punishment and discipline played in the early lives of people with these disorders. Presumably, these individuals formed a connection between sexual excitation and the experience of pain or chastisement. The attention they received in the process of being disciplined may have been the only caretaking they received from otherwise negligent parents. Perhaps even a beating was preferable to being ignored, leading to a later sexual preference for masochism. Another

Some people are so driven by masochistic needs that they will pay in order to be sexually humiliated.

scenario involves the pairing of physical punishment with subsequent parental cuddling and reassurance, leading the individual to associate pain with love. Sadists, conversely, may be driven by a wish to conquer others in the way that harsh parental figures controlled them early in life. The fact that sadists and masochists may switch roles complicates this analysis, but it is possible that the need for cooperating partners drives their reversal of sexual roles.

In rare cases, individuals who have sexual sadism commit sexual homicide. Based on an analysis of cases reported over the past century, one researcher proposed a typology of sexual murderers (Meloy, 2000). The first group consists of sexual sadists who also have antisocial or narcissistic personality disorders. These individuals have classic psychopathic traits such as emotional detachment, and they leave behind an organized crime scene. The second group is composed of individuals who have a mood disorder as well as personality disorders that involve schizoid and avoidant traits. Unlike the psychopathic sexual murderers, this second group has a history of early physical or sexual abuse. Although the "sample" in this study clearly was nonrandom and based on limited data, it is the only one of its kind to attempt to bring some sort of clarity into this otherwise almost inscrutable form of human behavior.

Most sadists and masochists do not seek professional help. In fact, the vast majority have no interest in changing their behaviors. They usually come to the attention of professionals only when their behavior results in physical injury or when they become distressed over ending a relationship with a partner. For the small number of people who spontaneously seek help and wish to change their sadistic or masochistic behaviors, group and individual therapy focusing on the behavioral principles of conditioning and reinforcement have been found most effective. Lutenizing hormone–releasing hormone (LHRH), mentioned earlier in the treatment of people with pedophilia, may also prove to have value in treating individuals with sexual sadism (Briken et al., 2001).

Transvestic Fetishism A syndrome found only in males is **transvestic fetishism,** in which a man has an uncontrollable urge to wear a woman's clothes (called cross-dressing) as his primary means of achieving sexual gratification. This sexual gratification has a compulsive quality, and it consumes a tremendous amount of the individual's emotional energy. Cross-dressing is often accompanied by masturbation or fantasies in which the man imagines that other men are attracted to him as a woman. When he is not cross-dressed, he looks like a typical man, and he may be sexually involved with a woman. In fact, the definition of this disorder implies that the man sees himself as a man and is heterosexual in orientation.

Transvestic behaviors vary widely. Some men wear only a single item of women's clothing, such as underwear, often under their masculine outer clothing. Others have complete feminine wardrobes and, while alone, put on an entire outfit, possibly including "breasts" made with water-filled balloons or padding, as well as makeup, wigs, shoes, and other accessories. Their experience while wearing these clothes is one of having assumed a different personality. They may also find that cross-dressing

while alone relaxes them or, when having sex with a partner, increases their level of excitement. A phenomenon related to transvestic fetishism is autogynephilia, in which a man derives sexual excitement from the thought or image of himself as having female anatomy or experiencing such biological functions as menstruation, childbirth, and breast-feeding (Blanchard, 1993).

Homosexual men who make themselves up as women are not transvestic fetishists because they are generally not dressing this way to gain sexual satisfaction. They do not have the same sense of compulsion that transvestic fetishists have. Rather, cross-dressing for some homosexual men has more to do with their participation in a subculture that they find inviting.

Individuals who develop transvestic fetishism often begin cross-dressing in childhood or adolescence. Some may have been forced to wear girls' clothes as a form of humiliation or to fulfill a parental fantasy that they were actually girls. Others ventured into cross-dressing out of curiosity and found the behavior to be enjoyable. Over time, the cross-dressing behavior seems to take on a life of its own, perhaps pleasurable at first but ultimately compulsive in nature. This behavior is not without

 MindMAP Segment 7.1 provides insight into the experience of transsexual individuals as they undergo a transformation from one sex to the other.

Some individuals with gender identity disorder are so uncomfortable in their bodies that they decide to undergo surgery so that they physically become the other sex.

Mini Case

TRANSVESTIC FETISHISM

In the evenings, when his wife leaves the house for her part-time job, Phil often goes to a secret hiding place in his workshop. In a locked cabinet, Phil keeps a small wardrobe of women's underwear, stockings, high heels, makeup, a wig, and dresses. Closing all the blinds in the house and taking the phone off the hook, Phil dresses in these clothes and fantasizes that he is being pursued by several men. After about 2 hours, he usually masturbates to the point of orgasm, as he imagines that he is being seduced by a sexual partner. Following this ritual, he secretly packs up the women's clothes and puts them away. Though primarily limiting his cross-dressing activities to the evenings, he thinks about it frequently during the day, which causes him to become sexually excited and to wish that he could get away from work, go home, and put on his special clothes. Knowing that he cannot, he wears women's underwear under his workclothes, and he sneaks off to the men's room to masturbate in response to the sexual stimulation he derives from feeling the silky sensation against his body.

Diagnostic Features

- For a period lasting at least 6 months, heterosexual men with this condition have recurrent, intense sexually arousing fantasies, sexual urges, or behaviors involving cross-dressing.

- The fantasies, sexual urges, or behaviors cause significant distress or impairment.

---

conflict; in fact, transvestic fetishists go through phases in which they destroy or give away all feminine clothing, swearing that they will give up this activity.

Relatively few transvestic fetishists seek professional help, because they are reluctant to give up their cross-dressing behavior. When these men do become distressed enough to seek help, it is usually attributable to another problem, such as depression or distress stemming from feeling that their behavior is out of control. Consequently, some therapists focus on helping the individual develop a sense of control rather than on extinguishing the behavior altogether. When a person is motivated to change, therapists use behavioral methods already described in the treatment of other paraphilias, such as aversive conditioning, covert sensitization, and orgasmic reconditioning. Keep in mind that cross-dressing usually serves the purpose of reducing anxiety for the individual; therefore, the therapist may encourage the client to try to gain insight into the stresses that precipitate the behavior through more traditional psychotherapy.

Voyeurism The word *voyeur* comes from the French word *voir* ("to see"). **Voyeurism** is a sexual disorder in which the individual has a compulsion to derive sexual gratification from observing the nudity or sexual activity of others who are unaware of being watched. The disorder is more common in men. The colloquial term "Peeping Tom" is often used to refer to a **voyeur**. This is a reference to the character Tom the Tailor, who was the

only one in town to violate Lady Godiva's request for privacy when she rode nude on horseback through her town.

Unlike people who become sexually aroused when watching a sexual partner undress or a performer in a sexually explicit movie, the voyeur has the recurrent and intense desire to observe unsuspecting people. The voyeur is sexually frustrated and feels incapable of establishing a regular sexual relationship with the person he observes. He prefers to masturbate either during or soon after the voyeuristic activity. "Peeping" provides him with a substitute form of sexual gratification.

As is the case with the other paraphilias we have discussed, very few voyeurs seek treatment voluntarily. Only when apprehended and coerced into treatment do they reluctantly obtain professional help. Once in therapy, many voyeurs are still unwilling to change. The preferred method of treatment for voyeurism includes behavioral techniques similar to those used for treating exhibitionists (Schwartz, 1994). For example, the voyeur may be told to imagine that he is apprehended and publicly humiliated as he is engaging in his voyeuristic behaviors. Therapy might also focus on self-esteem issues, because a poor self-image is thought to contribute to a predilection for voyeuristic activity (Rhoads, 1989).

Theories and Treatment of Paraphilias

In the preceding sections, you have read about the specific theories and treatment that relate to each of the paraphilias. Although each condition warrants an individualized approach, there are

Mini Case

VOYEURISM

Edward is a university senior who lives in a crowded dormitory complex. On most evenings, he sneaks around in the bushes, looking for a good vantage point from which to gaze into the windows of women students. Using binoculars, he is able to find at least one room in which a woman is undressing. The thrill of watching this unsuspecting victim brings Edward to the peak of excitement as he masturbates. Edward has been engaging in this behavior for the past 3 years, dating back to an incident when he walked past a window and inadvertently saw a naked woman. This event aroused him to such a degree that he became increasingly compelled to seek out the same excitement again and again.

Diagnostic Features

- For a period lasting at least 6 months, people with this condition have recurrent, intense sexually arousing fantasies, sexual urges, or behaviors involving the act of observing unsuspecting people who are naked, in the process of undressing, or engaging in sexual activity.

- The person has acted on these sexual urges, or the sexual urges or fantasies cause significant distress or impairment.

some general principles that apply across the board. Most paraphilias have their roots in childhood experiences, and they emerge during adolescent years as sexual forces within the body intensify. Once established, the paraphilia tends to be chronic.

One of the most prolific twentieth-century researchers in the area of human sexuality, John Money (Money & Ehrhardt, 1973/1996) theorized that paraphilias are due to distorted "lovemaps." According to Money, a **lovemap** is the representation of an individual's sexual fantasies and preferred practices. Lovemaps are formed early in life, during what Money considers to be a critical period of development: the late childhood years, when an individual first begins to discover and test ideas regarding sexuality. "Misprints" in this process can result in the establishment of sexual habits and practices that deviate from the norm. A paraphilia, according to this view, is due to a lovemap gone awry. The individual is, in a sense, programmed to act out fantasies that are socially unacceptable and potentially harmful. As discussed earlier, a paraphilia may occur in the context of sex with a partner. Such a behavior reflects a courtship disorder, a disturbed view of appropriate sexual behavior in relationships.

Although some theorists have suggested that individuals who become paraphilic are biologically predisposed to these behaviors through genetic, hormonal, or neurological abnormalities, as we saw in connection with pedophilia, a biological explanation alone is considered insufficient. According to a behavioral approach, one or more learning events have taken place in a person's childhood involving a conditioned response of sexual pleasure with an inappropriate stimulus object. Over time, the individual has become compulsively driven to pursue the gratification (reinforcement) associated with the object or experience. Often a sense of power accompanies this gratification. In other words, the voyeur experiences both sexual excitation and power when he is "peeping." Similarly, the exhibitionist, the frotteur, and the pedophile can satisfy both sexual and self-esteem needs through "successful" experiences with the object of desire. Another theory proposes that people with paraphilias have a general deficit of control. Rather than having acquired only one specific paraphilic behavior, they cross over from one paraphilia to another, or enact behaviors from more than one category (Abel & Osborn, 1992).

As we have seen, the treatment of people with paraphilias is particularly difficult, because these individuals are often reluctant to give up the pleasurable behavior or are too ashamed to seek help. Biological, psychological, and sociocultural interventions have been used in various combinations for these treatments. In the biological sphere, as we mentioned in our discussion of pedophilia, there are several forms of intervention, some much more extreme than others. The more commonly used medical interventions involve the prescription of pharmacological agents, such as antidepressant medications, SSRIs, and hormones, all of which are directed at reducing the individual's sexual desire (Bradford, 2001). Rarely would a clinician limit treatment to a medical intervention, however. Rather,

psychological and sociocultural components would play very important roles. In the psychological realm, the most commonly used techniques are behavioral and cognitive-behavioral. In the sociocultural sphere, clinicians often look for ways to involve the client in group therapy, in which other people with similar problems share their experiences and their efforts to achieve self-control. Furthermore, couple and family therapy may be recommended, with the goal of obtaining support and assistance from the individuals who are closest to the client.

The main goal of treatment of people with paraphilias who have committed criminal acts is to change the offender's desire to enact sexually deviant behaviors. Media attention to sexual crimes and frustration with the difficulty of treating sex offenders have led to the enactment of sexual predator laws in a number of states. These laws are intended to confine offenders who are considered at risk for committing similar crimes in the future (Noffsinger & Resnick, 2000). Similar laws mandating treatment and involuntary confinement were enacted in the 1940s and eventually repealed because treatment could not be proven to lower the rates of recidivism. Newer treatment methods, including cognitive-behavioral therapy, seem to hold greater promise, but it will be necessary to provide the resources to make these treatments more widely available (Wood, Grossman, & Fichtner, 2000).

Gender Identity Disorders

The term **gender identity** refers to the individual's self-perception as a male or female. However, an individual's gender identity may or may not match the **assigned** (or **biological**) sex that is recorded on the birth certificate. **Gender role** refers to a person's behaviors and attitudes that are indicative of maleness or femaleness in one's society.

Sexual orientation is the degree to which a person is erotically attracted to members of the same or opposite sex. Most people have a clear orientation to have sexual activity with members of the other sex, but some are attracted to members of the same sex, and yet others are attracted to members of both sexes. Constancy of sexual orientation is typical but not universal; some people change over time and due to circumstances.

Characteristics of Gender Identity Disorders

A **gender identity disorder** is a condition involving a discrepancy between an individual's assigned sex and the person's gender identity. People with gender identity disorders experience a strong and persistent cross-gender identification, which causes feelings of discomfort and a sense of inappropriateness about their assigned gender. Individuals with this condition have intense feelings of distress and usually have adjustment problems in social, occupational, and other areas of personal functioning. You may have heard the more commonly used term **transsexualism,** which also refers to this phenomenon in which a person has an inner feeling of belonging to the other sex. Some people with gender identity disorders wish to live as members of the other sex, and they act and dress accordingly. Unlike individuals with transvestic fetishism, these people do not derive sexual gratification from cross-dressing.

Considerable debate has emerged in recent years about the validity of characterizing dysphoria (i.e., extreme sadness) related to gender identity as a disorder, particularly when diagnosing children (Zucker, 2005; Zucker & Spitzer, 2005). Critics of such pathologizing make several arguments. First, they argue that gender identity disorder is nothing more than a normal variation, arguably extreme, in gender-related behavior. Second, they assert that children with this condition are not especially distressed or impaired, except in reaction to the social disapproval they face. Third, they point out that because gender identity disorder in children is a predictor of homosexual orientation in adulthood, the pathologizing of this condition in children is a veiled maneuver to prevent these individuals from becoming homosexual. In support of the notion of viewing these gender-related conditions as disorders is the belief that most people with such conditions do indeed experience an intense level of distress, far greater than one would expect just as a reaction to others. Their distress is understood as attributable to the marked disjunction between their bodily sex and their psychological gender and is intense enough to motivate many to seek professional help (Zucker, 2005).

As you can imagine, dialogue about gender identity disorder involves complex issues which have provoked emotionally charged arguments. Social attitudes have changed drastically during the past two decades with increased openness to viewing sexuality in dimensional rather than categorical terms. Because gender identity disorder remains in the formal diagnostic system, we discuss the condition in this text, but anticipate that many changes will take place in the years ahead regarding the extent to which this condition is regarded as an appropriate inclusion in *DSM-IV*.

A girl with gender identity disorder may refuse to acknowledge that she possesses a girl's body and, instead, insists that she will grow a penis. She may express this rejection of her female sex in various behaviors, such as standing while she urinates and refusing to have anything to do with normative feminine behavior or dress. When asked to wear a new dress, she may become angry and resentful and may choose to avoid social situations in which customs would dictate wearing feminine clothing. Similarly, a boy with gender identity disorder may disdain the fact that he is a male with a penis, and he may push it between his legs to make believe it is not part of his body. He may have an aversion to wearing pants and, instead, be attracted to more traditionally feminine clothing. Rather than play stereotypically male games, he may prefer, for example, to play house with other children and insist that he play the role of a female. This is a profoundly experienced psychological disorder. It does not refer to what some would call transient "tomboy" or "sissy" behaviors.

Distress over their assigned sex is usually evident before children with gender identity disorder reach their fourth birth-

day. When the child begins school, parents may become increasingly concerned about the ways in which their child acts differently from peers. For many of these children, the overt cross-gender behaviors become less evident as they grow into adolescence, but the disorder persists as the individual struggles with an ongoing feeling of inappropriateness about being male or female along with recurrent fantasies or cross-dressing behavior. In time, many individuals with gender identity disorder find themselves feeling deeply depressed because of the "prison" in which they must live. They may become increasingly isolated and may involve themselves only in activities in which gender has no bearing.

Some males with gender identity disorder are so disturbed by their ostensible sex characteristics that they resort to self-treatment by taking hormones or, in extreme cases, self-castration. There are reports, particularly in urban centers, of males with this disorder engaging in prostitution. The distress is so profound that some individuals get caught in a cycle of substance abuse and addiction in an effort to alleviate their emotional turmoil; when all else fails, some attempt suicide (American Psychiatric Association, 2000).

Researchers on the topic of gender identity disorder have devoted tremendous effort to gauging the developmental age during which this condition is first evident. The determination of dissatisfaction about gender is complicated by the fact that many young children act and speak in ways suggesting that they would prefer to be the other sex. In fact, there is not a great gender difference in such expressions; if anything, in normal children girls show a greater likelihood than boys of wishing to be the opposite sex. However, gender-conflicted boys are seven times more likely than gender-conflicted girls to be referred for professional help. This difference is attributed to the lower tolerance in society for boys dressing like girls (Bradley & Zucker, 1997). Even as gender-dysphoric individuals grow older, females report fewer emotional problems, perhaps because it is more acceptable for women to act and dress in stereotypically masculine ways than it is for men to act and dress in stereotypically feminine ways. Consequently, it is not surprising that men are more likely than women to seek professional psychological help (American Psychiatric Association, 2000).

In adult males, two considerably different pictures emerge regarding the development of gender identity disorder. In some, the condition is an extension of the gender identity disorder experienced during childhood. In others, however, cross-gender identification emerges more gradually later in life, sometimes associated with a history of transvestic fetishism. In these cases, the cross-gender identification tends to fluctuate as do the individuals' feelings about sex reassignment surgery (American Psychiatric Association, 2000).

Complicating efforts to understand gender identity disorder is the variable of sexual orientation. There is a strong relationship between childhood cross-gender behavior and later homosexual orientation in men and women (Bailey & Kucker, 1995). However, not all homosexual men and women have a history of cross-gender behavior in their childhood. The relationship

Kate Bornstein, a former heterosexual male and one-time Scientologist and IBM salesperson, is now a lesbian woman writer and actress who frequently appears on college campuses.

between gender identity disorder and adult sexual orientation becomes even fuzzier when the issue is raised as to whether a person with gender identity disorder has a homosexual or heterosexual orientation. A transsexual individual whose body is female and whose gender identity is male would reject the label of homosexual just because of an attraction to females. Rather, this person would want to be considered heterosexual, because the object of sexual desire is the "other sex." To deal with this issue, clinicians specify the gender of those to whom people with gender identity disorder are attracted: males, females, both, or neither.

It seems that males with gender identity disorder who are sexually attracted to males are more likely to have had a lifelong history of gender dysphoria. In contrast, those who are sexually attracted to females, or to both males and females, or to neither sex, are more likely to experience cross-gender identification later in life, and most typically following a history of transvestic fetishism (American Psychiatric Association, 2000).

Theories and Treatment of Gender Identity Disorders

The causes of gender identity disorder are not well understood, but, as in many of our discussions so far, biological, psychological, and sociocultural factors seem to play important roles. Biological research has focused on the effects of hormones that affect the development of the fetus during the prenatal period of life. Thus, females exposed to increased levels of androgens in the uterus are more likely to display stereotypically male gender role behaviors during childhood (Collaer & Hines, 1995). Most available research, however, has focused on biological males with gender identity disorder, although that is likely to

change with increasing attention to this condition. In rare cases, chromosomal abnormalities may exist, including an extra Y chromosome in the 23rd pair (47,XYY) in male-to-female transsexuals and an extra X chromosome (47,XXX) in female-to-males (Turan et al., 2000). Based on the assumption that children's play patterns are affected by hormonal factors, there is additional evidence that supports the biological approach to gender identity disorder. In one study, the males in treatment for gender identity disorder were described by their mothers as having been less likely to engage in so-called rough and tumble play than their peers. The girls in treatment for gender identity disorder were described as more likely to prefer rough play (Bradley & Zucker, 1997).

Carrying biological inquiry in another direction, researchers have been trying to understand findings about the relationship between birth order and the gender of siblings in individuals with gender identity disorder. For some reason, boys with this condition have a later birth order in the family than do boys in matched control groups (Blanchard & Bogaert, 1996), and they are more likely to have more brothers than sisters (Blanchard et al., 1996). Homosexual male-to-female transsexuals have a similar position in the family (Green, 2000). The precise ways in which these variables interact with gender identity remain unclear.

In contrast to the big-picture characteristics of birth order and sibling structure, researchers have also studied more subtle characteristics that differentiate individuals with gender identity disorder. Boys with gender identity disorder are acutely sensitive to various sensory stimuli and to the emotional expressiveness of their parents. Once again, it is difficult to understand how these characteristics influence gender identity, but somehow a vulnerability to high arousal and a sensitivity to parental affect are important factors in the development of gender identity disorder (Bradley & Zucker, 1997).

In the psychological realm, the picture is even murkier, as researchers have sorted through many hypotheses. In one avenue of study, investigators wondered about the importance of a parent's preference for a child of the other gender. There are no data to confirm that a parent's wish to have a girl can cause a boy to develop gender identity disorder (or vice versa), but there are some findings that suggest that, for some mothers of boys with gender identity disorder, disappointment with the birth of yet another son, rather than a daughter, may negatively influence her relationship with the boy (Bradley & Zucker, 1997). This is an interesting finding, but certainly not sufficient to explain the development of gender identity disorder. Researchers will continue to study other factors, such as early attachment experiences, parents' unintentional reinforcement of cross-gender behavior, and the powerful inner image that can result in which an individual develops a cross-gender identity.

The widely publicized case of David Reimer, described in *As Nature Made Him* (Colapinto, 2001), calls into question the premise that gender is determined by social influences. The case involves a 7-month-old baby boy whose surgery to correct a genital abnormality was botched, resulting in serious damage to his penis. After consulting with John Money, surgeons removed the baby's male genitals and constructed a vagina. The boy was then raised as a girl. The underlying premise was that children have no "gender" at birth and that biological sex plays no role in their psychosexual development. Initial reports on the child's adjustment during early childhood were favorable; however, as the years went by, the characteristics of this individual mirrored more stereotypically male interests and behaviors. The individual ultimately reached a crisis as she/he became more and more distressed with issues pertaining to sexual identity and developed serious psychological problems. When the individual was informed about his biological sex, he decided to undergo another series of surgeries to revert back to being a male (Diamond & Sigmundson, 1997).

Although sociocultural theories would not be sufficient for explaining the development of gender identity disorder, it is important to consider various ways in which American society idealizes men and women according to certain stereotypical variables. An impressionable child who is struggling with confusion that is biologically and psychologically rooted may be drawn to a resolution of the confusion by idealizing the attributes of attractive and successful members of the opposite sex.

Clinical work with individuals with gender identity disorder depends greatly on the age of the individual. Psychotherapy involving a child distressed about gender might involve the discouragement of cross-gender behavior and encouragement of the development of same-sex skills and friendships. The intervention would be primarily with the parents, if the identified client is a very young child, with an emphasis on helping the child develop greater self-value as either a boy or a girl. For older children and adolescents, the clinician would deal more directly with the client's cross-gender behavior and fantasy, as well as other distressing psychological experiences such as low self-esteem and fear of familial and peer rejection (Bradley & Zucker, 1997). Clinicians working with gender-disordered adults approach the therapy in much the same way they approach therapy with clients who are very dissatisfied with their lives. They help clients understand the causes of their distress, focusing on possible biological, psychological, and sociocultural origins. Most important, they provide support and help clients with gender identity disorder learn how to live with these feelings and experiences.

A small minority of individuals with gender identity disorder seek sex reassignment surgery; for these people, the term *transsexual* is appropriate in that they are "crossing over" to the other sex. In this process, individuals confront several complex issues. First, the procedure is available at only a few medical facilities and can cost hundreds of thousands of dollars. Second, the few surgeons who carry out these procedures insist that the individual complete a lengthy course of psychotherapy and a comprehensive psychological assessment prior to being accepted for surgery. Along with this, the individual must have lived as a member of the other sex during the evaluation period; this includes changes in legal name, clothing, and self-presentation.

Third, and perhaps most significant, the surgery is very complicated, and the physical results are never perfect. Female-to-male transsexuals cannot expect to have a penis that looks or functions normally. For example, a constructed penis may require artificial inflation to become erect. Although the male-to-female surgery is less complicated, there are still some risks, such as the possibility of the constructed vagina closing up following surgery. In addition, individuals also need hormonal supplements to facilitate the change and to maintain the secondary sex characteristics of the new gender (Asscheman & Gooren, 1992; Cohen-Kettenis & Gooren, 1992). Finally, although surgery changes a person's genitals, it cannot give a person the childbearing capability of the newly acquired gender. In Germany, there is evidence of a reduction in the ratio of male-to-female surgeries in the 1990s. A study of the nearly 1,800 patients studied from 1964 to 1998 who had undergone sex reassignment surgery showed that the 2:1 ratio decreased to a 1.2:1 ratio of male-to-female cases (Garrels et al., 2000).

Most studies evaluating the effectiveness of reassignment surgery provide evidence of psychological improvement following the surgery (Cohen-Kettenis & van Goozen, 1997). The people who are dissatisfied after treatment appear to be the male-to-female individuals who were disappointed with unalterable bodily characteristics, such as large hands and feet, the persistence of the Adam's apple, and the quality of their voice (Rakic, Starcevic, Maric, & Kelin, 1996).

It is also important to consider who should not be given sex reassignment surgery based on other clinical indicators. In a follow-up of nearly 50 adolescents with gender identity disorder, those who were treated were functioning well, psychologically and socially, 1 to 4 years after their surgery. Those who were rejected for treatment continued to show signs of psychological dysfunction. Yet it was considered appropriate for these individuals not to be treated with sex reassignment surgery, given their high levels of psychopathology (Smith, van Goozen, & Cohen-Kettenis, 2001).

The level of improvement in the lives of these people depends on a number of factors. First, satisfaction is usually greater when the transition is from female-to-male rather than male-to-female. Researchers are not sure why there is a difference, but they consider the possibility that men who become women may be surprised and troubled when they encounter some of the disadvantages that women experience in society as a result of sexist attitudes. Second, people who are better adjusted prior to the surgery are more likely to experience a favorable outcome. This is especially true if they encounter little difficulty in being accepted as a person of their newly assumed gender (Kuiper & Cohen-Kettenis, 1988). Third, the strength of the individual's commitment and identification as a member of the other sex prior to surgery is important, because this provides the motivation and determination to carry through with the procedures. Fourth, the quality of the surgery itself is related to successful adjustment. Individuals who receive high-quality surgical care with anatomically convincing results are likely to have an easier

Mini Case

GENDER IDENTITY DISORDER

Dale describes himself as a woman living in a man's body. His memories back to the age of 4 are of feeling discomfort with his assigned sex. When he was a young child, people often mistook him for a girl, because his mannerisms, style of play, and clothes were stereotypically feminine. He was glad he had an ambiguous name, and throughout adolescence he led others to believe he really was a girl. Schoolmates teased him at times, but this did not bother him, because he took pride in his feminine attributes. Dale's parents became increasingly alarmed, and they sent him to a psychologist when he was 15 years old. The psychologist recognized that Dale had a gender identity disorder, and she explained to Dale that he could not pursue sex reassignment surgery until adulthood, because a surgeon would insist that Dale have the maturity and life experience necessary for making such a dramatic decision. Now, at the age of 25, Dale is about to follow through on his wish to have the body of a woman and is consulting sex reassignment specialists at a major medical school to prepare for the surgery. After an initial evaluation, Dale was told that he needed to begin a presurgery evaluation process that would last for at least a year and a half. During this time, he would live publicly as a woman. This would involve dressing as a woman and changing all documentation that referred to him as a male (such as voting records, credit card applications, and driver's license). He would have to enter psychotherapy to evaluate his psychological health and readiness for surgery. Dale also had to begin taking hormones that would cause him to develop female secondary sex characteristics. After successfully completing the evaluation process, Dale would be able to enter the next phase of the sex reassignment process in which his physical characteristics would start to be transformed.

Diagnostic Features

- People with this condition have a strong and persistent cross-gender identification that is far greater than a desire for perceived cultural advantages associated with the opposite sex.
- In children, the disorder is evident by four of the following: (1) they repeatedly state their desire to be the other sex, or insist that they already are; (2) boys prefer cross-dressing, while girls insist on wearing only stereotypical masculine clothing; (3) they have a strong and persistent preference for cross-sex roles in make-believe play, or persistent fantasies of being the other sex; (4) they have an intense desire to participate in the games and activities stereotypically associated with the other sex; and (5) they have a strong preference for playmates of the other sex.
- In adolescents and adults, this disturbance is manifested by such symptoms as a stated desire to be the other sex, frequent passing as the other sex, and the conviction that he or she has the typical feelings and reactions of a person of the other sex.
- An individual with this condition has persistent discomfort with his or her sex or feels a sense of inappropriateness in the gender role of his or her biological sex.
- The disturbance is not concurrent with a physical condition involving ambiguous genitals.
- The disturbance causes significant distress or impairment.
- Sexual attraction may be to males, females, both, or neither.

---

time adapting to their lives as members of the opposite gender (Green et al., 1990; Rakic et al., 1996).

Despite the controversy surrounding this complicated and costly surgery, sex reassignment appears to be a valid alternative for individuals with severe gender identity disorder (Snaith, Tarsh, & Reid, 1993). Selection criteria have been developed to ensure that individuals seeking sex reassignment are appropriate candidates for the surgery (Cote & Wilchesky, 1996), and psychotherapy can assist the person to resolve other psychological problems and to adjust to the new gender role prior to surgery. A possible complication following surgery is that the person may have expected the operation to resolve many other life problems; psychotherapy can be useful at this point to help the person develop a more balanced outlook about his or her postoperative future. Advances in reproductive technology also enable people who have undergone sex reassignment surgery to have children who are biologically their own (De Sutter, 2001). Storing sperm or oocytes prior to the treatment allows for subsequent parenthood, enabling these individuals to maintain their reproductive potential. Finally, the growth and acceptance of the gender identity movement may help individuals adjust and live more happily in the context of a supportive and understanding community.

Sexual Dysfunctions

The disorders we will discuss in this section are very different from the paraphilias and gender identity disorder in that they are not considered deviant behaviors, and they involve no victimization of others. The term **sexual dysfunction** refers to an abnormality in an individual's sexual responsiveness and reactions.

The National Health and Social Life Survey (NHSLS) has revealed that a surprisingly high percentage of people living in the United States report symptoms of sexual dysfunction (Laumann, Paik, & Rosen, 1999). Overall, the rates of sexual dysfunction reported in this survey were 43 percent for women and 31 percent for men. The rates of sexual problems in the NHSLS varied somewhat by age, with 32 percent of women and 14 percent of men ages 18 to 29 reporting that they lacked interest in sex. In this age group, 26 percent of women and 7 percent of men stated that they were unable to achieve orgasm. Similar percentages were observed in the 30- to 39-year-old age group. These findings dispel the notion that only older adults report sexual dysfunction. Additional results indicated the importance of sexual functioning for quality of daily life. There were negative relationships between feelings of happiness and the presence of sexual dysfunction. Very few individuals with a sexual dysfunction sought professional help (10 percent of men and 20 percent of women).

Characteristics of Sexual Dysfunctions

Sexual dysfunctions are defined by the individual, often in terms of an intimate relationship and almost invariably in the context of cultural expectations and values about what constitutes normal sexual functioning. There is no one "correct" pattern of sexual activity; what one individual considers dysfunctional, another may regard as healthy and normal. Unfortunately, people may regard themselves as having a sexual dysfunction without being aware of the extent to which their behavior falls within the range of normal behavior. For example, in one study that queried people about reaching orgasm, three quarters of the men interviewed reported that they always reach orgasm during sexual intercourse, whereas the proportion of women was nearer to one fourth (Laumann et al., 1994). Looking at these figures in another way, does this mean that the remaining one fourth of men and three fourths of women are "abnormal"? Do they have a sexual dysfunction? An important factor to keep in mind as you read about each of the disorders in this section is whether or not a person feels distressed about the behavior.

Another feature of sexual dysfunctions that will become evident as you read the clinical descriptions and case histories is that sometimes sexual dysfunctions are signs or symptoms of problems in a person's life that do not directly pertain to sexuality. For example, a person who is very upset about job-related stresses or family problems may develop sexual performance problems. At times, people are not even aware of the connection between the sexual problem and other life stresses. On the other hand, some sexual problems are more clearly connected to problems within a particular relationship or to experiences in the person's past in which the foundation of a sexual problem was established. Clinicians refer to several distinctions in characterizing the nature of a sexual dysfunction. First, they question whether a dysfunction is attributable to a psychological factor, such as depression or relationship problems, or is due to a combination of psychological factors and physical factors, such as illness or substance use. They also distinguish between lifelong and acquired types, as well as between situational and generalized sexual dysfunctions. A lifelong dysfunction has been present since the beginning of active sexual functioning, whereas an acquired problem has developed following a period of normal functioning. Situational dysfunctions occur with only certain types of sexual stimulation, situations, or partners, whereas generalized dysfunctions are not limited.

Although our discussion refers to disturbances in heterosexual functioning, lesbians and gay men can also be affected by these disorders. Clinicians and researchers are increasing their attention to understanding and treating lesbians and gay men with sexual dysfunctions, but most of the publications to date have focused on heterosexuals.

Virginia Johnson and William Masters brought into the open the discussion of human sexual functioning and dysfunctions.

To understand sexual dysfunctions, it is helpful to gain a perspective on the factors that contribute to healthy sexual functioning. Masters and Johnson (1966, 1970), in their pioneering research on human sexuality, systematically observed the sexual responses of men and women under controlled laboratory conditions. Their research was widely publicized and helped dispel many myths regarding sexuality. For example, their observational studies of women provided more or less definitive proof that there is no physiological difference between vaginal and clitoral orgasms. This finding vindicated those who had disagreed with Freud's vigorous assertions that they differ. Not only did Masters and Johnson provide a more scientific basis for understanding sexual dysfunctions, but they also took a more humanistic approach to these disorders, treating them, insofar as possible, in the context of the interpersonal relationships in which they often develop.

The work of Masters and Johnson is not without its flaws, however. One criticism is that the laboratory setting they used was too artificial to provide a valid indicator of sexual functioning in naturalistic settings. Other criticisms are based on the selectivity of the sample. Think about whether you would want to

TABLE 7.2 Phases of Human Sexual Response Cycle and Associated Disorders

Phase	Male	Female
Sexual desire		
Normal response	Interest in sexual activity	Interest in sexual activity
Sexual dysfunctions	Hypoactive sexual desire disorder, sexual aversion disorder	Hypoactive sexual desire disorder, sexual aversion disorder
Sexual arousal		
Normal response	Penile erection	Lubrication and swelling of vagina
Sexual dysfunctions	Male erectile disorder	Female sexual arousal disorder
Orgasm		
Normal response	Feeling of inevitability of orgasm, followed by rhythmic contractions of prostate and urethra and expulsion of semen	Rhythmic contractions of vagina and uterus
Sexual dysfunctions	Male orgasmic disorder, premature ejaculation	Female orgasmic disorder

participate in this kind of research. Every aspect of a subject's sexual responses was monitored via electrophysiological recording devices, devices that obviously would be intrusive and uncomfortable. Even more to the point, the participants in this research had to be willing to allow a team of male and female researchers to observe them engaging in sexual acts. In addition, they had to be motivated enough to undergo the effort and expense of the therapy process. They also had to be willing to disclose highly personal details about their lives and sexual idiosyncrasies. Masters and Johnson have also been criticized for what some regard as a sex bias in some of their diagnostic criteria that tends to pathologize women who have few or no orgasms. Despite these limitations, the work of Masters and Johnson has received widespread recognition and continues to be used as the foundation for understanding the sexual dysfunctions.

Masters and Johnson identified four phases of the sexual response cycle: arousal, plateau, orgasm, and resolution. During the arousal stage, the individual's sexual interest heightens, and the body prepares for sexual intercourse (vaginal lubrication in the female, penile erection in the male). Sexual excitement continues to build during the plateau phase, and during the orgasm phase the individual experiences muscular contractions in the genital area that are associated with intense sensations of pleasure. The resolution phase is a period of return to a physiologically normal state. People differ in their typical patterns of sexual activity, in that some people progress more readily through the phases and others progress at a slower pace. Not every sexual encounter necessarily involves all phases, either; an individual may, for example, become sexually aroused but not have an orgasm.

Sexual dysfunctions are associated with the arousal and orgasm phases, as well as with a person's overall level of sexual desire (see Table 7.2). Some people with sexual dysfunctions have little or no interest in sex; others experience a

delay in a particular phase of sexual arousal or do not become aroused at all. Others may become highly aroused but are unable to experience the sexual release of orgasm. Still other people proceed too rapidly through the phases from arousal to orgasm and, therefore, feel that sexual relations lack the emotional meaning associated with a more relaxed approach. In some cases, an individual's partner may feel distressed over what seems like unacceptable deviations from a desired pattern of activity. Yet other sexual dysfunctions are the result of the experience of pain rather than pleasure during a sexual encounter.

You may wonder where to draw the line between ordinary variations in human sexual responsiveness and the pattern of psychological disorder represented by a sexual dysfunction. Sexual dysfunctions involve persistent and recurrent symptoms. To illustrate this point, consider two examples. Six weeks after the birth of her third child, Heather finds that she cannot regain her former interest in having sexual relations with her husband. At her sister's advice, Heather and her husband take a 5-day vacation during which Heather's sister will care for the baby. Although she still experiences occasional fatigue that dulls her sexual appetite, Heather regains her previous interest in sexual activity. She does not have a disorder because her symptoms are temporary and nonrecurrent. Treatment would not necessarily be indicated, other than her sister's commonsense advice.

Contrast Heather's situation with that of Christine, whose desire for sexual relations with her husband has dwindled for the past 5 years, until it is now very infrequent. Christine eventually seeks treatment when she realizes that, unless things change, her husband will give up on her and find sexual gratification elsewhere. Christine's loss of sexual desire has been persistent and is considered dysfunctional.

It is important to realize that, at times, other psychological problems are the basis of sexual difficulties. For example, abnormally low sexual desire in someone who is depressed would

Mini Case

HYPOACTIVE SEXUAL DESIRE DISORDER

With the pressures of managing a full-time advertising job and raising 3-year-old twins, Carol says that she has "no time or energy" for sexual relations with her husband, Bob. In fact, they have not been sexually intimate since the birth of their children. Initially, Bob tried to be understanding and to respect the fact that Carol was recovering from a very difficult pregnancy and delivery. As the months went by, however, he became increasingly impatient and critical. The more he pressured Carol for sexual closeness, the more angry and depressed she became. Carol feels that she loves Bob, but she has no interest in sexuality. She does not think about sex and can't imagine ever being sexual again. She is saddened by the effect that this change has had on her marriage but feels little motivation to try to change.

Diagnostic Features

- People with this condition have persistent or recurrently deficient sexual fantasies and desire for sexual activity, with consideration given to factors that affect sexual functioning, such as age and the context of the person's life.

- The disturbance causes significant distress or interpersonal difficulty.

- The disturbance is not accounted for by another disorder, medical condition, or substance.

- The disturbance may be lifelong or acquired; generalized or situational; and due to psychological factors or a combination of psychological and physical factors.

---

not be considered grounds for diagnosing a sexual dysfunction but, instead, would be regarded as part of the depression.

It is also important to keep in mind that sexual dysfunctions can be physically as well as psychologically based, and that often there is an interaction between physical and psychological factors. Many people with sexual dysfunctions, and even some professionals treating them, are quick to conclude that all sexual problems must be emotionally caused; they fail to consider that a sexual problem may be associated with physical illness, medication, or general level of health. For example, diabetes mellitus is a medical condition that affects millions of people in the world and is known to cause sexual dysfunction, particularly erectile problems in men (Thomas & LoPiccolo, 1994). Without an understanding of this connection and a comprehensive medical assessment, a clinician could draw an erroneous conclusion that a man's sexual problem is due to emotional or interpersonal causes.

One final point about sexual dysfunctions is that sexual problems can begin fairly innocuously but then develop into something more serious because of anxiety about the problem. For example, Roger, who is preoccupied with work problems, experiences difficulty one night in getting an erection with his partner, and he becomes worried that he is becoming impotent.

This concern may impair Roger's performance the next time he is sexually intimate, making it even more difficult the time after that. This process may soon escalate into a dysfunction. Masters and Johnson use the term **spectatoring** to refer to the experience in which the individual feels unduly self-conscious during sexual activity, as if evaluating and monitoring his or her performance during the sexual encounter.

Hypoactive Sexual Desire Disorder

The individual with **hypoactive sexual desire disorder** has an abnormally low level of interest in sexual activity. The individual neither seeks out actual sexual relationships, imagines having them, nor has the wish for a more active sex life. The distress associated with this disorder is usually in the realm of intimate relationships, which may be difficult to sustain. For some individuals, the condition applies to all potential sexual expression, while for others it is situational, perhaps occurring only in the context of a particular relationship. It is quite likely that

Mini Case

SEXUAL AVERSION DISORDER

Howard is a 25-year-old law school student who had done very well academically, but worries often about a sexual problem that has plagued him since adolescence. Although he yearns to be in an intimate relationship with a woman, he has steered away from dating because he dreads the prospect of being sexually intimate. Although he jokingly tells others, and himself, that he is asexual, he secretly acknowledges that he is disgusted by the idea of anyone touching his genitals. He feels sexual desire, and has no difficulty masturbating to orgasm. Although he feels attracted to women, the thoughts of sexual closeness cause him to feel anxious, distressed, and at times even nauseous. Howard dates the origin of his problem to an incident that took place when he was 14 years old when he was alone in a movie theater. Next to him sat a middle-aged woman who seductively pulled Howard's hand under her dress and rubbed her genitals with it. Shocked and repulsed, Howard ran out of the theater, carrying with him a powerful image and experience that would prove to be a lasting obstacle to sexual closeness.

Diagnostic Features

- People with this disorder experience recurrent extreme aversion to, and avoidance of, genital contact with a sexual partner.

- The disturbance causes significant distress or interpersonal difficulty.

- The disturbance is not accounted for by another disorder.

- The disturbance may be lifelong or acquired; generalized or situational; and due to psychological factors or a combination of psychological and physical factors.

people develop this disorder as the result of other psychological difficulties, such as depression, prior sexual trauma, poor body image or self-esteem, interpersonal hostility, or relationship power struggles. In some cases, the disorder may develop in association with a preexisting sexual dysfunction. For example, a man who lacks ejaculatory control may lose interest in sex because of embarrassment and anxiety about his problem.

Individuals with lifelong forms of hypoactive sexual desire disorder lack any interest in sexuality from the onset of puberty. Such cases are less common, however, than those cases of individuals who develop this condition in adulthood following a period of stress or interpersonal difficulties.

Sexual Aversion Disorder

Sexual aversion disorder is characterized by an active dislike and avoidance of genital contact with a sexual partner, which causes personal distress or interpersonal problems. The individual may be interested in sex and may enjoy sexual fantasies but is repulsed by the notion of sexual activity with another person. For some, the reaction is generalized and involves a disdain for all sexually intimate behavior, including kissing and hugging. For others, the aversion is to specific facets of interpersonal

sexuality, such as vaginal penetration or genital odors. Reactions range from moderate anxiety reactions to panic attacks. People with sexual aversion disorder are distressed by the disdain they feel about sexual behavior, and they find themselves feeling lonely and resistant to entering into intimate relationships. If already in a close relationship, they usually encounter discord with their partner because of their disturbed reaction to the prospect of sexual intercourse.

Masters and Johnson (Masters, Johnson, & Kolodny, 1982) specify four primary causes of this disorder: (1) severely negative parental sex attitudes, (2) a history of sexual trauma, such as rape or incest, (3) a pattern of constant sexual pressuring by a partner in a long-term relationship, and (4) gender identity confusion in men. In the typical case, the individual has sexual activity only once or twice a year, if that often, and this is a source of strain in a long-term, monogamous relationship.

Female Sexual Arousal Disorder

A woman with **female sexual arousal disorder** experiences the persistent or recurrent inability to attain or maintain the normal lubrication-swelling response of sexual excitement

Mini Case
FEMALE SEXUAL AROUSAL DISORDER

Permella is a 40-year-old married woman who has been frustrated for the past 5 years because of sexual nonresponsiveness. She describes her relationship with her husband in positive terms, and says that they love to caress and spend intimate time together. However, their positive feelings typically turn negative when they attempt intercourse. Permella states, "My mind is turned on, but my body doesn't respond." She elaborates by explaining that her vagina remains dry and uncomfortable throughout the sexual act. Although her husband manages penetration when using a genital lubricant, Permella does not find the experience to be pleasurable. She wants more from these sexual encounters, and has consulted her gynecologist about the problem.

Diagnostic Features

- Women with this condition experience persistent or recurrent inability to attain, or to maintain, adequate genital lubrication and swelling through or during sexual activity.

- The disturbance causes significant distress or interpersonal difficulty.

- The disturbance is not better accounted for by another disorder, medical condition, or substance.

- The disturbance may be lifelong or acquired; generalized or situational; and due to psychological factors or a combination of psychological and physical factors.

Mini Case
MALE ERECTILE DISORDER

Brian is 34 years old and has been dating the same woman for more than a year. This is his first serious relationship and the first person with whom he has been sexually intimate. During the past 6 months, they have frequently tried to have intercourse, but each time they have become frustrated by Brian's inability to maintain an erection for more than a few minutes. Every time this happens, Brian becomes very upset, despite his girlfriend's reassurance that things will work out better next time. His anxiety level heightens every time he thinks about the fact that he is in his midthirties, sexually active for the first time in his life, and encountering such frustrating difficulties. He fears he is "impotent" and will never be able to have a normal sex life.

Diagnostic Features

- Men with this condition experience persistent or recurrent inability to attain or to maintain an adequate erection until completion of sexual activity.

- The disturbance causes significant distress or interpersonal difficulty.

- The disturbance is not better accounted for by another disorder, medical condition, or substance.

- The disturbance may be lifelong or acquired; generalized or situational; and due to psychological factors or a combination of psychological and physical factors.

during sexual activity. The result is personal distress or interpersonal difficulty with her partner. The desire for sexual activity remains present, though, and some women with female sexual arousal disorder are able to have orgasms, especially when their clitoris is stimulated intensely, as with a vibrator. It is during normal intercourse that their bodies become unresponsive, and they do not experience the normal physiological reaction of vaginal swelling and lubrication. Consequently, penile penetration may cause considerable discomfort and possibly pain.

Male Erectile Disorder

Male erectile disorder involves the recurrent partial or complete failure to attain or maintain an erection during sexual activity, causing the man to feel distressed or to encounter interpersonal problems in his intimate relationship. (The term *impotence* was formerly used to refer to this disorder, but it is now considered inappropriate because it implies a defect in an individual's personality.)

Like women who experience female sexual arousal disorder, men with erectile disorder retain their interest in sex. Some men can ejaculate with a flaccid penis, although their level of pleasure is less intense than they would experience with an erection. Because their erectile difficulty causes emotional distress and embarrassment, men with this disorder may avoid sex with a partner altogether. Some men experience this difficulty from the outset of every sexual encounter; other men are able to attain an erection but lose it when they attempt penetration, or soon afterwards. What is interesting, and medically important, is the fact that men with this disorder usually have no erectile difficulty while masturbating.

As with other sexual dysfunctions, this condition can be lifelong or acquired, generalized or specific to one partner. For those men with acquired erectile disorder, approximately 15 to 30 percent will find that the problem goes away in time, often as the result of a change in the intensity or quality of a relationship.

Female Orgasmic Disorder

Inability to achieve orgasm, or a distressing delay in the achievement of orgasm, constitutes **female orgasmic disorder.** This condition causes considerable personal distress or interpersonal difficulty. Some women are unable to achieve orgasm in all situations; for others, the problem is situational. They may be able to reach orgasm by means of self-stimulation or with a partner engaging in sexual behaviors other than intercourse.

For many years, women with inhibited female orgasm and female sexual arousal disorder were labeled with the offensive and inappropriate term *frigid,* which implied a flawed personality style. To understand this disorder, it is important to realize that the female orgasm spans a range of experiences. Kaplan (1986) describes how at one extreme are a small number of women who can achieve orgasm merely by engaging in erotic fantasies, stimulation of the breasts, or kissing. Then there are the approximately 20 to 30 percent who are able to reach orgasm through intercourse alone, without direct stimulation of the clitoris. Some women can reach orgasm during intercourse, but only if assisted by manual stimulation of the clitoris. Next are those women who are unable to reach orgasm with a partner, but who are able to stimulate themselves to the point of orgasm. At the far end of the continuum are the approximately 8 percent of women who have never had an orgasm at all. Kaplan points out that the

Mini Case

FEMALE ORGASMIC DISORDER

Like many of her friends, when Margaret was a teenager, she often wondered what intercourse and orgasm would feel like. When she later became sexually active in college, Margaret realized that she was probably still missing something, since she did not feel "rockets going off" as she had imagined. In fact, she never could experience orgasm when she was with a man in any kind of sexual activity. When Margaret fell in love with Howard, she fervently hoped that things would improve. However, even though he made her feel more sensual pleasure than anyone else she had known, her response to him always stopped just short of climax. She approached every sexual encounter with anxiety, and, afterwards, tended to feel depressed and inadequate. To avoid making Howard worry, however, Margaret decided it would be better to "fake" orgasm than to be honest with him. After 5 years together, she still has not told him that she is not experiencing orgasms, and she feels too embarrassed to seek professional help, despite her ongoing distress.

Diagnostic Features

- Women with this condition experience persistent or recurrent delay in, or absence of, orgasm following a normal phase of sexual excitement. Taking into consideration the wide variability in the type and intensity of stimulation that triggers female orgasm, the diagnosis is only appropriate in cases in which a woman's orgasmic capacity is less than would be reasonable for her age, sexual experience, and adequacy of sexual stimulation.

- The disturbance causes significant distress or interpersonal difficulty.

- The disturbance is not better accounted for by another disorder, medical condition, or substance.

- The disturbance may be lifelong or acquired; generalized or situational; and due to psychological factors or a combination of psychological and physical factors.

demarcation between "normal" and "pathological" on this continuum is debatable, although most clinicians would regard individuals in the last two groups as having sexual dysfunctions.

Male Orgasmic Disorder

Male orgasmic disorder, also known as inhibited male orgasm, involves a specific difficulty in the orgasm stage. As with its female counterpart, this disorder may be generalized or situational. Men with generalized orgasmic disorder find it impossible to reach orgasm in any situation, whereas men with situational orgasmic disorder have difficulty in certain situations, such as intercourse, but not during masturbation. The most common complaint of men with this disorder is that, though fully aroused during intercourse, they find it impossible to reach orgasm with a partner at the point of desired release.

This disorder ranges from mild situational delays in ejaculating to total inability to reach orgasm. At the mild end of the

spectrum are men who take an exceptionally long time before they are able to ejaculate. Then there is a group of men who require added stimulation, either from a partner or themselves, in order to reach orgasm. Perhaps they can reach orgasm only when orally and manually stimulated. Next on the continuum are men who find it possible to reach orgasm only during masturbation. At the far extreme are men who find it impossible to reach orgasm regardless of the situation. In each of these cases, the man's concern over the problem or interpersonal difficulties that emerge in his close relationship result in psychological distress.

Premature Ejaculation

The man with **premature ejaculation** reaches orgasm in a sexual encounter long before he wishes to, perhaps even prior to penetration, and therefore feels little or no sexual satisfaction. The man may enjoy sexual intimacy and attraction to his partner, but as soon as he reaches a certain point of excitement he loses control. Usually, premature ejaculation occurs with all his partners, because the problem is that he has not learned voluntary control over his ejaculatory reflexes (Kaplan 1986, 1998). Responses to this problem vary, from the men who are mildly distressed by it to the men and their partners who are severely distressed and are unable to develop other mutually satisfying lovemaking patterns. Premature ejaculation is more commonly reported in young men, perhaps associated with their lack of maturation and experience.

Sexual Pain Disorders

Sexual pain disorders, which involve the experience of pain associated with intercourse, are diagnosed as either **dyspareunia** or **vaginismus.** Dyspareunia, which affects both males and females, involves recurrent or persistent genital pain before, during, or after sexual intercourse. Vaginismus, which affects only females, involves recurrent or persistent involuntary spasms of the outer muscles of the vagina. Ordinarily, a sexually aroused woman experiences a relaxing of the vaginal muscles, but the woman with vaginismus experiences a closing of the muscles such that penetration is impossible or painful. Many women with vaginismus experience similar muscle spasms in response to any attempt at vaginal penetration, including attempts to insert tampons and pelvic examinations by medical professionals.

Mini Case

MALE ORGASMIC DISORDER

Chen is now 42 years old and has not been able to have an orgasm during sexual intercourse with a woman for more than a decade. He has been involved in four intimate relationships during this period and has encountered the same problem with each of his partners. He is able to become intensely aroused during foreplay, but he is unable to reach orgasm during intercourse, even after prolonged, and usually very frustrating, attempts to climax. Particularly perplexing for Chen and his partner is the fact that he is able to reach orgasm by masturbating or having his partner stimulate him manually. He has consulted physicians about this problem, but they have been unable to find any medical basis for his sexual dysfunction.

Diagnostic Features

- With consideration given to age, this diagnosis is assigned to men who experience persistent or recurrent delay in, or absence of, orgasm following a phase of normal excitement during sexual activity that is considered to be adequate in terms of focus, intensity, and duration.

- The disturbance causes significant distress or interpersonal difficulty.

- The disturbance is not better accounted for by another disorder, medical condition, or substance.

- The disturbance may be lifelong or acquired; generalized or situational; and due to psychological factors or a combination of psychological and physical factors.

Theories and Treatment of Sexual Dysfunctions

Sexual dysfunction occurs for many different reasons. One man may experience inhibited male orgasm because of conflicts he has about physical intimacy; another man may experience the same problem because of a physical disorder, such as a prostate condition. Researchers now recognize that some sexual disorders result from physical problems, some from

Mini Case

PREMATURE EJACULATION

Jeremy is a 45-year-old investment broker who has struggled with the problem of premature ejaculation for as long as he can remember. Since his first experience with sexual intercourse as a college student, he has been unable to control his orgasms. He customarily ejaculates seconds after penetration. Because of this problem, his relationships over the years have been strained and difficult. In each instance, the person he was dating at the time became frustrated, and Jeremy felt too embarrassed to continue the relationship. For a period lasting several years, he avoided sexual relations completely, knowing that each experience of failure would leave him feeling depressed and furious.

Diagnostic Features

■ A man with this condition experiences persistent or recurrent ejaculation with minimal sexual stimulation before, on, or shortly after penetration, and before he wishes to ejaculate. Consideration is given to factors that affect the duration of the excitement phase, such as the man's age, novelty of his sexual partner or the situation, and the recent frequency of sexual activity.

■ The disturbance causes significant distress or interpersonal difficulty.

■ The condition is not due exclusively to the effects of a substance.

■ The disturbance may be lifelong or acquired; generalized or situational; and due to psychological factors or a combination of psychological and physical factors.

Frustrated by unsatisfying attempts at sexual intimacy, partners can feel hurt and rejected.

psychological problems, and others from an interaction between the two. Thus, once the disorder that is physiologically based has become established, psychological factors may come into play. In the example of the man with a prostate condition, you can imagine the emotional turmoil that might result from his sexual difficulty. Even knowing that his symptoms are physically based may not be particularly reassuring and might, in fact, cause other psychological problems, such as depression. Keeping in mind that most sexual dysfunctions arise from a complicated set of factors and interactions, let's now turn to the major theoretical approaches for understanding these disorders.

Biological Perspective   In recent years, increasing attention has been given to the fact that bodily processes, such as illness, reactions to medication, dietary factors, and even sleep, can cause or aggravate sexual difficulties. On the other hand, some physical experiences can enhance sexuality. For example, drinking a glass of wine makes some people feel more relaxed and open to sexual intimacy. In trying to understand the causes of a person's sexual dysfunction, the clinician must first conduct a comprehensive assessment of physical factors.

Various illnesses and diseases have direct connections to sexual problems. Some are quite obvious, such as a urinary infection, but others are not as evident and can involve a wide range of bodily systems, including neurological and cardiovascular disorders, liver or kidney disease, hormonal abnormalities, brain tumors, and hypothalamic-pituitary problems. As we mentioned earlier, diabetes mellitus is known to cause sexual dysfunction, particularly in men. Specific problems associated with the male and female reproductive systems can also cause sexual dysfunctions. For example, dyspareunia in women can be the result of inadequate vaginal lubrication, which might, in turn, result from a glandular disorder. Menstrual abnormalities can contribute to changes in the uterus that make it very sensitive to the contractions that occur during orgasm. A man's dyspareunia might result from an anatomical abnormality, such as foreskin tightness. Painful orgasms in men might be attributable to a variety of conditions that can affect the genital region. The *DSM-IV-TR* provides a separate category for sexual dysfunctions that are due to medical conditions. When treating people with such conditions, mental health professionals acknowledge the role of these physical factors, and they usually try to help the individual or couple expand the repertory of sexually intimate behaviors that take medical limitations into consideration.

These examples are just some of the many physical factors that can contribute to sexual functioning problems. But sexual problems can result from factors other than illnesses and physical abnormalities. For example, many chemical substances, both medications and illicit drugs, affect sexual functioning. For this reason, there is a *DSM-IV-TR* category called substance-induced sexual dysfunction. Earlier, we mentioned that a small amount of alcohol can enhance sexual interest; however, alcohol in

Mini Case

VAGINISMUS

Shirley is a 31-year-old single woman who has attempted to have sex with many different men over the past 10 years. Despite her ability to achieve orgasm through masturbation, she has found herself unable to tolerate penetration during intercourse. In her own mind, she feels a sense of readiness, but her vaginal muscles inevitably tighten up and her partner is unable to penetrate. It is clear to Shirley that this problem has its roots in a traumatic childhood experience; she was sexually abused by an older cousin. Although she recognizes that she should seek professional help, Shirley is too embarrassed and has convinced herself that the problem will go away if she can find the right man who will understand her problems.

Diagnostic Features

- Women with this condition experience recurrent or persistent involuntary spasm of the musculature of the outer third of the vagina, which interferes with sexual intercourse.

- The disturbance causes significant distress or interpersonal difficulty.

- The disturbance is not better accounted for by another disorder, or medical condition.

- The disturbance may be lifelong or acquired; generalized or situational; and due to psychological factors or a combination of psychological and physical factors.

---

excess depresses sexual responsivity. Amphetamines and cocaine produce similar phenomena but as the result of different drug actions. Both of these drugs stimulate dopamine and norepinephrine activity. A man taking large amounts of cocaine may feel sexually aroused due to the stimulating effects of dopamine activity, but he may experience erectile and orgasmic problems as the result of the stimulation of norepinephrine activity.

Medications for both physical and psychological disorders can also interfere with sexual functioning. For example, medications that have vasoconstrictive effects, which are used for treating hypertension, reduce the amount of blood supply to the genitals, causing a man taking these medications to experience erectile difficulties. With some medications, the connection between the drug's effects and sexual dysfunction is not as obvious. For example, tricyclic antidepressants, which can interfere with sexual functioning, depress the activity of the parasympathetic nervous system, which is involved in sexual arousal. Unfortunately, many physicians fail to consider such side effects or to warn their patients about them. They face the dilemma of wanting to prescribe a medication that is effective for the patient's medical problem, while risking the difficulties that this medication may create for the patient's sex life. In some cases, the side effect of a psychotropic medication can have beneficial therapeutic effects. Antidepressants such as serotonin reuptake

inhibitors cause ejaculatory delay (MacQueen, Born, & Steiner, 2001). Although this may be a distressing side effect for most men, a man with premature ejaculation would perceive this as beneficial, and it is one effective treatment option (Lee, Song, Kim, & Choi, 1996).

An important change has taken place in the scientific understanding of male erectile dysfunction in the past 20 years. In 1970, Masters and Johnson claimed that virtually all men (95 percent) with erectile dysfunction had psychological problems, such as anxiety and job stress, boredom with long-term sexual partners, and other relationship difficulties. During the 1970s and 1980s, researchers arrived at very different conclusions as a result of new and more sophisticated assessment devices sensitive to the presence of physiological abnormalities.

More than half the cases of erectile dysfunction are now viewed by health care professionals as attributable to physical problems of a vascular, neurological, or hormonal nature, or to impaired functioning caused by drugs, alcohol, and smoking.

The distinction between physical and psychological causes of erectile dysfunction is more than just of academic interest; it helps determine the appropriate treatment. For example, if a man's erectile problems are due to psychological factors, individual or couple therapy is recommended. When the cause of erectile dysfunction is found to be physical, one of several somatic interventions may be used. The most invasive treatment is the surgical implantation of a penile prosthesis, such as a rod or an inflatable device. The inflatable device has the advantage of being adjustable, and it has a higher postsurgical success rate than the rod (Mohr & Beutler, 1990). Even with the widespread prescription of Viagra, penile implant procedures continue to be conducted, primarily because of the perceived benefit of this intervention in an aging population (Stanley, Bivalacqua, & Hellstrom, 2000), although this approach would only be considered when other treatment options have failed. Another somatic treatment is an arterial bypass operation, which is intended to correct problems due to vascular disease, or blockage of the arteries leading to the penis. Alternatively, an injection of medication into the penis may be used to induce an erection (Segraves & Althof, 1998; Szasz, Stevenson, Lee, & Sanders, 1987). Specially designed vacuum devices are also occasionally recommended, especially for men whose problems are the result of vascular insufficiency (Althof & Seftel, 1995).

Viagra (sildanefil) has revolutionized the approach to this disorder, as it has a high effectiveness rate and is relatively noninvasive. The introduction of Viagra in 1998 brought to the spotlight a secret that millions of men had been harboring. In fact, in a very clever effort to publicize the prevalence of erectile dysfunction, the Pfizer pharmaceutical company hired as its spokesperson an internationally known politician, Bob Dole, following his unsuccessful bid for the presidency in 1996. In television commercials Dole introduced Americans to the term *ED* and spoke about the fact that he, like so many other men, had a problem that could successfully be treated by this remarkable new medication.

Even before Viagra was introduced, pharmaceutical company Pfizer Inc. was preparing for a financial windfall that would result from the international marketing of this new wonder drug. Even with the unusually high cost, this medication has been prescribed to millions of men worldwide. In addition to Viagra, other comparable products have been introduced, including vardenafil (Levitra) and tadalafil (Cialis).

What makes such medications appealing is the fact that they are so much less invasive than previous treatments for erectile dysfunction, such as surgery and implants, and so much less awkward than vacuum pumps or penile injections. These medications work when accompanied by the experience of sexual excitement, unlike other treatments in which an erection is achieved artificially and independent of what is going on sexually with the man or his partner.

In addition to being easy to use, medications for erectile dysfunction seem to be relatively safe, although initial cautions have been issued to men taking cardiac medications, such as nitroglycerine, since the combination of cardiac medications and those for erectile dysfunction can be fatal. Some minor side effects have been reported, such as impaired vision and headaches, but these are not troubling enough to scare most men away from the use of Viagra. Effectiveness rates have been remarkable, with the overwhelming majority of men reporting success (Boyce & Umland, 2001; Fagelman, Fagelman, & Shabsigh, 2001; R. Lewis et al., 2001; Muller et al., 2001). Even men whose erectile disorder is due to medical problems, such as diabetes, spinal cord injury, or surgery, have found that Viagra has helped them achieve an erection. Men who have concluded that their erectile difficulty is psychologically caused have also reported that, despite the feeling of emotional conflict, erectile difficulty subsides with the ingestion of this small pill.

With all this good news about the effectiveness of this medication, is there a downside? Some clinicians wonder whether this miracle pill is making it too easy for men to gloss over more deeply rooted emotional issues that are reflected in erectile difficulty. For example, a man's difficulty in achieving an erection may be a way in which his body is signaling hostility, resentment, or even fear that he feels toward his partner. Might it not be more beneficial for him to understand the reasons for his problem, rather than to ignore the alarm system being activated within his body?

Over the next decade, researchers and health care professionals will continue to monitor the impact of Viagra and similar medications, with particular attention to the influence of such treatments on intimate partnerships. While attending to the beneficial medical effects, it will be important that emotional and relationship issues also be addressed. Increased attention will also be given to the development of pharmacological interventions for women.

The other sexual dysfunctions do not have such clear-cut means of resolution. The clinician looks for possible physical causes and treatment routes and, in some cases, is able to recommend an effective medical intervention. For example, in cases involving side effects from medications, the physician may attempt to find substitutes that do not complicate sexual functioning. If a person has a physical disorder, treating this disorder would optimally resolve the sexual dysfunction. However, some medical problems are not easily treated. For example, a neurological impairment that results in sexual dysfunction may be incurable; consequently, the sexual problems will remain. In these instances, therapists may recommend other psychological interventions that help the individual develop alternative forms of sexual expression.

Increasing attention is being given to the treatment of sexual dysfunction in women. In the pharmacological realm, studies are being conducted with the aim of developing medications for women that are as effective as Viagra-like medications have been for men with erectile dysfunction. For some women, treatment with hormones is beneficial in increasing sexual desire and responsiveness, but no intervention has yet been developed that has had an impact as great as Viagra for male erectile dysfunction. In the nonpharmacological sphere, some technological devices have been introduced such as the Eros Clitoral Therapy Device, which is prescribed by physicians to women seeking help for sexual arousal disorder. The device, which is placed over the clitoris immediately before sex, consists of a small, soft plastic vacuum cup and a palm-sized battery-operated vacuum pump. When activated, the pump draws blood into the clitoris and causes engorgement and the feeling of sexual arousal.

Psychological Perspective   The biological perspective clearly provides insight into the causes of sexual dysfunction. However, psychosocial factors also contribute to these complex conditions. In women, sexual dysfunction is related to one's history of sexual abuse, overall well-being, and education as well as potential biological contributors such as physical health and one's history of sexually transmitted diseases (Goldstein, 2000). In men, psychological distress, troubled relationships, and specific psychosocial deficits in sexual situations play important roles in addition to physical factors such as illness, injury, and side effects of medication (Metz & Pryor, 2000). For both sexes, depression is associated with a reduction in sexual desire and performance; unfortunately, many antidepressants further diminish sexual drive (Ferguson, 2001). Physical and psychosocial changes in middle and later life also appear to be important for both women and men, as indicated by the higher rates of sexual dysfunction past midlife. Although most individuals continue to be interested in and enjoy sexual relationships as they age, older persons tend to be less sexually active—partly due to physical changes, but also due to social factors (such as fewer available partners) and cultural factors (such as the belief that older people aren't interested in sex) (Bartlik & Goldstein, 2001).

Unfortunately, knowledge about the causes and treatment of sexual dysfunction in women, particularly older women, lags behind understanding of male sexual dysfunction. Suggestions for treatment of women past menopausal age include a combination of hormonal supplements combined, if necessary, with psychosexual therapy (Bartlik & Goldstein, 2000).

Treatment of men, particularly in midlife and beyond, may involve hormonal treatment and medications targeted at erectile dysfunction along with psychosexual therapy focused at age-appropriate individual and relationship issues (Bartlik & Goldstein, 2001).

Presently, the methods for treating sexual dysfunctions rely on conceptual models that incorporate physical, educative, attitudinal, intrapsychic, and interpersonal factors (Kring, 2000; Metz & Pryor, 2000; Segraves & Althof, 1998). Most therapists treating clients with sexual dysfunctions rely at least in part on the methods originally developed by Masters and Johnson (Masters & Johnson, 1970), which have been refined over the past few decades. These methods typically focus on the couple's sexual behavior patterns and less on personality and relationship issues. Masters and Johnson conceptualized that much of the difficulty involved in sexual dysfunctions is due to spectatoring; hence, their treatment methods are attempts to reduce anxiety over sexual performance. For example, a man who is worried about losing his erection during intercourse may become so obsessed with his performance that he loses touch with the sexual experience itself. This objectification of the experience begins to interfere with his sexual arousal; consequently, he actually does lose his erection. His worst fears are then confirmed, and he approaches his next sexual encounter with increased anxiety (Barlow, 1986, 1988; Heimberg & Barlow, 1988; Segraves & Althof, 1998).

The treatment approach recommended by Masters and Johnson has several components. A primary objective is to refocus the individual's attention from anxiety over performance to the sensual pleasures of close physical contact with his or her partner. Also important is the need for the couple to clearly communicate their sexual wishes to each other. To achieve these two goals, Masters and Johnson recommend that couples use **sensate focus.** This method of treatment involves the partners taking turns stimulating each other in nonsexual but affectionate ways at first, then gradually progressing over a period of time toward genital stimulation. During the sensate focus exercise, individuals are instructed to focus on their own sensations, rather than on the partner's needs. During the early stage of treatment, intercourse is specifically forbidden, a fact that might seem surprising, given that this is a method of "sex" therapy. But the premise is that, when the option of having intercourse is eliminated, neither partner feels pressured to perform, thereby reducing the potential for failure. Further, the couple can learn to stimulate each other in a variety of new ways that they may never have tried before and, in the process, improve their communication about sex. The approaches developed by Masters and Johnson continue to be widely used in the treatment of sexual dysfunctions. For example, in one treatment program for men with hypoactive sexual desire disorder, the intervention focused on developing the individual's emotional aspects, increasing his sexual repertoire, and improving his attitude and response to these sexual experiences within the context of his relationship with his partner (McCabe, 1992).

Sex therapy often helps couples resolve their sexual problems and focus on the more pleasurable aspects of the relationship.

Originally, Masters and Johnson insisted that couples come to their St. Louis clinic for a 2-week treatment program in which they would be free from distractions and able to concentrate on the development of more satisfying sexual behaviors. Since the 1970s, numerous clinicians have modified these techniques so that the couple can practice between sessions in the privacy of their own home and over a longer period of time. Some sex therapists take a more moderate stand on the issue of whether intercourse prohibition is absolutely necessary; instead they recommend that a decision regarding this matter be made on the basis of an individualized assessment of each couple. An important aspect of sex therapy is the assumption that it take place with a sexual partner; however, a client with a sexual dysfunction may not have a partner or may have a partner who is unwilling to participate in the treatment program.

Numerous other behavioral methods have evolved from the work of Masters and Johnson. For example, for treating premature ejaculation, the **squeeze technique** and the **stop-start procedure** have been recommended. In the squeeze technique, the partner stimulates the man's penis during foreplay and squeezes it when he indicates that he is approaching orgasm. This delays the ejaculatory response and, in turn, shows the man that he may have more control over ejaculation than he had previously thought possible. In the stop-start procedure, which was introduced several decades ago (Semans, 1956), either the man or his partner stimulates him to sexual excitement, and, as he approaches the point of orgasmic inevitability, stimulation is stopped. He regains his composure, and stimulation is resumed and stopped repeatedly. With recurrent exercising of this procedure, the man develops greater control over his ejaculatory response.

For women, in addition to sensate focus, behavioral techniques have been developed to help treat such dysfunctions as orgasmic disorder and vaginismus. A woman who feels frustrated

REAL STORIES

RICHARD BERENDZEN: ENDURING EFFECTS OF SEXUAL ABUSE

The case of Richard Berendzen, former president of American University in Washington, D.C., highlights the fact that sexually disordered behavior can occur in anyone, even a person at the height of a successful professional career. Berendzen's inappropriate behavior involved his making sexually provocative phone calls to strangers, a bizarre endeavor that he later came to understand as a residual symptom of his own traumatic experiences of having been sexually abused as a child.

As president of American University, Berendzen was highly esteemed for his devoted efforts to bring the university to a new level of prestige and prosperity. As his successes accumulated, so also did his personal stress. Lacking healthy outlets for his stress, Berendzen turned to behaviors that would bring an abrupt and embarrassing end to his presidency. He began to make phone calls to day care centers asking about child sexual abuse, sometimes implying that he himself had engaged in sexual behavior with children, and at other times asking the people on the other end of the line about their own sexual behaviors with children. Berendzen's comments and questions became increasingly explicit, leading one caller to take action that resulted in his being apprehended after the authorities traced his calls.

The roots of Berendzen's inappropriate behavior can be traced back to childhood experiences in which he himself was victimized. He had been a sickly young child, suffering with serious asthma and rheumatic fever during several years when the family lived in the damp climate of Oregon. When Berendzen was 7, his family moved to

the warm, dry climate of Texas, where he regained his health and thrived socially. Everything seemed fine until one day when he was 8 years old. On this particular Sunday afternoon, he ran inside to get a drink of water and heard odd, panting noises coming from his parents' room. He heard his mother call out, "Come here!" and he obeyed. His mother told Richard to undress and to join her and her husband in sexual intercourse. Once it was over, Richard got up, dressed, and pretended that it had never happened. Unfortunately, this was only the first of many instances in which Richard would be sexually abused, although the subsequent experiences involved only his mother.

As Richard grew into adolescence, he tried to put the traumatic memories behind him. He was married briefly to a woman named Barbara, and they had a child, but the marriage ended when Barbara became frustrated with Richard's unavailability because of his commitment to work and study. Although devastated by the loss of his wife and child, Berendzen completed

his graduate work in astronomy at Harvard and went on to become a professor at Boston University. He married a woman, Gail, with whom he bore one child, and went on to a successful academic career, becoming a dean and eventually president of American University. Little did Berendzen anticipate that the ghosts of his traumatic experiences of childhood abuse would come back to haunt him during what should have been the best years of his life.

Berendzen's words from his autobiographical narrative, *Come Here,* capture the essence of his compulsive obscene phone calls:

> I called back with increasing frequency and we began to talk at length. I did not know that she was answering my questions in ways that she thought I wanted them answered so that I'd call back and my calls could be traced. So I described activities in my fabricated home, and asked about activities in hers. I said our children slept with us in the

Richard Berendzen

REAL STORIES

RICHARD BERENDZEN *(continued)*

nude, and asked if hers did too. I said my wife had sex with our son, and asked if she did with hers. I asked why she did it. I asked if she enjoyed it, if she ever wondered how the boy felt, if she cared. I asked why she did it. I described how we punished our children and asked how she did it in her home. I asked if she controlled her children through sex and intimidation. And I asked her what her husband knew about all this. . . .

On a conscious level at least, I didn't think about the abuse I had experienced as a child. Memories of that didn't intrude into my day-to-day life, and they didn't when I called. I never connected the calls to what had happened in my own childhood. I had no idea why I was doing what I did. When a call ended I sat in disbe-lief. My whole body ached, my hands shook, my vision blurred. I knew everything about the calls was profoundly wrong, yet I made them. Why? What was happening?

Source: From *Come Here* by Richard Berendzen. Copyright © 1993 Richard Berendzen. Used by permission of Villard Books, a division of Random House, Inc. and by International Creative Management, Inc.

---

because of her inability to reach orgasm may be instructed to begin a masturbation program (Heiman & LoPiccolo, 1988), in which she moves through a series of steps beginning with bodily exploration, progressing through masturbatory orgasm, and culminating in sexual intercourse while her partner stimulates her genitals manually or with a vibrator. A woman with vaginismus would be instructed to penetrate her vagina with small, prelubricated cylindrical objects (called dilators) while in a relaxed state. Gradually, she would use dilators that are larger in circumference and that ultimately approximate the size of a penis. This approach is based on the theory that, as she grows more comfortable with this experience, her muscles will become reconditioned to relax rather than to constrict during intercourse.

As you read about these behavioral methods, you may wonder whether more is involved than just learning new sexual responses. Although some sexual dysfunctions can be successfully treated by a specific behavioral intervention, most sexual problems are multifaceted and require an approach that incorporates attention to relational and intrapsychic factors. The late Helen Singer Kaplan, a specialist in the treatment of sexual problems, advocated this integrative approach (Kaplan, 1979, 1983, 1986, 1998). She recognized that, because many sexual problems are the result of intrapsychic conflicts, successful treatment of the problem necessitates exploring the conflict and its roots. For example, inhibited orgasm could be associated with such intrapsychic problems as a strict religious upbringing, strongly suppressed hostility, mixed feelings about one's partner, or unconscious conflicts about sex.

Cultural expectations can be translated into sexual difficulties for both men and women, as men feel they must be "masculine" to perform adequately in the sexual relationship and women feel they must accept the "feminine" role of passivity and dependence. Disparities between the individual's personal preferences and these cultural norms can create conflict and, thus, inhibit the individual's sexual functioning. The challenge for the therapist working with such individuals is to focus treatment both on the source of their conflict and on the unsatisfactory sexual behaviors. Therapists using Kaplan's approach usually limit the exploration of the conflict to the extent needed to resolve the sexual problem, while recommending certain sexual exercises and changes in sexual patterns that are geared toward more sexual intimacy.

When treating people with sexual dysfunctions, it is important to determine whether the sexual problem reflects a relationship gone sour (LoPiccolo & Stock, 1986). If the therapist determines that the relationship is really the source of the trouble, then trying to treat the sexual problem while ignoring the other difficulties between the partners is fruitless. The therapist would instead focus initially on improving communication between the partners and then move on to a sexual focus only when improved communication has been established.

As sensible and legitimate as the process of sex therapy appears, it does have some problems. For example, imagine yourself sharing very intimate details about your sexuality with a stranger. Most people would find this embarrassing enough to prevent them from seeking professional help. Thus, when considering the effectiveness of sex therapy methods, you must take into account that the people who have been studied are not representative of the population at large. The literature is filled with astounding claims of success in treating people with sexual dysfunctions, but these claims should be evaluated with considerable caution. Not only are the samples select, but the outcome measures are often poorly defined and the follow-up intervals too short to determine if the treatment has lasting effect

(O'Donohue, Dopke, & Swingen, 1997; O'Donohue, Swingen, Dopke, & Regev, 1999).

Even if the success rates are not as high as some claim, sex therapy techniques have created new treatment opportunities for many people whose difficulties would never have received attention otherwise. Furthermore, the widespread publicity associated with these techniques has made it much easier for people seeking self-help treatments to find resources and suggestions for dealing with their problems on their own.

Sexual Disorders: The Biopsychosocial Perspective

The sexual disorders constitute three discrete sets of difficulties involving varying aspects of sexual functioning and behavior. Although there are many unanswered questions concerning their causes, the behavioral perspective appears to hold the most promise as an explanation of how most of these diverse problems are acquired. Similarly, behavioral treatments of sexual disorders can be applied to the paraphilias and sexual dysfunctions. However, the biological perspective plays an important role as well, particularly with the gender identity disorders and the treatment of erectile dysfunction. Further, exploring personal history and relationship difficulties through insight-oriented and couple therapy seems to be an important adjunct to both the behavioral and biological approaches to treatment.

Interest in understanding and treating sexual disorders has a relatively recent history in the field of abnormal psychology. Even in this short time, though, significant advances have been made. We can expect these advances to continue as researchers and clinicians gain greater insight into the roles of biology and learning in these fascinating and often troubling conditions.

RETURN TO THE CASE

Case Report
Shaun Boyden

Shaun's History
In our second intake session, Shaun told me some of the details of his life history, which enabled me to gain a perspective on how an otherwise normal man would have acquired such a serious disorder.

As is so common in the story of adults who abuse children, Shaun himself had been abused as a child. Primarily, Shaun's father beat him frequently because he was so "slow to catch on to anything." It was true that Shaun was not an A or even a B student in school, mainly because he had difficulty concentrating on his work. Shaun's mother was a quiet woman who told Shaun there was nothing she could do to intervene because his father was so unreasonable. Rather than try to help Shaun, his father only came down harder on

him when his report card failed to live up to expectations. With a smirk on his face, Shaun pointed out the irony that his father was a dedicated volunteer in many social organizations yet was so cruel to Shaun.

His father's cruelty toward Shaun was compounded by the very different approach he took with Shaun's two brothers. It seemed to Shaun that the other two were spared their father's abuse by virtue of Shaun's "taking the rap" for them. If anything, they were inordinately treated to favorable attention. Later in life, the other two sons were to become partners in the father's furniture store, while Shaun was left to his own resources to make his way in the world.

Starting from the time Shaun was in high school, his main ambition in life, apart from finding a good job af-

ter graduation, was to help young boys in trouble and set them on the "right path." Unfortunately, before he knew what was happening, Shaun found himself drawn to sexual intimacy with young boys. Struggling with these impulses and fantasies during late adolescence, Shaun had naively hoped that, if he got married, his sexual preoccupation with young boys would disappear.

Assessment
Dr. Draper preferred to have the results of a comprehensive psychological assessment before planning a treatment, because pedophilia takes various forms and emerges for many different reasons. An understanding of the role of pedophilia in the conscious and unconscious realms of an individual's personality can facilitate

a more effective treatment. A standard battery of psychological tests was supplemented by several specialized assessment techniques. Shaun was administered the WAIS-III, the MMPI-2, the Rorschach, and the TAT. In addition, Shaun was given specialized sexual assessment inventories pertaining to functioning and preferences.

Shaun's IQ fell in the average range, with his performance IQ much higher than his verbal IQ. His pattern of subscale scores suggested an inability to temper impulses with more cautious reflection. Shaun seemed to be oblivious to socially acceptable behaviors and prone to acting on his own desires rather than taking the needs of others into consideration. On the MMPI-2, Shaun responded in the direction of appearing guarded and suspicious, possibly because of concern over how the scores would be used in court proceedings. The responses he produced to the Rorschach indicated impulsivity and a restricted ability to fantasize. Both of these tendencies could lead to his acting on his immediate needs without considering the consequences of his actions. His TAT stories contained themes of victimization, but there was also denial of interpersonal problems. Most of the TAT stories had unrealistic, "happily ever after" endings, suggesting a naive and unfounded optimism.

The sexual assessment inventories confirmed Shaun's preference for sex with young boys, almost to the exclusion of any other sexual acts. Shaun tolerated sexual intercourse with his wife to maintain harmony, but he lacked any real interest or desire for intimacy with her. Shaun was not interested in sexual intimacy with adult males and, in fact, found the notion of such activities to be repulsive.

Diagnosis
It was clear to me that Shaun met the diagnostic criteria for pedophilia in that he has had recurrent, intense sexual urges and fantasies involving sexual activity with children which he has acted on.

Axis I: Pedophilia, same sex, exclusive type, severe
Axis II: Deferred
Axis III: No medical diagnosis
Axis IV: Problems related to interactions with the legal system (charged with child molestation)
Axis V: Global Assessment of Functioning (past year): 48 serious symptoms as well as serious impairment in social functioning due to the disorder

Case Formulation
What would prompt a man who holds his own daughters so close to his heart to exploit children in order to satisfy his own cravings? Questions such as this are deeply perplexing. There are no clear answers, but, as I reviewed some of the facts about Shaun's life experiences, I began to develop a rudimentary understanding of why he might have developed along this path of deviance.

As a youngster, Shaun was subjected to very harsh treatment by his father and a not-so-benign neglect by his mother. Shaun could not live up to his father's unrealistic expectations of him and, consequently, was labeled a "failure." This label remained with him and eventually resulted in Shaun being left out of the favorable situation his younger brothers were to enjoy in the father's business. Although he managed to achieve a degree of material success and respect in the community, Shaun still longed for his father's approval and felt outraged at having been made to feel so worthless. He suppressed these powerful feelings through the very immature and fragile defense of denial. Shaun's poor ability to hold his impulses in check led him to act on the sexual desires he felt toward the boys he was ostensibly aiming to help. At the same time, Shaun's childlike view of himself caused him to identify with these boys, so that he did not see them as any different from himself. One remaining piece in the puzzle of Shaun's disorder concerned the possibility that he was sexually abused as a child. People with Shaun's disorder often have a background of sexual abuse.

Treatment Plan
In evaluating the context in which Shaun's treatment should take place, Dr. Draper and I concluded that outpatient care made sense. In some cases of pedophilia, inpatient care is warranted if there is concern that the individual may continue victimizing children. Shaun's mode of exploitation was limited to specific situations, which he would obviously have to avoid from that point forward. Dr. Draper agreed to accept Shaun into her treatment program, which consisted of intensive individual and group psychotherapy. Augmenting Shaun's psychotherapy would be his participation in an aversion therapy program aimed toward reducing and eventually eliminating his sexual responsiveness to children.

Outcome of the Case
Shaun responded to the aversion therapy offered by the sex offenders program, with minimal sexual arousal to stimuli involving young boys by the end of the 10-week treatment program. In his individual and group psychotherapy sessions, the story was much more complicated. Initially, Shaun was eager to impress Dr. Draper and the other members of the therapy group by showing what a "good patient" he was. However, Shaun revealed very little about himself, talking mostly in vague, superficial, and clichéd terms. This defensive style did not last very long, however, as the other men in the pedophile treatment group were harsh and direct in confronting Shaun. Once Shaun came to accept the reality of his behavior, he opened up remarkably in both group therapy and individual therapy. The real turning point came when Shaun publicly

shared the fact that, at the age of 12, he had been sexually abused by a neighbor, a "good friend" of his father. Shaun felt afraid and guilty and had never told anyone. By talking about this incident with Dr. Draper and the other group members, Shaun was able to gain some insight into the fact that his own behavior with young boys was a repetition of the pattern that had been enacted with him in his childhood.

Shaun's legal difficulties were not as great as they might have been. In judicial proceedings on the matter, a compromise was reached in which Shaun was given a 6-month prison sentence and was placed on 5 years probation and required to participate in a sex offenders treatment program. Of course, he was ordered to refrain from participating in any situations with young children in which private interactions might take place.

Shaun continued in therapy for that 2-year period, but, immediately after terminating with Dr. Draper, Shaun moved his family to another part of the state to "start a new life." He felt that the rumors about his child molestation would always haunt him and his family, and relocation was the only hope Shaun had of putting those rumors behind him.

Sarah Tobin, PhD

SUMMARY

- Sexual behavior is considered a psychological disorder if (1) it causes harm to others or (2) it causes an individual to experience persistent or recurrent distress, or impairment in important areas of functioning. Paraphilias are disorders, lasting at least 6 months, in which an individual has recurrent, intense sexually arousing fantasies, sexual urges, or behaviors involving (1) non-human objects, (2) children or other nonconsenting persons, or (3) the suffering or humiliation of self or partner. Pedophilia is a disorder in which an adult (16 years or over) has uncontrollable sexual urges toward sexually immature children. In exhibitionism, a person has intense sexual urges and arousing fantasies involving genital exposure to strangers. People with the paraphilia of fetishism are preoccupied with an object, and they become dependent on this object for achieving sexual gratification, actually preferring it over sexual intimacy with a partner. A frotteur has recurrent, intense sexual urges and sexually arousing fantasies of rubbing against or fondling another person. Sexual masochism is a disorder marked by an attraction to achieving sexual gratification by having painful stimulation applied to one's own body, either alone or with a partner. Sexual sadism is the converse of sexual masochism, in that it involves deriving sexual gratification from activities that harm, or from urges to harm, another person. Transvestic fetishism is a disorder in which a man has an uncontrollable urge to wear a woman's clothes (called cross-dressing) as his primary means of achieving sexual gratification. Voyeurism is a sexual disorder in which the individual has a compulsion to derive sexual gratification from observing the nudity or sexual activity of others who are unaware of being watched. Most paraphilias emerge during adolescence, although there is usually a connection with events or relationships in early childhood. Once established, they tend to be chronic. Although biological factors play a role in some paraphilias, psychological factors seem to be central; in most cases, one or more learning events have taken place in childhood involving a conditioned response that results in a paraphilia. Treatment depends on the nature of the paraphilia and may include a biological component (such as medication), a psychological component (such as psychotherapy), and a sociocultural component (such as group or family therapy).

- A gender identity disorder is a condition involving a discrepancy between an individual's assigned sex and his or her gender identity, in which the person experiences a strong and persistent cross-gender identification that causes feelings of discomfort and a sense of inappropriateness about his or her assigned sex. Various theories have been proposed to explain the development of gender identity disorder. One biological explanation focuses on the effects of hormones that affect fetal development. Psychological theories focus on factors such as the role of a parent's preference for a child of the other gender, the impact of early attachment experiences, and parents' unintentional reinforcement of cross-gender behavior. Sociocultural theories consider various ways in which American society idealizes men and women according to certain stereotypical variables. Various factors influence the choice of intervention, with the most extreme method involving sex reassignment surgery.

- Sexual dysfunctions involve conditions in which there is abnormality in an individual's sexual responsiveness and reactions. The individual with hypoactive sexual desire disorder has an abnormally low level of interest in sexual activity. Sexual aversion disorder is characterized by an active dislike and avoidance of genital contact with a sexual partner, which causes personal distress or interpersonal problems. A woman with female sexual arousal disorder experiences a persistent or recurrent inability to attain or maintain the normal lubrication-swelling response of sexual excitement during sexual activity. Male erectile disorder involves the recurrent partial or complete failure to attain or maintain an erection during sexual activity, causing the man to feel distressed or to encounter interpersonal problems in his intimate relationship. An inability to achieve orgasm, or a distressing delay in achievement of orgasm, constitutes female orgasmic disorder. Male orgasmic disorder, also known as inhibited male orgasm, involves a specific difficulty in the orgasm stage. The man with premature ejaculation reaches orgasm in a sexual encounter long before he wishes to, perhaps even prior to penetration; therefore, he feels little or no sexual satisfaction. Sexual pain disorders, which involve the experience of pain associated with intercourse, are diagnosed as either dyspareunia or vaginismus. Dyspareunia, which affects both males and females, involves recurrent or persistent genital pain before, during, or after sexual intercourse. Vaginismus, which affects only females, involves recurrent or persistent involuntary spasms of the outer muscles of the vagina. Sexual dysfunctions can be caused by physical or psychological problems, or an interaction of both. The treatment of sexual dysfunctions includes a range of physiological interventions, such as medication, as well as psychological interventions that include behavioral, cognitive-behavioral, and couple therapy techniques.

KEY TERMS

Assigned (biological) sex   227
Covert conditioning   221
Dyspareunia   237
Exhibitionism   221
Female orgasmic disorder   236
Female sexual arousal disorder   235
Fetish   221
Fetishism   221
Frotteur   222
Frotteurism   222
Gender identity   227
Gender identity disorder   227
Gender role   227

Hypoactive sexual desire disorder   234
Lovemap   227
Male erectile disorder   236
Male orgasmic disorder   237
Masochism   223
Orgasmic reconditioning   222
Paraphilias   216
Partialism   222
Pedophilia   217
Premature ejaculation   237
Sadomasochist   223
Sensate focus   241
Sexual aversion disorder   235

Sexual dysfunction   231
Sexual masochism   223
Sexual orientation   227
Sexual sadism   223
Spectatoring   234
Squeeze technique   241
Stop-start procedure   241
Transsexualism   227
Transvestic fetishism   225
Vaginismus   237
Voyeur   226
Voyeurism   226

INTERNET RESOURCE

To get more information on the material covered in this chapter, visit our website at **www.mhhe.com/halgin5.** There you will find more information, resources, and links to topics of interest.

Mood Disorders

I clearly recall the afternoon I received the phone call from a physician colleague, Eric Hampden. Frankly, I was surprised that Dr. Hampden was referring one of his patients to me in light of the fact that he had frequently reminded me of his lack of confidence in psychotherapy.

Eric Hampden explained to me that Janice had come to see him 2 months earlier with various bodily complaints, including ongoing exhaustion, sleep disturbance, and lack of appetite. She had described her feelings of sadness and gloom, as well as the difficulties that had emerged between her and her husband during the preceding 6 months. He was quite optimistic that a prescription of Prozac was all that Janice needed, but soon came to realize that he was wrong. Following 2 months of taking Prozac, Janice felt no better; in fact, she felt much worse and that very morning had made a suicide attempt. Apparently, wearing only her pajamas, Janice had gone into the garage after her husband had left for work and had turned on the car's ignition with the intention of asphyxiating herself. Having forgotten his briefcase, Janice's husband had returned to discover the disturbing scene of his wife trying to end her life. He called Dr. Hampden immediately, who in turn called me, admitting that this was a case beyond his competence to "cure." I instructed him to ask Janice's husband, Jed, to call me, so that I could explain the process of admitting Janice to a psychiatric hospital.

When I answered the phone a few moments later, it was not the voice of Jed Butterfield I heard, but rather, the faint whisper of a woman at the other end of the line. With a tremulous tone, Janice slowly spoke the words "Can you help me? Can you save me from myself?" With calmness and empathy, I assured Janice that I would do everything possible to help her, as long as she was willing to let me do so. I told her my emphatic opinion that it would be necessary for her to admit herself to a psychiatric hospital. At first, Janice said that she was unwilling to go to the "nut house" but didn't stop listening as I explained my reasoning. I told her, in no uncertain terms, that she had come dangerously close to death, a situation that warranted placing her in an environment in which she would be safe and cared for. Almost magically, Janice said, "I see what you mean. Yes, I am ready to go." In that momentary transition, the tone of her voice seemed to lighten a bit, as if a weighty burden had been lifted. I asked her to put Jed on the phone, to whom I could give instructions about hospital admission. I explained to both of them that I would meet with her later that afternoon to complete the intake interview.

As the day progressed, I felt harried and a bit weary myself. Suicidally depressed clients are never easy, so I knew that I had to summon the stamina prior to my initial meeting with Janice, which would be my last appointment of the day. There were five women among the dozen people sitting in the waiting room, but there was no question in my mind which one was Janice Butterfield. With a blank stare on her face and her eyes glazed over and cast down to the floor, Janice sat motionless as if in an altered state. Despite her ostensible depression, Janice was surprisingly well dressed and well groomed. Although everything seemed fine on the outside, it was clear from the expression on her face that she was suffering inner torment.

I escorted Janice and Jed to my office for the intake interview, where they shared with me the "nightmare" of the previous 6 months. Although it seemed difficult for Janice to participate actively in the interview, gradually she seemed to come to life. Janice explained that she felt like a "hopeless loser" who had no reason to live. She told me that, for at least 6 months, she had frequently been overcome by uncontrollable feelings of sadness. She repeated the bodily problems that Dr. Hampden had described and added that she had felt so weak that she could hardly find the energy to walk. When I inquired about the Prozac, she said that she had been taking the medication regularly but hated the edgy feelings it caused.

Both Janice and Jed told me how the depression had taken its toll on their relationship and home life. Jed said that he was finding himself complaining more and more about Janice's neglect of basic household responsibilities, her insensitivity to their 8-year-old daughter, and her total lack of interest in being affectionate or sexually intimate with him. The picture was painted of a woman who, for nearly a half year, had been spending the greater part of every day clothed in a bathrobe and slippers and staring at the walls. Even though Jed had begged Janice to see a mental health professional, her only concession was agreeing to see their family doctor for her "fatigue."

When I asked Janice how she felt about entering the hospital in order to treat her depression, she admitted, even to her own surprise, that it felt "good." She then smiled faintly and asked if she might go to her room to get some rest. After the day she had been through, the choice seemed a wise one, but, as I explained to Janice, it was hospital policy that she be observed for the first 24 hours to ensure her safety. As Janice left my office, escorted by an aide from the unit, I felt confident she would begin to feel better in the days ahead but, at the same time, knew that my work with her would be difficult. Interactions with depressed people are usually stressful for therapists, and the stress intensifies when the client has been suicidal. Even though my work with Janice would be challenging, I was hopeful I might play a role in relieving her feelings of despair.

Sarah Tobin, PhD

It is common for people to feel happy and energized at times and sad and apathetic at other times; almost everyone experiences periodic mood fluctuations. Thinking about your own variations in how you feel can give you insight into the nature of mood disorders.

The disorders presented in this chapter are far more painful and disruptive than the relatively normal day-to-day variations in mood. As you will read later in this chapter, people with mood disorders that involve elation act in ways that are out of character for them, possibly acting wild and uncontrolled. In mood disorders that involve serious depression, as in the case of Janice, individuals experience pain that is so intense that they feel immobilized and possibly suicidal.

General Characteristics of Mood Disorders

A mood disorder involves a disturbance in a person's emotional state, or mood. People can experience this disturbance in the form of extreme depression, excessive elation, or a combination of these emotional states. The primary characteristic of depressive disorders is that the individual feels overwhelming **dysphoria** or sadness. In another kind of mood disorder, called bipolar disorder, an individual has emotional experiences at the opposite "pole" from depression, feelings of elation called **euphoria.**

In MindMAP Segment 8.1, Tara discusses a number of different fantasies about committing suicide that fill her thoughts.

People who are suffering from major depressive disorder may experience all-consuming thoughts about death and dying.

As you will see later in this chapter, there are various subtypes of mood disorder involving dysphoria and euphoria.

To understand the nature of mood disorders, it is important to understand the concept of an **episode,** a time-limited period during which specific, intense symptoms of a disorder are evident. In some instances, an episode is quite lengthy, perhaps 2 years or more. People with mood disorders experience episodes of dysphoric or euphoric symptoms, or a mixture of both. Episodes differ in a number of important ways that clinicians document in their diagnosis (Keller et al., 1995). Following are some of the ways that a mood episode can be characterized.

First, the clinician documents the severity of the episode with a specifier, such as *mild, moderate,* or *severe.* Second, the clinician documents whether it is the first episode or a recurrence of symptoms. For recurrent episodes, the clinician notes whether or not the client has fully recovered between episodes. Third, specifiers can also reflect the nature of a prominent set of symptoms. For example, some people in the midst of a mood episode have bodily movements that are strikingly unusual, possibly even bizarre. The adjective *catatonic,* which we discussed in Chapter 3, describes odd body postures and movements, such as immobility, rigidity, or excessive purposeless motor activity. Another specifier pertains to whether the episode is postpartum, which indicates that a woman's mood disturbance is presumed to be related to the delivery of a baby within the preceding month. We will discuss other specifiers used to characterize mood episodes in the relevant sections that follow.

Depressive Disorders

Mental health professionals differentiate between two serious forms of depression. **Major depressive disorder** involves acute, but time-limited, periods of depressive symptoms which are called major depressive episodes (see box on page 251). People with **dysthymic disorder,** on the other hand, struggle with more chronic but less severe depression. The clinician diagnoses dysthymic disorder when these moderately depressive symptoms have lasted at least 2 years in adults and a year or more in children.

Major Depressive Disorder

Think of a time in your life when something very sad or tragic happened to you, and you felt overwhelmed with feelings of unhappiness, loss, or grief. Try to recall what those feelings were like and how despondent you were. As painful as this experience was, you probably could see the connection between the tragic event and your feelings, and you probably recovered after a period of time. Now imagine that these feelings just hit you without any obvious cause, or that you were unable to overcome your sense of loss. Then imagine feeling unremitting hopelessness, fatigue, worthlessness, and suicidality. This is comparable to what it's like for a person experiencing a major depressive episode.

Characteristics of a Major Depressive Episode The emotional symptoms of a **major depressive episode** involve a dysphoric mood of an intensity that far outweighs the ordinary disappointments and occasional sad emotions of everyday life. Such dysphoria may appear as extreme dejection or a dramatic loss of interest in previously pleasurable aspects of life. In some cases, the depression has its roots in an experience of bereavement following the loss of a loved one. Although intense depression following the death of a loved one is normal, it would be considered a mood disorder if the disabling sadness lasts inordinately long (more than 2 months). Many major depressive episodes are not precipitated by a particular event, however. The fact that this intense sadness can arise without a clear precipitant often causes people who experience one of these episodes to feel overwhelmed and perplexed. Usually the life of an individual in a major depressive episode is thrown into chaos because of the impairment experienced at work and home.

Physical signs of a major depressive episode are called somatic, or bodily, symptoms. Lethargic and listless, the person may experience a slowing down of bodily movement, called psychomotor retardation. Alternatively, some depressed people show the opposite symptom, psychomotor agitation; as a result, their behavior has a frenetic quality. As previously mentioned, when these behaviors are bizarre and extreme, they may be characterized as catatonic. Eating disturbances are also common, as the individual deviates from usual appetite patterns, either avoiding food or overindulging, usually with sweets or carbohydrates. People in a depressive episode also show a significant change in their sleeping patterns, either sleeping much more than usual or experiencing insomnia. In fact, in people experiencing a major depressive episode, dramatic changes in their EEG sleep patterns reflect disturbances in sleep continuity, intermittent wakefulness, and early-morning awakening. Disturbances in REM sleep are also commonly evident and take several forms. For example, there are more eye movements during REM sleep, and there is an increased duration of REM sleep early in the night. Such sleep abnormalities commonly precede the onset of the initial major depressive episode among people who are at high risk for developing a mood disorder, such as first-degree relatives of individuals who have experienced major depression (American Psychiatric Association, 2000).

In addition, people in a major depressive episode have cognitive symptoms that include an intensely negative self-view reflected by low self-esteem and feelings that they deserve to be punished. They may become tyrannized by guilt as they dwell unrelentingly on past mistakes. Unable to think clearly or to concentrate, they may find themselves indecisive about even the most insignificant matters. Activities that may have sparked their interest only weeks ago now lack any appeal. Feelings of hopelessness and negativity lead many people to become consumed by thoughts of death and to possibly look for escape by thinking about or actually committing suicide. We will look specifically at suicide later in this chapter.

The symptoms of a major depressive episode usually arise gradually over the course of several days or weeks. Some people

> **Diagnostic Features of a Major Depressive Episode**
>
> - For most of the time during a 2-week period, a person experiences at least five of the following symptoms, which involve a change from previous functioning (at least one of the first two symptoms must be present).
>   - Depressed mood
>   - Diminished interest or pleasure in all or most daily activities.
>   - Significant unintentional weight loss or appetite decrease or increase
>   - Insomnia or hypersomnia
>   - Psychomotor agitation or retardation
>   - Fatigue or energy loss
>   - Feelings of worthlessness or inappropriate guilt
>   - Concentration difficulty or indecisiveness
>   - Recurrent thoughts of death or suicidality
> - The symptoms are not part of a mixed (manic/depressive) episode and are not attributable to a medical condition, use of a substance, or bereavement.
> - The symptoms cause significant distress or impairment.

report that, prior to the full-blown symptoms of depression, they were noticeably anxious and mildly depressed, sometimes for months. Once the active episode of major depression begins, they may experience symptoms for 2 weeks to a period of months. If untreated, most major depressive episodes seem to run their course some time after 6 months, and most people return to normal functioning. However, for approximately one fourth of these severely depressed people, some symptoms continue for months or even years.

Types of Depression In addition to the specifiers used to characterize depressive and manic episodes, there are terms used only to describe the nature of depressive episodes. People whose depressive episodes have **melancholic features** lose interest in most activities or find it difficult to react to events in their lives that would customarily bring pleasure. Morning is a particularly difficult time of the day for people with this type of depression. They may wake up much earlier than usual, possibly feeling more gloomy throughout the morning and struggling with a number of other symptoms throughout the day, such as psychomotor agitation or retardation, significant appetite disturbance, and excessive or inappropriate guilt.

People whose episodes show a **seasonal pattern** develop a depressive episode at about the same time each year, usually for about 2 months during the fall or winter, but then they return to normal functioning. During these episodes, they lack energy, and they tend to sleep excessively, overeat, and crave carbohydrates. As you will see later, studies of people with seasonal depression have led some researchers to propose that an alteration in biological rhythms linked to seasonal variations in the amount of daylight causes depression in these individuals. In fact, this variant of major depressive disorder is more frequently diagnosed in people who live at higher latitudes, such as the more northerly states, where there is less sunlight.

Prevalence and Course of the Disorder   Major depressive disorder is a relatively common psychological disorder. Out of every 100 people, approximately 13 men and 21 women develop this disorder at some point in life (Kessler et al., 1994). The prevalence of major depressive disorder may be changing dramatically in the past few decades. Evidence from the National Comorbidity Study indicates that increasingly younger age groups, called *cohorts,* are showing a steeper rise in prevalence rates (Kessler et al., 2003). As shown in Figure 8.1, in the cohort of individuals ages 18–29, more people are likely to become depressed and at earlier ages than is the case with people ages 30–44. In turn, the current group of 30–44-year-olds develop depression earlier and in larger numbers than the people in the two older age groups. In other words, depression is surfacing at earlier ages and with greater frequency. These findings are cause for concern, because they imply that major depressive disorder will become an increasingly important public health concern in the coming decades.

In trying to define the course of major depressive disorder, researchers have come to realize that depression is a heterogeneous disorder with many possible courses. Approximately 40 percent of the people who have one episode never have another major depressive episode, meaning that approximately 60 percent will have a second episode. Among those who have experienced two episodes, 70 percent will have a third, and among those who have had three episodes, 90 percent will have a fourth (American Psychiatric Association, 2000).

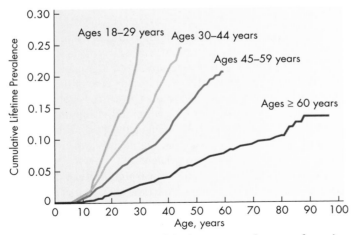

FIGURE 8.1 Cumulative lifetime prevalence of major depressive disorder by birth cohort
Source: Kessler, 2003.

Mini Case

MAJOR DEPRESSIVE DISORDER

Jonathan is a 37-year-old construction worker whose wife took him to a psychiatric facility. Although Jonathan has been functioning normally for the past several years, he suddenly became severely disturbed and depressed. At the time of admission, Jonathan was agitated, dysphoric, and suicidal, even going as far as to purchase a gun to kill himself. He had lost his appetite and had developed insomnia during the preceding 3 weeks. As each day went by, he found himself feeling more and more exhausted, less able to think clearly or to concentrate, and uninterested in anything or anyone. He had become hypersensitive in his dealings with neighbors, co-workers, and family, insisting that others were being too critical of him. This was the second such episode in Jonathan's history, the first having occurred 5 years earlier, following the loss of his job due to a massive layoff in his business.

Diagnostic Features

- This diagnosis is assigned to people who have either a single major depressive episode (see features on page 251) or recurrent episodes with 2 or more months intervening between episodes.

- The major depressive episode is not better explained by another disorder.

- The individual has never had a manic, mixed, or hypomanic episode.

This man's chronic depression interferes with his ability to concentrate and study for an exam.

Dysthymic Disorder

Not all forms of depression involve the severe symptoms we have discussed so far. For some people, depression involves sadness that is not as deep or intense as that of a major depressive episode but is nevertheless quite distressing and long-lasting. Keep in mind that we are not talking about normal blue moods that everyone experiences from time to time but a more serious, unrelenting depression. People with dysthymic disorder have, for at least 2 years, some of the same kinds of symptoms as those experienced by people with major depressive disorder, such as appetite disturbance, sleep disturbance, low energy or fatigue, low self-esteem, poor concentration, decision-making difficulty, and feelings of hopelessness. However, they do not experience as many symptoms, nor are these symptoms as severe. They feel inadequate in most of their endeavors and are unable to experience pleasure or interest in the events of life. As you can see, dysthymic disorder differs from major depressive disorder on the basis of its course, which is chronic. People with dysthymic disorder are likely to withdraw from others, to spend much of their time brooding or feeling guilty, and to act with anger and irritability toward others. During this extended depression, these individuals are never symptom-free for an interval longer than 2 months. They commonly have other serious psychological disorders as well. Approximately one tenth will go on to develop major depressive disorder. A sizable number also have a personality disorder, which makes accurate diagnosis difficult. Others are likely to develop a substance-abuse disorder, because they use drugs or alcohol excessively in misguided attempts to reduce their chronic feelings of depression and hopelessness. Hospitalization is uncommon for people with this disorder, except in cases in which the depression leads to suicidal behavior. The disorder is also diagnosed in children and adolescents. In these cases, however, the duration need only be 1 year, and the depression may be more evident in an intense, chronic irritability than in a depressed mood.

Approximately 8 percent of women and nearly 5 percent of men will develop this disorder in the course of their lives (Kessler et al., 1994). The rate of dysthymic disorder in the older

In MindMAP Segment 8.2, Roberto discusses his difficulty falling asleep, eating as a way to feel good, his chronic fatigue, and his difficulty getting things done at work.

People with dysthymic disorder experience a number of symptoms such as sleep disturbance, appetite disturbance, low energy or fatigue, and concentration difficulties.

Mini Case

DYSTHYMIC DISORDER

Miriam is a 34-year-old community college instructor who, for the past 3 years, has had persistent feelings of depressed mood, inferiority, and pessimism. She realizes that, since her graduation from college, she has never felt really happy and that, in recent years, her thoughts and feelings have been characterized as especially depressed. Her appetite is low, and she struggles with insomnia. During waking hours, she lacks energy and finds it very difficult to do her work. She often finds herself staring out the window of her office, consumed by thoughts of how inadequate she is. She fails to fulfill many of her responsibilities and, for the past 3 years, has received consistently poor teacher evaluations. Getting along with her colleagues has become increasingly difficult; consequently, she spends most of her free time alone in her office.

Diagnostic Features

- For a period lasting at least 2 years, people with this disorder experience depressed mood for most of the day, for more days than not, as indicated either by their own report or by the observation of others.

- While depressed, these individuals experience at least two of the following: poor appetite or overeating; insomnia or hypersomnia; low energy or fatigue; low self-esteem; poor concentration or difficulty making decisions; and feelings of hopelessness.

- During the 2-year period (1 year for children and adolescents), the individual has never been without these symptoms for 2 continuous months.

- The individual has not (1) had a major depressive episode during the first 2 years of the disturbance, (2) ever had a manic, mixed, or hypomanic episode, (3) met the criteria for cyclothymic disorder, (4) experienced the symptoms during the course of a chronic psychotic disorder, and (5) has not developed the symptoms as the direct result of a medical condition or use of a substance.

- The symptoms cause significant distress or impairment.

adult population is estimated to be 2 percent, and it is more prevalent among women than men in this age group as well (King & Markus, 2000). As is true for depression, the symptoms of dysthymia take on a different form in older adults, who are more likely to report disturbances in physical rather than psychological functioning (Oxman, Barrett, Sengupta, & Williams, 2000).

Disorders Involving Alternations in Mood

There are two forms of mood disorder in which alternations in mood are the primary characteristic: bipolar disorder and cyclothymic disorder. **Bipolar disorder** involves an intense and very disruptive experience of extreme elation, or euphoria, possibly alternating with major depressive episodes. A full-blown expression of extreme symptoms involving abnormally heightened levels of thinking, behavior, and emotionality that cause impairment in social or occupational functioning is called a **manic episode.** In some instances, the individual experiences psychotic symptoms, such as delusions and hallucinations. An individual may also experience a **mixed episode,** characterized by a period lasting at least a week, in which the symptoms of both a manic episode and a major depressive episode occur together in rapidly alternating fashion. **Cyclothymic disorder** involves alternations between dysphoria and briefer, less intense, and less disruptive states of euphoria called **hypomanic episodes.**

Bipolar Disorder

Think of a time when you felt unusually energetic and happy. You may have felt "on top of the world," with excitement filling your emotions and intense energy rushing through your body. During such a time, you may have slept and eaten less than usual, and you may have felt "hyped" to accomplish a remarkable task. You may have maintained this heightened energy level for several days but then suddenly "crashed," perhaps becoming exhausted or even a bit depressed. Experiences such as these, but in a much more extreme form, constitute the basis for manic episodes, the crucial component of bipolar disorder.

Characteristics of a Manic Episode   People who have manic episodes, even if they have never had a depressive episode, are diagnosed as having *bipolar disorder,* a term that has replaced *manic depression* in the diagnostic system. From what you may know about the more commonly used term, *manic depression,* you might expect that a bipolar disturbance would involve mood swings. The term *bipolar* does imply two poles, mania and depression; however, not all people with bipolar disorder show signs of depression. The assumption underlying the diagnostic

> ### Diagnostic Features of a Manic Episode
>
> - A period of abnormally and persistently elevated, expansive, or irritable mood lasting at least 1 week.
>
> - During this period, three or more of the following symptoms have persisted (four if the mood is only irritable):
>   - Inflated self-esteem or grandiosity
>   - Decreased need for sleep
>   - Increased talkativeness
>   - Flight of ideas or racing thoughts
>   - Distractibility
>   - Increase in goal-directed activity or psychomotor agitation
>   - Excessive involvement in pleasurable activities with potentially painful consequences
>
> - The symptoms are not part of a mixed (manic/depressive) episode and are not attributable to a medical condition or use of a substance.
>
> - The symptoms cause significant distress or impairment or necessitate hospitalization to prevent harm to self or others.

term is that, at some point, people with this disorder will become depressed.

A person in the midst of a manic episode may seem outgoing, alert, talkative, creative, witty, and self-confident. However, the experience of people in a manic episode is far more complicated. Their feelings of expansiveness and energy can cause serious dysfunction. Their self-esteem may be grossly inflated, and their thinking may be grandiose and even have a psychotic quality. For example, a manic man told his friends that he had just realized he possessed divine attributes and that soon he would be able to perform healing miracles. A manic woman asserted that the newspapers contained clues that suggested she would soon be called on by the White House to assume the vice presidency.

Most people in a manic episode do not have such bizarre thoughts, but they may have unusual ideas and bouts of uncharacteristic creativity. Their thoughts may race, and they may jump from idea to idea or activity to activity, easily distracted and craving stimulation. They may be more talkative and louder than usual, speaking with such rapidity that others find it difficult to keep up with them or to interrupt. They may make jokes, puns, and sexual comments, perhaps becoming theatrical and melodramatic, or hostile and aggressive. Strangers may view these individuals as being extraordinarily outgoing, friendly, and imaginative. Those who know them, however, recognize that something is seriously wrong and that their behavior and thinking are out of control.

People in a manic episode are unusually energetic, possibly getting by with only a few hours of rest each night. During this

MindMAP Segment 8.3 provides insight into the experience of bipolar disorder by showing the case of a man who discusses his symptoms and his frustration in finding treatment. The segment also illustrates the use of MRI as a research tool in understanding the disorder.

Scientists are seeking a variety of routes to understanding the biological basis of bipolar disorder and developing effective interventions.

Mini Case

BIPOLAR I DISORDER

Isabel is a 38-year-old realtor who, for the past week, has shown signs of uncharacteristically outlandish behavior. This behavior began with Isabel's development of an unrealistic plan to create her own real estate "empire." She went without sleep or food for 3 days, spending most of her time at her computer developing far-fetched financial plans. Within 3 days she put deposits on 7 houses, together valued at more than $3 million, although she had no financial resources to finance even one of them. She made several visits to local banks, where she was known and respected, and "made a scene" with each loan officer who expressed skepticism about her plan. In one instance she angrily pushed over the banker's desk, yanked his phone from the wall, and screamed at the top of her lungs that the bank was keeping her from earning a multimillion dollar profit. The police were summoned, and they brought her to the psychiatric emergency room, from which she was transferred for intensive evaluation and treatment.

Diagnostic Features

- People with this disorder have experienced at least 1 manic episode, with the possibility but not the necessity of a major depressive episode. (This contrasts with Bipolar II Disorder in which an individual experiences recurrent major depressive episodes, and a history of at least 1 hypomanic episode but no manic episodes.)
- The condition is not attributable to another disorder.
- The symptoms cause significant distress or impairment.

Diagnostic Features of a Hypomanic Episode

- A period of persistently elevated, expansive, or irritable mood lasting at least 4 days, which clearly differs from normal mood and is observable by others.
- During this period, three or more of the following symptoms have persisted (four if the mood is only irritable):
  - Inflated self-esteem or grandiosity
  - Decreased need for sleep
  - Increased talkativeness
  - Flight of ideas or racing thoughts
  - Distractibility
  - Increase in goal-directed activity or psychomotor agitation
  - Excessive involvement in pleasurable activities with potentially painful consequences
- There are no psychotic features, and the episode is not severe enough to cause marked impairment or to necessitate hospitalization.
- The symptoms are not attributable to a medical condition or the effects of a substance.

time, they feel driven in tireless pursuit of outlandish goals. When others ask them how they feel, they report feeling "on top of the world." However, there is also a downside to a manic episode: the euphoria may suddenly turn into extreme irritability, even aggressiveness and hostility, especially if other people thwart their unrealistic and grandiose plans. For example, Harry, a relatively unsuccessful dealer in rare coins, suddenly concocted a grand scheme to overhaul the U.S. monetary system. When he told his family that he was flying to Washington to present the plan to the president, his family and friends thought he was kidding, and he responded with rage. Manic individuals also tend to seek out pleasurable activities, disregarding the possibility of any negative consequences that may result from their sexual indiscretions, unrestrained buying sprees, and foolish investments. Manic individuals whose family and friends suggest that they obtain professional help often respond with annoyance and anger.

In contrast to a major depressive episode, which tends to emerge and diminish rather gradually, a manic episode typically appears and ends suddenly. Often the individual develops a range of symptoms in a period of only a few days. Manic

REAL STORIES

KAY REDFIELD JAMISON: BIPOLAR DISORDER

Kay Redfield Jamison

At the beginning of this chapter, you read the case of Janice Butterfield, a woman whose depression was so severe that she attempted suicide. Earlier in the book (Chapter 2), you read about Peter Dickinson, whose mood swings were so extreme that he had to be hospitalized for a condition called bipolar disorder. Although there are countless stories about people whose lives have been disrupted by painful bouts with mood disorders, the story of an eminent psychologist, Dr. Kay Redfield Jamison, is particularly compelling. Jamison courageously told the world about her personal struggle with bipolar disorder in her book *An Unquiet Mind: A Memoir of Moods and Madness.*

Jamison describes a relatively happy childhood. She grew up in a military family that moved frequently due to her father's Air Force assignments. At an early age, Jamison became fascinated by the field of medicine, and she looked for opportunities to follow Air Force physicians on rounds and occasionally assist with minor medical procedures. Teenage stresses then got the best of Jamison—when she was 15 her family moved, necessitating a breakup with her boyfriend and a move to a new school, where she experienced intense competition and social disappointments. Around this time, Jamison's father showed dramatic mood shifts; at times he struggled to get out of bed because of intense depression, and at other times he soared into episodes of gaiety. By the time Jamison was 16 or 17, it became clear that she also was prone to extreme moods, swinging from heightened energy and enthusiasm to intense emotional pain. During her senior

year in high school, Jamison experienced an episode in which she felt so wonderful that she thought she could accomplish anything she set her mind to. She raced around, played sports, stayed out all night with friends, and filled books with plays she had written. She describes feeling a sense of "cosmic relatedness," in which everything made sense to her. The episode was brief, however, and Jamison became tired, unenthusiastic, and unable to concentrate. Episodes like this recurred. At times they were so severe that she became emotionally devastated, and at one point suicidal.

Jamison managed to complete her undergraduate degree at UCLA despite her mood disturbances. Later she went on to study medicine and become a psychologist with appointments at prestigious medical schools, the first of which was UCLA, where she joined the faculty at the age of 27. Only 3 months into this job, Jamison experienced psychotic symptoms in her first full-blown manic episode. Ultimately she was diagnosed as having bipolar disorder, and she was treated with lithium, a medication about which she had mixed feelings because it prevented her from experiencing the soaring highs of mania. Jamison realized, however, that manic episodes can also be nightmar-

ish experiences, as reflected in her emotionally charged description:

In a rage I pulled the bathroom lamp off the wall and felt the violence go through me but not yet out of me. "For Christ's sake," he said, rushing in— and then stopping very quietly. Jesus, I must be crazy, I can see it in his eyes: a dreadful mix of concern, terror, irritation, resignation, and why me, Lord? "Are you hurt?" he asks. Turning my head with its fast-scanning eyes I see in the mirror blood running down my arms, collecting into the tight ribbing of my beautiful, erotic negligee, only an hour ago used in a passion of an altogether different and wonderful kind. "I can't help it. I can't help it," I chant to myself, but I can't say it; the words won't come out, and the thoughts are going by far too fast. I bang my head over and over against the bathroom door. God make it stop. I can't stand it, I know I'm insane again. He really cares, I think, but within ten minutes he too is screaming and his eyes have a wild look from contagious madness, from the lightning adrenaline between the two of us. "I can't leave you like this," but I say a few truly awful things and then go for his throat in a more literal way, and he does leave me, provoked beyond endurance and unable to see the devastation and desperation inside. I can't convey it and he can't see it; there's nothing to be done. I can't think, I can't calm this murderous cauldron, my grand ideas of an hour ago seem absurd and pathetic, my life is in ruins and—worse still—ruinous; my body is uninhabitable. It is raging and weeping and full of destruction and wild energy gone amok.

People with bipolar disorder can become hyperagitated and irritable. They may develop exaggerated views of their own importance and may behave in ways that reflect those views, such as directing traffic, unaware of the inappropriateness of their behavior.

episodes typically last from a few weeks to a few months, depending, in part, on whether or not professional treatment is obtained.

Types of Bipolar Disorder   There are several variations in the expression of bipolar disorder, with a primary distinction in the *DSM-IV-TR* between bipolar I disorder and bipolar II disorder. A diagnosis of **bipolar I disorder** describes a clinical course in which the individual experiences one or more manic episodes with the possibility, though not the necessity, of having experienced one or more major depressive episodes. In contrast, a diagnosis of **bipolar II disorder** means the individual has had one or more major depressive episodes and at least one hypomanic episode. In other words, those with bipolar II disorder have never experienced a full-blown manic episode but have become sufficiently energized to meet the criteria for a hypomanic episode.

Prevalence and Course of the Disorder   Bipolar disorder is much less common than major depressive disorder. Of the U.S. population, 1.6 percent have bipolar disorder at some point in life. Bipolar disorder is almost equally prevalent in males and females (Kessler et al., 1994), yet there is a gender difference in the way that the disorder first appears. The first episode for men is more likely to be manic, but for women it is more likely to be a major depressive episode. As in the case with major depressive disorder, women with bipolar disorder are at greater risk of developing a manic episode during the postpartum period than at other times in their lives (Leibenluft, 2000). Bipolar disorder most commonly appears in people in their twenties. In adults over 65 years of age, the prevalence rate is estimated to be 0.1 percent, although misdiagnosis may occur due to the coexistence of medical illness (King & Markus, 2000).

In recent years the diagnosis of bipolar disorder has been increasingly applied to children, some as young as 3 years of age (Kowatch et al., 2005). In fact, the term *pediatric bipolar disorder* has emerged in the psychiatric literature, although there is a lack of consistency about the diagnostic criteria and the appropriate methods for assessing this condition. Complicating the diagnostic process is the fact that many psychologically disturbed children present a range of symptoms and co-existing conditions, such as conduct disorder, attention-deficit/hyperactivity disorder, anxiety disorders, or depression (Schapiro, 2005). Much more research is needed before conclusions can confidently be drawn about the extent to which the mood and behavioral symptoms of distressed children meet the criteria for what is recognized as bipolar disorder among adults.

Following a single manic episode, there is a 90 percent probability that the individual will experience subsequent episodes. Once individuals have experienced a manic episode, they are at greater risk for experiencing another episode, even if they are taking medications to control the disorder; this phenomenon is called "kindling." Most subsequent manic episodes occur just prior to or soon after a major depressive episode. People who do not receive medication for the treatment of their bipolar disorder average about four episodes within the span of a decade, with the interval between these episodes decreasing as the individual grows older. A small percentage (less than 15 percent) of individuals with bipolar disorder have between four and eight mood episodes within the course of a single year; these individuals are referred to as **rapid cyclers,** and the specifier "rapid cycling" is part of the diagnosis. Approximately 10 to 30 percent of people with bipolar disorder experience rapid cycling; the majority of these individuals are women. Medical conditions such as hypothyroidism, disturbances in sleep-wake cycles, and even the use of antidepressant medications can contribute to the development of rapid cycling (Papadimitriou, Calabrese, Dikeos, & Christodoulou, 2005).

Most people with bipolar disorder act and feel normal between episodes, although approximately one fourth continue to show unstable mood and to have problems in their dealings with other people, both at home and at work (American Psychiatric Association, 2000). They are likely to have continuing difficulties at work following an initial episode, and less than half are

Mini Case

CYCLOTHYMIC DISORDER

Larry is a 32-year-old bank cashier who has sought treatment for his mood variations, which date back to the age of 26. For several years, co-workers, family, and friends have repeatedly told him that he is very "moody." He acknowledges that his mood never feels quite stable, although at times others tell him he seems more calm and pleasant than usual. Unfortunately, these intervals are quite brief, lasting for a few weeks and usually ending abruptly. Without warning, he may experience either a depressed mood or a period of elation. During his depressive periods, his confidence, energy, and motivation are very low. During his hypomanic periods, he willingly volunteers to extend his workday and to undertake unrealistic challenges at work. On weekends, he acts in promiscuous and provocative ways, often sitting outside his apartment building, making seductive comments and gestures to women walking by. Larry disregards the urging of his family members to get professional help, insisting that it is his nature to be a bit unpredictable. He also states that he

doesn't want some "shrink" to steal away the periods during which he feels "fantastic."

Diagnostic Features

- For at least 2 years, people with this disorder experience numerous periods with hypomanic symptoms and numerous periods with depressive symptoms that do not meet the criteria for a major depressive episode.

- During the 2-year period (1 year for children and adolescents), the individual has never been without these symptoms for 2 continuous months.

- No major depressive episode, manic episode, or mixed episode has been present during the first 2 years of the disturbance.

- The symptoms are not attributable to another disorder, medical condition, or substance.

- The symptoms cause significant distress or impairment.

---

fully adjusted within the 5 years after hospitalization (Goldberg, Harrow, & Grossman, 1995). Bipolar disorder is a very serious condition if untreated. In fact, the risk of suicide among people with bipolar disorder who do not receive treatment is estimated at 15 percent (Shastry, 2005).

Cyclothymic Disorder

Everyone experiences mood changes, but the mood shifts that people with cyclothymic disorder exhibit are unusually dramatic and recurrent, though not as intense as those experienced by people with bipolar disorder. The hypomania is never severe enough to be diagnosed as a manic episode, and the dysphoria is never severe enough to be diagnosed as a depressive episode. Still, the destabilizing effects of this disorder disrupt their lives.

Cyclothymic disorder is a chronic condition that lasts a minimum of 2 years (1 year in children and adolescents). On the surface, some people with cyclothymic disorder seem to get along satisfactorily, and they may claim that their periods of heightened energy are welcomed periods of creativity. Unfortunately, the individual with this disorder is actually more likely to feel some distress or impairment in work or interpersonal dealings due to the mood disorder. Problems are especially likely for individuals who struggle with unpredictable mood changes that recur in rapid cycles, because other people regard them as moody and unreliable. The onset of this disorder generally occurs when a person is in his or her twenties. The symptoms may not be apparent at first, but, over time, individuals with this disorder notice that their moods fluctuate dramatically, and people who know them find it increasingly difficult to deal with the individuals. People with cyclothymic disorder are at considerable risk of developing full-blown bipolar disorder. This disorder affects less than 1 percent of the population.

Theories and Treatments of Mood Disorders

For centuries, people have tried to gain an understanding of the causes of mood disorders and the ways in which people with these conditions should be treated. Due to the intense focus on these disorders, researchers and theorists have made considerable progress in recent years. Although no single perspective is sufficient, together they provide important insights into mood disorders which may lead to more effective treatments.

Biological Perspectives

From our discussion so far, you are already aware that biology is connected in an important way to mood disorders. On the very simplest level, mood disorders cause physical changes, such as disturbances of appetite and sleep patterns. More complex is the effect of biological processes on feelings of depression and elation.

Genetics   Compelling evidence of the importance of biological contributors to mood disorders comes from studies on genetics. The observation that these disorders run in families is well established. First-degree relatives of people with major depression are twice as likely to develop depressive disorders than are people in the general population (Sullivan, Neale, & Kendler, 2000b). The risk is even higher when these first-degree relatives are the offspring of these depressed individuals (Lieb et al., 2002). Adding weight to the genetic perspective are the findings from a large-scale investigation of three generations (children, parents, and grandparents). When major depressive disorder is present in the parent as well as the grandparent generation, children are more likely to show symptoms of psychopathology. Interestingly, this psychopathology takes the form of an anxiety disorder which, in turn, is predictive of the development of a depressive disorder in adulthood (Weissman et al., 2005). Thus, a child with an anxiety disorder who comes from a family in which depression has been diagnosed is at much greater risk of developing depression later in life.

The most compelling evidence in favor of a genetic basis of major depressive disorder comes from an analysis of the findings of five large-scale studies examining inheritance patterns in families. Based on these findings, the heritability of major depressive disorder is estimated to be 31 to 42 percent. However, the investigators were careful to explain that this heritability estimate applies to groups, not individuals. In other words, if someone you know has a parent or even a twin with major depressive disorder, this does not mean that this person has a 30 to 40 percent risk of developing the disorder. Instead, these estimates mean that among, for example, 100 individuals with a twin or close relative who has the disorder, 30 to 40 of them have a higher likelihood of developing major depression (Sullivan, Neale, & Kendler, 2000a).

In the area of bipolar disorder, researchers in a large NIMH study in five major research centers conducted genetic linkage analyses on over 500 individuals diagnosed with bipolar and other mood disorders (Faraone, Glatt, Su, & Tsuang, 2004). Even though this is the largest publicly available data set in existence on the genetics of bipolar disorder, the evidence is still far from clear regarding the involvement of specific genes (DePaulo, 2004). However, in trying to understand the genetic basis for bipolar disorder, investigators are looking at a range of psychopathology based on the finding of a possible link between bipolar disorder and schizophrenia. As more research in this area continues, investigators are exploring the possibility of a bipolar spectrum that includes schizophrenia (Berrettini, 2003).

Gender also appears to play a major role in influencing the gene-environment interaction in the development of mood disorders. In a major investigation of gender differences in depression, over 1,000 pairs of opposite-sex twins were interviewed 2 years apart to determine the effect of receiving social support on the development of depressive symptoms during this period of time (Kendler, Myers, & Prescott, 2005). As shown in Figure 8.2, the male members of the twin pair who received low levels of social support had a slightly higher rate of developing major depression within the 2-year period of the study compared to men who received more social support (the blue scatter points in the figure). By contrast, the female members of the twin pair who had low levels of social support were much more likely to develop major depression than the women who had higher levels of social support (the red scatter points in the figure). This finding adds to our understanding of the relative contributions of heredity and social context as influences on mood disorders. In support of the biopsychosocial model, we see that even powerful genetic risk factors can be influenced by environmental factors such as social relationships.

Biochemical Factors The biochemical mechanisms that genetically predispose high-risk people to become depressed or have manic episodes are still unknown. At present, the most

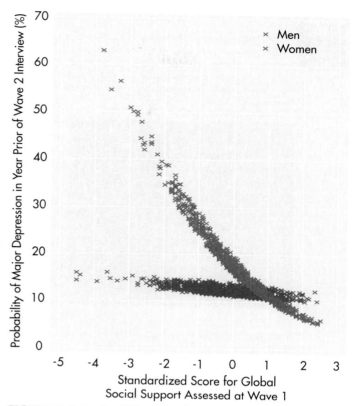

FIGURE 8.2 Probability of major depressive disorder in male and female twins as predicted by levels of social support.

Source: Kendler, K. S., Myers, J., & Prescott, C. A. (2005), "Sex differences in the relationship between social support and risk for major depression: A longitudinal study of opposite-sex twin pairs," *American Journal of Psychiatry*, 162, pp. 250–256. Copyright © 2005 American Psychiatric Association.

widely held biological theories focus on altered neurotransmitter functioning as the cause of mood disorders. Because scientists cannot directly observe the actions of neurotransmitters in the human brain, research in this area must involve studies of animals and observations of people who take certain types of drugs.

The earliest theory along these lines was the catecholamine hypothesis (Schildkraut, 1965), which asserted that a relative shortage of norepinephrine (a catecholamine) causes depression and an overabundance of norepinephrine causes mania. An alternative to the catecholamine hypothesis is the indolamine hypothesis (Glassman, 1969), which states that a deficiency of serotonin contributes to the behavioral symptoms of depression.

These neurotransmitter deficit hypotheses, referred to now as the **monoamine depletion model** (reflecting the name of this category of neurotransmitters), provided an important breakthrough in the understanding of the biological factors of mood disorders (Delgado, 2004). Norepinephrine and serotonin are the two monoamines that are thought to be most important in major depressive disorder (Elhwuegi, 2004). In fact, all antidepressant medications currently in use work to increase the availability of these neurotransmitters at the synapse.

Neuroendocrine research has also pointed out an important relationship between hormonal activity and depression. In

MindMAP Segment 8.4 highlights the case of a woman whose symptoms of severe depression did not respond to traditional treatments. However, when Prozac became available in 1987, this medication proved to be remarkably effective in her treatment.

The SSRIs brought about a revolution in the treatment of psychological disorders. By understanding the role of neurotransmitters in this disorder, researchers have made significant progress in alleviating the symptoms of depression.

particular, researchers have focused on the body's production of **cortisol,** a hormone involved in mobilizing the body's resources in times of stress. Researchers are attempting to determine whether there are reliable differences in cortisol levels in response to stress between depressed and nondepressed individuals. Although dozens of laboratory studies have shown a relationship between social stress and elevated cortisol, researchers have been unable to establish a clear link between naturally occurring stressors and depressive reactions (Hammen, 2005).

Although our understanding of the role of biology in mood disorders is still incomplete, multiple lines of research seem to point to a biological contribution to the causes and symptoms of mood disorders. Particularly compelling are the research findings in the area of genetics. As we discuss other theories of mood disorders, keep in mind the interaction among biological, psychological, and social factors. Regardless of what precipitates depression, depressed people experience biological changes. Any intervention must address the individual's physical as well as psychological state.

Psychological Perspectives

As important as biological factors appear to be in the understanding of mood disorders, it is clear that psychology plays a crucial role as well. Each of the major theoretical perspectives in the field has something to offer in understanding the causes of depression.

Psychodynamic Theories Early psychoanalytic theories of mood disorders reflected themes of loss and feelings of rejection (Abraham, 1911/1968). Later psychodynamic theories retain a focus on inner psychic processes as the basis for mood disturbances, although they involve less of an emphasis on loss. For example, well-known British psychoanalyst John Bowlby proposed that people can become depressed as adults if they were raised by parents who failed to provide them with a stable and secure relationship (Bowlby, 1980). Another variant on the theme of deficient parenting comes from Jules Bemporad (1985), who proposed that children in these families become preoccupied with the need to be loved by others. As adults, they form relationships in which they overvalue the support of their partners. When such relationships end, the depressed person becomes overwhelmed with feelings of inadequacy and loss. Psychoanalytic explanations of mania are similar to those of depression, in that mania is seen as a defensive response by which an individual staves off feelings of inadequacy, loss, and helplessness. Presumably, people develop feelings of grandiosity and elation or become hyperenergetic as an unconscious defense against sinking into a state of gloom and despair.

Behavioral and Cognitively Based Theories One of the earliest behavioral formulations of theories of depression was that the symptoms of depression are the result of a reduction in positive reinforcements (Lazarus, 1968; Skinner, 1953). According to this view, depressed people withdraw from life because they no longer have incentives to be active. Consider the example of a formerly successful athlete who suffers an injury. Lacking the positive reinforcement of the athletic successes to which he has become accustomed, he might retreat into a depressive state.

Contemporary behaviorist perspectives on depression (Kanter et al., 2004) are based on the model developed several

Neglectful parents can leave a child feeling unlovable.

decades ago by Lewinsohn (1974), who maintained that depressed people have a low rate of what he termed **response-contingent positive reinforcement,** behaviors that increase in frequency as the result of performing actions that produce pleasure. Take the example of Evelyn, a young woman who has relocated to a new town. Although she is in email contact with her friends from her former community, Evelyn finds herself spending her evenings and weekends alone. In an effort to meet new people, Evelyn decides to go to a neighborhood pub but realizes once she is there that everyone else seems to know each other. She feels awkward, leaves the pub, and spends the rest of the weekend watching television. After a few more unsuccessful tries, she gives up in frustration while becoming more and more sad, lonely, and pessimistic about her future. In behaviorist terms, Evelyn's depression is attributable to her lack of positive reinforcement in the form of socializing with other people. According to the behaviorist point of view, the symptoms of low self-esteem, guilt, and pessimism of people such as Evelyn eventually come to be elicited by their lack of positive reinforcement.

As you will recall from our discussion in Chapter 4, behavioral approaches have become integrated with cognitive approaches that focus on the role of cognitions in causing or aggravating symptoms. Let's take a look at contributions from the cognitive perspective. Think of a time when you were depressed, and try to recall the reasons for your depression. Perhaps you lost a close friend or felt pessimistic about your future. Maybe you misinterpreted something that someone said to you, which caused you to feel bad about yourself. Cognitively based approaches propose that serious mood changes can result from events in our lives or from our perceptions of events.

According to the cognitive perspective, people develop depressive disorders if they have been sensitized by early experiences to react in a particular way to a particular kind of loss or stressful event. Depressed people react to stressful experiences by activating a set of thoughts that Beck (Beck, 1967) called the **cognitive triad:** a negative view of the self, the world, and the future. Beck proposed that, once activated, this depressive way of viewing the self, the world, and the future (called a depressive schema) perpetuates itself through a cyclical process. For example, consider a young man, Anthony, who constantly looks at the negative side of life. Even when something good happens to him, he manages to see the downside of the situation. What is happening, according to theorists such as Beck, is that Anthony interprets every situation in terms of his schema, which prevents him from seeing anything but problems, hopelessness, and his own inadequacy. Because Anthony is so pessimistic, he can never take anything positive from his experiences, and his negative outlook proves to be a handicap. People become bored and irritated with Anthony and eventually give up trying to involve him in social activities. Thus, the cycle of depression is perpetuated.

Adding to the cycle of depressive thinking are **cognitive distortions,** errors that depressed people make in the way they draw conclusions from their experiences (Beck, Rush, Shaw, & Emery, 1979; Beck & Weishaar, 1989). These cognitive distortions involve applying illogical rules, such as making arbitrary

A parent who suddenly loses a spouse may have trouble adjusting to the doubling of household and family responsibilities, leading to depression and despondency.

inferences, jumping to conclusions, overgeneralizing, and taking a detail out of context (see Table 8.1). Using these rules makes the depressed person ascribe negative meanings to past and present events and make gloomy predictions about the future. The person is probably not even specifically aware of having these thoughts, because they have become such a constant feature of the individual's existence. The situation is comparable to what you might experience if you were sitting for a long time in a room with a noisy air conditioner. You do not actually notice how noisy the room is until someone else walks in and comments on it. Similarly, it takes a specific effort to isolate and identify automatic thoughts when they have become such permanent fixtures in the person's consciousness.

Contributing further to the unhappiness of depressed people, according to Beck, is the content of their thought. Depressed people feel sad because they believe they are deprived of something important that threatens their self-esteem. Further, depressed people are convinced that they are responsible for the loss. Their dysfunctional attitudes cause them to assume that they are worthless and helpless and that their efforts are doomed to fail. They distort any experience, including a positive one, so that it fits in with this generalized belief (Safran, 1990). As a consequence of these cognitive distortions, depressed individuals experience low feelings of well-being, energy, desire to be with others, and interest in the environment. These phenomena contribute to their depressed affect (Clark, Steer, & Beck, 1994).

Sociocultural and Interpersonal Perspectives

Some depressed people have had lifelong difficulties in their interactions with other people. Consider the case of Willy, a 40-year-old man who for most of his life has acted in abrasive ways that alienate others. As the years go by, Willy becomes increasingly saddened by the fact that he has no friends and realizes that it is unlikely that he will ever have a close relationship. For depressed

---

TABLE 8.1 Examples of Cognitive Distortions

Overgeneralizing

If it's true in one case, it applies to any case that is even slightly similar.	"I failed my first English exam so I'm probably going to fail all of them."

Selective Abstraction

The only events that the person takes seriously are those that represent failures, deprivation, loss, or frustration.	"Even though I won the election for school committee, I'm not really popular because not everyone voted for me."

Excessive Responsibility

I am responsible for all bad things that happen to me or others to whom I am close.	"It's my fault that my friend didn't get the job—I should've warned her about how hard the interview would be."

Assuming Temporal Causality

If it has been true in the past, then it's always going to be true.	"My last date was a wipeout, my next date will probably hate me too."

Making Excessive Self-References

I am the center of everyone else's attention, and they can all see when I mess up.	"When I spilled the coffee, everyone could see what a klutz I am!"

Catastrophizing

Always thinking the worst and being certain that it will happen.	"Because my sales figures were lower last quarter, I will never make it in the business world."

Dichotomous Thinking

Seeing everything as either one extreme or another rather than as mixed or in between.	"Everything about this school is rotten—the students, the professors, the dorms, and the food."

Source: Adapted from A. T. Beck, A. J. Bush, B. F. Shaw, & G. Emery in *Cognitive Therapy of Depression.* Copyright ©1979 Guilford Publications, Inc. Reprinted with permission.

---

people like Willy, whose social skills are so deficient, a cycle is created as their constant pessimism and self-deprecation make other people feel guilty and depressed. As a result, other people respond in unhelpful ways with criticism and rejection, and this further reinforces the depressed person's negative view of the world.

Expanding on these ideas, Columbia University researcher Myrna Weissman, with her late husband Gerald Klerman and their associates, developed a model of understanding mood disorders that emphasizes disturbed social functioning (Klerman, Weissman, Rounsaville, & Chevron, 1984; Weissman & Markowitz, 1994). This theory incorporates the ideas of behavioral psychologists who focus on the poor social skills of the depressed individual, but it goes one step further in looking at the origins of the depressed person's fundamental problems. The interpersonal theory of depression is rooted in the interpersonal approaches of Adolph Meyer (1957) and Harry Stack Sullivan (1953a, 1953b) and the attachment theory of John Bowlby. Meyer was known for his psychobiological approach to abnormal behavior, emphasizing how psychological problems might represent an individual's misguided attempts to adapt to the psychosocial environment. He believed that physical symptoms can also develop in association with psychological distress. Sullivan characterized abnormal behavior as a function of impaired

interpersonal relationships, including deficiencies in communication. Each of these theories could apply to a variety of psychological disorders, but Bowlby's theory, with its specific focus on disturbed attachment bonds in early childhood as the cause of unhappiness later in life, is particularly relevant to depression.

Interpersonal theory connects the ideas of these theorists with the behavioral and cognitively oriented theories by postulating a set of steps that leads to depression. The first step is the person's failure in childhood to acquire the skills needed to develop satisfying intimate relationships. This failure leads to a sense of despair, isolation, and resulting depression. Once a person's depression is established, it is maintained by poor social skills and impaired communication, which lead to further rejection by others. Reactive depressions in adulthood may arise when the individual experiences a stressful life event, such as the end of a relationship or death of a significant other. After the depressive symptoms begin, the individual's maladaptive social skills perpetuate them. For example, a man whose wife dies may become so distraught over an extended period of time that he alienates his friends and family members. In time, a vicious cycle establishes itself, in which his behavior causes people to stay away; because he is so lonely, he becomes even more difficult in his interactions with others. Although the individual circumstances differ in each case, it is this cycle of depression, lack of

Andrea Yates shocked the world when she methodically drowned each of her five children while she was in a state of mind characterized as postpartum depression. This photo was taken before the birth of her fifth child.

After Andrea Yates was found guilty of murder, she was sentenced to prison.

social interaction, and deterioration of social skills that interpersonal theory regards as the core problem of depression.

Stressful experiences are known to place individuals at risk for depression. These experiences can involve specific stress such as sexual victimization, chronic stress such as poverty and single parenting, and episodic stress such as bereavement or job loss. Women are more likely to be exposed to these stressors than are men, a fact that may account at least in part for the higher frequency in the diagnosis of depressive disorders in women (Hammen, 2005). An example of how these stressors may interact is provided by a study of over 700 African American women. Those who lived in impoverished neighborhoods characterized by high rates of crime and drug use were more likely to develop major depressive disorders. The highest rates of depression were found among women from these environments who had experienced specific recent negative life events (Cutrona et al., 2005).

Treatment

Biological Treatment Because of the strong support for biological influences on mood disorders, people with these disorders often receive somatic treatments. Antidepressant medication is the most common form of somatic treatment for people who

are depressed, and lithium carbonate (lithium) is the most widely used medication for people who have bipolar disorder. The most common medications used to treat depression are tricyclic antidepressants, monoamine oxidase inhibitors (MAOIs), and selective serotonin reuptake inhibitors (SSRIs).

Tricyclic antidepressants derive their name from the fact that they have a three-ring chemical structure. These medications, such as amitriptyline (Elavil, Endep), desipramine (Norpramin), imipramine (Tofranil), and nortriptyline (Aventyl, Pamelor), are particularly effective in alleviating depression in people who have some of the more common biological symptoms, such as disturbed appetite and sleep. Although the exact process by which tricyclic antidepressants work still remains unclear, it is known that they block the premature reuptake of biogenic amines back into the presynaptic neurons, thus increasing their excitatory effects on the postsynaptic neuron.

The antidepressant effects of MAOIs, such as phenelzine (Nardil) and tranylcypromine (Parnate), are believed to occur because the medications inhibit the enzyme monoamine oxidase, which converts the biogenic amines, such as norepinephrine and serotonin, into inert substances, so that they cannot excite the postsynaptic neurons. MAOIs prolong the life of neurotransmitters, thus increasing neuronal flow. These medications are particularly effective in treating depression in people with chronic depression that dates back many years and who have not responded to the tricyclics. However, MAOIs are not as commonly prescribed as the other two types of medications, because their interactions with certain other substances can cause serious complications. Specifically, people taking MAOIs are not able to take certain allergy medications or to ingest foods or beverages containing a substance called tyramine (for example, beer, cheese, and chocolate), because the combination can bring on a hypertensive crisis in which blood pressure rises dramatically and dangerously.

Selective serotonin reuptake inhibitors (SSRIs) have become very popular alternatives to the tricyclics and MAOIs. These medications block the uptake of serotonin, enabling more of this neurotransmitter to be available for action at the receptor sites. The SSRIs are distinguished from the tricyclics because of their selectivity. Unlike the other antidepressants, they do not block multiple receptors, which would cause unpleasant side effects, including sedation, weight gain, constipation, blood pressure changes, and dry mouth. The newer SSRI medications are not without side effects, however; the most commonly reported complaints are nausea, agitation, and sexual dysfunction. SSRIs such as fluoxetine (Prozac), sertraline (Zoloft), fluvoxamine (Luvox), paroxetine (Paxil), trazadone (Desyrel), citalopram (Celexa), and bupropion (Wellbutrin) have had a dramatic impact on the lives of millions of depressed people.

Although there have been reports in the media about the higher suicide risk associated with the SSRI category of medications, an investigation of all suicides in the years between 1996 and 1998 revealed a lower rate of suicide among individuals being treated with these medications compared to other forms of antidepressants. In part, this association was due to the generally better medical care provided in facilities that prescribe SSRIs compared to the older and less effective tricyclic antidepressants (TCA) (Gibbons, Hur, Bhaumik, & Mann, 2005). The beneficial effects of SSRIs are well documented; however, there is increasing concern about statistics showing that these medications can, in a small number of people, provoke extreme impulsive behaviors, including suicide attempts. Clinicians, as well as the U.S. Food and Drug Administration, have become quite concerned about the findings that suggest a link between suicide and the use of SSRI antidepressant medications, leading researchers to scrutinize these data. Attention has focused on a number of variables, including comorbid psychological disorders, gender, geographic location, and the role of psychotherapy. It is important to note that antidepressant medications are more likely to be prescribed to more severely disturbed patients, who are by the nature of their symptoms at higher risk for suicide (Rosack, 2005). Much more research is needed before conclusions can be drawn that antidepressant medications increase the risk of suicide among depressed individuals.

Antidepressant medications take time to work—from 2 to 6 weeks before a client's symptoms begin to lift. Once the depression has subsided, the client is usually urged to remain on the medication for 4 or 5 additional months, and much longer for clients with a history of recurrent, severe depressive episodes. Because of medication side effects and client concerns, clinicians have found it helpful to develop therapeutic programs that involve regular visits early in treatment, expanded efforts to educate clients about the medications, and continued monitoring of treatment compliance.

The traditional treatment for the manic symptoms of bipolar disorder is lithium carbonate, referred to as lithium. Lithium is a naturally occurring salt (found in small amounts in drinking water) that, when used medically, replaces sodium in the body. The psychopharmacological effect of this medication is to calm the manic individual by decreasing the catecholamine levels in the nervous system. Researchers have studied the efficacy of lithium in numerous studies over the past three decades, and the conclusion seems clear—lithium is effective in treating the symptoms of acute mania and in preventing the recurrence of manic episodes (Shastry, 2005).

People who have frequent manic episodes, such as two or more a year, are advised to remain on lithium continuously as a preventive measure. The drawback is that, even though lithium is a natural substance in the body, it can have side effects, such as mild central nervous system disturbances, gastrointestinal upsets, and more serious cardiac effects. Because of these side effects, some people who experience manic episodes are reluctant or even unwilling to take lithium continuously. Furthermore, lithium interferes with the "highs" associated with bipolar disorder, and manic individuals may be reluctant to take the medication because they enjoy the pleasurable feelings that accompany escalation into the manic episode. By the time a full-blown episode develops, these individuals may have become so grandiose that they deny they even have a problem. Those taking lithium face a difficult choice regarding whether or not to remain on maintenance doses of the medication. On the one hand, side effects must be considered. On the other hand, not taking the medication puts them at risk of having another episode. Some therapists encourage their clients to participate in lithium groups, in which members who use the medication on a regular basis provide support to each other regarding the importance of staying on the medication.

Because of the variable nature of bipolar disorder, additional medication is often beneficial in treating some symptoms. For example, people in a depressive episode may need to take an antidepressant medication in addition to the lithium for the duration of the episode. However, this can be problematic for a person who is prone to developing mania, because an antidepressant might provoke hypomania or mania. Those who have psychotic symptoms may benefit from taking antipsychotic medication until these disturbing symptoms subside. People who experience rapid cycling present a challenge for clinicians because of the sudden changes that take place in emotions and behavior. Psychopharmacologists have reported that rapid cyclers, especially those for whom lithium has not been sufficient, seem to respond positively to prescriptions of anticonvulsant medication, such as carbamazepine (Tegretol) or valproate (Depakote).

Much controversy has arisen about interventions for children who present symptoms of mood disorders. Because of continuing debate about whether very young children indeed suffer from depressive disorders or bipolar disorder that would be comparable to conditions diagnosed in adults, confusion has existed about the most appropriate mode of treatment. In recent years, there has been a marked increase in the prescription of medications, antidepressants as well as mood stabilizers, to children. However, alarm has been expressed about potential consequences of such prescriptions, including the ominous documentation of suicidality among some children and adolescents taking such medications. Much more research is needed in the years ahead which addresses the most appropriate interventions for children and adolescents with serious disturbances of mood.

For some clients with mood disorders, medication is either ineffective or slow in alleviating symptoms that are severe and possibly life-threatening. In cases involving incapacitating depression, the clinician may recommend electroconvulsive therapy (ECT). Although ECT is the most powerful somatic treatment for major depressive disorder, it is the least commonly used because of the negative connotations associated with it, as well as concern about short-term and long-term side effects. If you saw the movie *One Flew over the Cuckoo's Nest,* you will probably never forget the dramatic presentation of the misuse of ECT. Indeed, negative attitudes toward ECT are due mainly to historical misuse of this procedure as punishment rather than treatment. Today ECT continues to be administered, because it has been shown to be a lifesaving treatment for severely depressed people for whom medications alone are ineffective. This is especially true for people over the age of 60. In fact, this is the age group most likely to receive ECT for depression, probably because so many other treatments have been tried and discarded as ineffective (Niederehe & Schneider, 1998). In addition to being used for the treatment of depression, ECT is recommended for individuals in an acute state of mania who are not responding to medication (Mukherjee, Sackeim, & Schnur, 1994).

For depressed individuals, ECT is usually administered six to eight times, once every other day until the person's mood returns to normal. The person undergoing this treatment receives

In the dim days of winter, people with seasonal affective disorder are particularly prone to dysphoric moods.

anesthesia to reduce discomfort, a muscle relaxant, oxygen, and medication to help control heart rhythm. The lowest voltage needed to induce a convulsion is delivered to the client's head for less than a second. This is followed 2 to 3 seconds later by a tonic phase, lasting for 10 to 12 seconds, during which all muscles in the body under voluntary control undergo involuntary contractions. Last, there is a clonic phase, consisting of 30 to 50 seconds of convulsions, which appear more like a slight bodily tremor because of the muscle relaxant. A few minutes later, the individual emerges from the anesthesia, alert, without pain, and without recollection of what has transpired. Some seriously depressed individuals benefit from what is called "maintenance" ECT, in which the treatment is administered over a period of several months to prevent a recurrence of depressive symptoms.

One aspect of ECT that troubles some clinicians and clients is the fact that no one understands why ECT works. Most current hypotheses center on ECT-induced changes in neurotransmitter receptors and in the body's natural opiates. As for side effects, the primary complaints of clients following an ECT trial are short-term memory loss and confusion, which disappear within 2 weeks of the final treatment. No permanent brain damage or memory loss is known to result from ECT.

As discussed in Chapter 4, transcranial magnetic stimulation (TMS), when administered over repeated occasions, is being seen as an alternative to traditional ECT. Combining TMS with antidepressant medications appears to be a particularly promising approach to individuals whose depression does not respond to medications alone.

Light therapy is yet another intervention for people with depression that follows a seasonal pattern. Exposing some depressed individuals to special lights during the winter can alleviate depressive symptoms. In one version of light therapy, individuals with seasonal depression use a "dawn simulation"

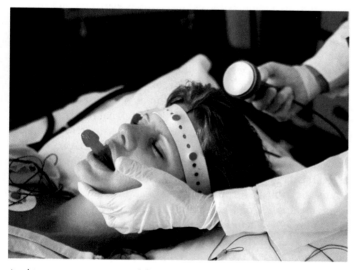

As this woman is prepared for ECT, precautions are taken to prevent injury. She is administered muscle relaxants, and a device is inserted into her mouth to prevent her from biting her tongue.

In behavioral interventions, clients are given homework assignments that encourage them to engage in more pleasurable activities.

procedure, in which they are exposed for a 2-hour period of gradual, dawnlike light each morning during the winter months (Golden et al., 2005). Another, less well-known but promising somatic treatment is sleep deprivation. Both methods work quickly to alleviate depressive symptoms and, when combined with antidepressant medication, can lead to long-lasting improvement (Wirz-Justice et al., 2004).

Although somatic interventions, such as medication, ECT, TMS, and light therapy, provide effective and sometimes life-saving help for many people, most therapists regard these treatments as insufficient by themselves. Consequently, clinicians typically recommend individual, family, or group psychotherapy as an adjunct to help the individual understand both the etiology of the disorder and the strategies for preventing recurrences. Let's turn now to the contributions of the various perspectives that address these psychological issues.

Psychological Treatment In recent decades, clinicians and researchers have demonstrated the effectiveness of behavioral and cognitively based techniques for treating people with mood disorders. Sometimes these techniques are part of a more comprehensive intervention, which also includes a somatic treatment (e.g., medication) or a sociocultural modality (e.g., couple therapy). In other instances, psychological interventions are sufficient.

Behavioral therapy for depression begins with a careful assessment of the frequency, quality, and range of activities and social interactions in the client's life. The clinician then implements a treatment involving a combination of helping the client change his or her environment, teaching the client certain social skills, and encouraging the client to seek out activities that help restore a proper mood balance. Specific reinforcements might be found from among activities that the client enjoyed in a nondepressed state.

Education is an essential component of behavioral intervention. Depressed clients often set unrealistic goals and then are unable to implement behaviors to reach these goals. The therapist gives regular homework assignments that help the client make gradual behavioral changes and that increase the probability of successful performance. Behavioral therapy also incorporates contracting and self-reinforcement procedures. For example, every time the client follows through on initiating a social activity, reward should follow. Such rewards may consist of self-congratulatory statements or may involve more concrete behaviors, such as having a favorite snack. If these procedures do not succeed, the behavioral therapist moves toward more extensive instruction, modeling, coaching, role-playing and rehearsal, and "real-world" trials.

Cognitively based therapy usually involves a short-term, structured approach that focuses on the client's negative thoughts and includes suggestions for activities that will improve the client's daily life. This technique involves an active collaboration between the client and the therapist and is oriented toward current problems and their resolution. The cognitive approach incorporates didactic work, cognitive restructuring, and behavioral techniques.

Didactic work involves explaining the theory to the client—teaching the client how depression results from faulty thinking. Cognitive restructuring (Sacco & Beck, 1985) involves a multistep approach. First, the client needs to identify and monitor dysfunctional automatic thoughts. Second, the client needs to recognize the connection between thoughts, emotions, and behavior. Third, the client must evaluate the reasonableness of the automatic thoughts. Fourth, the client must learn how to substitute more reasonable thoughts for the dysfunctional automatic thoughts. Finally, the client must identify and alter dysfunctional assumptions. In other words, the therapist attempts to break down the maladaptive thinking patterns that underlie the depressed individual's negative emotions.

Behavior change is needed in order to identify and alter dysfunctional cognitions. Behavioral methods include pleasure prediction experiments, weekly activity schedules, and graded task assignments. Pleasure prediction experiments involve planning an activity, predicting how much pleasure it will produce, and then observing how much it actually does produce. Such an exercise can help a depressed client see that he or she is mistaken about gloomy predictions. The weekly activity schedule helps the client monitor activities on an hour-by-hour basis, with the goal of showing the client that it is not true that he or she "never accomplishes anything." The client rates the mastery and pleasure of each activity. If the client really is inactive, then activities are planned hour-by-hour for each day of the week. Graded task assignments involve identifying a goal that the client wishes to attain but thinks is impossible, breaking the goal into simple component tasks, and helping the client experience the success of accomplishing a task, however simple.

The cognitively based method reduces the symptoms of depression by helping clients learn to restructure their thoughts.

Models of treatment for depression are increasingly moving toward the application of cognitive-behavioral techniques; however, there is also evidence of the beneficial effects of psychodynamically based therapy. Contemporary approaches within the psychodynamic perspective involve short (8- or 10-session) and focused treatments (Hilsenroth et al., 2003), possibly combined with medication (Dekker et al., 2005). In addition to the positive effects of short-term psychodynamic interventions on depressive symptoms and mood, these treatments may even have an effect at the level of brain functioning. In a fascinating report of a woman who was treated with psychodynamic therapy, a break-through in treatment was followed several months later not only by a reduction of depressive symptoms but also by normaliza-tion of serotonin functioning (Saarinen et al., 2005).

Although cognitive-behavioral therapy is often applied as a short-term method, perhaps lasting for 10 or 12 sessions, there are also advantages to long-term or maintenance cognitive-behavioral therapy for people with chronic major depressive disorder (Klein et al., 2004).

Although clinicians treating people with bipolar disorder customarily turn first to pharmacological interventions, they are also likely to incorporate psychological interventions designed to help clients develop better coping strategies in an effort to minimize the likelihood of relapse (Bowden, 2005). Psychoedu-cation is an especially important aspect of treating people with bipolar disorder in order to help clients with this condition un-derstand its nature, as well as the ways in which medication is so important in controlling symptoms. Many people who have experienced a manic episode are tempted to forgo taking their medication in the hope that they might once again experience the exciting highs of a manic episode. If they can develop insight into the risks involved in noncompliance, as well as an improved understanding of such medications as lithium, they are more likely to adhere to the treatment program.

Sociocultural and Interpersonal Intervention   Often in the treatment of people with mood disorders, clinicians find it ex-tremely valuable to involve people who are close to the client. Couple or family therapy may provide a therapeutic context in which partners and family members can come to understand the experiences of the mood-disordered loved one and develop strategies for dealing with this individual's symptoms and disor-der within the interpersonal system.

Interpersonal therapy was originally developed as a brief in-tervention, lasting between 12 and 16 weeks, which emerged from interpersonal theory. This approach adheres to a set of guidelines derived from research data. Although interpersonal therapy in-volves many of the techniques that most therapists use sponta-neously, it frames these techniques in a systematic approach, including manuals to guide therapists in applying the method.

Interpersonal therapy is divided into three broad phases. The first phase involves assessing the magnitude and nature of the individual's depression using quantitative assessment mea-sures. Interview methods are also used to determine the factors that precipitated the current episode. At that point, depending on the type of depressive symptoms the individual shows, the ther-apist considers treatment with antidepressant medications.

In the second phase, the therapist and the client collaborate in formulating a treatment plan that focuses on the primary prob-lem. Typically, these problems are related to grief, interpersonal

According to the interpersonal theory of depression, poor social skills can contribute to a cycle of disturbed relationships, which intensifies the individual's experience of depression.

disputes, role transitions, and problems in interpersonal relation-ships stemming from inadequate social skills. The treatment plan is then carried out in the third phase, with the methods vary-ing according to the precise nature of the client's primary prob-lem. In general, the therapist uses a combination of methods, such as encouraging self-exploration, providing support, educat-ing the client in the nature of depression, and providing feed-back on the client's ineffective social skills. Therapy focuses on the "here and now," rather than on past childhood or develop-mental issues. A large-scale analysis of studies conducted over 30 years on interpersonal therapy showed that, compared to cognitive-behavioral therapy and medications, interpersonal therapy was significantly more effective (Bowden, 2005).

Treatment options for depressive disorders have increased dramatically over the past decade. However, national surveys show that only 21 percent of people with major depressive dis-order receive adequate treatment (Kessler et al., 2003). Clearly, more emphasis must be placed on improving the screening and improving treatment quality.

Suicide

For some people, depression is so painful that their thoughts turn recurrently to ideas about escaping from the torment that char-acterizes every day. People who reach this point feel that they lack the resources to cope with their problems. Not all suicides are intended to be an end to life, however. Some suicide attempts are a "call for help" by people who believe the only way they can get help from others is by taking desperate actions. Rather than

Although the pain and depression of many people who commit suicide are usually evident to others, sometimes this is not the case. Scott Croteau, a 17-year-old from Lewiston, Maine, was a star football player, honor student, and popular classmate. He was found hanging from a tree with a bullet wound in his head, leading authorities to wonder why such a seemingly successful and happy person would take his own life. Portrait photographer Emmett Stuart, Jr., set up a window display in memory of Scott at his studio in Lewiston. Croteau had posed in his football jersey for a yearbook photo on the last day he was seen alive.

follow through on the act, they communicate their suicidal intent early enough so that they can be rescued.

Who Commits Suicide?

In the United States, about 30,000 people per year choose to end their lives (Hoyert, Kung, & Smith, 2005). In general, men are more likely to commit suicide than women, with the rate for adult men amounting to about four times the suicide rate for women. Women are more likely to *attempt* suicide, but they do not carry these attempts through to completion as often as men do. In turn, men are far more likely than women to take their own lives with firearms. When race is considered, White men are much more likely than are non-White men to commit suicide.

No formal diagnostic category in the *DSM* specifically applies to people who attempt suicide. However, nearly 90 percent of adults who commit suicide have a diagnosable psychological disorder. The most frequent are major depression, alcohol abuse or dependence, and schizophrenia (Duberstein & Conwell, 2000).

Suicidality is also a prominent feature in some personality disorders. Recall our discussion of people with borderline personality disorder who commonly make suicidal gestures and attempts.

There are international variations in suicide rates. The highest rates of suicide are found in Eastern Europe and the lowest rates in Latin America, the Muslim countries, and a few Asian countries (World Health Organization, 2004). Researchers characterize the geographic pattern in Europe of suicide risk as a *J* curve, which includes the countries starting in Finland in the northeast and extending to Slovenia in the south central part of Europe (Marusic, 2005).

Why Do People Commit Suicide?

Theories about the causes of suicide focus both on the experience of depression that often precedes a suicide attempt and on related conditions that may serve as predisposing factors (see Table 8.2).

Biological Perspective Statistics about family history of suicide support the notion that biological factors may predispose many individuals to the kinds of clinical states that lead to suicidality. In one of the largest investigations of the family patterns of suicide victims, nearly 250 relatives of 25 male suicide completers were compared with 171 relatives of matched controls, men who did not commit suicide. After controlling for the presence of other psychological disorders, the relatives of suicide completers were 10 times more likely than the relatives of the matched controls to have completed or attempted suicide (Kim et al., 2005).

Researchers working within the biological perspective are also beginning to gain an understanding of the complex interaction among personality, life events, and genetics. According to one hypothesis, there is a genetic vulnerability involving serotonin-related genes. This vulnerability is associated with certain personality traits which, in turn, interact with life events to increase a person's risk of attempting suicide (Baud, 2005).

A genetic vulnerability may also underlie the *J* curve discussed above in relation to the pattern of heightened suicidal risks in Europe. People living in the European countries that form the *J* may share genes that lower their tolerance for alcohol; the combination of this genetic vulnerability with alcohol consumption may place individuals at greater risk for committing suicide (Marusic, 2005).

Psychological Perspective One of the more compelling explanations of the psychological factors that predispose individuals to committing suicide is provided by Edwin Shneidman (1984), who views the act of taking one's own life as an attempt at interpersonal communication. According to Shneidman, people who attempt suicide are trying to communicate frustrated psychological needs to important people in their lives. Approaching the problem from a cognitively oriented view, Beck proposes that suicide is the expression of feelings of hopelessness triggered by perceiving one's stress to be insurmountable (Beck, Steer, Kovacs, & Garrison, 1985; Dixon, Heppner, & Rudd, 1994; Rudd, Rajab, &

TABLE 8.2 Risk and Protective Factors for Suicide

Risk Factors

Demographic or Social Factors

- Being a young or elderly male
- Being Native American or Caucasian
- Being single (especially if widowed)
- Social isolation, including new or worsening estrangement, and rural location
- Economic or occupational stress, losses, or humiliation
- New incarceration
- A history of gambling
- Easy access to a firearm

Clinical Factors

- Past and current major psychiatric illness (especially depressive)
- Personality disorder (borderline, narcissistic, antisocial)
- Impulsive or violent traits by history
- Current medical illness
- A family history of suicide
- Previous suicide attempts or other self-injurious or impulsive acts
- Current anger, agitation, or constricted preoccupation
- Current abuse of alcohol or drugs or heavy smoking
- Easy access to lethal toxins (including prescribed medicines)
- A formulated plan, preparations for death, or suicide note
- Low ambivalence about dying vs. living

Factors Specific to Youth

- All of the above, less racial difference
- Recent marriage, unwanted pregnancy
- A lack of family support
- A history of abuse
- School problems
- Social ostracism, humiliation
- A conduct disorder
- Homosexual orientation

Precipitants

- Recent stressors (especially losses of emotional, social, physical, or financial security)

Protective Factors

- Intact social supports, marriage
- Active religious affiliation or faith
- Presence of dependent young children
- Ongoing supportive relationship with a caregiver
- Absence of depression or substance abuse
- Living close to medical and mental health resources
- Awareness that suicide is a product of illness
- Proven problem-solving and coping skills

Source: From L. Tondo, L. and R. Baldessarini in *Suicide: An Overview*. Reprinted with permission from *Medscape*. http://www.medscape.com/viewprogram/353. © 2001 Medscape Portals, Inc.

Following the suicide of an adolescent, counselors often bring together high-school students to talk about their feelings. Such discussions are important to help teenagers cope with their sense of loss and to reduce the likelihood that they will see suicide as a way out of their problems.

Dahm, 1994). Beck (1996) and his colleagues (Rudd, 2000) use the term *suicidal mode* to describe the frame of mind of the person who has made multiple suicide attempts. According to this view, a previous suicidal experience sensitizes the individual to suicide-related thoughts and behaviors, which later become more accessible and active in the person's mind.

Impaired decision-making skills may also predispose an individual to committing suicide. Researchers believe there may be a neuropsychological basis for such deficits, possibly reflecting altered serotonin pathways in the parts of the brain involved in making complex choices. In one fascinating study, researchers recruited four groups of people—violent suicide attempters, nonviolent suicide attempters, men with mood disorders, and healthy controls. The participants were given a laboratory gambling task which taps emotional factors in decision making. Both groups of suicide attempters made unwise choices, but the violent suicide attempters were especially likely to do so (Jollant et al., 2005). Supporting the notion that there is a cognitive basis for suicidality is research on the relationship between intelligence and suicide risk. Of the nearly 100,000 Swedish men who were followed for up to a 25-year period, the 2,800 who committed suicide were found to have lower intelligence test scores. Interestingly, the highest rates occurred among men with low intelligence test scores from well-educated parents (Gunnell, Magnusson, & Rasmussen, 2005).

Sociocultural Perspective The earliest and most well-known sociocultural theory is that of French sociologist Emile Durkheim (1897/1952). A principal reason for suicide, according to Durkheim, is *anomie,* or a feeling of alienation from society. In the twentieth century, sociocultural theories have shifted to an emphasis on the role of the media in publicizing suicides, particularly among teenagers. In particular, concern about the role

of "copycat" suicides has increased in the past decade. There is no question that adolescent friends and acquaintances of suicide victims experience intense psychological reactions, grief that might be characterized as pathological (Brent et al., 1992). However, although grieving peers may have suicidal thoughts, they are not necessarily more likely to follow through with an attempt (Brent et al., 1993).

Researchers examining racial variations in suicide rates report that Whites are more likely than African Americans to commit suicide. Not only do the rates differ by race, but there are also differences in the age at which they are most likely to take their lives. For Blacks, the median age of suicide is 32, and for Whites the median age of suicide is 44 (Garlow, Purselle, & Heninger, 2005).

Although suicide rates are highest for White males 85 and older, individuals between the ages of 15 and 24 years are also at heightened risk of suicide. Approximately 3,900 late adolescents and young adults kill themselves in the United States each year, making intentional self-harm the third leading cause of death (Hoyert, Kung, & Smith, 2005). Thus, age, gender, and race are important factors to consider in understanding suicide.

Assessment and Treatment of Suicidality Although suicide statistics are alarming, they nevertheless reflect a low incidence in the population. When a clinician is attempting to evaluate whether a particular client is at high risk for committing suicide, this low probability must be factored into the assessment, because it means that few people are likely to carry through with a suicidal wish. Nevertheless, clinicians tend to err on the conservative side, and, if there is any chance that a client is suicidal, all precautions are taken to ensure the client's safety.

Various methods are available to improve the odds of predicting whether a client presents a serious suicide risk. First, the

A sense of hopelessness is one of the strongest predictors of suicide.

clinician assesses the individual's suicidal intent and lethality. **Suicidal intent** refers to how committed a person is to dying. A person who is committed to dying would be regarded as having a high degree of suicidal intent. In contrast, a person who is ambivalent about the wish to die would be regarded as having lower suicidal intent. **Suicidal lethality** refers to the dangerousness of the person's intended method of dying. Some examples of highly lethal methods include combining high doses of barbiturates with alcohol, hanging, shooting oneself, and jumping from high places. Methods that are low in lethality include taking over-the-counter medications and making superficial cuts on one's wrist.

Suicidal intent and lethality are usually linked, but not always, and the clinician must consider both factors when evaluating a person who is suicidal. One aid to assessing suicidality is asking the individual if he or she has a "plan"; a carefully worked out plan is usually a very worrisome indicator. Consider the example of Shari, who is convinced that she wants to die and chooses a method that would clearly be lethal, such as heavy overdosing on barbiturates. Shari figures out a way to obtain the drugs and sets a time and place where she can carry out her act without being interrupted. This is a carefully worked out plan, indicating a high risk of attempting suicide. Both the intent and the lethality of Shari's plan are high.

Many suicidal people are willing to tell others about their intentions, but they may find that other people become uncomfortable and are reluctant to discuss their concerns. There is a common misconception that asking a person if he or she is suicidal might suggest the idea to the individual. Many people conclude that it might be better to avoid the topic and even go as far as to ignore warning signs. However, asking depressed or troubled individuals direct questions about whether they are considering suicide does not seem to increase the likelihood that they will act on these thoughts. In a groundbreaking experimental study, over 2,000 high-school students were compared on distress levels after completing symptom surveys which in the experimental group contained questions about suicide intent and in the control group did not. There were no negative effects either on suicidality or distress following the survey, and in fact, the teens who were at high risk in terms of having previous depressive, substance abuse, or suicidal symptoms seemed less distressed after completing the survey (Gould et al., 2005).

Even trained health practitioners may not pick up on the signs that an individual is suicidal. In a 1-year "psychological autopsy" study conducted in Finland, in which researchers analyzed the apparent causes of suicidal deaths, close to half of the victims saw a health care professional prior to committing suicide (41 percent), most seeing a psychiatrist. Of those, only 22 percent of the victims discussed suicidal intent on their last office visit. In most of the cases, the office visit took place within a week of the suicide, and most of the victims had a diagnosed depressive disorder (Isometsä et al., 1995). Thus, even trained professionals may not take the opportunity to ask about suicidal intent when treating depressed clients.

Even if a person denies suicidal intent, behavioral clues can indicate a person's level of suicidality. For example, a depressed young man who gives away his stereo and mementos and puts his financial affairs in order might be preparing to end his life. However, it is easy to mistake the normal emotional and behavioral instability associated with puberty for signs of suicidality. Changes in mood, declining grades, recklessness, substance abuse, the giving up of former interests, and stormy relationships are frequently cited as suicide risk signs but are common experiences of adolescence, particularly during the early teen years. Poor coping strategies are another feature of the ways that high-risk adolescents deal with stress. They are less likely to ask for help from others and tend to use avoidance rather than confront their problems directly (Gould et al., 2004).

As you have probably realized by this point, each potential suicide involves a unique set of factors. For example, a teenage girl who is upset about her poor academic performance is quite different from an individual with a long history of bipolar disorder and multiple suicide attempts. Clinicians must evaluate a range of factors, such as the individual's age, gender, race, marital status, health, and family history; however, experienced clinicians know that these risk factors can be used only as guides, rather than as conclusive evidence of suicidality.

Suicidality is assessed in many contexts, including suicide hot lines, hospital emergency rooms, mental health clinics, and inpatient psychiatric facilities. The interventions offered in these settings vary considerably in their scope and depth. Cutting across the varying intervention contexts are two basic strategies for treating suicidal individuals: providing social support and helping these individuals regain a sense of control over their lives.

The need to provide social support is based on the idea that, when an individual is suicidal, he or she feels very alone; having

Providing comfort and support to a depressed person can help that person see alternatives to suicide.

other people around reduces that sense of isolation. Professionals follow through on this idea by establishing a formal connection to the suicidal individual by way of a "contract." This contract is a two-way agreement in which the client promises to contact the clinician on experiencing suicidal impulses. The clinician, in turn, agrees to be available in the event of such a crisis. If a client will not agree to these conditions, the clinician is likely to consider having the client hospitalized.

The therapist can use cognitive-behavioral techniques to help the individual gain control over suicidal feelings by thinking of alternative ways to deal with stress. The therapist might also encourage the client to consider reasons for living and to shift the focus away from death to life. In any case, having an opportunity to talk about suicidal feelings is important for the client, in order to develop some perspective on the situation and a sense of control (Boyer & Guthrie, 1985). A comprehensive model of treatment for adolescents is suggested by Brent (2001). This involves treatment of the underlying psychopathology, reduction of cognitive distortion, work on improvement of social skills, encouragement of problem solving, regulation of affect, and family intervention.

Researchers and clinicians are actively seeking ways to translate their understanding of suicide risk factors into successful intervention programs. Although there is now a greater understanding of the factors that can affect suicide risk in adolescents, there is a lack of controlled research on the effects of suicide prevention programs with this age group (Gould, Greenberg, Velting, & Shaffer, 2003). At the other end of the age spectrum, increased research attention has been given to older adults, another age group at risk for suicide. In one study, researchers found that depressed primary care patients over the age of 60 for whom intervention was provided had a lower risk of suicide than a control group receiving no treatment. The intervention, consisting of various components of medication and psychotherapy, reduced both suicidal ideation and depressive symptoms (Bruce et al., 2004).

People who seek professional help are likely to receive life-saving services. The bottom line is that serious depression and omens of suicide should be taken very seriously. Failure to respond can have devastating consequences; when you encounter someone who you think may be suicidal, do not be afraid to confront the situation and insist, as much as possible, that the individual seek intervention.

Mood Disorders: The Biopsychosocial Perspective

As you learned about each of the perspectives on mood disorders, you probably saw features that you felt were convincing, only to read on and find another approach that seemed equally compelling. This is because each approach has something valuable to offer in the way of understanding and treating mood disorders. You may be wondering how a clinician decides which techniques to use when treating clients with mood disorders. Many clinicians have preferences for one form of treatment over another, but, in addition to these preferences, they turn to the latest research findings to guide them in developing treatment plans responsive to each client's needs. For the most part, clinical decisions are based on the nature of the individual's problems. For example, a client having a manic episode would probably be prescribed medication, such as lithium, and this treatment would be supplemented by psychotherapy. A depressed client who has suffered a recent loss would be treated with psychotherapy; medication would be unlikely.

Much of what you have read should lead you to conclude that biology is an important contributor to mood disorders. Consequently, you may expect that somatic treatment approaches would be the most effective. Many experts in the field of depression would agree. However, as we have pointed out, medication alone has its limitations and in some instances may not be as effective as psychotherapy, or a combination of both.

It is encouraging to see the substantial progress being made in the understanding and treatment of mood disorders. Given the relatively high prevalence of these disorders, such progress will have a broad impact on many individuals and on society as a whole, and it is likely to enrich science's knowledge about the functioning of the brain and the role of genetics in human behavior as well. In the coming years, you will read and hear about many more advances in this heavily researched area.

Janice's History

Janice's voice quavered and tears streamed down her face as she recounted the story of her life, reminding me of her inner pain. The oldest daughter in a family of three girls, Janice described a harmonious family life during her early years that took a very sad turn when her father passed away when she was 14 years old. Prior to that unhappy date, Janice's mother had been a charming and energetic woman who devoted herself to the family. Everything changed dramatically following the death of Janice's father, when her mother became extremely withdrawn and uninvolved with her children. A few months later, Janice's mother was hospitalized for the first of several episodes of serious depression.

During each of her mother's hospitalizations, Janice was required to take over much of the family responsibilities, a pattern that continued throughout her remaining years in high school. On graduation, Janice realized that she couldn't leave home because of her mother's reliance on her, so she enrolled in a local community college and earned a degree in business administration. She continued to play an important role in caring for her two younger sisters until they left home.

Janice stayed with her mother and worked as a buyer for a local clothing store. She fell in love with a man named Jed, whom she had met at a church-sponsored function. Jed asked her to marry him, but she insisted that her mother needed her at home and that she could not possibly leave her. Several years later, Janice's mother became terminally ill, and Janice nursed her until her death. Janice was so distraught over her mother's death that she could not return to work for many months. The death was particularly traumatic for Janice, because it left her without a living parent. At this time, Janice was 30 years old. Jed had not yet gotten married, and he again proposed to her. Janice accepted and they were married.

Janice explained that, during the early years of her marriage, she felt relatively happy, despite occasional periods of sadness over the loss of her parents. Jed had used some of the insurance money Janice acquired after her mother's death to begin their own consulting firm, where she worked for more than a year, until the birth of her daughter. Although she had intended to quit working after her baby was born, she acquiesced to her husband's request that she continue working because they needed the money. She agreed to go along with this plan but harbored resentment about it.

Assessment

Although it was evident to me that Janice was depressed, I felt that psychological testing would provide me with some insight into her mood disorder. On each of the tests that Janice took, she showed evidence of deep sadness and discontent. Janice's MMPI-2 profile was that of a person experiencing serious depression and obsessional thinking. Her Rorschach and TAT responses reflected themes of emotional constriction, guilt, depression, and anxiety. On the WAIS-III, Janice received a performance IQ in the below average range as a result of her lethargy, in contrast to her verbal IQ, which was well above average. Her score on the Beck Depression Inventory-II confirmed my clinical impression that the depth of Janice's depression was extreme, warranting immediate and intensive treatment.

Diagnosis

The prominence of Janice's mood disturbance led me to feel certain that she had a serious form of depression. She showed no psychotic symptoms or any history of a manic episode. I was able to rule out dysthymic disorder as a diagnosis because of the relative brevity of her disturbance. All signs pointed to a diagnosis of major depressive disorder—depressed mood, diminished interest in ordinary activities, appetite disturbance, sleep disturbance, psychomotor retardation, fatigue, feelings of worthlessness and guilt, poor concentration, and suicidality.

Axis I: Major Depressive Disorder

Axis II: No evidence of personality disorder

Axis III: No physical disorders or conditions

Axis IV: Problems with primary support group (marital tensions)

Axis V: Current Global Assessment of Functioning: 45
Highest Global Assessment of Functioning (past year): 90

Case Formulation

In reviewing Janice's story in my attempt to understand why she became so severely depressed, my attention was first drawn to the fact that her mother had also experienced serious depression. Genetic factors, of course, have been shown to play an important role in the etiology of mood disorders but I also felt that there was more to Janice's story that warranted consideration. Specifically, she had experienced several major shifts in her life within the past decade. She felt a great deal of conflict about her mixed feelings regarding her mother's death. Janice felt her mother's death as a painful loss, yet she had contrasting feelings of elation, because she was freed from her mother's excessive demands. Any sense of relief that she felt in this regard caused her to feel guilty, and her guilt led Janice to berate herself for not having been more attentive to her mother.

Over the course of several years, events within Janice's current family

RETURN TO THE CASE
(continued)

added further stress to her already fragile level of emotional functioning. As Janice's daughter reached toddlerhood, Janice's conflict around the issue of mother-daughter relationships was reactivated. Furthermore, her husband's demands that she become more involved in their business affected her self-esteem, because she was thwarted from fulfilling her childrearing aspirations. I wondered whether her feelings of inadequacy, listlessness, and unhappiness were a turning-inward of the resentment she felt toward her husband. She saw suicide as her only escape from the unsatisfying trap of her life.

Treatment Plan

As with all cases involving a serious suicide attempt, Janice needed to be hospitalized, even if only for a brief period of time, for continued evaluation and mood stabilization. She remained in the hospital for 3 weeks. Following her discharge, I continued to see her weekly in individual psychotherapy for a year.

My work with Janice combined several approaches. Several factors about her current functioning and family history led me to the conclusion that antidepressant medication was warranted. Specifically, she was in a deep state of depression, involving both psychological and biological processes. In addition, the fact that her mother had had a mood disorder suggested to me that Janice was biologically predisposed to depression; therefore, biological intervention should be considered as a component of the treatment plan.

Regarding psychological intervention, I chose a combination of cognitive-behavioral and psychodynamically based techniques in my individual therapy, augmented by couple therapy provided by one of my colleagues.

I felt that cognitive-behavioral techniques would be effective in helping Janice reduce the frequency of her depressive thoughts and develop appropriately assertive interpersonal styles. In addition, I felt that Janice needed to explore her feelings about her mother to gain some insight into the ways in which unresolved mother-daughter issues had interfered with her own happiness. Also, couple therapy would allow Janice and Jed to begin working on some of the problems in their relationship—in particular, how he had stood in the way of Janice's feeling a greater sense of fulfillment in raising their child.

Outcome of the Case

During her stay in the hospital, Janice's mood improved as the antidepressant medication began to take effect. By the time she was ready to return home, she felt much more capable of handling her responsibilities.

In therapy, Janice learned to identify the ways in which her thinking was distorted and self-blaming, as well as to replace those thoughts with healthier ones. Focusing on becoming more assertive helped Janice become better able to express her needs to her husband. In time, Janice came to see how the conflicts she had harbored all these years about her relationships with her mother and her husband had seriously interfered with her achievement of happiness. Early in our work together, Janice came to the conclusion that she would work part-time, an idea with which I concurred. It seemed to me that Janice needed more time with her daughter and a reduction in her work responsibilities.

In couple therapy, Janice and Jed worked on developing clearer styles of communication. Jed came to recognize that his wife's depression was related to her loss of power in their relationship. Reluctantly, he began to accede to her requests for greater independence and more influence in their relationship. When he saw that these changes correlated with Janice's improved psychological functioning, he began to understand the impact of his behavior not only on Janice but also on the whole family system.

As I think back on my work with Janice, I feel a sense of satisfaction. When I first met Janice, she had just been rescued from a serious suicide attempt. Her self-esteem had been severely damaged, and her ability to live life as a happy and fulfilled person seemed only a remote possibility. That picture changed dramatically. Our work together, combined with the couple therapy, helped bring this woman from a period of despair to a state of fulfillment.

Sarah Tobin, PhD

SUMMARY

- A mood disorder involves a disturbance in a person's emotional state, or mood. People can experience this disturbance in the form of extreme depression, excessive elation, or a combination of these emotional states. An episode is a time-limited period during which specific intense symptoms of a disorder are evident. Major depressive disorder involves acute, but time-limited, episodes of depressive symptoms, such as feelings of extreme dejection, a loss of interest in previously pleasurable aspects of life, bodily symptoms, and disturbances in eating and sleeping behavior. Individuals with major depressive disorder also have cognitive symptoms, such as a negative self-view, feelings of guilt, an inability to concentrate, and indecisiveness. Depressive episodes can be characterized as melancholic or seasonal. Dysthymic disorder is characterized by depression that is not as deep or intense as experienced in major depressive disorder but that has a longer-lasting course. People with dysthymic disorder have, for at least 2 years, depressive symptoms, such as low energy, low self-esteem, poor concentration, decision-making difficulty, feelings of hopelessness, and disturbances of appetite and sleep.

- Bipolar disorder and cyclothymic disorder involve alternations in mood. Bipolar disorder involves an intense and very disruptive experience of extreme elation, or euphoria, called a manic episode, which is characterized by abnormally heightened levels of thinking, behavior, and emotionality that cause significant impairment. A mixed episode consists of symptoms of both a manic episode and a major depressive episode, which alternate rapidly. Cyclothymic disorder involves a vacillation between dysphoria and briefer, less intense, and less disruptive states called hypomanic episodes. In bipolar I disorder, an individual experiences one or more manic episodes, with the possibility, though not the necessity, of having experienced one or more major depressive episodes. In bipolar II disorder, the individual has had one or more major depressive episodes and at least one hypomanic episode.

- Mood disorders have been explained in terms of biological, psychological, and sociocultural approaches. The most compelling evidence supporting a biological model of mood disorders involves the role of genetics, with the well-established fact that these disorders run in families. Biological theories focus on neurotransmitter and hormonal functioning. Psychological theories have moved from early psychoanalytic approaches to more contemporary viewpoints that emphasize the behavioral, cognitive, and interpersonal aspects of mood disturbance. In the behavioral viewpoint, it is assumed that depression is the result of a reduction in positive reinforcements, deficient social skills, or the disruption caused by stressful life experiences. According to the cognitive perspective, depressed people react to stressful experiences by activating a set of thoughts called the cognitive triad: a negative view of the self, the world, and the future. Cognitive distortions are errors people make in the way they draw conclusions from their experiences, applying illogical rules, such as arbitrary inferences or overgeneralizing. Interpersonal theory involves a model of understanding mood disorders that emphasizes disturbed social functioning.

- Treatments for mood disorders are also based on biological, psychological, and sociocultural perspectives. Antidepressant medication is the most common form of somatic treatment for people who are depressed, and lithium carbonate is the most widely used medication for people who have bipolar disorder. In cases involving incapacitating depression and some extreme cases of acute mania, the clinician may recommend electroconvulsive therapy. The psychological interventions that are most effective for treating people with mood disorders are those rooted in the behavioral and cognitive approaches. Sociocultural and interpersonal interventions focus on the treatment of mood symptoms within the context of an interpersonal system, such as an intimate relationship.

- Although no formal diagnostic category specifically applies to people who commit suicide, many suicidal people have a mood disorder, and some suffer from other serious psychological disorders. The dramatic act of suicide is explained from biological, psychological, and sociocultural perspectives. The treatment of suicidal clients varies considerably, depending on the context, as well as intent and lethality. Most intervention approaches incorporate support and directive therapeutic involvement.

KEY TERMS

See Glossary for definitions

Bipolar disorder   254
Bipolar I disorder   257
Bipolar II disorder   257
Cognitive distortions   261
Cognitive triad   261
Cortisol   260
Cyclothymic disorder   254
Dysphoria   250

Dysthymic disorder   250
Episode   250
Euphoria   250
Hypomanic episodes   254
Major depressive disorder   250
Major depressive episode   251
Manic episode   254
Melancholic features   251

Mixed episode   254
Monoamine depletion model   259
Rapid cyclers   257
Response-contingent positive
   reinforcement   261
Seasonal pattern   251
Suicidal intent   271
Suicidal lethality   271

 INTERNET RESOURCE

To get more information on the material covered in this chapter, visit our website at **www.mhhe.com/halgin5.** There you will find more information, resources, and links to topics of interest.

CHAPTER 9

Schizophrenia and Related Disorders

I was on call in the Emergency Room on that afternoon when 22-year-old David Marshall was brought in by his parents who were deeply troubled by his odd thinking and behavior. As I approached the consulting room in which David was sitting with his parents, I could hear a booming but argumentative voice from within the room yell out, "I want to see Zoroaster. That's the only reason I've allowed you to bring me to this dump!" I opened the door and came on the curious sight of a large young man, sitting wedged between two adults, much smaller in stature. Dora and Alfred Marshall were apparently trying to restrain their son David, who seemed ready to bolt from the room any minute. Even though David was tightly cushioned by his parents, his left arm was extended outward from his body, as he made sweeping circular movements that seemed beyond his control. Before I was able to introduce myself, David said, with great annoyance in his voice, "You are not he! Where is he whom I have come to see?" I responded by explaining to David that I wasn't sure what he meant, but I would like to spend some time talking to him and to his parents.

As I sat in the chair across from David, my attention was drawn immediately to the look of torment on David's face, and the ways in which this look was mirrored in the eyes of both his father and his mother. At first, David said nothing, but permitted his parents to tell me about the events of the preceding several days. They explained that David had been uttering a string of bizarre statements, such as "You can't stop me from my mission! Zoroaster is coming to save us all!" As David's parents struggled to tell me the story, David continued to interrupt with loud, dramatic assertions that he had a mission to "protect humankind from the evil force of 'thools,' creatures from the planet Dortanus." Hearing just a few such comments led me to guess that he was in a psychotic state.

In a threatening tone of voice, David told his parents and me that anyone who stood in the way of his destiny might be at great risk. Mr. and Mrs. Marshall sat by quietly, allowing me to assess the severity of David's problem as he told me the story of how he had been chosen as a special envoy for Zoroaster, an alien god with an "intergalactic message of salvation." In response to my questioning, David told me that he had been informed of this special assignment by way of television commercials targeted especially at him, and by "the voice of Zoroaster," which spoke to him at two o'clock each afternoon. At that point, his parents interjected that, "in preparation for his mission," David had hoarded a roomful of spray cans to be used to break through the ozone layer in order to save the world from destruction.

I soon realized that, because of David's disordered state of mind and disruptive behavior, he would be unable to give me accurate information about his current emotional state or a clear sense of important experiences in his life. Consequently, I asked to meet privately with his parents to collect some of this very important information—a request that provoked a moment of rage from David. Warning me that they were "part of a plot" to suppress his message, he stormed out of the room and then bolted from the hospital. I was somewhat startled at the Marshalls' apparent lack of response to David's departure. Mr. Marshall explained that scenes like this took place every day. Sometimes David disappeared for a few days, but he always returned home, primarily because he wished to return to the private enclave of his room.

The Marshalls described David's deterioration during the course of his late adolescent years. David failed every course during the first semester of his first year in college, because he spent most of his time alone in his dormitory room, listening to rock music. After flunking out of college, David returned home, where he spent his time reading science fiction and esoteric religious writings. Mrs. Marshall noted that other oddities in his behavior became apparent around that time; she told of how David often attracted attention on the street because of his peculiar bodily movements and postures. For example, he would gaze heavenward, begin to wave his hand in a kind of spraying motion, and laugh with a sinister tone. Mrs. Marshall wept as she commented, "If only we had asked for help then, maybe David wouldn't have gotten so bad."

Three days after my initial meeting with the Marshalls, Mr. and Mrs. Marshall brought David back to the hospital. This time we took security precautions to prevent David from leaving again and made arrangements to have him involuntarily admitted. The events of the preceding few days had left the Marshalls feeling exhausted and deeply upset about David's poor judgment and bizarre behavior. They explained to me that David had not returned home the night following our last meeting. The Marshalls had become alarmed, because the weather had turned very cold and snowy. They knew that it was unlikely for David to seek shelter anywhere other than his own room. Consequently, they decided to notify the police.

Two nights passed without David being found, but, finally, in the early morning hours, the police located him. With the help of police dogs, David was tracked down deep in the woods a mile from the Marshall home. Perched on a rock, sitting in a lotus position, David was staring at the tops of the trees and speaking in a loud voice, apparently conversing with his "friends in the planets." He seemed unaffected by the dire weather conditions, despite his lightweight leather jacket, and appeared oblivious to the small group of searchers who tried to speak to him. He acquiesced to their request that he follow them to their nearby vehicle. As David spoke to his rescuers, it was clear that he believed they had been sent by Zoroaster and that it was his duty to adhere to their wishes. Moments after David was returned to his home, Mr. Marshall called for an ambulance to take David back to the psychiatric hospital.

Sarah Tobin, PhD

The disorders we will discuss in this chapter, including the one that afflicts David, are commonly referred to as falling in the category of psychosis. As you will discover in this chapter, the forms of psychotic disorders differ in a number of important ways, but they share the central feature of a severe disturbance in the individual's experience of reality about the world and the self. People with psychotic disorders may have difficulty thinking or speaking in a coherent manner and may be distracted, and possibly tormented, by vivid images or voices.

Psychotic episodes are among the most frightening and tormenting of human experiences, but perhaps even more frightening is their apparent uncontrollability. The distress of people going through psychotic episodes is made worse by the fear and aversion such behaviors create in other people. It is difficult for the ordinary person not to be disturbed by the eccentricities and strange ramblings of people in a psychotic state. Because people who have psychotic disorders are so often rejected by others, they frequently are isolated and have little opportunity for social interaction.

Characteristics of Schizophrenia

Have you ever seen a man on the street muttering to himself, gesturing oddly, and acting as though he is hearing voices that no one else can hear? You may have wondered what was wrong with him. Although such behaviors can be associated with a number of conditions, including drug reactions, in many cases they are symptoms of a form of psychosis called schizophrenia, which affects slightly more than 1 percent of the adult population.

Schizophrenia is a disorder with a range of symptoms involving disturbances in content of thought, form of thought, perception, affect, sense of self, motivation, behavior, and interpersonal functioning. Although statistically a small percentage of the population has this disorder, the 1 percent figure translates into a tremendous need for resources to care for these people. As the deinstitutionalization movement has taken hold, the burden of care has moved increasingly to families, and the costs, both in emotional and financial terms, are staggering. It is estimated that the direct cost of schizophrenia in the United States per year runs into the billions of dollars. This figure does not include indirect costs, such as family caregiving and lost income. As you read about this disorder, you will see that its symptoms are frightening and distressing, not only to the individuals who experience them but also to their families and friends who carry a tremendous burden in so many tangible and intangible ways.

The disorder that we currently call schizophrenia was first identified as a disease by a French physician, Benedict Morel (1809–1873), and was systematically defined by German psychiatrist Emil Kraepelin (1856–1926). **Dementia praecox,** as it was called, was thought to be a degeneration of the brain (*dementia*) that began at a relatively young age (*praecox*) and ultimately led to disintegration of the entire personality. Kraepelin believed that the hallucinations, delusions, and bizarre behavioral disturbances seen in people with schizophrenia could ultimately be traced to a physical abnormality or disease.

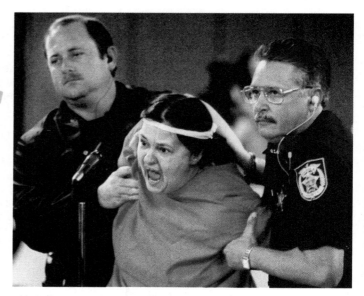

Although it is very unusual for people with schizophrenia to be dangerous, some high-profile cases have led the public to think otherwise. For example, Margaret Mary Ray stalked David Letterman. Following years of delusional pursuit of celebrities and multiple arrests and hospitalizations, Ray committed suicide in October 1998, when she stepped in front of a moving train.

Swiss psychologist Eugen Bleuler (1857–1939) challenged Kraepelin's views that dementia praecox was a disease of the brain. Bleuler (1911) proposed a dramatic change in both the name and the understanding of the disorder. According to Bleuler, a more appropriate name for the disorder was schizophrenia, a term that incorporated ideas central to his understanding of the disorder: a splitting of (*schiz*) or lack of integration among the individual's psychological functions. Unlike Kraepelin, Bleuler thought it was possible for people with schizophrenia to recover from the disorder. Furthermore, Bleuler considered schizophrenia to represent a group of disorders rather than a single entity. Even though he wrote about this disorder nearly a century ago, Bleuler's ideas about schizophrenia are still influential. The four fundamental features of the disorder that he identified are still commonly referred to as Bleuler's Four *A*'s:

1. *Association:* Thought disorder, as might be evident through rambling and incoherent speech
2. *Affect:* Disorder of the experience and expression of emotion—for example, inappropriate laughter in a sad situation
3. *Ambivalence:* The inability to make or follow through on decisions
4. *Autism:* The tendency to maintain an idiosyncratic style of egocentric thought and behavior

Disagreeing with Bleuler's broad characterization of schizophrenia was a German psychiatrist, Kurt Schneider (1887–1967), who introduced the idea that, for the diagnosis of schizophrenia, certain "first-rank" symptoms must be present (Schneider, 1959). These include hearing voices that comment on one's actions and believing that an outside agent is inserting thoughts into one's mind. We now know that first-rank symptoms are also associated with disorders other than schizophrenia, such as certain forms of mood disorder, so Schneider's idea about using these symptoms as the sole diagnostic indicators of schizophrenia is no longer considered valid. As you will see later in our discussion, debate about the nature of schizophrenia continues among contemporary researchers and clinicians.

Phases of Schizophrenia

Schizophrenia is a complex and multifaceted disorder that can take one of many forms. Essential to the diagnosis of schizophrenia is a marked disturbance lasting at least 6 months. During this 6-month period is an **active phase** of symptoms, such as delusions, hallucinations, disorganized speech, disturbed behavior, and negative symptoms (e.g., speechlessness or lack of initiative).

The active phase does not usually appear without warning signs. Most, but not all, cases have a **prodromal phase,** a period prior to the active phase during which the individual shows progressive deterioration in social and interpersonal functioning. This phase is characterized by several maladaptive behaviors, such as social withdrawal, inability to work productively, eccentricity, poor grooming, inappropriate emotionality, peculiar thought and speech, unusual beliefs, odd perceptual experiences, and decreased energy and initiative. For many people, the active phase is followed by a **residual phase,** in which there are continuing indications of disturbance similar to the behaviors of the prodromal phase. Throughout the duration of the disturbance, people with schizophrenia experience serious problems in work, relationships, and self-care.

The prodromal phase, as it is evidenced during childhood and adolescence, is of particular interest to researchers and clinicians for several reasons. First, deteriorative changes that emerge during this period of life shed light on the view of schizophrenia as a neurodevelopmental condition. In other words, changes are taking place in the brain of affected individuals which increase the likelihood that they will develop schizophrenia. If heightened vulnerability can be recognized, might interventions be introduced to protect the individual from developing the disorder? In studying young people at risk of developing schizophrenia, researchers have identified what they call the *CASIS cluster,* comprised of cognitive deficits (C), affective disturbances (A), social isolation (SI), and school failure (S). In addition to the CASIS cluster, researchers have documented other early signs of impending deterioration known as **positive symptoms,** exaggerations or distortions of normal thoughts, emotions, and behavior. Positive symptoms are viewed as direct lead-ins to the full expression of psychosis. The hope is that if the CASIS cluster or the initial emergence of positive symptoms can be recognized in vulnerable individuals, prevention programs can be introduced that reduce the risk of future psychosis

---

> ### Diagnostic Features of Schizophrenia
>
> - People with this disorder experience a disturbance that lasts at least 6 months and includes at least 1 month of active symptoms, including at least two of the following:
>   - Delusions
>   - Hallucinations
>   - Disorganized speech
>   - Disturbed or catatonic behavior
>   - Negative symptoms, such as flat affect or severe lack of motivation
> - For a significant portion of the time since symptom onset, they have experienced dysfunction in work, relationships, or self-care.
> - The symptoms are not due to another disorder, a medical condition, or substances.

---

while also eliminating the disability associated with the vulnerability deficits. For example, addressing the cognitive deficits, either pharmacologically or psychotherapeutically, could have profound positive effects. Research is still in beginning stages about which medications, if any, and which therapeutic interventions might be effective, but hope is held out for discoveries in the decade ahead (Cornblatt et al., 2003).

Symptoms of Schizophrenia

The mysterious and dramatic symptoms of schizophrenia cover a range of categories from extreme disturbances in thought content to bizarre behaviors. Let's take a look at some of the defining characteristics of this disorder.

Disturbance of Thought Content: Delusions Recall Dr. Tobin's interaction with David Marshall in the case study at the beginning of the chapter, and imagine yourself interacting with someone like David. What would you think if a friend were to tell you he had just received a message from someone named Zoroaster, telling him that he had been given the assignment to "protect humankind from the evil force of 'thools,' creatures from the planet Dortanus"? At first, you might think he was kidding around. Concluding that he was serious would cause you to become alarmed, because you would realize that your friend was delusional.

Delusions, or deeply entrenched false beliefs, are the most common disturbance of thought content associated with schizophrenia. David's false belief is an example of a delusion of grandeur. His delusion may also be persecutory, if he imagines that others are trying to harm him or prevent him from fulfilling his mission. David's thinking also seems to involve a delusion of reference, in that he believes that television commercials are targeted at him. As you recall from our discussion in Chapter 3,

REAL STORIES

JOHN FORBES NASH: SCHIZOPHRENIA

 MindMAP Segment 9.1 contains a provocative interview in which Nash and his son (both of whom have been diagnosed with schizophrenia) engage in a joint interview with Dr. Nancy Andreasen.

Schizophrenia can affect people from all walks of life including some with remarkable brilliance such as Nobel laureate John Forbes Nash, shown here with his son, John, who also has been diagnosed with schizophrenia.

When many people conjure up images of individuals with schizophrenia, they think of people such as David Marshall, whose story you began reading at the start of this chapter. Would you imagine that some people with this disabling condition accomplish great things in life? Would you imagine that a person who has suffered from severe personal disorganization and various symptoms of psychosis could go on to receive the Nobel Prize? This is the story of Nobel Laureate John Forbes Nash, a man regarded in the scientific community as a mathematical genius, whose life story was portrayed in the award winning film, *A Beautiful Mind.*

After graduating from Bluefield College in the 1950s, Nash was recruited for graduate study by Harvard, Princeton, Chicago, and Michigan. He chose Princeton and began working on his PhD when he was only 20. At the age of 21, he wrote a 27-page doctoral dissertation on game theory, or the mathematics of competition, a groundbreaking paper that drew the attention of many in the fields of mathematics and economics. After completing his doctorate, Nash went to MIT, where he worked for 8 years in economics and continued to impress the mathematical world. During this time he also invented the game Hex, marketed by Parker Brothers. In 1958, *Fortune* magazine called him America's brilliant young star of the "new mathematics."

He married Alicia Larde in 1957, and the successful young mathematician's life seemed nearly perfect. But shortly after his wife became pregnant, Nash's mental state deteriorated and he remained in emotional disarray for

nearly 30 years. During his most troubled days, he roamed the halls of Princeton in disheveled clothing, writing cryptic formulas on chalkboards, becoming known as the "phantom of Fine Hall." Although there were times when his delusions abated, and he would briefly return to rational thinking, at other times he required hospitalization. During his long illness, Nash and Alicia divorced. In the 1990s, when Nash's condition improved, he and Alicia were able to renew their relationship, and the two remarried.

While Nash was ill, game theory originating from his doctoral dissertation had become a staple tool in economics and business, and his

tremendous contributions several decades earlier were recognized in 1994 when he was awarded the Nobel Prize in economics.

Nash has spoken about his recovery and his battle with schizophrenia. In an article written for the Nobel Prize Foundation, Nash describes the onset of his illness:

The mental disturbances originated in the early months of 1959 at a time when Alicia happened to be pregnant. As a consequence I resigned my position as a faculty member at MIT and, ultimately, after spending 50 days under "observation" at McLean Hospital, traveled to Europe and attempted to gain status there as a refugee. I later spent times of the order of five to eight months in hospitals in New Jersey, always on an involuntary basis and always attempting a legal argument for release.

At the tenth World Congress of Psychiatry, Nash described some of his experiences during his illness: ". . . the staff at the Massachusetts Institute of Technology, and later all of Boston were behaving strangely towards me. . . . I started to see crypto-communists everywhere. . . . I started to think I was a man of great religious importance, and to hear voices all the time. I began to hear something like telephone calls in my head, from people opposed to my ideas. . . . The delirium was like a dream from which I never seemed to wake."

Nash, again in his brief autobiography written for the Nobel Prize Foundation, explains how the return of rationality is not always considered positive by those afflicted with psychosis: "So at the present moment I seem to be thinking rationally again in the style that is characteristic of scientists. However this is not entirely a matter of joy as if someone returned from physical disability to good physical health. One aspect of this is that

REAL STORIES

JOHN FORBES NASH *(continued)*

rationality of thought imposes a limit on a person's concept of his relation to the cosmos."

Following his recovery, Nash returned to lecturing and mathematical research, and he referred to his

"25 years of partially deluded thinking" as a sort of vacation that subsequently allowed him to pursue his interests with increased innovation, and to focus his energies on reconnecting to family, friends, and community.

Sources: Autobiography for the Nobel Prize Foundation: http:www.Nobel.se/economics/ laureates/1994/nashautobio.html, and from the site citing his paper at the Tenth World Congress of Psychiatry in 1996: http://www-groups.dcs. st-and.ac.uk/~history/Mathematicians/Nash.html

---

a delusion can take many forms, all of which are dramatic indicators of severe disturbance in a person's thinking.

Disturbance in Perception: Hallucinations   Have you ever had the experience, as you were falling asleep, of "hearing a voice" and thinking it was real? The mind often plays such tricks immediately before we fall asleep. But what if these voices, which no one else hears, were part of your everyday existence? What if you constantly heard the voice of an angry man telling you to hit someone sitting across from you or of someone telling you how stupid or unattractive you are? Certainly, you would be upset and frightened, and it might be a struggle for you to resist the commands. David Marshall reported that he had heard the "voice of Zoroaster," which had prompted him to take action to prepare for his "mission." David was experiencing an auditory hallucination. Recall that hallucinations are false perceptions involving one of the five senses. Although hallucinations do not correspond to actual stimuli, they are real to the person with schizophrenia. They are not under voluntary control but occur spontaneously, despite the individual's attempts to ward them off. As you can imagine, these experiences can be frightening and disruptive.

Disturbance of Thinking, Language, and Communication: Disorganized Speech   People with schizophrenia have such disorganized and dysfunctional cognitive processes that their thinking may lack cohesiveness and logic. Their language can be grossly distorted to the point of incomprehensibility. Attempting to communicate with a person who has a thought disorder is extremely perplexing. Dr. Tobin must have felt frustrated in her attempt to engage David Marshall in conversation. Because he was so consumed by his concerns about "Zoroaster" and the "evil forces," he was unable to interact in a normal conversation.

Some instances of disturbed communication in schizophrenia are not as dramatic; instead, some people with schizophrenia speak in a peculiar way and use awkward or pompous-sounding speech. For example, when casually asked about the weather,

one man said, "It is an auspicious day for a feast on the grass, but the cumulus meanderings above us seem oh so ominous." Some individuals speak with odd intonations and lack the usual expressiveness and gestures common in everyday talk. Even when they write, they may use language so stilted and formal that it sounds artificial. In some extreme cases, the individual may be mute, saying nothing for hours or days.

Disturbed Behavior   People with schizophrenia may move in odd and disturbing ways. For example, David Marshall's odd circular movement of his arm as he waited with his parents in

In MindMAP Segment 9.2, Peter speaks in ways that are difficult to follow, while hitting himself and making strange noises. He also shows inappropriate affect in his interactions with the interviewer.

People with schizophrenia, disorganized type, show symptoms of disorganized speech, disorganized behavior, and flat or inappropriate affect.

Mini Case

SCHIZOPHRENIA, CATATONIC TYPE

Maria is a 21-year-old college junior who has been psychiatrically hospitalized for a month. The resident assistant in Maria's dormitory brought her to the hospital in December, because she had grown increasingly concerned about Maria's deteriorating behavior over the course of the semester. When Maria returned to college in September, her roommate told others, including the resident assistant, that Maria was acting oddly. For example, she had an annoying habit of repeating other people's words, she stared listlessly out the window, and she ignored her personal hygiene. As the semester neared an end, Maria retreated more and more into her own world, until her behavior reached a point such that she was completely unresponsive to others. In the hospital, she maintains rigid posturing of her body, while staring at the ceiling and spending most of the day in a trance-like state that seems impenetrable. The treating staff are in a quandary about what intervention to use for Maria because of her hypersensitivity to most medications.

Diagnostic Features

In addition to meeting the general diagnostic criteria for schizophrenia (see page 279), people with this type of schizophrenia have a condition that is characterized by psychomotor disturbance that involves at least two of the following:

- Motor immobility or stupor
- Excessive purposeless motor activity
- Mutism or extreme negativism (e.g., rigid posturing or resistance to instructions)
- Peculiarities of movement (e.g., bizarre postures) or odd mannerisms or grimacing
- Echolalia (senseless repetition of words or phrases) or echopraxia (repetition by imitation of another's movements)

---

the consultation room was a visible behavioral symptom that would strike anyone as odd. At times, a person with schizophrenia may show signs of a catatonic disturbance, in the form of either stupor, rigidity, or excitement. Catatonic stupor is a state of being unresponsive to external stimuli, possibly to the point of being unaware of one's surroundings. Catatonic rigidity involves stiffened posturing of the body and resistance to pressure to move. Just as extreme is catatonic excitement, which involves apparently purposeless and repetitive bodily movements.

Negative Symptoms Many people with schizophrenia also have **negative symptoms,** those that involve functioning below the level of behavior regarded as normal. The most common negative symptoms are affective flattening, alogia, and avolition. In **affective flattening,** an individual seems unresponsive with relatively motionless body language and facial reactions and minimal eye contact. **Alogia** is a loss of words or notable lack of spontaneity or responsiveness in conversation. The symptom of **avolition** involves a lack of initiative and unwillingness to act. Staring out the window may be preferable to doing anything else, even something that might be pleasant.

Clinicians often find it difficult to diagnose negative symptoms, because, in fact, most people at one time or another act in these ways, as when they are fatigued or depressed. Although less commonly noted, some people with schizophrenia also experience **anhedonia,** a loss of interest in or ability to experience pleasure from activities that most people find appealing.

Social and Occupational Dysfunction The disturbing thoughts, feelings, and behaviors characteristic of schizophrenia affect every facet of functioning in people who have the disor-

 In MindMAP Segment 9.3, Isador speaks in a way that demonstrates disordered thinking while he discusses hallucinations such as religious and otherworldly phenomena.

The symptoms of undifferentiated schizophrenia include the essential features of schizophrenia but do not meet the criteria for any of the specific types of schizophrenia.

der. They have troubled and tumultuous interactions with relatives, acquaintances, and even strangers, particularly during the active phase of symptoms. In the case of David Marshall, his argumentative and threatening interactions with Dr. Tobin and with his parents would be disconcerting for anyone with whom he is interacting, and they would certainly cause problems in most realms of his life.

People with schizophrenia often express their emotions in ways that seem abnormal to others, possibly expressing outward affect that is inconsistent with how they are feeling or how they would be expected to feel in a given situation. This inconsistency may cause confusion in other people, who are bewildered by a person who is giggling in a setting that others regard as serious, or crying in a context that most people view as humorous. Because of such oddities, other people may shun individuals with schizophrenia, because being around them is confusing and uncomfortable. The social isolation that ensues can trigger a vicious cycle of impairment in relational style. Over time, the socially disturbed and isolated person is likely to be rejected and to retreat further into a world of fantasy and delusion.

Types of Schizophrenia

Although we speak of schizophrenia as a single disorder, it is actually diverse, taking on dramatically different forms from individual to individual, referred to in the *DSM-IV-TR* as types. When the prominent symptom in a person with schizophrenia is bizarre motor behaviors, the person is diagnosed as having **schizophrenia, catatonic type.**

Schizophrenia, disorganized type, is characterized by a combination of symptoms, including disorganized speech, disturbed behavior, and flat or inappropriate affect. Even the person's delusions and hallucinations, when present, lack any coherent theme. Individuals with this disorder are noticeably odd in their behavior and appearance and usually have serious impairment in work and other social contexts.

People with **schizophrenia, paranoid type,** are preoccupied with one or more bizarre delusions or have auditory hallucinations related to a theme of being persecuted or harassed, but without disorganized speech or disturbed behavior. The hallucinations are usually related to the content of the delusions; however, cognitive functioning and affect are reasonably normal. People with the paranoid type of schizophrenia have tremendous interpersonal problems, because of their suspicious and argumentative style.

In some people with schizophrenia, the symptoms are mixed, and the clinician cannot classify the disorder into one of the types just discussed; a diagnosis of **schizophrenia, undifferentiated type,** is used when a person shows a complex of schizophrenic symptoms, such as delusions, hallucinations, incoherence, and disturbed behavior, but does not meet the criteria for the paranoid (systematic bizarre delusions), catatonic (abnormalities of movement), or disorganized (disturbed or flat affect) types of schizophrenia.

Some people who have been diagnosed as having schizophrenia might no longer have prominent psychotic symptoms but might still show some lingering signs of the disorder. Although they are not delusional, hallucinating, incoherent, or disorganized, they might retain some symptoms, such as emotional dullness, social withdrawal, eccentric behavior, or illogical thinking. These individuals would be diagnosed as having **schizophrenia, residual type.**

Mini Cases

SCHIZOPHRENIA, DISORGANIZED TYPE

Joshua is a 43-year-old man who can be found daily standing near the steps of a local bank on a busy street corner. Every day, he wears a Red Sox baseball cap, a yellow T-shirt, worn-out hiking shorts, and orange sneakers. Rain or shine, day in and day out, Joshua maintains his "post" at the bank. Sometimes he can be seen "conversing" with imaginary people. Without provocation, he sobs miserably; sometimes he explodes in shrieks of laughter. Police and social workers keep taking him to shelters for the homeless, but Joshua manages to get back on the street before he can be treated. He has repeatedly insisted that these people have no right to keep bothering him.

Diagnostic Features

- In addition to meeting the general diagnostic criteria for schizophrenia (see page 279), people with this type of schizophrenia have (1) disorganized speech, (2) disturbed behavior, and (3) flat or inappropriate affect.

- The diagnosis is not given to people whose condition meets the criteria for the catatonic type of schizophrenia.

SCHIZOPHRENIA, PARANOID TYPE

Esther is a 31-year-old unmarried woman who lives with her elderly mother. A belief that the outside air is filled with radio waves that will insert evil thoughts into her head keeps Esther from leaving the house. The windows in her bedroom are "protected" with aluminum foil that "deflects the radio waves." She often hears voices that comment on these radio signals. For example, one comment is the slow, deep voice of an elderly man, who angrily states, "We're going to get these thoughts into your head. Give up your fight!"

Diagnostic Features

- In addition to meeting the general diagnostic criteria for schizophrenia (see page 279), people with this type of schizophrenia are preoccupied with frequent auditory hallucinations or with one or more delusions.

- The diagnosis is not given to individuals with any of the following prominent symptoms: disorganized speech, disturbed or catatonic behavior, or flat or inappropriate affect.

Dimensions of Schizophrenia

Researchers and clinicians have been exploring other ways, in addition to the types, of characterizing different presentations of schizophrenia. Many feel that the current categories fail to capture the essential dimensions underlying individual differences in symptoms. They are also concerned about the fact that the subtype categorization is not as valid in the real world as it may seem. In the most recent (2000) edition of the *DSM*, an

Mini Cases

SCHIZOPHRENIA, UNDIFFERENTIATED TYPE

Bruce, a 24-year-old maintenance worker, is considered "peculiar" by almost everyone he meets. He has a "strange" look in his eyes, and he often mumbles to himself, as if he were holding a conversation with someone. The words he uses sometimes sound like those of a foreign language, but no one else can understand them. At times, he stares out the window for hours, and he barks angrily at anyone who disturbs him. It seems as though he is lost in a world of fantasy, but he nevertheless manages to keep up with his custodial duties.

Diagnostic Features

- This diagnosis is assigned to individuals who have the general symptoms of schizophrenia but do not meet the diagnostic criteria for paranoid, disorganized, or catatonic type.

SCHIZOPHRENIA, RESIDUAL TYPE

Three years after her third hospitalization for schizophrenia, Joyce's condition seems to have stabilized. She has a set routine for taking her antipsychotic medications, for checking in regularly at the Center for Independent Living (which supervises her work placement in a glove factory), and for visiting with her sister and family. At 45, Joyce shows only occasional signs of the illness that, at one time, had totally incapacitated her. She still sometimes becomes preoccupied with the idea that her former mother-in-law is sending her poisoned envelopes in the mail. At other times, she cannot stop herself from pacing the floor. These symptoms never last very long, though, and she is soon able to resume her daily schedule without being unduly distressed.

Diagnostic Features

- This diagnosis is given to people who have had at least one episode of schizophrenia but currently lack prominent positive symptoms (i.e., delusions, hallucinations, disorganized speech, or grossly disorganized or catatonic behavior).

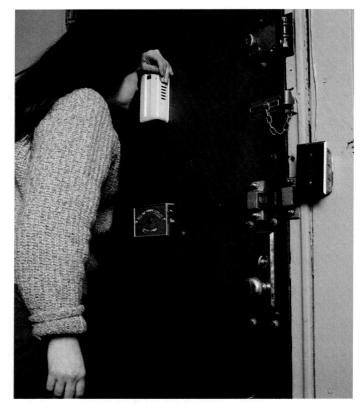

Convinced that assassins are in close pursuit, a person with paranoid schizophrenia might stay barricaded behind a heavily locked door.

alternative three-factor dimensional model has been proposed "because of the limited value of the schizophrenia subtypes in clinical and research settings" (p. 313). The three dimensions are (1) psychotic, (2) negative, and (3) disorganized. The psychotic factor is relevant in cases in which the individual experiences prominent delusions and hallucinations; the negative factor applies to conditions characterized by negative symptoms (e.g., affective flattening, alogia, and avolition, which we discussed in the section on negative symptoms). The disorganized factor includes disorganized speech, disorganized behavior, and inappropriate affect.

Courses of Schizophrenia

Schizophrenia may take one of several courses, or patterns. In the most serious of cases, the individual experiences continu- ous positive symptoms with no remission. Other people have episodes of positive symptoms, but, between these episodes, only negative symptoms are evident. In some cases, individuals who have had only a single episode of schizophrenia can live the rest of their lives without a recurrence of the disorder. These people are considered to be "in remission."

Estimates of recovery from schizophrenia range from a low of about 20 percent of people to a high of 67 percent, with the estimates varying according to how narrowly recovery is defined. Various factors are associated with prognosis for people with schizophrenia. As you can see in Table 9.1, a person's gender and age play important roles in determining prognosis, but also important are the individual's behaviors, such as taking antipsychotic medication soon after symptom onset and complying with the treatment program.

As you can imagine, people who do not recover at all are profoundly affected by their disorder in every facet of life. They experience troubled relationships, have difficulty maintaining stable employment, and often struggle with depression and loneliness. For many, their painful existence culminates in premature death due to suicide, violence, or impaired health. In one project, researchers studying the psychiatric histories of people who died suddenly found that sudden death was five times higher than normal in people with histories of psychiatric

The difference between the experiences of this woman and those of this man captures the distinction between the positive and negative symptoms of schizophrenia. The woman's hallucinations and bizarre delusions are positive symptoms. The man's flat affect and apathy are negative symptoms.

care. Although suicide accounted for part of the excess mortality, rates of death from natural causes and accidents were also elevated, especially among those who had misused substances. Findings such as these point to the importance of attending to the increased risk of death from inadequate care or suicide among people with schizophrenia (Ruschena et al., 1998).

TABLE 9.1 Factors Associated with More Favorable Prognosis in People with Schizophrenia

- Good adjustment prior to the development of the disorder
- Acute onset
- Later age at onset
- Good insight
- Being female
- A precipitating event associated with the onset of symptoms
- The presence of an associated mood disturbance
- Treatment with antipsychotic medication soon after the onset of the disorder
- Consistent compliance with medication recommendations
- Brief duration of active-phase symptoms
- Good functioning between episodes
- Absence of structural brain abnormalities
- Normal neurological functioning
- A family history of mood disorder
- No family history of schizophrenia

Source: American Psychiatric Association, 2000, p. 309.

Gender, Age, and Cultural Features

Extensive research on this disorder has led investigators to uncover some very interesting facts about the different ways schizophrenia is experienced and diagnosed in relation to gender, age, and cultural background (American Psychiatric Association, 2000). For example, men are most likely to develop the disorder between the ages of 18 and 25, whereas the modal age of onset for women is between 25 and the midthirties. In approximately 3 to 10 percent of women who develop this disorder, onset occurs after age 40; such a late onset is much less common in men. Even the kinds of symptoms differ along gender lines. Women are more likely to have paranoid delusions, hallucinations, and intense affective symptoms, whereas men are more likely to experience negative symptoms such as flat affect and social withdrawal. Further, the prognosis is better for women than for men, as measured by the number of rehospitalizations, length of hospital stays, overall duration of the symptoms, response to medication, and ability to function in social and work contexts.

Culture has a complex relation to the diagnosis of schizophrenia. For example, in the United States this disorder is more commonly diagnosed in African Americans and Asian Americans than in other racial groups. It is not clear whether these statistics reflect prevalence differences or are the result of clinician bias or cultural insensitivity (American Psychiatric Association, 2000).

Other Psychotic Disorders

At one time, the diagnosis of schizophrenia was applied so broadly to people with a wide range of maladaptive behaviors that most people living in institutions were labeled with this diagnosis. One of the most troubling facets of the overuse of this diagnosis was the corresponding notion that once a person was diagnosed as having schizophrenia, that person was doomed to carry that label for life. Even for people with only brief psychotic symptoms, clinicians mistakenly assumed that schizophrenia would subsequently lie dormant beneath the surface, waiting to burst out again in the form of new symptoms at any time. Many clinicians advised clients who had shown psychotic symptoms to take antipsychotic medication for life to prevent their symptoms from occurring again. This situation began to change during the 1970s, in part because researchers defined a group of disorders that shared some but not all symptoms with schizophrenia.

The schizophrenia-like disorders share three features: (1) each is a form of psychosis representing a serious break with reality, (2) the condition is not caused by a disorder of cognitive impairment (e.g., Alzheimer's disease), and (3) mood disturbance is not a primary symptom. Each disorder has aspects similar to certain features of schizophrenia, but other facets of the disorder, such as presumed cause and course, distinguish it from schizophrenia. Further, each of the schizophrenic-like disorders has a different set of proposed causes, symptom picture, and recommended course of treatment.

Brief Psychotic Disorder

Most people have heard the phrase "nervous breakdown" used to describe people who suddenly lose control, behave in bizarre ways, and have strange experiences, such as delusions or hallucinations. The term is actually a misnomer, because these symptoms are not due to a breakdown in nerves. The correct term is **brief psychotic disorder,** a disorder characterized by

Some people experience such intense personal stress that they develop brief psychotic disorder, with transient symptoms that resemble those of schizophrenia.

a sudden onset of psychotic symptoms that lasts less than a month. These symptoms are often reactive, appearing after a stressful event or set of events, and eventually the person returns to normal functioning. The stress may be something that others would clearly recognize as serious, such as the death of a spouse or a house fire; however, in some instances, the stressor is personally quite disturbing, though others might not construe it to be so serious (e.g., an academic or a financial problem). Some individuals become briefly psychotic without any apparent stressor, leaving clinicians and family members mystified about the cause of the dramatic change in the individual. Yet another variant of brief psychotic disorder involves women with postpartum onset. In Chapter 8 we mentioned that some women develop symptoms of major depression after giving birth. A very small percentage of women develop symptoms so severe during the month following birth that they meet the diagnostic

Mini Case

BRIEF PSYCHOTIC DISORDER

Anthony is a 22-year-old senior at a prestigious small college. His family has traditionally held high standards for Anthony, and his father had every expectation that his son would go on to enroll at Harvard Law School. Anthony felt intensely pressured as he worked day and night to maintain a high grade point average, while diligently preparing for the national examination for admission to law schools. His social life became devoid of any meaningful contact. He even began skipping meals, because he did not want to take time away from studying. When Anthony received his scores for the law school admission exam, he was devastated, because he knew that they were too low to allow him to get into any of the better law schools. He began crying uncontrollably, wandering around the dormitory hallways, screaming obscenities and telling people that there was a "plot" on the part of the college dean to keep him from getting into law school. After 2 days of this behavior, Anthony's resident adviser convinced him to go to the infirmary, where his

condition was diagnosed and treated. After a week of rest and some medication, Anthony returned to normal functioning and was able to assess his academic situation more rationally.

Diagnostic Features

- For at least 1 day, but less than a month, individuals with this disorder experience at least one of the following symptoms before returning to normal functioning:
  - ◆ Delusions
  - ◆ Hallucinations
  - ◆ Disorganized speech
  - ◆ Grossly disturbed or catatonic behavior
- The condition is not attributable to another disorder, a medical condition, or substances.
- The condition can be specified as (1) with marked stressor(s); (2) without marked stressor(s); or (3) with postpartum onset.

criteria for brief psychotic disorder. They may have bizarre delusions or troubling hallucinations or show disorganized or catatonic behavior.

Although experts believe that most cases of brief psychotic disorder are the result of psychological rather than biological factors, it is possible that certain people are biologically predisposed to develop this disorder when faced with considerable psychological stress. Most people have adequate resources for dealing with difficulties and anxiety. Some people, however, are more vulnerable, and, when their customary defenses fail or when a crisis is unusually stressful, they "fall apart."

This disorder can be terrifying for the individual who is experiencing intense and overwhelming changes in thoughts, feelings, and behavior. Individuals in such a state may act in ways that are completely uncharacteristic of their premorbid personality, failing to take care of themselves or interacting with others in ways that are incomprehensible to those who care about them. Particularly worrisome is the possibility that the individual will attempt suicide in an effort to escape psychological torment.

Treatment of brief psychotic disorder usually consists of a combination of medication and psychotherapy. Individuals often require short-term use of antianxiety or antipsychotic medication to help them return to normal functioning. The nature of the psychological intervention depends on the nature of the stressor, when one is evident. Sometimes removing the person from the stressful situation can reduce the disturbance. At other times, this may not be possible. In either case, effective psychotherapy integrates support, education, and the development of insight regarding the determinants of the person's disturbed reaction.

Schizophreniform Disorder

The term *schizophreniform* means that a disorder takes the form of schizophrenia but is somehow different. People with **schizophreniform disorder** have psychotic symptoms that are essentially the same as those found in schizophrenia, except for duration. The symptoms of schizophreniform disorder last longer than those of brief psychotic disorder, but not so long that the clinician would diagnose the person as having schizophrenia. Specifically, active symptoms last from 1 to 6 months. If the symptoms last longer than 6 months, the clinician is more likely to make a diagnosis of schizophrenia.

Most people with the diagnosis of schizophreniform disorder need medication to help bring their symptoms under control. For some, the symptoms will go away spontaneously, but the behavior of people with schizophreniform disorder is usually so disturbed that family and friends insist on an intervention. Most commonly, the clinician prescribes antipsychotic medication, particularly for the acute phase of the disorder. Because people with this disorder function normally when not experiencing a psychotic episode, most clinicians prefer to reduce and discontinue medication after a period of time. In cases in which the symptoms are dangerously out of control, electroconvulsive therapy can offer quick improvement. People with this disorder can also benefit from psychotherapy. Initially, the therapist helps the individual regain control, but eventually the focus shifts to possible causes of the disorder.

Schizoaffective Disorder

A major controversy pertains to the issue of whether schizophrenia and mood disorders are mutually exclusive or whether some

Mini Case

SCHIZOPHRENIFORM DISORDER

At the time that Edward developed a psychological disorder, he was 26 years old and worked for a convenience store chain. Although family and friends always regarded Edward as unusual, he had not experienced psychotic symptoms. This all changed as he grew more and more disturbed over the course of several months. His mother thought that he was just "stressed out" because of his financial problems, but Edward did not seem concerned about such matters. He gradually developed paranoid delusions and became preoccupied with reading the Bible. What brought his disturbance to the attention of his supervisors was the fact that he had submitted an order to the district office for 6,000 loaves of bread. He had scribbled at the bottom of the order form "Jesus will multiply the loaves." When his supervisors questioned this inappropriate order, Edward became enraged and insisted that they were plotting to prevent him from fighting world hunger. Paranoid themes and bizarre behaviors also surfaced in Edward's dealings with his wife and children. Following

2 months of increasingly disturbed behavior, Edward's boss urged him to see a psychiatrist. With rest and relatively low doses of antipsychotic medication, Edward returned to normal functioning after a few weeks of hospitalization.

Diagnostic Features

- People with this disorder experience an episode (at least 1 month but less than 6 months in duration) of at least two of the following schizophrenic symptoms:
  - ◆ Delusions
  - ◆ Hallucinations
  - ◆ Disorganized speech
  - ◆ Disturbed or catatonic behavior
  - ◆ Negative symptoms, such as flat affect or severe lack of motivation
- The symptoms are not due to another disorder, a medical condition, or substances.

Mini Case

SCHIZOAFFECTIVE DISORDER

At the time of her admission to a psychiatric hospital, Hazel was a 42-year-old mother of three children. She had a 20-year history of schizophrenia-like symptoms, and she experienced periodic episodes of mania. Her schizophrenia-like symptoms included delusions, hallucinations, and thought disorder. These symptoms were fairly well controlled by antipsychotic medications, which she received by injection every 2 weeks. She was also treated with lithium to control her manic episodes; however, she often skipped her daily dose because she liked "feeling high." On several occasions following extended periods of abstinence from the lithium, Hazel became manic. Accelerated speech and bodily activity, sleepless nights, and erratic behavior characterized these episodes. At the insistence of her husband and her therapist, Hazel would resume taking her lithium; and shortly thereafter her manic symptoms would subside, although her schizophrenia-like symptoms were still somewhat evident.

Diagnostic Features

- This diagnosis is appropriate for people who have experienced an uninterrupted period of disturbance, during which they have had either a major depressive episode, a manic episode, or a mixed episode concurrent with at least two of the following schizophrenic symptoms: (1) delusions, (2) hallucinations, (3) disorganized speech, (4) disturbed or catatonic behavior, or (5) negative symptoms, such as flat affect or severe lack of motivation.

- During the period of disturbance, the person has experienced delusions or hallucinations for at least 2 weeks in the absence of mood symptoms.

- The mood episode symptoms are present for a significant portion of the duration of the active and residual periods of the disturbance.

- The symptoms are not due to another disorder, a medical condition, or substances.

---

people have symptoms of both disorders. Bleuler believed that the diagnosis of schizophrenia should take precedence, regardless of how severe a client's mood disturbance might be. Many clinicians and researchers have moved away from this position, insisting that some individuals have both schizophrenic and mood symptoms. The diagnosis of **schizoaffective disorder** applies to people who experience either a major depressive episode, a manic episode, or a mixed episode at the same time that they meet the diagnostic criteria for schizophrenia. You may be wondering why this condition is not labeled a mood disorder if mood disturbance is so central to the diagnosis. This is because, during the period of active symptoms, there is a period of at least 2 weeks during which the person does not have prominent mood symptoms but continues to have psychotic symptoms, such as hallucinations or delusions.

Debate has focused on whether schizoaffective disorder is a variant of schizophrenia, with similar etiology, or whether it is a mood disorder. After reviewing the evidence on both sides of the issue, Nancy Andreasen, a prominent expert in the field, concluded that the term *schizoaffective disorder* most probably refers to a combination of schizophrenic and mood disorder symptoms that cannot clearly be separated (Andreasen, 1987b).

Clinicians are sometimes reluctant to use the diagnosis of schizoaffective disorder, because it has no systematic treatment protocol. Pharmacological intervention for people with this diagnosis usually involves a trial-and-error approach, which may include lithium, antidepressants, and antipsychotic medication, either alone or in various combinations. For the most part, antipsychotic medication is combined with lithium for clients with manic symptoms and with antidepressants for clients who are depressed. Psychotherapy needs to be individualized for each client with this diagnosis. The psychotherapist must be prepared to deal with abrupt symptom changes and with the client's unpredictable feelings and behaviors.

Delusional Disorders

People with **delusional disorders** have a single striking psychotic symptom—an organized system of nonbizarre false beliefs. Although they may have hallucinations, such symptoms are not prominent. They do not show the other symptoms that would make a diagnosis of schizophrenia or mood disorder an appropriate one. Their delusions are systematized and prominent but lack the bizarre quality commonly found in schizophrenia. In fact, it is sometimes initially difficult for others to determine whether these people are delusional, because they can be quite convincing and coherent in the expression of their beliefs. However, with continued contact, most people are able to discern that the beliefs of a person with a delusional disorder are very strange. Interestingly, these individuals are usually able to function satisfactorily, and they do not seem odd to others except when discussing the particular content of their delusion.

There are five types of delusional disorder. People with erotomanic type have a delusion that another person, usually of great prominence, is deeply in love with them. For example, an otherwise healthy woman may be firmly convinced that a famous talk show host is in love with her and that he communicates secret love messages to her in his monologue each night. Grandiose type is characterized by the delusion that one is an extremely important person. For example, a man may believe that he is the Messiah waiting for a sign from heaven to begin

Mini Case

DELUSIONAL DISORDER

Paul is a 28-year-old man who has recently experienced tremendous stress at his job. Although he has avoided dwelling on his job problems, he has begun to develop irrational beliefs about his lover, Elizabeth. Despite Elizabeth's repeated vows that she is consistently faithful in the relationship, Paul has become obsessed with the belief that Elizabeth is sexually involved with another person. Paul is suspicious of everyone with whom Elizabeth interacts, questioning her about every insignificant encounter. He searches her closet and drawers for mysterious items, looks for unexplained charges on the charge card bills, listens in on Elizabeth's phone calls, and has contacted a private investigator to follow Elizabeth. Paul is now insisting that they move to another state.

Diagnostic Features

- People with this disorder have nonbizarre delusions lasting at least 1 month.

- They have never had schizophrenic symptoms, other than possible tactile or olfactory hallucinations related to the delusional theme.

- For the most part, their functioning is not impaired; nor is their behavior bizarre.

- If mood disturbances have occurred concurrent with the delusions, the duration has been brief.

- The symptoms are not due to a medical condition or substance use.

- Types include erotomanic, grandiose, jealous, persecutory, somatic, mixed, and unspecified.

A person with delusional disorder, erotomanic type might develop an imagined love affair with a movie star and conceive a far-fetched explanation for why the celebrity is not responding to love letters and phone calls.

his active ministry. Jealous type is characterized by the delusion that one's sexual partner is being unfaithful. For example, a man may be mistakenly convinced that his wife is having an affair, and he may construct a set of "evidence" of routine domestic events (such as an unexplained charge on the phone bill) to "prove" her infidelity. People with persecutory type believe that they are being harassed or oppressed. For example, a woman may believe that she is the object of a government plot, and she may misconstrue insignificant events as evidence that she is a target for assassination. People with somatic type believe that they have a dreaded disease or that they are dying. Their adherence to such a belief is extreme and incorrigible. For example, a woman may believe that her teeth are turning to chalk, and that this deterioration process will then lead to the deterioration of her skull.

Shared Psychotic Disorder

In **shared psychotic disorder,** one or more people develop a delusional system as a result of a close relationship with a psychotic person who is delusional. Typically, two people are involved in this disorder, and the term *folie a deux* (folly of two) is applied to the pair. Occasionally, three or more people or the members of an entire family are involved.

Unlike schizophrenia, which develops with no apparent external provocation, shared psychotic disorder develops in the context of a close relationship in which there is a history of pathological dependence. The nonpsychotic person gets caught up in the delusional system of the psychotic person and becomes equally consumed by the irrational belief. If the two separate, the previously nonpsychotic person will very likely return to normal functioning and thinking.

This disorder is very rare. In the few instances that it is diagnosed, it is usually found among members of the same family, with the most common cases involving two sisters. This is followed in frequency by mother-child, father-child, and husband-wife combinations. Occasionally, it is found between two friends or lovers.

Shared psychotic disorder is explained primarily from a psychological perspective. The dominant person in these pairs feels desperately isolated from others due to numerous psychological problems. This person seeks out another person who can serve as an ally. The dependent person usually needs the dominant person for some reason, such as safety, financial security, or emotional support, and is therefore willing to surrender to the delusions of the dominant member.

People with shared psychotic disorder rarely seek treatment, because they do not perceive themselves as being disturbed. Occasionally, relatives or friends of the submissive partner urge this person to get professional help. Effective intervention involves separating the two people, at which point the submissive person sometimes becomes more open to rational discussion of the disturbed relationship. At that point, therapy can focus on personal issues that seem related to this person's

People with shared psychotic disorder develop a delusional system as a result of their relationship with a psychotic person who is delusional. This man shares the belief with the leader of his cult that aliens have visited the earth and will come again.

vulnerability to being dominated. The therapist would explore ways to bolster the client's self-esteem in order to prevent such a situation from occurring again.

Mini Case

SHARED PSYCHOTIC DISORDER

Julio and Carmen, both in their thirties, had been dating for 6 months. Having met at the accounting office where they both worked, they kept their intimate relationship a secret from co-workers at the insistence of Julio, the dominant partner in the relationship. Carmen submitted, and the couple kept exclusive company with each other. Most of their conversation centered around Julio's unwavering belief, which Carmen had come to share, that other people at their office did not like them and that several people wanted them fired. The two of them often stayed after work to search the desks and files of co-workers for evidence that would support Julio's notion. The slightest comment directed toward either of them was construed as evidence of this plot. On the rare occasions when they talked to co-workers, they immediately recorded the conversation in a secret log book. They refused to use the office computer, because they were convinced that it was programmed to keep tabs on them. Eventually, both lost their jobs, but not for the reasons they had constructed. Their odd behaviors aroused so much suspicion that the office routine was disrupted, and they had to be let go.

Diagnostic Features

- This diagnosis is appropriate in cases in which a person develops a delusion similar to an already established delusion held by a person with whom he or she shares a close relationship.

- The disturbance is not due to another disorder, a medical condition, or substance use.

Theories and Treatment of Schizophrenia

In the previous sections, you read about the nature of schizophrenia. We now turn our attention to explanations of how schizophrenia develops, and how people with this disorder are treated. As you prepare to read about views that may sound technical and theoretical, it is important to keep in mind that schizophrenia involves a disruptive and heartbreaking set of symptoms. Many people, when they hear about schizophrenia, think about a problem that happens only to other people, not to anyone they know. But, as you will discover as you proceed through life, schizophrenia touches the lives of millions of people—possibly someone in your own life. The experience of people with schizophrenia was stated well by William Carpenter, a prominent researcher (Carpenter, 1987): "This illness strikes at the very heart of what we consider the essence of the person. Yet, because its manifestations are so personal and social, it elicits fear, misunderstanding, and condemnation in society instead of sympathy and concern."

A review of the past century of research on schizophrenia shows that, despite major advances in our understanding of this disorder, we remain ignorant about its essence and causes. Experts still lack a reliable, valid set of diagnostic criteria for schizophrenia. When researchers attempt to identify the causes of this disorder, this lack of specificity makes their job far more difficult. Compounding the problem is the fact that the research on the causes of schizophrenia goes back over several decades, during which the definition of schizophrenia evolved from a very vague, broad concept to a specific, narrow set of criteria. Many people who were diagnosed as having schizophrenia in 1960 would not meet the current criteria for the disorder. Furthermore, evaluating the results of studies from the 1960s is difficult, because the people with "schizophrenia" who were studied constituted such a diverse group.

Some researchers have addressed these definitional problems by reanalyzing data from early studies using present-day criteria. Unfortunately, even this approach does not provide a solution, because the definition of schizophrenia still varies from researcher to researcher. As a way of dealing with these differences in definitions, many researchers decided to look at a broad cluster of associated conditions related to schizophrenia. The term *schizophrenic spectrum disorders* refers to schizophrenia-like conditions ranging from some of the personality disorders (for example, schizoid and schizotypal) to certain psychotic disorders (for example, delusional disorder, schizophreniform disorder, and schizoaffective disorder). At the extreme ends of the spectrum are schizophrenia and mood disorders with psychotic features; between these two poles are schizotypal personality disorder, other psychoses without prominent mood features, and schizoaffective disorder.

Theories accounting for the origin of schizophrenia have traditionally fallen into two categories: biological and psychological. In the first part of this century, a debate raged between proponents of both sides. More recently, researchers have begun to accept that both biology and experience interact in the determination of schizophrenia and have begun to build complex theoretical models that incorporate multiple factors (McGuffin, 2004). These models are based on the concept of vulnerability, proposing that individuals have a biologically determined predisposition to developing schizophrenia, but that the disorder develops only when certain environmental conditions are in place. As we look at each of the contributions to a vulnerability model, keep in mind that no single theory contains the entire explanation.

Biological Perspectives

Biological explanations of schizophrenia have their origins in the writings of Kraepelin, who thought of schizophrenia as a disease caused by a degeneration of brain tissue. Kraepelin's ideas paved the way for the later investigation of such factors as brain structure and genetics, which are now recognized as contributing to an individual's biological vulnerability to schizophrenia.

Brain Structure and Function   Interest in possible brain abnormalities in people with schizophrenia dates back to the nineteenth century, to the first scientific attempts to understand schizophrenia. Some of the early efforts to examine the brains of these individuals were crude and imprecise, because they could be examined only after the person died. Not until the latter half of the twentieth century were sophisticated techniques developed to enable researchers to study the living brain. The technologies of computerized tomography (CT, or CAT, scan) and magnetic resonance imaging (MRI) have enabled researchers in schizophrenia to take a picture of the brain and to analyze that picture quantitatively.

One of the most consistent discoveries using brain imaging methods has been that the brains of people with schizophrenia have enlarged ventricles (the cavities within the brain that hold cerebrospinal fluid). Ventricular enlargement is often accompanied by **cortical atrophy,** a wasting away of brain tissue. Loss of brain volume is particularly pronounced in the prefrontal lobes, the area of the brain responsible for planning as well as for inhibiting thoughts and behaviors (Molina et al., 2005). Decreases in brain volume are also found in the temporal lobes, the parts of the brain associated with processing auditory information (Kuperberg et al., 2003). Evidence of structural alterations in the brains of people with schizophrenia seems to support Kraepelin's belief that the disorder is a process of brain degeneration. However, it is important to keep in mind that studies of total brain size or volume are inherently limited in the information they can provide about the organic basis for schizophrenia. Decreases in brain volume could occur for any number of reasons; as impressive as the findings are, these decreases may reflect the result rather than the cause of

disease processes in the brain associated with schizophrenia (Keller et al., 2003).

Yet another path in the search for brain-behavior connections has been followed by researchers investigating the role of neurotransmitters, particularly dopamine. According to what is called the **dopamine hypothesis,** the delusions, hallucinations, and attentional deficits found in schizophrenia can be attributed to an overactivity of neurons that communicate with each other via the transmission of dopamine (Carlsson, 1988). This hypothesis emerged from two related lines of evidence. The first was the observation that antipsychotic medications reduce the frequency of hallucinations and delusions by blocking dopamine receptors. The second line of evidence was that certain drugs that are biochemically related to dopamine, such as amphetamines, increase the frequency of psychotic symptoms.

When first introduced, the dopamine hypothesis was heralded as a breakthrough in accounting for the more bizarre and puzzling symptoms of schizophrenia. Gradually, though, as with most explanations of schizophrenia, later findings caused researchers to temper their original enthusiasm and to refine the hypothesis. It is now believed that abnormalities in a specific dopamine receptor, the D2 receptor, are involved in schizophrenia (Hirvonen et al., 2005), particularly in cases involving a later age of onset (Dubertret et al., 2004). There is also evidence that deficits in the genes controlling serotonin levels in the brain are associated with schizophrenia (Dubertret et al., 2004), representing another neurotransmitter deficit possibly contributing to the development of this disorder.

Genetic Explanations   The family patterns of individuals who have schizophrenia provide convincing evidence in favor of a biological explanation. The closer a relative is to an individual with schizophrenia, the greater the likelihood of concordance. Identical twins have the highest concordance, close to 48 percent (Wong, Gottesman, & Petronis, 2005), and increasingly more distant relatives have correspondingly lower concordance rates (see Figure 9.1). Overall, the heritability of schizophrenia is very high, with some estimates reaching 85 percent (Craddock, O'Donovan, & Owen, 2005). In other words, the chances of schizophrenia emerging in a genetically predisposed person are 85 out of 100.

Having established that there is a high heritability to schizophrenia, researchers have since moved on to attempting to locate the specific genes involved and, secondly, to understanding the factors that increase the genetically vulnerable individual's chances of actually developing the disorder. One gene that has attracted considerable attention is on chromosome 22. Researchers have attempted to establish the existence of a relationship between schizophrenia and a condition known as *chromosome 22 deletion syndrome* (Horowitz et al., 2005). People with this condition are missing basic genetic information in a particular area near the middle region of chromosome 22. It is hypothesized that this syndrome is related to psychotic

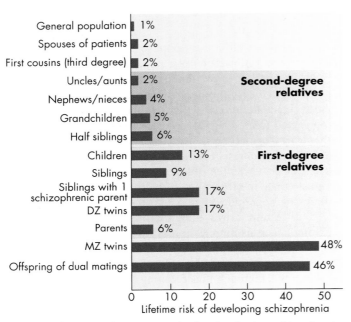

FIGURE 9.1 Grand average risks for developing schizophrenia, compiled from the family and twin studies conducted in European populations. The degree of risk correlates highly with the degree of genetic relatedness.

Source: From I. I. Gottesman in *Schizophrenia genesis: The origins of madness.* Copyright © 1991 by W. H. Freeman and Company/Werth Publishers. Used by permission.

symptoms, impairments in cognition, and communication deficits associated with schizophrenia (Zinkstok & van Amelsvoort, 2005). Another gene associated with higher risk of schizophrenia is on chromosome 5 (Pimm et al., 2005). It is thought that this gene is involved in the transport of neurotransmitters, including serotonin.

Of course, identifying the gene or genes involved in schizophrenia will be key to gaining an understanding of the biological basis for the disorder, but there are two cautions that must be taken into account. One is that there must ultimately be a connection between the genes thought to be involved in passing along the disorder and biochemical processes that would translate the genetic information into faulty brain functioning. Second, even though there is high heritability of schizophrenia, there remains an environmental component that must be explained. Even among monozygotic twins, whose genes are identical, the disorder may take different forms, run a different course, or even develop in one but not the other twin.

In their efforts to understand the reasons how and why people with schizophrenia differ from nonschizophrenic controls, researchers focus on the concepts of **endophenotypes,** biobehavioral abnormalities that are linked to genetic and neurobiological causes of mental illness (Gottesman & Gould, 2003). In other words, they are heritable traits or characteristics that are not direct symptoms of the disorder (e.g., delusion or hallucination), but have been found to be associated with the condition

(Heinrichs, 2005). In the section on the psychological perspective, we will discuss the fact that cognitive impairment has been found to be a characteristic that differentiates people with schizophrenia from controls without this disorder.

Biological Stressors and Vulnerability Although we tend to think of stress as a psychological event, there are many events that happen within the body, especially during development, that can be experienced as assaults with long-lasting consequences. Scientists are particularly interested in dramatic events during the prenatal period and delivery that may influence the development of schizophrenia among people who have a genetic vulnerability. These events include the exposure of pregnant women to harmful environmental conditions or the experience of birth complications. For example, the women who lived through the invasion of the Netherlands by Germany during World War II were more likely to bear children who later developed schizophrenia. Male offspring were particularly at risk (van Os & Selten, 1998). Other researchers examined the pregnancy and birth records of adults diagnosed with schizophrenia and found higher rates of problems during pregnancy, delivery, and the period immediately after birth (Ohman & Hultman, 1998). Presumably, these complications result in brain abnormalities that increase the likelihood of schizophrenia. Researchers have also been especially interested in statistics documenting the development of schizophrenia in the offspring of mothers who had influenza during the first

The Genain sisters were identical quadruplets born in the early 1930s. Although all four developed symptoms of schizophrenia in their 20s, as they entered later adulthood, their symptoms changed in severity, giving researchers unique opportunities to assess the relative contributions of genetics and environment.

trimester of pregnancy. The risk of schizophrenia was increased seven times in women who developed influenza in the first trimester of pregnancy (Brown et al., 2004). Seasonal variations in time of birth also appear to be related to the risk of developing schizophrenia, with higher rates among people born in the months of May and June (Selten et al., 2000).

However, it is important to realize that birth or pregnancy complications, without an underlying vulnerability, are unlikely to cause schizophrenia. This is where the diathesis-stress model becomes relevant. According to the diathesis-stress model, individuals may inherit a vulnerability to schizophrenia, which is expressed when the individual is exposed to stressors from the environment. This underlying vulnerability was called "schizotypy" by psychologist Paul Meehl (Meehl, 1962, 1990). The concept of a diathesis, or inherited, vulnerability to schizophrenia is one that underlies much of the current thinking regarding the causes of this complex disorder.

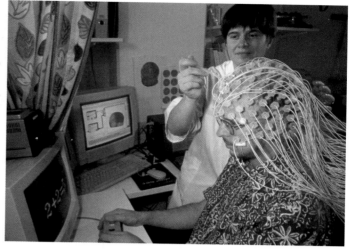

Studying attentional deficits in people with schizophrenia, a researcher records brain activity as the subject views stimuli on a monitor.

Psychological Perspective

There is no credible theory that proposes that schizophrenia develops exclusively as the result of psychological phenomena, such as life experiences, developmental difficulties, interpersonal problems, or emotional conflicts. Psychologists are increasingly accepting that schizophrenia is determined by a complex interaction of genetics, altered brain functioning, and environmental processes, all of which serve to cause changes in cognitive functioning and behavior (Beck & Rector, 2005). Impaired cognition in people with schizophrenia is evident in the form of defects that they exhibit in attention, memory, language, and reasoning. Research on the cognitive functioning of people with schizophrenia is regarded as one of the most important emerging avenues for understanding the phenomena of this disorder; in fact, one expert comments that "cognitive deficits are not only part of the schizophrenia syndrome; they are the primary expression of the schizophrenic brain" (Heinrichs, 2005, p. 229).

Abnormalities in cognitive processes provide important clues to the biological underpinnings of schizophrenia and are used in studies of biological markers. Researchers have used three measures of cognitive functioning as a way of identifying which individuals have inherited a vulnerability to schizophrenia: sustained attention, antisaccade eye movements, and smooth pursuit eye movements (Louchart–de la Chapelle et al., 2005). Laboratory measures of sustained attention (the Continuous Performance Test) involve having the person being tested make a response when a certain target stimulus is displayed. This target stimulus is presented along with other stimuli at unpredictable intervals. For instance, the researcher may instruct the person to push a button whenever the letter *A* appears from among a series of letters presented individually for very brief periods of time (on the order of milliseconds). This is a tedious task that requires constant vigilance by the participant in order to receive a high score. The researcher can also make the task more complex by adding other demands, such as requiring that

the person push the button only if the letter *A* is preceded by the letter *Q*. Typically, people with schizophrenia do very poorly on these tasks, especially when the demands of the task are increased, so that the individual's cognitive capacities are stretched to their limits (Elvevag, Weinberger, Suter, & Goldberg, 2000). The biological relatives of people with schizophrenia also show deficits on these tasks (Saoud et al., 2000). In the antisaccade task, the individual is instructed to look in the direction opposite to the side in which a stimulus is presented. This task is highly associated with a genetic predisposition to schizophrenia, as indicated by the poorer performance of people who are in the acute stage of schizophrenia and their first-degree relatives (Curtis et al., 2001). More to the point, the biological relatives of people with schizophrenia also show deficits.

Researchers measure the second biological marker, disturbance in smooth pursuit eye movements ("saccades"), by having participants visually follow a target, such as a small point of light on a dark background, and closely monitoring their eye movements with recording devices. In contrast to normal individuals, people with schizophrenia show irregular pursuit of a moving target, along with many interruptions by extraneous eye movements. First-degree relatives of people with schizophrenia also show this abnormality in the smooth pursuit function and related eye movement tasks (Karoumi et al., 2001).

A third behavioral abnormality that can serve as a biological marker is a defect in the ability to filter, or "tune out," auditory signals, a function known as sensory gating. This deficit is demonstrated by exposing individuals in the laboratory to repeated presentation of an auditory stimulus and measuring evoked brain potentials. People with schizophrenia do not show the sensory gating effect, meaning that they are more likely to have difficulty filtering out irrelevant distractions from the outside world. There is some evidence that this dysfunction is genetically based, as it is observed both in people with schizophrenia and in their relatives (Adler et al., 1998). Researchers are beginning to link this genetically based inability to filter out irrelevant stimuli with deficits in the hippocampus that result in poorer short-term memory (Waldo et al., 2000).

Although we are discussing cognitive impairment in the context of the psychological perspective, it is important to understand that researchers look at cognitive variables as being determined by a complex set of influences including pathophysiology (i.e., illness-related brain disturbance), genes, chronic stress and distress, medication, education, gender, sociocultural influences, and the content and structure of the cognitive task itself.

The impairments in cognitive functioning experienced by people with schizophrenia are varied and in many cases so debilitating that the individual's quality of life can be profoundly affected, thus setting up an unfortunate interaction of variables. Because of this form of impairment, people with schizophrenia are likely to encounter difficulties functioning in the world, interacting with other people, and achieving personal goals. Researchers are trying to zero in on the specific phenomena of cognitive impairment in people with schizophrenia. They are also trying to answer the question whether cognitive impairments reflect symptoms of the disorder or are more central to the diagnosis of schizophrenia (Barch, 2005). In other words, are problems with working memory due to the severity of disorganization in a person and to negative symptoms such as apathy? Or are such cognitive impairments attributable to specific brain pathways associated with memory deficits, which in turn contribute to the development of negative symptoms? As you can see from our discussion of the psychological perspective, there is no easy way to tease out psychological factors from biological factors, a realization that reminds us of the importance of looking for ways to bring together the various perspectives.

Sociocultural Perspective

Researchers working within the family systems perspective focus on the "system" of roles, interactions, and patterns of communication in the family environment in which the person with schizophrenia grew up. In studies on modes of communication and behavior within families with a schizophrenic member, researchers attempt to document deviant patterns of communication and inappropriate ways that parents interact with their children. These disturbances in family relationships are thought to lead to the development of defective emotional responsiveness and cognitive distortions fundamental to the psychological symptoms of schizophrenia.

Contemporary researchers have approached the issue by trying to predict outcome or recovery in adults hospitalized for schizophrenia. Instead of regarding a disturbed family as the cause of schizophrenia, these researchers view the family as a potential source of stress in the environment of the person who is trying to recover from a schizophrenic episode. The stress created by family members is reflected in the index of **expressed emotion (EE),** which provides a measure of the degree to which family members speak in ways that reflect criticism, hostile feelings, and emotional overinvolvement or overconcern. People living in families high in EE are more likely to suffer a relapse, particularly if they are exposed to high levels of criticism (Marom et al., 2005).

As mentioned earlier, EE may contribute to neuropsychological deficits in increasing the risk of schizophrenia in genetically susceptible individuals (Rosenfarb et al., 2000). An interactional, reciprocal relationship between EE and schizophrenia is also implied in research suggesting that EE is not simply the trigger for schizophrenic symptoms but also a response to unusual, disruptive, or poorly socialized behavior on the part of the schizophrenic individual (Woo, Goldstein, & Nuechterlein, 2004). Indeed, researchers are finding that EE seems to rise and fall along with the degree of burden represented by the disturbed child's presence in the home (Scazufca & Kuipers, 1998).

Moving beyond the family environment, broader social factors, such as social class and income, have also been studied in relationship to schizophrenia. In perhaps the first epidemiological study of mental illness to be conducted in the United States, Hollingshead and Redlich (1958) observed that schizophrenia was far more prevalent in the lowest socioeconomic classes, and numerous investigators since that time have supported the connection between lower social class and higher rates of schizophrenia (Gottesman, 1991). Over the years, this observation has been the source of a great deal of speculation about the role of social factors in either causing schizophrenia or influencing its course. Two principal explanations have been proposed: (1) the social causation hypothesis and (2) the downward social drift hypothesis.

According to the social causation hypothesis, membership in lower socioeconomic strata may actually cause schizophrenia. Members of the lowest classes of society experience numerous economic hardships and are often denied access to many of society's benefits, including high-quality education, health care, and employment. Because many are also members of ethnic or racial minorities, they may experience discrimination. These factors create a highly stressful environment, which might be conducive to the development of schizophrenia. Researchers in one study found that the poorer one's socioeconomic conditions, the higher the risk for mental disability and psychiatric hospitalization. Using sophisticated statistical techniques, they found compelling support for the social causation hypothesis, and concluded that the mental illness of people in the sample could not be attributed to geographic or economic downward mobility (Hudson, 2005). It is important to note that the social causation hypothesis need not contradict the diathesis-stress model; rather, the stresses of poverty and socioeconomic disadvantage may elicit schizophrenic symptoms at higher rates than in less disadvantaged social settings.

Many people with schizophrenia have difficulty readjusting to their families after a period of hospitalization. According to the theory of expressed emotion, returning to a family that is highly critical increases the chances that a relapse of the disorder will occur.

The other perspective, the downward social drift hypothesis, downplays the effects of socioeconomic stressors in the development of schizophrenia. Presumably, schizophrenia develops at equal rates across a variety of social, cultural, and economic backgrounds, but, once people develop the disorder, their economic standing declines precipitously. The debilitating symptoms of schizophrenia prevent individuals from pursuing economic success and preclude their living in more affluent areas. This perspective, therefore, downplays the potential stressors of poverty and lower social status in favor of a more directly biological approach to the causes of schizophrenia. The symptoms of the disorder are what account for the declining economic and social fortunes of people diagnosed with schizophrenia.

Overall, there is too little research to resolve the contrasting viewpoints of the social causation and downward social drift hypotheses. Tentative evidence exists to support the downward social drift hypothesis that individuals with schizophrenia are unable to achieve economic and social success due to the severity of their symptoms; however, if we return to the diathesis-stress model of causation, poverty and social disadvantage would seem powerful stressors capable of eliciting schizophrenic symptoms. These perspectives might clarify the distribution of schizophrenia within a society, but broader epidemiological studies have not indicated a clear relationship between the prevalence of schizophrenia and the level of economic development across societies.

The 2001 report on mental health by the U.S. Surgeon General concludes that genetics are a stronger influence in the causation of schizophrenia than cultural and societal factors (U.S. Surgeon General, 2001). We are left to conclude that the relationship of schizophrenia to socioeconomic status may extend beyond these two competing perspectives to include broader factors, such as societal values and beliefs about mental illness, among others.

Treatment of Schizophrenia

The vulnerability model we have just discussed implies that schizophrenia has no single cause. Although a particular theory may appear to be dominant, treatment must be based on a multifaceted approach that incorporates various theoretical components. Current comprehensive models of care include biological treatments, psychological interventions primarily in the form of behavioral techniques, and sociocultural interventions that focus on milieu therapy and family involvement.

Biological Treatments In the 1950s, effective medication was introduced for treating the symptoms of schizophrenia. This breakthrough had a massive impact on the mental health system, as you recall from our discussion in Chapter 1, helping to spur on the deinstitutionalization movement. The fact that medication could control the most debilitating symptoms of psychosis, at least to some extent, meant that hundreds of thousands of people could be treated on an outpatient basis rather than be confined and under constant supervision.

Prior to the 1950s, somatic interventions involved treatments intended to alter brain functioning, including ECT. The most extreme somatic intervention was the prefrontal lobotomy. Although this procedure helped reduce aggressive behaviors in people who experienced hallucinations and delusions, lobotomies also had many unfavorable outcomes for the individual, including a significant loss of motivation, creativity, and cognitive function. With the advent of antipsychotic medication in the 1950s, the procedure was all but abandoned. Similarly, medications have replaced the use of ECT in treating schizophrenia.

There are several categories of antipsychotic medication, also called major tranquilizers or **neuroleptics** (derived from the Greek words meaning "to seize the nerve"). In addition to their sedating qualities, neuroleptics reduce the frequency and severity of psychotic symptoms. The various neuroleptics differ in the dosage needed to achieve therapeutic effects, ranging from low-potency medications that require large dosages to high-potency medications that require comparatively smaller dosages. The low-potency class includes such medications as chlorpromazine (Thorazine) and thioridazine (Mellaril); middle-potency medications include trifluoperazine (Stelazine) and thiothixine (Navane); high-potency medications include haloperidol (Haldol) and fluphenazine (Prolixin). A physician would be more likely to prescribe a low-potency medication for a highly agitated patient, because low-potency medications tend to be more sedating than the high-potency ones. The high-potency medications may be preferable for a patient who is less agitated, but they do carry the risk of more serious side effects.

These traditionally prescribed antipsychotic medications have their effects through the blocking of dopamine receptors. In other words, these medications contain chemical substances that become attached to the sites on the neurons that would ordinarily respond to the neurotransmitter dopamine. This action has two behavioral results, one therapeutic and the other unintended and troublesome. The therapeutic result is reduced frequency and intensity of psychotic symptoms, as the dopamine receptors are deactivated in the sections of the brain that affect thoughts and feelings. On the negative side are consequences that can greatly interfere with the individual's movements and endocrine function. People taking such medications may suddenly experience such symptoms as uncontrollable shaking, muscle tightening, and involuntary eye movements. These side effects occur when dopamine accumulates because it is not being taken up by neurons whose receptor sites have been blocked by the medication. As the dopamine level rises, the neurons in the other areas of the brain that control motor movements are thrown into dysregulation. Interestingly, physicians treat people with Parkinson's disease, a nervous disease that is caused by an insufficiency of dopamine, with a medication that enhances dopamine activity. Thus, a commonly reported side effect of this anti-Parkinsonian medication is psychotic-like behavior and thinking.

One of the most troubling effects from the long-term use of neuroleptics is an irreversible neurological disorder called *tardive dyskinesia,* which affects 10 to 20 percent of people who take some of the neuroleptics for a year or more. People with tardive dyskinesia experience uncontrollable movements in various parts of their bodies, including the mouth, tongue, lips, fingers, arms, legs, and trunk. As you can imagine, these involuntary movements can seriously impair the person's ability to walk, breathe, eat, and talk, to say nothing of how embarrassing it is to be seen in this state.

Disturbed by the worrisome side effects of these traditional antipsychotic medications, as well as their ineffectiveness in treating negative symptoms, psychopharmacological researchers set out to develop new medications. In recent years, medications called *second-generation antipsychotics* (previously referred to as "atypical antipsychotics") have been more widely prescribed. Examples of second-generation antipsychotics (SGAs) include clozapine (Clozaril), amisulpride (Solian), risperidone (Risperdal), olanzapine (Zyprexa), quetiapine (Seroquel), and sertindole (Serlect). In a meta-analysis of studies comparing the efficacy of first-generation antipsychotics (FGAs) and second-generation antipsychotics, researchers found that some SGAs (i.e., clozapine, amisulpride, risperidone, olanzapine) are significantly more efficacious than FGAs, but some SGAs are no more effective than FGAs. Upon taking an even closer look at the particular symptoms that respond to specific medications, it was found that olanzapine and risperidone were slightly superior to FGAs for treating positive symptoms and moderately superior to FGAs for treating negative symptoms, thought disorder, mood disturbance, and impulse control (Davis, Chen, & Glick, 2003). As you can see, despite

Sometimes a person with schizophrenia becomes so impaired that hospitalization is necessary.

significant advances in psychopharamacological treatment of the symptoms of schizophrenia, scientific understanding remains limited about the most effective medications. What is known, sadly, is that these medications don't cure schizophrenia but are only effective in alleviating certain symptoms.

Complicating the issue about pharmacological intervention for treating people with schizophrenia are disturbing reports about the side effects of the second-generation antipsychotics. Metabolic disturbances, particularly weight gain, hyperlipidemia (elevation of fats in the bloodstream), and hyperglycemia (increase in plasma glucose) have been reported as adverse side effects of taking SGAs. Because of these risks, as well as a range of other potential problems, clinicians know that it is extremely important that all individuals taking these medications be carefully monitored for the early emergence of warning signs.

One dilemma that health care providers face when recommending antipsychotic medication is whether or not people with schizophrenia should be maintained on full doses of these medications when they are not experiencing the overt positive symptoms of the disorder. Some clinicians recommend to certain clients that they reduce or stop medication during extended periods of good functioning, as long as clients can be closely monitored for the reappearance of symptoms. Obviously, the clinician's decision to interrupt medication should only be done following a careful evaluation of the client's symptoms and history (Nuechterlein, Gitlin, & Subotnik, 1995).

Psychological Treatments The most common psychological interventions for people with schizophrenia are those derived from the behavioral perspective, in which it is assumed that much of the difficulty that many people with schizophrenia face is due to their having acquired bizarre and maladaptive behavior patterns. These treatments focus on the individual's symptoms that interfere with social adjustment and functioning.

In a token economy (Ayllon & Azrin, 1965), most often used in institutional settings, individuals are rewarded with plastic chips called "tokens" for acting in socially appropriate ways (see Table 9.2). They either do not earn tokens or must forfeit them when their behavior is inappropriate. The individual can use the tokens to acquire special privileges or opportunities. The expectation is that, over time, the new behaviors will become habitual and not dependent on being reinforced by tokens.

Consider the case of Cynthia, a woman with schizophrenia who is hospitalized and who has very poor personal hygiene and grooming. Her therapist might use a token economy system to encourage Cynthia to develop appropriate hygiene. For each privilege that she wishes to "purchase," she must cash in a fixed number of tokens. She may need 10 tokens to go on a weekend pass or 2 tokens to go to the hospital snack shop. Taking a daily shower may earn her 2 tokens, and combing her hair may be worth 1 token. The incentive to have these privileges would presumably be strong enough to motivate Cynthia to engage in appropriate grooming behaviors. Eventually, these behaviors become established and are reinforcing in their own right, so that the tokens are no longer necessary. Additionally, the attention and praise Cynthia receives when she earns each token can add to the reinforcement value of the tokens themselves. She learns to value such positive attention, making it more likely that she will work to maintain her grooming skills.

Social skills training is another behavioral intervention that involves reinforcing appropriate behaviors, especially those involved in interpersonal situations. People with schizophrenia often speak or act in ways that others regard as abnormal. In social skills training, an individual's inappropriate behaviors are identified and targeted, and reinforcement becomes dependent on the individual's acting in more socially acceptable ways. For example, a disturbed individual may speak loudly or with an unusual tone, move in peculiar ways, stare at others, or fail to maintain an appropriate distance when speaking to people. In social skills training, the therapist provides feedback to the individual about the inappropriateness of each of these behaviors. This may take place in the context of role-playing exercises, direct instruction, or a group setting in which participants are encouraged to comment openly on each other's behaviors.

Clinicians who implement social skills training programs strive to do the following: (1) help the individual set specific, personally relevant long- and short-term goals; (2) promote realistically favorable expectations; (3) help the individual create interpersonal situations that may be encountered in the near future; (4) build scenes that parallel anticipated situations by asking questions about the emotion or communication the person wants to convey, and to whom, where, and when; (5) develop role-playing scenarios that provide opportunities for behavioral rehearsal; (6) provide the individual with positive as well as corrective feedback regarding verbal and nonverbal behaviors, conversational style, and social perception; (7) coach the individual in the behavioral rehearsal of the scene with prompting, encouragement, and acknowledgment of appropriate verbal and nonverbal behaviors; (8) use behavioral shaping techniques to help the individual progress in small, attainable increments; (9) give specific, attainable, and functional homework assignments which the individual can practice in real-life situations; and (10) solicit reports from the individual about homework assignments, so that steps can then be made toward the attainment of new goals, the practicing of previously set goals, or problem solving to remove obstacles encountered by the individual (Liberman, 2005). Although social skills training programs are customarily done in mental health settings, family members of a person with schizophrenia can also receive training in techniques to help their relative acquire social skills that will enhance adjustment and interpersonal interactions.

Clinicians may also incorporate cognitive-behavioral techniques in helping the client to detect the early signs of a relapse, to take a more positive approach to evaluating the ability to cope with daily problems, and to develop a broader range of ways to handle emotional distress and anxiety. Disordered thinking processes and even delusions may be reduced through cognitive-behavioral interventions (Beck & Rector, 2005).

In an innovative approach to psychotherapy with schizophrenic individuals, one group of researchers developed an intervention called "personal therapy," in which clinicians tailor psychotherapy to strengthen interpersonal skills and control social stress (Hogarty et al., 1997). Personal therapy rests on the assumption that stress-related emotions aggravate positive symptoms, such as delusions and hallucinations, as well as negative symptoms, such as social withdrawal and apathy. Within

---

TABLE 9.2 Example of a Token Economy Used in Treating a Person with Schizophrenia

Earn tokens for the following behaviors:

  Eat with proper utensils

  Brush hair in the morning

  Keep clothing on during the day

  Answer when spoken to

  Participate in therapeutic activities

Lose tokens for the following behaviors:

  Shout at other people

  Take off clothes in public

  Eat with hands

  Refuse to participate in therapeutic activities

this framework, clinicians help clients study personal reactions to stress and develop coping strategies that facilitate relaxation in social contexts. Hogarty and his colleagues found that personal therapy was impressive for individuals living with their families in reducing the likelihood of relapse over a 3-year period. However, among those living independently of family, the individuals who participated in personal therapy had more psychotic relapses than did the individuals in a group receiving only supportive therapy. Research findings such as these point to the importance of therapeutic endeavors that involve those closest to the person with schizophrenia.

Sociocultural Treatments   From what you have read about schizophrenia, you can understand the way in which this disorder greatly involves other people in the life of the individual. Other people are certainly affected by the disturbing symptoms of a person with this condition, just as the person with schizophrenia is profoundly affected by others. Central to an integrative treatment is a therapeutic approach that includes a focus on interactions and relationships.

Milieu therapy is a model that involves social processes as a tool for changing the individual's behavior. In this approach, all staff and clients in a treatment setting work as a therapeutic community to promote positive functioning in the clients. Members of the community participate in group activities ranging from occupational therapy to training classes. The staff encourages clients to work with and spend time with other residents, even when leaving on passes. The entire community is involved in decision making, sometimes involving an executive council with elected members from units of the treatment setting. Every staff person, whether a therapist, nurse, or paraprofessional, takes part in the overall mission of providing an environment that supports positive change and appropriate social behaviors. The underlying idea of milieu therapy is that the pressure to conform to conventional social norms of behavior discourages the individual with schizophrenia from expressing problematic symptoms. The "normalizing" effects of such an environment are intended to help the individual make a smoother and more effective transition to life outside the therapeutic community. Education about symptoms and treatments, clarification of goals, aftercare planning, and coordination with family and other community supports are beneficial and therapeutic (Dhillon & Dollieslager, 2000).

Considerable information is now available for clinicians, families, and clients to draw on in their efforts to grope with this mysterious and devastating illness. Treatment programs that combine medication with psychosocial interventions appear to have the most promise for maximizing the day-to-day functioning of individuals with this disorder. These programs include residential or community facilities that provide training in coping with the stress of the disorder and its symptoms, rehabilitation through occupational training, and psychoeducation for families. Effective family programs, which usually last for 6 months or more, provide information to families about the psychotic disorder and its management, strive to decrease tension

and stress in the family, provide social support for the family, focus on the development of strategies for the future, improve functioning among all family members, and work to form a collaborative relationship between the treatment team and the family (Mueser et al., 2003).

The coordination of services is especially important in programs geared toward helping people with schizophrenia. One approach to integrating various services is Assertive Community Treatment (ACT), in which a team of professionals from psychiatry, psychology, nursing, and social work reach out to clients in their homes and workplaces. A team of a dozen or so professionals work together to help approximately 100 clients comply with medical recommendations, manage their finances, obtain adequate health care, and deal with crises when they arise. This approach involves bringing care to the clients, rather than waiting for them to come to a facility for help, a journey that may be too overwhelming for seriously impaired people. Although approaches such as ACT are expensive, the benefits are impressive. Researchers have conducted dozens of studies on the effectiveness of ACT and have concluded that ACT has had significant positive impact on reducing hospitalizations, stabilizing housing in the community, and lowering overall treatment costs. ACT is most beneficial for more severely disturbed individuals with a history of frequent or long-term hospitalizations or who have extremely limited psychosocial functioning skills and require daily assistance to live in the community (Mueser et al., 2003).

Schizophrenia: The Biopsychosocial Perspective

Schizophrenia is a disorder that has mystified people for centuries, although only within the past 100 years has the disorder had a name. As researchers attempt to gain a scientific understanding of the disorder, clinicians, family members, and individuals who have schizophrenia seek ways to cope on a daily basis with its many widespread effects.

As we begin the twenty-first century, relatively few conclusions about the causes of schizophrenia are evident. One fact does stand out, however; people do not develop schizophrenia solely as the result of troubled childhoods. Biology clearly plays a central role, although the precise nature and extent of this role remain unclear. We do know that differences exist in the brain structure and functioning of people with schizophrenia, as compared with those of others. We also know that there is a strong likelihood that people with schizophrenia have relatives with this disorder, and, the closer the relative, the greater the rate of concordance. Scientists have delineated specific biological markers that have assisted them in their efforts to understand which factors and genes are implicated in the acquisition of this disorder.

Even though few would contest the central role of biological factors in determining schizophrenia, biology cannot tell the whole story. Events happen in the life of the person predisposed to schizophrenia that trigger the disorder. Twin studies show us that environmental factors must play a role; otherwise, identical twins would have a 100 percent concordance rate for this disorder. However, it is not yet known what factors in life make one more vulnerable to schizophrenia. Numerous studies of early life relationships have failed to pinpoint a causal connection between faulty parenting and the development of this disorder. What does seem clear is that certain stresses might trigger the disorder, leading to a cycle of disturbance. The difficulty of raising a child with schizophrenia can lead to tension in the parents, and this increased familial tension can exacerbate the child's disturbance.

Although current understanding of the causes of schizophrenia remains incomplete, scientists continue to look for ways to alleviate its symptoms. The consensus is that an integrative intervention that includes medication, psychological treatment, and social support provides the best context for helping people with schizophrenia. Beginning with the biological approach, there is compelling evidence for the important role of medication in alleviating the distressing symptoms of this disorder. At

the same time, it is important to keep in mind that medication does not cure the disorder but only treats the symptoms.

Just as biology is an insufficient explanation for the disorder, medication is an incomplete intervention for treating people with schizophrenia. Individualized treatment plans range from tightly structured, institutionally affiliated programs to periodic psychotherapy that is provided when needed. Generally, those who are incapacitated by the disorder require comprehensive and permanent treatment and support. But many people with schizophrenia function adequately in the world and need active intervention only on occasion, when psychotic symptoms flare up.

Despite the inadequacy of current knowledge about this disorder, the tremendous gains made during the past decade are certainly cause for optimism. New research techniques have provided scientists with access to the human brain, where many of the secrets of this perplexing disorder lie. Refinements in genetic research have also provided hope that scientists soon will learn why some relatives develop schizophrenia, while others do not. In light of the speed of recent advances, it is possible that, within a decade, we will look back to the early years of the 21st century with disbelief about our limited knowledge.

Case Report
David Marshall

RETURN TO THE CASE

David's History

In part because they were so upset about David, Mr. and Mrs. Marshall found it difficult to remember many details about his early years. In response to my initial questions about his childhood, the Marshalls responded that he was a "normal kid." However, with further probing, they recalled that he was a "very quiet boy who kept most things to himself." David's subdued style stood in sharp contrast to the liveliness of his brother, Michael, who was a year older. When I asked about the family environment during David's early years, Mr. and Mrs. Marshall admitted that their marital relationship had been fairly "stormy" during those

years and that they had come close to divorce when David was about 2 years old. With the help of marriage counseling, they worked things out over the course of a year.

In recalling David's childhood personality, Mrs. Marshall pointed out an interesting contrast with his adolescent years, in that he was an exceptionally neat and clean child. She remembered how angry he became if for some reason he was unable to take his 7 P.M. bath. By the time he was in his late teens, however, David's finicky habits had changed entirely. He did not wash for several days at a time, and he finally did so only at the insistence of his mother, who practically

had to drag him into the shower. Mrs. Marshall said that she never would have believed that her formerly clean son would one day have greasy hair, unwashed for weeks at a time.

The Marshalls told me of their dismay and horror as they witnessed the almost total incapacitation of a once healthy young man. They spoke of the impact on their own lives, as they had come to worry about the safety of having such a disturbed young man living with them. I asked them to elaborate regarding this concern, and Mr. Marshall told me about David's nightly rituals in his room. With his door shut and locked, David each night lit two dozen candles as part of a "communication exercise with Zoroaster." Any use of fire by a man so disturbed was worrisome to his parents; the proximity of flames to the many spray cans in David's room increased their alarm even further.

Moving on to a discussion of family history, the Marshalls told me that the only relevant bit of information that came to mind was the fact that Mrs. Marshall's sister had a long history of psychological problems and had been hospitalized three times because she had "crazy beliefs, heard voices, and acted very strange."

Assessment

In light of David's severe disturbance, psychological testing was not viable. My assessment of David was, therefore, limited to a 30-minute mental status examination, in which his delusions and hallucinations were remarkable. Regardless of the question being asked, most of David's responses focused on his beliefs about Zoroaster and the aliens. His disorientation was apparent in his responses indicating that his name was "Brodo," that the date was the "36th of Fruen" in the "year of the next heaven, 9912," and that he was being held in a prison by the enemies of Zoroaster. After giving these answers, David laughed in a sinister way and then waved his arms high over his head in a spraying motion, both behaviors to which his mother had referred. He then stopped, as if he had heard something, and looked at his watch. The time was 11 A.M. Muttering to himself, "It's too early," he seemed to go off into a reverie. At that point, I concluded that David was hearing voices. When I asked him if this was the case, he said it was not a voice but a message telling him what he must do next to proceed on his mission. Further questioning at this point revealed David's beliefs about his secret mission and the daily messages he had been receiving from

the television set. I asked David to carry out some simple calculations, which he did adequately, and to copy some simple geometric figures. In the process of doing so, he wrote elaborate equations all over the piece of paper and drew pictures of what he called "hollow soft forms." He asked me if I knew the difference between these and "hollow hard forms," which he illustrated on another sheet of paper. These drawings consisted of squiggles and letter-like symbols that apparently contained a great deal of meaning to David but that made no sense to others. Despite my best efforts to communicate with David in a logical and clear manner, he did not tell me anything about himself other than to talk about his delusions.

Diagnosis

As I evaluated David's personal history and current symptoms, all signs pointed to a diagnosis of schizophrenia. In terms of personal history, David was in the age group during which schizophrenia most commonly surfaces, and he had a biological relative with a disorder suggestive of schizophrenia. Of course, these two facts were not sufficient to conclude that David had schizophrenia. The course and symptoms of his disorder provided the most telling evidence.

David was a young man with a progressively worsening course of functioning. He had deteriorated markedly from his high-school years in his academic performance, personal habits, and interpersonal relations. During the years preceding his hospitalization, David had become increasingly symptomatic.

David's symptoms were those of a person with psychosis. He had delusions, hallucinations, loosening of associations, and bizarre behaviors. He was impaired in most areas of everyday functioning, living a life of social isolation, behaving in a bizarre and idiosyncratic manner, and failing to take care of himself, even in regard to personal hygiene.

As for the particular kind of schizophrenia David had, the most tenable diagnosis was undifferentiated type. I assigned this diagnosis because David was not catatonic or prominently paranoid in his delusions, nor was his symptom presentation prominently disorganized.

Axis I: Schizophrenia, Undifferentiated Type

Axis II: Deferred

Axis III: No physical disorders or conditions

Axis IV: Problems related to the social environment (adjustment difficulties) Occupational problems (unemployed)

Axis V: Current Global Assessment of Functioning: 30 Highest Global Assessment of Functioning (past year): 45

Case Formulation

There was little question that David Marshall had schizophrenia, but I wondered what had caused this tragic set of symptoms to unfold in a young man who, as a child, was nothing other than a quiet and reserved boy, and I wondered what had taken place biologically and psychologically that had caused that transition from shyness to schizophrenia over the course of his adolescent years. I thought of the important biological fact that David's aunt, in all likelihood, had schizophrenia. The significance of this one fact, of course, lies in the current understanding of the critically important role that genetics plays in the etiology of this disorder. At the same time, experts know that biological predisposition is generally insufficient to determine whether or not a person will develop schizophrenia. Consequently, I turned to David's personal history for clues.

Throughout his early life, David was reticent and withdrawn, compared with his active and outgoing brother. On the one hand, David's behavior made him a target of his parents' scrutiny as they attempted to find out what he was feeling and thinking. On the other hand, David's parents clearly devoted most of their attention to his older brother, communicating to David the message that they really were less concerned with his well-being. I also wondered about the impact on David of the discord between his parents during the early years of his life.

Treatment Plan

The plan that I implemented for David took into account the need for decisive intervention over the short term and continued treatment for the years ahead. I realized that, even when his psychotic symptoms were under control, he would have residual problems requiring monitoring and treatment. David's parents concurred with me that his overt psychotic symptoms needed to be brought under control and that this could best be accomplished by medication, but they worried whether David would take the medication voluntarily. Much to their surprise, David did agree to give it a try. His decision to comply led me to wonder whether David, on some level, had come to recognize the seriousness of his problem and had become more willing to accept help.

I recommended that David remain in the hospital for 3 months, during which time he could be stabilized on his medication and the two of us could develop a working relationship. Ideally, we would continue to meet on an outpatient basis following his discharge. Our therapeutic work would center on several tasks. First, I wanted to help David develop an understanding of his disorder, as well as impress on him the importance of maintaining an ongoing relationship with a mental health professional. Second, I wanted to help him develop coping strategies to use in his everyday life. He needed to learn how to care for himself and to work on beginning to lead a more normal life.

During the initial weeks of David's hospitalization, the antipsychotic medication began to reduce the severity of his symptoms. As he became more lucid, he was able to carry on conversations without the intrusion of ideas about Zoroaster and a secret mission of saving the world. David told me of the despair he experienced about his symptoms and how incapable he felt of ever getting anywhere in his life. Gradually, David interacted more with other patients on the unit, though his preference was clearly to stay in his room alone, listening to rock music. At first, this preference for being alone caused his parents some distress, and they wondered whether he was really getting better or not. However, I felt less concerned, because his behavior seemed markedly different from his actions prior to his hospitalization. David clearly cherished his privacy, and being alone did not necessarily mean that he was lost in a delusional world.

After David had stabilized and his symptoms were under control, he and I talked about discharge from the hospital. I recommended to David that, instead of returning home, he should reside in a halfway house. He rejected this idea outright, on the grounds that such facilities do not afford much privacy. We arrived at a compromise that he would return home but attend a day treatment program for at least 6 months. In such a program, David's daily activities would be supervised, and he would have an opportunity to socialize and take part in vocational training. I agreed to continue seeing him in weekly psychotherapy sessions.

Outcome of the Case

Following David's discharge from the hospital, he moved back home and followed my recommendation that he participate in the hospital's day treatment program, where he thrived with the support of the treatment staff. As I might have predicted, he

remained a withdrawn young man who could feel content sitting alone in a corner and thinking. To the relief of his parents, David agreed to continue taking his medication, despite the fact that he complained about minor hand tremors.

After 12 months in the day treatment program, the treatment staff decided that David was ready for a trial run in a real job. He was placed in a position at a library, where he shelved books. He liked this job, because it involved so little contact with the public, and there was an orderliness about it which he found comforting. After a few months, David's supervisor noted his excellent performance and promoted him to a job at the circulation desk, which involved more contact with the public. This proved to be a mistake. The stress of exposure to many people over the course of the day was too much for David to handle, and within 2 weeks he had relapsed into a full-blown psychotic episode.

After a short hospital stay, in which he was restabilized on his medications, David returned to the day treatment program, where he remained for another 6 months. By this time, there was an opening in a group home, and David was finally able to move out of his parents' house. He now lives in this setting and has gone back to his former job at the library.

I have continued to see David over these past few years, but at present we meet only once a month, which seems most comfortable for David. Although we have worked together for more than 4 years, I have never gotten a clear message from David that he values our work or that he even cares about coming to psychotherapy. Nevertheless, it has become part of his life routine, and I hold on to the belief that our work together has played a role in his remaining relatively healthy for this long period.

Sarah Tobin, PhD

SUMMARY

- Schizophrenia is a disorder with a range of symptoms involving disturbances in content of thought, form of thought, perception, affect, sense of self, motivation, behavior, and interpersonal functioning. Essential to the diagnosis is a marked disturbance lasting at least 6 months. During this 6-month period is an active phase of symptoms, such as delusions, hallucinations, disorganized speech, disturbed behavior, and negative symptoms. The active phase is often preceded by a prodromal phase and followed by a residual phase. The prodromal phase is characterized by maladaptive behaviors, such as social withdrawal, inability to work productively, eccentricity, poor grooming, inappropriate emotionality, peculiar thought and speech, unusual beliefs, odd perceptual experiences, and decreased energy and initiative. The residual phase involves continuing indications of disturbance similar to the behaviors of the prodromal phase.

- Several types of schizophrenia have been delineated. Catatonic type is characterized by bizarre motor behaviors, while disorganized type consists of symptoms including disorganized speech, disturbed behavior, and flat or inappropriate affect. People with schizophrenia, paranoid type, are preoccupied with one or more bizarre delusions or have auditory hallucinations related to a theme of being persecuted or harassed, but without disorganized speech or disturbed behavior. The diagnosis of undifferentiated type is used when a person shows a complex of schizophrenic symptoms but does not meet the criteria for paranoid, catatonic, or disorganized type. The term *residual type* applies to people who have been diagnosed with schizophrenia and show lingering signs of the disorder other than psychotic symptoms.

- In addition to being categorized into types, schizophrenia is also viewed in terms of dimensions: (1) psychotic, (2) negative, and (3) disorganized. The psychotic factor is relevant in cases in which the individual experiences prominent delusions and hallucinations; the negative factor applies to those conditions characterized by negative symptoms (e.g., affective flattening, alogia, and avolition). The disorganized factor includes disorganized speech, disorganized behavior, and inappropriate affect.

- There are several disorders with symptoms like those of schizophrenia, including brief psychotic disorder, schizophreniform disorder, schizoaffective disorder, delusional disorders, and shared psychotic disorder. Brief psychotic disorder is characterized by a sudden onset of psychotic symptoms lasting between a day and a month; this disorder is specified as either with marked stressor, without marked stressor, or with postpartum onset. Schizophreniform disorder is a condition in which people experience a psychotic episode lasting 1 to 6 months. The diagnosis of schizoaffective disorder is given to people with a serious mood disturbance (major depressive episode, manic episode, or mixed episode) concurrent with at least two schizophrenic symptoms. Delusional disorder (erotomanic, grandiose, jealous, persecutory, somatic, mixed, or unspecified) is diagnosed in people who have nonbizarre delusions lasting at least a month, and whose functioning is not otherwise impaired. Shared psychotic disorder is a condition in which a person develops a delusion similar to an already established delusion held by a person with whom he or she shares a close relationship.

- Theories about the cause of schizophrenia focus on the interaction between biology and experience, with particular attention to the notion of vulnerability. Schizophrenia has a high degree of heritability, and researchers are actively attempting to identify the particular genes that lead to a vulnerability to the disorder. Biological researchers have focused on abnormalities of brain structure and function, genetic predispositions, biological markers, and biological stressors. Deficits in cognitive processing have been identified among people with schizophrenia, including abnormalities in sustained attention, sensory gating, and antisaccade eye movements. The most common psychological interventions for people with schizophrenia are those derived from the behavioral perspective, in which it is assumed that much of the difficulty that many people with schizophrenia face is due to their having acquired bizarre and maladaptive behavior patterns. Researchers working within the family systems perspective focus on the "system" of roles, interactions, and patterns of communication in the family environment in which the person with schizophrenia grew up. Current comprehensive models of care include biological treatments, psychological interventions primarily in the form of behavioral techniques, and sociocultural interventions that focus on milieu therapy and family involvement.

KEY TERMS

See Glossary for definitions

Active phase   279
Affective flattening   282
Alogia   282
Anhedonia   282
Avolition   282
Brief psychotic disorder   286
Cortical atrophy   291
Delusional disorders   289
Dementia praecox   278

Dopamine hypothesis   291
Endophenotypes   292
Expressed emotion (EE)   294
Negative symptoms   282
Neuroleptics   295
Positive symptoms   279
Prodromal phase   279
Residual phase   279
Schizoaffective disorder   288

Schizophrenia   278
Schizophrenia, catatonic type   283
Schizophrenia, disorganized type   283
Schizophrenia, paranoid type   283
Schizophrenia, residual type   283
Schizophrenia, undifferentiated type   283
Schizophreniform disorder   287
Shared psychotic disorder   289

 INTERNET RESOURCE

To get more information on the material covered in this chapter, visit our website at **www.mhhe.com/halgin5.** There you will find more information, resources, and links to topics of interest.

NOTHING TO HIDE

THE FRESE FAMILY

Fred speaks about coping with schizophrenia, working in the field of psychology, and the benefit of antipsychotic medication

I was diagnosed with paranoid schizophrenia when I was only twenty-five years old. For the next ten years I was in and out of various mental hospitals. I was told many times that I was insane, and I was given little hope that I could ever lead a dignified or reasonably normal life.

Today, I am the Director of Psychology at Western Reserve Psychiatric Hospital, a state hospital in Ohio. Ironically, I used to be a patient in the Ohio State mental health system. Traditionally, it has been taught that you don't recover from schizophrenia, that it is a degenerative brain disorder. I was told over thirty years ago that the symptoms of schizophrenia only get worse, not better. The thing is, people do recover, but because there is such a stigma about mental illness, people who get better often are reluctant to acknowledge that they have ever been sick.

• • • •

In the 1980s, mentally ill people who were in recovery began to be appointed to mental health boards around the country. I applied for this position in Ohio and became the first consumer on the Akron area mental health board. My identity as a recovering person was kept confidential. During my first meeting, it was mentioned that a mental health consumer was on the board, but it wasn't made clear which of us was the consumer. Later, when I was giving a talk to a group of graduate students, I got up and said, "If there's anyone here who has ever been locked up in a mental hospital, please stand up and identify yourself." Nobody stood up. Then I said, "Well, I guess I'm the only one standing." This was the first time I went public about my history of mental illness.

Now I speak to groups all over the country about surviving in the world of "normal." I am sometimes told that I have become a role model for others who have schizophrenia. I am an advocate for people with this illness, and I have written many articles about my experience with it. I've also appeared on several national radio and TV shows. When I'm interviewed, it never ceases to amaze me the number of times the interviewers themselves have grown up with schizophrenia somewhere in their families.

I still have to take antipsychotic medication, and I try to avoid stressful situations. Without these drugs, I would be back on a locked ward. With the help of my family and coworkers, I'm now able to know when my thoughts and behaviors are becoming abnormal. You really need someone else to tell you that you're beginning to get a little "schizzy." Several times a year, I have to stay home from work, increase my medication, and do what I call "cruising the cosmos," when I just sit and watch images that are like daydreams. I stay up late and weave intricate ideational relationships, often involving numbers and colors. After a few days of singing, dancing, and eating raw acorns, I return to a fairly normal life once again.

Source: Copyright © 2002 *Nothing to Hide: Mental Illness in the Family* by Peggy Gillespie and Jean J. Beard. Reprinted by permission of The New Press. www.thenewpress.com

Fred, Penny, Joe, and Claire

PAUL GOTTLIEB

Paul

Birthdays were always marvelous days for me, and they were enthusiastically celebrated in my family. As my fortieth birthday approached, however, I was dreading it for no particular reason. It would have been normal for me to plan a big celebration, but I just didn't want to do it that year. It didn't feel right. My natural emotions were being affected by something I didn't quite understand. In retrospect, I now know that I was experiencing the onset of a severe depression, which lasted from 1974 until 1981.

• • • •

Over time, the simplest, most practical things became extremely difficult. Little things became major decisions. For instance, I had trouble picking out a tie in the morning, or I would look at my messy desk and it would terrify me. I would think, "How can I go on like this? How can I go on so ineffectively and inefficiently?" I was worried that everyone would find out I was an empty shell and everything was falling apart inside me. I won't say that every day was like that, but the frequency of days like that accelerated.

• • • •

Before I began therapy, I felt that I knew myself quite well in all the dark interstices of my mind. Although there were a couple of insights and cathartic moments in therapy, there were no surprises and nothing that I didn't already know. I already understood my relationship with different members of my family, and I sort of understood who I was and what I was about. My treatment didn't touch the core of my increasingly depressive condition. My analyst was baffled. He didn't understand my case. We examined this and that, but unresolved psychological issues didn't seem to be the cause of my problem. It was

caused by something else, and neither he nor I knew what it was. Looking back on it all, psychoanalytic treatment was not a totally useless exercise, but it really had nothing to do with my particular kind of depression.

• • • •

Things continued to get worse for me emotionally. One day, I literally couldn't get myself to go to work. Instead, I rented a car and drove from Manhattan up to West Point and just walked around. I felt lost and separated from life. It was ghastly. When I was driving back home to the city, I stopped on the New Jersey side of the Hudson River just above the George Washington Bridge and stood at the edge of the cliffs overlooking the river. I don't remember if I was seriously thinking of hurling myself down. I don't even know if I could have done it. But I started screaming hysterically. Screaming. Just screaming into the air. I was desperate.

I spent about a week in the hospital, where I sank into a kind of oblivion while my doctor experimented with various antidepressant drugs. He explained that with mental illness, you can't just draw a blood sample and say, "Ah-ha! You need this, or you need that."

People have many different kinds of experiences with mental illness. My

doctor posited that at one end of the scale there are those who are suffering from psychological problems generated by relationship or parenting issues or whatever, and at the other end are people who are purely physiologically ill. I seemed to be in the latter category, because at the end of the period of experimentation the doctor finally mixed the right cocktail of medications for me. Miraculously, I was "myself" again, and after that, I never experienced a moment of the old depression.

This past year, I was interviewed by the *Wall Street Journal* for an article about executives who suffer from depression. When the article ran, I didn't get any negative responses. Instead, I received many letters and messages applauding what I had done and telling me, "Yes, I have suffered from depression, too, and have never spoken of it." Some of the most amazing responses I've had were from colleagues and friends whose stories I never would have guessed. They were "acting" at the same time as I was "acting," and we never knew about each other's suffering.

Sarah talks about coping with OCD

THE JOHNSON FAMILY

When I was three, I remember watching the movie *Pinocchio*. When Pinocchio lied, his nose would grow, and eventually he turned into a donkey. I was scared that my nose was going to grow, too. Whenever my parents thought I was lying, they'd joke, "Oh, your nose is growing, Sarah," and I'd scream and cry and run and look in the mirror to make sure it wasn't. My mom also used that old expression, "If you're lying, your tongue will turn black." Whenever she said that to me, I'd have to go to a mirror and check out my tongue.

When I was about thirteen, I started to get real depressed because of all my fears and rituals. I was acting different and taking a much longer time to do things. Mama noticed this and kept questioning me. She said, "If you don't stop this behavior by the time we go to Florida for Christmas, then I'm going to take you to a psychiatrist." I said, "No," because I wasn't sure what was going on. I knew there was something weird about my behavior.

When I became suicidal, my parents had me admitted to a hospital. The first hospital I was in didn't really help because I don't think I wanted to be helped. I was put on medication, but then I got depressed again and had to go back into the hospital. This happened over and over again. It's been almost a year since I was hospitalized, so I guess I'm doing a lot better.

I want people to know that I'm not "mental." There's nothing really wrong with me. This illness is just part of how my brain works. I'm a normal person.

I'm in an OCD chat group on the Internet. I talk to other kids who have this illness, and they understand me. When I talk to my mom and dad, they're like, "Why did you do that?" or, "How can you stop doing that?" It gets so confusing and frustrating. But when I talk to the kids in the chat room about things, they understand and give me advice.

I want other kids who have OCD to know that they're not alone. I was reading my e-mails today from my OCD chat group and one girl wrote that she feels like a freak and an outsider. We're not outsiders. There are so many kids who have OCD. I'm not the only one.

Source: Copyright © 2002 *Nothing to Hide: Mental Illness in the Family* by Peggy Gillespie and Jean J. Beard. Reprinted by permission of The New Press. www.thenewpress.com

Clockwise: Clifford, Mallory, Verna, and Sarah

Sarah and Mallory

Jane speaks about her depression and being the mother of children with mental illnesses

THE SCHNITTER FAMILY

In tree: Emily, Laquetta, and Megan. *Standing:* Paul, Brianna, Jane, Angelina, and Paul Jr.

Psychiatric illnesses run in my family. My father had paranoid schizophrenia. I suffer from a cyclical depression, and five of my seven children have been diagnosed with mental illness.

• • • •

There are times when I say, "This is too hard. What am I doing?" I have to keep reminding myself that although life is harder for me since the three girls arrived, their lives are much easier. When they arrived, they didn't know what cotton candy was or how to swim. They had never even been to a pool or a beach or an amusement park.

My husband and I often come from two different places about our children. Sometimes he feels that they should learn how to control their behavior and that all they need is better discipline. I feel that their behaviors are completely out of their control. Of course, I realize that it's always a mix of the two. Sometimes I tend to be too sympathetic, and he can be too harsh. Over the years, we've kind of blended our approach to them.

• • • •

As for me, my depression comes monthly, almost like severe PMS. When I ovulate, I start to go downhill until my period comes. I have three or four days when I cry all the time and can't function very well. In fact, I'm pretty much incapacitated. After a few days, I feel better.

I teach preschool three afternoons a week. When I was talking with the director a few months after I was hired, I casually mentioned to her that I took Prozac. She kind of panicked and said, "Jane, please don't let any of the parents or the other teachers know about this. If I had known this before I had actually known you personally, I never would have hired you. It would have scared me too much."

Source: Copyright © 2002 *Nothing to Hide: Mental Illness in the Family* by Peggy Gillespie and Jean J. Beard. Reprinted by permission of The New Press. www.thenewpress.com

THE YOUNGBLOOD/ANDREWS FAMILY

Standing: Winzer, Brandon, Vivian. *Seated:* Brandi, Eddie

When I first got sick, I forgot how to wash myself. I got to the point where I couldn't eat or sleep. I even forgot how to write. I didn't know how to do nothing. I was hospitalized in a mental institution, where I was diagnosed with schizophrenia.

I guess there were several reasons for my mental illness. My mother committed suicide in 1969 when she walked into a river and drowned herself. That hurt me terribly. My aunt, who was like a sister to me, died of cancer when she was only thirty. I didn't have much affection or companionship in my life because I was divorced, and I felt all alone. I withdrew, and unless I had to go somewhere, I just stayed in the house. I went to work and to church, but then I would come right back home and go to bed. That was it. I felt an emptiness in my soul, and there wasn't much joy in my life. At times, I still feel a deep loneliness that is hard to describe.

I'm doing pretty good now. I'm able to do all my affairs, like work and driving. I'm also more interactive with people, and I enjoy the kids I work with at Pizza Hut. I tell them, "Y'all keep me young." They be jiving and teasing me.

• • • •

In the midst of all my trials and tribulations, I still tried to serve the Lord. I joined my church when I was eight years old, and I started playing the piano there when I was only twelve. I've continued to play at the church for forty-six years. With the help of God and the mental health system, I'm doing just fine. I like sharing my experiences with others. As the song goes, "If I can help somebody as I pass along, then my living will not be in vain."

Like I say, mental illness is nothing to hide. I'm not "crazy" as some people might say; I simply have a mental illness. I'm going to be all right until God gives me a call.

THE SHEPARD FAMILY

I've heard of people who have lived with mental illness for many years and then they get cancer. Invariably, they say that cancer is easier to deal with than having a mental illness.

• • • •

I spent my fortieth birthday in a mental hospital. I had walked out of work in the middle of the day without telling anybody. On the way home, I stopped at a clinic to get some help. At the time, we had no crisis intervention services in our town, so the clinic staff told me to try to hold out until Monday, when I already had an appointment with a counselor. I didn't make it until Monday. By late Monday night, I was strapped to a bed in the state hospital.

• • • •

Since I've gotten better, I've been doing a lot of public speaking about mental illness. People often wonder how I can go up in front of groups like the Rotary Club and bare my soul. I sometimes wonder if I'm not daring the world to stigmatize me.

• • • •

I've been lucky. My family has been very understanding, and, fortunately,

Standing: Betty Lou, Rachel, and John. *Seated:* Muriel and Ruth

Betty Lou and I are still together. Many marriages break up when someone in the family has a mental illness. Everyone has their breaking point, and some people can take more than others can.

• • • •

Now I work in several group homes and in a homeless shelter for the mentally ill. I've heard that some mental health agencies have a rule against identifying yourself as a consumer when you're working with other consumers. I figured it would be easier to get close to the residents if they knew that I'd been through what they're going through. But the other day, I was talking with one of the ladies who is

new at the group home, and I had the feeling that it wouldn't be too wise to let her know that I'm a consumer. I didn't think she would appreciate being taken care of by another consumer.

I still don't have a whole lot of self-confidence, and I'm still introverted and bashful about approaching people. I know there are lots of people who are better at interacting with other people than I am. I still worry that I'm going to do something wrong, but all in all, it's been very satisfying to help others.

CHAPTER 10

Personality Disorders

My first interaction with Harold Morrill involved his phone call to schedule an intake session. Prior to initial sessions, it is common for prospective clients to ask about my clinical approach and to inquire about such issues as billing and scheduling. Although I was expecting such questions, I was not prepared for the kind of encounter we had in that 20-minute telephone exchange. Harold began the call by stating, "Dr. Tobin, I want to begin therapy with you as soon as possible. I've heard about your reputation from several people, so I know that you are probably the most skilled and sensitive therapist in the area." After speaking on the phone for only 10 or 15 minutes, Harold enthusiastically exclaimed, "Yes, you are exactly the kind of therapist I've been looking for. You seem like a person who is genuinely caring and would be able to understand all that I've been through in this miserable life. Please, please take me as your patient!"

As I listened to Harold's lush praise, I had to resist the temptation to be flattered, realizing that this kind of idealization is often a signal that there will be trouble in the relationship later on. I could think of a dozen clients whom I had treated over the years who began therapy with similar idealizing words but whose emotional responsiveness to me was at the other end of the continuum after only a session or two. I couldn't be sure, of course, if Harold would show such extremes in his dealings with me, but I knew that it would be important for me to watch out for this possibility. As a matter of fact, I caught a glimpse of this style of splitting as I explained to Harold that I had no openings until the following week. He responded with a tone of annoyance: "Busy little bee, aren't you?" Rather than take offense at Harold's comment, I tried to assure him that I was committed to working with him.

When I approached Harold Morrill in the waiting room, I immediately noticed the large gold loop dangling from his nostrils. His appearance caught my attention in other ways as well. Perhaps it was his shaggy, unkempt look or the fact that he appeared to be so much younger than 29, which was the age listed on his intake form.

Harold's initial description of his distress gave me a first glimpse into his confused state: "I feel lost and empty. I can't stand being alone, and yet I'm furious that people can't accept me for what I am. Sometimes I just want to kill myself to make other people feel some of the pain I feel all the time!" He then shared his long history of emotional problems—a life he characterized as filled with depression, anxiety, irritability, and uncontrollable anger. He spoke of the "emotional roller coaster" of his life, which had left others, as well as himself, feeling bewildered.

As Harold spoke of his dealings with other people, I found myself affected by the intensity of his interactions with others. When I asked about his numerous job changes, he described a series of bitter disputes with co-workers, most of which culminated in his abrupt departures from jobs, either because Harold was fired or because he stormed out in anger. In each situation, Harold rationalized his sudden departure by placing blame on an "airhead" supervisor or a "screwed up" company. To compensate for what he perceived to be his unjust treatment at each terminated job, Harold typically stole items from the workplace. Some items were relatively inexpensive office supplies, but Harold boasted that on one occasion he walked off with a laptop computer. He laughed as he explained, "Not only did they lose the computer, but I managed to walk away with some important inventory information that existed only on this computer. Guess they should've made a backup, and I guess they'll learn that it's a good idea to treat their employees better than they treated me."

His intimate relationships were similarly unstable. Moving from partner to partner every few months, Harold had a long string of relationships, most of which ended when he became enraged over seemingly small matters. Often, these episodes of rage were followed by violent outbursts. In discussing his most recent lover, for instance, Harold told me gleefully about the time he punctured the tires on her car in a fit of rage when she told him that she planned to take a vacation without him. Harold also described an experience during this incident that left him feeling a bit frightened that things were really getting out of control—he believed that a voice in his thoughts was telling him that his partner was a "she-demon who should be punished."

Although recognizing that desperate behaviors such as those had chased away previous lovers, Harold dreaded the pain of not being in an intimate relationship. Driven to panic and despair by these feelings of emptiness, Harold found himself rushing into new relationships with people whom he instantaneously idealized in his mind. Each time, the infatuation quickly deteriorated into vicious animosity.

When I asked Harold about his sexual orientation, he acknowledged that he was not sure whether he preferred intimate relationships with men or with women. He explained his ambivalence by stating that the gender of his partner was less important than was the person's ability to make a commitment to him.

After listening to Harold describe his chaotic and unsatisfying relationships, I became increasingly concerned about his ability to commit himself to a psychotherapy relationship. I also felt concerned about his capacity to act in abusive ways toward his therapist. My concerns intensified as Harold told me about his three prior experiences with psychotherapy, each of which he ended abruptly because of the "incompetence" of the professionals who were treating him. When I asked whether he could make a commitment to long-term therapy, Harold tried to assure me that he was now "ready" to get the help he needed to become happier in life.

Sarah Tobin, PhD

Think about a few people you know, and then think of four or five adjectives that describe each of their personalities. You might describe a well-adjusted friend as enthusiastic, talkative, pleasant, warm, and cooperative. Another acquaintance annoys everyone, because all she seems to care about is herself. You might describe her as egocentric, manipulative, selfish, and attention-seeking. These adjectives may not convey the subtle distinctions between these two people, but they give you a sense of the fundamental characteristics of each person—what psychologists call personality traits. A **personality trait** is an enduring pattern of perceiving, relating to, and thinking about the environment and others, a pattern that is ingrained in the matrix of the individual's psychological makeup. In this chapter, you will read about people whose patterns of behavior are so rigid and maladaptive that they experience significant psychological problems and interpersonal difficulties.

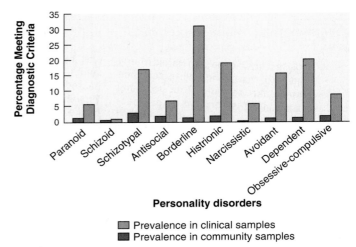

FIGURE 10.1 The lifetime prevalence of personality disorders in the general U.S. population and those in clinical samples.

Source: From M. T. Tsuang, M. Tohen, and G. E. P. Zuhner in *Textbook in Psychiatric Epidemiology*. Copyright © 1995. This material is used by permission of John Wiley & Sons, Inc.

The Nature of Personality Disorders

A **personality disorder** involves a long-lasting maladaptive pattern of inner experience and behavior, dating back to adolescence or young adulthood, that is manifested in at least two of the following areas: (1) cognition, (2) affectivity, (3) interpersonal functioning, and (4) impulse control. This inflexible pattern is evident in various personal and social situations, and it causes distress or impairment. The personality disorders represent a collection of diverse and complex patterns of behavior. The expression of psychological disturbance is quite different for each, yet the problems that people with personality disorders experience are present every day and in most of their interactions with others. Whether their problems involve excessive dependency, overwhelming fear of intimacy, intense worry, exploitative behavior, or uncontrollable rage, these individuals are usually unhappy and maladjusted. They become caught in a vicious cycle in which their disturbed personal style alienates others, thus intensifying their problematic styles of relating. Because personality disorders involve the whole fabric of an individual's being, clinicians typically perceive them as being the most challenging of the psychological disorders to treat.

In evaluating whether an individual has a personality disorder, a clinician considers the person's life history. Have the person's problems been long-term and pervasive throughout life? Or are they related to a particular event or relationship? If the problems appear to be deeply entrenched and long-standing, characteristic ways of feeling and acting, this person may have a personality disorder.

Consider a sensitive young woman who worries about whether the co-workers at her new job like her or not; she fears that they may be making critical comments about her work when she is out of the office. Assuming this is a one-time occurrence, she would not be considered to have a personality

disorder. By contrast, if the woman has lifelong concerns that others might talk about her, ridicule her, harm her, or try to stand in the way of her succeeding, this would be considered a rigid and maladaptive pattern indicative of a personality disorder.

As you can see in Figure 10.1, the lifetime prevalence of personality disorders in the general U.S. population ranges from 1 to 3 percent, with higher prevalence in people seen in clinical settings. However, estimates of prevalence vary according to age and sociodemographic factors. In one national survey of more than 500 adults, personality disorders were found to be diagnosed in younger individuals, students, and unemployed homemakers (Ekselius, Tillfors, Furmark, & Fredrikson, 2001). The prevalence of personality disorders is higher among individuals who have alcohol and drug abuse disorders. A national sample of over 43,000 individuals conducted in the United States in 2001–02 revealed 12-month prevalence rates of 26 percent among those with an alcohol use disorder and 48 percent with a current drug use disorder (Grant et al., 2004).

Diagnosing a personality disorder is difficult because many personality disorders have similar features (Grant et al., 2005). In addition, the U.S. prevalence study (Ekselius et al., 2001) found that there are high comorbidity rates of certain personality disorders. Although the authors of the *DSM-IV* used large-scale empirical studies to provide clearly delineated diagnostic criteria (Widiger & Shea, 1991), the reliability and validity of personality disorder diagnoses remain matters of concern, and specific criteria are defined in a variety of ways. For example, the *DSM-IV-TR* specifies "inappropriate, intense anger or difficulty controlling anger" as a criterion for diagnosing borderline personality disorder, Harold Morrill's condition. As you might imagine, one clinician might see outrageous acts of revenge (puncturing tires and stealing a computer) as expressions of inappropriate anger, while another clinician might see these behaviors as criminal behaviors that would relate more to a diagnosis of antisocial personality disorder. Further complicating issues of diagnosis is the fact that an individual may have an Axis I disorder that interacts with the symptoms of the personality disorder. What if Harold Morrill also suffers from a severe depression? It might be difficult to determine whether certain symptoms are due to Harold's depression or to long-lasting characteristics of his personality. Yet another problem is the fact that individuals tend to change over the adult years, as they adapt their personality traits to various life demands. As the symptoms change, the individuals may no longer meet the diagnostic criteria for the disorder. For example, people who are exploitative and impulsive during youth and the middle years of life may change as they develop a more mature understanding of the negative consequences of their behavior. We will discuss age-related shifts in personality disorder symptoms in more detail later in this chapter.

As we discussed in Chapter 2, considerable controversy exists over whether personality disorders should be conceptualized in terms of dimensions. In arguing in favor of a dimensional approach to personality disorders, some researchers point to the fact that the most commonly assigned Axis II diagnosis is "personality disorder not otherwise specified." This highlights the point that clinicians are much more likely to encounter clients with a composite of symptoms and characteristics which do not fit neatly into the *DSM-IV-TR* categories (Trull & Durrett, 2005). At present, though, the categorical system is being used and forms the basis for organizing this chapter. The *DSM-IV-TR* includes a set of separate diagnoses grouped into three clusters based on shared characteristics. Cluster A comprises paranoid, schizoid, and schizotypal

Ted Bundy, one of the most notorious serial killers in the United States, was an example of an extreme antisocial personality disorder. Some clinicians still use the term psychopath or sociopath to describe a person with this behavior.

personality disorders, which share the features of odd and eccentric behavior. Cluster B includes antisocial, borderline, histrionic, and narcissistic personality disorders. People with these disorders are overdramatic, emotional, and erratic or unpredictable. In Cluster C are avoidant, dependent, and obsessive-compulsive personality disorders. These are linked because they involve anxious and fearful behaviors. We will begin our discussion with Cluster B disorders—specifically, antisocial and borderline personality disorders. For each of these disorders, there is a relatively specific set of theoretical perspectives and treatment approaches. They are also the most extensively researched. Therefore, we will devote full sections to these two personality disorders before going on to describe the disorders that fall into Clusters A and C.

Antisocial Personality Disorder

When you hear a news story about a shocking crime in which the perpetrator has a long history of criminal behavior, you may wonder whether that individual has any sense of morality. Chances are that the people who commit these crimes have personality traits consistent with a diagnosis of **antisocial personality disorder,** which is characterized by a lack of regard for society's moral or legal standards.

Characteristics of Antisocial Personality Disorder

Although you may never have heard the label "antisocial personality disorder," you may have heard of people called

---

Diagnostic Features of Personality Disorder

- An enduring pattern of inner experience and behavior that differs markedly from what is expected in the person's culture. This pattern is manifested in at least two of the following areas:
    - Cognition—ways of perceiving self, other people, and events
    - Affectivity—range, intensity, and appropriateness of emotional expression
    - Interpersonal functioning
    - Impulse control
- The pattern is inflexible and pervasive across a range of personal and social situations.
- The pattern causes distress or impairment.
- The pattern is stable and of long duration, with an onset that can be traced back to adolescence or early adulthood.

When Dennis Rader was arrested in 2005 for the murder of 10 people over the course of several decades, the world was shocked not only by the gruesomeness of his murders but by his complete lack of emotion in describing his crimes. Lack of remorse is one of the most common criteria for a diagnosis of antisocial personality disorder.

psychopaths or sociopaths, terms commonly used to refer to people with a pattern of traits that would currently be labeled antisocial personality disorder. In 1801, Philippe Pinel first recognized this disorder as a form of madness in which the individual exhibited impulsive and even destructive behaviors while maintaining rational thought ("la folie raisonnante"). Several decades later, this disorder was labeled *moral insanity* (Millon et al., 2000).

Widespread publicity still is given to this disorder, particularly when it is reflected in violent crime. Consider the case of Ted Bundy, who sexually assaulted and ruthlessly murdered several dozen women during the years 1974 to 1978. Despite his brutal behavior, Bundy was able to deceive people with his charm. He showed no concern for right or wrong, or any remorse for his crimes.

The typical case of antisocial personality disorder is far less extreme than that of serial killers, such as Ted Bundy, yet all share a lack of concern for what is right or wrong. People with this disorder wreak havoc in our society, and for this reason they have been the focus of a great deal of research. Antisocial personality disorder is disturbingly common, with an estimated lifetime prevalence of 4.5 percent of the adult males and .8 percent of the adult females in the United States (Robins & Regier, 1991).

The diagnosis of antisocial behavior used today in the *DSM-IV-TR* has its origins in the work of Hervey Cleckley, whose 1941 book, *The Mask of Sanity,* represented the first scientific attempt to list and categorize the behaviors of the "psychopathic" personality, a work that appeared in its most recent edition more than 30 years later (Cleckley, 1976).

Cleckley developed a set of criteria for **psychopathy,** a personality type characterized by a cluster of traits that constitutes the core of what is now called antisocial personality disorder. He outlined more than a dozen characteristics of psychopathy, which have provided the foundation for current diagnostic criteria. Cleckley's characteristics of psychopathy include lack of remorse or shame for harmful acts committed to others; poor judgment and failure to learn from experience; extreme egocentricity and incapacity for love; lack of emotional responsiveness to others; impulsivity ("fantastic and uninviting behavior"); absence of "nervousness"; and unreliability, untruthfulness, and insincerity. Cleckley used the term *semantic dementia* to capture the psychopath's inability to react appropriately to expressions of emotionality. Cloaking these socially offensive behaviors is a veneer of superficial charm and seeming intelligence.

Cleckley's notion of psychopathy remains a key concept in descriptions of antisocial personality disorder. Building on Cleckley's work, Canadian psychologist Robert D. Hare developed an assessment instrument known as the Psychopathy Check List (PCL-R) (Hare, 1997), which has two factors: (1) core psychopathic personality traits and (2) antisocial lifestyle. The core personality traits include glibness and superficial charm, a grandiose sense of self-worth, a tendency toward pathological lying, a lack of empathy for others, a lack of remorse, and an unwillingness to accept responsibility for one's own actions. The antisocial-lifestyle trait revolves around impulsivity, a characteristic that can lead to behaviors expressed in an unstable lifestyle, juvenile delinquency, early behavioral problems, lack of realistic long-term goals, and a need for constant stimulation (Hare & Neumann, 2005). There is also evidence to support Cleckley's notion that psychopaths are intelligent in

Much research has focused on the relationship between juvenile delinquency and antisocial personality disorder.

Mini Case

ANTISOCIAL PERSONALITY DISORDER

Tommy was the leader of a teenage street gang that was reputed to be the most vicious in the neighborhood. He grew up in a chaotic home atmosphere, his mother having lived with a series of violent men who were heavily involved in drug dealing and prostitution. At the age of 18, Tommy was jailed for the brutal mugging and stabbing of an older adult woman. This was the first in a long series of arrests for offenses ranging from drug trafficking to car thefts to counterfeiting. At one point, between jail terms, he met a woman at a bar and married her the next day. Two weeks later, he beat her when she complained about his incessant drinking and involvement with shady characters. He left her when she became pregnant, and he refused to pay child support. From his vantage point now as a drug trafficker and leader of a child prostitution ring, Tommy shows no regret for what he has done, claiming that life has "sure given me a bum steer."

Diagnostic Features

This diagnosis is assigned to adults, who as children showed evidence of conduct disorder and who, from the age of 15, have shown a pervasive pattern of disregard for and violation of the rights of others, as indicated by three or more of the following:

- Repeated engagement in behaviors that are grounds for arrest
- Deceitfulness, such as lying, using false identities, or conning others for personal profit or pleasure
- Impulsivity, or failure to plan ahead
- Irritability and aggressiveness, such as repeated fights or assaults
- Reckless disregard for the safety of self or others
- Consistent irresponsibility, such as repeated failure to keep a job or honor financial obligations
- Lack of remorse, such as being indifferent to or rationalizing one's hurtful or dishonest behavior

---

terms of their verbal abilities and their ability to apply their intelligence to practical problems (Salekin, Neumann, Leistico, & Zalot, 2004).

The diagnostic criteria in the *DSM-IV-TR* go beyond the central traits of psychopathy and include the behavioral aspects of the disorder as reflected in a long list of chronic disreputable or manipulative behaviors. Consequently, not all individuals with psychopathic personalities meet the diagnostic criteria for antisocial personality disorder. These criteria involve a pervasive disregard for the rights of others as shown by such behaviors as unlawfulness, deceitfulness, and impulsivity. Individuals with this disorder may behave impulsively, aggressively, and recklessly without showing signs of remorse. At times, they may feign remorse with the intention of extricating themselves from a difficult situation. Rather than being outwardly aggressive, as indicated above, some are "smooth talkers," who are able to get what they want by presenting themselves in a favorable light. For example, a man with this disorder may persuade others to give him money by using manipulative sales tactics, or he may play on their sympathy by convincing them that he is a victim of circumstances and, in the process, get them to do something special for him.

It is important to distinguish between antisocial personality disorder and **adult antisocial behavior,** which refers to illegal or immoral behavior, such as stealing, lying, and cheating. A further distinction should be made between the terms *antisocial* and *criminal*. The term *criminal* has meaning in the legal system but is not a psychological concept. Nevertheless, many individuals who are sent to prison meet the psychological criteria for antisocial personality disorder. Estimates within prison populations of individuals with this disorder range from 40 to 75 percent (Hare, 1993; Widiger & Corbitt, 1995). Although some people tend to think only of men when discussing antisocial personality disorder, it is important to recognize that a significant number of women also have this condition, and many of them spend lengthy prison terms as convicted felons (Jordan, Schlenger, Fairbank, & Caddell, 1996). However, not all individuals with antisocial personality disorder are criminals. For many, the qualities of an antisocial personality disorder are reflected in acts that would not be considered violations of the law, such as job problems, promiscuity, and aggressiveness.

As is the case with all personality disorders, the problematic characteristics of people with antisocial personality disorder are enduring. That is, their problems begin in childhood and continue throughout most of their adulthood. In one fascinating study, researchers who assessed individuals at the age of 3 and again at the age of 21 found that undercontrolled young children (i.e., children who are impulsive, restless, and distractible) are more likely to meet the diagnostic criteria for antisocial personality disorder and to be involved in crime as adults (Caspi, Moffitt, Newman, & Silva 1996). As you will read in Chapter 11, problems with impulse control are common among children with conduct disorder, a condition that predisposes young people to develop antisocial personality disorder. Children and adolescents with conduct disorder get in trouble at home, in school, and in their neighborhoods. The more frequent and diverse the childhood antisocial acts are, the more likely the individual is to have a lifelong pattern of antisocial behavior (Lynam, 1997).

Although we have a good understanding of predisposing factors, we know less about the long-term prospects of individuals with antisocial personality disorder. Crime statistics suggest a reduction of antisocial behavior with age (Moran, 1999). The number of homicides committed by people over 50 is dramatically lower than the homicide rates of people under the age of 34 (Bureau of Justice Statistics, 2005). Overall, the rates for violent crime drop from approximately 1,000 per 100,000 in the population from the ages of 35–39 to 93 for people 60 and older (Federal

Bureau of Investigation, 2004). About 1 percent of all prisoners, federal and state, are over the age of 65; 2 percent of state and 6 percent of federal prisoners are 55 to 64 (Bureau of Justice Statistics, 2000).

The components of psychopathy involving impulsivity, social deviance, and antisocial behavior are less prominent in prison inmates who are older than the midforties (Harpur & Hare, 1994). Perhaps antisocial individuals experience "burnout" or have just become more adept at avoiding detection. Or perhaps some of the more extreme cases are eliminated from the population, because these people are killed or arrested in the course of their criminal activities.

It has been hypothesized that aging brings with it a reduction of Cluster B traits of acting out, impulsivity, and extreme behaviors; this is referred to as the **maturation hypothesis** (Segal, Coolidge, & Rosowsky, 2000). People with antisocial and the other Cluster B disorders, according to this view, become better able to manage their behaviors as they age. Supporting this hypothesis was a longitudinal study of men from adolescence to middle adulthood; a large majority of men decreased in personality traits related to antisocial behavior through midlife (Morizot & Le Blanc, 2005).

Theories and Treatment of Antisocial Personality Disorder

As you have seen, antisocial personality disorder represents a deeply entrenched pattern of behavior, with wide-ranging effects on both the individual and the people with whom the individual comes into contact. In this section, we will consider the most compelling explanations for the development of this personality disorder. It is important to remember that some of these investigations pertain to criminals, who may or may not have been diagnosed specifically with antisocial personality disorder.

Biological Perspectives   When you hear about a terrible crime, such as a vicious mugging or ruthless murder, you probably don't presume that a biologically based disorder caused the perpetrator to commit this act. You may be surprised, then, to learn that there are a number of biological hypotheses about criminal behavior. Various brain abnormalities are cited as possible causes of antisocial personality disorder, including defects in the prefrontal lobes of the cerebral cortex (Goethals et al., 2005), areas of the brain involved in planning future activities and in considering the moral implications of one's actions. In tasks that require interpreting affective stimuli, people with high psychopathy scores show altered responsiveness in parts of the brain responsible for interpreting emotion (Gordon, Baird, & End, 2004). MRI studies also reveal that they have difficulty processing conceptually abstract verbal information (Kiehl et al., 2004). Deficits in emotional processing are evident even in juveniles, supporting the notion that these are stable components of the psychopathy dimension that underlies antisocial personality disorder (Lynam & Gudonis, 2005).

These abnormalities in the brain may have genetic causes. It has been observed for decades that criminal behavior runs in families. As with other behaviors found to show such a pattern, scientists have questioned whether antisocial behavior is learned or is genetically acquired. We will turn next to adoption studies and the studies of family inheritance patterns used in research on criminal behavior as clues to understanding the roots of antisocial personality disorder.

Studies of family inheritance patterns show that there is a modest heritability of criminality and psychopathy (Kendler, Davis, & Kessler, 1997). Strong evidence in favor of the inheritance of antisocial personality disorder comes from a study of more than 3,200 male twin pairs (Lyons et al., 1995). The researchers assessed the relative contributions of sharing an environment and sharing the same genotype. Although the environment seemed to play a role in determining the antisocial behavior of these people as juveniles (under the age of 15), the expression of antisocial behaviors in the adults reflected the influence of inheritance. In other words, adults who engage in antisocial behavior are expressing a genetic predisposition. Antisocial behavior in juveniles, on the other hand, reflects the influence of external factors, such as peers and home life.

Although the study of twins provides an important perspective, adoption studies are able to control more effectively for the influence of shared environments on estimates of heritability. In a study of almost 200 male and female adoptees who had been separated shortly after birth from their biological parents, researchers found that the children of parents with documented antisocial personality disorder were more likely to develop this disorder, particularly if they were then raised in an adverse adoptive home environment. However, the children without a biological predisposition for the disorder did not develop symptoms, even if they were raised in similarly harsh settings (Cadoret et al., 1995).

On the basis of these and other studies, experts have concluded that genetics can explain over one half of the gene-environment equation, with one heritability estimate reaching as high as 56 percent (O'Connor et al., 1998). People who are genetically predisposed to antisocial personality disorder may be particularly vulnerable to family dysfunction, supporting the notion of gene-environment interactions (Button et al., 2005).

Psychological Perspectives   Closely related to the biological perspective is the hypothesis that antisocial personality disorder is due to neuropsychological deficits reflected in abnormal patterns of learning and attention. Following along the lines of Cleckley's characterization of the psychopath as lacking emotional reactivity was a pivotal study conducted by David Lykken (1957), in which psychopathic individuals failed to show the normal response of anxiety when they were subjected to aversive stimuli. Lykken's hypothesis that the psychopath is unable to "feel" fear or anxiety (Lykken, 1995) has continued to gather support (Day & Wong, 1996; Patrick,

Bradley, & Lang, 1993; Patrick, Cuthbert, & Lang, 1994). Studies of function of the hippocampus, a brain area involved in learning, suggest that there may be a biological basis for this psychological deficit. In a sample of habitually violent offenders, high psychopathy checklist (PCL-R) scores were strongly related to hippocampal brain volumes (Laakso et al., 2001). Further evidence in support of this notion comes from studies showing amygdala dysfunction in antisocial men who were especially aggressive. The amygdala is a part of the brain involved in processing emotion that plays a role in aversive conditioning (Blair, 2004).

The fearlessness hypothesis has evolved into a more general proposition called the response modulation hypothesis, which proposes that psychopaths are unable to process any information that is not relevant to their primary goals (Bernstein, Newman, Wallace, & Luh, 2000). According to the response modulation hypothesis, psychopaths are able to learn to avoid punishment when this is their main goal. However, if their attention is focused elsewhere, they do not pay attention to information that would allow them to avoid aversive consequences. This hypothesis would explain many aspects of the core psychopathic traits Cleckley identified, such as the inability to think about someone else's needs when one is focused on one's own personal interests. It might also explain the lack of remorse when causing pain to victims.

Another psychological perspective based on social cognitive theory regards low self-esteem as a causal factor in antisocial personality disorder. As children, people who develop this disorder feel the need to prove their competence by engaging in aggressive acts (Lochman & Dodge, 1994).

Sociocultural Perspectives Sociocultural perspectives on antisocial personality disorder focus on factors in the family, early environment, and socialization experiences that can lead individuals to develop a psychopathic lifestyle. It is clear that the transmission of antisocial personality disorder occurs over multiple generations. Children who are aggressive themselves are more likely to fail in school, become involved in high-risk behavior including adolescent pregnancy, and then place their own offspring at risk due to poverty and poor parenting (Serbin & Karp, 2004). One of the landmark studies investigating the role of early life influences was a 30-year follow-up study of juvenile delinquents carried out by Washington University psychologist Lee Robins (1966). Although it is commonly assumed that children of divorce later develop problems because of a lack of adequate discipline, Robins found that it is not the divorce itself but disharmony between parents that precede the child's development of antisocial behavior. According to Robins, this may be because the type of parents who are likely to argue excessively, especially fathers, may have psychological difficulties, including antisocial tendencies.

In the research by Robins and others on the effect on a child of different kinds of childrearing, inconsistent discipline appears to be especially problematic. When parents vacillate between unreasonable harshness and extreme laxity, they send confusing messages to the child about what is right and what is wrong, or what is acceptable and what is unacceptable. Children with such parents fail to make a connection between their actions, bad or good, and the consequences.

The relationship between childhood abuse and the development of antisocial personality disorder has become the focus of some very important research. Luntz and Widom (1994) tracked more than 400 individuals with substantiated histories of having been abused or neglected during childhood. When they interviewed and assessed these people in

One of the most graphic expressions of antisocial behavior is reflected in the wanton violence that has become all too common in American schools.

Inmates participating in group therapy, such as the Lifeline Recovery Program, confront each other while openly admitting their own problems and maladaptive behaviors.

early adulthood, they found that the experiences of childhood victimization played a major role in influencing the likelihood that they would become antisocial adults. In a related study, Widom found that adults who had been neglected during childhood went on to have 50 percent more arrests for violent crimes than did matched subjects. Even more startling was the finding that physical abuse during childhood led to a rate that was double that of those in the comparison group. Malnutrition in early life may serve as another risk factor for the development of antisocial personality disorder. In a study of children tested from ages 3 to 17, those who suffered from poor nutrition at the age of 3 showed more aggressiveness and motor activity as they grew up; by the age of 17 they had a higher likelihood of conduct disorder (Liu, Raine, Venables, & Mednick, 2004).

In summing up the research on the impact of life experiences on the development of sociopathic behavior, Lykken (2000) views many of the parents of sociopathic individuals to have been overburdened, incompetent, and sociopathic themselves. To compensate for parental inadequacy, greater attention could be given to placement in foster care, group homes, and boarding schools. The suggestion has been raised that parents should be "licensed," or at least given greater training in childrearing, especially when dealing with high-risk children.

Treatment of Antisocial Personality Disorder From our discussion of antisocial personality disorder, you could conclude that people with this disorder do not change easily. For that matter, they are unlikely to seek professional help voluntarily,

because they see no reason to change (Hare, 1993; Widiger, 1998). If they do see a clinician, it is often because treatment is mandated by a court order. Furthermore, by attending therapy sessions, the client may simply be attempting to impress a judge or a probation officer of a serious intent to reform. In such a situation, the clinician may have difficulty knowing whether or not to believe the client. Without giving up on the client or operating on the basis of preconceived biases, the clinician must be careful not to become unduly optimistic.

Given the difficulty of working with people with antisocial personality disorder, how can a clinician achieve a satisfactory treatment goal? Experts maintain that these people change their behavior only when they realize that what they have done is wrong. Therefore, the goal of therapy, ironically, is not to help these individuals feel better but, rather, to get them to feel worse about themselves and their situation. To do so, the clinician must initially adopt a confrontational approach, showing ostensible disbelief regarding the client's presumed fabrications, while continually reflecting back to the client the selfish and self-defeating nature of such behavior. Group therapy can be helpful in this process, because feedback from peers, who cannot be easily deceived, can have a forceful impact.

When the therapeutic process is "successful," the client begins to feel remorse and guilt about his or her behavior, followed by feelings of hopelessness and despondency, which, it is hoped, will lead to behavior change. Keep in mind, though, that such a "positive" outcome is extremely difficult to achieve.

Borderline Personality Disorder

The names of most of the personality disorders include words that convey the essence of the disorder, such as "antisocial" and "paranoid." What does it mean to be "borderline"? In the

The movie *Fatal Attraction* portrayed many of the symptoms and behaviors associated with borderline personality disorder, such as this scene following a suicidal gesture of Alex in response to her rage about being abandoned.

Mini Case

BORDERLINE PERSONALITY DISORDER

Lisa is a 28-year-old account executive with a long history of interpersonal problems. At the office, her co-workers see her as being intensely moody and unpredictable. On some days, she is pleasant and high-spirited, but on others she exhibits uncontrollable anger. People are often struck by her inconsistent attitudes toward her supervisors. She vacillates between idealizing them and devaluing them. For example, she may boast about the "brilliance" of her supervisor one day, only to deliver a burning criticism the next day. Her co-workers keep their distance from her, because they have become annoyed with her constant demands for attention. She has also gained a reputation in the office for her promiscuous involvements with a variety of people, male and female. On several occasions, she has been reprimanded for becoming inappropriately involved in the personal lives of her clients. One day, after losing one of her accounts, she became so distraught that she slashed her wrists. This incident prompted her supervisor to insist that Lisa obtain professional help.

Diagnostic Features

This diagnosis is assigned to people who show recurrent impulsivity and a pervasive pattern of instability of interpersonal relationships, self-image, and affects, as indicated by five or more of the following:

- Frantic efforts to avoid real or imagined abandonment
- A pattern of unstable and intense interpersonal relationships characterized by changes between idealizing and devaluing others
- Identity disturbance—unstable self-image or sense of self
- Impulsivity in at least two areas, such as spending, sex, substance abuse, and reckless driving
- Recurrent suicidal behavior, gestures, or threats or self-mutilating behavior
- Emotional instability, such as intense episodes of sadness, irritability, or anxiety, usually lasting a few hours and sometimes several days
- Chronic feelings of emptiness
- Inappropriate, intense anger or difficulty controlling anger, such as frequent displays of temper, constant anger, or recurrent physical fights
- Occasional stress-related paranoid thinking or dissociative symptoms

---

current *DSM-IV-TR* terminology, **borderline personality disorder** is characterized by a pervasive pattern of instability, most evident in relationships, mood, and sense of identity (Burgmer, Jessen, & Freyberger, 2000). Because this is a somewhat elusive diagnosis, the authors of the *DSM-IV-TR* have specified observable behaviors and symptoms that characterize the disorder.

Characteristics of Borderline Personality Disorder

When the term *borderline* first became popular in psychiatry, it was used as a catchall for the most difficult and treatment-resistant clients (Stern, 1938). These individuals were felt to be functioning somewhere at the "border" between neurosis and psychosis, on the fringes of schizophrenia (Knight, 1953). Despite the vagueness of the concept of borderline, the term remained in use because it described a subgroup of clients that did not seem to fit into the existing diagnostic categories. Efforts to clarify and define the nature of the disorder continued through the 1980s. Some researchers have maintained that borderline personality disorder is a variant of schizophrenia or mood disorder, or possibly a hybrid. However, by the time the *DSM-IV* was in its final stages of preparation, most experts had come to regard it as a singular personality disorder (Berelowitz & Tarnopolsky, 1993).

The female character Alex in the movie *Fatal Attraction* is a good example of what a person with borderline personality is

like. In a very dramatic scene in the movie, Alex becomes overwhelmingly distraught following a one-night sexual encounter, and she slashes her wrists at the moment her sexual partner is preparing to leave. In the weeks that follow, Alex obsessively pursues this man. Her intense emotionality and rage terrify him, as she acts out many outrageous and disturbing behaviors, such as boiling the pet rabbit that belongs to the man's family. The intensity of this relationship, even one so brief, gives you a glimpse into a central characteristic of people with this disorder—unstable interpersonal relationships.

People with borderline personality disorder often experience a distinct kind of depression that is characterized by feelings of emptiness and variable negative emotionality (Southwick, Yehuda, & Giller, 1995; Westen & Cohen, 1993). Although they rarely go as far as to harass other people, they tend to be deeply affected by interpersonal incidents that most other people would let pass. It is common for people with this disorder to form suddenly intense, demanding relationships with others and to perceive other people as being all good or all bad—a phenomenon referred to as **splitting.** The inappropriate intensity of their relationships results in recurrent experiences of distress and rage. In fact, anger and hostility are enduring characteristics found in many people with this disorder.

In addition to having disturbed relationships, people with borderline personality disorder are often confused about their own **identity,** or concept of who they are. Even after they have passed through the customary time of identity questioning in adolescence, they are unsure of what they want out of life and, at a deeper level, lack a firm grasp of their sense of self. Their uncertainty about who they are may be expressed in sudden shifts in life choices, such as career plans, values, goals, and types of friends. This identity confusion may reach a point at which they become unclear about the boundaries between themselves and others. For example, in close relationships, they may have difficulty distinguishing between their own feelings and the feelings of the other person. Other identity problems appear in the area of sexual orientation; these individuals may shift between identifying as homosexual or heterosexual, perhaps going through phases in which they abruptly redefine their own sexuality (Munich, 1993).

Chronic feelings of boredom lead people with borderline personality disorder to seek stimulation. In part, the drama of their relationships reflects this search for intense emotional experiences. In their attempt to fend off boredom, they may engage in impulsive behaviors, such as promiscuity, careless spending, reckless driving, binge eating, substance abuse, or shoplifting. The excitement from these activities makes them feel alive. Furthermore, their moods are as unstable as their behavior. They may vacillate between extreme emotional states, one day feeling on top of the world and the next feeling depressed, anxious, and irritable.

The extremes of feelings that people with borderline personality disorder experience may drive them precipitously into a state of suicidal thinking and self-injurious behavior. As was illustrated in the discussion in Chapter 8, p. 268, sometimes they are not intent on killing themselves, and their behavior—called **parasuicide**—is considered a gesture to get attention from family, a lover, or professionals. In other cases, they may actually hurt themselves with a knife or razor in an act of self-directed aggression. For people with borderline personality disorder, such behavior sometimes serves as a test of whether they are actually alive, a concept that most people take for granted but one that becomes a source of uncertainty for these individuals. The sight of blood and the physical pain reassure them that their bodies have substance. Some of these individuals do not experience pain while cutting themselves. These individuals seem to constitute a subtype of borderline personality disorder involving especially severe symptoms of depression, anxiety, impulsiveness, and dissociation; furthermore, many in this high-risk group have histories of early abuse. It is not surprising that the intensity of emotional pain leads to serious suicide attempts (Kemperman, Russ, & Shearin, 1997; Russ, Shearin, Clakin, & Harrison, 1993). The risk of suicide is especially high in individuals with deficient problem-solving ability who may see suicide as the only way out of a difficult situation (Kehrer & Linehan, 1996), and is also especially high in borderline disordered individuals with poor social adjustment (Kelly et al., 2000).

Many individuals with borderline personality disorder seem intensely angry much of the time. Even without provocation, they fly into a fury. A friend's seemingly innocent comment may cause them to lash out sarcastically or to become bitter for an unreasonable length of time. A common trigger for their rage is the feeling that they have been neglected or abandoned by a lover or another important person. At times, their intense anger may lead them to express physical violence against others. After their angry outbursts, they may feel ashamed and guilty and become convinced of their inherent evil nature.

Stress is particularly problematic for people with borderline personality disorder. During stressful experiences, their vulnerability intensifies, causing them to feel highly suspicious and untrusting of others to the point of being paranoid. They may also develop dissociative symptoms, such as feeling disconnected from others and even their own conscious self.

Although many aspects of their functioning are disturbed, most people with this disorder can manage the responsibilities of everyday life. Some are actually successful in various contexts (for instance, the character Alex in *Fatal Attraction* had a well-paid, important job). However, for many there is a constant undercurrent of interpersonal conflict and the risk that their unpredictability, dependency, and moodiness may drive away people they are close to. At times, the demands of their lives may become overwhelming. They may experience a transient, psychotic-like state, possibly characterized by delusional thinking or dissociative symptoms, which can necessitate hospitalization.

Theories and Treatment of Borderline Personality Disorder

Tremendous effort has been devoted to the development of theories and treatment for people with this condition, perhaps because these individuals create so much chaos in the lives of everyone with whom they interact. It is also an inherently fascinating disorder, because it revolves around a disturbance in the very essence of self-definition.

The biopsychosocial model is particularly well-suited to understanding this disorder. Researchers are increasingly recognizing that the disorder evolves from a combination of a vulnerable temperament, traumatic early experiences in childhood, and a triggering event or set of events in adulthood (Zanarini & Frankenburg, 1997). Together, these influences interact to create the volatile behaviors and difficulties in identity and relationships that plague the life of the individual with the disorder.

Biological Perspectives Researchers studying possible biological contributors to this disorder are trying to identify physiological markers that distinguish borderline personality disorder from mood disorders and schizophrenia. Although most theories regarding this disorder are psychological, some investigators have examined the possibility that some of the psychological factors thought to be involved in the development of this disorder have biological correlates, such as neurotransmitter dysregulation (Gurvits, Koenigsberg, & Siever, 2000). As you will see, early childhood trauma in the form of

REAL STORIES

SUSANNA KAYSEN: BORDERLINE SYMPTOMS

Susanna Kaysen

The case which you began reading at the start of this chapter gives you a glimpse into the life and behaviors of a person with borderline personality disorder. Rarely do people who have been given this diagnosis speak publicly about their symptoms, because the diagnosis implies that the person has many negative characteristics. Susanna Kaysen chose to speak openly about her experience of borderline symptoms in her best-selling book, *Girl, Interrupted,* a compelling autobiographical account of harrowing emotional experiences during her 2-year inpatient stay at a psychiatric hospital outside of Boston. The book was subsequently made into a highly successful movie. Although Kaysen's symptoms might not meet current diagnostic criteria for borderline personality disorder, her story captures the essence of the emotional turmoil experienced by people with this personality disorder.

Kaysen grew up in a middle-class family. Her father was a successful economics professor. Although it was assumed that Kaysen, like most of her peers, would immediately go on to a prestigious college following high school graduation, she had an intense disdain for school at the time and instead chose to go live in a commune. At the age of 18, Kaysen tried to kill herself by swallowing 50 aspirins. She was placed in McLean Hospital, where she was told she would need just a few weeks' rest. A few weeks turned into 2 years of barred windows, vinyl armchairs, constant observations and examinations, and a ban on sharp objects.

Following her 2-year hospital stay, Kaysen found a job as a copy editor with aspirations to become a writer, a goal that she achieved with great success. For the most part, Kaysen has resisted becoming involved in debates about mental health issues, preferring to remain more private.

In *Girl, Interrupted* Kaysen discusses her diagnosis of borderline personality disorder:

So these were the charges against me. I didn't read them until twenty-five years later. A "character disorder" is what they'd told me then.

I had to find a lawyer to help me get my records from the hospital . . . then I had to locate a copy of the *Diagnostic and Statistical Manual of Mental Disorders* and look up Borderline Personality to see what they really thought of me.

It's a fairly accurate picture of me at eighteen, minus a few quirks like reckless driving and eating binges. It's accurate but it isn't profound. Of course, it doesn't aim to be profound. It's not even a case study. It's a set of guidelines, a generalization.

I'm tempted to try refuting it, but then I would be open to the further charges of "defensiveness" and "resistance."

All I can do is give particulars: an annotated diagnosis.

"Uncertainty about several life issues, such as self-image, sexual orientation, long-term goals or career choice, types of friends or lovers to have. . . ." I still have that uncertainty. Is this the type of friend or lover I want to have? I ask myself every time I meet someone new. Charming but shallow; good-hearted but a bit conventional; too handsome for his own good; fascinating but probably unreliable; and so forth. I guess I've had my share of unreliables. More than my share? How many would constitute more than my share?

Fewer than somebody else—somebody who'd never been called a borderline personality?

"Self-mutilating behavior (e.g. wrist scratching) . . ." I've skipped forward a bit. This is the one that caught me by surprise as I sat on the floor of the bookstore reading my diagnosis. Wrist scratching! I thought I'd invented it.

sexual abuse is regarded as a prime suspect in the search for psychological factors. The possibility that such abuse leaves an imprint on the individual's brain led researchers to suggest that sexual abuse in childhood may make the noradrenergic (sympathetic nervous system) pathways hypersensitive, so that the individual is constantly primed to overreact to experiences of any kind later in adulthood. This altered sympathetic functioning may interact with a predisposition toward

In MindMAP Segment 10.1, Becky describes two of the characteristic symptoms of this disorder including inappropriate and intense anger, and recurrent self-mutilating behavior.

People with borderline personality disorder commonly engage in self-mutilating behavior and feel unable to control expressions of rage.

impulsivity, due to abnormalities in serotonergic receptors in the brain. The self-destructive and impulsive behaviors of people with this disorder, combined with the distress they experience due to their tendency to overreact to life events, may produce the characteristics of borderline personality disorder (Figueroa & Silk, 1997).

Researchers using magnetic resonance imaging (MRI) techniques have uncovered some intriguing differences in the brains of people diagnosed with borderline personality disorder (Driessen et al., 2000). For instance, a study of 21 women with borderline personality disorder found that in these women the hippocampus was 16 percent smaller than in healthy control subjects, and the amygdala was 8 percent smaller.

Psychological Perspectives A growing body of research evidence points to the fact that extreme negative experiences within the family are very common in the childhood histories of most adults with borderline personality disorder. Three classes of variables have emerged as especially compelling predictors for the development of borderline personality disorder: disturbed childhood family environment, parental psychopathology, and the experience of childhood abuse. Of these variables, childhood sexual abuse is the most significant predictor of borderline symptomatology, with childhood physical abuse also showing a trend in the same direction (Bradley, Jenei, & Westen, 2005). It is important to keep in mind, of course, that abuse would typically take place within the context of a disturbed home and be perpetrated by dysfunctional parents or guardians, thus making it challenging to tease out specific causal factors. Theories regarding the basis for the relationship between early abuse and neglect and the development of borderline personality disorder propose that these experiences cause children to expect that others will harm them (Silk, Lee, Hill, & Lohr 1995). As adults, people with borderline personality disorder report that their caretakers withdrew from them emotionally, treated them inconsistently, denied the validity of their thoughts and feelings, and did not carry out their roles as parents in terms of providing them with protection from abuse (Zanarini et al., 1997).

Clinical observations led the psychodynamic theorists who first described the characteristics of borderline personality disorder to propose a different model of parent-child relationships to explain the development of borderline pathology (Gunderson, 1984; Kernberg, 1967; Masterson, 1981). These theorists believed that deficits in the formation of the self were the underlying pathology of this disorder. One disturbed pattern of parenting they identified is that of a mother who is overinvolved with her child but also inconsistent in her emotional responsiveness. By failing to bolster the child's independent sense of self, she sets the stage for her child's later lack of an identity and a sense of commitment to life goals. The individual fails to develop a healthy "real" self that can form the basis for intimate, sharing, and committed relationships with others or that can be creative, spontaneous, and assertive. The individual perceives other people in a distorted way and builds a false self that is fused with these distorted perceptions of others (Masterson & Klein, 1989).

In contrast to theories that emphasize abnormalities in parenting, cognitive-behavioral approaches to understanding people with borderline personality disorder focus on their maladaptive thoughts. According to Beck's cognitive approach (Beck, Freeman, & Davis, 2004), people with this disorder have a tendency to dichotomize their thinking about themselves and other people; in other words, they think in terms of "all or nothing." Such thinking could account for the individual's tendency to shift moods so readily and to use splitting in relationships with others. For example, if an individual with borderline personality disorder originally perceives someone as all good, and that person then fails to follow through on a promise, the person immediately appears to become all bad. People with borderline personality disorder also apply this limited set of standards when evaluating themselves; when they perceive themselves as falling short, even on minor grounds, their entire self-evaluation becomes negative. Finally, a low sense of self-efficacy related to their weak identity causes a lack of confidence in their decisions, low motivation, and an inability to seek long-term goals.

Sociocultural Perspectives Millon contends that the pressures of contemporary society that have placed a strain on families and individuals may exacerbate the deficient parenting that can give rise to this disorder (Millon & Davis, 1996). People with borderline personality disorder are particularly vulnerable to the diminished cohesion in society that is associated with urbanization and modernization in contemporary culture. Their lack of psychic cohesion reflects the instability within society and a lack of clearly defined cultural norms and expectations. Further contributing to their development of this disorder is a pattern of instability within their family. A child who is subjected to parental conflict comes to feel internally divided and, furthermore, starts to question basic assumptions about life's predictability and stability. From another perspective, family difficulties, including depression, substance abuse, and antisocial behavior, can lead to the development of this disorder through the perpetuation of childrearing patterns that are carried from generation to generation (Goldman, D'Angelo, & DeMaso, 1993). An adult with borderline personality disorder who was abused as a child passes on this pattern of parenting to the next generation, who then become vulnerable to developing the disorder (Stone, 1990).

Treatment of Borderline Personality Disorder Clinicians working with clients who have borderline personality disorder face a number of treatment challenges. Treatment difficulties are usually apparent from the very outset of therapy, in part due to the confusing nature of the client's initial presentation. Individuals with borderline personality disorder "often appear more healthy at first glance than they really are" (Millon et al., 2000, p. 445). Consequently, clinicians are likely to focus on some apparently simple issue, only to realize over time the very complex nature of the client's problems.

Due to their volatility, inconsistency, and intensity, people with borderline personality disorder have difficulty remaining in therapy long enough to make progress. Also, these individuals commonly become pathologically dependent on their therapist; as a result, they may feel uncontrollably enraged when the therapist fails to live up to their idealizations. Consequently, therapists are watchful of their own emotional reactions, recognizing that these clients may evoke intense feelings of anger or helplessness. Furthermore, since these clients are prone to distort their relationship with the therapist, it is necessary to try to keep the client grounded in reality (Kernberg et al., 1989).

Especially important in the treatment of clients with borderline personality disorder is the establishment of a clear treatment framework (Goin, 2001). In setting up this framework, the clinician discusses and clarifies the goals of treatment and the roles that the client and the therapist are expected to play. Explicit goals, such as improvement in relationships and reduction of symptoms, are formulated. In this treatment framework, the client is expected to discuss inner thoughts, problems in functioning, and anticipated behavior. Within the treatment framework the therapist commits to efforts to provide understanding, consistency, and empathic feedback.

People with borderline personality disorder often have a difficult time with good-byes. Reluctant to end the session, such a client may bring up an "important" new issue, ignoring the therapist's cues that it is time to get up and leave.

Practical matters are also specified, such as the time and place of sessions, procedures for handling emergencies, and methods of billing and payment.

Although clinicians agree on certain key facets of therapy for people with borderline personality disorder, controversy remains about whether to focus more on confrontive or supportive approaches (Gunderson, 1989). Some clinicians believe that the client's manipulative behavior can be held in check only by confrontation (Gunderson, 1984; Kernberg, 1984; Masterson & Klein, 1989). In contrast, other clinicians recommend a more supportive, nurturant technique. For example, Millon (1998) suggests that, once clear limits have been established early in the therapy relationship, the therapist should be as responsive and supportive as possible within those limits; he contends that a failure to be responsive causes the client to feel abandoned. Consider the situation in the case study at the beginning of the chapter, when Harold Morrill made a sarcastic comment to Dr. Tobin about her inability to schedule an immediate appointment. When Harold stated, "Busy little bee, aren't you?" Dr. Tobin felt that it would be therapeutically wiser for her to assure Harold of her commitment to helping him than to confront his sarcasm. In the course of therapy, a client may make derogatory remarks about the therapist, which the therapist can then use as opportunities to show the client the inappropriateness and destructiveness of misdirected anger. The therapist, then, would respond to the client's anger with concern and understanding. This approach is based on the assumptions that the client's disorder is the result of poor parenting and that the therapist can provide a positive parental role. As Millon notes, much can be gained as the client comes to realize that others need not be perceived as people who are dangerous or likely to abandon the client out of an unwillingness to put up with the client's problems and difficult interpersonal style.

Some clinicians integrate supportive and cognitive-behavioral techniques to reduce the frequency of self-destructive acts and to improve the client's ability to handle disturbing emotions, such as anger and dependency. Psychologist Marsha Linehan has developed a treatment method that she calls "Dialectical Behavioral Therapy (DBT)," in which the term *dialectical* refers to systematically combining opposed ideas with the goal of reconciling them (Heard & Linehan, 1994; Linehan, 1993a). Thus, the therapist's strategy is to alternate between accepting clients as they are and confronting their disturbing behavior to help them change. In a detailed manual, Linehan provides guidelines for therapists working with clients who have borderline personality disorder (Linehan, 1993b). These guidelines are based on the underlying principle that therapists should move between acceptance and change within the context of a supportive therapeutic relationship. Much of Linehan's work is based on therapy with suicidal individuals, in which the relationship becomes a crucial factor, not only for keeping the client in therapy but also for keeping the client alive. In her work with suicidal clients, Linehan applies the dialectical approach by "reframing" suicidal behaviors as dysfunctional, maladaptive efforts to solve problems. This reframing constitutes acceptance or an attempt to understand the origins of the behavior. At the same time, she focuses therapy on new ways to analyze the problem and to develop healthier solutions, a process that stimulates change. Specific methods used within this framework are regulating emotions, developing interpersonal effectiveness, learning to tolerate emotional distress, and developing self-management skills. One process, called "core mindfulness," teaches clients to balance emotions, reason, and intuition in their approach to life's problems.

Research findings support the effectiveness of DBT. Clients who participate in DBT show considerable improvement in symptoms of depression, dissociation, anxiety, and anger. Quite importantly, they are also much less prone to engage in suicidal or parasuicidal behaviors than are individuals with this disorder who are participating in other forms of treatment (Bohus et al., 2000; Shearin & Linehan, 1994). The DBT clients describe themselves as more emotionally adjusted, describe their interpersonal relationships in more positive terms, and experience fewer problems in social and vocational settings. Furthermore, the DBT clients remain in therapy for longer periods of time, are hospitalized less frequently, and maintain improved functioning for 1 year after treatment.

Because DBT often involves a considerable amount of staff resources, variations have been developed in which the program is provided in a briefer format. In one study of 87 patients admitted to a 3-week intensive outpatient program following suicidal or parasuicidal behavior, significant benefits were evident in the majority of participants, particularly on measures of depression and hopelessness (McQuillan et al., 2005).

As an adjunct to the psychological treatment of people with borderline personality disorder, some clinicians recommend medication. Although no medication can effectively treat borderline personality disorder, several pharmacological interventions have been shown to be effective in treating specific symptoms. The group of medications used to target borderline symptoms includes antidepressants, antipsychotics, anticonvulsants, lithium, and minor tranquilizers. Physicians realize that these medications must be prescribed with careful assessment of the specific symptoms that are most problematic for the client. For example, serotonergic medications, such as fluoxetine (Prozac), have been shown to be especially effective in controlling depression and impulsive aggression while helping the client manage anxiety, sensitivity about possible rejection, psychotic-like thinking, and obsessive-compulsive symptoms (Coccaro & Kavoussi, 1997). Clinical evidence is also emerging about the possible effectiveness of second-generation antipsychotic medications, particularly with individuals with psychotic-like, extremely impulsive, or suicidal symptoms (Grootens & Verkes, 2005).

Clearly, both the symptoms and the treatment of people with borderline personality disorder are challenging and complex. In severe cases, successful treatment can be undertaken only in an inpatient or partial hospitalization setting. This is particularly true when clients are suicidal, experience psychotic-like episodes, or threaten harm to other people. The hospital or partial care program provides a safe and secure setting, in which limits are established and maintained. Day treatment partial hospitalization is sometimes preferable to inpatient care because it provides intensified treatment that is less likely to cultivate too much dependency (Bateman & Fonagy, 2001; Miller, 1995).

Histrionic Personality Disorder

Some people tend to express themselves in very dramatic ways. When carried to an extreme, these tendencies form the basis for **histrionic personality disorder.** The term *histrionic* is derived from a Latin word meaning "actor." People with this disorder display theatrical qualities in their everyday behavior. For example, someone with this disorder may put on a "show" of being overwhelmed with tears and sentimentality at the wedding of a distant relative or may greet an acquaintance at a party with ostentatious and attention-getting hugs and exclamations of affection. What differentiates people with this disorder from those who show appropriate emotionality is the fleeting nature of their emotional states and the fact that they use excessive emotions to manipulate others rather than to express their genuine feelings. This disorder is more commonly diagnosed in women, though it is not clear whether this is because the disorder is more common in women or because those who are assigning the label regard histrionic behaviors as stereotypically feminine.

People with histrionic personality disorder enjoy being the center of attention and behave in whatever way necessary to

Mini Case

HISTRIONIC PERSONALITY DISORDER

Lynnette is a 44-year-old high-school teacher who is notorious for her outlandish behavior and inappropriate flirtatiousness. Several of her students have complained to the principal about her seductive behavior during individual meetings. She often greets students with overwhelming warmth and apparent concern over their welfare, which leads some to find her appealing and engaging at first; however, they invariably become disenchanted, once they realize how shallow she is. To her colleagues, she brags about her minor accomplishments, as if they were major victories, yet, if she fails to achieve a desired objective, she sulks and breaks down into tears. She is so desperate for the approval of others that she will change her story to suit whomever she is talking to at the time. Because she is always creating "crises," and never reciprocates the concern of others, people have become immune and unresponsive to her frequent pleas for help and attention.

Diagnostic Features

This diagnosis is given to people who show a pervasive pattern of excessive emotionality and attention seeking, as indicated by five or more of the following:

- Discomfort when not the center of attention
- Interactions characterized by inappropriate sexually seductive or provocative behavior
- Rapid shifts and shallow expression of emotions
- Use of physical appearance to draw attention
- Speech that is excessively impressionistic and lacking in detail
- Self-dramatization, theatricality, and exaggerated expression of emotion
- High suggestibility
- Misinterpretation of relationships as being more intimate than they are

---

ensure that this happens. They are excessively concerned with their own physical appearance, often trying to draw attention to themselves in such extreme ways that their behavior seems ludicrous. Furthermore, they are likely to be seen as flirtatious and seductive, demanding the reassurance, praise, and approval of others and becoming furious if they don't get it. They want immediate gratification of their wishes and overreact to even minor provocations, usually in an exaggerated way, such as by weeping or fainting. Although their relationships are superficial, they assume them to be intimate and refer to acquaintances as "dear" friends. They are easily influenced by others, lack analytic ability, and see the world in broad, impressionistic terms.

You can imagine how such histrionic behaviors would cause others to keep their distance; being in a relationship with a person with a histrionic personality disorder can be exasperating and unsatisfying. The result, of course, is that people with this disorder have few, if any, close and reciprocal relationships. In keeping with this clinical picture, individuals with histrionic personality disorder are more likely to have an insecure attachment type. They are constantly seeking support and approval from their partners (Lopez & Brennan, 2000).

Cognitive-behavioral theorists propose that people with this personality disorder suffer from mistaken assumptions underlying their approach to life (Freeman, Pretzer, Fleming, & Simon, 1990). One basic belief of the person with this disorder is that "I am inadequate and unable to handle life on my own," which leads to the next step of assuming that it is necessary to find someone else to make up this deficit (Millon, 1991; Millon et al., 2000). These individuals seek attention and approval by acting in ways that are stereotypes of hyperfemininity or

Trying to catch other people's attention is a common characteristic of people with histrionic personality disorder.

Mini Case

NARCISSISTIC PERSONALITY DISORDER

Chad is a 26-year-old man who has been desperately trying to succeed as an actor. However, he has had only minor acting jobs and has been forced to support himself by working as a waiter. Despite his lack of success, he brags to others about all the roles he rejects because they aren't good enough for him. Trying to make inroads into acting, he has been selfishly exploitive of any person whom he sees as a possible connection. He has intense resentment for acquaintances who have obtained acting roles and devalues their achievements by commenting that they are just "lucky," yet, if anyone tries to give him constructive criticism, Chad reacts with outrage, refusing to talk to the person for weeks. Because of what he regards as his "terrific" looks, he thinks he deserves special treatment from everyone. At the restaurant, Chad has recurrent arguments with his supervisor, because he insists that he is a "professional" and that he should not have to demean himself by clearing dirty dishes from the tables. He annoys others, because he always seeks compliments on his clothes, hair, intelligence, and wit. He is so caught up with himself, that he barely notices other people and is grossly insensitive to their needs and problems.

Diagnostic Features

This diagnosis applies to people who show a pervasive pattern of grandiosity, need for admiration, and lack of empathy, as evidenced by five or more of the following:

- Grandiose sense of self-importance
- Preoccupation with fantasies of success, power, brilliance, beauty, or ideal love
- Belief that they are so "special" that they should associate only with other special people, who can understand them
- Need for excessive admiration
- Sense of entitlement
- Exploitive interpersonal style
- Lack of empathy
- Envy of others or belief that others are envious
- Arrogant behaviors and attitudes

---

hypermasculinity, believing that this will elicit admiration and support from others. Given the cognitive-behavioral position that emotions are a product of one's thoughts, it follows that the global nature of the histrionic individual's thinking style leads also to diffuse, exaggerated, and rapidly changing emotional states. The way these individuals evaluate people and situations is equally imprecise and subject to distortion; therefore, their opinions can change on a daily basis from one extreme to another.

A therapist using cognitive-behavioral techniques would help the client develop more effective ways of approaching problems and situations, would work with the client to focus on goals, and would teach the client how to think more precisely and objectively. By taking this approach, the therapist models good problem-solving behavior and gives the client practical help in dealing with various life issues. Clients also learn self-monitoring strategies to keep their impulsive tendencies in check, as well as assertiveness skills to improve interpersonal relationships.

Narcissistic Personality Disorder

People with **narcissistic personality disorder** have an unrealistic, inflated sense of their own importance, a trait known as **grandiosity.** The name of this disorder comes from the Greek legend of Narcissus, the youth who fell in love with his own reflection in a pond. Although people with this disorder expect others to compliment them and gratify all their wishes and demands, they lack sensitivity to the needs of others. Because they perceive themselves as being so special, they feel that only high-status people can appreciate their special needs and problems. They possess excessive aspirations for their own lives and intense resentment for others whom they perceive as more successful, beautiful, or brilliant. They are preoccupied with and driven to achieve their own goals and think nothing of exploiting others in order to do so. Despite their show of grand self-importance, they are often troubled by self-doubt. Relationships with others, whether social, occupational, or romantic, are distorted by the perception of other people as tools for self-gratification. Furthermore, they can be haughty and arrogant, characteristics that interfere with their interpersonal relationships.

Noting the many types of behaviors incorporated into the definition of narcissistic personality disorder, Millon and his colleagues (2000) proposed subtypes: the elitist, the amorous, the unprincipled, and the compensatory narcissist. Elitists feel privileged and empowered and tend to flaunt their status and achievements. Usually upwardly mobile, the elitist desperately engages in self-promotion and tries to cultivate special status and any opportunity to be recognized. The amorous narcissist tends to be sexually seductive, yet avoids real intimacy. Such individuals are especially drawn to tempting naive and emotionally needy people, with whom they play a game in which they deceptively imply that they are interested in pursuing a close relationship; however, their only real interest is temporarily exploiting the other's warm body. Unprincipled narcissists are much like antisocial individuals in that they tend to be unscrupulous, deceptive, arrogant, and exploitive. Even when found guilty of illegal behavior, they convey an attitude of nonchalance, acting as if the victim were to blame for not having caught on to what was happening. Compensatory narcissists tend to be negativistic, seeking to counteract their deep feelings of inferiority. They try to create illusions of being superior and exceptional.

The construct of narcissism is an interesting one and has stimulated some important theoretical analyses regarding its origins and development. The traditional Freudian psychoanalytic approach regards narcissism as the failure to progress beyond the early stages of psychosexual development. More current object relations conceptualizations focus on the effect of disturbances in the parent-child relationship on the developing child's sense of self. Every child needs parents to provide reassurance and positive responses to accomplishments. Without these, the child becomes insecure. This insecurity is expressed, paradoxically, in an inflated sense of self-importance that can be understood as the individual's attempt to make up for what was missing earlier in life (Kohut, 1966, 1971). Lacking a firm foundation of a healthy self, these individuals develop a false self that is precariously based on grandiose and unrealistic notions about their competence and desirability (Masterson & Klein, 1989). Narcissistic personality disorder can be understood, then, as the adult's expression of this childhood insecurity and need for attention.

Cognitive-behavioral theorists (Beck et al., 2004) contend that people with narcissistic personality disorder hold maladaptive ideas about themselves, including the view that they are exceptional people who deserve to be treated far better than ordinary humans. They lack insight into or concern for the feelings of other people, because they consider themselves to be superior to others. These beliefs hamper their ability to perceive their experiences realistically, and they encounter problems when their grandiose ideas about themselves clash with their experiences of failure in the real world.

The psychodynamic approach to treating individuals with narcissistic personality disorder is based on the notion that they lack early experiences of admiration for their positive qualities. Therapy is intended to provide a corrective developmental experience, in which the therapist uses empathy to support the client's search for recognition and admiration but, at the same time, attempts to guide the client toward a more realistic appreciation that no one is flawless. Somewhat paradoxically, the more recognition and support the therapist gives the client, the less grandiose and self-centered the client becomes (Kohut, 1971).

Cognitive-behavioral therapy for narcissistic personality disorder also is oriented toward reducing the client's grandiosity and enhancing the client's ability to relate to others. In working toward this goal, the therapist structures interventions that work with, rather than against, the client's self-aggrandizing and egocentric tendencies. For example, rather than try to convince the client to be less selfish, the therapist might try to show that there are better ways to reach important personal goals. At the same time, the therapist avoids giving in to the client's demands for special favors and attention. When the therapist establishes and follows an agenda with clear treatment goals, the client may learn how to set limits in other areas of life (Freeman et al., 1990).

Paranoid Personality Disorder

The term *paranoia,* as you have already learned, means suspiciousness, guardedness, and vigilance toward other people, based on the belief that others intend harm. As you will see later in this book, paranoid thinking is present in various psychological disorders. In this section, we will look at the personality disorder that is characterized by paranoia.

People with **paranoid personality disorder** are extremely suspicious of others and are always on guard against potential danger or harm. Their view of the world is very narrowly focused, in that they seek to confirm their expectations that others will take advantage of them, making it virtually impossible for them to trust even their friends and associates. They may accuse a spouse or partner of being unfaithful, even if no substantiating evidence exists. For example, they may believe that an unexplained toll call that appears on a telephone bill is proof of an extramarital affair. They are unable to take responsibility for their mistakes and, instead, project blame onto others. If others criticize them, they become hostile. They are also prone to misconstrue innocent comments and minor events as having a hidden or threatening meaning. They may hold grudges for years, based on

A person with narcissistic personality disorder is preoccupied with appearance and extremely concerned about impressing others with an attractive and suave presentation.

Mini Case

PARANOID PERSONALITY DISORDER

Anita is a computer programmer who constantly worries that other people will exploit her knowledge. She regards as "top secret" the new database management program she is writing. She even fears that, when she leaves the office at night, someone will sneak into her desk and steal her notes. Her distrust of others pervades all her interpersonal dealings. Her suspicions that she is being cheated even taint routine transactions in banks and stores. Anita likes to think of herself as rational and able to make objective decisions; she regards her inability to trust other people as a natural reaction to a world filled with opportunistic and insincere corporate ladder climbers.

Diagnostic Features

People with this personality disorder show pervasive distrust and suspiciousness of others whose motives they interpret as malevolent, as indicated by four or more of the following:

- Unjustified suspicion that others are exploiting, harming, or deceiving them
- Preoccupation with unjustified doubts about others' loyalty or trustworthiness
- Reluctance to confide in others, for fear that the information will be used against them
- Tendency to read hidden demeaning or threatening meanings into harmless remarks or events
- Tendency to bear grudges
- Perception of personal attacks that are not apparent to others and tendency to respond with angry counterattacks
- Recurrent unjustified suspicions about the faithfulness of spouse or sexual partner

---

a real or an imagined slight by another person. Although individuals with this disorder might be relatively successful in certain kinds of jobs requiring heightened vigilance, their emotional life tends to be isolated and constrained.

As you can imagine, people with paranoid personality disorder have problematic relationships. They keep other people at a distance because of irrational fears that others will harm them, and they are particularly sensitive to people in positions of power. Supporting this clinical evidence, people with paranoid personality disorder are characterized by a fearful attachment style (Lopez & Brennan, 2000).

A certain amount of paranoid thinking and behavior might be appropriate in some situations, such as in dangerous political climates in which people must be on guard just to stay alive; however, people with paranoid personality disorder think and behave in ways that are unrelated to their environment.

Particularly frustrating to the relatives and acquaintances of these people is the fact that they refuse to seek professional help, because they don't acknowledge the nature of their problem. In the unlikely event they do seek therapy, their rigidity and defensiveness make it very difficult for the clinician to make inroads and work toward any kind of lasting change.

Psychodynamic theorists have explained paranoid personality disorder as a style of viewing the world in which the individual relies heavily on the defense mechanism of projection, meaning that other people, rather than the self, are perceived as having negative or damaging motives (Shapiro, 1965). In contrast, cognitive-behavioral theorists (Beck et al., 2004) regard the person with paranoid personality disorder as someone who suffers from mistaken assumptions about the world and who attributes personal problems and mistakes to others.

The cognitive-behavioral perspective (Freeman et al., 1990) incorporates these ideas but presents an alternate view, emphasizing the three basic mistaken assumptions that people

with paranoid personality disorder hold: "People are malevolent and deceptive," "They'll attack you if they get the chance," and "You can be OK only if you stay on your toes." The difficulty these assumptions create is that the behavior of others inevitably causes them to conclude that their impressions are correct. If a woman is primed to suspect other people's motives, she is likely to interpret what they do as proof. For instance, Caroline believes that retail merchants deliberately take advantage of consumers. The next time a salesperson gives her the wrong change, she will interpret this not as a casual error but as confirmation of her fears. According to the cognitive-behavioral view, the third mistaken assumption, that people have to be vigilant to avoid being harmed, is related to feelings of low self-efficacy, leading paranoid people to believe that they cannot detect the harmful intentions of others and, therefore, must perpetually stay on guard.

The treatment of paranoid personality disorder that follows from the cognitive-behavioral perspective (Freeman et al., 1990) involves countering the client's mistaken assumptions in an atmosphere aimed at establishing a sense of trust. The therapist attempts to increase the client's feelings of self-efficacy, so that the client feels able to handle situations without resorting to a defensive and vigilant stance. Because the client with paranoid personality disorder is likely to enter therapy feeling distrustful of the therapist, the therapist must make a special effort to help the client feel that therapy is a collaborative process. Direct confrontation with the paranoid client usually backfires, because the client is likely to construe this as yet another attack (Millon et al., 2000). Other beneficial interventions involve helping the client become more aware of other points of view and develop a more assertive approach to conflict with others. These increased interpersonal skills improve the quality of the client's interactions outside therapy and eventually contribute to disproving the client's mistaken assumptions.

Mini Case

SCHIZOID PERSONALITY DISORDER

Pedro, who works as a night security guard at a bank, likes his job, because he can enter the private world of his thoughts without interruptions from other people. Even though his numerous years of service make him eligible for a daytime security position, Pedro has repeatedly turned down these opportunities, because daytime work would require him to deal with bank employees and customers. Pedro has resided for more than 20 years in a small room at a rooming house. He has no television or radio, and he has resisted any attempts by other house residents to involve him in social activities. He has made it clear that he is not interested in "small talk" and that he prefers to be left alone. Neighbors, co-workers, and even his own family members (whom he also avoids) perceive Pedro as a very peculiar person who seems strikingly cold and detached. When his brother died, Pedro decided not to attend the funeral, because he did not want to be

bothered by all the "carrying on" and sympathetic wishes of relatives and others.

Diagnostic Features

This diagnosis applies to people who show a pervasive pattern of detachment from relationships and a restricted emotional range, as indicated by four or more of the following:

- Lack of desire for or enjoyment of close relationships
- Strong preference for solitary activities
- Little or no interest in sexual experiences with another person
- Lack of pleasure in few, if any, activities
- Lack of close friends or confidants, other than immediate relatives
- Indifference to praise or criticism
- Emotional coldness, detachment, or flat emotionality

Schizoid Personality Disorder

The term *schizophrenia,* as discussed in Chapter 2, refers to a psychological disorder in which the individual experiences severe disturbances in thought, affect, and behavior. Two personality disorders, schizoid and schizotypal, involve disturbances in personality that have schizophrenia-like qualities but do not take on the psychotic form seen in schizophrenia. As you saw in Chapter 9, researchers are studying the relationship between these personality disorders and schizophrenia. In fact, some researchers refer to these three disorders as **schizophrenia spectrum disorders,** implying that all three are on a continuum of psychological disturbance and may be related. For the present, we will describe the characteristics of the two personality disorders that share some aspects of the symptoms found in schizophrenia.

Schizoid personality disorder is characterized by an indifference to social and sexual relationships, as well as a very limited range of emotional experience and expression. Individuals with this disorder prefer to be by themselves rather than with others, and they appear to lack any desire to be accepted or loved, even by their families. Sexual involvement with others holds little appeal. As you might expect, others perceive them as cold, reserved, withdrawn, and seclusive, yet the schizoid individual is unaware of, and typically insensitive to, the feelings and thoughts of others.

Throughout their lives, people with schizoid personality disorder seek out situations that involve minimal interaction with others. Employment is problematic for these individuals, and they are unlikely to retain jobs for more than a few months (Fulton & Winokur, 1993). Those who are able to tolerate work are usually drawn to jobs in which they spend all of their work hours alone. They rarely marry but, rather, choose solitary

living, possibly in a single room, where they guard their privacy and avoid any dealings with neighbors. Although they are not particularly distressed or a risk to others, their self-imposed isolation and emotional constriction can be considered maladaptive. They take pleasure in few, if any, activities. As maladaptive as their behavior may seem, people with schizoid personality disorder are not likely to seek psychotherapy. If they do enter therapy, perhaps for another psychological disorder, such as a mood disorder or substance abuse, these people are difficult to treat because of their lack of interest in interpersonal relationships.

The construct of schizoid personality disorder is closely tied to the schizophrenia spectrum concept (Rodriguez Solano & Gonzalez De Chavez, 2000). In an interesting examination of possible risk factors for the development of this particular personality disorder, a team of researchers investigating the effect of early life experiences found that nutritional deficiency during the prenatal period was a risk factor for the development of schizoid personality disorder by the age of 18 years. This study was conducted in the Netherlands, on men born during the famine of 1944–1946. Schizophrenia was also more prevalent in men whose mothers suffered through the famine (Hoek et al., 1996).

Treating people with schizoid personality disorder is extremely difficult, because they lack the normal patterns of emotional responsiveness that play a role in human communication. The therapist must be careful to avoid setting unrealistically high goals for therapy, because progress with these individuals is likely to be slow and limited in scope. Most promising is an approach geared toward helping them work on their styles of communication (Freeman et al., 1990). To accomplish this goal, the therapist might use role playing and in vivo exposure techniques (Millon et al., 2000).

Mini Case

SCHIZOTYPAL PERSONALITY DISORDER

Joe is a college junior who has devised an elaborate system for deciding which courses to take, depending on the course number. He will not take a course with the number 5 in it, because he believes that, if he does so, he might have to "plead the Fifth Amendment." Rarely does he talk to people in his dormitory, believing that others are intent on stealing his term paper ideas. He has acquired a reputation for being "kind of flaky" because of his odd manner of dress, his reclusive tendencies, and his ominous drawings of sinister animals displayed on the door of his room. The sound of the nearby elevator, he claims, is actually a set of voices singing a monastic chant.

Diagnostic Features

This diagnosis is given to people who show a pervasive pattern of social and interpersonal deficits marked by acute discomfort with, and reduced capacity for, close relationships and who experience cognitive or perceptual distortions and behavioral eccentricities, as indicated by five or more of the following:

- Ideas of reference
- Odd beliefs or magical thinking, which influences their behavior (e.g., belief in mind reading)
- Unusual perceptual experiences, including bodily illusions
- Odd thinking and speech
- Suspiciousness or paranoid ideation
- Inappropriate or constricted affect
- Behavior or appearance that is odd or eccentric
- Lack of close friends or confidants other than immediate relatives
- Excessive social anxiety that tends to be associated with paranoid fears

Schizotypal Personality Disorder

People with **schizotypal personality disorder** are peculiar, eccentric, and oddly bizarre in the way they think, behave, and relate to others, even in how they dress. Their peculiar ideas may include magical thinking and beliefs in psychic phenomena, such as clairvoyance and telepathy. They may have unusual perceptual experiences in the form of illusions. Though their speech is not incoherent, the content sounds strange to others. Their affect is constricted and inappropriate. They are often suspicious of other people and may have ideas of reference, beliefs that the behavior of others or a random object or event refers to them. Unable to experience pleasure, their lives are characterized by a sense of blandness, which robs them of the capacity for enthusiasm. Like people with schizoid personality disorder, these individuals find it difficult to establish close relationships, because they experience discomfort around others—in part, due to their suspiciousness. In fact, the characteristics of oddness, aloofness, and social withdrawal have been found by researchers to be the most striking features defining this disorder (Fossati et al., 2001).

The symptoms of social isolation, eccentricity, peculiar communication, and poor social adaptation associated with schizotypal personality disorder place it within the schizophrenic spectrum (Camisa et al., 2005). According to this view, the symptoms of schizotypal personality disorder represent a **latent** form of schizophrenia, meaning that people with schizotypal symptoms are vulnerable to developing a full-blown psychosis if exposed to difficult life circumstances that challenge their ability to maintain contact with reality. This position was first developed in the early 1980s after the publication of a 15-year follow-up study of people who met the criteria for schizotypal personality disorder, schizophrenia, and borderline personality disorder. At the end of the follow-up period, the schizotypal individuals were functioning more like people

Odd behavior and appearance are characteristics of people with schizotypal personality disorder.

diagnosed with schizophrenia than like those with borderline personality disorder (McGlashan, 1983). Two decades later, researchers continue to look at the relationship between

Mini Case

AVOIDANT PERSONALITY DISORDER

Max is a delivery person for a large equipment corporation. His co-workers describe Max as a loner, because he does not spend time in casual conversation and avoids going out to lunch with others. Little do they know that every day he struggles with the desire to interact with them but is too intimidated to follow through. Recently, he turned down a promotion to become manager, because he realized that the position would require a considerable amount of day-to-day contact with others. What bothered him most about this position was not just that it would require interaction with people but also that he might make mistakes that would be noticed by others. Although he is 42 years old, Max has hardly ever dated. Every time he feels interested in a woman, he becomes paralyzed with anxiety over the prospect of talking to her, much less asking her for a date. When female co-workers talk to him, he blushes and nervously tries to end the conversation as soon as possible.

Diagnostic Features

This diagnosis applies to people with a pattern of social inhibition, feelings of inadequacy, and hypersensitivity to negative evaluation, as indicated by four or more of the following:

- Avoidance of activities that involve significant interpersonal contact because of fears of criticism, disapproval, or rejection
- Unwillingness to get involved with others unless certain of being liked
- Restraint within intimate relationships due to fear of being shamed or ridiculed
- Preoccupation with being criticized or rejected in social situations
- Inhibition in new interpersonal situations because of feelings of inadequacy
- Self-view as socially inept, personally unappealing, or inferior to others
- Reluctance to take personal risks or new activities due to fear of being embarrassed

---

schizotypal symptoms and the subsequent development of schizophrenia, with particular attention to learning why these individuals do not develop full-blown psychosis in the form of schizophrenia (Seeber & Cadenhead, 2005).

There is also evidence that people with schizotypal personality disorder have some of the same biological anomalies as people with schizophrenia, such as memory deficits (Roitman et al., 2000), enlarged brain ventricles (Kurokawa et al., 2000), and abnormalities of eye movements (Larrison, Ferrante, Briand, & Sereno, 2000). Subtle differences appear, however, in the thalamic area of the brain within specific structures involved in the transmission of sensory information to corresponding areas in the cortex (Byne et al., 2001).

Evidence in support for the schizophrenia spectrum concept also comes from genetic studies. In one investigation, the offspring of women with schizophrenia were found to be more likely to have schizotypal personality disorder along with other disorders along the theoretical schizophrenia spectrum (Tienari et al., 2000). In another large investigation of the relatives of individuals with an onset of schizophrenia in childhood, schizotypal personality disorder was found to be more prevalent in patients' parents (Asarnow et al., 2001).

Treatment for people with schizotypal personality disorder parallels the interventions commonly used in treating schizophrenia. For example, many individuals with schizotypal personality disorder experience cognitive and perceptual distortions, symptoms that seem to respond to neuroleptic antipsychotic medications (Coccaro, 1998). Clinicians working with these clients strive to establish a therapeutic alliance prior to confronting their distortions of reality (Millon et al., 2000), or before trying to persuade them to take antipsychotic medication.

Avoidant Personality Disorder

Most people feel some degree of shyness on occasion—for example, in an unfamiliar situation in which they do not know other people. They may be concerned about committing a social blunder and appearing foolish; however, if a person is always

Although wanting to do so, a person with avoidant personality disorder cannot join in a lively conversation, due to the fear of saying something embarrassing.

intimidated by social situations, fearful of any kind of involvement with others, and terrified by the prospect of being publicly embarrassed, he or she may have **avoidant personality disorder.**

People with avoidant personality disorder refrain almost entirely from social encounters, especially avoiding any situation with the potential for personal harm or embarrassment, and they steer clear of an activity that is not part of their usual, everyday routine. Sometimes they imagine terrible calamities resulting from novel activities and use this concern as a reason to avoid new situations where they can be seen by other people. Convinced that they are socially inferior to others, they become extremely sensitive to rejection and ridicule, interpreting the most innocent remark as criticism. As a result of their desire to avoid the imagined disapproval of others, they tend to be loners. Their job preferences reflect this desire to keep away from others; they avoid occupations that would involve interacting with people. If they can be assured of unconditional acceptance, they can enter into close and even intimate relationships. However, they remain restrained in their relationships, guarding against possible criticism, embarrassment, or rejection.

This disorder shares some characteristics with schizoid personality disorder. In both disorders, the person tends to stay away from intimate relationships. However, the person with the avoidant disorder truly desires closeness and feels a great deal of emotional pain about the seeming inability to make connections with others. By contrast, the schizoid individual prefers to be alone and lacks a sense of distress about being uninvolved with others.

Avoidant personality disorder is thought to exist along a continuum extending from the normal personality trait of shyness to the anxiety disorder known as social phobia (which we discussed in Chapter 5). According to this view, avoidant personality disorder is a more severe form of social phobia (Rettew, 2000), possibly distinguished from social phobia by the presence of introversion and depressive symptoms (van Velzen, Emmelkamp, & Scholing, 2000). Data from the relatives of people with social phobia further support the notion of a link with avoidant personality disorder. In a study that explored genetic links among these disorders, relatives of people with social phobia with and without avoidant personality disorder were at higher risk for experiencing excessive social anxiety (Tillfors, Furmark, Ekselius, & Fredrikson, 2001). Avoidant personality disorder was also found to be more prevalent in the parents of people who developed schizophrenia in childhood (Asarnow et al., 2001).

Contemporary psychodynamic explanations of this disorder emphasize the individual's fear of attachment in relationships (Sheldon & West, 1990), while cognitive-behavioral approaches regard the individual as hypersensitive to rejection, due to childhood experiences of extreme parental criticism (Beck et al., 2004; Freeman et al., 1990). According to this approach, the dysfunctional attitudes these individuals hold center around the core belief that they are flawed and unworthy of other people's regard. Because of their perceived unworthiness, they expect that people will not like them; therefore, they avoid getting close to others to protect themselves from what they believe to be inevitable rejection. Contributing to their dilemma are their distorted perceptions of experiences with others. Their sensitivity to rejection causes them to misinterpret seemingly neutral and even positive remarks. Hurt by this presumed rejection, they retreat inward, placing further distance between themselves and others.

The main goal of cognitive-behavioral therapy is to break the negative cycle of avoidance. The client learns to articulate the automatic thoughts and dysfunctional attitudes that are interfering with interpersonal relations and to see the irrationality of these beliefs, but in a supportive atmosphere. These interventions are most successfully accomplished after the client has come to trust the therapist. Other therapeutic measures based on a cognitive-behavioral model include graduated exposure to increasingly threatening social situations and the training of specific skills to improve intimate relationships. The very nature of the avoidant condition makes the treatment prognosis poor, primarily because these clients tend to be intensely sensitive to the possibility of any form of negative evaluation. Therapists, regardless of orientation, must be extremely patient in their attempts to build a therapeutic relationship, because it is only within a context of trust that there is any hope of making therapeutic progress (Millon et al., 2000).

Dependent Personality Disorder

Unlike people with avoidant personality disorder, individuals with **dependent personality disorder** are strongly drawn to others. However, they are so clinging and passive that they may achieve the opposite of their desires as others become impatient with their lack of autonomy. Convinced of their own inadequacy, they cannot make even the most trivial decisions on their own. For example, a man may feel incapable of selecting his clothes each day without consulting his live-in partner. In more important spheres, he may rely on his partner to tell him what kind of job to seek, whom he should be friends with, and how he should plan his life.

Others may characterize individuals with this disorder as "clingy." Without others near them, people with dependent personality disorder feel despondent and abandoned. They become preoccupied with the fear that close ones will leave them. They cannot initiate new activities on their own, because they feel that they will make mistakes unless others guide their actions. They go to extremes to avoid being disliked—for example, by agreeing with other people's opinions, even when they believe these opinions to be misguided. Sometimes they take on responsibilities that no one else wants, so that others will approve of and like them. If anyone criticizes them, they feel shattered. They are likely to throw themselves wholeheartedly into relationships and, therefore, become devastated when relationships end. This extreme dependence causes them to seek another relationship urgently to fill the void.

Mini Case

DEPENDENT PERSONALITY DISORDER

Betty has never lived on her own; even while a college student, 30 years ago, she commuted from home. She was known by her classmates as someone who was dependent on others. Relying on others to make choices for her, she did whatever her friends advised, whether it involved the choice of courses or the clothes she should wear each day. The week after graduation, she married Ken, whom she had dated all senior year. She was particularly attracted to Ken, because his domineering style relieved her of the responsibility to make decisions. As she has customarily done with all the close people in her life, Betty goes along with whatever Ken suggests, even if she does not fully agree. She fears that he will become angry with her and leave her if she rocks the boat. Although she wants to get a job outside the home, Ken has insisted that she remain a full-time homemaker, and she has complied with his wishes. However, when she is home alone, she calls friends and desperately pleads with them to come over for coffee. The slightest criticism from Ken, her friends, or anyone else can leave her feeling depressed and upset for the whole day.

Diagnostic Features

People with this disorder have a pervasive and excessive need to be taken care of, which leads to their submissive, clinging behavior and fears of separation, as indicated by five or more of the following:

- Difficulty making everyday decisions without advice and reassurance
- Need for others to assume responsibility for most major areas of life
- Difficulty expressing disagreement with others due to fear of loss of support or approval
- Difficulty initiating projects or tasks because of low self-confidence in judgment or abilities
- Tendency to go to excessive lengths to obtain nurturance and support to the point of volunteering to do things that are unpleasant
- Feelings of discomfort or helplessness when alone due to fear of being unable to care for themselves
- Pursuit of another relationship as a source of care and support immediately following the end of a close relationship
- Preoccupation with fears of being left to take care of themselves

Psychodynamic theory has traditionally regarded individuals with dependent personality disorder as having regressed to or become fixated at the oral stage of development because of parental overindulgence or parental neglect of dependency needs. Object relations theorists regard such individuals as being insecurely attached, constantly fearing abandonment (West & Sheldon, 1988). Because of their low self-esteem, they rely on others for guidance and support (Livesly, Schroeder, & Jackson, 1990). Consistent with these theories, researchers using the Family Environment Scale have found that the families of people with dependent personality disorder tend to have high ratings on the factor of control but low ratings on the factor of independence (Baker, Capron, & Azorlosa, 1996).

A cognitive-behavioral approach to dependent personality disorder maintains that resting at the heart of the disorder are unassertiveness and anxiety over making independent decisions. Dependent individuals believe that they are inadequate and helpless and, therefore, are unable to deal with problems on their own. For them, the natural solution is to find someone else who will "take care" of them and relieve them of the obligation to make independent decisions. Having arrived at this solution, they dare not act in assertive ways that might challenge the relationship's security.

Unlike for most of the other personality disorders, there is much greater cause for optimism regarding treatment of people with dependent personality disorder. Most people with this condition are motivated to change (Millon et al., 2000). In psychotherapy based on cognitive-behavioral principles, the therapist provides structured ways for the client to practice increasing levels of independence in carrying out daily activities.

When waiting to meet a late-arriving friend, a person with dependent personality disorder may feel helpless, not knowing what to do.

The client also learns to identify actual areas of skill deficits and then to acquire the abilities necessary to perform these skills. However, while helping the client, the therapist avoids becoming an authority figure to the client. Clearly, it would be counterproductive for the client to become as dependent on the therapist as on others in his or her life (Beck et al., 2004; Freeman et al., 1990).

Obsessive-Compulsive Personality Disorder

People with obsessive-compulsive personality disorder struggle continuously with an overwhelming concern about neatness and the minor details of everyday life. You can probably think of instances in your own life when you have found it very difficult to make a decision. Perhaps you worried about the matter for days, going back and forth between two choices, somewhat tormented by the process of evaluating the pros and cons of each choice. Imagine what it would be like to go through life this way. People with **obsessive-compulsive personality disorder** feel immobilized by their inability to make a decision. (The words *obsessive* and *compulsive* in this context have a different meaning from the way you will see them used in the next chapter, when we discuss the anxiety disorder known as obsessive-compulsive disorder, a condition in which the individual suffers with the kind of diagnosable obsessions or compulsions we discussed in Chapter 3.) In addition, people with obsessive-compulsive personality disorder are intensely perfectionistic and inflexible and express these attributes in a number of maladaptive ways. In striving for unattainable perfection, they become caught up in a worried style of thinking, and their behavior is inflexible to the point of being rigid.

The disturbance of people with obsessive-compulsive personality disorder is also evident in how they act. They have an inordinate concern with neatness and detail, often to the point of losing perspective on what is important and what is not. This style is both irksome to others and inefficient for the individual with the disorder, because it makes it impossible to complete a project. Every single detail must come out just right, and, by the time these details are handled, the person has run out of time or resources. Similarly, these individuals' daily lives are ruled by a fanatical concern with schedules. For example, they might refuse to start a meeting until precisely the second it is scheduled to begin, or they might insist on seating each person in a room in alphabetical order. They are stingy with time and money and tend to hoard even worn-out and worthless objects. People with this disorder have a poor ability to express emotion, and they have few intimate relationships. Their intense involvement in their work contributes to this pattern, because they have little time for leisure or socializing. When they do interact with other people, they tend to be so rigid that they will not concede or compromise when there is disagreement. Others may regard them as excessively moralistic or prudish because of their narrow views on social, religious, and political issues.

Mini Case

OBSESSIVE-COMPULSIVE PERSONALITY DISORDER

For as long as he can remember, Trevor has been preoccupied with neatness and order. As a child, his room was meticulously clean. Friends and relatives chided him for excessive organization; for example, he insisted on arranging the toys in his toy closet according to color and category. In college, his rigid housekeeping regimens both amazed and annoyed his roommates. He was tyrannical in his insistence on keeping the room orderly and free from clutter. Trevor has continued this pattern into his adult life. He is unhappy that he has not found a woman who shares his personal habits but consoles himself by becoming immersed in his collection of rare record albums featuring music of the 1940s. Trevor, a file clerk, prides himself on never having missed a day of work, regardless of health problems and family crises. However, his boss will not offer him a promotion, because she feels he is overattentive to details, thus slowing up the work of the office as he checks and rechecks everything he does. He enhances his sense of self-importance by looking for opportunities in the office to take control. For example, when his co-workers are planning a party, Trevor tends to slow down matters because of his annoying concerns about every detail about the event. More often than not, his co-workers try to avoid letting him get involved, because they object to his rigidity even in such trivial matters.

Diagnostic Features

This diagnosis applies to people with a pervasive pattern of preoccupation with orderliness, perfectionism, and mental and interpersonal control, at the expense of flexibility, openness, and efficiency, as indicated by four or more of the following:

- Preoccupation with details, rules, order, organization, or schedules to such an extent that the major point of the activity is lost
- Perfectionism that interferes with task completion
- Excessive devotion to work and productivity to the exclusion of leisure activities and friendships (not due to economic necessity)
- Tendency to be overconscientious, scrupulous, and inflexible about matters of morality, ethics, or values (not due to culture or religion)
- Inability to discard worn-out or worthless objects
- Reluctance to delegate tasks to others unless they agree to an exact way of doing things
- Miserly spending style toward self and others
- Rigidity and stubbornness

It is important to keep in mind that there is a difference between the hard-working, well-organized person with high standards and a concern about getting a job done right and the person with an obsessive-compulsive personality disorder. People with this disorder are unproductive, and their pursuit of perfectionism becomes self-defeating rather than constructive. Obsessive-compulsive personality disorder is one of the more common personality disorders (Weissman, 1993), and it is more common in men than women (Golomb, Fava, Abraham, & Rosenbaum, 1995).

Freud believed that the obsessive-compulsive style represented fixation at or regression to the anal stage of psychosexual development. Psychodynamic thinking about this disorder has advanced somewhat from the time of Freud, however, with more attention given to cognitive factors and prior learning experiences as central in its development.

From the standpoint of cognitive-behavioral theory, people with this disorder have unrealistic expectations about being perfect and avoiding mistakes (Beck et al., 2004; Freeman et al., 1990). Their feelings of self-worth depend on their behaving in ways that conform to an abstract ideal of perfectionism; if they fail to achieve that ideal (which, inevitably, they must), they regard themselves as worthless. In this framework, obsessive-compulsive personality disorder is based on a problematic way of viewing the self. Supporting the importance of cognitive factors, researchers have identified among people with this disorder a greater tendency to be distracted by small details unimportant to the processing of visual stimuli (Yovel, Revelle, & Mineka, 2005).

Cognitive-behavioral treatment can be made more difficult due to characteristic features of this personality disorder. The person with obsessive-compulsive personality disorder tends to intellectualize (Millon et al., 2000), to go over past actions constantly, and to consider further actions in light of whether or not there is a danger of making a mistake. Cognitive-behavioral therapy, with its focus on examining the client's thought processes, may reinforce this ruminative tendency. Consequently, some therapists use more traditional behavioral techniques, such as thought stopping—instructing the client to reduce the amount of time spent in ruminative worry (Millon et al., 2000).

Personality Disorders: The Biopsychosocial Perspective

Now that you have read about the wide variety of ingrained patterns represented in the personality disorders, you can appreciate that it is difficult to make general statements about the causes and treatment of this diverse group. As we have seen throughout this chapter, researchers working in the field of personality disorders have struggled with the issue of overlap among these disorders (Bornstein, 1998). The jury is still out on whether the *DSM-IV-TR* has brought about greater refinement.

While researchers continue to investigate the best system for diagnosing personality disorders, clinicians continue to look for the most effective methods for treating people whose symptoms have endured over many years and whose problems have been resistant to change. Not surprisingly, people with personality disorders, particularly borderline, make extensive use of interventions ranging from medications to various forms of therapy (Bender et al., 2001). Given the uncertainties regarding the causes and nature of these personality disorders, clinicians focus their therapeutic efforts on the primary causes of the client's current distress, a more realistic goal than bringing about total change. Although some clinicians follow a set of specific ideas about treatment, most individualize their treatment to respond to the particular problems of each client. For example, when treating a person with a dependent personality disorder, the clinician can help the client understand the roots of this dependency and then intervene in ways to reinforce autonomy. In contrast, when treating a client with avoidant personality disorder, the therapist focuses on helping the client develop more satisfying interpersonal relations. Some theorists recommend particular attention to the therapeutic alliance when working with personality disordered individuals, especially in light of the fact that impairment in interpersonal relationships is so central to the disturbance of these individuals. Specifically, those with Cluster A personality disorders (schizotypal, schizoid, and paranoid) suffer from a profound impairment in interpersonal relationships. Those with Cluster B personality disorders (antisocial, borderline, histrionic, and narcissistic) tend to push the limits, thus requiring clinicians to exercise great care to avoid crossing inappropriate lines in their efforts to build an alliance. Individuals with Cluster C personality disorders (avoidant, dependent, and obsessive-compulsive) are emotionally inhibited and averse to interpersonal conflict; they are prone to feelings of guilt, and tend to internalize blame for situations. Clinicians working with these clients may find it easier to build an alliance because of their greater willingness to engage (Bender, 2005).

At times, the clinician may rely more heavily on particular theoretical perspectives if they seem pertinent to the client's history and current symptoms. For example, when treating clients with borderline personality disorder, more and more clinicians are finding that cognitive-behavioral approaches, such as Dialectical Behavior Therapy, are quite helpful. Even clinicians who identify with other approaches may incorporate some of these techniques in treating clients with this personality disorder.

Another feature of the personality disorders reflecting biopsychosocial factors is that they evolve over the period of adulthood. Table 10.1 presents a summary of the main features of these disorders as they are thought to appear in later adulthood. These are important to keep in mind in attempting to understand and treat individuals with these disorders as they move into old age.

TABLE 10.1 Theorized Patterns in Later Life of Axis II Disorders of the *DSM-IV-TR*

Disorder	Theorized patterns in later life
Antisocial personality disorder	Underlying trait of psychopathy does not seem to change with age. There is a reduction of impulsive and deviant behaviors.
Borderline personality disorder	Prevalence in older adults not well-established. Risky behaviors and suicide of individuals when young may lead to apparent decline in prevalence.
Histrionic personality disorder	Physical changes that signify to them a loss of attractiveness and sexuality may lead to difficult adaptation to aging.
Narcissistic personality disorder	"Narcissistic injuries" due to loss of power and prestige and general ageism in society may lead to increases in symptoms.
Paranoid personality disorder	Age-related deficits in vision and hearing, along with cognitive changes, may lead to isolation as the individual grows to believe that others are threatening or talking about him or her in negative ways.
Schizoid personality disorder	The need to depend on others for care with physical or cognitive infirmities creates stress due to lifelong patterns of social isolation.
Schizotypal personality disorder	No clear prevalence data. However, odd and disorganized behavior in a person who does not have dementia may indicate the presence of this disorder.
Avoidant personality disorder	People with this disorder resist applying for and receiving needed social and supportive services. Without such support, they can become lonely, anxious, and frightened.
Dependent personality disorder	Older adults with this disorder experience extreme difficulty adjusting to widowhood. They become helpless, lost, and vulnerable and might turn to children to replace the spouse.
Obsessive-compulsive personality disorder	This disorder can become worse in later adulthood due to a greater need for control over the environment in the face of physical, cognitive, and social losses.

Source: Adapted from D. L. Segal, F. L. Coolidge, and E. Rosowsky in S. K. Whitbourne (Ed.) *Psychopathology in Later Life*, pp. 89–116. Copyright © 2000. Reprinted with permission of John Wiley & Sons, Inc.

Because of the chronic and persistent nature of personality disorders, as well as the difficulty in precisely identifying their qualities, these disorders are likely to remain a challenging area for researchers and clinicians. It is also quite likely that the diagnostic criteria for these disorders, and even their names, will undergo continued revision in future editions of the *DSM*, as theorists and researchers continue to refine and elaborate on their scientific base. In this process, mental health professionals will develop not only a better understanding of this form of disturbance, but also perhaps a richer appreciation for the factors that contribute to normal personality growth and change through life.

Harold's History

The story Harold told about his life helped me make sense of the turmoil of the past few years. The only child of middle-class parents, Harold spent much of his childhood seeking a compromise between his mother's demands that he stay "out of trouble" and his own desires to play and explore in his backyard and neighborhood. When explaining even relatively minor incidents that occurred, the words he used to describe his mother reflected the intensity of his feelings about her, as well as his pained ambivalence toward her. She was a "bitch . . . always yelling at me for anything I did. She controlled my every move, yelled at me for playing too long with my friends, going too far from the house, leaving her home all alone. If I stayed in the backyard and near her, I was the good boy, and she praised me and rewarded me with candy and cookies. But, if I strayed for an hour, even when I was a teenager, she yelled down the street and humiliated me. Maybe it was her way of showing she loved me and worried about me, but it was a tough thing to deal with."

Harold's description of his father was certainly no more positive than that of his mother. He spoke of his resentment about the fact that his father was hardly ever home and that, when he was there, he virtually ignored Harold. The message his mother repeated so often to Harold haunts him to the present day. She told him that she needed him to be the "man of the house." According to Harold, this was how she rationalized her need for him to stay so close to her—he had "important responsibilities, after all."

Harold told me that during adolescence he desperately tried to flee his mother's clutches. He became caught up in substance abuse, which seemed like his only chance "to escape." Introduced to the world of street drugs, Harold became involved in a promiscuous and dangerous lifestyle, as he became caught up in drug trafficking and petty thiev-

ery. He finally moved out of his mother's apartment to a squalid room in a boarding house, and he hasn't spoken to his mother in more than 5 years. Occasionally, he sees his father but is not interested in maintaining a relationship with him.

Throughout most of his twenties, Harold drifted from job to job, without any sense of purpose. He tried college several times but dropped out, because the "teachers were such losers." Harold contended that his employment instability was due mostly to a series of health problems. He told me about three hospitalizations, each of which resulted from a serious motorcycle accident. He enumerated a long list of broken bones, concussions, and internal injuries he had sustained and, with a laugh in his voice, commented, "You'd think I was trying to kill myself, wouldn't you?"

Relationships have been terribly unhappy for Harold. Throughout adolescence and adulthood, he has moved from one relationship to another, abruptly walking out on people who have been unable to satisfy his insatiable demands for love and affection. As Harold described the many stormy relationships of his life, he found it difficult to acknowledge the possibility that he might have played a role in their failure.

Assessment

I told Harold that a psychological assessment battery would help me derive a clearer understanding of the nature of his problem. Initially, he responded with irritation, but he finally agreed. This ambivalence was evident throughout the testing sessions. At times, he was cooperative and pleasant, but he became irascible and impatient a short while later.

Harold's IQ is above average, but his IQ score alone did not tell the whole story about Harold's intelligence. The variability among the WAIS-III subtest scores reflected the unevenness in his cognitive functioning, with impressive strengths on certain tasks (such as vocabulary)

but notable deficits on others (such as comprehension). Harold's problem with comprehension tasks revealed his inadequate understanding of appropriate behavior in common situations. For instance, he responded to a question about why stoplights are needed by saying, "So that people won't murder each other." Although the essence of Harold's response to this question suggested that he understood the issue, I noted the angry content of what he said and how he said it.

Harold's profile on the MMPI-2 revealed serious personality disorganization, with some psychotic-like features. This impression was supported by his performance on the Rorschach test, in which he gave many unusual responses, describing images that are rarely reported by others who take the test. In the color cards, Harold saw fire, explosions, and bursts of ammunition, coupled with sadistic human destruction: "a grenade blowing up in the middle of a Sunday picnic." Themes of rage in the face of abandonment were particularly pronounced in Harold's TAT stories. He described people's moods as changing suddenly and chaotically, and the plots of his stories were similarly disorganized.

Diagnosis

Most striking about Harold's story is the chaos that has permeated most facets of his life. His relationships have been turbulent and unfulfilling, his emotions volatile, his behavior self-destructive and impulsive, and his sense of self seriously confused.

My initial interaction with Harold left me with a fairly certain diagnostic impression of borderline personality disorder. In part, my inference was based on his presenting problems and history, but I was also deeply affected by my personal reactions to Harold. I found myself feeling sympathetic toward him at times and at times feeling disturbed by his abusive responses to my efforts to understand and help him.

I was tuning in to the process by which Harold was "splitting" in his dealings with me, at times complimenting me about my clinical skillfulness but soon thereafter questioning my competence and ability to establish rapport with him.

As I considered the diagnostic criteria for borderline personality disorder, I confirmed my initial diagnostic hunch. Harold has a history of unstable and intense interpersonal relationships in which he responded to people in dramatically different ways, vacillating between idealization and devaluation of anyone close to him. This was commonly intertwined with affective instability, in which he felt tossed from one emotional state to another, feeling extremes of depression, anxiety, and irritability. At times, his mood escalated into inappropriate and intense expressions of anger in the form of temper tantrums and victimizing behavior. At other times, the anger was self-directed and took the form of impulsive and self-destructive pursuits—such as reckless motorcycle driving, promiscuity, and drug abuse. Never really sure about his own identity, he wandered from lifestyle to lifestyle, from lover to lover, and from job to job, in a desperate attempt to fill the void that he painfully carried with him everywhere.

Axis I: Rule out cocaine dependence

Axis II: Borderline personality disorder

Axis III: History of motorcycle injury that may include head trauma

Axis IV: Problems with primary support group (lack of contact with parents) Occupational problems (discord and job instability)

Axis V: Current Global Assessment of Functioning: 32 Highest Global Assessment of Functioning (past year): 32

Case Formulation

My diagnosis of Harold seemed clear and accurate, in that he met the criteria for borderline personality disorder. But how did Harold develop this personality structure? By putting together the information from my interview, the psychological assessment, and Harold's history and current presenting problems, I was able to formulate hypotheses based on what clinicians and researchers know about this personality disorder.

When trying to understand the etiology of an individual's personality disorder, it is common to consider the family's contributions, both genetic and environmental. According to Harold, both his parents were "troubled people." We can see this disturbance in his mother's overprotective and anxious interactions with Harold and in his father's aloofness and emotional unavailability. Could these personality disturbances have been transmitted genetically? Scientific understanding of this possibility remains limited, but it is reasonable to conclude that, as a result of his parents' disturbance, Harold grew up in an emotionally unhealthy home environment.

Looking at these issues more closely, we see a family system ripe for the development of a personality disorder. Harold's father was distant, rejecting, and ineffective in moderating his wife's overcontrol of their son. Moreover, at a time when children need to be able to exercise some autonomy, Harold's mother was over-controlling. She punished him by withdrawing her love if he ventured away from her. The only way he could gain her love was by not leaving her in the first place. Harold's mother exerted similar pressure on him during his adolescence. Under these circumstances, Harold's ability to differentiate himself psychologically from his mother would have been extremely impeded, contributing to his current identity confusion.

Behavioral and systems perspectives help augment this understanding of Harold's problems. For example, it is reasonable to imagine that Harold modeled his interpersonal relationships after the disturbed relationships he observed in his home life. Perhaps Harold "learned" negative attitudes about himself and inadequate strategies for coping with stresses, particularly those his mother imposed on him.

Harold's difficulties may also be seen as resulting from a disturbed family system in which an overinvolved mother formed a unit with Harold that excluded his father. Her overinvolvement continued into adolescence, a time when he should have been allowed to break away from the family. His involvement in the world of street drugs could be seen as the result of his mother having placed him in an impossible situation of not being able to satisfy her and his own needs simultaneously. Perhaps he saw drugs as the only escape from this dilemma. In addition, Harold's inability to develop an adult identity reflects his mother's reluctance to let Harold grow up. He went on to substitute dependence on lovers for the pathological relationship with his mother.

Treatment Plan

After my initial evaluation of Harold, I felt that intervention should involve an attempt at restructuring his personality, while attending to his current stresses and self-defeating behaviors. Had Harold been suicidal or more seriously self-destructive, I might have recommended that he admit himself to an inpatient treatment program, which is sometimes beneficial for people with borderline personality disorder. This is especially true for those who seem to need the security and stability of the milieu. Although I considered this for Harold, his limited financial resources made hospitalization impossible. Therefore, I recommended outpatient psychotherapy.

Harold asked me if I would be his psychotherapist, stating that I was the "only person to seem to understand" his problems. Having treated a number of people with borderline personality disorder, I was alert to the probability that Harold's positive response involved idealization, commonly noted in people with this personality disorder. At the same time, I found myself feeling interested in treating Harold. Something about him affected me deeply. Perhaps I was moved by the belief that I could help him undertake major life changes. Some might call this a "rescue fantasy"—the notion that psychotherapists can rescue clients from the unhappiness that has become so much a part of their lives. With a bit of apprehension, and following a consultation with my colleagues about the wisdom of my treating Harold, I agreed to accept him into treatment and recommended that we schedule two sessions weekly for the first 3 months. I believed that the increased frequency of sessions would facilitate the development of rapport.

The treatment approach I have found to be most effective in treating people like Harold involves an integration of psychodynamic and cognitive-behavioral approaches. Within the psychodynamic perspective, I planned an intense psychotherapy, in which the pattern of Harold's early life relationships could be brought to the surface and re-examined. I was not so naive as to consider such an approach with Harold to be simple. I expected that his initial laudatory comments about my clinical expertise would very likely be replaced by devaluing critiques of my "incompetence." I was prepared for the likelihood that he would act and speak in provocative ways, perhaps testing me to see if I would angrily reject him, thereby proving that I wasn't really concerned about him. I knew that there was a strong possibility that he would end treatment precipitously and go to another therapist, to whom he might describe me in very unflattering ways. In addition to the psychodynamic framework, I planned to incorporate some cognitive-behavioral techniques with which Harold could learn appropriate styles of interacting with others, more constructive ways of perceiving himself, and more effective strategies for dealing with ordinary life stresses.

Outcome of the Case

To no one's surprise, including mine, Harold's treatment did not go very well. The first few months were difficult and, frankly, fairly stressful for me. Harold became increasingly demanding of my attention and time, making emergency telephone calls on weekends, asking for extra sessions, and ruminating in therapy sessions about how frustrating it was not to be able to find out more about my personal life. One incident troubled me greatly. It took place on a Friday afternoon as I was leaving my office, several hours after a session with Harold. As I got into my car, I noticed in the rearview mirror that Harold was sitting in his car across the parking lot, ostensibly ready to follow me home. Feeling both alarmed and angry, I walked over and spoke to Harold; he acknowledged that my hunch was correct but became very angry with me when I pointed out the inappropriateness of this plan. When he didn't show up for either of our sessions the following week, I felt greatly relieved. At the same time, I recognized my responsibility to reach out to Harold in a therapeutic manner, so I decided to drop him a note, urging him to come to our regularly scheduled sessions.

Harold returned to therapy, but his response to me remained troubling from that point on. His expressions of anger were more aptly characterized as rage, as he derided many of my efforts to help. By contrast, there were numerous times when he seemed responsive, and he made temporary changes in his life that reflected a more healthy way of thinking and acting. We continued our therapy sessions for another year, during which our work could best be described as rocky.

Another crisis unfolded when I informed Harold that I would be taking a 3-week vacation several weeks hence. Once again, he failed to show up for our sessions, and I tried to reach out to him by urging him to resume therapy sessions. A week after I mailed my letter to him, I received a disturbing phone call from the emergency room physician in the hospital where I worked. Harold had taken an overdose of heroin and wanted to see me. I did see Harold and made arrangements for him to be admitted to the inpatient psychiatric unit. He told me how grateful he felt about my expression of concern and how relieved he felt that our sessions would resume, this time on the inpatient unit. I wondered whether he had manipulated me, but I felt that the seriousness of his self-destructive behavior warranted inpatient treatment.

Harold remained on the unit for 2 weeks and seemed to stabilize, both physically and emotionally. However, in our session just prior to his discharge from the hospital, Harold angrily told me of his plans never to return to therapy with me. He stated that he wanted to find a therapist who would be "more giving" than I was. My efforts to work through this issue with Harold failed, and I never did see him again. Several months after our termination, I read in the newspaper that Harold had been arrested and charged with reckless driving while intoxicated. The photograph accompanying the newspaper story showed Harold staring into the camera with knifelike intensity. I could see the rage in his eyes, yet at the same time I knew that underlying his rage were feelings of confusion, loneliness, and desperation.

Sarah Tobin, PhD

SUMMARY

- A personality disorder involves a long-lasting, maladaptive pattern of inner experience and behavior, dating back to adolescence or young adulthood, that is manifested in at least two of the following areas: (1) cognition, (2) affectivity, (3) interpersonal functioning, and (4) impulse control. This inflexible pattern is evident in various personal and social situations, and it causes distress or impairment. Because personality disorders involve the whole fabric of an individual's being, clinicians typically perceive these as being the most challenging of the psychological disorders to treat. Personality disorders cause major intrapsychic and interpersonal difficulty, leading to long-lasting impairment. The diagnosis of personality disorders is difficult, because many personality disorders share similar features, causing some concerns about the reliability and validity of these diagnoses. The *DSM-IV-TR* uses separate diagnoses that are grouped into three clusters based on shared characteristics. Cluster A comprises paranoid, schizoid, and schizotypal personality disorders, which share the features of odd and eccentric behavior. Cluster B includes antisocial, borderline, histrionic, and narcissistic personality disorders. People with these disorders are overdramatic, emotional, erratic, or unpredictable. In Cluster C are avoidant, dependent, and obsessive-compulsive personality disorders. These are linked because they involve anxious and fearful behaviors.

- People with antisocial personality disorder lack regard for society's moral or legal standards. This diagnosis has its origins in Cleckley's notion of psychopathy, a personality type characterized by several features, such as lack of remorse, extreme egocentricity, lack of emotional expressiveness, impulsivity, and untruthfulness. *DSM-IV-TR* diagnostic criteria add behavioral aspects involving disreputable and manipulative behaviors. Biological theories have focused on brain abnormalities, such as defects in the prefrontal lobes of the cerebral cortex. There is considerable support for the notion that genetic makeup plays an important, though not exclusive, role. Psychological theories have focused on the notion that these individuals are unable to feel fear or anxiety or to process any information that is not relevant to their immediate goals. Sociocultural perspectives focus on family, early environment, and socialization experiences. As for treatment, experts recommend confrontation, especially in group therapy.

- Borderline personality disorder is characterized by a pervasive pattern of poor impulse control, fluctuating self-image, and unstable mood and interpersonal relationships. Many people with this condition engage in splitting and parasuicidal behavior. An interesting biological theory focuses on brain differences, particularly hypersensitive noradrenergic pathways, that may have evolved as a result of earlier trauma. Psychological theories have dwelled on trauma and abuse as predisposing factors. Sociocultural views focus on the possibility that many people develop this disorder as a result of diminished cohesion in contemporary society. As for treatment, clinicians try to balance levels of support and confrontation, while giving special attention to issues of stability and boundaries. Linehan's Dialectical Behavior Therapy involves components of acceptance and confrontation. As an adjunct to psychological treatment, some clinicians recommend medication.

- In addition to antisocial and borderline personality disorders, which have received extensive attention in the research and clinical literature, there are eight other personality disorders. The diagnosis of histrionic personality disorder is given to people who show a pattern of excessive emotionality and attention seeking, while narcissistic personality disorder applies to people who show a pervasive pattern of grandiosity, need for admiration, and lack of empathy. Paranoid personality disorder is characterized by extreme suspiciousness of others. People with schizoid personality disorder show a pattern of detachment from relationships and a restricted range of emotional expression in their dealings with others. Those with schizotypal personality disorder show a pattern of social and interpersonal deficits marked by acute discomfort with, and reduced capacity for, close relationships; they also experience cognitive or perceptual distortions and behavioral eccentricities. Avoidant personality disorder is characterized by a pattern of social inhibition, feelings of inadequacy, and hypersensitivity to negative evaluation. People with dependent personality disorder have an excessive need to be taken care of, which leads to their submissive and clinging behavior and fears of separation. The diagnosis of obsessive-compulsive personality disorder is characterized by a preoccupation with orderliness, perfectionism, and mental and interpersonal control, at the expense of flexibility, openness, and efficiency. Given the lack of certainty about the causes of personality disorders, clinicians tend to focus efforts on improving the client's current life experiences, rather than attempts to bring about total change; consequently, most therapists individualize treatments to respond to the particular present needs and difficulties of each client.

KEY TERMS

See Glossary for definitions

INTERNET RESOURCE

To get more information on the material covered in this chapter, visit our website at **www.mhhe.com/halgin5.** There you will find more information, resources, and links to topics of interest.

CHAPTER II

Development-Related Disorders

From the moment I entered the waiting room to greet 8-year-old Jason Newman and his parents, I could tell that my intake session would be a challenge. Jason's father, Marvin, was kneeling on the floor, trying to sponge up several gallons of water leaking from the water cooler that Jason had just knocked over. His mother, Janet, stood nearby and, with audible exasperation, scolded Jason for his carelessness. With a mixture of tearfulness and rage, Mrs. Newman sternly lashed out at Jason with the words "Why can't you be more careful?! Get over there and help your father clean up the mess you just made!" Instead of paying any attention to her, however, Jason was intensely committed to playing a game on his handheld Nintendo Gameboy. He made popping noises with his mouth, interspersed with cheers about his video accomplishments. Feeling like an intruder in a tense family scene, I awkwardly introduced myself. Even before responding to my introduction, Mrs. Newman crisply commented, "I'm glad you arrived when you did, so that you can see firsthand the kind of frustrations we face with Jason a dozen times every day!" I tried to offer calming and reassuring words, but I realized how upsetting such experiences must be for the entire family, including Jason.

As soon as we began the interview, Jason's parents eagerly proceeded to tell me the ways in which Jason had been creating havoc for most of his life. Neighbors had complained about his behavior for years, each of his classroom teachers had urged the Newmans to get help for him, and most of their relatives had explicitly conveyed their concern about Jason's behavior during family gatherings.

Mrs. Newman's voice was tense as she described her years of struggling with Jason's problems. She explained that, although he had been a quiet child during his infancy, this began to change around Jason's first birthday. As soon as he began walking, Jason became a "terror." When describing a day at home with Jason, Mrs. Newman said she often felt as though she were locked up with an unmanned motorcycle that roared through the house, wrecking everything in its path. Although I had heard many descriptions of attention-deficit/hyperactivity disorder, the words Janet Newman chose had tremendous power, leaving me with the sense that this was an exhausted and exasperated parent.

Mrs. Newman frequently used the term hyper in describing her son. Jason was a fidgeter, always squirming in his seat, frequently jumping up and running around, regardless of whether they were in church, at a movie, or at dinner at home. Jason was a constant source of aggravation to his playmates, because he caused trouble in any game they were playing. Even in the simplest of games, such as basketball, Jason broke the rules, stole the ball from other children, refused to wait his turn, or intentionally provoked others to the point that all the children on the playground yelled at him and told him to go home.

Mrs. Newman had lost count of the number of special teacher conferences to which she had been summoned. In every meeting, the story was the same: Jason did not pay attention in school; he disrupted virtually every classroom activity; he threw things at other children; he played tricks on the teachers; and he talked out loud even during quiet reading time. Each of Jason's teachers had observed that Jason was bright, but they could not get him to do his assignments, either for classroom activities or homework. Even when Jason did complete his homework, he usually lost it on his way to school, along with his books and pencils. The teachers had developed several intervention plans that included behavioral strategies, but the effectiveness of these attempts was limited. As Mr. Newman admitted, "We never followed through with the plan when Jason was home, so I guess that's why he hasn't changed very much."

The Newmans then explained what finally prompted them to seek professional help for Jason. His behavior had gotten so out of control that he was risking the safety of others. At school one day during the previous week, Jason was caught setting fires. Taking a box of wooden matches he had brought from home, Jason went into the boys' lavatory, ignited a roll of toilet paper and some paper towels, and threw a lit match into the wastebasket. The smoke detector set off the school fire alarm, and everyone was evacuated. This was the final straw for the school principal, who called the Newmans and made it clear that Jason could not return to school until a professional treatment plan was in place.

After talking with the Newmans, I asked Jason to meet with me for 15 minutes alone. This was a difficult session, but it gave me the opportunity to interact with Jason in a way that would reduce distractions and interruptions. He answered some of my questions, ignored others, and often abruptly changed the topic. I did get the sense that Jason was upset about his lack of friends. He told me that his teachers were "boring" and that he would rather stay home and practice basketball, because he wanted to play professional basketball when he grew up. After our talk, I could understand the ambivalence that clearly characterized his own mother's response to him. He was an attractive child with some very endearing qualities. At the same time, he engaged in many annoying behaviors that made even brief interactions with him feel exhausting.

Sarah Tobin, PhD

The disorders discussed in this chapter are conceptually related, because they first appear at birth or during youth. Because they strike so early, disorders that begin in childhood are of great concern to the adults who have a role in the child's life. Imagine what it would be like if, as a parent, you faced problems like Jason's on a daily basis. You would probably feel a great deal of personal distress as you struggled to deal with his needs. The emotional burden of having a disturbed child can be great for those who are close to the child, and the pain that the atypical child experiences can last throughout life. Some cases of disturbance are so serious that even the best efforts to bring these children into the mainstream of society have limited positive impact. In recent years, the mental health problems of children have become such a focus of concern that the U.S. surgeon general convened a national conference to develop a national action agenda from which specific recommendations emerged (*Report of the Surgeon General's Conference on Children's Mental Health*, 2000).

Introductory Issues

As you are reading about the conditions described in this chapter, you may wonder at times why mental retardation and learning disabilities, for example, are considered psychological disorders. Some would contend that it is inappropriate to include these conditions in a list of "disorders." Along related lines, some so-called disorders may actually represent developmental aberrations rather than psychiatric abnormalities. For example, you will read about a disorder called oppositional defiant disorder, which involves a pattern of disruptive and uncooperative behavior. You may question if it is right to give a psychiatric diagnosis to a boy who frequently loses his temper, argues with his parents, refuses to obey rules, acts in annoying ways, swears, and lies. However, it is important to keep in mind that these are conditions that result in maladjustment or experiences of

Most children are stubborn at times, but chronically difficult behavior becomes a source of distress and a burden to parents.

distress. Consequently, it makes sense that these conditions are included in the *DSM-IV* for many of the same reasons that other disorders are included.

Mental Retardation

Mental retardation, a condition present from childhood, is characterized by significantly below average general intellectual functioning (an IQ of 70 or below). Approximately 1 percent of the population has mental retardation, and it is more common in males. Mental retardation is a broad term that encompasses several gradations of intellectual functioning and adaptive behavior, which are reflected in the categorization system developed by the American Association of Mental Deficiency and incorporated into the psychiatric nomenclature.

Characteristics of Mental Retardation

In addition to intellectual deficits, people with mental retardation have significant impairments in various abilities involved in adapting to everyday life. For example, they may lack social skills and judgment, have difficulty communicating, or be unable to care for themselves. Many mentally retarded individuals depend on others for their personal care and well-being. Table 11.1 summarizes the common social and academic capabilities at each level of retardation.

Theories and Treatment of Mental Retardation

Mental retardation may result from an inherited condition or from an event or illness that takes place during the course of development at any point from conception through adolescence.

Inherited Causes   Some forms of mental retardation are genetically transmitted from the parents to the child at the time of conception. For example, infants with phenylketonuria (PKU) are born with an inability to utilize phenylalanine, an amino acid essential to the manufacturing of proteins. Phenylalanine builds up in the body's tissues and blood, leading to severe neural damage. Tay-Sachs disease is a metabolic disorder caused by the absence of a vital enzyme (hexosamindase A, or hex-A), which leads to the accumulation of lipid in nerve cells, leading to neural degeneration and early death, usually before the age of 5. Tay-Sachs disease is most commonly found in descendants of Eastern European (Ashkenazi) Jews. Fragile X syndrome, which derives its name from the fact that it is transmitted through the "Fragile X gene (FMR1)" on the X chromosome, is associated with severe forms of retardation, particularly in males.

Other forms of inherited disorders are the result of a chromosomal aberration during conception. **Down syndrome** is the most well known of these forms of mental retardation (named after the English physician who first described the disorder). As we pointed

TABLE 11.1 Classification of Mental Retardation by IQ Scores and Behavioral Competencies

Degree of Retardation	IQ Range	Behavioral Competencies	
		Preschool (0–5)	School Age (6–19)
Mild	50/55–70	Can develop social and communication skills; minimal retardation in sensory-motor area; often not distinguished until later ages	Can learn academic skills up to sixth-grade level; can be guided toward social conformity
Moderate	35/40–50/55	Can talk or learn to communicate; poor social awareness; fair motor skills; profits from self-help skill training; requires some supervision	Can profit from training in social and occupational skills; unlikely to progress beyond second-grade level; some independence in familiar places possible
Severe	20/25–35/40	Poor motor development and minimal language skill; generally cannot profit from training in self-help; little communication	Can learn to talk or communicate; can be trained in elemental self-help skills; profits from systematic habit training
Profound	Under 20 or 25	Gross retardation, with minimal capacity for functioning in sensory-motor areas; requires intense care	Some motor development present; may respond to very limited range of training in self-help

Source: From E. J. Mash & L. G. Terdal (Eds.), *Behavioral Assessment of Childhood Disorders,* 2nd ed. Copyright © Guilford Publications, Inc. Reprinted by permission.

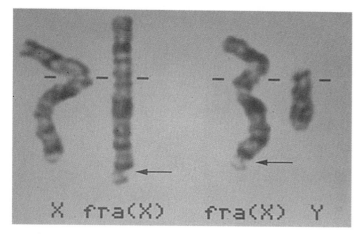

Fragile X syndrome. This is a micrograph of two X chromosomes of a female (*left*) and an X and a Y chromosome of a male (*right*). The two arrows point to the region known as a fragile site. Note that the indentation at the bottom of each looks as if it is ready to break.

out in Chapter 4, Down syndrome is caused by an extra twenty-first chromosome. People with Down syndrome have a characteristic facial structure and one or more physical disabilities. All individuals with Down syndrome have mental retardation, generally ranging from mild to moderate. Compared with other children, their motor, cognitive, and social skills develop at a slower rate. Early in the twentieth century, people with Down syndrome

were fated to live in institutions and rarely lived past the age of 9 years. Improvements in therapeutic and educational interventions, such as better medical treatment and the integration of children into schools and communities, have contributed to increases in life expectancy. Currently, most people with Down syndrome live into their fifties. However, the health of those living to this age is usually poor, and nearly all develop brain changes resembling those of Alzheimer's disease (see Chapter 12).

Environmental Causes Environmental hazards are a second cause of mental retardation. These include exposure to certain drugs or toxic chemicals, maternal malnutrition, and infections in the mother during critical phases of fetal development. For example, researchers have determined that mothers who contract rubella ("German measles") during the first 3 months of pregnancy are likely to have a child with mental retardation. Problems during the baby's delivery that can cause mental retardation include infections, anoxia (loss of oxygen, leading to brain damage), and injury to the brain. Premature birth can also be associated with mental retardation. After birth and all during childhood, mental retardation can result from diseases, head injuries caused by accidents or child abuse, and exposure to toxic substances, such as lead or carbon monoxide.

Fetal alcohol syndrome (FAS) is a set of physical and mental birth defects that results from a mother's alcohol consumption during pregnancy. FAS is considered by some to be the leading cause of mental retardation, affecting approximately

Mini Case

MENTAL RETARDATION

Juanita is a 5-year-old girl with Down syndrome. Her mother was 43 when she and her husband decided to start their family. Because of her age, Juanita's mother was advised to have prenatal testing for any abnormalities in the chromosomal makeup of the developing fetus. Juanita's parents were shocked and distressed when they learned the test results. When Juanita was born, her parents were prepared for what to expect in terms of the child's appearance, behavior, and possible medical problems. Fortunately, Juanita needed no special medical attention. Very early in Juanita's life, her parents consulted with educational specialists, who recommended an enrichment program designed to maximize cognitive functioning. From the age of 6 months, Juanita attended a program each morning in which the staff made intensive efforts to facilitate her motor and intellectual development. Now that she is school-age, Juanita will enter kindergarten at the local public school, where efforts will be made to bring her into the mainstream of education. Fortunately, Juanita lives in a school district in which the administrators recognize the importance of providing resources for pupils like Juanita, so that they will have the opportunity to learn and grow as normally as possible.

Diagnostic Features

- With an onset prior to age 18, people with mental retardation have subaverage intellectual functioning, as demonstrated by such measures as IQ, which is approximately 70 or below.

- They have concurrent deficits or impairments in adaptive functioning in at least two of the following areas: communication, self-care, home living, social/interpersonal skills, use of community resources, self-direction, functional academic skills, work, leisure, health, and safety.

- Degree of severity is either mild, moderate, severe, or profound.

---

1 of every 1,000 live births (Sampson et al., 1997). The condition is of particular concern among certain high-risk groups, such as African Americans, Native Americans, and Canadian Indians (U.S. Department of Health and Human Services, 1993).

At birth, infants with fetal alcohol syndrome are smaller in weight and length, and these deficiencies persist into childhood. Their IQ is usually in the mildly retarded range, although some are severely retarded. Many have a characteristic set of facial abnormalities involving the eyes, nose, jaw, and middle region of the face. Their internal organs may also be affected, particularly the cardiovascular system. Motor and cognitive deficits are also associated with the syndrome, including a lack of coordination, an inability to concentrate, and impairments in speech and hearing. Furthermore, they may be unable to form friendships, and they can become socially withdrawn and isolated.

There appears to be a direct connection between the amount of alcohol ingested by the mother and the degree of physical and behavioral problems in the child. It is not clear just how much alcohol is needed to cause this condition, though researchers have determined that drinking even relatively moderate amounts of alcohol during pregnancy can result in lower birth weight and can place the newborn at risk of dying (National Institute of Alcoholism, 2005). Heavy alcohol intake during pregnancy can also cause a wide range of neuropsychological deficits, including dysfunctions in visuospatial processing, verbal and nonverbal learning, attention, and executive control processes (Riley & McGee, 2005). To reflect the fact that the disorders caused by prenatal exposure to alcohol run along a continuum from mild to severe, experts in the field are now referring to FAS as a spectrum disorder (Hoyme et al., 2005). Prenatal exposure to cocaine also has detrimental effects on the developing fetus, particularly in the area of motor development (Miller-Loncar et al., 2005).

Children born with fetal alcohol syndrome have a constellation of behavioral and physical characteristics reflecting the detrimental effects of alcohol on their prenatal development.

As you can see, the developing human is vulnerable to toxic influences and requires adequate nutrition and nurturance for normal development to take place. In addition, many other factors can impair normal development during childhood and can play a role in causing mental retardation. Poor nutrition in the early years, particularly the first year of life, can cause mental retardation, leading to long-term deficits in cognitive and behavioral functions. Inadequate prenatal care or grossly inattentive parenting also can contribute to **failure to thrive,** a condition in which the child fails to grow physically and cognitively at a normal rate.

Treatment   Although there is no cure for mental retardation, early intervention can enrich the intellectual and physical development of people with this condition. Some people with mental retardation can learn the skills needed to live in a productive way in society. With educative interventions early in life, they can develop better motor abilities, coordination, language usage, and social skills. Through the process of **mainstreaming,** in which people with cognitive and physical disabilities are integrated with nondisabled individuals, they participate in ordinary school classrooms, where they are provided with assistance geared to their particular needs.

Behavioral interventions are the most useful in producing motor, language, social, and cognitive gains. Parents can participate in this process by rewarding a child for appropriate behaviors and by responding negatively to inappropriate behaviors. Family-based interventions provide parents with a context within which to discuss family problems and issues related to the family member who has mental retardation. Such interventions can provide an important source of support.

To see how a combined behavioral-family approach might work, consider the case of Lucy's parents, who are reluctant to take her out of the house, even to go grocery shopping. When they do, she pulls things off the shelves, cries when food items are taken away from her, and sits in the aisle, refusing to get up. A behavioral approach to treating the problem would involve training the parents to respond immediately to undesirable behaviors with verbal reprimands and to provide positive reinforcement for desirable ones. They might be instructed to yell forcefully when Lucy sits in the aisle and to touch and praise her when she acts appropriately.

Because of increased public awareness, more attention is being given to preventing the physical disorders that lead to mental retardation. The most straightforward form of prevention is the early detection of PKU by testing the baby for this disorder immediately after delivery. If the baby tests positive, steps are taken to correct the disorder by means of a special diet. The other genetic causes of mental retardation, however, cannot be reversed.

In contrast to genetically caused mental retardation, many environmentally caused forms of mental retardation can be prevented. In fact, fetal alcohol syndrome is the most preventable form of mental retardation (Miller-Loncar et al., 2005). In recent years, attempts have been made to teach people ways to improve conditions of prenatal development and to make the birth process safer. For example, alcoholic beverage containers and cigarette packages now have warning labels about the relationship between congenital disabilities and drinking alcohol or smoking during pregnancy. Community education programs within specific populations can be influential in changing alcohol-related behaviors among pregnant women in particular high-risk groups (Hankin, 1994). Counseling pregnant women who abuse or are dependent on alcohol or other substances can also help limit the damage to the developing fetus. Important technological advances have brought about improved conditions for childbirth, such as more effective measures for preventing oxygen deprivation during the birth process. Parents are also being alerted to the importance of protecting children from head injuries; for example, using bicycle helmets, children's car seats, and automobile seatbelts can prevent potentially debilitating traumas to the brain. In recent years, psychologists have been called upon to raise awareness that environmental toxicants play a major role in causing a variety of developmental disabilities (Koger, Schettler, & Weiss, 2005).

Pervasive Developmental Disorders

In this section, we will turn our attention to conditions that seem to permeate every facet of a child's existence. Because of the encompassing nature of these conditions, they are referred to as **pervasive developmental disorders** and are characterized by severe impairment in several areas of development (e.g., social interaction or communication skills) or the presence of extremely odd behavior, interests, and activities. We will focus on the most common of these conditions, **autistic disorder,** which is characterized by a massive impairment in an individual's ability to communicate and relate emotionally to others.

Although we will not dwell on the other pervasive developmental disorders, you should be familiar with some of the conditions that have received considerable scientific attention. In **Rett's disorder,** which occurs only in females, the child develops normally through the first 5 months of life; however, between the age of 5 months and 4 years, some changes indicative of neurological and cognitive impairments occur. The growth of the child's head slows; this is accompanied by a loss of hand skills, followed by odd hand movements (e.g., hand-wringing), a loss of social engagement with others, poorly coordinated walking and bodily movements, psychomotor retardation, and severely impaired language. A child with **childhood disintegrative disorder** develops normally for the first 2 years but, before the age of 10, starts to lose language and motor skills as well as other adaptive functions, including bowel and bladder control. Serious deterioration also becomes evident in the child's social interaction and communication, which is accompanied by repetitive and stereotyped patterns of behavior, interests, and activities. Children with **Asperger's disorder** maintain adequate cognitive and language development but become severely impaired in social interaction. In addition, they develop restricted, repetitive, and stereotyped patterns of behavior, interests, and activities.

From their earliest years, people with Asperger's disorder commonly have disturbed interpersonal experiences that result

 MindMAP Segment 11.1 features the unusual story of Amanda and Tim, two children in the same family with Asperger's disorder, and describes their efforts to cope with their condition. The segment includes an interview with their mother.

Children who have Asperger's disorder demonstrate disturbances in communication and social interaction.

in maladjustment and impaired relationships. This condition has received increasing attention in recent years, as experts have come to recognize that there are marked differences between Asperger's disorder and autistic disorder. They have also realized that if parents and professionals understand the experiences of children with Asperger's disorder, they can initiate specialized interventions to reduce the impact of social dysfunction. The interpersonal disturbance that is part of the very nature of the disorder results in social exclusion, sometimes so extreme that even children in early grades of primary school are cruelly victimized by peers.

Children with this pervasive developmental disorder maintain adequate cognitive and language development but become severely impaired in social interaction as they grow up. Despite the fact that these children develop restricted, repetitive, and stereotyped patterns of behavior, interests, and activities, Asperger's disorder can go undetected in the first years of life due to the unremarkable development of language and cognitive functioning. However, by the time the child reaches school, the child's social dysfunction becomes so prominent that social exclusion becomes a distressing fact of life.

This disorder is named after Hans Asperger, a Viennese physician who, during World War II, described a group of boys who possessed rather good language and cognitive skills but had marked social problems because they acted like pompous "little professors" and were physically awkward. Many individuals with this condition have a remarkable interest in and knowledge about a very specific topic that is so all-consuming for them that it interferes with their overall development.

In one case described in the literature (Volkmar et al., 2000), an 11-year-old boy, Robert, had the verbal abilities of a 17-year-old but the social skills of a 3-year-old. Although Robert had a remarkable knowledge about the stars, planets, and time, his exclusive intellectual devotion to these subjects kept him from acquiring other kinds of knowledge. Peers rejected him because of his one-sided and naive overtures. The case of Robert serves to highlight the complex nature of this diagnosis. In the early years of life, parents are more likely to view their child as being especially gifted rather than as suffering from a serious impairment. As these children develop, their problems become more prominent.

Learning about people with Asperger's is crucially important for professionals who are trying to understand the various expressions of pervasive developmental disorder. With the knowledge that Asperger's disorder is markedly different from autistic disorder, appropriate assessment and intervention protocols can be developed as soon as there is diagnostic evidence of Asperger's disorder. In other words, parents and educators with responsibility for children with Asperger's disorder can focus on the acquisition of more adaptive interpersonal skills early in life. Otherwise, these children are at increased risk for profound discrimination and extremely demeaning social experiences, ranging from name-calling and pranks to alarming forms of abuse and victimization.

Characteristics of Autistic Disorder

Before the age of 3, usually in infancy, individuals with autistic disorder show oddities in several spheres that other people easily detect. Although in approximately 20 percent of cases, autistic disturbance is not evident during the first or even second year of life, the more common picture involves notable abnormalities from the early months of infancy, with parents of these infants becoming aware that the child seems somehow different (American Psychiatric Association, 2000). The parents might mistakenly attribute the child's unresponsiveness to deafness. In time, however, they come to realize that their child is able to hear but lacks the ability to respond like other children of that age. At this point, they are likely to turn to a pediatrician or clinician with developmental expertise. Clinicians assign the diagnosis of autistic disorder based on symptoms that fall into three groups: impairment in social interaction; impairment in communication; and oddities of behavior, interests, and activities. Although the media have given more attention to autistic disorder in recent years, this condition is rare, occurring in perhaps 2 to 20 per 10,000 children (American Psychiatric Association, 2000).

Individuals with autistic disorder show impaired social interaction in several ways. Their nonverbal behaviors convey a sense of emotional distancing, which is evidenced by avoiding eye contact, making odd facial expressions, posturing, and using gestures as a way of controlling interactions. Unlike most children, who are inclined to play with other children, children with autistic disorder refrain from peer relationships. Further, they seem to lack the ability to share thoughts, feelings, or interests with others. Their world is characterized by a preference for isolation, in which they lack an awareness of others, possibly even being oblivious to their own parents and siblings. As infants, they resist the cuddling or tickling of a parent. Unlike nonautistic babies, who smile when they are happy or in response to an adult's laughter, the autistic child remains aloof and unresponsive. To the extent that they do interact with people, they lack emotion and sensitivity.

Communication for the individual with autistic disorder is abnormal in several ways, both verbally and nonverbally. Many

This 7-year-old boy with autistic disorder is seen with his aide, who is giving him assistance with classroom activities.

with the disorder either are unable to speak or show serious delays in language acquisition. Those who do speak are unlikely to initiate a conversation or remain involved in one. The language they use and the style of their speech make them sound very strange, because the tone, pitch, rate, and rhythm are unusual. For example, they may speak in a monotone voice and end sentences with a question-like rise; grammar may be of the sort that one would expect from a much younger child; and they may repeat words or phrases. They may confuse pronouns, such as *I* and *you,* saying, "You am hungry," for instance. Their speech is often characterized by **echolalia,** or the repetition of words or phrases that they hear. In response to the question "What is your name?" the person might say, "Your name, your name, your name." In less severe cases, the person with autistic disorder may be able to use speech normally but be unable to maintain a normal conversational exchange, instead speaking incessantly in a monologue. Even in inner communication, usually evidenced in the make-believe play of most children, the child with autistic disorder lacks the ability to engage in play that is age-appropriate.

Several behavioral oddities are characteristic of individuals with autistic disorder. They may be intensely preoccupied with one or more fixed interests, possibly to the exclusion of just about anything else. They may be particularly interested in the parts of objects, such as the buttons on sweaters, or moving objects, such as the rotating blade of an electric fan. They usually adhere to rituals and rigid daily routines, and they may become very disturbed at the slightest change. For example, when opening a can of soda, a boy with autistic disorder may insist that the tab be at a particular position and, if it is not, refuse to drink the soda. Bodily movements are often bizarre and include repetitive mannerisms. They may shake their arms, spin around repetitively, rock back and forth, or engage in harmful, self-damaging behavior, such as head-banging. Regressive behaviors are very common, such as temper tantrums, childish expressions of anger, and the soiling of clothes by defecating or urinating.

People with Asperger's disorder often interact with others in unusual ways, possibly showing odd facial expressions, unusual posturing or gesturing, or inappropriate eye-to-eye gaze. Further, their interests, activities, and behaviors are often rigid and repetitive.

The unusual characteristics of autistic disorder become more prominent as the infant grows into the toddler and school-age years, and this disorder continues throughout the individual's life, taking one of a number of forms varying in symptoms and severity. Mental retardation is common, affecting three fourths of those with autistic disorder. The majority suffer long-lasting impairments that interfere with their ability to live independently as adults (Nordin & Gillberg, 1998).

In an unusual variant of this disorder, called autistic savant syndrome, the individual possesses, in addition to severe limitations, an extraordinary skill, such as the ability to perform extremely complicated numerical operations (for example, correctly naming the day of the week on which a date thousands of years away would fall) (Treffert, 1988). Some autistic savants have exceptional musical talents, such as the remarkable case of one who, at the age of 6 months, could hum complex operatic arias (Treffert, 1989). In fact, the autistic savant syndrome typically appears at an early age, when the young child with autistic disorder appears to have exceptional musical skills, artistic talent, or the ability to solve extremely challenging puzzles (Hou et al., 2000; Koegel, Valdez-Menchaca, & Koegel, 1994). The autistic savant syndrome was dramatized in the movie *Rain Man,* in which the central character had an astounding mathematical ability, as well as an incredible knowledge of baseball trivia.

Public legislation in 1975 set a federal mandate for children with serious developmental disorders to be integrated into regular classrooms in the public schools.

Theories and Treatment of Autistic Disorder

The theory that autistic disorder is biologically caused is supported by evidence pointing to patterns of familial inheritance. Based on these investigations, the heritability of autistic disorder is estimated to be approximately 90 percent, with genetic abnormalities suspected to exist on chromosomes 7, 2, and 15. No clear evidence exists regarding specific deficits in brain structure, but researchers have focused on the cerebellum, frontal cortex, hippocampus, and amygdala. There is some evidence that overall brain size is increased in some individuals with autistic disorder (Santangelo & Tsatsanis, 2005). Abnormalities in the neural circuitry of people with autistic disorder exist as reflected by their particular difficulty in processing facial stimuli (Dalton et al., 2005). These brain alterations may account for the fact that people with autistic disorder are less likely to gaze into other people's eyes when communicating with them and less able to use emotional cues when processing information from other people's facial expressions (Bayliss & Tipper, 2005; Dawson et al., 2004).

Although it is evident that neurological differences exist between normal people and people with autistic disorder, the basis for these differences and their implications are not clear. Some researchers suggest that there is a continuum or spectrum of autistic disorders, with different causes and distinct patterns of symptoms and neurological deficits. According to this view, Asperger's disorder is regarded as a variant of so-called high-functioning autism.

The earliest psychological explanations of autistic disorder focused on psychodynamic processes as being at the root of the disturbance in the child's attachment to the parents (Bettelheim, 1967; Kanner, 1943). The term *refrigerator mother* was used to describe the cold and detached type of parenting theorized to cause autistic disorder. In the 1970s, psychologists shifted to a more cognitive explanation of autistic disorder, regarding it as a disorder of language, attention, and perception (Rutter, 1984). Many theorists still believe that people develop autistic disorder because they lack an innate ability to form emotional bonds with others, beginning with their parents. This lack of an ability to form emotional attachment leads the individual to develop serious flaws in the ability to relate socially to others.

According to the behavioral perspective, the primary issue is not what causes autistic disorder but how to reduce the parents' frustration as well as the emotional distance between the child and caregivers that the child's symptoms create. A cycle becomes established, in which the caregivers find it difficult to interact positively with the child, who recoils from their touch and their attempts to establish emotional warmth. The child's self-injurious behaviors are reinforced by attention from adults or by the escape such behaviors provide from situations the child finds even more aversive.

Although the treatment of autistic disorder, with its severe and broad range of deficits, can appear to have little promise, clinicians are making inroads into ways that the behavior of these children can be successfully changed through medication and behavioral treatment programs. The underlying premise of behavioral treatments for autistic disorder is that, when the child can communicate his or her needs more effectively, some of the disruptive and self-stimulatory behaviors will decrease (Jensen & Sinclair, 2002). If children with autistic disorder are given reinforcement for appropriate behaviors, such as asking for help or feedback, they are less likely to engage in self-injurious or

Mini Case

AUTISTIC DISORDER

Brian is a 6-year-old child being treated at a residential school for mentally disabled children. As an infant, Brian did not respond well to his parents' efforts to play with and hold him. His mother noticed that his whole body seemed to stiffen when she picked him up out of his crib. No matter how much she tried, she could not entice Brian to smile. When she tried to play games by tickling his toes or touching his nose, he averted his eyes and looked out the window. Not until Brian was 18 months old did his mother first realize that his behavior reflected more than just a quiet temperament—that he, in fact, was developing abnormally. Brian never did develop an attachment to people; instead, he clung to a small piece of wood he carried with him everywhere. His mother often found Brian rocking his body in a corner, clinging to this piece of wood. Brian's language, though, finally indicated serious disturbance. At an age when most children start to put together short sentences, Brian was still babbling incoherently. His babbling did not sound like that of a normal infant. He said the same syllable over and over again—usually the last syllable of something that had just been said to him—in a high-pitched, monotone voice. Perhaps the most bizarre feature of Brian's "speech" was that it was not directed at the listener. Brian seemed to be communicating in a world of his own.

Diagnostic Features

With onset prior to age 3, individuals with this disorder experience serious delays or abnormal functioning in social interaction, communicative language, or play; furthermore, they show at least six symptoms from the following three groups:

- Qualitative impairment in social interaction manifested by at least two of the following:
  - Impairment in the use of several nonverbal behaviors, such as facial expression, body postures, and eye contact
  - Failure to develop appropriate peer relationships
  - Lack of spontaneous sharing of enjoyment, interests, or achievements with others
  - Lack of social or emotional reciprocity
- Qualitative impairments in communication as manifested by at least one of the following:
  - Delay in or lack of spoken language development
  - Impairment in the ability to initiate or sustain a conversation
  - Stereotyped and repetitive use of language or idiosyncratic language
  - Lack of spontaneous make-believe play or social imitative play
- Restricted repetitive and stereotyped patterns of behavior, interests, and activities manifested by at least one of the following:
  - Preoccupation with stereotyped or restricted patterns of interest
  - Inflexible adherence to nonfunctional routines or rituals
  - Stereotyped and repetitive motor mannerisms (e.g. hand flapping or complex body movements)
  - Preoccupation with parts of objects

aggressive behaviors. In this type of treatment, clinicians find it more useful to focus on changing pivotal behaviors, with the goal of bringing about improvements in other behaviors, rather than focusing on changing isolated behavioral disturbances. The therapist may also help the child develop new learning skills that will give him or her some experiences of success in problem solving; for example, the therapist might teach the child to break down a large problem, such as getting dressed, into smaller tasks that the child can accomplish. This is an important aspect of treatment, because the child with autistic disorder, when frustrated, is likely to regress to problem behaviors, such as rocking and head-banging. Clinicians also focus on the need to motivate the child to communicate more effectively. Within this framework, increasing the child's motivation to respond to social and environmental stimuli is seen as the key to treatment (Koegel, Koegel, & McNerney, 2001). Such an approach is most effective if children with autism can be encouraged to regulate and initiate behaviors on their own. Simple changes can increase motivation, such as having children choose the materials, toys, and activities that are used in the intervention rather than that choice being made by the clinician.

Other behavioral strategies that clinicians use to treat people with autistic disorder are self-control procedures, such as self-monitoring of language, relaxation training, and covert condi-

tioning. As simple as it seems, it also may be possible to help children with autistic disorder perform behavioral sequences as simple as touching an icon to indicate rejection rather than engaging in more aggressive ways to indicate displeasure (Martin, Drasgow, & Haller, 2005). The most well-known—and, in some ways, radical—interventions were developed by psychologist Ivar Lovaas (2003), whose behavioral treatments are intended to eliminate all odd behaviors, including those that involve self-harm. Clinicians teach children with autistic disorder appropriate eye contact and responsiveness to instructions as necessary preconditions for other therapeutic and educational interventions. This program targets undesirable behaviors and then reduces them through the operant conditioning methods of positive reinforcement, extinction, negative reinforcement, and, in some cases, punishment. The principles and techniques of Lovaas' method can be applied in a variety of settings in addition to the laboratory, including the home and the school (Lovaas, 2003).

To illustrate the way in which behavioral principles can be applied, consider the case of Dexter, a young boy who is aggressive toward other people and engages in disruptive behaviors, such as shouting. The therapist might ignore Dexter (extinction), thereby withdrawing the attention that has presumably reinforced his engaging in these behaviors. At the same time, the therapist gives Dexter positive reinforcement for engaging in desirable behaviors, such as interacting with other children and playing appropriately with toys. If extinction does not produce results, the therapist may remove Dexter from the play area and send him to a "time-out" room. For more resistant and dangerous behaviors, such as head-banging, the therapist may give verbal punishment (a loud "no") or, even more extreme, a slap on the thigh. The important point about this kind of treatment is that the consequence of the child's behavior occurs very soon after the behavior is performed. Shaping is another operant principle that is used in this therapy; it involves positive reinforcement for behaviors that increasingly approximate the desirable target behaviors. A child who cannot sit still in a chair must be rewarded first for sitting before the therapist can move on to more complex interactive skills.

An important fact to realize is that, for these behavioral programs to be effective, they must be carried out intensively for a long period of time, beginning early in the child's life (less than 4 years of age). In a long-term follow-up of a research project begun in 1970, Lovaas (1987) reported that a high rate of success was achieved only after years of 40-hour-per-week treatment. Almost one half of the children treated with this intensive program went on to achieve normal intellectual and educational functioning by the time they reached first grade. This success rate is particularly striking in light of the fact that only 2 percent of the control group (who were treated for 10 hours or less per week) showed improvement.

In another long-term follow-up using archival records, Lovaas and his collaborators found that early intervention was effective in improving language and intelligence test scores. Nevertheless, even intensively treated children continued to exhibit developmental delays (Smith, Eikeseth, Klevstrand, & Lovaas, 1997).

Intervention to improve language and communication during the early years of a child's life would seem to be particularly important. The findings of a longitudinal study conducted at UCLA tracing children starting when they were ages 2 to 6 showed that those children who had better skills in the areas of communication and play had better language and social skills in their early preteen years (Sigman et al., 1999). Teaching adaptive skills that will help children manage everyday tasks and interactions is also an important early intervention. To be most effective, such treatment should focus on generalizing across social contexts to give children the tools they need to interact across a wider range of settings.

Another approach to intervention is to have peers rather than adults interact with the child. This approach is based on the belief that children with autistic disorder can derive some very important benefits from appropriate interactions with other children. This situation approximates a more normal type of social environment, in which children typically serve a powerful role in modifying a peer's behavior. In contrast to interventions in which adults provide the reinforcement, peer-mediated interventions have the advantage of allowing children to carry on with their ordinary activities without adult interruption (Kohler, Strain, & Goldstein, 2005). Playgroups, in which children with autism interact under adult guidance, can also be beneficial in helping these children normalize their interactions (Wolfberg & Schuler, 1999).

Given the complexity and seriousness of autistic disorder, its treatment requires a comprehensive program of intervention. This program must involve work with the family, peers, and the schools, as well as the individual with the disorder. In addition, institutional placement may be required, at least until the more dangerous behaviors are brought under control.

Learning, Communication, and Motor Skills Disorders

Perhaps you know someone who has a "block" about math. Even doing simple calculations causes this person to feel frustrated. Or you may have a classmate who has trouble reading and needs assistance with course assignments. In extreme forms, these problems may reflect a specific developmental disorder, which is a delay or deficit in an area of functioning, such as academic skills, language and speech, or motor coordination.

You may be wondering why a person's difficulty with math or reading is regarded as a psychological disorder. This is actually a very controversial issue. Some clinicians feel it is inappropriate to include learning difficulties in a classification system designed for the diagnosis of psychological disorders. However, the rationale for including these conditions is that they are often associated with emotional distress, and they may seriously interfere with the person's everyday life and social relationships. For example, an eighth-grader who is having difficulty completing his homework assignments because of a reading disorder will probably feel ashamed and anxious. Over time, these emotions will have a cumulative impact on the individual's self-esteem and sense of well-being.

Learning Disorders

A **learning disorder** is a delay or deficit in an academic skill that is evident when an individual's achievement on standardized tests is substantially below what would be expected for others of comparable age, education, and level of intelligence. These disorders, which cause significant impairment in functioning, are estimated to affect 2 to 10 percent of Americans, and approximately 5 percent of public school children are currently diagnosed (American Psychiatric Association, 2000). Learning disorders are evident in three areas, each associated with a given academic skill: mathematics, writing, and reading.

The individual with **mathematics disorder** has difficulty with mathematical tasks and concepts. Impairment may be evident in linguistic skills (for example, understanding mathematical terms, symbols, or concepts), perceptual skills (such as reading arithmetic signs), attention skills (for example, copying numbers correctly), and mathematical skills (for example, learning multiplication tables). A school-age child with this disorder may have

Children with learning disorders find the classroom a frustrating place when they are unable to follow directions or to understand what they are reading.

problems in these areas. An adult with this disorder might be unable to balance a checkbook because of difficulty performing simple mathematical calculations. In a **disorder of written expression,** the individual's writing is characterized by poor spelling, grammatical or punctuation errors, and disorganization of paragraphs, which creates serious problems for children in many academic subjects. For adults, this disorder can be very embarrassing, perhaps limiting the person's range of job opportunities. **Reading disorder,** commonly called **dyslexia,** is a learning disorder in which the individual omits, distorts, or substitutes words when reading and reads in a slow, halting fashion. This inability to read inhibits the child's progress in a variety of school subjects. As with the disorder of written expression, adults with dyslexia face embarrassment and restrictions in the type of employment for which they may qualify. Epidemiological studies show that, at least in English-speaking countries, boys are more likely than girls to develop reading disability (Rutter et al., 2004).

Adolescence is the peak time during which behavioral and emotional problems associated with learning disorders are particularly evident. As many as 40 percent of those with learning disorders drop out of school before finishing high school. Even outside the school context, however, many people with learning disorders have low self-esteem and feelings of incompetence and shame. On the other hand, a learning disorder does not necessarily sentence a person to a life of failure; in fact, some

extremely famous people overcame a childhood learning disorder, including Albert Einstein, Thomas Edison, Woodrow Wilson, Nelson Rockefeller, Winston Churchill, Charles Darwin, General George Patton, and John F. Kennedy (see Table 11.2).

Communication Disorders

If you have ever tried to communicate an idea that others couldn't understand or have been so inarticulate that even your speech was incomprehensible, you have an idea about the experiences of people with disturbances in speech and language. What is difficult to imagine, however, is the emotional pain and frustration that people with communication disorders confront on a daily basis. **Communication disorders** are conditions characterized by impairment in the expression or understanding of language.

Expressive language disorder is a developmental disorder characterized by obvious problems of verbal expression. Children with this disorder do not have the ability to express themselves in ways appropriate to their age group. This may be evident in a language style that includes using limited and faulty vocabulary, speaking in short sentences with simplified grammatical structures, omitting critical words or phrases, and putting words together in peculiar order. A person with this disorder may, for example, always use the present tense, referring to activities of the previous day by saying, "I have a good time yesterday." For some children, expressive language disorders are developmental conditions in which speaking abilities occur at a later age than normal, and progress more slowly than average. Others acquire this disorder, perhaps as a result of a medical illness or a neurological problem resulting from a head trauma.

Children with **mixed receptive-expressive language disorder** have difficulty in both expressing and understanding certain kinds of words or phrases, such as directions, or, in more severe forms, basic vocabulary or entire sentences. Even simple directions, such as "take the third door on the right," might confuse an individual with this disorder. When speaking, children with this disorder show some of the same communication problems as children with expressive language disorder. Mixed receptive-expressive language disorder can also be either developmental or acquired.

The expressive difficulties of some people are characterized not by their ability to understand or express language but by difficulties specific to speech. A person with **phonological disorder** substitutes, omits, or incorrectly articulates speech sounds. For example, a child may use a *t* sound for words containing the letter *k,* saying *tiss* rather than *kiss.* People often regard the mispronunciations of children as cute; however, these childhood speech patterns are likely to cause academic problems as the child grows older and may evoke ridicule from peers.

Stuttering involves a disturbance in the normal fluency and patterning of speech that is characterized by such verbalizations as sound repetitions and prolongations, broken words, the blocking out of sounds, word substitutions to avoid problematic words, and words expressed with an excess of tension.

TABLE 11.2 Famous People Who Had Problems in School

Winston Churchill (1874–1965)	Described as a "dull youth" by his father, who thought he would not be able to make a living, this legendary British statesman was also seen as hyperactive in childhood. Although Churchill enjoyed history and literature, he refused to study Latin, Greek, or math, and he repeatedly failed his school exams.
Charles Darwin (1809–1882)	When he was a child, his father told Darwin that he cared for nothing but "shooting, dogs, and rat-catching." Darwin failed in his medical studies and marked time in college until he took the trip on the *H.M.S. Beagle* that changed his life.
Thomas Edison (1874–1931)	In school, Edison's performance was so poor that his headmaster warned that he "would never make a success of anything." His mother helped him learn to read, and he soon began inventing.
Albert Einstein (1879–1955)	Einstein's parents feared that he was retarded because of his delayed speech and language development. His school performance on all subjects except mathematics was dismal, and he failed his college entrance exams. While in the process of developing his relativity theory, he had trouble holding down a job.
Henry Ford (1863–1947)	A poor reader in school, Ford always preferred working with machines. He achieved early prowess in fixing tools and building waterwheels and steam engines.
Isaac Newton (1642–1727)	Described as an "idler" and "mechanical dabbler," Newton proved to be so inefficient that he could not run the family farm. A poor student, he suddenly came to life after a fight with a bully motivated him to advance himself.

Source: From Wallace, Wallechinsky, Wallace, & Wallace in *The Book of Lists 2* (1980). Copyright © 1980 David Wallechinsky. Reprinted by permission of David Wallechinsky.

Motor Skills Disorders

The primary form of motor skills disorder is **developmental coordination disorder,** which is characterized by marked impairment in the development of motor coordination. Children with this disorder encounter problems in academic achievement and daily living because of their severe lack of coordination, unassociated with another developmental disability (for example, cerebral palsy). In the early stages of life, children with developmental coordination disorder have trouble crawling, walking, and sitting. As they develop, other age-related tasks are also below average. They may be unable to tie shoelaces, play ball, complete a puzzle, or even write legibly. This disorder is also relatively common, with as many as 6 percent of children between the ages of 5 and 11 meeting the diagnostic criteria (American Psychiatric Association, 2000).

Theories and Treatment of Learning, Communication, and Motor Skills Disorders

The most widely accepted explanation of the learning, communication, and motor skills disorders involves neurological abnormalities. Experts believe that damage to various brain sites responsible for the affected functions has occurred during fetal development or during the birth process, or as a result of a neurological condition caused by a physical trauma or medical disorder.

One possible cause of certain kinds of developmental disorders is that the brain areas involved in vision, speech, and language comprehension cannot integrate information. For example, a child whose ability to remember sequences of letters or words is impaired may have difficulties in comprehending speech. An 8-year-old child should be able to remember the following sentences: "Joe asked his mother to take him to see the cows in the barn. Luis carved a handsome statue out of wood with his sharp knife." However, an 8-year-old child with auditory memory problems would most likely confuse the sequence of events and forget most of the details. Impairment in the central nervous system that results in deficits in cognitive processing can result in serious social and emotional disturbance.

The school environment is usually the primary site of treatment for specific developmental disorders. A treatment plan is designed by an interdisciplinary team consisting of various professionals, such as a school psychologist, a special education teacher, the classroom teacher, a speech language therapist, and possibly a neurologist. Typically, children with these disorders require more structure, fewer distractions, and the presentation of new material that uses more than one sensory modality at a time. For example, the instructor may teach math concepts by using oral presentation combined with hands-on manipulation of objects. Perhaps most important is building on the child's strengths, so that he or she can feel a sense of accomplishment and increased self-esteem.

Attention Deficit and Disruptive Behavior Disorders

Think back to your days in grade school and try to recall classmates whom your teachers and peers regarded as constant nuisances. Perhaps they were so restless that they could not stay seated, or perhaps they were always getting into fights and causing trouble. Quite possibly these youths had one of the behavior disorders that we will discuss in this section. Children with these disorders commonly act in ways that are so disruptive and provocative that caretakers and peers respond with anger, impatience, punishment, or avoidance.

Attention-Deficit/Hyperactivity Disorder (ADHD)

Attention-deficit/hyperactivity disorder (ADHD) is a disorder involving inattentiveness and hyperactivity-impulsivity. Each of these two components of the disorder is defined in terms of several behavioral criteria. Inattentiveness is characterized by such behaviors as carelessness, forgetfulness in daily activities, and other attentional problems. Inattentive children commonly lose their belongings, are easily distracted, cannot follow through on instructions, and have difficulty organizing tasks. The hyperactive-impulsive component is further divided into the subtypes of hyperactivity and impulsivity. Hyperactivity is characterized by fidgeting, restlessness, running about inappropriately, difficulty in playing quietly, and talking excessively. Impulsivity is evident in individuals who blurt out answers, cannot wait their turn, and interrupt or intrude on others. Children can be diagnosed as having ADHD with a predominant characteristic of inattentiveness, hyperactivity-impulsivity, or a combination of the two. Not surprisingly, the children with the predominantly inattentive type develop serious academic deficits and school-related problems, whereas those with the predominantly hyperactive-impulsive type have more peer rejection and accidental injuries (American Psychiatric Association, 2000).

The recognition that a child has ADHD usually occurs fairly early in the child's life. Prior to school age, children with ADHD are usually regarded as "difficult" by their parents, relatives, and friends, who are responding to the child's impulsivity and hyperactivity. During the grade school years, children with ADHD show deficits in educational performance, have repeated discipline problems, are commonly left back, and often require tutoring and placement in special classes (Wilens, Faraone, & Biederman, 2004). Problems associated with ADHD continue and often intensify as the individual grows older, creating serious emotional and behavioral problems that persist throughout life.

Although it was once thought that ADHD symptoms subside by adolescence, this view has been discarded, as increasing attention has been given to the ways in which ADHD is experienced during adolescence and adulthood. The symptom picture changes from childhood to adolescence, such that the hyperactivity that is so evident during preschool and early childhood years declines by adolescence, yet attentional problems remain, and overt difficulties in executive functions become prominent. Executive functions include tasks such as self-reflection, self-control, planning, forethought, delay of gratification, affect regulation, and resistance to distraction (Wasserstein, 2005).

Teenagers with ADHD can have a wide range of behavioral, academic, and interpersonal problems that create emotional

In MindMAP Segment 11.2, David, a young man with ADHD, talks about his learning disabilities as well as difficulties behaving in the classroom.

High energy levels can cause children and teenagers with ADHD to behave in ways that seem out of control.

havoc for them and serious difficulties in their relationships with family, friends, and educators. Teens with ADHD are much more likely than their peers to drink caffeinated drinks excessively and to use nicotine, substances that increase arousal in underactive parts of the brain. They tend to be especially immature, more likely to engage in conflict with their parents, have strikingly poor social skills, and engage in more high-risk activities such as substance abuse, unprotected sex, and reckless driving (Resnick, 2005).

The diagnosis of ADHD in teenage girls is especially complicated, and often missed by educators and clinicians because their symptoms tend to be less overt than the symptoms of boys, possibly taking the form of forgetfulness, disorganization, low self-esteem, and demoralization; their tendency to internalize symptoms may cause them to become anxious, depressed, and socially withdrawn. Alternatively, some teenage girls show a different symptom picture in that they are hypertalkative or emotionally overreactive (Quinn, 2005), characteristics that can be mistaken as reflecting typical adolescent volatility. Teenage girls with ADHD often experience an intensification of symptoms because of hormonal changes at puberty, and they are likely to act out in ways different from male counterparts and put themselves at risk for unplanned and unwanted pregnancies (Resnick, 2005).

REAL STORIES

EDWARD HALLOWELL: ATTENTION DEFICIT SYMPTOMS

At the beginning of this chapter you began reading about Jason Newman, a child whose hyperactivity and impatience caused great frustration for his parents and made it difficult for him to become friends with other children. The case of Jason involves the story of a child with attention-deficit/hyperactivity disorder, or ADHD (sometimes referred to as ADD). Although most people have known people or heard about individuals with such conditions, the usual picture involves a troubled child who continues to experience challenges and frustrations throughout life. It might surprise you to learn that some prominent and successful individuals have struggled through life with ADHD but have found ways to manage their problematic symptoms. Such has been the experience of Dr. Edward Hallowell, a highly respected physician who is a member of the Harvard Medical School faculty. Hallowell has been able to use his own difficult life experiences to help others understand and treat people with ADHD. He has also brought attention to the fact that ADHD is a condition that lasts beyond the childhood years and continues to cause havoc in the lives of thousands of adults.

Edward Hallowell's childhood could be referred to as turbulent, at best. His mother suffered from alcoholism and was divorced twice. His father, who had bipolar disorder requiring hospitalization, left the family when Hallowell was only 3 years old. Hallowell's mother then married a man whom he describes as a "sadistic alcoholic" who antagonized him and abused his mother.

At the age of 10, Hallowell was sent to a boarding school. Here he struggled academically because he had difficulties concentrating, but nevertheless he felt relieved to be away from his turbulent home life. He remembers lying awake at night wondering if he would ever find happiness in his life, and fearing that the answer would probably be no, considering his troubles at home and in school.

In the years that followed, however, Hallowell's life unfolded in ways that were much more positive than he had ever anticipated. Although his childhood was less than perfect, he received love and support from many people, including friends, teachers, and extended family. Hallowell went on to a successful college career followed by admission to medical school and a prominent career as an instructor at Harvard Medical School and as director of the Hallowell Center for Cognitive and Emotional Health in Massachusetts.

Here, in his own words, Edward Hallowell describes some of his difficulties in school and some of the people who helped him through the rough times:

The first teacher I can remember is Mrs. Eldridge, whom I met when I was six and in first grade in Chatham. I was unable to learn to read. As my classmates started to catch on to phonics and the sounds that letters stand for, I didn't catch on. I was unable to look at letters and make words. I was unable to keep up with the other children in class.[1]

In another classroom, I might have been labeled stupid or slow or even retarded. After all, during the years of my growing up—the 1950's and 1960's—there were only two descriptors of a child's mental ability: "smart" and "stupid." Because I was very slow to read, I qualified as stupid. As a result, I might have been ridiculed, put in a corner, told to try harder or simply forgotten about. In a public school in

Edward (Ned) Hallowell, M. D.

REAL STORIES

EDWARD HALLOWELL
(continued)

a small town in Cape Cod in those days, people didn't know much about diagnosing children beyond identifying them as smart or stupid, good or bad. Along with stupid and bad, came the standard treatments of shame, pain, and humiliation. But Mrs. Eldridge was not a shamer. . . .

She made it safe for me to fail. She made it safe for me to have the brain I had.

Throughout his often-troubled grade school years, Hallowell was unaware that he had both dyslexia and ADHD. Here, he describes his great feeling of relief when, much later in his life, he discovered that there was a reason for the many problems he had concentrating:

I discovered I had ADD when I was thirty-one years old, near the end of my training in child psychiatry at the Massachusetts Mental Health Center in Boston. As my teacher in neuropsychiatry began to describe ADD in a series of morning lectures dur-

ing a steamy Boston summer, I had one of the great "Aha!" experiences of my life.[2]

"There are some children," she said, "who chronically daydream. They are often very bright, but they have trouble attending to any one topic for very long. They are full of energy and have trouble staying put. They can be quite impulsive in saying or doing whatever comes to mind, and they find distractions impossible to resist."

So there's a name for what I am! I thought to myself with relief and mounting excitement. There's a term for it, a diagnosis, an actual condition, when all along I'd just thought I was slightly daft. . . . I wasn't all the names I'd been called in grade school—"a daydreamer," "lazy," "an underachiever," "a spaceshot,"—and I didn't have some repressed unconscious conflict that made me impatient and action-oriented. . . .

At last there was a term to explain the conversations I tuned out of, involuntarily, for apparently no reason. For the rage I felt and the times I threw books and pencils around the room when I didn't immediately grasp a concept in grade school. For the seven attempts it can take me to read a page of a novel. For the nonsequiturs my wife says I've offered in the midst of intimate conversation. . . . Now with a name rooted in neurobiology that I could make sense of, in a forgiving way, parts of myself that had often scared or frustrated me.

Sources: [1]From *Human Moments. How to Find Meaning and Love in Your Everyday Life* by Edward M. Hallowell. Copyright © 2001 Health Communications, Inc. Reprinted with permission. [2]From *Driven to Distraction* by Edward M. Hallowell, M. D. and John J. Raley, M. D. Copyright © 1994 by Edward M. Hallowell, M. D. and John R. Raley, M. D. Used by permission of Pantheon Books, a division of Random House, Inc.

Now that it is known that ADHD continues into adulthood, a considerable amount of research has been conducted in an effort to assess the specific ways in which this condition manifests itself beyond the adolescent years. Experts believe that there are no cases in which ADHD first emerges during adulthood, but there are many instances in which it is first accurately diagnosed at this stage of life; the assumption is that childhood symptoms were overlooked or misdiagnosed particularly in those individuals who, as children, had inattentive but not disruptive symptoms. Although there are no precise statistics about the number of adults with ADHD, estimates range from 2 to 7 percent with 4 percent being the generally accepted rate, with nearly equal numbers of men and women having this condition (Resnick, 2005; Wender, 2000).

Adults with ADHD tend to be chronic procrastinators who are repeatedly forgetful and grossly disorganized regardless of the task, even activities that they find enjoyable. They tend to be intolerant of stress, emotionally volatile, and almost incapable

of meeting deadlines. Hyperactivity is likely to be experienced as a sensation of tension or restlessness, and interpersonal communication brief and intense (Resnick, 2005). They may fidget, pace, shake their legs, play with nearby objects, or rustle papers (Wasserstein, 2005). Multitasking is common, but is usually inefficient, error-laden, and exasperating for others with whom they are interacting.

Because of all their psychological and interpersonal problems, adults with ADHD have tremendous difficulty with routines, are haphazard in their management of time and money, and have a very hard time completing academic work or holding down jobs. They miss appointments, even dates with their own partners, and they forget to pay bills or follow through on commitments. Because of their craving for stimulation, they are likely to engage in high-risk behaviors, some of which have serious consequences, such as automobile accidents (Wasserstein, 2005). A small percentage of adults with ADHD manage to channel their excessive energy and restlessness into creative

Mini Case

ATTENTION-DEFICIT/HYPERACTIVITY DISORDER

Joshua's mother has just had a conference with her son's teacher, who related that Joshua, age 7, has been extremely restless and distractible in class. Every few minutes, he is out of his desk, exploring something on a bookshelf or looking out the window. When in his seat, he kicks his feet back and forth, drums his fingers on the table, shifts around, and generally keeps up a constant high level of movement. He may ask to go to the bathroom three times in an hour. He speaks very quickly, and his ideas are poorly organized. During recess, Joshua is aggressive and violates many of the playground rules. Joshua's mother corroborated the teacher's description of Joshua with similar stories about his behavior at home. Although Joshua is of normal intelligence, he is unable to sustain concentrated attention on any one activity for more than a few minutes.

Diagnostic Features

■ With an onset of serious symptoms before the age of 7 that cause impairment in at least two settings, individuals with this condition show either a pattern of inattention or hyperactivity-impulsivity.

■ Inattention is characterized by a pattern consisting of at least six of the following symptoms, which have persisted for at least 6 months: (1) makes careless mistakes or fails to attend to details; (2) has difficulty sustaining attention; (3) doesn't listen when spoken to; (4) doesn't follow through on instructions or responsibilities; (5) has difficulty organizing activities; (6) avoids tasks requiring sustained mental effort; (7) loses items necessary for tasks; (8) is easily distracted; (9) is often forgetful.

■ Hyperactivity-impulsivity is characterized by at least six of the following symptoms, which have persisted for at least 6 months and which fall in the subgroup of hyperactivity or the subgroup of impulsivity.

◆ Hyperactivity is characterized by symptoms including (1) often fidgets or squirms; (2) often leaves seat inappropriately; (3) often runs about or climbs excessively when it is inappropriate; (4) often has difficulty playing or engaging in leisure activities; (5) is often "on the go" or acts as if "driven by a motor"; (6) often talks excessively.

◆ Impulsivity is characterized by symptoms including (1) often blurts out answers before questions have been completed; (2) often has difficulty awaiting turn; (3) often interrupts or intrudes.

■ Types include (1) combined type, (2) predominantly inattentive type, and (3) predominantly hyperactive-impulsive type.

---

endeavors, such as entrepreneurial ventures (Weiss & Murray, 2003), although the likelihood of their succeeding for any extended period of time is slim due to their inability to sustain their attention and commitment to a project.

The symptom picture in women with ADHD differs from what is most commonly found in men. Rather than showing the kinds of conduct problems that are more evident in men, women with this condition are more likely to experience dysphoria, organization problems, impulsivity, and inattention, characteristics that are of particular concern if they interfere with consistent parenting (Quinn, 2005).

Adults with ADHD typically have serious problems in relationships, whether the relationship is with an intimate partner, a co-worker, an acquaintance, or even a stranger. Somewhat ironically, because they are always seeking stimulation, they may do so by provoking conflict in their interactions with others by starting arguments, refusing to end arguments, or insisting that they have the last word. They find it difficult to listen to others, they may hear only parts of a conversation, they are prone to interrupting, and they speak while others are trying to speak. They tend to be very high strung, which is evident in their tendency to be hypersensitive and overreactive, expressed at times in outbursts and intense moodiness. Their intimate partners become exasperated by their impulsivity, propensity for overcommitment, poor decision making, and inept management of money. Conflicts and arguments often arise because of their disorganization, forgetfulness, chronic lateness, repeated misplacement of keys and other important items, and overall undependability (Robbins, 2005).

Conduct Disorder

You have probably read or heard stories about teenage gang wars, juvenile delinquency, criminal behavior, and drug use. Many of the youths involved in these criminal activities have **conduct disorder,** a condition characterized by the repetitive and persistent violation of the rights of other people.

Individuals with conduct disorder violate the rights of others and society's norms or laws. Their delinquent behaviors include stealing, truancy, running away from home, lying, fire-setting, breaking and entering, physical cruelty to people and animals, sexual assault, and mugging. These individuals, many of whom also abuse drugs or alcohol, may act alone or in groups. When caught, they deny their guilt, shift blame onto others, and lack remorse about the consequences of their actions.

Clinicians differentiate between conduct disorder with childhood onset (prior to the age of 10) and conduct disorder with adolescent onset. Conduct disorder is one of the most frequently diagnosed disorders in outpatient and inpatient treatment programs for children: estimates range from 1 percent to more than 10 percent of the general population, with prevalence rates higher among males than among females (American Psychiatric Association, 2000). There are differing degrees of conduct disorder, with more serious cases involving arrest and stable delinquent behavior. Mild cases of conduct disorder involve pranks, insignificant lying, or group mischief.

Researchers attempting to understand the causes of conduct disorder focus on gene-environment interactions based on the assumption, as is true for antisocial personality disorder, that a

Mini Case

CONDUCT DISORDER

Bert, a 16-year-old high-school dropout, took pride in his ability to burglarize homes and to shoplift without getting caught. He bragged about his special skill in breaking into places and about his collection of computers and expensive stereo and video equipment. He was skilled at finding buyers for many of the items he stole, and he liked to brag about all his money by flashing big bills in his friends' faces. Bert lived with his mother, who spent most of her days and evenings at a local bar, not particularly interested in what he was doing. She was not even aware of the fact that he spent most of his time on the streets, trying to entice his peers to "rock" with him, which involved throwing rocks at animals, store windows, and cars. If property destruction was not their aim, they taunted people by laughing at passersby and calling out hurtful names. Recently, Bert has decided to move to a more sophisticated kind of crime. Rather than breaking and entering, he has begun to talk his way into the homes of unsuspecting victims. He goes from door to door, neatly dressed and pleasant in his interactions, offering to do odd jobs around the house. After conning his way in, Bert "cases" the house and walks off with valuables, such as jewelry, that are unlikely to be missed right away.

Diagnostic Features

Individuals with this disorder show a repetitive and persistent pattern of behavior in which they violate social norms or the rights of others, as evidenced by at least three of the following:

- Aggression to people and animals, including (1) often bullies, threatens, or intimidates; (2) often initiates physical fights; (3) has used a weapon; (4) has been physically cruel to people; (5) has been physically cruel to animals; (6) has stolen while confronting a victim; (7) has forced someone into sexual activity

- Destruction of property, including (1) has set fires to cause serious damage; (2) has destroyed others' property

- Deceitfulness or theft, including (1) has broken into a house, building, or car; (2) often "cons" others by lying in order to obtain goods or favors; (3) has stolen, as in shoplifting or forgery

- Serious violations of rules, including (1) stays out at night, despite parental prohibitions, beginning before age 13; (2) has run away from home overnight at least twice; (3) is often truant from school, beginning before age 13

---

genetic predisposition heightens the individual's risk when exposed to certain harsh environments. The development of conduct problems in over 1,100 five-year-old twin pairs and their families was studied as a function of the contributions of genetics and physical maltreatment by parents. Among identical twins whose co-twin had conduct problems (i.e., those at high genetic risk), the probability of a conduct disorder diagnosis was nearly 25 percent when their parents physically maltreated them. In contrast, those children at low genetic risk who were subject to physical maltreatment had only a 2 percent chance of developing conduct disorder (Jaffee et al., 2005). Other investigations examining specific symptoms within the conduct disorder diagnosis, separating aggressive from nonaggressive behaviors, point to heritability estimates of .49 for aggressive and .53 for nonaggressive behaviors. Although high, these estimates leave about one-half the variance unaccounted for in explaining the development of this disorder. Clearly, the gene-environment interaction clearly makes sense when attempting to understand the roots of this troubling disorder.

Unfortunately, we know that aggressive and antisocial children are likely to have serious problems as adults. Furthermore, the more severe the antisocial behavior during childhood, the more likely it is that the individual encounters serious problems in adulthood. These problems can include marital difficulties, reduced occupational and economic opportunities, impoverished social relationships, heavy alcohol use, and poor physical health. In a classic longitudinal study, only one in six of the original sample was completely free of psychological disorder in adulthood; more than one quarter had antisocial personality disorder (Robins, 1966). Subsequent studies have confirmed this pes-

simistic outlook, with results indicating that at least 50 percent of children with conduct disorder develop antisocial personality disorder, a likelihood that is increased further in the presence of other diagnoses, such as major depressive disorder (Fombonne et al., 2001).

Oppositional Defiant Disorder

Most children go through periods of negativism and mild defiance, particularly in adolescence, and most parents complain of occasional hostility or argumentativeness in their children; however, what if such behaviors are present most of the time? Children and adolescents with **oppositional defiant disorder** show a pattern of negative, hostile, and defiant behavior that results in significant family or school problems. This disorder is much more extreme than the typical childhood or adolescent rebelliousness, and it is more than a "phase." Youths with this disorder repeatedly lose their temper, argue, refuse to do what they are told, and deliberately annoy other people. They are touchy, resentful, belligerent, spiteful, and self-righteous. Rather than seeing themselves as the cause of their problems, they blame other people or insist that they are a victim of circumstances. Some young people who behave in this way are more oppositional with their parents than with outsiders, but most have problems in every sphere. To the extent that their behavior interferes with their school performance and social relationships, they lose the respect of teachers and the friendship of peers. These losses can lead them to feel inadequate and depressed.

Oppositional defiant disorder typically becomes evident between the ages of 8 and 12. Preadolescent boys are more likely

Mini Case

OPPOSITIONAL DEFIANT DISORDER

Mindy, at age 13, has changed in the past year from a relatively reserved and socially isolated young teenager to what her father now calls "a little tramp." Apart from her behavior, which includes staying out late at night, visiting the college dormitories in town, and cutting most of her classes during the day, Mindy's looks suggest those of a much older and street-wise adolescent. Mindy dyed her hair orange, wears heavy makeup, and dresses in provocative clothes. The more her parents tell Mindy to behave and dress like a "normal" girl, the more Mindy seems driven to defy them. The expression of her anger toward her parents has reached such a level that they have lost sleep at night, fearing that Mindy might run away with one of the motorcyclists whom she has recently befriended.

Diagnostic Features

Individuals with this condition experience significant impairment because of their pattern of negative, hostile, and defiant behavior. This pattern lasts at least 6 months, during which they show four or more of the following criteria:

- Often lose temper
- Often argue with adults
- Often actively defy or refuse to comply with adults' requests or rules
- Often deliberately annoy others
- Often blame others for their mistakes or misbehavior
- Are easily annoyed by others
- Are often angry and resentful
- Are often spiteful or vindictive

to develop this disorder than are girls of the same age, but after puberty it tends to be equally common in males and females. In some cases, oppositional defiant disorder progresses to conduct disorder; in fact, most children with conduct disorder have histories of oppositional defiance. However, many children with oppositional defiant disorder "grow out of" the disorder by the time they reach adolescence as long as they do not have another disorder such as ADHD (Mannuzza, Klein, Abikoff, & Moulton, 2004).

Theories and Treatment of ADHD and Disruptive Behavior Disorders

The search for what causes some children to develop ADHD and disruptive behavior disorders is complicated by many factors, the most central of which involves the difficulty of separating environmental from biological influences on development. In our discussion of theories and treatment, we will focus on ADHD, because this condition has received the greatest amount of research attention.

Theories The attentional deficit and hyperactivity associated with ADHD reflect the fact that these problems involve an abnormality of brain functioning. The biological determination of ADHD is well established, as indicated by family, twin, adoption, and molecular genetic studies. The heritability of ADHD is approximately 70 percent and is among the highest rates of all psychiatric disorders. Studies of individuals with ADHD have found evidence for the involvement of several genes related to dopamine. Structural brain abnormalities in people with ADHD have also been found, and researchers believe that a network of interrelated brain areas is involved in the impairment of attentional-executive functions of these individuals (Wilens et al., 2004). Neuroimaging studies have found such structural brain abnormalities as smaller volumes in the frontal cortex, the cerebellum, and subcortical structures. Adding more weight to theories pointing to brain abnormalities are functional imaging studies suggesting abnormal functioning in the circuits that provide feedback to the cortex for the regulation of behavior (Seidman, Valera, & Bush, 2004).

Although researchers have found functional and structural abnormalities in the brains of people with ADHD, they are uncertain about causal factors other than genetics. Research continues to focus on other biological factors such as birth complications, acquired brain damage, exposure to toxic substances, and infectious diseases. Researchers also suspect that there may be subtypes of ADHD, depending on whether it occurs with other disorders, such as mood or anxiety disorders, learning disabilities, or conduct or oppositional defiant disorder. Each of these subtypes may have a different pattern of family inheritance, risk factors, neurobiology, and responses to medications (Biederman, Mick, Faraone, & Burback, 2001).

In trying to explain the relationship between biological abnormalities and behavioral problems in ADHD, Barkley (1998) focuses on impaired behavioral inhibition and self-control. This impairment is evidenced in four realms of functioning: (1) nonverbal working memory, (2) the internalization of self-directed speech, (3) the self-regulation of mood, motivation, and level of arousal, and (4) reconstitution—the ability to break down observed behaviors into component parts that can be recombined into new behaviors directed toward a goal. Consider how each of these impairments is expressed in a child's behavior. Problems with working memory cause the child to have difficulty keeping track of time or remembering such things as deadlines and commitments. Having an impaired internalization of self-directed speech means that these children fail to keep their thoughts to themselves or engage in private self-questioning or self-guidance; rather, they tend to talk too much and lack a sense of rule-governed behavior. Their impaired self-regulation of mood and motivation causes them to display all their emotions outwardly without censorship, while being unable to self-regulate their drive and motivation. An impaired ability to reconstitute results in a limited capacity to solve problems, because they are unable to analyze behaviors and synthesize new behaviors.

In addition to biological and psychological factors, sociocultural influences also play a role in the aggravation of the

ADHD symptom picture. Many children with ADHD have grown up in a disturbed family environment and have had failure experiences in school, conditions that could contribute to attentional deficits and behavioral problems. On the other hand, the disruptive behavior of this disorder may contribute to these family and school problems. Raising a child with ADHD is more difficult than raising a non-ADHD child, and this stress on the family could lead to family disturbances. Similarly, the child's experiences of failure in school may be the result, rather than the cause, of attentional disturbances.

By the time that individuals with ADHD reach adulthood, they have experienced so many frustrations in life, particularly in relationships, that they become caught in a vicious trap of dysfunction. The very nature of their disorder causes them to have difficulty relating to others, even those to whom they are closest. Partners become exasperated and may give up on the relationship, causing the individual with ADHD to become even more depressed and more inclined to seek self-energizing behaviors that ultimately prove to be counterproductive.

Treatment Treatment typically includes medications which are effective in helping a large proportion of people with ADHD. Although there are more than a dozen brand names under which prescriptions are written, most medications are based on methylphenidate. Over the past few decades, pharmaceutical companies have made significant advances in developing effective medications for ADHD, such that more recently produced medications are longer-lasting, in what are known as extended-release formulations. The first class of stimulant medications, which included methylphenidate (Ritalin), was effective for very brief durations (3 to 5 hours) and required multiple, well-timed doses throughout the day. Subsequently, extended-release formulations were developed, and work in one of two ways: (1) back-loaded delivery systems and (2) beaded 50-50 delivery systems. Concerta is an example of a back-loaded product; 22 percent of the dose is composed of the immediate release overcoat, and 78 percent of the dose is first delivered about 4 hours after ingestion. Adderall XR is an example of a 50-50 beaded delivery product and is designed to mimic what would happen if the patient took two equal doses at the right time; the duration of action is 7 to 9 hours in adults (Dodson, 2005).

As an alternative to methylphenidate, antidepressant medications are sometimes prescribed for people with ADHD. These include buproprion (Wellbutrin SR), pemoline (Cylert), atomoxetine (Strattera), and imipramine. This second line of medications is used to treat mild to moderate ADHD, with some effects apparent in 2 to 3 days, long before antidepressants would be expected to be effective; full benefits develop over the course of 8 to 10 weeks. This group of medications would typically be considered for individuals with mild ADHD symptoms and co-existing symptoms, such as anxiety or depression, for individuals with medical conditions that contraindicate stimulant use, for individuals with tic disorder or Tourette's syndrome (discussed later in this chapter), and for people with drug abuse histories (Dodson, 2005).

Some people are understandably concerned about the side effects associated with stimulant use. For example, some children on the medication have trouble sleeping and have a reduced appetite. More serious side effects involve the development of uncontrollable bodily twitches and verbalizations, as well as temporary growth suppression.

Put yourself in the place of parents trying to decide whether to follow the recommendation of putting a hyperactive child on medications that have worrisome side effects. In agreeing to go along with such a recommendation, parents are hoping that the benefits of the child's improved attentional control and decreased hyperactive behavior will make such a choice worthwhile. Experts in this field (Barkley & Edwards, 1998) believe that the benefits clearly outweigh the costs, in that children who feel more in control of themselves tend to be happier, to be more academically successful, and to behave in more socially appropriate ways. Further, they are more likely to have positive interactions with their parents, because the medications make it more likely that they will behave themselves.

Although the use of medication as been well established for treating individuals with ADHD, its use is not without controversy. Some critics contend that such medications are overprescribed and that medication is being used as the primary, and often only, intervention for dealing with individuals, particularly children, with behavior problems. The one issue regarding which most experts agree is the notion that interventions for individuals with ADHD should involve far more than medication.

In the nonpharmacological realm, a number of interventions are effective in reducing the symptoms of ADHD and helping individuals with this condition function better interpersonally and feel better about themselves. Murphy (2005) enumerates a multipronged approach to psychosocial treatment. Although he focuses on the treatment of teens and adults with ADHD, some of the strategies can also be applied in families of children with ADHD.

1. Psychoeducation is the starting point. The more people with ADHD know about their condition and how it affects them, the better they will be able to understand the impact of this disorder on their daily functioning and, therefore, develop coping strategies for dealing with the challenges they face. One aspect of psychoeducation is the instilling of hope and optimism, such that the individual frames the condition as treatable and develops an expectation that life will become better once he or she begins making changes.

2. Psychological therapies, such as individual therapy, provide a context in which treatment goals can be set, conflicts can be resolved, problems can be solved, life transitions can be managed, and co-existing problems such as depression and anxiety can be treated. Specific techniques, such as cognitive-behavioral strategies, can help clients change maladaptive behavior and thought patterns that interfere with daily functioning. Maladaptive thought patterns have commonly become entrenched as the result of recurrent negative messages from teachers, parents, and peers.

3. Compensatory behavioral and self-management training provides the opportunity to build skills by incorporating more structure and routine into one's life. Simple strategies can make day-to-day tasks and responsibilities more manageable. These include making to-do lists, using appointment books, keeping notepads in useful locations, having multiple sets of keys, and so on.

4. Other such psychological therapies, as marital counseling, family therapy, career counseling, group therapy, and college planning also provide opportunities to assess the various ways in which ADHD symptoms affect life choices and the people with whom the individual is involved.

5. Coaching, a more recently developed intervention, involves consulting with a professional who can assist the individual with ADHD focus on the practical implementation of goals; in other words, the coach helps the person find ways to get things done in a pragmatic, behavioral, results-oriented approach.

6. Technology (e.g., computer programs or personal digital assistants, PDAs) can be used to help individuals with ADHD access tools and devices that help them more effectively communicate, write, spell, stay organized, remember information, stay on schedule, and keep track of time.

7. School and workplace accommodations can be sought that facilitate productivity and minimize distraction. Students or employees with ADHD usually work better in quiet, nondistracting environments. They are also more likely to succeed when they receive more frequent performance reviews to help shape their performance and establish priorities. Tasks may be restructured in ways that capitalize on their strengths and talents.

8. Advocacy, particularly in the form of advocating for oneself, is especially important in attaining success. Although it is difficult for most people to disclose the disabling aspects of ADHD to others, they may find that explaining their condition to others improves the situation for everyone involved.

The multipronged approach discussed above is obviously most appropriate for teens and adults who can take more managerial responsibility for their own lives. Some of these strategies can be adapted by clinicians, parents, and teachers who are dealing with children with ADHD.

A therapist working with a child might use self-reinforcement to encourage the child to regulate such behaviors as settling into a task, delaying gratification, maintaining self-motivation, and monitoring progress toward goals. Implicit in the behavioral approach is the notion that the family must learn to use behavioral methods and be directly involved in helping the child reduce disruptive behaviors. Coordinating these efforts with comparable intervention by classroom teachers improves the odds for helping the child gain better self-control. Again, no one method is necessarily going to provide all the solutions; a multifaceted treatment approach involving medication, educational interventions, behavior modification, social skills training, and counseling is likely to produce the most successful outcomes.

Some of the interventions used for treating young people with ADHD are also applied when working with individuals with oppositional defiant disorder or conduct disorder, although conduct disorder commonly provides even greater challenges. The reason for this is that the home environment of many children with conduct disorder is characterized by severe problems, such as alcoholism and abuse. The children and adolescents themselves are often involved in serious drug abuse, while the stage is being set for their subsequent development of antisocial personality disorder (Myers, Stewart, & Brown, 1998).

A combination of behavioral, cognitive, and social learning approaches appears to be the most useful strategy in working with youths with disruptive behavior disorders (Pelham & Fabiano, 2000). The goal of treatment is to help the child learn appropriate behaviors, such as cooperation and self-control, and to unlearn problem behaviors, such as aggression, stealing, and lying. Therapy focuses on reinforcement, behavioral contracting, modeling, and relaxation training and may take place in the context of peer therapy groups and parent training. Unfortunately, intervention with youths who have disruptive behavior disorders is often initiated during adolescence, a developmental stage that some experts in this field consider to be too late. Behavioral interventions that begin during the earlier years of development are usually more promising.

Separation Anxiety Disorder

Every child experiences anxiety. If you think back to your own childhood, you can probably remember times when you felt nervous or fearful. Perhaps you felt apprehensive on the first day of school or extremely shy when you first met a new playmate. These are common childhood reactions. For some children, though, anxiety becomes a very powerful and disruptive force. They cannot leave home without panicking, they cling to their parents, they are mute with strangers, or they worry obsessively about being hurt. In most cases, anxiety in children is diagnosed according to the same criteria as in adults (see Chapter 6). One anxiety disorder, separation anxiety disorder, is diagnosed only in children, with a prevalence rate of approximately 4 percent of all children and adolescents (American Psychiatric Association, 2000).

Characteristics of Separation Anxiety Disorder

Children with **separation anxiety disorder** have intense and inappropriate anxiety concerning separation from home or caregivers. To understand the nature of this disorder, let's take a look at the role of separation anxiety in normal childhood development.

Mini Case

SEPARATION ANXIETY DISORDER

Six weeks have gone by since the beginning of the school year, and 8-year-old Kira has not yet attended a full day of school. Each morning, she pleads with her mother to let her stay home, some days complaining of stomachaches and other days saying she feels so weak she fears she will faint on her walk to school. Kira's parents are perplexed by her behavior, because she did well in school during second grade and had a circle of good friends. On the few days that she has ventured to school, Kira has insisted that the school nurse call home to report her health problem of the day. While at home, Kira becomes alarmed if her mother leaves on an errand and insists that she be allowed to go along. Even sleep time is disturbed; Kira frequently wanders into her parents' bedroom in the middle of the night, complaining of nightmares involving her parents being killed. Concern about Kira's problems has prompted her mother to ask the school guidance counselor to help develop a plan of intervention for Kira and the family.

Diagnostic Features

With onset prior to age 18, individuals with this condition experience developmentally inappropriate and excessive anxiety for at least 4 weeks concerning separation from home or from people to whom they are attached, as evidenced by at least three of the following:

- Recurrent excessive distress when they anticipate separation from home or important attachment figures
- Worry that harm may befall important attachment figures or that they will lose these people
- Worry that a bad event, such as being kidnapped, will cause a separation from a major attachment figure
- Reluctance or refusal to go to places, such as school, because of fear of separation
- Fear or reluctance to be alone or without attachment figures
- Reluctance or refusal to go to sleep without being near an attachment figure
- Repeated nightmares involving separation
- Repeated complaints of physical symptoms when separation is anticipated

From the moment of birth, any infant's cries usually evoke caregiving behavior in adults. As infants develop in the first year of life, they are able to communicate their needs to caregivers in new ways, as they learn to reach, crawl, grasp, and use verbal utterances. At the same time, children begin to develop a psychological attachment to their parents and become distressed when their parents are not present (Ainsworth, 1989). Although most children maintain a strong attachment to their parents, they become less distressed at separation at around the age of 18 months (Emde, Gaensbauer, & Harmon, 1976). However, a small percentage of children do not overcome the experience of separation anxiety but go on to develop symptoms of separation anxiety disorder. For example, Jennie wavers briefly and then skips happily into the classroom of her day care center when her father drops her off in the morning. In contrast, Emily is terrified when her parents leave her for any period of time.

Children like Emily experience severe reactions when confronted with the prospect of being apart from their parents. They become upset and often physically ill when facing a normal separation, such as when a parent leaves for work or when they go to a relative's house for a visit. Some may refuse to sleep overnight at a friend's house or to go to camp or school. When separated, they fear that something terrible will happen to their parents or to themselves—for example, that they will be kidnapped. When separated from their caretaker, they are likely to complain of physical maladies, such as headaches or stomachaches. Even going to sleep may represent a traumatic separation. They may insist that a parent stay with them until they fall asleep or may plead to sleep in their parents' bed because of nightmares involving separation. When not with an attachment figure, they become panicky, miserable, homesick, socially withdrawn, and sad. They are also demanding, intrusive, and in need of constant attention. Sometimes they cling so closely to a parent that they will not let the parent out of their sight.

Theories and Treatment of Separation Anxiety Disorder

As you know, anxiety is an experience that involves both physical and psychological reactions. Recalling our discussion from Chapter 5, in which we explored anxiety disorders in adults, it is important to consider both of these factors in trying to explain and treat anxiety disorders in children. When looking at the biological component of anxiety, investigators have turned to such sources of information as familial patterns and responsiveness to antianxiety medication. As is the case in other areas of research, familial patterns provide information about the possible role of genetics.

Some children with separation anxiety disorder have a family history of anxiety (Bernstein, Layne, Egan, & Nelson, 2005). A large-scale study of nearly 1,200 female twin pairs yielded evidence of strong heritability (Cronk et al., 2004). However, the same study produced evidence that there are also important environmental contributions to the development of this disorder.

The absence of a father in the home was significantly associated with separation anxiety regardless of socioeconomic status. Children may also develop this disorder in response to natural or manmade disasters. In the aftermath of the September 11 attacks on the World Trade Center, estimates were that nearly 13 percent of New York City schoolchildren had a probable diagnosis of separation anxiety disorder (Hoven et al., 2005). It is possible that temperamental differences rooted in biology cause some children to experience heightened reactivity in these kinds of situations. From the psychodynamic and family systems perspectives, anxiety disorders are seen as the result of children's being held back and failing to learn how to negotiate the normal developmental tasks of separating from parents.

The majority of children diagnosed with separation anxiety disorder experience remission and are completely free of any psychological symptoms even within as short a period as 18 months (Foley et al., 2004). For those who do not, the clinician's primary task is to help the child gain control over anxiety-provoking situations. As with most childhood disorders, behavioral treatments have been demonstrated to be particularly effective. Behavioral techniques used for treating fears and anxieties in children include systematic desensitization, prolonged exposure, and modeling. Contingency management and self-management are also useful in teaching the child to react more positively and competently to a fear-provoking situation. These various behavioral techniques may be applied either individually or in combinations. For example, a child with separation anxiety disorder may learn relaxation techniques along with cognitive strategies for thinking more positively about separation (Jurbergs & Ledley, 2005). Although traditional antianxiety medications are generally not effective (Graae, Milner, Rizzotto, & Klein, 1994), fluoxetine may reduce anxiety symptoms in children (Birmaher et al., 1994). For several years, SSRIs such as fluoxetine were the psychopharmacological treatment of choice for children with separation anxiety disorder (Birmaher et al., 2003). Recently, however, serious concerns have been raised about the prescription of these medications to children, particularly in light of several reports of extreme impulsive reactions, including suicidal attempts, among a small number of children taking SSRIs (Ramchandani, 2004).

Regardless of the specific modality, at some point parents become involved in the child's treatment. Family therapists, in particular, give the greatest emphasis to the parents' role in helping the anxious child, but therapists from all perspectives recommend that treatment involve the family.

Other Disorders that Originate in Childhood

There is a set of relatively rare and unusual disorders that are limited to the childhood years. For the most part, these disappear by adulthood, but the symptoms may linger and have a profound impact on the individual's psychological well-being and social functioning.

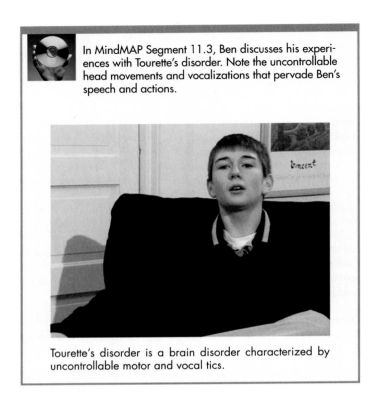

In MindMAP Segment 11.3, Ben discusses his experiences with Tourette's disorder. Note the uncontrollable head movements and vocalizations that pervade Ben's speech and actions.

Tourette's disorder is a brain disorder characterized by uncontrollable motor and vocal tics.

Childhood Eating Disorders

Children with **pica,** a condition commonly associated with mental retardation, eat inedible substances, such as paint, string, hair, animal droppings, and paper. By contrast, in **feeding disorder of infancy or early childhood,** the individual persistently fails to eat, leading to a loss of weight and failure to gain weight. Another form of eating disorder is **rumination disorder,** in which the infant or child regurgitates and rechews food after it has been swallowed. Each of these eating disorders lasts at least 1 month and is not associated with transient stomach distress.

Tic Disorders

A **tic** is a rapid, recurring involuntary movement or vocalization. There are several kinds of tic disorders involving bodily movements or vocalizations. Examples of motor tics include eye blinking, facial twitches, and shoulder shrugging. Vocal tics include coughing, grunting, snorting, the uttering of obscenities (called **coprolalia**), and tongue clicking.

The tic disorder you are most likely to hear about is **Tourette's disorder,** a combination of chronic movement and vocal tics that is much more commonly reported in males. For most, the disorder begins gradually, usually with a single tic, such as eye blinking, which over time grows into more complex behaviors. People with Tourette's disorder usually make uncontrollable movements of the head and sometimes parts of the upper body. In some cases, individuals engage in complex bodily movements involving touching, squatting, twirling, or retracing steps. At the same time, they utter vocalizations that sound very odd to others; for example, an individual may have a complex tic behavior in which he rolls his head around his neck while making sniffing and barking noises. In only a small percentage of cases do people with Tourette's disorder utter obscenities. This is not a passing condition but, rather, one that is usually lifelong, with onset in childhood or adolescence. Young people with this disorder commonly have other psychological symptoms as well, the most common of which are obsessive-compulsive symptoms, speech difficulties, and attentional problems. Deficits in brain inhibitory mechanisms in the prefrontal cortex are thought to be involved in Tourette's disorder, a feature that is shared with obsessive-compulsive disorder and ADHD (Wright et al., 2005).

Elimination Disorders

Children with elimination disorders have not become "toilet-trained," long past the time when they were physiologically capable of maintaining continence and using the toilet properly. In **encopresis,** the child, who is at least 4 years old, repeatedly has bowel movements either in clothes or in another inappropriate place. Children with **enuresis** urinate in clothes or in bed after the age when they are expected to be continent; this is not an infrequent event but, rather, one that takes place at least twice a week for a minimum of 3 consecutive months in children who are at least 5 years old.

Reactive Attachment Disorder

Reactive attachment disorder of infancy or childhood is a severe disturbance in the individual's ability to relate to others. Some children with this disorder do not initiate social interactions or respond when it is appropriate; they may act extremely inhibited and avoidant. Other children show a very different symptom picture, in that they do not discriminate in their sociability but show inappropriate familiarity with strangers. This disturbed style of interpersonal relating arises from pathological caregiving; perhaps the parent or caregiver disregarded the child's emotional or physical needs during the early years of development. Alternatively, there might be so many changes in primary caregivers during early development that the child fails to develop stable attachments.

Stereotypic Movement Disorder

People with **stereotypic movement disorder** engage in repetitive, seemingly driven behaviors, such as waving, body rocking, head-banging, self-biting, and picking at their bodies. These behaviors interfere with normal functioning and sometimes cause bodily injury.

Selective Mutism

In **selective mutism,** the individual consciously refuses to talk in certain situations, usually when there is an expectation for interaction, such as at school. The condition is evident for an extended period of time, at least 1 month, and interferes significantly with normal functioning. Children with this disorder may speak spontaneously in some situations but refuse to speak in other settings.

Development-Related Disorders: The Biopsychosocial Perspective

Now that you have read about the various forms of childhood disorders, you can appreciate our opening comments about the complexities involved in diagnosing and treating children. Perhaps you have also gained some insight into how painful it is for parents and teachers to see a child experience such problems. You can also understand the dilemmas faced by the adults in a child's life about the best course of action to follow in making treatment decisions.

In some ways, the disorders of childhood are like a microcosm of all abnormal psychology. In fact, there is considerable debate among researchers and clinicians about whether separate diagnostic categories should exist for children in the areas of schizophrenia and depression. The question of overlap between childhood and adult forms of psychological disorder is one that is likely to remain unresolved for some time, as researchers continue to explore whether these really are separate entities.

Questions might also be raised about the origin of a child's referral for psychological evaluation or treatment. A parent's reporting of a child's "symptoms" may be a cry for help from an overburdened parent of a normal but difficult child, or it may be the reflection of a disturbance that lies outside the child and instead within the parent, the family, the school, or the larger social milieu. Nevertheless, when children experience these symptoms, they are real, painful, and a legitimate cause of concern. If they are not treated seriously, the problems can accompany the child into adulthood, causing many years of prolonged unhappiness. Because of the relationship between early life difficulties and later adjustments, researchers are actively pursuing a number of intriguing leads for understanding and intervening in the disorders of childhood. Fortunately, therapeutic interventions, particularly involving behavioral methods, can have positive and significant effects on reducing many childhood symptoms (Weisz et al., 1994).

Jason's History

At the second intake session, I first met with Jason and his parents, and then later I discussed Jason's history alone with Mr. and Mrs. Newman. I also spent some time alone with Jason. At first, Mr. Newman expressed reservations about going into detail, because I had told the Newmans in the initial meetings, before having a grasp of Jason's problem, that I may not continue as the clinician following the intake. I explained that I could take the case if family therapy would be sufficient; however, I would recommend another therapist if Jason's needs would be better served by a specialist in child treatment, but, in response to Mrs. Newman's urgings, he agreed. They proceeded to share with me the pain and distress of the past 7 years.

Although only 8 years old, Jason had for most of his life been unable to control his behavior. He had antagonized every important person in his life, time and time again. The older of two children, Jason had a 7-year-old sister, Anna, who showed none of the disturbance that was so much a part of Jason.

Jason's father was 34 years old; he owned and managed a small but successful local card store, where 32-year-old Mrs. Newman worked as a part-time salesperson while the children were in school. The Newmans had been married for 10 years, and they had been relatively happy prior to the onset of Jason's problems. For the past 7 years, however, the tension between Mr. and Mrs. Newman had intensified greatly. From what I could tell, it seemed as though Mr. Newman had denied the seriousness of Jason's problems, usually minimizing the troubles by making such comments as "He's just a typical boy." Alternatively, Mr. Newman blamed teachers for not having enough structure in the classroom.

As Jason's problems grew, Mr. Newman spent less and less time at home, contending that it was necessary to devote his energy to the family business. Thus, Mrs. Newman often felt isolated. She tried to turn to her friends, but over time she began to sense that they did not want to maintain the relationship, because they also found it difficult to interact with Jason. Mrs. Newman told me how she prayed every day that Jason would become normal. She knew he was an intelligent and attractive child but that acquaintances had come to detest him and teachers to dread him.

Assessment

Because Jason had recently taken an IQ test in school, it was not necessary to repeat intelligence testing. The report from the school psychologist indicated that Jason's IQ, as assessed with the WISC-III, placed him in the above-average range of intelligence for both verbal and performance IQ. I felt that it would be helpful to have some quantitative data about Jason's behavioral problems, however, so I asked his parents to complete a child behavior checklist and provided them with some other scales to be completed by Jason's teachers. Both assessment instruments confirmed the picture that Mr. and Mrs. Newman had conveyed in our discussions. Jason's scores were those found in hyperactive children. For example, on the Conners scale, Jason received scores that were more than a full standard deviation above the mean of the subscales of Learning Problems and Impulsivity-Hyperactivity, as well as the Hyperactivity Index.

Diagnosis

There was little question in my mind that Jason met the criteria for attention-deficit/hyperactivity disorder. His current behaviors and his long history of behavioral disturbance made such a conclusion fairly obvious. No one involved with Jason was surprised with this diagnosis—including parents, teachers, and mental health professionals.

Axis I:	Attention-Deficit/ Hyperactivity Disorder, Combined Type
Axis II:	None
Axis III:	No physical disorders or conditions
Axis IV:	Problems with primary support group (family tension) Educational problems
Axis V:	Current Global Assessment of Functioning: 55 Highest Global Assessment of Functioning (past year): 55

Case Formulation

Although in all likelihood biological factors played an important role in Jason's problem, there was certainly more to the picture. Jason's disruptive behavior was serving a function, both at home and in school. Perhaps, somewhat unconsciously, Jason was trying to seek attention. Feeling unable to control his own behavior or thoughts, Jason became increasingly hurt by his lack of friends, but, at the same time, he felt incapable of modifying his behavior in positive directions. His failure to obtain the nurturance that he craved led Jason to an escalation of his behavior, which culminated in the dangerous firesetting at school.

Jason's problem was not one limited to his behavior alone; it had become a family and school problem and required intervention in both contexts.

Treatment Plan

Focusing first on Jason, I recommended that he participate in individual therapy with Dr. Clara Hill, a child psychiatrist highly regarded

RETURN TO THE CASE

(continued)

for her expertise in treating hyperactive children. My recommendation was based on two assumptions. First, I believed that Jason would benefit from medication. Second, I felt that Jason would respond positively to the idea that he would have his own private therapist, who would spend time alone with him each week. Regarding Mr. and Mrs. Newman, I suggested that they meet with Dr. Hill's colleague, a psychologist named Dr. Albert Kennedy, who would develop a contingency management program that could be implemented both at home and in school. Dr. Kennedy had ample experience with hyperactive children, and he was respected by the local school administrators and teachers for the interventions he had developed for other children. Dr. Kennedy would also meet with Mr. and Mrs. Newman on a regular basis to help them through the process and to give them an oppor-

tunity to work on their own relationship, focusing on the ways in which Jason's problem had so deeply affected both of them.

Outcome of the Case

Two years have passed since I first evaluated Jason, and the news so far has been promising. Jason started taking Ritalin shortly after seeing Dr. Hill, and the changes in his behavior were dramatic and quick. He settled down both at school and at home in ways that caused everyone who knew him to sigh with relief. Of course, he did not turn from urchin to angel overnight. In fact, he continued to be provocative and somewhat disruptive at times, but rarely to the extreme of his pretreatment days. Mr. and Mrs. Newman learned from Dr. Kennedy the importance both of being swift with repercussions for inappropriate behavior and of rewarding positive changes. Through

meetings with the Newmans and consultations with school staff, Dr. Kennedy developed a comprehensive intervention program that was consistent and clear. Dr. Hill informed me that, after 6 months of weekly sessions with Jason, she reduced the frequency to bimonthly and then monthly meetings. At the point of each reduction in frequency, Jason's disruptive behaviors flared up temporarily, but in time he settled back into his new routine.

I was glad to learn of Jason's progress and felt confident that his prognosis could now be considered improved. It is difficult to know, however, what scars will remain with this boy from the turbulent years that preceded his treatment. I am hopeful that Jason's positive personality traits will serve as resources to help him continue to grow, unburdened by the hurts of his childhood years.

Sarah Tobin, PhD

SUMMARY

- The category of development-related disorders is comprised of several sets of disorders that first appear at birth or during youth. Mental retardation is characterized by significantly below average general intellectual functioning, indicated by an IQ of 70 or below. In addition to intellectual deficits, people with mental retardation have significant impairments in various abilities, such as social skills, judgment, communication, and capacity for self-care. Mental retardation can result from an inherited condition or from an event or illness that takes place during development. Although there is no cure, early intervention can enrich the intellectual and physical development of people with this condition.

- Pervasive developmental disorders are characterized by severe impairment in several areas of development (e.g., social interaction or communication skills) or the presence of extremely odd behavior, interests, and activities. The most common of these conditions is autistic disorder, which is

characterized by massive impairment in an individual's ability to communicate and relate emotionally to others. The theory that autistic disorder is biologically caused is supported by evidence pointing to patterns of familial inheritance, as well as studies of brain size and structure. Although psychological theories cannot explain the causes of autistic disorder, these approaches are valuable in regard to interventions, particularly those aimed at providing parents and teachers with the tools needed for modifying the maladaptive behaviors of autistic individuals.

- Another set of development-related disorders is comprised of conditions characterized by problems with learning, communication, or motor skills. A learning disorder is a delay or deficit in an academic skill that is evident when an individual's achievement on standardized tests is substantially below what would be expected for others of comparable age, education, and level of intelligence. Communication disorders are conditions characterized by impairment in the expression or understanding of language. The primary form of motor skills disorder is developmental coordination disorder, a condition characterized by marked impairment in the development of motor coordination. Most developmental disorders in these categories are viewed as neurologically based, with various causes, such as damage during fetal development, birth, or as the result of physical trauma or a medical disorder. The school setting is the most likely context for intervening with children who have these conditions.

■ Attention-deficit-hyperactivity disorder (ADHD) involves inattentiveness and hyperactivity-impulsivity. Inattentiveness is characterized by behaviors such as carelessness, forgetfulness in daily activities, and other attentional problems. The hyperactive-impulsive component is further divided into the subtypes of hyperactivity and impulsivity. Hyperactivity is characterized by fidgeting, restlessness, inappropriate running about, difficulty in playing quietly, and excessively talking. Impulsivity is evident in individuals who blurt out answers, cannot wait their turn, and interrupt or intrude on others. Theories that once held that children outgrow ADHD have been discarded in light of the recognition of this condition in approximately 4 percent of adults. Although many of the symptoms of ADHD typically found in children are also found in adults, other symptoms also emerge, such as procrastination, problems with the management of time and money, and difficulties fulfilling work and personal commitments. Other conditions that involve children's disruptive behavior include conduct disorder and oppositional defiant disorder. Young people with conduct disorder repeatedly and persistently violate the rights of others, while those with oppositional defiant disorder show a pattern of negativistic, hostile, and defiant behavior, which results in family or school problems. Extensive research has focused on the causes and interventions for ADHD, with special attention given to neurological abnormality, possibly associated with genetic factors. Neurological abnormality presumably results in impaired behavioral inhibition and self-control. Over time, the individual experiences a number of failure experiences and interpersonal disturbances, which aggravate personal difficulties. Treatment typically includes medications, the most common of which is methylphenidate. Psychological techniques, especially those based on behavioral and cognitive principles, are also regarded as important aspects of interventions aimed at helping individuals with ADHD gain control over their behavior and attention.

■ Several other psychological disorders have received extensive attention by researchers and clinicians. Separation anxiety disorder involves the experience of intense and inappropriate anxiety concerning separation from home or caregivers. Childhood eating disorders include such conditions as pica, feeding disorder of infancy or early childhood, and rumination disorder. Tic disorders, such as Tourette's disorder, involve bodily movements or vocalizations. Elimination disorders, such as encopresis and enuresis, are characterized by a failure to maintain continence at an age-appropriate stage. Reactive attachment disorder is a severe disturbance in the individual's ability to relate to others. Individuals with stereotypic movement disorders engage in repetitive, seemingly driven bodily movements. Those with selective mutism refuse to talk in certain situations, such as at school.

KEY TERMS

See Glossary for definitions

INTERNET RESOURCE

To get more information on the material covered in this chapter, visit our website at **www.mhhe.com/halgin5.** There you will find more information, resources, and links to topics of interest.

CHAPTER 12

Aging-Related and Cognitive Disorders

As I prepared to leave my office to meet Irene Heller, the receptionist called on the intercom to tell me that this new client was "causing a stir in the waiting room." Irene was reportedly yelling at her son that he had no business taking her to the clinic. When I entered the waiting room, however, there was no turmoil but, rather, the sight of a serene-looking gray-haired woman sitting next to a man in his midforties.

It seemed a sad irony that it was on her sixty-seventh birthday that Irene Heller was brought to the mental health clinic by her son Jonathan. As I went to meet her, my eyes were drawn immediately to the corsage she had pinned to her jacket; amid the small bouquet emerged a sign reading "Happy Birthday." Realizing that my attention was drawn to the flowers, Irene commented, "Aren't they a beautiful expression of my son's thoughtfulness?"

After some small talk, I suggested that we proceed to my office. Everything seemed relatively routine until Irene asked me if I was the same Sarah Tobin who had stolen her bicycle when she was 8 years old. Since we were in the middle of the hallway, I was perplexed about how to respond. The question was absurd in several ways, not the least of which was the fact that I was nearly two decades younger than Mrs. Heller. My initial response was to suggest that we wait until we reached my office to discuss her concerns, but Mrs. Heller didn't give me the opportunity to complete my sentence. Rather, she angrily threw her purse on the floor and shouted, "I will not move another step until you acknowledge what you did to me!" At that point, her son pleaded with his mother to cooperate. In a soothing voice, he tried to reassure her by saying, "Mother, this is Dr. Tobin. She is a psychologist who wants to help us find ways to make you feel better. Let's go to her office and tell her what has been going on." Fortunately, Irene agreed and began walking toward my office. On entering, she noticed my diploma hanging on the wall. In a matter-of-fact manner, she quickly translated the five lines of Latin as if she were a fluent speaker of the language. At that point, Jonathan interjected by mentioning that Mrs. Heller had, in recent years, taken up the study of Latin and Greek as a pastime. He then went on to explain that her ability to retain classical Greek and Latin vocabulary and grammar was remarkable, despite the fact that she couldn't recall her address and phone number or the names of her grandchildren.

As Jonathan attempted to tell me the sad story of Irene's debilitating condition, she launched into a monologue, trying to convince me that nothing was wrong with her. Fortunately, she agreed to permit Jonathan to continue to explain his version of events before interrupting again. According to Jonathan, his mother had changed over the past few years from an intellectually alert, vibrant, and active woman who loved teaching into a forgetful, easily distracted, unhappy individual. Her memory problems had become so serious that Jonathan worried about her safety. Would she remember to lock her door at night, to turn off the gas stove, or to take her medicine? He knew that, despite regular phone calls from him and from her friends, Irene was unable to stay on top of things. In fact, she was often unable to recall what a person had said just moments earlier, much less attend to her personal needs.

Jonathan explained that he had noticed alarming changes in his mother during the previous several months. Recently, Jonathan had been expecting his mother to visit his family in their new home. When she failed to show up at the appointed time, he telephoned her and she indignantly responded that he was trying to trick her. Apparently, Irene had gone to his former residence, ostensibly oblivious to the fact that he had moved nearly 2 months ago. Despite his insistence that he had reminded her of his new address just the day before, Irene claimed to have no recollection and insisted that he must be trying to free himself from any obligations to her. The following day, Irene called Jonathan as if nothing unusual had taken place between the two of them. Clearly, she had forgotten all the turmoil that had taken place less than 24 hours ago.

Jonathan went on to describe other situations in which Irene's loss of memory was accompanied by increasingly disruptive and uncharacteristic behaviors. For example, one day the manager of a local department store called Jonathan to complain that Irene was roaming aimlessly through the store, muttering the phrase "a stitch in time, a stitch in time." When the manager asked if he could be of help, Irene began to yell obscenities at him and tried to assault him. As the manager attempted to take her to the office, she screamed, "Murderer! Take your hands off me!" In anguish and embarrassment, Jonathan rushed to the store to find his mother sobbing quietly in a corner of the office. Although occasional peculiar events involving his mother had occurred during the year, none was this extreme. Jonathan had downplayed each one until it became obvious that Irene needed professional attention.

When I asked Irene about her understanding of what Jonathan was talking about, she acknowledged that she had become "a bit forgetful." To Jonathan's surprise, as well as mine, Irene then said, "Perhaps it would be a good idea for someone to help me, so that I don't do something dangerous." I was relieved to hear Irene say this, because her comment gave me reason to feel confident that she would go along with my recommendation that we conduct a comprehensive assessment of her condition.

Sarah Tobin, PhD

What would you think if someone in your life were to begin acting in the ways that Irene Heller did? Like Jonathan, you might first assume that she had an emotional problem, possibly related to an upsetting event in her life. Few people consider that a person's behavioral difficulties might be caused by brain damage or a disease that affects the nervous system, yet, as you will learn in this chapter, there are many ways in which neurological disorders can cause people to experience major changes in their intellectual functioning, mood, and perceptions. You will also see that a variety of physical conditions can cause cognitive impairments through damage to the central nervous system.

The Nature of Cognitive Disorders

Cognitive functions include the processing of thoughts, the capacity of memory, and the ability to be attentive. In the disorders we will discuss in this chapter, cognitive impairment is the central characteristic. This kind of impairment arises from various causes, including brain trauma, disease, or exposure to toxic substances (possibly including drugs). In *DSM-IV-TR*, the formal name for the group of disorders characterized by this set of symptoms is *delirium, dementia, amnestic, and other cognitive disorders*. For the sake of brevity, we will use the term *cognitive disorders* as a comprehensive label.

It may not be obvious that physical abnormalities can cause a set of presumably psychological symptoms, such as hallucinations and delusions. In fact, various physically based syndromes mimic schizophrenia, mood disorders, and personality disorders. People can develop delusions, hallucinations, mood disturbances, and extreme personality changes due to abnormalities in the body resulting from disease, reactions to medication, and exposure to toxic substances. People with disorders involving the brain are frequently found to be suffering from depression either due to the disabling effects of the illness or as a result of physiological changes that underlie both the physical and psychological abnormalities (McNamara, 1991). As you will see in Chapter 13, drugs and alcohol can also cause a person to think, feel, and act in ways that mimic serious psychological disturbances.

Differentiating symptoms that are associated with a psychological disorder from those arising in response to a physical disorder can be very difficult. Fortunately, this process has been facilitated by advances in neuropsychological assessment and the development of new technologies to assess brain structure and function (see Chapter 3). However, even in an age of sophisticated diagnostic technology, determining whether a person's psychological problems are attributable to physical factors can sometimes be very difficult. Consider the case of Flora, a 59-year-old woman who had been hospitalized many times for what appeared to be bipolar disorder. Her symptoms included suicide attempts, extreme belligerence toward her family, and grandiose beliefs about herself. Only after several psychiatric

hospitalizations did an astute clinician determine that Flora's symptoms were caused by an endocrine disorder. After only a few weeks of treatment, Flora's medical condition improved, and her "psychiatric" symptoms diminished.

Another physical disorder with symptoms that appear to be psychological is **epilepsy,** a neurological condition that involves recurring bodily seizures with associated changes in EEG patterns. Because people with epilepsy may act in ways that strike others as being odd, or even psychotic, they may mistakenly be regarded as having a psychological disorder. Epilepsy has been misunderstood for centuries, and many people with this condition have experienced discrimination because of society's lack of understanding about epilepsy.

Epilepsy is classified into two groups according to the extent of brain involvement in the seizure: one type involves generalized seizures, and the other involves partial, or focal, seizures. People with generalized convulsive seizures may have what are called grand-mal seizures, during which they lose consciousness, stop breathing for a brief period, and undergo uncontrollable bodily jerking. Following the seizure, they feel drowsy and confused. Another form of generalized seizure consists of petit-mal seizures, in which the individual experiences a temporary loss of consciousness, possibly accompanied by rhythmic movements of the lips, mouth, head, and eyelids, but does not undergo the full-body spasms that occur with grand-mal seizures.

In contrast to generalized seizures, partial, or focal, seizures involve abnormal EEG patterns that are localized in a cortical or subcortical region of one cerebral hemisphere. Of particular interest to our discussion are seizures that arise from the temporal lobe or nearby limbic areas, because these seizures result in symptoms that have the appearance of psychological disturbances. For example, people with this condition, called temporal lobe epilepsy, may experience a number of symptoms, such as increased fear, mood swings, inappropriate affect, bursts of anger, illusions or hallucinations, altered thought processes, and bizarre behavior. A small percentage of people with temporal lobe epilepsy undergo a disturbing period of psychotic-like behavior following a seizure that can last from a few moments to as long as a few days.

As you can see, careful and precise diagnosis is necessary so that the clinician does not overlook an organic condition, such as epilepsy or endocrine disease, and treat an individual with such a disorder for an emotional disturbance.

Delirium

You have probably heard the term *delirious* used many times, possibly to describe someone who is in a state of uncontrolled excitement. Or perhaps you have personally experienced delirium in a different form while in the grips of a high fever or following an injury. You may have awakened from your sleep, not knowing where you were or what time it was. Family members

A person in a state of delirium experiences numerous cognitive, emotional, and behavioral disturbances. Elderly hospital patients are particularly prone to delirium.

Mini Case

DELIRIUM

Jack is a 23-year-old carpenter whose co-workers brought him to the emergency room when he collapsed at work with a fever that seemed to be burning up his body. Although Jack was not ostensibly injured, it was obvious to Jack's co-workers that something was wrong. When they asked whether he was hurt, Jack repeatedly responded with the nonsensical answer, "The hammer's no good." Jack's co-workers were startled and perplexed by his bizarre suggestions that they were trying to steal his tools and by his various other paranoid-sounding remarks. Grabbing at things in the air, Jack insisted that objects were being thrown at him. Jack couldn't remember the names of anyone at the site; in fact, he was unsure of where he was. Initially, he resisted his co-workers' attempts to take him to the hospital because of his concern that they had formed a plot to harm him.

Diagnostic Features

- People in this state experience a disturbance of consciousness with a reduced ability to focus, sustain, or shift their attention that develops over a short period of time (hours to days) and fluctuates during the day.

- They experience a change in cognition (e.g., memory problems, disorientation, language disturbance), or they develop a perceptual disturbance not better accounted for by dementia.

- The delirium is specified as being due to either a medical condition, substance intoxication, substance withdrawal, or multiple causes.

may have been perplexed by your inability to respond to them in conversation. Perhaps you had some strange thoughts or perceptions that you later realized were hallucinations. If you have ever had such an experience, you know firsthand how a bodily disturbance can result in an altered state of consciousness accompanied by bizarre symptoms.

Delirium is a temporary state in which individuals experience a clouding of consciousness, in which they are unaware of what is happening around them and are unable to focus or pay attention. In addition, they experience cognitive changes, in which their memory is foggy and they are disoriented. A person in a state of delirium may forget what he or she had eaten for lunch only an hour earlier or be unaware of the day of the week, or even the season of the year. The speech of individuals experiencing delirium may be rambling or incoherent as they shift from one topic to another. These individuals may also experience delusions, illusions, or hallucinations, as well as emotional disturbances, such as anxiety, euphoria, or irritability. As you can imagine, such symptoms can be very frightening, both for the person who is experiencing them and for anyone who is observing. Not surprisingly, delirious individuals may do things that are physically dangerous, such as walking into traffic or falling down stairs. Health professionals are therefore concerned about the possibility that the delirious medical patient will get out of bed, unaware of being connected to medical equipment, such as a respiratory tube or urinary catheter.

Delirium is caused by a change in the brain's metabolism and usually reflects something abnormal occurring in the body. A variety of factors can cause delirium, including substance intoxication or withdrawal, head injury, high fever, and vitamin deficiency. People of any age can experience delirium, but it is more common among medically or psychiatrically hospitalized older adult patients, particularly among

surgical patients with pre-existing cognitive impairment and depressive symptoms (Minden et al., 2005). The higher incidence among older people is due to the fact that they are more prone to falls and are more likely to have undergone surgery, experiences that can provoke a state of delirium (Curyto et al., 2001; Marcantonio, Flacker, Wright, & Resnick, 2001). Older adults are also more susceptible to experiencing adverse reactions from medications due to noncompliance and omission or early cessation of treatment (Chan, Nicklason, & Vial, 2001). Even after the symptoms of delirium subside, older hospitalized patients who experience this condition are likely to have continued difficulties for at least a year, and are more likely to experience complications, rehospitalization, and be at greater risk of dying (Marcantonio et al., 2005).

Although delirium has no typical course, it follows some general trends. Delirium typically has a rapid onset, developing over a period of a few days at most, and its duration is brief. Rarely does delirium last for more than a month. Some individuals do show a slower, more subtle manifestation of symptoms, however. Over the course of a day, a delirious individual may experience a variety of emotional disturbances, such as anxiety, fear, depression, irritability, euphoria, restlessness, difficulty in thinking clearly, and hypersensitivity to auditory and visual stimuli. As the delirium continues, these symptoms can fluctuate considerably by time of day, diminishing in the morning and worsening during the nights, when sleep may be disturbed by vivid dreams or nightmares.

Health care professionals differentiate psychomotor disturbances commonly associated with delirium as either hyperactive or hypoactive. Hyperactive individuals manifest restless and agitated behavior, possibly groping or picking at bedclothes, trying to get out of bed when it is unsafe, and making sudden bodily movements. Hypoactive individuals, on the other hand, are slowed down, acting in ways that reflect their feelings of lethargy and stupor. Sometimes there is a shift from one extreme to the other. Hallucinations, delusions, and agitation are most likely during a hyperactive phase (American Psychiatric Association, 2000).

Testing does not usually reveal distinct neurological deficits in a person with delirium, but abnormal bodily movements, such as tremor or shaking, are often evident. Signs of autonomic nervous system disturbance are often present, such as tachycardia (rapid heartbeat), sweating, flushed face, dilated pupils, and elevated blood pressure. The individual either naturally recovers, is effectively treated, develops a progressive neurological deficit, or dies from the underlying physical condition.

Interventions that follow a multidimensional approach may help foster recovery from delirium. Such an approach focuses on educating staff in assessment, prevention, and treatment and in particular the importance of attending to the needs for individualized care of the patient with delirium (Lundstrom et al., 2005). Educating medical and psychiatric personnel about the symptoms of delirium is particularly important for prevention and early detection, both of which can reduce the negative consequences for the older patient (Weber, Coverdale, & Kunik, 2004).

Amnestic Disorders

As you have learned from our discussion of dissociative amnesia in Chapter 6, psychological factors can cause memory loss. There are biological causes for loss of memory as well; such conditions are referred to as **amnestic disorders.** People with amnestic disorders are unable to recall previously learned information or to register new memories. This inability to incorporate recent events into memory or to recall important information can be very disturbing, because the individual loses a sense of personal identity. The individual may try to cover up the social problems caused by memory loss through denial or confabulation, the fabrication of facts or events to fill a memory void. However, these tactics cannot compensate for the feeling of a lack of connectedness with one's own daily and past experiences.

The *DSM-IV-TR* includes two major categories of amnestic disorders: those due to a general medical condition and those that are substance-induced. Amnestic disorders due

---

Mini Case

AMNESTIC DISORDER

Harvey is a 57-year-old music teacher in a public high school. While bicycling to work one day, he was struck by a car and was rushed to the emergency room. In addition to receiving a broken leg, Harvey suffered a head injury and was unable to remember anything that had happened during the preceding 2 weeks. Furthermore, he had no idea how old he was, where he was born, or whether he was married. This inability to remember his personal past was a source of great distress to Harvey. By contrast, Harvey had no trouble remembering the ambulance ride to the hospital or the name of the emergency room physician who first examined him. Following a 3-day hospital stay, Harvey was transferred to a rehabilitation facility for 3 months, where memory therapy helped him learn mnemonic strategies for recalling important information.

Diagnostic Features

- People with this condition develop memory impairment evidenced by an inability to recall previously learned information or by an impaired ability to learn new information.

- The memory disturbance causes significant impairment and represents a decline from a previous level of functioning.

- The memory disturbance does not occur exclusively during the course of delirium or dementia.

- The condition is specified as being due to a medical condition, the use of a substance, or uncertain cause.

---

to medical conditions may be chronic (lasting a month or more) or transient. They can result from a wide variety of medical problems, such as head trauma, loss of oxygen, or herpes simplex. When drugs or medications cause serious memory impairment, the condition is referred to as **substance-induced persisting amnestic disorder.** This condition may be caused by an array of substances, including medications, illicit drugs, or environmental toxins, such as lead, mercury, insecticides, and industrial solvents. The most common cause of amnestic disorder is chronic alcohol use, as you will see in Chapter 13. Note the use of the word *persisting* in the diagnosis to distinguish this condition from the passing effects of substance intoxication or substance withdrawal. When assigning this diagnosis, the clinician indicates the problematic substance (for example, "barbiturate-induced persisting amnestic disorder").

Regardless of the specific reason for the amnesia, memory loss is the result of damage to the subcortical regions of the brain responsible for consolidating and retrieving memories. For some people, especially chronic abusers of alcohol, amnestic disorder persists for life, and impairment is quite severe, possibly requiring custodial care. For others, such as those whose condition results from medications, full recovery is possible.

Traumatic Brain Injury

Damage to the brain caused by exposure to trauma, known as **traumatic brain injury (TBI),** is increasingly being recognized as an important cause of mental and physical dysfunction. Brain tissue is highly sensitive to damage caused by intense pressure to the head, such as that which occurs in an automobile accident, contact sports, or combat. In the Afghanistan and Iraq wars, it is estimated that as many as 22 percent of wounded soldiers have suffered TBI (Okie, 2005). Although a similar number of soldiers in the Vietnam War received brain injuries, more of the soldiers fighting in Afghanistan and Iraq have survived because of the improvements in treatment that have occurred in the decades since the Vietnam War. Furthermore, modern-day helmets made out of Kevlar provide greater protection, contributing to the higher survival rates. However, the victims of these combat brain injuries are now more likely to suffer closed brain injuries when exposed to the blasts produced by improvised explosive devices (IEDs). Injuries caused by IED blasts include concussions, contusions, cerebral infarctions (cutting off of blood), and the intrusion into the brain of fragments of weaponry, bodies, or even vehicles.

Although the victims of TBI receive immediate treatment on the battlefield and then further care in military hospitals, symptoms persist and can involve permanent damage. Some of these symptoms include headaches, sleep disturbances, sensitivity to light and noise, and diminished cognitive performance on tests of attention, memory, language, and reaction time. These soldiers may also suffer depression, anxiety, emotional outbursts, mood changes, or inappropriate affect.

When these TBI victims return to their communities, they also face challenges in daily life as they continue to cope with these cognitive, affective, and personality changes. Some of these changes may produce subtle effects that are not immediately observable (Vanderploeg, Curtiss, & Belanger, 2005); in some ways, these changes are more insidious because they are not as obvious as injuries to other parts of the body. Although many veterans are actively working to rehabilitate themselves, there is concern among public health officials about those veterans who are either less motivated or less able, due to the nature of their injuries, to recover their lost functions (Okie, 2005).

Dementia

The word *dementia* comes from the Latin words *de* (meaning "away from") and *mens* (meaning "mind"). **Dementia** is a form of cognitive impairment involving generalized progressive deficits in a person's memory and learning of new information, ability to communicate, judgment, and motor coordination. In addition to experiencing cognitive changes, people with dementia undergo changes in their personality and emotional state. As you might guess, such disturbances have a profound impact on a person's ability to work and interact normally with other people.

The main cause of dementia is profuse and progressive brain damage. Other physical conditions that can cause this dementia include vascular (circulatory) diseases, AIDS, head trauma, psychoactive substances, and various neurological disorders that we will discuss later in this chapter. Dementias are found in people of all ages, including children, but the most well known is Alzheimer's disease, which we will discuss in detail shortly.

Characteristics of Dementia

The symptoms of dementia may begin with mild forgetfulness, only slightly noticeable and annoying. However, if the underlying brain disorder that causes the dementia cannot be treated, the person's symptoms will become increasingly obvious and distressing. As the condition of people with dementia worsens, so does their capacity for caring for themselves, for staying in touch with what is going on around them, and for living a normal life.

The diagnosis of dementia involves a thorough physical and psychological assessment to evaluate such symptoms as aphasia, apraxia, and memory loss.

Memory Loss The first sign of dementia is slight memory impairment. In fact, a common but insensitive joke made by many people whose memory occasionally falters is that they must have Alzheimer's disease. Fortunately, most people who fear they are developing Alzheimer's disease are likely to be wrong. For those who do have the disease, however, memory loss becomes increasingly pronounced. Eventually the person is incapable of retaining any new information. As time goes on, people with the disorder become unable to remember even the basic facts about themselves and their lives.

Aphasia, Apraxia, and Agnosia The term **aphasia** refers to a loss of the ability to use language. Aphasia is caused by damage to the brain's speech and language area, and this damage influences the production and understanding of language. Two forms of aphasia are Wernicke's aphasia and Broca's aphasia, both named after the people who discovered them. In **Wernicke's aphasia,** the individual is able to produce words but has lost the ability to comprehend them, so that these verbalizations have no meaning. In contrast to the person with Wernicke's aphasia, the person with **Broca's aphasia** has a disturbance of language production, but comprehension abilities are intact. In other words, the individual knows the rules of sentence construction and can grasp the meaning of language, but he or she is unable to produce complete sentences; verbal production is reduced to the fundamental communication of content with all modifiers left out.

A person with **apraxia** has lost the ability to carry out coordinated bodily movements that he or she could previously perform without difficulty. This impairment is not due to physical weakness or decreased muscle tone but, rather, to brain deterioration. **Agnosia** is the inability to recognize familiar objects or experiences, despite the ability to perceive their basic elements.

Disturbance in Executive Functioning **Executive functioning** includes cognitive abilities, such as abstract thinking, planning, organizing, and carrying out behaviors. Executive dysfunction is evident in many everyday activities. Consider the case of Max. The relatively simple task of boiling a pan of water becomes a frustrating event each day, because Max fails to turn on the burner. When the phone rings, he does not know which end of the phone to speak into. When asked to write down a phone number, he confuses the digits. In addition to obvious behavioral manifestations of executive dysfunction, the individual's abstract thinking is impaired. For example, when asked "In what way are a watermelon and a honeydew alike?" Max responded, "I'm not sure, but I guess it's because water and dew are both wet."

Alzheimer's Disease (Dementia of the Alzheimer's Type)

Many people fear as they get older that they will lose control of their mental functioning. However, only a very small percentage of older adults develop the form of dementia known as Alzheimer's disease, or dementia of the Alzheimer's type. The term *senile* is sometimes mistakenly used to refer to this disorder, or more generally to the process of growing old. This is an unfortunate misnomer, as it implies that the aging process involves an inevitable loss of cognitive functions. The odds are actually low that a person will develop Alzheimer's disease later in life, but, for those who do, the disorder has tragic consequences.

Alzheimer's disease was first reported in 1907 by a German psychiatrist and neuropathologist, Alois Alzheimer (1864–1915), who documented the case of a 51-year-old woman complaining of poor memory and disorientation to time and place (Alzheimer, 1907/1987). Eventually, the woman became depressed and began

Mini Case
DEMENTIA OF THE ALZHEIMER'S TYPE

Ellen is a 69-year-old woman who was taken to her family physician by her husband, who was becoming increasingly concerned by her failing memory and strange behavior. Ellen's husband first became concerned a few months earlier when Ellen couldn't remember the names of basic household items, such as *spoon* and *dishwasher.* Her day-to-day forgetfulness became so problematic that she would repeatedly forget to feed or walk the dog. As the weeks went by, Ellen seemed to get worse; she would leave food burning on the stove and water overflowing the bathtub. A review of Ellen's medical history found no physical problems that could account for her deterioration; nor could her physician or a neurologist determine any current medical basis for her behavior.

Diagnostic Features

- People with this disorder develop multiple cognitive deficits manifested by memory impairment, and at least one of the following cognitive disturbances: (a) language disturbance; (b) impaired ability to carry out motor activities; (c) failure to recognize or identify objects; (d) disturbance in executive functioning, such as planning, organizing, or abstracting.

- The course is characterized by gradual onset and continuing cognitive decline.

- The cognitive deficits cause significant impairment and represent a decline from the previous level of functioning.

- The deficits are not due to other disorders, medical conditions, or substance use and do not occur exclusively during the course of a delirium.

to hallucinate. She showed the classic cognitive symptoms of dementia, including loss of language and lack of recognition of familiar objects, as well as an inability to perform voluntary movements. Alzheimer was unable to explain this process of deterioration until after the woman died, when an autopsy revealed that most of the tissue in this woman's cerebral cortex had degenerated. On examining the brain tissue under a microscope, Alzheimer also found that individual neurons had degenerated and had formed abnormal clumps of neural tissue. Ninety years later, a discovery of brain slides from this woman confirmed that the changes seen in her brain were similar to those typically found in current cases of the disease (Enserink, 1998). Although there is still no explanation for what causes the process of brain deterioration that forms the core of this disease, the term **Alzheimer's disease** has come to be associated with this severe cerebral atrophy, as well as the characteristic microscopic changes in brain tissue.

Several subtypes of Alzheimer's disease are identified by the prominent feature of the clinical presentation. When clinicians diagnose Alzheimer's disease, they specify one of the following subtypes: (1) with delirium, (2) with delusions, (3) with depressed mood, or (4) uncomplicated (for cases in which none of these other characteristics apply).

The prevalence of Alzheimer's disease is widely but inaccurately reported in the popular press as 4.5 million, amounting to 12 percent of the population over the age of 65 and 50 percent of those over the age of 85. These figures are intended to document the seriousness of this disorder, but recent efforts at more precise prevalence estimates indicate a much lower number of people afflicted with the disorder. Analyses of data from the United States, as well as U.S. mortality records, place the prevalence at 1.7 to 1.9 million cases, which is closer to 5 to 7 percent of the over-65 population (Hy & Keller, 2000). The prevalence rises among those over 85 to about 29 percent (Brookmeyer & Kawas, 1998). Autopsy studies confirm the lower percentage estimate. In one rural Pennsylvania community, Alzheimer's disease was found to be the cause of death in 4.9 percent of people 65 years and older (Ganguli et al., 2005). Of course this estimate includes only those whose deaths are confirmed to have resulted from Alzheimer's disease; in many cases, another disease, such as pneumonia, is actually the immediate cause of death in people with advanced Alzheimer's disease. Nevertheless, this percentage is substantially lower than what would be expected on the basis of figures published in the media. Perhaps somewhat amazingly, among centenarians (people who live to 100 years and older), approximately 90 percent were symptom-free until the age of 92 (Perls, 2004).

Alzheimer's disease progresses in stages marked by the deterioration of cognitive functioning, along with changes in personality and interpersonal relationships. As you can see from Table 12.1 on page 379, the behavioral symptoms of dementia due to Alzheimer's disease are memory loss, disorientation, decline of judgment, deterioration of social skills, and extreme flatness or changeability of affect. Other psychological symptoms include agitation, wandering, hallucinations, delusions,

aggressiveness, insomnia, demandingness, and an inability to adapt to new routines or surroundings.

These symptoms evolve over time, but their rate of progress varies from person to person and according to the stage of the disease, with the most rapid deterioration occuring during the middle phase. The progression from early to late dementia in people with Alzheimer's usually occurs over a 5- to 10-year period, ending in death through the development of complicating diseases, such as pneumonia.

Dementia Caused by Other Conditions

Clinicians attempting to diagnose Alzheimer's disease are faced with the difficult task of determining whether the cognitive impairment shown by the individual is caused by other physical disorders producing similar symptoms. In addition, depression may produce cognitive impairment in older people causing them to appear as though they have Alzheimer's disease when in fact they have a treatable psychological disorder.

Physical Conditions Dementia can result from a variety of physical conditions, including infectious diseases such as neurosyphilis, encephalitis, tuberculosis, meningitis, or localized infections in the brain. People who experience kidney failure may have symptoms of dementia as a result of the toxic accumulation of substances that the kidneys cannot cleanse from the blood. People with certain kinds of brain tumors also experience cognitive impairments and other symptoms of dementia.

Dementia can also result from anoxia (oxygen deprivation to the brain), which may occur during surgery under general anesthesia or may result from carbon monoxide poisoning. Anoxia can have severe effects on many brain functions, because neurons quickly die if they are deprived of oxygen. Because neurons in the brain do not replace themselves, the loss of a significant number of neurons can lead to concrete thinking and permanent impairments in such functions as new learning ability, attention, concentration, and tracking. The emotional effects of brain damage due to anoxia can include affective dulling and disinhibition, as well as depression. The person's ability to plan, initiate, and carry out activities can be drastically reduced.

Even the substances that a person ingests, such as drugs, and exposure to environmental toxins, such as industrial chemicals, intense fumes from house paint, styrene used in plastics manufacturing, and petroleum-distilled fuels, can cause brain damage and result in a condition called **substance-induced persisting dementia.**

Severe nutritional deficiencies can also cause dementia. People who are severely undernourished are prone to develop a deficiency of folate, a critical nutrient; this can lead to progressive cerebral atrophy. If the deficiency is not counteracted by dietary improvements, the individual can become depressed and show various cognitive impairments, such as poor memory and abstract reasoning. Many chronic heavy users of alcohol develop a thiamine deficiency, which leads to an organic disorder known as Korsakoff's syndrome, which we will discuss in Chapter 13.

REAL STORIES

JOHN BAYLEY AND IRIS MURDOCH: CARING FOR A PERSON WITH ALZHEIMER'S DISEASE

The case of Irene Heller, which opens this chapter, tells the story of a woman affected by forgetfulness, distractibility, and unhappiness—symptoms that pointed to her developing dementia. The lives of people with dementia dramatically change as symptoms worsen. The lives of those who are closest to them change as well. In *Elegy for Iris,* John Bayley, an eminent literary critic and Oxford professor, wrote about his experience of caring for his beloved wife Iris Murdoch, who developed Alzheimer's disease in her midseventies.

The early years of John's relationship with Iris seem much like the story of many couples of the era. John recalls that when he first caught sight of Iris as she rode her bicycle one day through Oxford, he felt an immediate sense of intrigue regarding this special woman, who at the time was a philosophy professor. When they began seeing each other, John was 28 and Iris 34 years old. Iris went on to become a successful novelist, writing 26 works of fiction in addition to her publications in the field of philosophy.

John initially became concerned about Iris' cognitive functioning in 1994 when Iris was giving a talk at a university in Israel. During this speech, Iris had difficulty finding the words to convey her thoughts, and later she seemed unaware of the problem and of the awkward reaction of the audience. Over time, Iris' condition deteriorated and John began to take on more and more responsibility caring for his wife.

In *Elegy for Iris,* John describes how even seemingly small tasks became confusing, sometimes frightening, for both him and his wife. On one occasion he took Iris to a stream for a swim,

John Bayley and Iris Murdoch

an activity she had always cherished—but one that would become impossible for her because of her failing cognitive and physical abilities:

> Iris was never keen on swimming as such. She never swam fast and noisily or did fancy strokes. What she loved was being in the water. Twice she came quite close to drowning. I thought of that, with the anxiety that had now invaded both our lives, as we approached the riverbank again to scramble out. . . . I pulled myself out first and turned to help Iris. As she took my hands, her face contracted into that look of childlike dread which so often comes over it now, filling me, too, with worry and fear. Suppose her arm muscles failed her, and she slipped back into the deep water, forgetting how to swim and letting water pour into her mouth as she opened it in a soundless appeal to me? I knew on the spot that we must never come to bathe here again.

Bayley also describes the difficulty of communicating with an Alzheimer's sufferer:

> An Alzheimer's sufferer begins many sentences, usually with an anxious, repetitive query, but they remain unfinished, the want unexpressed. . . .

REAL STORIES

JOHN BAYLEY AND IRIS MURDOCH: CARING FOR A PERSON WITH ALZHEIMER'S DISEASE (continued)

Often they remain totally enigmatic, related to some unidentifiable man or woman in the past who has swum up to the surface of her mind as if encountered yesterday. At such times, I feel my own mind and memory faltering, as if required to perform a function too far outside their own beat and practice. . . .

Our mode of communication seems like underwater sonar, each bouncing pulsations off the other, then listening for an echo. The baffling moments when I cannot understand what Iris is saying, or about whom or what— moments which can produce tears and anxieties, though never, thank goodness, the raging frustration typi-

cal of many Alzheimer's sufferers— can sometimes be dispelled by embarking on a joky parody of helplessness, and trying to make it mutual, both of us at a loss for words.

Source: From *Elegy for Iris* by John Bayley. Copyright © 1998 by John Bayley. Reprinted with permission from St. Martin's Press.

TABLE 12.1 Stages of Alzheimer's Disease

Stage	Cognitive Deficits	Personality Changes
Forgetfulness	Forgetting names and where one has placed things	Appropriate concern with mild forgetfulness of familiar objects, but no objective deficits in work or social situations
Early confusional	Getting lost when going to familiar place; colleagues and family notice forgetfulness of names and words; poor reading comprehension; inability to concentrate	Denial of memory problems but anxiety accompanies symptoms of forgetfulness and confusion
Late confusional	Decreased knowledge of current events; forgetting of one's personal history; decreased ability to travel or handle finances	Very obvious use of denial regarding memory problems; flattening of affect and withdrawal from challenging situations
Early dementia	Cannot recall some important features of current life, such as address or telephone number and names of grandchildren; inability to recall some personal facts, such as the name of one's high school; some disorientation with regard to time or date	No assistance needed for toileting or eating but possible difficulty choosing proper clothing
Middle dementia	May occasionally forget name of spouse; largely unaware of all recent events and experiences and many events of life; unaware of surroundings or the season of year but can distinguish familiar from unfamiliar people in their environment	Totally dependent on spouse or caregiver for survival; many personality and emotional changes occur, including becoming delusional, obsessive, and anxious; fails to follow through on intentions due to forgetfulness of these intentions
Late dementia	Loss of all verbal abilities; incontinent of urine and requires assistance in toileting and feeding; loses basic psychomotor skills, including ability to walk	Complete deterioration of personality and social skills, as individual is almost totally unresponsive to all but the simplest form of communication

Source: Adapted with the permission of The Free Press, a division of Simon & Schuster, Publishing Group, from *Alzheimer's Disease: The Standard Reference* by Barry Reisberg, M.D. Copyright © 1983 by Barry Reisberg, M.D. All rights reserved.

Elderly people are often victims of the stereotype that they are prone to developing dementia. However, most elderly people are in good physical and psychological health and are able to enjoy productive lives.

Sometimes dementia associated with physical disorders and toxic reactions can be reversed if the person receives prompt and appropriate medical treatment. However, if no intervention for a treatable dementia takes place in the early stages, the brain damage becomes irreversible. The more widespread the structural damage to the brain, the lower the chances the person with dementia will ever regain lost functions.

Often clinicians can pinpoint that the cause of dementia is one of several medical diseases or conditions that affect neurological functioning. For example, dementia due to head trauma is a condition in which an individual has sustained an injury to the brain, such as in an automobile accident. People who have traumatic brain injury typically develop amnesia and persisting memory problems. Various other common symptoms include sensory and motor deficits, language disturbance, attentional problems, irritability, anxiety, emotional upheaval, increased aggression, and other personality changes.

In recent years, particular attention has focused on the fact that many people with AIDS develop dementia; in fact, subtle deterioration in cognitive functioning is sometimes the first clue that a person has AIDS. As the disease progresses, cognitive deterioration usually becomes more obvious, leading to a diag-

nosis of dementia due to AIDS. People with this form of dementia are likely to become forgetful and unable to concentrate or solve problems. Movement disturbances include such symptoms as tremor, imbalance, and loss of coordination. Psychological symptoms may include delusions and hallucinations. Over time, the loss of control over emotions, behavior, and thought becomes so pervasive that many individuals become deeply depressed, apathetic, and socially withdrawn. Complicating the psychological and physical difficulties experienced by people with AIDS is the societal discrimination they encounter.

Pick's disease is a relatively rare progressive degenerative disease that affects the frontal and temporal lobes of the cerebral cortex. It is caused by the accumulation in neurons of unusual protein deposits called Pick bodies. In addition to having memory problems, people with this disorder become socially disinhibited, acting either inappropriately and impulsively or apathetic and unmotivated. In contrast to the sequence of changes shown by people with Alzheimer's disease, people with Pick's disease undergo personality alterations before they begin to have memory problems. For example, they may experience deterioration in social skills, language abnormalities, flat emotionality, and a loss of inhibition.

Parkinson's disease involves neuronal degeneration of the basal ganglia, the subcortical structures that control motor movements. Deterioration of diffuse areas of the cerebral cortex may occur. Dementia does not occur in all people with Parkinson's disease, but rates are estimated as high as 60 percent, mostly involving those who are older and at a more advanced stage of the disease. Parkinson's disease is usually progressive, with the most striking feature of the disorder being various motor disturbances. At rest, the person's hands, ankles, or head may shake involuntarily. The person's muscles become rigid, and it is difficult for him or her to initiate movement, a symptom referred to as **akinesia.** A general slowing of motor activity, known as **bradykinesia,** also occurs, as does a loss of fine motor coordination. For example, some people with Parkinson's disease walk with a slowed, shuffling gait; they have difficulty starting to walk and, once started, have difficulty stopping. In addition to these motor abnormalities, they show signs of cognitive deterioration, such as slowed scanning on visual recognition tasks, diminished conceptual flexibility, and slowing on motor response tests. The individual's face also appears expressionless and speech becomes stilted, losing its normal rhythmic quality. They have difficulty producing words on tests that demand verbal fluency. However, many cognitive functions, such as attention, concentration, and immediate memory remain intact.

Lewy body dementia, first identified in 1961, is very similar to Alzheimer's disease, with progressive loss of memory, language, calculation, and reasoning, as well as other higher mental functions. However, the progress of the illness may be more rapid than seen in Alzheimer's disease. Lewy bodies are tiny, spherical structures consisting of deposits of protein found in dying nerve cells found in damaged regions deep within the brains of people with Parkinson's disease. Lewy body dementia is diagnosed when Lewy bodies are found more diffusely

At the age of 37, Michael J. Fox disclosed his 6-year struggle with Parkinson's disease and the fact that he had undergone surgery to control the symptoms of the disorder.

dispersed throughout the brain. It is not clear whether the condition called Lewy body dementia is a distinct illness or a variant of either Alzheimer's or Parkinson's disease (Serby & Samuels, 2004), although some claim that this is the second most common form of dementia (McKeith et al., 2004). Researchers are beginning to differentiate Lewy body dementia from Alzheimer's disease, however, based on neurological evidence. In one study, using both PET scan and autopsies, investigators found that deficits in the visual cortex were specific to the brains of people with Lewy body dementia (Gilman et al., 2005).

Yet another form of dementia specifically involves the frontal lobes of the brain, and therefore is known as **frontotemporal dementia.** Rather than involving a decline in memory, as is seen in Alzheimer's disease, frontotemporal dementia is reflected in personality changes, such as apathy, lack of inhibition, obsessiveness, and loss of judgment. Eventually, the individual becomes neglectful of personal habits and loses the ability to communicate. The onset of the dementia is slow and insidious. On autopsy, the brain shows atrophy in the frontal and temporal cortex, but there are no amyloid plaques or arterial damage. Some evidence supports the notion that this form of dementia is linked to a gene located on chromosome 17 (Cruts et al., 2005).

Although primarily a disease involving loss of motor control, **Huntington's disease** is a degenerative neurological disorder that can also affect personality and cognitive functioning. Huntington's disease is a genetic disease involving an abnormality on chromosome 4 that causes a protein, now known as huntington, to accumulate and reach toxic levels. The symptoms first appear during adulthood, usually in people in their forties but sometimes as early as the age of 20. The disease involves the death of neurons in subcortical motor control structures, as well as decreases in the neurotransmitters GABA, acetylcholine, and substance P.

A number of disturbances are associated with Huntington's disease, ranging from altered cognitive functioning to social and personality changes. The disease is associated with mood disturbances, changes in personality, irritability and explosiveness, suicidality, changes in sexuality, and a range of specific cognitive deficits. Because of these symptoms, the disorder may be incorrectly diagnosed as schizophrenia or a mood disorder, even if the individual has no history suggestive of these disorders. People with Huntington's disease can also appear apathetic because of their decreased ability to plan, initiate, or carry out complex activities. Their uncontrolled motor movement interferes with sustained performance of any behavior, even maintaining an upright posture, and eventually most people with Huntington's disease become bedridden.

Creutzfeldt-Jakob disease is a rare neurological disease thought to be caused by an infectious agent that results in abnormal protein accumulations in the brain. Initial symptoms include fatigue, appetite disturbance, sleep problems, and concentration difficulties. As the disease progresses, the individual shows increasing signs of dementia and eventually dies. Underlying these symptoms is widespread damage known as spongiform encephalopathy, meaning that large holes develop in brain tissue. The disease appears to be transmitted to humans from cattle who have been fed the body parts of dead farm animals infected with the disease (particularly sheep, in whom the disease is known as scrapies). In 1996, an epidemic in England of "mad cow disease," along with reported cases of the disease in humans, led to a ban against British beef. Concerns about this disease continue to exist in European countries, as well as in the United States.

Another possible cause of dementia is cardiovascular disease affecting the supply of blood to the brain. Such a condition is called **vascular dementia.** Dementia can follow a stroke, in which case it is called acute onset vascular dementia, but the most common form of vascular dementia is multi-infarct dementia, or MID, caused by transient attacks in which blood flow to the brain is interrupted by a clogged or burst artery. The damage to the artery deprives the surrounding neurons of blood and oxygen, which causes the neurons to die. Although each infarct is too small to be noticed at first, over time the progressive damage caused by the infarcts leads the individual to lose cognitive abilities.

Vascular dementia resembles the dementia due to Alzheimer's disease in some ways. People with vascular dementia experience memory impairment, as well as one of the following: (1) aphasia, (2) apraxia, (3) agnosia, or (4) disturbance in executive functioning. However, there are some significant differences between these two forms of dementia. People with vascular dementia show a particular set of physical abnormalities, such as walking difficulties and weakness in the arms and legs. Furthermore, people with vascular dementia show a pattern of cognitive functioning that is distinctly different from that found in people with Alzheimer's. In the typical clinical picture of vascular dementia, certain cognitive functions remain intact and others show significant loss, a pattern called patchy deterioration. Another unique feature of vascular dementia is that it shows a stepwise deterioration in cognitive functioning: a function that was relatively unimpaired is suddenly lost or severely deteriorates. This is in contrast to the gradual pattern of deterioration in Alzheimer's disease.

As is true for Alzheimer's disease, there is no treatment to reverse the cognitive losses in MID. However, individuals can take preventive actions throughout adulthood to protect themselves from the subsequent onset of vascular dementia. Reducing the risk of hypertension and diabetes is one important way to lower the chances of developing cognitive disorders in later life (Papademetriou, 2005).

Depression   Adding to the complexity of separating the causes of dementia in disorders other than Alzheimer's is the fact that depression can lead to symptoms that mimic those apparent in the early stages of Alzheimer's disease. These cognitive changes constitute a condition known as **pseudodementia,** or false dementia. Depression may also co-exist with Alzheimer's disease, particularly during the early to middle phases, when the individual is still cognitively intact enough to be aware of the onset of the disorder and to foresee the deterioration that lies ahead. Although depressive symptoms are distinct from Alzheimer's disease, these symptoms may serve to heighten the risk of an individual's developing Alzheimer's disease, particularly men. In a 40-year longitudinal study of nearly 1,400 older adults, men who were depressed had twice the risk of developing Alzheimer's disease as men who were not depressed (Dal Forno et al., 2005). Based on these and other findings, it appears that a useful indicator of early stage Alzheimer's disease might be symptoms of depression (Bartolini et al., 2005).

Clinicians treating a person with cognitive impairment who is also depressed have the difficult task of trying to determine if the depression is caused by Alzheimer's disease or whether the cognitive impairment is caused by depression. Distinguishing between pseudodementia and Alzheimer's disease is important, because depression can be successfully treated. Several indicators can help the clinician differentiate depression from dementia. For example, depressed individuals are more keenly aware of their impaired cognition and frequently complain about their faulty memory. In contrast, the individual with Alzheimer's usually tries to hide or minimize the extent of impairment or explain it away when the loss cannot be concealed. As the disorder progresses, people with Alzheimer's disease lose awareness of the extent of their cognitive deficits and may even report improvement as they lose their capacity for critical self-awareness. The order of symptom development also differs between Alzheimer's disease and depression. In depressed elderly people, mood changes precede memory loss; the reverse is true for people with Alzheimer's disease.

Clinicians can also distinguish pseudodementia by the nature of the individual's symptoms, which follow the classic pattern seen in people with major depressive disorders. The person with depression is anxious, has difficulty sleeping, shows disturbed appetite patterns, and experiences suicidal thoughts, low self-esteem,

In MindMAP Segment 12.1, Helen, a woman with Alzheimer's disease, demonstrates difficulties associated with this disorder in memory and orientation. Her daughter confirms the memory problems and describes what her mother was like prior to developing the disorder.

Caring for an older adult friend or relative with Alzheimer's disease can be emotionally stressful.

guilt, and lack of motivation. People with dementia, in contrast, experience unsociability, uncooperativeness, hostility, emotional instability, confusion, disorientation, and reduced alertness. People with pseudodementia also are likely to have a history of prior depressive episodes that may have been undiagnosed. Their memory problems and other cognitive complaints have a very abrupt onset, compared with those of people with dementia, who experience a more slowly developing downward course. Another clue that can help clinicians distinguish between Alzheimer's and pseudodementia may be found by exploring the individual's recent past to determine whether a stressful event has occurred that may have precipitated the onset of depression. Sensitive tests of memory may also enable the clinician to distinguish pseudodementia from Alzheimer's disease. People with pseudodementia are likely not to respond when they are unsure of the correct answer; by contrast, individuals with Alzheimer's adopt a fairly liberal criterion for making responses and, as a result, give many incorrect answers.

Diagnosis of Alzheimer's Disease

Because of the importance of early diagnosis to rule out treatable dementias, researchers and clinicians have devoted significant energy and attention to the development of behavioral tests for diagnosing Alzheimer's disease in its initial stages. An erroneous diagnosis would be a fatal mistake if the person had a dementia that would have been reversible if the proper treatment had been applied when the symptoms first became

TABLE 12.2 Mini-Mental State Examination

Orientation to time	"What is the date?"
Registration	"Listen carefully. I am going to say three words. You say them back after I stop. Ready? Here they are . . . HOUSE (pause), CAR (pause), LAKE (pause). Now repeat those words back to me." [Repeat up to 5 times, but score only the first trial.]
Naming	"What is this?"
Reading	"Please read this and do what it says." [Show examinee the words on the stimulus form.] CLOSE YOUR EYES

evident. Similarly, if the individual had a disorder with a nonorganic basis, a crucial opportunity to intervene would have been missed. Unfortunately, the early symptoms of Alzheimer's do not provide a sufficient basis for diagnosis. A definitive diagnosis of Alzheimer's disease can be made only in an autopsy by studying microscopic changes in brain tissue, leaving clinicians with the only option of conducting diagnosis by exclusion. However, in the later stages of the disease, there are diagnostic guidelines that can be applied and are claimed to have 85 to 90 percent accuracy. These guidelines were developed in 1984 by a joint commission of the National Institute of Neurological and Communicative Disorders and Stroke and the Alzheimer's Disease and Related Diseases Association and are therefore referred to as the NINCDS/ADRDA Guidelines (McKhann et al., 1984). The diagnosis of Alzheimer's disease based on the NINCDS/ADRDA criteria involves thorough medical and neuropsychological screenings. Even with these very stringent and complete guidelines, however, the diagnosis they lead to is at best one of "probable" Alzheimer's disease, reflecting the fact that the only certain diagnosis can be obtained through autopsy.

Brain imaging techniques are increasingly being used for diagnosing Alzheimer's disease. Although such measures have been regarded as assisting in the process of diagnosis by exclusion, evidence is accumulating to support the use of brain scans (CAT and MRI) to provide more positive indicators of the disease as well. For example, such measures detect atrophy in the hippocampus, the first area to be affected by the disease. Neuron loss in this area seems to be a good prediction of the development of the disease (Csernansky et al., 2004). Later in the disease, brain scans can reveal the presence of more marked abnormalities characteristic of the disease, such as areas of widespread atrophy and enlarged cerebral ventricles. Alterations in brain circuits within the areas of the cortex that are involved in memory, including the temporal and prefrontal lobes, have been detected with MRI and PET scans (Hirono et al., 2004). Biological markers are providing another diagnostic tool. Tests are being developed to assess the presence in cerebrospinal fluid of certain proteins that reach elevated levels in the brains of people with Alzheimer's disease. These tests appear to have potential as diagnostic tools, particularly for making diagnoses during the early stages of the disease, during which phase it is important to differentiate Alzheimer's disease from depression and other cognitive disorders (Andreasen & Blennow, 2005).

The clinical tool most commonly used for diagnosing Alzheimer's disease is a specialized form of the mental status examination known as the Mini-Mental State Examination (MMSE) (Folstein, Folstein, & McHugh, 1975) (see Table 12.2). People with Alzheimer's disease respond in particular ways to several of the items on this instrument; they tend to be circumstantial, repeat themselves, and lack richness of detail when describing objects, people, and events. Obviously, more intense workups are required following abnormal MMSE performance, but the MMSE is a useful screening tool.

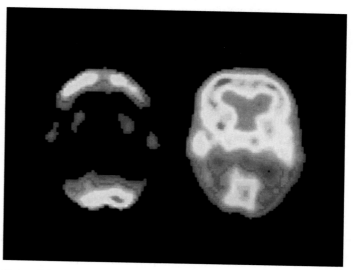

Pictured here are PET scans of the brains of an individual with Alzheimer's disease (on the left), and a normal control subject (on the right). Darker areas indicate lower brain activity.

In diagnosing a person thought to have Alzheimer's disease, clinicians use a variety of approaches, including psychological testing. A primary focus of such testing includes an evaluation of the individual's cognitive functions, with particular attention to memory.

Theories and Treatment of Alzheimer's Disease

All theories regarding the cause of Alzheimer's disease focus on biological abnormalities involving the nervous system. Other theoretical perspectives, however, can offer insight into the impact of the disease on the individual's life and relationships with others.

Biological Perspective   Two major types of changes occur in the brains of people with Alzheimer's disease. The first is the formation of **neurofibrillary tangles,** in which the cellular material within the cell bodies of neurons becomes replaced by densely packed, twisted microfibrils, or tiny strands, of protein. Neurofibrillary tangles are made up of one form of a protein called **tau,** which normally helps maintain the internal support structure of the axons. The collapse of the transport system within the neuron leads to altered communication between neurons and, ultimately, perhaps to the neuron's death. Neurofibrillary tangles develop early in the disease and may become quite widespread before the individual shows any behavioral symptoms.

The second change that occurs in the brains of people with Alzheimer's disease is the development of **amyloid plaques,** which are clusters of dead or dying neurons mixed with fragments of protein molecules. They are called "amyloid" because their core is composed of a substance called beta amyloid. There are several types of beta amyloid; the one linked with Alzheimer's disease is referred to as "beta amyloid-42."

Beta amyloid is formed from a larger protein found in the normal brain, referred to as amyloid precursor protein (APP). Researchers believe that APP, which is manufactured by neurons, plays a role in the growth of neurons and their communication

with each other, and perhaps contributes to the repair of injured brain cells. Beta amyloid is formed when APP is being manufactured in the cell. Enzymes called proteases snip the APP into fragments. If the APP is snipped at the wrong place, beta amyloid-42 is formed (Vassar et al., 1999). The fragments eventually clump together into abnormal deposits that the body cannot dispose of or recycle. In addition to its tendency to form insoluble plaques, beta amyloid seems to be toxic to neurons.

A relatively new theory, called the **caspase theory of Alzheimer's disease,** proposes that beta amyloid stimulates substances called caspases, which become enzymes that destroy neurons. The destruction of neurons, called apoptosis, is what then ultimately leads to the loss of cognitive functioning that occurs in Alzheimer's disease (Cotman, Poon, Rissman, & Blurton-Jones, 2005) (see Figure 12.1).

Until the late 1980s, biological theories focused on changes in levels of neurotransmitters or in structures that were thought to account for the degeneration of the brain and behavioral losses associated with Alzheimer's. The most prominent of these theories proposed that the primary disturbances involved in Alzheimer's disease are in the acetylcholine neurotransmitter system, which is involved in the processes of learning and memory (Coyle, Price, & DeLong, 1983). According to this view, people with Alzheimer's disease have insufficient amounts of **choline acetyltransferase (CAT),** which is essential for the synthesis of acetylcholine. Particularly important in this account of Alzheimer's disease is the fact that many of the biochemical and structural changes found in the brains of people with this disorder are in the hippocampus, a structure in the limbic system involved in memory and the learning of new information. Changes in this area of the brain are presumed to play a major role in the cognitive deficits associated with Alzheimer's disease.

Although there are various theories being tested to understand the causes of Alzheimer's disease, the most probable is that an underlying defect in the genetic programming of neural activity triggers whatever changes may take place within the brain as a result of degenerative processes. The genetic theory was given impetus from the discovery that a form of the disease called early-onset familial Alzheimer's disease, which begins at the unusually young age of 40 to 50 years, occurs with higher than expected prevalence in certain families. Other genes appear to be involved in a form of late-onset familial Alzheimer's disease that starts at the more expected age of 60 or 65 years. These genes are postulated to lead to excess amounts of beta amyloid protein.

With the discovery of familial patterns of early-onset Alzheimer's disease along with advances in genetic engineering, researchers have identified several genes that may hold the key to understanding the cause of the disease. The apoE gene on chromosome 19 has three common forms, $\epsilon 2$, $\epsilon 3$, and $\epsilon 4$. Each one produces a corresponding form of apolipoprotein E (apoE) called "E2," "E3," and "E4." The presence of the $\epsilon 4$ allele sets up the mechanism for production of the E4 form of apoE, which is thought to damage the microtubules within the neuron, which probably play an essential role in the activity of the cell. Ordinarily, apoE2 and apoE3 protect the tau protein, which helps stabilize the microtubules. The theory is that, if the tau protein is unprotected

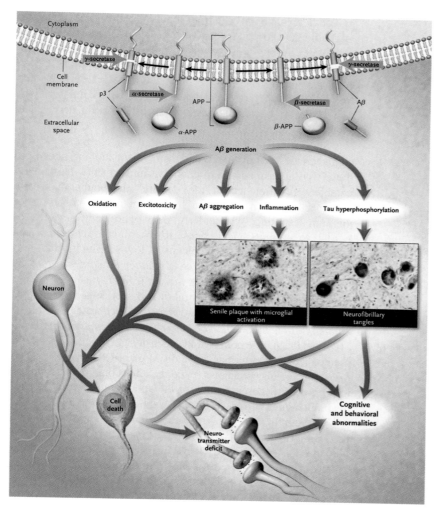

FIGURE 12.1 Putative amyloid cascade
The amyloid cascade hypothesis is illustrated here. The hypothesis proposes that beta-amyloid peptide is generated from the amyloid precursor protein, and eventually leads to cell death. APP denotes amyloid precursor protein, and Aβ beta-amyloid.

Source: From J. L. Cummings (2004). "Alzheimer's Disease." *New England Journal of Medicine,* 351, pp. 56–57. Figure 1. Copyright © 2004 Massachusetts Medical Society. All rights reserved. Used with permission.

by apoE2 and apoE3, the microtubules will degenerate, eventually leading to the destruction of the neuron. (See Figure 12.1.)

Most early-onset familial Alzheimer's disease cases are associated with defects in the so-called presenilin genes (PS1 and PS2), which, as the name implies, are thought to be involved in causing the brain to "age" prematurely. The mean age of onset in families with mutations in the PS1 gene is 45 years (ranging from 32 to 56 years) and 52 years for people with PS2 gene mutations (40 to 85 years). The pattern of inheritance for the presenilin genes is autosomal dominant, meaning that, if one parent carries the allele that is associated with the disease, the offspring has a 50 percent chance of developing the disorder. Researchers are attempting to determine how presenilin genes 1 and 2 interact with APP, beta amyloid, plaques, and tangles. Researchers estimate that the four genes, presenilin 1 and 2, APP, and apoE, account for approximately half the genetic risk for Alzheimer's disease (St. George-Hyslop & Petit, 2005).

Environmental Perspective As compelling as the genetic theory is, as discussed above, it accounts for at most 50 percent of Alzheimer's cases. Mechanisms other than genetics are apparently needed to explain the so-called sporadic (nonfamilial) form of the disease.

Health-related behaviors are increasingly being viewed as important moderators of genetic risk. One important behavioral risk factor is cigarette smoking. In the Honolulu-Asia Aging Study, a large longitudinal study of Japanese American men studied from midlife to later adulthood, heavy smoking at midlife was associated with a higher risk of developing Alzheimer's disease. Even more impressive was the fact that there was a

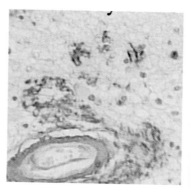
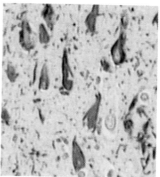

The major microscopic signs of Alzheimer's disease include beta amyloid deposits shown on the left and neurofibrillary tangles shown on the right.

The School Sisters of Notre Dame in Minnesota are participating in a groundbreaking epidemiological study of the predictors of Alzheimer's disease.

positive relationship between the amount of cigarette smoking and the number of plaques discovered in the brains at autopsy (Tyas et al., 2003). Similar findings were obtained in a 2-year follow-up of over 2,800 individuals living in China (Juan et al., 2004). A second behavioral risk factor is obesity. In a longitudinal investigation of older adults in Sweden, there was a 36 percent increase in the risk of developing Alzheimer's disease by the age of 79 for every unit of increase in body mass index (BMI) at the age of 70 (Gustafson et al., 2003). A third behavioral risk factor that may increase the individual's risk of developing Alzheimer's disease is a sedentary lifestyle. In the Honolulu-Asia Aging Study, men who walked more than two miles a day had a lower risk of dementia than those who walked one-quarter to one mile a day (Abbott et al., 2004). Although the forms of dementia included causes other than Alzheimer's disease, the findings nevertheless point to a potentially important lifestyle factor.

An unusual study provides a somewhat different perspective on possible environmental contributions to Alzheimer's disease. The "Nun Study" was begun in 1986 and is one of the most intriguing studies in the field of psychology and aging (Snowdon, 2001). The project has involved 678 nuns, ranging in age from 75 to 106, who have given the research team unprecedented access to their personal and medical histories, who have agreed to undergo intensive annual cognitive and physical testing, and who have pledged to donate their postmortem brains to this scientific endeavor. At the heart of Snowdon's inquiry were questions about what factors helped so many of these elderly women remain cognitively vibrant and live such long and healthy lives.

Snowdon received a gold mine of data when he was given access to the personal records of the nuns, dating back to their initial entry into the religious community. In each nun's file was a relatively standardized set of forms including an autobiography which she had written decades earlier. What made this set of data so valuable was the fact that Snowdon would be able to assess the nun's cognitive functioning during her youth, and then look for connections with how she fared many years later.

For decades researchers in this area have been frustrated by the fact that autopsy has been the only reliable method for confirming a diagnosis of Alzheimer's disease. Snowdon's research project has generated considerable excitement because it has the potential to yield information about factors in early life that might predict subsequent onset of Alzheimer's, with the ultimate goal of developing preventive measures. For example, in one investigation of over 50 of the nuns whose brains were studied at autopsy, there was a positive association found between performance on a memory test about one year before death and the size of the hippocampus, the portion of the brain involved in short-term memory (Mortimer et al., 2004).

Snowdon and his colleagues noted some very interesting characteristics that differentiated the high-functioning nuns from those who developed severe cognitive impairments. Particularly notable were differences in "idea density" (the number of discrete ideas per 10 written words) and the "grammatical complexity" of the nun's writing. The elderly nuns who showed signs of Alzheimer's disease had decades earlier written essays low in idea density and grammatical complexity. A low-scoring writing sample would include sentences like *My father Edward was born in Chicago, Illinois, and is now a factory worker in Gary, Indiana.* High-scoring writing includes more complex sentences like *My father is a well-read man, whose principal occupation is that of a builder, a trade that he had begun prior to marrying my mother.*

That the simple notion of idea density can be such a powerful predictor of dementia has engendered great excitement. In fact, Snowdon and his colleagues found that they could predict with 85 to 90 percent accuracy which of the young nuns would develop the brain damage characteristic of Alzheimer's six decades later.

The significance of this research extends well beyond accurate prediction of later-life cognitive problems. What is especially important is the realization that the brain can be "exercised," resulting in benefits akin to those resulting from bodily exercise. In other words, the nuns who had been cognitively active throughout life, perhaps as teachers, showed much less cognitive decline than their peers who had been employed in service roles involving minimal cognitive challenge. It appears continuous intellectual activity stimulates the brain in ways that have lifelong benefits.

When they looked not only at the style of writing but also at the content of what the nuns had written, Snowdon and his colleagues came upon other fascinating findings, such as a startling statistical correlation between the expression of positive emotions and longevity. For example, Sister Genevieve Kunkel, at 90 years old, describes herself as "up and grateful" because she spent her life teaching young people. The expression of positive emotions (such as happiness, love, hope, gratitude, and contentment) even early in life provide a lens through which the future may be viewed in terms of long-term health and happiness. Similarly, negative emotional expression early in life sets the stage for a life that will likely be abbreviated and unhealthy.

From this fascinating scientific inquiry, Snowdon and his colleagues have begun to answer some of the most perplexing questions in the field of aging and have brought to the attention of researchers and mental health professionals the importance of emphasizing health-oriented behaviors early in life. We now know that healthful behaviors not only take care of the rest of the body but also include cognitive exercise and positive emotionality that benefit the brain.

Some older people are able to take advantage of computer networks that provide information and support for relatives of Alzheimer's patients.

Medical Treatment of Alzheimer's Disease Clearly, the ultimate goal of the intense research on Alzheimer's disease is to find effective treatment, if not a cure. There is a great deal of optimism in the scientific community that this treatment, when it is found, will also benefit those who suffer from other degenerative diseases of the brain (Hardy & Gwinn-Hardy, 1998). As the search for the cause of Alzheimer's disease proceeds, researchers are attempting to find medications that will alleviate its symptoms.

Two medications are approved by the U.S. Food and Drug Administration for use in the treatment of Alzheimer's disease symptoms. These medications, which target the neurotransmitter acetylcholine, are THA, or tetrahydroaminoacridine (also called tacrine and given the brand name Cognex) and donepezil hydrochloride (Aricept). Both fall in the category of anticholinesterase medications, because they work by inhibiting the action of acetylcholinesterase (also called cholinesterase), the enzyme that normally destroys acetylcholine after its release into the synaptic cleft. Because they inhibit the action of acetylcholinesterase, these medications slow the breakdown of acetylcholine; therefore, higher levels remain in the brain. Unfortunately, both medications have side effects. Tacrine can produce toxic effects in the liver, and the required doses are too high for some people. Aricept is as effective as tacrine in targeting cognitive symptoms, although it has gastrointestinal side effects related to the effects of acetylcholinesterase inhibitors (diarrhea and nausea). However, its required dose is lower, and it does not interfere with liver function (Corey-Bloom, 2000). Both med-

ications have the advantage that they give the patient a period of relief from the disturbing cognitive symptoms that occur in the early stages of the disease. While these are the only approved medications on the market, there are other acetylcholinesterase agents (citicoline, arecoline, and ENA 713, also called Exelon), as well as medications that work on other neurotransmitters.

A second category of medications targets the so-called free radicals, which are molecules formed when beta amyloid breaks into fragments; free radicals are thought to damage neurons in the surrounding brain tissue. Antioxidants are agents that can disarm free radicals and, therefore, may be another treatment for Alzheimer's disease.

Several therapeutic approaches are now being tested that target the formation of beta amyloid plaques. Clioquinol is an antibiotic that breaks up the chemical bonds that hold the amyloid protein together (Raman et al., 2005). Antioxidants are also being experimented with, based on the theory that when beta amyloid breaks into fragments, free radicals are formed that damage the surrounding neurons. One form of antioxidant is bioflavonoid, a substance that occurs naturally in wine, tea, fruits, and vegetables. Naturally occurring bioflavonoids (found in, for example, blueberries) are seen by some researchers as having important preventive roles in reducing the extent of memory loss in later adulthood (Joseph, Shukitt-Hale, & Casadesus, 2005). A longitudinal study of over 1,300 French people found benefits associated with bioflavonoids in reducing the risk of Alzheimer's disease (Commenges et al., 2000). Perhaps the most exciting research in

President Ronald Reagan was diagnosed with Alzheimer's disease in 1994 and died in 2004.

TABLE 12.3 Examples of Caregiver Burden

The following items from the Screen for Caregiver Burden illustrate the kinds of concerns that caregivers experience. The prevalence of each concern among a representative sample of caregivers is indicated across from each item:

Item	Prevalence (%)
My spouse continues to drive when he/she shouldn't.	43
I have little control over my spouse's behavior.	87
I have to do too many jobs/chores (feeding, shopping, paying bills) that my spouse used to do.	67
I am upset that I cannot communicate with my spouse.	73
I feel so alone—as if I have the world on my shoulders.	43
I have to cover up for my spouse's mistakes.	60
I am totally responsible for keeping our household in order.	70

Source: Republished with permission of Gerontological Society of America, from P. P. Vitaliano, et. al., "The Screen for Caregiver Burden" in *The Gerontologist*, 1991, 31: 76–83; permission conveyed in the format Textbook via Copyright Clearance Center, Inc.

this area is on the development of an Alzheimer's vaccine that would increase the body's immune response against beta amyloid to prevent or reduce plaque formation (Chauhan & Siegel, 2005). So far, however, no medications have been found that substantially alter the progression of the disease.

Behavioral Management of Symptoms As biomedical researchers continue their search for treatments to cure or alleviate the symptoms, behavioral psychologists are developing strategies to maximize the daily functioning of people with Alzheimer's disease. These efforts are often targeted at the **caregivers,** who are the people (usually family members) primarily responsible for caring for the person with the disease. Caregivers often suffer adverse effects from the constant demands placed on them, effects known as **caregiver burden** (see Table 12.3). However, caregivers can be taught behavioral strategies that can promote the patient's independence and reduce his or her distressing behaviors. Support groups can also provide a forum in which caregivers learn ways to manage the emotional stress associated with their role.

Behavioral strategies aimed at increasing the patient's independence include giving prompts, cues, and guidance in the steps involved in self-maintenance. For example, the patient can be encouraged to relearn the steps involved in getting dressed and then be positively rewarded with praise and attention for having completed those steps. Modeling can be used, so that the client relearns previous skills through imitation. Finally, time management can be helpful in that, if the caregiver is taught to follow a strict daily schedule, the client is more likely to be able to fall into a regular routine of everyday activities. All of these methods benefit both the client and the caregiver. The client regains some measure of independence, and the caregiver's burden is reduced to the extent that the client can engage in self-care tasks.

Behavioral strategies can also eliminate, or at least reduce

the frequency of, wandering and aggression in an Alzheimer's patient. One possible approach, which is not always practical, involves extinction. The caregiver ignores certain disruptive behaviors, with the intention of eliminating the reinforcement that has helped maintain them. However, extinction is not practical for behaviors that may lead to harm in the client, such as wan-

 MindMAP Segment 12.2 focuses on the New England Centenarian Study in which people 100 years old and older are given a variety of neuropsychological and cognitive tests. The elders in this study are healthy and active, and it is hoped that by examining them closely, we can learn more about how to prevent Alzheimer's disease and other cognitive disorders.

Studies on long-living older adults can help provide the key to understanding the causes of cognitive disorders such as Alzheimer's disease.

dering if it involves leaving the house and walking into the street. One possibility is to give the client positive reinforcement for staying within certain boundaries. However, this may not be sufficient, and, at that point, protective barriers need to be installed. Another possible approach is for the caregiver to identify situations that are particularly problematic for the patient, such as in the bathtub or at the table. Behavioral methods can then be used in these circumstances. For example, if the problem occurs while eating, it may be that the patient can be encouraged to relearn how to use a knife and fork, rather than needing to be fed. Again, such an intervention can reduce caregiver burden, as well as increase the patient's functional skills.

These behavioral interventions can be implemented through individual therapy or in a support group. The support group facilitator can teach these methods to participants. Furthermore, caregivers can share strategies among themselves based on their own experiences. The emotional support that caregivers can provide for each other can be just as valuable as the actual instruction they receive. Ultimately, better-quality care is provided to the Alzheimer's patient when caregiver burden is minimized.

You can see, then, that although the prospect of Alzheimer's is frightening and painful for all individuals involved, a number of interventions are available. Until a cure for the disorder is found, however, clinicians must be content to see their gains measured less as progress toward a cure and more as success in prolonging the period of maximum functioning for the individual and the individual's family.

Cognitive Disorders: The Biopsychosocial Perspective

The cognitive impairments associated with the disorders discussed in this chapter are, by definition, best understood from a biological perspective. However, the biological perspective has not yet produced a viable treatment for one of the most devastating of these disorders, Alzheimer's disease. Until a cure is found, individuals and their families whose lives are touched by the disease must be willing to try a variety of approaches to alleviate the suffering caused by Alzheimer's. Many research programs are currently underway to explore strategies for reducing the stress placed on caregivers. Some of these approaches involve innovative, high-technology methods, such as computer networks; others take the more traditional approach of providing emotional support to individuals with Alzheimer's disease and their families. The application of cognitive-behavioral and other methods of therapy to helping people cope with Alzheimer's is another useful approach. It seems that the bottom line in all this research on understanding and treating those affected by Alzheimer's disease is that it is not necessary for psychologists to wait until biomedical researchers discover a cure. Much can be done to improve the quality of life for people with Alzheimer's and to maintain their functioning and their dignity as long as possible.

RETURN TO THE CASE

Case Report
Irene Heller

Irene's History

In order to put together a picture of Irene Heller's life history, I had to rely on her as well as Jonathan for details. For parts of the story, she was coherent and accurate in her recall. For other parts, however, she left out pieces of information, which Jonathan had to fill in. Fortunately, Jonathan had collected a considerable amount of information about his mother from relatives and her friends. When he joined in telling the story, his voice was filled with sadness.

Irene grew up in a poor family in a small mining town in the Appalachians. Despite the family's poverty, she attended a state university and on graduation was offered a fellowship to pursue a doctorate in mathemat-

ics, an unusual opportunity for a woman in the 1930s. However, Irene declined the fellowship, because she met and fell in love with Jonathan's father and they decided to get married. The couple had three sons in short succession. After the birth of their third child, Irene's husband became caught up in gambling and drinking, eventually leaving his wife and moving across the country, never to be heard from again.

Over the years, Irene managed to get by, struggling as a poorly paid teacher. All three boys did well academically, going on to college and successful careers, one in New York City and the other two in the same city as Irene. By the time she retired from teaching, she had gained enor-

mous respect from the people in her community, from her fellow teachers, and from the many students she helped in her role as teacher and adviser. She had accumulated a large enough pension to allow her to fulfill her life's dream of being able to travel, pursue her interests in gardening and needlework, and "just plain relax." However, her deterioration over the course of the past year had made those plans impossible.

Jonathan repeatedly noted that the onset of his mother's problems seemed to coincide with her retirement. He had come to recognize that her problems were far more serious than adjustment difficulties, but he couldn't help wondering whether the major life change had triggered something that was waiting to happen. When I asked Jonathan to be more specific about his mother's problems, he discussed her memory difficulties, her poor judgment, and her inappropriate behaviors.

Assessment

Irene agreed to take a battery of tests, and I referred her to Dr. Furcolo, the staff neuropsychologist. Dr. Furcolo's report indicated that Irene had moderate cognitive deficits, including the inaccurate naming of objects, poor performance on tests of abstract reasoning and verbal fluency, disorientation as to time and place, and impairment of recent memory. Her intellectual abilities were relatively intact on scales of well-learned abilities measured in a familiar format and on scales of immediate memory recall not requiring any encoding processes. In contrast, she performed poorly on intelligence test scales involving unfamiliar, abstract, speed-dependent tasks that strained her capacity for attention and learning. Irene showed no signs of a psychotic disorder, nor did she suffer from specific symptoms of depression. Her symptoms appeared to have had a gradual onset and to have progressed over at least a 2 year period. Irene's annoyance when she described her symptoms reinforced my impression, and Dr. Furcolo's, that her irritability was related to frustration over her declining mental faculties.

In a case such as Irene's, in which there is a strong likelihood of a medical problem, a comprehensive medical workup is necessary, including laboratory tests and brain imaging. Irene agreed to my recommendation that she be admitted to the hospital for 3 days of testing. The test results showed that her endocrine and metabolic functioning were normal, and there was no evidence of excessive alcohol or substance use. Irene's EKG, blood pressure, cerebral angiography (X-ray of cerebral blood vessels), and measure of cerebral blood flow showed no evidence of cardiovascular or cerebrovas-

cular abnormalities. The CT scan revealed some atrophy and enlargement of ventricles, but there was no evidence of focal lesions or trauma. Her EEG pattern showed some evidence of slowing but no evidence of focal abnormalities.

Diagnosis

I assumed that Irene was experiencing more than just emotional problems related to her retirement. The medical workup and the nature of her symptoms pointed to a physically based disorder involving dementia; specifically, all signs pointed to a diagnosis of dementia of the Alzheimer's type.

Axis I:	Dementia of the Alzheimer's Type
Axis II:	Deferred
Axis III:	Alzheimer's disease
Axis IV:	Problems related to the social environment (living alone in unsupervised housing)
Axis V:	Current Global Assessment of Functioning: 28 Highest Global Assessment of Functioning (past year): 60

Case Formulation

I formed the diagnosis of dementia of the Alzheimer's type for this 67-year-old retired schoolteacher after extensive medical and neuropsychological testing and observation on an inpatient unit by an interdisciplinary team of professionals. Irene had had symptoms of dementia for an undetermined period of time, possibly as long as 2 years, when she apparently first noted long-term memory loss and difficulty registering new information into short-term memory. Although Irene's retirement occurred around the time her symptoms first appeared, it is not likely that the retirement caused the onset of the disorder. It did not appear that retirement in and of itself presented a stress to Irene, who was looking forward to spending her time in travel and other leisure pursuits.

Treatment Planning

Irene's dementia was sufficiently advanced so that a return to her home without any supervision or assistance was out of the question. I consulted with Mary Lyon, the hospital's social worker, about the options that were available locally for Irene. Ms. Lyon recommended that Irene move into an apartment complex that provided supervised living arrangements for elderly people. The income from the sale of her house, plus her retirement pension, would give her the financial resources to live in a reasonably large and comfortable apartment without the responsibilities of owning a home. In addition to helping with Irene's residential arrangements, Ms. Lyon consulted with Irene, Jonathan, and me about treatment options. We all agreed that a multidisciplinary treatment team was needed, including a psychologist, a social worker, and a counselor from the local Council on Aging. In particular, Irene needed help with developing methods of self-care and independent living.

Outcome of the Case

More than 3 years have passed since my consultation with Irene and her son. Sadly but predictably, matters have not improved in Irene's life. She initially moved into a supervised apartment and attended a day program at a local nursing home, but her deterioration was rapid and unyielding. After only 6 months, Irene had to move into a nursing home, because she repeatedly endangered herself by carelessly disposing of matches and by wandering out of her apartment at night and getting lost.

In a recent note I received from Jonathan, he explained how impaired his mother had become. Although she had some good days in which they could converse satisfactorily, on most days she seemed unaware that he was her son. Jonathan ended his note with the expression of a faint hope that science might find some of the answers to this tragic disease.

Sarah Tobin, PhD

SUMMARY

- Cognitive disorders (formally called "delirium, dementia, amnestic, and other cognitive disorders") are those in which the central characteristic is cognitive impairment that results from such causes as brain trauma, disease, or exposure to toxic substances.

- Delirium is a temporary state in which individuals experience a clouding of consciousness in which they are unaware of what is happening and are unable to focus or pay attention. They experience cognitive changes in which their memory is foggy and they are disoriented, and they may have various other symptoms, such as rambling speech, delusions, hallucinations, and emotional disturbances. Delirium, which is caused by a change in the metabolism of the brain, can result from various factors, including substance intoxication or withdrawal, head injury, high fever, and vitamin deficiency. The onset is generally rapid and the duration brief.

- Amnestic disorders are conditions in which people are unable to recall previously learned information or to register new memories. These disorders are due either to the use of substances or to such medical conditions as head trauma, loss of oxygen, and herpes simplex.

- Traumatic brain injury (TBI) is increasingly being recognized as an important cause of mental and physical dysfunction. Some of these symptoms include headaches, sleep disturbances, sensitivity to light and noise, and diminished cognitive performance on tests of attention, memory, language, and reaction time. These individuals may also suffer depression, anxiety, emotional outbursts, mood changes, or inappropriate affect.

- Dementia is a form of cognitive impairment involving generalized progressive deficits in a person's memory and learning of new information, ability to communicate, judgment, and motor coordination. In addition to experiencing cognitive changes, individuals with this condition undergo changes in their personality and emotional state. Dementia results from profuse and progressive brain damage associated with physical conditions, such as vascular diseases, AIDS, head trauma, psychoactive substances, and various neurological disorders. The most well-known form of dementia is Alzheimer's disease, a condition associated with severe cerebral atrophy as well as characteristic microscopic changes in the brain. Alzheimer's disease is specified according to subtypes: (1) with delirium, (2) with delusions, (3) with depressed mood, or (4) uncomplicated. The diagnosis of Alzheimer's is challenging for several reasons. Some conditions, such as vascular dementia, have symptoms similar to those of Alzheimer's. Other conditions, such as depression, can lead to symptoms that mimic those in the early stages of Alzheimer's. All theories regarding the cause of Alzheimer's disease focus on biological abnormalities involving the nervous system—specifically, two types of brain changes. The first is the formation of neurofibrillary tangles, in which the cellular material within the cell bodies of neurons becomes replaced by densely packed, twisted microfibrils, or tiny strands, of protein. The second change involves the development of amyloid plaques, which are clusters of dead or dying neurons mixed with fragments of protein molecules. In addition to biological explanations, researchers have also focused on environmental contributors to Alzheimer's, as well as the role of certain behaviors in preventing the development of the disease. Although there is no cure for this disease, researchers are attempting to find medications, such as anticholinesterase agents, that alleviate its symptoms. At the same time, experts have focused their attention on refining behavioral techniques for managing symptoms and have given particular attention to strategies for alleviating caregiver burden.

KEY TERMS

See Glossary for definitions

Agnosia 376
Akinesia 380
Alzheimer's disease 377
Amnestic disorders 374
Amyloid plaques 384
Aphasia 376
Apraxia 376
Bradykinesia 380
Broca's aphasia 376
Caregiver burden 388
Caregivers 388

Caspase theory of Alzheimer's disease 384
Choline acetyltransferase (CAT) 384
Creutzfeldt-Jakob disease 381
Delirium 373
Dementia 375
Epilepsy 372
Executive functioning 376
Frontotemporal dementia 381
Huntington's disease 381
Lewy body dementia 380
Neurofibrillary tangles 384

Parkinson's disease 380
Pick's disease 380
Pseudodementia 382
Substance-induced persisting amnestic disorder 374
Substance-induced persisting dementia 377
Tau 384
Traumatic brain injury (TBI) 375
Vascular dementia 381
Wernicke's aphasia 376

INTERNET RESOURCE

To get more information on the material covered in this chapter, visit our website at **www.mhhe.com/halgin5.** There you will find more information, resources, and links to topics of interest.

CHAPTER 13

Substance-Related Disorders

One morning, our receptionist gave me a message to call Dr. Elaine Golden, the director of residency training in the medical school, and I called her back as soon as I found a free moment that afternoon. Dr. Golden told me that she was looking for a psychotherapist to treat one of the physicians in the surgical residency program. It was not unusual for physicians in training to be referred for treatment of depression or anxiety, but neither of those was a problem for 31-year-old Dr. Carl Wadsworth. I sensed even in the tone of Elaine's voice that the case of Carl Wadsworth was unusual, an impression that was confirmed when Elaine emphasized the importance of keeping the case absolutely confidential. Before Elaine proceeded to tell me the details, however, I felt that it would be important for me to remind her about the standards of confidentiality, as well as the exceptions to these standards. I explained that I would, of course, keep the case confidential, unless there was serious reason to believe that a client was in danger of harming himself or another person, or was involved in the abuse of a child, an elder, or a person with a disability. Elaine assured me that none of these issues pertained to the case of Carl Wadsworth. Rather, her concern pertained more to the reputation of this young doctor and that of the medical school. As it turned out, Carl Wadsworth was addicted to cocaine. Not only was he using the substance on a daily basis, but he had begun to sell drugs to fellow medical residents and medical students in order to pay for his own habit.

After hearing Elaine share this disturbing information about a physician-in-training, I asked her point blank, "Why aren't you throwing this guy out of the program?" Elaine responded nondefensively, "I've thought seriously about that possibility. However, I think we have a case of a young man who can be salvaged from his self-destructive behavior." She went on to explain, "Carl is a gifted physician, who has, sadly, become caught in a trap, from which he is pleading for help to be released. Sarah, I think that you can help him."

Elaine explained that Carl had called her at home late the previous night, with his wife, Anne, sitting by his side. With a trembling voice, he had begun the phone discussion with the startling words, "Dr. Golden, I desperately need your help. I'm a junkie." As Elaine told me this story, I thought about how fortunate Carl was to have a relationship with such a caring and concerned mentor. Elaine listened carefully to Carl's story and arranged to see him the next morning. In that appointment she told Carl that it was imperative that he contact me that day to set up an appointment, which he did. That afternoon, I received a call from Carl, who urgently pleaded that I see him as soon as possible. We agreed to meet the next morning.

When I first met Carl Wadsworth, I was struck by the fact that he seemed so young and unsure of himself. Rather than wearing his hospital uniform, or any clothing suggestive of his profession, Carl wore a college sweatshirt and matching sweatpants. My guess was that he would have felt embarrassed sitting in the waiting room of the mental health clinic in medical attire. Carl's face was gaunt and haggard, suggesting that he was run down, perhaps to the point of exhaustion. My suspicions were confirmed. After introducing himself, he apologized for his ostensible weariness, explaining that he hadn't slept much in recent days. After entering my office, Carl proceeded to tell me the painful story of his seduction by cocaine and the eventual hold it took over his whole life. He acknowledged that the problem had become so serious that he risked destroying his family and ruining his career. These realizations became startlingly apparent to him when Anne, pregnant with their second child, told Carl that she would divorce him if he did not obtain professional help.

Carl explained that, when he first began using cocaine 1 year ago, he fully believed that he could control his use, and maintain it as a harmless pastime. Predictably, though, Carl began to rely on the drug more and more heavily. Money problems began to accumulate, and, rather than attribute these to the expense of his cocaine habit, he blamed them on his inadequate salary. It became necessary to draw on the family bank account to pay the household bills. Carl soon began to spend more and more time away from home. Telling Anne that he was at work, he spent hours each day seeking ways to pick up extra cash. At the hospital, his work had become sloppy, and Elaine had let him know that he was at risk of being dismissed from the hospital. His patients complained to the nursing staff about his abrupt and insensitive manner.

As we talked about the changes in Carl's professional behavior, I could see that he was becoming increasingly distraught, and, when I asked him about his family life, he fought to hold back tears. He explained that he loved his wife and daughter very much but that he found himself losing control in his interactions with them. He had become irritable and impatient with them and occasionally so angry that he had come close to physical violence.

When Carl first came to see me, he was in serious trouble. He was accurate in his perception that his personal life and his career were on the line and that he needed help immediately.

Sarah Tobin, PhD

We live in a society in which the use of mind-altering substances has become a central part of the culture. Leafing through any popular magazine, you are certain to see advertisements with successful, attractive people using cigarettes. Watching a sporting event on television, you will surely see commercials with fun-loving, happy people consuming alcohol. These legal drugs represent only a small fraction of the substances that Americans ingest each day. As you will see, both legal and illegal drugs affect all sectors of the population, including well-educated and professional people such as Carl.

The Nature of Substance Abuse and Dependence

A **substance** is a chemical that alters a person's mood or behavior when it is smoked, injected, drunk, inhaled, snorted, or swallowed in pill form. Although most of our discussion will focus on drugs of abuse, it is important to realize that people often use medications and toxic chemicals to induce altered psychological states. Because substances are so much a part of everyday life, most people take them for granted. A glass of wine at dinner, a cup of coffee in the morning, a beer or two at a party, a sleeping pill at night—none of these may seem particularly unusual or troublesome. Although most people are able to regulate their use of such substances, many drugs pose high risks. In this chapter, we will focus most of our attention on the ways in which alcohol, as well as illicit drugs, adversely affect individuals, families, communities, and society. The most reliable source of information about substance use and abuse in the United States is the Substance Abuse and Mental Health Services Administration (SAMHSA), which publishes data from national surveys of nearly 20 million Americans 12 years and older (SAMHSA, 2004). In the most recent survey, approximately 8 percent of the population had used illicit drugs in the past 30 days (i.e., were "current" users). Marijuana is the most commonly used illicit drug, with 14.6 million Americans (6.2 percent) reporting current use at the time of the survey. An estimated 2.3 million Americans (1.0 percent) were current cocaine users, 604,000 of whom used crack. Approximately one million Americans had recently used hallucinogens, and approximately 119,000 were heroin users. In recent years, the nonmedical abuse of prescription drugs has become especially problematic, with 4.7 million Americans abusing pain relievers, 1.8 million abusing tranquilizers, 1.2 million taking stimulants, and 0.3 million using sedatives. Of particular note is the dramatic increase in the abuse of pain relievers, with lifetime nonmedical use leaping significantly from 29.6 million to 31.3 million Americans aged 12 or older within a 1-year period (SAMHSA, 2004).

Rates of current illicit drug use vary significantly among the major ethnic and racial groups with the highest rates found among American Indians and Alaska Natives (12.1 percent), followed by people who report being of two or more races (12.0 percent), Native Hawaiians and other Pacific Islanders (11.1 percent), Blacks (8.7 percent), Whites (8.3 percent), and Hispanics (8.0 percent), with Asians showing the lowest rate (3.8 percent). When considering the groups with higher rates, it is important to assess the role of poverty and unemployment. It has been well established that economically disadvantaged people are at particularly high risk for having problems with drugs. Nearly one of every five unemployed adults (18.2 percent) is a current illicit drug user, as compared with 7.9 percent of those employed full-time, and 10.7 percent of those employed part-time (SAMHSA, 2004).

In addition to the devastating psychological costs to individuals and families, the economic costs of substance abuse to society are astronomical, with estimates running into the hundreds of billions of dollars (Horgan, 2001). In one recent year, the rate of Americans who were arrested for driving under the influence of alcohol or narcotics was startling: 1.4 million arrests, which amounts to 1 of every 137 licensed U.S. drivers. (http://www.cdc.gov/alcohol/factsheets/general_information.htm). The number of deaths that can be attributed to alcohol is also remarkable. In a given year, there are more than 75,000 alcohol-attributed deaths associated with such health problems as cirrhosis of the liver and various cancers, as well as injuries or violence. Researchers have used statistical methods to assess the years of potential life lost because of these deaths, and estimate that for each person who dies as a result of alcohol, 30 years of life are sacrificed ("Alcohol-Attributable Deaths," 2004).

In this chapter, for the sake of simplicity, we will discuss each of the major substances associated with serious psychological and physical impairment in a way that might imply that the abuse of a particular substance takes place independent of other forms of substance abuse or psychological disturbance. In reality, however, many people who abuse one substance also abuse others, thus making it difficult for clinicians and researchers to tease out the specific detrimental effects of any given substance in isolation. A second important consideration is the fact that many

For many people, addictive behavior involves the use of more than one substance.

individuals with substance-related disorders also suffer with comorbid conditions, particularly anxiety disorders and mood disorders (Grant et al., 2004). Because of the co-occurrence of substance-related disorders with other psychiatric conditions, such as mood disorders, assessment and treatment are especially challenging (Nunes & Levin, 2004). As you read this chapter and learn about the various conditions directly associated with substance use, it will be important for you to be aware of the ways in which substance-related conditions are often connected to other psychological disorders.

Behaviors Associated with Substance-Related Disorders

In this section, we will discuss the ways in which substances affect human behavior. Although each substance has specific effects, which depend on its chemical composition and its effects on the brain or body, you will find it helpful to have an overview of how substances in general affect behavior.

Substance-Induced Disorders

Substance intoxication is the temporary maladaptive experience of behavioral or psychological changes due to the accumulation of a substance in the body. Let's take a closer look at this definition. A condition of substance intoxication is a transient phenomenon that is limited to the period that the substance is biologically potent in the body. The behavior of an intoxicated person is maladaptive, which means that his or her functioning is impaired significantly. In the case of alcohol intoxication, the individual experiences impaired judgment and attention, slurred speech, abnormal eye movements, slowed reflexes, unsteady walking, and changeable moods. By contrast, the person who becomes intoxicated following the ingestion of amphetamines experiences accelerated bodily functioning, as well as perspiration or chills. Even people who drink a great amount of a caffeinated beverage can experience troubling bodily sensations, such as nervousness, twitching, insomnia, and agitation.

In addition to the effects that follow the ingestion of substances, psychological and physical changes also occur when some substances are discontinued, a reaction that is referred to as **substance withdrawal.** A person in a state of substance withdrawal experiences significant distress or impairment at home, at work, or in other important life contexts. Withdrawal takes different forms, according to the actual substance involved. For example, nicotine withdrawal commonly includes anxiety and irritability. People taking substances with higher potency can undergo such severe psychological and physical withdrawal symptoms that they need medical care. A phenomenon called **tolerance** is related to substance withdrawal. This occurs when an individual requires larger and larger amounts of the substance in order to achieve its desired effects or when the person feels less of its effects after using the same amount of the substance.

For example, a man may find that he now needs to drink two six-packs of beer in order to achieve the same state of relaxation that was previously attained with a single six-pack. You will see as you read this chapter that tolerance can develop in different ways—in some instances, tolerance is caused by changes in the body's metabolism of the drug; in others, it results from the way the drug affects the nervous system.

As you will see later in the chapter, when we discuss specific substances, the extent of substance intoxication and the distress associated with substance withdrawal are influenced by the way in which individuals take a specific drug into the body, how rapidly acting the substance is, and how lasting the effect of the drug is. Drugs that are efficiently absorbed into the bloodstream due to intravenous injection or smoking are likely to lead to a more intense kind of intoxication than are drugs taken in pill form. Drugs that have an immediate impact on the person are more seductive than those that take longer to take effect. Further, drugs that have a powerful, but short-lived, effect are more likely to lead to patterns of abuse, because the person craves to repeat the experience time and again within a short time frame.

In addition to the diagnostic categories of substance intoxication and substance withdrawal, there are several other substance-induced disorders that have symptoms that are quite similar to the psychological disorders we discussed in previous chapters. For example, there are several cognitive disorders (Chapter 12) related to substances, such as substance-induced delirium, substance-induced persisting dementia, and substance-induced persisting amnestic disorder. In addition to these cognitive disorders, the *DSM-IV-TR* lists the following substance-induced conditions: psychotic disorder, mood disorder, anxiety disorder, sexual dysfunction, and sleep disorder. Therefore, clinicians conducting their initial assessment of clients realize that it is important to consider the possibility that the symptoms might be the result of substance use. For example, the clinician considers whether manic symptoms are due to bipolar disorder or amphetamines, or whether bizarre symptoms are due to psychosis or hallucinogenic drugs. Or, as we discussed above, there may be a comorbidity of the substance-related disorder and another condition, such as an anxiety disorder or a mood disorder. In such cases, the individual may have gotten caught up in the abuse of substances in an attempt to alleviate the psychological distress associated with emotional dysfunction.

Substance Use Disorders

When does a person's use of substances become abuse? When does a person's need for substances reach the point of dependency and become an addiction? These are questions that researchers and clinicians have struggled with for decades. Currently, **substance abuse** is defined as the maladaptive pattern of substance use occurring within a 12-month period that leads to significant impairment or distress evidenced by one or more of the following: (1) failure to meet obligations, (2) use of substances in physically hazardous situations, (3) legal problems, or (4) interpersonal problems.

People who abuse substances find that their lives are affected in many ways. They neglect obligations at work, and their commitments to home and family start to erode. In addition to letting their work and family life slide, they may begin to take risks that are personally dangerous and put others in jeopardy, such as driving or operating powerful machinery while intoxicated. Legal problems arise for many people who abuse substances, because their behavior puts them into positions in which they violate the law. In addition to arrests for driving while intoxicated, they may face charges of disorderly conduct or assaultive behavior. Last, and most common, the life of the substance-abusing person is often characterized by interpersonal problems. During episodes of intoxication, they may become argumentative and possibly violent with close ones. Even when the substance-abusing person is sober, his or her relationships are commonly strained and unhappy.

The main feature of abuse, then, is a pattern of behavior in which the individual continues to use substances, even when it is clear that such behavior entails significant risks or creates problems in living. For example, a college professor may insist on having three martinis at lunch, despite the fact that this interferes with her ability to teach her afternoon seminar. Her behavior is characterized as abuse, because her drinking interferes with her work responsibilities. By contrast, her sister, who occasionally has a glass of wine with dinner, would not be regarded as abusing alcohol, because there is no evidence of impairment.

The notion of substance abuse carries with it no implication that the individual is addicted to the substance. Continuing with the example of the three-martini professor, the question is to what extent she "needs" to have those drinks in order to get through the day. If she has reached the point at which she relies on this form of drinking, she would be considered dependent on alcohol. **Substance dependence** is a maladaptive pattern of substance use manifested by a cluster of cognitive, behavioral, and physiological symptoms during a 12-month period and caused by the continued use of a substance.

Experts also strive to understand the roles that psychological and physiological factors play in determining dependence on or tolerance to a substance. Physiological dependence is determined when an individual shows signs of either tolerance or withdrawal. As you will see later in this chapter, clinicians treating people with substance problems must understand these physiological patterns, especially when monitoring the symptoms of withdrawal or when recommending somatic interventions such as medication.

Alcohol

We begin our discussion of disorders by focusing on alcohol, a substance that has received increased attention in recent years because of the tremendous personal and societal costs associated with the abuse of this mind-altering drug.

Patterns of Use and Abuse

Although the amount of alcohol consumed per person in the United States has steadily decreased since reaching a peak in 1980, many people use alcohol on a regular basis. Over half of all Americans over the age of 12 admit that they had had at least one drink in the month prior to being surveyed (SAMHSA, 2005). About 22 percent of Americans report that they engage in binge drinking, meaning that they have had five drinks on one occasion in the past 30 days. Heavy drinking, which is defined as consuming five or more drinks on the same occasion on at least five days in the month, is found in 7 percent of the adult population of Americans (Bouza, Angeles, Munoz, & Amate, 2004). Higher rates of alcohol consumption are associated with the following variables: male gender, being White, being married, having a higher educational level, having a higher income, being employed, and being a smoker (Moore et al., 2005).

As can be seen from Figure 13.1, there are variations in alcohol use by age, with consumption typically declining as people

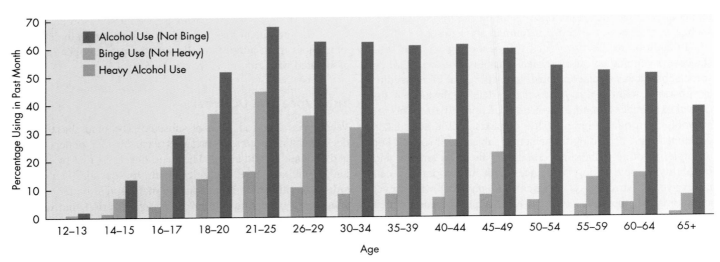

FIGURE 13.1 Alcohol use by age group
Source: SAMHSA, 2004.

REAL STORIES

BEN AFFLECK: SUBSTANCE ABUSE

At the beginning of this chapter you read about Carl Wadsworth, a young man whose cocaine dependence was wreaking havoc in his family and medical career. Some people are surprised and disturbed when they learn that an individual who seemingly "has it all" would resort to such self-destructive behavior. Yet the media is filled with stories of eminently successful people who stray down the path of substance abuse and lose so much as they become obsessed with satisfying addictive cravings. Such a sad story of self-destructive addiction has been told by Ben Affleck, the successful actor and screenwriter.

Like so many people struggling with addiction, Affleck grew up in a home in which substance abuse caused considerable family turbulence, leading to parental divorce when Affleck was 12 years old. Soon after the divorce, Affleck's father entered a rehabilitation center where he obtained treatment for his alcohol problem; he subsequently pursued work as a recovery counselor.

Affleck describes his high-school years in Cambridge, Massachusetts, as a wild time when he engaged in "underage drinking, pot smoking, and all the attendant shenanigans." Even during these youthful days, Affleck devoted himself to some remarkable creative endeavors with his close friend Matt Damon, with whom he wrote the screenplay for the critically acclaimed

Ben Affleck

movie *Good Will Hunting.* Although Affleck graduated from high school, he dropped out of college after only one semester to pursue an acting career. He was in several small, low-budget movies before landing the starring role in the 1997 hit *Chasing Amy.*

After the explosive success of *Good Will Hunting* and *Chasing Amy,* Affleck's life changed dramatically. Although he was experiencing many wonderful things, he was also encountering some demons. On the positive side, he became romantically involved with another prominent star, Gwyneth Paltrow, and also immersed himself in exciting and successful creative endeavors. He also became socially proactive, as evident in

his public efforts to increase research funding for neurological disease. But there was also the negative side of Affleck's life in which he turned increasingly to alcohol for relief from the pressures of life.

"My life changed so quickly I lost any sense of who exactly I was. . . . I made some poor choices." Affleck describes the impact of gross intoxication:

> The next morning, my head was throbbing, it was all I could do to find the car. . . .
>
> I started regretting some of the things I did when I was drunk. It's funny to be obnoxious or out of control, but then it's like, "I think I hurt that person's feelings. I made a fool of myself," or "I didn't want to kiss that girl. . . ." Now it's kind of depressing to be bombed at 3 in the morning.

Affleck also talks about the ineffectiveness of his reliance on partying and alcohol to get through rough times: "I had broken up with Gwyneth . . . and I felt very adrift. . . . So I thought, . . . 'Okay, I'll go to these parties. I'll try to embrace this life people think I have.' . . . And I found myself even more miserable." The good news is that Affleck has come to terms with his addiction and has found the courage to seek treatment and to speak publicly about the perils associated with the abuse of substances. He is now committed to a healthier lifestyle without alcohol, and he is grateful for the support of his family and friends.

Source: Excerpts from Anne-Marie O'Neill, "Reality Check" in *People Weekly,* August 20, 2001. Reprinted with permission.

get older (Moore et al., 2005). Young adults aged 18 to 25 have the highest rates of binge drinking and heavy drinking. Age 21 is associated with the highest rates of drinking, with 47.8 percent of 21-year-olds engaging in binge drinking and 18.7 percent in heavy drinking. The rates of binge and heavy drinking decline sharply throughout adulthood; by the age period 45 to 49, 23.2 percent engage in binge drinking and 6.8 percent drink heavily. Those over 60 are the least likely to drink heavily, and people over 65 are the least likely to use alcohol at all. Full-time college students aged 18 to 22 are more likely to use alcohol, binge drink, and drink heavily than peers who are not enrolled full-time.[1]

Effects of Alcohol Use

One of the reasons people consume alcohol is to achieve an altered mood and state of awareness. Before examining the long-term effects of chronic alcohol use, we will look first at its immediate effects on the user and the mechanisms thought to be responsible for these effects.

Immediate Effects In small amounts, alcohol has sedating effects, leading to feelings of warmth, comfort, and relaxation. In larger amounts, alcohol may lead the drinker to feel more outgoing, self-confident, and uninhibited. Some people stop drinking when they have achieved the positive mood they were seeking from alcohol. If an individual continues to drink beyond that point, though, the effects of alcohol as a **depressant** drug become more apparent, as feelings of sleepiness, uncoordination, dysphoria, and irritability set in. Excessive drinking affects a person's vital functions and can be fatal. The mixture of alcohol with other drugs is referred to as **potentiation,** meaning that

the effect of two drugs taken together is greater than the effect of either substance alone. For example, combining alcohol, which is a depressant, with another depressant would exaggerate the effects on the body and possibly would be fatal.

The rate at which alcohol is absorbed into the bloodstream depends in part on the concentration of alcohol in the particular beverage, the amount of alcohol consumed, the rate at which it is consumed, and the amount of food present in the stomach. The rate of alcohol absorption also depends on individual characteristics, including gender and a person's metabolic rate, or the rate at which the body converts nutrients to energy (in this case, the "nutrient" is alcohol). The rate at which alcohol is metabolized determines how long the person will continue to experience the effects of alcohol. The average person metabolizes alcohol at a rate of one third of an ounce of 100 percent alcohol per hour, which is equivalent to an ounce of whiskey per hour. A guide to blood alcohol levels is shown in Table 13.1 on page 399.

Following a bout of extensive intake of alcohol, a person is likely to experience an abstinence syndrome, what everyone knows as a "hangover." The symptoms of hangover include nausea and vomiting, tremors, extreme thirst, headache, tiredness, irritability, depression, and dizziness. The extent of a person's hangover depends on how much alcohol he or she has consumed and over what period of time. Metabolic rate also affects the duration of a person's hangover. Contrary to whatever advice one hears about homemade remedies, there is no cure for a hangover other than to wait for the body to recover.

Long-Term Effects In part, alcohol's harmful long-term effects may be attributed to the factor of tolerance. The more a person consumes, the more alcohol that person needs to achieve the

The unpredictability and dysfunctional behavior of an alcoholic parent or spouse create tension and insecurity for all family members.

TABLE 13.1 Alcohol Impairment Chart

Men: Approximate Blood Alcohol Percentage

Drinks*	Body Weight in Pounds								Effect on Person
	100	120	140	160	180	200	220	240	
0	.00	.00	.00	.00	.00	.00	.00	.00	Only safe driving limit.
1	.04	.03	.03	.02	.02	.02	.02	.02	
2	.08	.06	.05	.05	.04	.04	.03	.03	Impairment begins.
3	.11	.09	.08	.07	.06	.06	.05	.05	
4	.15	.12	.11	.09	.08	.08	.07	.06	Driving skills significantly affected.
5	.19	.16	.13	.12	.11	.09	.09	.08	Possible criminal penalties.
6	.23	.19	.16	.14	.13	.11	.10	.09	
7	.26	.22	.19	.16	.15	.13	.12	.11	
8	.30	.25	.21	.19	.17	.15	.14	.13	Legally intoxicated.
9	.34	.28	.24	.21	.19	.17	.15	.14	Criminal penalties imposed.
10	.38	.31	.27	.23	.21	.19	.17	.16	

Women: Approximate Blood Alcohol Percentage

Drinks*	Body Weight in Pounds									Effect on Person
	90	100	120	140	160	180	200	220	240	
0	.00	.00	.00	.00	.00	.00	.00	.00	.00	Only safe driving limit.
1	.05	.05	.04	.03	.03	.03	.02	.02	.02	Impairment begins.
2	.10	.09	.08	.07	.06	.05	.05	.04	.04	
3	.15	.14	.11	.11	.09	.08	.07	.06	.06	Driving skills significantly affected.
4	.20	.18	.15	.13	.11	.10	.09	.08	.08	Possible criminal penalties.
5	.25	.23	.19	.16	.14	.13	.11	.10	.09	
6	.30	.27	.23	.19	.17	.15	.14	.12	.11	
7	.35	.32	.27	.23	.20	.18	.16	.14	.13	
8	.40	.36	.30	.26	.23	.20	.18	.17	.15	Legally intoxicated.
9	.45	.41	.34	.29	.26	.23	.20	.19	.17	Criminal penalties imposed.
10	.51	.45	.38	.32	.28	.25	.23	.21	.19	

Subtract .01% for each 40 minutes of drinking.

*One drink is equal to 1¼ oz. of 80 proof liquor, 12 oz. of beer, or 4 oz. of table wine.

Source: National Clearinghouse for Drug and Alcohol Information, SAMHSA, http://www.samhsa.gov/centers/clearinghouse/clearinghouses.html, Accessed 12/20/01.

desired impact. Heavy drinkers tend to increase their intake of alcohol over time, thereby increasing the likelihood of bodily damage. As we will see later, scientists are attempting to understand the biochemical changes associated with long-term heavy alcohol use as a way of comprehending the factors leading to tolerance and dependence.

Alcohol affects almost every organ system in the body, either directly or indirectly. Long-term use of alcohol can lead to permanent brain damage, with symptoms of dementia, blackouts, seizures, hallucinations, and damage to the peripheral parts of the nervous system. Two forms of dementia are associated with long-term, heavy alcohol use: Wernicke's disease and Korsakoff's syndrome. **Wernicke's encephalopathy** is an acute condition involving delirium, eye movement disturbances, difficulties in movement and balance, and deterioration of the peripheral nerves to the hands and feet. The cause of Wernicke's encephalopathy is not alcohol itself, but a thiamine (Vitamin B) deficiency due to the deleterious effects of alcohol on the metabolism of nutrients, as well as an overall pattern of poor nutrition. Adequate thiamine intake can reverse Wernicke's encephalopathy. People who develop Wernicke's disease are likely to develop **Korsakoff's syndrome,** a permanent form of dementia in which the individual develops retrograde and anterograde amnesia, leading to an inability to remember recent events or to learn new information. It is thought that both disorders represent the same underlying disease process, with Wernicke's being the acute form and Korsakoff's being the chronic form of the disorder. The chances of recovering from Korsakoff's syndrome are less than one in four, and about one quarter of those who have this disorder require permanent institutionalization.

Death from long-term, heavy alcohol use is often associated with liver disease. Most chronic alcohol users develop fatty liver, a condition characterized by abnormal changes in the blood vessels in the liver. This condition develops in 90 to 100 percent of heavy drinkers and may be a precursor to cirrhosis, a degenerative disease that results in progressive and irreversible liver damage. Cirrhosis is one of the primary factors associated with death due to chronic alcohol use. Although the death rate for this disease has diminished over the past few decades, cirrhosis is the twelfth leading cause of death in the United States (Hoyert, Kung, & Smith, 2005). Heavy alcohol consumption also causes a number of harmful changes in the gastrointestinal system, including inflammation of the esophagus, stomach lining, and pancreas, and a slowing down of smooth muscle contractions throughout the gastrointestinal tract. These conditions can interfere with the process of digestion and can lead to serious nutritional imbalances, including thiamine deficiency, as mentioned earlier, and even malnutrition. A diet that is deficient in zinc may lead to a decrease in the activity of **alcohol dehydrogenase (ADH),** a zinc-containing enzyme in the stomach. ADH breaks down a portion of the alcohol into fatty acids, carbon dioxide, and water before it enters the bloodstream. As a result of lowered ADH activity, a greater portion of the alcohol enters the bloodstream without first being broken down, increasing its effect throughout the body. Women appear to be more vulnerable to the effects of alcohol because of their lower amounts of ADH, leading to the dispersion of greater amounts of undigested alcohol throughout the body's tissues. As a result, women reach higher blood alcohol concentrations for a given amount of alcohol consumption, and they are more susceptible to liver disease caused by excessive alcohol intake.

The list of damaging effects of alcohol is long. Chronic alcohol consumption lowers a person's bone strength and puts the individual at risk for developing chronic muscle injury due to atrophy and a bone-weakening disease called osteoporosis.

MindMAP Segment 13.1 presents the case of a woman with a history of alcohol addiction who discusses the nature of her addiction and the detoxification treatment she went through.

People who are severely addicted to alcohol must go through a period of detoxification in the process of becoming sober.

Alcohol can increase a person's risk of developing various forms of cancer, a risk that grows if the individual also smokes cigarettes. A reduction in the functioning of the immune system, which helps fight off cancer as well as infectious diseases, appears to play a role in the deteriorative process. Because of the effects of alcohol on the immune system, people infected with HIV who drink heavily are more likely to accelerate the progression of AIDS. Finally, the abrupt withdrawal of alcohol after chronic usage can result in such symptoms as severe hangover, sleep disturbances, profound anxiety, tremulousness, sympathetic hyperactivity, psychosis, seizures, and even death.

Theories of Alcohol Dependence

Researchers in the field of alcohol dependence were among the first in abnormal psychology to recognize the need for a biopsychosocial model to explain why some people develop alcoholism (Zucker & Gomberg, 1986). This model, as applied to alcohol dependence, emphasizes genetic vulnerability in interaction with influences from the home and peer environments.

Biological Perspective Researchers are making major advances in understanding the important role that biology plays in determining whether a person becomes dependent on alcohol. Especially noteworthy is the finding that alcohol dependence tends to aggregate within families. In one study comparing the relatives of people with alcoholism (probands) to controls, researchers found lifetime risk rates of developing alcohol dependence to be 28.8 percent in the relatives of the probands, compared to 14.4 percent in the relatives of the controls (Nurnberger et al., 2004). Siblings of alcohol-dependent individuals have a three to eight times greater risk of becoming dependent themselves. Based on research with twins, the heritability of alcohol dependence is estimated to be 50 to 60 percent, meaning that at least half of the tendency to develop alcohol dependence is due to genetic factors (Reich et al., 1998).

Given the inherited component of alcohol dependence, it seems likely that biological markers could be identified that would help indicate a person's predisposition to the disorder. One potential marker is the individual's subjective reaction to alcohol, or how much alcohol is needed to produce the feeling of being under the influence of the substance. Researchers have found that genetically predisposed people who have less of a subjective reaction following the intake of alcohol in a laboratory seem to be at higher risk of becoming dependent themselves. The low subjective response to alcohol is most predictive of development of alcohol dependence in men who have poor coping strategies and low levels of social support (Schuckit & Smith, 2001). Another possible biological marker is the event-related brain potential (ERP), the positive voltage charge that occurs 300 to 500 milliseconds after exposure to a stimulus. An abnormal ERP response is an inherited characteristic linked to a high genetic risk for alcohol dependence (Hesselbrock et al., 2001).

Although there is strong evidence that predisposition to alcohol dependence has a genetic basis, there is much that is not known, such as the number of genes, their locations, and the way in which they lead to vulnerability. It is hoped that the process of genetic mapping will identify genetic markers of alcohol susceptibility that can be linked to behavioral responses to alcohol. Researchers have identified a gene or genes involved in alcohol susceptibility on chromosomes 1, 4, and 8 (Corbett et al., 2005). It is thought that genetic mechanisms play a role in causing abnormalities in several neurotransmitters, including gamma-aminobutyric acid (GABA), dopamine, serotonin, and opioids (Rader & Goldman, 2001).

Psychological Perspective Proponents of the behavioral perspective view alcohol dependence as resulting from a process in which classical conditioning plays a role in the development of cravings (O'Brien, Childress, Ehrman, & Robbins, 1998). However, theorists and researchers realize that alcohol dependence must be due to a broader range of factors. One model that is gaining considerable support is the **expectancy model,** which has evolved from cognitive-behavioral and social learning perspectives (Parks, Anderson, & Marlatt, 2001). According to this model, people with alcohol dependence develop problematic beliefs about alcohol relatively early in life

through a combination of reinforcement and observational learning.

Concepts central to the expectancy model are self-efficacy and coping. Self-efficacy, as you will recall from Chapter 4, refers to an individual's perception that he or she has the ability to meet the challenges of a difficult situation. The concept of coping, as used in the cognitive-behavioral model, refers to the strategies that an individual uses to reduce the perception of a threat or danger. According to the expectancy model, these cognitive factors, along with the individual's ideas or expectations about the effects of alcohol, presumably play a role in determining whether or not an individual will relapse to problem drinking. A sample of an assessment inventory based on the model is shown in Table 13.2 on page 402.

The expectancy model describes a series of reactions that occurs when an alcohol-dependent individual attempts to remain abstinent. Consider the contrasting cases of Marlene, who has been successful in remaining abstinent, and Edward, who has been unsuccessful. Both Marlene and Edward encounter high-risk situations, such as parties at which other people are consuming alcohol. Marlene is able to abstain from drinking at the party, because she has learned how to cope with such situations, and she feels capable of carrying through with her intention not to drink alcohol. Each successful episode of abstinence reinforces her sense of self-efficacy, causing her to feel more capable of abstaining in subsequent situations. Unlike Marlene, some individuals, such as Edward,

MindMAP Segment 13.2 features a man whose alcohol abuse was treated by a combination of naltrexone and therapy. As pointed out in this segment, education also plays an important role in the treatment of addictions.

As a way of treating addiction, drugs such as naltrexone help an individual overcome cravings for the substance.

TABLE 13.2 Sample Items from Expectancy-Based Assessment Measures

The Inventory of Drinking Situations is used to determine which situations represent a high risk for the alcohol-dependent individual. Each item is rated on the following 4-point scale: "I DRANK HEAVILY—Never, Rarely, Frequently, Almost Always." The items on the Situational Confidence Questionnaire (Annis, 1984) are the same but are rated according to the scale of "I WOULD BE ABLE TO RESIST THE URGE TO DRINK HEAVILY," with percentages ranging from Not at All Confident (0 percent) to Very Confident (100 percent).

Determinants	Item	Scale
Intrapersonal	When I felt that I had let myself down	Negative emotional state
	When I had trouble sleeping	Negative physical state
	When I felt confident and relaxed	Positive emotional state
	When I convinced myself that I was a new person now and could take a few drinks	Testing personal control
	When I remembered how good it tasted	Urges and temptations
Interpersonal	When other people treated me unfairly	Social rejection
	When pressure built up at work because of the demands of my superior	Work problems
	When I felt uneasy in the presence of someone	Tension
	When I had an argument with a friend	Family/friends problems
	When I was out with friends and they stopped by for a drink	Social pressure to drink
	When I was out with friends "on the town" and wanted to increase my enjoyment	Social drinking
	When I wanted to heighten my sexual enjoyment	Intimacy

Source: From H. M. Annis in *Inventory of Drinking Situations: Short Form.* Copyright © 1984 Center for Addiction and Mental Health. Reprinted with permission.

lack a satisfactory coping response. The actual consumption of alcohol is not what leads to a relapse but, rather, the individual's interpretation of the act of drinking as a sign of loss of self-control. Thus, when Edward enters a high-risk situation, he feels incapable of staying away from alcohol because of his low sense of self-efficacy. A compelling expectation that alcohol will have a positive mood-altering effect adds to his low sense of self-efficacy and leads him to take the first drink. The positive sensations the alcohol produces further undermine Edward's resolve, but cognitive factors enter at this point in the process as well. Having violated the self-imposed rule of remaining abstinent, he now is subject to the **abstinence violation effect,** a sense of loss of control over one's behavior that has an overwhelming and demoralizing effect. Thus, Edward's self-efficacy is further eroded, initiating a downward spiral, which eventually ends in renewed alcohol dependence.

Sociocultural Perspective Researchers and theorists working within the sociocultural perspective regard stressors within the family, community, and culture as factors that, when combined with genetic vulnerability, lead the individual to develop alcohol dependence. The sociocultural perspective was given support in a landmark longitudinal study conducted in the early 1980s. Researchers followed individuals from childhood or adolescence to adulthood, the time when most individuals who become alcohol dependent make the transition from social or occasional alcohol use to dependence (Zucker & Gomberg, 1986). Those most likely to become alcohol dependent in adulthood had a history of childhood antisocial behavior, including aggressive and sadistic behavior, trouble with the law, rebelliousness, lower achievement in school, completion of fewer years of school, and a higher truancy rate. These individuals also showed a variety of behaviors possibly indicative of early neural dysfunction, including nervousness and fretfulness as infants, hyperactivity as children, and poor physical coordination. It was thought that these characteristics reflect a genetically based vulnerability, which, when combined with environmental stresses, leads to the development of alcohol dependence. More recent studies have continued to support the role of family environment as influenced by larger sociocultural factors. In one 2-year study of more than 800 suburban adolescents, the teenagers who received high levels of social support from their families at home were less likely to consume alcohol. The effect of social support seemed to be due primarily to the fact that families providing high levels of social support were also more likely to have a strong religious emphasis in the home. School grades also correlated with lower teen use of alcohol. Teens who got good grades were more likely to receive higher levels of social support from their families, which in turn was associated with lower rates of alcohol use. The teens who used alcohol were more likely to show poorer school performance over the course of the study (Mason & Windle, 2001).

You may be wondering about the extent to which growing up in a home with parental alcoholism might predispose children to develop such problems themselves. As we have discussed elsewhere, the question is especially complicated by virtue of the fact that genetic loading plays so prominent a role in the development of alcoholism. Nevertheless, some theorists and researchers have explored the sociocultural impact of such environments and have put forth some interesting notions. A few decades ago the notion of adult children of alcoholics (ACOAs) was proposed (Woititz, 1983), in which it was suggested that the offspring of alcoholic parents are at high risk of developing alcoholism themselves, and also prone to developing a range of interpersonal difficulties as a result of their dysfunctional home life during childhood. Although research has generally not validated the specific characteristics originally associated with the ACOA personality, a number of investigators have documented the detrimental impact of psychological development that results from growing up in a home in which alcohol abuse plays a prominent role. Children in such homes are likely to find it difficult to comprehend and adjust to what is going on around them. Conflicts are common between parents during periods of drinking as well as times of recovery. Home life is experienced as unpredictable and uncontrollable, thus setting the stage for the development of a range of problems, including possible substance abuse, in the children who grow up in such chaotic family environments (Haugland, 2005).

Critics may raise questions about the legitimacy of general characterizations of the family members of alcoholics, but there is no question that alcohol-related disorders create emotional stress for individuals and families. In addition, there is a wider social cost. Besides the damaging effects of substances on the fabric of society, there are the exorbitant financial costs associated with medical treatment for alcohol-related conditions, lost work time, the loss of human life, and the treatment of children with fetal alcohol syndrome.

Treatment of Alcohol Dependence

The search for the effective treatment of alcohol dependence has been a difficult and challenging process. Alcohol use is so much a part of Western culture that many people who abuse or are dependent on alcohol do not realize that their behavior is problematic. There are no legal sanctions against the use of alcohol other than a minimum drinking age; in fact, endorsements of drinking as a socially acceptable behavior frequently appear in advertising. Little consideration is given to the downside of alcohol consumption—namely, that it can involve a serious disorder. Nor is much attention given to the fact that alcohol-related disorders are treatable.

Due to denial, most alcohol-dependent individuals do not seek treatment voluntarily. Therefore, developing strategies for health care and social service institutions, families, and informal service providers aimed at changing social networks and referring people to treatment is an important goal (Weisner, Matzger & Kaskutas, 2003).

Biological Treatment   Medications are becoming increasingly used as biological treatment for alcohol dependence. Medications that seem to have the most success are those that block or interact with the brain mechanisms thought to be the causes of alcohol dependence. Naltrexone (ReVia) is prescribed as an aid in preventing relapse among people with alcohol dependence. Naltrexone originally was used as a treatment for opioid dependence. The way in which naltrexone works is not well understood, but researchers believe that it blocks the pleasurable effects of opioids, both those produced by the body as well as those that are ingested. As a result, a person taking naltrexone who then drinks alcohol will find the experience much less reinforcing and is therefore more likely to abstain. At that point, the individual is better able to take advantage of psychotherapy. Clinicians recommending naltrexone to clients have found that adherence to daily use of the medication can be problematic, and are therefore more likely to recommend longer lasting injectable administrations, which have been found to result in significant reductions in heavy drinking among alcohol-dependent individuals who seek treatment (Garbutt et al., 2005).

Another medication used to treat alcohol dependence is acamprosate, which was approved by the U.S. FDA in 2004 and released to pharmacies in early 2005, although it had been marketed in several other countries since the late 1980s and used with very promising results. Studies conducted in European countries where the medication has been widely used have found consistent increases in abstinence rates, particularly when it is paired with psychological interventions. For individuals taking acamprosate, significant improvements in quality of life have been observed, such that their functioning has increased to levels comparable to that found in healthy individuals (Morgan, Landron, & Lehert, 2004). Although the precise mechanism that makes acamprosate effective in the treatment of alcohol-dependent individuals is unclear, researchers hypothesize that this medication restores the balance between inhibitory and excitatory neurotransmission in the central nervous system (Overman, Teter, & Guthrie, 2003).

In comparing the efficacy of acamprosate and naltrexone, researchers have found that both medications are effective, but acamprosate appears especially useful in a therapeutic approach targeting the goal of abstinence, whereas naltrexone seems preferable in treatment programs aimed at controlled consumption (Bouza et al., 2004).

Some medications are used to control symptoms of coexisting conditions: for example, benzodiazepines can manage the symptoms of withdrawal and prevent the development of **delirium tremens,** a physical condition consisting of autonomic

Mini Case

SUBSTANCE DEPENDENCE (ALCOHOL)

Rhona is a 55-year-old homemaker married to a successful builder. Every afternoon, she makes herself the first of a series of daiquiris. On many evenings, she has passed out on the couch by the time her husband arrives home from work. Rhona lost her driver's license a year ago after being arrested three times on charges of driving while intoxicated. Although Rhona's family has urged her to obtain treatment for her disorder, she denies that she has a problem because she can "control" her drinking. The mother of three grown children, Rhona began to drink around the age of 45, when her youngest child left for college. Prior to this time, Rhona kept herself extremely busy through her children's extracurricular activities. When she found herself alone every afternoon, she took solace in having an early cocktail. Over a period of several years, the "cocktail" developed into a series of five or six strong drinks. Rhona's oldest daughter has lately begun to insist that something be done for her mother. She does not want to see Rhona develop the fatal alcohol-related illness that caused the premature death of her grandmother.

Diagnostic Features

During a 12-month period, people with substance dependence show at least three of the following:

- Tolerance
- Withdrawal
- Use of the substance in larger amounts or over a longer period than intended
- Persistent desire or unsuccessful efforts to cut down or control substance use
- Extensive time devoted to activities involved in obtaining, using, or recovering from substance use
- A giving up of or reduction in important activities because of substance use
- Continued use despite knowledge of a substance-caused physical or psychological problem

---

nervous system dysfunction, confusion, and possibly seizures. Other antianxiety medications, and antidepressants, may help reduce the individual's dependence on alcohol by alleviating the symptoms of anxiety and depression, which can foster the need for alcohol. Because antianxiety medications carry the risk of dependence, these must be carefully monitored.

Another category of medications used to treat alcohol dependence consists of those that are intended to produce a strongly aversive physiological reaction when a person drinks. This method relies on an aversive conditioning process, in which the unpleasant reaction to alcohol provoked by the medication causes the individual to form a negative association to alcohol intake, providing a strong incentive for not drinking. The medication used in this form of treatment is **disulfiram,** known popularly as Antabuse. Disulfiram inhibits **aldehyde dehydrogenase (ALDH),** an enzyme that, along with ADH, is responsible for metabolizing alcohol. When ALDH is inhibited, the level of blood acetaldehyde, a toxic substance, rises, and within 30 minutes the individual experiences a severe physical reaction lasting for as long as 1 hour. Depending on the amount of alcohol in the body, this reaction includes a headache, hot and flushed face, chest pain, weakness, sweating, thirst, blurred vision, confusion, rapid heart rate and palpitations, a drop in blood pressure, difficulty breathing, nausea, and vomiting. Although disulfiram has been used for decades, controlled studies have failed to validate its efficacy. This is due to the fact that people, expecting negative side effects from drinking on disulfiram, resist the medication rather than continue to abstain from drinking alcohol (MacKillop et al., 2003). It is generally agreed that treatment with disulfiram is usually only effective when done within a supervised setting.

Psychological Treatment   Relapse prevention therapy is a psychological treatment based on the cognitive-behavioral model of relapse in which the goal is to identify and prevent high-risk situations for relapse. In other words, when people try to change problematic behavior such as the chronic abuse of alcohol, they are likely to have a setback (lapse), following which they are at greater risk of returning to the problematic behavior (relapse). For some individuals, however, another outcome is possible—they may get back on track in the direction of positive change (prolapse). When alcohol-dependent individuals trip up and resume drinking, they are vulnerable to the abstinence violation effect which we discussed earlier in this chapter; they tend to blame themselves and feel a loss of perceived control following such a violation of their self-imposed rules (Witkiewitz & Marlatt, 2004). As you can imagine, such inner thoughts and experiences present challenges for the individual struggling to change and for the clinicians trying to help them.

Clinicians working within the conceptual framework of the relapse prevention model begin their work by assessing the high-risk situations, or those circumstances in which the individual may relapse. These circumstances include associating with people such as drinking buddies, going to places such as favorite bars, and attending events such as parties. The therapist challenges the client's expectations regarding the perceived positive effects of drinking or using other substances, and discusses the psychological components of the substance use so that the client can make more informed choices in threatening situations. By explicitly discussing the abstinence violation effect and preparing clients for possible lapses, the clinician may help the client avoid a major relapse (Witkiewitz & Marlatt, 2004). According to the notion of the abstinence violation effect, if the lapse is seen as a sign of weakness, or a character flaw, this will damage the individual's sense of self-efficacy so severely that the possibility of future abstinence seems out of the question. If, instead, the individual can learn to interpret the drinking episode as a single incident that was unfortunate but not a permanent failing, the individual's self-efficacy can remain intact and a relapse can be prevented.

In relapse prevention, the individual learns decision-making abilities that make it possible for him or her to analyze a high-risk situation and determine which coping skills would work best to prevent a relapse. Skill training can also help individuals learn how to express and receive positive and negative feelings, how to initiate contact, and how to reply to criticism. For example, consider the case of a woman named Sheila, who knows that going to a party will put her in a high-risk situation. For years, Sheila believed that she needed alcohol in such situations so that she could "loosen up," thereby appearing more likable and lively. Now that she is trying to maintain abstinence, she can make alternative plans prior to going to a party that will prepare her with coping skills, such as staying away from the bar and asking a friend to keep her glass full with a nonalcoholic beverage. Cognitive restructuring would help Sheila interpret high-risk situations more productively. If she believes that it is necessary to have alcohol to be popular and lively, she can learn to reframe this belief, so she can see that people like her even if she is not high on alcohol. Maintenance is an important part of the treatment approach as well; there is a need for continued therapeutic contacts, social support from friends and family, and changes in lifestyle to find alternate sources of gratification. Sheila needs to keep in periodic contact with her therapist, to find new friends and seek help from her family, and to find other ways to socialize, such as joining a health club. Skill training and the development of alternate coping methods can also be combined with behavioral techniques, such as cue exposure.

The goal of relapse prevention cannot be achieved in one step; rather, it requires a graded program that exposes the individual to high-risk situations in greater and greater increments. At each step, the therapist encourages the individual to draw inferences from successful behavior that will reinforce feelings of self-efficacy.

Another approach to the treatment of alcohol-dependent clients is associated with motivated interviewing, which we discussed in Chapter 4. Motivational interviewing is a directive, client-centered therapeutic approach for eliciting behavior change by helping clients explore and resolve their ambivalence. Clinicians rely on reflective listening in which they seek to stimulate change within the client, and they attempt to elicit the client's own intrinsic motivation for change by emphasizing autonomy and the ability to choose whether, when, and how to change (Hettema, Steele, & Miller, 2005).

Alcoholics Anonymous While biologists and psychologists continue to explore treatment approaches based on scientific models of alcohol dependence, one intervention model, whose

Meetings are central to the Alcoholics Anonymous movement. Members describe their experiences with alcohol dependence, hoping to inspire others to resist the omnipresent temptations of the addiction.

roots are in spirituality rather than science, continues to be used on a widespread basis: Alcoholics Anonymous, or AA. This movement was founded in 1935 by Bill W., a Wall Street stockbroker, and Dr. Bob, a surgeon from Akron, Ohio, and from these humble beginnings AA has grown to worldwide proportions. More than 2 million members participate in approximately 98,000 AA groups throughout the world (www.aa.org). The value of this approach has become generally accepted, and AA is now a component of most treatment programs in the United States.

The standard recovery program in AA involves a strong commitment to participate in AA-related activities, with the most important component being the AA meeting. Many AA meetings begin with an introduction of members, who state their first names, followed by the statement "I am an alcoholic." This ritual is the basis for the name of the program, Alcoholics Anonymous, meaning that members never consider themselves not to be alcoholics and that they are not required to divulge their identities. During the meeting, one or more members share their experiences about how they developed drinking problems, the suffering their drinking caused, the personal debasement they may have felt when they lied and cheated, and how they "hit bottom" and began to turn around their drinking patterns and their lives. The 12 steps to recovery form the heart of AA's philosophy. This emphasis on honesty, confrontation, and storytelling is seen as the essential element of the 12-step program. (See Table 13.3 on page 406.)

The second component of AA is the constant availability of another member, called a sponsor, who can provide support during times of crisis, when the urge to drink becomes overpowering. Round-the-clock hot lines staffed by AA volunteers also help make such assistance continuously available. Third, the spiritual element is a major factor within the AA movement, in that members admit that they are powerless over alcohol and turn over their lives to a power greater than themselves. The AA experience differs considerably from person to person, with some people deriving benefit from attendance at meetings, and others from adherence to the spiritual principles.

TABLE 13.3 Is AA for You?

This is AA General Service
Conference-approved literature
Copyright © 1973, 1998 by AA World Services, Inc.
All Rights Reserved

Answer "yes" or "no" to the following questions.

1. Have you ever decided to stop drinking for a week or so, but lasted for only a couple of days?

2. Do you wish people would mind their own business about your drinking—stop telling you what to do?

3. Have you ever switched from one kind of drink to another in the hope that this would keep you from getting drunk?

4. Have you had to have an eye-opener on awakening during the past year?

5. Do you envy people who can drink without getting into trouble?

6. Have you had problems connected with drinking during the past year?

7. Has your drinking caused trouble at home?

8. Do you ever try to get "extra" drinks at a party because you do not get enough?

9. Do you tell yourself you can stop drinking any time you want to, even though you keep getting drunk when you don't mean to?

10. Have you missed days of work or school because of drinking?

11. Do you have "blackouts"?

12. Have you ever felt that your life would be better if you did not drink?

What's Your Score?

Did you answer "yes" four or more times? If so, you are probably in trouble with alcohol. Why do we say this? Because thousands of people in AA have said so for many years. They found out the truth about themselves—the hard way. But, again, only you can decide whether you think AA is for you. Try to keep an open mind on the subject. If the answer is yes, we will be glad to show you how we stopped drinking ourselves. Just call. AA does not promise to solve your life's problems. But we can show you how we are learning to live without drinking "one day at a time." We stay away from that "first drink." If there is no first one, there cannot be a tenth one. And, when we got rid of alcohol, we found that life became much more manageable.

ALCOHOLICS ANONYMOUS ® is a fellowship of men and women who share their experience, strength and hope with each other that they may solve their common problem and help others to recover from alcoholism.
• The only requirement for membership is a desire to stop drinking. There are no dues or fees for AA membership; we are self-supporting through our own contributions.
• AA is not allied with any sect, denomination, politics, organization or institution; does not wish to engage in any controversy; neither endorses nor opposes any causes.
• Our primary purpose is to stay sober and help other alcoholics to achieve sobriety.
The twelve questions have been excerpted from material appearing in the pamphlet "Is AA for You?" and has been reprinted with permission of Alcoholics Anonymous World Services, Inc. (AAWS). Permission to reprint this material does not mean that AAWS has reviewed and/or endorses this publication. AA is a program of recovery from alcoholism *only*—use of AA material in any non-AA context does not imply otherwise.

Source: Copyright © 1973, 1988 by Alcoholics Anonymous World Services, Inc. All rights reserved. Reprinted with permission.

The fundamental approach that AA fosters with regard to understanding alcohol dependence is that alcoholism is a disease that prevents those who have it from controlling their drinking. If the alcoholic does succumb to temptation and goes on a drinking binge, this is attributed within the AA model not to a moral failing but to a biological process. A second tenet of AA is that alcoholics are never cured; they are "recovering." The goal of AA treatment is total abstinence. According to the AA philosophy, one drink is enough to send the individual back into a state of alcohol dependence.

An offshoot of AA was formed in the early 1950s for relatives and friends of people with alcohol dependence. Called Al-Anon, to distinguish it from AA, this program provides support for people who are close to alcoholics and need help to cope with the problems alcoholism creates in their lives. A later movement, called Alateen, is specifically designed for teenagers whose lives have been affected by alcoholism in the family. As we mentioned earlier, there are also groups for adult children of alcoholics, which focus on the psychological problems that result from growing up in a family with an alcoholic parent. There are currently 30,000 Al-Anon and Alateen groups existing in 112 countries (http://www.al-anon.alateen.org/helppro.html).

Millions of people credit AA for their sobriety; in addition, proponents of AA cite glowing outcome figures, which, if correct, would make it the most successful approach to treating alcohol dependence. According to AA, the average length of abstinence is slightly over 4 years; 29 percent have been abstinent for more than 5 years, 38 percent from 1 to 5 years, and 33 percent for less than a year. A recent study confirmed that AA participation causes subsequent decreases in drinking and related problems and that comorbid psychiatric disorders do not necessarily change the relationship between AA involvement and alcohol problems (McKellar et al., 2003).

What lessons can researchers and clinicians learn from AA? We can see from the elements involved in this program that AA has much in common with a cognitive-behavioral approach. AA encourages the alcohol-dependent individual to avoid self-blame for failures and to develop alternative coping skills, features shared with the expectancy model that may also enhance the outcome of AA (Morgenstern et al., 1997). Similarly, AA encourages the individual to use coping skills that rely on seeking help from outside the self rather than from within. Both approaches, however, share the element of recommending continued contact with the treatment provider. They also include an emphasis on social support, one of the most striking elements in the AA model (National Institute on Alcohol Abuse [NIAA], 2000).

The benefits of AA participation have been well documented, yet some alcohol-dependent individuals do not feel comfortable with this approach, and seek alternatives. Many such individuals who are interested in a spiritually based approach have found that meditation and techniques based on mindfulness are especially beneficial. Mindfulness is an intentional focused awareness, a way of paying attention on purpose in the present moment, non-judgmentally (www.umassmed.edu/cfm/history.cfm). This approach emphasizes the value of being aware of the present moment; rather than judging, reflecting, or thinking, you simply observe the moment in which you find yourself. Mindfulness or meditation is believed to affect the cognitive, behavioral, and neurobiological mechanisms that can be helpful to the individual who is striving to control the use of substances (Marlatt et al., 2004). All alcohol treatment programs, however, share the major limitation of appealing to and being effective with only those who are motivated to change. Without that motivation, neither medication nor the most elaborate psychological treatment strategy will have a lasting impact.

Substances Other Than Alcohol

Various substances other than alcohol have the potential for abuse and dependence. In the following sections, we will review the major categories of substances and examine their effects on behavior and their mechanisms of action. Many of these drugs share features, however, in that they alter the neurons in an area of the brain involved in the regulation of pleasure or reward.

Dopamine is one of the major neurotransmitters involved in this pleasure pathway. The functions associated with dopamine in addition to the sensation of pleasure include motor activity, awareness, judgment, and motivation. A circuit of dopamine-producing neurons located at the top of the brainstem in an area called the ventral tegmental area (VTA) plays a particularly important role in regulating the sensation of pleasure (see Figure 13.2).

These neurons relay messages about pleasure to neurons in a structure within the limbic system called the nucleus accumbens. They also project to the frontal cortex. This entire circuit is known as the mesolimbic dopamine system. It is thought to play a role in survival, in that the sensation of pleasure associated with such activities as eating and sexual arousal helps ensure that organisms engage in activities that maintain life and perpetuate the species.

Psychoactive drugs seem to activate the mesolimbic dopamine system. Substances such as heroin and LSD mimic the effects of a natural neurotransmitter on the neurons in the brain's pleasure center. Others, such as PCP, block the synaptic receptors and, consequently, interfere with normal transmission. Such drugs as cocaine interfere with the molecules responsible for ensuring that dopamine is absorbed from the synapse back to the neurons that released them. Drugs such as methamphetamine stimulate the excess release of neurotransmitters, resulting in heightened stimulation and arousal. Thus, many drugs with abuse potential become addictive by virtue of their actions on the dopamine system in the mesolimbic pathway, even though each drug may operate according to a different mechanism.

Over a prolonged period of time, the constant use of one of these substances produces permanent changes in the brain. If the substance is not present in the individual's nervous system, the neurons change their functioning. For example, in the case of cocaine, dopamine accumulates in the synapses because cocaine blocks the reabsorption of dopamine by the presynaptic neurons. As the dopamine accumulates, the neurons with dopamine receptors decrease the number of receptors they produce, a process called "down regulation." If the individual stops taking cocaine, dopamine levels eventually return to normal, but now there are fewer dopamine receptors available to be stimulated. The individual experiences this state as a craving for higher levels of dopamine, leading to a desire for more cocaine. Another change that occurs in the brain is the destruction of neurons as a result of long-term or heavy substance use.

In attempting to understand the role of biology in drug dependence, researchers have searched for genes that control levels of dopamine, the neurotransmitter thought to play a primary role in the brain's response to drugs. For various reasons, researchers must rely on evidence from animal models. Of particular interest is the gene for the protein known as Nurr1. This protein appears to play a key role in the development of excessive reward-seeking behaviors that characterize addiction (Werme et al., 2003). One approach involves removing a specific gene in mice and observing the results (these mice are appropriately called "knockout" mice). Such a manipulation was performed on the gene for Nurr1. When this happened, the mice failed to generate neurons containing dopamine in the midbrain area involved in the brain's pleasure circuit. One effect of such a manipulation was that the mice continued to have reduced

The brain

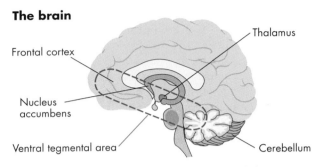

Addicts become accustomed to high levels of dopamine, which plays an important role in the regulation of pleasure. Dopamine is manufactured in nerve cells within the ventral tegmental area and is released in the nucleus accumbens and the frontal cortex.

Dopamine's normal action

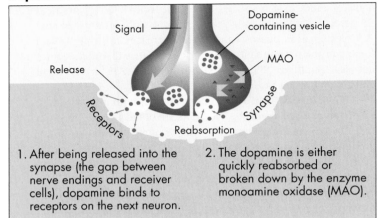

1. After being released into the synapse (the gap between nerve endings and receiver cells), dopamine binds to receptors on the next neuron.

2. The dopamine is either quickly reabsorbed or broken down by the enzyme monoamine oxidase (MAO).

How drugs affect dopamine levels

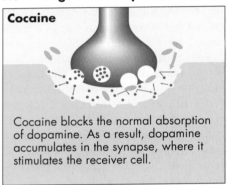

Cocaine

Cocaine blocks the normal absorption of dopamine. As a result, dopamine accumulates in the synapse, where it stimulates the receiver cell.

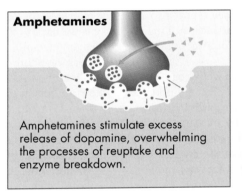

Amphetamines

Amphetamines stimulate excess release of dopamine, overwhelming the processes of reuptake and enzyme breakdown.

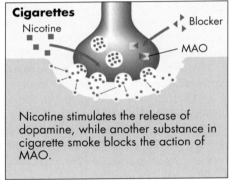

Cigarettes

Nicotine stimulates the release of dopamine, while another substance in cigarette smoke blocks the action of MAO.

FIGURE 13.2 Normal action of dopamine Dopamine is released into the synapse and binds to receptors on the postsynaptic neuron. The dopamine is either reabsorbed or broken down by monoamine oxidase (MAO).

dopamine levels into adulthood (Zetterstrom et al., 1997). If this result is generalized to humans, it would mean that such an abnormality may cause a craving for drugs to counteract the dopamine deficiency. A second approach involves studying the response to drugs among inbred mice with identical genetic makeups. Using this strategy, researchers have found differences among these mice strains in their responses to drugs, with some strains refusing most drugs and others showing preferences for many drugs of abuse (Crabbe, Gallagher, Cross, & Belknap, 1998; Grisel et al., 1997).

Among humans, the situation is obviously far more complicated. However, some progress has been made by comparing the DNA of people who abuse drugs with the DNA of people who do not. This method has resulted in the identification of a gene that leads to the production of the COMT enzyme (catechol-o-methyl-transferase). This enzyme, found throughout the body, is involved in breaking down and inactivating dopamine. The version of the gene that produces higher levels of COMT is found more often in individuals who are drug abusers (Vandenbergh et al., 1997). In another approach, researchers investigated the role of subjective responses to drugs. In an unusual study of subjective responses to marijuana in identical twins and fraternal twins, researchers found

that identical twin pairs were more likely than fraternal twin pairs to have similar reactions to the drug, a finding that supports the notion that there is a genetic component involved in the ways people experience the effects of drugs (Lyons et al., 1997).

Research evidence clearly supports the importance of genetics in the development of serious substance problems. Specifically, genetic susceptibility plays a significant role in the transition from substance use to dependence, and from chronic use to addiction (Hiroi & Agatsuma, 2005).

Clearly, more research on humans is needed to understand the contribution of biological factors to drug abuse and dependence. Researchers attempting to integrate various empirical findings believe that emerging evidence suggests that addiction may result from a "hijacked brain reward pathway" involving most of the structures in the reward circuitry of the brain. Repeated drug exposure has a number of consequences, including causing changes in gene expression, intracellular signaling, and synaptic plasticity in the structures of the reward circuitry. Researchers are investigating the relationship between molecular and cellular mechanisms and the behavioral manifestations of addiction, such as tolerance, dependence, craving, compulsive drug taking, and relapses (Mohn, Yao, & Caron, 2004).

Mini Case

AMPHETAMINE DEPENDENCE

Catherine is a 23-year-old salesperson who tried for 3 years to lose weight. Her physician prescribed amphetamines but cautioned her about the possibility that she might become dependent on them. She did begin to lose weight, but she also discovered that she liked the extra energy and good feelings caused by the diet pills. When Catherine returned to her doctor after having lost the desired weight, she asked him for a refill of her prescription to help her maintain her new figure. When he refused, Catherine asked around among her friends until she found the name of a physician who was willing to accommodate her wishes for ongoing refills of the prescription. Over the course of a year, Catherine has developed a number of psychological problems, including depression, paranoid thinking, and irritability. Despite the fact that she realizes that something is wrong, she feels driven to continue using the drug.

Diagnostic Features

During a 12-month period, people with amphetamine dependence show at least three of the following:

- Tolerance
- Withdrawal
- Use of amphetamines in larger amounts or over a longer period than intended
- Persistent desire or unsuccessful efforts to cut down or control amphetamine use
- Extensive time devoted to activities involved in obtaining, using, or recovering from amphetamine use
- A giving up of or reduction in important activities because of amphetamine use
- Continued use despite knowledge of an amphetamine-caused physical or psychological problem

---

In addition to the role of biological factors, learning and environmental factors are also influential in the acquisition and maintenance of substance-related conditions. For example, in one comprehensive long-term study of more than 650 teenagers, the use of alcohol, cigarettes, and marijuana was tracked. Various factors were found to be powerful influences associated with increased substance use; these factors included the failure of parents to monitor their children, conflict between parents and children, academic failure, and the influential behavior of their peers (Duncan, Duncan, Biglan, & Ary, 1998).

Current treatment programs rely heavily on psychosocial factors (in conjunction with medical treatments), but, in the future, treatment based on insights gained from genetic research may also hold important potential for curbing the cravings that initially predispose an individual to a life of drug dependence.

Stimulants

You have perhaps on occasion wished you could be more alert and energetic. You may have sought a "pick-me-up," such as a cup of coffee. Caffeine is just one substance in a category of drugs called **stimulants**—substances that have an activating effect on the nervous system. The stimulants associated with psychological disorders are amphetamines, cocaine, and caffeine. These differ in their chemical structure, their specific physical and psychological effects, and their potential danger to the user. In the following sections, we will discuss the major stimulant drugs.

Amphetamines Amphetamines are stimulants, or "uppers," that cause a range of effects, depending on the amount, method, and duration of use, as well as the specific form of the drug that is taken. In moderate amounts taken orally, amphetamines and related drugs cause euphoria, increased confidence, talkativeness, and energy. When taken intravenously, amphetamines have more powerful effects. Immediately after injection, the user feels a surge, or "rush," of extremely pleasurable sensations that some describe as similar to orgasm. A smokeable methamphetamine called "ice" (because of its crystalline appearance) is a highly addictive and toxic amphetamine.

One reason amphetamines become a problem for users is that people quickly build up tolerance. For example, people who use them for dieting find that, after a certain period (as brief as 4 to 6 weeks), they must use higher doses to maintain the same appetite suppressant effect. At that point, they have become dependent on the drug's mood-altering results. Tolerance to amphetamines also extends to psychological effects. In order to achieve the same "high," long-term users must take greater doses of the drug. A debate exists about whether amphetamines cause physical dependence, but most researchers agree that these drugs are psychologically addictive.

Although an overdose of amphetamines rarely results in death, many medical problems can occur, such as stroke, heart irregularity, kidney failure, temporary paralysis, circulatory collapse, seizures, and even coma. Some users develop psychotic symptoms, including delusions, hallucinations, or profound mood disturbance. Paranoid delusions may develop, as well as tactile hallucinations, such as feeling that bugs are crawling on the skin. People in this state may have little control over their behavior; feeling terrified or out of control, they may act in violent or self-destructive ways.

When people discontinue amphetamines after heavy usage, they exhibit withdrawal symptoms, called "crashing," that include profound depression, extreme hunger, craving for the drug, exhaustion, and disturbed sleep. These symptoms can last for 2 weeks or more, and some residual problems may last for a year.

There are two principal routes to amphetamine dependence: medical abuse and street abuse. In medical abuse, the individual begins taking amphetamines for a medical reason, such

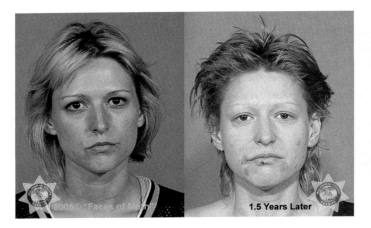

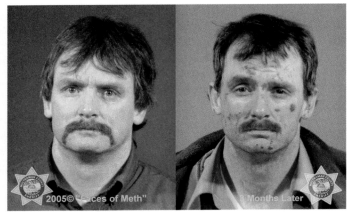

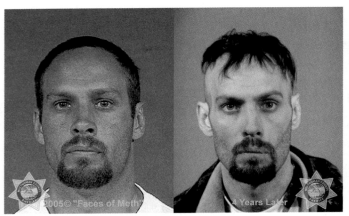

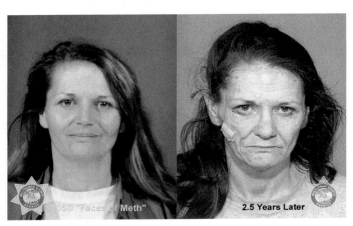

The devastating effects of methamphetamine are evident in these before-and-after photos of four individuals who were chronic users of the drug. "Faces of Meth"™ is a project which began when Deputy Bret King put together mug shots of persons booked into the Oregon Multnomah County Detention Center.

as to reduce weight or to treat fatigue, increasing the dose as tolerance develops and obtaining the drug by seeking multiple or refillable prescriptions. Efforts to stop taking the drug result in an increase of the symptoms it was intended to reduce, leading the individual to increase dosages to harmful levels. Because of these worrisome effects, physicians are reluctant to prescribe these medications. Street abusers take amphetamines deliberately to alter their state of consciousness, perhaps in alternation with depressants. An even more dangerous mode of amphetamine use involves taking the drug in "runs" of continuous ingestion for 2 to 4 days, a pattern that often results in withdrawal and psychosis.

The abuse of methamphetamine has emerged as a major drug of abuse worldwide. Methamphetamine is an addictive stimulant drug that is related to amphetamine, but provokes more intense central nervous system effects. This drug releases high levels of dopamine which stimulates brain cells and enhances mood and body movement. At the same time, methamphetamine damages brain cells containing dopamine and serotonin, and over time can result in symptoms similar to the movement disorder, Parkinson's disease. Methamphetamine, which is taken orally, intranasally, intravenously, or by smoking, causes a rush or feeling of euphoria,

and becomes addictive very quickly (http://www.nida.nih.gov/Infofacts/methamphetamine. html). In addition to the adverse physical consequences resulting from methamphetamine use, significant cognitive impairments have also been found. Especially alarming to public health officials is the relationship between the use of methamphetamine and unprotected sexual activity that has put large numbers of people at risk for developing sexually related diseases (Chang, Ernst, Speck, & Grob, 2005).

Cocaine Cocaine became the drug of choice for recreational users during the 1980s and spread to every segment of the population. The widespread availability of **crack cocaine,** a crystallized, inexpensive form of street cocaine that is usually smoked, has added to the problem.

Cocaine has a fascinating history that dates back thousands of years. In the United States, its popular use can be traced to the late 1800s, when it was marketed as a cure for everything from fatigue to malaria. A major pharmaceutical company, Parke-Davis, sold tablets, sprays, and cigarettes that contained cocaine. Coca-Cola was developed in the 1880s, and its stimulating mixture of cocaine and caffeine made it a popular beverage. The cocaine was eliminated from Coca-Cola in 1905.

TABLE 13.4 Sample Items from the Cocaine Abuse Assessment Profile: Addiction/Dependency Self-Test

Each item receives a "yes" or "no" answer; a "yes" counts toward a positive cocaine abuse score.

1. Do you tend to use whatever supplies of cocaine you have on hand, even though you try to save some for another time?
2. Do you go on cocaine binges for 24 hours or longer?
3. Do you need to be high on cocaine in order to have a good time?
4. Does the sight, thought, or mention of cocaine trigger urges and cravings for the drug?
5. Do you feel guilty and ashamed of using cocaine and like yourself less for doing it?
6. Have your values and priorities been distorted by cocaine use?
7. Do you tend to spend time with certain people or go to certain places because you know that cocaine will be available?
8. Do you hide your cocaine use from "straight" friends or family because you're afraid of their reactions?
9. Have you become less involved in your job or career due to cocaine use?
10. Do you worry about whether you are capable of living a normal and satisfying life without cocaine?

Source: From *800-COCAINE* by Mark S. Gold, M. D. Copyright © 1984 by Mark S. Gold, M. D. Used by permission of Bantam Books, a division of Random House, Inc.

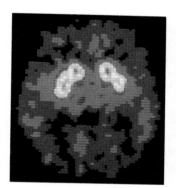 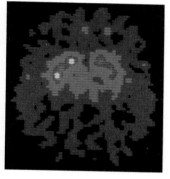

Following the prolonged use of cocaine, nerve endings deaden in the brain's system of pleasure regulation. A brain scan (*right*) provides a graphic image of the drop in the number of functioning dopamine receptors.

In the early 1900s, as the use of cocaine continued to spread, authorities in medicine and government began to question the medicinal value of the drug and the harm it could cause. Reports of addiction, death, and associated crime circulated throughout the United States, resulting in legislation prohibiting the interstate shipment of cocaine-containing products. Government controls continued to tighten on the distribution of cocaine for medicinal purposes until it was banned. The drug then became so expensive and difficult to obtain that its use sharply declined for several decades.

During the 1960s and 1970s, a resurgence of cocaine use occurred, because the drug became inaccurately perceived once again as relatively harmless. When crack cocaine became available in the 1980s, a new set of social problems developed that continues today. A significant proportion of the population struggles with cocaine dependence. According to the National Household Survey (SAMHSA, 2005), approximately 2.3 million Americans 12 years and older (0.9 percent of the population) are cocaine users, meaning that they use cocaine at least once per month. Of these cocaine users, about 604,000 use crack. The highest rate of cocaine use is among the 18 to 25 age group. No longer is cocaine viewed as an innocuous recreational drug; rather, cocaine is now implicated in various social problems, such as increased crime committed by drug-dependent individuals and/or the neglect and abuse of children by parents who are incapacitated. It is estimated that about half a million "crack" babies are born prematurely to crack-addicted mothers.

Compared with amphetamines, the stimulating effects of cocaine last for a shorter period of time but are much more intense. Users experience the strongest effects within the first 10 minutes after administration, and these effects quickly subside. In moderate doses, cocaine leads to feelings of euphoria, sexual excitement, potency, energy, and talkativeness. At higher doses, users may experience psychotic symptoms; for example, they may become delusional, hallucinate, and feel confused, suspicious, and agitated. Their paranoid delusions tend to include suspicions that the police or drug dealers are about to apprehend them or that others who are nearby plan to attack them and steal their cocaine. They may have illusory experiences, perhaps misinterpreting an unexplained noise or misperceiving an object in ways that coincide with their delusional thinking. They may also hallucinate that bugs or foreign objects are on their skin and try desperately to scratch off these objects. Violence is a common part of the scenario; these people may become dangerously out of control and lash out at others, including those who are closest to them.

Mini Case

CAFFEINE INTOXICATION

Carla is a 19-year-old college sophomore who felt compelled to excel at every endeavor and to become involved in as many activities as time and energy would permit. As her commitments increased and her studies became more burdensome, Carla became more and more reliant on coffee, soda, and over-the-counter stimulants to reduce her need for sleep. During final examination week, Carla overdid it. For 3 days straight, she consumed approximately 10 cups of coffee a day, along with a box of No-Doz. In addition to her bodily symptoms of restlessness, twitching muscles, flushed face, stomach disturbance, and heart irregularities, Carla began to ramble when she spoke. At first, Carla thought she was having a heart attack, or possibly an anxiety attack associated with her final exams. At her roommate's insistence, Carla went to the health service, where the treating physician recognized her condition as caffeine intoxication.

Diagnostic Features

This condition, which follows recent consumption in excess of 250 mg of caffeine (more than two or three cups of brewed coffee),

causes significant impairment or distress, as evidenced by at least five of the following:

- Restlessness
- Nervousness
- Excitement
- Insomnia
- Flushed face
- Frequent urination
- Gastrointestinal disturbance
- Muscle twitching
- Rambling speech
- Rapid or irregular heart rate
- Periods of inexhaustibility
- Psychomotor agitation

Needless to say, the psychotic-like states that result from cocaine use are distressing and even terrifying. When the effects of cocaine wear off, the user "comes down," or "crashes," experiencing a depressed mood, sleep disturbance, agitation, craving, and fatigue. Chronic heavy users experience these symptoms intensely for up to 3 or 4 days, and for a month afterward they may still feel some effects of withdrawal.

In addition to its powerful, addictive effects, cocaine poses a significant danger to a person's vital functions of breathing and blood circulation. The risks associated with cocaine are the result of the drug's actions as a local anesthetic and as a stimulant to the central nervous system and sympathetic nervous system. Cocaine simultaneously increases the sympathetic nervous system stimulation to the heart and anesthetizes the heart muscle, so that it is less able to contract and pump blood. During a binge, the individual seeks an ever greater high by taking in more and more cocaine, leading to higher and higher blood levels of the drug. At such levels, the pumping of the heart becomes impaired, and it becomes unable to contract to force blood into the arteries. Also, high blood levels of cocaine have a paradoxical effect on the way it is eliminated from the blood. Rather than being eliminated in higher amounts, as you might expect, the elimination rate actually is reduced, further contributing to a rise in cocaine blood levels. Other calamitous changes in the heart also occur during a binge: oxygen can be cut off to the heart muscle, further impairing its ability to contract, and changes in the heart's electrophysiological functioning lead to irregular rhythms. Cocaine may also produce the effect of kindling, through which the user develops convulsions, because the brain's threshold for seizures has been lowered by repeated exposure to cocaine.

Caffeine Caffeine is a drug that has been used or at least tried by virtually everyone. In fact, most Americans ingest caffeine daily, either in coffee, tea, chocolate candy, or caffeinated soft drinks. It is also an ingredient in many prescription and nonprescription medications, including headache remedies and diet pills.

Although people may not think of caffeine as a substance of abuse, it is in the category of psychoactive drugs. Caffeine's effect on mood and alertness occurs through its activation of the sympathetic nervous system. Even half a cup of coffee can bring about slight improvements in mood, alertness, and clarity of thought; however, as the amount of caffeine ingested on one occasion increases (up to three to four cups of coffee), more symptoms of anxiety and irritability similar to those seen in amphetamine use begin to appear. After four to six cups of coffee, an individual can develop symptoms that resemble those of a panic attack and may experience overstimulation, anxiety, dizziness, ringing in the ears, feelings of unreality, visual hallucinations, and confusion. People who are susceptible to panic attacks may experience these symptoms even after consuming relatively small amounts of caffeine.

Unlike other substance-related disorders, it is uncommon for people to consult clinicians because of problems associated with caffeine intake. However, sometimes people seek help because they are experiencing some disturbing symptoms, not realizing the possibility that caffeine might cause them. The diagnosis of caffeine intoxication is assigned when the individual is distressed or functionally impaired and experiences a set of at least five symptoms following caffeine ingestion. These symptoms include restlessness, nervousness, excitement, insomnia, flushed face, frequent urination, stomach disturbance,

Mini Case

CANNABIS (MARIJUANA) DEPENDENCE

Gary, a 22-year-old man, has lived with his parents since dropping out of college 3 years ago, midway through his freshman year. Gary was an average student in high school and, although popular, was not involved in many extracurricular activities. When he entered college, Gary became interested in the enticing opportunities for new experiences, and he began to smoke marijuana casually with his roommates. However, unlike his roommates, who limited their smoking to parties, Gary found that a nightly "hit" helped him relax. He started to rationalize that it also helped him study, because his thinking was more creative. As his first semester went by, he gradually lost interest in his studies, preferring to stay in his room and listen to music while getting high. He realized that it was easy to support his habit by selling marijuana to other people in the dorm. Although he convinced himself that he was not really a dealer, Gary became one of the primary suppliers of marijuana on campus. When he received his first-semester grades, he did not feel particularly discouraged about the fact that he had flunked out. Rather, he felt that he could benefit from having more time to himself. He moved home and became friendly with some local teenagers who frequented a nearby park and shared drugs there. Gary's parents have all but given up

on him, having become deeply discouraged by his laziness and unproductivity. They know that he is using drugs, but they feel helpless in their efforts to get him to seek professional help. They have learned that it is better to avoid discussing the matter with Gary, because violent arguments always ensue.

Diagnostic Features
During a 12-month period, people with cannabis dependence show at least three of the following:

- Tolerance
- Withdrawal
- Use of cannabis in larger amounts or over a longer period than intended
- Persistent desire or unsuccessful efforts to cut down or control cannabis use
- Extensive time devoted to activities involved in obtaining, using, or recovering from cannabis use
- A giving up of or reduction in important activities because of cannabis use
- Continued use despite knowledge of a cannabis-caused physical or psychological problem

---

muscle twitching, rambling thoughts, heartbeat irregularity, periods of inexhaustible energy, and psychomotor agitation. In some cases, caffeine can cause symptoms similar to those of anxiety disorders and sleep disorders. When this occurs, the clinician assigns the diagnosis of caffeine-induced anxiety disorder or caffeine-induced sleep disorder.

You might think that only large quantities of caffeine at one time can bring on physical symptoms, but, in fact, the regular consumption of two to three cups a day can cause the symptoms of intoxication. A person who drinks up to six cups of coffee a day on a regular basis may develop delirium. Over the course of years of such heavy consumption, the individual may develop such medical conditions as high blood pressure, rapid and irregular heartbeat, increased respiration rate, and peptic ulcers.

If we know caffeine has so many negative physical and psychological effects, why do people consume it regularly? Part of the reason that many people continue to consume caffeine is that they experience unpleasant withdrawal symptoms when they stop, such as headache, fatigue, decreased energy, decreased alertness, drowsiness, depressed mood, difficulty concentrating, and irritability (Juliano & Griffiths, 2004).

Cannabis

Marijuana (also called "grass," "pot," and "weed") is the most widely used illegal drug in the country. More than 40 percent of all Americans over the age of 12 have tried marijuana (Bouza

et al., 2004). Although during the decade of the 1990s the prevalence of marijuana use remained stable, there was a significant increase in marijuana abuse and dependence. Of particular interest is the fact that the frequency and quantity of marijuana use did not increase, suggesting that the stronger potency of the drug may have contributed to the rising rates of abuse and dependency (Compton et al., 2004).

Two factors seem to be of central importance in accounting for the relative popularity of marijuana. First, only 40 percent of the Americans surveyed by the National Institute of Drug Abuse regard trying marijuana as harmful—a far smaller number than those who perceive cocaine use to be risky. Among high-school seniors, marijuana has the lowest perceived risk of all illegal drugs. Second, marijuana is the most widely available illegal drug, and it is perceived as easily available, as indicated by the fact that 86 percent of high-school seniors regard this drug as relatively easy to obtain (Johnson, O'Malley, Bachman, & Schulenberg, 2005).

Marijuana has been used for more than 4,000 years in many cultures throughout the world. The active drug in marijuana, delta-9-tetrahydrocannabinol (THC), comes from cannabis sativa, a tall, leafy, green plant that thrives in warm climates. The more sunlight the plant receives, the higher the percentage of active THC it produces. Marijuana comes from the dried leaves of the plant, and hashish, containing a more potent form of THC, comes from the resins of the plant's flowers. The marijuana or hashish that reaches the street is never pure THC; other substances, such as tobacco, are always mixed in with it. Synthetic forms of THC are used for medicinal purposes, such as treating

Some young people feel that they can achieve social acceptance by agreeing with those who pressure them to try drugs. Researchers have found that marijuana users are much more likely to abuse other substances as well.

asthma and glaucoma and reducing nausea in cancer patients undergoing chemotherapy.

The most common way to take marijuana is to smoke it, but it can also be eaten or injected intravenously. When a person smokes marijuana, the peak blood levels are reached in about 10 minutes, but the subjective effects of the drug do not become apparent for another 20 to 30 minutes. The effects of intoxication last for 2 to 3 hours, but the metabolites of THC may remain in the body for 8 or more days.

People take marijuana in order to alter their perceptions of their environment and their bodily sensations. The desired effects include relaxation, a heightened sense of sensuality and sexuality, and an increased awareness of internal and external stimuli. However, a number of maladaptive behavioral and psychological changes may occur, including impaired coordination, increased anxiety, the sensation of slowed time, impaired judgment, and social withdrawal. Other disturbing conditions, including delirium, cannabis-induced anxiety disorder, and cannabis-induced psychotic disorder, may also develop. Bodily changes associated with marijuana use include watery eyes, increased appetite, dry mouth, and faster heart rate. The quality and intensity of the experience depend on the purity and form of the drug, on how much is ingested, and on what the user's expectations are about the drug's effects.

Most of the acute effects of cannabis intoxication are reversible, but, when marijuana is taken over long periods, abuse is likely to lead to dependence and to have a number of adverse effects on a person's bodily functioning and psychological stability. Nasal and respiratory problems, such as those encountered by tobacco smokers, can develop, including chronic sinus inflammation, bronchial constriction, breathing difficulty, and loss of lung capacity. After years of heavy marijuana use, as with all forms of smoking, the risk of cancer and cardiovascular disease

increases. Marijuana can also have negative effects on immunological and reproductive functioning. Men who use the drug regularly have a lower sperm count and are more likely to produce defective sperm, and women may experience delayed ovulation.

There is considerable controversy over the psychological effects of marijuana use. In the short term, it appears that marijuana can interfere with attentional processes and memory (Ilan, Smith, & Gevins, 2004). Researchers followed for an average of 20 years monozygotic twin pairs in which one twin had been a marijuana user and the co-twin had not used marijuana. The twins took a variety of neuropsychological tests, and there were virtually no cognitive differences between those who had used marijuana and those who had not (Lyons et al., 2004). However, the story becomes more complicated when factoring in the age of onset and the lifetime use of cannabis. Individuals who began using marijuana at an early age and continue to use it throughout their lives are more likely to experience cognitive deficits (Pope & Yurgelun-Todd, 2004).

Hallucinogens

Hallucinogens are drugs that cause abnormal perceptual experiences in the form of illusions or hallucinations, which are usually visual. Hallucinogen intoxication causes maladaptive behavioral and psychological changes, such as anxiety, depression, ideas of reference, the fear of losing one's mind, paranoid thinking, and generally impaired functioning. Also prominent are perceptual changes, such as the intensification of perceptions,

In MindMAP Segment 13.3, Bobbie tells how she started smoking at the age of 12 and soon thereafter moved on to alcohol and marijuana abuse. By the time she turned 15, abuse of these drugs had led to the use of cocaine, LSD, speed, and heroin.

Many substance abusers move from the abuse of legal substances such as nicotine and alcohol to illegal substances such as marijuana, cocaine, hallucinogens and heroin.

Mini Case

HALLUCINOGEN DEPENDENCE (LSD)

Candace is a 45-year-old artist who has used LSD for a number of years, because she feels that doing so enhances her paintings and makes them more visually exciting. Although she claims to know how much LSD she can handle, she is occasionally caught off guard and experiences disturbing side effects. She begins sweating, has blurred vision, is uncoordinated, and shakes all over. She commonly becomes paranoid and anxious, and she may act in strange ways, such as running out of her studio and into the street, ranting incoherently. On more than one occasion, she has been picked up by the police and taken to an emergency room, where she was given antipsychotic medication.

Diagnostic Features

During a 12-month period, people with hallucinogen dependence show at least three of the following:

- Tolerance
- Withdrawal
- Use of hallucinogens in larger amounts or over a longer period than intended
- Persistent desire or unsuccessful efforts to cut down or control hallucinogen use
- Extensive time devoted to activities involved in obtaining, using, or recovering from hallucinogen use
- A giving up of or reduction in important activities because of hallucinogen use
- Continued use despite knowledge of a hallucinogen-caused physical or psychological problem

feelings of depersonalization, hallucinations, and illusions. Physiological responses include dilation of the pupils, increased heart rate, sweating, heart palpitations, blurred vision, tremors, and uncoordination. For some individuals, the reaction is especially severe and may cause hallucinogen-induced disorders, including delirium, psychotic disorder, mood disorder, and anxiety disorder.

Hallucinogens come in a number of forms, both naturally occurring and synthetic. The most frequently used hallucinogens are lysergic acid diethylamide (LSD), psilocybin (found in hallucinogenic mushrooms), dimethyltryptamine (DMT), mescaline (peyote), dimethoxymethylamphetamine (DOM or STP, which stands for "serenity, tranquility, and peace"), methylene dioxymethamphetamine (MDMA), and phencyclidine (PCP).

LSD was discovered in a pharmaceutical laboratory in the late 1930s, when a scientist named Albert Hofmann was working with a fungus that was accidentally absorbed into his skin, causing him to have an hallucinogenic experience. A few days after this experience, he thought he would take a small amount to study the effects. This "small" amount was actually many times larger than what is now known to be a sufficient dose to trigger hallucinations, and Hofmann experienced intense and frightening effects. For example, he reported thinking that he was losing his mind, that he was outside his own body, and that time was standing still. Everything around him seemed distorted, and he became terrified of what he saw—experiences now known to be typical effects of LSD ingestion. As reports of this powerful drug spread through the scientific community, researchers wondered whether LSD could be used to understand the symptoms of schizophrenia, which the drug seemed to mimic. This gave rise to a new theory of schizophrenia, but researchers later determined that the LSD actions are quite different from those occurring in people with schizophrenia. Another

theory was that LSD could break down the individual's ego defenses and thus make psychotherapy more effective. This theory was also abandoned, however. In the 1960s, LSD became the central component of a nationwide drug "culture" started by two former Harvard professors, Timothy Leary and Richard Alpert (Alpert now calls himself Baba Ram Dass). Many of the "flower children" of the 1960s celebrated the effects of LSD in art, music, and theater.

LSD is an extremely potent drug. After ingesting LSD, which is usually taken orally, the user experiences hallucinogen intoxication with dizziness, weakness, and various physiological changes that lead to euphoria and hallucinations. This experience can last from 4 to 12 hours, with the "high" depending on such factors as the dose, the individual's expectations, the user's prior drug experiences, the setting, and the person's psychiatric history. During the period of LSD intoxication (or "trip"), individuals risk engaging in bizarre, and even dangerous, behaviors. They may injure themselves, have an accident, or attempt to "fly" from a high place, for example.

Other hallucinogens differ from LSD in various ways, although they all stimulate visual and sometimes auditory hallucinations. Psilocybin (hallucinogenic mushrooms), in low doses, also produces relaxation and feelings of euphoria. PCP, also called "angel dust," "rocket fuel," and "purple," has very unpredictable effects when smoked. In low doses, it acts as a depressant, and the user feels effects similar to alcohol intoxication. Larger doses cause distorted perceptions of the self and the environment, sometimes causing users to become aggressive and irrational, even violent. Unlike LSD, PCP can precipitate a temporary psychotic state, with symptoms that are virtually indistinguishable from those of schizophrenia. Through a combination of effects on the autonomic nervous system, PCP can also produce severely toxic, life-threatening effects, including coma, convulsions, and high blood pressure, progressing to severe brain damage with psychotic symptoms. Very disturbing cases have been reported of PCP users becoming so disoriented that they died as a result of accidental falls, drowning, or self-inflicted injuries.

Some people who use hallucinogens develop a condition called hallucinogen persisting perception disorder, in which they experience flashbacks or spontaneous hallucinations, delusions, or disturbances in mood similar to the changes that took place while they were intoxicated with the drug. Their perceptual experiences may include sights of geometric figures, flashes of color, halos around objects, and false perceptions of movement. Some people report that they can induce these experiences voluntarily, while others find that they occur spontaneously, possibly when they are stressed, are weary, are using another drug, or even entering a darkened room. These experiences can occur as long as 5 years after ingestion of the hallucinogen.

MDMA

MDMA—whose street name is Ecstasy and chemical name is 3,4-methylenedioxymethamphetamine—continues to be a problem drug, although use of this drug has decreased in recent years as a result of alarming effects reported in the media. Experts in the field of substance abuse have responded with considerable alarm to prevalent misconceptions about this drug and the increase in use among the many grade school and high-school youth who consider Ecstasy to be a harmless recreational substance that livens up parties. In addition to the easy availability of MDMA at raves and dance parties, young people have access to the drug in various social settings frequented by young adults, adolescents, and even children.

MDMA is an illegal synthetic drug that is manufactured in a capsule or tablet, and is most commonly ingested orally. The effects of the drug last 3 to 6 hours, depending on the dosage, with peak effects usually achieved within an hour. The sensations caused by the drug are variable and are influenced by the presence of other mind-altering agents commonly mixed with the MDMA.

MDMA is especially popular because of its appealing physical and psychological effects. Users refer to Ecstasy as the "hug drug" or "love drug" because it gives them a mellow glow and feelings of physical and emotional warmth; it also sparks a surge in energy that enables all-night dancing. The good feelings don't last very long, and the drug can provoke serious medical complications. Because MDMA causes bodily temperature to rise, often in an already heated environment, users can end up in the emergency room suffering hyperthermia and even convulsions. The consequences can be fatal due to the body's inability to thermally regulate itself (Kalant, 2001).

MDMA increases the activity levels of serotonin, dopamine, and norepinephrine and causes these substances to be released from their neuronal storage sites, resulting in increased brain activity. As you have read, serotonin plays a prominent role in the regulation of mood, sleep, pain, and appetite. The release of large amounts of serotonin causes a significant depletion of this neurotransmitter in the brain; it then takes some time for these neurotransmitters to be restored in the brain. When individuals take moderate to high doses of MDMA, serotonin depletion can be long-lasting and result in abnormal behavioral effects. Researchers have found that MDMA users have difficulty coding information into long-term memory, experience impaired verbal learning, have short-term memory deficits, are more easily distracted, and are less efficient at focusing attention on complex tasks (McCardle et al., 2004; Wareing, Fisk, Murphy, & Montgomery, 2004). Over time, heavy users of MDMA experience residual cognitive impairments which appear even when researchers control for such other factors as verbal intelligence, depression, and time since last use of the drug (Halpern et al., 2004).

Heroin and Opioids

Opioids are drugs that include naturally occurring substances and semisynthetic and synthetic drugs. Morphine and opium are naturally occurring opioids derived from the opium poppy. Semisynthetic opioids, such as heroin, are produced by slight chemical alterations in the basic poppy drug. Most heroin sold on the street is in the form of powder that is mixed, or "cut," with other drugs or other powdered substances. Although most users inject heroin directly into their bloodstream, increasingly users are sniffing or snorting the drug. There are also synthetic opioids, including methadone, codeine, and other manufactured drugs that have morphine-like effects. **Methadone** is prescribed to heroin-dependent individuals to help them get control over their addiction with a safer and more controlled reaction.

The fatal drug overdose of comedian Chris Farley at the height of his career renewed public awareness of the danger involved in using drugs such as heroin.

Mini Case

OPIOID DEPENDENCE (HEROIN)

Jimmy is a 38-year-old homeless man who has been addicted to heroin for the past 10 years. He began to use the drug at the suggestion of a friend who told him it would help relieve the pressure Jimmy was feeling from his unhappy marriage and financial problems. In a short period of time, he became dependent on the drug and got involved in a theft ring in order to support his habit. Ultimately, he lost his home and moved to a shelter, where he was assigned to a methadone treatment program.

Diagnostic Features
During a 12-month period, people with heroin dependence show at least three of the following:

- Tolerance

- Withdrawal

- Use of heroin in larger amounts or over a longer period than intended

- Persistent desire or unsuccessful efforts to cut down or control heroin use

- Extensive time devoted to activities involved in obtaining, using, or recovering from heroin use

- A giving up of or reduction in important activities because of heroin use

- Continued use despite knowledge of a heroin-caused physical or psychological problem

Codeine is a commonly prescribed painkiller and cough suppressant.

Some 3.7 million people in the United States used heroin at some time in their lives, and more than 119,000 people admitted to using heroin within the 30 days prior to the survey (SAMHSA, 2003). One of the most disturbing features of these statistics on heroin use is the fact that drug overdoses are common. Yet it is important to note that heroin and the combination of other drugs and/or impurities are primarily responsible for overdoses, especially when heroin is combined with cocaine. The number of fatalities associated with the use of heroin and other narcotics is startling. In some areas of the country, more people die from drug-related causes than from traffic accidents, a picture much different from what was seen a decade earlier. For example, in one recent year in the state of Massachusetts there were 574 deaths caused by narcotics, compared with 521 automobile fatalities; the number of narcotics-related deaths was six times what it had been only 15 years earlier (www.mass.gov/dph/bhsre/death/2003/report.pdf). The overdose rates due to multidrug use suggest that public health interventions might benefit from discussing the risks associated with the combinations of drugs. And furthermore, findings demonstrate that different drug combinations vary with racial/ethnic backgrounds, which emphasizes the understanding of multidrug use for risk reduction efforts in different populations (Coffin et al., 2003).

Following its injection or inhalation, heroin reaches the brain, where it is converted to morphine and binds to opioid receptors. Its effects are perceived by the user as a "rush," a feeling that varies according to the amount of drug taken in and the speed with which it binds to opioid receptors. Along with pleasurable feelings, however, the user also experiences a set of undesirable side effects, including warm flushing of the skin, dry mouth, a heavy feeling in the extremities, nausea, vomiting, and severe itching. Following these initial effects, there are residual psychological and physiological changes, including drowsiness, a clouding of cognitive functions, and a slowing of cardiac and respiratory functions, which can be fatal.

There are many undesirable long-term effects of heroin use, not the least of which is heroin dependence. People who suffer from heroin dependence compulsively seek the substance, as their life purpose becomes totally fixated on seeking and using the drug. In part, these behavioral effects result from changes in their brains, as their bodies adapt to the presence of the drug, and go through withdrawal if the drug supply is cut off. Withdrawal can occur anywhere from 6 to 24 hours after the last administration of heroin. The symptoms of withdrawal include restlessness, muscle and bone pain, insomnia, diarrhea, vomiting, cold flashes with goose bumps ("cold turkey"), and leg movements. These symptoms typically peak between 24 and 48 hours after the last dose and diminish after 7 days. However, for some people, withdrawal is a process that persists for many months. Oddly enough, addicted individuals may choose to go through withdrawal in an effort to reduce their tolerance for the drug, so that they can again experience the intense rush they feel when their bodies are exposed to it.

There are a number of additional long-term psychological and physical effects of heroin use. As with some of the other disorders discussed in this chapter, long-term heroin use can also induce other serious conditions, including delirium, psychotic disorder, mood disorder, sexual dysfunction, and sleep disorder. There are also serious physical effects, including scarred or collapsed veins, bacterial infections of blood vessels and heart valves, skin infections, and liver or kidney disease. The individual's poor health condition and heroin's negative effects on respiratory functioning can cause lung complications, including pneumonia and tuberculosis. In addition, the additives mixed into heroin include insoluble substances that can clog the major arteries in the body. Arthritis and other rheumatologic problems may occur as the result of immune reactions to these substances. Some of the most serious effects of heroin use come about as the result of sharing needles among heroin users. These effects include infections from hepatitis, HIV, and other viruses passed through the blood. The sexual partners and children of heroin users then become susceptible to these diseases (NIDA, 1997).

In recent years there has been a surge in the abuse of the prescription medications that have been diverted to illegal, nonmedical uses. Opioid pain relievers, in particular, have become popular substances among those who abuse drugs. Raising special concern among legal authorities as well as health professionals is OxyContin, which first appeared in federal drug abuse reports in 2001. Approximately 2.8 million adults or 1.2 percent of the population in the United States (SAMHSA, 2004) report having used OxyContin at some point in their lives. The problem is particularly pronounced among young people, with 5 percent of high-school seniors reporting that they have used OxyContin, a drug that is gaining a greater following than heroin or amphetamines (Johnston et al., 2005). Unlike other drugs we have discussed, OxyContin is a legitimately prescribed semisynthetic opioid medication for treating people with chronic pain. The medication's active ingredient, oxycodone, is found in other pain-killing medications, but OxyContin contains much higher levels, and in a time-release tablet. Because of the intense high that OxyContin causes, a high that is compared to the euphoria provided by heroin, it has become an exceptionally popular street drug.

OxyContin users either crush the tablet and ingest or snort it, or they may dilute it in water and inject it. An intense high is achieved when the drug is crushed and diluted, because the time-release action is disarmed. Although the cost of OxyContin is not exceptionally great when legitimately prescribed, the street value is exorbitant, thus causing this drug to be associated with criminal activity, as addicted individuals go to great lengths to get the drug. Some get caught up in a lifestyle in which they steal in order to pay for their expensive habit, and some begin dealing the drug in order to pay the expense of their own habit. The risks associated with OxyContin abuse are great. In addition to the psychological deterioration that commonly results from opioid abuse, those who abuse OxyContin put their lives in jeopardy, especially when they mix this drug with other substances, which is commonly done (Wolf, Lavezzi, Sullivan, & Flannagan, 2005).

Sedatives, Hypnotics, and Anxiolytics

Sedatives, hypnotics, and anxiolytics (antianxiety medications) include a wide range of substances that induce relaxation, sleep, tranquility, and reduced awareness of the environment. They are brain depressants. All have medical value and are manufactured by pharmaceutical companies; therefore, they are not illegal. However, because these drugs have high potential for abuse, much tighter federal controls have been placed on them since the 1970s. The term **sedative** refers to a drug that has a calming effect on the central nervous system, and the term **hypnotic** refers to sleep-inducing qualities. Anxiolytics are antianxiety agents that induce a calmer mental state in the user.

Intoxication resulting from the use of these drugs involves maladaptive behavioral or psychological changes, such as inappropriate sexual or aggressive behavior, unstable mood, impaired judgment, and generally impaired functioning. Other changes include symptoms such as slurred speech, incoordination, unsteady walking, impaired attention and memory, and stupor or possibly coma. Withdrawal symptoms may include trembling, insomnia, nausea, sweating, psychomotor agitation, anxiety, transient illusions or hallucinations, and possibly even grand-mal seizures. In severe cases, the use of this group of drugs can result in a range of induced disorders, such as mood, anxiety, sleep, and psychotic disorders.

Barbiturates Barbiturates are widely prescribed medications that serve important medical functions as anesthetics and anticonvulsants. They were also once widely used to induce sleep, although such prescriptions are now unusual, due to public awareness about the dangers of these drugs. People who use these substances recreationally are seeking a dulling of consciousness similar to the effects of alcohol use. In low doses, these drugs give the individual both a feeling of calm and sedation and a sense of increased outgoingness, talkativeness, and euphoria. In higher doses, barbiturates induce sleep.

Barbiturate users find that they quickly become tolerant to these drugs and need larger and larger doses to achieve the desired effects, not realizing the hazards of such abuse, such as the risk of respiratory failure. Many users increase the risk of death by combining these drugs with alcohol, which potentiates the effects of barbiturates.

The barbiturates most frequently abused are ones whose effects persist for several hours, including secobarbital (Seconal), pentobarbitol (Nembutal), amobarbital (Amytal), butabarbitol (Butisol), and combinations of these substances, amobarbital and tuinal. (The street names for these drugs are "blue heavens," "blue devils," "blue angels," "goofballs," and "rainbows.") The sedative effects of barbiturates are due to their action on the GABA and benzodiazepine receptors in the brain.

Barbiturate-Like Substances When the nonbarbiturate sedative-hypnotics were introduced in the 1970s, it was thought that they would be nonaddictive and safe substitutes for the barbiturates. They were originally intended to resolve some of the barbiturates' side effects, such as sleep disturbances and the feelings of morning-after "hangovers" (Schuckit, 1989). However, it was soon found that the nonbarbiturates have equally addicting effects. They have since been withdrawn from medical use because of their high abuse potential and because nonaddictive substitutes are now available.

One frequently used drug in the category of barbiturate-like substances is methaqualone, once marketed as Quaalude and popularly called "lude." Users of methaqualone report that the "high" they experience is more pleasant than that achieved from barbiturate use, because there is less of a "knock-out" effect. The feeling that users desire is total dissociation from their physical and mental selves, loss of inhibitions, and greater euphoria during sexual encounters. This last effect is an illusion, because in reality the user's sexual performance is impaired. Tolerance and dependence develop in ways similar to that for barbiturate use.

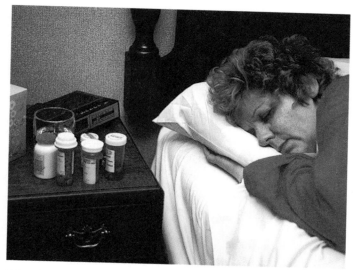

What begins as a seemingly harmless use of barbiturates to induce sleep can quickly become a serious problem of dependence and abuse.

Another group of nonbarbiturate medications, sold over the counter, are used to induce sleep. The most common brands are NyTol and Sominex. These are actually antihistamines, whose efficacy in inducing sleep is variable from person to person.

Anxiolytics The antianxiety medications include diazepam (Valium), clonazepam (Clonopin), chlordiazepoxide (Librium), flurazepam (Dalmane), and temazepam (Restoril). These medications are used specifically to treat anxiety, although they do have other medical uses. They are the most widely prescribed of all medicines. Only in recent years has the extent of the legal abuse of antianxiety medications become evident. At one time, prescriptions for these medications were open-ended; that is, physicians prescribed them without limits on the length of time they could be taken, in the belief that tolerance and dependence did not develop. We now know that these drugs have the potential for both responses. In the years since these problems were recognized, the federal government has placed tighter controls on these substances.

Abusers of antianxiety medications seek the sense of calm and relaxation that these substances produce; over time, some people increase their intake and become dependent. People who use them for more than a year usually have withdrawal symptoms when they stop. These symptoms include restlessness, irritability, insomnia, muscle tension, and occasionally other bodily sensations, such as weakness, visual problems, and various aches and pains. They may have troubling nightmares and become hypersensitive to light and sound.

Other Drugs of Abuse

So far in this chapter, we have discussed the more commonly used substances, but other substances cause serious psycho-logical problems for millions of people and are tremendously costly for society. For example, although people do not become intoxicated from smoking or chewing nicotine products, many are physiologically dependent on this substance. As the confirmed health risks of nicotine use become known, many people have tried to give up the habit, but they find themselves tormented by a craving for nicotine, as well as such symptoms as depression, insomnia, irritability, anxiety, restlessness, decreased heart rate, weight gain, and concentration difficulty.

In addition to nicotine, other legal and easily available products are associated with substance-related disorders. Inhalants have received increasing attention in recent years, because some people intentionally use such products as gasoline, glue, paint, and other chemical substances to create altered psychological states, such as euphoria. Deeply breathing the fumes from these substances, abusers develop maladaptive behavioral and psychological changes. Symptoms include dizziness, uncoordination, slurred speech, tremor, blurred vision, and stupor. Tolerance develops fairly quickly.

The use of anabolic steroids to enhance strength and musculature, particularly among athletes, has become an international concern that is generally brought to the attention of the public every time the Olympic games are held. However, steroid use has become more of a fact of life in the average U.S. high school. Nearly 3 percent of high-school seniors report having used those drugs at least once in their lives (Johnston, O'Malley, & Bachman, 2001). The most likely user is a teenage boy who wants to improve his appearance and sports performance. Using anabolic steroids along with engaging in intensive physical workouts does accelerate the growth of muscles, but at a great psychological and physical cost. Abusers tend to be irritable, aggressive, and moody, while their bodies develop a wide array of problems, ranging from kidney and liver diseases to deterioration of the reproductive system.

Another substance that people sometimes abuse is nitrous oxide, or laughing gas, which many dentists use to help patients relax in preparation for a dental procedure. This substance induces a state that is characterized by feelings of lightheadedness and a sensation of floating that lasts for a few minutes. Although extensive research has not been conducted on the consequences of nitrous oxide use, there is concern about the abuse of nitrite inhalants (aerosols and anesthetics), more commonly known as "poppers." These inhalants create a mild euphoria, a change in the perception of time, feelings of relaxation, and intensification of sexual feelings. They are considered dangerous, however, because they are thought to irritate the respiratory system and impair immune functioning.

By this point in the chapter, you have probably come to realize that there is no end to the list of substances that people are likely to use in their efforts to alter consciousness. The *DSM-IV-TR* even includes catnip as a substance to which some individuals turn in their efforts to produce experiences that are likened to intoxication with marijuana or LSD. For an overview of commonly abused drugs, see Table 13.5 on page 420.

TABLE 13.5 Commonly Abused Drugs

Substance: Category and Name	Examples of Commercial and Street Names	DEA Schedule/ How Administered	Intoxication Effects/Potential Health Consequences
Cannabinoids			Euphoria, slowed thinking and reaction time, confusion, impaired balance and coordination/cough, frequent respiratory infections; impaired memory and learning; increased heart rate, anxiety; panic attacks; tolerance, addiction
Hashish	Boom, chronic, gangster, hash, hash oil, hemp	I/swallowed, smoked	
Marijuana	Blunt, dope, ganja, grass, herb, joints, Mary Jane, pot, reefer, sinsemilla, skunk, weed	I/swallowed, smoked	
Depressants			Reduced anxiety; feeling of well-being; lowered inhibitions; slowed pulse and breathing; lowered blood pressure; poor concentration/fatigue; confusion; impaired coordination, memory, judgment; addiction; respiratory depression and arrest, death
Barbiturates	Amytal, Nembutal, Seconal, Phenobarbital; barbs, reds, red birds, phennies, tooies, yellows, yellow jackets	II, III, V/injected, swallowed	Sedation, drowsiness/depression, unusual excitement, fever, irritability, poor judgment, slurred speech, dizziness, life-threatening withdrawal
Benzodiazepines (other than flunitrazepam)	Ativan, Halcion, Librium, Valium, Xanax; candy, downers, sleeping pills, tranks	IV/swallowed, injected	Sedation, drowsiness/dizziness
Flunitrazepam	Rohypnol; forget-me pill, Mexican Valium, R2, Roche, roofies, roofinol, rope, rophies	IV/swallowed, snorted	Visual and gastrointestinal disturbances, urinary retention, memory loss for the time under the drug's effects
GHB	Gamma-hydroxybutyrate; G, Georgia home boy, grievous bodily harm, liquid ecstasy	I/swallowed	Drowsiness, nausea/vomiting, headache, loss of consciousness, loss of reflexes, seizures, coma, death
Methaqualone	Quaalude, Sopor, Parest; ludes, mandrex, quad, quay	I/injected, swallowed	Euphoria/depression, poor reflexes, slurred speech, coma
Dissociative Anesthetics			Increased heart rate and blood pressure, impaired motor function/memory loss; numbness; nausea/vomiting
Ketamine	Ketalar SV; cat Valiums, K, Special K, vitamin K	III/injected, snorted, smoked	At high doses, delirium, depression, respiratory depression and arrest
PCP and analogs	Phencyclidine; angel dust, boat, hog, love boat, peace pill	I, II/injected, swallowed, smoked	Possible decrease in blood pressure and heart rate, panic, aggression, violence/loss of appetite, depression

TABLE 13.5 Commonly Abused Drugs *(continued)*

Substance: Category and Name	Examples of Commercial and Street Names	DEA Schedule/ How Administered	Intoxication Effects/Potential Health Consequences
Hallucinogens			Altered states of perception and feeling; nausea; persisting perception disorder (flashbacks)
LSD	lysergic acid diethylamide; acid, blotter, boomers, cubes, microdot, yellow sunshines	I/swallowed, absorbed through mouth tissues	LSD and mescaline—increased body temperature, heart rate, blood pressure; loss of appetite, sleeplessness, numbness, weakness, tremors
Mescaline	buttons, cactus, mesc, peyote	I/swallowed, smoked	For LSD—persistent mental disorders
Psilocybin	magic mushroom, purple passion, shrooms	I/swallowed	Nervousness, paranoia
Opioids and Morphine Derivatives			Pain relief, euphoria, drowsiness/nausea, constipation, confusion, sedation, respiratory depression and arrest, tolerance, addiction, unconsciousness, coma, death
Codeine	Empirin with Codeine, Fiorinal with Codeine, Robitussin A-C, Tylenol with Codeine; Captain Cody, Cody, schoolboy; (with glutethimide) doors & fours, loads, pancakes and syrup	II, III, IV/injected, swallowed	Less analgesia, sedation, and respiratory depression than morphine
Fentanyl and fentanyl analogs	Actiq, Duragesic, Sublimaze; Apache, China girl, China white, dance fever, friend, goodfella, jackpot, murder 8, TNT, Tango and Cash	I, II/injected, smoked, snorted	
Heroin	Diacetylmorphine; brown sugar, dope, H, horse, junk, skag, skunk, smack, white horse	I/injected, smoked, snorted	Staggering gait
Morphine	Roxanol, Duramorph; M, Miss Emma, monkey, white stuff	II, III/injected, swallowed, smoked	
Opium	Laudanum, paregoric; big O, black stuff, block, gum, hop	II, III, V/swallowed, smoked	
Oxycodone HCL	OxyContin; Oxy, O.C., killer	II/swallowed, snorted, injected	
Hydrocodone bitartrate, acetaminophen	Vicodin; vike, Watson-387	II/swallowed	
Stimulants			Increased heart rate, blood pressure, metabolism; feelings of exhilaration, energy, increased mental alertness/rapid or irregular heart beat; reduced appetite, weight loss, heart failure, nervousness, insomnia

(continued)

TABLE 13.5 Commonly Abused Drugs (continued)

Substance: Category and Name	Examples of Commercial and Street Names	DEA Schedule/ How Administered	Intoxication Effects/Potential Health Consequences
Amphetamine	Biphetamine, Dexedrine; bennies, black beauties, crosses, hearts, LA turnaround, speed, truck drivers, uppers	II/injected, swallowed, smoked, snorted	Also, for amphetamine—rapid breathing/ tremor, loss of coordination; irritability, anxiousness, restlessness, delirium, panic, paranoia, impulsive behavior, aggressiveness, tolerance, addiction, psychosis
Cocaine	Cocaine hydrochloride; blow, bump, C, candy, Charlie, coke, crack, flake, rock, snow, toot	II/injected, smoked, snorted	Increased temperature/chest pain, respiratory failure, nausea, abdominal pain, strokes, seizures, headaches, malnutrition, panic attacks
MDMA (methylenedioxy-methamphetamine)	Adam, clarity, ecstasy, Eve, lover's speed, peace, STP, X, XTC	I/swallowed	Mild hallucinogenic effects, increased tactile sensitivity, empathic feelings/impaired memory and learning, hyperthermia, cardiac toxicity, renal failure, liver toxicity
Methamphetamine	Desoxyn; chalk, crank, crystal, fire, glass, go fast, ice, meth, speed	II/injected, swallowed, smoked, snorted	
Methylphenidate (safe and effective for treatment of ADHD)	Ritalin; JIF, MPH, R-ball, Skippy, the smart drug, vitamin R	II/injected, swallowed, snorted	
Nicotine	Cigarettes, cigars, smokeless tobacco, snuff, spit tobacco, bidis, chew	Not scheduled/smoked, snorted, taken in snuff and spit tobacco	Aggression, violence, psychotic behavior/ memory loss, cardiac and neurological damage; impaired memory and learning, tolerance, addiction
			Additional effects attributable to tobacco exposure, adverse pregnancy outcomes, chronic lung disease, cardiovascular disease, stroke, cancer, tolerance, addiction
Other Compounds			
Anabolic steroids	Anadrol, Oxandrin, Durabolin, Depo-Testosterone, Equipoise; roids, juice	III/injected, swallowed, applied to skin	No intoxication effects/hypertension, blood clotting and cholesterol changes, liver cysts and cancer, kidney cancer, hostility and aggression, acne; in adolescents, premature stoppage of growth; in males, prostate cancer, reduced sperm production, shrunken testicles, breast enlargement; in females, menstrual irregularities, development of beard and other masculine characteristics

Source: http://www.nida.nih.gov/DrugPages/DrugsofAbuse.html

Treatment for Substance Abuse and Dependence

As the high cost of drug dependence to society and individuals became more and more apparent in the 1980s and 1990s, researchers searched for effective treatment methods. The Drug Abuse Treatment Outcome Study (DATOS) was conducted from 1995 to 2003 to evaluate the effectiveness of four common drug

treatment approaches (http://www.datos.org/). Researchers followed more than 10,000 patients in almost 100 programs in 11 cities over a 3-year period. In contrast to the more generally discouraging estimates of drug treatment effectiveness available prior to this study, evidence has been accumulating from DATOS that some of the more commonly used methods can have very positive outcomes.

The four major categories of drug treatment studied by DATOS included outpatient methadone programs, long-term residential programs, outpatient drug-free programs, and short-term inpatient programs. In outpatient methadone programs, clients are given methadone to reduce cravings for heroin and block its effects. They also receive counseling and vocational skills development to help them rebuild their lives. In long-term residential programs, clients are given continual drug-free treatment in a residential community they share with counselors and fellow recovering addicts (sometimes called a therapeutic community). In outpatient drug-free programs, a wide range of psychosocial approaches are used, including 12-step programs. Finally, in short-term inpatient programs, clients are stabilized medically and then are encouraged to remain abstinent through taking steps to change their lifestyle.

The methods used in these treatment formats rely on one or more components of biological treatment combined with psychotherapy and efforts to provide clients with social supports and improvements in their occupational and family functioning.

Biological Treatment

In biological treatments, clients are given substances that block or reduce the craving for drugs. One of the oldest forms of treatment for heroin dependence is the provision of methadone which, as we described earlier, is a synthetic opioid. Methadone blocks the effects of heroin and eliminates withdrawal symptoms. When correctly prescribed, methadone is neither intoxicating nor sedating, and it does not interfere with everyday activities. The symptoms of withdrawal are suppressed for 1 to 3 days, and the craving associated with heroin dependence is relieved. Furthermore, should the individual take heroin when on methadone treatment, the "rush" is greatly reduced. Although methadone can be taken safely for 10 years or longer, ideally, this form of treatment is combined with behavioral therapy or supportive treatment. A side benefit of methadone treatment is a reduction in illnesses associated with heroin use. Unfortunately, individuals taking methadone become physically dependent on it and cannot easily discontinue use.

Another pharmaceutical approach involves the provision of LAAM (levo-alpha-acetyl-methadol), which, like methadone, is a synthetic opioid that can be used to treat heroin addiction. However, LAAM has longer-lasting effect, and needs to be administered only three times per week, rather than daily. Naltrexone is another medication used in treating heroin dependence; rather than simply reducing craving, it actually blocks the effects of opioids. A person taking naltrexone cannot experience the pleasurable effects of heroin and, therefore, would be less likely to seek it. Because naltrexone does not reduce craving, alternative medications have been developed that serve that important function. Buprenorphine alone (Subutex) or in combination with the opiate agonist naloxone (Suboxone) has become a very popular medication for treating opioid-dependent individuals. The buprenorphine medications are especially appealing because they can be prescribed in an outpatient setting, thus providing a take-home treatment for opioid dependence that is regarded as safe and effective (Fudala et al., 2003). This medication is similar to methadone, but it has a far lower potential of inducing physical dependence. An individual can discontinue buprenorphine without experiencing the withdrawal symptoms associated with methadone discontinuation.

Nonmedical Therapies

Several of the interventions we discussed earlier in the chapter in our discussion of alcoholism also apply when treating individuals who are dependent on other substances. For example, Narcotics Anonymous (NA), like Alcoholics Anonymous, is a nonprofit fellowship for individuals for whom drugs have become a major problem. In the 12 steps of NA, the word "addiction" is used instead of the word "alcohol," and the recovery process includes admitting that there is a problem, seeking help, engaging in a thorough self-examination, engaging in confidential self-disclosure, making amends for harm done, and helping other drug addicts who want to recover. Central to the NA program is an emphasis on practicing spiritual principles (www.na.org).

Traditional psychotherapeutic methods also play an important role in recovery for many people with substance-related disorders. For some people, inpatient care is necessary at least for a brief duration while they proceed through a process of detoxification; during a period lasting from a few weeks to several months of residential care, some individuals stabilize physically and psychologically by participating in a multimodal program.

For many people, outpatient treatment helps them attain their goals, although many psychotherapists strongly recommend that recovering clients also participate in a 12-step program in which they have access to ongoing support on a regular and consistent basis. Behavioral and cognitive techniques are often incorporated in the psychotherapeutic treatment. One of these is contingency management, in which the client earns "points" for producing negative drug tests. These points can then be traded for desired items or participation in activities. Cognitive-behavioral therapy involves providing clients with interventions that modify their thoughts, expectancies, and behaviors associated with drug use. This treatment can also include training in coping strategies. Relapse prevention strategies similar to those in alcohol treatment programs can also be used.

Many experts recommend combining psychological treatment with biological interventions. Psychosocial services, such as vocational counseling, psychotherapy, and family therapy, are important adjuncts to increase the effectiveness of medical interventions. In addition to the method of intervention itself, however, a major factor predicting the success of treatment is the client's motivation to remain in treatment.

Substance Abuse and Dependence: The Biopsychosocial Perspective

The biopsychosocial model is extremely useful for understanding substance dependence and approaches to treatment. Scientists have made remarkable leaps in the past decade in understanding how people come to abuse substances, as well as the most effective interventions for treating those with substance problems. Unfortunately, treatment programs for people with substance problems have encountered serious obstacles in recent years. The National Institute of Drug Abuse reports that, during the 1990s, there was a drop in services provided to substance-dependent individuals. Managed care has played a role in this process, reducing the number of covered days in treatment from 28 to 14 or fewer—far less time than the 3 months that researchers recommended as the minimum. Most people in short-term inpatient programs report that they feel they are not getting the psychological support they need (NIDA, 1997).

In the years ahead, society will continue to deal with the tremendous costs of substance abuse. The emotional havoc experienced by millions of people who have suffered privately with addictions will continue to expand from within the person to the social contexts in which Americans work and live. Dramatic social initiatives will be needed to respond to the powerful biological, psychological, and sociocultural forces involved in the development and maintenance of abuse and dependence.

Case Report

Carl Wadsworth

RETURN TO THE CASE

Carl's History

After meeting with Carl for an initial intake session, I asked him to return 2 days later, so that I could take some additional history. When Carl returned for our second meeting, he seemed relieved and said that acknowledging the fact that he had a problem was tremendously comforting to him. I explained to Carl that I wanted to get a clearer picture of his life history, and he proceeded to tell the story that would later help me understand how he had gotten to this point of desperation.

An only child, Carl grew up in a small Midwestern town, where his father was a well-loved and respected "family doctor." Carl's father had himself been the son of a physician, and Carl's parents generally assumed throughout his childhood that he would carry on the family tradition. This meant that Carl had to devote himself entirely to his schoolwork, because math and science did not come easily to him. In college, he became desperate about his studies and repeatedly sought help from his classmates. After he entered medical school, this pattern of dependence

continued, and he found one or two older students to help him through his exams, lab work, and hospital duties because they felt sorry for him. Even though Carl felt guilty about his reliance on others, he contended that it was necessary, because his parents would be crushed if he failed. In his third year of medical school, Carl met Anne, a nurse at the medical school, and they married after a few months of dating. Shortly after their marriage, Anne became pregnant, and they mutually agreed that she would stay home and care for their baby after the birth.

Assessment

The only psychological test I administered to Carl was the MMPI-2. The diagnostic picture seemed fairly clear to me, but I usually find it helpful to have the quantitative data that the MMPI-2 provides to formulate my treatment recommendations. Carl's profile was that of a man struggling with dependency issues and having a propensity for acting out, particularly when confronted with difficult or demanding situations. I was not surprised to see that Carl

scored very high on indicators of addiction proneness.

Diagnosis

Carl's Axis I diagnosis was clear. Carl was using large amounts of cocaine, he had begun to undermine successful life pursuits in his attempt to satisfy his cravings, cocaine use was interfering with his work and family life, and he had become more and more withdrawn from others as he compulsively pursued satisfaction for his cravings. As apparent as the diagnosis of cocaine dependence was, this single diagnostic label could not tell the whole story. It was apparent to me that Carl also had a personality disorder, a style of functioning that led him to define himself according to the wishes of his parents and to deal with difficult problems by becoming pathologically dependent on others.

Axis I:	Cocaine Dependence
Axis II:	Dependent Personality Disorder
Axis III:	Deferred
Axis IV:	Problems with primary support group (marital tensions) Occupational problems

Axis V: Current Global Assessment of Functioning: 50.
Serious impairment.
Highest Global Assess-
ment of Functioning
(past year): 70

Case Formulation

What would lead a young man to risk such a promising career and potentially happy family life just to get high on cocaine? Obviously, there is no simple explanation for why Carl could have become so compulsively involved in a world of drugs. Looking back to Carl's youth, I saw a boy growing up in a family in which intense pressure to become a doctor not only determined his career choice but also set the stage for him to become reliant on others to reach his goal. It was as if Carl had absorbed a message from his father that a medical career was the only acceptable option and that his failure to achieve such a goal would result in rejection. Desperate to avoid this, Carl resorted to any means necessary to succeed, rationalizing that his dependence on others was necessary for the good of other people. As the pressures of medical training mounted and his own feelings of inadequacy grew, Carl sought out someone on whom to rely. His marriage to Anne probably was more of an expression of his need for a caretaker than an expression of love and mutuality. As time went by, Anne could not save Carl from his own feelings of low self-esteem, so he felt compelled to find something that would make him feel better about himself. Unfortunately, that something was cocaine, an insidious substance that would delude Carl into believing that he was happy, competent, and successful.

Treatment Plan

Carl Wadsworth had both immediate and long-term treatment needs. First and foremost, his cocaine dependence required aggressive intervention. I knew that Carl would not receive my recommendation enthusiastically, but I felt that a 4-week inpatient stay would be necessary in order for him to receive the multidisciplinary attention that a severe substance-abuse problem requires. The long-term plan would involve intensive psychotherapy, probably lasting at least a year following his discharge from the substance-abuse treatment program. As I expected, Carl raised a number of concerns about the interruption of his medical training, the disruption of his family life, and one other concern that was at the heart of his objections—what would other people think? In response, I impressed on Carl the seriousness and urgency of his problem. I also convinced him that this was a good time for him to begin to work on being more honest with other people. Initially, Carl took offense at this observation, but he soon began to see my point. Furthermore, I pointed out to Carl that he needed to come to grips with the issues in his life that had led him to become involved in using drugs, and he needed to develop autonomy and an improved sense of self-esteem. Perhaps he could begin to set his own goals in life; perhaps he could tap his own inner resources to achieve those goals; and perhaps he could develop new cognitive strategies that would result in his feeling better about himself. All this would require intensive confrontational psychotherapy.

Outcome of the Case

Carl did follow through on my recommendations, although initially it seemed to me that his compliance was dictated by a fear of being expelled from residency training. On entering the treatment center, Carl was not completely prepared for the rigor and vigilance shown by the staff in preventing the patients from gaining access to drugs. He made unsuccessful attempts to obtain cocaine, and other patients and staff harshly confronted this behavior. The harshness of the confrontation apparently awakened Carl to the depth of his problem; this proved to be a major turning point in Carl's recovery.

By the time of his discharge, Carl had shown a good deal of psychological growth and was prepared to move to the next step of treatment; intensive psychotherapy. Carl was referred to a psychologist who specializes in treating professionals with substance-abuse problems. A part of Carl's treatment involved participation in weekly meetings of a local group of physicians who had similar problems with substance abuse. The changes in Carl over the course of a year were dramatic. By the time his second child was born, Carl's priorities had evolved to a point at which he was able to recognize how central his wife and children were in his life. At work, he consciously devoted his efforts to resuming a bedside manner with his patients. Carl began to think in more constructive ways, looking for solutions to life's problems, rather than escape, and feeling that he had the personal competence to work toward these solutions.

As I recall the case of Carl Wadsworth, I think of a man who was on the verge of self-destruction. Had he not encountered an understanding supervisor who responded to his crisis with firm insistence that he get help, I fear that Carl's fate would have been tragic.

Sarah Tobin, PhD

SUMMARY

- A substance is a chemical that alters a person's mood or behavior when smoked, injected, drunk, inhaled, or swallowed in pill form. Substance intoxication is the temporary maladaptive experience of behavioral or psychological changes that are due to the accumulation of a substance in the body. When some substances are discontinued, people may experience symptoms of substance withdrawal that involve a set of physical and psychological disturbances. To counteract withdrawal symptoms, people are inclined to use more of the substance, causing them to develop tolerance. Substance abuse is a maladaptive pattern of substance use that leads to significant impairment or distress.

- Approximately one in seven Americans has a history of alcohol abuse or dependence. The short-term effects of alcohol use are appealing to many people because of the sedating qualities of this substance, although side effects, such as hangovers, are distressing. The long-term effects of heavy use are worrisome and involve serious harm to many organs of the body, possibly resulting in medical problems and dementia. Researchers in the field of alcohol dependence were among the first to propose the biopsychosocial model to explain the development of a psychological disorder. In the realm of biological contributors, researchers have focused on the role of genetics in light of the fact that dependence runs in families. This line of research has focused on markers and genetic mapping. Psychological theories focus on concepts derived from behavioral theory, as well as cognitive-behavioral and social learning perspectives. For example, according to the widely accepted expectancy model, people with alcohol dependence develop problematic beliefs about alcohol early in life through reinforcement and observational learning. Researchers and theorists working within the sociocultural perspective regard stressors within the family, community, and culture as factors that lead the person to develop alcohol dependence.

- Treatment for alcohol problems may be derived in varying degrees from each of three perspectives. In biological terms, medications may be used to control symptoms of withdrawal, to control symptoms associated with co-existing conditions, or to provoke nausea following alcohol ingestion. Various psychological interventions are used, some of which are based on behavioral

and cognitive-behavioral techniques. Alcoholics Anonymous is a 12-step recovery program built on the premise that alcoholism is a disease.

- Stimulants have an activating effect on the nervous system. Amphetamines in moderate amounts cause euphoria, increased confidence, talkativeness, and energy. In higher doses, the user has more intense reactions and, over time, can become addicted and develop psychotic symptoms. Cocaine users experience stimulating effects for a shorter period of time that are nevertheless quite intense. In moderate doses, cocaine leads to euphoria, sexual excitement, potency, energy, and talkativeness. At higher doses, psychotic symptoms may develop. In addition to the disturbing psychological symptoms, serious medical problems can arise from the use of cocaine. Although not typically regarded as an abused substance, high levels of caffeine can cause a number of psychological and physical problems. Cannabis, or marijuana, causes altered perception and bodily sensations, as well as maladaptive behavioral and psychological reactions. Most of the acute effects of cannabis intoxication are reversible, but a long period of abuse is likely to lead to dependence and to have adverse psychological and physical effects. Hallucinogens cause abnormal perceptual experiences in the form of illusions and hallucinations. Opioids include naturally occurring substances (e.g., morphine and opium) as well as semisynthetic (e.g., heroin) and synthetic (e.g., methadone) drugs. Opioid users experience a rush, involving a range of psychological reactions as well as intense bodily sensations, some of which reflect life-threatening symptoms, particularly during episodes of withdrawal. Sedatives, hypnotics, and anxiolytics are substances that induce relaxation, sleep, tranquility, and reduced awareness.

- Various treatment programs for people with substance-related disorders have emerged within the biopsychosocial perspective. Biological treatment may involve the prescription of substances that block or reduce craving. Behavioral treatment involves such techniques as contingency management, while cognitive behavioral techniques are used to help clients modify their thoughts, expectancies, and behaviors associated with drug use.

KEY TERMS

See Glossary for definitions

Abstinence violation effect   402
Alcohol dehydrogenase (ADH)   400
Aldehyde dehydrogenase
  (ALDH)   404
Crack cocaine   410
Delirium tremens   403
Depressant   398
Disulfiram   404

Expectancy model   401
Hallucinogens   414
Hypnotic   418
Korsakoff's syndrome   400
Methadone   416
Potentiation   398
Relapse prevention therapy   404
Sedative   418

Stimulant   409
Substance   394
Substance abuse   395
Substance dependence   396
Substance intoxication   395
Substance withdrawal   395
Tolerance   395
Wernicke's encephalopathy   400

 INTERNET RESOURCE

To get more information on the material covered in this chapter, visit our website at **www.mhhe.com/halgin5.** There you will find more information, resources, and links to topics of interest.

CHAPTER 14

Eating Disorders and Impulse-Control Disorders

Stories such as the one of 19-year-old Rosa had become all too familiar at the clinic, with the spreading epidemic of eating disorders among girls and young women. It was not Rosa who first contacted me, nor was it one of her family members. Rather, Rosa's varsity tennis coach, Joannie Lyons, called me that October morning to speak to me about one of her freshman players, who seemed to be "withering away."

Coach Lyons acknowledged that she didn't really know that much about Rosa, because of Rosa's preference for remaining very private about her life. What she did know was what she had observed during the 5 weeks Rosa had been on campus, participating on the tennis team. In that brief period of time, Rosa had lost nearly 20 pounds and was now down to a weight of 87 pounds. Coach Lyons explained to me that, when she expressed her concern about the weight loss in mid-September, Rosa downplayed the issue by saying that she had been having some problems adjusting to the campus food.

Two weeks later, Rosa's weight continued to dwindle. When Coach Lyons once again asked about her weight loss, Rosa minimized the issue and insisted that she was just trying to lose a few more pounds, so that she would look better in her tennis uniform. The coach didn't buy this story but confronted Rosa with a stern statement of alarm. She went a step further and suspended Rosa from the team until she had undergone a complete physical examination. This brought the problem to a crisis point for Rosa, which led to a tearful admission that she had been starving herself and forcing herself to exercise several extra hours each day. When she did eat, she occasionally induced vomiting. After I heard this disturbing story, I urged Coach Lyons to have Rosa contact me immediately.

Several days went by before I received Rosa's voice-mail message. As I listened to her faint voice, I found it difficult to understand what she was saying. After listening three times, I was able to discern the words "Coach Lyons suspended me, but it's not my fault. She wants me to see you soon." I didn't feel particularly comforted by what seemed like Rosa's ambivalent attitude about obtaining help. Having dealt with numerous eating-disordered clients in the past, I was prepared for a struggle, and that is initially what I encountered.

When Rosa came in for her first appointment, I was taken by the fact that she was dressed in baggy pants and an oversized sweatshirt, which concealed her bodily profile. Her face seemed gaunt, but not dramatically different from what I've seen among contemporary college women. It was clear to me that the task of getting things going would rest on my shoulders, since Rosa volunteered very little. In response to my questioning about her eating, Rosa initially responded with irritation in her voice. She claimed that she had "merely been trying to lose a few pounds," because she hated looking "overweight." She claimed that she was trying to shed all her "baby fat," so that she would "feel better" about herself. The thought of going back to being a "117-pound hippo" was terrifying, and she was prepared to do everything she could to stay slim. With a challenging look and tone of voice, she asked, "Is there really anything wrong with wanting to be attractive? What's the big deal?" When I asked her about her admitting a problem to Coach Lyons, she downplayed the interaction, claiming that she was simply trying to get the coach off her back.

I wasn't sure how to respond to Rosa in light of the depth of her denial and the rigidity of her resistance to accepting professional help. I chose to refrain from a confrontation with Rosa; instead, I asked if I might review the medical report of her physical examination. Reluctantly, she handed me Dr. Kennedy's report, which I reviewed quickly. Although I was inclined to react strongly about the dramatic contents of the report, I remained calm and asked Rosa what she thought about Dr. Kennedy's recommendation that, if she were to lose another 5 pounds, medical hospitalization would be necessary. For nearly a minute, Rosa stared at me. In the silence of that minute, much was communicated. The quiet was punctuated by tears that began to flow down Rosa's face, accompanied by the strained words "I'm scared."

Once the barrier of Rosa's resistance had been penetrated, she was prepared to tell me her story. We spent another 2 hours together that afternoon, during which Rosa told me about the emotional battle that had been going on in her thoughts and the havoc that had been taking place in her body. Apparently, in the months prior to coming to college, Rosa's anxiety had escalated to such a point that she was worrying each day. Although many athletic scholarship offers came her way, she also felt an inner pressure that began to frighten her. She explained that choosing a college was extremely difficult for her. Throughout her senior year, she had been told that she was a "star." What seemed so flattering at first came to feel distressing and worrisome. Would she be able to live up to the high expectations of others?

As the start of college came close, Rosa began to "worry about everything." She feared that she would struggle with academic demands as well as athletic pressures. Over the course of those months, she also began to see her body in distorted ways. Rather than seeing the muscular development of a premier athlete, she saw bulges that she equated with obesity. Distorted thoughts about her competence became intertwined with distorted images of her body.

Following this intense 2-hour session, my initial doubts about Rosa's receptivity to psychotherapy faded. I came to realize that Rosa was opening the door to her emotions, and it was important for me to take advantage of this special opportunity to help Rosa get her life back on track.

Sarah Tobin, PhD

The story of Rosa Nomirez is disturbing and provocative. Why would a young woman with so much going for her place her physical health in such jeopardy? What thoughts might have been going through the mind of this talented athlete that resulted in such gross distortions about herself? How did things reach such a dangerous point that, on a daily basis, she found herself unable to control a condition that was overtaking her mind and body? In this chapter, we will cover various conditions that involve a loss of self-control. In the first section, we will discuss conditions in which the loss of control results in disorders characterized by conflicts about food, eating, exercise, and body image. In the second section of the chapter, we will discuss the conditions in which the loss of control is experienced in a variety of other ways, all of which are characterized by behaviors that are in response to seemingly irresistible impulses. Let's turn our attention first to eating disorders.

Eating Disorders

The psychological meaning of food extends far beyond its nutritive powers. It is common for people to devote many hours and much effort to choosing, preparing, and serving food. In addition to physical dependence on food, humans have strong emotional associations with food. Hungry people feel irritable and unhappy; by contrast, a good meal can cause people to feel contented and nurtured.

For some people, food takes on inordinate significance, and they find themselves enslaved to bizarre and unhealthy rituals that revolve around the process of eating. People with eating disorders struggle to control their disturbed attitudes and behaviors regarding food, and, to the distress of those who are close to them, many put their lives at risk. We will look at two disorders associated with eating: anorexia nervosa and bulimia nervosa. Although they are distinct disorders, they have important similarities. Consequently, we will combine our discussion of the theories and treatment of these disorders.

Characteristics of Anorexia Nervosa

Many people in Western society diet to lose weight at some point in their lives. However, people with the eating disorder anorexia nervosa carry this to an extreme. They develop an intense fear of becoming fat that leads them to diet to the point of emaciation.

Four symptoms characterize anorexia nervosa. First, people with **anorexia nervosa** refuse or are unable to maintain normal

MindMAP Segment 14.1: Perception of Body Shape

weight, defined as weight less than 85 percent of that expected for a person of that height and body frame. Second, people with anorexia nervosa have an intense fear of gaining weight or becoming fat, even if they are grossly underweight. Third, they have a distorted perception of the weight or shape of their body, possibly denying the seriousness of abnormally low body weight. Fourth, postpubescent females with anorexia nervosa experience amenorrhea, the absence of at least three consecutive menstrual cycles.

The Eating Attitudes Test (Garner, Olmsted, & Bohr, 1982), shown in Table 14.1, provides a measure of preoccupation with dieting and food, bulimic behaviors, and the ability to control eating. This instrument has been used in numerous studies across a variety of cultures to understand the correlates of disordered eating as well as to identify individuals with eating disorder symptoms for further study.

Some anorexic individuals (restricting type) engage in various behaviors geared toward weight loss, such as abusing laxatives or diet pills and becoming compulsive exercisers. Others (binge eating/purging type) overeat and then force themselves to **purge,** or rid themselves of whatever they have just eaten. The starvation associated with anorexia nervosa causes a number of physical abnormalities, such as menstrual disturbance, dry and cracking skin, slowed heartbeat, reduced gastrointestinal activity, and muscular weakness. As the self-starvation continues, the bodily signs of physical disturbance become more evident. For example, some people with this disorder begin to grow fine, downy hair on the trunk of the body, and for some a yellowing of the skin occurs. Those who induce vomiting commonly experience abnormalities of the salivary glands, dental enamel erosion, and scarring of hand skin from contact with teeth. The extreme results of self-starvation are catastrophic and include anemia, impaired kidney functioning, heart problems, and bone deterioration. Death is alarmingly common; in one carefully conducted follow-up study spanning a 35-year period, the mortality estimate was 4.4 percent (Millar et al., 2005). Although the majority of deaths from anorexia nervosa occur in young adults, a Norwegian study of anorexia nervosa–related deaths found that a substantial portion, perhaps as high as 40 percent, occurred in people 65 years and older (Reas et al., 2005). Approximately 15 percent of women with an eating disorder attempt suicide (Franko et al., 2004).

The word *anorexia* literally means "without appetite," a somewhat misleading term in light of the fact that loss of appetite is not the key feature of this disorder, at least not initially. On the contrary, people with this disorder are very interested in eating and having normal appetites, although they have difficulty reading their hunger cues. Some anorexic individuals go to great lengths to prepare high-calorie meals and baked goods for other people, taking great delight in handling the food as they prepare it. Others develop compulsive rituals involving food. For example, they may hide food around the house, eat meals in a ritualistic fashion, and take many hours to eat a small portion of food. Aware of how unusual such behaviors will seem to others, they go to extremes to conceal their eccentric eating habits.

TABLE 14.1 Eating Attitudes Test—Eating Disorder

The Eating Attitudes Test (EAT-26) was the screening instrument used in the 1998 National Eating Disorders Screening program. The EAT-26 is probably the most widely used standardized measure of symptoms and concerns characteristics of eating disorders. The EAT-26 alone does not yield a specific diagnosis of an eating disorder. Neither the EAT-26 nor any other screening instrument has been established as highly efficient as the sole means for identifying eating disorders. However, studies have shown that the EAT-26 can be an efficient screening instrument as part of a two-stage screening process in which those who score at or above a cutoff score of 20 are referred for a diagnostic interview. If you score above 20 on the EAT-26, please contact your doctor or an eating disorders treatment specialist for a follow-up evaluation.

Age ☐ Sex: F ☐ M ☐ Height: ☐ Current weight: ☐
Highest weight: ☐ Lowest adult weight: ☐

Education: If currently enrolled in college/university, are you a:

Freshman ☐ Sophomore ☐ Junior ☐ Senior ☐ Grad student ☐

If not enrolled in school, level of education completed:

Jr. high/middle school ☐ High school ☐ College ☐ Postcollege ☐

Ethnic/racial group:

African American ☐ Asian American ☐ European American ☐ Hispanic ☐
American Indian ☐ Other ☐

Do you participate in athletics at any of the following levels:

Intramural ☐ Intercollegiate ☐ Recreational ☐ High-school teams ☐

Please Circle a Response for Each of the Following Statements:

Question	Always	Usually	Often	Sometimes	Rarely	Never
1. Am terrified about being overweight	3	2	1	0	0	0
2. Avoid eating when I am hungry	3	2	1	0	0	0
3. Find myself preoccupied with food	3	2	1	0	0	0
4. Have gone on eating binges where I feel I may not be able to stop	3	2	1	0	0	0
5. Cut my food into small pieces	3	2	1	0	0	0
6. Aware of the calorie content of foods I eat	3	2	1	0	0	0
7. Particularly avoid food with a high carbohydrate content (bread, rice, potatoes, etc.)	3	2	1	0	0	0
8. Feel that others would prefer if I ate more	3	2	1	0	0	0
9. Vomit after I have eaten	3	2	1	0	0	0
10. Feel extremely guilty after eating	3	2	1	0	0	0
11. Am preoccupied with a desire to be thinner	3	2	1	0	0	0
12. Think about burning up calories when I exercise	3	2	1	0	0	0
13. Other people think I'm too thin	3	2	1	0	0	0
14. Am preoccupied with the thought of having fat on my body	3	2	1	0	0	0
15. Take longer than others to eat my meals	3	2	1	0	0	0
16. Avoid foods with sugar in them	3	2	1	0	0	0

(continued)

TABLE 14.1 Eating Attitudes Test—Eating Disorder (continued)

Question	Always	Usually	Often	Sometimes	Rarely	Never
17. Eat diet foods	3	2	1	0	0	0
18. Feel that food controls my life	3	2	1	0	0	0
19. Display self-control around food	3	2	1	0	0	0
20. Feel that other pressure me to eat	3	2	1	0	0	0
21. Give too much time and thought to food	3	2	1	0	0	0
22. Feel uncomfortable after eating sweets	3	2	1	0	0	0
23. Engage in dieting behavior	3	2	1	0	0	0
24. Like my stomach to be empty	3	2	1	0	0	0
25. Have the impulse to vomit after meals	3	2	1	0	0	0
26. Enjoy trying new rich foods	0	0	0	1	2	3

Please Respond to Each of the Following Questions:

1. Have you gone on eating binges where you feel that you may not be able to stop?
   (Eating much more than most people would eat under the circumstances.) No ☐ Yes ☐
   If yes, on average, how many times per month in the last 6 months? ☐☐☐

2. Have you ever made yourself sick (vomited) to control your weight or shape? No ☐ Yes ☐
   If yes, on average, how many times per month in the last 6 months? ☐☐☐

3. Have you ever used laxatives, diet pills, or diuretics (water pills) to control your weight or shape? No ☐ Yes ☐
   If yes, on average, how many times per month in the last 6 months? ☐☐☐

4. Have you ever been treated for an eating disorder? No ☐ Yes ☐, If yes, when? ☐☐☐

5. Have you recently thought of or attempted suicide? No ☐ Yes ☐, If yes, when? ☐☐☐

Scoring System for the EAT-26

Responses for each item (1–26) are weighted from zero to three, with a score of 3 assigned to the responses farthest in the "symptomatic" direction, a score of 2 for the immediately adjacent response, a score of 1 for the next adjacent response, and a 0 score assigned to the three responses farthest in the "asymptomatic" direction.

Total Score: Add the values circled for questions 1–26 above:

EAT Score
TOTAL _____

Items are assigned to three subscales as follows:

Dieting subscale items: 1, 6, 7, 10, 11, 12, 14, 16, 17, 22, 23, 24, 25

Subscale Score:
_____

Bulimia and food preoccupation subscale items: 3, 4, 9, 18, 21, 26

Subscale Score:
_____

Oral control subscale items: 2, 5, 8, 13, 15, 19, 20
To determine subscale scores, add together all item scores for that particular subscale.

Subscale Score:
_____

Source: From D. M. Garner, M. P. Olmsted, and Y. Bohr (1982). "The Eating Attitudes Test: Psychometric Features and Clinical Correlates," *Psychological Medicine*, 12, pp. 871–878. Reprinted with permission of Cambridge University Press.

REAL STORIES

TRACEY GOLD: EATING DISORDER

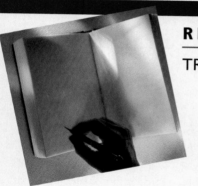

Tracey Gold in her anorexic and post-anorexic states.

Most contemporary college students are well aware that eating disorders have become epidemic, particularly among female adolescents. Experts analyzing the reasons for this social problem often focus on media images of celebrities that idealize extremely thin bodies. Girls who are struggling to define their own identity during the turbulent years of adolescence commonly emulate the behavior and look of these media idols. Although rumors abound that many of these celebrities achieved their emaciated figures by means of self-starvation, few have been willing to share their stories. Tracey Gold is one celebrity, however, who did speak openly about her struggle with anorexia. During the 7 years when Gold starred in the popular television series *Growing Pains,* she was adored by millions of people who admired her character, her style, and her beautiful looks. Little did they know that beneath the surface were inner turmoil and medical danger.

Gold's life story seems like it is straight from a novel or movie. She grew up in southern California in a tightly knit family that included four younger sisters. Because her father owned a talent agency, Gold was surrounded for much of her youth by famous actors and actresses. Within this world of celebrities, Gold had access to many opportunities, and at the age of 5 she began making television commercials and movies. Her fame skyrocketed during the years she played the role of bookish Carol Seaver on *Growing Pains.* Those years were thrilling, yet demanding, particularly in light of the challenges she experienced trying to balance her acting career and her academic responsibilities as a high school student who was also diagnosed with ADHD.

At the age of 12, Gold developed eating issues that were serious enough to catch the attention of her pediatrician, who diagnosed her as having anorexia nervosa. With good medical attention, she recovered and was fine throughout much of her adolescence. However, when she was 19, the producers of *Growing Pains* instructed her to lose 20 pounds. Gold went on an extreme diet, and her weight plunged from 133 pounds to 113. She then felt unable to stop dieting, and her eating disorder reappeared. Gold was exhausted, often sick, and felt dizzy when she stood up. In 1992 her weight had plunged to 90 pounds, and she was forced to leave the show to seek medical attention. Following some therapeutic intervention, Gold's weight stabilized for a few months, but once again fell dangerously low, to 83 pounds, and her emotions took a similarly worrisome downturn. Her mother noticed that her daughter had stopped laughing and had begun to experience terrible mood swings. This caused so much alarm in Gold's mother that she would sneak into her bedroom during the night to check Tracey's pulse and make sure that she was still breathing. A turning point came for Gold one day when she looked into a mirror, saw how thin she was, and realized that she did not want to die.

Before Gold developed anorexia nervosa, the *Growing Pains* writers occasionally poked some fun at her character's "chubbiness," even though she was certainly not overweight. This kind of humor made Gold extremely uncomfortable during the time that her body was going through the changes of puberty. She explains: "I would call the producers, and I'd say, 'You've got to take it out, I can't rehearse with it, it's hurting me and I have a real problem with this and maybe I'm oversensitive to it, maybe it's funny, but I'm not finding it funny.'"

REAL STORIES

TRACEY GOLD (continued)

When she was struggling with anorexia nervosa, Gold obsessed over anything she ate, as is evident from this quote: "I had a cup of cereal for breakfast and a cup of cereal for lunch and a cup is 100 calories and, like, one gram of fat. An apple has no fat. . . ." Gold realized that although food may seem to be the main issue, anorexia often is a symptom of other problems. Some people with anorexia become focused on what they perceive to be the benefits of their engaging in this disordered eating behavior. For example, Gold yearned for a sense of security in her life, which she felt that she received when she became a frail and childlike girl whom others wanted to take care of. Tracey explains,

> If you've gone through what I've gone through, you would know that it's not so simple as eating; it has nothing nearly to do with food . . .

there's a security in it because you're taken care of and protected because you look frail and breakable and I get cold easily. I'm not really a comfortable body to be in right now, physically, but emotionally it's my security blanket.

Gold felt that her eating disorder gave her some control over her family and producers. The importance of controlling her own life became increasingly significant to Gold, despite the irony that she was so out of control in terms of what was happening to her body.

In characterizing the experience of anorexia, Gold states,

> I used to explain it like you're drowning, and my hand was reaching above the surface and I was just trying to get somebody to help me. The hardest thing with this disease is that there is no real cure. . . . You can't feel pretty, there's no way

you're going to feel good; it's uncomfortable. I couldn't sleep. I couldn't lie down.

She also describes the turning point in her battle with the disease:

> I looked in the mirror and I didn't have any clothes on and I was scared. . . . I saw what I saw in pictures of people that I've seen die of anorexia. So that's what scared me. I saw myself actually dying of it. . . . I was a skeleton. I would move and I would get a bruise. I had to go to the doctor because I had all these bumps all along my hip area. . . . I'm still afraid but every day I'm less afraid. I feel the most free that I have felt in a long time.

Source: From Tracey Gold in *Tracey's Diary*, produced by Shelly Ross; edited by Jack Pyle. Interview by Diane Sawyer, ABC 20/20. Reproduced with permission.

Mini Case

ANOREXIA NERVOSA

Lorraine is an 18-year-old first-year college student who, since leaving home to go to school, has been losing weight steadily. Initially, Lorraine wanted to lose a few pounds, thinking this would make her look sexier. She stopped eating at the cafeteria, because they served too many starchy foods, choosing instead to prepare her own low-calorie meals. Within 2 months, she became obsessed with dieting and exercise and with a fear that she might gain weight and become fat. She stopped menstruating, and her weight dropped from 110 to 80 pounds. Regardless of the repeated expressions of concern by her friends that she appeared emaciated, Lorraine insisted that she was fat. When Lorraine went home for Thanksgiving break, her parents were so alarmed that they insisted she go for professional help.

Diagnostic Features

People with anorexia nervosa fall into two groups (restricting type and binge eating/purging type) with the following characteristics:

■ They refuse to maintain body weight at or above minimally normal weight for their age and height.

■ They have an intense fear of gaining weight or becoming fat, even though they are underweight.

■ They experience a disturbance in the way they experience body weight, or their self-evaluation is unduly influenced by body weight or shape, or they deny the seriousness of their deficient weight.

■ Females who are beyond puberty miss at least three consecutive menstrual cycles.

Body image disturbance is a core feature of anorexia nervosa. As anorexics look in the mirror, they see an obese person, rather than the skin and bones so evident to everyone else. In fact, family members of people with this disorder experience a great deal of frustration, because they are unable to convince them that they are actually horrendously thin.

Estimates of the prevalence of this disorder range from a low of 0.5 percent to a high of 3.7 percent in women, depending on whether diagnostic criteria are narrowly or broadly defined. Apart from differences in the basis for these estimates, it is also likely that there is a spectrum of anorexic syndromes in women. Along this spectrum, certain forms of the disorder show familial patterns of inheritance, as well as comorbidity with obsessive-compulsive disorder and social phobia. Even people without one of these disorders have a tendency to be anxious, perfectionistic, and cautious. Many of the individuals who have an eating disorder in adulthood report having the symptoms of an anxiety disorder in childhood prior to the onset of their eating disorder (Kaye et al., 2004).

Although these statistics indicate that the problem of eating disorders is a serious one, research on the long-term duration of eating disorders offers some hope. Heatherton and his colleagues (Heatherton et al., 1997; Vohs, Heatherton, & Herrin, 2001) conducted a 10-year longitudinal study in which they found that rates of eating-disordered behavior in women dropped by more than half over that period. Maturing into adulthood and escaping from intense social pressures that emphasize thinness among college women seem to make the difference. However, eating disorders still afflicted one in five women and more than half the men in the study after ten years. Body image problems can persist not only into early adulthood (Rizvi, Stice, & Agras, 1999) but even into old age. Middle-aged women in one study exhibited high scores on a measure of drive for thinness and older adults possessed disordered body images similar to those of young women (Lewis & Cachelin, 2001). In a 5-year study examining the persistence of bulimia, one third to one half of the sample still exhibited a clinical eating disorder with 10 to 25 percent still suffering from bulimia at the study's end. History of childhood obesity, degree of overvaluation of shape and weight, and level of social maladjustment were all shown to be predictors of persistent disordered eating (Fairburn et al., 2003). With the aging of the baby-boomer generation and the preoccupation with a youthful appearance that many possess, it is likely that patterns of disordered body image will become increasingly prevalent (Jones, Whitbourne, & Skultety, in press).

Characteristics of Bulimia Nervosa

People with the eating disorder known as **bulimia nervosa** alternate between the extremes of eating large amounts of food in a short time and then compensating for the added calories by vomiting or other extreme actions. Episodes of overeating are known as **binges** and are characterized by (1) eating an amount of food within a 2-hour period that is much greater than most people would eat under similar circumstances and (2) feeling a lack of

control over what or how much is being eaten. People with bulimia nervosa also engage in inappropriate behaviors that are intended to prevent weight gain. Those with the **purging type** try to force out of their bodies what they have just eaten; to do this, they induce vomiting, administer an enema, or take laxatives or diuretics. Those with the **nonpurging type** try to compensate for what they eat by fasting or engaging in excessive exercise. In both cases, these individuals get caught up in a vicious cycle of binging, followed by desperate attempts to cleanse themselves of the foods that were so gratifying during the eating episode. Following the purging, hunger returns and the cycle begins again.

In MindMAP Segment 14.2, Nancy talks about feeling that food has total control over her. After binging, she then purges by vomiting, but still worries that she might not have gotten all the food out of her.

People with bulimia nervosa engage in episodes of binge eating in which they eat an excessive amount of food in a short period of time and experience a lack of control over eating during these episodes. They then engage in behaviors that, in their minds, help to compensate for their overeating.

BULIMIA NERVOSA

Cynthia is a 26-year-old dance teacher. Cynthia has struggled with her weight since adolescence. A particular problem for Cynthia has been her love of high-calorie carbohydrates. She regularly binges on a variety of sweets and then forces herself to vomit. Over the years, Cynthia has developed a number of physical problems from the frequent cycles of binging and purging. She recently went to her physician, complaining of severe stomach cramps that had bothered her for several weeks.

Diagnostic Features

People with bulimia nervosa fall into two groups (purging type or nonpurging type) with the following characteristics:

- They engage in recurrent episodes of binge eating that are characterized by (1) eating an amount of food in a 2-hour period that is substantially larger than what most people would eat and (2) experiencing a lack of control over eating during these episodes.

- They engage in recurrent compensatory behavior aimed at preventing weight gain (e.g., self-induced vomiting, fasting, excessive exercise, or misuse of laxatives, diuretics, or enemas).

- The binge eating and compensatory behaviors both occur on average at least twice a week for 3 months.

- Their self-evaluation is unduly influenced by body weight and shape.

Many people find it difficult to imagine what would motivate a person to engage in behaviors that are usually regarded as disgusting. Again, it is important to keep in mind that this is a disorder in which a person feels out of control. Resisting the urge to binge seems impossible. The individual derives satisfaction from relieving the ensuing feelings of discomfort. Most people with bulimia nervosa prefer to use vomiting in order to gain this relief. Over time, the vomiting behavior may become a goal in itself, because for many of these individuals it begins to provide an odd sort of pleasure. Experienced individuals can induce vomiting at will.

Although some people have both anorexia nervosa and bulimia nervosa, two critical features distinguish these disorders. The first is body image. People with anorexia nervosa have very distorted perceptions of their body size. Even when close to a chronic state of starvation, anorexics see themselves as overweight. By contrast, the individual with bulimia nervosa has an accurate body perception, but still worries about gaining weight. The second difference is the amount of weight that the individual has lost. People with anorexia nervosa weigh significantly below the norm for height and build, whereas many people with bulimia nervosa have weight that is average or above average.

Many medical complications commonly develop in individuals with bulimia nervosa. The most serious of these problems are the life-threatening complications associated with purging. For example, the medication ipecac syrup, which is used to induce vomiting in people who have swallowed a poisonous substance, has severe toxic effects when taken regularly and in large doses by people with eating disorders. These effects occur throughout the gastrointestinal, cardiovascular, and nervous systems. Dental decay, which results from recurrent vomiting, is common, as cavities develop and teeth take on a ragged appearance. The salivary glands become enlarged, and skin calluses develop on hands that brush against teeth in the vomiting process. In females, menstrual irregularity is common. Toxic effects can also result from the laxatives, diuretics, and diet pills that bulimics use to induce weight loss. Some with bulimia nervosa also engage in harmful behaviors, such as using enemas, regurgitating and then rechewing their food, or overusing saunas in efforts to lose weight. In addition to the effects of dehydration caused by binging and purging, the bulimic individual runs the risk of permanent gastrointestinal damage, fluid retention in the hands and feet, and destruction of the heart muscle or collapse of the heart valves.

Diagnosable cases of bulimia nervosa are relatively uncommon (1 to 2 percent of high-school and college women and 0.2 percent of college men), yet a disturbingly large percentage of young people have some symptoms of this disorder. Stice and his colleagues (Stice, Killen, Hayward, & Taylor, 1998) have found that, for girls, the age of highest risk for the development of binge behavior is around 16, while it is nearly 2 years later, around age 18, that purging is most likely to develop. These researchers believe that it takes approximately that long for teens who get caught up in dieting/binge eating behavior to abandon dieting in favor of more extreme weight loss measures, such as vomiting.

Compared to the attention given to the study of eating disorders in girls and women, relatively little research has taken place involving males, yet investigations have turned up some interesting findings. Among a group of 135 males hospitalized at Massachusetts General Hospital between 1980 and 1994, 62 (46 percent) had bulimia nervosa, 30 (22 percent) anorexia nervosa, and the remaining 43 (32 percent) an unspecified eating disorder. Researchers uncovered interesting data about sexual orientation among these patients, with 42 percent of the bulimic individuals identifying themselves as either homosexual or bisexual, and 58 percent of the anorexic patients considering themselves asexual. As is the case with eating-disordered girls and women, many of the males also had co-existing psychological disorders, such as major depressive disorder (54 percent), substance abuse (37 percent), and personality disorder (26 percent) (Carlat, Camargo, & Herzog, 1997).

In a large-scale Canadian investigation, men with eating disorders were found to be more similar to women with eating disorders than to men who had no history of dysfunction (Woodside et al., 2001). Although the prevalence may be very different, then, it appears likely that the core disturbance in eating disorders may transcend gender.

Theories and Treatment of Eating Disorders

Food is important to us for biological, psychological, and sociocultural reasons. In explanations of the development of eating disorder, each of these factors is seen as playing an important role. Clearly, this is an area within the field of abnormal psychology to which a biopsychosocial perspective aptly applies.

Theories Evidence is accumulating that suggests that people with eating disorders have altered dopamine and serotonin neurotransmitter systems. Abnormalities in dopamine receptors have been identified in people with eating disorders, reflecting an inherited vulnerability (Bergen et al., 2005; Levitan et al., 2004; Shinohara et al., 2004). Dopamine, which plays a role in feelings of reward and pleasure related to food could therefore be involved in binge eating. Serotonin, in particular, seems to play a role in the regulation of feelings of hunger or satiety. A deficiency of serotonin appears to be related to feelings of hunger (leading to binging), and an excess is related to feelings of fullness (leading to anorexia).

From the psychological perspective, eating disorders are seen as developing in young people who suffer a great deal of inner turmoil and pain and become obsessed with bodily issues, often turning to food for feelings of comfort and nurturance. Individuals with eating disorders tend to have difficulty understanding and labeling their emotions, and over time they learn that eating can provide a means for dealing with unpleasant and unclear emotional states (Leon, Fulkerson, Perry, & Early-Zald, 1995). In trying to understand the development of an eating-disordered response to inner pain, researchers have been particularly interested in the fact that some women with bulimia nervosa have a history of being abused sexually or physically during childhood (Katerndahl, Burge, & Kellogg, 2005). Researchers studying connections between the experiences of being hurt during childhood and self-inflicted bodily harm later in life are beginning to understand possible biochemical links between childhood abuse and eating disorders. Both appear to involve serotonin disturbances, but abuse also appears to be linked to reductions in cortisol, the stress hormone (Steiger et al., 2001).

Cognitive factors are considered relevant within the psychological perspective as an explanation of eating disorders. According to cognitive theories, over time people with eating disorders become trapped in their pathological patterns because of a resistance to change that commonly characterizes their thought processes (Mizes & Christiano, 1995). They avoid problems rather than resolve them; they resort to wishful thinking rather than realistic appraisal; and they tend not to seek social support, even when they are in serious trouble (Troop, Holbrey, Trowler, & Treasure, 1994). For both boys and girls, negative affect also plays a role in moderating the relationship between concerns about body size and bulimic behavior (Ricciardelli & McCabe, 2001).

The pursuit of emotional comfort through eating may also be seen as a desperate expression of the individual's unresolved feelings of dependency on his or her parents (Bornstein & Greenberg, 1991). The personality trait of dependency along with obsessiveness appears to be closely related to bulimic symptoms (Rogers & Petrie, 2001). Along related theoretical lines, women with eating disorders have been found to have an insecure, anxious style of attachment along with more symptoms of separation anxiety disorder in childhood (Troisi, Massaroni, & Cuzzolaro, 2005). Among women with bulimia nervosa who have personality disorders, borderline personality disorder is the most common, as it is among women with the binging/purging type of anorexia nervosa (Sansone, Levitt, & Sansone, 2005). It appears, then, that people in a certain subgroup of individuals with eating disorders have fundamental difficulties in the development of their identities.

Our discussion of the individual's conflict over separation from the family is an appropriate lead-in to a consideration of family theories within the sociocultural perspective. A traditional view of family systems theorists has been that some girls develop anorexia nervosa in an effort to assert their independence from an overly involved family (Minuchin, Rosman, & Baker, 1978). According to this view, girls who feel that their families are standing in the way of their becoming autonomous develop abnormal eating patterns as a way to become separated from their parents. Other disturbances in the family may also contribute to the development of eating disorders, including a family that is chaotic, incapable of resolving conflict, unaffectionate, and unempathic to the child's needs (Strober & Humphrey, 1987). The family environment can also influence the evolution of an eating disorder; that is, a person's moving from anorexia to bulimia and vice versa. Women with anorexia nervosa living in families characterized by a high degree of criticism have a greater likelihood of crossing over to developing bulimia nervosa. By contrast, women crossing over from bulimia to anorexia are more likely to live in family environments characterized by alcohol abuse and dependence (Tozzi et al., 2005).

From a broader sociocultural perspective, a primary influence on the development of eating disorders is society's attitudes toward eating and diet. Society's idealization of thinness leads many adolescent girls to equate beauty with a slim figure. As an adolescent girl matures, she reads magazines, talks to her friends, and watches television and movies, repeatedly confronting the glamorization of thinness. All of this is happening during a period of development in which individuals become preoccupied with the way they are perceived by others, a concept called the "social self" (Striegel-Moore, Silberstein, & Rodin, 1993). Those who feel inadequate about their appearance develop a social self that focuses inordinately on inadequacies of their body. This relationship between body image dissatisfaction and social anxiety presumably serves as the basis from which eating disorders emerge. Interestingly, although eating disorders are thought of as afflicting primarily White, middle- or upper-middle class girls, a large-scale study of Latina teenagers revealed prevalence rates of eating disorder–related variables comparable to those of the United States as a whole (Granillo,

Jones-Rodriguez, & Carvajal, 2005). Disturbed eating patterns in the form of self-starvation have even been observed to occur in remote areas of Ghana, where the pressure to be thin is not culturally transmitted (Bennett, Sharpe, Freeman, & Carson, 2004). Nevertheless, researchers regard young White females or highly acculturated ethnic minority females as being at highest risk for eating disorders (Jacobi et al., 2004).

Each of the two major forms of eating disorder develops, then, as the result of a complex interaction among biological, psychological, and sociological factors (see Table 14.2). In the case of anorexia nervosa, it seems that biological factors, dieting, and psychosocial influences come together and set the stage for developing this disorder. Once the stage is set, the individual becomes trapped in a cycle of physiological changes that leads to the desire for more dieting and weight loss. For those with bulimia nervosa, physiological influences also play a prominent role in the maintenance of binging and purging behaviors. The extreme behaviors of excessive food intake followed by purging provoke neurochemical changes that cause the individual to become addicted to these abnormal eating patterns (Heebink & Halmi, 1994). Clients who show the greatest improvement initially in terms of reducing the frequency of purging are the most likely to benefit from treatment,

In MindMAP Segment 14.3, Julie talks about dieting to fit in with a popular crowd in high school and losing control over her eating.

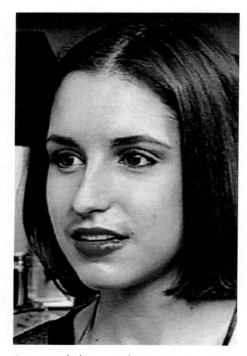

Anorexia, bulimia, and excessive exercising often reflect multiple influences from societal pressures and low self-esteem.

maintaining their gains for at least an 8-month period (Fairburn et al., 2004).

Treatment   Given the multiple perspectives on the causes of eating disorders, it follows that effective treatment usually requires a combination of approaches. Medications affecting serotonin are effective in treating people with eating disorders. In a double-blind placebo-controlled study involving people who were assessed a year after being discharged from inpatient treatment, fluoxetine was more effective than a placebo in controlling relapse, maintaining weight gains, and reducing other symptoms (Kaye et al., 2001). Researchers will continue to investigate the short-term and long-term benefits of such medications for people with anorexia nervosa. The picture for bulimia nervosa is similar, in that fluoxetine has also proved helpful in reducing the symptoms of this disorder (Schatzberg, 2000).

Regardless of the potential effectiveness of medications, it is clear from a biopsychosocial perspective that psychotherapy is necessary in treating people with eating disorders. Christopher Fairburn and his colleagues at Oxford University compared three interventions for people with bulimia nervosa: cognitive-behavioral therapy, behavioral therapy, and focal interpersonal therapy in which emphasis was placed on current interpersonal problems rather than the eating disorder. At the 1-year follow-up, 86 percent of the clients treated with behavioral therapy techniques still had bulimia nervosa, compared with only 37 percent of those treated with cognitive-behavioral therapy and 28 percent of those treated with focal interpersonal therapy (Fairburn, 1997). Similar findings regarding the efficacy of both cognitive-behavioral therapy and interpersonal therapy have been reported by Stewart Agras and his colleagues at Stanford University (Agras & Apple, 1998). For both cognitive-behavioral therapy and interpersonal therapy, the quality of the therapeutic alliance is an important key to the success of the intervention. Particularly crucial are the expectations that clients have about the likelihood that they will improve (Constantino, Arnow, Blasey, & Agras, 2005).

The techniques of cognitive-behavioral therapy for the treatment of eating disorders are fairly straightforward. As proposed by Fairburn (1997), the treatment involves 12 elements for each disorder. Building on a good therapeutic relationship, the clinician teaches the client self-monitoring techniques, an understanding of the cognitive model, the importance of weekly weighing and regular eating patterns, and other techniques designed to bring about healthy eating habits. The client learns self-control strategies, problem-solving techniques, cognitive restructuring, and ways to prevent relapse.

Interpersonal therapy uses techniques similar to those used for treating depression, with a focus on helping the client cope with stress in interpersonal situations and with feelings of low self-esteem. The client learns to recognize emotions as triggers of disordered eating, particularly binge eating. Presumably, interpersonal therapy can reduce these emotional triggers (Agras & Apple, 1998). Unfortunately, even among women who recover from an eating disorder in adolescence, difficulties in

TABLE 14.2 Main Risk Factors for Anorexia Nervosa and Bulimia Nervosa

General Factors

Female

Adolescence and early adulthood

Living in a Western society

Individual-Specific Factors

Family history

- Eating disorder of any type
- Depression
- Substance misuse, especially alcoholism (bulimia nervosa)
- Obesity (bulimia nervosa)

Premorbid experiences

- Adverse parenting (especially low contact, high expectations, parental discord)
- Sexual abuse
- Family dieting
- Critical comments about eating, shape, or weight from family and others
- Occupational and recreational pressure to be slim

Premorbid characteristics

- Low self esteem
- Perfectionism (anorexia nervosa and to a lesser extent bulimia nervosa)
- Anxiety and anxiety disorders
- Obesity (bulimia nervosa)
- Early menarche (bulimia nervosa)

Source: From C. G. Fairburn and P. J. Harrison (2003). "Eating Disorders," *The Lancet, 361*, pp. 407–416. Used by permission of Elsevier.

adjustment and self-image may persist for several years thereafter (Striegel-Moore, Seeley, & Lewinsohn, 2003).

Group therapy can also be helpful in the treatment of eating disorders although success rates fall well below those of individual therapy (Thompson-Brenner, Glass, & Westen, 2003). In cognitive-behavioral groups, clients receive help in changing their thoughts and behaviors concerning eating. Self-help manuals, focusing on specific symptoms of bulimia or on self-assertion skills, have been shown to reduce the frequency of symptoms among those placed on treatment waiting lists (Carter et al., 2003).

Within the sociocultural perspective, interventions incorporating a family component are used for clients with eating disorders who are still in their teens and whose condition has been relatively brief in duration (Eisler et al., 1997). Although there has been debate among family therapists about whether this intervention should include all family members, a review of research points to the conclusion that involvement of the parents

and the teen is sufficient to bring about positive change (Wilson & Fairburn, 1998). In fact, therapists have found a multifamily therapy group to be particularly effective for eating disorders. In this type of therapy, several families participate in group sessions simultaneously. One positive factor in this intervention is the reduction of feelings of stigmatization and isolation that occur when a family member suffers from an eating disorder (Schmidt & Asen, 2005).

In conclusion, eating disorders are conditions in which there is a complex interaction of biological, psychological, and sociocultural factors. Unlike some disorders we have discussed, in which biology seems to set the stage for the disorder, eating disorders seem more likely to arise as a result of interpersonal and intrapersonal conflict. Interpersonal influences, most notably within the family system and the peer network, evoke intense concerns about body image and attractiveness. Distorted self-perception and disturbed thinking compound the problem, and in time bodily changes become part of the overall picture. Biopsychosocial intervention approaches bring together techniques from all three spheres. In the biological sphere, the treatment may involve medication, but not necessarily. What is necessary, however, is a medical component that focuses on healthy bodily functioning and eating behaviors. The most effective psychological techniques are those emphasizing distorted thinking and perception. The sociocultural component may include family or group therapy. Aggressive intervention, especially at an early stage of eating-disordered behavior, can change the course of these potentially devastating disorders.

Impulse-Control Disorders

We will turn our attention now to a set of disorders in which people repeatedly lose control of behavior in response to irresistible impulses. Most people have had experiences involving impulses to do something they later regretted. Some people yell at drivers who cut them off in traffic; others yell angrily at people who are annoying them. These are relatively common responses, although they can be disturbing or even dangerous at times. However, imagine behaviors that are repeatedly taken to an extreme, which a person feels unable to control. In this section, we will discuss disorders that are characterized by a seeming inability to resist the urge to engage in certain unacceptable and harmful behaviors. These disorders involve disturbances in the ability to regulate an **impulse**—an urge to take an action. People with **impulse-control disorders** repeatedly engage in behaviors that are potentially harmful, feeling unable to stop themselves and experiencing a sense of desperation if they are thwarted from carrying out their impulsive behavior. Impulsive behavior in and of itself is not necessarily harmful; in fact, we all act impulsively on occasion. Usually our impulsive acts have no ill effects, but in some instances they may involve risk. Consider the following example. While walking through a clothing store, Yolanda decides on the spur of the moment to charge an expensive sweater that is beyond her budget; she may regret her decision later, but

Mini Case

KLEPTOMANIA

Gloria is a 45-year-old well-dressed and attractive executive with a comfortable salary and a busy lifestyle. For the past few years, she has been under considerable stress and has worked long hours as the result of reorganizations in her company. As a teenager, Gloria occasionally took small, inexpensive items, such as hair barrettes and nail polish, from the drug store, even though she could afford to pay for them. Lately, Gloria has started shoplifting again. This time, her behavior has an intensity that she cannot control. During her lunch hour, Gloria often visits one of the large department stores near her office building, walks around until she finds something that catches her eye, and then slips it into her purse or pocket. Although she has sworn to herself that she will never steal again, every few days she finds the tension so great that she cannot stay out of the stores.

Diagnostic Features

- People with this condition have irresistible, recurrent urges to steal, not out of anger or vengeance, or in response to a delusion or hallucination, or to obtain objects for personal use or monetary value.

- They experience an increasing sense of tension immediately prior to the theft.

- They feel pleasure, gratification, or relief at the time they are committing the theft.

---

few serious consequences will result. Were Yolanda to use all her financial resources to buy an expensive sports car, the consequences would be considerably more serious. This pattern of "compulsive buying," although not a diagnosis in the *DSM-IV-TR,* gives you a sense of what the impulse-control disorders are like. In fact, some researchers have studied compulsive buying and have found that 2 to 8 percent of U.S. adults, most of whom are women, experience irresistible urges to shop and spend to the point of incurring serious debt (Black, 2001).

Impulse-control disorders have three essential features. First, people with these disorders are unable to refrain from acting on impulses that are harmful to themselves or others. Some people attempt to fight their impulses, and others give in when they feel the urge to act. The act can be either spontaneous or planned. Second, before they act on their impulses, people with these disorders feel pressured to act, experiencing tension and anxiety that can be relieved only by following through on their impulses. Some people with these disorders experience a feeling of arousal that they liken to sexual excitement. Third, on acting on their impulses, they experience a sense of pleasure or gratification, also likened to the release of sexual tension (American Psychiatric Association, 2000).

Individuals with impulse-control disorders are not usually conflicted at the moment of choosing to engage in the behavior, because they are not inclined to proceed through a rational decision-making process. Conflict, regret, and remorse, if they do occur, happen afterward.

Kleptomania

You may have heard the term *kleptomaniac* used to describe a person who shoplifts or takes things from other people's houses. People with the impulse-control disorder called **kleptomania** are driven by a persistent urge to steal, although their theft is not motivated by a wish to own the object or by the monetary value of the item they have stolen.

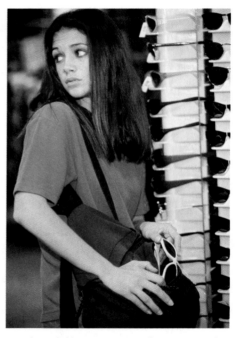

People with kleptomania are less interested in what they steal than in the act of stealing itself.

Characteristics of Kleptomania   There is a common misconception that people with kleptomania are driven by the wish to acquire possessions; in fact, that is not the case. It is not the idea of having the object that is appealing but, rather, the excitement of engaging in the act of stealing the object. In the process of stealing, they sense a release of tension that feels gratifying, as they experience a temporary thrill. Despite the transient positive sensation, the urge to steal feels unpleasant, unwanted, intrusive, and senseless. People with kleptomania steal just about anything, although the most common objects are food, clothes, jewelry, cosmetics, compact discs, toys, pens and paper, and money. Most people with kleptomania steal from a store or workplace, but for some the behavior is limited to stealing from a particular person, perhaps someone for whom they have intense feelings of attraction or jealousy. Keep in mind that it is not the intrinsic value of these objects that motivates the person with kleptomania to steal but, rather, the urge to release tension. In fact, most people with kleptomania are perplexed about what to do with their acquired items. Some hoard the objects, as in the case of a woman whose closet was overflowing with thousands of inexpensive plastic combs and brushes that she took over the course of several years. Others give away or even throw away the items. This lack of interest in the stolen items is the main feature that differentiates a typical shoplifter or burglar from a person with kleptomania.

Theories and Treatment of Kleptomania Although kleptomania is a fascinating psychological disorder, researchers have given it relatively little attention, perhaps because relatively few cases come to professional attention, except for those referred to forensic psychologists. Clinicians usually become aware that a person has kleptomania only when he or she is in treatment for another psychological problem, such as an anxiety, psychoactive substance abuse, eating, or mood disorder. This comorbidity raises an interesting question: Is kleptomanic behavior a symptom of another disorder, possibly biologically caused? With this possibility in mind, some researchers have speculated that a serotonin deficiency underlies kleptomania. Their data suggest that kleptomania constitutes a variant of obsessive-compulsive disorder, as people with kleptomania have a compulsion to steal. Like obsessive-compulsive disorder, kleptomania responds to SSRIs (Durst et al., 2001).

In addition to using pharmacological interventions, clinicians also employ behavioral treatments to help individuals control their urge to steal. In covert sensitization, the client is instructed to conjure up aversive images (vomit, for example) when the compulsion to steal emerges. Alternatively, the clinician may instruct the client to use thought-stopping techniques, in which dramatic internal cries to resist thinking about the stealing behavior prevent the person from following through on the urge.

Pathological Gambling

Gambling is a common activity. Even if you do not consider yourself a "gambler," you have probably bought a raffle ticket, scratched off the disk on a game card in a cereal package, sent a card in the mail to a sweepstakes contest, bet on your home team, or wagered a dollar with a friend that your answer to a test question was correct. Perhaps you have been to a gambling casino and have played the slot machines or have sat at the blackjack table for an hour or two. If you have had any of these experiences, you know how thrilling it can be to see your bet pay off. People who are troubled by **pathological gambling** have an urge to gamble that is much stronger than that of the average person, and they often end up spending their entire lives in pursuit of big wins. Table 14.3 contains some questions that are helpful in determining whether a person's gambling behavior is a cause for concern.

TABLE 14.3 Questions to Assess Pathological Gambling

Gamblers Anonymous offers the following questions to anyone who may have a gambling problem. These questions are provided to help the individual decide if he or she is a compulsive gambler and wants to stop gambling.

1. Did you ever lose time from work or school due to gambling?
2. Has gambling ever made your home life unhappy?
3. Did gambling affect your reputation?
4. Have you ever felt remorse after gambling?
5. Did you ever gamble to get money with which to pay debts or otherwise solve financial difficulties?
6. Did gambling cause a decrease in your ambition or efficiency?
7. After losing did you feel you must return as soon as possible and win back your losses?
8. After a win did you have a strong urge to return and win more?
9. Did you often gamble until your last dollar was gone?
10. Did you ever borrow to finance your gambling?
11. Have you ever sold anything to finance gambling?
12. Were you reluctant to use "gambling money" for normal expenditures?
13. Did gambling make you careless of the welfare of your family?
14. Did you ever gamble longer than you had planned?
15. Have you ever gambled to escape worry or trouble?
16. Have you ever committed, or considered committing, an illegal act to finance gambling?
17. Did gambling cause you to have difficulty in sleeping?
18. Do arguments, disappointments, or frustrations create within you an urge to gamble?
19. Did you ever have an urge to celebrate any good fortune by a few hours of gambling?
20. Have you ever considered self-destruction as a result of your gambling?

Most compulsive gamblers will answer yes to at least seven of these questions.

Source: Gamblers Anonymous at http://www.gamblersanonymous.org/20questions.html. Reprinted with permission.

Characteristics of Pathological Gambling During the late 1980s, the sports world was shaken by the story that one of the leading baseball figures of all time, Pete Rose, had been betting thousands of dollars a day on baseball games. Admitting his guilt, Rose publicly acknowledged that he was unable to control his gambling, despite his realization that this would lead to his

Mini Case

PATHOLOGICAL GAMBLING

Wayne is a 22-year-old auto mechanic, a father of two, married to a factory worker. Two years ago, he went to the local race track with a friend, who showed him how to bet on horses. To his surprise, Wayne made some good bets and came home with a $50 profit. Buoyed by his success, he made repeated trips to the track and, in time, began taking days off from work to bet on the races. On one of these occasions, Wayne won $5,000. This made him feel extremely proud of his betting expertise and convinced him that he had special skills at picking the right horse. Even though he was losing many of his bets, he now felt certain that his winnings would more than compensate. He had a feeling of self-confidence that, for once in his life, he was a success. To keep up his image, Wayne started to make larger and larger bets on long shots that failed to pay off. As his losses accumulated into the tens of thousands of dollars, he grew panicky and felt driven to bet even more.

Diagnostic Features

People with this disorder engage in persistent and recurrent maladaptive gambling characterized by at least five of the following:

- They are preoccupied with gambling.
- They need to gamble increasing amounts of money to achieve the desired level of excitement.
- They are repeatedly unsuccessful in their attempts to control or stop gambling.
- They are restless or irritable when they try to cut down or stop.
- They gamble in an effort to escape problems or relieve unpleasant emotions.
- After losing money, they often return to gambling in an effort to gain back what they have lost.
- They lie to family members, therapists, or other people in order to conceal the extent of their gambling.
- They commit illegal acts, such as forgery, fraud, or theft, to finance their gambling.
- They jeopardize or lose a significant relationship, job, or educational or career opportunity because of gambling.
- They rely on others for money to help out with desperate financial problems caused by their gambling.

Many pathological gamblers get started through rather harmless ventures, such as a neighborhood poker game. Most people gamble recreationally with no ill effects; by contrast, pathological gamblers get caught up in a cycle they are unable to control.

banishment from baseball. Pete Rose's problem brought attention to a disorder with which few Americans were familiar.

During this same time period, federal laws were changed in ways that would increase the availability of high-stakes gambling to many Americans. For example, the Indian Gaming Regulatory Act of 1988 permitted the establishment of casino gambling on Native American lands. Towns and cities around the nation built casinos and placed gambling boats in nearby waters, attracting people to legal gambling who had never in their lives entered a gambling establishment. State lotteries became very popular during the 1980s, as did off-track betting. Pathological gambling is becoming a serious problem in U.S. society, affecting millions of Americans. It is estimated that the lifetime prevalence of this disorder is slightly less that 1 percent. Pathological gamblers are more likely than nongamblers to be male, non-White, and unmarried. They are likely to have comorbid disorders, including mood, alcohol abuse, and substance abuse disorders (Dannon et al., 2004). Low education levels and middle income levels are also risk factors for pathological gambling (Wong & So, 2003).

Pathological gambling is a more serious condition than the occasional buying of a lottery ticket or involvement in an office betting pool. Pathological gamblers are preoccupied with gambling to such an extent that it is difficult for them to get the idea of betting out of their mind. Repeated efforts to control their gambling are usually unsuccessful; during these attempts, they are likely to be restless and irritable. They become caught up in a pattern of "chasing," in which they return to betting following a loss in an effort to make back what they have lost. The higher the degree of disturbance the individual experiences, the greater the variety of gambling activities in which he or she engages. Casino gambling is associated with the highest risk of pathology, and lottery, cards, and bingo with a moderate risk. However, people with severe pathological gambling will gamble almost indiscriminately in a variety of ways, regardless of whether or how much they win or lose (Welte et al., 2004).

From the day that Pete Rose was discovered to be a pathological gambler, controversy has brewed about his eligibility to be inducted into the Baseball Hall of Fame. Rose's betting on baseball was especially self-defeating due to the fact that he was still actively involved in managing a major league baseball team.

Eventually, the gambling lifestyle takes its toll not only on the individual's finances but on psychological health. Among a study of twin pairs discordant for pathological gambling, there were no differences in how well they rated their physical well-being. The pathological gamblers, however, had lower scores across a variety of mental health indexes pertaining to quality of life (Scherrer et al., 2005).

Although U.S. society presents many opportunities for gambling, not everyone who gambles becomes a pathological gambler. How does such a seemingly harmless pastime develop into a compulsive, self-destructive pattern? According to the late psychiatrist Robert L. Custer (1982), who in the 1970s established the first clinic for the treatment of pathological gambling in the United States, gambling progresses through a series of stages. In the first stage, the individual is simply a recreational gambler who enjoys gambling as a social activity. Movement into the next stage, which is the beginning of a pathological gambling pattern, occurs when the individual begins to win. At

this point, the gambler gains an identity as a "winner," and, the more often that success is encountered in gambling, the more this identity becomes reinforced. If at this point the gambler encounters a **big win,** a gain of large amounts of money in one bet, he or she is propelled into a pattern of addiction that inevitably becomes almost impossible to break. This event is so reinforcing, both financially and psychologically, that the individual is obsessed with the need to re-experience it. In the doomed search for another big win, a cycle becomes established in which the pathological gambler has periodic wins that maintain an unreasonable optimism; however, these gains never erase the debt, because, for every win experienced, continued gambling leads to heavier losses. In time, the gambler's physical, psychological, and financial resources are depleted, and the person considers drastic action, such as committing suicide, running away, or embarking on a life of crime.

Theories and Treatment of Pathological Gambling We have just seen the stages that lead from recreational to pathological gambling. These stages seem to involve some of the same factors that play a role in alcohol and drug addiction, in that the individual continually seeks pleasure from a behavior that, although leading to trouble, possesses strong reward potential. Interestingly, a biopsychosocial perspective is also becoming viewed as an appropriate model to use in understanding the causes of this disorder.

From a biological perspective, the gambler's perpetual pursuit of the big win can be seen as similar to the alcohol-dependent person's search for stimulation and pleasurable feelings through alcohol use, though there are some differences between the two in that the spending of money does not have the same intrinsically rewarding quality as the taking of a psychoactive substance. However, researchers are finding that people with pathological gambling have abnormalities in the brain that lead them to seek excess stimulation, be it through drugs, food, or gambling. Such a deficiency may have a genetic basis (Goudriaan, Oosterlaan, de Beurs, & Van den Brink, 2004), as indicated by studies on pathological gamblers who possess genetic abnormalities affecting a number of neurotransmitter systems, including dopamine, serotonin, and MAOI (Ibanez et al., 2003). Researchers believe that dopamine abnormalities, in particular, affect the reward system of the brain that lead pathological gamblers to seek excess stimulation (Reuter et al., 2005). These gamblers also show deficiencies in areas of the brain involved in decision making, possibly contributing to their tendencies to make risky bets (Brand et al., 2005).

Cognitive factors may also play a role in the transmission of pathological gambling from one generation to the next. In one investigation of parents and their teenage children, researchers found that the ways in which children thought about gambling were heavily influenced by the way their parents, particularly their fathers, thought about gambling (Oei & Raylu, 2004).

Another factor that contributes to a person's likelihood of becoming a pathological gambler is the experience of gambling during childhood and adolescence. Public health researchers fear that people who begin gambling in adolescence and young adulthood are at the highest risk for developing lifelong patterns of gambling addiction (Messerlian, Derevensky, & Gupta, 2005). In a large-scale investigation of adolescents and young adult gamblers, researchers found that those who began to gamble early in adolescence were more likely to report high levels of depression, alcohol, and drug use. The lifestyle associated with gambling is thus associated among young people with a life of high-risk behaviors that in turn creates further mental health impairments.

Some researchers suggest that individuals with certain personality characteristics may have a predisposition to developing the disorder. In particular, a high level of the trait of impulsivity or a combination of high levels of impulsivity and psychopathy are thought to predispose individuals to seek the excitement provided by involvement in gambling (Petry, 2001).

Sociocultural factors are also involved in the acquisition and maintenance of pathological gambling. Exposure to a culture of gambling, in which parents and peers are heavily engaged in gambling activities themselves, can also increase the individual's chances of developing this disorder (Langhinrichsen-Rohling, Rohde, Seeley, & Rohling, 2004). As we mentioned earlier, the 1980s saw an increased availability of legalized gambling through state lotteries, off-track betting, and casinos, a trend that continues into the present with no signs of abating. Internet addiction is becoming the newest context for pathological gambling, and although more common among young people, it is also becoming prevalent among the adult population. Individuals with a vulnerability to this disorder are therefore more likely to be in situations in which they will be unable to resist the urge to gamble.

Persuading pathological gamblers to enter treatment is challenging because of their tendency to deny the seriousness of their problem. Only a small percentage of pathological gamblers seek help for their problem, as most tend to deny the seriousness of their disorder. Therefore, for any intervention to work, clinicians must first deal with the gambler's resistance to treatment.

Online gambling has become an irresistible temptation to many individuals because of its ease of access and immediate reinforcement potential.

In keeping with the biopsychosocial model of understanding the disorders, treatment methods that combine elements of the various perspectives seem to have the greatest chance of success. Clinical trials are pointing to the effectiveness of serotonin reuptake inhibitors (such as clomipramine and fluvoxamine) as biological interventions (Kuzma & Black, 2004). In one fascinating intervention study, naltrexone (used for treating substance abuse disorders) led to reduced symptoms of pathological gambling (Kim, Grant, Adson, & Shin, 2001). As the evidence on these interventions continues to be gathered, clinicians are also finding success in the use of behavioral and cognitive-behavioral methods of treatment (Toneatto & Ladoceur, 2003). Such interventions may include correcting the gambler's inaccurate perceptions of gambling, providing training in problem solving and social skills, and incorporating elements of motivational telephone interventions (Hodgins, Currie, el-Guebaly, & Peden, 2004). In addition to traditional psychotherapy approaches, many pathological gamblers benefit from the confrontation and support that peers provide in such programs as Gamblers Anonymous.

Pyromania

The sight of fire is fascinating to many people. If a building is on fire, most passersby stop and watch while it is brought under control. Candles and fireplaces are commonly regarded as backdrops to a romantic or an intimate evening. For the very small percentage of the population who have the impulse-control disorder called pyromania, fascination with fire goes beyond this normal degree of interest and becomes a compulsive and dangerous urge to set fires deliberately.

Characteristics of Pyromania As is true for all people with impulse-control disorders, people with **pyromania** cannot restrain themselves from acting on strong and compelling urges; in this case, the urges involve the intense desire to prepare, set, and watch fires. Before the fire, these people become tense and aroused; on setting the fire, they experience intense feelings of pleasure, gratification, or relief. Even when not actively involved in firesetting, they are fascinated with, interested in, and curious about fire and anything to do with it. For example, they may have police scanners that alert them to ongoing fires, so that they can rush out immediately to watch the fire. Some even find ways to become involved with firefighting, so that they can be more personally involved in the excitement of witnessing a raging fire close up. The behavior of the person with pyromania differs from that of an arsonist, who starts fires for an ulterior motive, such as financial gain, political dissent, vengeance, or the concealment of a crime. Unfortunately, the research evidence in this field is based largely on findings with chronic firesetters and individuals incarcerated for the crime of arson (Barnett, Richter, Sigmund, & Spitzer, 1997). The potential significance of this disorder is indicated by statistics showing that arson is the second leading cause of fire-related deaths in the United States (United States Fire Administration, 2001).

As with pathological gambling, pyromania is more common in males, with most showing the first signs of a pathological interest in fire during childhood and early adolescence (Hanson, MacKay-Soroka, Staley, & Poulton, 1994).

Theories and Treatment of Pyromania   Most individuals with pyromania have one or more other problems or disorders, and in most cases the disorder is rooted in childhood problems and firesetting behavior. Firesetting children have a compelling attraction to and curiosity about fire, which develops as a result of their observation and modeling of adult firesetting behavior. They have access to firestarting materials, lack remorse over firesetting, and feel motivated to start fires out of curiosity and a view of the act as fun. Furthermore, their parents are ineffective or uninterested in disciplining their children for this behavior (Kolko & Kazdin, 1994). These children also tend to be highly aggressive, have higher levels of psychopathology, show evidence of antisocial behavior and have difficulties in school (Martin, Bergen, Richardson, Roeger, & Allison, 2004). Emotional neglect and abuse are additional factors found within the homes of these children.

As adults, individuals who engage in firesetting behavior continue to show other disturbances, including schizophrenia, bipolar disorder, and alcohol or substance abuse (Ritchie & Huff, 1999). Furthermore, pointing perhaps to the role of sociocultural factors, individuals with a history of firesetting have low levels of education and employment (Rasanen, Hakko, & Vaisanen, 1995). Biological factors also play a role. Abnormally low levels of serotonin have been identified in individuals with a long history of firesetting (Virkkunen, Eggert, Rawlings, & Linnoila, 1996).

Given the evidence that chronic firesetting has its roots in childhood, treatment programs aimed at youths would seem to have the most potential for success. Thus, programs developed

The lure of a fire proves to be so fascinating for the pyromaniac that the urge to start fires is irresistible.

Diagnostic Features

People with this condition show evidence of the following characteristics:

- They deliberately and repeatedly set fires.

- They experience a sense of tension or affective arousal before the firesetting.

- They are fascinated with, interested in, curious about, or attracted to fire and things associated with fire.

- They feel pleasure, gratification, or relief when setting fires or when watching or participating in the events following a fire.

- Their firesetting is not done for ulterior motives, such as monetary gain, an expression of political ideology, the concealment of criminal activity, or an expression of anger or vengeance.

Mini Case

SEXUAL IMPULSIVITY

Raj is a 24-year-old clerk who lives alone in an apartment in a large city. A loner since high school, Raj nevertheless is intensely preoccupied with the pursuit of sex. At work, he constantly thinks about each person he meets as a potential sexual partner. Repeatedly on his mind are plans to find new places where he can have sex. On a typical day, Raj goes to a pornographic movie theater during his lunch hour, where he seeks to have oral sexual activities with as many different men as he can find. On his way home from work, he often stops at a highway rest area, where he once again seeks anonymous sex partners. During the weekend, he frequents singles bars, where he usually succeeds in picking up women. Although he continues to involve himself in these sexual activities, Raj is quite distressed by his behavior. Guilt and negative feelings about himself cause him to feel depressed, and even suicidal at times. However, his behavior seems to him to be beyond his control. Although he has thought of obtaining professional help, he is too embarrassed to admit his problem to anyone.

Diagnostic Features

- People with this condition are unable to control their sexual behavior, and they feel driven to engage in frequent and indiscriminate sexual activity.

- They experience an increasing sense of tension prior to engaging in a sexual act.

- They feel a great deal of distress about their behavior and, following sexual encounters, are likely to feel dejected, hopeless, and ashamed.

- Their compulsive pursuit of sexual encounters interferes with their ability to carry out normal social and occupational responsibilities.

---

for children and adolescents in psychiatric hospitals focus on prevention by incorporating didactic techniques regarding fire safety, as well as interventions that focus on self-esteem. Outreach and community prevention are additional strategies that are recommended to reduce the likelihood of a child becoming a firesetter (Kolko, 2001).

Sexual Impulsivity

People with **sexual impulsivity** are unable to control their sexual behavior, and they feel driven to engage in frequent and indiscriminate sexual activity. Although this condition is not an official *DSM-IV-TR* diagnosis, the symptoms and behaviors of people with sexual impulsivity are quite similar to those associated with impulse-control disorders. During the past few decades, clinicians have seen increasing numbers of clients looking for help to contain uncontrollable sexuality. Some experts believe that the easy availability of sexuality on the Internet has pulled some people into a world where they desperately seek sexual gratification—addictedly viewing sexual images, participating in sexually oriented chat rooms, or contacting other people seeking sexual encounters (Carnes, Delmonico, Griffin, & Moriarty, 2001).

Characteristics of Sexual Impulsivity People with the disorder of sexual impulsivity are preoccupied with sex, feeling uncontrollably driven to seek out sexual encounters, which they later regret. This drive is similar to that reported in other impulse-control disorders, involving a state in which the individual is transfixed by the need for sex. People with sexual impulsivity feel that they cannot control the number of their sexual encounters, or even the contexts in which they are likely to initiate sexual behavior. Terms such as "sexual addiction," "sexual compulsivity," and "sexual dependency" are also used to characterize this disorder, indicating the pervasive effects that the drive for

To a person with sexual impulsivity, each social interaction is perceived as an opportunity for another sexual conquest.

sexuality has on the lives of these individuals.

As is true in other impulse-control disorders, the uncontrollable behavior of people with sexual impulsivity interferes with their ability to carry out normal social and occupational responsibilities and can place their social status in jeopardy (Gordon, Fargason, & Kramer, 1995). They feel a great deal of distress about their behavior; following sexual encounters, they are likely to feel dejected, hopeless, and ashamed. Although a few are consumed by the constant need to masturbate, most seek out partners, usually people they do not know or care to know following the anonymous sexual encounter. In extreme cases, sexual impulsivity may extend into very serious deviant and violent behavior, including "lust" murders and serial killing (Blanchard, 1995).

One of the first detailed investigations of sexual impulsivity, which was conducted with a male homosexual and bisexual sample, provides an indication of the extreme nature of this disorder (Quadland, 1985). In this group, individuals with sexual impulsivity averaged more than 29 partners per month and more than 2,000 sexual encounters over their lifetimes. They frequently sought sex in public settings and used alcohol or drugs with sex, and they typically had a history of few long-term relationships. Although the disorder is more common in men, women also have this condition, although it is expressed in different ways; women tend to be more passive in their openness to sexual encounters, while men are more likely to be intrusive, possibly exploitive, in their pursuits (Ross, 1996).

Individuals with sexual impulsivity commonly suffer with a co-existing condition, such as depression, substance abuse, or anxiety; in fact, episodes of strong sexual interest seem to occur when these individuals are feeling depressed or anxious (Bancroft & Vukadinovic, 2004). Some people with this condition experience dissociative symptoms linked to their sexual impulsivity. They describe going into an altered state of consciousness, even while consumed with the pursuit of sexual excitement on the Internet, which we will discuss later in the chapter. Researchers believe that the traits of impulsivity associated with this disorder place sexual impulsivity in the spectrum with other impulsive-compulsive spectrum disorders (Raymond, Coleman, & Miner, 2003).

Theories and Treatment of Sexual Impulsivity   A disorder as potentially dangerous as sexual impulsivity calls for a comprehensive approach to understanding and treatment. As in other disorders we have seen in this chapter, a biopsychosocial model provides an excellent starting point for such an integrated approach (Price, 2004). Those working within the biological perspective suggest that sexual impulsivity is comparable to the other addictions, with a similar biochemical basis (Sunderwirth, Milkman, & Jenks, 1996). However, in trying to understand the origins of sexual impulsivity, researchers have focused primarily on the roots of the disorder within the early life experiences of the individual. Psychodynamic theorists view sexually addictive behavior as an intimacy disorder rooted in early attachment experiences (Adams & Robinson, 2001). According to this view, impaired bonding between infant and caregiver can cause some individuals to experience difficulties regulating their affect as adults. Consequently, they get caught in a compulsive cycle in which they try to soothe themselves and regulate internal struggles by engaging in sexual behaviors. Unfortunately, such efforts tend to create more shame and dysregulation of affect. Exposure to an abusive family environment is one of the key factors thought to predispose an individual toward this behavior (Carnes & Delmonico, 1996). In adulthood, this relationship between violence and sexuality may persist as the perpetrator uses sex as a hostile activity directed toward the partner (Irons, 1996).

Like other disorders in the obsessive-compulsive spectrum, sexual impulsivity responds to SSRIs (Hollander & Rosen, 2000). Treatment for sexual impulsivity involves a combination of psychological components derived from the insight-oriented, behavioral, and family systems approaches. Insight-oriented

therapy focuses on bringing to the surface the individual's underlying conflicts that motivate the behavior. These conflicts include resolving nonsexual problems through sexual means, needing reassurance, and feeling insecure about one's sex role (Longo, 2004). The therapist may also help the client learn how to regulate affect and establish adaptive sexual boundaries (Adams & Robinson, 2001). Behavioral techniques include aversive covert conditioning (McConaghy, Armstrong, & Blaszczynski, 1985), imaginal desensitization (McConaghy, Blaszczynski, & Frankova, 1991), and behavioral contracting (Schwartz & Brasted, 1985). If sexual impulsivity is associated with other psychological disorders, such as mood disorder or obsessive-compulsive disorder, treatment of these associated conditions with medications may also be warranted (Sealy, 1995). Family or couples therapy is also an important component of therapy for clients whose excessive sexual behavior occurs in the context of long-term close relationships. The early involvement of partners in this process is seen as crucial to the success of the intervention (Matheny, 1998).

Trichotillomania

The urge to pull out one's hair, which becomes a compulsion in people with the rare disorder called **trichotillomania,** may seem bizarre and far removed from the realm of everyday human behavior. In American culture, for example, many people, especially women, are self-conscious about body hair and go to some trouble to remove it. However, for some people, the act of hair-pulling develops a compulsive quality, causing them to become so preoccupied with pulling out their hair that they are oblivious to the fact that they may actually be marring their appearance. Estimates of prevalence are generally in the range of 1 to 2 percent of the population (American Psychiatric Association, 2000), although some figures are as high as 5 percent (Graber & Arndt, 1993), particularly among female adolescents and young adults. For some, the condition is relatively transient, while for others it lasts for decades.

Characteristics of Trichotillomania   Like people with other impulse-control disorders, the person with trichotillomania experiences an increasing sense of tension immediately prior to pulling out the hair or when trying to resist the urge to pull. The experience of hair-pulling results in feelings of relief, pleasure, or gratification. People with trichotillomania are upset by their uncontrollable behavior and may find that their social, occupational, or other areas of functioning are impaired because of this disorder. They feel unable to stop this behavior, even when the pulling results in bald patches and lost eyebrows, eyelashes, armpit hair, and pubic hair. In extreme cases, some individuals swallow the hair after they have pulled it out, risking the danger that it will solidify in the stomach or intestines (a condition referred to as a trichobezoar or "Rapunzel syndrome").

People with this disorder are secretive about what they are doing and tend to engage in hair-pulling only when alone. For

Mini Case

TRICHOTILLOMANIA

For most of her childhood and adolescence, 15-year-old Janet lived a fairly isolated existence, with no close friends. Although Janet never discussed her unhappiness with anyone, she often felt very depressed and hopeless. As a young child, Janet lay in bed on many nights, secretly tugging at her hair. Over time, this behavior increased to the point at which she plucked the hair, strand by strand, from her scalp. Typically, she pulled out a hair, examined it, bit it, and either threw it away or swallowed it. Because her hair was thick and curly, her hair loss was not initially evident, and Janet kept it carefully combed to conceal the bald spots. One of her teachers noticed that Janet was pulling her hair in class, and, in looking more closely, she saw these patches on Janet's head. She referred Janet to the school psychologist, who called Janet's mother and recommended professional help.

Diagnostic Features

People with this condition show evidence of the following characteristics:

- They recurrently pull out hair, which causes considerable hair loss.

- They experience an increasing sense of tension immediately before pulling out hair or when they try to resist hair-pulling behavior.

- They feel pleasure, gratification, or relief when pulling out hair.

- Their behavior causes significant distress or impairment.

---

some, the interest goes beyond their own bodily hair and may involve pulling the hair from another person, or even from pets, dolls, and materials, such as carpets and sweaters. Even when clear physical evidence suggests intentional hair-pulling, people with this disorder tend to deny that they are engaging in the behavior. They may even conceal the damage they have done by wearing hats or rearranging their hair to cover bald spots. In cases involving children and adolescents, parents may become alarmed at the mysterious hair loss and take the child to a dermatologist or pediatrician with a concern about a medical problem. On examination, the health professional may notice many short, broken hairs around the bald areas on the skin, indicating that the hairs have been plucked. In other cases, it is not a dermatological concern that brings clinical attention but, rather, another psychological problem, such as depression, anxiety, or an eating disorder.

Trichotillomania often co-exists with other disorders, including depression, obsessive-compulsive disorder, substance abuse, or an eating disorder (Folks & Warnock, 2001). These conditions may bring the individual into treatment, at which point the hair-pulling compulsion may be disclosed.

Theories and Treatment of Trichotillomania Trichotillomania is an intriguing disorder that is not well understood; however, each of the major perspectives offers some insights. From a biological perspective, trichotillomania is seen as sharing some characteristics with obsessive-compulsive disorder. Supporting this notion are the observations that, in both disorders, behavior is driven by anxiety or tension, and people with both disorders respond to medication. However, some researchers see trichotillomania as having more in common with the other impulse control disorders than with obsessive-compulsive disorder (Lochner et al., 2005).

Behavioral theorists regard the disorder as a complex interaction among environmental cues, hair-pulling, and the consequences of pulling (Mansueto, Stemberger, Thomas, & Golomb,

Trichotillomania often goes undetected, because those suffering from the irresistible urge to pull out their own hair usually deny their behavior.

1997). Individuals with this disorder learn to associate hair-pulling behavior with relief from tension. Thus, a young woman who becomes anxious while studying may experience transient relief when she tugs on her hair. Over time, she may return to the hair-pulling behavior in an effort to regain the sense of relief she experienced the last time.

Finally, from the sociocultural perspective, trichotillomania affects the individual's social relationships. The disorder exacts a toll in feelings of shame and unattractiveness and in disturbed interactions with others (Stemberger, Thomas, Mansueto, & Carter, 2000).

Pharmacological treatments for this disorder include paroxetine (Paxil) (Ravindran, Lapierre, & Anisman, 1999), ven-

INTERMITTENT EXPLOSIVE DISORDER

Ed, a 28-year-old high-school teacher, has unprovoked, violent outbursts of aggressive and assaultive behavior. During these episodes, Ed throws whatever objects he can get his hands on and yells profanities. He soon calms down, though, and feels intense regret for whatever damage he has caused, explaining that he didn't know what came over him. In the most recent episode, he threw a coffeepot at another teacher in the faculty lounge, inflicting serious injury. After the ambulance took the injured man to the hospital, Ed's supervisor called the police.

Diagnostic Features

People with this condition show evidence of the following characteristics:

- During several separate episodes, they are unable to resist aggressive impulses, which result in serious acts of assault or destruction.

- Their level of aggressiveness during these episodes is grossly out of proportion to any precipitating stressors.

- Their aggressive episodes are not associated with another mental or physical disorder.

A sudden eruption of rage causes people with intermittent explosive disorder to lose control over what they say and do.

laflaxine (Effexor) (Ninan, 2000), fluvoxamine (Luvox) (Figgit & McClellan, 2000), and olanzapine, which is an atypical antipsychotic (Stewart & Nejtek, 2003).

Although this disorder might have a biological component, learning also appears to play a role. In a waiting-list control group investigation comparing fluoxetine with behavioral therapy, a greater reduction in hair-pulling symptoms was observed for the group receiving behavioral treatment (van Minnen et al., 2003). Habit reversal is a particularly effective behavioral technique; in this method the individual is trained to be more aware of the behavior and then is taught a new response to compete with hair-pulling. Combining habit reversal with methods that provide social and emotional support to clients can be particularly effective (Twohig & Woods, 2004).

Intermittent Explosive Disorder

All people lose their tempers on occasion, but most are able to let off steam without causing any harm. In contrast, people with **intermittent explosive disorder** feel a recurrent inability to resist assaultive or destructive acts of aggression.

Characteristics of Intermittent Explosive Disorder The behaviors found in people with intermittent explosive disorder are occasional bouts of extreme rage, in which they become assaultive or destructive without serious provocation or verbally threaten to physically assault another individual. During

these episodes, these people can cause serious physical harm to themselves, other people, and property. While in the midst of an episode, they feel as if they are under a spell, and some have even used terms that suggest that it is like a seizure state. Just prior to the outburst, they may feel an impending sense that something is about to happen, an experience that has been compared to the aura, or anticipatory state, that people with epilepsy experience prior to a seizure. Some individuals state that their aggressive episodes are often preceded or accompanied by symptoms such as tingling, tremor, heart palpitations, head pressure, or even hearing echoes. Between episodes, they may be somewhat impulsive or aggressive by nature, but not to such a degree that their behavior is harmful. Because of their outbursts, most individuals with this disorder have difficulties at work and at home. They may lose their jobs, and their partners may become intolerant. This rare disorder is more common among men, some of whom are imprisoned for their destructive or assaultive behavior. Women with this disorder are more likely to be sent to a mental health facility for treatment. This disorder is often associated with other clinical disorders, particularly mood disorders, which are estimated to occur in over 90 percent of individuals with the diagnosis. Other comorbid conditions include substance use disorders and anxiety disorders, which are found in nearly half of the individuals diagnosed with intermittent explosive disorder (McElroy et al., 1998).

Although thought of as a relatively rare disorder, researchers have begun to rethink its prevalence. One-month incidence estimates place the possible number in the United States at 1.4 million, which would translate to an estimated lifetime prevalence of 10 million people (Coccaro, Schmidt, Samuels, & Nestadt, 2004).

Theories and Treatment of Intermittent Explosive Disorder
Many features of intermittent explosive disorder suggest that a complex interaction of biological and environmental factors lead an individual to develop an inability to control aggressive outbursts (Kavoussi, Armstead, & Coccaro, 1997). In terms of spe-

cific biological factors, alterations in the serotonergic system are suggested as providing a possible vulnerability to the disorder (Hollander & Rosen, 2000). Researchers have observed abnormalities in brain circuits involved in impulsive aggressiveness (Best, Williams, & Coccaro, 2002).

In terms of psychological factors, learning theorists would point to the concepts of operant conditioning to explain the behavior of people who explode occasionally. In such circumstances, they probably provoke intense reactions, possibly of fear and submission, in people around them, leading to a powerful form of reinforcement. This conceptualization can be carried into the realm of sociocultural theory as well, as we consider the influence on family systems and intimate relationships when a person's behavior is so threatening and violent. Although not considered a psychological disorder, "road rage," in which an individual loses control while driving in an aggressive outburst, may bear some similarities to intermittent explosive disorder (Galovski & Blanchard, 2004). Another form of uncontrolled impulsive aggression can be found in the angry and violent outbursts in the workplace that have become the source of tragic instances of multiple homicides.

Based on the findings of serotonergic abnormalities among people with this disorder, clinicians advocate the use of medications in treatment, particularly citalopram (Reist et al., 2003). However, it is recognized that psychotherapeutic methods must be combined with somatic approaches. For example, people with this disorder can be taught to monitor their levels of anger and find verbal rather than physical outlets, an approach that has worked successfully in reducing aggressive driving behaviors (Galovski & Blanchard, 2002).

Internet Addiction

Since the emergence of the World Wide Web during the past two decades, clinicians and researchers have become aware of a condition that seems related in many ways to the impulse-control disorders discussed in this chapter. The condition, referred to as **Internet addiction,** is an impulse-control condition in which an individual feels an irresistible need to be involved in Internet-based activities. Internet addiction is not included in *DSM-IV-TR,* but shares many of the characteristics of the impulse-control disorders and creates substantial intrapsychic and interpersonal turmoil for people with this seemingly uncontrollable condition. Some experts are beginning to make the case for adding Internet addiction to the *DSM* (Warden, Phillips, & Ogloff, 2004).

Characteristics of Internet Addiction

Because the Internet provides a world of anonymity in which individuals have access to a cyber-world where censorship is absent and fantasy can run wild, some individuals get caught up in Internet-related activities that consume an inordinate amount of time, energy, and money. Over time, as is the case

with the pathological gambler or the individual with sexual impulsivity, the person who is addicted to the Internet experiences irresistible urges to be on the Internet in chat rooms, engaging in gambling activities, or perusing pornographic websites. The informal diagnostic term, "cyber-disorders," has developed among practitioners seeing clients whose primary clinical problem involves the Internet, and includes the following subtypes: (1) cyber-sexual addiction involving the compulsive use of sexually oriented websites; (2) cyber-relationship addiction characterized by overinvolvement in online relationships; (3) net compulsions such as online gambling, shopping, or trading; (4) information overload which involves compulsive Web surfing or database searches; and (5) computer addiction, which consists of compulsive involvement in online game playing (Young, 2004).

The demographics associated with Internet addiction have changed in recent years. In the early days of the Internet, addicted individuals were predominantly young, introverted, and computer-oriented males. As computer access has become more common and as increasing numbers of girls and women have become computer savvy, the demographics of addiction have correspondingly changed. There are also high personal and social costs associated with Internet addiction. College administrators are reporting that high dropout rates, even among students with strong academic skills, are associated with extensive patterns of Internet use. In the workplace, surveys have established that nearly one third of companies in the United States have fired employees for inappropriate Internet use. Online affairs, which can progress to secret meetings offline, are becoming a growing cause for concern as well, with lawyers reporting that the Internet has played a role in a growing number of divorces (Young, 2004).

Theories and Treatment

The biopsychosocial model can be used to conceptualize Internet addiction (Beard, 2005). In biological terms, as with the other disorders discussed in this chapter, changes occur at the level of neurotransmitters in the brain while people engage in addictive behavior. These changes create altered physiological states that result in a sense of euphoria. In terms of psychological processes, classical conditioning occurs as physiological arousal becomes conditioned to such cues as seeing a computer, turning it on, or waiting for information to be downloaded. Internally, addicted individuals have sensations such as excitement, stimulation, pleasure, hope, and surprise, such that in time they become psychologically dependent on the computer. Operant conditioning principles also apply in that the Internet-oriented behaviors of addicted individuals provide quick reinforcement that is rewarding in terms of feelings of excitement or the provision of relief from states of dysphoria. The sociocultural perspective on Internet addiction focuses on the familial, social, and cultural dynamics of this behavior. Some people use the Internet to escape family or relationship conflict, a choice which ironically often compounds such conflict. As mentioned above, there are a number of significant interpersonal problems that arise from Internet use, particularly when individuals cut off social relationships, become consumed with their private Internet activities, and become increasingly alienated. A vicious cycle then develops in which the dysphoria created by these problems intensifies, leading to even more addictive behavior.

As with the impulse-control disorders discussed in this chapter, people who are addicted to the Internet usually resist seeking treatment. It is usually only at the insistence of loved ones that they seek help. Researchers in this area have urged clinicians to take this problem seriously and to resist underestimating the extent to which excessive Internet use has caused havoc in the lives of many people. In recent years, there has been an increase in professional training and access to educational resources on Internet addiction such as the Center for Online Addiction (www.netaddiction.com). Many of the techniques used in the treatment of impulse-control disorders also apply to the treatment of clients involved in uncontrollable Internet use. In addition to individual psychotherapy, couples therapy may also be recommended, particularly in cases in which there has been serious detrimental impact of this behavior on a relationship.

Eating Disorders and Impulse-Control Disorders: The Biopsychosocial Perspective

In this chapter, we have discussed several disorders that involve people's struggles to control strong urges to act in ways that are destructive or detrimental to their existence. Some of these disorders represent behaviors that, in moderation, are not problematic. Nothing is wrong with dieting, gambling, or having sexual interests. It is also normal to lose one's temper on occasion. However, when these behaviors are carried to an extreme, they can become a source of distress to the individual and to others. In contrast, firestarting and stealing are outside the realm of what society regards as acceptable behavior, because these actions violate the rights of others and are against the law. Regardless of the degree of acceptability of the behavior, the main issue in understanding these disorders is that the individual feels powerless to control the impulse to act.

A number of the disorders we have covered in this chapter cause considerable harm to other people in addition to the client. Even if the client does not recognize a need for treatment, interventions may be mandated by legal authorities or may be insisted on by family members. Unfortunately, the nature of these disorders makes it particularly difficult for these individuals to seek help and, even when they do, to seize control over their behavior.

In their attempt to explain impulse-control disorders, experts have proposed that these conditions fall on an "affective spectrum" that includes mood disorders, obsessive-compulsive disorder, substance abuse disorders, eating disorders, and anxiety disorders. All these conditions share certain symptoms, hypothesized biological mechanisms, and treatments. As researchers continue to explore these links, we can look forward to improved understanding of these mysterious and disabling psychological phenomena.

Case Report
Rosa Ramirez

RETURN TO THE CASE

Rosa's History

I had been relieved at the end of our intake session when Rosa agreed to initiate psychotherapy. She approached our first psychotherapy session with a style that was considerably different from that which she showed during her first meeting with me. She seemed more open, as well as more eager to deal with the issues that had been troubling her. As soon as we sat down, Rosa launched into telling me about her life.

Rosa began to tell me about her 19 years of life, which were filled with countless experiences of success. She explained that she felt she had been "blessed with good fortune," causing her to feel at times as though she was "living under a lucky star." She was the only child of a middle-class Puerto Rican family that resided in a wealthy suburb of San Juan. Both of Rosa's parents were successful business executives who had risen to positions of prominence in the banking field. She spoke of them with deep affection, while alluding to the intense levels of pressure they placed on her to succeed.

Rosa had learned that the pressure she felt from her parents began to emerge even prior to her birth. Even though she was an only child, she knew that she was the second-born in the family, with her birth taking place 2 years after the tragic death of her brother, Juan, on his fifth birth-day. Juan had died in a freak acci-dent when the bike he had just received for his birthday careened down a hillside and slammed into a tree. Although Rosa's parents never spoke of the accident, and rarely mentioned Juan's name, her Uncle Rico shared with Rosa the details of the event and the emotional devasta-tion that followed for her parents.

According to Rico, Rosa's parents had mourned the death of Juan for a year, after which they decided to try to have another child. This time, however, they promised that they "would be more careful." Rico had told Rosa about the overprotective-ness of her parents. From the day that Rosa was carried into the home for the first time, she was treated like a fragile work of art. Rarely was she left unattended, even for a few moments. When her parents were at work, she was left in the hands of her grandmother, who doted over her with solicitous affection.

Rosa was sent to the finest schools, and she excelled in aca-demics as well as athletics. From an early age, she was nurtured to be a tennis pro, with private lessons be-ginning in early childhood. Rosa's parents' expectations for her were very high. If she did poorly in a com-petitive tennis match, more tennis lessons were added to her weekly schedule. If she received any grade less than an A in school, her parents lectured her about the importance of her studies and took away some privileges until she attained perfect grades.

As Rosa told me about her par-ents' childrearing practices, I in-quired about her feelings growing up in a family with such high expecta-tions. To my surprise, Rosa did not speak negatively about these experi-ences. Rather, she stated, "I felt so fortunate to know, on a daily basis, how much my parents loved me." She stated that she never resented their demands but shared their val-ues to make her life the best it could possibly be. She explained that she has always loved her parents deeply and, in fact, missed them intensely since coming to college, feeling "desperately homesick."

When we turned our attention to Rosa's eating disorder, I could per-ceive a tensing of her body. It was obvious that she was reluctant to talk about how this horrendous prob-lem had developed, but she realized that it was important for me to know the history, so that I could help her. In beginning to tell me about the roots of her eating disorder, Rosa began with the emphatic statement, "I want you to understand that this problem had nothing to do with my parents. They never said a word about my weight or my appearance." Although I thought it odd that she would begin with that disclaimer, I decided to leave the parental issue aside and to proceed to a direct questioning about when and how Rosa had gotten caught up in this self-destructive behavior.

Rosa recalled the day she associ-ates with the development of her eating problem. In the fall of her se-nior year, she was being contacted by college tennis coaches who had heard about her remarkable athletic skills. She was told by more than a dozen colleges that she would be awarded a 4-year scholarship, based on her athletic and academic accomplishments. Rather than feel jubilant, Rosa suddenly felt intense self-consciousness. One December night, following a dinnertime discus-sion about which college Rosa was intending to choose, she rushed from the table in tears to an upstairs bath-room and vomited. Feeling a sense of relief, Rosa then went to her bed-room and fell asleep.

In the weeks and months that followed, Rosa outwardly seemed fine. She had made a choice about college and had resumed her suc-cessful endeavors in school and ten-nis. However, as Rosa explained, the facade masked inner turmoil. Self-doubts tormented her, and she wor-ried most of the time about whether she would be able to fulfill the high expectations everyone seemed to have for her. As high school gradua-tion approached, she realized that she would be the class valedictorian. As commencement day approached, Rosa was increasingly getting caught up in a cycle of self-starvation and excessive exercise. She had con-vinced herself that these behaviors were temporary and that she would "return to normal" right after gradu-ation. The summer months flew by, and she left for college at the end of August. Rosa hoped and prayed that she could board the plane in San Juan and leave her "sick" behaviors on the island, beginning college with a healthy sense of herself and opti-mism about her future. When her tennis coach confronted her about the problem, Rosa realized, however, that she had carried with her a "suit-case of worries" that was killing her.

Assessment

Although the diagnosis of Rosa's problem seemed straightforward, I recommended that she complete the MMPI-2, to shed some more light on her personality. As expected, Rosa's profile was that of a young woman who was markedly defensive and striving to present herself in a favor-able light. Even though Rosa's defen-siveness was evident, so also was a profile characterized as perfectionis-tic, hypersensitive, and depressive—features commonly found in individu-als with eating disorders.

Besides the data from the clinical interview and the MMPI-2, I also had Dr. Kennedy's medical report, which highlighted a number of health prob-lems commonly associated with eat-ing disorders. Rosa had lost nearly 20 percent of her body weight in the past several months. She had stopped menstruating and showed signs of anemia, dehydration, and electrolyte disturbance. Dr. Kennedy's medical conclusions were stated in frank and stern language. He recommended regular medical monitoring by university health personnel and stated that he considered hospitalization imperative if there was not an immediate improvement in Rosa's eating behavior.

Diagnosis

The psychological as well as the medical symptoms shown by Rosa pointed directly to an eating disorder. Although some clients with obsessive concerns about weight and compulsive behaviors pertaining to eating meet the criteria for obsessive-compulsive disorder, Rosa's clinical picture was focused exclusively on body image issues. She had not been engaging in binge eating, thus ruling out a diagnosis of bulimia nervosa. Rather, Rosa's condition met all the criteria for anorexia nervosa. She had been refusing to maintain appropriate body weight; she had an intense fear of gaining weight, even though dramatically underweight; she had a disturbed perception of her body weight and figure, while denying the seriousness of her dangerously low weight; and she had not menstruated in several months. Characteristics involving self-starvation and excessive exercise supported a subclassification of "restricting type."

Axis I: Anorexia Nervosa, Restricting Type
Axis II: No evidence of personality disorder
Axis III: Anemia, dehydration, electrolyte disturbance, amenorrhea
Axis IV: Educational problems, problems related to social environment (homesickness), and athletic pressures
Axis V: Current Global Assessment of Functioning: 60 Highest Global Assessment of Functioning (past year): 90

Case Formulation

Rosa's history reads like a textbook case of a young woman at risk for developing an eating disorder. Constantly striving for perfection in every facet of her life, Rosa came to define herself in terms of the highest standards in each of her endeavors. She internalized her parents' high expectations and accepted nothing less than perfection in academic and athletic pursuits. As pressures mounted, and the expectations of others continued to intensify, Rosa reached a point at which her defenses began to break down. Being told that she was a "star" was gratifying at first, but Rosa began to worry that she would be unable to fulfill the dreams that so many people had for her. As her self-doubts increased, her distortions about her intelligence, personality, and attractiveness also increased. In a desperate attempt to make things right, she began to starve herself in a misguided attempt to appear more attractive to others and, in turn, possibly to feel better about herself.

Treatment Plan

When treating clients with serious eating disorders, I have learned over the years to attend first and foremost to their medical status. Even with the best of psychotherapeutic intervention, the health dangers require professional medical monitoring and intervention. I was relieved to know that Rosa was willing to cooperate with Dr. Kennedy's recommendations, the first of which was an emergency consultation with the staff nutritionist, Shelley Hatch, who put together a nutritional plan for Rosa. Ms. Hatch realized, just as well as I, that there was considerable risk that Rosa might pay lip service to complying with the nutritional plan, while secretly engaging in some of the self-destructive behaviors that had become so deeply entrenched. Ms. Hatch joined forces with me in conveying the dangerousness of Rosa's health condition, and the fact that hospitalization would be necessary if

Rosa failed to regain some weight. Further, Rosa was expected to go for a medical checkup with Dr. Kennedy three times during the first week, then gradually move to less frequent appointments.

The medical and nutritional interventions were absolutely necessary in Rosa's case, but she would certainly need more. I recommended that she see me weekly in psychotherapy and that she participate in a group for eating-disordered women that met on campus. Rosa agreed to the weekly individual psychotherapy sessions but vehemently resisted the notion of participating in group therapy. Despite my strong recommendation, she made it clear that she would feel exposed and ashamed sharing her problems with other people, even those with the very same concerns. She reminded me of a cultural factor that I should have been more sensitive to: in Puerto Rican culture, seeking professional psychological help for problems carries a great stigma. It was difficult enough for her to admit to herself and to health professionals that she had problems; to tell her peers would be catastrophic. I respected the intensity of her feelings about the group and backed off with that idea. At the same time, however, I emphasized the importance of her compliance with the intervention plan involving regular psychotherapy sessions in addition to the health interventions. She agreed.

As soon as we began our regular sessions, Rosa seemed to plunge right into the issues. In fact, I recall being startled by her insight into the development of her problems. Rosa realized that her emotional difficulties did not have their roots in her adolescence but, rather, dated back to the early years of her life. Rosa began the second session with the profound statement, "I had to be perfect to erase the pain my parents felt following Juan's death." She proceeded to explain that, following Juan's bicycle accident, he remained a powerful presence in the family, even though he was rarely discussed. In her childhood, Rosa found herself wishing that she could find ways to make her parents happy and to help them put the tragedy behind them. She recalled wonderful memories of gratification when they celebrated her athletic and academic accomplishments, as well as memories of inner pain when they expressed any disappointments. As she approached adulthood, her striving for perfection intensified. She wanted to attend a prestigious college, and wanted to be as beautiful as possible. In a matter of months, many of these issues became confused, and Rosa was responding in unhealthy and desperate attempts to cope.

Much of my work with Rosa involved cognitive techniques, in which I tried to help her develop more accurate views of herself, the world, and her future potential. At the same time, I realized that it was important for her to have a good understanding of her family dynamics and the ways in which early life experiences influenced the development of her eating disorder. Our work did not involve "blaming" her parents, as Rosa feared that it might. Rather, she came to understand the ways in which their pain, and their needs, played a role in her pathological pursuit of perfection.

Outcome of the Case
Much to my relief, Rosa did comply with the medical and nutritional regimen proposed by Dr. Kennedy and Ms. Hatch. In fact, during the early weeks of treatment, Rosa was not only eating balanced meals but she also was allowing herself to indulge in an occasional milkshake, with the goal of returning to the target weight she had set. She was also working with her coach to establish an exercise program that made sense for conditioning purposes but was not excessive.

With the health components of the treatment plan working so smoothly, Rosa was in the right frame of mind to make optimal use of psychotherapy. I continued to see Rosa weekly for 6 months, during which she made major advances in self-understanding as well as behavior change. She came to realize that, not only did she not have to be perfect, but relentless striving for perfection would lead her to misery. She came to realize that she couldn't win every tennis match, nor did she need to. She realized that she needn't be devastated if she did not attain a 4.0 grade point average each semester. And she realized that her body did not have to look like that of a fashion model. Central to Rosa's growth was her gentle confrontation with her parents when she returned home between semesters. In a loving way, she found the words to express her appreciation for all they had given her, while at the same time conveying her need to have the pressure lessened at this point in her life. Rosa told me that, at first, they seemed defensive but seemed to "wake up" when she told them about the serious health problems she had developed a few months earlier due to her disordered eating. This discussion seemed to be a turning point for Rosa, enabling her to move from the confining demands imposed by her parents to a point at which she could set goals and expectations for herself.

Rosa developed a close working alliance with me during those 6 months. At the end of February, when I suggested that we consider terminating, she seemed genuinely sad at first, yet she recognized the importance of taking the work she had been doing in psychotherapy into her own hands. She felt confident that she could stay healthy, and she promised to contact me should she find herself slipping back into unhealthy behaviors. In fact, in mid-April, the pressures of the tennis season seemed a bit overwhelming for Rosa, and she found herself having some of the same obsessions. After a few days of skipping meals, she realized that she was in danger, so she called me for an appointment. In that 50-minute session, Rosa did virtually all the talking. She explained what was going on in her thoughts and in her behavior, and she laid out a treatment plan for herself. Feeling confident that she could take care of this issue before it worsened, she left the session in good spirits, stating that there was no need for further meetings at that time. I trusted her judgment.

The next time I heard from Rosa was the following September, in a note telling me how well things were going. The tennis team had lost the championship game in May, but, rather than fret about it, Rosa explained that she had found a way to leave it behind her and have a great summer at home, working in a day care center with children in poverty worse than any challenge she had ever faced. That was the last time Rosa ever contacted me, although I did see occasional stories in the campus newspaper about the ups and downs of the tennis team. In each of the accompanying photos, Rosa looked healthy and happy.

Sarah Tobin, PhD

SUMMARY

- People with anorexia nervosa experience four kinds of symptoms. They (1) refuse or are unable to maintain normal weight, (2) have an intense fear of gaining weight or becoming fat, even though they may be grossly underweight, (3) have a distorted perception of the weight or shape of their body, and (4) experience amenorrhea, if postpubertal. People with bulimia nervosa alternate between the extremes of eating large amounts of food in a short time (binges) and then compensating for the added calories by vomiting or performing other extreme actions. Those with the purging type try to force out of their bodies what they have just eaten, while those with the nonpurging type try to compensate for what they eat by fasting or exercising excessively. Biochemical abnormalities in the norepinephrine and serotonin neurotransmitter systems, perhaps with a genetic basis, are thought to be involved in eating disorders. The psychological perspective views eating disorders as developing in people who suffer a great deal of inner turmoil and pain, and who become obsessed with body issues, often turning to food for comfort and nurturance. According to cognitive theories, over time people with eating disorders become trapped in their pathological patterns because of resistance to change. Within the sociocultural perspective, eating disorders have been explained in terms of family systems theories and, more broadly, in terms of society's attitudes toward eating and diet. Treatment of eating disorders requires a combination of approaches. While medications, particularly those affecting serotonin, are sometimes prescribed, it is also clear that psychotherapy is necessary, particularly those using cognitive-behavioral and interpersonal techniques. Family therapy, particularly when the client is a teen, can also be an important component of an intervention plan.

- People with impulse-control disorders repeatedly engage in behaviors that are potentially harmful, feeling unable to stop themselves and experiencing a sense of desperation if they are thwarted from carrying out their impulsive behavior. People with kleptomania are driven by a persistent urge to steal, not because they wish to have the stolen objects but because they experience a thrill while engaging in the act of stealing. In addition to recommending medication, clinicians commonly treat people with kleptomania with behavioral treatments, such as covert sensitization, to help them control the urge to steal.

- People with pathological gambling have an intense urge to gamble, causing them to become preoccupied with such risk-taking behaviors. From a biological perspective, the gambler's perpetual pursuit of the big win can be seen as a drive for stimulation and pleasurable feelings. Certain personality characteristics, such as impulsivity and psychopathy, also seem to predispose people to developing this condition. Sociocultural factors, such as the spread of legalized gambling, may aggravate the tendency of some vulnerable individuals to become immersed in such behavior. Treatment methods that combine various approaches seem most effective. Medications, such as SSRIs, are helpful with some clients, as are behavioral and cognitive-behavioral techniques. Many pathological gamblers also benefit from participation in peer groups, such as Gamblers Anonymous.

- People with pyromania are driven by the intense desire to prepare, set, and watch fires. This disorder seems to be rooted in childhood problems and firesetting behavior. In adulthood, people with pyromania typically have various dysfunctional characteristics, such as problems with substance abuse as well as relationship difficulties. Some treatment programs focus on children showing early signs of developing this disorder. With adults, various approaches are used, with the aim of focusing on the client's broader psychological problems, such as low self-esteem, depression, communication problems, and inability to control anger.

- People with sexual impulsivity are unable to control their sexual behavior and feel driven to engage in frequent and indiscriminate sexual activity, which they later regret. Individuals with this condition commonly suffer with a co-existing condition, such as depression, phobic disorder, or substance abuse, and some experience dissociative symptoms. Although this condition can be understood as related to a biochemical disturbance, most experts focus on early life experiences. Treatment usually combines components derived from insight-oriented, behavioral, and family systems approaches.

- People with trichotillomania have an irresistible urge to pull out their hair. Certain brain abnormalities have been implicated. Behavioral theorists regard the disorder as resulting from the reinforcement associated with tension relief following random hair-pulling. Sociocultural theorists focus on the development of this condition within the context of disturbed parent-child relationships, in which an upset child resorts to this kind of behavior in an attempt to gain attention. Various medications for treating this disorder are being tested, although clinicians would usually recommend that treatment include behavioral therapy, such as habit reversal.

- People with intermittent explosive disorder feel a recurrent inability to resist assaultive or destructive acts of aggression. Theorists propose that an interaction of biological and environmental factors lead to this condition. In terms of biology, serotonin seems to be implicated. In terms of psychological and sociocultural factors, theorists focus on the reinforcing qualities of emotional outbursts, as well as the effects of such behaviors on family systems and intimate relationships. Treatment may involve the prescription of medication, although psychotherapeutic methods would also be included in the intervention.

- Internet addiction is an impulse-control condition in which an individual feels an irresistible need to be involved in Internet-based activities. The biopsychosocial model can be used to conceptualize Internet addiction. Most people with this condition resist treatment, but some are coerced into seeking help by their loved ones. Treatment involves individual therapy and, at times, couples therapy.

KEY TERMS

See Glossary for definitions

Anorexia nervosa   430
Big win   443
Binges   435
Bulimia nervosa   435
Impulse   439
Impulse-control disorders   439

Intermittent explosive disorder   449
Internet addiction   450
Kleptomania   440
Nonpurging type   435
Pathological gambling   441
Purge   430

Purging type   435
Pyromania   444
Sexual impulsivity   446
Trichotillomania   447

 INTERNET RESOURCE

To get more information on the material covered in this chapter, visit our website at **www.mhhe.com/halgin5.** There you will find more information, resources, and links to topics of interest.

THE McDOWELL FAMILY

Jake speaks about his OCD and the benefit of reaching out to other children with OCD

Some people say they are "obsessed" with things like baseball. I have obsessive-compulsive disorder, and I used to be obsessed with germs.

I wouldn't let anyone other than my family members touch me. If they did, I would lick my hands and rub a certain spot on my face until it was raw. At home, I used to sit on my mom's lap and line my legs up perfectly with hers so that I wouldn't touch the furniture. I did this because I was afraid of lice. When I did go to school, I wouldn't sit near anyone because I was afraid they had lice. I was also scared of chemicals. I couldn't even walk on grass because of the fertilizer. My brother, Luke, had a Power Wheels car and he would ask me to play with him in the backyard. I would just say, "You go ahead without me."

There was a time when I wouldn't go to school because I couldn't put my socks on. The creases in them felt like rocks. My parents had a system where I would get a poker chip worth a certain amount of money for each time I would wear them. I could save up to buy myself a toy. It was bribery. It was like, "I'm going to wear my socks today so I can get paid."

Back row: Andrew, Bill, and Debbie. *Front row:* Jake and Luke

I didn't talk much about my thoughts and obsessions because I didn't understand them. I couldn't figure out what was wrong; I was just being me. After a while, I thought I was completely insane. I would slam my head against the wall and say to myself, "I'm crazy and I want to die. I hate my life." When I was finally diagnosed with OCD, the doctor told me that I had a mental illness, but that I wasn't crazy. I was a bit happier after hearing that. I still worried and obsessed, but my fear that I was crazy was gone.

I am real open about having OCD. After I was diagnosed, I spoke about my illness to my class at school. A couple of other kids were diagnosed with it, too. It helped them to meet someone else who had OCD.

I met one kid who had OCD really bad. He wouldn't let anyone play with his LEGOs or go into his room at all. I asked him, "What are your obsessions and what do you need help with?" He let me play with him and he let me go into his room. He trusted me. Now we hang out together.

I've gotten much better because I'm on medication and in treatment. My life was screwed up before, and I wasn't a happy person at all. Now I have a lot of things to live for. When I grow up, I want to help other people who have OCD.

NOTHING TO HIDE

JUAN INEGUEZ

Juan speaks about having bipolar disorder and the experiences of violent tendencies; he also discusses cultural gaps in mental health agencies and the problem of stigmatization

Juan

I came from skid row all the way up to where I'm at today. When I first went to a mental health clinic about fifteen years ago, I had no place to live. I had been wandering in the streets for years with hardly any money coming in. Now I live in my own apartment, which is something I worked very hard to make happen.

• • • •

When I first found out about having hydrocephalus, I was really depressed. They had me see one of the psychiatrists in the hospital, and he told me, "You have bipolar disorder." I said, "You're telling me that on top of all that I'm going through, I also have to deal with having a mental illness?" But then he told me about what bipolar disorder was, and I felt at ease with the diagnosis. I knew that my behavior was kind of weird. I'd feel real depressed one day, and then the next day or so, I would be real manicky and sometimes violent. Once I understood what was wrong with me, I said, "Okay, what do I do now?" The doctor gave me some meds and told me to go to a mental health clinic.

• • • •

I haven't attacked anybody in maybe a good four or five years now. That's a miracle! It's a long time for me because I have an urge to fight. Now it's more like if you piss me off, I say, "Okay, fine." I might cuss under my breath or something, but I've learned to control my temper.

I've found out that I'm very good with people who have mental illness, because I understand their pain and what they're going through. Over time, I've come to realize that there is something I was put here on earth to do. I'm meant to help people, whether it's to be a listening ear or a shoulder to cry on. I want to help my fellow man.

• • • •

A lot of Latinos fear that if they come into these mental health places, they're going to be stripped of their dignity and their beliefs. As Latinos, we do our own thing. We were raised differently from Anglos. For instance, let's say an Anglo grandmother comes in for some medication, and the doctor gives her a prescription for a pill to take three times a day; she's probably going to take the meds. But let's say a Latino grandmother comes in. Even if she believes in her doctor, she probably won't take the medicine. If the doctor doesn't spend the time finding out why she won't take it, then we're defeating the purpose. I know a lot of Latino grandmothers who are second- or third-generation immigrants who won't take their medication. On the other hand, a friend of mine has a grandmother who believes in the Virgin Mary. She keeps all of her medicines right in front of the statue of the Virgin Mary, and she believes that if she takes her pills right there, Mary will protect her.

If we can get the professionals to understand that, with Latinos, they're dealing with a different culture, we'll be much better off. Doctors have to sit down and try to find out what their clients believe in and what their culture is like. A lot of Latino people think that if someone in their family is stricken with mental illness, somewhere down the line, one of their relatives did something bad and God is punishing them by making this person sick.

• • • •

I don't know if the stigma of mental illness will be reduced during my generation, but I hope with the help of the young people who are being educated about it, there will be some kind of a breakthrough. I just want to get something started, and if I get to see the finished product, it would be wonderful. I want to see the stigma stop. Hopefully, it will.

Celeste talks about having bipolar disorder and speaks about her struggle with addictions, faith, and caring for her daughter

NOTHING TO HIDE

THE CHAPMAN/SIRMONS FAMILY

Carol, Celeste, Antoine (Carol's great-grandson), and Wilma

I was sick for the first seven years of my daughter's life. It all started right after my baby girl, Rahshedia, was born. I ended up in a hospital and I missed her first birthday.

The stress of trying to work and raise a child as a single mother was just too much for me. Rahshedia had her days and nights mixed up, and I was exhausted. I'd get up early every morning, take her to my parents or to daycare, smoke a joint, go to work, pick up the baby, and come home and try and cook dinner and get her to bed. It was hell. At the end of the day, it was like, "I deserve a drink. I need a drink." I'd go straight to the bar and stay there all night long till I closed the bar. Then I'd go to the nightclubs. I was drinking and drugging every day. My mother had to raise my child because I was never around.

• • • •

My problem was with this bipolar thing. I just couldn't accept the fact that I had a mental illness, and I didn't want to be labeled as mentally ill. It wasn't until I started taking my medication fourteen years ago that I was able to comprehend the things that had happened to me. At Alcoholics Anonymous I got into recovery from my addictions. I met this woman there named Dot, and she helped save my life.

Dot was a beautiful person. I would call her in the middle of the night crying and complaining and she always listened and had words of wisdom for me. "Pray," she said, "let's pray!" Dot would pray with me right then and there on the phone. "Skig, honey" she would say, calling me by my nickname, "the reason why you can't get this program is because you won't take your medication." I said, "Oh, yeah?" But I really wanted to work with this woman, and so I started taking my meds every day. I got my life back.

• • • •

My daughter is twenty-one years old now and she lives with me. We're thick as thieves! Rahshedia calls me up like I'm one of her girlfriends. "Ma," she says, "I just called to see how you're doing." I'll say, "I ain't doing nothing, you know?" And we talk. I know that she loves me, and that's the best thing.

Where I was putting love into men and other things, God gave me a child to truly love me.

At first I thought I had something to hide, but if you start hiding things, you'll never get to the root of your problems. If I can step up and say, "Yes, I suffer with a mental illness, but I've been helped through medication and therapy to deal with the real world," maybe it will help some folks. If there's anyone I can help by sharing my story, I would be real happy. People should know to take their medicine, give it a chance, get into therapy, talk about everything, and get it out! That's what really helped me. I have nothing to hide.

NOTHING TO HIDE

THE BEARD FAMILY

My daughter, Ashley, may have severe psychiatric problems, but if she's having a good day, she can be fabulous. She's got a great sense of humor and shows unusual sensitivity to others. She can deal with her symptoms now in a better way. She no longer gets aggressive or psychotic like she did when she was younger. She used to throw things, hurt herself, or break windows out of frustration and terror. Her craziness got into the whole family. You're always thinking, "What's going to explode in your face next?"

For years and years, our family never had a joyful holiday. When Ashley was still living at home, things were always very tense, and when she was in various locked units, all of us would spend holidays with her there. It's only been in the last four or five years that all of us Beards have been able to celebrate relatively peaceful and happy holidays at home together.

It takes so little to please Ashley. If she wants something and we say, "No, you can't have it," she accepts it. She's never argumentative. And she is so thrilled by the simplest of things in life, like a candlelight dinner at home with just her and me. Being with Ashley is very refreshing. She and I have an incredible relationship, and I thoroughly enjoy it. I never say, "Oh, this is the weekend Ashley's coming home. I've got to take care of my sick daughter." Ashley can't wait to come home on her monthly pass, and I look forward to her visits, too. We have so much fun together.

The way I approach life, you have to play the hand you're dealt. You can't just run around wringing your hands, thinking, "Why did this have to happen? Why did lightning have to strike me?" That's the wrong way to go through life. The most important thing is to have a positive attitude and look for the good in things as opposed to the bad. Having a daughter like Ashley has probably made us a more caring family. It certainly makes you more respectful of other people who have problems.

I once read that more money is spent on the prevention of tooth decay in this country than on research for schizophrenia. These priorities don't seem straight to me. The issue of mental illness must be raised to the level of a national problem so that this country can allocate appropriate funds to help. Our family is privileged, and we've been able to give Ashley the best life we possibly can. I'm not covered by insurance for her care any longer. How many people in the world can afford the price of good mental health care? It's a fraction of one percent. This situation has to change.

Source: Copyright © 2002 *Nothing to Hide: Mental Illness in the Family* by Peggy Gillespie and Jean J. Beard. Reprinted by permission of The New Press. www.thenewpress.com

Standing: Ashley and Jamie. *Seated:* Anson H., Jean, and Anson M.

Jean and Ashley

THE MOSER FAMILY

Jane speaks about her son David's schizophrenia and the family's struggle with the legal system in their attempt to get help for their son

My husband, Tex, and I have four sons, all of whom are grown. When we tell the story of our oldest son, David, we say that the real tragedy is that his story is not unique. David, who is now forty-eight, has schizo-affective disorder. He has been sick ever since he was seventeen.

When David moved to Michigan, Tex and I began to get bizarre letters from him. These letters were beautifully written, but filled with strange ideas. David would mention people who were beaming messages down to him, and tell us how he had just exorcised his dog. It was all very odd. For the first time, I acknowledged to myself that he might be psychotic.

As parents, we had to make the decision to go to court so that our son would receive treatment. If David had been diagnosed with a life-threatening medical condition and was resisting treatment or surgery for it, we would have done the same thing. The psychiatrist warned us that we might become the enemy in David's eyes. He was right. We hoped that if David was required to take medication, he would get better and understand why we had taken this action. Unfortunately, this didn't happen.

• • • •

One night, David broke into our house while Tex and I were asleep. He beat us badly and almost killed me. We had a large house, and the neighbors couldn't hear us calling for help. Fortunately, our son Stephen and his wife were living with us at the time on the third floor of the house. When they

Jane and Tex

heard us screaming, they were terrified and called the police. Stephen finally subdued his brother. After the assault, the court sent David to a state prison hospital for evaluation. The medical staff there wanted him hospitalized, but a court-appointed psychologist, who had only met with David for twenty minutes, found him competent to stand trial on several felony counts. David had to go to Superior Court and stand trial. It was out of our hands.

• • • •

Mental illnesses are brain disorders. If you accept that basic fact, then our laws should reflect that understanding. They don't. What this country does is tell a person whose decision-making parts of their brain are damaged and dysfunctional that they can make their own rational decision about whether or not to get treatment. This is simply not right.

• • • •

When our own son assaulted us, there was so much media attention that we had no choice but to speak out. We said to ourselves, "Okay, so this has happened. Let's try to make it understandable to the public." As a result, a lot of people have contacted us and have literally whispered, "This has happened in our family, too." Not only did they feel the stigma of mental illness, but they also felt tremendous shame around the issue of violence.

CHAPTER 15

Ethical and Legal Issues

It had been more than 10 years since I treated Mark Chen. At the time, he was an undergraduate student who came to see me in his senior year for serious depression. In fact, he had been so depressed that he had to be hospitalized for 2 weeks and treated with electroconvulsive therapy. I hadn't heard from him since that time and occasionally wondered how he might be doing. One unusually warm January afternoon, I received a phone call from Mark's wife, Tanya, urgently asking for my assistance. Apparently, Mark was experiencing a recurrence of his depression with intensity so great that Tanya feared he might kill himself. Tanya recalled that Mark had seen me a decade earlier and explained that she didn't know where to turn. Her emotion-packed words alerted me to the frightening situation she was facing: "Dr. Tobin, he's been sitting home for the past 2 days, holding a knife to his wrist. What should I do?"

I asked Tanya whether she felt she would be able to persuade Mark to go with her to the emergency room, where I could conduct an evaluation. As I held the phone, I could hear Tanya murmuring to Mark, but I heard no response. She spoke louder to him and soon began to cry with impassioned pleas for him to answer. Still no response.

Given the seriousness of the situation, I discussed with Tanya ways that she might get Mark to the hospital. Since she was alone and he was immobilized, she didn't think it would be possible for her to take him without assistance. I suggested she call an ambulance service, and I gave her the name of a local company with expertise in dealing with individuals in psychiatric crisis. I also suggested that she contact a relative or friend to come to her apartment and help her deal with the situation. She followed both recommendations, first summoning an ambulance and then calling her best friend, Anita, who was able to provide her with support in this troubling situation.

Two hours after we ended our phone contact, I received a call from the emergency room with a request that I come down to do an evaluation on Mark Chen. Knowing that I was walking into a stressful situation, I braced myself for the likelihood that I might have to make some difficult decisions about hospitalizing Mark.

When I entered the consulting room, I came upon Tanya and a man I didn't recognize. Admittedly, 10 years had passed since my brief treatment of Mark Chen. But how could this man be only 32 years old? Perhaps it was his unshaven face, his unkempt hair, and his weary look that made him seem so much older. I extended my hand to greet Mark, but my words fell on seemingly deaf ears. Sitting in the chair like a lump of flesh, Mark was immobile. He uttered no words and made absolutely no movements. Then, suddenly, he grabbed the pen from the nearby desk and gouged at his wrist. With a split-second reaction, I pulled the pen from his hand and in a strong but calming voice said, "Mark, you are in the hospital. I am Dr. Sarah Tobin. Remember, I treated you 10 years ago when you were in college. You need help again, and Tanya and I are trying to help you. Please cooperate with us. You mustn't hurt yourself."

The decisions that I dreaded were now before me. Mark was clearly in danger of hurting himself. Ideally, he would be able to recognize the depth of his depression and comply with my recommendation that he sign himself into the hospital. Realistically, however, Mark did not seem to comprehend a word I was saying. I placed the Informed Consent form before him, but he stared blankly at the paper with absolutely no responsiveness. There was no other choice for me but to commit Mark to the hospital. The process of taking away a person's voluntary control over personal choices is one of the most unpleasant aspects of the work of a mental health professional. Every time I face the task of committing a person to the hospital, I am temporarily paralyzed by questions about how I would feel if I were in that person's place. Would I be enraged? Would I be frightened? Would I feel relieved?

I discussed the dilemma with Tanya and asked her how she felt participating in committing Mark to the hospital. Choking on her own emotion, she found it difficult to speak in a way that I could understand. She did nod her agreement, however, so I proceeded to complete the legal forms documenting the need to take this decision out of Mark's hands.

The next decision I faced pertained to the nature of the initial intervention for Mark's profound depression. Mark had not eaten in days and had gotten only a minimal amount of sleep. Furthermore, Tanya reported with some embarrassment, Mark had urinated and defecated in his clothing, almost unaware of what was happening. With a symptom picture as serious as Mark's, we did not have the luxury of waiting for antidepressant medications to take effect. Mark's condition called for electroconvulsive therapy, a treatment that had been tremendously helpful for Mark 10 years earlier. When I raised this suggestion with Tanya, she seemed initially irritated, stating, "Isn't there a less dangerous treatment you can use?" After I reassured Tanya about the safety of ECT, as well as the urgency of Mark's condition, she agreed to sign the forms granting permission for this treatment. Once again, we were facing the troubling task of deciding on a course of action for a person deemed incapable of making such important choices for himself.

After all the necessary forms were completed, I summoned psychiatric aides to bring a wheelchair to escort Mark Chen to the treatment unit. A hospital wristband was placed on Mark, indicating that he should remain under 24-hour watch and that all "dangerous objects" should be kept out of his reach. As Mark was wheeled out of the consulting room, I tried to reassure Tanya that I believed he would show improvement within a few days and that these difficult choices were necessary and wise.

Sarah Tobin, PhD

The case of Mark Chen is indeed provocative. You might find it disturbing to confront the fact that profoundly important choices about hospitalization and treatment are sometimes made by people other than the client. In some instances, these decisions are made by strangers, such as police officers or emergency room physicians, who have little or no information about the person other than the behavior they are observing. However, even staunch protectors of personal freedom and individual rights realize that, in certain situations, people are incapable of acting in their own best interest; in some cases, they are so impaired that their lives or the safety of others is at risk. In this chapter, we will discuss the ways in which the work of mental health professionals is affected by and informed by ethical and legal issues.

Ethical Issues

When most people think about psychological interventions, they focus on the helping nature of the therapeutic relationship. From the chapters you have read so far, you might conclude that psychotherapy is usually a voluntary process in which a person willingly seeks help and therapy proceeds in a straightforward manner. We will now turn our attention to some of the complexities associated with the delivery of professional services. These complexities relate to the responsibilities of mental health professionals, the ethical issues in the provision of mental health care, the legal issues pertaining to the rights of clients in treatment, and the responsibilities of a society to ensure the protection of its citizens. These issues have emerged in the context of broader social and historical changes in the mental health system, such as deinstitutionalization, increased attention to potential abuses in psychotherapy, and heightened publicity regarding medical malpractice.

Roles and Responsibilities of Clinicians

As you are reading this final chapter of the text, think back to our discussion in Chapter 2 about the work and responsibilities of clinicians. In that chapter, we spoke of the clinician as an expert in human relations with a range of responsibilities for assessing and helping people with psychological problems. Throughout the book, you have read about the cases of Dr. Tobin, as well as many other clinical examples involving the work of clinicians with their clients. By now, you have developed an appreciation for how demanding and difficult this work must be. Adding to the challenges involved in diagnosis and treatment, clinicians also contend with a number of difficult issues pertaining to professional and ethical practice. In the sections that follow, we will examine some of the concerns that mental health professionals face in their efforts to maintain the highest standards of practice.

Therapist Competence It would be naive to think that possessing a doctorate in clinical psychology or a degree in medicine is a guarantee that a professional is capable of treating every client requesting services. Mental health professionals are guided by standards that specify that they possess the skills needed to treat people who approach them for professional services. In other words, they should have the intellectual competence to assess, conceptualize, and treat clients whom they accept into treatment. Furthermore, they need to be emotionally capable of managing the clinical issues that emerge in treatment.

Consider how inappropriate it would be for a clinician without any training or experience in the treatment of people with severe eating disorders to advertise that he is opening a specialty practice in treating women with anorexia nervosa. Obviously, he would be practicing in a field in which he lacks the competence to treat people with specialized treatment needs, and his behavior would be unethical. In a case such as this, the absurdity is evident. However, there are other cases in which the clinician may have the training and experience, but not the emotional competence, to deal with certain kinds of clinical issues. An example of this is the case of a profoundly depressed clinician who is treating clients also suffering from severe mood disturbance. Although this clinician's training may be sufficient, the active nature of the clinician's own psychological disorder could impede his or her ability to be a wise and constructive consultant in the life of a client suffering with the same problem.

Mental health professionals are expected to conduct regular self-scrutiny, in which they make an effort to objectively evaluate their competence to carry out their work. When faced with prospective clients whose needs are beyond the clinician's competence, a referral should be made, or the clinician should obtain appropriate supervision. Self-assessment of emotional competence is a bit more difficult, in that it can be difficult to recognize the depth or extent of one's own problems. Astute clinicians regularly seek out the advice of senior or peer consultants to help them make such evaluations. Competency is a multifaceted phenomenon that includes a clinician's sensitivity to people of diverse backgrounds and the clinician's effort to understand and acquire knowledge about individuals from differing backgrounds (White Kress, Eriksen, Rayle, & Ford, 2005). For example, in recent years the American Psychological Association has developed Guidelines for Psychotherapy with Lesbian, Gay, and Bisexual Clients (Table 15.1), Guidelines for Psychological Evaluations in Child Protection Matters (Table 15.2, p. 466), and Guidelines for Psychological Practice with Older Adults (Table 15.3, p. 467).

Informed Consent Assuming that the clinician has the intellectual and emotional competence to treat, the next set of issues pertains to obligations within the treatment context. Although it would be unusual to have a legalistic contract for therapy, experts in the field recommend some form of a therapeutic understanding. In other words, clinicians should provide clients with the information they will need to make decisions about therapy.

TABLE 15.1 Guidelines for Psychotherapy with Lesbian, Gay, and Bisexual Clients

1. Psychologists understand that homosexuality and bisexuality are not indicative of mental illness.
2. Psychologists are encouraged to recognize how their attitudes and knowledge about lesbian, gay, and bisexual issues may be relevant to assessment and treatment and seek consultation or make appropriate referrals when indicated.
3. Psychologists strive to understand the ways in which social stigmatization (i.e., prejudice, discrimination, and violence) poses risks to the mental health and well-being of lesbian, gay, and bisexual clients.
4. Psychologists strive to understand how inaccurate or prejudicial views of homosexuality or bisexuality may affect the client's presentation in treatment and the therapeutic process.
5. Psychologists strive to be knowledgeable about and respect the importance of lesbian, gay, and bisexual relationships.
6. Psychologists strive to understand the particular circumstances and challenges faced by lesbian, gay, and bisexual clients.
7. Psychologists recognize that the families of lesbian, gay, and bisexual people may include people who are not legally or biologically related.
8. Psychologists strive to understand how a person's homosexual or bisexual orientation may have an impact on his or her family of origin and the relationship to that family of origin.
9. Psychologists are encouraged to recognize the particular life issues or challenges that are related to multiple and often conflicting cultural norms, values, and beliefs that lesbian, gay, and bisexual members of racial and ethnic minorities face.
10. Psychologists are encouraged to recognize the particular challenges that bisexual individuals experience.
11. Psychologists strive to understand the special problems and risks that exist for lesbian, gay, and bisexual youth.
12. Psychologists consider generational differences within lesbian, gay, and bisexual populations and the particular challenges that lesbian, gay, and bisexual older adults may experience.
13. Psychologists are encouraged to recognize the particular challenges that lesbian, gay, and bisexual individuals experience with physical, sensory, and cognitive-emotional difficulties.
14. Psychologists support the provision of professional education and training on lesbian, gay, and bisexual issues.
15. Psychologists are encouraged to increase their knowledge and understanding of homosexuality and bisexuality through continuing education, training, supervision, and consultation.
16. Psychologists make reasonable efforts to familiarize themselves with relevant mental health, educational, and community resources for lesbian, gay, and bisexual people.

Source: Guidelines for psychotherapy with lesbian, gay, and bisexual clients (Division 44, 2000) by American Psychological Association. Copyright © by the American Psychological Association. Reprinted with permission.

According to Koocher and Keith-Spiegel (1998), there are several key elements in the sound therapeutic contract. At the outset of therapy, clinicians should discuss the goals of treatment, the process of therapy, the client's rights, the therapist's responsibilities, the treatment risks, the techniques that will be used, financial issues, and the limits of confidentiality. When these matters have been discussed, the client gives **informed consent,** an indication that he or she has participated in setting the treatment goals, understands and agrees to the treatment plan, and knows the clinician's credentials (Koocher, 1994). Generally, clients are given a written statement containing this information. In cases in which a risk is involved in treatment, such as when medication or electroconvulsive therapy is recommended, the client should understand the possible short-term and long-term side effects. The clinician has a responsibility to ensure that the client is made aware of these issues, is given answers to these questions, and is given the opportunity to refuse treatment.

Even though a person may be in extreme distress, upon his or her admission to a psychiatric hospital, the clinician must obtain informed consent.

TABLE 15.2 Guidelines for Psychological Evaluations in Child Protection Matters

1. The primary purpose of the evaluation is to provide relevant, professionally sound results or opinions in matters where a child's health and welfare may have been and/or may in the future be harmed.
2. In child protection cases, the child's interest and well-being are paramount.
3. The evaluation addresses the particular psychological and developmental needs of the child and/or parent(s) that are relevant to child protection issues, such as physical abuse, sexual abuse, neglect, and/or serious emotional harm.
4. The role of the psychologist conducting evaluations is that of a professional expert who strives to maintain an unbiased, objective stance.
5. The serious consequences of psychological assessment in child protection matters place a heavy burden on psychologists.
6. Psychologists gain specialized competence.
7. Psychologists are aware of personal and societal biases and engage in nondiscriminatory practice.
8. Psychologists avoid multiple relationships.
9. Based on the nature of the referral questions, the scope of the evaluation is determined by the evaluator.
10. Psychologists performing psychological evaluations in child protection matters obtain appropriate informed consent from all adult participants and, as appropriate, inform the child participant. Psychologists need to be particularly sensitive to consent issues.
11. Psychologists inform participants about the disclosure of information and the limits of confidentiality.
12. Psychologists use multiple methods of data gathering.
13. Psychologists neither overinterpret nor inappropriately interpret clinical or assessment data.
14. Psychologists conducting a psychological evaluation in child protection matters provide an opinion regarding the psychological functioning of an individual only after conducting an evaluation of the individual adequate to support their statements or conclusions.
15. Recommendations, if offered, are based on whether the child's health and welfare have been and/or may be seriously harmed.
16. Psychologists clarify financial arrangements.
17. Psychologists maintain appropriate records.

Source: Committee on Professional Practice and Standards Board of Professional Affairs, 1998 (published report). Copyright © by the American Psychological Association. Reprinted with permission.

This process has some complications. Psychotherapy is an imprecise procedure, and it is not always possible to predict its course, risks, or benefits. The clinician's job, however, is to give a best estimate at the onset of therapy and to provide further information as therapy proceeds. Most people are able to discuss these matters with the clinician and to make an informed choice. However, what happens when prospective clients are unable to understand the issues in order to make informed consent? This is the case with people who are out of touch with reality, people who are mentally retarded, and children. In these cases, the clinician must work with the individual's family or other legally appointed guardians, as Dr. Tobin did in her dealings with Mark Chen. Because he was so depressed and catatonic, she found it necessary to turn to Mark's wife to obtain consent for the administration of electroconvulsive therapy. The clinician must make every effort to ensure that the client's rights are protected.

Confidentiality   Part of the informed consent process involves informing the client that what takes place in therapy is private. **Confidentiality,** long regarded as a sacred part of the clinician-client relationship, refers to the principle that the therapist must safeguard disclosures in therapy as private. Why is confidentiality so important? In order for clients to feel comfortable disclosing intimate details, they need to have the assurance that the clinician will protect this information (Dolan, 2004). For example, if a man tells his therapist that he is having an extramarital affair, he would do so with the understanding that the therapist would not divulge this information to others. In fact, safeguards against the disclosure of confidential information exist within the laws of most states.

The content of therapy is legally considered **privileged communication.** In other words, the clinician may not disclose any information about the client in a court of law without the client's expressed permission. This issue would arise in a court proceeding; for example, a therapist might be summoned to appear in a divorce case and be asked to divulge information about a client's sexual dysfunction that had been discussed in therapy. Because the content of therapy is "privileged communication," the therapist must have the client's permission before discussing any information that had emerged in therapy. In the context of the courts, privileged communication differs from the general notion that the public is entitled to relevant evidence pertaining to a case (Smith-Bell & Winslade, 1994). However, there are certain kinds of cases in which the court is entitled to information shared within the therapy context. For example, in certain

TABLE 15.3 Guidelines for Psychological Practice with Older Adults

Attitudes

Guideline 1. Psychologists are encouraged to work with older adults within their scope of competence, and to seek consultation or make appropriate referrals when indicated.

Guideline 2. Psychologists are encouraged to recognize how their attitudes and beliefs about aging and about older individuals may be relevant to their assessment and treatment of older adults, and to seek consultation or further education about these issues when indicated.

General Knowledge about Adult Development, Aging, and Older Adults

Guideline 3. Psychologists strive to gain knowledge about theory and research in aging.

Guideline 4. Psychologists strive to be aware of the social/psychological dynamics of the aging process.

Guideline 5. Psychologists strive to understand diversity in the aging process, particularly how sociocultural factors such as gender, ethnicity, socioeconomic status, sexual orientation, disability status, and urban/rural residence may influence the experience and expression of health and of psychological problems in later life.

Guideline 6. Psychologists strive to be familiar with current information about biological and health-related aspects of aging.

Clinical Issues

Guideline 7. Psychologists strive to be familiar with current knowledge about cognitive changes in older adults.

Guideline 8. Psychologists strive to understand problems in daily living among older adults.

Guideline 9. Psychologists strive to be knowledgeable about psychopathology within the aging population and cognizant of the prevalence and nature of that psychopathology when providing services to older adults.

Assessment

Guideline 10. Psychologists strive to be familiar with the theory, research, and practice of various methods of assessment with older adults, and knowledgeable of assessment instruments that are psychometrically suitable for use with them.

Guideline 11. Psychologists strive to understand the problems of using assessment instruments created for younger individuals when assessing older adults, and to develop skill in tailoring assessments to accommodate older adults' specific characteristics and contexts.

Guideline 12. Psychologists strive to develop skill at recognizing cognitive changes in older adults, and in conducting and interpreting cognitive screening and functional ability evaluations.

Intervention, Consultation, and Other Service Provision

Guideline 13. Psychologists strive to be familiar with the theory, research, and practice of various methods of intervention with older adults, particularly with current research evidence about their efficacy with this age group.

Guideline 14. Psychologists strive to be familiar with and develop skill in applying specific psychotherapeutic interventions and environmental modifications with older adults and their families, including adapting interventions for use with this age group.

Guideline 15. Psychologists strive to understand the issues pertaining to the provision of services in the specific settings in which older adults are typically located or encountered.

Guideline 16. Psychologists strive to recognize issues related to the provision of prevention and health promotion services with older adults.

Guideline 17. Psychologists strive to understand issues pertaining to the provision of consultation services in assisting older adults.

Guideline 18. In working with older adults, psychologists are encouraged to understand the importance of interfacing with other disciplines, and to make referrals to other disciplines and/or to work with them in collaborative teams and across a range of sites, as appropriate.

Guideline 19. Psychologists strive to understand the special ethical and/or legal issues entailed in providing services to older adults.

Education

Guideline 20. Psychologists are encouraged to increase their knowledge, understanding, and skills with respect to working with older adults through continuing education, training, supervision, and consultation.

Source: Guidelines for Psychological Practice with Older Adults 2004, (published report). Copyright © by the American Psychological Association. Reprinted by permission.

kinds of child custody cases, a judge may deem that therapy information is crucial in order to protect the welfare of the child. Other exceptions to privilege involve cases in which a defendant is using mental disability as a defense in a criminal trial; in this kind of case, the court would likely rule that the defendant has waived the psychologist-client privilege as it relates to the defendant's mental state at the time of the alleged crime. Along similar lines, an exception to privilege applies in a case in which a psychologist is appointed by a court to determine whether the defendant is competent to stand trial; obviously, the psychologist would be expected to share findings from such an evaluation with the court. However, the psychologist would not necessarily have blanket permission to share all that was communicated during the evaluation; the psychologist cannot disclose any statements by the defendant regarding the offense, unless the individual gives explicit permission (Brant, 1998).

As you can see, the work of a mental health professional involves many challenges in cases in which there is a legal aspect. For the most part, the legal system is committed to protecting the sanctity of private communication between a mental health professional and a client who has turned to that professional for help. In some instances, however, the client's rights must be overlooked for the good of society and the welfare of other people, such as children, who might be at risk of harm.

There are some important exceptions to the principle of confidentiality, such as cases involving abuse. Every state requires some form of **mandated reporting** by professionals when they learn firsthand of cases involving child abuse or neglect. Abuse, which may be physical or sexual, is defined as an act by a caretaker that causes serious physical or emotional injury. Neglect is characterized as the intentional withholding of food, clothing, shelter, or medical care (Brant, 1998). In recent years, many states have expanded mandated reporting statutes to include a wider range of vulnerable people, such as those who are handicapped or developmentally disabled as well as impaired elders who cannot otherwise protect themselves. One variation of mandated reporting that has been enacted in some states is the requirement to report self-neglect of older persons (60 or older) who are not attending to essential needs for food, clothing, safe and secure shelter, personal care, and medical needs.

Clinicians as well as teachers and other health professionals are required by law to notify the appropriate authorities about cases in which vulnerable individuals are being abused or neglected. The purpose of mandated reporting is to protect victims from continuing abuse and neglect, to initiate steps toward clinical intervention with the abused individual, and to deter, punish, and rehabilitate abusers.

Another exception to the principle of confidentiality involves instances in which the clinician learns that a client is planning to hurt another person. In such cases, the clinician has a **duty to warn** (sometimes referred to as "duty to protect"). This means that the clinician is required to inform the intended victim that the client plans to harm him or her. Duty to warn laws have their origins in a famous case that took place in 1969 in California. The "Tarasoff" case (*Tarasoff v. Regents of the*

University of California et al., 1976) involved a young woman named Tatiana Tarasoff, who was a student at the University of California at Berkeley. She was shot and fatally stabbed by a man named Prosenjit Poddar, whom she had dated the previous year and with whom she had broken off relations. Her parents successfully sued the university following her murder on the grounds that she was not properly warned about the fact that Poddar, who was a client at the counseling center, intended to kill her. The psychologist who treated the murderer had become alarmed when Poddar told him that he was going to go after Tarasoff and kill her. The psychologist informed the police, who then interviewed Poddar. After assurances from Poddar, the police let him go. The court ruled that the psychologist had not gone far enough in preventing Tarasoff's murder. He should have told her that Poddar was intent on killing her. It took several years for this case to proceed through the legal system, and its ramifications continue to be felt by psychotherapists who struggle to differentiate between their clients' serious threats and random fantasies. In trying to make these distinctions, clinicians recurrently weigh the client's right of confidentiality against concern for the rights of other people.

When you hear about a clinician's duty to warn, you may feel that it is a logical precaution worth taking. After all, if another person's life is at stake, you would think that a clinician would certainly want to do everything to let that person know. However, the situation is more complicated than it seems. There are a number of complications associated with the *Tarasoff* ruling that have come to light within the past 35 years. Some forensic psychologists assert that the ruling led to an erosion of client-therapist privilege and expressed concern that therapists may be open to criminal rather than civil charges for not taking action (Weinstock, Leong, & Silva, 2001). Other experts maintain that *Tarasoff* rulings have diminished in recent years, thus limiting the impact on confidentiality (Walcott, Cerundolo, & Beck, 2001). Yet a third point of view is that therapists who invoke the *Tarasoff* ruling notice an improvement in the therapeutic

Tatiana Tarasoff (*left*), a junior at the University of California, was stabbed to death on the doorstep of her home by Prosenjit Poddar (*right*), who had told his therapist that he intended to kill her.

relationship (Noffsinger & Saleh, 2000). Whatever the impact on therapy, it is clear that therapists who decide to warn or protect a possible target of harm must do so after careful assessment of the risks and benefits (Borum & Reddy, 2001). Complicating the matter even further is the imprecise nature of predicting dangerousness, which we will discuss later in the chapter.

Duty to warn statutes vary considerably in the United States, with some state statutes specifying that this duty only arises when there is an identifiable victim and the intended violence is imminent. Other statutes, however, do not require there to be an identifiable victim, but may apply to a more general threat not limited to a specified person or persons, as would be the case when a client intends to commit a violent act in a public place, or when the client indicates the intention to harm a particular person but refuses to say whom.

Duty to protect standards are especially complicated for clinicians who are treating suicidal clients. It is generally accepted that the duty to protect should apply whenever a client is engaging in a behavior that may lead to self-harm or death. What about situations in which a client is making a seemingly thoughtful decision to end life, as in cases in which an individual is fatally ill? Obviously, many ethical and moral issues pertain to such situations, and each clinician's decision about how to respond must be based on personal and professional standards of behavior, as well as a carefully elucidated assessment protocol and consultation with colleagues (Werth, 2005).

Relationships with Clients As you were reading the case studies in this book, you probably noticed that, in addition to speaking about the client, Dr. Tobin also spoke about herself in terms of her emotional reactions to her clients. In a few instances, she spoke about how difficult and exasperating her work with some clients can be. The therapeutic relationship is, by definition, intense and intimate. Because of the charged nature of this relationship, clinicians know that they must proceed with utmost vigilance in their interactions with clients. Clear roles and boundaries are essential in order for the client to feel safe and trusting, and for the clinician to maintain objectivity and effectiveness. When boundaries are violated within a therapeutic relationship, the consequences can be catastrophic for clients.

The most extreme form of violation of the therapeutic relationship involves sexual intimacy with clients, which is explicitly forbidden in the ethical codes of the mental health professions. Other forms of involvement with clients can fall into gray areas, however. While clinicians are urged to maintain neutrality and distance in their dealings with clients, these efforts are at times complicated, as is the case for clinicians working in small towns. What should the only psychologist in town do when it turns out that a prospective new client is also her son's sixth-grade teacher or baseball coach? Ethical codes in the mental health professions urge clinicians to avoid developing such dual relationships and to look for alternatives, if at all possible. Certain kinds of relationships with clients would always be considered inappropriate. In addition to sexual or romantic involvements, it would be inappropriate for clinicians to become involved in business

relationships with clients, because the boundaries, and thus the clinician's objectivity, would be blurred (Koocher & Keith-Spiegel, 1998).

The Business of Psychotherapy As we have discussed the mental health field throughout this book, we have focused on the helping aspects of the profession. It is the opportunity to touch positively the lives of those in need that draws people to such a career. It is only a matter of time, however, before idealistic helpers find that they depend for their livelihood on a complex health care system characterized by intense pressures to control costs. It sometimes feels like a jarring experience for beginning practitioners to confront the reality that success in the field of psychotherapy requires them to come to terms with the fact that they are running a business in which they will have to consider issues related to marketing, fee collection, and risk management (Rogers, 2004).

Although some clients are able to pay for their therapy, most are reliant on a third-party payor, such as a public assistance program or an insurance policy. In terms of health insurance, during recent decades major changes in the American health care system took place involving the introduction and expansion of managed health care programs. In principle, such institutions as health maintenance organizations and managed care mental health systems made sense, because they emerged from efforts to contain costs in order to keep insurance premiums affordable. As managed health care has expanded, however, many clinicians have found that they struggle with recurring ethical dilemmas, as they try to "balance the needs and best interests of their clients with an array of rewards, sanctions, and other inducements" (Koocher & Keith-Spiegel, 1998, p. 251). In some cases, clinicians are given financial incentives to limit care. When the case involves psychiatric hospitalization, an expensive proposition, pressures may be placed on the clinician to make the inpatient stay unreasonably brief, possibly placing the client at risk.

In order to adhere to the highest standards of ethical practice, good clinicians are alert to the financial pressures that affect their work. The American health care system will continue to evolve, and unexpected ethical challenges are likely to emerge in response to technological changes in society and in the delivery of mental health services (DeLeon, Vandenbos, Sammons, & Frank, 1998). As these changes take place, good clinicians will continue to strive to adhere to the principles that hold the good of their clients and of society above their own needs and wishes.

Special Roles for Clinicians In addition to their work as psychotherapists, clinicians are sometimes called on for special roles, each with its own set of ethical challenges. Among these special roles are the instances in which a clinician is an expert witness in court, becomes involved in a child custody case, or evaluates people with dementia. Expert witnesses have special value to the court because they have extensive knowledge in a specific area that is not within the common knowledge of the court. Such experts are invited to give evidence because of their qualifications and experience in their field of specialty (Lewis, 2004).

Former heavyweight boxing champion Mike Tyson leaves Massachusetts General Hospital in September 1998 following a psychological evaluation ordered by the Nevada Athletic Commission, as a result of his biting his opponent's ear during a boxing match.

The role of expert witness has a number of challenges, in that the clinician is called on to provide specialized information not commonly known by people outside the mental health profession. For example, a psychologist may be asked to conduct a specialized examination of a defendant or to critique the assessment findings of another professional. In such instances, the psychologist is expected to be an unbiased professional who is helping the court understand technical information pertinent to court deliberations. The process becomes ethically challenging, however, due to the fact that one of the parties involved in the legal proceeding is paying for the psychologist's services and opinions. In such contexts, the ethical clinician strives to be thoughtful, cautious, nondefensive, and scientifically rigorous (Koocher & Keith-Spiegel, 1998).

Even more complicated than the role of expert witness is the task of conducting evaluations in child protection cases. Such evaluations are deemed necessary in situations in which there are concerns about the child's welfare. For example, if there has been evidence or charges involving abuse, a mental health professional may be called on to make recommendations about the child's care. A clinician may be appointed as an agent of the court or a child protection agency, or may be hired by one of the parents. In some instances, the clinician is appointed as a **guardian ad litem,** a person appointed by the court to represent or make decisions for a person (e.g., minor or incapacitated adult) who is legally incapable of doing so in a civil legal proceeding.

As evaluators in child protection cases, clinicians may be asked to address such concerns as the extent to which the child's psychological well-being is being affected, the nature of the therapeutic interventions that are warranted, the psychological effect of a child being given over to one or both parents, and the psychological effect on the child if separated from the parents (Committee on Professional Practice and Standards Board of Professional Affairs, 1998). Table 15.3 specifies the guidelines that psychologists are expected to follow when conducting such evaluations. As you can see, clinicians willing to take on such responsibilities find themselves in positions where they must manage various kinds of pressure. The heightened tensions involved in these cases make it much more likely that clinicians will be faced with charges of ethical violations than is true in other areas of practice (Kirkland & Kirkland, 2001). Fortunately, however, most therapists conducting child custody evaluations have become increasingly skilled at handling these highly sensitive cases (Bow & Quinnell, 2001).

Clinicians may also be called on to conduct evaluations of people suffering with various symptoms reflective of cognitive decline. Such evaluations are most commonly conducted by psychologists, because, among the mental health professionals, they have the unique training and experience to administer neuropsychological tests that assess memory and cognitive functioning in order to differentiate normal changes from symptoms of serious deterioration. As is the case with evaluations involving child protection cases, guidelines have been published to alert psychologists to the special issues involved in the evaluation of cognitive decline.

Commitment of Clients

The case of Mark Chen at the beginning of this chapter highlights one of the most disturbing aspects of the work of mental health professionals—making a decision to involuntarily detain an individual in a psychiatric hospital. Imagine how you might feel and what you might do if a loved one told you that he is so despondent that he is going to kill himself? Obviously, you would be very alarmed and would want to do anything possible to stop him from hurting or killing himself. In order to deal with situations such as this, all states have laws designed to protect mentally ill individuals from harming themselves or other people. **Commitment** is an emergency procedure for the involuntary hospitalization of a person who, if not hospitalized, is deemed to be likely to create harm for self or other people as a result of mental illness (Brant, 1998).

The concept of commitment stems from the legal principle that the state has the authority to protect those who are unable to protect themselves; in the law, this authority is referred to as **parens patriae.** This responsibility is vested in various professionals, such as psychologists, physicians, and nurse specialists, who are authorized to sign an application for a time-limited commitment (usually 10 days); if a health professional is not accessible, a police officer may file commitment papers. In this application, the professional states why the failure to hospitalize the individual would result in the likelihood of serious harm due to mental illness. In some instances, application is made to a district court judge, perhaps by a family member; after hearing the reasons for commitment, the judge may issue a warrant to apprehend the mentally ill person in order for that individual to be assessed by a qualified professional. Once the individual is hospitalized, subsequent applications and hearings may be necessary to extend the period of commitment.

As you think about the concept of involuntary commitment, it is probably clear to you that it is a very complex issue. Does one person have the right to interfere with another's decisions or freedom of action? If your friend wants to kill himself, what right have you or anyone else to stop him? Consider the question of dangerousness. Your friend's threats are very serious, but what if his risk is less obvious? Perhaps he has stopped eating for the past few days, or perhaps he has been drinking and driving. Would these behaviors be considered dangerous enough to warrant his involuntary hospitalization?

Clinicians and legal experts have struggled with questions regarding involuntary commitment for the past two decades, and standards have alternated between being overly restrictive and overly liberal. For example, when commitment procedures have been very stringent, it was difficult to keep all but the most extremely disturbed individuals in the hospital. More recently, the trend has been toward less strict requirements for commitment, as public officials have reinterpreted commitment laws to make it easier to place seriously disturbed individuals in hospitals. Even with more flexible interpretation of statutes regarding involuntary commitment, many clinicians are reluctant to take such action unless there is a clear and imminent risk of harm. Although the standard of clear and imminent harm may seem straightforward enough, the situation becomes more complex when we consider individuals who are engaging in high-risk substance abuse. In one study, researchers found that psychiatrists were much more likely to consider the involuntary commitment for individuals with schizophrenia and bipolar disorder than for those who are dangerously dependent on substances. There are a number of reasons for such different treatment, but one factor that emerges is the view of some clinicians that people with schizophrenia and bipolar disorder usually respond well to treatment in a psychiatric setting. By contrast, psychiatric hospitalization for individuals with substance dependence is viewed as less effective (Luchins, Cooper, Hanrahan, & Rasinski, 2004).

The move to relax the criteria for involuntary commitment was, in part, a response to the increase in the numbers of mentally ill homeless people living on the streets of large cities. In the United States there are hundreds of thousands of homeless people, a large percentage of whom have psychological disorders. In some American cities, debate has raged over the legality of involuntarily hospitalizing disturbed homeless people for the purpose of ensuring that they have shelter. As you can imagine, there are many complex issues involved in such a debate, not the least of which pertain to the individual rights of citizens to make personal choices, including how and where they live.

Sometimes questions regarding commitment involve evaluations of dangerousness by professionals who do commitment evaluations. Forensic psychologists are often called on to assess dangerousness, usually in the context of predicting whether a person will be dangerous in the future. As you might imagine, this is often a difficult determination to make. Most psychologists agree that the best prediction of future dangerousness is the level of dangerousness shown by the person in the past. An individual who has murdered several times is more likely to

harm someone in the future than is an individual with no homicidal history. Even when the probability of dangerousness is high, however, there is still room for error in the prediction of future behavior. The consequences of erroneous predictions are, of course, very significant. The supposedly dangerous individual might be institutionalized unnecessarily, or the person deemed nondangerous might go on to commit serious harm.

Right to Treatment   The admission to psychiatric hospitals, whether voluntary or involuntary, is only the beginning of the story for people entering these facilities. Once admitted, the client enters a world that is unfamiliar to most people. They may feel frightened; if hospitalized against their will, they may feel outraged. Such reactions are understandable, and health professionals try to ensure that clients are given appropriate care and that they understand their legal rights. We have already discussed the importance of obtaining informed consent, when possible, prior to beginning treatment to ensure that clients understand the nature of treatment, the options available, and the client's rights.

Perhaps the most important legal right of the person entering a psychiatric hospital is the right to treatment. It may seem odd that laws are needed to ensure that patients in hospitals be provided with treatment, but, as you read the legal history of these statutes, you will understand why they are necessary. The right to treatment emerged as the outcome of a landmark legal

 In MindMAP Segment 15.1, Valerie speaks about how her bizarre thinking and behavior led her to be committed to a psychiatric hospital.

When people act in ways that endanger themselves or others, commitment to a psychiatric hospital may be deemed necessary.

case, *Wyatt v. Stickney* (1971, 1972). In this case, a patient named Ricky Wyatt instituted a class action suit against the commissioner of mental health for the state of Alabama, Dr. Stickney, in response to the horrifying conditions in psychiatric and mental retardation facilities. These institutions failed to provide even a minimum of treatment and, indeed, were so inhumane that they were actually detrimental to the patient's mental health. At the time, the court relied on a principle put forth by a legal scholar (Birnbaum, 1960), invoking the constitutional right to due process in making the ruling against Alabama. In other words, the court ruled that people cannot be committed to an institution that is supposed to help them unless they can be guaranteed that they will be helped. Otherwise, their commitment constitutes the equivalent of imprisonment without a trial. Along these lines, patients have the right to a "humane" environment, including privacy, appropriate clothing, opportunities for social interaction, mail, telephone and visitation privileges, comfortable furnishings, physical exercise, and adequate diet. Another related right is that of liberty and safety (*Youngberg v. Romeo*, 1982), a right that includes the right to move about the ward and to be protected from violent patients. Seclusion and mechanical restraints cannot be used unless medically indicated and, when used, can be used only for a limited amount of time and only for appropriate purposes (La Fond, 1994).

An alternative to involuntary institutionalization is outpatient commitment, in which the patient is not forced to reside within the institution but lives in the community. Outpatient commitment is particularly appropriate in mandating that patients take prescribed medications and keep mental health appointments to prevent their psychological condition from deteriorating to a point at which hospitalization would otherwise be necessary. Support for the idea of outpatient commitment dwindled with the budget cuts for community services in the 1980s, but access to outpatient treatment was given support in connection with the Americans with Disabilities Act of 1990 (Perlin, 1994). According to this act, individuals with disabilities cannot be discriminated against and are entitled to be brought into the mainstream of society (House Committee on Energy and Commerce, 1990). People with psychiatric disorders are, therefore, entitled to be treated in the community, rather than relegated to institutions. In order to fulfill the conditions of this act, the government is obligated to provide funding for community-based treatment.

In recent years, the tides have changed such that there has been increased interest in the notion of outpatient commitment. In fact, more than two dozen states now give courts, police officers, psychiatrists, mental health professionals, and families the option to coerce mentally ill individuals who have broken the law into treatment rather than to have them arrested. Those supporting legislation permitting outpatient commitment assert that the benefits to society, in addition to the therapeutic benefits for the individual, outweigh the risks. In fact, states that have enacted legislation for outpatient commitment report dramatic decreases in arrests and homelessness, accompanied by increases in medication compliance among people ordered to receive treatment (Milne, 2005).

Refusal of Treatment   One client right that has engendered considerable controversy is the right to refuse unwanted treatment. It is accepted in our society that competent adults have the right to either accept or decline medical treatment. If a physician tells a woman that she has breast cancer that warrants immediate surgery, the patient has the right to accept or ignore the recommendation. It would be unfathomable that the court would become involved in taking away this woman's right to determine her own health choices. In the realm of psychiatry, the issue is more complicated, however, primarily because some psychologically disturbed individuals are cognitively incapable of deciding what is best for them. This was the case with Mark Chen, whose case you read at the beginning of the chapter. Because Mark's mental status was characterized by intense depression with catatonic features, his wife was called on to grant permission for this dramatic procedure. On the other hand, had Mark been cognitively alert and responsive, he would have had the right to make this decision and would have had the legal right to decline Dr. Tobin's recommendation. This right is based on the principle that a competent person has the right to control interventions involving his or her body.

 In MindMAP Segment 15.3, defense attorneys for Brandon Wilson assert that Wilson was psychotic when he brutally murdered a young boy and was therefore unable to differentiate right from wrong, a position that the jury did not accept.

A central issue involved in insanity pleas is that of determining whether a defendant knew the difference between right and wrong when the crime was committed.

The case involving the prescription of psychoactive medications is a bit more complex, however, because medications are not generally regarded as being as risky as ECT or psychosurgery. Nevertheless, many states have enacted laws that give the client the right to refuse unwanted medications. But what happens when a client's disorder is putting the individual or others at great risk? In these cases, the clinician must obtain a written order from a court of law, documenting the need for medication. This procedure is based on landmark cases (*Rennie v. Klein,* 1979; *Rogers v. Okin,* 1979) that assert the right of clients to refuse psychoactive medications.

In recent years, increasing legal attention has been given to the regulation of treatments that are considered harsh and controversial. Such treatments as the application of aversive noise or unpleasant shock would be regarded as extreme by most people and, therefore, would be refused by people capable of making an informed choice. However, some clients are incapable of making informed decisions about such interventions. Consequently, many states have enacted legal protections for clients being treated with aversive and avoidance conditioning; a court applies a doctrine called "substituted judgment" for people deemed incompetent of making such treatment decisions themselves. Substituted judgment is a subjective analysis of what the client would decide if he or she were cognitively capable of making the decision (Brant, 1998). A judge might be faced with the difficulty of trying to imagine whether he or she would willingly approve the administration of aversive shock as a treatment designed to extinguish life-threatening headbanging behavior. As in so many of the issues we have discussed so far, the issues are complicated and ambiguous. Efforts are continually being made, by the legal and mental health professions, to balance the issue of human freedoms with the issue of caring for those incapable of caring for themselves.

Clients also have the right to be placed in what is called the **least restrictive alternative** to treatment in an institution. This evolved from several legal cases brought to trial on behalf of mental patients in various states. One U.S. Supreme Court ruling in particular received national attention. This case (*O'Connor v. Donaldson,* 1975) involved several issues relevant to the commitment and treatment of mental patients, including the right to refuse treatment and the right to a humane environment. Donaldson was committed at the age of 49 to a mental hospital in Chattahoochee, Florida, on the basis of his father's contention that Donaldson was dangerous. However, Donaldson never exhibited signs of threatening behavior. His disorder, which was diagnosed as paranoid schizophrenia, went into remission soon after his commitment. Nevertheless, Donaldson was kept in the hospital for nearly two decades, during which time he was denied many fundamental privileges, such as the right to send and receive mail. Donaldson's successful lawsuit, along with several less well-known cases, paved the way for major changes in the mental health system. Society was forced to recognize that the presence of mental illness in a person is not sufficient reason for confinement to a mental hospital.

MindMAP Segment 15.2: The Insanity Defense

Forensic Issues in Psychological Treatment

During the past decade, several legal cases received remarkable attention from the media, because they involved difficult questions about the psychological functioning of people who had carried out horrific acts of violence. Consider the case of Jeffrey Dahmer, a meek-sounding Milwaukee candy factory worker, who brutally murdered 17 boys and young men, engaged in sexual acts with corpses, and ate the flesh of those he had sacrificed. Would any sane person have carried out such outrageous acts? Did Dahmer understand the nature of his acts? Was he competent to stand trial? Questions such as these, which perplexed the public as well as the courts, fall within the field of forensic psychology. In this rapidly growing field, professionals with backgrounds in law and mental health tackle a variety of questions regarding the relationship between criminal behavior and psychological disturbance.

Insanity Defense

Contrary to popular belief, insanity is not a psychological term but, rather, a legal term that refers to the individual's lack of moral responsibility for committing criminal acts. The **insanity defense** refers to the argument presented by a lawyer acting on behalf of the client that, because of the existence of a mental disorder, the client should not be held legally responsible for criminal actions. The insanity defense has a long history dating back to the 1800s. To understand the basis of the insanity defense, it is important to know the assumptions on which criminal law is based—that people have free choice in their actions and that, if they break the law, they must be held responsible. People who are "insane," however, are considered to lack freedom of choice over controlling their behavior, as well as the mental competence to distinguish right from wrong. The insanity defense originated as an attempt to protect people with mental disorders from being punished for harmful behavior resulting from their disturbed psychological state.

The insanity defense emerged from various legal precedents and the legal profession's attempts at clarification (Caplan, 1984). In 1843, the M'Naghten Rule was handed down in a landmark case involving a Scottish woodcutter named Daniel M'Naghten. Under the delusional belief that he was being commanded by God, M'Naghten killed an official of the English government. When he went to trial, the argument was presented that he should not be held responsible for the murder, because his mental disorder prevented him from knowing the difference between right and wrong. He believed that he was following the commands of a higher power and, therefore, saw nothing wrong in his behavior. This is why the M'Naghten Rule is often referred to as the "right-wrong test."

The M'Naghten Rule was criticized, because it did not address the question of the individual's capacity to control harmful behavior. About 30 years later, the irresistible impulse test went a step further to add the notion that some disturbed behaviors may result from people's inability to inhibit actions they feel compelled to carry out. They may "know" that an act is wrong but be unable to stop themselves from acting on their impulses. You can imagine how difficult it is to make the determination of irresistible impulse. It may not be possible to establish that the defendant's criminal behavior resulted from an inability to distinguish right from wrong or an inability to control impulses.

Other changes in the mid-twentieth century broadened the scope of the insanity defense. The first, known as the Durham Rule, emerged from a court decision in 1954, asserting that a person is not criminally responsible if the "unlawful act was the product of mental disease or defect." This rule is significant, because it allows for the insanity defense to be used in cases involving many forms of mental disorders. Its intent was to protect individuals with disturbed psychological functioning due to any of a variety of conditions, including personality disorders. As you can imagine, this rule, although well-intentioned, created tremendous legal difficulties, because it put the burden on mental health experts to prove whether or not a defendant is mentally disturbed, even when there is not overt psychosis.

In an attempt to develop uniform standards for the insanity defense, the American Law Institute (ALI) published guidelines in 1962 (Sec. 4.01) that take a middle position between the pre-Durham Rule codes and the liberal standing taken by the Durham Rule. According to the ALI, people are not responsible for criminal behavior if their mental disorder prevents them from "appreciating" the wrongfulness of their behavior (a variation of the M'Naghten right-wrong rule) or from exerting the necessary willpower to control their acts (the irresistible impulse rule). The important term here is *appreciating*. In other words, knowing what is right and wrong is not equivalent to "understanding" that one's behavior is wrong (Gutheil & Appelbaum, 1982). An important feature of the ALI code is the exclusion from the insanity defense of people whose only maladaptive behavior is repeated criminal or otherwise antisocial conduct. The ALI guideline is considered a more viable standard of insanity than the Durham Rule, because it takes the question of guilt or innocence away from mental health experts and places it in the hands of the jury, who can then make a determination based on the evidence related to the crime itself. Despite this improvement, the ALI guidelines remain problematic.

In the years following the publication of the ALI standards, the insanity defense became much more widely used up to the point of the case of John Hinckley, a young man who attempted to assassinate President Reagan soon after his inauguration in 1981. At the time, Hinckley was obsessed with actress Jodie Foster. Hinckley believed that, if he killed the president, Jodie Foster would be so impressed that she would fall in love with him and marry him. He even thought that they would live in the White House someday. When the case went to trial, the jury confronted a very difficult question—was John Hinckley's behavior that of an "insane" person or that of a cold-blooded assassin? They ruled that he was insane, and he was sent to a mental hospital rather than a prison. This case brought to the nation's attention the rarely used but controversial insanity plea as it had been broadened through the Durham and ALI standards. The public was particularly outraged about the possibility that an assassin could get away with murder on the grounds of having a mental disorder.

To tighten the standards of the insanity defense, Congress passed the Insanity Defense Reform Act of 1984 (Shapiro, 1986). This act was an attempt to clear up the ambiguity inherent in the ALI standards regarding the severity and nature of an accused person's mental disorder. In order for people to be designated as insane according to the reform act, they must meet criteria of severe disturbance. In other words, people with personality disorders would probably not be considered insane according to the new law. This law also changed the nature of the legal arguments used to establish the insanity defense. Instead of the prosecuting attorney having the responsibility of proving that the defendant was sane, the defense must show that the defendant was insane. This means that the defense must provide a stronger case to convince the jury that the defendant should not go to jail. Prior to this law, the defense needed only to provide "reasonable doubt" regarding the prosecution's argument that the defendant was sane.

The upshot of these changes in insanity guidelines is that it is now harder for a defendant to be acquitted on the basis of the insanity plea. This is a federal law that applies in federal cases, and individual states vary in the nature of the insanity defense used in criminal proceedings at the state level. Some states have moved toward separating the question of guilt from that of mental disorder by allowing the plea of "guilty, but mentally ill" (Simon & Aaronson, 1988). The defendant is not then exonerated from the crime but is given special consideration by virtue of having a mental disorder. Another important feature of the reform act was developed in response to criticisms that "insane" people were often released from mental hospitals after a much shorter period of time than they would have spent in a jail. With the reform act, people who are guilty, but mentally ill, are treated in a psychiatric institution. Should their psychological condition improve, they would then be moved to a prison for the duration of the "sentence."

In the decade following these reforms, controversy surrounding the insanity plea resurfaced, and once again the U.S. judicial system struggled with some of the thorny legal issues raised in the case of John Hinckley. Partly because of the storm of criticism following the Hinckley case, however, a very different route was taken in 1992. This time, the case involved a 31-year-old man, Jeffrey Dahmer, mentioned earlier. Dahmer confessed to murdering and dismembering 17 boys and young men and explained that he was driven to kill out of a compulsion

REAL STORIES

JOHN HINCKLEY: INSANITY DEFENSE

In March 1981, a young man named John Hinckley shocked the nation when he attempted to assassinate President Ronald Reagan. As President Reagan left the Washington Hilton, Hinckley fired off six shots, wounding the president and three other men in his party. Although President Reagan was seriously injured by Hinckley's gunshot, he recovered and returned to his presidential duties relatively soon. The fate for James Brady, Mr. Reagan's press secretary, was not so positive—he suffered irreversible brain damage and paralysis.

One thing that made the assassination attempt particularly notable was the fact that Hinckley lacked a political motivation. Rather, he was motivated by a set of fantasies pertaining to an imagined relationship with actress Jodie Foster, whom he believed he could impress by assassinating the president. Immediately after Hinckley was arrested, his serious psychological problems were evident; consequently, it was not surprising that when the case went to trial his defense attorneys used the insanity defense. The ultimate verdict—not guilty by reason of insanity—engendered tremendous social and political debate and ultimately led to significant legislative changes, which are discussed in this chapter.

Instead of receiving a death sentence or life imprisonment, Hinckley was sent to a Washington, D.C., psychiatric institution, St. Elizabeth's Hospital, where he remains to the present time. The case of John Hinckley continues to evoke heated discussions among forensic specialists and mental health experts, who continue to discuss

The case of John Hinckley, who in 1981 tried to assassinate President Ronald Reagan, raised public concern over possible misuse of the insanity defense. Hinckley, who was declared insane by the courts, was not imprisoned; instead, he was committed to treatment at St. Elizabeth's Hospital in Washington, D.C., where he still resides.

whether Hinckley can recover and, if he does, what should become of this once-troubled man.

Hinckley was born in Oklahoma, the youngest of three children of well-to-do religious parents. Although mental health problems were not evident during John's childhood, during his teenage years he withdrew emotionally from other people and became obsessed with famous figures such as the Beatle John Lennon. He left home at age 21 and moved to Hollywood with hopes of becoming a famous songwriter.

While living in Hollywood, Hinckley saw the movie *Taxi Driver* numerous times and seemed to identify with the character Travis, a man who became obsessed with a political campaign worker. In the movie, Travis shot the political candidate for whom this woman worked, in hopes of attracting

her attention. Travis failed to assassinate the candidate, and later shifted his attention to a young prostitute played by Jodie Foster. He shot the prostitute's pimp to make himself a hero to the girl and to the public.

Hinckley began to imitate Travis, accumulating weapons and becoming obsessed with Jodie Foster. He first tried to gain Foster's attention by planning to assassinate President Jimmy Carter, but was arrested for possession of firearms in a Nashville airport where Carter was making a campaign stop. Following this arrest, Hinckley's parents sent John to a psychiatrist, who diagnosed his problems as "emotional immaturity." When Hinckley learned that Foster would be attending Yale University, he traveled to Connecticut to be near her. He did make contact with her on a couple of occasions, and ultimately he decided to

REAL STORIES

JOHN HINCKLEY: *(continued)*

take a drastic measure to gain her attention—attempt to assassinate the new president, Ronald Reagan.

John Hinckley's own words, written by him in a March 1981 letter to Jodie Foster, capture the intensity of his feelings and the disturbance of his thinking:

Dear Jodie,
There is a possibility that I will be killed in my attempt to get Reagan. It is for this reason that I am writing you this letter now.

As you well know by now I love you very much. Over the past seven months I've left you dozens of poems, letters, and love messages in the faint hope that you could develop an interest in me. Although we talked on the phone a couple of times I never had the nerve to simply approach you and introduce myself. Besides my shyness, I honestly did not wish to bother you with my constant presence. I know the many messages left at your door and in your mailbox were a nuisance, but I felt that it was the most painless way for me to express my love for you.

I feel very good about the fact that you at least know my name and know how I feel about you. And by hanging around your dormitory I've come to realize that I'm the topic of more than a little conversation, however full of ridicule it may be. At least you know that I'll always love you.

Jodie, I would abandon this idea of getting Reagan in a second if I could only win your heart and live out the rest of my life with you, whether it be in total obscurity or whatever. . . .

Jodie, I'm asking you to please look into your heart and at least give

me the chance, with this historical deed, to gain your respect and love.
I love you forever,
John Hinckley[1]

Two years later, following his treatment in the psychiatric hospital, Hinckley wrote in a manner reflecting a very different frame of mind. Hinckley was requesting that he be given expanded privileges in the hospital, such as being permitted to walk on the hospital grounds with a staff member or being allowed to use the telephone.

When I arrived at St. Elizabeth's Hospital on June 22, 1982, I did have mental problems. I was out of control two years ago and the restrictions placed upon me at that time were appropriate. Looking back now, I can see that I definitely needed mail and telephone and interview restrictions because my illness led me to do and write and say some very stupid and very sick things. At the time, I didn't appreciate these restrictions on me, but now I can see that they were necessary and protected me from myself. I no longer need protection from myself. These severe restrictions have become severe and unnecessary. . . . Your honor, I can see now that I did need that interview restriction in the summer of '82 because my judgment was so poor and my delusions about Jodie Foster were so strong that I was capable of saying some very dangerous things. But now my doctors and I believe that my judgment is much better and my obsession with Jodie Foster has been over for 19 months. . . .

All I want is the chance to have my therapy in the sunshine for a change away from the walls and fences and bars and every other

depressing thing. The atmosphere at John Howard Pavilion can be suffocating at times and it would be the best therapy in the world for me to breathe fresh air away from the building an hour a day or an hour a week if the court feels that is more appropriate.[2]

Two decades have passed since that fateful day in March 1981, and John Hinckley and his family continue to plead with the courts for expanded freedoms pertaining to John's status. For example, in November 2004, Hinckley's lawyers told the court that he is no longer mentally ill and should be allowed to make longer, unsupervised visits to his parents' home. Although prosecutors objected, U.S. District Judge Paul Friedman did allow Hinckley to continue making overnight visits to his parents without supervision, but these visits would be limited to six 32-hour visits with his parents at a Washington area hotel, with hospital assessments required after each visit. In objecting to Hinckley's request for more freedom, government lawyers pointed to the fact that Hinckley had a romantic relationship with a woman while both were confined to the hospital, but the woman broke it off several years after she was released in 1990. Since her release, she has remained a close friend of Hinckley, but prosecutors said it is unclear whether Hinckley has come to terms with the breakup. They are concerned that he may stalk her just as he stalked Jodie Foster prior to the assassination attempt on Reagan.

Sources: [1] http://www.law.umkc.edu/faculty/ projects/ftrials/hinckley/jfostercommun.htm. [2] http://www.law.umkc.edu/faculty/projects/ ftrials/hinckley/hinckleyeliz.htm.

to have sex with dead bodies. The trial took place in Milwaukee for the 15 murders that Dahmer claimed to have committed in Wisconsin. Dahmer's defense attorney argued that Dahmer's bizarre acts could only be those of someone who was insane.

The effects of the reform act could be seen in the outcome of the Dahmer case (Glynn, 1992). Unlike Hinckley, who was sent to a psychiatric hospital for treatment, Dahmer was sent to prison in February 1992, with a sentence of 15 consecutive life terms. A sixteenth life term was added later for his first murder, that of an Ohio hitchhiker in 1978. His plea of "guilty but insane" was rejected by the jury, who believed him to be responsible for his crimes and able to appreciate the wrongfulness of his conduct. At numerous points during the trial, questions were raised about the exact nature of his disorder. In the end, it was decided that he was not psychotic but, rather, had a sexual disorder; however, this was not considered sufficient grounds for absolving him of responsibility. Two years after his imprisonment, publicity surrounding the publication of *A Father's Story* by his father, Lionel Dahmer, drew national attention once again to Dahmer's mental state and psychological problems throughout his life. The sadistic murders he committed were apparently responses to tormenting thoughts and urges linking sex and mutilation. The final chapter of this tragic story was the brutal slaying of Dahmer himself at the age of 34 by another Wisconsin prison inmate in November 1994. Although Dahmer had been heavily guarded, a lapse in security one night allowed a seriously disturbed fellow prisoner to attack and beat him to death.

Other highly publicized cases since Dahmer's have brought out other subtleties in the insanity defense as it is currently construed. In both cases, the accused confessed that they had committed murder but claimed that they had been driven to these drastic actions as a result of abuse by their "victims." Lyle and Erik Menendez, two young men in California, admitted to the premeditated murder of their parents in response, they claimed, to years of sexual and emotional abuse. Erik, 23 years old, and Lyle, 26, were accused of having shot their parents, Jose and Kitty Menendez, as the couple watched television and ate ice cream in their Beverly Hills mansion in late August 1989. Both brothers admitted to the killings but claimed they had acted in self-defense. Their defense attorneys presented the argument of "imperfect self-defense," asserting that they acted out of the mistaken belief that their parents were about to kill them, a belief that stemmed from a lifelong history of physical, emotional, and sexual abuse. According to defense attorneys, 12 years of abuse led Erik, at the age of 18, to be tormented by feelings of powerlessness, hopelessness, helplessness, and fear. These feelings led him to believe that his parents, with their violent tendencies, could and would kill the sons to keep the molestation secret. The defense claimed that, on the night of the killings, a family argument was the stimulus for Erik to enter an altered state. Without conscious thought, he retrieved his shotgun, loaded it, and burst in on his parents. The prosecution claimed that the brothers' actions were motivated by their wish to collect a $14 million inheritance. Supporting this argument was the fact that Lyle spent $15,000 a few days after the shootings on expensive jewelry for himself and his brother.

Another dramatic example, specifically focused on the irresistible impulse defense, was the highly publicized case of Lorena Bobbitt, a Virginia woman who committed the unthinkable act of cutting off her husband's penis. Her defense attorneys used the irresistible impulse defense for Lorena Bobbitt, claiming that she was temporarily insane as the result of years of physical and psychological abuse by her husband, John Wayne Bobbitt. At the time that she committed the act, she reported having gone to the refrigerator for a glass of water when she spotted a large kitchen knife. She claimed that at that point she became overcome with what she called "pictures," or mental images, of having been abused by him. According to Lorena Bobbitt, she remembered nothing of what happened until after the incident. While fleeing in her car, she discovered she was holding the knife in one hand and the dismembered body part in the other. During the 8-day trial, the defense and prosecution debated her psychological state during the episode and whether the act was intentional and premeditated. The jury concluded that she was temporarily insane and acquitted her of all charges of malicious and unlawful wounding. As mandated by Virginia law, the judge in the case committed Lorena Bobbitt to a state psychiatric hospital to determine whether or not she posed a danger to herself or others. After the 45-day period, she was released.

Adding to the complex debate about the insanity defense was the perplexing case of Theodore Kaczynski, more commonly known as the Unabomber. After being apprehended by federal authorities from his wilderness cabin in Montana, Kaczynski admitted that he had killed three people and had maimed many others with package bombs in a solitary 18-year campaign aimed at bringing down the technological system. From his history and extensive clinical evaluation, fairly compelling evidence pointed toward a diagnosis of schizophrenia, paranoid type. Rather than follow the advice of his attorneys to consider using an insanity defense, however, Kaczynski was outspoken in his rejection of such efforts. He did not consider himself to be psychologically disturbed, nor did he consider his acts to be those of an insane person. Many of those involved in the trial sighed with relief when Kaczynski agreed to plead guilty. By doing so, a thorny judicial debate was avoided. What did emerge from this trial, however, was the realization among forensic experts that more precision is needed in determining the competency of a person who is on trial for bizarre acts, such as those committed by Kaczynski.

Perhaps no story in recent memory has provoked more discussion about the insanity defense than the case of Andrea Yates, whom we discussed in Chapter 8. In June 2001, Yates methodically drowned her five children in the bathtub of her Texas home, and then called her husband at work and asked him to come home. The case of Andrea Yates stands apart from other insanity pleas because her story is that of a loving mother with a clear history of mental disturbance. In fact, prior to the tragic murder of her children, Andrea Yates had suffered episodes of profound postpartum depression following the births of her fourth and fifth children. With her history of psychiatric hospitalizations and suicide attempts, the stage was set for what would seem to be a compelling case for an insanity plea. However, as was evident from the March 2002 guilty verdict, society is reluctant to excuse homicide, regardless of the mental state of the perpetrator.

Yet another complicated issue pertaining to the insanity defense was brought to light in the trials of Lee Boyd Malvo and John Allen Muhammed. These individuals were arrested in October 2002 in connection with sniper attacks in the Washington, D.C. area during the preceding summer when they shot and killed 10 strangers. At the time of the murders, 17-year-old Malvo had become involved with Muhammed (a man in his forties), who became powerfully controlling in his relationship with Malvo. It was asserted that Muhammed had undertaken the shooting spree and ordered Malvo to help carry it out. Malvo's defense attorneys pleaded the insanity defense on the grounds that he was indoctrinated, and that such indoctrination could be considered a form of mental illness. Malvo's attorneys insisted that his intense indoctrination by Muhammed made it impossible for this teenager to know right from wrong. The jury rejected the insanity defense for Malvo and convicted him of capital murder in the state of Virginia. Muhammed was sentenced to death. The case did not end there because both men were extradited to Maryland where they will be tried for the murders that took place in that state. The interesting point about this case is the notion that the control of one person over another could be used as a basis for the insanity defense.

From the cases we have just discussed, you can see how many complex issues pertain to the insanity defense. One major question concerns the process by which forensic mental health evaluations of insanity are actually conducted. Keep in mind that the task involves determining a defendant's sanity at the time of the offense, which may have been months or even years prior to the trial. Researchers attempting to understand the process that takes place when professionals evaluate the sanity of defendants have examined a number of possible variables. In one study involving 5,175 sanity evaluations conduced in Virginia over a 10-year period, researchers focused on (1) the clinical, criminal, and demographic attributes of the defendants who were determined to have met the criteria for insanity; (2) the forensic process and legal criteria used by the evaluating clinician in reaching a psycholegal opinion; (3) differences in sanity evaluations conducted by psychologists and psychiatrists in terms of process and outcome; and (4) the consistency in these opinions over the 10-year period. The researchers found that the overall model that best predicted an opinion of insanity was most likely to be found in an individual who had an Axis I (not an Axis II) diagnosis as the primary diagnosis, had a history of prior hospitalizations, was not under the influence of substances at the time of the offense, and had not been charged with a drug offense. Those individuals with a history of serious mental illness, not surprisingly, were the most likely to meet the criteria associated with insanity. Significant differences pertaining to the professional

discipline of the evaluator were not found, leading the researchers to conclude that well-trained psychiatrists and psychologists, although using different assessment methods, are fairly consistent. One finding with considerable social significance was that minority status had a significant negative association with the opinion of insanity (8.5 percent of minorities versus 11.4 percent of Whites were opined to be insane), a finding that highlights some of the racial disparities in the American justice system (Best, Williams, & Coccaro, 2002). In terms of assessing trends over the 10-year period, the researchers found no significant changes in the proportion of defendants evaluated as insane from one year to the next. In teasing out other significant influences on the designation of a perpetrator as insane, the researchers differentiated "cognitive" from "volitional" prongs. Cognitive prongs include (1) the ability to understand the nature, character, and consequences of the act and (2) the ability to distinguish right from wrong. A volitional prong is the ability to resist the impulse of the act. In the analyses of the cases in which insanity was determined, it was clear that the cognitive prongs played a much more significant role than was played by volitional prongs. In other words, evaluators have a difficult time ascertaining the extent to which an individual acted in response to an irresistible impulse (volitional prong), but find less difficulty concluding that psychotic delusions may have interfered with the individual's ability to differentiate right from wrong (cognitive prong).

Joining the debate about the insanity defense is the National Alliance for the Mentally Ill (NAMI), which has undertaken lobbying efforts aimed at educating the public about the relationship between mental illness and some criminal behaviors. In strongly worded statements, NAMI supports the retention of the insanity defense that incorporates the ALI two-prong test using both volitional and cognitive standards. NAMI opposes the "guilty but mentally ill" statutes, which it views as attempts to punish rather than treat individuals with "brain disorders who have committed crimes as a consequence of their brain disorders" (http://www.nami.org/update/platform/criminal.htm). In the years to come, cases such as the one involving Andrea Yates will add to judicial and legislative deliberations regarding the most appropriate ways to view the homicidal behavior of mentally disturbed individuals.

Competency to Stand Trial

The case of Theodore Kaczynski involved a man whose history and behavior at the time of the trial raised many questions about the extent to which he was competent to participate in legal proceedings with an informed understanding of what was taking place in the trial and to participate in his own defense. The determination of **competency to stand trial** pertains to the question of whether a defendant is aware of and able to participate in criminal proceedings against him or her. In other words, a person should not be tried, convicted, sentenced, or punished while, as a result of mental illness, he or she is not able to understand the legal proceedings or assist in his or her own defense (Brant,

After many years of eluding capture, Theodore Kaczynski, commonly known as the Unabomber, was apprehended by law enforcement officers working on a tip from his brother who recognized Theodore Kaczynski's disordered style of thought in the anonymous manifesto published by the *New York Times* and the *Washington Post*.

1998). To make this determination, the judge calls on a psychologist or psychiatrist to conduct an examination of the defendant and to testify about the defendant's competency. This decision is never taken lightly; in fact, a finding of incompetency must be based on a preponderance of the evidence; in other words, both the quantity and the quality of the evidence clearly point to a conclusion that the defendant is suffering from mental illness or defect and that the defendant is unable to understand or participate in the court proceedings (Brant, 1998). The job of the mental health expert is to evaluate the defendant's cognitive capacity, emotional stamina, and ongoing symptoms. For example, if a man is hallucinating and evidently delusional, he will probably have a very difficult time participating in the court proceedings. In other cases, however, defendants whose crime was committed while they were in a disturbed mental state may appear "normal" when interviewed about the crime. The forensic expert must determine, though, whether the stress of the criminal trial would precipitate a psychotic episode.

In efforts to increase the precision of competency assessments, forensic experts have developed standardized instruments to be used in such evaluations. One such instrument is the MacArthur Structured Assessment of the Competencies of Criminal Defendants (MacSAC-CD) (Bonnie et al., 1997; Hoge

et al., 1997a, 1997b). The MacSAC-CD was developed to replace imprecise assessment techniques that have been common for years. Rather than rely on the defendant's answers to such questions as "Where does the judge sit in the courtroom?" the MacSAC-CD tries to measure the extent to which the defendant is able to understand more cognitively complex information. For example, the defendant may be told a story about two men, Fred and Reggie, who get into a barroom fight during a game of pool. Fred hits Reggie so hard with a pool stick that Reggie falls, injuring his head and nearly dying. The tester then describes the legal system and the roles of a lawyer, prosecutor, and judge; then the tester asks the defendant questions in order to assess his or her understanding of the legal process. Instruments such as the MacSAC-CD have considerable appeal, because they establish national norms that can be used in court evaluations throughout the country.

As you can see from our discussion of forensic issues, there is a whole body of knowledge and practice regarding mental disorders that has very little to do with psychology per se. Mental health professionals are playing an increasingly important role in the legal system and, at the same time, are finding that they must familiarize themselves with a whole array of forensic issues. Clearly, the areas of intersection between psychology and the law will continue to grow as society looks for interventions that are humane, ethical, and effective.

Courts often rely on the testimony of psychologists for guidance in determining issues of insanity or competency.

Mark's History

Gathering information about Mark's life history was challenging, due to the fact that he was too emotionally incapacitated to tell me the story himself. I had to rely on the clinical record from his hospitalization a decade ago, as well as the information provided by his wife. Prior to meeting with Tanya the afternoon of Mark's admission, I obtained Mark's chart from the Medical Records Department and quickly read it in order to refresh my memory of that previous treatment. Then, when I met with Tanya, I was able to ask questions about Mark's life and experiences during the 10 intervening years.

Mark was born in San Francisco, the only son of parents who had immigrated to the United States from Taiwan a year prior to his birth. Although they spoke very little English, they chose to give their son a Western-sounding name in the hope that he would be perceived as American. Both parents worked in the garment industry, in circumstances that were harsh. Mark's mother operated a sewing machine, and his father was a technician responsible for maintaining industrial equipment in the factory. Although the Chens had little affection for their jobs, they felt fortunate to obtain work permits in positions with benefits, such as life insurance. Little did they realize how important those benefits would prove to be. Just before Mark's fifth birthday, Mr. Chen was killed in a gruesome machine accident at work.

Alone and emotionally devastated, Mrs. Chen wanted to pack up her belongings and take Mark back to Taiwan, feeling that her dream of a better life in the States had been an unrealistic fantasy. Although she had once intended to gain American citizenship, this goal suddenly seemed pointless. With the support of caring relatives, Mrs. Chen reconsidered and remained in San Francisco. She quit her job in the factory and began working as a maid in a luxury hotel.

Mark was educated in public schools, where he was regarded as a model student. His mother was able to manage the household with the earnings from her job and the interest from the $50,000 life insurance money. The road was not an easy one for her, however, in that she began to suffer from recurring episodes of depression in her late twenties. Fortunately, she had access to good health care and found a physician who prescribed effective antidepressant medication. Although Mrs. Chen's doctor had urged her to see a clinical psychologist or psychiatrist, Mrs. Chen refused, because she would feel too ashamed. In fact, Mrs. Chen didn't like the idea of taking medication, either. Periodically, she stopped taking her meds and, within a month or two, became depressed, stopped going to work, and felt incapable of caring for Mark. Fortunately, she had a sister who lived nearby, who swung into action each time, to make sure that Mrs. Chen was taken for help and Mark was adequately cared for.

Even though Mark's life had been filled with much emotional stress, including the untimely death of his father and the depressive episodes of his mother, he seemed to manage. He occasionally became moody and felt a bit sorry for himself, but those feelings subsided in a few days. He excelled in his high-school classes and won a full scholarship to the university, where he chose to pursue a degree in management.

By the time Mark had reached his senior year, he had found that there was an emotional storm raging within him that caused him to experience periods of despair and hopelessness. His customary optimism and good cheer suddenly gave way to expressions of pessimism and gloom. There were ups and downs during his freshman and sophomore years, but life seemed to feel great for Mark during his junior year. He had begun dating Tanya and had found a great sense of peace and security in that relationship. They decided to live together during their senior year, with the expectation that they would consider marriage later on. Mark's mother disapproved of this plan but decided to go along with it, believing that his positive state of mental health was probably due to his happy relationship with Tanya.

During Mark's senior year, he took a turn for the worse during the final exam period at the end of the first semester. Feeling stressed and overwhelmed, he slipped into a depression far more intense than he had ever experienced, or ever observed in his mother. When it became apparent that Mark's symptoms could not be managed on an outpatient basis, he agreed to enter the hospital and agreed to the administration of ECT.

Mark recovered quickly from that depression and went on to marry Tanya and obtain a well-paying job as an account executive. He continued to take antidepressant medication for several years, then decided to try life without meds. He realized that his thinking was remarkably similar to his mother's unwise decision about medication but, nevertheless, felt that he wanted to try this path himself. Several years went by, during which Mark was psychologically healthy. Other than the customary mood swings of life, he experienced no worrisome signs of a mood disorder. All that changed the week before he was brought in for this hospitalization.

When I asked Tanya in the admission interview about any recent stressors in their lives, she responded, "No, not at all. Things have been going great. In fact, we have both been so happy in recent weeks since learning that I'm pregnant." When Tanya spoke those words, she was not even imagining the possibility that good news can also cause stress. Some people with a history of severe emotional disturbance respond in ways far different from what others might expect.

Assessment

Assessing a client in such a severe state of depression is obviously difficult. Not only were traditional psychological tests out of the question, but it was even impossible to engage Mark in an interview. My assessment would have to rest on behavioral observations and the reports of other people. Mark's immobilization reflected a depth of depression that was so great that his body seemed to have shut down in a self-protective maneuver.

Although I could see that Mark was immobilized, I could not conclude with certainty that he was depressed. Drugs can cause a person to be immobilized. So can certain medical conditions. Consequently, I had to rely on Tanya's report about Mark's behavior during the past several days. I asked her directly whether it was possible that Mark had used any drugs, to which she responded with an emphatic "no." Explaining that they were both "health fanatics," she assured me that he did not, and would not, put anything into his body other than prescription medication—even those he didn't like to take. She had been with him for the entire period during which he had become symptomatic, and was certain that nothing had happened to Mark out of the ordinary. The only spark for Mark's depression seemed to be the good news about their impending parenthood.

Diagnosis
Based on Mark's symptom picture and history, it was safe to conclude that he was suffering from a mood disturbance. I had ruled out drugs as the cause for his state of stupor, and there was no evidence of a medical condition that could explain what he was experiencing. (Of course, a complete medical examination would still be conducted by a hospital physician.) Had I not had so much information about Mark's psychiatric and family history, I would have considered several diagnostic possibilities. However, the fact that he had a previous episode of major depression, and that his mother also had a history of depression, the conclusion seemed clear that Mark's symptom picture

was that of a person with major depressive disorder. His bodily immobility pointed to further specificity—namely, that his condition involved catatonic features.

Axis I: Major Depressive Disorder, Recurrent, with Catatonic Features
Axis II: No personality disorder
Axis III: None
Axis IV: Familial stressor—recent news of his wife's pregnancy (planned)
Axis V: Current Global Assessment of Functioning: 20 Highest Global Assessment of Functioning (past year): 95

Case Formulation
Mark's history, in both biological and psychological terms, contained several aspects that would predispose a person to a mood disorder. The fact that his mother suffered from recurrent depression was an important clue regarding the potential role of genetics in causing Mark's depression. In addition to a possible biological predisposition, some of Mark's life experiences could also have influenced the development of his mood disorder. The death of his father when Mark was only 5 years old apparently evoked a powerful emotional reaction within the family that would have an impact on Mark for the rest of his life. As Mark grew older, he found it difficult to manage intense stress. His personal difficulty managing stress was compounded by the fact that he felt that it would be culturally unacceptable to seek professional help to deal with his emotional problems. As a college student facing seemingly insurmountable pressures, Mark fell into a deep depression requiring an extreme intervention. Although he found ways to cope following his recovery from the first depressive episode, he lacked sufficient coping resources to thwart a recurrence of his depression. Even though a decade had passed between episodes, a

new stressor—anxiety about becoming a parent—sent him into a state of emotional havoc. This occurrence was especially salient for Mark, in light of his unresolved feelings of loss about the premature death of his father during Mark's childhood.

Treatment Plan
My intervention plan for Mark required special attention to issues of immediate management before turning my attention to longer-term treatment planning. Mark needed a dramatic intervention to help him recover from the depth of immobilizing depression that had overtaken him. His inability to take care of himself and his self-injurious behavior justified the recommendation of electroconvulsive therapy. It was fortunate that his wife was willing to sign forms giving permission for the multiple administrations recommended by the medical professionals.

Following Mark's emergence from his incapacitating state, a course of antidepressant medication and psychotherapy would be recommended. In individual treatment, Mark could attempt to understand the factors in his life that might have sparked the current mood episode, while paying special attention to cognitive strategies he could develop to reduce the likelihood of subsequent episodes.

Outcome of the Case
In textbook fashion, Mark's response to the course of six ECT treatments involved a seemingly miraculous recovery. In fact, after only three treatments, Mark was saying that he was feeling great. His thinking had become clearer, and his catatonic-like behaviors had subsided. Although he expressed some reservations about completing the full course of ECT, he went along with the recommendation of the treatment team. He also agreed to begin a regimen of antidepressant medication and to continue working with me in individual psychotherapy.

One of the first issues I felt it important to address in our therapy was Mark's feelings about having been committed to the hospital and administered ECT without his making an informed choice about these decisions. Mark's response in this discussion consisted of a perplexing mixture of gratitude and anger. He acknowledged that he felt markedly better, and that he was deeply thankful to me and to his wife for our willingness to make the hospitalization and treatment choice for him. At the same time, however, he said, "I don't ever want to be in this position again, of having someone else take control over such important decisions." I could see his point and could empathize with the emotionality of his reaction, but I also felt a bit defensive. Rather than getting into a lecture justifying these choices, I suggested that we move our focus to the task of helping Mark develop strategies to minimize the likelihood of a recurrence of incapacitating depression.

I saw Mark weekly for 8 months, and all seemed to be going well. Matters took a turn for the worse, however, shortly after Tanya delivered their baby. Although their new son was healthy and normal, Mark once again found that deep emotions were being stirred up in response to the increasing demands of being a new parent. A week after his wife and son came home from the hospital, Mark found that he was becoming unexplainably sad and tearful each day. His symptoms were evident in one of our sessions, and we talked about what he was going through. We increased the frequency of our sessions to twice weekly for the next few weeks, and Mark's psychiatrist also raised the dosage of his medication. Mark responded quite positively to these added efforts and gradually returned to a normal mood. We resumed weekly meetings, which we continued for another year. We then reduced the frequency of sessions to monthly meetings, and more recently to twice yearly. Mark has remained stabilized on a relatively low dose of antidepressant medication. Although all has seemed fine for the past several years, Mark and his wife both realize the importance of their vigilance for any signs of deepening depression. Mark knows that he is vulnerable to a recurrence, but, if action can be taken quickly, the development of disturbing symptoms surrounding his previous hospitalizations might be avoidable.

Sarah Tobin, PhD

SUMMARY

- Clinicians have various roles and responsibilities. They are expected to have the intellectual competence to assess, conceptualize, and treat clients whom they accept into treatment, in addition to being emotionally capable of managing the clinical issues that emerge. When beginning work with clients, they should obtain the client's informed consent to ensure that the client understands the goals of treatment, the process of therapy, the client's rights, the therapist's responsibilities, the treatment risks, the techniques that will be used, financial issues, and the limits of confidentiality.

- Confidentiality is the principle that the therapist must safeguard disclosures in therapy as private. With only a few exceptions, the content of therapy is considered privileged communication; that is, the clinician may not disclose any information about the client in a court without the client's expressed permission. Exceptions to the principle of confidentiality include instances involving mandated reporting and duty to warn. Mental health professionals are mandated by law to report information involving the abuse or neglect of a child or people who are unable to protect themselves. The duty to warn involves the clinician's responsibility to take action to inform a possible victim of a client's intention to do harm to that person.

- In their relationships with clients, clinicians are expected to adhere to the highest standards of ethical and professional conduct. They are to avoid inappropriate relationships, such as sexual intimacy with clients, and are expected to maintain neutrality and distance in their dealings with clients. In overseeing the business aspects of psychotherapy practice, mental health professionals face various challenges, particularly when operating within managed health care delivery systems. Sometimes clinicians are called on for special roles that present unique ethical challenges (e.g., expert witness, child custody evaluations, and evaluations of people with dementia).

- Clinicians are sometimes involved in the process of commitment, an emergency procedure for the involuntary hospitalization of a person who, if not hospitalized, is deemed to be likely to create harm for self or other people as a result of mental illness. Clients who are hospitalized have the right to treatment—the right to a humane environment with appropriate amenities, in addition to liberty and safety. Clients also have the right to refuse unwanted treatment, unless a court deems that the client is at risk of harming self or others without needed intervention. Clients also have the right to be placed in the least restrictive alternative to treatment in an institution.

■ The major forensic issues that pertain to the field of mental health involve the insanity defense and the competency to stand trial. The insanity defense is the argument presented by a lawyer acting on behalf of the client that, because of the existence of a mental disorder, the client should not be held legally responsible for criminal actions. Various controversies have emerged during the past two decades regarding the insanity defense, as courts have struggled with issues of assessing a defendant's responsibility in well-publicized cases involving violent assault and murder. The determination of competency to stand trial pertains to the question of whether a defendant is aware of and able to participate in criminal proceedings against him or her.

KEY TERMS

See Glossary for definitions

Commitment   470
Competency to stand trial   478
Confidentiality   466
Duty to warn   468

Guardian ad litem   470
Informed consent   465
Insanity defense   473
Least restrictive alternative   473

Mandated reporting   468
Parens patriae   470
Privileged communication   466

INTERNET RESOURCE

To get more information on the material covered in this chapter, visit our website at **www.mhhe.com/halgin5.** There you will find more information, resources, and links to topics of interest.

A

Abstinence violation effect: A sense of loss of control over one's behavior that has an overwhelming and demoralizing effect. 402

Active phase: A period in the course of schizophrenia in which psychotic symptoms are present. 279

Acute stress disorder: An anxiety disorder that develops after a traumatic event with symptoms such as depersonalization, numbing, dissociative amnesia, intense anxiety, hypervigilance, and impairment of everyday functioning. People with this disorder may reexperience the event and desperately avoid reminders of the trauma. These symptoms arise within the month following the trauma and last from 2 days to 4 weeks. 166

Adoption study: A method of comparing genetic versus environmental contributions to a disorder by tracking the incidence of disorders in children whose biological parents have diagnosed psychological disorders but whose rearing parents do not. 28

Adult antisocial behavior: Illegal or immoral behavior such as stealing, lying, or cheating. 315

Affect: An individual's outward expression of emotion. 75

Affective flattening: A symptom of schizophrenia in which an individual seems unresponsive and which is reflected in relatively motionless body language and facial reactions, as well as minimal eye contact. 282

Agnosia: The inability to recognize familiar objects or experiences, despite the ability to perceive their basic elements. 376

Agoraphobia: Intense anxiety about being trapped or stranded in a situation without help if a panic attack occurs. 150

Akinesia: A motor disturbance in which a person's muscles become rigid and movement is difficult to initiate. 380

Alcohol dehydrogenase (ADH): A zinc containing enzyme that breaks down alcohol into fatty acids, carbon dioxide, and water before it enters the bloodstream. 400

Aldehyde dehydrogenase (ALDH): An enzyme that is involved in metabolizing alcohol. 404

Alogia: Speechlessness or a notable lack of spontaneity or responsiveness in conversation. 282

Alters: The alternative personalities that develop in an individual with dissociative identity disorder. 198

Alzheimer's disease: A form of dementia characterized by progressive and gradual cognitive deficits due to severe cerebral atrophy. 377

Amnestic disorders: Cognitive disorders involving the inability to recall previously learned information or to register new memories. 374

Amyloid plaques: A characteristic of Alzheimer's disease in which clusters of dead or dying neurons become mixed together with fragments of protein molecules. 384

Anal stage: A period of psychosexual development in which the toddler's pleasure focuses on anal stimulation from holding onto and expelling feces. 106

Anhedonia: A loss of interest in or ability to experience pleasure from activities that most people find appealing. 282

Anorexia nervosa: An eating disorder characterized by an inability to maintain normal weight, an intense fear of gaining weight, and distorted body perception. 430

Antisocial personality disorder: A personality disorder characterized by a lack of regard for society's moral or legal standards. 313

Anxiety: A future-oriented and global response, involving both cognitive and emotional components, in which an individual is inordinately apprehensive, tense, and uneasy about the prospect of something terrible happening. 148

Anxiety disorders: Disorders characterized by intense, irrational, and incapacitating apprehension. 148

Anxiety sensitivity theory: The belief that panic disorder is caused in part by the tendency to interpret cognitive and somatic manifestations of stress and anxiety in a catastrophic manner. 151

Aphasia: A loss of the ability to use language. 376

Apraxia: A loss of the ability to carry out coordinated bodily movements that the individual could previously perform without difficulty. 376

Asperger's disorder: A pervasive developmental disorder in which a child maintains adequate cognitive and language development but becomes severely impaired in social interaction. Children with this disorder also develop restricted, repetitive, and stereotyped patterns of behavior, interests, and activities. 347

Assessment: The evaluation of a person in terms of the psychological, physical, and social factors that have the most influence on the individual's functioning. 68

Assigned (biological) sex: The sex of the individual that is recorded on the birth certificate. 227

Asylum: Literally a place of refuge or safety, the term was originally used to describe a psychiatric facility and later came to have negative connotations. 12

Attachment style: The way a person relates to a caregiver figure. 110

Attention-deficit/hyperactivity disorder (ADHD): A behavior disorder of childhood involving problems with inattentiveness, hyperactivity, and impulsivity. 355

Auditory hallucination: An hallucination that involves hearing sounds, often voices or even entire conversations. 76

Autistic disorder: A pervasive developmental disorder involving massive impairment in an individual's ability to communicate and relate emotionally to others. 347

Automatic thoughts: Ideas so deeply entrenched that the individual is not even aware that they lead to feelings of unhappiness and discouragement. 122

Aversions: Responses of discomfort or dislike to a particular object or situation. 153

Aversive conditioning: A form of conditioning in which a painful stimulus is paired with an initially neutral stimulus. 119

Avoidant personality disorder: A personality disorder whose most prominent feature is that the individual desires, but is fearful of, any involvement with other people and is terrified at the prospect of being publicly embarrassed. 332

Avolition: A lack of initiative, either not wanting to take any action or lacking the energy and will to take action. 282

Axis: A class of information in *DSM-IV* regarding an aspect of the individual's functioning. 45

B

Base rate: The frequency with which a disorder occurs in the general population. 41

Baseline: The period in which a participant is observed prior to being given treatment, the purpose being to document the frequency of the target behavior. 27

Behavioral assessment: A form of measurement based on objective recording of the individual's behavior. 87

Behavioral medicine: An interdisciplinary approach to medical conditions affected by psychological factors that is rooted in learning theory. 196

Behavioral observation: A behavioral method of assessment in which the clinician observes the individual and records the frequency of specific behaviors along with any relevant situational factors. 90

Behavioral perspective: A theoretical perspective in which it is assumed that abnormality is caused by faulty learning experiences. 118

Behavioral self-report: A method of behavioral assessment in which the individual provides information about the frequency of particular behaviors. 88

Benzodiazepines: Medications that slow down central nervous system reactions that are thought to contribute to anxiety. 152

Big win: A gain of large amounts of money in one bet which propels the pathological gambler into a pattern of uncontrollable gambling. 443

Binges: The ingestion of large amounts of food during a short period of time, even after reaching a point of feeling full, and a lack of control over what or how much is eaten. 435

Biofeedback: A procedure in which people learn to monitor and control their autonomic responses, such as blood pressure, heart rate, skin conductance, and muscular tension. 130

Biological markers: Measurable characteristics or traits whose patterns parallel the inheritance of a disorder or other characteristic. 28

Biological perspective: A theoretical perspective in which it is assumed that disturbances in emotions, behavior, and cognitive processes are caused by abnormalities in the functioning of the body. 125

Biopsychosocial: A model in which the interaction of biological, psychological, and sociocultural factors is seen as influencing the development of the individual. 9

Bipolar disorder: A mood disorder involving manic episodes—intense and very disruptive experiences of heightened mood, possibly alternating with major depressive episodes. 254

Bipolar I disorder: The diagnosis used to describe a clinical course in which the individual experiences one or more manic episodes with the possibility, though not the necessity, of having experienced one or more major depressive episodes. 257

Bipolar II disorder: The diagnosis used to describe a clinical course in which the individual experiences one or more major depressive episodes and at least one hypomanic episode. 257

Body dysmorphic disorder: A somatoform disorder in which individuals are preoccupied with the idea that a part of their body is ugly or defective. 184

Borderline personality disorder: A personality disorder characterized by a pervasive pattern of poor impulse control and instability in mood, interpersonal relationships, and self-image. 319

Bradykinesia: A motor disturbance involving a general slowing of motor activity. 380

Brief psychotic disorder: A disorder characterized by the sudden onset of psychotic symptoms that are limited to a period of less than a month. 286

Broca's aphasia: A form of aphasia that involves a disturbance in language production but intact comprehension abilities. 376

Bulimia nervosa: An eating disorder involving the alternation between the extremes of eating large amounts of food in a short time, and then compensating for the added calories either by vomiting or other extreme actions to avoid gaining weight. 435

C

Caregiver burden: The adverse effects on caregivers from the constant demands placed on them by their role. 388

Caregivers: The people (usually family members) primarily responsible for caring for a person with a chronic disease, such as Alzheimer's disease. 388

Case formulation: A clinician's analysis of the factors that might have influenced the client's current psychological status. 52

Case study method: An intensive study of a single person described in detail. 26

Caspase theory of Alzheimer's disease: The proposal that beta amyloid stimulates substances called caspases, which become enzymes that destroy neurons. 384

Catatonia: Extreme motor disturbances in a psychotic disorder not attributable to physiological causes. 73

Childhood disintegrative disorder: A pervasive developmental disorder in which the child develops normally for the first 2 years and then starts to lose language, social, and motor skills, as well as other adaptive functions, including bowel and bladder control. 347

Choline acetyltransferase (CAT): An enzyme that is essential for the synthesis of acetylcholine. 384

Chromosomes: Structures found in each cell of the body that contain the genes and exist in a pair, with one chromosome contributed from each parent at conception. 127

Classical conditioning: The learning of a connection between an originally neutral stimulus and a naturally evoking stimulus that produces an automatic reflexive reaction. 119

Client: A person seeking psychological treatment. 38

Client-centered: An approach based on the belief held by Rogers that people are innately good and that the potential for self-improvement lies within the individual. 112

Clinical psychologist: A mental health professional with training in the behavioral sciences who provides direct service to clients. 40

Cognitive-behavioral perspective: A theoretical perspective in which it is assumed that abnormality is caused by maladaptive thought processes that result in dysfunctional behavior. 119

Cognitive distortions: Errors that depressed people make in the way they draw conclusions from their experiences. 261

Cognitive restructuring: One of the fundamental techniques of cognitive behavioral therapy in which clients learn to reframe negative ideas into more positive ones. 124

Cognitive triad: A negative view of the self, the world, and the future. 261

Command hallucination: An hallucination in which the individual hears an instruction to take an action. 76

Commitment: Legal procedure designed to protect individuals from doing harm to themselves or others through involuntary institutionalization or other forms of mental health treatment. 470

Communication disorders: Conditions involving impaired expression or understanding of language. 353

Community mental health center (CMHC): Outpatient clinic that provides psychological services on a sliding fee scale to serve individuals who live within a certain geographic area. 59

Comorbid: Multiple diagnostic conditions that occur simultaneously within the same individual. 39

Competency to stand trial: A prediction by a mental health expert of the defendant's cognitive and emotional stability during the period of the trial. 478

Compulsion: A repetitive and seemingly purposeful behavior performed in response to uncontrollable urges or according to a ritualistic or stereotyped set of rules. 74, 161

Computed axial tomography (CAT or CT scan): A series of X-rays taken from various angles around the body which are integrated by a computer to produce a composite picture. 93

Concordance rate: Agreement ratios between people diagnosed as having a particular disorder and their relatives. 28

Conditioned fear reactions: Acquired associations between an internal or external cue and feelings of intense anxiety. 151

Conditioned response: An acquired response to a stimulus that was previously neutral. 119

Conditioned stimulus: A previously neutral stimulus that, after repeated pairings with the unconditioned stimulus, elicits a conditioned response. 119

Conduct disorder: A development-related disorder that involves repeated violations of the rights of others and society's norms and laws; the childhood precursor of antisocial personality disorder in adulthood. 358

Confidentiality: The principle that disclosures in therapy must be safeguarded by the therapist as private. 466

Content of thought: Ideas that fill a client's mind. 73

Contingency management: A form of behavioral therapy that involves the principle of rewarding a client for desired behaviors and not providing rewards for undesired behaviors. 124

Continuous amnesia: Inability to recall past events from a particular date up to and including the present time. 207

Control group: The group of participants that does not receive the "treatment" thought to influence the behavior under study. 23

Conversion disorder: A somatoform disorder involving the translation of unacceptable drives or troubling conflicts into physical symptoms. 181

Coping: The process through which people reduce stress. 192

Coprolalia: The involuntary uttering of obscenities. 364

Correlation: An association, or correlation, between two variables, that can range in value from +1.0 to −1.0. 25

Cortical atrophy: A wasting away of tissue in the cerebral cortex of the brain. 291

Cortisol: A hormone involved in the mobilization of the body's resources in times of stress. 260

Counterconditioning: The process of replacing an undesired response to a stimulus with an acceptable response. 123

Covert conditioning: A behavioral intervention in which the therapist instructs the client to imagine a highly negative experience when engaging in an undesirable behavior. 221

Crack cocaine: A crystallized form of cocaine that is usually smoked. 410

Creutzfeldt-Jakob disease: A neurological disease transmitted from animals to humans that leads to dementia and death resulting from abnormal protein accumulations in the brain. 381

Crossfostering study: A method of comparing genetic versus environmental contributions to a disorder by tracking the incidence of disorders in children who are adopted by parents with psychological disorders but whose biological parents are psychologically healthy. 28

Culture-bound syndromes: Recurrent patterns of abnormal behavior or experience that are limited to specific societies or cultural areas. 53

Cyclothymic disorder: A mood disorder that, compared with bipolar disorder, involves a less intense vacillation between states of euphoria and dysphoria. 254

D

Day treatment program: A structured program in a community treatment facility that provides activities similar to those provided in a psychiatric hospital. 59

Decision tree: A strategy used for diagnosis, consisting of yes/no questions that guide clinicians in ruling in or out psychological disorders. 51

Defense mechanisms: Tactics that keep unacceptable thoughts, instincts, and feelings out of conscious awareness and thus protect the ego against anxiety. 103

Deinstitutionalization movement: The release of psychiatric patients into community treatment sites as a result of dramatic changes in public policy. 19

Delirium: A temporary state in which individuals experience a clouding of consciousness in which they are unaware of what is happening around them and are unable to focus or pay attention. 373

Delirium tremens: A physical condition consisting of autonomic nervous system dysfunction, confusion, and possible seizures associated with alcohol withdrawal. 403

Delusional disorders: Disorders marked by a single striking psychotic symptom—an organized system of nonbizarre false beliefs. 289

Delusions: Deeply entrenched false beliefs not consistent with the client's intelligence or cultural background. 73

Demand characteristics: The expectations of participants in an experiment about what is going to happen to them or the proper way to respond. 24

Dementia: A form of cognitive impairment involving generalized progressive deficits in a person's memory and learning of new information, ability to communicate, judgment, and motor coordination. 375

Dementia praecox: The term coined by Kraepelin to describe what is currently known as schizophrenia. According to Kraepelin, this condition involves a degeneration of the brain that begins at a young age and ultimately leads to a disintegration of the entire personality. 278

Deoxyribonucleic acid (DNA): A molecule containing a sequence of nucleotides that forms the structure of the chromosome. 127

Dependent personality disorder: A personality disorder whose main characteristic is that the individual is extremely passive and tends to cling to other people, to the point of being unable to make any decisions or to take independent action. 332

Dependent variable: The variable whose value is the outcome of the experimenter's manipulation of the independent variable. 23

Depersonalization: An altered experience of the self, ranging from feeling that one's body is not connected to one's mind to the feeling that one is not real. 77

Depersonalization disorder: A dissociative disorder in which the individual experiences recurrent and persistent episodes of depersonalization. 208

Depressant: A psychoactive substance that causes the depression of central nervous system activity. 398

Developmental coordination disorder: A condition characterized by marked impairment in the development of motor coordination. 354

Deviation IQ: An index of intelligence derived from comparing the individual's score on an intelligence test with the mean score for that individual's reference group. 80

Diagnostic and Statistical Manual of Mental Disorders (DSM): A book published by the American Psychiatric Association that contains standard terms and definitions of psychological disorders. 40

Diathesis-stress model: The proposal that people are born with a predisposition (or "diathesis") that places them at risk for developing a psychological disorder if exposed to certain extremely stressful life experiences. 10, 129

Differential diagnosis: The process of systematically ruling out alternative diagnoses. 51

Disorder of written expression: A learning disorder in which the individual's writing is characterized by poor spelling, grammatical or punctuation errors, and disorganization of paragraphs. 353

Dissociative amnesia: An inability to remember important personal details and experiences; is usually associated with traumatic or very stressful events. 206

Dissociative fugue: A dissociative disorder in which a person, confused about personal identity, suddenly and unexpectedly travels to another place and is unable to recall past history or identity. 207

Dissociative identity disorder: A dissociative disorder, formerly called multiple personality disorder, in which an individual develops more than one self or personality. 198

Disulfiram: Known popularly as Antabuse, a medication used in the treatment of alcoholism that inhibits aldehyde dehydrogenase (ALDH) and causes severe physical reactions when combined with alcohol. 404

Dizygotic twins: Nonidentical, or fraternal, twins who are genetically alike only to the same degree as other siblings. 28

Dopamine hypothesis: The biological hypothesis that the delusions, hallucinations, and attentional deficits of schizophrenia result from overactivity of neurons that communicate with each other via the transmission of dopamine. 291

Double-blind technique: An experimental procedure in which neither the person giving the treatment nor the person receiving the treatment knows whether the participant is in the experimental or control group. 24

Down syndrome: A form of mental retardation caused by abnormal chromosomal formation during conception. 344

Dream analysis: A method used in psychoanalysis in which the client relates the events of a dream to the clinician and free associates these events. 108

Duty to warn: The clinician's responsibility to notify a potential victim of a client's harmful intent toward that individual. 468

Dysfunctional attitudes: Personal rules or values people hold that interfere with adequate adjustment. 122

Dyslexia: A learning disorder in which the individual omits, distorts, or substitutes words when reading and reads in a slow, halting fashion. 353

Dyspareunia: A sexual dysfunction affecting both males and females that involves recurrent or persistent genital pain before, during, or after sexual intercourse. 237

Dysphoria: The emotion of sadness. 250

Dysphoric mood: Unpleasant feelings, such as sadness or irritability. 76

Dysthymic disorder: A mood disorder involving chronic depression of less intensity than major depressive disorders. 250

E

Echolalia: Repetition of words or phrases in the speech of a person with autistic disorder. 349

Ego: In psychoanalytic theory, the structure of personality that gives the individual the mental powers of judgment, memory, perception, and decision making, enabling the individual to adapt to the realities of the external world. 103

Electroconvulsive therapy (ECT): The application of electrical shock to the head for the purpose of inducing therapeutically beneficial seizures. 130

Electroencephalogram (EEG): A measure of changes in the electrical activity of the brain. 92

Emotion-focused coping: A type of coping in which a person does not change anything about the situation itself, but instead tries to improve feelings about the situation. 194

Encopresis: An elimination disorder in which the child is incontinent of feces and has bowel movements either in clothes or in another inappropriate place. 365

Endophenotypes: Biobehavioral abnormalities that are linked to genetic and neurobiological causes of mental illness. 292

Enuresis: An elimination disorder in which the child is incontinent of urine and urinates in clothes or in bed after the age when the child is expected to be continent. 365

Environmental assessment scales: Measures of key environmental dimensions hypothesized to influence behavior. 91

Epilepsy: A neurological condition that involves recurring bodily seizures with associated changes in EEG patterns. 372

Episode: A time-limited period during which specific symptoms of a disorder are present. 250

Euphoria: The emotion of elation. 250

Euphoric mood: A feeling state that is more cheerful and elated than average, possibly even ecstatic. 76

Executive functioning: Cognitive abilities such as abstract thinking, planning, organizing, and carrying out of behaviors. 376

Exhibitionism: A paraphilia in which a person has intense sexual urges and arousing fantasies involving the exposure of genitals to a stranger. 221

Expectancy model: An approach to alcohol dependence that focuses on cognitive-behavioral and social learning perspectives. According to this view, people acquire the belief that alcohol will reduce stress; will make them feel more competent socially, physically, and sexually; and will give them feelings of pleasure. 401

Experimental group: The group of participants that receives the "treatment" thought to influence the behavior under study. 23

Experimental method: A research method that involves altering or changing the conditions to which participants are exposed (independent variable) and observing the effects of this manipulation on the participants' behavior (dependent variable). 23

Expressed emotion (EE): An index of the degree to which family members speak in ways that reflect criticism, hostile feelings, and emotional overinvolvement or overconcern with regard to the schizophrenic individual. 294

Expressive language disorder: A communication disorder characterized by having a limited and faulty vocabulary, speaking in short sentences with simplified grammatical structures, omitting critical words or phrases, or putting words together in peculiar order. 353

Extinction: The cessation of behavior in the absence of reinforcement. 121

F

Factitious disorder: A disorder in which people fake symptoms or disorders not for the purpose of any particular gain, but because of an inner need to maintain a sick role. 187

Factitious disorder by proxy (or Munchausen's syndrome by proxy): A condition in which a person induces physical symptoms in another person who is under that person's care. 188

Failure to thrive: A condition in which the child does not grow physically and cognitively at a normal rate due to poor prenatal care or grossly inadequate and inattentive parenting. 346

Family dynamics: The pattern of interactions among the members of a family. 114

Family history: Information gathered in a psychological assessment regarding the sequence of major events in the lives of the client's relatives, including those who are closest to the client as well as more distantly related family members. 69

Family perspective: A theoretical perspective in which it is assumed that abnormality is caused by disturbances in the pattern of interactions and relationships within the family. 114

Family therapy: Psychological treatment in which the therapist works with several or all members of the family. 60

Fear: An innate, almost biologically based alarm response to a dangerous or life-threatening situation. 148

Feeding disorder of infancy or early childhood: A disorder involving the persistent failure to eat, leading to a loss of weight or failure to gain weight. 364

Female orgasmic disorder: A sexual dysfunction in which a woman experiences problems in having an orgasm during sexual activity. 236

Female sexual arousal disorder: A sexual dysfunction characterized by a persistent or recurrent inability to attain or maintain the normal physiological and psychological arousal responses during sexual activity. 235

Fetal alcohol syndrome (FAS): A condition associated with mental retardation in a child whose mother consumed large amounts of alcohol on a regular basis while pregnant. 345

Fetish: A strong, recurrent sexual attraction to a nonliving object. 221

Fetishism: A paraphilia in which the individual is preoccupied with an object and depends on this object rather than sexual intimacy with a partner for achieving sexual gratification. 221

Fixation: Arrested development at a particular stage of psychosexual development attributable to excessive or inadequate gratification at that stage. 106

Flooding: A behavioral technique in which the client is immersed in the sensation of anxiety by being exposed to the feared situation in its entirety. 155

Free association: A method used in psychoanalysis in which the client speaks freely, saying whatever comes to mind. 108

Frontotemporal dementias: Dementias that involve the frontotemporal area of the brain. 381

Frotteur: A person with the paraphilia of frotteurism. 222

Frotteurism: A paraphilia in which the individual has intense sexual urges and sexually arousing fantasies of rubbing against or fondling an unsuspecting stranger. 222

Functional magnetic resonance imaging (FMRI): A variant of the traditional MRI, which makes it possible to construct a picture of activity in the brain. 93

G

Galvanic skin response (GSR): Minor electrical changes in the skin that result from sweating. 92

Gender identity: The individual's self-perception as a male or female. 227

Gender identity disorder: A condition in which there is a discrepancy between an individual's assigned sex and gender identity, involving a strong and persistent identification with the other gender. 227

Gender role: The behaviors and attitudes a person has that are indicative of maleness or femaleness in one's society. 227

Gene: The basic unit of heredity. 137

Generalized amnesia: Inability to remember anything from one's past life. 206

Generalized anxiety disorder: An anxiety disorder characterized by anxiety that is not associated with a particular object, situation, or event but seems to be a constant feature of a person's day-to-day existence. 160

Genetic mapping: The attempt by biological researchers to identify the structure of a gene and the characteristics it controls. 28

Genital stage: A period of psychosexual development coinciding with the resurfacing of sexual energy just prior to puberty. 106

Genome: The complete set of instructions for "building" all the cells that make up an organism. 127

Global Assessment of Functioning (GAF) scale: Axis V of the *DSM-IV*, a scale that rates the individual's overall level of psychological health. 49

Graduated exposure: A procedure in which clients gradually expose themselves to increasingly greater anxiety-provoking situations. 156

Grandiosity: An exaggerated view of oneself as possessing special and extremely favorable personal qualities and abilities. 326

Group therapy: Psychological treatment in which the therapist facilitates discussion among several clients who talk together about their problems. 60

Guardian ad litem: A person appointed by the court to represent or make decisions for a person (e.g., a minor or an incapacitated adult) who is legally incapable of doing so in a civil legal proceeding. 470

Gustatory hallucination: An hallucination involving the false sensation of taste, usually unpleasant. 76

H

Halfway house: A community treatment facility designed for deinstitutionalized clients leaving a hospital who are not yet ready for independent living. 59

Hallucination: A false perception not corresponding to the objective stimuli present in the environment. 414

Hallucinogens: Psychoactive substances that cause abnormal perceptual experiences in the form of illusions or hallucinations, usually visual in nature. 414

Heritability: The proportion of the offspring's phenotype that is due to genetic causes. 129

Hierarchy of needs: According to Maslow, the order in which human needs must be fulfilled. 112

Histrionic personality disorder: A personality disorder characterized by exaggerated emotional reactions, approaching theatricality, in everyday behavior. 324

Host: The central personality of an individual with dissociative identity disorder. 198

Humanistic: An approach to personality and psychological disorder that regards people as motivated by the need to understand themselves and the world and to derive greater enrichment from their experiences by fulfilling their unique individual potential. 114

Huntington's disease: A hereditary condition causing dementia that involves a widespread deterioration of the subcortical brain structures and parts of the frontal cortex that control motor movements. 381

Hyperactivity: A motor pattern involving abnormally energized physical activity, often characterized by quick movements and fast talking. 72

Hypnotherapy: A method of therapy in which hypnosis is used for various purposes, such as helping a person recall repressed memories. 203

Hypnotic: A substance that induces sedation. 418

Hypnotism: The process of inducing a trance state. 17

Hypoactive sexual desire disorder: A sexual dysfunction in which the individual has an abnormally low level of interest in sexual activity. 234

Hypochondriasis: A somatoform disorder characterized by the misinterpretation of normal bodily functions as signs of serious illness. 185

Hypomanic episode: A period of elated mood not as extreme as a manic episode. 254

Hypothesis formation process: The stage of research in which the researcher generates ideas about a cause-effect relationship between the behaviors under study. 21

Hysteria: A disorder in which psychological problems become expressed in physical form. 17

Hysterical neurosis: A term used by Freud to describe conversion disorder, implying that it is a reaction to anxiety. 181

I

Id: In psychoanalytic theory, the structure of personality that contains the sexual and aggressive instincts. 102

Identity: One's self-concept or sense of who one is. 319

Identity confusion: A lack of clear sense of who one is, ranging from confusion about one's role in the world to actual delusional thinking. 77

Imaginal flooding: A behavioral technique in which the client is immersed through imagination in the feared situation. 156

Impulse: An urge to act. 439

Impulse-control disorders: Psychological disorders in which people repeatedly engage in behaviors that are potentially harmful, feeling unable to stop themselves and experiencing a sense of desperation if their attempts to carry out the behaviors are thwarted. 439

In vivo **observation:** A form of behavioral assessment in which the individual is observed in the natural context in which the target behavior occurs. 91

Inappropriate affect: The extent to which a person's emotional expressiveness fails to correspond to the content of what is being discussed. 75

Incidence: The frequency of new cases within a given time period. 26

Independent variable: The variable whose level is adjusted or controlled by the experimenter. 23

Individual psychotherapy: Psychological treatment in which the therapist works on a one-to-one basis with the client. 59

Informed consent: The process, often in the form of a written statement, in which a client participates in setting treatment goals, understands and agrees to the treatment plan, and knows the credentials of the clinician. 465

Insanity defense: The argument, presented by a lawyer acting on behalf of the client, that, because of the existence of a mental disorder, the client should not be held legally responsible for criminal actions. 473

Insight: A sense of understanding and awareness about oneself and one's world. 77

Intelligence quotient (IQ): A method of quantifying performance on an intelligence test, originally calculated according to the ratio of a person's tested age to that person's chronological age, and changed in the 1960 revision of the Stanford-Binet to the deviation IQ. 80

Intensity of affect: Strength of emotional expression. 76

Intermittent explosive disorder: An impulse-control disorder involving an inability to hold back urges to express strong angry feelings and associated violent behaviors. 449

Internet addiction: An impulse-control condition in which an individual feels an irresistible need to be involved in Internet-based activities. 450

K

Kleptomania: An impulse-control disorder that involves the persistent urge to steal. 440

Korsakoff's syndrome: A permanent form of dementia associated with long-term alcohol use in which the individual develops retrograde and anterograde amnesia, leading to an inability to remember recent events or learn new information. 400

L

La belle indifférence: Lack of concern by some people with a conversion disorder over what might otherwise be construed as very disturbing physical problems. 181

Latency: In psychoanalytic theory, a period of psychosexual development during which the child interacts with peers and imitates the behavior of parents and other adults of the same biological sex as the child. 106

Latent: A state in which a disorder is present and capable of becoming evident but is not yet obvious or active. 330

Learning disorder: A delay or deficit in an academic skill that is evident when an individual's achievement on standardized tests is substantially below what would be expected for others of comparable age, education, and level of intelligence. 352

Least restrictive alternative: A treatment setting that provides the fewest constraints on the client's freedom. 473

Lewy body dementia: A form of dementia similar to Alzheimer's disease with progressive loss of memory, language, calculation, and reasoning, as well as other higher mental functions. 380

Libido: An instinctual pressure for gratification of sexual and aggressive desires. 107

Localized amnesia: Inability to remember all events that occurred in a specific time period. 206

Lovemap: The representation of an individual's sexual fantasies and preferred practices. 227

M

Magical thinking: A peculiarity of thinking in which an individual makes a connection between two objects or events that other people would see as unrelated. 74

Magnetic resonance imaging (MRI): The use of radiowaves rather than X-rays to construct a picture of the living brain based on the water content of various tissues. 93

Mainstreaming: A governmental policy to integrate fully into society people with cognitive and physical disabilities. 347

Major depressive disorder: A mood disorder in which the individual experiences acute, but time-limited, episodes of depressive symptoms. 250

Major depressive episode: A period in which the individual experiences intense psychological and physical symptoms related to a dysphoric mood. 251

Male erectile disorder: A sexual dysfunction marked by a recurrent partial or complete failure to attain or maintain an erection during sexual activity. 236

Male orgasmic disorder: A sexual dysfunction in which a man experiences problems having an orgasm during sexual activity; also known as inhibited male orgasm. 237

Malingering: The fabrication of physical or psychological symptoms for some ulterior motive. 187

Mandated reporting: The legal requirement that professionals notify appropriate authorities about cases in which children and certain other groups of vulnerable individuals are being abused. 468

Manic episode: A period of euphoric mood with symptoms involving abnormally heightened levels of thinking, behavior, and emotionality. 254

Masochism: The seeking of pleasure from being subjected to pain. 223

Mathematics disorder: A learning disorder in which the individual has difficulty with mathematical tasks and concepts. 352

Maturation hypothesis: The proposition that people with antisocial personality and the other Cluster B disorders become better able to manage their behaviors as they age. 316

Medical model: The view that abnormal behaviors result from physical problems and should be treated medically. 16

Melancholic features: A specifier for a depressive episode in which the individual loses interest in most activities, awakens much earlier than usual in the morning, has significant loss of appetite, and possibly experiences psychomotor agitation or retardation and excessive or inappropriate guilt feelings. 251

Mental retardation: A condition, present from childhood, characterized by significantly below-average general intellectual functioning (an IQ of 70 or below). 344

Mental status examination: A method of objectively assessing a client's behavior and functioning in a number of spheres, with particular attention to the symptoms associated with psychological disturbance. 72

Mesmerized: Derived from the name Mesmer; a process of bringing about a state of heightened suggestibility through the words and actions of a charismatic individual. 17

Methadone: A synthetic opioid that produces a safer and more controlled reaction than heroin and that is used in treating heroin addiction. 416

Milieu therapy: A treatment approach, used in an inpatient psychiatric facility, in which all facets of the milieu, or environment, are components of the treatment. 59, 117

Mixed episode: A period of at least a week during which the symptoms of both a manic episode and a major depressive episode occur in rapidly alternating fashion. 254

Mixed receptive-expressive language disorder: A communication disorder in which the individual has difficulty understanding and expressing certain kinds of words or phrases, such as directions, or, in more severe forms, basic vocabulary or entire sentences. 353

Modality: The form in which psychotherapy is offered. 59

Modeling: Acquiring new behavior by imitating that of another person. 121

Monoamine depletion model: The proposal that deficits in monoamine neurotransmitters are the cause of depression. 259

Monozygotic twins: Identical twins, who share the same genetic inheritance. 28

Mood: A person's experience of emotion. 76

Moral treatment: The philosophy popular in the mid-19th century that people can, with the proper care, develop self-control over their own disturbed behaviors. 14

Motivational interviewing (MI): A directive, client-centered style for eliciting behavior change by helping clients explore and resolve ambivalence. 114

Multiaxial system: A multidimensional classification and diagnostic system that summarizes a variety of relevant information about an individual's physical and psychological functioning. 45

Multifactorial polygenic threshold: The position that several genes with varying influence are involved in the transmission of a disorder or characteristic. 129

Multiple baseline approach: In behavioral research, the observation of different dependent variables in a person over the course of treatment, or observing the behavior as it occurs under different conditions. 27

Munchausen's syndrome: An extreme form of factitious disorder in which the individual goes to great lengths to maintain a sick role. 188

N

Narcissistic personality disorder: A personality disorder primarily characterized by an unrealistic, inflated sense of self-importance and a lack of sensitivity to the needs of other people. 326

Negative reinforcement: The removal of aversive conditions when certain behaviors are performed. 121

Negative symptoms: The symptoms of schizophrenia, including affective flattening, alogia, avolition, and anhedonia, that involve functioning below the level of normal behavior. 282

Neurofibrillary tangles: A characteristic of Alzheimer's disease in which the material within the cell bodies of neurons becomes filled with densely packed, twisted protein microfibrils, or tiny strands. 384

Neuroleptics: A category of medications used to reduce the frequency and intensity of psychotic symptoms; also called major tranquilizers. 295

Neuropsychological assessment: A process of gathering information about a client's brain functioning on the basis of performance on psychological tests. 95

Neurosis: Behavior that involves symptoms that are distressing to an individual and that the person recognizes as unacceptable; unofficially used to characterize psychological disorders considered to be less severe than psychosis. 44

Nonpurging type: A form of bulimia nervosa in which individuals compensate for what they eat by fasting or engaging in excessive exercise. 435

Normal mood (euthymic mood): A feeling state that is neither unduly happy nor sad but shows day-to-day variations within a relatively limited range considered to be appropriate. 76

O

Object relations: One's unconscious representations of important people in one's life. 107

Observation process: The stage of research in which the researcher watches and records the behavior of interest. 21

Obsession: An unwanted thought, word, phrase, or image that persistently and repeatedly comes into a person's mind and causes distress. 75, 161

Obsessive-compulsive disorder (OCD): An anxiety disorder characterized by recurrent obsessions or compulsions that are inordinately time-consuming or that cause significant distress or impairment. 161

Obsessive-compulsive personality disorder: Intense perfectionism and inflexibility manifested in worrying, indecisiveness, and behavioral rigidity. 334

Olfactory hallucination: An hallucination involving the perception of a smell. 76

Operant conditioning: A learning process in which an individual acquires behaviors through reinforcement. 120

Oppositional defiant disorder: A disruptive behavior disorder of childhood that is characterized by undue hostility, stubbornness, strong temper, belligerence, spitefulness, and self-righteousness. 359

Oral stage: A period of psychosexual development in which the infant's pleasure comes from stimulation of the mouth. 106

Orgasmic reconditioning: A behavioral intervention geared toward a relearning process in which the individual associates sexual gratification with appropriate stimuli. 222

Orientation: A person's awareness of time, place, and identity. 73

Overvalued idea: A thought that has an odd and absurd quality but is not usually bizarre or deeply entrenched. 73

P

Pain disorder: A somatoform disorder in which the only symptom is pain that has no physiological basis. 183

Panic attack: A period of intense fear and physical discomfort accompanied by the feeling that one is being overwhelmed and is about to lose control. 149

Panic control therapy (PCT): Treatment that consists of cognitive restructuring, exposure to bodily cues associated with panic attacks, and breathing retraining. 153

Panic disorder: An anxiety disorder in which an individual has panic attacks on a recurrent basis or has constant apprehension and worry about the possibility of recurring attacks. 149

Paranoid personality disorder: A personality disorder whose outstanding feature is that the individual is extremely suspicious of others and is always on guard against potential danger or harm. 327

Paraphilias: A disorder in which an individual has recurrent, intense sexually arousing fantasies, sexual urges, or behaviors involving (1) nonhuman objects, (2) children or other nonconsenting persons, or (3) the suffering or humiliation of self or partner. 216

Parasuicide: A suicidal gesture to get attention from loved ones, family, or professionals. 320

Parens patriae: The state's authority to protect those who are unable to protect themselves. 470

Parkinson's disease: A disease that can cause dementia and that involves the degeneration of neurons in the subcortical structures that control motor movements. 380

Partialism: A paraphilia in which the person is interested solely in sexual gratification from a specific body part, such as feet. 222

Participant modeling: A form of therapy in which the therapist first shows the client a desired behavior and then guides the client through the behavioral change. 124

Pathological gambling: An impulse-control disorder involving the persistent urge to gamble. 441

Patient: In the medical model, a person who receives treatment. 38

Pedophilia: A paraphilia in which an adult's sexual urges are directed toward children. 217

Penetrance: The extent to which a genotype is expressed in the individual's phenotype. 129

Personality disorder: Ingrained patterns of relating to other people, situations, and events with a rigid and maladaptive pattern of inner experience and behavior, dating back to adolescence or early adulthood. 312

Personality trait: An enduring pattern of perceiving, relating to, and thinking about the environment and others. 312

Person-centered theory: The humanistic theory that focuses on the uniqueness of each individual, the importance of allowing each individual to achieve maximum fulfillment of potential, and the need for the individual to confront honestly the reality of his or her experiences in the world. 112

Pervasive developmental disorders: Conditions that begin in childhood and have a major impact on social and cognitive functioning; involve serious deficits in social interaction and communication skills, as well as odd behavior, interests, and activities. 347

Phallic stage: A period of psychosexual development in which the genital area of the body is the focus of the child's sexual feelings. 106

Phenotype: The expression of the genetic program in the individual's physical and psychological attributes. 127

Phonological disorder: A communication disorder in which the individual misarticulates, substitutes, or omits speech sounds. 353

Pica: A condition in which a person eats inedible substances, such as dirt or feces; commonly associated with mental retardation. 364

Pick's disease: A relatively rare degenerative disease that affects the frontal and temporal lobes of the cerebral cortex and that can cause dementia. 380

Placebo condition: The condition used in experimental research in which people are given an inert substance or treatment that is similar in all other ways to the experimental treatment. 23

Pleasure principle: In psychoanalytic theory, a motivating force oriented toward the immediate and total gratification of sensual needs and desires. 102

Polygenic: A model of inheritance in which more than one gene participates in the process of determining a given characteristic. 129

Population: The entire group of individuals sharing a particular characteristic. 23

Positive reinforcement: Providing reward when certain behaviors are performed. 121

Positive symptoms: The symptoms of schizophrenia, including delusions, hallucinations, disturbed speech, and disturbed behavior, that are exaggerations or distortions of normal thoughts, emotions, and behavior. 279

Positron emission tomography (PET) scan: A measure of brain activity in which a small amount of radioactive sugar is injected into an individual's bloodstream, following which a computer measures the varying levels of radiation in different parts of the brain and yields a multicolored image. 93

Post-traumatic stress disorder (PTSD): An anxiety disorder in which the individual experiences several distressing symptoms for more than a month following a traumatic event, such as a reexperiencing of the traumatic event, an avoidance of reminders of the trauma, a numbing of general responsiveness, and increased arousal. 167

Potentiation: The combination of the effects of two or more psychoactive substances such that the total effect is greater than the effect of either substance alone. 398

Pragmatic case study: An organized approach for the development and accumulation of case study material that focuses on practical results. 26

Premature ejaculation: A sexual dysfunction in which a man reaches orgasm well before he wishes to, perhaps even prior to penetration. 237

Prevalence: The number of people who have ever had a disorder at a given time or over a specified period. 26

Primary gain: The relief from anxiety or responsibility due to the development of physical or psychological symptoms. 189

Primary process thinking: In psychoanalytic theory, loosely associated, idiosyncratic, and distorted cognitive representation of the world. 103

Primary reinforcers: Rewards that satisfy a biological need, making them intrinsically rewarding. 120

Principal diagnosis: The disorder that is considered to be the primary reason the individual seeks professional help. 52

Privileged communication: Information provided by a client to a clinician that cannot be disclosed in a court of law without the client's expressed permission. 466

Probability: The odds or likelihood that an event will happen. 23

Problem-focused coping: Coping in which the individual takes action to reduce stress by changing whatever it is about the situation that makes it stressful. 194

Prodromal phase: A period in the course of schizophrenia, prior to the active phase of symptoms, during which the individual shows progressive deterioration in social and interpersonal functioning. 279

Prognosis: A client's likelihood of recovering from a disorder. 49

Projective test: A technique in which the test-taker is presented with an ambiguous item or task and is asked to respond by providing his or her own meaning or perception. 85

Pseudodementia: Literally, false dementia, or a set of symptoms caused by depression that mimic those apparent in the early stages of Alzheimer's. 382

Psychiatrist: A medical doctor (MD) with advanced training in treating people with psychological disorders. 40

Psychoanalysis: A theory and system of practice that relies heavily on the concepts of the unconscious mind, inhibited sexual impulses, early development, and the use of the "free association" technique and dream analysis. 18

Psychoanalytic model: An approach that seeks explanations of abnormal behavior in the workings of unconscious psychological processes. 16

Psychodynamic perspective: The theoretical orientation in psychology that emphasizes unconscious determinants of behavior. 102

Psychodynamics: The processes of interaction among personality structures that lie beneath the surface of observable behavior. 102

Psychological factors affecting medical condition: Situations in which psychological or behavioral factors have an adverse effect on a medical condition. 191

Psychological testing: A broad range of measurement techniques, all of which involve having people provide scorable information about their psychological functioning. 40

Psychometrics: Literally, "measurement of the mind," reflecting the goal of finding the most suitable tests for psychological variables under study. 78

Psychomotor agitation: A motor pattern involving an obvious level of personal discomfort in which the individual appears to be restless and stirred up. 72

Psychomotor retardation: A motor pattern involving abnormally slow movements and lethargy. 72

Psychoneuroimmunology: The study of connections among psychological stress, nervous system functioning, and the immune system. 194

Psychopathy: A personality type characterized by a cluster of traits that constitutes the core of what is now called *antisocial personality disorder.* 314

Psychosexual stages: According to psychoanalytic theory, the normal sequence of development through which each individual passes between infancy and adulthood. 103

Psychosis: Behavior involving loss of contact with reality. 44

Psychosurgery: A form of brain surgery, the purpose of which is to reduce psychological disturbance. 130

Psychotherapy: The treatment of abnormal behavior through psychological techniques. 18

Punishment: The application of an aversive stimulus. 121

Purge: To eliminate food through unnatural methods, such as vomiting or the excessive use of laxatives. 430

Purging type: A form of bulimia nervosa in which individuals force out of their bodies what they have just eaten. 435

Pyromania: An impulse-control disorder involving the persistent and compelling urge to start fires. 444

Q

Quasi-experimental design: A design that is like an experimental design but lacks the key ingredient of random assignment to groups. 25

R

Range of affect: The extent and variety of an individual's emotional expression. 76

Rapid cyclers: Individuals with bipolar disorder who have four to eight mood episodes within the course of a year. 257

Reactive attachment disorder of infancy or childhood: A disorder involving a severe disturbance in the ability to relate to others in which the individual is unresponsive to people, is apathetic, and prefers to be alone rather than to interact with friends or family. 365

Reading disorder: A learning disorder in which the individual omits, distorts, or substitutes words when reading and reads in a slow and halting fashion. 353

Reality principle: In psychoanalyic theory, motivational force that leads the individual to confront the constraints of the external world. 103

Reinforcement: The "strengthening" of a behavior. 120

Relapse prevention therapy: A treatment method based on the expectancy model, in which individuals are encouraged not to view lapses from abstinence as signs of certain failure. 404

Relaxation training: A behavioral technique used in the treatment of anxiety disorders that involves progressive and systematic patterns of muscle tensing and relaxing. 152

Reliability: The consistency of measurements or diagnoses. 41, 78

Representativeness: The extent to which a sample adequately reflects the characteristics of the population from which it is drawn. 23

Residual phase: A period in the course of schizophrenia, following the active phase, in which there are continuing indications of disturbance, evidenced by the same kinds of behaviors that characterize the prodromal phase. 279

Resistance: The unconscious blocking of anxiety-provoking thoughts or feelings. 108

Response-contingent positive reinforcement: Behaviors that increase in frequency as the result of performing actions that produce pleasure. 261

Rett's disorder: A pervasive developmental disorder, occurring only in females, in which the child develops normally until between 5 months and 4 years of age and then begins to show a number of neurological and cognitive impairments, including a deceleration of head growth, stereotyped movements of the hand, a lack of bodily coordination, language impairments, and social withdrawal. 347

Rumination disorder: An eating disorder in which the infant or child regurgitates food after it has been swallowed and then either spits it out or reswallows it. 364

S

Sadomasochist: A person who derives sexual pleasure from both inflicting and receiving pain. 223

Sample: A selection of individuals from a larger group. 23

Schizoaffective disorder: A psychotic disorder involving the experience of a major depressive episode, a manic episode, or a mixed episode while also meeting the diagnostic criteria for schizophrenia. 288

Schizoid personality disorder: A personality disorder primarily characterized by an indifference to social relationships, as well as a very limited range of emotional experience and expression. 329

Schizophrenia: A disorder with a range of symptoms involving disturbances in content of thought, form of thought, perception, affect, sense of self, motivation, behavior, and interpersonal functioning. 278

Schizophrenia, catatonic type: A type of schizophrenia characterized by a variety of bodily movement abnormalities. 283

Schizophrenia, disorganized type: A type of schizophrenia characterized by a combination of symptoms, including disorganized speech and behavior and flat or inappropriate affect. Even delusions and hallucinations lack a coherent theme. 283

Schizophrenia, paranoid type: A type of schizophrenia characterized by preoccupation with one or more bizarre delusions or with auditory hallucinations that are related to a particular theme of being persecuted or harassed. 283

Schizophrenia, residual type: A type of schizophrenia in which people who have previously been diagnosed as having schizophrenia may no longer have prominent psychotic symptoms but still show some lingering signs of the disorder, such as emotional dullness, social withdrawal, eccentric behavior, or illogical thinking. 283

Schizophrenia, undifferentiated type: A type of schizophrenia characterized by a complex of schizophrenic symptoms, such as delusions, hallucinations, incoherence, or disorganized behavior, that does not meet the criteria for other types of schizophrenia. 283

Schizophrenia spectrum disorders: A term used by some researchers to characterize a continuum of disorders, including schizophrenia, schizoid personality disorder, and schizotypal personality disorder. 329

Schizophreniform disorder: A disorder characterized by psychotic symptoms that are essentially the same as those found in schizophrenia, except for the duration and chronic nature of the symptoms; specifically, symptoms usually last from 1 to 6 months. 287

Schizotypal personality disorder: A personality disorder that primarily involves peculiarities and eccentricities of thought, behavior, appearance, and interpersonal style. People with this disorder may have peculiar ideas, such as magical thinking and beliefs in psychic phenomena. 330

Seasonal pattern: A specifier for a depressive episode in which the individual has varying symptoms according to time of year, with symptoms usually developing during the same months every year. 251

Secondary gain: The sympathy and attention that a sick person receives from other people. 190

Secondary process thinking: In psychoanalytic theory, the kind of thinking involved in logical and rational problem solving. 103

Secondary reinforcers: Rewards that derive their value from association with primary reinforcers. 120

Sedative: A psychoactive substance that has a calming effect on the central nervous system. 418

Selective amnesia: Inability to remember some, but not all, events that occurred in a specified time period. 206

Selective mutism: A disorder originating in childhood in which the individual consciously refuses to talk, sometimes accompanying this refusal by oppositional or avoidant behavior. 365

Selective serotonin reuptake inhibitors (SSRI): Medications that block the reuptake of serotonin at the synapse, enabling more of this neurotransmitter to be available at the receptor sites. 130

Self-actualization: In humanistic theory, the maximum realization of the individual's potential for psychological growth. 112

Self-efficacy: The individual's perception of competence in various life situations. 122

Self-monitoring: A self-report technique in which the client keeps a record of the frequency of specified behaviors. 88

Self-report clinical inventory: A psychological test with standardized questions having fixed response categories that the test-taker completes independently, self-reporting the extent to which the responses are accurate characterizations. 82

Semistructured interview: A standardized series of questions in which the interviewer has the discretion to ask follow-up questions that will clarify the person's responses. 69

Sensate focus: A method of treatment for sexual dysfunctions that involves the partners' taking turns stimulating each other in nonsexual but affectionate ways at first, then gradually progressing over a period of time toward genital stimulation. 241

Separation anxiety disorder: A childhood disorder characterized by intense and inappropriate anxiety, lasting at least 4 weeks, concerning separation from home or caregivers. 362

Sexual aversion disorder: A sexual dysfunction characterized by an active dislike of intercourse or related sexual activities. 235

Sexual dysfunction: An abnormality in an individual's sexual responsiveness and reactions. 231

Sexual impulsivity: An impulse-control disorder in which people feel uncontrollably driven to seek out sexual encounters and to engage in frequent and indiscriminate sexual activity. 446

Sexual masochism: A paraphilia marked by an attraction to achieving sexual gratification by having painful stimulation applied to one's own body. 223

Sexual orientation: The degree to which a person is erotically attracted to members of the same or opposite sex. 227

Sexual sadism: A paraphilia in which sexual gratification is derived from activities that harm, or from urges to harm, another person. 223

Shaping: A learning technique in which reinforcement is provided for behaviors that increasingly resemble a desired outcome. 121

Shared psychotic disorder: A psychotic disorder in which one or more people develop a delusional system as a result of a close relationship with a psychotic person who is delusional. 289

Single photon emission computed tomography (SPECT): A variant of the PET scan that permits a longer and more detailed imaging analysis. 93

Single-subject design: An experimental procedure in which one person at a time is studied in both the experimental and control conditions. 26

Situationally bound (cued) panic attack: A panic attack that is triggered by anticipation of or exposure to a specific situation or cue. 149

Situationally predisposed panic attack: A panic attack that is usually but not invariably triggered by exposure to a situational cue. 149

Social phobia: An anxiety disorder characterized by irrational and unabating fear that one's behavior will be scrutinized by others, causing the individual to feel embarrassed and humiliated. 157

Sociocognitive model of dissociative identity disorder: The view that an individual who appears to have dissociative identity disorder might be enacting a social role. 202

Sociocultural perspective: The theoretical perspective that emphasizes the ways that individuals are influenced by people, social institutions, and social forces in the world around them. 114

Somatic hallucination: An hallucination involving the false perception of bodily sensation. 76

Somatic therapies: Biologically based treatments that act upon known or presumed immediate causes of a psychological disorder. 129

Somatization disorder: A somatoform disorder in which multiple and recurrent bodily symptoms, which lack a physiological basis, are the expression of psychological issues. 182

Somatoform disorders: A variety of conditions in which psychological conflicts become translated into physical problems or complaints. 180

Specific phobia: An irrational and unabating fear of a particular object, activity, or situation. 153

Spectatoring: The experience in which the individual feels unduly self-conscious during sexual activity, as if evaluating and monitoring his or her performance during the sexual encounter. 234

Splitting: A defense, common in people with borderline personality disorder, in which individuals perceive others, or themselves, as being all good or all bad, usually resulting in disturbed interpersonal relationships. 319

Squeeze technique: A method of treatment for premature ejaculation in which the partner stimulates the man's penis during foreplay and squeezes it when he indicates he is approaching orgasm. 241

Stereotypic movement disorder: A disorder in which the individual voluntarily repeats nonfunctional behaviors, such as rocking or head-banging, that can be damaging to his or her physical well-being. 365

Stimulant: A psychoactive substance that has an activating effect on the central nervous system. 409

Stimulus discrimination: Differentiation between two stimuli that possess similar but essentially different characteristics. 119

Stimulus generalization: The process of learning to respond in the same way to stimuli that share common properties. 119

Stop-start procedure: A method of treatment for premature ejaculation in which the man or his partner stimulates him to sexual excitement, and, as he approaches the point of orgasmic inevitability, stimulation is stopped. When this procedure is repeated over time, the man can develop greater control over his orgasmic response. 241

Stress: The unpleasant emotional reaction that a person has when an event is perceived by an individual as threatening. 192

Stressor: An event that disrupts the individual's life; also called a *stressful life event.* 192

Structured interview: A standardized series of assessment questions, with a predetermined wording and order. 69

Stuttering: A communication disorder that involves a disturbance in the normal fluency and patterning of speech that is characterized by such verbalizations as sound repetitions or prolongations, broken words, the blocking out of sounds, word substitutions to avoid problematic words, or words expressed with an excess of tension. 353

Substance: A chemical that alters a person's mood or behavior when it is smoked, injected, drunk, inhaled, or swallowed in pill form. 394

Substance abuse: The pattern of maladaptive substance use that leads to significant impairment or distress. 395

Substance dependence: A maladaptive pattern of substance use manifested by a cluster of cognitive, behavioral, and physiological symptoms during a 12-month period and caused by the continued use of a substance. 396

Substance-induced persisting amnestic disorder: An amnestic disorder caused by drugs or environmental toxins. 374

Substance-induced persisting dementia: A form of dementia caused by the ingestion of substances, such as drugs, or exposure to toxins. 377

Substance intoxication: The temporary maladaptive experience of behavioral or psychological changes that are due to the accumulation of a substance in the body. 395

Substance withdrawal: Psychological and physical changes that occur when some substances are discontinued. 395

Suicidal intent: The level of commitment to taking one's own life. 271

Suicidal lethality: The dangerousness of a suicidal person's intended method of dying. 271

Superego: In psychoanalytic theory, the structure of personality that includes the conscience and the ego ideal; it incorporates societal prohibitions and exerts control over the seeking of instinctual gratification. 103

Survey method: A research tool, used to gather information from a sample of people considered representative of a particular population, in which participants are asked to answer questions about the topic of concern. 25

Synapses

Synaptic cleft

Syndrome: A collection of symptoms that form a definable pattern. 43

Systematic desensitization: A variant of counterconditioning that involves presenting the client with progressively more anxiety-provoking images while in a relaxed state. 123

T

Target behavior: A behavior of interest or concern in an assessment. 88

Tau: A protein that normally helps maintain the internal support structure of the axons. 384

Theoretical perspective: An orientation to understanding the causes of human behavior and the treatment of abnormality. 102

Thinking style and language: A term used in a mental status exam to indicate how a person thinks. This includes information on the client's vocabulary use and sentence structure. 74

Thought stopping: A cognitive-behavioral method in which the client learns to stop having anxiety-provoking thoughts. 156

Tic: A rapid, recurring, involuntary movement or vocalization. 364

Token economy: A form of contingency management in which a client who performs desired activities earns chips or tokens that can later be exchanged for tangible benefits. 124

Tolerance: The extent to which the individual requires larger and larger amounts of a substance in order to achieve its desired effects, or the extent to which the individual feels less of its effects after using the same amount of the substance. 395

Tourette's disorder: A tic disorder involving a combination of chronic movement and vocal tics. 364

Transcranial magnetic stimulation (TMS): Treatment in which a powerful electromagnet is placed on the individual's scalp and a current is passed through the cortex. 130

Transference: The carrying over toward the therapist of the feelings the client had toward parents or other significant people in the client's life. 108

Transsexualism: A term sometimes used to refer to gender identity disorder, specifically pertaining to individuals choosing to undergo sex reassignment surgery. 227

Transvestic fetishism: A paraphilia in which a man has an uncontrollable craving to dress in women's clothing in order to derive sexual gratification. 225

Traumatic brain injury (TBI): Damage to the brain caused by exposure to trauma. 375

Traumatic experience: A disastrous or an extremely painful event that has severe psychological and physiological effects. 166

Trephining: The drilling of a hole in the skull, presumably as a way of treating psychological disorders during prehistoric times. 11

Trichotillomania: An impulse-control disorder involving the compulsive, persistent urge to pull out one's own hair. 447

U

Unconditional positive regard: A method in client-centered therapy in which the clinician gives total acceptance of what the client says, does, and feels. 113

Unconditioned response: A reflexive response that occurs naturally in the presence of the unconditioned stimulus without having been learned. 119

Unconditioned stimulus: The stimulus that naturally produces a response without having been learned. 119

Unexpected (uncued) panic attack: A panic attack that occurs in the absence of a specific situation or cue. 149

Unstructured interview: A series of open-ended questions aimed at determining the client's reasons for being in treatment, symptoms, health status, family background, and life history. 68

V

Vaginismus: A sexual dysfunction that involves recurrent or persistent involuntary spasms of the musculature of the outer part of the vagina. 237

Validity: The extent to which a test, diagnosis, or rating accurately and distinctly characterizes a person's psychological status. 41, 78

Variable: A dimension along which people, things, or events differ. 23

Vascular dementia: A form of dementia resulting from a vascular disease that causes deprivation of the blood supply to the brain. 381

Vicarious reinforcement: A form of learning in which a new behavior is acquired through the process of watching someone else receive reinforcement for the same behavior. 121

Visual hallucination: A hallucination involving the false visual perception of objects or persons. 76

Voyeur: A person with the paraphilia of voyeurism. 226

Voyeurism: A paraphilia in which the individual has a compulsion to derive sexual gratification from observing the nudity or sexual activity of others. 226

W

Wernicke's aphasia: A form of aphasia in which the individual is able to produce language but has lost the ability to comprehend, so that these verbal productions have no meaning. 375

Wernicke's encephalopathy: An acute condition—associated with long-term, heavy alcohol use—involving delirium, eye movement disturbances, difficulties in movement and balance, and deterioration of the peripheral nerves to the hands and feet. 400

Working through: A phase of psychoanalytic treatment in which the clinician helps the client achieve a healthier resolution of issues than had occurred in the client's early childhood environment. 108

REFERENCES

A

Abbott, M. J., & Rapee, R. M. (2004). Post-event rumination and negative self-appraisal in social phobia before and after treatment. *Journal of Abnormal Psychology, 113,* 136–144.

Abbott, R. D., White, L. R., Ross, G. W., Masaki, K. H., Curb, J. D., & Petrovitch, H. (2004). Walking and dementia in physically capable elderly men. *Journal of the American Medical Association, 292,* 1447–1453.

Abel, G. G., & Osborn, C. (1992). The paraphilias: The extent and nature of sexually deviant and criminal behavior. *Psychiatric Clinics of North America, 15,* 675–687.

Abouesh, A., & Clayton, A. (1999). Compulsive voyeurism and exhibitionism: A clinical response to paroxetine. *Archives of Sexual Behavior, 28,* 23–30.

Abraham, K. (1911/1968). Notes on the psychoanalytic investigation and treatment of manic-depressive insanity and allied conditions. In K. Abraham (Ed.), *Selected papers of Karl Abraham.* New York: Basic Books.

Adams, K. M., & Robinson, D. W. (2001). Shame reduction, affect regulation, and sexual boundary development: Essential building blocks of sexual addiction treatment. *Sexual Addiction and Compulsivity, 8,* 23–44.

Adebimpe, V. R. (1994). Race, racism, and epidemiological surveys. *Hospital and Community Psychiatry, 45,* 27–31.

Adler, A. (1931/1958). *What life should mean to you.* New York: Capricorn.

Adler, L. E., Olincy, A., Waldo, M., Harris, J. G., Griffith, J., et al. (1998). Schizophrenia, sensory gating, and nicotinic receptors. *Schizophrenia Bulletin, 24,* 189–202.

Agras, W. S., & Apple, R. F. (1998). Sally and her eating disorder: A case of bulimia nervosa. In R. P. Halgin & S. K. Whitbourne (Eds.), *A casebook in abnormal psychology: From the files of experts* (pp. 268–283). New York: Oxford University Press.

Aikins, D. E., & Craske, M. G. (2001). Cognitive theories of generalized anxiety disorder. *Psychiatric Clinics of North America, 24,* 57–74.

Ainsworth, M. D. S. (1989). Attachments beyond infancy. *American Psychologist, 44,* 709–716.

Ainsworth, M. D. S., Blehar, M., Waters, E., & Wall, S. (1978). *Patterns of attachment.* Hillsdale, NJ: Erlbaum.

Alcohol-attributable deaths and years of potential life lost—United States, 2001. (2004). *Journal of the American Medical Association, 292,* 2831–2832.

Alexander, P. C. (1992). Application of attachment theory to the study of sexual abuse. *Journal of Consulting and Clinical Psychology, 60,* 185–195.

Allen, A., & Hollander, E. (2000). Body dysmorphic disorder. *Psychiatric Clinics of North America, 23,* 617–628.

Allgulander, C., Dahl, A. A., Austin, C., Morris, P. L., Sogaard, J. A., Fayyad, R., et al. (2004). Efficacy of sertraline in a 12-week trial for generalized anxiety disorder. *American Journal of Psychiatry, 161,* 1642–1649.

Althof, S. E., & Seftel, A. D. (1995). The evaluation and treatment of erectile dysfunction. *Psychiatric Clinics of North America,* 171–192.

Alzheimer, A. (1907/1987). About a peculiar disease of the cerebral cortex. *Alzheimer's Disease and Associated Disorders, 1,* 7–8.

American Psychiatric Association. (1994). *DSM-IV Diagnostic and Statistical Manual.* Washington, DC: American Psychiatric Association.

American Psychiatric Association. (2000). *Diagnostic and statistical manual of mental disorders* (4th ed., text rev.). Washington DC: Author.

Anderson, P. L., Rothbaum, B. O., & Hodges, L. (2001). Virtual reality: Using the virtual world to improve quality of life in the real world. *Bulletin of the Menninger Clinic, 65,* 78–91.

Anderson, S. C., & Hibbs, V. K. (1992). Alcoholism in the Soviet Union. *Social Work, 35,* 441–453.

Andreasen, N., & Blennow, K. (2005). CSF biomarkers for mild cognitive impairment and early Alzheimer's disease. *Clinical Neurology and Neurosurgery, 107,* 165–173.

Andreasen, N. C. (1987a). Creativity and mental illness: Prevalence rates in writers and their first-degree relatives. *American Journal of Psychiatry, 144,* 1288–1292.

Andreasen, N. C. (1987b). The diagnosis of schizophrenia. *Schizophrenia Bulletin, 13,* 9–22.

Annis, H. M. (1984). *Inventory of drinking situations.* Toronto: Addition Research Foundation.

Armfield, J. M., & Mattiske, J. K. (1996). Vulnerability representation: The role of perceived dangerousness, uncontrollability, unpredictability and disgustingness in spider fear. *Behaviour Research & Therapy, 34,* 899–909.

Asarnow, R. F., Nuechterlein, K. H., Fogelson, D., Subotnik, K. L., Payne, D. A., et al. (2001). Schizophrenia and schizophrenia-spectrum personality disorders in the first-degree relatives of children with schizophrenia: The UCLA Family Study. *Archives of General Psychiatry, 58,* 581–588.

Asher, R. (1951). Munchausen's syndrome. *Lancet, 1,* 339–341.

Asmundson, G. J., Larsen, D. K., & Stein, M. B. (1998). Panic disorder and vestibular disturbance: An overview of empirical findings and clinical implications. *Journal of Psychosomatic Research, 44,* 107–120.

Asscheman, H., & Gooren, L. J. (1992). Hormone treatment in transsexuals. *Journal of Psychology and Human Sexuality, 5,* 39–54.

Ayllon, T., & Azrin, N. H. (1965). The measurement and reinforcement of behavior of psychotics. *Journal of Experimental Analysis of Behavior, 8,* 351–383.

B

Baer, L., Rauch, S. L., Ballantine, T., Martuza, R., Cosgrove, R., et al. (1995). Cingulotomy for intractable obsessive-compulsive disorder. *Archives of General Psychiatry, 52,* 384–392.

Bagley, C., Wood, M., & Young, L. (1994). Victim to abuser: Mental health and behavioral sequels of child sexual abuse in a community survey of young adult males. *Child Abuse & Neglect, 18,* 683–697.

Bailey, J. M., & Kucker, K. J. (1995). Childhood sex-typed behavior and sexual orientation: A conceptual analysis and quantitative review. *Developmental Psychology, 31,* 43–45.

Baker, G. A., Hanley, J. R., Jackson, H. F., Kimmance, S., & Slade, P. (1993). Detecting the faking of amnesia: Performance differences between simulators and patients with memory impairment. *Journal of Clinical and Experimental Neuropsychology, 15,* 668–684.

Baker, J. D., Capron, E. W., & Azorlosa, J. (1996). Family environment characteristics of persons with histrionic and dependent personality disorders. *Journal of Personality Disorders, 10,* 82–87.

Baker, R. A. (1990). *They call it hypnosis.* Buffalo: Prometheus Books.

Bancroft, J., & Vukadinovic, Z. (2004). Sexual addiction, sexual compulsivity, sexual impulsivity, or what? Toward a theoretical model. *Journal of Sex Research, 41,* 225–234.

Bandura, A. (1971). Psychotherapy based upon modeling principles. In A. E. Bergin & S. L. Garfield (Eds.), *Handbook of psychotherapy and behavior change* (pp. 653–708). New York: Wiley.

Bandura, A. (1986). *Social foundations of thought and action: A social cognitive theory.* Englewood Cliffs, NJ: Prentice Hall.

Bandura, A. (1991). Human agency: The rhetoric and the reality. *American Psychologist, 46,* 157–162.

Bandura, A. (2004). Health promotion by social cognitive means. *Health Education and Behavior, 31,* 143–164.

Bandura, A., & Locke, E. A. (2003). Negative self-efficacy and goal effects revisited. *Journal of Applied Psychology, 88,* 87–99.

Bandura, A., Caprara, G. V., Barbaranelli, C., Gerbino, M., & Pastorelli, C. (2003). Role of affective self-regulatory efficacy in diverse spheres of psychosocial functioning. *Child Development, 74,* 769–782.

Banzato, C. E. M. (2004). Classification in psychiatry: The move towards ICD-II and DSM-V. *Current Opinions in Psychiatry, 17,* 497–501.

Barbaree, H., & Seto, M. C. (1997). Pedophilia: Assessment and treatment. In D. R. Laws & W. T. O'Donohue (Eds.), *Sexual deviance: Theory, assessment, and treatment* (pp. 175–193). New York: Guilford Press.

Barch, D. M. (2005). The cognitive neuroscience of schizophrenia. *Annual Review of Clinical Psychology, 1,* 321–353.

Barkley, R. A. (1998). Attention-deficit hyperactivity disorder. *Scientific American, 279,* 66–71.

Barkley, R. A., & Edwards, G. (1998). Paul: An instructive case of attention-deficit/hyperactivity disorder. In R. P. Halgin & S. K. Whitbourne (Eds.), *A casebook in abnormal psychology: From the files of experts* (pp. 212–235). New York: Oxford University Press.

Barlow, D. H. (1986). Causes of sexual dysfunction: The role of anxiety and cognitive interference. *Journal of Consulting and Clinical Psychology, 54,* 140–148.

Barlow, D. H. (1988). *Anxiety and its disorders: The nature and treatment of anxiety and panic.* New York: Guilford Press.

Barlow, D. H. (2002). *Anxiety and its disorders: The nature and treatment of anxiety and panic* (2nd ed.). New York: Guilford Press.

Barlow, D. H., Craske, M. G., Cerny, J. A., & Klosko, J. S. (1989). Behavioral treatment of panic disorder. *Behavior Therapy, 20,* 261–282.

Barlow, D. H., Esler, J. L., & Vitali, A. E. (1998). Psychosocial treatments for panic disorders, phobias, and generalized anxiety disorder. In P. E. Nathan & J. M. Gorman (Eds.), *A guide to treatments that work* (pp. 288–318). New York: Oxford University Press.

Barnett, W., Richter, P., Sigmund, D., & Spitzer, M. (1997). Recidivism and concomitant criminality in pathological firesetters. *Journal of Forensic Sciences, 42,* 879–883.

Barnoya, J., & Glantz, S. A. (2004). Modifiable behavioral factors as causes of death. *Journal of the American Medical Association, 291,* 2941–2942; author reply 2942–2943.

Barsky, A. J. (1996). Hypochondriasis: Medical management and psychiatric treatment. *Psychosomatics, 37,* 48–56.

Barsky, A. J., & Ahern, D. K. (2004). Cognitive behavior therapy for hypochondriasis: A randomized controlled trial. *Journal of the American Medical Association, 291,* 1464–1470.

Barsky, A. J., Ahern, D. K., Bailey, E. D., Saintfort, R., Liu, E. B., & Peekna, H. M. (2001). Hypochondriacal patients' appraisal of health and physical risks. *American Journal of Psychiatry, 158,* 783–787.

Barsky, A. J., Brener, J., Coeytaux, R. R., & Cleary, P. D. (1995). Accurate awareness of heartbeat in hypochondriacal and nonhypochondriacal patients. *Journal of Psychosomatic Research, 39,* 489–497.

Bartholomew, K. (1997). Adult attachment processes: Individual and couple perspectives. *British Journal of Medical Psychology, 70,* 249–263.

Bartholomew, K., & Horowitz, L. M. (1991). Attachment styles among young adults: A test of a four-category model. *Journal of Personality and Social Psychology, 61,* 226–244.

Bartlik, B., & Goldstein, M. Z. (2000). Practical geriatrics: Maintaining sexual health after menopause. *Psychiatric Services, 51,* 751–753.

Bartlik, B., & Goldstein, M. Z. (2001). Men's sexual health after midlife. *Psychiatric Services, 52,* 291–306.

Bartolini, M., Coccia, M., Luzzi, S., Provinciali, L., & Ceravolo, M. G. (2005). Motivational symptoms of depression mask preclinical Alzheimer's disease in elderly subjects. *Dementia and Geriatric Cognitive Disorders, 19,* 31–36.

Bassuk, E. L., Dawson, R., Perloff, J., & Weinreb, L. (2001). Post-traumatic stress disorder in extremely poor women: Implications for health care clinicians. *Journal of the American Medical Women's Association, 56,* 79–85.

Bateman, A., & Fonagy, P. (2001). Treatment of borderline personality disorder with psychoanalytically oriented partial hospitalization: An 18-month follow-up. *American Journal of Psychiatry, 158,* 36–42.

Baud, P. (2005). Personality traits as intermediary phenotypes in suicidal behavior: genetic issues. *American Journal of Medical Genetics C: Seminar in Medical Genetics, 133,* 34–42.

Bayliss, A. P., & Tipper, S. P. (2005). Gaze and arrow cueing of attention reveals individual differences along the autism spectrum as a function of target context. *British Journal of Psychology, 96,* 95–114.

Beard, K. W. (2005). Internet addiction: A review of current assessment techniques and potential assessment questions. *Cyberpsychology and Behavior, 8,* 7–14.

Bech, P., & Angst, J. (1996). Quality of life in anxiety and social phobia. *International Clinical Psychopharmacology, 3,* 97–100.

Beck, A. T. (1967). *Depression: Clinical, experimental, and theoretical aspects.* New York: Harper & Row.

Beck, A. T. (1996). Beyond belief: A theory of modes, personality, and psychopathology. In P. M. Salkovskis (Ed.), *Frontiers of cognitive therapy* (pp. 1–25). New York: Guilford Press.

Beck, A. T., & Rector, N. A. (2005). Cognitive approaches to schizophrenia: Theory and therapy. *Annual Review of Clinical Psychology, 1,* 577–606.

Beck, A. T., Emery, G., & Greenberg, R. L. (1985). *Anxiety disorders and phobias: A cognitive perspective.* New York: Basic Books.

Beck, A. T., Freeman, A., & Davis, D. D. (2004). *Cognitive therapy of personality disorders.* New York: Guilford Press.

Beck, A. T., Rush, A. J., Shaw, B. F., & Emery, G. (1979). *Cognitive therapy of depression: A treatment manual.* New York: Guilford Press.

Beck, A. T., Steer, R. A., Kovacs, M., & Garrison, B. (1985). Hopelessness and eventual suicide: A 10-year prospective study of patients hospitalized with suicidal ideation. *American Journal of Psychiatry, 142,* 559–563.

Beck, A. T., & Weishaar, M. (1989). Cognitive therapy. In A. Freeman, K. M. Simon, L. E. Beutler, & H. Arkowitz (Eds.), *Comprehensive handbook of cognitive therapy* (pp. 21–36). New York: Plenum Press.

Beere, D. (1995). Loss of "background": A perceptual theory of dissociation. *Dissociation: Progress in the Dissociative Disorders, 8,* 165–174.

Bellodi, L., Cavallini, M. C., Bertelli, S., Chiapparino, D., Riboldi, C., & Smeraldi, E. (2001). Morbidity risk for obsessive-compulsive spectrum disorders in first-degree relatives of patients with eating disorders. *American Journal of Psychiatry, 158,* 563–569.

Bemporad, J. R. (1985). Long-term analytic treatment of depression. In E. E. Beckham & W. R. Leber (Eds.), *Handbook of depression: Treatment, assessment, and research* (pp. 82–89). Homewood, IL: Dorsey Press.

Bender, D. S. (2005). The therapeutic alliance in the treatment of personality disorders. *Journal of Psychiatric Practice, 11,* 73–87.

Bender, D. S., Dolan, R. T., Skodol, A. E., Sanislow, C. A., Dyck, I. R., et al. (2001). Treatment utilization by patients with personality disorders. *American Journal of Psychiatry, 158,* 295–302.

Bennett, D., Sharpe, M., Freeman, C., & Carson, A. (2004). Anorexia nervosa among female secondary school students in Ghana. *British Journal of Psychiatry, 185,* 312–317.

Berelowitz, M., & Tamopolsky, S. (1993). The validity of borderline personality disorder: An updated review of recent research. In P. Tyrer & G. Stein (Eds.), *Personality disorder reviewed* (pp. 90–112). London: Gaskell.

Bergen, A. W., Yeager, M., Welch, R. A., Haque, K., Ganjei, J. K., van den Bree, M. B., et al. (2005). Association of multiple DRD2 polymorphisms with anorexia nervosa. *Neuropsychopharmacology, 30,* 1703–1710.

Berlin, F. S. (1998). Hal, driven by an invisible force: A case of pedophilia. In R. P. Halgin & S. K. Whitbourne (Eds.), *A casebook in abnormal psychology: From the files of experts* (pp. 114–126). New York: Oxford University Press.

Bernstein, A., Newman, J. P., Wallace, J. F., & Luh, K. E. (2000). Left-hemisphere activation and deficient response modulation in psychopaths. *Psychological Science, 11,* 414–418.

Bernstein, G. A., Layne, A. E., Egan, E. A., & Nelson, L. P. (2005). Maternal phobic anxiety and child anxiety. *Journal of Anxiety Disorders, 19,* 658–672.

Berrettini, W. (2003). Evidence for shared susceptibility in bipolar disorder and schizophrenia. *American Journal of Medical Genetics C: Seminar in Medical Genetics, 123,* 59–64.

Besson, J., Aeby, F., Kasas, A., Lehert, P., & Potgieter, A. (1998). Combined efficacy of acamprosate and disulfiram in the treatment of alcoholism: A controlled study. *Alcoholism, Clinical & Experimental Research, 22,* 573–579.

Best, M., Williams, J. M., & Coccaro, E. F. (2002). Evidence for a dysfunctional prefrontal circuit in patients with an impulsive aggressive disorder. *Proceedings of the National Academy of Sciences USA, 99,* 8448–8453.

Bettelheim, B. (1967). *The empty fortress.* New York: Free Press.

Beutler, L. E., Consoli, A. J., & Williams, R. E. (1995). Integrative and eclectic therapies in practice. In B. Bongar & L. E. Beutler (Eds.), *Comprehensive textbook of psychotherapy: Theory and practice* (pp. 274–292). New York: Oxford University Press.

Biederman, J., Faraone, S. V., Hirshfeld-Becker, D. R., Friedman, D., Robin, J. A., & Rosenbaum, J. F. (2001). Patterns of psychopathology and dysfunction in high-risk children of parents with panic disorder and major depression. *American Journal of Psychiatry, 158,* 49–57.

Biederman, J., Faraone, S. V., Mick, E., Spencer, T., Wilens, T., et al. (1995). High risk for attention deficit hyperactivity disorder among children of parents with childhood onset of the disorder: A pilot study. *American Journal of Psychiatry, 152,* 431–435.

Biederman, J., Mick, E., Faraone, S. V., & Burback, M. (2001). Patterns of remission and symptom decline in conduct disorder: A four-year prospective study of an ADHD sample. *Journal of the American Academy of Child and Adolescent Psychiatry, 40,* 290–298.

Bieling, P. J., & Alden, L. E. (1997). The consequences of perfectionism for patients with social phobia. *British Journal of Clinical Psychology, 36,* 387–395.

Binder, R. L., McNiel, D. E., & Goldstone, R. L. (1996). Is adaptive coping possible for adult survivors of childhood sexual abuse? *Psychiatric Services, 47,* 186–188.

Birmaher, B., Axelson, D. A., Monk, K., Kalas, C., Clark, D. B., Ehmann, M., et al. (2003). Fluoxetine for the treatment of childhood anxiety disorders. *Journal of the American Academy of Child and Adolescent Psychiatry, 42,* 415–423.

Birmaher, B., Waterman, G. S., Ryan, N., Cully, M., Balach, L., Ingram, J., & Brodsky, M. (1994). Fluoxetine for childhood anxiety disorders. *Journal of the American Academy of Child and Adolescent Psychiatry, 33,* 993–999.

Birnbaum, M. (1960). The right to treatment. *American Bar Association Journal, 46,* 499–503.

Black, D. W. (2001). Compulsive buying disorder: Definition, assessment, epidemiology and clinical management. *CNS Drugs, 15,* 17–27.

Blair, R. J. (2004). The roles of orbital frontal cortex in the modulation of antisocial behavior. *Brain and Cognition, 55,* 198–208.

Blanchard, E. B., Zucker, K. J., Cohen-Kettenis, P. T., Gooren, L. J. G., & Bailey, J. M. (1996). Birth order and sibling sex ratio in two samples of Dutch gender-dysphoric homosexual males. *Archives of Sexual Behavior, 25,* 495–514.

Blanchard, G. T. (1995). Sexually addicted lust murderers. *Sexual Addiction and Compulsivity, 2,* 62–71.

Blanchard, R. (1993). Varieties of autogynephilia and their relationship to gender dysphoria. *Archives of Sexual Behavior, 22,* 241–251.

Blanchard, R., Barbaree, H. E., Bogaert, A. F., Dickey, R., Klassen, P., Kuban, M. E., & Zucker, K. J. (2000). Fraternal birth order and sexual orientation in pedophiles. *Archives of Sexual Behavior, 29,* 463–478.

Blanchard, R., & Bogaert, A. F. (1996). Homosexuality in men and number of older brothers. *American Journal of Psychiatry, 153,* 27–31.

Blanchard, R., Klassen, P., Dickey, R., Kuban, M. E., & Blak, T. (2001). Sensitivity and specificity of the phallometric test for pedophilia in nonadmitting sex offenders. *Psychological Assessment, 13,* 118–126.

Bleuler, E. (1911). *Dementia praeco oder gruppe der schizophrenien.* (Dementia praecox or the group of schizophrenias). Leipzig: F. Deuticke.

Bliss, E. L. (1980). Multiple personalities: A report of 14 cases with implications for schizophrenia and hysteria. *Archives of General Psychiatry, 37,* 1388–1397.

Bohus, M., Haaf, B., Stiglmayr, C., Pohl, U., Bohme, R., & Linehan, M. (2000). Evaluation of inpatient dialectical-behavioral therapy for borderline personality disorder—A prospective study. *Behaviour Research and Therapy, 38,* 875–887.

Bonnie, R. J., Hoge, S. K., Monahan, J., Poythress, N., Eisenberg, M., & Feucht-Haviar, T. (1997). The MacArthur Adjudicative Competence Study: A comparison of criteria for assessing the competence of criminal defendants. *Journal of the American Academy of Psychiatry and the Law, 25,* 249–259.

Boor, M. (1982). The multiple personality epidemic: Additional cases and inferences regarding diagnosis, etiology, dynamics, and treatment. *Journal of Nervous and Mental Disease, 170,* 302–304.

Borkovec, T. D., & Ruscio, A. M. (2001). Psychotherapy for generalized anxiety disorder. *Journal of Clinical Psychiatry, 62* (Suppl. 11), 37–42.

Bornstein, R. F. (1998). Reconceptualizing personality disorder diagnosis in the *DSM-V;* The discriminant validity challenge. *Clinical Psychology: Science and Practice, 5,* 333–343.

Bornstein, R. F., & Greenberg, R. P. (1991). Dependency and eating disorders in female psychiatric patients. *Journal of Nervous and Mental Disease, 179,* 148–152.

Borum, R. & Reddy, M., (2001). Assessing violence risk in *Tarasoff* situations: A fact-based model of inquiry. *Behavioral Sciences and the Law, 19,* 375–385.

Bouchard, T. J., Jr., Lykken, D. T., McGue, M., Segal, N. L., & Tellegen, A. (1990). Sources of human psychological differences: The Minnesota study of twins reared apart. *Science, 250,* 223–228.

Bourin, M., Baker, G. B., & Bradwejn, J. (1998). Neurobiology of panic disorder. *Journal of Psychosomatic Research, 44,* 163–180.

Bouton, M. E., Mineka, S., & Barlow, D. H. (2001). A modern learning theory perspective on the etiology of panic disorder. *Psychological Review, 108,* 4–32.

Bouza, C., Angeles, M., Munoz, A., & Amate, J. M. (2004). Efficacy and safety of naltrexone and acamprosate in the treatment of alcohol dependence: A systematic review. *Addiction, 99,* 811–828.

Bow, J. N., & Quinnell, F. A. (2001). Psychologists' current practices and procedures in child custody evaluations: Five years after American Psychological Association guidelines. *Professional Psychology Research and Practice, 32,* 261–268.

Bowden, C. L. (2005). Treatment options for bipolar depression. *Journal of Clinical Psychiatry, 66* (Supplement 1), 3–6.

Bowlby, J. (1980). *Attachment and loss: Volume III: Loss: Sadness and depression.* New York: Basic Books.

Bowman, E. S., & Coons, P. M. (2000). The differential diagnosis of epilepsy, pseudoseizures, dissociative identity disorder, and dissociative disorder not otherwise specified. *Bulletins of the Menninger Clinic, 64,* 164–180.

Boyce, E. G., & Umland, E. M. (2001). Sildenafil citrate: A therapeutic update. *Clinical Therapeutics, 23,* 2–23.

Boyer, J. L., & Guthrie, L. (1985). Assessment and treatment of the suicidal patient. In E. E. Beckham & W. R. Leber (Eds.), *Handbook of depression: Treatment, assessment, and research* (pp. 606–633). Homewood, IL: Dorsey Press.

Bracero, W. (1998). Intimidades: Confianza, gender, and hierarchy in the construction of Latino-Latina therapeutic relationships. *Cultural Diversity and Ethnic Minority Psychology, 4,* 264–277.

Bradford, J. M. (2001). The neurobiology, neuropharmacology, and pharmacological treatment of the paraphilias and compulsive sexual behaviour. *Canadian Journal of Psychiatry, 46,* 26–34.

Bradley, R., Greene, J., Russ, E., Dutra, L., & Westen, D. (2005). A multidimensional meta-analysis of psychotherapy for PTSD. *American Journal of Psychiatry, 162,* 214–227.

Bradley, R., Jenei, J., & Westen, D. (2005). Etiology of borderline personality disorder: Disentangling the contributions of intercorrelated antecedents. *Journal of Nervous & Mental Disease, 193,* 24–31.

Bradley, S. J., & Zucker, K. J. (1997). Gender identity disorder: A review of the past 10 years. *Journal of the Academy of Child and Adolescent Psychiatry, 36,* 872–880.

Brand, M., Kalbe, E., Labudda, K., Fujiwara, E., Kessler, J., & Markowitsch, H. J. (2005). Decision-making impairments in patients with pathological gambling. *Psychiatry Research, 133,* 91–99.

Brant, J. (1998). *Law and mental health professionals: Massachusetts.* Washington, DC: American Psychological Association.

Bremner, J. D., Krystal, J. H., Charney, D. S., & Southwick, S. M. (1996). Neural mechanisms in dissociative amnesia for childhood abuse: Relevance to the current controversy surrounding the "false memory syndrome." *American Journal of Psychiatry, 153,* 71–82.

Brent, D. A. (2001). Assessment and treatment of the youthful suicidal patient. *Annals of the New York Academy of Sciences, 932,* 106–128; discussion 128–131.

Brent, D. A., Perper, J. A., Moritz, G., Allman, C., Schweers, J., Roth, C., Balach, L., Canobbio, R., & Liotus, L. (1993). Psychiatric sequelae to the loss of an adolescent peer to suicide. *Journal of the American Academy of Child and Adolescent Psychiatry, 32,* 509–517.

Brent, D. A., Perper, J. A., Moritz, G., Baugher, M., & Allman, C. (1993). Suicide in adolescents with no apparent psychopathology. *Journal of the American Academy of Child and Adolescent Psychiatry, 32,* 494–500.

Brent, D. A., Perper, J., Moritz, G., Allman, C., Friend, A., Schweers, J., Roth, C., Balach, L., & Harrington, K. (1992). Psychiatric effects of exposure to suicide among the friends and acquaintances of adolescent suicide victims. *Journal of the American Academy of Child and Adolescent Psychiatry, 31,* 629–639.

Breslow, N., Evans, L., & Langley, J. (1985). On the prevalence and roles of females in the sadomasochistic subculture: Report of an empirical study. *Archives of Sexual Behavior, 14,* 303–317.

Breuer, J., & Freud, S. (1892/1982). *Studies in hysteria* (J. Strachey, A. Freud, Trans.) New York: Basic Books.

Brick, S. S., & Chu, J. A. (1991). The simulation of multiple personalities: A case report. *Psychotherapy, 28,* 267–272.

Briken, P., Nika, E., & Berner, W. (2001). Treatment of paraphilia with luteinizing hormone-releasing hormone agonists. *Journal of Sexual and Marital Therapy, 27,* 45–55.

Brodsky, B. S., Cloitre, M., & Dulit, R. A. (1995). Relationship of dissociation to self-mutilation and childhood abuse in borderline personality disorder. *American Journal of Psychiatry, 152,* 1788–1792.

Brookmeyer, R., & Kawas, C. (1998). Projections of Alzheimer's disease in the United States and the public health impact of delaying disease onset. *American Journal of Public Health, 88,* 1337–1342.

Brown, A. S., Begg, M. D., Gravenstein, S., Schaefer, C. A., Wyatt, R. J., Bresnahan, M., et al. (2004). Serologic evidence of prenatal influenza in the etiology of schizophrenia. *Archives of General Psychiatry, 61,* 774–780.

Brown, L., Sherbenou, R. J., & Johnsen, S. K. (1997). *Test of Nonverbal Intelligence-3 (TONI-3).* Minneapolis: American Guidance Service.

Bruce, M. L., Ten Have, T. R., Reynolds, C. F., 3rd, Katz, II, Schulberg, H. C., Mulsant, B. H., et al. (2004). Reducing suicidal ideation and depressive symptoms in depressed older primary care patients: A randomized controlled trial. *Journal of the American Medical Association, 291,* 1081–1091.

Bruder, G. E., Schneier, F. R., Stewart, J. W., McGrath, P. J., & Quitkin, F. (2004). Left hemisphere dysfunction during verbal dichotic listening tests in patients who have social phobia with or without comorbid depressive disorder. *American Journal of Psychiatry, 161,* 72–78.

Bureau of Justice Statistics (2005). *Homicide trends in the U.S.,* from http://www.ojp.usdoj.gov/bjs/homicide/teens.htm.

Burgmer, M., Jessen, F., & Freyberger, H. J. (2000). Polythetic diagnostic approach to the borderline personality disorder: The valency of the single criterion in the concept of professional therapists. *Psychopathology, 33,* 119–124.

Butler, L. D., Duran, R. E., Jasiukaitis, P., Koopman, C., & Spiegel, D. (1996). Hypnotizability and traumatic experience: A diathesis-stress model of dissociative symptomatology. *American Journal of Psychiatry, 153,* 42–63.

Button, T. M., Scourfield, J., Martin, N., Purcell, S., & McGuffin, P. (2005). Family dysfunction interacts with genes in the causation of antisocial symptoms. *Behavioral Genetics, 35,* 115–120.

Byne, W., Buchsbaum, M. S., Kemether, E., Hazlett, E. A., Shinwari, A., Mitropoulou, V., & Siever, L. J. (2001). Magnetic resonance imaging of the thalamic mediodorsal nucleus and pulvinar in schizophrenia and schizotypal personality disorder. *Archives of General Psychiatry, 58,* 133–140.

C

Cadoret, R. J., Yates, W. R., Troughton, E., Woodworth, G., & Stewart, M. A. (1995). Genetic-environmental interaction in the genesis of aggressivity and conduct disorders. *Archives of General Psychiatry, 52,* 916–924.

Caldirola, D., Bellodi, L., Caumo, A., Migliarese, G., & Perna, G. (2004). Approximate entropy of respiratory patterns in panic disorder. *American Journal of Psychiatry, 161,* 79–87.

Callahan, D. (1999). Balancing efficiency and need in allocating resources to the care of persons with serious mental illness. *Psychiatric Services, 50,* 664–666

Camisa, K. M., Bockbrader, M. A., Lysaker, P., Rae, L. L., Brenner, C. A., & O'Donnell, B. F. (2005). Personality traits in schizophrenia and related personality disorders. *Psychiatry Research, 133,* 23–33.

Campo, J. V., & Negrini, B. J. (2000). Case study: Negative reinforcement and behavioral management of conversion disorder. *Journal of the American Academy of Child and Adolescent Psychiatry, 39,* 787–790.

Canino, G. (1994). Alcohol use and misuse among Hispanic women: Selected factors, processes, and studies. *International Journal of the Addictions, 29,* 1083–1100.

Caplan, L. (1984). *The insanity defense and the trial of John W. Hinckley, Jr.* Boston: David R. Godin.

Cardena, E., & Spiegel, D. (1996). Diagnostic issues, criteria, and comorbidity of dissociative disorders. In L. K. Michelson & W. J. Ray (Eds.), *Handbook of dissociation: Theoretical, empirical, and clinical perspectives* (pp. 227–250). New York: Plenum Press.

Carlat, D. J., & Camargo, C. A., Jr., & Herzog, D. B. (1997). Eating disorders in males: A report on 135 patients. *American Journal of Psychiatry, 154,* 1127–1132.

Carlson, C. R., & Hoyle, R. H. (1993). Efficacy of abbreviated progressive muscle relaxation training: A quantitative review of behavioral medicine research. *Journal of Consulting and Clinical Psychology, 61,* 1059–1067.

Carlsson, A. (1988). The current status of the dopamine hypothesis of schizophrenia. *Neuropsychopharmacology, 1,* 179–186.

Carlsson, A., Waters, N., Holm-Waters, S., Tedroff, J., Nilsson, M., & Carlsson, M. L. (2001). Interactions between monoamines, glutamate, and GABA in schizophrenia: New evidence. *Annual Review of Pharmacology and Toxicology, 41,* 237–260.

Carlsson, M. L. (2001). On the role of prefrontal cortex glutamate for the antithetical phenomenology of obsessive compulsive disorder and attention deficit hyperactivity disorder. *Prog. Neuropsychopharmacol. Biol. Psychiatry, 25,* 5–26.

Carnes, P. J., & Delmonico, D. L. (1996). Childhood abuse and multiple addictions: Research findings in a sample of self-identified sexual addicts. *Sexual Addiction and Compulsivity, 3,* 258–268.

Carnes, P. J., Delmonico, D., Griffin, E., & Moriarty, J. (2001). *In the shadows of the net: Breaking free of compulsive online sexual behavior.* Center City, MN: Hazelden.

Carpenter, W. T. (1987). Approaches to knowledge and understanding of schizophrenia. *Schizophrenia Bulletin, 13,* 1–7.

Carr, R. E. (1998). Panic disorder and asthma: Causes, effects and research implications. *Journal of Psychosomatic Research, 44,* 43–52.

Carstensen, L. L., Gottman, J. M., & Levenson, R. W. (1995). Emotional behavior in long-term marriage. *Psychology and Aging, 10,* 140–149.

Carter, J. C., Olmsted, M. P., Kaplan, A. S., McCabe, R. E., Mills, J. S., & Aime, A. (2003). Self-help for bulimia nervosa: a randomized controlled trial. *American Journal of Psychiatry, 160,* 973–978.

Caspi, A., Moffitt, T. E., Newman, D. L., & Silva, P. A. (1996). Behavioral observations at age 3 years predict adult psychiatric disorders. Longitudinal evidence from a birth cohort. *Archives of General Psychiatry, 53,* 1033–1039.

Cath, D. C., Spinhoven, P., van Woerkom, T. C., van de Wetering, B. J., Hoogduin, C. A., Landman, A. D., Roos, R. A., & Rooijmans, H. G. (2001). Gilles de la Tourette's syndrome with and without obsessive-compulsive disorder compared with obsessive-compulsive disorder without tics: Which symptoms discriminate? *Journal of Nervous and Mental Disease, 189,* 219–228.

Centers for Disease Control and Prevention. (1993). Fetal alcohol syndrome United States, 1979–1992. *Morbidity and Mortality Weekly Reports, 42,* 339–341.

Chambless, D. L., & Ollendick, T. H. (2001). Empirically supported psychological interventions: Controversies and evidence. *Annual Review of Psychology, 52,* 685–716.

Chan, M., Nicklason, F., & Vial, J. H. (2001). Adverse drug events as a cause of hospital admission in the elderly. *Internal Medicine Journal, 31,* 199–205.

Chang, L., Ernst, T., Speck, O., & Grob, C. S. (2005). Additive effects of HIV and chronic methamphetamine use on brain metabolite abnormalities. *American Journal of Psychiatry, 162,* 361–369.

Charney, D. S. (2004). Psychobiological mechanisms of resilience and vulnerability: Implications for successful adaptation to extreme stress. *American Journal of Psychiatry, 161,* 195–216.

Chartier, M. J., Walker, J. R., & Stein, M. B. (2001). Social phobia and potential childhood risk factors in a community sample. *Psychological Medicine, 31,* 307–315.

Chauhan, N. B., & Siegel, G. J. (2005). Efficacy of anti-Abeta antibody isotypes used for intracerebroventricular immunization in TgCRND8. *Neuroscience Letters, 375,* 143–147.

Chioqueta, A. P., & Stiles, T. C. (2004). Suicide risk in patients with somatization disorder. *Crisis, 25,* 3–7.

Chodorow, N. (1978). *The reproduction of mothering.* Berkeley: University of California Press.

Christensen, G. A., Mackenzie, T. B., & Mitchell, J. E. (1991). Characteristics of 60 adult chronic hair pullers. *American Journal of Psychiatry, 148,* 365–370.

Clark, D. A., Steer, R. A., & Beck, A. T. (1994). Common and specific dimensions of self-reported anxiety and depression: Implications for the cognitive and tripartite models. *Journal of Abnormal Behavior, 103,* 645–654.

Clark, D. B. (1989). Performance-related medical and psychological disorders in instrumental musicians. *Annals of Behavioral Medicine, 11,* 28–34.

Clark, D. B., & Agras, W. S. (1991). The assessment and treatment of performance anxiety in musicians. *American Journal of Psychiatry, 148,* 598–605.

Classen, C., Koopman, C., & Spiegel, D. (1993). Trauma and dissociation. *Bulletin of the Menninger Clinic, 57,* 178–194.

Cleckley, H. M. (1976). *The mask of sanity* (5th ed.). St. Louis: Mosby.

Coccaro, E. F. (1998). Clinical outcome of psychopharmacologic treatment of borderline and schizotypal personality disordered subjects. *Journal of Clinical Psychiatry, 59* (Suppl. 1), 30–357.

Coccaro, E. F., & Kavoussi, R. J. (1997). Fluoxetine and impulsive aggressive behavior in personality-disordered subjects. *Archives of General Psychiatry, 54,* 1081–1088.

Coccaro, E. F., Schmidt, C. A., Samuels, J. F., & Nestadt, G. (2004). Lifetime and 1-month prevalence rates of intermittent explosive disorder in a community sample. *Journal of Clinical Psychiatry, 65,* 820–824.

Coffey, B. J., Miguel, E. C., Biederman, J., Baer, L., Rauch, S. L., et al. (1998). Tourette's disorder with and without obsessive-compulsive disorder in adults: Are they different? *Journal of Nervous and Mental Disease, 186,* 201–206.

Coffin, P. O., Galea, S., Ahern, J., Leon, A. C., Vlahov, D. & Tardiff, K. (2003). Opiates, cocaine and alcohol combinations in accidental drug overdose deaths in New York City, 1990–98. *Addiction, 98,* 739–747.

Cohen, S., & Williamson, G. M. (1991). Stress and infectious disease in humans. *Psychological Bulletin, 109,* 5–24.

Cohen, S., Doyle, W. J., Turner, R., Alper, C. M., & Skoner, D. P. (2003). Sociability and susceptibility to the common cold. *Psychological Science, 14,* 389–395.

Cohen, S., Frank, E., Doyle, W. J., Skoner, D. P., Rabin, B. S., & Gwaltney, J. M. J. (1998). Types of stressors that increase susceptibility to the common cold in healthy adults. *Health Psychology, 17,* 214–223.

Cohen-Kettenis, P. T., & Gooren, L. J. (1992). The influence of hormone treatment on psychological functioning of transsexuals. Special issue: Gender dysphoria: Interdisciplinary approaches in clinical management. *Journal of Psychology and Human Sexuality, 5,* 55–67.

Cohen-Kettenis, P. T., & van Goozen, S. H. M. (1997). Sex reassignment of adolescent transsexuals: A follow-up study. *Journal of the*

American Academy of Child and Adolescent Psychiatry, 36, 263–271.

Colapinto, J. (2001). *As nature made him.* New York: Harper Perennial.

Collaer, M. L., & Hines, M. (1995). Human behavioral sex differences: A role for gonadal hormones during early development? *Psychological Bulletin, 118,* 55–107

Commenges, D., Scotet, V., Renaud, S., Jacqmin-Gadda, H., Barberger-Gateau, P., & Dartigues, J. F. (2000). Intake of flavonoids and risk of dementia. *European Journal of Epidemiology, 16,* 357–363.

Committee on Professional Practice and Standards Board of Professional Affairs. (1998). *Guidelines for psychological evaluations in child protection matters.* Washington, DC: American Psychological Association.

Compas, B. E., Haaga, D. A., Keefe, F. J., Leitenberg, H., & Williams, D. A. (1998). Sampling of empirically supported psychological treatments from health psychology: Smoking, chronic pain, cancer, and bulimia nervosa. *Journal of Consulting and Clinical Psychology, 66,* 89–112.

Compton, W. M., Grant, B. F., Colliver, J. D., Glantz, M. D., & Stinson, F. S. (2004). Prevalence of marijuana use disorders in the United States: 1991–1992 and 2001–2002. *Journal of the American Medical Association, 291,* 2114–2121.

Conners, C. K., Erhardt, D., & Sparrow, E. (1997). *Conners' Adult ADHD Rating Scales.* Eagen, MN: Pearson Assessments.

Constantino, M. J., Arnow, B. A., Blasey, C., & Agras, W. S. (2005). The association between patient characteristics and the therapeutic alliance in cognitive-behavioral and interpersonal therapy for bulimia nervosa. *Journal of Consulting and Clinical Psychology, 73,* 203–211.

Cook, T. D., & Campbell, D. T. (1979). *Quasi-experimentation: Design and analysis for field settings.* Chicago: Rand McNally

Cook, T. D., Campbell D. T., & Peracchio, L. (1990). Quasi-experimentation. In M. D. Dunnette & L. M. Hough (Eds.), *Handbook of industrial and organizational psychology* (2nd ed., Vol. 1, pp 491–576). Palo Alto, CA: Consulting Psychologists Press.

Coons, P. M. (1980). Multiple personality: Diagnostic considerations. *Journal of Clinical Psychiatry, 41,* 330–336.

Coons, P. M., Bowman, E. S., Pellow, T. A., & Schneider, P. (1989). Post-traumatic aspects of the treatment of victims of sexual abuse and incest. *Psychiatric Clinics of North America, 12,* 325–335.

Cooper, R. S., Rotimi, C. N., & Ward, R. (1999). The puzzle of hypertension in African-Americans. *Scientific American.*

Coplan, J. D., Goetz, R., Klein, D. F., Papp, L. A., Fyer, A. J., Liebowitz, M. R., Davies, S. O., & Gorman, J. M. (1998). Plasma cortisol concentrations preceding lactate-induced panic. Psychological, biochemical, and physiological correlates. *Archives of General Psychiatry, 55,* 130–136.

Corbett, J., Saccone, N. L., Foroud, T., Goate, A., Edenberg, H., Nurnberger, J., et al. (2005). A sex-adjusted and age-adjusted genome screen for nested alcohol dependence diagnoses. *Psychiatrics Genetics, 15,* 25–30.

Corey-Bloom, J. (2000). Dementia. In S. K. Whitbourne (Ed.), *Psychopathology in later life* (pp. 217–243). New York: Wiley.

Cornblatt, B. A., Lencz, T., Smith, C. W., Correll, C. U., Auther, A. M., & Nakayama, E. (2003). The schizophrenia prodrome revisited: A neurodevelopmental perspective. *Schizophrenia Bulletin, 29,* 633–651.

Cornelius, J. R., Salloum, I. M., Mezzich, J., Cornelius, M. D., Fabrega, H., et al. (1995). Disproportionate suicidality in patients with comorbid major depression and alcoholism. *American Journal of Psychiatry, 152,* 358–364.

Corrigan, P. (2004). *On the stigma of mental illness: Practical strategies for research and social change.* Washington, DC: American Psychological Association.

Corrigan, P. W., & Penn, D. L. (1999). Lessons from social psychology on discrediting psychiatric stigma. *American Psychologist, 54,* 765–776.

Coryell, W. (1998). The treatment of psychotic depression. *Journal of Clinical Psychiatry, 1,* 22–27.

Costa, P. T., Jr., & McCrae, R. R. (1992). *NEO-PI-R manual.* Odessa, FL: Psychological Assessment Resources.

Costa, P. T., Jr., & VandenBos, G. R. (Eds.). (1996). *Psychological aspects of serious illness: Chronic conditions, fatal diseases, and clinical care.* Washington, DC: American Psychological Association.

Cote, H., & Wilchensky, M. (1996). The use of sexoanalysis for patients with gender identity disorder. *Canadian Journal of Human Sexuality, 5,* 261–270.

Cotman, C. W., Poon, W. W., Rissman, R. A., & Blurton-Jones, M. (2005). The role of caspase cleavage of tau in Alzheimer disease neuropathology. *Journal of Neuropathology and Experimental Neurology, 64,* 104–112.

Couprie, W., Wijdicks, E. F. M., Rooijmans, H. G. M., & van Gijn, J. (1995). Outcome in conversion disorder: A follow-up study. *Journal of Neurology, Neurosurgery and Psychiatry, 58,* 750–752.

Couturier, J. L. (2005). Efficacy of rapid-rate repetitive transcranial magnetic stimulation in the treatment of depression: A systematic review and meta-analysis. *Journal of Psychiatry and Neuroscience, 30,* 83–90.

Cowley, D. S., & Arana, G. W. (1990). The diagnostic utility of lactate sensitivity in panic disorder. *Archives of General Psychiatry, 47,* 277–284.

Coyle, J. T., Price, D. L., DeLong, M. R. (1983). Alzheimer's disease: A disorder of cortical cholinergic innervation. *Science, 219,* 1184–1190.

Crabbe, J. C., Gallaher, E. J., Cross, S. J., & Belknap, J. K. (1998). Genetic determinants of sensitivity to diazepam in inbred mice. *Behavioral Neuroscience, 112,* 668–677.

Craddock, N., O'Donovan, M. C., & Owen, M. J. (2005). The genetics of schizophrenia and bipolar disorder: Dissecting psychosis. *Journal of Medical Genetics, 42,* 193–204.

Craighead, L. W., Craighead, W. E., Kazdin, A. E., & Mahoney, M. J. (1994). Cognitive and behavioral perspectives: An introduction. In L. W. Craighead, W. E. Craighead, A. E. Kazdin, & M. J. Mahoney (Eds.), *Cognitive and behavioral interventions: An empirical approach to mental health problems* (pp. 1–14). Boston: Allyn & Bacon.

Craske, M., & Rowe, M. (1997). A comparison of behavioral and cognitive treatments of phobias. In G. Davey (Ed.), *Phobias: A handbook of theory, research, and treatment* (pp. 247–280). Chichester, UK: Wiley.

Craske, M. G., Glover, D., & DeCola, J. (1995). Predicted versus unpredicted panic attacks: Acute vs. general distress. *Journal of Abnormal Psychology, 104,* 214–223.

Cronk, N. J., Slutske, W. S., Madden, P. A., Bucholz, K. K., & Heath, A. C. (2004). Risk for separation anxiety disorder among girls: Paternal absence, socioeconomic disadvantage, and genetic vulnerability. *Journal of Abnormal Psychology, 113,* 237–247.

Crum, T. A., Teichner, G., Bradley, J. D., & Golden, C. J. (2000). Prediction of WAIS-R indices based on performance on the Luria Nebraska Neuropsychological Battery-III. *International Journal of Neuroscience, 101,* 157–163.

Cruts, M., Rademakers, R., Gijselinck, I., van der Zee, J., Dermaut, B., de Pooter, T., et al. (2005). Genomic architecture of human 17q21 linked to frontotemporal dementia uncovers a highly homologous family of low-copy repeats in the tau region. *Human Molecular Genetics, 14,* 1753–1762.

Csernansky, J. G., Hamstra, J., Wang, L., McKeel, D., Price, J. L., Gado, M., et al. (2004). Correlations between antemortem hippocampal volume and postmortem neuropathology in AD subjects. *Alzheimer Disease and Associated Disorders, 18,* 190–195.

Cummings, J. L. (2004). Alzheimer's disease. *New England Journal of Medicine, 351,* 56–67.

Curtis, C. E., Calkins, M. E., Grove, W. M., Feil, K. J., & Iacono, W. G. (2001). Saccadic disinhibition in patients with acute and remitted schizophrenia and their first-degree biological relatives. *American Journal of Psychiatry, 158,* 100–106.

Curyto, K. J., Johnson, J., TenHave, T., Mossey, J., Knott, K., & Katz, I. R. (2001). Survival of hospitalized elderly patients with delirium: A prospective study. *American Journal of Geriatric Psychiatry, 9,* 141–147.

Custer, R. L. (1982). An overview of compulsive gambling. In S. Kieffer (Ed.), *Addictive disorders update.* New York: Human Sciences Press.

Cutrona, C. E., Russell, D. W., Brown, P. A., Clark, L. A., Hessling, R. M., & Gardner, K. A. (2005). Neighborhood context, personality, and stressful life events as predictors of depression among African American women. *Journal of Abnormal Psychology, 114,* 3–15.

D

Dal Forno, G., Palermo, M. T., Donohue, J. E., Karagiozis, H., Zonderman, A. B., & Kawas, C. H. (2005). Depressive symptoms, sex, and risk for Alzheimer's disease. *Annals of Neurology, 57,* 381–387.

Dalton, K. M., Nacewicz, B. M., Johnstone, T., Schaefer, H. S., Gernsbacher, M. A., Goldsmith, H. H., et al. (2005). Gaze fixation and the neural circuitry of face processing in autism. *Nature Neuroscience, 8,* 519–526.

Dannon, P. N., Lowengrub, K., Sasson, M., Shalgi, B., Tuson, L., Saphir, Y., et al. (2004). Comorbid psychiatric diagnoses in kleptomania and pathological gambling: A preliminary comparison study. *European Psychiatry, 19,* 299–302.

Davidson, J. R. (2001). Pharmacotherapy of generalized anxiety disorder. *Journal of Clinical Psychiatry, 62* (Suppl. 11), 46–50.

Davidson, J. R. T., & Foa, E. B. (1991). Diagnostic issues in post-traumatic stress disorder: Considerations for the *DSM-IV. Journal of Abnormal Psychology, 100,* 346–355.

Davidson, J. R., Stein, D. J., Shalev, A. Y., & Yehuda, R. (2004). Posttraumatic stress disorder: Acquisition, recognition, course, and treatment. *Journal of Neuropsychiatry and Clinical Neuroscience, 16,* 135–147.

Davis, J. M., Chen, N., & Glick, I. D. (2003). A meta-analysis of the efficacy of second-generation antipsychotics. *Archives of General Psychiatry, 60,* 553–564.

Davis, S. F., Pierce, M. C., Yandell, L. R., Arnow, P. S., & Loree, A. (1995). Cheating in college and the Type A personality: A reevaluation. *College Student Journal, 29,* 493–497.

Dawson, G., Webb, S. J., Carver, L., Panagiotides, H., & McPartland, J. (2004). Young children with autism show atypical brain responses to fearful versus neutral facial expressions of emotion. *Developmental Science, 7,* 340–359.

Day, R., & Wong, S. (1996). Anomalous perceptual asymmetries for negative emotional stimuli in the psychopath. *Journal of Abnormal Psychology, 105,* 648–652.

de Jong, P. J., & Merckelbach, H. (2000). Phobia-relevant illusory correlations: The role of phobic responsivity. *Journal of Abnormal Psychology, 109,* 597–601.

Dekker, J., Molenaar, P. J., Kool, S., Van Aalst, G., Peen, J., & de Jonghe, F. (2005). Dose-effect relations in time-limited combined psycho-pharmacological treatment for depression. *Psychological Medicine, 35,* 47–58.

DeLeon, P. H., Vandenbos, G. R., Sammons, M. T., & Frank, R. G. (1998). Changing health care environment in the United States: Steadily evolving into the twenty-first century. In A. N. Weins (Ed.), *Comprehensive clinical psychology: Volume 2: Professional Issues* (pp. 393–409). Oxford, U.K.: Elsevier.

Delgado, P. L. (2000). Depression: The case for a monoamine deficiency. *Journal of Clinical Psychiatry, 61,* 7–11.

Delgado, P. L. (2004). How antidepressants help depression: Mechanisms of action and clinical response. *Journal of Clinical Psychiatry, 65* (Supplement 4), 25–30.

DeLongis, A., Folkman, S., & Lazarus, R. S. (1988). The impact of daily stress on health and mood: Psychological and social resources as mediators. *Journal of Personality and Social Psychology, 54,* 486–495.

Demopulos, C., Fava, M., McLean, N. E., Alpert, J. E., Nierenberg, A. A., & Rosenbaum, J. F. (1996). Hypochondriacal concerns in depressed outpatients. *Psychosomatic Medicine, 58,* 314–320.

DePaulo, J. R., Jr. (2004). Genetics of bipolar disorder: Where do we stand? *American Journal of Psychiatry, 161,* 595–597.

Derogatis, L. R. (1994). *Manual for the Symptom Check List-90 Revised (SCL-90-R).* Minneapolis: National Computer Systems.

DeRubeis, R. J., & Crits-Cristoph, P. (1998). Empirically supported individual and group psychological treatments for adult mental disorders. *Journal of Consulting and Clinical Psychology, 66,* 17–52.

de Silva, P. (1993). Post-traumatic stress disorder: Cross-cultural aspects. *International Review of Psychiatry, 5,* 217–229.

De Sutter, P. (2001). Gender reassignment and assisted reproduction: Present and future reproductive options for transsexual people. *Human Reproduction, 16,* 612–614.

de Waal, M. W., Arnold, I. A., Eekhof, J. A., & van Hemert, A. M. (2004). Somatoform disorders in general practice: Prevalence, functional impairment and comorbidity with anxiety and depressive disorders. *British Journal of Psychiatry, 184,* 470–476.

Dearth, C. S., Berry, D. T., Vickery, C. D., Vagnini, V. L., Baser, R. E., Orey, S. A., et al. (2005). Detection of feigned head injury symptoms on the MMPI-2 in head injured patients and community controls. *Archives of Clinical Neuropsychology, 20,* 95–110.

Deutsch, A. (1949). *The mentally ill in America* (2nd ed.). New York: Columbia University Press.

Devinsky, O., Putnam, F., Grafman, J., Bromfield, E., & Theodore, W. H. (1989). Dissociative states and epilepsy. *Neurology, 39,* 835–840.

Dhillon, A. S., & Dollieslager, L. P. (2000). Rehab rounds: Overcoming barriers to individualized psychosocial rehabilitation in an acute treatment unit of a state hospital. *Psychiatric Services, 51,* 313–317.

Diaferia, G., Bianchi, I., Bianchi, M. L., Cavedini, P., Erzegovesi, S., & Bellodi, L. (1997). Relationship between obsessive-compulsive personality disorder and obsessive-compulsive disorder. *Comprehensive Psychiatry, 38,* 38–42.

Diamond, M., & Sigmundson, H. K. (1997). Sex reassignment at birth: A long-term review and clinical implications. *Archives of Pediatric and Adolescent Medicine, 151,* 298–304.

Dick, C. L., Bland, R. C., & Newman, S. C. (1994). Panic disorder. *Acta Psychiatrica Scandinavica, 89,* 45–53.

Diehl, M., Elnick, A. B., Bourbeau, L. S., & Labouvie-Vief, G. (1998). Adult attachment styles: Their relations to family context and personality. *Journal of Personality and Social Psychology, 74,* 1656–1669.

Diener, E., & Lucas, R. E. (1999). Personality and subjective well-being. In D. Kahneman & E. Diener (Eds.), *Well-being: The foundations of hedonic psychology* (pp. 213–229). New York: Russell Sage Foundation.

DiLalla, D. L., Gottesman, I. I., & Carey, G. (2000). Madness beyond the threshold? Associations between personality and psychopathology. In V. J. Molfese & D. L. Molfese (Eds.), *Temperament and personality development across the life span* (pp. 177–210). Mahwah, NJ: Erlbaum.

Dinardo, P. A., Brown, T. A., & Barlow, D. H. (1994). *Anxiety interview schedule for DSM-IV (DIS-IV).* Albany, NY: Graywind.

Dinnerstein, D. (1976). *The mermaid and the minotaur: Sexual arrangements and human malaise.* New York: Harper.

Dixon, W. A., Heppner, P. P., & Rudd, M. D. (1994). Problem-solving appraisal, hopelessness, and suicide ideation: Evidence for a mediational model. *Journal of Counseling Psychiatry, 41,* 91–98.

Dodson, W. W. (2005). Pharmacotherapy of adult ADHD. *Journal of Clinical Psychology, 61,* 589–606.

Dolan, B. (2004). Medical records: Disclosing confidential clinical information. *Psychiatric Bulletin, 28,* 53–56.

Dougall, A. L., Hyman, K. B., Hayward, M. C., McFeeley, S., & Baum, A. (2001). Optimism and traumatic stress: The importance of social support and coping. *Journal of Applied Social Psychology, 31* (U.S.: Bellwether).

Driessen, M., Herrmann, J., Stahl, K., Zwaan, M., Meier, S., et al. (2000). Magnetic resonance imaging volumes of the hippocampus and the amygdala in women with borderline personality disorder and early traumatization. *Archives of General Psychiatry, 57,* 1115–1122.

Duberstein, P. R., & Conwell, Y. (2000). Suicide. In S. K. Whitbourne (Ed.), *Psychopathology in later life* (pp. 245–275). New York: Wiley.

Dubertret, C., Hanoun, N., Ades, J., Hamon, M., & Gorwood, P. (2004). Family-based association studies between 5-HT5A receptor gene and schizophrenia. *Journal of Psychiatric Research, 38,* 371–376.

Duckworth, A. L., Steen, T. A., & Seligman, M. E. P. (2005). Positive psychology in clinical practice. *Annual Review in Clinical Psychology, 1,* 629–651.

Duncan, S. C., Duncan, T. E., Biglan, A., & Ary, D. V. (1998). Contributions of the social context to the development of adolescent substance use: A multivariate latent growth modeling approach. *Drug and Alcohol Dependence, 50,* 57–71.

Durkheim, E. (1897/1952). *Suicide: A study in sociology* (J. A. Spaulding, C. Simpson, Trans.). London: Routledge & Kegan Paul.

Durst, R., Katz, G., Teitelbaum, A., Zislin, J., & Dannon, P. N. (2001). Kleptomania: Diagnosis and treatment options. *CNS Drugs, 15,* 185–195.

E

Eaton, W. W., Kessler, R. C., Wittchen, H. U., & Magee, W. J. (1994). Panic and panic disorder in the United States. *American Journal of Psychiatry, 151,* 413–420.

Edelstein, B. (2000). Assessment. In S. K. Whitbourne (Ed.), *Psychopathology in later life* (pp. 61–87). New York: Wiley.

Eisen, J. L., Phillips, K. A., Coles, M. E., & Rasmussen, S. A. (2004). Insight in obsessive compulsive disorder and body dysmorphic disorder. *Comprehensive Psychiatry, 45,* 10–15.

Eisler, I., Dare, C., Russell, G. F., Szmukler, G., le Grange, D., & Dodge, E. (1997). Family and individual therapy in anorexia nervosa. A 5-year follow-up. *Archives of General Psychiatry, 54,* 1025–1030.

Ekselius, L., Tillfors, M., Furmark, T., & Fredrikson, M. (2001). Personality disorders in the general population: DSM-IV and ICD-10 defined prevalence as related to sociodemographic profile. *Personality and Individual Differences, 30,* 467–471.

Elhwuegi, A. S. (2004). Central monoamines and their role in major depression. *Progress in Neuropsychopharmacology and Biological Psychiatry, 28,* 435–451.

El-khatib, H. E., & Dickey, T. O. (1995). Sertraline for body dysmorphic disorder. *Journal of the American Academy of Child and Adolescent Psychiatry, 34,* 1404–1405.

Ellason, J. W., & Ross, C. A. (1997). Two-year follow-up of inpatients with dissociative identity disorder. *American Journal of Psychiatry, 154,* 832–839.

Ellason, J. W., Ross, C. A., & Fuchs, D. L. (1996). Lifetime Axis I and II comorbidity and childhood trauma history in dissociative identity disorder. *Psychiatry: Interpersonal & Biological Processes, 59,* 255–266.

Elliott, R. (2001). Contemporary brief experiential psychotherapy. *Clinical Psychology Science and Practice, 8,* 38–51.

Elvevag, B., Weinberger, D. R., Suter, J. C., & Goldberg, T. E. (2000). Continuous performance test and schizophrenia: A test of stimulus-response compatibility, working memory, response readiness, or none of the above? *American Journal of Psychiatry, 157,* 772–780.

Emde, R. N., Gaensbauer, R. J., & Harmon, R. J. (1976). *Emotional expressions in infancy: A biobehavioral study.* New York: International Universities Press.

Emmelkamp, P. M. G. (1982). *Phobic and obsessive-compulsive disorders.* New York: Plenum Press.

Enserink, M. (1998). First Alzheimer's disease confirmed. *Science, 279,* 2037.

Ensink, K., Robertson, B. A., Zissis, C., & Leger, P. (1997). Post-traumatic stress disorder in children exposed to violence. *South African Medical Journal, 87,* 1526–1530.

Erikson, E. H. (1963). *Childhood and society* (2nd ed.). New York: Norton.

Etherton, J. L., Bianchini, K. J., Greve, K. W., & Ciota, M. A. (2005). Test of Memory Malingering Performance is unaffected by laboratory-induced pain: Implications for clinical use. *Archives of Clinical Neuropsychology, 20,* 375–384.

Evans, D. L., Leserman, J., Perkins, D. O., Stern, R. A., Murphy, C., et al. (1997). Severe life stress as a predictor of early disease progression in HIV infection. *American Journal of Psychiatry, 154,* 630–634.

Eysenck, H. J. (1967). *The biological basis of personality.* Springfield, IL: Charles C. Thomas Press.

F

Fagelman, E., Fagelman, A., & Shabsigh, R. (2001). Efficacy, safety, and use of sildenafil in urologic practice. *Urology, 57,* 1141–1144.

Fairburn, C. G. (1997). Eating disorders. In D. M. Clark & C. G. Fairburn (Eds.), *The science and practice of cognitive behaviour therapy.* Oxford, U.K.: Oxford University Press.

Fairburn, C. G., Agras, W. S., Walsh, B. T., Wilson, G. T., & Stice, E. (2004). Prediction of outcome in bulimia nervosa by early change in treatment. *American Journal of Psychiatry, 161,* 2322–2324.

Fairburn, C. G., Stice, E., Cooper, Z., Doll, H. A., Norman, P. A., & O'Connor, M. E. Understanding persistence in bulimia nervosa: a 5-year naturalistic study. *Journal of Consulting and Clinical Psychology, 71,* 103–109.

Fallon, B. A. (2004). Pharmacotherapy of somatoform disorders. *Journal of Psychosomatic Research, 56,* 455–460.

Falsetti, S. A., & Davis, J. (2001). The non-pharmacologic treatment of generalized anxiety disorder. *Psychiatric Clinics of North America, 24,* 99–117.

Faraone, S. V., Glatt, S. J., Su, J., & Tsuang, M. T. (2004). Three potential susceptibility loci shown by a genome-wide scan for regions influencing the age at onset of mania. *American Journal of Psychiatry, 161,* 625–630.

Faravelli, C., Giugni, A., Salvatori, S., & Ricca, V. (2004). Psychopathology after rape. *American Journal of Psychiatry, 161,* 1483–1485.

Farber, I. E. (1975). Sane and insane constructions and misconstructions. *Journal of Abnormal Psychology, 84,* 589–620.

Federal Bureau of Investigation (2004). *Age-specific arrest rates and race-specific arrest rates for selected offenses 1993–2001: Uniform crime reports.* Washington, DC: Federal Bureau of Investigation.

Fedoroff, I. C., & Taylor, S. (2001). Psychological and pharmacological treatments of social phobia: A meta-analysis. *Journal of Clinical Psychopharmacology, 21,* 311–324.

Ferguson, J. M. (2001). The effects of antidepressants on sexual functioning in depressed patients: A review. *Journal of Clinical Psychiatry, 62,* 22–34.

Figgitt, D. P., & McClellan, K. J. (2000). Fluvoxamine: An updated review of its use in the management of adults with anxiety disorders. *Drugs, 60,* 925–954.

Figueroa, E., & Silk, K. R. (1997). Biological implications of childhood sexual abuse in borderline personality disorder. *Journal of Personality Disorders, 11,* 71–92.

Figueroa, R. A., & Sassenrath, J. M. (1989). A longitudinal study of the predictive validity of the System of Multicultural Assessment (SOMPA). *Psychology in the Schools, 26,* 5–19.

Fine, C. G. (1996). A cognitively based treatment model for DSM-IV dissociative identity disorder. In L. K. Michelson & W. J. Ray (Eds.), *Handbook of dissociation: Theoretical, empirical, and clinical perspectives* (pp. 401–411). New York: Plenum Press.

Fink, P., Ornbol, E., Toft, T., Sparle, K. C., Frostholm, L., & Olesen, F. (2004). A new, empirically established hypochondriasis diagnosis. *American Journal of Psychiatry, 161,* 1680–1691.

Finn, P. R., Sharkansky, E. J., Brandt, K. M., & Turcotte, N. (2000). The effects of familial risk, personality, and expectancies on alcohol use and abuse. *Journal of Abnormal Psychology, 109,* 122–133.

Firestone, P., Bradford, J. M., Greenberg, D. M., & Nunes, K. L. (2000). Differentiation of homicidal child molesters, nonhomicidal child molesters, and nonoffenders by phallometry. *American Journal of Psychiatry, 157,* 1847–1850.

First, M. B., Gibbon, M., Spitzer, R. L., & Williams, J. B. W. (1997). *Structured Clinical Interview for DSM-IV Axis II Personality Disorders (SCID-II).* Washington, DC: America Psychiatric Association.

First, M. B., Pincus, H. A., Levine, J. B., Williams, J. B., Ustun, B., & Peele, R. (2004). Clinical utility as a criterion for revising psychiatric diagnoses. *American Journal of Psychiatry, 161,* 946–954.

First, M. B., Spitzer, R. L., Gibbon, M., & Williams, J. B. W. (1997). *SCID-I/P (for DSM-IV) patient edition structured clinical interview for DSM-IV Axis I disorders, research version, patient/non-patient edition.* New York: Biometrics Research, New York State Psychiatric Institute.

First, M. B., Spitzer, R. L., Gibbon, M., & Williams, J. B. W. (2002). *Structured clinical interview for DSM-IV-TR Axis I disorders (SCID-I).* New York: Biometrics Research, New York State Psychiatric Institute.

Firstman, R., & Talan, J. (1997). *The death of innocents.* New York: Bantam.

Fishman, D. B. (1999). *The case for pragmatic psychology.* New York: NYU Press.

Fishman, D. B. (2001). From single case to database: A new method for enhancing psychotherapy, forensic, and other psychological practice. *Applied and Preventive Psychology, 10,* 275–304.

Fishman, D. B., & Messer, S. B. (2004). Case-based studies as a source of unity in applied psychology. In R. J. Sternberg (Ed.), *The unification of psychology: Prospect or pipedream?* Washington, DC: American Psychological Association.

Fitts, S. N., Gibson, P., Redding, C. A., & Deiter, P. J. (1989). Body dysmorphic disorder: Implications for its validity as a DSM-III-R clinical syndrome. *Psychological Reports, 64,* 655–658.

Flakierska-Praquin, N., Lindstrom, M., & Gillberg, C. (1997). School phobia with separation anxiety disorder: A comparative 20- to 29-year follow-up study of 35 school refusers. *Comprehensive Psychiatry, 38,* 17–22.

Foa, E. B., Liebowitz, M. R., Kozak, M. J., Davies, S., Campeas, R., Franklin, M. E., et al. (2005). Randomized, placebo-controlled trial of exposure and ritual prevention, clomipramine, and their combination in the treatment of obsessive-compulsive disorder. *American Journal of Psychiatry, 162,* 151–161.

Foa, E. B., Steketee, G., & Rothbaum, B. O. (1989). Behavioral/cognitive conceptualizations of post-traumatic stress disorder. *Behavior Therapy, 20,* 155–176.

Foa, E. B., Steketee, G. S., & Ozarow, B. J. (1985). Behavior therapy with obsessive-compulsives: From theory to treatment. In M. Mavissakalian, S. M. Turner, & L. Michelson (Eds.), *Obsessive-compulsive disorder: Psychological and pharmacological treatment* (pp. 49–129). New York: Plenum Press.

Foley, D. L., Pickles, A., Maes, H. M., Silberg, J. L., & Eaves, L. J. (2004). Course and short-term outcomes of separation anxiety disorder in a community sample of twins. *Journal of the American Academy of Child & Adolescent Psychiatry, 43,* 1107–1114.

Folkman, S., Lazarus, R. S., Gruen, R. J., & DeLongis, A. (1986). Appraisal, coping, health status, and psychological symptoms. *Journal of Personality and Social Psychology, 50,* 571–579.

Folks, D. G., & Warnock, J. K. (2001). Psychocutaneous disorders. *Current Psychiatry Reports, 3,* 219–225.

Folstein, M. F., & Folstein, S. E. (2000). Chapter 38. Mental Status Examination. In M. H. Beers & R. Berkow (Eds.), *The Merck Manual of Geriatrics.* Whitehouse Station, NJ: Merck.

Folstein, M. F., Folstein, S. E., & McHugh, P. R. (1975). Mini-Mental State: A practical method for grading the cognitive state of patients for the clinician. *Journal of Psychiatric Research, 12,* 189–198.

Fombonne, E., Wostear, G., Cooper, V., Harrington, R., & Rutter, M. (2001). The Maudsley long-term follow-up of child and adolescent depression: 1. Psychiatric outcomes in adulthood. *British Journal of Psychiatry, 179,* 210–217.

Fossati, A., Maffei, C., Battaglia, M., Bagnato, M., Donati, D., et al. (2001). Latent class analysis of DSM-IV schizotypal personality disorder criteria in psychiatric patients. *Schizophrenia Bulletin, 27,* 59–71.

Foster, P. S., & Eisler, R. M. (2001). An integrative approach to the treatment of obsessive-compulsive disorder. *Comprehensive Psychiatry, 42,* 24–31.

Frankel, F. H. (1996). Dissociation: The clinical realities. *American Journal of Psychiatry, 153,* 64–70.

Frankl, V. (1963). *Man's search for meaning.* New York: Simon & Schuster.

Franklin, M. E., Abramowitz, J. S., Kozak, M. J., Levitt, J. T., & Foa, E. B. (2000). Effectiveness of exposure and ritual prevention for obsessive-compulsive disorder: Randomized compared with nonrandomized samples. *Journal of Consulting and Clinical Psychology, 68,* 594–602.

Franko, D. L., Keel, P. K., Dorer, D. J., Blais, M. A., Delinsky, S. S., Eddy, K. T., et al. (2004). What predicts suicide attempts in women with eating disorders? *Psychological Medicine, 34,* 843–853.

Frederick, R. I. (1998). *Validity indicator profile.* Minnetonka, MN: National Computer System.

Fredrikson, M., Annas, P., & Wik, G. (1997). Parental history, aversive exposure and the development of snake and spider phobia in women. *Behaviour Research and Therapy, 35,* 23–28.

Freeman, A., Pretzer, J., Fleming, B., & Simon, K. M. (1990). *Clinical applications of cognitive therapy.* New York: Plenum Press.

Freud, S. (1900). The interpretation of dreams. In J. Strachey (Ed.), *The standard*

edition of the complete psychological works of Sigmund Freud* (Vols. 4 and 5). London: Hogarth.

Freud, S. (1905). Three essays on the theory of sexuality. In J. Strachey (Ed.), *The standard edition of the complete psychological works of Sigmund Freud* (Vol. 7). London: Hogarth.

Freud, S. (1911). Formulations of the two principles of mental functioning. In J. Strachey (Ed.), *The standard edition of the complete psychological works of Sigmund Freud* (Vol. 12). London: Hogarth.

Freud, S. (1913). Totem and taboo. In J. Strachey (Ed.), *The standard edition of the complete psychological works of Sigmund Freud* (Vol. 13). London: Hogarth.

Freud, S. (1913–14/1963). Further recommendations in the technique of psychoanalysis. In S. Freud (Ed.), *Therapy and technique.* New York: Collier.

Freud, S. (1917). Mourning and melancholia. In J. Strachey (Ed.), *The standard edition of the complete psychological works of Sigmund Freud* (Vol. 14, pp. 151–169). London: Hogarth.

Freud, S. (1923). The ego and the id. In J. Strachey (Ed.), *The standard edition of the complete psychological works of Sigmund Freud* (Vol. 19). London: Hogarth.

Freud, S. (1925). An autobiographical study. In J. Strachey (Ed.), *The standard edition of the complete psychological works of Sigmund Freud* (Vol. 20). London: Hogarth.

Freund, K., Watson, R., & Dickey, R. (1990). Does sexual abuse in childhood cause pedophilia? An exploratory study. *Archives of Sexual Behavior, 19,* 557–568.

Fricchione, G. (2004). Clinical practice: Generalized anxiety disorder. *New England Journal of Medicine, 351,* 675–682.

Friedman, M. J. (2004). Acknowledging the psychiatric cost of war. *New England Journal of Medicine, 351,* 75–77.

Friedman, M., Breall, W. S., Goodwin, M. L., Sparagon, B. J., Ghandour, G., & Fleischmann, N. (1996). Effect of Type A behavioral counseling on frequency of episodes of silent myocardial ischemia in coronary patients. *American Heart Journal, 132,* 933–937.

Frost, R. O., Krause, M. S., & Steketee, G. (1996). Hoarding and obsessive-compulsive symptoms. *Behavior Modification, 20,* 116–132.

Fudala, P. J., Bridge, T. P., Herbert, S., Williford, W. O., Chiang, C. N., Jones, K., et al. (2003). Office-based treatment of opiate addiction with a sublingual-tablet formulation of buprenorphine and naloxone. *New England Journal of Medicine, 349,* 949–958.

Fulton, M., & Winokur, G. (1993). A comparative study of paranoid and schizoid personality disorder. *American Journal of Psychiatry, 150,* 1363–1367.

Furmark, T., Tillfors, M., Garpenstrand, H., Marteinsdottir, I., Langstrom, B., Oreland, L., et al. (2004). Serotonin transporter polymor-

phism related to amygdala excitability and symptom severity in patients with social phobia. *Neuroscience Letters, 362,* 189–192.

G

Gacono, C. B., Meloy, J. R., & Bridges, M. R. (2000). A Rorschach comparison of psychopaths, sexual homicide perpetrators, and nonviolent pedophiles: Where angels fear to tread. *Journal of Clinical Psychology, 56,* 757–777.

Gagné, G. G. J., Furman, M. J., Carpenter, L. L., & Price, L. H. (2000). Efficacy of continuation ECT and antidepressant drugs compared to long-term antidepressants alone in depressed patients. *American Journal of Psychiatry, 157,* 1960–1965.

Gallacher, J. E., Sweetnam, P. M., Yarnell, J. W., Elwood, P. C., & Stansfeld, S. A. (2003). Is type A behavior really a trigger for coronary heart disease events? *Psychosomatic Medicine, 65,* 339–346.

Galovski, T. E., & Blanchard, E. B. (2002). The effectiveness of a brief psychological intervention on court-referred and self-referred aggressive drivers. *Behaviour Research & Therapy, 40,* 1385–1402.

Galovski, T. E., & Blanchard, E. B. (2004). Road rage: A domain for psychological intervention? *Aggression and Violent Behavior, 9,* 105–127.

Ganguli, M., Dodge, H. H., Shen, C., Pandav, R. S., & DeKosky, S. T. (2005). Alzheimer's disease and mortality: A 15-year epidemiological study. *Archives of Neurology, 62,* 779–784.

Garb, H. N. (2005). Clinical judgment and decision making. *Annual Review in Clinical Psychology, 1,* 67–89.

Garbutt, J. C., Kranzler, H. R., O'Malley, S. S., Gastfriend, D. R., Pettinati, H. M., Silverman, B. L., et al. (2005). Efficacy and tolerability of long-acting injectable naltrexone for alcohol dependence: A randomized controlled trial. *Journal of the American Medical Association, 293,* 1617–1625.

Garlow, S. J., Purselle, D., & Heninger, M. (2005). Ethnic differences in patterns of suicide across the life cycle. *American Journal of Psychiatry, 162,* 319–323.

Garner, D. M., Olmsted, M. P., & Bohr, Y. (1982). The Eating Attitudes Test: Psychometric features and clinical correlates. *Psychological Medicine, 12,* 871–878.

Garrels, L., Kockott, G., Michael, N., Preuss, W., Renter, K., Schmidt, G., Sigusch, V., & Windgassen, K. (2000). Sex ratio of transsexuals in Germany: The development over three decades. *Acta Psychiatrica Scandinavica, 102,* 445–448.

Gavett, B. E., O'Bryant, S. E., Fisher, J. M., & McCaffrey, R. J. (2005). Hit rates of adequate performance based on the Test of Memory Malingering (TOMM) Trial 1. *Applied Neuropsychology, 12,* 1–4.

Gay, P. (1988). *Freud: A life for our time.* New York: Norton.

Gelernter, J., Page, G. P., Stein, M. B., & Woods, S. W. (2004). Genome-wide linkage scan for loci predisposing to social phobia: Evidence for a chromosome 16 risk locus. *American Journal of Psychiatry, 161,* 59–66.

Geller, D., Biederman, J., Jones, J., Park, K., Schwartz, S., Shapiro, S., & Coffey, B. (1998). Is juvenile obsessive-compulsive disorder a developmental subtype of the disorder? A review of the pediatric literature. *Journal of the American Academy of Child & Adolescent Psychiatry, 37,* 420–427.

Gentry, W. D. (1984). *Handbook of behavioral medicine.* New York: Guilford Press.

Gibbons, R. D., Hur, K., Bhaumik, D. K., & Mann, J. J. (2005). The relationship between antidepressant medication use and rate of suicide. *Archives of General Psychiatry, 62,* 165–172.

Gilman, S., Koeppe, R. A., Little, R., An, H., Junck, L., Giordani, B., et al. (2005). Differentiation of Alzheimer's disease from dementia with Lewy bodies utilizing positron emission tomography with [18F]fluoro-deoxyglucose and neuropsychological testing. *Experimental Neurology, 191 (Suppl. 1),* S95–S103.

Gilroy, L. J., Kirkby, K. C., Daniels, B. A., Menzies, R. G., & Montgomery, I. M. (2000). Controlled comparison of computer-aided vicarious exposure versus live exposure in the treatment of spider phobia. *Behavior Therapy, 31* (U.S.: Association for the Advancement of Behavior Therapy).

Glassman, J. N. S., Magulac, M., & Darko, D. F. (1987). Folie à famille: Shared paranoid disorder in a Vietnam veteran and his family. *American Journal of Psychiatry, 144,* 658–660.

Gleaves, D. H., Smith, S. M., Butler, L. D., & Spiegel, D. (2004). False and recovered memories in the laboratory and clinic: A review of experimental and clinical evidence. *Clinical Psychology: Science & Practice, 11,* 3–28.

Glynn, S. M. (1992). If Dahmer's not crazy, who is? *National Law Journal, 14,* 13–25.

Goddard, A. W., Mason, G. F., Appel, M., Rothman, D. L., Gueorguieva, R., Behar, K. L., & Krystal. (2004). Impaired GABA neuronal response to acute benzodiazepine administration in panic disorder. *American Journal of Psychiatry, 161,* 2186–2193.

Goethals, I., Audenaert, K., Jacobs, F., Van den Eynde, F., Bernagie, K., Kolindou, A., et al. (2005). Brain perfusion SPECT in impulsivity-related personality disorders. *Behavioural Brain Research, 157,* 187–192.

Goin, M. K. (2001). Borderline personality disorder: The importance of establishing a treatment framework. *Psychiatric Services, 52,* 167–168.

Goisman, R. M., Warshaw, M. G., Peterson, L. G., Rogers, M. P., Cuneo, P., et al. (1994). Panic, agoraphobia, and panic disorder with agoraphobia: Data from a multicenter anxiety disorders study. *Journal of Nervous and Mental Disease, 182,* 72–79.

Gojer, J., & Berman, T. (2000). Postpartum depression and factitious disorder: A new presentation. *International Journal of Psychiatry in Medicine, 30,* 287–293.

Goldberg, J. F., Harrow, M., & Grossman, L. S. (1995). Course and outcome in bipolar affective disorder: A longitudinal follow-up study. *American Journal of Psychiatry, 152,* 379–384.

Golden, C. J., Purisch, A. D., & Hammeke, T. A. (1985). *Luria-Nebraska neuropsychological battery: Forms I and II.* Los Angeles: Western Psychological Corporation.

Golden, R. N., Gaynes, B. N., Ekstrom, R. D., Hamer, R. M., Jacobsen, F. M., Suppes, T., et al. (2005). The efficacy of light therapy in the treatment of mood disorders: A review and meta-analysis of the evidence. *American Journal of Psychiatry, 162,* 656–662.

Goldfried, M. R., & Norcross, J. C. (1995). Integrative and eclectic therapies in historical perspective. In B. Bongar & L. E. Beutler (Eds.), *Comprehensive textbook of psychotherapy: Theory and practice* (pp. 254–273). New York: Oxford University Press.

Goldman, S. J., D'Angelo, E. J., & DeMaso, D. R. (1993). Psychopathology in the families of children and adolescents with borderline personality disorder. *American Journal of Psychiatry, 150,* 1832–1835.

Goldstein, I. (2000). Female sexual arousal disorder: New insights. *International Journal of Impotence Research, 12* (Suppl. 4), S152–157.

Golomb, M., Fava, M., Abraham, M., & Rosenbaum, J. F. (1995). Gender differences in personality disorders. *American Journal of Psychiatry, 152,* 579–582.

Goodman, W. K., Price, L. H., Rasmussen, S. A., Mazure, C., Delgado, P., Heninger, G. R., & Charney, D. S. (1989a). The Yale-Brown Obsessive Compulsive Scale. II. Validity. *Archives of General Psychiatry, 46,* 1012–1016.

Goodman, W. K., Price, L. H., Rasmussen, S. A., Mazure, C., Fleischmann, R. L., Hill, C. L., Heninger, G. R., & Charney, D. S. (1989b). The Yale-Brown Obsessive Compulsive Scale. I. Development, use, and reliability. *Archives of General Psychiatry, 46,* 1006–1011.

Goodwin, R. D., Fergusson, D. M., & Horwood, L. J. (2004). Panic attacks and psychoticism. *American Journal of Psychiatry, 161,* 88–92.

Gordon, H. L., Baird, A. A., & End, A. (2004). Functional differences among those high and low on a trait measure of psychopathy. *Biological Psychiatry, 56,* 516–521.

Gordon, L. J., III, Fargason, P. J., & Kramer, J. J. (1995). Sexual behaviors of patients in a residential chemical dependency program: Comparison of sexually compulsive physicians and nonphysicians with non-sexually compulsive physicians and nonphysicians. *Sexual Addiction and Compulsivity, 2,* 233–255.

Gottesman, I. I. (1991). *Schizophrenia genesis: The origins of madness.* New York: Freeman.

Gottesman, I. I., & Gould, T. D. (2003). The endophenotype concept in psychiatry: Etymology and strategic intentions. *American Journal of Psychiatry, 160,* 636–645.

Goudriaan, A. E., Oosterlaan, J., de Beurs, E., & Van den Brink, W. (2004). Pathological gambling: A comprehensive review of biobehavioral findings. *Neuroscience and Biobehavioral Review, 28,* 123–141.

Gould, M. S., Greenberg, T., Velting, D. M., & Shaffer, D. (2003). Youth suicide risk and preventive interventions: A review of the past 10 years. *Journal of the American Academy of Child and Adolescent Psychiatry, 42,* 386–405.

Gould, M. S., Marrocco, F. A., Kleinman, M., Thomas, J. G., Mostkoff, K., Cote, J., et al. (2005). Evaluating iatrogenic risk of youth suicide screening programs: A randomized controlled trial. *Journal of the American Medical Association, 293,* 1635–1643.

Gould, M. S., Velting, D., Kleinman, M., Lucas, C., Thomas, J. G., & Chung, M. (2004). Teenagers' attitudes about coping strategies and help-seeking behavior for suicidality. *Journal of the American Academy of Child and Adolescent Psychiatry, 43,* 1124–1133.

Graae, F., Milner, J., Rizzotto, L., & Klein, R. G. (1994). Clonazepam in childhood anxiety disorder. *Journal of the American Academy of Child and Adolescent Psychiatry, 33,* 372–376.

Graber, J., & Arndt, W. B. (1993). Trichotillomania. *Comprehensive Psychiatry, 34,* 340–346.

Grammer, K. (1996). *So Far. . . .* New York: Penguin Books.

Granillo, T., Jones-Rodriguez, G., & Carvajal, S. C. (2005). Prevalence of eating disorders in Latina adolescents: Associations with substance use and other correlates. *Journal of Adolescent Health, 36,* 214–220.

Grant, B. F., Hasin, D. S., Stinson, F. S., Dawson, D. A., Patricia Chou, S., June Ruan, W., et al. (2005). Co-occurrence of 12-month mood and anxiety disorders and personality disorders in the US: Results from the national epidemiologic survey on alcohol and related conditions. *Journal of Psychiatric Research, 39,* 1–9.

Grant, B. F., Stinson, F. S., Dawson, D. A., Chou, S. P., Dufour, M. C., Compton, W., et al. (2004). Prevalence and co-occurrence of substance use disorders and independent mood and anxiety disorders: Results from the National Epidemiologic Survey on Alcohol and Related Conditions. *Archives of General Psychiatry, 61,* 807–816.

Grant, B. F., Stinson, F. S., Dawson, D. A., Chou, S. P., Ruan, W. J., & Pickering, R. P. (2004). Co-occurrence of 12-month alcohol and drug use disorders and personality disorders in the United States: Results from the National Epidemiologic Survey on Alcohol and Related Conditions. *Archives of General Psychiatry, 61,* 361–368.

Grant, J. E., Menard, W., Pagano, M. E., Fay, C., & Phillips, K. A. (2005). Substance use disorders in individuals with body dysmorphic disorder. *Journal of Clinical Psychiatry, 66,* 309–316.

Greaves, G. B. (1980). Multiple personality: 165 years after Mary Reynolds. *Journal of Nervous and Mental Disease, 168,* 577–596.

Green, B. L., Grace, M. C., Lindy, J. D., Gleser, G. C., & Leonard, A. (1990). Risk factors for PTSD and other diagnoses in a general sample of Vietnam veterans. *American Journal of Psychiatry, 147,* 729–733.

Green, R. (2000). Birth order and ratio of brothers to sisters in transsexuals. *Psychological Medicine, 30,* 789–795.

Greenberg, J. R., & Mitchell, S. A. (1983). *Object relations in psychoanalytic theory.* Cambridge, MA: Harvard University Press.

Grenyer, B. F., & Luborsky, L. (1996). Dynamic change in psychotherapy: Mastery of interpersonal conflicts. *Journal of Consulting and Clinical Psychology, 64,* 411–416.

Grisel, J. E., Belknap, J. K., O'Toole, L. A., Helms, M. L., Wenger, C. D., & Crabbe, J. C. (1997). Quantitative trait loci affecting methamphetamine responses in BXD recombinant inbred mouse strains. *Journal of Neuroscience, 17,* 745–754.

Grootens, K. P., & Verkes, R. J. (2005). Emerging evidence for the use of atypical antipsychotics in borderline personality disorder. *Pharmacopsychiatry, 38,* 20–23.

Gross, C. G. (1999). 'Psychosurgery' in renaissance art. *Trends in Neurosciences, 22,* 429–431.

Gunderson, J. G. (1984). *Borderline personality disorders.* Washington, DC: American Psychiatric Press.

Gunderson, J. G. (1989). Borderline personality disorders. In American Psychiatric Association Task Force on Treatments of Psychiatric Disorders (Eds.), *Treatments of psychiatric disorders* (Vol. 3, pp. 2749–2759). Washington, DC: American Psychiatric Association.

Gunnell, D., Magnusson, P. K., & Rasmussen, F. (2005). Low intelligence test scores in 18 year old men and risk of suicide: Cohort study. *British Medical Journal, 330,* 167.

Gunstad, J., & Phillips, K. A. (2003). Axis I comorbidity in body dysmorphic disorder. *Comprehensive Psychiatry, 44,* 270–276.

Gureje, O., Ustun, T. B., & Simon, G. E. (1997). The syndrome of hypochondriasis: A cross-national study in primary care. *Psychological Medicine, 27,* 1001–1010.

Gurman, A. S. (2001). Brief therapy and family/couple therapy: An essential redundancy. *Clinical Psychology Science and Practice, 8,* 51–65.

Gurvits, I. G., Koenigsberg, H. W., & Siever, L. J. (2000). Neurotransmitter dysfunction

in patients with borderline personality disorder. *Psychiatric Clinics of North America, 23.*

Gushurst, C. A. (2003). Child abuse: Behavioral aspects and other associated problems. *Pediatric Clinics of North America, 50,* 919–938.

Gustafson, D., Rothenberg, E., Blennow, K., Steen, B., & Skoog, I. (2003). An 18-year follow-up of overweight and risk of Alzheimer disease. *Archives of Internal Medicine, 163,* 1524–1528.

Gutheil, T. G., & Appelbaum, P. S. (1982). *Clinical handbook of psychiatry and the law.* New York: McGraw-Hill.

Guthrie, R. M., & Bryant, R. A. (2005). Auditory startle response in firefighters before and after trauma exposure. *American Journal of Psychiatry, 162,* 283–290.

Guziec, J., Lazarus, A., & Harding, J. J. (1994). Case of a 29-year-old nurse with factitious disorder: The utility of psychiatric intervention on a general medical floor. *General Hospital Psychiatry, 16,* 47–53.

H

Haenen, M. A., Schmidt, A. J. M., Kroeze, S., & van den Hout, M. A. (1996). Hypochondriasis and symptom reporting—The effect of attention versus distraction. *Psychotherapy and Psychosomatics, 65,* 43–48.

Hall, G. C. N., Shondrick, D. D., & Hirschman, R. (1993). Conceptually derived treatments for sexual aggressors. *Professional Psychology: Research and Practice, 24,* 2–69.

Hallowell, E. M. (1994). *Driven to Distraction.* New York: Pantheon Books.

Hallowell, E. M. (2001). *Human moments: how to find meaning and love in your everyday life.* Deerfield Beach, FL: Health Communications, Inc.

Halpern, J. H., Pope, H. G., Jr., Sherwood, A. R., Barry, S., Hudson, J. I., & Yurgelun-Todd, D. (2004). Residual neuropsychological effects of illicit 3,4-methylenedioxymethamphetamine (MDMA) in individuals with minimal exposure to other drugs. *Drug and Alcohol Dependence, 75,* 135–147.

Halstead, W. C. (1947). *Brain and intelligence: A quantitative study of the frontal lobes.* Chicago: University of Chicago Press.

Hammen, C. (2005). Stress and depression. *Annual Review in Clinical Psychology, 1,* 293–319.

Hankin, J. R. (1994). FAS prevention strategies: Passive and active measures. *Alcohol Health and Research World, 18,* 62–66.

Hanna, G. L. (1997). Trichotillomania and related disorders in children and adolescents. *Child Psychiatry and Human Development, 27,* 255–268.

Hanson, M., MacKay-Soroka, S., Staley, S., & Poulton, L. (1994). Delinquent firesetters: A comparative study of delinquency and fireset-

ting histories. *Canadian Journal of Psychiatry, 39,* 230–232.

Happe, F., Ehlers, S., Fletcher, P., Frith, U., Johansson, M., Gillberg, C., Dolan, R., Frackowiak, R., & Frith, C. (1996). "Theory of mind" in the brain. Evidence from a PET scan study of Asperger syndrome. *Neuroreport, 8,* 197–201.

Hardy, J., & Gwinn-Hardy, K. (1998). Genetic classification of primary neurodegenerative disease. *Science, 282,* 1075–1083.

Hare, R. D. (1993). *Without conscience: The disturbing world of the psychopaths among us.* New York: Simon & Schuster.

Hare, R. D. (1997). *Hare Psychopathy Checklist-Revised (PCL-R).* Odessa, FL: Personality Assessment Resources.

Hare, R. D., & Neumann, C. S. (2005). Structural models of psychopathy. *Current Psychiatry Reports, 7,* 57–64.

Harpur, T. J., & Hare, R. D. (1994). Assessment of psychopathy as a function of age. *Journal of Abnormal Psychology, 103,* 604–609.

Harris, D. L., & Carr, A. T. (2001). Prevalence of concern about physical appearance in the general population. *British Journal of Plastic Surgery, 54,* 223–226.

Hatfield, E., & Rapson, R. (1994). Love and attachment processes. In M. Lewis & J. M. Haviland (Eds.), *Handbook of emotions* (pp. 595–604). New York: Guilford Press.

Hathaway, S. R., & McKinley, J. C. (1989). *The Minnesota Multiphasic Personality Inventory-2.* Minneapolis: University of Minnesota Press.

Hattori, M., Fujiyama, A., Taylor, T. D., Watanabe, H., et al. (2000). The DNA sequence of human chromosome 21. *Nature, 405,* 311–319.

Haugland, B. S. M. (2005). Recurrent disruptions of rituals and routines in families with paternal alcohol abuse. *Family Relations, 54,* 225–241.

Haugland, G., Siegel, C., Hopper, K., & Alexander, M. J. (1997). Mental illness among homeless individuals in a suburban county. *Psychiatric Services, 48,* 504–509.

Haywood, T. W., Kravitz, H. M., Wasyliw, O. E., Goldberg, J., & Cavanaugh, J. L., Jr. (1996). Cycle of abuse and psychopathology in cleric and noncleric molesters of children and adolescents. *Child Abuse and Neglect, 20,* 1233–1243.

Hazan, C., & Shaver, P. (1987). Romantic love conceptualized as an attachment process. *Journal of Personality and Social Psychology, 52,* 511–524.

Hazan, C., & Shaver, P. R. (1994). Attachment as an organizational framework for research on close relationships. *Psychological Inquiry, 5,* 1–22.

Heard, H. L., & Linehan, M. M. (1994). Dialectical behavior therapy: An integrative approach to the treatment of borderline personality disorder. *Journal of Psychotherapy Integration, 4,* 55–82.

Heatherton, T. F., Mahamedi, F., Striepe, M., Field, A. E., & Keel, P. (1997). A 10-year longitudinal study of body weight, dieting, and eating disorder symptoms. *Journal of Abnormal Psychology, 106,* 117–125.

Heebink, D. M., & Halmi, K. A. (1994). Eating disorders. In J. M. Oldham & M. B. Riba (Eds.), *Review of psychiatry* (pp. 227–252). Washington, DC: American Psychiatric Press.

Heiman, J. R., & LoPiccolo, J. (1988). *Becoming orgasmic: A sexual and personal growth program for women.* New York: Prentice Hall.

Heimann, S. W. (1997). SSRI for body dysmorphic disorder. *Journal of the American Academy of Child and Adolescent Psychiatry, 36,* 868.

Heimberg, R. G. (2001). Current status of psychotherapeutic interventions for social phobia. *Journal of Clinical Psychiatry, 62* (Suppl. 1), 36–42.

Heimberg, R. G., & Barlow, D. H. (1988). Psychosocial treatments for social phobia. *Psychosomatics, 29,* 27–37.

Heinrichs, R. W. (2005). The primacy of cognition in schizophrenia. *American Psychologist, 60,* 229–242.

Heldring, M. (1998). Fighting for health care on the hill: A tale of a senator, a psychologist, and the American people. *Professional Psychology: Research and Practice, 29,* 3–4.

Helzer, J. E., Burnam, A., & McEvoy, L. T. (1991). Alcohol abuse and dependence. In L. N. Robins & D. A. Regier (Eds.), *Psychiatric disorders in America* (pp. 81–115). New York: Free Press.

Helzer, J. E., Canino, G. J., Yeh, E. K. Bland, R. C., Lee, C. K., Hwu, H. G., & Newman, S. (1990). Alcoholism—North America and Asia. A comparison of population surveys with the Diagnostic Interview Schedule. *Archives of General Psychiatry, 47,* 313–319.

Herd, D. (1994). Predicting drinking problems among black and white men: Results from a national survey. *Journal of Studies on Alcohol, 55,* 61–71.

Hesselbrock, V., Begleiter, H., Porjesz, B., O'Connor, S., & Bauer, L. (2001). P300 event-related potential amplitude as an endophenotype of alcoholism—Evidence from the collaborative study on the genetics of alcoholism. *Journal of Biomedical Sciences, 8,* 77–82.

Hettema, J. M., Prescott, C. A., & Kendler, K. S. (2004). Genetic and environmental sources of covariation between generalized anxiety disorder and neuroticism. *American Journal of Psychiatry, 161,* 1581–1587.

Hettema, J. M., Steele, J., & Miller, W. R. (2005). Motivational interviewing. *Annual Reviews in Psychology, 105,* 91–111.

Hettema, J. M., Steele, J., & Miller, W. R. (2005). Motivational interviewing. *Annual Review in Clinical Psychology, 1,* 91–111.

Hiller, W., Leibbrand, R., Rief, W., & Fichter, M. M. (2005). Differentiating hypochondriasis from panic disorder. *Journal of Anxiety Disorders, 19,* 29–49.

Hilsenroth, M. J., Ackerman, S. J., Blagys, M. D., Baity, M. R., & Mooney, M. A. (2003). Short-term psychodynamic psychotherapy for depression: An examination of statistical, clinically significant, and technique-specific change. *Journal of Nervous and Mental Disease, 191,* 349–357.

Hiroi, N., & Agatsuma, S. (2005). Genetic susceptibility to substance dependence. *Molecular Psychiatry, 10,* 336–344.

Hirono, N., Hashimoto, M., Ishii, K., Kazui, H., & Mori, E. (2004). One-year change in cerebral glucose metabolism in patients with Alzheimer's disease. *Journal of Neuropsychiatry and Clinical Neuroscience, 16,* 488–492.

Hirvonen, J., van Erp, T. G., Huttunen, J., Aalto, S., Nagren, K., Huttunen, M., et al. (2005). Increased caudate dopamine D2 receptor availability as a genetic marker for schizophrenia. *Archives of General Psychiatry, 62,* 371–378.

Hobfall, S. E., Spielberger, C. D., Breznitz, S., Figley, C., Folkman, S., et al. (1991). War-related stress: Addressing the stress of war and other traumatic events. *American Psychologist, 46,* 848–855.

Hodgins, D. C., Currie, S., el-Guebaly, N., & Peden, N. (2004). Brief motivational treatment for problem gambling: A 24-month follow-up. *Psychology of Addictive Behaviors, 18,* 293–296.

Hodgins, D. C., el-Guebaly, N., & Armstrong, S. (1995). Prospective and retrospective reports of mood states before relapse to substance abuse. *Journal of Consulting and Clinical Psychology, 63,* 400–407.

Hoehn, T., Braune, S., Scheibe, G., & Albus, M. (1997). Physiological, biochemical and subjective parameters in anxiety patients with panic disorder during stress exposure as compared with healthy controls. *European Archives of Psychiatry and Clinical Neuroscience, 247,* 264–274.

Hoek, H. W., Susser, E., Buck, K. A., Lumey, L. H., Lin, S. P., & Gorman, J. M. (1996). Schizoid personality disorder after prenatal exposure to famine. *American Journal of Psychiatry, 153,* 1637–1639.

Hogan, M. F. (2003). The President's New Freedom Commission: Recommendations to transform mental health care in America. *Psychiatric Services, 54,* 1467–1474.

Hogarty, G. E., Greenwald, D., Ulrich, R. F., Kornblith, S. J., DiBarry, A. L., Cooley, S., Carter, M., & Flesher, S. (1997). Three-year trials of personal therapy among schizophrenia patients living with or independent of family, II: Effects on adjustment of patients. *American Journal of Psychiatry, 154,* 1514–1524.

Hoge, C. W., Castro, C. A., Messer, S. C., McGurk, D., Cotting, D. I., & Koffman, R. L. (2004). Combat duty in Iraq and Afghanistan, mental health problems, and barriers to care. *New England Journal of Medicine, 351,* 13–22.

Hoge, S. K., Poythress, N., Bonnie, R. J., Monahan, J., Eisenberg, M., & Feucht-Haviar, T. (1997a). The MacArthur Adjudicative Competence Study: Development and validation of a research instrument. *Law and Human Behavior, 21,* 141–179.

Hoge, S. K., Poythress, N., Bonnie, R. J., Monahan, J., Eisenberg, M., & Feucht-Haviar, T. (1997b). The MacArthur Adjudicative Competence Study: Diagnosis, psychopathology, and competence-related abilities. *Behavioral Sciences and the Law, 15,* 329–345.

Hollander, E., & Rosen, J. (2000). Impulsivity. *Journal of Psychopharmacology, 14* (Suppl. 1), S39–44.

Hollander, E., & Rosen, J. (2000). Impulsivity. *Journal of Psychopharmacology, 14,* S39–44.

Hollender, M. H. (1997). Genital exhibitionism in men and women. In L. B. Schlesinger & E. Revitch (Eds.), *Sexual dynamics of anti-social behavior* (2nd ed.). Springfield, IL: Charles C. Thomas Press.

Hollingshead, A. B., & Redlich, F. C. (1958). *Social class and mental illness: A community study.* New York: Wiley.

Holmes, T. H., & Rahe, R. H. (1967). The social readjustment rating scale. *Journal of Psychosomatic Research, 11,* 213–218.

Honigman, R. J., Phillips, K. A., & Castle, D. J. (2004). A review of psychosocial outcomes for patients seeking cosmetic surgery. *Plastic and Reconstructive Surgery, 113,* 1229–1237.

Hopko, D. R., Bourland, S. L., Stanley, M. A., Beck, J. G., Novy, D. M., Averill, P. M., & Swann, A. C. (2000). Generalized anxiety disorder in older adults: Examining the relation between clinician severity ratings and patient self-report measures. *Depression and Anxiety, 12,* 217–225.

Horger, B. A., & Roth, R. H. (1996). The role of mesoprefrontal dopamine neurons in stress. *Critical Reviews in Neurobiology, 10,* 395–418.

Horney, K., & Paris, B. J. (2000). *The unknown Karen Horney: Essays on gender, culture, and psychoanalysis.* New Haven: Yale University Press.

Horowitz, A., Shifman, S., Rivlin, N., Pisante, A., & Darvasi, A. (2005). A survey of the 22q11 microdeletion in a large cohort of schizophrenia patients. *Schizophrenia Research, 73,* 263–267.

Hou, C., Miller, B. L., Cummings, J. L., Goldberg, M., Mychack, P., Bottino, V., & Benson, D. F. (2000). Autistic savants. *Neuropsychiatry, Neuropsychology, and Behavioral Neurology, 13,* 29–38.

House Committee on Energy and Commerce. (1990). H.R. Rep. No 485, 101st Cong., 101st., 2d Sess., pt. 4.

Hoven, C. W., Duarte, C. S., Lucas, C. P., Wu, P., Mandell, D. J., Goodwin, R. D., et al. (2005). Psychopathology among New York City public school children 6 months after

September 11. *Archives of General Psychiatry, 62,* 545–552.

Hoyert, D. L., Kung, H. C., & Smith, B. L. (2005). Deaths: Preliminary data for 2003. *National Vital Stat Rep, 53,* 1–48.

Hoyert, D. L., Kung, H.-C., & Smith, B. L. (2005). *Deaths: Preliminary data for 2003.* Hyattsville, MD: National Center for Health Statistics.

Hoyme, H. E., May, P. A., Kalberg, W. O., Kodituwakku, P., Gossage, J. P., Trujillo, P. M., et al. (2005). A practical clinical approach to diagnosis of fetal alcohol spectrum disorders: Clarification of the 1996 Institute of Medicine criteria. *Pediatrics, 115,* 39–47.

Hudson, C. G. (2005). Socioeconomic status and mental illness: Tests of the social causation and selection hypotheses. *American Journal of Orthopsychiatry, 75,* 3–18.

Hughes, J. R., Oliveto, A. H., Helzer, J. E., Higgins, S. T., & Bickel, W. K. (1992). Should caffeine abuse, dependence, or withdrawal be added to *DSM-IV* and ICD-10? *American Journal of Psychiatry, 149,* 33–40.

Hurwitz, T. A. (2004). Somatization and conversion disorder. *Canadian Journal of Psychiatry, 49,* 172–178.

Hy, L. X., & Keller, D. M. (2000). Prevalence of AD among whites: A summary by levels of severity. *Neurology, 55,* 198–204.

Hyams, K. C., Wignall, F. S., & Roswell, R. (1996). War syndromes and their evaluation: From the U.S. Civil War to the Persian Gulf War. *Annals of Internal Medicine, 125,* 398–405.

I

Ibanez, A., Blanco, C., de Castro, I. P., Fernandez-Piqueras, J., & Saiz-Ruiz, J. (2003). Genetics of pathological gambling. *Journal of Gambling Studies, 19,* 11–22.

Ilan, A. B., Smith, M. E., & Gevins, A. (2004). Effects of marijuana on neurophysiological signals of working and episodic memory. *Psychopharmacology (Berlin), 176,* 214–222.

International Human Genome Sequencing Consortium. (2001). Initial sequencing and analysis of the human genome. *Nature, 409,* 860–921.

Irons, R. R. (1996). Comorbidity between violence and addictive disease. *Sexual Addiction and Compulsivity, 3,* 85–96.

Isometsä, E. T., Heikkinen, M. E., Marttunen, M. J., Henriksson, M. M., Aro, H. M., & Lönnqvist, J. K. (1995). The last appointment before: Is suicide intent communicated? *American Journal of Psychiatry, 152,* 919–922.

J

Jacobi, C., Hayward, C., de Zwaan, M., Kraemer, H. C., & Agras, W. S. (2004). Coming to terms with risk factors for eating disorders: Application of risk terminology and suggestions for a general taxonomy. *Psychological Bulletin, 130,* 19–65.

Jacobs, G. D., Benson, H., & Friedman, R. (1996). Perceived benefits in a behavioral-medicine insomnia program: A clinical report. *American Journal of Medicine, 100,* 212–216.

Jaffee, S. R., Caspi, A., Moffitt, T. E., Dodge, K. A., Rutter, M., Taylor, A., et al. (2005). Nature × nurture: Genetic vulnerabilities interact with physical maltreatment to promote conduct problems. *Development and Psychopathology, 17,* 67–84.

Janszky, I., Szedmak, S., Istok, R., & Kopp, M. (1997). Possible role of sweating in the pathophysiology of panic attacks. *International Journal of Psychophysiology, 27,* 249–252.

Jenike, M. A. (2004). Clinical practice. Obsessive-compulsive disorder. *New England Journal of Medicine, 350,* 259–265.

Jenkins, C. D. (1995). An integrated behavioral medicine approach to improving care of patients with diabetes mellitus. *Behavioral Medicine, 21,* 53–65.

Jensen, P. S., Hinshaw, S. P., Swanson, J. M., Greenhill, L. L., Conners, C. K., et al. (2001). Findings from the NIMH Multimodal Treatment Study of ADHD (MTA): Implications and applications for primary care providers. *Journal of Developmental and Behavioral Pediatrics, 22,* 60–73.

Jensen, V. K., & Sinclair, L. V. (2002). Treatment of autism in young children: Behavioral intervention and applied behavior analysis. *Infants and Young Children, 14,* 42–52.

Johnson, J. G., Cohen, P., Kasen, S., Smailes, E., & Brook, J. S. (2001). Association of maladaptive parental behavior with psychiatric disorder among parents and their offspring. *Archives of General Psychiatry, 58,* 453–460.

Johnston, L. D., O'Malley, P. M., & Bachman, J. G. (2001a). *Monitoring the Future national survey results on drug use, 1975–2000. Volume I: Secondary school students* (NIH Publication No. 01-4924). Bethesda, MD: National Institute on Drug Abuse.

Johnston, L. D., O'Malley, P. M., & Bachman, J. G. (2001b). *National survey results on drug use from the Monitoring the Future study, 1975–1998. Volume I: Secondary school students.* Rockville, MD: National Institute on Drug Abuse.

Johnston, L. D., O'Malley, P. M., Bachman, J. G., & Schulenberg, J. E. (2005). *Monitoring the future national results on adolescent drug use: Overview of key findings, 2004* (NIH Publication No. 05–5726). Bethesda, MD: National Institute on Drug Abuse.

Jollant, F., Bellivier, F., Leboyer, M., Astruc, B., Torres, S., Verdier, R., et al. (2005). Impaired decision making in suicide attempters. *American Journal of Psychiatry, 162,* 304–310.

Jones, E. (1953). *The life and work of Sigmund Freud: The formative years and the great discoveries.* New York: Basic Books.

Jones, K. M., Whitbourne, S. K., & Skultety, K. M. (in press). Identity in midlife. In S. K.

Whitbourne & S. L. Willis (Eds.), *The baby boomers grow up: Contemporary perspectives on midlife development.* Mahwah, NJ: Lawrence Erlbaum.

Jones, M. K., & Menzies, R. G. (1997). The cognitive mediation of obsessive-compulsive handwashing. *Behaviour Research and Therapy, 35,* 843–850.

Jones, V. F., Badgett, J. T., Minella, J. L., & Schuschke, L. A. (1993). The role of the male caretaker in Munchausen syndrome by proxy. *Clinical Pediatrics, 32,* 245–247.

Jonnal, A. H., Gardner, C. O., Prescott, C. A., & Kendler, K. S. (2000). Obsessive and compulsive symptoms in a general population sample of female twins. *American Journal of Medical Genetics, 96,* 791–796.

Jordan, B. K., Schlenger, W. E., Fairbank, J. A., & Caddell, J. M. (1996). Prevalence of psychiatric disorders among incarcerated women. II. Convicted felons entering prison. *Archives of General Psychiatry, 53,* 513–519.

Joseph, J. A., Shukitt-Hale, B., & Casadesus, G. (2005). Reversing the deleterious effects of aging on neuronal communication and behavior: Beneficial properties of fruit polyphenolic compounds. *American Journal of Clinical Nutrition, 81,* 313S–316S.

Juan, D., Zhou, D. H., Li, J., Wang, J. Y., Gao, C., & Chen, M. (2004). A 2-year follow-up study of cigarette smoking and risk of dementia. *European Journal of Neurology, 11,* 277–282.

Juliano, L. M., & Griffiths, R. R. (2004). A critical review of caffeine withdrawal: Empirical validation of symptoms and signs, incidence, severity, and associated features. *Psychopharmacology (Berlin), 176,* 1–29.

Jung, C. G. (1916). General aspects of dream psychology. In H. Read, M. Fordham, & G. Alder (Eds.), *The collected works of C. G. Jung* (Vol. 8, pp. 237–280). Princeton, NJ: Princeton University Press.

Jung, C. G. (1961). *Memories, dreams, reflections.* New York: Pantheon.

Jurbergs, N., & Ledley, D. R. (2005). Separation anxiety disorder. *Pediatric Annals, 34,* 108–115.

K

Kahn, E., & Rachman, A. W. (2000). Carl Rogers and Heinz Kohut: A historical perspective. *Psychoanalytic Psychology, 17,* 294–312.

Kalant, H. (2001). The pharmacology and toxicology of "Ecstasy" (MDMA) and related drugs. *Canadian Medical Journal, 165,* 917–928.

Kanner, L. (1943). Autistic disturbances of affective contact. *Nervous Child, 2,* 217–250.

Kanter, J. W., Callaghan, G. M., Landes, S. J., Busch, A. M., & Brown, K. R. (2004). Behavior analytic conceptualization and treatment of depression: Traditional models and recent advances. *The Behavior Analyst Today, 5,* 255–274.

Kaplan, H. S. (1979). *Disorders of sexual desire: The new sex therapy* (Vol. 2). New York: Brunner/Mazel.

Kaplan, H. S. (1983). *The evaluation of sexual disorders: Psychological and medical aspects.* New York: Brunner/Mazel.

Kaplan, H. S. (1986). Psychosexual dysfunctions. In A. M. Cooper, A. J. Frances, & M. H. Sacks (Eds.), *The personality disorders and neuroses* (pp. 467–479). New York: Basic Books.

Kaplan, H. S. (1998). Ernie: A complicated case of premature ejaculation. In R. P. Halgin & S. K. Whitbourne (Eds.), *A casebook in abnormal psychology: From the files of experts* (pp. 128–142). New York: Oxford University Press.

Karasz, A. (2005). Cultural differences in conceptual models of depression. *Social Science in Medicine, 60,* 1625–1635.

Kardiner, A., & Spiegel, H. (1947). *War stress and neurotic illness* (2nd ed.) New York: P. E. Hoeber.

Karon, B. P. (1995). Provision of psychotherapy under managed health care: A growing crisis and national nightmare. *Professional Psychology: Research and Practice, 26,* 5–9.

Karoumi, B., Saoud, M., d'Amato, T., Rosenfeld, F., Denise, P., et al. (2001). Poor performance in smooth pursuit and antisaccadic eye-movement tasks in healthy siblings of patients with schizophrenia. *Psychiatry Research, 101,* 209–219.

Katerndahl, D., Burge, S., & Kellogg, N. (2005). Predictors of development of adult psychopathology in female victims of childhood sexual abuse. *Journal of Nervous and Mental Disorders, 193,* 258–264.

Kavoussi, R., Armstead, P., & Coccaro, E. (1997). The neurobiology of impulsive aggression. *Psychiatric Clinics of North America, 20,* 395–403.

Kaye, W. H., Bulik, C. M., Thornton, L., Barbarich, N., & Masters, K. (2004). Comorbidity of anxiety disorders with anorexia and bulimia nervosa. *American Journal of Psychiatry, 161,* 2215–2221.

Kaye, W. H., Nagata, T., Weltzin, T. E., Hsu, L. K., Sokol, M. S., et al. (2001). Double-blind placebo-controlled administration of fluoxetine in restricting- and restricting-purging-type anorexia nervosa. *Biological Psychiatry, 49,* 644–652.

Kehrer, C. A., & Linehan, M. M. (1996). Interpersonal and emotional problem solving skills and parasuicide among women with borderline personality disorder. *Journal of Personality Disorders, 10,* 153–163.

Keller, A., Castellanos, F. X., Vaituzis, A. C., Jeffries, N. O., Giedd, J. N., & Rapoport, J. L. (2003). Progressive loss of cerebellar volume in childhood-onset schizophrenia. *American Journal of Psychiatry, 160,* 128–133.

Keller, M. B., Herzog, D. B., Lavori, P. W., Bradburn, I. S., & Mahoney, E. M. (1995). A prospective study of outcome in bulimia nervosa and the long-term effects of three psychological treatments. *Archives of General Psychiatry, 52,* 304–312.

Keller, M. B., Lavori, P. W., Wunder, J., Beardslee, W. R., Schwartz, C. E., & Roth, J. (1992). Chronic course of anxiety disorders in children and adolescents. *Journal of the American Academy of Child and Adolescent Psychiatry, 31,* 595–599.

Kelly, K. G., & Zisselman, M. (2000). Update on electroconvulsive therapy (ECT) in older adults. *Journal of the American Geriatrics Society, 48,* 560–566.

Kelly, T. M., Soloff, P. H., Lynch, K. G., Haas, G. L., & Mann, J. J. (2000). Recent life events, social adjustment, and suicide attempts in patients with major depression and borderline personality disorder. *Journal of Personality Disorders, 14,* 316–326.

Kemperman, I., Russ, M. J., & Shearin, E. (1997). Self-injurious behavior and mood regulation in borderline patients. *Journal of Personality Disorders, 11,* 146–157.

Kendler, K. S., Davis, C. G., & Kessler, R. C. (1997). The familial aggregation of common psychiatric and substance use disorders in the National Comorbidity Survey: A family history study. *British Journal of Psychiatry, 170,* 541–548.

Kendler, K. S., Myers, J., & Prescott, C. A. (2005). Sex differences in the relationship between social support and risk for major depression: A longitudinal study of opposite-sex twin pairs. *American Journal of Psychiatry, 162,* 250–256.

Kendler, K. S., Myers, J., Prescott, C. A., & Neale, M. C. (2001). The genetic epidemiology of irrational fears and phobias in men. *Archives of General Psychiatry, 58,* 257–265.

Kernberg, O. F. (1967). Borderline personality organization. *Journal of the American Psychoanalytic Association, 15,* 641–685.

Kernberg, O. F. (1984). *Severe personality disorders: Psychotherapeutic strategies.* New Haven, CT: Yale University Press.

Kernberg, O. F., Selzer, M. A., Koenigsberg, H. W., Carr, A. C., & Applebaum, A. H. (1989). *Psychodynamic psychotherapy of borderline patients.* New York: Basic Books.

Kessler, R. C. (1997). The prevalence of psychiatric comorbidity. In S. Wetzler & W. C. Sanderson (Eds.), *Treatment strategies for patients with psychiatric comorbidity* (pp. 23–48). New York: Wiley.

Kessler, R. C., & Ustun, T. B. (2004). The World Mental Health (WMH) Survey Initiative Version of the World Health Organization (WHO) Composite International Diagnostic Interview (CIDI). *International Journal of Methods in Psychiatric Research, 13,* 93–121.

Kessler, R. C., Abelson, J., Demler, O., Escobar, J. I., Gibbon, M., Guyer, M. E., et al. (2004). Clinical calibration of DSM-IV diagnoses in the World Mental Health (WMH) version of the World Health Organization (WHO) Composite International Diagnostic Interview (WMHCIDI). *International Journal of Methods in Psychiatric Research, 13,* 122–139.

Kessler, R. C., Berglund, P., Demler, O., Jin, R., Koretz, D., Merikangas, K. R., Rush, A. J., Walters, E. E. & Wang, P. S. (2003). The epidemiology of major depressive disorder: Results from the national comorbidity survey replication. *Journal of the American Medical Association, 289,* 3095–3105.

Kessler, R. C., McGonagle, K. A., Zhao, S., Nelson, C. B., Hughes, M., Eshleman, S., Wittchen, H., & Kendler, K. S. (1994). Lifetime and 12-month prevalence of *DSM-III*-R psychiatric disorders in the United States: Results from the National Comorbidity Survey. *Archives of General Psychiatry, 51,* 8–19.

Kessler, R. C., Stein, M. B., & Berglund, P. (1998). Social phobia subtypes in the National Comorbidity Survey. *American Journal of Psychiatry, 155,* 613–619.

Kiehl, K. A., Smith, A. M., Mendrek, A., Forster, B. B., Hare, R. D., & Liddle, P. F. (2004). Temporal lobe abnormalities in semantic processing by criminal psychopaths as revealed by functional magnetic resonance imaging. *Psychiatry Research, 130,* 297–312.

Kihlstrom, J. F. (2005). Dissociative disorders. *Annual Review in Clinical Psychology, 1,* 227–253.

Kim, C. D., Seguin, M., Therrien, N., Riopel, G., Chawky, N., Lesage, A. D., et al. (2005). Familial aggregation of suicidal behavior: A family study of male suicide completers from the general population. *American Journal of Psychiatry, 162,* 1017–1019.

Kim, S. W., Grant, J. E., Adson, D. E., & Shin, Y. C. (2001). Double-blind naltrexone and placebo comparison study in the treatment of pathological gambling. *Biological Psychiatry, 49,* 914–921.

King, D. A., & Markus, H. E. (2000). Mood disorders in older adults. In S. K. Whitbourne (Ed.), *Psychopathology in later life.* New York: Wiley.

Kinsey, A. C., Pomeroy, W. B., & Martin, C. E. (1948). *Sexual behavior in the human male.* Philadelphia: Saunders.

Kinsey, A. C., Pomeroy, W. B., Martin, C. E., & Gebhard, P. H. (1953). *Sexual behavior in the human female.* Philadelphia: Saunders.

Kirk, S. A., & Kutchins, H. (1992). *The selling of DSM: The rhetoric of science in psychiatry.* New York: A. de Gruyter.

Kirkland, K., & Kirkland, K. L. (2001). Frequency of child custody evaluation complaints and related disciplinary action: A survey of the Association of State and Provincial Psychology Boards. *Professional Psychology: Research and Practice, 32,* 171–174.

Klein, D. F. (1993). False suffocation alarms, spontaneous panics, and related conditions: An integrative hypothesis. *Archives of General Psychiatry, 50,* 306–317.

Klein, D. N., Santiago, N. J., Vivian, D., Blalock, J. A., Kocsis, J. H., Markowitz, J. C., et al. (2004). Cognitive-behavioral analysis system of psychotherapy as a maintenance treatment for chronic depression. *Journal of Consulting and Clinical Psychology, 72,* 681–688.

Kleinknecht, R. A., Dinnel, D. L., Kleinknecht, E. E., Hiruma, N., & Harada, N. (1997). Cultural factors in social anxiety: A comparison of social phobia symptoms and Taijin Kyofusho. *Journal of Anxiety Disorders, 11,* 157–177.

Klerman, G. L., Weissman, M. M., Rounsaville, B. J., & Chevron, E. S. (1984). *Interpersonal psychotherapy of depression.* New York: Basic Books.

Klosko, J. S., Barlow, D. H., Tassinari, R., & Cerny, J. A. (1990). A comparison of alprazolam and behavior therapy in treatment of panic disorder. *Journal of Consulting and Clinical Psychology, 58,* 77–84.

Kluft, R. P. (1984a). Aspects of the treatment of multiple personality disorder. *Psychiatric Annals, 14,* 51–55.

Kluft, R. P. (1984b). An introduction to multiple personality disorder. *Psychiatric Annals, 14,* 19–24.

Kluft, R. P. (1986). High functioning multiple personality disorders. *Journal of Nervous and Mental Disease, 174,* 722–726.

Kluft, R. P. (1987a). First-rank symptoms as a diagnostic clue to multiple personality disorder. *American Journal of Psychiatry, 144,* 293–298.

Kluft, R. P. (1987b). The simulation and dissimulation of multiple personality disorder. *American Journal of Clinical Hypnosis, 30,* 104–118.

Kluft, R. P. (1989). Playing for time: Temporizing techniques in the treatment of multiple personality disorder. *American Journal of Clinical Hypnosis, 32,* 90–98.

Kluft, R. P. (1997). The argument for the reality of delayed recall of trauma. In L. A. U. M. R. E. Paul S. Appelbaum (Ed.), *Trauma and memory: Clinical and legal controversies* (pp. 25–57). New York: Oxford University Press.

Kluft, R. P. (1998). Joe: A case of dissociative identity disorder. In R. P. Halgin & S. K. Whitbourne (Eds.), *A casebook in abnormal psychology: From the files of experts* (pp. 90–112). New York: Oxford University Press.

Knight, R. (1953). Borderline states. *Bulletin of the Menninger Clinic, 17,* 1–12.

Koegel, L. K., Valdez-Menchaca, M. C., & Koegel, R. L. (1994). Autism: Social communication difficulties and related behaviors. In V. B. V. Hasselt & M. Hersen (Eds.), *Advanced abnormal psychology* (pp. 165–187). New York: Plenum Press.

Koegel, R. L., Koegel, L. K., & McNerney, E. K. (2001). Pivotal areas in intervention for autism. *Journal of Clinical Child Psychology, 30,* 19–32.

Koger, S. M., Schettler, T., & Weiss, B. (2005). Environmental toxicants and developmental disabilities. *American Psychologist, 60,* 243–255.

Kohler, F. W., Strain, P. S., & Goldstein, H. (2005). Learning experiences . . . an alternative program for preschoolers and parents: Peer-mediated interventions for young children with autism. In E. D. Hibbs & P. S. Jensen (Eds.), *Psychosocial treatments for child and adolescent disorders: Empirically based strategies for clinical practice* (2nd ed., pp. 659–657). Washington DC: American Psychological Association.

Kohut, H. (1966). Forms and transformations of narcissism. *Journal of the American Psychoanalytic Association, 14,* 243–272.

Kohut, H. (1971). *The analysis of the self.* New York: International Universities Press.

Kolko, D. J. (2001). Efficacy of cognitive-behavioral treatment and fire safety education for children who set fires: Initial and follow-up outcomes. *Journal of Child Psychology and Psychiatry, 42,* 359–369.

Kolko, D. J., & Kazdin, A. E. (1994). Children's descriptions of their firesetting incidents: Characteristics and relationship to recidivism. *Journal of the American Academy of Child and Adolescent Psychiatry, 33,* 114–122.

Koocher, G. P. (1994). The commerce of professional psychology and the new ethics code. *Professional Psychology: Research and Practice, 25,* 355–361.

Koocher, G. P., & Keith-Spiegel, P. (1998). *Ethics in psychology: Professional standards and cases.* New York: Oxford University Press.

Koopman, C., Classen, C., & Spiegel, D. A. (1994). Predictors of posttraumatic stress symptoms among survivors of the Oakland/Berkeley, Calif., firestorm. *American Journal of Psychiatry, 151,* 888–894.

Koren, D., Norman, D., Cohen, A., Berman, J., & Klein, E. M. (2005). Increased PTSD risk with combat-related injury: A matched comparison study of injured and uninjured soldiers experiencing the same combat events. *American Journal of Psychiatry, 162,* 276–228.

Koster, A., Bosma, H., van Lenthe, F. J., Kempen, G. I., Mackenbach, J. P., & van Eijk, J. T. (2005). The role of psychosocial factors in explaining socio-economic differences in mobility decline in a chronically ill population: Results from the GLOBE study. *Social Science & Medicine, 61,* 123–132.

Kowatch, R. A., Fristad, M., Birmaher, B., Wagner, K. D., Findling, R. L., & Hellander, M. (2005). Treatment guidelines for children and adolescents with bipolar disorder. *Journal of the American Academy of Child and Adolescent Psychiatry, 44,* 213–235.

Krafft-Ebing, R. V. (1886/1950). *Psychopathia sexualis.* New York: Pioneer.

Krahn, L. E., Li, H., & O'Connor, M. K. (2003). Patients who strive to be ill: Factitious disorder with physical symptoms. *American Journal of Psychiatry, 160,* 1163–1168.

Kring, B. (2000). Psychotherapy of sexual dysfunction. *American Journal of Psychotherapy, 54,* 97–101.

Kristenson, M., Eriksen, H. R., Sluiter, J. K., Starke, D., & Ursin, H. (2004). Psychobiological mechanisms of socioeconomic differences in health. *Social Science & Medicine, 58,* 1511–1522.

Kropp, P., Gerber, W. D., Keinath-Specht, A., Kopal, T., & Niederberger, U. (1997). Behavioral treatment in migraine. Cognitive-behavioral therapy and blood-volume-pulse biofeedback: A cross-over study with a two-year follow-up. *Functional Neurology, 12,* 17–24.

Krueger, R. F., Tackett, J. L., & Markon, K. E. (2004). Structural models of comorbidity among common mental disorders: Connections to chronic pain. *Advances in Psychosomatic Medicine, 25,* 63–77.

Kubany, E. S. (1994). A cognitive model of guilt typology in combat-related PTSD. *Journal of Traumatic Stress, 7,* 3–19.

Kuiper, B., & Cohen-Kettenis, P. (1988). Sex reassignment surgery: A study of 141 Dutch transsexuals. *Archives of Sexual Behavior, 17,* 439–457.

Kumari, V., Kaviani, H., Raven, P. W., Gray, J. A., & Checkley, S. A. (2001). Enhanced startle reactions to acoustic stimuli in patients with obsessive-compulsive disorder. *American Journal of Psychiatry, 158,* 134–136.

Kuperberg, G. R., Broome, M. R., McGuire, P. K., David, A. S., Eddy, M., Ozawa, F., et al. (2003). Regionally localized thinning of the cerebral cortex in schizophrenia. *Archives of General Psychiatry, 60,* 878–888.

Kupers, T. A. (1997). The politics of psychiatry: Gender and sexual preference in *DSM-IV.* In M. R. Walsh (Ed.), *Women, men, and gender: Ongoing debates* (pp. 340–347). New Haven: Yale University Press.

Kupfer, M. B., First, D. J., & Regier, D. A. (2002). *A research agenda for DSM-V.* Washington DC: American Psychiatric Association.

Kurokawa, K., Nakamura, K., Sumiyoshi, T., Hagino, H., Yotsutsuji, T., et al. (2000). Ventricular enlargement in schizophrenia spectrum patients with prodromal symptoms of obsessive-compulsive disorder. *Psychiatry Research, 99,* 83–91.

Kusumakar, V., Yatham, L. N., Haslam, D. R., Parikh, S. V., Matte, R., Silverstone, P. H., & Sharma, V. (1997). Treatment of mania, mixed state, and rapid cycling. *Canadian Journal of Psychiatry, 42,* 79S–85S.

Kutchins, H., & Kirk, S. A. (1997). *DSM: The psychiatric bible and the creation of mental disorders.* New York: Free Press.

Kuzma, J. M., & Black, D. W. (2004). Compulsive disorders. *Current Psychiatry Reports, 6,* 58–65.

L

Laakso, M. P., Vaurio, O., Koivisto, E., Savolainen, L., Eronen, M., et al. (2001). Psychopathy and the posterior hippocampus. *Behavioural Brain Research, 118* (Netherlands).

Labouvie-Vief, G., & Diehl, M. (2000). Cognitive complexity and cognitive-affective integration: Related or separate domains of adult development? *Psychology & Aging, 15,* 490–504.

La Fond, J. Q. (1994). Law and the delivery of involuntary mental health services. *American Journal of Orthopsychiatry, 64,* 209–222.

Laing, R. D. (1959). *The divided self.* New York: Penguin.

Laing, R. D. (1964). Is schizophrenia a disease? *International Journal of Social Psychiatry, 10,* 184–193.

Laird, L. K. (1995). Luvox joins growing list of approved obsessive-compulsive treatment. *Psychopharmacology Update, 6,* 1–2.

Lalonde, J. K., Hudson, J. I., Gigante, R. A., & Pope, H. G., Jr. (2001). Canadian and American psychiatrists' attitudes toward dissociative disorders diagnoses. *Canadian Journal of Psychiatry, 46,* 407–412.

Lamberg, L. (2004). Efforts grow to keep mentally ill out of jails. *Journal of the American Medical Association, 292,* 555–556.

Lamberg, L. (2004). Military psychiatrists strive to quell soldiers' nightmares of war. *Journal of the American Medical Association, 292,* 1539–1540.

Lambert, M. V., Senior, C., Fewtrell, W. D., Phillips, M. L., & David, A. S. (2001). Primary and secondary depersonalisation disorder: A psychometric study. *Journal of Affective Disorders, 63,* 249–256.

Lang, A. J., & Stein, M. B. (2001). Social phobia: Prevalence and diagnostic threshold. *Journal of Clinical Psychiatry, 62* (Suppl. 1), 5–10.

Lang, P. J., Davis, M., & Ohman, A. (2000). Fear and anxiety: Animal models and human cognitive psychophysiology. *Journal of Affective Disorders, 61,* 137–159.

Langhinrichsen-Rohling, J., Rohde, P., Seeley, J. R., & Rohling, M. L. (2004). Individual, family, and peer correlates of adolescent gambling. *Journal of Gambling Studies, 20,* 23–46.

Lantz, P. M., House, J. S., Lepkowski, J. M., Williams, D. R., Mero, R. P., & Chen, J. (1998). Socioeconomic factors, health behaviors, and mortality: Results from a nationally representative prospective study of U.S. adults. *Journal of the American Medical Association, 279,* 1703–1708.

Lanyon, R. I. (1986). Theory and treatment of child molestation. *Journal of Consulting and Clinical Psychology, 54,* 176–182.

Larrison, A. L., Ferrante, C. F., Briand, K. A., & Sereno, A. B. (2000). Schizotypal traits, attention and eye movements. *Progress in Neuro-Psychopharmacology and Biological Psychiatry, 24,* 357–372.

Lauer, J., Black, D. W., & Keen, P. (1993). Multiple personality disorder and borderline personality disorder: Distinct entities of variations on a common theme? *Annals of Clinical Psychiatry, 5,* 129–134.

Laumann, E. O., Gagnon, J. H., Michael, R. T., & Michaels, S. (1994). *The social organization of sexuality.* Chicago: University of Chicago Press.

Laumann, E. O., Paik, A., & Rosen, R. C. (1999). Sexual dysfunction in the United States. *Journal of the American Medical Association, 281,* 537–544.

Lazarus, A. A. (1968). Learning theory and the treatment of depression. *Behaviour Research and Therapy, 6,* 83–89.

Lazarus, R. S., & Folkman, S. (1984). *Stress, appraisal, and coping.* New York: Springer.

Lecci, L., Karoly, P., Ruehlman, L. S., & Lanyon, R. I. (1996). Goal-relevant dimensions of hypochondriacal tendencies and their relation to symptom manifestation and psychological distress. *Journal of Abnormal Psychology, 105,* 42–52.

Lecrubier, Y., & Weiller, E. (1997). Comorbidities in social phobia. *International Clinical Psychopharmacology, 12,* S17–21.

Lee, H. S., Song, D. H., Kim, C. H., & Choi, H. K. (1996). An open clinical trial of fluoxetine in the treatment of premature ejaculation. *Journal of Clinical Psychopharmacology, 16,* 379–382.

Lejuez, C. W., Eifert, G. H., Zvolensky, M. J., & Richards, J. B. (2000). Preference between onset predictable and unpredictable administrations of 20% carbon-dioxide-enriched air: Implications for better understanding the etiology and treatment of panic disorder. *Journal of Experimental Psychology: Applied, 6,* 349–358.

Lenzenweger, M. F., Loranger, A. W., Korfine, L., & Neff, C. (1997). Detecting personality disorders in a nonclinical population. Application of a 2-stage procedure for case identification. *Archives of General Psychiatry, 54,* 345–351.

Leocani, L., Locatelli, M., Bellodi, L., Fornara, C., Henin, M., Magnani, G., Mennea, S., & Comi, G. (2001). Abnormal pattern of cortical activation associated with voluntary movement in obsessive-compulsive disorder: An EEG study. *American Journal of Psychiatry, 158,* 140–142.

Leon, G. R., Fulkerson, J. A., Perry, C. L., & Early-Zald, M. B. (1995). Prospective analysis of personality and behavioral vulnerabilities and gender influences in the later development of disordered eating. *Journal of Abnormal Psychology, 104,* 140–149.

Lee, V. M., Goedert, M., & Trojanowski, J. Q. (2001). Neurodegenerative tauopathies. *Annual Review of Neuroscience, 24,* 1121–1159.

Leibenluft, E. (2000). Women and bipolar disorder: An update. *Bulletin of the Menninger Clinic, 64,* 5–17.

Leibenluft, E., Moul, D. E., Schwartz, P. J., Madder, P. A., & Wehr, T. A. (1993). A clinical trial of sleep deprivation in combination with antidepressant medication. *Psychiatry Research, 46,* 213–227.

Lenzenweger, M. F. (1999). Stability and change in personality disorder features: The Longitudinal Study of Personality Disorders. *Archives of General Psychiatry, 56,* 1009–1015.

Leserman, J., Petitto, J. M., Perkins, D. O., Folds, J. D., Golden, R. N., & Evans, D. L. (1997). Severe stress, depressive symptoms, and changes in lymphocyte subsets in human immunodeficiency virus-infected men. A 2-year follow-up study. *Archives of General Psychiatry, 54,* 279–285.

Levitan, R. D., Masellis, M., Basile, V. S., Lam, R. W., Kaplan, A. S., Davis, C., et al. (2004). The dopamine-4 receptor gene associated with binge eating and weight gain in women with seasonal affective disorder: An evolutionary perspective. *Biological Psychiatry, 56,* 665–669.

Lewinsohn, P. M. (1974). A behavioral approach to depression. In R. J. Friedman & M. M. Katz (Eds.), *Psychology of depression: Contemporary theory and research* (pp. 157–178). Oxford, England: John Wiley & Sons.

Lewis, A. (2004). Training psychiatrists to be expert witnesses. *Psychiatric Bulletin, 28,* 143–144.

Lewis, D. M., & Cachelin, F. M. (2001). Body image, body dissatisfaction, and eating attitudes in midlife and elderly women. *Eating Disorders, 9,* 29–39.

Lewis, D. O., Yeager, C. A., Swica, Y., Pincus, J. H., & Lewis, M. (1997). Objective documentation of child abuse and dissociation in 12 murderers with dissociative identity disorder. *American Journal of Psychiatry, 154,* 1703–1710.

Lewis, R., Bennett, C. J., Borkon, W. D., Boykin, W. H., Althof, S. E., Stecher, V. J., & Siegel, R. L. (2001). Patient and partner satisfaction with Viagra (sildenafil citrate) treatment as determined by the Erectile Dysfunction Inventory of Treatment Satisfaction Questionnaire. *Urology, 57,* 960–965.

Li, D., Chokka, P., & Tibbo, P. (2001). Toward an integrative understanding of social phobia. *Journal of Psychiatry and Neuroscience, 26,* 190–202.

Liberman, R. P. (2005). Rehab rounds: Drug and psychosocial curricula for psychiatry residents for treatment of schizophrenia: Part II. *Psychiatric Services, 56,* 28–30.

Liberman, R. P., Massel, H. K., Mosk, M. D., & Wong, S. E. (1985). Social skills training for chronic mental patients. *Hospital and Community Psychiatry, 36,* 396–403.

Lichtenstein, P., & Annas, P. (2000). Heritability and prevalence of specific fears and phobias in childhood. *Journal of Child Psychology and Psychiatry, 41,* 927–937.

Lidbeck, J. (2003). Group therapy for somatization disorders in primary care: Maintenance of treatment goals of short cognitive-behavioural treatment one-and-a-half-year follow-up. *Acta Psychiatrica Scandinavica, 107,* 449–456.

Lieb, R., Isensee, B., Hofler, M., Pfister, H., & Wittchen, H.-U. (2002). Parental major depression and the risk of depression and other mental disorders in offspring: A prospective-longitudinal community study. *Archives of General Psychiatry, 59,* 365–374.

Liebowitz, M. R., Fyer, A. J., Gorman, J. M., Dillon, D., Appleby, I. L., et al. (1984). Lactate provocation of panic attacks: I. Clinical behavioral findings. *Archives of General Psychiatry, 31,* 764–770.

Lilienfeld, S. O., Lynn, S. J., Kirsch, I., Chaves, J. F., Sarbin, T. R., Ganaway, G. K., & Powell, R. A. (1999). Dissociative identity disorder and the sociocognitive model: Recalling the lessons of the past. *Psychological Bulletin, 125,* 507–523.

Lilienfeld, S. O., Wood, J. M., & Garb, H. N. (2000). The scientific status of projective techniques. *Psychological Science in the Public Interest, 1,* 27–66.

Lima, B. R., Pai, S., Santacruz, H., & Lozano, J. (1991). Psychiatric disorders among poor victims following a major disaster: Armero, Colombia. *Journal of Nervous and Mental Disease, 179,* 420–427.

Linehan, M. M. (1993a). *Cognitive-behavioral treatment of borderline personality disorder.* New York: Guilford Press.

Linehan, M. M. (1993b). *Skills training manual for treating borderline personality disorder.* New York: Guilford Press.

Link, B. G., Phelan, J. C., Bresnahan, M., Stueve, A., & Pescosolido, B. A. (1999). Public conceptions of mental illness: Labels, causes, dangerousness, and social distance. *American Journal of Public Health, 89,* 1328–1333.

Lipowski, Z. J. (1988). Somatization: The concept and its clinical application. *American Journal of Psychiatry, 145,* 1358–1368.

Lisanby, S. H., Maddox, J. H., Prudic, J., Devanand, D. P., & Sackeim, H. A. (2000). The effects of electroconvulsive therapy on memory of autobiographical and public events. *Archives of General Psychiatry, 57,* 581–590.

Liu, J., Raine, A., Venables, P. H., & Mednick, S. A. (2004). Malnutrition at age 3 years and externalizing behavior problems at ages 8, 11, and 17 years. *American Journal of Psychiatry, 161,* 2005–2013.

Livesley, W. J., Schroeder, M. L., & Jackson, D. N. (1990). Dependent personality disorder and attachment problems. *Journal of Personality Disorders, 4,* 131–140.

Livesley, W. J., Schroeder, M. L., Jackson, D. N., & Jang, K. L. (1994). Categorical distinctions in the study of personality disorder:

Implications for classification. *Journal of Abnormal Psychology, 103,* 6–17.

Lochman, J. E., & Dodge, K. A. (1994). Social-cognitive processes of severely violent, moderately aggressive, and nonaggressive boys. *Journal of Consulting and Clinical Psychology, 62,* 366–374.

Lochner, C., Hemmings, S. M., Kinnear, C. J., Niehaus, D. J., Nel, D. G., Corfield, V. A., et al. (2005). Cluster analysis of obsessive-compulsive spectrum disorders in patients with obsessive-compulsive disorder: Clinical and genetic correlates. *Comprehensive Psychiatry, 46,* 14–19.

Loehlin, J. C., McCrae, R. R., Costa, P. T., Jr., & John, O. P. (1998). Heritabilities of common and measure-specific components of the Big Five personality factors. *Journal of Research in Personality, 32,* 431–453.

Londborg, P. D., Hegel, M. T., Goldstein, S., Goldstein, D., Himmelhoch, J. M., et al. (2001). Sertraline treatment of posttraumatic stress disorder: Results of 24 weeks of open-label continuation treatment. *Journal of Clinical Psychiatry, 62,* 325–331.

Longo, R. E. (2004). Using experiential exercises in treating adolescents with sexual behavior problems. *Sexual Addiction and Compulsivity, 11,* 249–263.

Lopez, F. G., & Brennan, K. A. (2000). Dynamic processes underlying adult attachment organization: Toward an attachment theoretical perspective on the healthy and effective self. *Journal of Counseling Psychology, 47,* 283–300.

Lopez, S. R., & Guarnaccia, P. J. (2000). Cultural psychopathology: Uncovering the social world of mental illness. *Annual Review of Psychology, 51,* 571–716.

LoPiccolo, J., & Stock, W. E. (1986). Treatment of sexual dysfunction. *Journal of Consulting and Clinical Psychology, 54,* 158–167.

Loranger, A. W., Sartorius, N., Andreoli, A., Berger, P., Buchheim, P., et al. (1994). The International Personality Disorder Examination. *Archives of General Psychiatry, 51,* 215–224.

Louchart–de la Chapelle, S., Nkam, I., Houy, E., Belmont, A., Menard, J. F., Roussignol, A. C., et al. (2005). A concordance study of three electrophysiological measures in schizophrenia. *American Journal of Psychiatry, 162,* 466–474.

Lovaas, O. I. (1987). Behavior treatment and normal educational and intellectual functioning in young autistic children. *Journal of Consulting and Clinical Psychology, 55,* 3–9.

Lovaas, O. I. (2003). *Teaching individuals with developmental delays: Basic intervention.* Austin, TX: PRO-ED.

Luchins, D. J., Cooper, A. E., Hanrahan, P., & Rasinski, K. (2004). Psychiatrists' attitudes toward involuntary hospitalization. *Psychiatric Services, 55,* 1058–1060.

Lundstrom, M., Edlund, A., Karlsson, S., Brannstrom, B., Bucht, G., & Gustafson, Y.

(2005). A multifactorial intervention program reduces the duration of delirium, length of hospitalization, and mortality in delirious patients. *Journal of the American Geriatrics Society, 53,* 622–628.

Luntz, B. K., & Widom, C. S. (1994). Antisocial personality disorder in abused and neglected children grown up. *American Journal of Psychiatry, 151,* 670–674.

Lussier, R. G., Steiner, J., Grey, A., & Hansen, C. (1997). Prevalence of dissociative disorders in an acute care day hospital population. *Psychiatric Services, 48,* 244–246.

Lykken, D. I. (1957). A study of anxiety in the sociopathic personality. *Journal of Abnormal and Social Psychology, 55,* 6–10.

Lykken, D. T. (1995). *The antisocial personalities.* Hillsdale, NJ: Erlbaum.

Lykken, D. T. (2000). The causes and costs of crime and a controversial cure. *Journal of Personality, 68.*

Lynam, D. R. (1997). Pursuing the psychopath: Capturing the fledgling psychopath in a nomological net. *Journal of Abnormal Psychology, 106,* 425–438.

Lynam, D. R., & Gudonis, L. (2005). The development of psychopathy. *Annual Review in Clinical Psychology, 1,* 381–407.

Lyons, M. J., Bar, J. L., Panizzon, M. S., Toomey, R., Eisen, S., Xian, H., et al. (2004). Neuropsychological consequences of regular marijuana use: A twin study. *Psychological Medicine, 34,* 1239–1250.

Lyons, M. J., Toomey, R., Meyer, J. M., Green, A. I., Eisen, S. A., Goldberg, J., True, W. R., & Tsuang, M. T. (1997). How do genes influence marijuana use? The role of subjective effects. *Addiction, 92,* 409–417.

Lyons, M. J., True, W. R., Eisen, S. A., Goldberg, J., Meyer, J. M., Faraone, S. V., Eaves, L. J. & Tsuang, M. T. (1995). Differential heritability of adult and juvenile antisocial traits. *Archives of General Psychiatry, 52,* 906–915.

M

MacDonald, M. (1981). *Mystical bedlam: Madness, anxiety, and healing in seventeenth-century England.* New York: Cambridge University Press.

MacKillop, J., Lisman, S. A., Weinstein, A., Rosenbaum, D. (2003). Controversial treatments for alcoholism. In S. O. Lilienfeld, S. J. Lynn, & J. M. Lohr (Eds.) *Science and pseudoscience in clinical psychology* (pp. 273–305). New York: Guilford Press.

MacQueen, G., Born, L., & Steiner, M. (2001). The selective serotonin reuptake inhibitor sertraline: Its profile and use in psychiatric disorders. *CNS Drug Reviews, 7,* 1–24.

Magnavita, N., Narda, R., Sani, L., Carbone, A., De Lorenzo, G., & Sacco, A. (1997). Type A behaviour pattern and traffic accidents. *British Journal of Medical Psychology, 70,* 103–107.

Maher, W. B., & Maher, B. A. (1985). Psychopathology: I. From ancient times to the eighteenth century. In G. A. Kimble & K. Schlesinger (Eds.), *Topics in the history of psychology* (Vol. 2, pp. 251–294). Hillsdale, NJ: Lawrence Erlbaum.

Mahler, M., Bergman, A., & Pine, F. (1975). *The psychological birth of the infant: Symbiosis and individuation.* New York: Basic Books.

Mai, F. (2004). Somatization disorder: A practical review. *Canadian Journal of Psychiatry, 49,* 652–662.

Maldonado, J. R., Butler, L. D., & Spiegel, D. (1998). Treatments for dissociative disorders. In P. E. Nathan & J. M. Gorman (Eds.), *A guide to treatments that work* (pp. 423–446). New York: Oxford University Press.

Maletzky, B. M. (1997). Exhibitionism: Assessment and treatment. In R. D. Laws & W. T. O'Donohue (Eds.), *Sexual deviance: Theory, assessment, and treatment* (pp. 40–74). New York: Guilford Press.

Mannuzza, S., Klein, R. G., Abikoff, H., & Moulton, J. L., 3rd. (2004). Significance of childhood conduct problems to later development of conduct disorder among children with ADHD: A prospective follow-up study. *Journal of Abnormal Child Psychology, 32,* 565–573.

Mansueto, C. S., Stemberger, R. M., Thomas, A. M., & Golomb, R. G. (1997). Trichotillomania: A comprehensive behavioral model. *Clinical Psychology Review, 17,* 567–577.

Marcantonio, E. R., Flacker, J. M., Wright, R. J., & Resnick, N. M. (2001). Reducing delirium after hip fracture: A randomized trial. *Journal of the American Geriatrics Society, 49,* 516–522.

Marcantonio, E. R., Kiely, D. K., Simon, S. E., John Orav, E., Jones, R. N., Murphy, K. M., et al. (2005). Outcomes of older people admitted to postacute facilities with delirium. *Journal of the American Geriatrics Society, 53,* 963–969.

Marlatt, G. A., Witkiewitz, K., Bowen, S. W., Parks, G. A., MacPherson, L. M., Lonczak, H. S., et al. (2004). Vipassana meditation as a treatment for alcohol and drug use disorders. In S. C. Hayes, V. M. Follette & M. M. Linehan (Eds.), *Mindfulness and acceptance: Expanding the cognitive-behavioral tradition* (pp. 261–287). New York: Guilford Press.

Marmar, C. R., Weiss, D. S., Schlenger-William, E., Fairbank, J. A., Jordan, B. K., Kulka, R. A., & Hough, R. L. (1994). Peritraumatic dissociation and post-traumatic stress in male Vietnam theater veterans. *American Journal of Psychiatry, 151,* 902–907.

Marino Junior, R., & Cosgrove, G. R. (1997). Neurosurgical treatment of neuropsychiatric illness. *Psychiatric Clinics of North America, 20,* 933–943.

Marom, S., Munitz, H., Jones, P. B., Weizman, A., & Hermesh, H. (2005). Expressed emotion: Relevance to rehospitalization in schizophrenia over 7 years. *Schizophrenia Bulletin.*

Marshall, W. L., & Fernandez, Y. M. (2000). Phallometric testing with sexual offenders: Limits to its value. *Clinical Psychology Review, 20,* 807–822.

Martin, C. A., Drasgow, E., & Halle, J. W. (2005). Teaching a child with autism and severe language delays to reject: Direct and indirect effects of functional communication training. *Educational Psychology, 25,* 287–304.

Martin, G., Bergen, H. A., Richardson, A. S., Roeger, L., & Allison, S. (2004). Correlates of firesetting in a community sample of young adolescents. *Australian and New Zealand Journal of Psychiatry, 38,* 148–154.

Marusic, A. (2005). History and geography of suicide: Could genetic risk factors account for the variation in suicide rates? *American Journal of Medical Genetics C: Seminars in Medical Genetics, 133,* 43–47.

Maslow, A. (1962). *Toward a psychology of being.* Princeton, NJ: Van Nostrand.

Maslow, A. (1971). *The farther reaches of human nature.* New York: Viking.

Mason, W. A., & Windle, M. (2001). Family, religious, school and peer influences on adolescent alcohol use: A longitudinal study. *Journal of Studies on Alcohol, 62,* 44–53.

Mason, W. A., Kosterman, R., Hawkins, J. D., Herrenkohl, T. I., Lengua, L. J., & McCauley, E. (2004). Predicting depression, social phobia, and violence in early adulthood from childhood behavior problems. *Journal of the American Academy of Child & Adolescent Psychiatry, 43,* 307–315.

Masters, W. H., & Johnson, V. E. (1966). *Human sexual response.* Boston: Little, Brown.

Masters, W. H., & Johnson, V. E. (1970). *Human sexual inadequacy.* Boston: Little, Brown.

Masters, W. H., Johnson, V. E., & Kolodny, R. C. (1982). *Human sexuality.* Boston: Little, Brown.

Masterson, J. F. (1981). *The narcissistic and borderline disorders: An integrated developmental approach.* New York: Brunner/Mazel.

Masterson, J. F., & Klein, R. (1989). *Psychotherapy of the disorders of the self.* New York: Brunner/Mazel.

Mataix-Cols, D., do Rosario-Campos, M. C., & Leckman, J. F. (2005). A multidimensional model of obsessive-compulsive disorder. *American Journal of Psychiatry, 162,* 228–238.

Mataix-Cols, D., Wooderson, S., Lawrence, N., Brammer, M. J., Speckens, A., & Phillips, M. L. (2004). Distinct neural correlates of washing, checking, and hoarding symptom dimensions in obsessive-compulsive disorder. *Archives of General Psychiatry, 61,* 564–576.

Matheny, J. C. H. (1998). Strategies for assessment and early treatment with sexually addicted families. *Sexual Addiction and Compulsivity, 5,* 27–48.

May, R. (1983). *The discovery of being: Writings in existential psychology.* New York: Norton.

McCabe, M. P. (1992). A program for the treatment of inhibited sexual desire in males. *Psychotherapy, 29,* 288–296.

McCabe, O. L. (2004). Crossing the quality chasm in behavioral health care: The role of evidence-based practice. *Professional Psychology: Research & Practice, 35,* 571–579.

McCardle, K., Luebbers, S., Carter, J. D., Croft, R. J., & Stough, C. (2004). Chronic MDMA (Ecstasy) use, cognition and mood. *Psychopharmacology (Berlin), 173,* 434–439.

McConaghy, N., Armstrong, M. S., & Blaszczynski, A. (1985). Expectancy, covert sensitization and imaginal desensitization in compulsive sexuality. *Acta Psychiatrica Scandinavica, 72,* 176–187.

McConaghy, N., Blaszczynski, A., & Frankova, A. (1991). Comparison of imaginal desensitization with other behavioural treatments of pathological gambling: A two- to nine-year follow-up. *British Journal of Psychiatry, 159,* 390–393.

McCullough, L., & Andrews, S. (2001). Assimilative integration: Short-term dynamic psychotherapy for treating affect phobias. *Clinical Psychology Science and Practice, 8,* 82–97.

McCullough-Vaillant, L. (1997). *Changing character.* New York: Basic Books.

McDermut, W., Miller, I. W., & Brown, R. A. (2001). The efficacy of group psychotherapy for depression: A meta-analysis and review of the empirical research. *Clinical Psychology Science and Practice, 8,* 98–116.

McDougle, C. J., Epperson, C. N., Pelton, G. H., Wasylink, S., & Price, L. H. (2000). A double-blind, placebo-controlled study of risperidone addition in serotonin reuptake inhibitor-refractory obsessive-compulsive disorder. *Archives of General Psychiatry, 57,* 794–801.

McElroy, S. L., Soutullo, C. A., Beckman, D. A., Taylor, P., Jr., & Keck, P. E., Jr. (1998). DSM-IV intermittent explosive disorder: A report of 27 cases. *Journal of Clinical Psychiatry, 59,* 203–210.

McGlashan, T. H. (1983). The borderline syndromes: II. Is it a variant of schizophrenia or affective disorder? *Archives of General Psychiatry, 40,* 1319–1323.

McGue, M., & Bouchard, T. J., Jr. (1998). Genetic and environmental influences on human behavioral differences. *Annual Review of Neuroscience, 21,* 1–24.

McGue, M., Hirsch, B., & Lykken, D. T. (1993). Age and the self-perception of ability: A twin study analysis. *Psychology and Aging, 8,* 72–80.

McGuffin, P. (2004). Nature and nurture interplay: Schizophrenia. *Psychiatrische Praxis, 31* (Supplement 2), S189–193.

McKay, D., Todaro, J., Neziroglu, F., & Campisi, T. (1997). Body dysmorphic disorder: A preliminary evaluation of treatment and maintenance using exposure with response prevention. *Behaviour Research and Therapy, 35,* 67–70.

McKeith, I., Mintzer, J., Aarsland, D., Burn, D., Chiu, H., Cohen-Mansfield, J., et al. (2004). Dementia with Lewy bodies. *Lancet Neurology, 3,* 19–28.

McKellar, J., Stewart, E., Humphreys, K. (2003). Alcoholics Anonymous involvement and positive alcohol-related outcomes: Cause, consequence, or just a correlate? A prospective 2-year study of 2,319 alcohol-dependent men. *Journal of Consulting & Clinical Psychology, 71,* 302–308.

McKhann, G., Drachman, D., Folstein, M., Katzman, R., Price, D., & Stadlan, E. M. (1984). Clinical diagnosis of Alzheimer's disease: Report of the NINCDS-ADRDA Work Group under the auspices of Department of Health and Human Services Task Force on Alzheimer's Disease. *Neurology, 34,* 939–944.

McNally, R. J. (1994). Choking phobia: A review of the literature. *Comprehensive Psychiatry, 35,* 83–89.

McNally, R. J. (2004). The science and folklore of traumatic amnesia. *Clinical Psychology: Science & Practice, 11,* 29–33.

McNamara, M. E. (1991). Psychological factors affecting neurological conditions: Depression and stroke, multiple sclerosis, Parkinson's disease, and epilepsy. *Psychosomatics, 32,* 255–267.

McQuillan, A., Nicastro, R., Guenot, F., Girard, M., Lissner, C., & Ferrero, F. (2005). Intensive dialectical behavior therapy for outpatients with borderline personality disorder who are in crisis. *Psychiatric Services, 56,* 193–197.

McWilliams, N., & Weinberger, J. (2003). Handbook of psychology: Clinical psychology. In G. Stricker & T. A. Widiger (Eds.), *Handbook of psychology: Clinical psychology* (Vol. 8). New York: John Wiley & Sons.

Meehl, P. E. (1962). Schizotaxia, schizotypy, schizophrenia. *American Psychologist, 17,* 827–828.

Meehl, P. E. (1990). Toward an integrated theory of schizotaxia, schizotypy, and schizophrenia. *Journal of Personality Disorders, 4,* 1–99.

Meichenbaum, D. (1985). *Stress inoculation training.* New York: Pergamon Press.

Meichenbaum, D. (1998). Sheila and Karen: Two cases of post-traumatic stress. In R. P. Halgin & S. K. Whitbourne (Eds.), *A casebook in abnormal psychology: From the files of experts* (pp. 72–87). New York: Oxford University Press.

Meloy, J. R. (2000). The nature and dynamics of sexual homicide: An integrative review. *Aggression and Violent Behavior, 5,* 1–22.

Mercer, J. R. (1979). *The System of Multicultural Pluralistic Assessment: Conceptual and technical manual.* New York: Psychological Corporation.

Merckelbach, H., & Muris, P. (1997). The etiology of childhood spider phobia. *Behaviour Research and Therapy, 35,* 1031–1034.

Merskey, H. (1992). The manufacture of personalities: The production of multiple personality disorder. *British Journal of Psychiatry, 160,* 327–340.

Messer, S. B. (2000). Applying the visions of reality to a case of brief therapy. *Journal of Psychotherapy Integration, 10,* 55–69.

Messer, S. B. (2001). What makes brief psychodynamic therapy time efficient. *Clinical Psychology: Science and Practice, 8,* 1–4.

Messerlian, C., Derevensky, J., & Gupta, R. (2005). Youth gambling problems: A public health perspective. *Health Promotion International, 20,* 69–79.

Metz, M. E., & Pryor, J. L. (2000). Premature ejaculation: A psychophysiological approach for assessment and management. *Journal of Sex and Marital Therapy, 26,* 293–320.

Mezzich, J. E., Kirmayer, L. J., Kleinman, A., Fabrega, H., Jr., Parron, D. L., Good, B. J., Lin, K.-M., & Manson, S. M. (1999). The place of culture in *DSM-IV. Journal of Nervous and Mental Disease, 187,* 457–464.

Meyer, A. (1957). *Psychobiology: A science of man.* Springfield, IL: Charles C. Thomas Press.

Mickelson, K. D., Kessler, R. C., & Shaver, P. R. (1997). Adult attachment in a nationally representative sample. *Journal of Personality and Social Psychology, 73,* 1092–1106.

Millar, H. R., Wardell, F., Vyvyan, J. P., Naji, S. A., Prescott, G. J., & Eagles, J. M. (2005). Anorexia nervosa mortality in northeast Scotland, 1965–1999. *American Journal of Psychiatry, 162,* 753–757.

Miller, B. C. (1995). Characteristics of effective day treatment programming for persons with borderline personality disorder. *Psychiatric Services, 46,* 605–608.

Miller, G. E., & Cohen, S. (2001). Psychological interventions and the immune system: A meta-analytic review and critique. *Health Psychology, 20,* 47–63.

Miller, N. E., & Banuazizi, A. L. I. (1968). Instrumental learning by curarized rats of a specific visceral response, intestinal or cardiac. *Journal of Comparative and Physiological Psychology, 65,* 1–7.

Miller, N. E., & Dworkin, B. R. (1977). Effects of learning on visceral functions: Biofeedback. *New England Journal of Medicine, 296,* 1274–1278.

Miller-Loncar, C., Lester, B. M., Seifer, R., Lagasse, L. L., Bauer, C. R., Shankaran, S., et al. (2005). Predictors of motor development in children prenatally exposed to cocaine. *Neurotoxicology and Teratology, 27,* 213–220.

Millon, T. (1991). Classification in psychopathology: Rationale, alternatives, and standards. *Journal of Abnormal Psychology, 100,* 245–261.

Millon, T. (1998). Ann: My first case of borderline personality disorder. In R. P. Halgin

& S. K. Whitbourne (Eds.), *A casebook in abnormal psychology: From the files of experts* (pp. 8–22). New York: Oxford University Press.

Millon, T., & Davis, R. D. (1996). *Disorders of personality: DSM-IV and beyond* (2nd ed.). New York: John Wiley & Sons.

Millon, T., Davis, R., Millon, C., Escovar, L., & Meagher, S. (2000). *Personality disorders in modern life.* New York: Wiley.

Milne, D. (2005). Outpatient commitment garners broad support. *Psychiatric News, 40,* 14.

Minden, S. L., Carbone, L. A., Barsky, A., Borus, J. F., Fife, A., Fricchione, G. L., et al. (2005). Predictors and outcomes of delirium. *General Hospital Psychiatry, 27,* 209–214.

Minuchin, S., Rosman, B. L., & Baker, L. (1978). *Psychosomatic families: Anorexia nervosa in context.* Cambridge, MA: Harvard University Press.

Mitchell, J. (1974). *Psychoanalysis and feminism.* New York: Pantheon.

Mizes, J. S., & Christiano, B. A. (1995). Assessment of cognitive variables relevant to cognitive behavioral perspectives on anorexia nervosa and bulimia nervosa. *Behaviour Research and Therapy, 33,* 95–105.

Mohn, A. R., Yao, W. D., & Caron, M. G. (2004). Genetic and genomic approaches to reward and addiction. *Neuropharmacology, 47 (Suppl. 1),* 101–110.

Mohr, D. C., & Beutler, L. E. (1990). Erectile dysfunction: A review of diagnostic and treatment procedures. *Clinical Psychology Review, 10,* 123–150.

Moldin, S. O., & Gottesman, I. I. (1997). At issue: Genes, experience, and chance in schizophrenia-positioning for the 21st century. *Schizophrenia Bulletin, 23,* 547–561.

Molina, V., Sanz, J., Sarramea, F., Benito, C., & Palomo, T. (2005). Prefrontal atrophy in first episodes of schizophrenia associated with limbic metabolic hyperactivity. *Journal of Psychiatric Research, 39,* 117–127.

Money, J. (1984). Paraphilias: Phenomenology and classification. *American Journal of Psychotherapy, 38,* 164–179.

Money, J., & Ehrhardt, A. (1973/1996). *Man and woman, boy and girl.* Northvale, NJ: Jason Aronson.

Moore, A. A., Gould, R., Reuben, D. B., Greendale, G. A., Carter, M. K., Zhou, K., et al. (2005). Longitudinal patterns and predictors of alcohol consumption in the United States. *American Journal of Public Health, 95,* 458–465.

Moos, R. H., & Moos, B. S. (1986). *Family Environment Scale Manual* (2nd ed.). Palo Alto, CA: Consulting Psychologists Press.

Moran, P. (1999). The epidemiology of antisocial personality disorder. *Social Psychiatry and Psychiatric Epidemiology, 34,* 231–242.

Morey, L. C. (1991). *Personality Assessment Inventory professional manual.* Odessa, FL: Psychological Assessment Resources.

Morey, L. C. (1996). *An interpretive guide to the Personality Assessment Inventory (PAI).* Odessa, FL: Psychological Assessment Resources.

Morgan, C. D., & Murray, H. A. (1935). A method for investigating fantasies: The Thematic Apperception test. *American Medical Association Archives of Neurology and Psychiatry, 34,* 289–306.

Morgan, D. L., & Morgan, R. K. (2001). Single-participant research design: Bringing science to managed care. *American Psychologist, 56,* 119–127.

Morgan, M. Y., Landron, F., & Lehert, P. (2004). Improvement in quality of life after treatment for alcohol dependence with acamprosate and psychosocial support. *Alcoholism: Clinical and Experimental Research, 28,* 64–77.

Morgenstern, J., Langenbucher, J., Labouvie, E., & Miller, K. J. (1997). The comorbidity of alcoholism and personality disorders in a clinical population: Prevalence rates and relation to alcohol typology variables. *Journal of Abnormal Psychology, 106,* 74–84.

Morizot, J., & Le Blanc, M. (2005). Searching for a developmental typology of personality and its relations to antisocial behavior: A longitudinal study of a representative sample of men. *Journal of Personality, 73,* 139–182.

Morris, A., Baker, B., Devins, G. M., & Shapiro, C. M. (1997). Prevalence of panic disorder in cardiac outpatients. *Canadian Journal of Psychiatry, 42,* 185–190.

Mortimer, J. A., Gosche, K. M., Riley, K. P., Markesbery, W. R., & Snowdon, D. A. (2004). Delayed recall, hippocampal volume and Alzheimer neuropathology: Findings from the Nun Study. *Neurology, 62,* 428–432.

Mueser, K. T., & Liberman, R. P. (1995). Behavior therapy in practice. In B. Bongar & L. E. Beutler (Eds.), *Comprehensive textbook of psychotherapy: Theory and practice* (pp. 84–110). New York: Oxford University Press.

Mueser, K. T., Torrey, W. C., Lynde, D., Singer, P., & Drake, R. E. (2003). Implementing evidence-based practices for people with severe mental illness. *Behavior Modification, 27,* 387–411.

Mukherjee, S., Sackeim, H. A., & Schnur, D. B. (1994). Electroconvulsive therapy of acute manic episodes: A review of 50 years' experience. *American Journal of Psychiatry, 151,* 169–176.

Muller, M. J., Ruof, J., Graf-Morgenstern, M., Porst, H., & Benkert, O. (2001). Quality of partnership in patients with erectile dysfunction after sildenafil treatment. *Pharmacopsychiatry, 34,* 91–95.

Munich, R. L. (1993). Conceptual issues in the psychoanalytic psychotherapy of patients with borderline personality disorder. In W. H. Sledge & A. Tasman (Eds.), *Clinical challenges in psychiatry* (pp. 61–88). Washington, DC: American Psychiatric Press.

Muris, P., & Merckelbach, H. (2000). How serious are common childhood fears? II. The parent's point of view. *Behavior Research and Therapy, 38,* 813–818.

Murphy, K. (2005). Psychosocial treatments for ADHD in teens and adults: A practice-friendly review. *Journal of Clinical Psychology, 61,* 607–619.

Murphy, M. J., DeBernardo, C. R., & Shoemaker, W. E. (1998). Impact of managed care on independent practice and professional ethics: A survey of independent practitioners. *Professional Psychology: Research and Practice, 29,* 43–51.

Murray, H. A. (1938). *Explorations in personality.* New York: Oxford University Press.

Murray, H. A. (1943). *Thematic Apperception Test manual.* Cambridge, MA: Harvard University Press.

Myers, M. G., Stewart, D. G., & Brown, S. A. (1998). Progression from conduct disorder to antisocial personality disorder following treatment for adolescent substance abuse. *American Journal of Psychiatry, 155,* 479–485.

N

Narrow, W. E., Regier, D. A., Rae, D. S., Manderscheid, R. W., & Locke, B. Z. (1993). Use of services by persons with mental and addictive disorders: Findings from the National Institute of Mental Health Epidemiologic Catchment Area Program. *Archives of General Psychiatry, 50,* 95–107.

Nathan, P. E. (1998). Practice guidelines: Not yet ideal. *American Psychologist, 53,* 290–299.

National Institute on Alcohol Abuse. (2000). New advances in alcoholism treatment. *Alcohol Alert,* No. 49.

National Institute of Alcoholism. (2005). *Fetal alcohol exposure.*

National Institute on Drug Abuse. (1997) *NIDA research report—Heroin abuse and addiction* (NIH Publication No. 97-4165). Rockville, MD: Author.

National Institute of Mental Health. (2001). *NIMH research on treatment for attention deficit hyperactivity disorder (ADHD): The Multimodal Treatment Study—Questions and answers.* Available on the World Wide Web at www.nimh.nih.gov/events/mtaqa.cfm.

National Institutes of Health. (1985). *Electroconvulsive therapy. NIH Consensus Statement* (5[11]: 1–23). Bethesda, MD.

Nelson, E., & Rice, J. (1997). Stability of diagnosis of obsessive-compulsive disorder in the Epidemiologic Catchment Area study. *American Journal of Psychiatry, 154,* 826–831.

Nestadt, G., Addington, A., Samuels, J., Liang, K. Y., Bienvenu, O. J., Riddle, M., et al. (2003). The identification of OCD-related subgroups based on comorbidity. *Biological Psychiatry, 53,* 914–920.

Neziroglu, F. A., & Yaryura-Tobias, J. A. (1993). Exposure, response prevention, and cognitive therapy in the treatment of body dysmorphic disorder. *Behavior Therapy, 24,* 431–438.

Niederehe, G., & Schneider, L. S. (1998). Treatments for depression and anxiety in the aged. In P. E. Nathan & J. M. Gorman (Eds.), *A guide to treatments that work* (pp. 270–287). New York: Oxford University Press.

Nierenberg, A. A., Phillips, K. A., Petersen, T. J., Kelly, K. E., Alpert, J. E., Worthington, J. J., et al. (2002). Body dysmorphic disorder in outpatients with major depression. *Journal of Affective Disorders, 69,* 141–148.

Ninan, P. T. (2000). Use of venlafaxine in other psychiatric disorders. *Depression and Anxiety, 12,* 90–94.

Noffsinger, S. G., & Resnick, P. J. (2000). Sexual predator laws and offenders with addictions. *Psychiatric Annals, 30,* 602–608.

Noffsinger, S. G., & Saleh, F. M. (2000). Ideas of reference about newscasters. *Psychiatric Services, 51,* 679.

Nordin, V., & Gillberg, C. (1998). The long-term course of autistic disorders: Update on follow-up studies. *Acta Psychiatrica Scandinavica, 97,* 99–108.

Noyes, R., Jr., Watson, D. B., Letuchy, E. M., Longley, S. L., Black, D. W., Carney, C. P., et al. (2005). Relationship between hypochondriacal concerns and personality dimensions and traits in a military population. *Journal of Nervous and Mental Disease, 193,* 110–118.

Noyes, R., Watson, D. B., Carney, C. P., Letuchy, E. M., Peloso, P. M., Black, D. W., et al. (2004). Risk factors for hypochondriacal concerns in a sample of military veterans. *Journal of Psychosomatic Research, 57,* 529–539.

Nuechterlein, K. H., Gitlin, M. J., & Subotnik, K. L. (1995). The early course of schizophrenia and long-term maintenance neuroleptic therapy. *Archives of General Psychiatry, 52,* 203–205.

Nunes, E. V., & Levin, F. R. (2004). Treatment of depression in patients with alcohol or other drug dependence: A meta-analysis. *Journal of the American Medical Association, 291,* 1887–1896.

Nunes, E. V., Frank, K. A., & Kornfeld, D. S. (1987). Psychologic treatment for the Type A behavior pattern and for coronary heart disease: A meta-analysis of the literature. *Psychosomatic Medicine, 48,* 159–173.

Nurnberger, J. I., Jr., Wiegand, R., Bucholz, K., O'Connor, S., Meyer, E. T., Reich, T., et al. (2004). A family study of alcohol dependence: Coaggregation of multiple disorders in relatives of alcohol-dependent probands. *Archives of General Psychiatry, 61,* 1246–1256.

Nutt, D. J. (2001). Neurobiological mechanisms in generalized anxiety disorder. *Journal of Clinical Psychiatry, 62* (Suppl. 11), 22–27.

O

O'Brien, C. P., Childress, A. R., Ehrman, R., & Robbins, S. J. (1998). Conditioning factors in drug abuse: Can they explain compulsion? *Journal of Psychopharmacology, 12,* 15–22.

O'Connor, T. G., McGuire, S., Reiss, D., Hetherington, E. M., & Plomin, R. (1998). Co-occurrence of depressive symptoms and antisocial behavior in adolescence: A common genetic liability. *Journal of Abnormal Psychology, 107,* 27–37.

O'Connor v. Donaldson. (1975). 95 S. Ct. 2486.

O'Donohue, W., Dopke, C. A., & Swingen, D. N. (1997). Psychotherapy for female sexual dysfunction: A review. *Clinical Psychology Review, 17,* 537–566.

O'Donohue, W. T., Swingen, D. N., Dopke, C. A., & Regev, L. G. (1999). Psychotherapy for male sexual dysfunction: A review. *Clinical Psychology Review, 19,* 591–630.

Oei, T. P., & Raylu, N. (2004). Familial influence on offspring gambling: A cognitive mechanism for transmission of gambling behavior in families. *Psychological Medicine, 34,* 1279–1288.

Official position of the division of clinical neuropsychology (APA division 40) on the role of neuropsychologists in clinical use of fMri: Approved by the Division 40 Executive Committee July 28, 2004. (2004). *Clin Neuropsychol, 18,* 349–351.

Ohman, A., & Hultman, C. M. (1998). Electrodermal activity and obstetric complications in schizophrenia. *Journal of Abnormal Psychology, 107,* 228–237.

Okie, S. (2005). Traumatic brain injury in the war zone. *New England Journal of Medicine, 352,* 2043–2047.

Okin, R. L. (1995). Testing the limits of deinstitutionalization. *Psychiatric Services, 46,* 73–78.

Okin, R. L., Borus, J. F., & Baer, L. (1995). Long-term outcome of state hospital patients discharged into structured community residential settings. *Psychiatric Services, 46,* 73–78.

O'Reilly, R. (2004). Why are community treatment orders controversial? *Canadian Journal of Psychiatry, 49,* 579–584.

Orne, M. T., Dinges, D. F., & Orne, E. C. (1984). On the differential diagnosis of multiple personality in the forensic context. *International Journal of Clinical and Experimental Hypnosis, 32,* 118–169.

Ost, L. G., Jerremalm, A., & Johansson, J. (1984). Individual response patterns and the effects of different behavioral methods on the treatment of social phobia. *Behaviour Research and Therapy, 22,* 697–708.

Overman, G. P., Teter, C. J., & Guthrie, S. K. (2003). Acamprosate for the adjunctive treatment of alcohol dependence. *Annals of Pharmacotherapy, 37,* 1090–1099.

Oxman, T. E., Barrett, J. E., Sengupta, A., & Williams, J. W., Jr. (2000). The relationship of aging and dysthymia in primary care. *American Journal of Geriatric Psychiatry, 8,* 318–326.

P

Papademetriou, V. (2005). Hypertension and cognitive function. Blood pressure regulation and cognitive function: A review of the literature. *Geriatrics, 60,* 20–22, 24.

Papadimitriou, G. N., Calabrese, J. R., Dikeos, D. G., & Christodoulou, G. N. (2005). Rapid cycling bipolar disorder: Biology and pathogenesis. *International Journal of Neuropsychopharmacology, 8,* 281–292.

Papp, L. A., Coplan, J., & Gorman, J. M. (1994). Anxiety disorders, In J. M. Oldham & M. B. Riba (Eds.), *Review of psychiatric disorders.* Washington, DC: American Psychiatric Press.

Papp, L. A., Martinez, J. M., Klein, D. F., Coplan, J. D., Norman, R. G., et al. (1997). Respiratory psychophysiology of panic disorder: Three respiratory challenges in 98 subjects. *American Journal of Psychiatry, 154,* 1557–1565.

Parker, P. E. (1993). A case report of Munchausen syndrome with mixed psychological features. *Psychosomatics, 34,* 360–364.

Parks, G. A., Anderson, B. K., & Marlatt, G. A. (2001). Relapse prevention therapy. In N. Heather & T. J. Peters (Eds.), *International handbook of alcohol dependence and problems* (pp. 575–592). New York: John Wiley.

Pato, M. T., Schindler, K. M., & Pato, C. N. (2001). The genetics of obsessive-compulsive disorder. *Current Psychiatry Reports, 3,* 163–168.

Patrick, C. J., Bradley, M. M. & Lang, P. J. (1993). Emotion in the criminal psychopath: Startle reflex modulation. *Journal of Abnormal Psychology, 102,* 82–92.

Patrick, C. J., Cuthbert, B. N., & Lang, P. J. (1994). Emotion in the criminal psychopath: Fear image processing. *Journal of Abnormal Psychology, 103,* 523–534.

Pedersen, S. S., & Denollet, J. (2003). Type D personality, cardiac events, and impaired quality of life: A review. *European Journal of Cardiovascular Prevention & Rehabilitation, 10,* 241–248.

Pelham, W. E., Jr. & Fabiano, G. A. (2000). Behavior modification. *Child and Adolescent Psychiatric Clinics of North America, 9,* 671–688, ix.

Penn, D. L., & Martin, J. (1998). The stigma of severe mental illness: Some potential solutions for a recalcitrant problem. *Psychiatric Quarterly, 69,* 235–247.

Pennebaker, J. W. (1997a). *Opening up: The healing power of expressing emotions* (rev. ed.). New York: Guilford Press.

Pennebaker, J. W. (1997b). Writing about emotional experiences as a therapeutic process. *Psychological Science, 8,* 162–166.

Pennebaker, J. W., Colder, M., & Sharp, L. K. (1990). Accelerating the coping process. *Journal of Personality and Social Psychology, 58,* 528–537.

Pereg, D., & Mikulincer, M. (2004). Attachment style and the regulation of negative affect: Exploring individual differences in mood congruency effects on memory and judgment. *Personality and Social Psychology Bulletin, 30,* 67–80.

Perlin, M. L. (1994). Law and the delivery of mental health services in the community. *American Journal of Orthopsychiatry, 64,* 194–208.

Perls, T. (2004). Centenarians who avoid dementia. *Trends in Neuroscience, 27,* 633–636.

Peterson, A., & Halstead, T. (1998). Group cognitive behavior therapy for depression in a community setting: A clinical replication series. *Behavior Therapy, 29,* 3–18.

Petry, N. M. (2001). Substance abuse, pathological gambling, and impulsiveness. *Drug and Alcohol Dependency, 63,* 29–38.

Phelps, R., Eisman, E. J., & Kohout, J. (1998). Psychological practice and managed care: Results of the CAPP Practitioner Survey. *Professional Psychology: Research and Practice, 29,* 31–36.

Phillips, K. A. (1996). Body dysmorphic disorder: Diagnosis and treatment of imagined ugliness. *Journal of Clinical Psychiatry, 57,* 61–65.

Phillips, K. A., & Diaz, S. F. (1997). Gender differences in body dysmorphic disorder. *Journal of Nervous and Mental Disease, 185,* 570–577.

Phillips, K. A., & Najjar, F. (2003). An open-label study of citalopram in body dysmorphic disorder. *Journal of Clinical Psychiatry, 64,* 715–720.

Phillips, K. A., & McElroy, S. L. (2000). Personality disorders and traits in patients with body dysmorphic disorder. *Comprehensive Psychiatry, 41,* 229–236.

Phillips, K. A., McElroy, S. L., Keck, P. E., & Pope, H. G. (1993). Body dysmorphic disorder: 30 cases of imagined ugliness. *American Journal of Psychiatry, 150,* 302–308.

Phillips, K. A., Nierenberg, A. A., Brendel, G., & Fava, M. (1996). Prevalence and clinical features of body dysmorphic disorder in a typical major depression. *Journal of Nervous and Mental Disease, 184,* 125–129.

Phillips, K. A., & Taub, S. L. (1995). Skin picking as a symptom of body dysmorphic disorder. *Psychopharmacology Bulletin, 31,* 279–288.

Phillips, K. A., Siniscalchi, J. M., & McElroy, S. L. (2004). Depression, anxiety, anger, and somatic symptoms in patients with body dysmorphic disorder. *Psychiatry Quarterly, 75,* 309–320.

Piek, J., Lidke, G., Terberger, T., von Smekal, U., & Gaab, M. R. (1999). Stone age skull surgery in Mecklenburg-Vorpommern: A systematic study. *Neurosurgery, 45,* 147–151.

Pimm, J., McQuillin, A., Thirumalai, S., Lawrence, J., Quested, D., Bass, N., et al. (2005). The Epsin 4 gene on chromosome 5q, which encodes the clathrin-associated protein enthoprotin, is involved in the genetic susceptibility to schizophrenia. *American Journal of Human Genetics, 76,* 902–907.

Pine, D. S., Cohen, P., Gurley, D., Brook, J., & Ma, Y. (1998). The risk for early-adulthood anxiety and depressive disorders in adolescents with anxiety and depressive disorders. *Archives of General Psychiatry, 55,* 56–64.

Pine, D. S., Klein, R. G., Roberson-Nay, R., Mannuzza, S., Moulton, J. L., 3rd, Wolde-hawariat, G., & Guardino. (2005). Response to 5% carbon dioxide in children and adolescents: Relationship to panic disorder in parents and anxiety disorders in subjects. *Archives of General Psychiatry, 62,* 73–80.

Pini, S., Cassano, G. B., Simonini, E., Savino, M., Russo, A., & Montgomery, S. A. (1997). Prevalence of anxiety disorders comorbidity in bipolar depression, unipolar depression and dysthymia. *Journal of Affective Disorders, 42,* 145–153.

Piotrowski, C. (2000). How popular is the Personality Assessment Inventory in practice and training? *Psychological Reports, 86,* 65–66.

Pitts, F. N., Jr., & McClure, J. N., Jr. (1967). Lactate metabolism in anxiety neurosis. *New England Journal of Medicine, 277,* 1329–1336.

Piven, J., Bailey, J., Ranson, B. J., & Arndt, S. (1997). An MRI study of the corpus callosum in autism. *American Journal of Psychiatry, 154,* 1051–1056.

Plomin, R., & Caspi, A. (1999). Behavioral genetics and personality. In L. A. Pervin & O. P. John (Eds.), *Handbook of personality: Theory and research* (2nd ed.), (pp. 251–276). New York: Guilford Press.

Pollack, M. H., Rapaport, M. H., Clary, C. M., Mardekian, J., & Wolkow, R. (2000). Sertraline treatment of panic disorder: Response in patients at risk for poor outcome. *Journal of Clinical Psychiatry, 61,* 922–927.

Pollack, M. H., Zaninelli, R., Goddard, A., McCafferty, J. P., Bellew, K. M., Burnham, D. B., & Iyengar, M. K. (2001). Paroxetine in the treatment of generalized anxiety disorder: Results of a placebo-controlled, flexible-dosage trial. *Journal of Clinical Psychiatry, 62,* 350–357.

Pope, H. G., Jr., & Yurgelun-Todd, D. (2004). Residual cognitive effects of long-term cannabis use. In D. Castle & R. Murray (Eds.), *Marijuana and Madness.* Cambridge, England: Cambridge University Press.

Porter, S., Birt, A. R., Yuille, J. C., & Herve, H. F. (2001). Memory for murder: A psychological perspective on dissociative amnesia in legal contexts. *International Journal of Law Psychiatry, 24,* 23–42.

Powell, R. A., & Gee, T. L. (1999). The effects of hypnosis on dissociative identity disorder: A reexamination of the evidence. *Canadian Journal of Psychiatry, 44,* 914–916.

Powell, R. A., & Gee, T. L. (2000). Re: Powell, Gee, and Ross—The effects of hypnosis on

dissociative identity disorder. *Canadian Journal of Psychiatry, 45,* 848–849.

Prentky, R. A. (1997). Arousal reduction in sexual offenders: A review of antiandrogen interventions. *Sexual Abuse: Journal of Research and Treatment, 9,* 335–347.

Prentky, R. A., Knight, R. A., Sims-Knight, J. E., Straus, H., Rokous, F., & Cerce, D. (1989). Developmental antecedents of sexual aggression. *Development and Psychopathology, 1,* 153–169.

Prentky, R. A., Knight, R., & Lee, A. F. (1997). Risk factors associated with recidivism among extrafamilial child molesters. *Journal of Consulting and Clinical Psychology, 65,* 141–149.

President's New Freedom Commission on Mental Health (2003). Achieving the Promise: Transforming Mental Health Care in America. Available on the World Wide Web at www.mentalhealthcommission.gov/reports/Finalreport/downloads/FinalReport.pdf

Price, D. (2004). Youth with problem sexual behaviors: Integrating diverse models of treatment. *Sexual Addiction and Compulsivity, 11,* 183–186.

Proulx, J., Pellerin, B., Paradis, Y., McKibben, A., Aubut, J., & Ouimet, M. (1997). Static and dynamic predictors of recidivism in sexual aggressors. *Sexual Abuse: Journal of Research and Treatment, 9,* 7–27.

Putnam, F. W., Guroff, J. J., Silberman, E. K., Barban, L. & Post, R. M. (1986). The clinical phenomenology of multiple personality disorder: Review of 100 recent cases. *Journal of Clinical Psychiatry, 47,* 285–293.

Q

Quadland, M. C. (1985). Compulsive sexual behavior: Definition of a problem and approach to treatment. *Journal of Sex and Marital Therapy, 11,* 121–132.

Quinn, P. O. (2005). Treating adolescent girls and women with ADHD: Gender-specific issues. *Journal of Clinical Psychology, 61,* 579–587.

R

Rachman, S. (1966). Sexual fetishism: An experimental analog. *Psychological Record, 16,* 293–296.

Rachman, S., & Hodgson, R. J. (1968). Experimentally induced "sexual fetishism" replication and development. *Psychological Record, 18,* 25–27.

Radel, M., & Goldman, D. (2001). Pharmacogenetics of alcohol response and alcoholism: The interplay of genes and environmental factors in thresholds for alcoholism. *Drug Metabolism and Disposition, 29,* 489–494.

Rakic, Z., Starcevic, V., Maric, J., & Kelin, K. (1996). The outcome of sex reassignment surgery in Belgrade: 32 patients of both sexes. *Archives of Sexual Behavior, 25,* 515–525.

Raman, B., Ban, T., Yamaguchi, K., Sakai, M., Kawai, T., Naiki, H., et al. (2005). Metal ion-dependent effects of clioquinol on the fibril growth of an amyloid {beta} peptide. *Journal of Biological Chemistry, 280,* 16157–16162.

Ramchandani, P. (2004). Treatment of major depressive disorder in children and adolescents. *British Medical Journal, 328,* 3–4.

Ramsay, R., Gorst-Unsworth, C., & Turner, S. W. (1993). Psychiatric morbidity in survivors of organised state violence including torture: A retrospective series. *British Journal of Psychiatry, 162,* 55–59.

Rapoport, J. L. (1990). The waking nightmare: An overview of obsessive-compulsive disorder. *Journal of Clinical Psychiatry, 51,* 25–28.

Rasanen, P., Hakko, H., & Vaisanen, E. (1995). Arson trend increasing: A real challenge to psychiatry. *Journal of Forensic Sciences, 40,* 976–979.

Rassovsky, Y., Kushner, M. G., Schwarze, N. J., & Wangensteen, O. D. (2000). Psychological and physiological predictors of response to carbon dioxide challenge in individuals with panic disorder. *Journal of Abnormal Psychology, 109,* 616–623.

Rauch, S. L., & Jenike, M. A. (1998). Pharmacologic treatment of obsessive-compulsive disorder. In P. E. Nathan & J. M. Gorman (Eds.), *A guide to treatments that work* (pp. 358–376). New York: Oxford University Press.

Ravindran, A. V., Lapierre, Y. D., & Anisman, H. (1999). Obsessive-compulsive spectrum disorders: Effective treatment with paroxetine. *Canadian Journal of Psychiatry, 44,* 805–807.

Raymond, N. C., Coleman, E., & Miner, M. H. (2003). Psychiatric comorbidity and compulsive/impulsive traits in compulsive sexual behavior. *Comprehensive Psychiatry, 44,* 370–380.

Reas, D. L., Kjelsas, E., Heggestad, T., Eriksen, L., Nielsen, S., Gjertsen, F., et al. (2005). Characteristics of anorexia nervosa–related deaths in Norway (1992–2000): Data from the National Patient Register and the Causes of Death Register. *International Journal of Eating Disorders, 37,* 181–187.

Reich, T., Edenberg, H. J., Goate, A., Williams, J. T., Rice, J. P., et al. (1998). Genome-wide search for genes affecting the risk for alcohol dependence. *American Journal of Medical Genetics, 81,* 207–215.

Reidy, D. E. (1994). The mental health system as an agent of stigma. Resources: *Workforce Issues in Mental Health Systems, 6,* 3–10.

Reis, S., & Grenyer, B. F. (2004). Fear of intimacy in women: Relationship between attachment styles and depressive symptoms. *Psychopathology, 37,* 299–303.

Reisberg, B. (1983). Clinical presentation, diagnosis, and symptomatology of age-associated cognitive decline and Alzheimer's disease. In B. Reisberg (Ed.), *Alzheimer's disease* (pp. 173–187). New York: Free Press.

Reist, C., Nakamura, K., Sagart, E., Sokolski, K. N., & Fujimoto, K. A. (2003). Impulsive aggressive behavior: Open-label treatment with citalopram. *Journal of Clinical Psychiatry, 64,* 81–85.

Renner, M. J., & Mackin, R. S. (1998). A life stress instrument for classroom use. *Teaching of Psychology, 25,* 46–48.

Rennie v. Klein. 462 F. Supp. 1131 (1979).

Report of the Surgeon General's Conference on Children's Mental Health: A National Action Agenda. (2000). Available on the World Wide Web at www.surgeongeneral.gov/ cmh/ childreport.htm9/25/01.

Resnick, R. J. (2005). Attention deficit hyperactivity disorder in teens and adults: They don't all outgrow it. *Journal of Clinical Psychology, 61,* 529–533.

Rettew, D. C. (2000). Avoidant personality disorder, generalized social phobia, and shyness: Putting the personality back into personality disorders. *Harvard Review of Psychiatry, 8.*

Reuter, J., Raedler, T., Rose, M., Hand, I., Glascher, J., & Buchel, C. (2005). Pathological gambling is linked to reduced activation of the mesolimbic reward system. *Nature Neuroscience, 8,* 147–148.

Rey, J. M., Peng, R., Morales-Blanquez, C., Widyawati, I., Peralta, V., & Walter, G. (2000). Rating the quality of the family environment in different cultures. *Journal of the American Academy of Child and Adolescent Psychiatry, 39,* 1168–1174.

Rey, J. M., Singh, M., Hung, S. F., Dossetor, D. R., Newman, L., Plapp, J. M., et al. (1997). A global scale to measure the quality of the family environment. *Archives of General Psychiatry, 54,* 817–822.

Rhoads, J. M. (1989). Exhibitionism and voyeurism. In T. S. Karasu (Ed.), *Treatment of psychiatric disorders* (Vol. 1, pp. 670–673). Washington, DC: American Psychiatric Association.

Ricciardelli, L. A., & McCabe, M. P. (2001). Dietary restraint and negative affect as mediators of body dissatisfaction and bulimic behavior in adolescent girls and boys. *Behaviour Research and Therapy, 39,* 1317–1328.

Richards, J. M., Beal, W. E., Seagal, J. D., & Pennebaker, J. W. (2000). Effects of disclosure of traumatic events on illness behavior among psychiatric prison inmates. *Journal of Abnormal Psychology, 109,* 156–160.

Richardson, R. D., & Engel, C. C., Jr. (2004). Evaluation and management of medically unexplained physical symptoms. *Neurologist, 10,* 18–30.

Rickels, K., DeMartinis, N., Garcia-Espana, F., Greenblatt, D. J., Mandos, L. A., & Rynn, M. (2000). Imipramine and buspirone in treatment of patients with generalized anxiety disorder who are discontinuing long-term benzodiazepine therapy. *American Journal of Psychiatry, 157,* 1973–1979.

Riley, E. P., & McGee, C. L. (2005). Fetal alcohol spectrum disorders: An overview with emphasis on changes in brain and behavior. *Experimental Biology and Medicine, 230,* 357–365.

Ritchie, E. C., & Huff, T. G. (1999). Psychiatric aspects of arsonists. *Journal of Forensic Science, 44,* 733–740.

Rizvi, S. L., Stice, E., & Agras, W. S. (1999). Natural history of disordered eating attitudes and behaviors over a 6-year period. *International Journal of Eating Disorders, 26,* 406–413.

Robbins, C. A. (2005). ADHD couple and family relationships: Enhancing communication and understanding through Imago Relationship Therapy. *Journal of Clinical Psychology, 61,* 565–577.

Roberts, R. E., Alegria, M., Roberts, C. R., & Chen, I. G. (2005). Mental health problems of adolescents as reported by their caregivers: A comparison of European, African, and Latino Americans. *Journal of Behavior and Health Services Research, 32,* 1–13.

Robins, L. N., (1966). *Deviant children grow up: A sociological and psychiatric study of sociopathic personality.* Baltimore: Williams & Wilkins.

Robins, L. N., & Regier, D. A. (1991). *Psychiatric disorders in America.* New York: Free Press.

Rodriguez Solano, J. J., & Gonzalez De Chavez, M. (2000). Premorbid personality disorders in schizophrenia. *Schizophrenia Research, 44,* 137–144.

Rogers, C. (2004). *Psychotherapy and counseling: A professional business.* London: Whurr.

Rogers, C. R. (1951). *Client-centered therapy: Its current practice implications and theory.* Boston: Houghton Mifflin.

Rogers, C. R. (1959). A theory of therapy, personality, and interpersonal relationships as developed in the client-centered framework. In S. Koch (Ed.), *Psychology: A study of a science* (Vol. 3, pp. 184–256). New York: McGraw-Hill.

Rogers, R. L., & Petrie, T. A. (2001). Psychological correlates of anorexia and bulimic symptomatology. *Journal of Counseling and Development, 79,* 178–187.

Rogers v. Okin. 478 F. Supp. 1342 (D Mass) 1979.

Roid, G. H. (2003). *Stanford-Binet Intelligence Scales (fifth edition).* Itsaca, IL.

Roitman, S. E., Cornblatt, B. A., Bergman, A., Obuchowski, M., Mitropoulou, V., Keefe, R. S., et al. (1997). Attentional functioning in schizotypal personality disorder. *American Journal of Psychiatry, 154,* 655–660.

Rosack, J. (2005). New analysis disputes antidepressant, suicide risk. *Psychiatric News, 40,* 1.

Rosen, J. C., Reiter, J., & Orosan, P. (1995). Cognitive-behavioral body image therapy for body dysmorphic disorder. *Journal of*

Consulting and Clinical Psychology, 63, 263–269.

Rosenbaum, M. (1980). The role of the term schizophrenia in the decline of diagnoses of multiple personality. *Archives of General Psychiatry, 37,* 1383–1385.

Rosenberg, D. R., Dick, E. L., O'Hearn, K. M., & Sweeney, J. A. (1997). Response-inhibition deficits in obsessive-compulsive disorder: An indicator of dysfunction in frontostriatal circuits. *Journal of Psychiatry & Neuroscience, 22,* 29–38.

Rosenfarb, I. S., Nuechterlein, K. H., Goldstein, M. J., & Subotnik, K. L. (2000). Neurocognitive vulnerability, interpersonal criticism, and the emergence of unusual thinking by schizophrenic patients during family transactions. *Archives of General Psychiatry, 57,* 1174–1179.

Rosenhan, D. L. (1973). On being sane in insane places. *Science, 179,* 250–258.

Roskies, E., Seraganian, P., Oseasohn, R., Smilga, C., Martin, N., & Hanley, J. A. (1989). Treatment of psychological stress responses in healthy Type A men. In R. W. J. Neufeld (Ed.), *Advances in the investigation of psychological stress* (pp. 284–304). New York: Wiley.

Rosler, A., & Witztum, E. (2000). Pharmacotherapy of paraphilias in the next millennium. *Behavioral Sciences and the Law, 18,* 43–56.

Ross, C. A. (1989). *Multiple personality disorder: Diagnosis, clinical features, and treatment.* New York: Wiley.

Ross, C. A. (1997a). Cognitive therapy of dissociative identity disorder. In P. S. Appelbaum, L. A. Uyehara, & M. R. Elin (Eds.), *Trauma and memory: Clinical and legal controversies* (pp. 360–377). New York: Oxford University Press.

Ross, C. A. (1997b). *Dissociative identity disorder: Diagnosis, clinical features, and treatment of multiple personality* (2nd ed.). New York: John Wiley & Sons.

Ross, C. A., Miller, S. D., Reagor, P., Bjornson, L., Fraser, G. A., & Anderson, G. (1990). Structured interview data on 102 cases of multiple personality disorder from four centers. *American Journal of Psychiatry, 147,* 596–601.

Ross, C. J. (1996). A qualitative study of sexually addicted women. *Sexual Addiction and Compulsivity, 3,* 43–53.

Ross, R., Frances, A., & Widiger, T. A. (1997). Gender issues in the *DSM-IV.* In M. R. Walsh (Ed.), *Women, men, and gender: Ongoing debates* (pp. 340–347). New Haven: Yale University Press.

Roth, T., Roehrs, T. A., & Rosenthal, L. (1994). Normative and pathological aspects of daytime sleepiness. In J. M. Oldham & M. B. Riba (Eds.), *Review of Psychiatry* (Vol. 13, pp. 707–728). Washington DC: American Psychiatric Press.

Rothbaum, F., Weisz, J., Pott, M., Miyake, K., & Morelli, G. (2000). Attachment and culture: Security in the United States and Japan. *American Psychologist, 55,* 1093–1104.

Rothbaum, P. A., Bernstein, D.M., Haller, O., Phelps, R., & Kohout, J. (1998). New Jersey psychologists' report on managed mental health care. *Professional Psychology: Research and Practice, 29,* 37–42.

Rounsaville, B. J., O'Malley, S., Foley, S., & Weisman, M. M. (1988). Role of manual-guided training in the conduct and efficacy of interpersonal psychotherapy for depression. *Journal of Consulting and Clinical Psychology, 56,* 681–688.

Rounsaville, R. J., Alarcon, R. D., Andrews, G., Jackson, J. S., Kendell, R. E., & Kendler, K. S. (2002). Basic nomenclature issues for DSM-V. In M. B. Kupfer, D. J. First & D. A. Regier (Eds.), *A research agenda for DSM-V.* Washington, DC: American Psychiatric Association.

Rudd, M. D. (2000). The suicidal mode: A cognitive-behavioral model of suicidality. *Suicide and Life Threatening Behavior, 30,* 18–33.

Rudd, M. D., Rajab, M. H., & Dahm, P. F. (1994). Problem-solving appraisal in suicide ideators and attempters. *American Journal of Orthopsychiatry, 64,* 136–149.

Rumi, D. O., Gattaz, W. F., Rigonatti, S. P., Rosa, M. A., Fregni, F., Rosa, M. O., et al. (2005). Transcranial magnetic stimulation accelerates the antidepressant effect of amitriptyline in severe depression: A double-blind placebo-controlled study. *Biological Psychiatry, 57,* 162–166.

Ruschena, D., Mullen, P. E., Burgess, P., Cordner, S. M., Barry-Walsh, J., et al. (1998). Sudden death in psychiatric patients. *British Journal of Psychiatry, 172,* 331–336.

Russ, M. J., Shearin, E. N., Clarkin, J. F., & Harrison, K. (1993). Subtypes of self-injurious patients with borderline personality disorder. *American Journal of Psychiatry, 150,* 1869–1871.

Rutter, M. (1984). Psychopathology and development: II. Childhood experiences and personality development. *Australian and New Zealand Journal of Psychiatry, 18,* 314–327.

Rutter, M., Caspi, A., Fergusson, D., Horwood, L. J., Goodman, R., Maughan, B., et al. (2004). Sex differences in developmental reading disability: New findings from 4 epidemiological studies. *Journal of the American Medical Association, 291,* 2007–2012.

S

Saarinen, P. I., Lehtonen, J., Joensuu, M., Tolmunen, T., Ahola, P., Vanninen, R., et al. (2005). An outcome of psychodynamic psychotherapy: A case study of the change in serotonin transporter binding and the activation of the dream screen. *American Journal of Psychotherapy, 59,* 61–73.

Sacco, W. P., & Beck, A. T. (1985). Cognitive therapy of depression. In E. E. Beckhan & W. R. Leber (Eds.), *Handbook of depression: Treatment, assessment, and research* (pp. 3–38). Homewood, IL: Dorsey Press.

Safran, J. D. (1990). Towards a refinement of cognitive therapy in light of interpersonal theory: I. Theory. *Clinical Psychology Review, 10,* 87–105.

Safran, J. D., & Muran, J. C. (2000). *Negotiating the therapeutic alliance: A relational treatment guide.* New York: Guilford Press.

Salekin, R. T., Neumann, C. S., Leistico, A. M., & Zalot, A. A. (2004). Psychopathy in youth and intelligence: An investigation of Cleckley's hypothesis. *Journal of Clinical Child & Adolescent Psychology, 33,* 731–742.

Salkovskis, P. M., & Westbrook, D. (1989). Behavior therapy and obsessional ruminations: Can failure be turned into success? *Behaviour Research and Therapy, 24,* 597–602.

Salkovskis, P. M., Westbrook, D., Davis, J., Jeavons, A., & Gledhill, A. (1997). Effects of neutralizing on intrusive thoughts: An experiment investigating the etiology of obsessive-compulsive disorder. *Behaviour Research and Therapy, 35,* 211–219.

Salkovskis, P. M., Wroe, A. L., Gledhill, A., Morrison, N., Forrester, E., Richards, C., Reynolds, M., & Thorpe, S. (2000). Responsibility attitudes and interpretations are characteristic of obsessive compulsive disorder. *Behaviour Research and Therapy, 38,* 347–372.

Salter, M., & Byrne, P. (2000). The stigma of mental illness: How you can use the media to reduce it. *Psychiatric Bulletin, 24,* 281–283.

SAMHSA (2004). *Results from the 2003 National Survey on Drug Use and Health: National Findings. NSDUH Series H-25, DHHS Publication No. SMA 04-3964.* Rockville MD: Substance Abuse and Mental Health Services Administration, Office of Applied Studies.

SAMHSA (2005). Healthy people 2010 (conference edition). At http://www.mentalhealth.samhsa.gov/features/hp2010/18Mental.asp.

Sampson, P. D., Streissguth, A. P., Bookstein, F. L., Little, R. E., Clarren, S. K., et al. (1997). Incidence of fetal alcohol syndrome and prevalence of alcohol-related neurodevelopmental disorder. *Teratology, 56,* 317–326.

Sanderson, W. C., & Barlow, D. H. (1990). A description of patients diagnosed with DSM-III-R generalized anxiety disorder. *Journal of Nervous and Mental Disease, 178,* 588–591.

Sansone, R. A., Levitt, J. L., & Sansone, L. A. (2005). The prevalence of personality disorders among those with eating disorders. *Eating Disorders: The Journal of Treatment & Prevention. Special issue: Personality Disorders & Eating Disorders, 13,* 7–21.

Santangelo, S. L., & Tsatsanis, K. (2005).

What is known about autism: Genes, brain, and behavior. *American Journal of Pharmacogenomics, 5,* 71–92.

Saoud, M., d'Amato, T., Gutknecht, C., Triboulet, P., Bertaud, J. P., et al. (2000). Neuropsychological deficit in siblings discordant for schizophrenia. *Schizophrenia Bulletin, 26,* 893–902.

Sar, V., Akyuz, G., Kundakci, T., Kiziltan, E., & Dogan, O. (2004). Childhood trauma, dissociation, and psychiatric comorbidity in patients with conversion disorder. *American Journal of Psychiatry, 161,* 2271–2276.

Sasson, Y., Zohar, J., Chopra, M., Lustig, M., Iancu, I., & Hendler, T. (1997). Epidemiology of obsessive-compulsive disorder: A world view. *Journal of Clinical Psychiatry, 12,* 7–10.

Saudino, K. J., Gagné, J. R., Grant, J., Ibatoulina, A., Marytuina, T., Ravich-Scherbo, I., & Whitfield, K. (1999). Genetic and environmental influences on personality in adult Russian twins. *International Journal of Behavioral Development, 23,* 375–389.

Sawchuk, C. N., Lohr, J. M., Tolin, D. F., Lee, T. C., & Kleinknecht, R. A. (2000). Disgust sensitivity and contamination fears in spider and blood-injection-injury phobias. *Behavior Research and Therapy, 38,* 753–762.

Saxena, S., & Rauch, S. L. (2000). Functional neuroimaging and the neuroanatomy of obsessive-compulsive disorder. *Psychiatric Clinics of North America, 23,* 563–586.

Sayers, J. (1991). *Mothers of psychoanalysis.* New York: Norton.

Scarr, S. (1992). Developmental theories for the 1990s: Development and individual differences. *Child Development, 63,* 1–19.

Scazufca, M., & Kuipers, E. (1998). Stability of expressed emotion in relatives of those with schizophrenia and its relationship with burden of care and perception of patients' social functioning. *Psychological Medicine, 28,* 453–461.

Schapiro, N. A. (2005). Bipolar disorders in children and adolescents. *Journal of Pediatric Health Care, 19,* 131–141.

Schatzberg, A. F. (2000). New indications for antidepressants. *Journal of Clinical Psychiatry, 61,* 9–17.

Scherrer, J. F., Xian, H., Shah, K. R., Volberg, R., Slutske, W., & Eisen, S. A. (2005). Effect of genes, environment, and lifetime co-occurring disorders on health-related quality of life in problem and pathological gamblers. *Archives of General Psychiatry, 62,* 677–683.

Schildkraut, J. J. (1965). The catecholamine hypothesis of affective disorders: A review of supporting evidence. *American Journal of Psychiatry, 122,* 509–522.

Schlenger, W. E., Caddell, J. M., Ebert, L., Jordan, B. K., Rourke, K. M., Wilson, D., et al. (2002). Psychological reactions to terrorist attacks: Findings from the National Study of Americans' Reactions to September 11. *Journal of the American Medical Association, 288,* 581–588.

Schmidt, U., & Asen, E. (2005). Editorial: Does multi-family day treatment hit the spot that other treatments cannot reach? *Journal of Family Therapy. Special issue: Multi-family Therapy in Anorexia Nervosa, 27.*

Schneider, K. (1959). *Clinical psychopathology.* New York: Grune & Stratton.

Schneiderman, N., Ironson, G., & Siegel, S. D. (2005). Stress and health: Psychological, behavioral, and biological determinants. *Annual Review in Clinical Psychology, 1,* 607–628.

Schneier, F. R. (2001). Treatment of social phobia with antidepressants. *Journal of Clinical Psychiatry, 62* (Suppl. 1), 43–48.

Schneier, F. R., Blanco, C., Antia, S. X., & Liebowitz, M. R. (2002). The social anxiety spectrum. *Psychiatric Clinics of North America, 25,* 757–774.

Schreiber, F. R. (1973). *Sybil.* Chicago: Henry Regnery.

Schuckit, M. A. (1989). *Drug and alcohol abuse: A clinical guide to diagnosis and treatment.* New York: Plenum Medical Book.

Schuckit, M. A., & Smith, T. L. (2001). Correlates of unpredicted outcomes in sons of alcoholics and controls. *Journal of Studies on Alcohol, 62,* 477–485.

Schwartz, M. F. (1994). The Masters and Johnson treatment program for sex offenders: Intimacy, empathy and trauma resolution. *Sexual Addiction and Compulsivity, 1,* 261–277.

Schwartz, M. F., & Brasted, W. S. (1985). Sexual addiction. *Medical Aspects of Human Sexuality, 19,* 106–107.

Scogin, F., Floyd, M., & Forde, J. (2000). Anxiety in older adults. In S. K. Whitbourne (Ed.), *Psychopathology in later life* (pp. 117–140). New York: Wiley.

Scribner, C. M. (2001). Rosenhan revisted. *Professional Psychology: Research and Practice, 32,* 215–216.

Scroppo, J. C., Drob, S. L., Weinberger, J. L., & Eagle, P. (1998). Identifying dissociative identity disorder: A self-report and projective study. *Journal of Abnormal Psychology, 107,* 272–284.

Sealy, J. R. (1995). Psychopharmacologic intervention in addictive sexual behavior. *Sexual Addiction and Compulsivity, 2,* 257–276.

Seeber, K., & Cadenhead, K. S. (2005). How does studying schizotypal personality disorder inform us about the prodrome of schizophrenia? *Current Psychiatry Reports, 7,* 41–50.

Seedat, S., Lockhat, R, Kaminer, D., Dirwayi-Zungu, N., & Stein, D. J. (2001). An open trial of citalopram in adolescents with post-traumatic stress disorder. *International Clinical Psychopharmacology, 16,* 21–25.

Segal, D. L., Coolidge, F. L., & Rosowsky, E. (2000). Personality disorders. In S. K. Whitbourne (Ed.), *Psychopathology in later life.* New York: Wiley.

Segal, D. L., Hook, J. N., & Coolidge, F. L. (2001). Personality dysfunction, coping styles, and clinical symptoms in younger and older adults. *Journal of Clinical Geropsychiatry, 7,* 201–212.

Segraves, R. T., & Althof, S. (1998). Psychotherapy and pharmacotherapy of sexual dysfunctions. In P. E. Nathan & J. M. Gorman (Eds.), *A guide to treatments that work* (pp. 447–471). New York: Oxford University Press.

Seidman, L. J., Valera, E. M., & Bush, G. (2004). Brain function and structure in adults with attention-deficit/hyperactivity disorder. *Psychiatric Clinics of North America, 27,* 323–347.

Seligman, M. E. P. (1971). Phobias and preparedness. *Behavior Therapy, 2,* 307–320.

Seligman, M. E. P. (1995). The effectiveness of psychotherapy: The Consumer Reports study. *American Psychologist, 50,* 965–975.

Selten, J. P., van der Graaf, Y., Dijkgraaf, M., Edlinger, M., & Kahn, R. (2000). Seasonality of schizophrenia and stillbirths in the Netherlands. *Schizophrenia Research, 44,* 105–111.

Semans, J. H. (1956). Premature ejaculation: A new approach. *Southern Medical Journal, 49,* 353–361.

Serban, G. (1992). Multiple personality: An issue for forensic psychiatry. *American Journal of Psychotherapy, 46,* 269–280.

Serbin, L. A., & Karp, J. (2004). The intergenerational transfer of psychosocial risk: Mediators of vulnerability and resilience. *Annual Review of Psychology, 55,* 333–363.

Serby, M., & Samuels, S. C. (2004). Diagnostic criteria for dementia with Lewy bodies reconsidered. *Focus, 2,* 309–313.

Serin, R. C., Malcolm, P. B., Khanna, A., & Barbaree, H. E. (1994). Psychopathy and deviant sexual arousal in incarcerated sexual offenders. *Journal of Interpersonal Violence, 9,* 3–11.

Shader, R. I., & Scharfman, E. L. (1989). Depersonalization disorder. In T. B. Karasu (Ed.), *Treatments of psychiatric disorders* (pp. 2217–2222). Washington, DC: American Psychiatric Press.

Shadish, W. R., Matt, G. E., Navarro, A. M., & Phillips, G. (2000). The effects of psychological therapies under clinically representative conditions: A meta-analysis. *Psychological Bulletin, 126,* 512–529.

Shafran, R. (1997). The manipulation of responsibility in obsessive-compulsive disorder. *British Journal of Clinical Psychology, 36,* 397–407.

Shalev, A. Y., Freedman, S., Peri, T., Brandes, D., Sahar, T., Orr, S. P., & Pitman, R. K. (1998). Prospective study of post-traumatic stress disorder and depression following trauma. *American Journal of Psychiatry, 155,* 630–637.

Shalev, A. Y., Peri, T., Canetti, L., & Schreiber, S. (1996). Predictors of PTSD in injured trauma survivors: A prospective study. *American Journal of Psychiatry, 153,* 219–225.

Shapiro, D. (1965). *Neurotic styles.* New York: Basic Books.

Shapiro, D. (1986). The insanity defense reform act of 1984. *Bulletin of the American Academy of Forensic Psychology, 1,* 1–6.

Sharf, R. S. (1996). *Theories of psychotherapy and counseling: Concepts and cases.* Pacific Grove, CA: Brooks/Cole.

Shastry, B. S. (2005). Bipolar disorder: An update. *Neurochemistry International, 46,* 273–279.

Shaver, P. R., Schachner, D. A., & Mikulincer, M. (2005). Attachment style, excessive reassurance seeking, relationship processes, and depression. *Personality and Social Psychology Bulletin, 31,* 343–359.

Shearin, E. N., & Linehan, M. M. (1994). Dialectical behavior therapy for borderline personality disorder: Theoretical and empirical foundations. *Acta Psychiatrica Scandinavica, 89,* 61–68.

Sheldon, A. E., & West, M. (1990). Attachment pathology and low social skills in avoidant personality disorder: An exploratory study. *Canadian Journal of Psychiatry, 35,* 596–599.

Sher, L. (2005). Type D personality: The heart, stress, and cortisol. *QJM, 98,* 323–329.

Shiffman, S., Balabanis, M. H., Paty, J. A., Engberg, J., Gwaltney, C. J., et al. (2000). Dynamic effects of self-efficacy on smoking lapse and relapse. *Health Psychology, 19,* 315–323.

Shinohara, M., Mizushima, H., Hirano, M., Shioe, K., Nakazawa, M., Hiejima, Y., et al. (2004). Eating disorders with binge-eating behaviour are associated with the s allele of the 3′-UTR VNTR polymorphism of the dopamine transporter gene. *Journal of Psychiatry and Neuroscience, 29,* 134–137.

Shneidman, E. S. (1984). Aphorisms of suicide and some implications for psychotherapy. *American Journal of Psychotherapy, 38,* 319–328.

Shulman, I. D., Cox, B. J., Swinson, R. P., Kuch, K., & Reichman, J. T. (1994). Precipitating events, locations and reactions associated with initial unexpected panic attacks. *Behaviour Research and Therapy, 32,* 17–20.

Siegman, A. W. (1994). From Type A to hostility to anger: Reflections on the history of coronary-prone behavior. In A. W. Siegman & T. W. Smith (Eds.), *Anger, hostility, and the heart* (pp. 1–21). Hillsdale, NJ: Erlbaum.

Sigman, M., Ruskin, E., Arbeile, S., Corona, R., Dissanayake, C., et al. (1999). Continuity and change in the social competence of children with autism, Down syndrome, and developmental delays. *Monographs of the Society for Research in Child Development, 64,* 1–114.

Silk, K. R., Lee, S., Hill, E. M., & Lohr, N. E. (1995). Borderline personality disorder symptoms and severity of sexual abuse. *American Journal of Psychiatry, 152,* 1059–1064.

Silverstein, J. L. (1996). Exhibitionism as countershame. *Sexual Addiction and Compulsivity, 3,* 33–42.

Simeon, D., Guralnik, O., Schmeidler, J., Sirof, B., & Knutelska, M. (2001). The role of childhood interpersonal trauma in depersonalization disorder. *American Journal of Psychiatry, 158,* 1027–1033.

Simon, G. E., Gureje, O., & Fullerton, C. (2001). Course of hypochondriasis in an international primary care study. *General Hospital Psychiatry, 23,* 51–55.

Simon, R. J., & Aaronson, E. E. (1988). *The insanity defense: A critical assessment of law and policy in the post-Hinckley era.* New York: Praeger.

Simpson, M. (1989). Multiple personality disorder. *British Journal of Psychiatry, 155,* 565.

Skinner, B. F. (1953). *Science and human behavior.* New York: Free Press.

Slater, L. (2004). *Opening Skinner's box.* New York: Norton.

Slovenko, R. (1993). The multiple personality and the criminal law. *Medicine and Law, 12,* 329–340.

Smith, R. C., Gardiner, J. C., Lyles, J. S., Sirbu, C., Dwamena, F. C., Hodges, A., et al. (2005). Exploration of DSM-IV criteria in primary care patients with medically unexplained symptoms. *Psychosomatic Medicine, 67,* 123–129.

Smith, T., Eikeseth, S., Klevstrand, M., & Lovaas, O. I. (1997). Intensive behavioral treatment for preschoolers with severe mental retardation and pervasive developmental disorder. *American Journal of Mental Retardation, 102,* 238–249.

Smith, T. W. (1996). *American sexual behavior: Trends, socio-demographic differences, and risk behavior* (GSS Topical Report No. 25). Chicago: National Opinion Research Center, University of Chicago.

Smith, T. W., Glazer, K., Ruiz, J. M., & Gallo, L. C. (2004). Hostility, anger, aggressiveness, and coronary heart disease: An interpersonal perspective on personality, emotion, and health. *Journal of Personality, 72,* 1217–1270.

Smith, Y. L., van Goozen, S. H., & Cohen-Kettenis, P. T. (2001). Adolescents with gender identity disorder who were accepted or rejected for sex reassignment surgery: A prospective follow-up study. *Journal of the American Academy of Child and Adolescent Psychiatry, 40,* 472–481.

Smith-Bell, M., & Winslade, W. J. (1994). Privacy, confidentiality, and privilege in psychotherapeutic relationships. *American Journal of Orthopsychiatry, 64,* 180–193.

Snaith, P., Tarsh, M. J., & Reid, R. W. (1993). Sex reassignment surgery: A study of 141 Dutch transsexuals. *British Journal of Psychiatry, 162,* 681–685.

Snowden, L. R., & Yamada, A.-M. (2005). Cultural differences in access to care. *Annual Reviews in Psychology, 56.*

Snowdon, D. A. (2001). *Aging with grace: What the nun study teaches us about leading longer, healthier, and more meaningful lives.* New York: Bantam Books.

Snyder, A. G., Stanley, M. A., Novy, D. M., Averill, P. M., & Beck, J. G. (2000). Measures of depression in older adults with generalized anxiety disorder: A psychometric evaluation. *Depression and Anxiety, 11,* 114–120.

Snyder, H. N. (2000). Sexual assault of young children as reported to law enforcement: Victim, incident, and offender characteristics. *National Center for Juvenile Justice.*

Sobin, C., Prudic, J., Devanand, D. P., Nobler, M. S., & Sackeim, H. A. (1996). Who responds to electroconvulsive therapy? A comparison of effective and ineffective forms of treatment. *British Journal of Psychiatry, 169,* 322–329.

Solms, M. (2004). Freud returns. *Scientific American, 290,* 82–88.

Southall, D. P., Plunkett, M. C., Banks, M. W., Falkov, A. F., & Samuels, M. P. (1997). Covert video recordings of life-threatening child abuse: Lessons for child protection. *Pediatrics, 100,* 735–760.

Southwick, S. M., Krystal, J. H., Bremner, J. D., Morgan, C. A., III, Nicolaou, A. L., et al. (1997). Noradrenergic and serotonergic function in post-traumatic stress disorder. *Archives of General Psychiatry, 54,* 749–758.

Southwick, S. M., & Yehuda, R., Giller, E. L. (1995). Psychological dimensions of depression in borderline personality disorder. *American Journal of Psychiatry, 152,* 789–791.

Spanos, N. P. (1996). *Multiple identities and false memories: A sociocognitive perspective.* Washington, DC: American Psychological Association.

Sparr, L., & Pankratz, L. D. (1983). Factitious post-traumatic stress disorder. *American Journal of Psychiatry, 140,* 1016–1019.

Spearman, C. (1904). General Intelligence: Objectively determined and measured. *American Journal of Psychology, 15,* 201–292.

Spiegel, D., & Cardena, E. (1991). Disintegrated experience: The dissociative disorders revisited. *Journal of Abnormal Psychology, 100,* 366–378.

Spinelli, M. G. (2001). A systematic investigation of 16 cases of neonaticide. *American Journal of Psychiatry, 158,* 811–813.

Spitzer, R. L. (1975). On pseudoscience in science, logic in remission, and psychiatric diagnosis: A critique of D. L. Rosenhan's "On Being Sane in Insane Places." *Journal of Abnormal Psychology, 84,* 442–452.

St. George-Hyslop, P. H., & Petit, A. (2005). Molecular biology and genetics of Alzheimer's disease. *Comptes Rendus Biologies, 328,* 119–130.

Stanley, G. E., Bivalacqua, T. J., & Hellstrom, W. J. (2000). Penile prosthetic trends in the era of effective oral erectogenic agents. *Southern Medical Journal, 93,* 1153–1156.

Steiger, H., Gauvin, L., Israel, M., Koerner, N., et al. (2001). Association of serotonin and cortisol indices with childhood abuse in bulimia nervosa. *Archives of General Psychiatry, 58,* 837–850.

Stein, D. J. (2000). Advances in the neurobiology of obsessive-compulsive disorder: Implications for conceptualizing putative obsessive-compulsive and spectrum disorders. *Psychiatric Clinics of North America, 23,* 545–562.

Stein, M. B., Forde, D. R., Anderson, G., & Walker, J. R. (1997). Obsessive-compulsive disorder in the community: An epidemiologic survey with clinical reappraisal. *American Journal of Psychiatry, 154,* 1120–1126.

Stein, M. B., Walker, J. R., & Forde, D. R. (1996). Public-speaking fears in a community sample. Prevalence, impact on functioning, and diagnostic classification. *Archives of General Psychiatry, 53,* 169–174.

Steinberg, M. (1991). The spectrum of depersonalization: Assessment and treatment. *Annual Review of Psychiatry, 10,* 223–247.

Steinberg, M. (1994). *Structured Clinical Interview for DSM-IV Dissociative Disorders–Revised (SCID-D-R).* Washington DC: American Psychiatric Press.

Steinberg, M. (2000). Advances in the clinical assessment of dissociation: The SCID-D-R. *Bulletin of the Menninger Clinic, 64,* 146–163.

Steinberg, M., Bancroft, J., & Buchanan, J. (1993). Multiple personality disorder in criminal law. *Bulletin of the American Academy of Psychiatry and the Law, 21,* 345–356.

Steinberg, M., & Hall, P. (1997). The SCID-D diagnostic interview and treatment planning in dissociative disorders. *Bulletin of the Menninger Clinic, 61,* 108–120.

Steinberg, M., Hall, P., Lareau, C., & Cicchetti, D. (2001). Recognizing the validity of dissociative symptoms using the SCID-D-R: Guidelines for clinical and forensic evaluations. *Southern California Interdisciplinary Law Journal, 10,* 225–242.

Steinberg, M., Hall, P., Lareau, C., & Cicchetti, D. (2001). Recognizing the validity of dissociative symptoms and disorders using the SCID-D-R: Guidelines for clinical and forensic evaluations. *The University of Southern California Interdisciplinary Law Journal.*

Steketee, G. (1994). Behavioral assessment and treatment planning with obsessive-compulsive disorder: A review emphasizing clinical application. *Behavior Therapy, 25,* 613–633.

Steketee, G. (1998). Judy: A compelling case of obsessive-compulsive disorder. In R. P. Halgin & S. K. Whitbourne (Eds.), *A casebook in abnormal psychology: From the files of experts* (pp. 58–71). New York: Oxford University Press.

Steketee, G., & Frost, R. (2003). Compulsive hoarding: Current status of the research. *Clinical Psychology Review, 23,* 905–927.

Stemberger, R. M., Thomas, A. M., Mansueto, C. S., & Carter, J. G. (2000). Personal toll of trichotillomania: Behavioral and interpersonal sequelae. *Journal of Anxiety Disorders, 14,* 97–104.

Stern, A. (1938). Psychoanalytic investigation of therapy in the borderline group of neuroses. *Psychoanalytic Quarterly, 7,* 467–489.

Stern, R. A., & White, T. (2003). *Neuropsychological Assessment Battery (NAB).* Odessa, FL: Psychological Assessment Resources.

Stewart, R. S., & Nejtek, V. A. (2003). An open-label, flexible-dose study of olanzapine in the treatment of trichotillomania. *Journal of Clinical Psychiatry, 64,* 49–52.

Stice, E., Killen, J. D., Hayward, C., & Taylor, C. B. (1998). Age of onset for binge eating and purging during late adolescence: A 4-year survival analysis. *Journal of Abnormal Psychology, 107,* 671–675.

Stone, A. (1990). *The fate of borderline patients: Successful outcome and psychiatric practice.* New York: Guilford Press.

Street, L. L., & Barlow, D. H. (1994). Anxiety disorders. In L. W. Craighead, W. E. Craighead, A. E. Kazdin, & M. J. Mahoney (Eds.), *Cognitive and behavioral interventions: An empirical approach to mental health problems* (pp. 71–87). Boston: Allyn & Bacon.

Stretch, R. H., Marlowe, D. H., Wright, K. M., Bliese, P. D., Knudson, K. H., & Hoover, C. H. (1996). Post-traumatic stress disorder symptoms among Gulf War veterans. *Military Medicine, 161,* 407–410.

Striegel-Moore, R. H., Seeley, J. R., & Lewinsohn, P. M. (2003). Psychosocial adjustment in young adulthood of women who experienced an eating disorder during adolescence. *Journal of the American Academy of Child and Adolescent Psychiatry, 42,* 587–593.

Striegel-Moore, R. H., Silberstein, L. R., & Rodin, J. (1993). The social self in bulimia nervosa: Public self-consciousness, social anxiety, and perceived fraudulence. *Journal of Abnormal Psychology, 102,* 297–303.

Strober, M., & Humphrey, L. L. (1987). Familial contributions to the etiology and course of anorexia nervosa and bulimia. *Journal of Consulting and Clinical Psychology, 55,* 654–659.

Strohle, A., Kellner, M., Yassouridis, A., Holsboer, F., & Wiedemann, K. (1998). Effect of flumazenil in lactate-sensitive patients with panic disorder. *American Journal of Psychiatry, 155,* 610–612.

Substance Abuse and Mental Health Services Administration, Office of Applied Studies. (2001a). Drug Abuse Warning Network detailed emergency department (ED) tables. http://www. samhsa.gov/oas/dawn.htm, accessed 11/29/01.

Substance Abuse and Mental Health Services Administration. (2001b). *Summary of findings from the 2000 National Household Survey on Drug Abuse.* Washington DC: U.S. Department of Health and Human Services.

Sullivan, H. S. (1953a). *Conceptions of modern psychiatry.* New York: Norton.

Sullivan, H. S. (1953b). *The interpersonal theory of psychiatry.* New York: Norton.

Sullivan, P. F., Neale, M. C., & Kendler, K. S. (2000a). Genetic epidemiology of major depression: Review and meta-analysis. *American Journal of Psychiatry, 157,* 1552–1562.

Sullivan, P. F., Neale, M. C., & Kendler, K. S. (2000b). Genetic epidemiology of major depression: Review and meta-analysis. *American Journal of Psychiatry, 157,* 1552–1562.

Summers, F. (1994). *Object relations theory and psychopathology: A comprehensive text.* Hillsdale, NJ: Analytic Press.

Sunderwirth, S., Milkman, H., & Jenks, N. (1996). Neurochemistry and sexual addiction. *Sexual Addiction and Compulsivity, 3,* 22–32.

Swartz, M. S., & Swanson, J. W. (2004). Involuntary outpatient commitment, community treatment orders, and assisted outpatient treatment: What's in the data? *Canadian Journal of Psychiatry, 49,* 585–591.

Swartz, M., Landerman, R., George, L. K., Blazer, D. G., & Escobar, J. (1991). Somatization disorder. In L. N. Robins & D. A. Regier (Eds.), *Psychiatric disorders in America: The epidemiologic catchment area study* (pp. 220–257). New York: Free Press.

Szasz, G., Stevenson, R. W. D., Lee, L., & Sanders, H. D. (1987). Induction of penile erection by intracavernosal injection: A double-blind comparison of phenoxybenzamine versus papaverine-phentolamine versus saline. *Archives of Sexual Behavior, 16,* 371–378.

Szasz, T. (1961). *The myth of mental illness.* New York: Harper & Row.

T

Tarasoff v. Regents of the University of California et al., Cal. Rep., 14, 551 Pg., 2d, 334 (1976).

Taylor, S., Kuch, K., Koch, W. J., Crockett, D. J., & Passey, G. (1998). The structure of post-traumatic stress syndrome. *Journal of Abnormal Psychology, 107,* 154–160.

Teichner, G., Golden, C. J., Bradley, J. D. D., & Crum, T. A. (1999). Internal consistency and discriminant validity of the Luria Nebraska Neuropsychological Battery-III. *International Journal of Neuroscience, 98,* 141–152.

Tennen, H., Affleck, G., Armeli, S., & Carney, M. A. (2000). A daily process approach to coping: Linking theory, research, and practice. *American Psychologist, 55,* 626–636.

Terr, L. C. (1991). Childhood traumas: An outline and overview. *American Journal of Psychiatry, 148,* 10–20.

Tharyan, P. (2000). Electroconvulsive therapy for schizophrenia. *Cochrane Database of Systematic Reviews* [computer file], CD000076.

Thase, M. E., & Kupfer, D. J. (1996). Recent developments in the pharmacotherapy of mood disorders. *Journal of Consulting and Clinical Psychology, 64,* 646–659.

Thigpen, C. H., & Cleckley, H. M. (1957). *The three faces of Eve.* New York: McGraw-Hill.

Thomas, A. M., & LoPiccolo, J. (1994). Sexual functioning in persons with diabetes: Issues in research, treatment, and education. *Clinical Psychology Review, 14,* 61–85.

Thompson-Brenner, H., Glass, S., & Westen, D. (2003). A multidimensional meta-analysis of psychotherapy for bulimia nervosa. *Clinical Psychology: Science and Practice, 10,* 269–287.

Tienari, P., Wynne, L. C., Moring, J., Laksy, K., Nieminen, P., et al. (2000). Finnish adoptive family study: Sample selection and adoptee DSM-III-R diagnoses. *Acta Psychiatrica Scandinavica, 101,* 433–443.

Tillfors, M., Furmark, T., Ekselius, L., & Fredrikson, M. (2001). Social phobia and avoidant personality disorder as related to parental history of social anxiety: A general population study. *Behavior Research and Therapy, 39,* 289–298.

Tinsley, J. A., Finlayson, R. E., & Morse, R. M. (1998). Developments in the treatment of alcoholism. *Mayo Clinic Proceedings, 73,* 857–863.

Tondo, L., & Baldessarini, R. J. (2001). *Suicide: An overview* [website]. Accessed August 16, 2001 on the World Wide Web at http:// psychiatry.medscape.com/Medscape/ psychiatry/ ClinicalMgmt/CM.v03/ pnt-CM.v03.html.

Toneatto, T., & Ladoceur, R. (2003). Treatment of pathological gambling: A critical review of the literature. *Psychology of Addictive Behaviors, 17,* 284–292.

Torrey, E. F. (1995). *Surviving schizophrenia: A manual for families, consumers, and providers* (3rd ed.). New York: Free Press.

Tozzi, F., Thornton, L. M., Klump, K. L., Fichter, M. M., Halmi, K. A., Kaplan, A. S., et al. (2005). Symptom fluctuation in eating disorders: Correlates of diagnostic crossover. *American Journal of Psychiatry, 162,* 732–740.

Trask, P. C., & Sigmon, S. T. (1997). Munchausen syndrome: A review and new conceptualization. *Clinical Psychology— Science and Practice, 4,* 346–358.

Treffert, D. (1988). The idiot savant: A review of the syndrome. *American Journal of Psychiatry, 145,* 563–572.

Treffert, D. A. (1989). Balancing legal realities: The courts, the legislature, and public psychiatry. *New Directions for Mental Health Services, 42* (Summer), 63–74.

Treiber, F. A., Kamarck, T., Schneiderman, N., Sheffield, D., Kapuku, G., & Taylor, T. (2003).

Cardiovascular reactivity and development of preclinical and clinical disease states. *Psychosomatic Medicine, 65,* 46–62.

Troisi, A., Massaroni, P., & Cuzzolaro, M. (2005). Early separation anxiety and adult attachment style in women with eating disorders. *British Journal of Clinical Psychology, 44,* 89–97.

Troop, N. A., Holbrey, A., Trowler, R., & Treasure, J. L. (1994). Ways of coping in women with eating disorders. *Journal of Nervous and Mental Disease, 182,* 535–540.

True, W. R., Rice, J., Eisen, S. A., Heath, A. C., Goldberg, J., Lyons, M. J., & Nowak, J. (1993). A twin study of genetic and environmental contributions to liability for post-traumatic stress symptoms. *Archives of General Psychiatry, 50,* 257–264.

Trull, T. J., & Durrett, C. A. (2005). Categorical and dimensional models of personality disorder. *Annual Review of Clinical Psychology, 1,* 355–380.

Trzepacz, P. T., & Baker, R. W. (1993). *The psychiatric mental status examination.* New York: Oxford University Press.

Turan, M. T., Esel, E., Dundar, M., Candemir, Z., Basturk, M., Sofuoglu, S., & Ozkul, Y. (2000). Female-to-male transsexual with 47, XXX karyotype. *Biological Psychiatry, 48,* 1116–1117.

Twohig, M. P., & Woods, D. W. (2004). A preliminary investigation of acceptance and commitment therapy and habit reversal as a treatment for trichotillomania. *Behavior Therapy, 35,* 803–820.

Tyas, S. L., White, L. R., Petrovitch, H., Webster Ross, G., Foley, D. J., Heimovitz, H. K., et al. (2003). Mid-life smoking and late-life dementia: The Honolulu-Asia Aging Study. *Neurobiology of Aging, 24,* 589–596.

U

Uhde, T. W., Tancer, M. E., Black, B., & Brown, T. M. (1991) Phenomenology and neurobiology of social phobia: Comparison with panic disorder. *Journal of Clinical Psychiatry, 52,* 31–40.

U.S. Department of Health and Human Services, Administration on Children, Youth, and Families. (2005). Child maltreatment 2003. Washington, DC: U.S. Government Printing Office.

U.S. Department of Health and Human Services. (1999). *Mental health: A report of the Surgeon General.* Bethesda MD: U.S. Public Health Service.

U.S. Fire Administration, (2001). *Arson in the United States.* Emmitsburg, MD: United States Fire Administration, at www.usfa.fema.gov/downloads/pdf/tfrs/v1i8-508.pdf.

U.S. Surgeon General. (2001). *Mental health: Culture, race, and ethnicity.* Washington, DC: U.S. Government Printing Office.

V

Vaillant, G. E. (1994). Ego mechanisms of defense and personality psychopathology. *Journal of Abnormal Psychology, 103,* 44–50.

Van Ameringen, M. A., Lane, R. M., Walter, J. R., Bowen, R. C., Chokka, P. R., Goldner, E. M., Johnston, D. G., Lavallee, Y. J., Nandy, S., Pecknold, J. C., Hadrava, V., & Swinson, R. P. (2001). Sertraline treatment of generalized social phobia: A 20-week, double-blind, placebo-controlled study. *American Journal of Psychiatry, 158,* 275–281.

Vandenbergh, D. J., Rodriguez, L. A., Miller, I. T., Uhl, G. R., & Lachman, H. M. (1997). High-activity catechol-O-methyltransferase allele is more prevalent in polysubstance abusers. *American Journal of Medical Genetics, 74,* 439–442.

van der Hart, O., Boon, S., & Heijtmajer Jansen, O. (1997). Ritual abuse in European countries: A clinician's perspective. In A. F. George (Ed.), *The dilemma of ritual abuse: Cautions and guides for therapists. Clinical practice, No. 41* (pp. 137–163). Washington, DC: American Psychiatric Press.

Vanderploeg, R. D., Curtiss, G., & Belanger, H. G. (2005). Long-term neuropsychological outcomes following mild traumatic brain injury. *Journal of the International Neuropsychological Society, 11,* 228–236.

van Minnen, A., Hoogduin, K. A., Keijsers, G. P., Hellenbrand, I., & Hendriks, G. J. (2003). Treatment of trichotillomania with behavioral therapy or fluoxetine: A randomized, waiting-list controlled study. *Archives of General Psychiatry, 60,* 517–522.

van Os, J., & Selten, J. P. (1998). Prenatal exposure to maternal stress and subsequent schizophrenia. The May 1940 invasion of The Netherlands. *British Journal of Psychiatry, 172,* 324–326.

van Velzen, C. J., Emmelkamp, P. M., & Scholing, A. (2000). Generalized social phobia versus avoidant personality disorder: Differences in psychopathology, personality traits, and social and occupational functioning. *Journal of Anxiety Disorders, 14,* 395–411.

Vassar, R., Bennett, B. D., Babu-Khan, S., Kahn, S., Mendiaz, E. A., Denis, P., et al. (1999). Beta-secretase cleavage of Alzheimer's amyloid precursor protein by the transmembrane aspartic protease BACE. *Science, 286,* 735–741.

Veale, D., De Haro, L., & Lambrou, C. (2003). Cosmetic rhinoplasty in body dysmorphic disorder. *British Journal of Plastic Surgery, 56,* 546–551.

Veale, D., Ennis, M., & Lambrou, C. (2002). Possible association of body dysmorphic disorder with an occupation or education in art and design. *American Journal of Psychiatry, 159,* 1788–1790.

Venter, J. C., Adams, M. D., Myers, E. W., Li, P. W., et al. (2001). The sequence of the human genome. *Science, 291,* 1304–1351.

Verger, P., Dab, W., Lamping, D. L., Loze, J. Y., Deschaseaux-Voinet, C., Abenhaim, L., & Rouillon. (2004). The psychological impact of terrorism: An epidemiologic study of post-traumatic stress disorder and associated factors in victims of the 1995–1996 bombings in France. *American Journal of Psychiatry, 161,* 1384–1389.

Verrier, R. L., & Mittleman, M. A. (1996). Life-threatening cardiovascular consequences of anger in patients with coronary heart disease. *Cardiology Clinics, 14,* 289–307.

Villarreal, G., & King, C. Y. (2001). Brain imaging in post-traumatic stress disorder. *Seminars in Clinical Neuropsychiatry, 6,* 131–145.

Viola, J. M., Hicks, R., & Porter, T. (1993). Gulf War veterans with PTSD. *Military Medicine, 158,* A4.

Virkkunen, M., Eggert, M., Rawlings, R., & Linnoila, M. (1996). A prospective follow-up study of alcoholic violent offenders and fire-setters. *Archives of General Psychiatry, 53,* 523–529.

Vohs, K. D., Heatherton, T. F., & Herrin, M. (2001). Disordered eating and the transition to college: A prospective study. *International Journal of Eating Disorders, 29,* 280–288.

Volkmar, F. R., Klin, A., Schultz, R. T., Rubin, E., & Bronen, R. (2000). Asperger's disorder. *American Journal of Psychiatry, 157,* 262–267.

W

Wachtel, P. L. (1977). *Psychoanalysis and behavior therapy: Toward an integration.* New York: Basic Books.

Wachtel, P. L. (1997). *Psychoanalysis, behavior therapy, and the relational world.* Washington, DC: American Psychological Association.

Walcott, D. M., Cerundolo, P., & Beck, J. C. (2001). Current analysis of the *Tarasoff* duty: An evolution towards the limitation of the duty to protect. *Behavioral Sciences and the Law, 19,* 325–343.

Waldo, M. C., Adler, L. E., Leonard, S., Olincy, A., Ross, R. G., Harris, J. G., & Freedman, R. (2000). Familial transmission of risk factors in the first-degree relatives of schizophrenic people. *Biological Psychiatry, 47,* 231–239.

Wallace, S. T., & Alden, L. E. (1997). Social phobia and positive social events: The price of success. *Journal of Abnormal Psychology, 106,* 416–424.

Wampold, B. E. (2001). *The great psychotherapy debate: Models, methods, and findings.* Mahwah, NJ: Erlbaum.

Wampold, B. E., & Bhati, K. S. (2004). Attending to the omissions: A historical examination of evidence-based practice movements. *Professional Psychology: Research & Practice, 35,* 563–570.

Wandersman, A., & Nation, M. (1998). Urban neighborhoods and mental health: Psychological contributions to understanding toxicity, resilience, and interventions. *American Psychologist, 53,* 647–656.

Warden, N. L., Phillips, J. G., & Ogloff, J. R. P. (2004). Internet addiction. *Psychiatry, Psychology and Law, 11,* 280–295.

Wareing, M., Fisk, J. E., Murphy, P., & Montgomery, C. (2004). Verbal working memory deficits in current and previous users of MDMA. *Human Psychopharmacology, 19,* 225–234.

Warren, S. L., Huston, L., Egeland, B., & Sroufe, L. A. (1997). Child and adolescent anxiety disorders and early attachment. *Journal of the American Academy of Child and Adolescent Psychiatry, 36,* 637–644.

Wasserstein, J. (2005). Diagnostic issues for adolescents and adults with ADHD. *Journal of Clinical Psychology, 61,* 535–547.

Watkins, J. G. (1984). The Bianchi (L. A. Hillside Strangler) case: Sociopath or multiple personality? *International Journal of Clinical Experimental Hypnosis, 32,* 67–101.

Weber, J. B., Coverdale, J. H., & Kunik, M. E. (2004). Delirium: Current trends in prevention and treatment. *Internal Medicine Journal, 34,* 115–121.

Wechsler, D. (1997). *Wechsler Adult Intelligence Scale–Third Edition.* San Antonio, TX: Psychological Corporation.

Wechsler, D. (2002). *Wechsler Preschool and Primary Scale of Intelligence (WIPPSI-III).* San Antonio, TX: Psychological Corporation.

Wechsler, D. (2003). *Wechsler Intelligence Scale for Children-IV (WISC-IV).* San Antonio, TX: Psychological Corporation.

Weinberger, L. E., Sreenivasan, S., Garrick, T., & Osran, H. (2005). The impact of surgical castration on sexual recidivism risk among sexually violent predatory offenders. *Journal of the American Academy of Psychiatry and the Law, 33,* 16–36.

Weinstock, R., Leong, G. B., & Silva, J. A. (2001). Potential erosion of psychotherapist-patient privilege beyond California: Dangers of "criminalizing" *Tarasoff. Behavioral Sciences and the Law, 19,* 437–449.

Weisner, C., Matzger, H., & Kaskutas, L. A. (2003). How important is treatment? One-year outcomes of treated and untreated alcohol-dependent individuals. *Addiction, 98,* 901–911.

Weiss, M., & Murray, C. (2003). Assessment and management of attention-deficit hyperactivity disorder in adults. *Canadian Medical Association Journal, 168,* 715–722.

Weissman, M. M. (1993). The epidemiology of personality disorders: A 1990 update. *Journal of Personality Disorders, 7* (Supplement, Spring), 44–62.

Weissman, M. M., Bland, R. C., Canino, G. J., Faravelli, C., Greenwald, S., et al. (1997). The cross-national epidemiology of panic disorder. *Archives of General Psychiatry, 54,* 305–309.

Weissman, M. M., Bland, R. C., Canino, G. J., Greenwald, S., Lee, C. K., et al. (1996). The cross-national epidemiology of social phobia: A preliminary report. *International Clinical Psychopharmacology, 3,* 9–14.

Weissman, M. M., Wickramaratne, P., Nomura, Y., Warner, V., Verdeli, H., Pilowsky, D. J., et al. (2005). Families at high and low risk for depression: A 3-generation study. *Archives of General Psychiatry, 62,* 29–36.

Weissman, M. M., & Markowitz, J. C. (1994). Interpersonal psychotherapy: Current status. *Archives of General Psychiatry, 51* (Suppl.), 599–606.

Weisz, J. R., Weiss, B., Han, S. S., Granger, D. A., & Morton, T. (1994). Effects of psychotherapy with children and adolescents revisited: A meta-analysis of treatment outcome studies. *Psychological Bulletin, 117,* 450–468.

Welte, J. W., Barnes, G. M., Wieczorek, W. F., Tidwell, M. C., & Parker, J. C. (2004). Risk factors for pathological gambling. *Addictive Behavior, 29,* 323–335.

Wender, P. H. (2000). *Attention-deficit hyperactivity disorder in children and adults.* New York: Oxford University Press.

Werme, M., Hermanson, E., Carmine, A., Buervenich, S., Zetterstrom, R. H., Thoren, P., et al. (2003). Decreased ethanol preference and wheel running in Nurr1-deficient mice. *European Journal of Neuroscience, 17,* 2418–2424.

Werth, J. L. (2005). Assessing for impaired judgment as a means of meeting the "duty to protect" when a client is a potential harm-to-self: Implications for clients making end-of-life decisions. *Mortality, 10,* 7–21.

West, M., & Sheldon, A. E. R. (1988). Classification of pathological attachment patterns in adults. *Journal of Personality Disorders, 2,* 153–159.

Westen, D. (1991a). Clinical assessment of object relations using the TAT. *Journal of Personality Assessment, 56,* 56–74.

Westen, D. (1991b). Social cognition and object relations. *Psychological Bulletin, 109,* 429–455.

Westen, D., & Cohen, R. P. (1993). The self in borderline personality disorder: A psychodynamic perspective. In Z. V. Segal & S. J. Blatt (Eds.), *The self in emotional distress: Cognitive and psychodynamic perspectives* (pp. 334–368). New York: Guilford Press.

Westen, D., Lohr, N. E., Silk, K., & Kerber, K. (1994). *Measuring object relations and social cognition using the TAT: Scoring manual* (Vol. 2). Ann Arbor: University of Michigan.

White Kress, V. E., Eriksen, K. P., Rayle, A. D., & Ford, S. J. W. (2005). The *DSM-IV-TR* and culture: Considerations for counselors. *Journal of Counseling and Development, 83,* 97–104.

Widiger, T. A. (1998). Murray: A challenging case of antisocial personality disorder. In R. P. Halgin & S. K. Whitbourne (Eds.), *A casebook in abnormal psychology: From the files of experts* (pp. 24–36). New York: Oxford University Press.

Widiger, T. A. (2004). Looking ahead to DSM-V. *The Clinical Psychologist, 57 (1&2),* 8–15.

Widiger, T. A., & Corbitt, E. M. (1995). Are personality disorders well-classified in DSM-IV? In W. J. Livesley (Ed.), *The DSM-IV personality disorders* (pp. 103–126). New York: Guilford Press.

Widiger, T. A., & Shea, T. (1991). Differentiation of Axis I and Axis II disorders. *Journal of Abnormal Psychology, 100,* 399–406.

Wilbur, C. B., & Kluft, R. P. (1989). Multiple personality disorder. In T. B. Karasu (Ed.), *Treatment of psychiatric disorders* (pp. 2197–2216). Washington, DC: American Psychiatric Association.

Wilens, T. E., Faraone, S. V., & Biederman, J. (2004). Attention-deficit/hyperactivity disorder in adults. *Journal of the American Medical Association, 292,* 619–623.

Wilson, G. T., & Fairburn, C. G. (1998). Treatments for eating disorders. In P. E. Nathan & J. M. Gorman (Eds.), *A guide to treatments that work* (pp. 501–530). New York: Oxford University Press.

Wirz-Justice, A., Terman, M., Oren, D. A., Goodwin, F. K., Kripke, D. F., Whybrow, P. C., et al. (2004). Brightening depression. *Science, 303,* 467–469.

Witkiewitz, K., & Marlatt, G. A. (2004). Relapse prevention for alcohol and drug problems: That was Zen, this is Tao. *American Psychologist, 59,* 224–235.

Wittchen, H. U., & Beloch, E. (1996). The impact of social phobia on quality of life. *International Clinical Psychopharmacology, 3,* 15–23.

Wittchen, H. U., Zhao, S., Kessler, R. C., & Eaton, W. W. (1994). DSM-III-R generalized anxiety disorder in the National Comorbidity Survey. *Archives of General Psychiatry, 51,* 355–364.

Wolf, B. C., Lavezzi, W. A., Sullivan, L. M., & Flannagan, L. M. (2005). One hundred seventy two deaths involving the use of oxycodone in Palm Beach County. *Journal of Forensic Science, 50,* 192–195.

Wolfberg, P. J., & Schuler, A. L. (1999). Fostering peer interaction, imaginative play and spontaneous language in children with autism. *Child Language Teaching and Therapy, 15,* 41–52.

Wolpe, J. (1958). *Psychotherapy by reciprocal inhibition.* Stanford: Stanford University Press.

Wolpe, J. (1973). *The practice of behavior therapy.* Elmsford, NY: Pergamon.

Wolpe, J., & Lang, J. (1977). *Manual for the Fear Survey Schedule.* San Diego: EdITS.

Wong, A. H. C., Gottesman, I. I., & Petronis, A. (2005). Phenotypic differences in genetically identical organisms: The epigenetic perspective. *Human Molecular Genetics, 14,* R11–18.

Wong, I. L., & So, E. M. (2003). Prevalence estimates of problem and pathological gambling in Hong Kong. *American Journal of Psychiatry, 160,* 1353–1354.

Woo, S. M., Goldstein, M. J., & Nuechterlein, K. H. (2004). Relatives' affective style and the expression of subclinical psychopathology in patients with schizophrenia. *Family Process, 43,* 233–247.

Wood, R. M., Grossman, L. S., & Fichtner, C. G. (2000). Psychological assessment, treatment, and outcome with sex offenders. *Behavioral Sciences and the Law, 18,* 23–41.

Woodside, D. B., Garfinkel, P. E., Lin, E., Goering, P., Kaplan, A. S., Goldbloom, D. S., & Kennedy, S. H. (2001). Comparisons of men with full or partial eating disorders, men without eating disorders, and women with eating disorders in the community. *American Journal of Psychiatry, 158,* 570–574.

World Health Organization (2004). *Suicide prevention.* Retrieved May 23, 2005, from www.who.int/mental_health/prevention/suicide/suicideprevent/en/

World Health Organization. (1997). *Composite International Diagnostic Interview* (CIDI). Geneva, Switzerland: World Health Organization.

Wright, C. I., McMullin, K., Martis, B., Fischer, H., & Rauch, S. L. (2005). Brain correlates of negative visuospatial priming in healthy children. *Psychiatry Research: Neuroimaging, 139,* 41–52.

Wright, E. R., Gronfein, W. P., & Owens, T. J. (2000). Deinstitutionalization, social rejection, and the self-esteem of former mental patients. *Journal of Health and Social Behavior, 41,* 68–90.

Wyatt v. Stickney, 325 F. Supp. 781 (M.D. Ala. 1971); 344 F. Supp. (M.D. Ala. 1972).

Y

Yalom, I. D. (1995). *The theory and practice of group psychotherapy* (4th ed.). New York: Basic Books.

Yonkers, K. A., Dyck, I. R., & Keller, M. B. (2001). An eight-year longitudinal comparison of clinical course and characteristics of social phobia among men and women. *Psychiatric Services, 52,* 637–643.

Yonkers, K. A., Zlotnick, C., Allsworth, J., Warshaw, M., Shea, T., & Keller, M. B. (1998). Is the course of panic disorder the same in women and men? *American Journal of Psychiatry, 155,* 596–602.

Young, K. S. (2004). Internet addiction: A new clinical phenomenon and its consequences. *American Behavioral Scientist, 48,* 402–415.

Youngberg v. Romeo, 457 U.S. 307 (1982).

Yovel, I., Revelle, W., & Mineka, S. (2005). Who sees trees before forest? The obsessive-compulsive style of visual attention. *Psychological Science, 16,* 123–129.

Z

Zanarini, M. C., & Frankenburg, F. R. (1997). Pathways to the development of borderline personality disorder. *Journal of Personality Disorders, 11,* 93–104.

Zanarini, M. C., Williams, A. A., Lewis, R. E., Reich, R. B., Vera, S. C., et al. (1997). Reported pathological childhood experiences associated with the development of borderline personality disorder. *American Journal of Psychiatry, 154,* 1101–1106.

Zatzick, D. F., Weiss, D. S., Marmar, C. R., Metzler, T. J., Wells, K., et al. (1997). Post-traumatic stress disorder and functioning and quality of life outcomes in female Vietnam veterans. *Military Medicine, 162,* 661–665.

Zetterstrom, R. H., Solomin, L., Jansson, L., Hoffer, B. J., Olson, L., & Perlmann, T. (1997). Dopamine neuron agenesis in Nurr1-deficient mice. *Science, 276,* 248–250.

Zhang, F., & Labouvie-Vief, G. (2004). Stability and fluctuation in adult attachment style over a 6-year period. *Attachment and Human Development, 6,* 419–437.

Zinkstok, J., & van Amelsvoort, T. (2005). Neuropsychological profile and neuroimaging in patients with 22Q11.2 deletion syndrome: A review. *Child Neuropsychology (Neuropsychology, Development and Cognition: Section C), 11,* 21–37.

Zohar, A. H., & Bruno, R. (1997). Normative and pathological obsessive-compulsive behavior and ideation in childhood: A question of timing. *Journal of Child Psychology and Psychiatry & Allied Disciplines, 38,* 993–999.

Zohar, A. H., Pauls, D. L., Ratzoni, G., Apter, A., Dycian, A., et al. (1997). Obsessive-compulsive disorder with and without tics in an epidemiological sample of adolescents. *American Journal of Psychiatry, 154,* 274–276.

Zubin, J., & Spring, B. (1977). Vulnerability—A new view of schizophrenia. *Journal of Abnormal Psychology, 86,* 103–126.

Zucker, K. J. (2005). Gender identity disorder in children and adolescents. *Annual Review of Clinical Psychology, 1,* 467–492.

Zucker, K. J., & Spitzer, R. L. (2005). Was the gender identity disorder of childhood diagnosis introduced into DSM-III as a backdoor maneuver to replace homosexuality? A historical note. *Journal of Sex and Marriage Therapy 31,* 31–42.

Zucker, R. A., & Gomberg, E. S. L. (1986). Etiology of alcoholism reconsidered: The case for biopsychosocial process. *American Psychologist, 41,* 783–793.

© Mary Kate Denny/Photo Edit; p. 411(left): © Transparencies; p. 411 (right): Courtesy of Brookhaven National Laboratory; p. 413: © Richard Hutchings/Photo Edit; p. 414: Multnomah County Sheriff's Office www.facesofmeth.us; p. 417: © David Rohmer/Gamma; p. 418: © Deneve Bundle/Unicorn Stock Photos

CHAPTER 14
p. 428: McGraw-Hill Companies/Lars A. Niki, photographer; p. 433 (left): © Everett Collection, Inc.; p. 433 (right): © Everett Collection, Inc.; p. 440: David Young-Wolff/Getty Images; p. 442: © Chris Ware/The Image Works; p. 443: AP/Wide World Photos; p. 444: © Park Street/Photo Edit; p. 445: Miro Vintoniv/StockBoston; p. 446: Yellow Dog Productions/Getty Images; p. 448: Bannor/Custom Medical Stock Photo; p. 449: Jim Boorman/Pixland/Getty Images; pp. 457–461: Copyright © 2002 Nothing to Hide: Mental Illness in the Family by Jean J Beard and Peggy Gillespie. Photographs by Gigi Kaeser. Reprinted by permission of The New Press. www.thenewpress.com

CHAPTER 15
p. 462: McGraw-Hill Companies/Lars A. Niki, photographer; p. 465: © SPL/Photo Researchers, Inc.; p. 469 (left): AP/Wide World Photos; p. 469 (right): AP/Wide World Photos; p. 471: AP/Wide World Photos; p. 476: AP/Wide World Photos; p. 480 (top): AP/Wide World Photos; p. 480 (bottom): © Reuters/Corbis

INDEXES

Note: Page numbers in *italics* indicate figures and illustrations; page numbers followed by *t* indicate tables. This index contains reference names and names of persons discussed in the text.

Name Index

A

Aalto, S., 291
Aaronson, E.E., 475
Aarsland, D., 381
Abbott, M.J., 157
Abbott, R.D., 386
Abel, G.G., 227
Abikoff, H., 360
Abouesh, A., 221
Abraham, K., 260
Abraham, M., 335
Abramowitz, J.S., 165
Ackerman, S.J., 267
Adams, K.M., 447
Adams, M.D., 128
Addington, A., 185
Adebimpe, V.R., 39
Adelson, J., 71
Ades, J., 291
Adler, A., 107, 138
Adler, L.E., 294
Adson, D.E., 444
Aesclepiades, 11
Affleck, B., 397
Affleck, G., 27
Agatsuma, S., 408
Agras, W.S., 160, 435, 438, 443
Ahern, D.K., 186, 187
Ahern, J., 417
Ahola, P., 267
Aikins, D.E., 161
Aime, A., 439
Ainsworth, M., 110, *110*
Ainsworth, M.D.S., 363
Akyuz, G., 182
Alarcon, R.D., 42
Albus, M., 151
Alden, L.E., 157
Alegria, M., 31
Alexander, P.C., 219
Allen, A., 185
Allgulander, C., 161
Allison, S., 445
Allman, C., 270
Allsworth, J., 150
Alper, C.M., 195
Alpert, J.E., 185
Alpert, R., 415
Althof, S., 239, 241
Alzheimer, A., 376
Amate, J.M., 396, 403, 412
An, H., 381
Anderson, B.K., 401
Anderson, G., 202
Anderson, P.L., 156
Andreasen, N., 383
Andreoli, A., 71
Andrews, G., 42
Andrews, S., 134
Angeles M., 396, 403, 412
Anisman, H., 448
Annas, P., 155

Antia, S.X., 185
Appel, M., 151
Appelbaum, P.S., 475
Apple, R.F., 438
Applebaum, A.H., 323
Arbeile, S., 352
Armeli, S., 27
Armfield, J.M., 155
Armstead, P., 449
Armstrong, M.S., 447
Arnold, I.A., 181
Arnow, B.A., 438
Arnow, P.S., 195
Aro, H.M., 271
Ary, D.V., 409
Asarnow, R.F., 332
Asen, E., 439
Asher, R., 188
Asperger, H., 348
Asscheman, H., 230
Astruc, B., 270
Aubut, J., 220
Audenaert, K., 316
Austin, C., 161
Auther, A.M., 279
Axelson, D.A., 364
Ayllon, T., 124
Azorlosa, J., 333
Azrin, N.H., 124

B

Baba Ram Dass, 415
Babu-Khan, S., 384
Bachman, J.G., 413, 418, 419
Badgett, J.T., 189
Baer, L., 19, 164
Bagley, C., 219
Bailey, E.D., 186
Bailey, J.M., 228, 229
Baird, A.A., 316
Baity, M.R., 267
Baker, G.A., 187
Baker, J.D., 333
Baker, L., 437
Baker, R.A., 16
Baker, R.W., 72
Balabanis, M.H., 124
Balach, L., 270, 364
Ban, T., 387
Bancroft, J., 205, 447
Bandura, A., 18, 121–122, 122, 124, 157
Banks, M.W., 189
Banuazizi, A.L.I., 132
Banzato, C.E..M, 42
Baptiste Family, 144
Bar, J.L., 414
Barban, L., 202
Barbaranelli, C., 122
Barbaree, H., 219, 220
Barbaree, H.E., 219
Barbarich, N., 435, 437
Barberger-Gateau, P., 387
Barch, D.M., 294

Barkley, R.A., 360, 361
Barlow, D.H., 69, 71, 122, 123, 124, 148, 152, 153, 156, 160, 241
Barnes, G.M., 442
Barnett, W., 444
Barrett, J.E., 254
Barry, S., 416
Barry-Walsh, J., 285
Barsky, A., 373
Barsky, A.J., 186, 187
Bartholomew, K., 110
Bartlik, B., 240, 241
Bartolini, M., 382
Baser, R.E., 187
Basile, V.S., 437
Bass, N., 292
Bassuk, E.L., 171
Basturk, M., 229
Bateman, A., 324
Baud, P., 268
Bauer, C.R., 346, 347
Bauer, L., 401
Bayliss, A.P., 350
Beal, W.E., 195
Beard family, 460
Beard, J.J., 141, 142, 143, 144, 145
Beard, K.W., 450
Beck, A.T., 18, 122, 139, 155, 261, 266, 268, 270, 293, 297, 322, 327, 328, 332, 334, 335
Beck, J.C., 468
Beckman, D.A., 449
Beere, D., 202
Beers, C., 16
Begg, M.D., 293
Begleiter, H., 401
Behar, K.L., 151
Belanger, H.G., 375
Belknap, J.K., 408
Bellew, K.M., 161
Bellivier, F., 270
Bellodi, L., 151, 164
Belmont, A., 293
Bemporad, J., 260
Bender, D.S., 335
Benito, C., 291
Bennett, B.D., 384
Bennett, D., 438
Benson, D.F., 350
Benson, H., 197
Berelowitz, M., 319
Berendzen, R., 243–244
Bergen, A.W., 437
Bergen, H.A., 445
Berger, P., 71
Berglund, P., 159, 252, 267
Berlin, F.S., 117, 220
Berman, J., 170
Berman, T., 189
Bernagie, K., 316
Berner, W., 225
Bernheim, H., 17
Bernstein, A., 317
Bernstein, D.M., 21

Bernstein, G.A., 363
Berrettini, W., 259
Berry, D.T., 187
Bertaud, J.P., 293
Bertelli, S., 164
Best, M., 450, 479
Bettelheim, B., 350
Beutler, L.E., 134, 239
Bhati, K.S., 61
Bhaumik, D.K., 264
Bianchini, K.J., 187
Biederman, J., 159, 163, 164, 355, 360
Bieling, P.J., 157
Bienvenu, O.J., 185
Biglan, A., 409
Binder, R.L., 202
Binet, A., 80, 86
Birmaher, B., 257, 364
Birt, A.R., 207
Bjornson, L., 202
Black, B., 157
Black, D.W., 187, 440, 444
Blagys, M.D., 267
Blair, R.J., 317
Blais, M.A., 438
Blak, T., 220
Blalock, J.A., 267
Blanchard, E.B., 229, 450
Blanchard, G.T., 446
Blanchard, R., 219, 220, 225, 229
Blanco, C., 185, 443
Bland, R.C., 149, 154
Blasey, C., 438
Blaszczynski, A., 447
Blazer, D.G., 182
Blennow, K., 383, 386
Bleuler, E., 278
Bliese, P.D., 170
Bliss, E.L., 200
Blurton-Jones, M., 384
Bobbitt, L., 478
Bobbitt, W., 478
Bockbrader, M.A., 330
Bogaert, A.F., 219, 229
Bohr, Y., 430
Bonnie, R.J., 479
Bookstein, F.L., 346
Boon, S., 202
Boor, M., 200
Borkovec, T.D., 161
Born, L., 239
Bornstein, K., *229*
Bornstein, R.F., 335, 437
Borum, R., 469
Borus, J.F., 19, 373
Bosma, H., 196
Bottino, V., 350
Bouchard, T.J., Jr., 10, 27, 129
Bourbeau, L.S., 110
Bourland, S.L., 161
Bouton, M.E., 152
Bouza, C., 396, 403, 412
Bow, J.N., 471
Bowden, C.L., 267
Bowen, M., 114

Robers, C., 470
Roberson-Nay, R., 151
Roberts, C.R., 31
Roberts, R.E., 31
Robertson, B.A., 170
Robin, J.A., 360
Robins, D.A., 38
Robins, L.N., 314, 359
Robinson, D.W., 447
Rodriguez, L.A., 408
Rodriguez Solano, J.J., 329
Roeger, L., 445
Roehrs, T. A., 191
Rogers, C., 111, 112, 113, 114, 139
Rogers, M.P., 150
Rogers, R.L., 437
Rohde, P., 444
Rohling, M.L., 444
Roid, G.H., 80
Rokous, F., 219
Rooijmans, H.G., 164
Roos, R.A., 164
Rorschach, H., 85–86
Rosa, M.A., 130
Rosa, M.O., 130
Rosack, J., 264
Rose, M., 443
Rose, P., 441–442
Rosen, J., 447, 450
Rosenbaum, D., 404
Rosenbaum, J.F., 335, 360
Rosenbaum, M., 200
Rosenberg, D.R., 164
Rosenfarb, I.S., 294
Rosenfeld, F., 293
Rosenhan, D., 6, 7, 9
Rosenthal, L., 191
Roskies, E., 197
Rosler, A., 218
Rosman, B.L., 437
Rosowsky, E., 316
Ross, C.A., 202, 204, 205
Ross, C.J., 447
Ross, E., 57
Ross, G.W., 386
Ross, J., 57
Ross, R., 42
Ross, R.G., 294
Roswell, R., 168
Roth, C., 270
Roth, R.H., 169
Roth, T., 191
Rothbaum, B.O., 156, 169
Rothbaum, F., 111
Rothbaum, P.A., 21
Rothenberg, E., 386
Rothman, D.L., 151
Rotimi, C.N., 196
Rounsaville, R.J., 42, 262
Rourke, K.M., 168
Roussignol, A.C., 293
Ruan, W.J., 312
Rubin, E., 348
Rudd, M.D., 268, 270
Ruiz, J.M., 195
Rumi, D.O., 130
Ruschena, D., 285
Ruscio, A.M., 161

Rush, A.J., 122, 252, 261
Rush, B., 14, *15*
Ruskin, E., 352
Russ, E., 172
Russ, M.J., 319, 320
Russell, D.W., 263
Russell, G.F., 439
Russo, A., 160
Rutter, M., 350, 353, 359
Ryan, N., 364
Rynn, M., 161

S

Saarinen, P.I., 267
Sacco, A., 196
Sacco, W.P., 266
Saccone, N.L., 401
Sacher-Masoch, L., 223
Sackeim, H.A., 130, 265
Safran, J.D., 114, 261
Sagart, E., 450
Sainfort, R., 186
Saiz-Ruiz, J., 443
Sakai, M., 387
Saleh, F.M., 469
Salekin, R.T., 315
Salkovskis, P.M., 164, 165
Salter, M., 28
Salvatori, S., 170
Sammons, M.T., 469
Sampson, P.D., 346
Samuels, J., 185
Samuels, J.F., 449
Samuels, M.P., 189
Samuels, S.C., 381
Sanders, H.D., 239
Sani, L., 196
Sansone, L.A., 437
Sansone, R.A., 437
Santacruz, H., 171
Santangelo, S.L., 350
Santiago, N.J., 267
Sanz, J., 291
Saoud, M., 293
Saphir, Y., 442
Sar, V., 182
Sarbin, T.R., 202
Sarramea, F, 291
Sartorius, N., 71
Sassenrath, J.M., 82
Sasson, M., 442
Sasson, Y., 163
Saudino, K.J., 129
Savino, M., 160
Savolainen, L., 317
Sawchuk, C.N., 155
Saxena, S., 164
Sayers, J., 110
Scarr, S., 129
Scazufca, M., 294
Schachner, D.A., 110
Schaefer, C.A., 293
Schaefer, H.S., 350
Schapiro, N.A., 257
Schatzberg, A.F., 438
Scheibe, G., 151
Scherrer, J.F., 443
Schettler, T., 347

Schildkraut, J.J., 259
Schlenger, W.E., 168, 315
Schlenger-William, E., 170
Schmidt, A.J.M., 186
Schmidt, C.A., 449
Schmidt, G., 230
Schmidt, U., 439
Schneider, K., 278, 279
Schneider, L.S., 265
Schneiderman, N., 194, 195
Schneier, F.R., 159, 160, 185
Schnur, D.B., 265
Schreiber, F.R., 197
Schreiber, S., 170
Schroeder, M.L., 45, 333
Schuckit, M.A., 401, 418
Schulberg, H.C., 272
Schulenberg, J.E., 413, 418, 419
Schuler, A.L., 352
Schultz, R.T., 348
Schuschke, L.A., 189
Schwartz, M.F., 226
Schwartz, S., 163
Schwarze, N.J., 151
Schweers, J., 270
Scogin, F., 150, 161
Scot, R., 13
Scotet, V., 387
Scourfield, J., 316
Scribner, C.M., 7
Seagal, J.D., 195
Sealy, J.R., 447
Seeber, K., 331
Seeley, J.R., 437, 439, 444
Segal, D.L., 194, 316
Segal, N.L., 129
Segraves, R.T., 239, 241
Seidman, L.J., 360
Seifer, R., 346, 347
Seiver, L.J., 320
Seligman, M., 60
Seligman, M.E.P., 155, 197
Selten, J.P., 292, 293
Selzer, M.A., 323
Semans, J.H., 241
Sengupta, A., 254
Senior, C., 208
Sequin, M., 268
Seraganian, P., 197
Serban, G., 205
Serbin, L.A., 317
Serby, M., 381
Sereno, A.B., 331
Serin, R.C., 219
Shadish, W.R., 25
Shaffer, D., 272
Shah, K.R., 443
Shalev, A.Y., 170, 171
Shalgi, B., 442
Shankaran, S., 346, 347
Shapiro, D., 328, 474
Shapiro, S., 163
Sharf, R.S., 114
Sharkansky, E.J., 25
Sharma, V., 130
Sharpe, M., 438
Shastry, B.S., 258, 264
Shaver, P., 110
Shaver, P.R., 110

Shaw, B.F., 122, 261
Shea, T., 150, 312
Shearin, E., 319
Shearin, E.N., 320
Sheffield, D., 195
Sheldon, A.E., 332
Sheldon, A.E.R., 333
Shen, C., 378
Sher, L., 196
Sherbenou, R. J., 82
Sherwood, A.R., 416
Shiffman, S., 124, 291
Shin, Y.C., 444
Shinohara, M., 437
Shinwari, A., 331
Shioe, K., 437
Shoemaker, W.E., 21
Shondrick, D.D., 218
Shukitt-Hale, B., 387
Shulman, I.D., 150
Siegel, G.J., 388
Siegel, S.D., 194
Siever, L.J., 331
Sigman, M., 352
Sigmon, S.T., 189
Sigmund, D., 444
Sigmundson, H.K., 230
Sigusch, V., 230
Silberg, J.L., 364
Silberman, E.K., 202
Silk, K., 87
Silk, K.R., 322
Silva, J.A., 468
Silva, P.A., 315
Silverstein, J.L., 221
Silverstone, P.H., 130
Simon, G.E., 187, 208
Simon, K.M., 327, 328, 332, 334, 335
Simon, R.J., 475
Simon, S.E., 373
Simon, T., 80
Simonini, E., 160
Sims-Knight, J.E., 219
Sinclair, L.V., 350
Singer, P., 298
Siniscalchi, J.M., 185
Sirbu, C., 181
Sirmons family, 459
Skinner, B.F., 18, 120, *120*, 139, 260
Skoner, D.P., 195
Skoog, I., 386
Skultety, K.M., 435
Slater, L., 7
Slovenko, R., 205
Sluiter, J.K., 196
Slutske, W., 443
Slutske, W.S., 363
Smeraldi, E., 164
Smilga, C., 197
Smith, A.M., 316
Smith, B.L., 268, 270, 400
Smith, C.W., 279
Smith, M.E., 414
Smith, R.C., 181
Smith, S.M., 203
Smith, T., 352
Smith, T.L., 401

Subject Index
A

situationally bound panic attack, **149**
situationally predisposed panic attack, **149**
Six Days, Seven Nights, 200
sleep
 disorders, 47*t,* 191*t*
 inducing, *419*
 terror disorder, 191*t*
sleepwalking disorder, 191*t*
Social Cognition and Object Relations Scale (SCORS), 87
social cognitive theory, 121
social discrimination, 116
social introversion, 84*t*
social learning and social cognition, 121–122
social phobia, **157–160,** 176
 behavioral techniques, 160
 best-estimate 1-year prevalence rates based on ECA and NCS, for persons 18–54 years old, 148*f*
 characteristics of, 157–160
 psychological perspectives on, 159
 theories and treatment of, 159–160
sociocognitive model of dissociative identity disorder, **202**
sociocultural, 9
 scales, 82
sociocultural causes
 of abnormality, 9
sociocultural perspectives, **114**–118, 139
 of abnormal behavior, 114–118
 of alcohol dependence, 402–403
 of borderline personality disorder, 323
 evaluation of, 118
 family perspective, **114, 116**
 of mood disorders, 261–263
 of post-traumatic stress disorder (PTSD), 170–171
 of schizophrenia, 294–295
 of social discrimination, 116
 of social influences and historical events, 116
 of suicide, 270
 of treating eating disorders, 439
 treatments, 116–118
somatic
 delusion of, 74*t*
 hallucinations, **76**
 interventions, 139
 obsessions, 165*t*
 therapies, **129–130**
somatization disorder, **182,** 183, 212
somatoform disorders, 47*t,* **180,** 180–190, 212
 biopsychosocial perspective, 209
 body dysmorphic disorder, 184–185
 conditions related to, 187–189
 conversion disorder, 181–182
 hypochondriasis, **185–187**
 malingering, 187–189
 somatization disorder and related conditions, **182**
 theories and treatment of, 189–190
somnophilia, 217*t*

SOMPA. *See* System of Multicultural Pluralistic Assessment
Sophie's Choice (Styron), 115
specific phobias, **153,** 153–157, 176
SPECT. *See* single photon emission computed tomography
spectatoring, **234**
Speech-Sounds Perception Test, 95
spell, 55*t*
spiritual possession, 12, *13*
splitting, 105*t,* **319**
spouse, loss of, *261*
squeeze technique, **241**
SSRIs. *See* selective serotonin reuptake inhibitors; serotonin reuptake inhibitors
standardization, 78
standardized tests, *79*
Standord-Binet Fifth Edition (SB5), 80
Stanford-Binet Intelligence Test, 80–81
stereotypes, 29, 44. *See also* stigma
stereotypic movement disorder, **365,** 368
stigma, 28–30, 32
stigmatophilia, 217*t*
stimulants, 132*t,* **409,** 421*t,* 426
stimulus discrimination, **119**
stimulus generalization, **119**
stop-start procedure, **241**
stress, *192,* 192–195
 borderline personality disorder and, 320
stressful life event, **192**
stressor, **192**
Structured Clinical Interview for *DSM-IV* Dissociative Disorders-Revised (SCID-D-R), 201, 205, 206
Structured Clinical Interview for *DSM-IV* Personality Disorders (SCID-II), 69
Structured Clinical Interview for *DSM-IV-TR* Axis I disorders (SCID-I), 69
structured interviews, **69–72**
Studies in Hysteria (Breuer & Freud), 17
stuttering, **353**
substance, **394,** 426
substance abuse, **395**
 dependence and, 422–424
 nature of, 394–395
substance dependence, **396**
 diagnostic features of alcohol, 404
 other than alcohol, 407–422
substance intoxication, **395**
substance use disorders, 395–396
substance withdrawal, **395**
substance-induced disorders, 395
substance-induced persisting amnestic disorder, 374
substance-induced persisting dementia, **377**
substance-related disorders, 46*t,* 392–427
 alcohol, 396–407
 behaviors associated with, 395–396
 treatment for, 426
subway, crowded, *223*

sudden infant death syndrome (SIDS), 189
suicidal intent, **271**
suicidal lethality, **271**
suicidal mode, 270
suicide, 43, 74, 267–272, 275
 of adolescent, *270*
 alternatives, *272*
 assessment and treatment, 270–272
 biological perspective, 268
 hotline, *58*
 psychological perspective, 268, 270
 risk and protective factors for, 269*t*
 sociocultural perspective, 270
 who commits, 268
 why people commit, 268–272
superego, 102, **103**
superstition, 12
suppression, 104*t*
survey method, **25–26**
susto, 55*t*
symptoms, *43*
symptoms of schizophrenia
 delusions, 279, 281
 disorganized speech, 281–282
 hallucinations, 281
 negative symptoms, 282
 social and occupational dysfunction, 282–283
synapses, 125
synaptic cleft, 126
syndrome, **43**
System of Multicultural Pluralistic Assessment (SOMPA), 82
systematic desensitization, **123**

T

Tactual Performance Test, 95
Taijin Kyofusho (TKS), 55*t,* 159
talk therapy, 60
talking cure, 18
Tarasoff v. Regents of the University of California, 469
tardive dyskinesia, 296
target behavior, **88**
TAT. *See* Thematic Apperception Test
TAT card, *87*
tau, **384**
Taxi Driver, 476
Tay-Sachs disease, 344
TBI. *See* traumatic brain injury
teenagers, with ADHD, 355
terminology, appropriate, 38
terror, of family violence, *203*
terrorism, 168
Test of Nonverbal Intelligence-3 (TONI-3), 82
test-retest, 79*t*
Thematic Apperception Test (TAT), 86–87
theoretical perspectives, **102,** 138
 purpose of, in abnormal psychology, 102
Theorized Patterns in Later Life of Axis II Disorders of the *DSM-IV-TR,* 336*f*
therapist competence, 464
therapy, *38*
 issues disrupting, 62

thinking style and language, **74–75**
thioridazine (Mellaril), 132*t,* 295
thiothixene (Navane), 132*t,* 295
third force, 111
thought broadcasting, delusion of, 74*t*
thought insertion, delusion of, 74*t*
thought stopping, **156**
tic, **364**
tic disorders, 364–365
Till Eulenspiegel Society, 223
Titanic, 119
TKS. *See* Taijin Kyofusho
TMS. *See* transcranial magnetic stimulation
token economy, **124,** *124*
 example of, used in treating schizophrenia, 297*t*
tolerance, **395**
TONI-3. *See* Test of Nonverbal Intelligence-3
Tourette's disorder, **364,** *364,* 368
Tracey's Diary (Gold), 433–434
tranquilizer chair, 15
transcranial magnetic stimulation (TMS), 130
transference, **108**
transsexual, 230
transsexualism, **227**
transvestic fetishism, **225,** 246
 diagnostic features of, 226
tranylcypromine (Parnate), 131*t*
trauma, 8
traumatic brain injury (TBI), 391
traumatic experience, **166**
trazodone (Desyrel), 132*t,* 264
treatment implementation, 61–62
 course of, 61–62
 four-step approach to, 61
 modality of, 59–60
 outcome of, 62
treatment planning, 56, 58–61, 65
 determining best approach, 60–61
 goals of, 56, 58
 modality of, 59–60
 site of, 58–59
treatments
 family therapy, 116–117
 group therapy, 117
 milieu therapy, 117–118
 multicultural approach, 117
 refusal of, 473–474
trephining, **11**
trichotillomania, **447,** 455
 characteristics of, 447–448
 theories and treatment of, *448,* 448–449
tricyclic antidepressants, 131*t*
trifluoperazine (Stelazine), 132*t,* 295
trifluopromazine (Vesprin), 132*t*
Twelve-Month Prevalence of World Mental Health Composite International Diagnostic Interview, 39*t*
twins. *See also* dizygotic twins; monozygotic twins
 probability of major depressive disorder in, *259f*
 schizophrenia and, 299
 studies, *81*